LITERATURE IN NEW ENGLAND

VAN WYCK BROOKS

HAS WRITTEN:

THE FLOWERING OF NEW ENGLAND

THE LIFE OF EMERSON

THE ORDEAL OF MARK TWAIN

THE PILGRIMAGE OF HENRY JAMES

EMERSON AND OTHERS

THREE ESSAYS ON AMERICA
America's Coming-of-age
Letters and Leadership
The Literary Life in America

SKETCHES IN CRITICISM

LITERATURE
IN
NEW ENGLAND

THE FLOWERING OF NEW ENGLAND
1815–1865

NEW ENGLAND: INDIAN SUMMER
1865–1915

BY
VAN WYCK BROOKS

GARDEN CITY PUBLISHING CO., INC.

GARDEN CITY, NEW YORK

1944

GARDEN CITY PUBLISHING CO., INC.

PREFACE

PREFACE

THE two volumes here reprinted belong together naturally. They are complementary and uniform in style, method and feeling alike, and they relate the literary history of New England over a period of just one hundred years. The year 1815 marked the beginning of a "golden age" in the intellectual life of the Western world, while a century later, in 1915, a new group of New England writers bore witness to the tenacity of the Yankee mind. It appeared, however, that the "genial period,"—one of those "heats," as Emerson put it, "by which high tides are caused in the human spirit,"—had come to a definite conclusion. This was New England's great hundred years.

The Flowering of New England and New England: Indian Summer may thus be said to form a single work. But they are also parts of a larger work that is not yet finished, a literary history of the United States. They are episodes of a more inclusive cycle, and I mention this because it explains the omission of various New England authors whose lives are more properly seen in other connections. Among these are the poet Bryant and "Artemus Ward." It also explains the choice of subjects in New England: Indian Summer, which might otherwise seem somewhat arbitrary, for, after all, Henry James thought of himself as a New Yorker and Howells was a man of the Middle West. Which of my authors were New Englanders, and which were not? With the gradual merging of New England in the rest of the nation, during the years that followed the Civil War, it was by no means easy to draw the line; and in consequence I have included numbers born outside New England, who were yet in essential ways identified with it, while omitting others who were New Englanders in the stricter sense. But any sectional treatment of our literary history is bound, as it seems to me, to be arbitrary, and this question can only be judged in relation to the total effect. I have left out certain figures who might have been included here, feeling that in some future volume they could be treated to better advantage. Perhaps this is the place to add that I am not myself a New Englander, except in part by heredity and in part by adoption.

Regarding recent and living authors, except in two or three cases, I have been necessarily brief in my treatment. I have been more concerned with the background from which they emerged, and this I have tried to treat with fullness. It may strike some readers that I have made too much of Boston, too much especially of Harvard, at the expense of other New England centres; but, considering that this is a literary history, I cannot feel that I have done so. Harvard has retained an extraordinarily close connection with literature in this region, if not in the nation, while Boston remains the regional capital in most things intellectual. Aside from this, my emphasis on Boston has served to give these volumes a "unity of place." This was indispensable in any attempt to picture a phase of literary history as confused and complex and marked by such multifarious comings and goings as the phase described especially in the second volume. It must be added that I have not ventured to discuss philosophical writers at length. I am not competent to do so, and, besides, I feel that these writers are related to my subject somewhat obliquely. This must be my excuse for treating so inadequately the beautiful mind and spirit of William James.

It remains to be added that this is a moment when

PREFACE

writers on the American past have a real function to perform, a valuable function. Countless Americans of the old stock have grown up, in recent years, without any of that immediate acquaintance with the history of their forbears which the older Americans drank in with their mothers' milk, while millions of foreign-born citizens and children of the foreign-born have never even become aware that America has a past. At a time when the world has lost its memory, this is peculiarly true of America, and no doubt this fact explains the flood of books in the last two decades the purpose of which has been to restore this or that cell of the national memory. Yet many influential writers still talk of a certain "tradition" which never by chance includes the American tradition, and it seems to me high time to affirm, without exaggerating this, that it ought to constitute for Americans the foreground of all tradition. What past can have any reality for us that does not flow through *our* past, if we as living Americans are true to ourselves? As one who lives in the continuing stream of the past, the present and the future, with at least an imaginative affection for all its parts, I hope I have thrown light on one small section of tradition that is for us the gate of all the rest.

V. W. B.

Westport, Conn., Nov. 1943.

THE FLOWERING
OF NEW ENGLAND
1815-1865

To

MAXWELL EVARTS PERKINS

CONTENTS

CONTENTS

CHAPTER I

THE BOSTON OF GILBERT STUART

AT THE time of the Peace of Ghent, which brought to a close the War of 1812, Gilbert Stuart, the portrait-painter, was an old inhabitant of Boston. He had lived in the town,—for it was still a town, not to become a city for almost a decade,—nine good years. The son of a Rhode Island snuff-grinder, he had made his way up in the world of art until nobody questioned his eminence. He was famous in London and Dublin, where he had been a rival of Lawrence and Beechey. In all American circles, his word was law. No one dared to praise an American poet until the *Edinburgh Review* had done so, but Stuart was the arbiter in painting. In his careless way, he had neglected to answer the letter from the Academy of Florence asking for a portrait of himself. He did not need these testimonials. In the capital of New England, whither he had come to live and die, everyone praised and admired him. Even John Adams, the patriarch of Quincy, who said he would not give sixpence for a Raphael, yielded to the spell of the genial artist. The old man had rejoiced, with a Puritan's fervour, that the age of painting and sculpture had not arrived to corrupt his beloved country. But Gilbert Stuart's witty anecdotes charmed away his prejudices. After his first sitting, he exclaimed that he would be glad to sit to Stuart from one year's end to another.

Times had undoubtedly changed in the Christian Sparta, as John Adams's cousin, Samuel Adams, had called the town of Boston. Gilbert Stuart, who was a notable

wag, liked to begin his anecdotes by saying, "When I
lived in the Athens of America." Everyone knew what he
meant by the phrase: he was referring to Philadelphia.
And every Bostonian knew that he was mistaken. William
Penn's town had taken the lead in all these matters of
enlightenment—thanks to a good Bostonian, Benjamin
Franklin; but that was in days past. The real American
Athens was the Christian Sparta. At least, it was advancing towards this position, with large and rapid strides;
and Stuart knew it. He was only indulging a taste for
mischief. In England, when people had asked him where
he was born, he had said, by way of explaining Narragansett, "six miles from Pottawome and ten miles from
Poppasquash." His sitters were little the wiser when he
added that he had spent his early years at Newport,
where, in some of the old merchants' houses, he had seen
portraits by Van Dyck and Kneller, real or supposititious.
And if he liked to tease the men of Boston, who suffered
from no lack of self-esteem, it was not because he found
them dull. He laughed at blue laws and blue noses, but so
did many of his Boston sitters, those who had not lost
their Tory ways and some of those who belonged to the
younger circles. For the dominant Boston nose was far
from blue: it was a Roman nose, flanked by a full-blown
complexion. Stuart, with his lordly style, his fresh, ruddy
face and downright manners,—not to mention his taste
for the best Madeira, which he poured from a half-gallon
ewer, throwing off tumblers like cider in haying-time,—
was quite at home with the great East India merchants,
whose ships had sometimes carried the Madeira twice
round the Cape, to give it a good rocking. They liked the
hearty freedom of a man who, when one of his sitters fell
asleep, painted him with ass's ears. They liked a man
who, if he used snuff, used half a pound of it a day. They
liked his high spirits and his flowing talk, as well as the
claret he seemed to mix with his paint. And they liked the

uncanny skill with which he dived into their own thoughts, —for they were proud of their thoughts,—and made them live and speak on his eloquent canvas.

This was the golden age of portrait-painting. It was an age of public men. It was an age of family pride, nowhere more marked than in Boston. It was an age of modest wealth, which the recent war had checked but not extinguished. For three generations, since the days of Smibert, Boston had supported its portrait-painters, and Gilbert Stuart was another Copley. It was true that the town had little feeling for art. Stuart was to die as obscure and poor as any tippling poet in the gutter. The Boston people did not cherish him—much as they enjoyed his company—because they were proud that one of the world's artists had chosen to live in Boston. They cherished him because he so greatly added to their own pride in themselves; and when they finally buried him in the Common, near the famous Julien of the "soup," they did not even mark his grave. Boston was torpid in aesthetic matters. Stuart had refused to exhibit his pictures because they had been hung so badly. Boston was congenitally obtuse in all that concerned the senses, except Madeira; and this was still to be true a century later, when, with little more aesthetic feeling, the town possessed so much aesthetic knowledge. It was always to look on the plastic arts, instinctively, as a clever woman said, in the days when New Yorkers liked to tease Bostonians, merely as branches of literature. There was something cold and dry in its perceptions. But the very elements in its social life that nourished the portrait-painters,—the family pride, the wealth, the public spirit,—were obviously creating a situation that fostered all its natural faculties. The merchant-patricians, like those of Holland and Flanders, in times gone by, wished to perpetuate their names and glorify their capital not only in the elegance of their mansions but also in churches, parks and public buildings, in professorial chairs at Harvard College, in schools and asylums and hospitals. Such were the desires and thoughts that Stuart caught in the faces of his sitters.

All the omens favoured these intentions. The recent war had cleared the atmosphere. For twenty years after the Revolution, Boston had been poor and apprehensive. The nation was torn with sectional dissensions. Everyone feared the interference of England. Napoleon was abroad like a wolf in the night. But Waterloo and Commodore Perry had quieted these anxieties. England had ceased to be a menace. The abhorrent career of Napoleon had broken the old connection with France. Europe had become engrossed in problems that had little meaning across the ocean. America, united and free at last, with all its problems solved, as it seemed at the moment, faced a future that was almost dazzling. The "era of good feeling" was beginning, and circumstances had been kind to Boston. The war, which had largely destroyed the commerce of the smaller New England ports, had had no lasting effect on the capital. Strong enough, in fact, to survive the crisis, it prospered with the ruin of so many rivals; and it was attracting more and more the younger merchants of the rural regions who had taken advantage of the decline of shipping, during the years of war, and the boycott of English goods that followed the war, to build up a manufacturing system and supply the American people with native products. Factory-towns were rising on every hand, in eastern Massachusetts and New Hampshire,—Lawrence, Lowell, Fitchburg, Manchester, Lynn. Every village with a waterfall set up a textile-mill or a paper-mill, a shoe-factory or an iron-foundry; and as Boston remained the financial centre, as well for manufacturing as for shipping, the mercantile fortunes of the inland counties were joined with those of the magnates of the seaboard.

Boston was rich, in short, as never before; and, hav-

ing the means, the leading citizens could not imagine why
their little town should not be the finest in the world. No
one challenged this prepossession. New England was an
isolated region, and Boston had some right to its self-
esteem. It had taken the lead in the Revolution, with the
statesmen of Virginia, and played a large part in both
the wars in which the United States had defeated Eng·
land. The boast of the Boston poet, —

> We have the guns,
> We have the ships,—

was justified by the British themselves. All their commentators had asserted that the American cruisers were
the best and that the Yankee rifle in Yankee hands had
set a new standard of marksmanship. No one could guess
what happy fortunes lay before the valiant young republic, and Boston hoped for a special dispensation. The old
dream of a Puritan commonwealth, a true city of God,
lingered in the New England mind, and it seemed as if
the appointed hour had come. Cotton Mather had foretold this hour. Jonathan Edwards, on his lonely rides
over the forest hills of leafy Stockbridge, had seen the
millennium approaching. Bishop Berkeley, on his farm at
Newport, had prophesied the golden age. The hard conditions of life in earlier days had yielded to more propitious circumstances. The time was surely ripe; and what
wealth was unable to compass might be left to piety and
reason. The Boston people had only themselves to blame,
or so, at least, they felt, if the kingdom of heaven, a sober
New England kingdom,—not built of the gaudy materials that vulgarized the Book of Revelation,—were
not, at last, at hand.

They meant to do their best. The Lowells, the Cabots,
the Appletons, the Jacksons, the "codfish aristocracy" and
the "Essex Junto,"—the members of which had wished

to break the Union, in favour of their New England separatism,—the Perkinses, Higginsons, Cushings, the brothers Lawrence, who had made their fortunes on the sea, along with the Hong merchants of the Flowery Kingdom, or from the whirring of their wheels and spindles, united in a passion for the *genius loci*. Some of them suggested in their faces, faithfully painted by Stuart, the florid merchants of colonial times, their grandsires and uncles, in velvet cap and flowered robe, flushed with wine and generosity. Others recalled the Puritan cast, the lean, shrewd, nervous Yankee type, cautious, with a turn for metaphysics, dried by the American atmosphere. All of them lived and moved, walked and spoke as if their little town were a holy city and Rome, Paris and London were their suburbs. For this there were certain reasons. Boston was only a regional capital, but a Boston man could say to himself, quite truly, that it was much more a capital than either New York or Philadelphia; for the people were more homogeneous. A visitor from New York, observing the crowd in the streets, exclaimed, "Why, all these people are of one race. They behave like members of one family, whereas with us a crowd is an assembly of all the nations upon earth." As one of the results of this homogeneity, the institutions of the town and country had a greater similarity than in other regions,—a fact that was full of meaning for the future. It favoured the growth of the region in all its parts. For, while Boston attracted the master-minds and took them away from the smaller towns, it rendered them more active and efficient; and, precisely because of this concentration of powers, it was able to send forth influences that were beneficial to the rural districts. It was able to do so and it wished to do so, more and more as the century advanced. The older patrician families, those that had come over in the "Arbella," and those of whom it was said that, at the time of the Deluge, they had a boat to themselves, possessed a sense of responsibility that sometimes seemed acute. The eminent men who had come from the country, or from the smaller ports and county-seats, and who mingled on equal terms with the patricians, were loyal to their rustic antecedents. One and all felt, as the Boston orators were always saying, in the old "cradle of liberty," Faneuil Hall, that they were the heirs of the Revolution. They were determined to carry out, in every sphere in which their interests lay, their duties as American citizens. They meant to make Boston a model town. They meant to make New England a model region.

Boston was another Edinburgh, with marked variations of its own. It resembled Edinburgh in many ways, as New England resembled Scotland. The bitter climate and the hard soil, the ice, the granite and the Calvinism, yielding to more gracious forms of faith, the common schools, the thrifty farmer-folk, the coast-line, with its ports and sailors' customs, the abundant lakes and mountains, the geological aspects of the region, all suggested the land of Sir Walter Scott, as well as the adjacent land of Wordsworth, whose bareness and simplicity, together with his loftiness and depth,—proofs, as Hazlitt said, that his work was written in a mountainous country,—commended him to the young New England mind; and if, in this mind, there was something cold and hard that recalled the ice and the granite, there were reserves of feeling and perception that were to find expression in the years to come. A well-known Scottish traveller * remarked of Boston, "I could scarcely believe I was not in Scotland." One found there, as in Edinburgh, the same wealth, similarly earned, the same regard for manners and decorum, the same respect for learning, the same religious point of view, alike in its antecedents and in its liberal modifications, the same scrupulous conscientious-

* Sir Charles Lyell,—some years later.

ness, the same punctiliousness and the same pride, even the
same prudence. One found the same exactions in matters
of taste, the same aristocratic prepossessions and the
same democratic feeling underneath them. The golden
calf the Bostonians worshipped was a mere pygmy, as
Dickens said, a generation later, beside the giant effigies
one found in the other American cities.

Not that the Boston people were other-worldly, for all
their messianic expectations, except as compared with the
profane New Yorkers. Some of them lived in magnificent
style. Many of them were accomplished in the art of living. The Cushing house in Summer Street was surrounded
with a wall of Chinese porcelain. Peacocks strutted about
the garden. The Chinese servants wore their native dress.
The older folk, sedate, a little complacent, dwelling in
the solid garden-houses that stood about the Common,
each with its flagged walk and spacious court-yard, filled
with fragrant shrubs, shaded by its over-arching elms,
were genial and pleasure-loving, as a rule. Here and there
one found a Sybarite. Harrison Gray Otis, at the age of
eighty, after forty years of gout, breakfasted every morning on *pâté de foie gras.* Every afternoon, at the Otis
house, ten gallons of punch evaporated out of the Lowe-
stoft bowl that was placed on the landing. One of the
Perkins brothers, challenged by a rigorous pastor, who
had come out for total abstinence, doubled his children's
ration of Madeira. Even the young girls, in some of these
houses, where they maintained the royalist traditions and
sometimes toasted "the King," under the rose, read *Tom
Jones,* Smollett and *Tristram Shandy,* as if they had
never heard of a Pilgrim Father. In every house one
found the standard authors, Hume, Gibbon, Shakespeare,
Milton, Dryden, Addison, the *Arabian Nights, Don
Quixote,* Sir William Temple's works in folio, a set of
Hogarth's original plates, perhaps, or two or three first

editions of Pope, books that were worthy of their calf bindings, on shelves that might have been carved by Grinling Gibbons, surmounted by marble busts. The children were brought up on Maria Edgeworth and the writings of Mrs. Barbauld and Fanny Burney. Sons who came home from abroad with too many airs were greeted with an almost crushing composure. The Boston people were willing to learn, but only if one recognized how much they knew already. Their minds were closed on certain lines, and they did not like "originality." But, as a generation that knew the world, they were prepared to humour their sons and daughters.

There were many strains in the Boston mind, a warm and chivalrous Tory strain, a passionate strain of rebelliousness, a strain of religious fervour, a marked and even general disposition,—despite the sybaritic Mr. Otis, who, for the rest, was public-spirited,—to sacrifice at other than mundane altars. The town abounded in quixotic souls, "unmanageable" Adamses, younger sons who refused the social uniform, visionaries, *exaltés,* nonconformists. The future was to provide them with their causes. It was true that these idealists, who spoke for "impossible loyalties," found Beacon Hill a mountain of ice. Principle was a reality in Boston. Conscience was a large reality. Everyone knew the story of the merchant who, when one of his ships was overdue, found that he was more anxious about his thoughts than about the money he was losing. Was it possible, he asked himself, that he had really grown to love his money more for itself than for its noble uses? To settle the point in his own mind, he reckoned the value of the ship and cargo and gave the sum to his favourite charity. The story was typical of the Boston merchants who, within a space of thirty years, from 1810 to 1840, established thirty benevolent institutions. And yet there were those who said

that Boston had a double intellect and only half a heart.
The prevailing mind was cautious, excessively formal,
singularly obsessed with its own importance, bigoted in
its fear of political change. The mother of "Athenæum"
Shaw enjoined upon him, during his early travels, the
virtues of silence, secrecy and circumspection, quoting the
counsel of an experienced father, that one should keep
one's countenance open but one's thoughts close. The
Puritans had learned this art in their days of persecu-
tion, and a trading community had found it useful. Moreover, the prevailing mind was legalistic. Burke—with Dr.
Johnson, its favourite author—noted that more than half
of the first edition of Blackstone's Commentaries found
its way to America. A large proportion had remained in
Boston, where it served as an arsenal of logic against the
Jacobins and their bob-tailed crew. For Boston was controlled by an oligarchy, an unofficial caste of leading men
for whom a "republic" and a "democracy" had next to
nothing in common. Hamiltonian Federalists to a man,
Whigs after the fall of Federalism, they had found that
the doctrines of Burke and Johnson admirably supported
their property-interests. For the rest, they had "looked
at France," as Fisher Ames had advised them to do, and
witnessed the results of a red revolution,—anarchy, in-
fidelity, just as Burke had prophesied, with a lord of mis-
rule, Napoleon, as the end of all things.

Stability at any price! They had had too many wars
and altercations. The first French Republic had gone to
the dogs. They could not believe that their own would
fare much better. In days of debt and disunitedness, it
was a natural assumption that power ought to go with
property. The theory had a special justification in days
when *not* to have property, if one wished it, was almost
a certain sign of shiftlessness. "Where are your poor?"
said Lafayette, when, a few years later, he scrutinized
the crowds in the Boston streets. The slum was a thing of

the future,* and most of the rich men had acquired their
wealth by the superior exercise of traits that almost every
Yankee shared and applauded. Besides, if their minds
were closed in political matters, they were more than
liberal in religion. They took a lenient view of human
nature. Few traces of Puritanism were left among them.
Most of them had seen the world, as supercargoes, merchants, statesmen, students. They had fought with Tri-
politan pirates, visited Canton, India and Egypt, bought
skins in Canada and sold them in China, carried ice from
Labrador to Java, taken the grand tour to Rome and
Naples and had themselves measured by London tailors,
who continued to make their clothes when they had shrunk
within the measurements. The fact that the clothes were
made in London was more important than that they did
not fit. If their views were not loose, like their clothes,
at least they were enlarged, as people said. They no
longer looked on their fellow-beings with the eyes of
Puritan deacons. Indeed, the human nature they found
about them, far from being totally depraved, seemed, in
the light of these wider circumstances, compared with
Chinese coolies and Italian beggars, singularly innocent
and good. Who had measured its capacity? Boston boys
believed in themselves. They grew up alert and self-
reliant,† battling with the east winds, coasting over the
frozen snow, convinced that they were able to "lick creation." ‡ How could they accept the ancestral doctrine of

* There was, however, one region in Boston, on the Cambridge side of
Beacon Hill, that is said to have been extremely squalid and vicious. It was
filled with crowded, tumble-down tenements where crime ran riot. The
population was largely black, with a worse white intermixture. This region greatly exercised the Boston and Cambridge humanitarians, notably
the fathers of Lowell the poet and Charles Eliot Norton.

† A rule of the household of Wendell Phillips's father, the first mayor of
the city of Boston: "Ask no man to do for you anything that you are not
able and willing to do for yourself."

‡ All classes in New England shared this assurance. See Emerson's Journal, at sea, 1833: "The captain believes in the superiority of the American
to every other countryman. 'You will see,' he says, 'when you get out here
how they manage in Europe; they do everything by main strength and ignorance. Four truckmen and four stevedores at Long Wharf will load my
brig quicker than a hundred men at any port in the Mediterranean.' "

the worthlessness of human efforts and motives? How could they hear themselves described as "vipers"? Were Boston boys "little fallen wretches," even worse than vipers? They were more ready to think that, having succeeded in so many things, they could succeed in everything. In short, they believed in perfectibility.

This change in their religious point of view, gradual, scarcely perceptible at first, signified an emotional revolution as marked as the events of '76. Absorbed as they were in politics and trade, the Boston folk were hardly aware that the old faith had vanished from their horizon. Twenty years before, the well-known wit, Robert Treat Paine, had cursed the "Vandal spirit of Puritanism,"— a levity of the fashionable circles, savouring of the colonial governor's court, that had grown to be a commonplace. In 1809, the most popular preacher in Boston, referring to the creed of the Pilgrim Fathers,—Calvinism, with its "revolting forms,"—spoke of Milton's eyes as having been "quenched in the service of a vulgar and usurping faction." A mild and tolerant Unitarianism, rationalistic, torpid, utilitarian, had been set up as the State Church. Known far and wide as the "Boston religion," it still possessed a frail dogmatic structure, of which it was only conscious when it was challenged. The ministers were graceful rhetoricians. Calling themselves Arminians or Arians, sometimes Moderate Calvinists, they still believed in the supernatural; and, having "disproved" the Trinitarian doctrine, with most of the other doctrines of their forbears, they clung to the Christian miracles, as the proper evidences of the faith.

Negative and pallid as it was, the new religion sprang from an atmosphere that was favourable to the flowering of the mind. The ministers, learned, cultivated men, lovers of music and eloquence, had introduced the literary sermon. Their models were Bossuet and Massillon. They had abandoned the older pulpit methods, the texts, the arguments and the commentaries. Their sermons were glowing essays, dealing with the interests of daily life. Joseph Stevens Buckminster, the melodious preacher, the "Chrysostom of America," as he was called, who had read his Greek Testament at five, had prophesied the birth of a great school of American letters. Poets and historians, he had said, in one of his discourses at Harvard College, were soon to appear, to direct American taste and mould the genius of the young republic, men of whom posterity was to stand in awe. "You, my young friends," he had exclaimed, "are destined to witness the dawn of our Augustan age, and to contribute to its glory,"—a very different note from Fisher Ames's, the spokesman of the previous decade, who had never missed a chance to say that the American genius was foredoomed to fail. Buckminster's successor, William Ellery Channing, the great ethical leader of the future, equally sanguine, was more critical. The impassioned little saint with the burning heart, whose intellect was the conscience of New England, felt that the hour had struck for American thinkers. Mind, mind required all one's care! In his youth he had had a sudden illumination, a vision of human nature, which seemed to him a godhead in the making. He ceaselessly preached the gospel of self-improvement. "We want great minds," he said, "to be formed among us. We want the human intellect to do its utmost here."

Boston corresponded to Plato's city, a population that was not too large to hear the voice of a single orator. The people were prepared for these stirring sermons. With Faneuil Hall as their Acropolis, they were accustomed to public speaking, and oratory had filled them with exalted thoughts. At school they learned to recite the swelling strains of the *Life of William Tell:* "Friends of liberty, sons of sensibility, ye who know how to die for your independence!" Bombast, in a sense, but they believed it. Their fathers and uncles had fought in a similar cause, swept along by a tide of eloquence. Moreover, Plutarch was their second Bible, together with Pope's Homer. Deep in their hearts they cherished the conviction that they could emulate these heroic models and reproduce the deeds of history. The sons of William Emerson, for instance, the former minister of the First Church, who had founded the Philosophical Society, were born with these convictions in their blood, and one of them, a boy of twelve named Ralph, a chubby little spouter of Scott and Campbell, who had recently trundled his hoop about the Common, where he pastured the family cow, was to express them later in his essays. The Emerson boys, "born to be educated,"—the object of a Boston childhood seemed to be to prepare for the Latin School,—were typical of a ministerial household, heirs of a long line of divines and scholars, one of whom had prayed every evening that none of his descendants might ever be rich. Their mother, like all the devout New England matrons, enjoyed her morning hour of meditation. Their aunt, the minister's sister, Mary Moody Emerson of Concord, who despised the new religion, poor, low, thin, as she thought it was, dwelt in the fiery depths of a Calvinism which, although she only half believed it, filled her with a sombre poetry. She prophesied that her nephews were to be called of men Rabbis and Fathers. Ralph already had a mind of his own. He carried the *Pensées* of Pascal to church, to read during the sermon. At night, in his cold upper chamber, covered with woollen blankets to the chin, he read his precious Dialogues of Plato. He associated Plato, ever after, with the smell of wool.

Under its placid surface, Boston tingled with a new ambition. Half the boys expected to go to sea. They hovered about the ships and the wharves, scenting the salt air, the ropes and the tar, listening to tales of Chinese pirates, greeting some cousin, home from Spanish Manila,

in white trousers and jacket of sky-blue silk, marvelling
over an older brother who, for a lark, on his way back
from Cairo, had travelled the length of Italy, in his carriage, dressed as an Oriental potentate. As many others
dreamed of a life of letters. Here and there, some poor
young man, who could not go to the Latin School, bought
his own Andrews and Stoddard's grammar, from which
every proper Boston boy supposed the Latin language
had been derived, and spent his nights over a commonplace-book, copying his favourite passages from Gibbon.
Learning was endemic in the Boston mind, as befitted a
town whose first inhabitant, the Cambridge scholar Blaxton,—who had built his thatched cottage, with a garden
and spring, on the site of Louisburg Square,—had
brought his library with him. There had been books on
the slope of Beacon Hill when the wolves still howled
on the summit. There had always been some Boston man
who could address in Arabic or Persian a merchant or
diplomat from the land of Xerxes; and now that the war
was over, and the nation seemed to be on a solid footing,
the intellectual life grew apace. The clever Frenchmen,
with their godless notions, had made all thought suspicious for a while. The Boston people preferred to settle
questions by thumping the table, or by whacks and
blows,* in the manner of Dr. Johnson. But subtlety had
grown with confidence. The argand lamp, improved by
Jefferson, had furthered the habit of reading. It was observed at once that dinner-parties, formerly lighted by
candles, ceased to be as brilliant as of old. Those who
had excelled in talking took to their books and writing-
desks. It was true that this intellectual life was timid,
cautious and derivative. In short, it was still colonial,

* Not, however, delivered on the person. In spite of the downright ways
of the old Bostonians, New England was noted for its mildness. Timothy
Dwight reported that he had never heard of a New England man using
arms in a private quarrel. Josiah Quincy said that only five duels were known
to have taken place in New England up to 1820.

forty years after Bunker Hill. English culture had a right
of way that no one thought of challenging, and every
Boston boy was taught to regard Pope and Burke as unapproachable. The literary government of Europe was a
more potent yoke than the political government had been.
But the ferment of the rising generation might be expected to break it.

As if to provide the future with a proper setting, the
Boston people had rebuilt the town. The architect,
Charles Bulfinch, the son of a doctor, had appeared with
providential promptness. A man of sensibility, he had
been moved to tears, on a tour of Europe, when he had
entered St. Peter's at Rome. He had been obliged to
teach himself. Among so many carpenters and builders,
skilful, well-trained craftsmen, schooled in the styles of
Wren and Inigo Jones, there was not an architect in Boston when he returned in 1787; and, search as one might,
high and low, one could not find a book on architecture.
Bulfinch, who had bought some books in Europe and
found his taste and talent in demand, soon developed a
style,—an outgrowth of the prevailing style, more
delicate than the colonial Georgian, quite without the
English massiveness,—that caught the temper of the Boston people. It was modestly elegant, somewhat prim, but
dignified and simple. He had built the first theatre in the
town, as far back as 1793, where all Boston rejoiced in
The School for Scandal, disguised as a "moral lecture."
He had built the admirable State House, which was to
serve as a model for so many others. He had filled Boston
with his works, houses and blocks of houses, crescents,
churches, which, with their grace and propriety, struck
the note of an epoch, an outward and visible sign that the
new Boston mind had crystallized and found its appropriate form. Various institutions of learning followed in
rapid succession, a Library of Law in 1806, a Theological
Library in 1807,—in the same year, the Boston Athe-

næum. Modelled on the Liverpool Athenæum, this was
largely the work of Buckminster, who had spent most of
his little fortune buying books in Paris. He had sent three
thousand volumes home, sets of the British essayists and
poets, the Botanical Magazine, topographical works on
Greece and Rome that brought the classical world before
one's eyes, works in unknown realms, Roscoe's *Lorenzo
de' Medici,* Duppa's *Life of Michael Angelo,* Italian and
Spanish dictionaries. The first wistaria vine, the first
mimosa was scarcely more of a novelty in Boston than
some of these intellectual plants and vines that were to
scatter their seeds across New England.

Two other institutions, the Handel and Haydn Society and the *North American Review*—founded, both, in
1815—marked the coming-of-age of the Boston mind.
For music and for letters, these were of the future. The
culture of the immediate past and present found expression through another organ. For several years there had
existed, from 1803 to the outbreak of the war, a club
devoted to literary interests. The Anthology Society, as
it was called, numbered among its members Buckminster,
Channing, William Emerson, Dr. Gardiner, the rector of
Trinity Church, William Tudor, the merchant, President
Kirkland of Harvard, John Lowell and other well-known
men. The members met one evening every week to discuss the manuscripts for their magazine, the *Monthly
Anthology,* over a modest supper of widgeons and teal,
brants or a mongrel goose, with a little good claret.
There was too little intercourse, they felt, among Americans who cared for letters. They even hoped that their
review, the first of its kind in the country, which had succeeded many feebler efforts, might foster the growth of a
national literature.

The members were not professional men of letters, a
species that was still unknown in Boston. Moreover, their
expectations were not excessive, or much beyond the

pleasures of their task. William Emerson was the editor.
William Tudor, who had established the club, had made a
small fortune, with his brother, shipping ice, cut from
their pond at Saugus, to Martinique and South America.
Indeed, the Tudors introduced, throughout the equatorial
world, even as far as Calcutta, the custom of using ice in
table-drinks.* Dr. Gardiner, an Episcopalian, conducted
a little school in his spacious study, instructing a chosen
handful in Latin and Greek, following the methods of his
master, the great English scholar, Samuel Parr. Among
the other contributors or members, some of them correspondents from a distance, were the rising Portsmouth
lawyer, Daniel Webster, who had not yet moved to Boston, the Reverend Aaron Bancroft, who lived in Worcester, a theologian of the older school, the father of a
son who was soon to be famous, Joseph Story of Salem,
the notable jurist, the greatest writer on the law since
Blackstone, as the Lord Chief Justice of England called
him later, and various younger men of ample promise,
Alexander Everett and George Ticknor. Judge Story, a
classmate of Dr. Channing, had published a poem, *The
Power of Solitude,* suggested by the writings of Zimmer-
mann. Although he had taken a "lawyer's farewell of the
muse," he often entertained himself in court by making
his notes of arguments in verse.

The magazine, though somewhat staid in manner, **de-**
cidedly starched and impersonal, was yet an enterprise
that promised much, in days when "Who wrote Junius?"
was still an exciting topic of conversation. In style it resembled the British reviews, not yet irradiated by Lamb
and Hazlitt,—the English Unitarian minister's son who
had spent three years, as a boy, in Massachusetts, who
had seen Boston before he saw London and never forgot
the Yankee barberry-bushes. Far from calling a spade a

* It was to William Tudor, when he was presented to George the Fourth,
that the king remarked, "What, one of us?"

spade, it always called a name an appellation. Behind
these traits of Johnsonese, moreover, might have been
discerned the self-distrust that marks the colonial mind,
a mind that has no centre of its own and clings to the
well-tried ways of the mother-country after the mother-
country has thrown them off. It abounded in Addisonian
bric-a-brac, playful bits on toast and cranberry sauce,
worthy of a Grandison's hours of ease, accounts of visits
to Dr. Johnson's birthplace, continuations of Collins's
Ode to the Passions, reviews of *The Gamesters: or Ruins
of Innocence,* Beresford's *The Miseries of Human Life*
and *A Wreath for the Rev. Daniel Dow.* It defended
Pope against all comers, especially Coleridge's nonsense.
Even in Boston there were even lawyers who thought its
tone was pompous and said that Dr. Gardiner was a snob.
This was a little severe. The magazine was well-informed.
It reviewed the museums, the theatres, the social assemblies, and criticized the state of Harvard College.
It noticed the important publications, Washington Irving's *Knickerbocker,* Aaron Bancroft's *Washington,*
Madame de Staël's *Corinne,* Wilson's *American Orni-
thology.* It published intelligent essays on Erasmus, the
Carelessness of Dryden, Sir Walter Scott, whose poems
stirred the Boston breast and who was supposed to be
writing the Waverley novels: "Who writes the Waverley
novels?" was almost as thrilling a question as "Who
wrote Junius?" It attacked Blair's *Grave,* for the mortu-
ary vein was running out.* It printed papers on Italian
painters, Luca Giordano, the Carracci, and even a version
of the *Sakuntala,* the first Hindu work to appear in the

* "Sixty years ago," said Emerson, referring to this period, "the books
read, the sermons and prayers heard, the habits of thought of religious
persons were all directed on death. All were under the shadow of Calvinism, and of the Roman Catholic purgatory, and death was dreadful.
The emphasis of all the good books given to young people was on death.
We were all taught that we were born to die; and, over that, all the terrors that theology could gather from savage nations were added to increase the gloom."—*Letters and Social Aims.*

country. It deplored the backward state of American letters, the servile imitation of England, the fruits of a
superficial education. Whatever the future might produce,
the writers of the review showed that the Boston of Gilbert Stuart had roused itself out of its ancient slumbers.

Some of these writers, in fact, prefigured the future.
Buckminster professed the daring notion that there was
a higher poetry than the "mere language of reason." He
had himself taken as much delight in the ragged splendours of a western sunset, rich, disorderly, indistinct in
shape, as in the seven colours of the rainbow, properly
disposed in a semicircle, as if a good Bostonian had arranged them. This was quite absurd, Dr. Gardiner said.
Heaven could only tell what it betokened, in a world that
persisted in moving and changing its mind.

CHAPTER II

HARVARD COLLEGE IN 1815

ALL ABOUT Boston, to the north, west and south, there still dwelt, in these days of Gilbert Stuart, many a veteran of the Revolution, protagonists, masterminds and lesser worthies. In Cambridge, in Concord, up and down the coast, in every port and village, one found survivors of the stirring hour, with their firelocks over their chimney-pieces. They recalled the brave days of the Roman republic, when the chief men of the State stayed on their farms, awaiting some summons for a public council to call them from their villas to the Senate.

At Pepperell, near the New Hampshire line, Colonel William Prescott had his farm, which he held by its original Indian title. The hero of Bunker Hill, like Cincinnatus, had taken up the plough again where he had left it standing in the furrow. Passing through Dorchester southward, or driving through the quiet lanes of Brookline, where the great East India merchants had their villas, with spreading lawns and airy parlours, filled with plaster casts and Italian paintings, and summer-houses in the Chinese style, one came at last to Quincy, where John Adams lived. There, like Thomas Jefferson at Monticello, with whom he had resumed his correspondence, on his ancient terms of good will,—since all passion was spent now,—the patriarch cheerfully sat for the painters and sculptors and studied the greater art of growing old. Once a year, together with his Bible, he read and pondered Cicero's *De Senectute*. He liked to talk with his friends on

subjects suggested by his reading, such as the merits of
Alexander the Great; and, as the years passed, he waited
calmly for a better world, where he expected to meet
all the great and good who had gone before him.

Close by, his kinsfolk, the Quincy family dwelt. Josiah
Quincy, now in the prime of life, the ancient doge of later
times whose mind had been formed in the stress of the
previous age, also spent his leisure hours, those he could
spare from active politics, either in Boston or Washington, or from the toils of his farm, reading his three editions of Cicero, one for the shelf, one for the table and
one, in twenty volumes, for the pocket, along with his
Plutarch and his well-conned Horace. For generations, on
their ancestral acres, where, with his six servants, the
first American forbear of the family had raised his honoured roof-tree, the Quincys had lived as magistrates and
squires, loving their field-sports as they loved their country
and poring over the Tusculan Disputations: for Cicero,
the defender of liberty, stirred a responsive chord in the
Quincy bosom, Cicero, the instructor of every profession,
the friend of every age! If the present master of the
house, a house as ample as those of the Brookline merchants, overflowing with cousins and friends and public
men of half a dozen countries,—if the present Josiah
Quincy was not himself a man of the Revolution, he
might, equally well, have been his father, whose life he
had seen mirrored in Pope's Homer. He was the happy
warrior who, for a long generation to come, was to fight
for all the Revolution had stood for. He was the *integer
vitae* who, like the Romans, in his inmost heart, had built
twin temples to virtue and honour, so joined that one
could enter the temple of honour only by passing first
through the temple of virtue. He knew and loved the ancients, as Harvard knew them, not so much because he
cared for learning as for their noble patterns of behaviour.

The happiest moments of the Adams household, few as they were at present, snatched from the busiest life that America knew, were those that John Quincy Adams, the rising hope of the old President's heart, was able to spend with his aging father and mother. Already in train for the White House, Minister to England, Secretary of State, almost a popular hero, like Andrew Jackson, thanks to his work in concluding the recent war, he, too, was a man of the Revolution. At eight, he had watched the Battle of Bunker Hill; at nine, he had served as a little post-rider; at fourteen, he had entered public life as secretary to the Minister to Russia. He had known Washington, Franklin, Jefferson, Jay, as a younger member of their constellation, and had followed a proud, unmanageable course that had won him the hatred of his own party and the gratitude of the nation. Against the interests of his Federalist friends, for whom money counted more than country, he had fought for Jefferson's Embargo, as later, in the teeth of the cotton-interests, he was to fight the slave-power. For the selfish claims of his class and breed he cared no more than he cared for his own popularity; and yet, by the force of his intellect and will, he had carved for himself a career that every common politician envied. It was a career that his father understood and Abigail Adams rejoiced in, for he had never compromised his faith that statesmanship was the noblest of human callings. And if, at times, his methods were those of the hedgehog, at Quincy the quills were always folded in.

There, in the peaceful homestead, where later generations of Adamses were to sit in the old President's chair, in the quiet upstairs study, and write their memoirs and their histories, father and son, at these propitious moments, discussed the great problems of their country. John Quincy Adams, now turning fifty, short, stout and bald, less florid than his father,—for the English type was gradually dying out,—had passed his earliest years there, and there, in later years, still fighting, in the House at Washington, for justice, for improvement, justice for the negroes, justice for the outraged Indians, for science, for the Smithsonian Institution, with both feet planted on the Rock of Ages,—there he was to pass his long vacations, always writing, writing, with ink-spots on his fingers, notes on Plutarch, notes on the Book of Leviticus, speeches, essays, poems, nodding in his chair, wandering about the garden and the ragged orchard, with hatchet and saw in hand, pruning his pear and cherry-trees, hoeing and plucking weeds, bending over his plants in their pots and boxes or using his wife's best tumblers to cover the caterpillars that were supposed to turn into butterflies but—as his grandsons noticed—never did so. At Quincy, as a little boy, with his thoughts filled with birds' eggs and trifles, he had begun his famous Diary, enjoined thereto by his austere papa, so that he might later be able to note the stages by which he had advanced in taste, knowledge and judgment. There he had read his fairy-tales and revelled in the *Arabian Nights* and Shakespeare. In all the furious years he had passed in Holland, Prussia, Russia, France and England, as well as in Boston and Washington, since, as a boy, he had gone to school in Paris, in Amsterdam and Leyden, the charm of his life had been literature. Rising at four or five, lighting his fire and candle, reading his Bible first, with English, French and German commentaries, reading his Homer and his Latin authors, without whom he could not have endured existence, reading Evelyn's *Sylva* for his garden, reading all the new books on science, bent on his own improvement, bent on the improvement of his children before he undertook to improve his country, he had mastered Dutch and Russian as well as the tongues that other people knew. And the summit of his ambition was to write, to serve his country, at its feeblest point, by some enduring work of literature.

One work he was to write that served his country, the celebrated *Report on Weights and Measures.* But this was not the work he had in mind. Nor was the Pepysian Diary, incomparable in American letters, the living portrait of his wilful mind, with malice towards all, with charity for none, least of all himself. He had written a volume of *Letters on Silesia* that showed what gifts he had for observation. His *Lectures on Rhetoric and Oratory,* delivered at Harvard College in 1806, revealed his powers of organized reflection. He had heard the greatest orators of the previous age, Fox, Pitt and Burke, as well as their American contemporaries, and Harvard was prepared to hear the doctrine, sanctioned by Cicero and Demosthenes, that, while liberty was the parent of eloquence, eloquence was the stay of liberty. It was a doctrine that Harvard wished to hear, in an age when the art of the pulpit, the art of the forum, the art of the judge and the lawyer, soon to be followed by that of the lecture-platform,—all one art, in its several branches,—was the only literary art that performed a vital function; and Adams, with his experience and his learning, his gifts for perspicuity and order, was certainly the most competent instructor the college could have found. His lectures served as a textbook for the rising generation of public speakers.* But this was not the writing he had dreamed of, and dreamed of still, when, on a Christmas morning, he read Pope's *Messiah* to his household, or when he noted that an

---

* "When he read his first lectures in 1806, not only the students heard him with delight, but the hall was crowded by the professors and by unusual visitors. I remember when, long after, I entered college, hearing the story of the numbers of coaches in which his friends came from Boston to hear him. On his return in the winter to the Senate at Washington, he took such ground in the debates of the following session as to lose the sympathy of many of his constituents in Boston. When, on his return from Washington, he resumed his lectures in Cambridge, his class attended, but the coaches from Boston did not come."—Emerson, *Letters and Social Aims.*

actor's letter, asking for his analysis of *Othello,* pleased him more than all his political honours. Like his own grandson, Henry Adams, who, longing to think like Benvenuto, knew that his instinct was "blighted from babyhood," he longed to think and feel as Shakespeare felt, or as the Germans Wieland and Bürger felt, whom he had read so many years before, as far back as 1800, when he was living in Germany, the first of all Americans to do so. But his instinct also had been blighted by the long winter of Puritanism. The time had not yet come for New England poets.

The time had not yet come, but the time was coming, and Adams, in his pertinacity, represented the chill before the dawn. During those years in Germany, he had translated Wieland's *Oberon.* The poet, to whom his tutor sent the version, compared it with the English Sotheby's version. Adams's was more accurate, he said, but Sotheby's was more poetical. Alas, the more Adams had written since, the more he realized that, with poetry, there was a certain point that one might reach, by means of the virtues that New England knew, beyond which no vigils or vows would take one. But he was under a spell. What was he to do? Riding, walking, musing, he poured the verses forth, odes to Lucinda, Narcissa, Belinda, whose charms he could not refuse to acknowledge, translations of Juvenal's Satires, elegiac stanzas, versifications of La Fontaine's Fables, versions of the Psalms in rhyme, even a long poem, *Dermot McMorrogh,* a satire in the eighteenth-century mode that filled his mind for weeks and left him, at the end, like a pleasant dream, to dull and distressing realities. What could he do when the rhymes insisted on coming and he found he could sometimes hold in his mind fifty lines at once? Throw his poems behind the fire? Or suffer a few, at least, to appear in print? Certainly one of the greatest statesmen living, he was content to be known as one of the smallest poets of his country. Meanwhile, as a

searcher of the skies, who knew that there are many kinds
of stars and who liked to promote astronomy, he scanned
the horizon every day for other and better poets than
himself.

*

* *

Cambridge, across the Charles, was a quiet village, so
quiet that one could hear in Harvard Square the booming
of the guns in the navy-yard in Boston. One even heard
the murmur of the waves breaking on the far-away sea-
beaches. Cambridgeport was a huckleberry-pasture, with
a few wharves and houses. Thence the sloop "Harvard,"
moored to its dock, a Viking ship in the eyes of the village
boys, sailed once a year to the coast of Maine to bring
back wood for the college.

Through the port, as first through the village centre,
passed the white-topped wagons that brought to the Boston market the wares and products of the inland regions.
They filled the yards of the inns, the Porter House, for
one, beyond the village, and the shouts and oaths of the
teamsters rang through the tranquil air. Around the un-
garnished Common, where the dust and the snow blew
unchecked, a few old houses stood amid their ample gardens. One of them, a gambrel-roofed dwelling, General
Ward's headquarters in the Revolution, was the house of
the Reverend Abiel Holmes, the author of the *Annals of
America,* a work, sufficiently bald, that was yet the first
of its kind. The house next door was that of the Higginson
family. On Dana Hill stood the Dana mansion. The family
of Chief Justice Dana, the first American minister to Russia, had owned their Cambridge farm for six generations.
On Brattle Street stood the Craigie house, one of a line of
spacious Georgian villas that were known as Tory Row.
They had been built before the Revolution by opulent
loyalist families, who owned slave-plantations in the West
Indies. In the careless eighteenth-century days, the great

halls and chambers of these houses had echoed with the
sounds of music and dancing. "Elmwood" stood a mile or
so beyond, the last house in the row, formerly the home
of Elbridge Gerry. It had been occupied for several years
by the Reverend Charles Lowell and his household. Widespread lawns encircled these dwellings, covered with wine-
glass elms and willows, with orchards at the rear. The
windows of the Craigie house overlooked the placid meadows to the river Charles.

From these Cambridge windows peered,—one saw them
from the street,—the faces of aging women, now and
then with turbans on their heads and massive silver spectacles, eyes that had witnessed and remembered the passing of guns and troops in the Revolution. Mrs. Craigie's
head was often seen, as she sat at her parlour window.
Her house had been Washington's headquarters, in the
winter of '76, and there Mrs. Washington had come,
with a coach and servants in scarlet livery, to celebrate
her wedding-day. The late Mr. Craigie, the Boston merchant, had been famous for his entertainments; and
among his guests, in this house, had been Talleyrand *
and Queen Victoria's father. But the days of Queen Victoria had not arrived, nor the days of a Cambridge poet
who was to make the house more famous still. Mrs.
Craigie, once a well-known beauty, a widow now, much
reduced in fortune, even to the point of taking lodgers,
spent her days reading her favourite authors, Voltaire and
the British reviewers. Her house was well-stocked with
books, like all the other liberal Cambridge houses. Hume,
Addison, Gibbon, Swift stood on every shelf, along with
Milton and *Evelina,* Richardson, perhaps a polyglot
Bible, Casaubon's Polybius, two or three Elzevirs. The
library of the Reverend Charles Lowell, who had a
church in Boston, numbered nearly four thousand volumes.

* Of whom Miss Mary Moody Emerson said, "I fear he is not organized
for a future state."

Mr. Lowell had exiled to the attic the old prints that had filled his grandfather's study, heads of the ancient wise men, Plato, Pythagoras, Socrates, Cicero, Seneca; for, without thinking less of the ancients, he thought more of the moderns. He had studied his theology in Scotland and had visited Southey and Wordsworth, the new English poets, whose work he enjoyed discussing; and facing his chair in the dining-room hung a portrait of Wilberforce, the symbol of his humanitarian interests. The Reverend Mr. Holmes, who also made the most of the art of living, had yet maintained the ancient faith. Indeed, he was deposed for doing so, although he was only mildly Orthodox, for the Cambridge people were Unitarians. They had settled this great question for good and all, along with the Boston people. They were Unitarians as they were Whigs. Here and there one found a Calvinist, as here and there one found a Democrat, like Mr. Timothy Fuller of Cambridgeport. But one had to be a personage, a Member of Congress or a magistrate, a man who could afford his coach and pair, to carry off these odious opinions. The Cambridge people knew what they believed, and they did not propose to discuss it. But Mr. Holmes had literary compensations. His house overflowed with books. Amid the lumber in the attic, one found Erasmus's *Colloquies* and queer old Latin works on alchemy. Sometimes, in the evening, Mr. and Mrs. Holmes and their sons and daughters gathered about the London-made piano, and one of the daughters, who was the family minstrel, sang the *Irish Melodies* of Thomas Moore.

All of these ampler houses, those of the ministerial and legal families, and some of the merchant families, abounded in family portraits. They were the work of so many journeyman painters, at ten, twenty or forty dollars a head, that they represented only a decent regard for fathers and mothers who would have thought themselves passing rich on a thousand dollars a year. If one

had a Copley or a Stuart, one had the right to lift one's
chin a little. On the shelves of the closets lay bundles of
mint and catnip, lavender, sweet-marjoram, pennyroyal.
Apples were stored there, and peaches spread their fragrance on the darkness, as if waiting to inspire strains and
strophes. For little boys were growing up in Cambridge
who were to be known as "household poets," and often
as something better. Their parents even wished them to
be poets. The Cambridge fathers and mothers were not
poetic, but they respected poetry. Their gardens were
full of marigolds, hollyhocks, larkspurs, with the humbler
vegetables of the working kind, carrots, parsnips, beets,—
as if to remind the sons of the Revolution that classes
were provisional in republics, that a deserving carrot was
better than an undeserving lupin, that hollyhocks were
only hollyhocks when they were plucky enough to withstand the wind, each on its own stalk (which made them
pleasing vegetables indeed), and that the man who had
the family portraits must always prove himself on other
grounds. One of the "household poets" * was to make
this clear. The Cambridge flowers had a moral meaning,
as good New England flowers ought to have; but they
had a poetical meaning that was even more apparent. So
did the sounds one heard on summer evenings, the bells
of the cows ambling home at twilight, the lullaby of the
crickets in early autumn, the hymns of the frogs, in
spring, in some neighbouring swamp, not to speak of the
creaking of the winter wood-sleds, dragging their loads
of walnut over the complaining snow. Every sound and
odour had its value. One heard the carpenter smoothing
his knotty boards, and the whips of the four-horse
coaches rattling by; one heard the ticks in the joints of
the old bedsteads; one smelt the salt of the sea in the
summer breeze. What a store of allusions and similes,
drawn from the homely facts of his daily living, a Cam-

* Oliver Wendell Holmes.

bridge boy might pack into his poems! When it came to associations and recollections, such as all New England boys shared in common, buried under the leaves of many summers, the Cambridge boys who were to write their poems were to understand the meaning of Byron's line about "striking the electric chain."

In Cambridge, other facts pressed themselves upon one's attention. There was the village church-yard, where one puzzled over the Latin inscriptions on the grave-stones of old theologians and presidents of the college, the diamond-shaped cavities in the stones from which the leaden escutcheons had been removed to be used for bullets in the Revolution, the graves of ancient scholars, with virtues ending in *issimus* and *errimus*. One somehow acquired the sense that learning was a very distinguished object, which made the scholar a natural leader of men. The spot where Washington took command of the army was near the spot where President Langdon of Harvard had offered prayers, before the assembled troops, and sped them on their way to Bunker Hill. Learning might indeed be quaint and queer, as, for instance, with those living tutors who had so steeped themselves in Latin that their English was a foreign babble, men who said "in-tramural aestivation" when what they meant was town-life in summer, men who might have written a poem begin-ning—

> In candent ire the solar splendour flames;
> The foles, languescent, pend from arid rames.*

But all the New England statesmen were also scholars, and most of them had come to nurse in Cambridge. There had been set up, in the year the town received its name, the first printing-press in the commonwealth, brought from England in 1638, the press that had produced for two-

* Holmes.

score years all the printing in the colonies, including
Eliot's Bible and the *Freeman's Oath.* Learning was immemorial in Cambridge. Learning was omnipresent. In
a population wholly derived from England, one counted
the foreigners on a single hand: two Scotch gardeners,
a hair-cutter of nebulous antecedents, one Irishman, the
master of a spade. And the Irishman knew his Latin,
like everyone else: he had learned his Horace at a hedge-
school and was always ready to lean on his spade and
test a boy's knowledge of the *Quo me, Bacche.* The shop-
keepers around the square added tags of Latin to their
signs. The janitor of the newly-established Law School
was a notable spouter of Virgil. The height of wit in all
the Cambridge circles was a thoroughly sound Latin-
English pun.

The schoolmasters in Cambridge, as in Boston, were
cut on the ancient pattern. They drove the boys with
switch and ferule, and even drove the girls, all the more
when the boys and girls were children of the learned
families; for everyone in Cambridge was precocious, and
only a dunce could fail to be ready for college at fourteen
or fifteen. The best-known school, soon to be opened, for
Greek and Latin only, was that of William Wells, an
Englishman. It was he who had published in Boston the
Cicero in twenty volumes. He had also edited Tacitus.
His school was a Gehenna of blood and tears.* At Cambridgeport, there was another school where, in the process
of flogging the Latin in, and pulling the boys about by the
ears, the master almost pulled their ears off. One of the
little Dana boys, the grandson of the old Chief Justice,
never forgot how his ear had felt. He had his mind made
up in regard to floggers, especially when he sailed before
the mast and saw the sailors flogged; and in days to come
he was to speak his mind. But the boys had pleasures,

---

* "My dears, it was hell," said Charles C. Perkins, the art-critic of later
days.

too. They pitched hay with the hired men, and even with their fathers, on occasion. They knew all the trees by their bark and leaves, and all the birds by their notes and manner of flying. They scoured the country in search of flowers and insects; they fished for pouts and waded for water-lilies; they searched for powder-mills and old redoubts, left from the Revolution. They lay and chattered on the grassy slopes and fought the battles over again. They haunted the Boston wharves, redolent of the ocean and swarming with ear-ringed seamen. Moreover, they had their parties with the Cambridge girls. Strangers who came from less heroic regions sometimes found these parties a little chilly. One of them said that, during the quadrille, his partner touched his hand as if she were feeling for cucumbers in the dark.

Harvard College was the heart of Cambridge. Seven generations before, every New England household had given the college twelvepence, or a peck of corn, or its value in unadulterated wampum peag. But those were the good old days when the Orthodox faith reigned in every mind. Established now on a Unitarian basis,—for the founding of the Divinity School, with Dr. Henry Ware as its chief professor, settled the character of the new regime,—the college was considered, in the country districts, dangerously lax and liberal. West of Worcester, and up the Connecticut Valley, the clergy, Calvinist almost to a man, united in condemning the Cambridge collegians, in the very words of Whitefield, as "close Pharisees, resting on head knowledge,"—the same collegians who had called Whitefield "low." But as for this "head knowledge," no one denied that they possessed it. More than a few of the Orthodox admitted that it was what collegians ought to possess. Harvard still had an exalted prestige. The patrician families of Boston and Cambridge regarded it as more than a family affair. It was a family responsibility. They sent their sons to the

college, as a matter of course. But they considered it a
public duty, not only to endow and foster it, in the interests of the meritorious poor, but to maintain its standards
and oversee it. They founded chairs that bore their
names, the Boylston chair, the Eliot chair, the Smith
professorship.* They watched and brooded over its progress and welfare. Who would have respected wealth in
Boston if wealth had not, in turn, respected learning?
And, if the professors' salaries were very small, everyone knew they were partly paid in honour.

It was true that the standard of learning was not too
lofty. In this, as in certain other respects, the well-known
"Harvard indifference" resembled that of Oxford and
Madrid. Intellectual things took second place. The object
of study was to form the mind, but this was to form the
character; and Massachusetts knew what its character
was and took a certain satisfaction in it. Everyone was
aware of the best Boston and Cambridge type, the type
that Josiah Quincy represented, or the late Chief Justice
Dana, formed on the classic models. A clear, distinct
mentality, a strong distaste for nonsense, steady composure, a calm and gentle demeanour, stability, good principles, intelligence, a habit of under-statement,† a slow
and cautious way of reasoning, contempt for extravagance, vanity and affectation, kindness of heart, purity,
decorum, profound affections, filial and paternal. A noble
type, severely limited, which Boston celebrated in its
marble busts. Comparing it, trait for trait, with half of
Plutarch's characters, one might have felt that Boston

---

* The Boylston chair has been held, among others, by John Quincy
Adams, Edward Tyrrel Channing and Charles Townsend Copeland. The
line of the Smith professors is as follows: George Ticknor, Longfellow,
Lowell, Bliss Perry. Of Adams, Emerson says: "I have heard that no man
could read the Bible with such powerful effect." (*Letters and Social Aims.*)
This has been a distinction also of Adams's successor, Mr. Copeland.

† See Jonathan Phillips's remark about his saintly friend, Dr. Channing:
"I have known him long, I have studied his character, and I believe him
capable of virtue."

deserved its busts. Moreover, beneath its cold and tranquil surface, burned, though the fires were low, the passions and convictions of the Revolution, ready to flame
forth on a fresh occasion. But would the occasion ever
recur? That was what a stranger might have asked, face
to face with the marble busts. The surface, at least,
seemed somewhat tame, suited for the merchant and the
lawyer, and the man of God after the Boston fashion.

This was the type, and almost the only type, the curriculum of Harvard contemplated. Whatever studies favoured its formation, whatever were the best ways to
form it, these were the ways and the studies that Harvard
knew. Whatever studies did not favour it, or favoured the
formation of other types that Boston did not like or had
never heard of, these were no concern of Harvard, or
its concern only to oppose them. Josiah Quincy was not
enthusiastic. Why should Harvard be? Mr. Dana was
eminently decorous. He had caused the arrest, for contempt of court, of a butcher who, appearing at the bar,
had left his coat behind him. Decorum was a Harvard
characteristic.* Neither Mr. Quincy nor Mr. Dana cared
a button for the German language, which had been spoken
by the Hessian troops, a half-barbarous tribe of Europeans who had been hired out to the British king. German, from the point of view of Harvard, always excepting John Quincy Adams, who, as everyone knew, was a
little queer,†—German was an outlandish dialect; and,
while it was not improper to speak French, the language
of Lafayette, which it was quite improper not to know,
more than a few felt that Bonaparte had destroyed its

* In time, it even became, with Irving Babbitt, one of the many Harvard
religions.
† Concerning the Adams family, the popular view remained unchanged
for four generations. "I think them all . . . exhibiting a combination of
talent and good moral character with passions and prejudices, etc. . . .
that would puzzle La Bruyère to describe and which has no prototype in
Shakespeare or Molière."—Harrison Gray Otis on Charles Francis Adams
the first.

respectability. Greek was esteemed as the tongue of a group of ancient republics that possessed some of the virtues of New England. Greece had produced a number of orators who were more eloquent even than Samuel Adams. Search as one might, however, in Massachusetts, one could not find a play of Euripides; besides, compared with Latin, which everyone drank in with his mother's milk, Greek was a little dubious. The Roman word "convivium" meant "living together." "Symposium" had a similar sense in Greek, but what did "symposium" imply? "Drinking together." Was not this alone enough to prove that the Romans were more respectable than the Greeks? Cicero had made the point, and everyone knew that Cicero must be right.

These were the days of the genial President Kirkland, who, after conducting an examination, regaled the boys with a fine dish of pears. He was an easy-going man, a Unitarian minister, like most of the professors, sympathetic and of the gentlest temper, naturally frank and cordial, with all the delicate feeling for human behaviour that characterized the best New Englanders. It was said that he threw his sermons into a barrel, as the farmers threw their corn into the silo, and that on Sunday morning he fished out enough for a discourse and patched the leaves together. The story had a symbolic truth, at least. It signified the president's "Harvard indifference," which was accompanied by the best intentions and a notably warm heart. He never took the narrow view. Hearing that the flip at the Porter House had proved to be too attractive to the students, he dropped in to see the proprietor. "And so, Mr. Porter," he said, "the young gentlemen come to drink your flip, do they?"—"Yes, sir," said Mr. Porter, "sometimes."—"Well, I should think they would," the president said. "Good day, Mr. Porter." Any sort of illumination, physical or spiritual, might have taken place under his eye. He was kind to the rich young men whose fathers, at their graduation, gave them dinners in a great marquee, with five hundred guests and dancing in the Yard. He was kinder to the poor young men whose black coats were turning green. He was not a man to oppose any important change in the system of studies; and before the end of his long reign, in fact, certain changes were to occur that were eventually to transform the college. But he could not see why changes should occur. He thought the old ways were good enough, and he played into the hands of firmer men who thought that all other ways were bad. Four hours a day for study and recitation were quite enough for anyone. A library of twenty thousand books was certainly large enough. In fact, the Harvard library was a wonder. No other American library was larger, except perhaps one. A young man with literary tastes could find Hakluyt's *Voyages* there, Cotton's Montaigne and Dodsley's *Old Plays,* as well as the books that he ought to have at home; and the window-sills were broad enough to sit on, if he was too fidgety to keep his chair. What more, in reason, could one ask for? For the rest, the teaching consisted of recitations. No nonsense on the part of the professors, no lectures, no unnecessary comments, no flowery illustrations. One ground in one's Latin and mathematics, under a pair of candles, and the next day one ground them out again. Professors were not nurses, neither were they dancing-masters. One did not go to Harvard to stimulate a dubious fancy. One went to learn to deserve a marble bust.

A few imaginative persons had their doubts. The college was dying of antiquated notions,—so, at least, they thought. Twenty years before, one of the students, who was known later as a writer,* had printed certain strictures on the college. He had called it "the death-bed of genius." How many immortals, he asked, had Harvard educated?—and how could it expect to produce immor-

* William Austin, author of *Peter Rugg, the Missing Man.*

tals? The delicate muse of belles-lettres could never be induced to visit Harvard. "No, she would recoil at the sight of our walls." And very properly, the professors thought. The college was not for ladies, neither was it meant for men of genius, or any other sort of extravagant creature. For a thorough Boston lawyer, a merchant who desired a well-trained mind, a minister who did not indulge in raptures, Harvard had proved to be an adequate nest. It fostered polite, if not beautiful letters, it sent one back to Plutarch for one's models, it sharpened the reasoning faculties, it settled one's grounds for accepting a Christian faith that always knew where to draw the line.

In short, the college was a little realm as fixed and final as a checker-board. The squares of the various studies were plainly marked, with straight lines and indisputable corners. All one had to do was to play the game. Dr. Popkin, "Pop," was Professor of Greek. Over his cocked hat he carried a circular canopy that Cambridge learned to know as an umbrella. The doctor was a sound grammarian. He found his poetry in the Greek roots; he did not need to seek it in the flowers. A second umbrella appeared in the Cambridge streets, in the hands of Professor Hedge, who had written a famous *Logic*. He had spent seventeen years composing this work, with the aid of the other members of his household. No Logic could have been better, and he hoped his students would learn it word for word. For logic was important. Unless one knew logic, one could not read Locke; and who that had not read Locke could ever be certain that his Christian faith had a solid bottom? Logic was the Golden Calf of Cambridge, the muse of Theology, the muse of Law. For Hebrew, one went to Professor Willard; for Latin, to Brazer or Otis; for Natural Religion, to Professor Frisbie, whose taste for the ethically severe was modified by his love of graceful ease. He enjoyed Maria Edgeworth as well as the rigours of Tacitus. Dr. Ware presided over

Divinity. Dr. Ware's favourite phrase was "on the one hand, on the other hand." He knew he possessed the truth, but he did not wish to slight its minor aspects. He was famous for the accuracy of his definitions. No one could distinguish better than he between "genuineness" and "authenticity"; and, although he had nineteen children, he never used the rod. He punished infractions of the household law by the hydropathic treatment.

Towering modestly over the other professors, Andrews Norton symbolized the *zeitgeist,* a word that he would have deprecated. It savoured of those antic tricks which the young men were beginning to play with language (or were so soon to begin to play),—German barbarisms, exclamations, inversions, coarse and violent metaphors, innovations which, to Mr. Norton, seemed both *outré* and *bizarre,* much as he disliked to use two foreign words in a single sentence. His own greatest days had not arrived, but Cambridge was prepared for his fortunate marriage. The heir of John Norton, who had proclaimed his line a "royal priesthood," not himself ordained, was yet a potent theologian, the Dexter Professor of Sacred Literature. He was more than a match for the daughter of a Boston merchant who kept a variety-store on Dock Square and who, after sending his son to Europe, to make the grand tour in his own carriage, wished his daughter to live in becoming style. Mr. Norton's father-in-law purchased "Shady Hill" for the promising couple, made a gentleman's house of it and bought the fifty acres of "Norton's Woods," as the domain was henceforth to be called, an elegant park, unrivalled in homely Cambridge, where, in time, were to blossom, along with little Charles Eliot Norton, the handsome daughters whom the college knew as the "Evidences of Christianity," a reference to their father's famous book. "Shady Hill" was to have a notable history long after its first lord, the "Unitarian Pope," as Carlyle was to call him, who, for a generation, was to fight, on behalf of Harvard and common sense, against the Germanizing radicals, the Transcendentalists and their noxious crew, metaphysicians of the wilder sort, —long after the great Andrews Norton had laid his cold head in the colder tomb.

These days were still remote. Professor Norton was not married yet. He was not yet the "tyrant of the Cambridge Parnassus," nor was there an Emerson to call him so. He had not yet edited Mrs. Hemans, although he had written his own devotional poems. He had not visited his English readers; nor had he produced his commanding work, the *Evidences of the Genuineness of the Gospels,* which proved, to the satisfaction of honest men,— whatever the Germans might say, in their so-called higher criticism,—that Matthew, Mark, Luke and John had really written the books that bore their names, a demonstration as clear as Hedge's *Logic.* The four great volumes were still unborn, but Mr. Norton had won his spurs already. His head was long, his head was firm, his mind never wavered or misgave him. In Cambridge, *chiaroscuro,* a word unknown, would have been thought to savour of corruption; and the man who had put the Calvinists to rout, by sheer force of reasoning, was not the man to be upset by any other appeal to the vulgar "feelings," that of the pantheist Schleiermacher, for instance, with his notion that the verities of religion rested, not on the letter of the Scriptures, but on "the soul's sense of things divine." Odious phrase, how German! Mr. Norton's lectures had spread his fame. There was not a lawyer in Boston or Cambridge who could find a crack in his chain of logic. No one could prove that he was mistaken; and, inasmuch as a lawyer-proof religion was exactly what Boston wished for, Mr. Norton's eminence was uncontested. Was he a little petulant and vain? That was beside the point. And if he was called a Pharisee by certain ill-bred persons, that was wholly a matter of definition. Mr. Norton, like Professor Ware, was a master of definition. He was benevolent, he was conscientious. Moreover, he was the only professor,—or he was soon to be,—who had his private carriage. One saw it every Sunday, drawn up beside the president's carriage at the entrance of the college chapel.

Such was Harvard College, as it might have appeared in the eyes of a travelling Persian. It resembled Paley's watch. One found the watch on the seashore and instantly inferred that some intelligent mind must have designed it. One found Harvard College in the village of Cambridge: the evidences of design were also there, the wheels and all the parts in perfect order. The mainspring was useful common sense, based on a thrifty view of Christian ethics; and, if it resembled the watch in other ways, if it was small, cold and mechanical, was it more mechanical than Oxford, where they also put the Apostles in the witness-box and drowsed over their bottles of port? Oxford was torpid also, droning along in its eighteenth-century grooves, waiting for its great awakening. Harvard was only a more provincial Oxford, as the travelling Persian would have seen at once. A sympathetic stranger, an aspiring student, especially one who had been born in Cambridge, would have seen it in a rosier light. The Cambridge boy would have known the "Cambridge elm," with its suggestions of the Revolution, the old houses with their charming customs, the gracious lawns, the birds, the luxuriant flowers, stuff for a dozen poets, especially when the naturalist Thomas Nuttall became curator of the Botanic Garden and wrote his books on birds and plants, drawn largely from observations of the local scene. The Cambridge folk were intelligent and kind; and, if it was one of their foibles to put other people in their places, this was an indication, after all, that other people's places were not Cambridge. They were serious, devout, cultivated, stable. They were not given to excesses, even

on the side of righteousness. The "ministers' sons" who
became proverbial were the sons of the brimstone God
of the inland regions. The ministers' sons of Cambridge
never knew repression and therefore had no wild oats to
sow. Neither in its action nor in its reaction was the
Cambridge mind marked by a waste of force. Its only
danger was a certain smugness. Its only excess was an
excess of caution.

Harvard, moreover, was on the brink of change. Woe
to the student, woe to the youthful tutor who counted
overmuch on the signs of the times, who interlarded his
speech with foreign phrases, sported embroidered waistcoats or even thought that modern languages ought to be
included in the course of studies. Harvard was intellectually sound, and the sound intellect makes its changes
slowly. But the changes were plainly imminent. President
Kirkland might have been indifferent, but he was also
liberal in temper. The ethics that Professor Frisbie
taught might have been cold and dry, but the warmth with
which he taught it,—he was a poet himself, in a modest
way,—gave his pupils an impulse to study ethics instead
of accepting it on authority. The Harvard philosophy was
not exciting,—Locke, Paley, Reid,—but one became excited over it. One acquired a taste for philosophy. One
acquired a sceptical attitude that opened the way for
other points of view. Even Andrews Norton promoted
this sceptical attitude. He had no sympathy with the new
ideas that were dawning in people's minds, but he had demolished the old ideas. One could not, after hearing Mr.
Norton, revert to the Calvinist view; and if one had disposed of Nortonism, to one's own satisfaction, at least,
one was obliged to go forward to something else. And
Mr. Norton's positive tone aroused the desire for combat
in his pupils. They learned to fight, in the world of the
mind. Their intellectual life was filled with zest.

In a word, the students learned to think. Moreover,

they learned to write. Whatever might have been said of
the Harvard professors, their taste could not have been
impugned. Their taste was as refined as their ethical instincts. Their standards were severe. Their students might
have certain limitations, but certain others they could
hardly have. Their style was almost sure to be marked by
grace and, as often as not, by force. Their scholarship
was sure to be exacting, especially when Edward Tyrrel
Channing, the younger brother of Dr. Channing, became
professor of Rhetoric,—two years after the birth of a
Concord boy, Henry Thoreau by name, who was to acknowledge, in later years, that he had learned to write as
Channing's pupil. In fact, the whole New England "renaissance" was to spring so largely from Channing's pupils,
Emerson, Holmes, Dana, Motley, Parkman, to name only
a few, that the question might have been asked, Did
Channing cause it?—

> Channing, with his bland, superior look,
> Cold as a moonbeam on a frozen brook,
> While the pale student, shivering in his shoes,
> Sees from his theme the turgid rhetoric ooze.*

That the rhetoric oozed from his pupils' themes, under
his bland eye,—that is to say, the "turgid" rhetoric,—
was one of the secrets of his influence; for turgid rhetoric
was the bane of letters in the days of the Boston orators,
the orators whom every boy adored. He had a remorseless
eye for the high-falutin, the swelling period, the em-
phatic word, morbid tissue to this ruthless surgeon whose
Puritan instincts had been clarified by a sensible classical
culture. None of his pupils grew the sort of feathers that
required the ministrations of Artemus Ward.

One of these pupils † kept his college themes, and a

* Holmes.
† Thoreau.

list of some of the subjects that Channing set might go
as far as any other fact to explain why his pupils were to
go so far. Bearing in mind the careers of his pupils, poets,
historians, essayists or whatever, one asks oneself what
must have been the effect, on adolescent minds, prepared
and eager, of questions like the following,—on which
they were obliged to write, and to write with perspicuity,
whether they shivered in their shoes or not: on keeping
a private journal, the anxieties and delights of a discov-
erer, the cultivation of the imagination, the pleasures and
privileges of a literary man, the duty and dangers of conformity, the superior and the common man. These were
the subjects that Channing discussed and urged his little
classes to discuss, these and the topics of his brilliant
*Lectures,** a writer's preparation, a writer's habits, permanent literary fame. The literary life, as he described
it, seemed very important and very exciting. Moreover,
he spoke of its problems in a way that brought it home
to the rising generation. He referred to the confident freedom of thought and style that comes from a writer's
pride in his own people and gives him a fine "bravery and
indifference to foreign doubts and censure." He showed
how the world in general values most the writers who
bear the unmistakable stamp, the pungency and native
sincerity, of their own time and place. The early Roman
writers—like the American writers of the past—depended
on foreign examples and supplies. In Rome, at least, this
question had found an answer in the praise the Romans
bestowed upon their writers for turning home at last for
their themes and their style.

Judging by the fruits of his instruction, one might
almost say that Channing sowed more of the seeds that
make a man of letters—when the seeds fall on a fortunate
soil—than all the other teachers of composition and all
the writers of ingenious text-books that have ever taught

* Edited by Richard Henry Dana, author of *Two Years Before the Mast.*

a much-taught country. A Harvard student of his generation had certain advantages of an inward kind that were not likely to be soon repeated. One of them was that, reading Plutarch, in this sympathetic atmosphere, he might have understood Cicero's youth,—how, consulting the Delphic oracle, he listened to the pythoness who advised him not to regard the opinion of other people, but to make his own genius the guide of his life.

CHAPTER III

THE COAST AND THE HINTERLAND

IN EVERY corner of this New England country, where the ways of the eighteenth century lingered on, a fresh and more vigorous spirit was plainly astir. On the granite ledges of New Hampshire, along the Merrimac River, in Essex and Middlesex counties, where the spindles whirred, or westward, on the lovely Housatonic, life was filled with a kind of electric excitement. The air resounded with the saw and hammer, the blows of the forge, the bells in the factory-towers. In all directions the people were building turnpikes, hundreds of miles of straight lines that cut athwart the old winding roads. The Green Mountain boys had erected their State House. Dwellings were going up in clearings and meadows, or, being up, were carted bodily off to better sites. Churches grew like snowdrops in early March. Villages, towns sprang from the fields. A current of ambition had galvanized New England. The "era of good feeling" was on its way.

As yet there were no signs of a similar movement in the intellectual life of this buzzing region. No poets, no historians had arisen, none or few, feeble as they were few, to celebrate and record men's thoughts and feelings. The mind of the country, torn, since the Revolution, with other anxieties and preoccupations, was tired and too busy with the present. It had no use for its own imagination. The ways of the folk, the deeds of the past, of the notable sires and grandsires of New England, if

surely not unhonoured, were unsung. The seaports, like
the inland villages, bristled with their legendary lore,
tales of the wars, tales of Indian fights, of painted Indian
faces at the farmhouse window, of the war-dance, the
pow-wow and the forest, of great snows in which men
had lost their lives, of haunted bridges, buccaneers and
redcoats, of Yankee maidens and their Tory lovers, of
shipwrecks and battles,—themes for a New England
Scott or Byron. One heard of the "screeching woman" of
Marblehead. One heard of "witches' hollows," groves of
beech and hemlock, where the Indians had held their
demon-worship and burning crosses appeared in a greenish light. There were popular ballads and folk-songs,—
"Skipper Ireson's Ride," for one,—sailors' chanties
along the coast, ballads of village murders, rockaby
songs, sugar-makers' songs, sung by weavers and carpenters, by farm-wives and wandering fiddlers, by hunters,
trappers, guides and lumbermen, snatches and refrains
and longer pieces, brought from the old world or natural outgrowths of the American soil. But the rhymesters,
for there were plenty of these,—the rural colleges and
academies were turning them out in hundreds,—the
rhymesters, unmindful of Burns, whom they imitated, ignored these rude materials of their art, as they were
unaware of the greater themes the history of their country offered them.

They felt, these rhymesters, one and all, as later writers felt,—as Hawthorne was to feel, in his earlier days,
—that the American scene was too prosaic. How could
one write poems and romances about a world that seemed
so spick-and-span?—a country that had no shadow, no
picturesqueness, no mystery, no pageantry of the past,
none of those romantic associations that gathered like
moss about every roof and tree, about every hill and
valley of the older countries? A land where everything
sprawled on the same dull level, in the broad, simple,

garish light of day? It required a vision that no one as
yet possessed to detect the stores of poetic interest that
lay beneath this commonplace appearance. Among these
living poetasters, whose style and tone were so flat and
thin, whose only thought was to follow the current fashion, or who were busy translating Horace's Odes, or giving new twists to the Psalms, there was not one who had
the diviner's eye. But for two hundred years the New
England people had been actively working their minds.
They had been striving to educate themselves, thinking,
brooding, keeping their journals, reading their Bibles,
their classics, their books of sermons; and all this life
was preparing to bear its fruit. In the country schools, no
doubt, in the grammar schools, even in Boston, Cambridge and New Haven, the masters droned along in
their ancient ruts. No business of theirs to produce Vir-
gils and Livys! They made the scholars spell aloud in
chorus. One learned, at the rod's end, the longest words
in the language, learned them to the last sad syllable, a
method which, if it failed to rouse one's mind, taught one
that every error meant a rap. One saw the schoolmarm,
with her willow switch, pinning the boys and girls to her
terrible apron, when they were restless and unruly. One
found, in many a village, the methods of some old
"Ma'am Betty," who kept school in her bedroom and
chewed tobacco and drank from the nose of her tea-
kettle. But other, more promising methods were rapidly
growing, in the Latin schools about the capital, as well as
in the towns along the seaboard.

At Newport, Salem, Portsmouth, where the great
square mansions faced the sea or lined the stately streets,
with their beautiful gardens, cultivated by Scotch and
Irish gardeners, there were notable scholars in charge of
the young, Harvard men or Englishmen, French tutors,
Italian dancing-masters, the dim dawn of a cosmopolitan
culture. There were public reading-rooms in Newport

and Portsmouth. Salem, like Boston, had its Athenæum
and a Philosophical Library, one of the prizes of the late
war, second to that of Philadelphia. In Portland, in the
cultivated circles, where many spoke French and a few
Italian, they were beginning to criticize Dr. Johnson,
whom no one had ever criticized before and who had
been so unjust to the poet Gray. Music, so long the symbol of the ne'er-do-well, began to be heard on summer
nights. The strains of the harp and the flute had ceased
to suggest the danger of a drunkard's grave. Here and
there some carver of figureheads, or of pumpheads and
wooden urns for gate-posts, some young whittler, fired by
a book on Rome, which he had found in the reading-
room, dreamed of a sculptor's life. If he could carve
these eagles for McIntire doorways, these heads of
Galen for the apothecaries, why should he not create a
marble group that would fill the portico of the county
court-house?

In all these bustling ports, or ports that had recently
bustled, where the forests of masts rose at the wharves
and Portuguese sailors sauntered through the streets, the
wide world was omnipresent. Everyone talked about voyages "up the Straits," or to Hong Kong and Calcutta,
towns that seemed closer to Salem or Portsmouth than
Hartford or New York had ever seemed. The lofty
chambers of the great dwellings, hung with French or
English tapestry, adorned with arches and columns and
carved Italian mantel-pieces, were papered with bold designs, brilliantly coloured birds and tropical flowers and
scenes from the Mediterranean lands. The massive bedsteads in the upper rooms were draped with curious curtains of India linen, covered with quaint pagodas and
figures in turbans. Canton shawls and Smyrna silks were
as common as linsey-woolsey. There were parrots and
pet monkeys in half the houses. The children played with
cocoanuts and coral and spent their pennies for tama-

rinds and ginger, or spent their Russian kopeks and their British coppers, which circulated as freely as American coins. The men wore Chinese gowns at the Salem assemblies, and the horn-pipe was taught in the dancing-schools. At the great merchants' houses there were formal parties, where the heads of the Federal government came to dine, with ambassadors from the European countries. One of the Salem magnates of the previous decade was the largest shipowner in the world.

All these towns abounded in interesting persons, sometimes droll and quaint, often witty, almost always learned. At Salem, the most imposing of the seaports, dwelt a circle of distinguished men who were to leave their mark in American history. One of them was Joseph Story, already Mr. Justice Story, who wrote for the *Monthly Anthology* in Boston. Judge William Prescott was another, the son of the old hero of Bunker Hill, who lived on his farm at Pepperell. Both these worthies were men of renown and both the fathers of sons who were famous later. Another was John Pickering, the son of Timothy Pickering, who had learned Arabic in his youth, while travelling with his father, and had mastered twenty other tongues. He had refused, as a busy lawyer, the chairs of Greek and Hebrew at Harvard and was at work on a philological project, for the spelling of the American Indian tongues, that was to lead to a world-wide movement for the study of all the primitive languages.* Presently, Rufus Choate joined the circle, the great Boston orator of the future, a weirdly exotic creature in appearance who might have come over in one of the ships from Java. All the members of this Salem group,—like Daniel Webster of Portsmouth, Choate's more famous fellow-orator, who had already made his mark in Congress,—were soon to move to Boston, as the

* John Pickering, the first president of the American Oriental Society, was the author, among other works, of a pioneer book on Americanisms.

fortunes of Salem waned and the capital spread its tentacles through New England.

So was the most illustrious of the Salem worthies, the great mathematician, Nathaniel Bowditch, the author of *The Practical Navigator,* a little, nimble man with burning eyes, with silky hair prematurely white, who darted about, rubbing his hands with excitement. This second Benjamin Franklin, the son of a poor cooper and mechanic, who had learned his Latin as a boy in order to read Newton's *Principia*—in which he found an error—had found eight thousand errors in the best English book on navigation. The book he had written himself, the *Navigator,* had saved countless lives and made the American ships the swiftest that had ever sailed. Everyone knew that, as a supercargo, bound for Sumatra and Manila, Bowditch had mastered astronomy so well—between the stars that he watched from the deck and the books he carried with him in his berth—that he was able to revise Laplace. Everyone knew how, on a Christmas night, in the midst of a blinding snow-storm, when he was captain of his own ship and there was not a landmark to be seen, Bowditch had sailed straight to his Salem wharf, as if it had been a sunny day in June. He had taught all his sailors navigation, and every one of them became a captain. And what a work was this *Practical Navigator,* a work that was still to be in active use a century after his death. The literary circles in Boston and Cambridge blushed over the taunts of the British reviewers, the clever men in London who were always asking, "Who reads an American book?" They felt so helplessly mortified. But here was an American book that every British seaman had to read if he hoped to get ahead of the Yankee skippers. It was a classic in its realm, as stoutly built as one of the clipper-ships for which Dr. Bowditch had prepared the way. If the Yankee mind could produce a work like this, what could not the Yankee mind produce when it turned its faculties in other directions? Even here in Salem, where the Prescotts lived, where a little boy, also called Nathaniel, the son of another skipper, was reading his *Pilgrim's Progress.*

In all these centres of the seaboard life, there had arisen a buffer generation that lay between the hard old Puritan ways and the minds of the younger people. Alive itself to literature and thought, prosperous, interested in a larger world, creative, though only, or mainly, in practical spheres, it was a kind of *cordon sanitaire* against the repressive habits of the past. The lawyers, merchants, ministers and scholars who formed the society of these towns preserved the faith in discipline and standards that had marked the older culture, and yet they encouraged in their sons and daughters a free mind, a knowledge of mundane things, the study of languages, music, drawing, dancing, an education of the eye and ear which, from the point of view of the inland regions, savoured of the frankest paganism. The Unitarian cause had won the day all along the sea-line. The leading families professed the "Boston religion." Their intercourse with other lands and peoples had mollified their mental habits; indeed, almost as much as their wide-flung commerce, a little good Madeira softened the old rigidities. They smiled at the faith of their forbears, when they were not shocked by its consequences. For which of them had not seen, in some neighbouring farmhouse, or even in one of the mansions or beside the wharves, some poor crazy woman, chained to a bed, or held by a staple in the floor, driven mad by some hysterical sermon about some unpardonable sin? Wherever one turned, in these prosperous ports, far more in the towns of the hinterland, one seemed to encounter simpletons, and worse, idiots and harmless lunatics, freely walking about, as if the supply of chains were insufficient; and the young people drew their own conclusions. They respected the old ways and the old religion. But they felt there was something unwholesome in this life from which their own minds had been liberated.

For among the younger folk of all these towns, on the sunny side of this buffer generation, these lawyers and merchants and scholars and experienced skippers, there were boys, growing up in dozens, who were to thrive on these new influences. Newport was already reaping its harvest, for there the Channing family lived. William Ellery Channing, the Boston preacher, had spent half the hours of his childhood wandering about the beach and the towering rocks, listening to the music of the waves, with the wide ocean before him, filled with a sense of awe and rapture; and there he spent all his vacations now, in the house surrounded by the charming garden, which had been laid out by the son of Gilpin, the famous writer on the picturesque. At Newport, on winter days, the air was soft and springlike, tempered by the Gulf Stream. There the northern blizzard seldom came, and the English ivy grew on the old stone walls and covered the well-known Mill. Legends throve in the languid atmosphere, and the British arms still hung in Trinity Church, near Bishop Berkeley's organ. And there, in a setting half rustic, half cosmopolitan, the Southern planters brought their families and mingled with the New York and Boston merchants. One could almost see in imagination the Brighton or Baden-Baden of the future. On the promenade, as if it were Europe, the men took off their hats to one another; and the ships set sail from the strange little wharves for Mozambique, Fayal or Zanzibar. The sailors talked of the East and the West Cape and a voyage to the Indian Ocean, perhaps in some fishing-smack of fifty tons.

Newport, the "American Eden," so like the Isle of Wight, had fostered in Channing a feeling for Wordsworth and Byron, those two romantic poets who had shared his moods. There, as a boy, after some sulphurous sermon, dealing with infant damnation, he had heard his father whistle. That was the end of the old faith for Channing. If his father did not believe in it, life was not so dismal, after all. Mingling with the Southern families, he had come to dislike what he called the avarice of the North, the selfish prudence of his fellow-Yankees. He loved the spontaneous ways of the Southern folk, who took no thought for the morrow, ways that fostered poetry and art. He had spent a year as a tutor in Virginia, and it was the Jeffersonians there who had weaned him away from his Federalist prepossessions, strong enough, at first, in a Newport boy whose father had entertained, as he well remembered, Washington, Jay and the other Federalist leaders. In the South, he had read the French philosophers, Godwin's books and Mary Wollstonecraft, and first conceived those dreams of social justice that were to find a voice in his later years. His health had never been strong since those early days when, with a stoic desire for self-improvement, he had slept on the bare floor, subjected himself to a rigid system of diet and prolonged his studies till two or three in the morning. But the slender, pallid, nervous little man, grave, reflective, fond of lonely rambles, teemed with the new ideas that were slowly coming to birth along the seacoast. All thanks to Newport!—where the South and Europe seemed so close at hand. And if Newport had also sheltered the great, grim author of the *System of Doctrines,* Dr. Samuel Hopkins's views had gradually melted away from people's minds. They were no longer "willing to be damned." All that the Newport people wished to recall was the doctor's prediction that the millennium was bound to occur within two hundred years.

In this little corner of New England, Roger Williams too had lived and toiled for the cause of religious liberty. Channing's brother, Edward Tyrrel Channing, had also spent his childhood there. So had the cousin of the Channing brothers, Richard Henry Dana, the poet and critic, the son of the old Chief Justice. So had Washington Allston, the painter and poet, the child of one of the South Carolina families who flocked to Newport for the summer season. His father and mother, distressed by his early talent, and fearing that he would disgrace a planter's household, had sent him North to cure him of his folly; and at Newport he had fallen in with Malbone, the unrivalled painter of miniatures. Allston, whose first wife was Channing's sister and who was later to marry the sister of Dana, had played as a boy with both of his brothers-in-law, both his friends at Harvard and both the inseparable friends of his Boston years. At Newport, Gilbert Stuart had lived, and there the great Berkeley had dwelt for a while. In his house, "Whitehall," near the sea, he had planned his new-world university. He had written his *Minute Philosopher* among the rocks where the Channings, Allston and Dana had dreamed and wandered. One might have imagined that Berkeley's benign spirit still lingered in the gracious Newport air.*

Other writers and poets were to draw from Newport the themes of poems and stories. There were themes enough,—the writers had only to pluck them,—in the burying-ground of the Portuguese Jews who had settled there after the Lisbon earthquake, in the Mill, which, as people supposed, the Norsemen had built, in the old black houses and rough-stone mansions, in the anomalous figures, vaguely savouring of the great world, whom one saw on the promenade or behind the curtained windows, one the reputed sister of an English queen, one the heroine of a strange romance, an impoverished lady of title who paid her washerwoman with costly lace. There were

* Most, if not all of the fashionable American watering-places were first "found" and colonized by writers and artists,—Newport, Bar Harbour, Southampton, East Hampton, Monterey, etc.

themes near by on the Providence Plantations, where
lingered, and were to linger for many years, the great
feudal dwellings of the rural magnates, households of
seventy, eighty, ninety persons, where the master of his
twelve thousand acres, his fox-hounds and his four thousand sheep kept twelve dairy-maids at work, each with
another girl to wait upon her, and two dozen cheeses, as
big as cart-wheels, vanished into the void every day.
There were stories enough to the north and west, in the
valleys and plains of Connecticut, on the green hill-slopes
of Vermont, where the Scottish ballads, on the lips of
immigrant weavers and shepherds, bloomed again as in
their native air, and the farmers and hunters were building a commonwealth. Themes enough for the novels and
the poems, waiting for the novelists and the poets.

But still, or more than ever, in these inland regions,
not poetry, or history, or romance, but a more sombre
form of exercise possessed the people's minds. They did
not care for stories. They thought that fiction was a
fraud, and worse. Religion was their only poetry. The
cultivated few, the "mansion people," those who had seen
something of the world, or knew at least Boston or New
York, the families of the rural magistrates, the squires,
the village notables who had connections in the capitals,
made an exception of Scott, whose Waverley novels
were in every house. They read Scott for his moral tone,
just as they read Richardson's *Clarissa* and the tales of
Maria Edgeworth, which all the leading families enjoyed
and discussed,—often with the families of the Boston
merchants, who, in their travelling-carriages, constantly
made tours across New England, to Stafford Springs,
through the Berkshire hills, to Round Hill, Mount Hol-
yoke or Graylock, perhaps on their way to Niagara or
Trenton Falls, for a little holiday outing, stopping to see
their cousins on the way. These novels, so moderate and
so elevating, served them as patterns of manners. Scott,

who adorned and beautified all that was growing old and
passing away, appealed to their conservative feelings,
and Richardson's Grandison was their beau ideal. Many
a girl said she would never marry until she found his
like. Novels like these were hardly "fiction." One read
them without loss of self-respect, as one read the works
of Hannah More, or Mrs. Chapone on the bringing-up of
girls.

This was only in the mansion-houses. The mansion
people formed an invisible chain, stretching across the
country, through which the currents of the great world
passed. Outside, the village life continued in its primal
innocence. Even the rural aristocracy, touched as it was
by foreign influences, retained its strong indigenous character. America was the only land it knew, or that its
forbears had known for seven generations. In towns near
the seaboard, one found a loyalist family here and there.
A few old ladies lingered on who spoke of themselves as
"eating the King's bread," because their father had
fought on the Tory side and they still received a British
pension. Miss Debby Barker of Hingham, a town that
was much like "Cranford,"—as everyone saw at once
when the book came out,—went into mourning, donned a
purple dress, at the death of George the Fourth. There
were many Miss Debby Barkers in Boston and Newport,
but most of the country aristocracy had always opposed
the crown. The village folk in general, mainly of the
purest English stock, carried on their ancient village
ways, not in a spirit of Anglophobia, but rather as if
England had never existed.* They formed a self-sufficing

* Anglomania, in all its forms, social or poetic, was confined to the
fashionable urban classes. The British, from the rural point of view, were
as foreign as any other foreigners, and most of the country-people, high
and low, deprecated intermarriage with them. Miss Fortune, in *The Wide,
Wide World,* undoubtedly expressed their attitude: "I wish Morgan could
have had the gumption to marry in his own country; but he must go running after a Scotchwoman! A Yankee would have brought up his child to
be worth something. Give me Yankees!"

Yankee world, separated by a pathless ocean from the ways of the mother-country. They were farmers almost to a man, aside from a few mechanics. Most of the ministers tilled their own soil. Each village had its Indian population, a cluster of huts on the outskirts, a few negroes who had once been slaves, sometimes two or three Irishmen and one or two beggars and paupers. The larger towns had public reading-rooms, possibly a Franklin Institute, where a few odd volumes of Shakespeare, Hume and Milton, Young's *Night Thoughts,* Thomson's *Seasons,* Rollin's *Ancient History,* filled the shelves with old books of sermons, Owen on Sin or *An Arrow Against Profane and Promiscuous Dancing.*

Every village had its squire and parson, a Deacon Hart, living on the turnpike, where he raised the golden squashes, the full-orbed pumpkins, the rustling Indian corn and the crimson currants that straggled by the painted picket fence. Further on, dwelt some Abihu Peters. An Ebenezer Camp contrived the shoes. A Patience Mosely made the village bonnets, hard by Comfort Scran's general store. There were always two or three hired men, a handy-andy, usually a fiddler, who had made his violin from the bole of a maple and strung his bow from the tail of the family horse. Now and then one found a village drunkard, who might have been a poet, perhaps some scalawag of a Stephen Burroughs, the worst boy in the town, who was often kept in chains in the county jail. There were a few Yankees of the swindling kind who found their proper sphere in the peddling business. Sometimes they were caught as counterfeiters. The Yankee mind was quick and sharp, but mainly it was singularly honest,—as honest as the men of Maine a hundred years later. Everyone who travelled through the country marvelled that the New England farmers' doors were seldom locked or barred, even at night; and, while the land flowed with rum, and even overflowed,* the great popular drink was homely cider. The cider-barrel was never empty at weddings and ordinations, on training-days, at huskings, at Thanksgiving, when the sounds of chopping and pounding and baking and brewing rose from the smoke-browned walls of the farmhouse kitchen. Those who grew up in these inland regions, looking back on the old village life, saw it in the light of Goldsmith's Auburn, abounding in mild virtues, faithful swains, rural virgins, peace and innocence. The goodman's daughters made his shirts and stockings; his garments were provided by his flocks and herds. So were those of the women-folk, who, as they spun and knitted, discussed the weekly sermon.

For religion filled the horizon of the village people, all that was left by politics and law. On Sunday morning, in the church, one heard the Psalms repeated, in Sternhold and Hopkins's version, which some of the old women believed were the very strains King David had sung to his harp,—"The Lord will come, and he will not," and, after a pause, another line, which most of the children thought was another idea, "Keep silence, but speak out." The old-fashioned polemical sermon followed, fortified with texts and garnished with quotations in Greek and Hebrew, for most of the clergy were still learned men. Perhaps only the week before, the minister had driven in his one-horse chaise twenty or thirty miles across the country to meet some reverend brother and settle some nice point in theology on which he was writing a treatise: he could not agree with Dr. Stern that God had created sin deliberately, and he wished to lay his case before his flock. Many of the village ministers, whose cocked hats and gold-headed canes were symbols of their unques-

---

* When the Reverend John Pierpont made his pilgrimage to the Holy Land, the first object he saw, on the wharf at Beirut, was a hogshead of New England rum.

tioned authority, as shepherds and judges of the people,
devoted their lives to writing these treatises. The farmers
discussed them over their ploughs, and the farm-wives
over their spinning-wheels. For religion was their romance. They named their children after the biblical
heroes, **and the Bible places,** Chittim and the Isles, Dan
and Beersheba, Kedar and Tarshish were stations on the
map of their El Dorado. The congregations followed the
web of the sermons with a keen and anxious watchful-
ness, eager to learn the terms of their damnation. And
they talked about fate and freedom and how evil came,
and what death is, and the life to come, as familiarly as
they talked of their crops and the weather.

All New England seethed with these discussions. One
heard about "potential presence" and "representative
presence" and "representative identity," and Dr. Bancroft's sermon on the fourth commandment. Blacksmiths
and farriers, youths and maidens argued about free will
and predestination, about "natural ability" and "moral
ability" and "God's efficiency" and "man's agency."
Sometimes it was a morbid interest, when the children sat
on "anxious seats" and wept over their wicked little
hearts. The conscience of New England was precocious.
Even Cotton Mather had observed that "splenetic maladies" throve among the people, maladies that were
scarcely allayed by some of the more emotional preachers. One heard of "sweating" sermons and "fainting"
sermons, followed by "convulsion-fit" sermons, in the
best tradition of Whitefield.* Sometimes, in the frontier
settlements, on the borders of the wilderness, in the forests of New Hampshire and Vermont, where men almost
forgot that they had voices, and only the axe and the
hammer broke the silence, where, on the frozen slopes,
the snow fell for days together, strange and terrible
thoughts rose in the mind. A Green Mountain boy with

* See the Reverend Mr. Stoker, in Holmes's *The Guardian Angel.*

an axe in his hand might sing his happy songs in the busy summer, rejoicing in the Alpine air, scented with fir and hemlock, for the Green Mountain boys had their mountain freedom. But when the snow began to fall, and he sat brooding beside the stove, over his calfskin Bible, in the close, foul air of the farmhouse kitchen, digesting food that was never meant for man, then, as he conned the mystical Revelations and the savage mythology of the ancient Jews, visions of blood-atonement swept his brain. Among the native ballads of the Vermonters, bloodshed was an omnipresent theme. They felt the presence of the God of Vengeance. They heard voices that were not benign. From them was to spring, a few years hence, the cult of Joseph Smith and Brigham Young,* where flourished now, as foretastes of the Mormons, the quiet murder and the loud revival.

Sometimes, on the other hand, these wrestlings over sublime abstractions rose, in some lonely soul, to the loftiest heights, where the mind was lost in mystical raptures over the universe and its great Architect, and men conversed with angels. Here and there, in the woods of Maine or among the hills of western Massachusetts, some spinster or some godly man, like Benedict in his solitary cell, seated on the mount of transfiguration, kept his days of appointment with the Eternal. What hopes, what rhapsodies possessed his soul, what meditations on a time and space in which all transient ills were engulfed or muted! He saw the whirling of the puppet-world with the eye of the mounting eagle that faces the sun. What mattered this changing planet with its petty cares, lost in the unfading light of moons and stars? † There was a fire in the New England heart, in the intellectual depths of Calvinism, which the cold minds of Unitarian Cambridge possessed no knowledge of, a hunger for right-

* Both born in Vermont.
† See the journals and letters of Mary Moody Emerson.

eousness and a thirst for truth, a passionate dream of
perfection. Concord knew this dream, and Concord was
to express it. Not for nothing had this vigorous race invested in its flaming ancient faith all the treasures of its
thought and feeling. Deep in its mental caverns lingered
still the spiritual passions of the Middle Ages. Deep in
its mental caverns lingered the passions of the Roundheads, who had suffered and fought for freedom and
human rights. Let the trumpet sound again, let the God
of Hosts unfurl his banners! New England was prepared, when the time was ripe, for another holy war.

At the moment, the state of mind of these inland
regions,—even Connecticut, which faced the sea,—
seemed hardly auspicious for the man of letters. It was
not quickened by the mental currents that brought new
light to the towns of the Eastern seaboard. It was
wrapped in an atmosphere of gloom; and its doctrines of
total depravity and the utter vanity of human effort
paralyzed the literary sense. Whatever mobility this mind
possessed was all but confined to the theological sphere.

One could only say that in this sphere its mobility was
surprising. The great New England schism had broken
out, thirty years later than in Boston. The theocratic
Church was giving way. Many of the farmers were moving westward; others were in revolt against the blue
laws. The Church had been forced to yield in its main
positions, as the democratic movement grew apace, for
the democratic movement, with its faith in equality, could
and would no longer tolerate the aristocratic doctrine of
"election"; and, breaking at the centre, it had begun to
branch at the outer edges into forms that were often
fantastic. Many of the congregations were held together
by the prestige of some ancient minister, who still ruled
the village as of old. But as these ministers vanished, one
by one, the congregations fell apart in factions, and
hundreds of conventicles arose,—poor little ugly scraps

of wooden Gothic,—in the shadows of the village churches. The mansion people, up and down the country, had begun to be touched by the Unitarian movement. Some of them, as in Boston, were Episcopalians. All of them had lost their taste for the Orthodox phraseology; and to please them, or to express their own views, which were also rapidly changing, numbers of the Orthodox clergy let down the bars of the old religion. Their sermons wandered from the ancestral standards. The humbler folk, meanwhile, who were breaking away, the farmers, mechanics, factory-hands, were offered a wide choice of isms, some of them brand-new, an assortment as appetizing and variegated as that of any Connecticut pedlar's pack. The more emotional sects, the Methodists, throve on the sudden reaction against the logical sermons of the past. The Universalists promised salvation to all. For the Adventists, Christ was coming at once: they did not have to wait for a far-away judgment. Perfectionism captured some; Restorationism captured others. According to the Come-outers of Cape Cod, the word was written in the human heart, a doctrine that pleased the unlettered who had heard too many texts in Greek and Hebrew. As for the question of punishment after death, one could choose between No Punishment, Eternal Punishment, good for most of one's neighbours, or a strictly limited punishment that stopped after the first million years.

All this represented a movement of mind that was to find expression in other spheres, the practical sphere, the scientific sphere,—for it promoted enquiry and the feeling for action,—but whether in the sphere of literature was rather open to question. At present, the intellect of the rural regions was largely confined to two of these factions: the mansion people, with their broader leanings, and the still potent Orthodox party. The sects, appealing to the simpler-minded, contributed to the Abolition movement, which was to make its appearance presently; but they had little to give to thought or letters. The Unitarians were still few and scattered. There remained the Orthodox leaders who, to regain their power, as the dissolution of the Church advanced, redoubled their ancient threats of hell-fire. To stop the Unitarian movement, the "icy system," as Lyman Beecher called it, they founded the Andover Seminary and built the Park Street Church in the centre of Boston, fortresses of the old faith, in the heart of the enemy's country, from which to pelt the enemy with their sermons,—"each one fresh, like bullets from a mould." * They denounced the "vandal spirit of innovation," as Robert Treat Paine had denounced the "vandal spirit of Puritanism." They reaffirmed the glory of the Pilgrim Fathers. As far back as New England history went, the "Connecticut school" had had its own tone, distinct from that of the "Massachusetts school"; and now more than ever, with Lyman Beecher,—as erstwhile with "old Pope Dwight," Timothy Dwight, the president of Yale, who died in 1817,—the Connecticut school was conscious of its strength. Its efforts were futile to capture the stronghold of Boston, but on its own ground it stood firm. The ancient Puritan faith had been revived in a new and powerful cult.

This energy seemed to promise an abundant life in various other realms. At Yale, for instance, the great centre of learning, the second capital of the New England mind, a notable school of science had arisen, with Benjamin Silliman as its presiding spirit. Harvard, with all its literary prospects, had nothing to show as yet, or for years to come, beside this genius of the laboratory, who formed for Yale its collection of minerals and its physical and chemical apparatus, along with the *American Journal of Science*. Silliman's pioneer work in science might have been expected to offset the obscurantist the-

* Lyman Beecher.

ology of the college, for Yale, like the other and lesser
centres of learning, Williams, Amherst, Bowdoin, Brown
and Dartmouth, those minor Paley's watches, continued
to be stoutly Orthodox. Through Silliman's *Journal,* the
science of the world passed into the mind of the nation;
and Yale was in other respects nationally-minded, with
broader political sympathies than Harvard and a much
more all-American student-body. But it was isolated from
the great-world interests, outside the field of science, that
were so soon to stir Boston and Cambridge; and this, in
addition to its religious thinking and the relative poverty
of the institution, portended little good for literature.
Certainly there was little enough at present. Timothy
Dwight, the "last of the Puritans,"—as people had
called him once, before they became aware of Lyman
Beecher,—Timothy Dwight, Jonathan Edwards's grandson, a mighty man, a prodigy of learning, even a poet
himself in earlier times, had frowned on "song" and the
"arts of the pencil and chisel." He had made every effort
to restore the Puritan modes and methods. Of the New
Haven poets of the hour, James A. Hillhouse was symptomatic. The son of a well-known senator, a college-mate
of the novelist Cooper, he wrote long poems, correct but
decidedly dismal, on biblical themes.*

At Hartford, the political capital, the second New
England seat of the Federalists, which had grown in
about the same proportion as Boston, the literary scene
was scarcely brighter. A few of the "Hartford Wits"
lingered on. Humphreys, Barlow and Lemuel Hopkins
were gone, but Theodore Dwight remained, the "old
Pope's" brother. One saw him strolling about the Hart-

---

* "Yale has never put its football relish into letters or followers of letters. All that related to rhetoric or composition in my day was most shab-
bily pursued or methodized; nor, indeed, has Yale ever put its foot strongly
in that direction."—Note by "Ik Marvel," in Dunn's *Life of Donald G.
Mitchell,* page 71. See also President Hadley's remarks in *Four American
Universities.* Naturally, all this was changed later.

ford streets, filled to the brim with anecdote and learning, Dwight who had once pursued the Jacobins with the
vigilance of a beagle in the brush. John Trumbull still
lived in Hartford, the once-famous author of *MacFingal,*
old, small, emaciated, bent, tottering on his cane, his fine
little face alive with Erasmian humour. One could not
forget that the Hartford Wits, whatever their faults and
limitations were, had laughed away the popular taste for
bombast, at least for a generation. They had had a vigorous interest in poetry which the Boston of their day
could only match in the bilious rhymes of Robert Treat
Paine. But their day was already remote. Hartford had
lost its tincture of intellectual life, and Mrs. Sigourney
and her little *salon* still belonged to the future. A youthful poet* who, at this moment, oscillated between Hartford and New Haven, cried to the empty air for someone
with whom he could talk. A mere author had no place
here. The only society that he could find was a handful
of indolent and dyspeptic tutors, one or two lawyers
without ambition and the illiterate mistress of a boarding-
house.

The Connecticut mind, as travellers often noted, was
keen, strong and witty, but usually narrow, educated
rather than cultivated. It abounded in prejudices that
were often small, like most of the "Yankee notions." It
lacked, as a rule, the power of generalizing, which had
been marked in New York, in Virginia and in Boston. It
was a village mind, in short, that had never breathed a
larger atmosphere. It bore few of the fruits that spring
from an intercourse and collision with other minds from
other mental regions. The only important Connecticut
man of letters, a man of great importance, a symbol of
his world in many ways, was the famous lexicographer,

---

* James Gates Percival. It was characteristic of these years at Yale
that Percival, whose failure as a poet almost became proverbial, was
eminently successful as a man of science.

Noah Webster, who was more concerned with "education" than he was ever concerned with "cultivation," but who was doing more with his education than all the American pedagogues put together. A tall, lean, black-coated man, with black small-clothes and black silk stockings, with the oddest, quaintest, old-fashioned air,—if you had met him in China, you would have known that he hailed from Connecticut,—always a farmer's son in his heart of hearts, a busy-body, self-important, vain, but upright and honest, aggressive, enterprising, pertinacious, a schoolmaster, lawyer, journalist, who had written on banking, medicine and statistics, and yet, for all these multifarious interests, possessed a vast and accurate fund of learning, he was at work, at New Haven, writing his Dictionary, for which his Spelling-book had prepared the way,—a new Declaration of Independence. His object was to establish a national language as a bond of "national union," for Webster, with his democratic tastes, was an old-school Federalist in politics. Already an elderly man, he had lived through the Revolution; and, filled as he was with patriotic fervour, he had not failed to note that, while the Americans boasted of their freedom, nevertheless their arts, their dress, their customs still aped the ways of the mother-country. Why should they receive, in this supine way, everything that came from a foreign press? A spirit of the blindest imitation stifled all American enquiry, benumbed the intellectual faculties. During the years of war, when the intercourse with England was interrupted and American school-books had to be improvised, he had supplanted Dilworth's Spelling-book with his own popular speller. He saw no reason why American children should learn that the letters "Ast. P. G. C." meant "Astronomy Professor of Gresham College," on the other side of the ocean. He had worked up his own vernacular word-book, based on the common usage of New England. The store-keepers,

up and down the country, laid in supplies of Webster's
Speller, along with their hogsheads of rum and their kegs
of molasses. The pedlars carried it from door to door,
until, as the decades passed, fifty million copies had been
sold. It had given the population a uniform spelling.

The irrepressible Cobbett, in his will, bequeathed five
pounds to Noah Webster to pay for a new engraving of
his portrait, so that the children who used his speller
might no longer be frightened out of their wits by the
grim Websterian visage. But the visage had its work to
do. Webster was a fighter. He had fought for an author's
copyright law, travelling through the South and the
Middle States, working on the minds of the legislatures.
He spoke in terms that farmers understood. The copyright, he said, was the "author's soil." Only the products
belonged to the purchaser; the soil should be vested in
the owner. He fought for his mother-tongue in a similar
fashion. He toiled along the road from village to village,
visiting every country printing-house, handing the com-
positor a printed slip, saying, as he did so, "My lad, when
you use these words, oblige me by spelling them as here,"
—*theater, center, honor,* etc. He had such a passion for
detail, for the fruits and even the process of enumera-
tion, that he often counted the houses in the village,
counting up one side of a street and down the other
side. For the rest, he saw no reason why the language
should not be spelled as the average man pronounced it,
even,—he had his little crotchets,—dropping the final *e* in
fugitive; for he had no use for the formal grammarians.
As a patriotic gesture of a wholesome kind, he used, as
illustrations in his work, quotations from the American
fathers, Hancock, Barlow, Livingston, along with Burke
and Johnson. It happened that all his own affiliations, in
spite of his prodigious store of learning, had been with
the plain people: a fact which, accounting for his suc-

cess, also indicated his limitations. For he had little literary feeling; he had no sense, or only a primitive sense, of the flavour and the history of words, well as he knew his etymology. He had a somewhat arid emotional nature, and the relatively thin, pale speech that had come to prevail among the Yankee farmers, who had lost, in the dry American air, much of their ancestral heartiness,* sounded as rich and full in Webster's ears as the deep chest-notes of the men of old, whose tones were maintained in cultivated usage. His temper, as befitted a man of Yale, was rather scientific than humanistic; and his influence, as a result of this, was very far from happy. When it came to the niceties of language, whether in spelling or pronunciation, Webster's work was always to be challenged. But he did his task so well, within his limits, adding his thousands of words, adding his tens of thousands of definitions, which no previous book had ever contained, that "Webster," with its countless modifications, was destined to remain a standard work for the English-speaking peoples of the world.

In short, the great Connecticut Dictionary stood, as a monument of New England learning, beside Bowditch's *Practical Navigator.* Only by courtesy works of literature, these two solid books rose like a pair of imposing gate-posts at the opening of an epoch. Indeed, the lonely scholar, Noah Webster, who, for a generation, prowled round and round his study-table, shaped in a hollow circle and piled with dictionaries of Greek and Latin, Hebrew, Arabic, twenty other tongues, was a highly symbolic figure; for learning, at this moment in New

---

* Emerson often remarked on this phenomenon, in its various aspects, e.g., "In America I grieve to miss the strong black blood of the English race; ours is a pale, diluted stream . . . Our American lives are somewhat poor and pallid, no fiery grain; staid men, like our pale and timid flora . . . The Englishman speaks with all his body. His elocution is stomachic,—as the American's is labial."

England, was in a very active state. The new sects paid
less attention to it, but there were many country ministers like Mr. Taylor of Westfield, who took such delight
in Origen's works that, not being able to purchase them,
he copied them out in four quarto volumes. One heard of
ministers who, rebuked for heresy by a group of others,
defended themselves in Latin, Greek and Hebrew, and,
when they were cornered in all these tongues, retreated
into Arabic, where they were safe from pursuit. Here and
there, some secular scholar, dressed in his decent black
coat,—old but not untidy, neatly bound at the cuffs,—
conned his Christian fathers and his Cave and Stanley
while he composed his work on the Universe. The children of the ministerial households, whose mother, as
often as not, read Virgil aloud in the afternoon, talked
about Homer and the ancient myths while they were
milking or learning to bake, or, in New Hampshire and
Vermont, sugaring-off in the spring. Serving-women were
not unknown who read their Latin with the boys and
girls and heard them recite, after washing the dishes.
Young girls, who rose at five and asked themselves,
"What hard good work have I to do today?" began
with two or three books of *Paradise Lost,* to give them
the proper tone. They talked about Dugald Stewart and
Alison on Taste, or perhaps about the *Life of Sir William Jones,* which was spreading an interest in Oriental
studies. Older sisters advised their younger sisters, who
were filled with the *furor scribendi,* to discipline their
minds by studying Butler's *Analogy.* One little girl of
seven, who had read a book on the ancient gods, telling
how much they had been loved and honoured, they whom
no one worshipped any more, felt her heart fill with pity.
Entering the woods near by, she built a little altar of
stones, decked it with flowers and shells and laid her
favourite toys on the summit. Then she apostrophized
the god of gods: "Poor old Jupiter, I love you! Nobody

else worships you, but I will, dear old god. You shall have my doll, and I will bring you flowers every day."

All over New England, not only in the "Literary Emporium," as Boston was called far and wide, there was a passionate interest in self-culture. Countless households followed Miss Edgeworth's theories, or some other theory of education, and practised on their friends and youthful cousins. All the sons and daughters of the well-to-do were sent to the "literary institutions," the colleges and academies. Children of the poorer families, who could not afford to buy paper and ink, made their own, or used chalk or charcoal, and learned to write on the kitchen floor; and here and there some group of boys and girls, who had read Washington Irving's *Salmagundi*, edited a family magazine. This interest in reading and study, in books and authors, laid trains of feeling in the general mind that were about to burst into expression. Throughout the region, as throughout the nation, there was a widely spread presentiment that a great native American literature was about to make its appearance. Everyone read English books, histories, poems, essays, in which people found the moulds of their minds and manners; but they already felt that these English authors described a world that had ceased to be their own. They read about beggars, in the British novels, just as they read about kings, but few had seen a beggar, no one had seen a king. They read about skylarks and nightingales, but a skylark was as rare as a "pampered menial." Who had seen a pampered menial? Most of the distinctions and conventions which they found in the European writers were foreign to their own experience. They were ready to welcome tales and poems without the kings, the menials and the beggars,—with bobolinks instead of larks, with the blue-bird and the wood-thrush where the nightingale had been, and fresh American flowers instead of the far-away verdure of the British poets,—whenever the authors appeared who were able to write them.* They were ready for historians and poets who might prove to be as independent as their statesmen had already been.

Of this frame of mind it was symptomatic that a New England author of the future, describing the generation that preceded his own, wrote a story about a valley in which the people cared so much for greatness that they were watching for the man to come, the child born in the valley, who was to be the greatest of his time. The story of *The Great Stone Face* had its prophetic element. It also had a foundation in fact, which it could not have had a century later; for it was true that the New England air was filled with a sense of expectation.

* Within a few years, almost all Americans felt as Hosea Biglow felt:
    "Why, I'd give more for one live bobolink
        Than a square mile o' larks in printer's ink."

CHAPTER IV

GEORGE TICKNOR'S WANDERJAHRE

IN THE spring of 1815, two young Boston men had embarked on a voyage of discovery. Not content with the state of affairs at Harvard, they had made up their minds to go to Germany and investigate the reports that had come to Boston about the prodigious progress of the German scholars. Was the German tongue obscure and artificial, as everyone supposed in Massachusetts? Were the Germans merely a race of barbarous pedants, as almost everyone thought in England also? George Ticknor, a lawyer, a Dartmouth man with a great respect for Harvard, had serious doubts about it. So did Edward Everett, a brilliant young minister of twenty, with whom and two or three other friends, Everett's older brother Alexander, Edward Tyrrel Channing and Nathan Hale,* who had married Everett's sister, Ticknor had formed a reading club. At the meetings, they shared their Latin compositions, largely aimed at one another's foibles, and ended up with a hasty-pudding frolic.

These two enquiring spirits had sailed for Liverpool, the first stage for Germany, along with a party of other Boston friends and two sons of John Quincy Adams. George Ticknor was a rich young man, with very engaging manners, vivacious, with a melodious voice, with large, dark, velvety eyes and hair that curled and might have been romantic. He was positive, self-assured in the Boston way, not by any means a man of genius, or

* The father of Edward Everett Hale.

he would not have been so self-assured,—that is to say, at
twenty-three, but certainly a man of remarkable talents,
and talents of a useful kind. The son of a notable merchant who, before he acquired his wealth, had written
an English grammar and who shared his son's scholarly
aspirations, the young man was favourably known in
Boston, as a member of the Anthology Club and the editor of Buckminster's posthumous papers. Everett was
even better known. He was an intellectual prodigy. At
twenty, he had already preached for a year in the most
fashionable of the Boston pulpits. The son of another
minister who had composed a famous "Eulogy on Washington," which Everett was to repeat for fifty years, with
variations and modulations,—or so his enemies said,—he
had been highly praised for his school orations. He was
the prize boy as a speaker of pieces and had once inter-
rogated the listening air with a question that was soon to
have an answer. Why were there no American poets?
Why was not New England what it should be, a "nest of
singing birds"? Everett sang in prose. His florid and
affluent fancy was greatly admired. He was compared to
Massillon.* John Adams called him "our most celebrated
youth." Moreover, Everett really knew his classics; and,
when he was asked to become Professor of Greek,—one
of those Harvard chairs that were almost as important

* See the comment of John Quincy Adams on a sermon of Edward
Everett's: "It was without comparison the most splendid composition as a
sermon that I ever heard delivered. . . . His composition is more rich,
more varied, more copious, more magnificent, than was that of Buckminster. There were passages that reminded me perhaps too much of Massillon, but the whole sermon was equal to any of the best that Massillon
ever wrote. It abounded in splendid imagery, in deep pathos, in cutting
satire, in profound reflections of morals, in coruscations of wit, in thunder-
bolts of feeling."—J. Q. Adams's *Diary*, February 13, 1820.

It may be said of Adams that, while he shared the taste for the rococo
that was common among his contemporaries, he knew, by comparison with
the best in the world, what oratory was. Boston abounded in connoisseurs
of sermons. They knew all the points of oratory, as Haydn's audience
knew a fine concerto. They enjoyed it so luxuriously for itself that they
were glad to overlook its frequent emptiness of content.

as a seat in the Senate,—he accepted the nomination
without reluctance, on one condition only, that he might
prepare himself in Europe.

The two friends had much in common. Both were
model students. Both had an ample share of the Boston
sense of responsibility. Everett was considered the
brightest student who had ever passed through Harvard.
Ticknor had had less opportunity to show what he was
made of; but anyone could see that he was solid, whatever his limitations were, while there were several persons who suspected that Everett might be hollow. This
was quite unjust. Everett was a little spoiled, perhaps.
How could he not have been spoiled when President
Kirkland said that he resembled the bust of Apollo? He
was a little vain, but he was unquestionably gifted. He
was a little ambitious, in every sense of the word; but
he had his own way to make in the world, while Ticknor
had been born on the upper crust. If he had abandoned,
with little scruple, the career of the man of God, everyone
knew that half the ministers were only men of God because the pulpit, which was highly honoured, also gave
them time to read and write. No one denied that he was
conscientious. He was a helpful friend. Besides, his
Greek was really something to boast of; it could only
have been more surprising if he had studied in Germany.
So, at least, Everett surmised. That was why he had
sailed away with Ticknor.

But how had it all happened? Who had put the notion
of Germany into the heads of these two exemplary students? Madame de Staël, of course, the lady who owned
the land in upper New York, bordering on Lake Ontario.
They had read her famous book, *De l'Allemagne,* which
had just appeared in an English version. They were predisposed to like the book, since everyone knew that
Napoleon did not like it. He had suppressed the book and
driven Madame de Staël out of France. Moreover, they

had read a remarkable pamphlet defending the University of Göttingen against the evil intentions of Napoleon's brother, the ill-famed King of Westphalia. Everyone knew that a thing must be good, whether a university or a book, if the Bonapartes disliked it. The University of Göttingen was plainly good, almost too good to be true, Ticknor thought, when a travelling Englishman who had actually seen it,—he must have been one of the first,— described the library to one of his friends. Ticknor, having time to spare, set to work to learn the German language. But where was he to find the books he needed? Several young men in Boston had heard of a Mr. Goethe, who was said to have written a few respectable pages. They had even heard of Dante, the Italian bard, who had been almost forgotten even in England.* But of either tongue, German or Italian, who possessed a grammar? Everett's clever brother, Alexander, produced a German grammar from his desk, and Ticknor remembered that one of his friends in New Hampshire had spoken of a German dictionary. Then he found that John Quincy Adams had bought and kept a copy of *The Sorrows of Werther*. He puzzled it out and made a translation of it.†

Whatever Ticknor did was sure to be thorough. Everett was thorough, too, in all these scholarly matters. Much as he might have been thought a Laodicean, in

* The popular knowledge of Dante, among the English-speaking peoples, dates from the publication of Cary's translation at about this moment, 1814.

† Carlyle's experience in Scotland, at just this moment,—as related by him to Charles Eliot Norton,—was a parallel case. Having become aware of German thought through Madame de Staël's book, he could find only two persons in Edinburgh who had any knowledge of the German language. There was not a German book to be bought in the city. He finally procured a set of Schiller through the skipper of a trading-ship at Leith. This was about 1815.—See *Letters of Charles Eliot Norton*, I, 480-481.

Although German was so little known in Boston, there were a few students of the language elsewhere in New England. Dr. Bentley of Salem and Professor Moses Stuart of Andover both owned collections of German books.

certain aspects of his later life, he was bent on the welfare of Boston and Harvard, as afterwards, no doubt, of
a larger world. He was convinced that the scholar had a
mission. Going to Germany was not a lark, for such a
mind as his; it was a novitiate, to be taken strictly. Ticknor felt this even more profoundly, or had the time and
means to appear to do so. His country, he felt, would
never lack good lawyers, but it was in urgent need of
scholars, not the musty theologues of old but well-
trained teachers and men of letters. In this capacity he
could be more useful, especially if he had seen the world.
And he was well-equipped for seeing the world. In fact,
he was a man of the world already, with a shrewd eye
for the traits of human nature. He could recognize at
sight a man of genius, or, if not genius, animated talent.
Real genius might be another matter: the fact that one
is actually in its presence "dawns slowly on a Boston
mind," as one of the Adamses remarked later. To this
rule, Ticknor was no exception. He was to meet several
men of genius, both in his own country and in Europe,
who never dawned on his mind at all, unless they were
his friends or men of high breeding.* But his eye for
talent served him well. When the famous Francis Jeffrey
came to Boston,—the editor of the *Edinburgh Review,*
—in pursuit of a young lady of New York whom he had
met in Scotland, most of the Bostonians disliked him.
They did not know what to make of the stout, little, red-
faced man who seemed to have none of the dignity for
which his magazine was so respected. They thought he
was a merry-andrew, frivolous, vain, far too free and
familiar, who had obviously not grown up in a well-bred
circle. But Ticknor liked him thoroughly. Why expect
from a foreigner the decorum that could only spring

---

* See the remarks in his *Journal* about Lamb, Hazlitt and other English
"bohemians," together with his marked indifference to the later movement of mind in Boston and Concord.

from an early discipline,—that is to say, a Boston discipline? Jeffrey's impatience and abruptness, which
wounded the self-esteem of the Boston people, seemed to
him rapidity of mind. It was prodigious. It was wholly
pleasing. If this was the sort of torrential eloquence, torrential and yet logical and compact, that characterized
the foreign intellect, Ticknor was prepared to see it
twice.

Not, however, before he had taken pains to see what
the American intellect yielded. The American mind had
produced the Revolution; and everyone knew, not in
Boston only, that there was no event in modern times
with which to compare the American Revolution. The
French Revolution, perhaps, but in Boston one did not
dwell on this fiasco. Besides, everyone knew, even in
France, that the French would never have had a revolution unless the Americans had had one first. The men
who made the American Revolution were world-heroes
of the first order. Even in London, nobody questioned
this; and as two or three of these men were still alive,
Ticknor proposed to see them. Adams and Jefferson were
a pair of yardsticks with which to measure any man in
Europe,—for Jefferson had risen in the Boston mind,
now that he had abandoned politics and found his Horace
and his Tacitus much more interesting than the daily papers. A journey through the other American cities would
surely give a young Bostonian that proper notion of his
own country which Dr. Johnson said a man should have
before he travelled abroad.* Moreover, he might encounter a few persons who, having been to Europe,
could give him a little useful information about the
universities and means of study. With a number of

* It was the rule, at this period, for young Americans, e.g., Josiah
Quincy, to make the grand tour of the United States, through Virginia and
the Carolinas to Charleston, and sometimes Savannah, before they went
abroad. This sensible classical custom was later indicated in the well-
known tag, "See America first."

letters that Adams placed in his hand, Ticknor had
set out for New York and the South; and before many
months or weeks had passed, he could almost have said,
—he would not have said it,—that he knew John Randolph, Madison and Marshall. The old philosopher of
Monticello was more than pleased with this ardent
neophyte, who offered to purchase books for him in
Europe,—the new German editions of the classics,—and
who was so ready to discuss his plans for the education of
the Southern people. Not since his own years abroad had
Jefferson seen such an eager student; and, seated in his
beautiful study, surrounded by his seven thousand books,
he talked of the days when, on his foreign missions, he
had escaped, when he could, from his public business to
spend his time with the continental scholars. Twice, a few
years later, he was to invite the young Bostonian to teach
in the university he had founded, offering him an unheard-
of salary. And he gave Ticknor letters to his friends in
Europe, scholars and men of affairs, that almost con-
ferred on him the rank of an unofficial ambassador.

Everett, too, had made the American tour and called
on President Madison. He, too, was equipped with letters that opened every European door. In fact, amid all
the adventures that lay before them, the heads of these
two young men might well have been turned. For what
young men of any other country,—during this year that
followed the Peace of Ghent,—could have had quite their
opportunities, as the first young scholars, with attractive
manners, or, rather, the first after Washington Irving,
representing the new American nation, upon which so
many hopes of humanity rested, at a time when humanity
was full of hopes, a nation that interested every sentient
being, not least, because, for the second time, it was the
victor in a war with England? What were they to say
and feel when Madame de Staël remarked to them, "You
are the advance-guard of the human race," when Lafay-

ette, Chateaubriand, Benjamin Constant greeted them in
the same soul-stirring fashion? They were to find that in
Germany all the great writers of the previous age,
Lessing, Herder, Klopstock, had sympathized with the
American Revolution,—which they themselves were felt
to represent,—that even the old courtier-poet Goethe,
whose name had reached their friends at home, recol-
lected the Boston Tea-Party as one of the symbolic events
that had stamped itself on his mind as a child. What was
a young man to say when the Pope told him that in a
few years the new world would dictate to the old? However it might have been with Everett, Ticknor's head
was not to be turned; and he quite agreed with those who
praised his country. When the Grand Duke of Tuscany
asked him where, among all the nations, he thought a
man could live most happily, and Ticknor replied, "In
America," he did not spare the Grand Duke's blushes,
which became visible as he explained—as only a Bostonian can explain such matters—that America was more
elevating than other countries.

These were the fortunate days of the youthful republic, when the good old Anglo-American sang-froid had
solid facts to base itself upon,—when young men, heirs
of the Great Event, knew that they had beaten England
twice, although they were too well-bred to mention it,
and felt, if they were students and men of letters, that
they were volunteers in a nobler war, as builders of a
great new civilization. If Ticknor, and even Everett, in
his way, stood so calmly in their own shoes, and used their
heads so shrewdly, during a four-years' tour of observation that might have flattered a diplomat,—as Ticknor's
Journal was to prove in time, a picture of the Europe of
these years that could hardly have been more full or more
discerning,—it was because, with the Revolution behind
them, they were engaged, and they knew it, and everyone knew it, in serving the purposes of the Revolution.

They were serving the cause in their studies and travels, a fact they were not likely to forget, with Washington Irving on the ground before them. For wherever they went, they were to meet Irving, who never seemed to weary of discoursing on the prospects and the duties of their country: he liked to tell his young compatriots that, at their time of life, they ought to set aside all other cares and lay up a solid stock of knowledge. Follow their ends, at any cost; scramble, if they had to scramble; buy books, whatever else they lacked. Learning,—this was the sense of Irving's counsel,—was the first of patriotic duties. The touching letters of Ticknor's merchant-father breathed the same spirit. The old man, who had fitted his son for college, longed to see him in a professor's chair. And how would any son have wished to respond to such a letter as the following, so filled with everything that was good in Boston?—

I can look forward and see you, every week, and every month, employed in some part of Europe, in acquiring something which will be useful and pleasant to you in after life. So long as you continue to be the kind, discreet, wise and dutiful son . . . so long I shall . . . continue, even to the end of my life, to aid and assist you, and make the path of life easy and pleasant to you . . . The great object of your journey I am sure you will keep in mind, and never turn to the right hand nor to the left, viz., to improve in solid science, the arts, and literature, and in the knowledge of men . . . You have not left your home for the sole purpose of describing the lawns, the hills, the valleys, the tops of mountains, the columns of smoke, the villages,—except for amusement, and as shades to ornament your other improvements, which may be often and happily interspersed; but you have left your father to grow wiser and better,—to learn how to be more useful to yourself, your friends and your country.*

With a letter like this in his pocket, a letter worthy of a Roman parent, a young man knows how to behave when

* *Life, Letters and Journals of George Ticknor.* II, 410.

he meets Lord Byron and Sir Humphry Davy, when Byron tells him about his love-affairs, tells him the story of his life,—as Englishmen are prone to do, in the presence of a sympathetic stranger,—gives him a beautiful copy of his poems, gives him a letter to Ali Pasha, in case he wishes to go to Greece, and a splendidly mounted pistol with which to defend himself there. And when Sir Humphry Davy presented Ticknor with another handful of letters, one to Canova, one to Madame de Staël,— to whom he already had two letters,—he might have felt that he was fairly launched. The young men were quite at home in England, which was only a larger and livelier Massachusetts. Indeed, their first celebrity, Mr. Roscoe, the Liverpool banker-scholar, a sound Whig and patron of learning who had been the smith of his own fortunes, had been exactly like a Boston man, one of the founders of the Athenæum. Southey also had a Puritan conscience and the same laborious habits one knew at home; and the grand old Dr. Parr, Dr. Johnson's ancient friend and the master of Ticknor's master, Dr. Gardiner, received the young men as if they had had a volume of introductions. He said he had turned on his heel, in the days of the Revolution, when he heard the Americans described as rebels. He added, in his hearty way, "I was always glad that you beat us."

But Ticknor and Everett had not crossed the ocean to find another Boston, with improvements. As for the English universities, Oxford was only a larger and livelier Harvard, far from having had its own reforms. In Germany they were soon to meet a scholar who had put the English Latinists to the blush. He had pointed out several grammatical errors in the Latin notes of a posthumous work of Porson, the pride of the Cambridge scholars. In fact, these German professors were something new under the sun, as formidable in the field of studies as Frederick the Great had been in the field of arms; and

Ticknor and Everett, once in Göttingen, found themselves
on their mettle. What a mortification, the grievous distance between an American and a German scholar!
America had never known, not only what a Greek scholar
was, but even the process by which a man became one. At
Harvard, they thought they knew how to work, heirs of
the Puritans as they were, but it was plain enough that,
beside these Germans, they cared for nothing but their
own convenience. They were more indolent than the
English scholars. They thought two years sufficient to
make a Grecian, and here was little Dissen of Göttingen
who had spent no less than eighteen years, at sixteen
hours a day, on Greek and nothing but Greek, and who
said that even now he could not read Æschylus without
a dictionary. It all depended on what one meant by "knowing." No one who had ever seen a German could ever
again call a man a scholar unless he was willing to follow
Eichhorn's programme: 5 A.M. to 9 P.M., with half-
hour intervals for meals. As for the poor little Harvard
library, it was a good half-century behind the times.

All this became painfully evident as Ticknor and
Everett pegged away, for twenty solid months, at a
typical Göttingen schedule: 5-8, Greek, 8-9, German,
9-10, exegesis, 10-12, Greek, 1½-4, Latin and French,
4-5, philology, 5-7, Greek, 7-8, the drill-sergeant, 9-11,
résumé of lectures, varied, perhaps, by Hebrew and
Syriac, a little natural history and a four-mile walk. No
man ever died of study, Eichhorn often said, though he
thought that perhaps for soft young Yankees twelve
hours a day might answer, at first. Harvard was a school
for ministers, and Harvard men could hardly be expected to know what a scholar was. Who had ever seen
an American scholar? While everyone knew that the
Yankees were enterprising, the wonder was, not that
they studied badly, but that they studied at all. And
Ticknor and Everett did not study badly. Full-grown as

they were, they were glad to go to school again, with their big portfolios under their arms, just like two boys who fear the birch. So was their friend, Joseph Green Cogswell, another Harvard man who joined them shortly, and who was also to play a historic role: for as Ticknor was to become, in America later, the father of modern-language studies, as Everett was to give an unparalleled impulse to the study of Greek mythology and letters, so Cogswell was destined to become, as head of the Astor Library in New York, a founder of the modern library-system. Cogswell, who was thirty, had already had a varied life. His work as a lawyer had taken him to Marseilles, where he had found himself regarded as an authority on books. In the length and breadth of this great commercial city, one looked in vain for a book that was not connected with trade; and, whenever a stray volume in Latin or Hebrew turned up in the hands of the dealers, Cogswell was asked to examine it. The town was more benighted than New York. It was dangerous to be thought a savant there, as the president of the Marseilles Academy told him, and he might well have died of ennui if he had not happened to fall in with two or three learned Spanish exiles. In Göttingen, along with his other studies, Cogswell pursued his bibliographical work, going over the shelves and catalogues of the university library. On their walking-tours, in vacation-time, the three young men visited and examined the great German libraries and several universities. At Weimar, at various times, they called upon Goethe, who gave them fresh sheaves of letters. The old poet was living much alone. He was glad to hear their news from America and eager for their recent impressions of Byron. Cogswell especially touched him. He thanked the young man for taking an interest in his old age and kissed him with affection. He sent Cogswell several presents after he had returned to his own country. *

As for Edward Everett, Cousin said, before he set out for home, that, for Greek, he had never seen Everett's equal. He was at least so competent in German that Eichhorn asked him for contributions to the Göttingen magazine. Before his visit to Greece, he had spent several days with Sir Walter Scott, who had neglected his old German studies and was glad to talk them over again. He had given the little Scotts a lesson in Tasso. He had heard Moore and Béranger sing their songs, passed a day with Ugo Foscolo and dined with the Bonaparte family, assembled in Rome. He had taken the first steps of his later life as a diplomat; and, when he went to Greece, with Byron's letters,—for he wished, in his way, to consult the oracle, too,—he was received and passed on, from one official to another, as if he had been a diplomat already.

Ticknor's studies, after Göttingen, still lay before him. He had been appointed, in his absence, the Smith Professor of Belles-Lettres at Harvard. He was expected to teach Popular Latin, Old French, Provençal, Spanish and Portuguese. For this he had to prepare in the southern countries. He had formed certain habits as a student that were to make his teaching influential. One of them was to choose, for his private instructors, in Germany first, then elsewhere, in France, Italy, Spain and even Scotland, scholars who were typical of their nations, men with round, full, musical voices who could direct his reading and share it with him, and give him, along with the grammar and the literary history, the overtones and the intimacies of feeling, a sense of the popular spirit from which each literature had sprung. The scholar Conde, who, for all his fame, was dying of starvation at Madrid, —for Spain was in a sad state, and most of the men of letters were so wretched that they were ashamed to re-

* It was through Cogswell that Goethe presented to Harvard College a set of his works in twenty volumes.

ceive a stranger,—Conde was one of these instructors.*
With him, during a spring and summer, Ticknor spent
several hours a day, reading the old Castilian authors.
In Rome, for four months, a well-known archæologist
was his cicerone. In Edinburgh, he read the Scottish poets
with Robert Jamieson. Scott, who was glad to give him
several days, walking with him about the countryside and
telling him stories of the Scottish border, spoke of him
to Southey in a letter as a "wonderful fellow for romantic
lore."

All this was to have its effect on the rising generation
of American poets, so many of whom were to study under him. For Ticknor was not only to sow at Harvard,
in a ground already prepared, the seeds of the modern
literatures of Europe; he was to stimulate, in some of his
pupils,—by opening up these veins of popular legend, the
balladry of Spain, Provence and Scotland,—a feeling
that was already half awake for the legendary lore of
their own country. Scott had renewed the literature of
his people by building on this ancient balladry; and Scott
had conceived his idea of doing so by reading Bürger's
Lenore, which had had the same effect in Germany. Why
should not America follow Scott, as Scott had followed
Bürger? Washington Irving had already done so. He
had shaped, in charming prose, the legends of the Hudson River; and every river-valley in New England
teemed with similar legends, waiting for other Irvings,
in prose or verse. Ticknor did not need to make the point.
Boys who had grown up among the ballads of the Revolution, the folk-tales of Marblehead and Portsmouth, could
hardly fail to draw the inference, especially when Ticknor was able to tell them how interesting Southey had

---

* Ticknor visited Spain at a moment when, under the despot, Ferdinand
VII, the country, ravaged by the Peninsular War, had sunk to the depths
of poverty. It was the depressed condition of Spanish letters that gave
Ticknor,—as later his friend Prescott,—an opportunity to make himself a
world-authority in things Spanish.

found the New England legends. For, to Southey, Mather's *Magnalia* was enthralling; he knew more about Roger Williams than anyone in Boston cared to remember; he had written a long poem on King Philip's War. This was to mean as much to renascent Harvard, with its instinctive respect for an English poet, even a dull poet, as if New England had produced a Shakespeare. And it was to come with force from Ticknor because of his gift for lecturing. Not for nothing had he observed, in the midst of his other studies, the world-famous lecturers of Paris, Cousin and Lacretelle, with all their art and grace of execution.

In fact, as one followed Ticknor on his travels, one could imagine already how he was destined to stir his Harvard class-room. Although his main concerns were prosaic enough, philological data, sober facts of literary history, still the lives that he was to talk about, Cervantes, Lope de Vega, Dante, Petrarch, Froissart, Calderon, the old explorers and soldier and sailor poets, were quite enough to excite a roomful of boys who were able to do their own embroidering. They opened up vistas of adventure, unheard-of prospects for a poet's life. And if, without wishing to spread the peacock's feathers, he dropped, in those years to come, into reminiscence, he could unfold a world-panorama such as few in Cambridge had ever dreamed of. He seemed to have met, and more than met, every famous living personage. He had pleased Byron, on a later encounter, by telling him how Goethe admired his work. He had spent three days at La Grange with Lafayette, and Humboldt had read to him from his book of travels. Chateaubriand had told him again and again about his wanderings in the United States, through the unbroken forests.* He had known Canova and

* Chateaubriand remarked to Ticknor that, in a hundred years, when all the legitimate sovereigns had vanished, Europe would be full of despotisms. He knew what happens after world-wars.

Thorwaldsen, the sculptors, and Bunsen and Niebuhr in Rome, as well as he knew Sismondi and Madame de Staël, with whom he had often talked beside her death-bed. He had met the Countess of Albany many times, the wife of the last Pretender, who had liked his frankness when he said that England was better off without the Stuarts. He had travelled about Spain with a band of smugglers. At Naples, he had spent all his evenings at the *salon* of the old archbishop, where a group of Italian cognoscenti read Alfieri and Poliziano, in the Attic fashion of the Renaissance. With Washington Irving he had gone to Windsor: his pupils had read of this excursion if they knew *The Sketch Book*. He had met, among a hundred others, Lord Brougham's "bare, bold, bullion talent,"—for Ticknor was a master of the phrase, when it came to judging character. He had spent an evening with Godwin's circle, Hazlitt, Lamb and Hunt, and had never seen Sydney Smith's equal,—this was at Lord Holland's house, where he felt more at home,—for floating down the stream of conversation, and, without seeming to influence it, giving it all his own hue and charm.

In days to come, the young men at Harvard were to reap the fruits of Ticknor's *wanderjahre*. Here and there, as they followed his lectures, they were to catch a phrase or an allusion that opened up the picture. What patterns of the literary life the great professor, cold as he was, and distant, was able to place before them!—Humboldt, with his fifteen hours of study, pursued in the midst of all his social duties; Schlegel, who spent his evenings in the drawing-rooms, but rose at four and worked again till midnight; Madame de Staël, whose pen, lifted against Napoleon, was almost mightier than Wellington's sword. Never before, in America, had anyone invested with such glamour the life of the poet and the man of letters; and Harvard was ready for the new evangel.

CHAPTER V

THE NEW AGE IN BOSTON AND CAMBRIDGE

IT WAS 1819 when Ticknor returned to America, a youthful master of the grand style. Safe in his father's house, he felt rewarded for all these years he had spent away from Boston. He unpacked his collections of books, acquired at such expense, with the aid of half the booksellers in Europe, especially the Spanish collection, which was later to become so famous. There was no room in his mind for that malaise which, in after times, was to affect so many Americans, newly returned from the old world. The sense of an enthralling purpose dominated all his other thoughts.

It was a fortunate moment. "We are living," said the great Dr. Bowditch, who had come to live in Boston, "in the best days of the republic." He said this in his most impressive manner, and Dr. Bowditch was always impressive, partly because he was Dr. Bowditch and partly because of his reputation, which was already international. He felt obliged to add, as one who was accustomed to calculation, that worse days were bound to follow. But that worse days were to follow, even remotely, few Bostonians were prepared to think.* The nation was on the march, moving with equal tread towards unknown splendours; and a young man with a ruling passion, that of reforming Harvard College and making it worthy of

* Josiah Quincy was one of the few. Always cheerful and hopeful,—insomuch that at eighty-two, in 1854, unable to agree with most of his friends, who thought the world was going to the dogs, he said, "Almost everything at the present time seems to me to be better," even religion and morals,—he yet foresaw, through the "era of good feeling," the great convulsion coming, the Civil War.

the new day, had some reason to be happy. With Daniel
Webster as one of his intimate circle,—for Webster, too,
had settled in Boston,—with Bowditch as another, and
Dr. Channing, with the Prescotts, father and son, Judge
Prescott and William Hickling Prescott, Ticknor's
younger friend, with Edward and Alexander Everett,
recently the Minister to Spain, he could watch the wheels
of progress turning and even give the wheels a push himself; for all these men, whatever their interests were, had
a touch of the statesman in their composition. So did the
great East India and China merchants and the men who
were building up the factory-system and believed they
were building up the country. Their public aims and their
known distinction, which carried them into diplomatic
posts, attracted to the little capital,—larger in its littleness than it was to be when it was big,—every traveller
from the old world; and at their tables one met, from
week to week, members of the German and Russian lega-
tions, Spanish grandees and Danish princes, Chancellor
Kent from New York and Lafayette, scientists and historians from England. The Liverpool packets discharged
their passengers in Boston, which, for a while, with the
Cunard Line, became the main American port of entry.

Boston was more than ever like Edinburgh, the Edinburgh of the last few decades, when the Scottish metropolis was in its heyday. Later, these days of renown were
to pass, or to pass, at least, in a measure, when London
overshadowed Edinburgh and much of the glory of Boston passed to New York. But the social world of Scott,
Gifford and Jeffrey, of the Waverley novels, *Blackwood's* and the great *Review,* was reproduced, and more
than reproduced, in the New England capital, for a generation. The intellectual life was the fashion there, just
as it had been in Edinburgh, where university professors
and men of letters, judges and learned lawyers, lowland
lairds and Highland chieftains gathered for evening

routs in the winter season. Chalmers had his counterpart
in Channing, the shepherd of the Boston flock; nor was
there any lack of superior women, cultivated, witty and
devout, enough to meet the exactions of Abigail Adams.*
The greatest mind that was ever born in Boston was able
to feel that the town, in its spirit of emulation, suggested
Florence. Everyone with talent was impelled to struggle.
Everyone laboured to be foremost.†

"I meet in London occasionally," Stuart Newton, the
painter, wrote, "such society as I meet all the time in Boston." There were many people in Boston who took this
for granted. They did not give the British capital the
benefit of a doubt, whether their correspondent had met
all London. "The true Bostonian," Henry Adams said,
"always knelt in self-abasement before the majesty of
English standards"; but this was less the case at the present time than at any time earlier or later. No doubt, in
the Boston soul, politically American, there was a sub-
stratum of Anglicism that was never to be eradicated; and
this grew stronger, rather than weaker, as New England
lost its control in politics. The more the centre of gravity
of the nation shifted towards the West, the more the Boston mind, thrown back upon itself, resumed its old colonial allegiance. Boston, at present, was dominant and
potent. It was not Persepolis, of course: one did not find
there, or wish to find, the "courts where Jamshyd gloried
and drank deep." What one did find, or what the Bostonians found, was a singular situation, together with the
will to cope with it. They had received a nation from

---

* "If we mean to have heroes, statesmen and philosophers, we should have
learned women."—Abigail Adams.
† "What Vasari said, three hundred years ago, of the republican city
of Florence might be said of Boston: 'that the desire for glory and honour
is powerfully generated by the air of that place, in the men of every profession; whereby all who possess talent are impelled to struggle that they
may not remain in the same grade with those whom they perceive to be
only men like themselves, even though they may acknowledge such indeed
to be masters; but all labour by every means to be foremost.' "—Emerson
Natural History of Intellect.

their fathers, and they proposed to make it a great nation. This was a notable school of self-respect,* even of
the self-sufficiency for which the Boston people were
celebrated; † and, if there were many Pharisees among
them, others deserved the phrase, uttered by Benjamin
Constant,—they had all the virtues they affected. No one
spoke of provinciality. The word had not yet come into
use; there was even no occasion for it.‡ The word provinciality implies a centre, and nations that are in process
of building themselves are always self-centred. That
"the mind is its own place" no one doubts when people
are occupied with important matters. The Bostonians
were absorbed in public interests, and they had another
centre in the classics, which they shared with all Western
Europe. Moreover, having known great things at home,
they knew a great thing when they saw it elsewhere.§

* Ticknor, to whom Metternich said that he found the present state of
Europe "disgusting" and who discovered everywhere abroad the seeds of
decay and "moral degradation," expressed the feeling of all his contemporaries in writing, "A man is much more truly a *man* with us than he is
elsewhere . . . It is much more gratifying and satisfying to the mind, the
affections, the soul, to live in our state of society."

† See the remark of President Eliot's mother, addressed to a friend who
had joined the Episcopal Church: "Eliza, do you kneel down in church
and call yourself a miserable sinner? Neither I nor any of my family will
ever do that."—Henry James, *Charles W. Eliot,* I, 33.

‡ "Americans of that generation hadn't that snobbish shamefacedness
about their country,—and especially if they were well-born as you represent
Wentworth to have been. It is a vice of the *nuova gente* altogether. The
older men took their country as naturally as they did a sunrise. There
was no question . . . as to whether their country were the best in the world
or no—they *knew* it was."—Letter of Lowell to Henry James, 1878, apropos
of the latter's novel, *The Europeans.*

§ "A noble school," wrote Channing, in one of his note-books, "is profitable only to noble spirits. The learner must have something great in order
to receive great lessons." Today, in many large American cities, a man may
enjoy every material advantage, and even the advantages of travel, yet
still remain as unconscious of the great currents of contemporary thought
as any European peasant. But when, a hundred years ago, the *zeitgeist*
penetrated New England, with its train of world-ideas, it found a sensibility prepared for it; and a man like Thoreau, who scarcely stirred out of
his little Concord, instinctively understood Mazzini and Kossuth,—the
Gandhis and the Trotskys of his time. Those who have in their minds the
pattern of greatness recognize this pattern wherever they find it. They belong to the freemasonry of the enlightened, whatever their condition may
be or wherever they live.

The republic had proved to be a triumphant success, for the clouds had not yet risen in the Southern sky; the wealth and population of the country were growing at a prodigious rate, most of all, perhaps, in Massachusetts. By virtue of their experience and cultivation, the Boston people saw themselves as leaders in a great forward movement of the race.* No wonder their portrait-painters throve. "How rages the Harding fever?" asked Gilbert Stuart, in 1823, referring to Chester Harding, the admirable backwoods artist, who was luring away his own clients. Harding was to know as well as Stuart what Boston was willing to pay for its *amour-propre*. He had so many orders that he could not fill them. The Boston people thronged his studio, sometimes fifty in an afternoon. He had to book them like a racing-tout.†

Of this little statesmanly world, of which Ticknor was to be *pars magna,* Webster was the great political figure. A demon of a man, a full-blooded, exuberant Philistine, with a demiurgic brain and a bull's body, a Philistine in all but his devotion to the welfare of the State, his deep strain of racial piety,—this was the grand thing in Webster,—with an all-subduing personal force, an eye as black as death and a look like a lion's, as the farmers in his native New Hampshire said, almost a foreigner, with his rustic manners, among these Boston lovers of ele-

---

* Emerson expressed the general feeling when, some years later, he wrote: "I do not speak with any fondness, but the language of coldest history, when I say that Boston commands attention as the town which was appointed in the destiny of nations to lead the civilization of North America." —*Natural History of Intellect.*

† One readily understands how Ticknor, who had been received as an honoured junior by Humboldt, Madame de Staël and so many others, asked for nothing better than an opportunity to address the hard benches of a Cambridge class-room. Similarly, John Quincy Adams, aged eighteen, after having served abroad as Secretary of Legation, had been only too happy to resume his place as a Harvard sophomore. These facts imply a variety of conditions that make the place and time unique. They are certainly not remarkable, from the point of view of a sensible man. But few professors and students in the great universities of our day are sensible in quite this fashion.

gance, he was fighting, in and out of Congress, first for the Constitution, for the Union, imperilled by so many factions, and secondly for the manufacturing interests that lay behind New England's rising fortunes. With an oratorical gift as great as Burke's, in learning, in unction, if not in cultivation,—for, while Webster had a feeling for the sublime, he had little feeling for the beautiful,— he fought for the solid facts of property and the good old Yankee motive of self-interest. His politics, his economic doctrines were those of any sound New Hampshire farmer who owned a dam and a mill and turned his dollars over to the Boston bankers. These doctrines naturally pleased the Boston bankers. As a lawyer, he was unapproachable. When he talked about other lawyers, he made them seem like characters in Plutarch. He could invest a common murder-case with the atmosphere of an Æschylean drama.

A hunter, fisherman, farmer, who gloried in his rural avocations, in which the traits of the backwoods pioneer were mingled with those of an old border baron, Webster was to become, as the years went by, a legendary figure in New England. In Boston, he was the rock of the Constitution, as kings had been defenders of the faith. Throughout the country districts, he was "Dan'l," whose every word, as a farmer remarked, seemed to weigh a pound. People said that Dan'l was made of granite, and they knew he had learned his American history from old Captain Webster of the minute-men, who had guarded Washington's tent on the battle-field and for whom Liberty and the Union, far from being phrases, were facts that represented blood and steel. Everyone knew the great squire of Marshfield, where he had a farm as large as half a county. Everyone had heard him on the platform, every boy and girl had seen his picture, the dark brow that looked like Mount Monadnock, the wide-brimmed hat and the knee-high boots, the linsey-woolsey coat and the flowing necktie, the walking-stick that was said to be ten feet long. There was something elemental in his composition, something large and lavish. Even his faults were ample. Webster despised the traditional virtues.* He spent money in a grand way, borrowing and lending with equal freedom. He was far from sober, or would have been if two tumblers of brandy had been enough to put him under the table. He could be surly enough, when he had his moods of God-Almightiness, or when he wished to insult some sycophant. The thunder-clouds would gather on his brow and the lightning flash from his eye, and he would tell a committee that their town was the dullest place on earth. No one could be more truculent, especially in the hay-fever season; but he was always good-natured with the farmers, who liked to think of him as their man. They knew what Webster meant when he said that his oxen were better company than the men in the Senate. They knew all his ways and the names of his guns and animals, as the Jews of old knew the weapons of Nimrod, or Abraham's flocks and herds,—his great ram Goliath, his shot-guns, "Mrs. Patrick" and "Wilmot Proviso," his trout-rod, "Old Killall." They knew he had written the Bunker Hill oration, composed it word by word, with Old Killall in his hand, wading in the Marshfield River. They had heard of his tens of thousands of swine and sheep, his herds of Peruvian llamas and blooded cattle, the hundreds of thousands of trees he had raised from seed. They knew that while his guests were still asleep,—the scores of guests who were always visiting Marshfield,—he rose at four o'clock and lighted the fires, roused the cocks with his early-morning

---

* "Thirty years ago, when Mr. Webster at the bar or in the Senate filled the eyes and minds of young men, you might often hear cited as Mr. Webster's three rules: first, never to do today what he could defer till tomorrow; secondly, never to do himself what he could make another do for him; and, thirdly, never to pay any debt today."—Emerson, *Letters and Social Aims.*

candles, milked and fed the stock and chatted in the kitchen with his farm-hands, quoting Mr. Virgil, the Roman farmer. And at Marshfield, as everyone knew, his horses were buried in a special graveyard, with all the honours of war, standing upright, with their shoes and halters.

From Boston, across New England, across the nation, Webster's fame spread, as the years advanced. Boston men who had seen Garrick and Foote and heard Burke and Sheridan, the masters of the spoken word, were satisfied that Webster was their equal. Countless thousands, bankers, lawyers, farmers, read his orations aloud by the evening fire. They felt as if the woods and the fields and the ocean had found a worthy voice in Webster's words; and Captain Thomas, his neighbour, was not the only man who longed for death when Webster met defeat. This faithful follower, fearing that all was lost, after Senator Hayne's second speech, cast away his boots, saying he would never want them more, and took to his bed for days. New England had never known a public man with such a Jovian personality,* whose words, when he chose to deploy them in a diplomatic encounter, had the force of a fleet of battle-ships. He could make the United States appear the mightiest of all historic empires. Who knew better than he, or could say it better, that America was the hope of liberty, as those who had visited Europe could see for themselves, as Ticknor and Everett had already seen, when the old regime had been restored in force, in Italy, France and Germany, when liberal ideas, even in England, were still in doubtful debate? Who was more the symbol of his country? Were the Boston people, with all their self-possession, still, in a measure, tinged with colonialism? Were they prone to ask the

---

* "There was the monument, and there was Webster," Emerson wrote, referring to the Bunker Hill oration. Sydney Smith exclaimed, when he saw Webster in London, in 1839, "Good heavens, he is a small cathedral by himself."

visiting European what he thought of American institutions? Were the countryfolk too ready to protest that
they had whipped the redcoats? Were the gentry still
English in their customs? Webster was the universal answer. Noah Webster, with his dictionary,—whether for
better or worse,—had established American usage in the
matter of words. Daniel Webster was equally potent in
matters of personality. All his traits, his references, his
habits bore witness to the national character and but-
tressed it with the kind of authority that could not be
gainsaid. When he spoke of the Bay State and Bunker
Hill, of Plymouth Rock, Lexington and Concord, one
felt that to belong to Massachusetts was the noblest
privilege of history. *Civis Romanus sum.* "Thank God, I
also am an American!"

With Webster as the great political figure, Channing
was the great religious figure, another member of Ticknor's circle,—for Channing had not yet embarked on his
later career as a social reformer, which was to divide the
Boston household. As Webster spoke for the outer life of
the town, its property-sense and a kind of patriotism that
largely represented its mundane pride, Channing spoke
for the inner life of Boston, with a charm and glow of
intellectual goodness that triumphed over its prejudices.
Although he was a Unitarian, the only man of genius in
the movement, who had defined the faith and even defended it in controversy, when the Orthodox party attacked the "Boston religion," he was a poet in his theology, for whom a creed was only a vestibule. He was not
at home with the Cambridge logic-choppers, whose ways
he found repellent. His fluid mind, suspicious of every
dogma, wished to live "under the open sky." The adora-
tion of goodness was his religion. He hungered and
thirsted for it; and the great, wide, ingenuous eyes that
beamed under his broad-brimmed hat and lighted up the
little figure, wasted by so many sufferings, proclaimed his

inextinguishable faith in the natural possibilities of men. He detested the jealous caution of New England, the insane love of money that pervaded the trading world, the coldness of the calculating mind, the dullness and timidity of provincial manners. Oh, for a Burns to shock the Boston burghers out of their staid decorum! Under the crust of American life, so frigid on the surface, was to be found, he thought, if one looked for it, the simple, wild stock of human nature, with all its natural feelings and social instincts, the seeds of every noble attribute. It required stimulus, it required affection. Channing was always young for liberty,* not the mere terrestrial liberty that Webster represented, but a liberty of the intellect and spirit that tended to form a superior race of men.

In days to come, Channing's ideas, which had their own logic, were to be expressed in certain ways that Ticknor and his circle did not like. These were the days,—one saw them in advance,—when Ticknor, with Everett as his only rival, was the great intellectual and social figure, as potent as Webster and Channing in their spheres, the host of every visitor to Boston, the one man who had seen all the world, where others had seen only portions of it, and numbered among his countless correspondents the preëminent minds of half a dozen countries. These were the days after he had married one of the daughters of the well-known merchant whose other daughter had married Andrews Norton, and people spoke of him with bated breath; for wealth united with learning, and learning with prestige, and prestige crowned with conscientiousness,—

* George S. Hillard recalled that, at the time of his graduation from Harvard, Channing, to whom he was introduced, remarked: "I see that you young gentlemen of Cambridge were quite too wise to be thrown out of your accustomed serenity by the new revolution in France! I was in college in the days of the first French Republic, and at every crisis of its history our dignity was wholly upset. We were rushing to meetings of sympathy, or kindling bonfires of congratulation, and walking in torch-light processions. But now the young American has come to years of discretion and may not give way to such unseemly excitements." Channing, in spite of his early Federalism, always felt at heart as he had felt in college.

all these formed a constellation that would have dazzled
any other town. By virtue of a similar constellation,
Andrews Norton reigned over Cambridge; and Ticknor's great house at the head of Park Street, dominating
the Common from Beacon Hill, soon became the symbol
of his renown. There he kept his famous library, the
amplest private library in Boston, housed in the largest
and most elegant room, approached through a marble
hall by a marble stairway, about which the butler dis-
creetly hovered. Over the mantel hung the Leslie portrait
for which Sir Walter had sat at Abbotsford, and the
walls of the stately apartment were covered with books,
methodically arranged and richly bound. And there, with
his air of the scholar-nobleman, gracious but somewhat
marmoreal, like his hall and mantel, Ticknor dispensed
his counsels to aspiring students. He was ready to give
advice about the various versions of Cervantes, if someone wished to make a new translation. He was happy to
lend his books, as many as two or three hundred, to any
qualified applicant, even in Maine or New Hampshire, or
the South. Everyone knew that, where books were concerned, he knew, as no one else, all the resources of Europe, from Naples and Spain to Scotland, from Holland
House in London to the cabinet of Prince John of Saxony, where his own portrait hung in later years. He had
seen all the books, even the lumber-rooms of the Escorial,
even the Medical Library at Madrid, where he had been
the first enquiring student for three-and-twenty years to
break the rust on the locks and the wire nettings. He
knew, or was to know, even the little bookcase that stood
near the window in Tieck's parlour; and if, as befitted
one whose knowledge of Spanish literature was greater
than that of any man in Spain, he was especially rich in
Spanish works, he was a great collector in other fields.
Under the mantel, beside the fire, he held frequent classes

for young ladies, the daughters of his friends, in Dante, Milton and Shakespeare.

This was a type that Boston understood, the magnanimous man who passed its peculiar tests. Correct himself, and willing to diffuse correctness, he was able to correct a duchess, when the case called for correction, without disturbing the poise of a drawing-room. Moreover, in addition to his wealth and learning, he was a faithful adherent of Dr. Channing, as long as Channing did not go too far. His pamphlet on Lafayette passed through three editions in the French translation. But in his teaching he was most the statesman; for, although he continued to live in his Boston house, he had at once assumed his post at Harvard. Jefferson, as everyone knew, had tried to induce him to go to Charlottesville: all he desired was that God might send him two or three Ticknors. But Ticknor was not to be drawn aside. The Harvard library, which had seemed so large, seemed to him now a closetful of books. The college could scarcely be called a respectable high school. To turn it into a university, one that could bear the name and deserve the name, and set the intellectual pace of the country, was the Jeffersonian task that lay before him.

Meanwhile, Everett and Cogswell had also returned to Cambridge. Cogswell, the master-bibliographer, took the college library in hand and rearranged the books on the Göttingen plan. Everett began his career as Professor of Greek, a notable career, alas, too brief. The old grammarians, who had taught the classics, might have had warmer hearts than Everett, but they had colder minds. They had no feeling for the Greek myths, no feeling for the poetry of Homer, and Everett was another Abélard, or so the Harvard students were convinced. But there were other irons in Everett's fire, as time was soon to show. On his arrival from Europe, he had preached a sermon in Washington, where no one had ever heard such magical words. Senators, justices, cabinet members praised him as the prince of orators and asked him to remain as the chaplain of Congress. He had come back to Cambridge with a halo, but with his mind torn with a new ambition. The incident had unsettled him for life. As the years passed and he carried on his lectures, he watched the rising star of his friend Webster. Webster had risen by oratory, and he was as good an orator as Webster. Why should not he too enter Congress and meet his college classes between the sessions? Why should he not be Minister to Greece, as his brother had been Minister to Spain?—especially when, like Ticknor and Andrews Norton, he had formed a fortunate marital alliance, with the daughter of the richest man in Boston? Not that he craved the splendid burdens of office! But were not the splendid burdens of office, painful as they were, more in the line of a man's public duty than teaching a roomful of boys? Others who have been known to ask this question have answered it as Everett answered it. He complained, in a letter to Justice Story, which he asked Story to burn, that he found the life and duties of a professor far too humble for him. They were not, he said, respectable enough.

The roomful of boys at Harvard knew nothing of the professor's doubts and dilemmas. That he was discontented never entered the head of one of these boys, Ralph Waldo Emerson, who thought of Everett as "our Cicero" and took it for granted that, like his prototype, Everett scorned the opinion of the vulgar, those that held a man in low esteem who, side by side with the politicians, was known merely as a "Greek and scholar." Everett held the students spellbound. He was severe and precise in his college class-rooms, eager to impart, in detail, the wealth of the new German learning, Wolf's theory of the Homeric writings, the exegesis of Voss and Ruhaker, the criticism of the ante-Homeric remains.* Outside, in his public lectures and speeches, to which the students flocked, he let his fancy soar. His Greek brought back the days of Pericles, his imagery was opulently Persian. That he was magniloquent they did not know. That he was theatrical they did not care, for oratory was their theatre. His elegance, his confidence, his ease stirred their imagination. What pictures he could present of Scott and Byron, the reigning British poets, whose Harolds and Manfreds and Marmions were on every lip, of Humboldt, Madame de Staël and Lafayette! Standing before the panorama of Athens, which had been presented to the college, he discoursed on Greece as one who had seen it. His multifarious quotations were so apt, his style so fluent and graceful, he uttered such inspiring reflections on the future of American literature! The fame of his foreign training, the glamour of his adventures attracted students from the remotest parts, from Georgia and Tennessee.

It was a triumph of style and fantasy. In later years, some of Everett's pupils, seeing how vacuous his career had been, wondered that he had so beguiled their minds. Too tender-minded for a statesman,—as they perceived, looking back,—he had followed Webster as an understudy. He had been Governor of the Commonwealth, Secretary of State and Senator, but always, as one of these pupils said, a "dangler;" and the more he elaborated his outward graces, the more he became a shaken reed within.† And yet he had not really beguiled the students.

* "During the present century, I believe that Harvard received and welcomed the new learning from Germany . . . before it had been accepted by the more conservative universities of the Old Home. Everett's translation of Buttmann's Greek Grammar was reprinted in England, with the 'Massachusetts' omitted after 'Cambridge,' at the end of the preface, to conceal its American origin."—Lowell, *Literary and Political Addresses.*

† Emerson said of Everett, in his journal: "Webster has done him incalculable harm by Everett's too much admiration of his iron nature; warped him from his true bias all these twenty years, and sent him cloud-

Empty as so much of his rhetoric was, it stirred the adolescent imagination. False, or largely false, it communicated an impulse that was true. A student who imitated Everett's style was sure to be corrected by Edward Channing, who hated a purple patch as he hated the devil; and meanwhile Everett waved a wand that opened up the magical world of Homer. Some of the boys who saw the wand waving were always to have a foothold in that world, with all its wild beauty, even while the dour Professor Channing kept their other foot in Yankee-land. And with Ticknor busy, with unsleeping eye, over his new department, that of the modern languages, and lecturing, with all of Everett's verve, on French and Spanish literature, a student might well have found himself alert. For Ticknor was a scholar born, as Webster was a statesman born and Dr. Channing was a born priest, never tempted to stray from his natural sphere. He fought for his reforms. He did his best to substitute thorough teaching for the old sing-song ways the college loved. There was a brief flutter. Then the old system was resumed, except in Ticknor's own field. There he had his way. He gath-

---

hunting at Washington and London, to the ruin of his solid scholarship, and fatal diversion from the pursuit of his right prizes."

In later times, Everett, in contradistinction to Webster,—the oratorical "Michael Angelo," as Everett was the "Raphael," so called,—became the classic example of all that was bad in American oratory. One marvelled over the bursts of applause that followed his apostrophe to Stuart's portrait of Washington in Faneuil Hall: "Speak, glorious Washington! Break the long silence of that votive canvas!" But Everett's style was the style of his age in all but the greatest men. Italy, France and Ireland, in the eighteen-twenties, afforded similar examples. Even Victor Hugo, and even a generation later, abounded in this vein. Everett was a master of calculation. John Bartlett of Cambridge,—"Familiar Quotations" Bartlett,—saw him drilling a group of old Revolutionary soldiers who were to sit on the platform during his Concord oration. The poor old souls were expected to rise when Everett exclaimed, "Noble men!" and bob up and down in their seats at various other points in the oration. He was once observed in a country book-store asking for a pocket Bible, which he wished to produce dramatically during a speech. As the Bible was not forthcoming, he took a copy of Hoyle's *Games* instead. It served just as well, and nobody knew the difference. In fact, there was so much "theatre" in Everett's speeches that people soon wondered whether there had ever been anything else.

ered together a staff of foreign instructors, French, Italian, German. And there he established a path for the university to follow later.

During these years of change and growth at Harvard, Dr. Channing's mind was also growing. Shortly after Ticknor's return, he too had reappeared in Boston, after a year of travel and rest in Europe, charged with fresh life. In England, he had found many admirers, for the great Boston preacher's reputation had spread beyond the sea; but the doctor, ill and depressed, had fled from all these kindly ministrations and sought the solitude of the English lakes and the conversation of Wordsworth. He had read the poet's *Excursion* again and again; indeed, he had never read anything but Shakespeare more. Ever since his early youth at Newport, he had shared this mystical sense of the universe as the outer garment of God; and the landscape of New England had prepared him for the charms of the Cumberland country. For Channing was a lover of lakes and mountains. He had studied their contours under various skies; he knew all the effects of atmosphere, of mist and cloud and dry and watery sunlight. The grandeur of New Hampshire, the gentle, pastoral beauty of Vermont had swayed and attuned his feelings. He could form a friendship with a mountain; and he knew the interminable depths of the virgin forests as well as he knew the ocean, beside whose crashing waves he had leaped for joy. These temperamental sympathies had drawn him to the new German *Naturphilosophie*. Through Madame de Staël, at first,—whom he had read with different eyes from Ticknor's,—and then through Wordsworth's friend, the poet Coleridge, he had been introduced to the writings of Schelling, in whose intimations of a divine life, manifested in nature and the soul, he had found his mental home. He had been roused as well by Fichte's heroic stoicism, which spoke of the grandeur of the human will. These prophets seemed to him to corroborate the great hopes of the French Revolution, which he had shared in his youth. In deference to the feelings of his congregation, the richest and most respectable in Massachusetts, practically-minded Whigs, with little taste for nonsense, he had suppressed his natural sympathies. But he belonged to the race of the older and bolder. He looked askance at the reigning thoughts of Boston, with its "scared and petrified" conservatism.

His year in Europe, spent with congenial friends, in England, among the Alps, in Rome and Florence, had quickened all his apostolic instincts. Wordsworth had read to him passages from *The Prelude*. He had communed with Coleridge, who described him later as the "very rarest character" he had known. He had formed the friendship with Lucy Aikin that was to result in so many relations between the old world and the new; and it was observed, on his return, that a change had taken place in his mental horizon. The preacher who had delighted everyone with his penetrating discourses on ethical questions, dear to the Boston heart, seemed at once more literary and more social. Not that he ceased to be a moralist, one of those rare artists of human behaviour,—like his own Fénelon, for instance,—who, by virtue of some inward grace, constantly flowing through the intellect, purge the mind of cant and win the imagination of untold thousands to the beauty of their own unworldly goodness. Channing was a poet and a saint; and he shared and led, as no one else could lead them, the deeply devout religious conversations that occupied so many Boston minds. He did not care to discuss theological matters, the question of Particular Providence, the Evidences of Christianity, the Genuineness of the Gospels, all those special, textual, technical problems that exercised the learned men of Cambridge. But he was often present at those reading parties where they talked over a chapter of *Rasselas,* or a passage from Plato or Milton, and the topic set for the evening was the distinction between natural and moral happiness. Whether the performance of one's duty should have any connection with one's self-regard. Whether the moral nature was immortal or would be swallowed up in the divine. Gratitude, personal obligation. If one saw two persons in grave danger, which should one save first, one's benefactor and private friend or the person of most use to humanity? In these Boston parlour-conversations, carried on by scholarly casuists, blue-stockings and others, Miss C. defending Paley, Mrs. S. taking the side of Kant, Channing was a frequent arbitrator.

But the focus of his mind had been gradually shifting, along with the general focus of the Boston mind. The serious atmosphere of these discussions,—so like the discussions of similar circles in England, those that surrounded Macaulay, Mill and Ruskin, the rising generation of British authors,*—assumed another aspect as the years advanced. The great problems of the factory-system, which was so rapidly growing, the problems of the poor forced themselves on these conscientious minds. They could no longer ignore the social questions that complicated the ethical point of view. What was the effect of an occupation with wholly mechanical things? What was the moral difference between workers in mills and those who worked by themselves? How much taste and judgment were involved in making a handsome shoe? What were the obligations of the rich in regard to the education of the poor? Unitarianism, it was noted, had always been accompanied by radical movements. Even in far-away Poland, the Unitarians had been non-resistants

* Also the discussions of the Jansenist circles of seventeenth-century France. The atmosphere of Geneva, in the eighteen-thirties and forties, as reflected in Amiel's *Journal Intime,* was strikingly similar to that of Boston.

For this aspect of the New England mind, see *Memoir of W. E. Channing,* by W. H. Channing, the *Memoir of Mary L. Ware,* by E. B. Hall and *The Life of Charles Follen,* by E. L. Follen.

and pacifists, conscientious objectors, communists, trouble-makers for the powers that be. The Boston Unitarians, as a group, cared for none of these things. They had made a State Church of their religion, and, with their shrewd sense of the interests of trade and their temperamental self-complacency, they were opposed to any further changes. But the Unitarian leaven that worked in Channing was of a much more fundamental kind. He pondered all these questions in his heart, and, as the years passed and his fame grew, the rift grew wider and wider between the doctor and the respectable classes he represented. Living in his beautiful house, the property of his wife, he slept in a cold and cheerless attic, struggling to solve the problems that weighed upon him. How to destroy the worship of money. How to elevate the depressed classes. How to remove the evils of competition. How to convince human beings that they were parts of a great whole, bound to work for the welfare of this whole. The union of labour and culture. Slavery in the South. He could not please the Abolitionists, for he saw things in too complex a light; nor could he please his parishioners, who began to cut him on the street. Only his fame and his saintly character kept for him the respect of the practically-minded.

This was in the future, when his name had travelled round the world and he had readers in India.* Now already, in these early twenties, he had begun to play the part of a leader in the renaissance that was evidently at hand. Were there not seasons of spring in the moral world, and was not the present age such a season? Could one fail to see on every side the signs of an unparalleled energy? And yet the mind of the nation was still asleep. As a boy, Channing had been a famous wrestler. He had loved adventurous sports and had borne well the name

* It was Channing's secular essays, on Milton, Fénelon and Napoleon, that gave him, at first, this larger reputation.

of "little King Pepin." He had climbed the mastheads of all the ships at Newport. For twenty years he had wrestled with himself; and who was better prepared than he to wrestle, in the name of enlightened reason, with all the dark forces, inward and outward, that cramped the spirit of his countrymen? Had not theology laboured without ceasing to cover human nature with infamy, to crush its energy and confidence, so that men had almost ceased to believe in their mental and moral powers? They idolized wealth because they did not know what other and greater goods they were capable of. They looked to what was profitable first and only on second thoughts to what was right, for their natural feelings were masked and petrified by caution, policy, prudence. Their lives were needlessly joyless. For himself, he thought the ancients were too solemn in calling the earth Mother, the earth, so youthful, so exuberant, so living and rejoicing. The first of all the wonder-signs of Jesus was that in which he blessed a wedding-feast and heightened all its pleasures, even its pleasures of sense. Was not the intemperance of New England a signal judgment on the Puritans, who had tried to banish pleasure from the world? To rid society of its sordid vices, music should be taught in the common schools. Dancing should be encouraged and festivals fostered, so that old and young might share in sports and pastimes. There should be picture-galleries and halls of sculpture. Boston should develop the sense of beauty by creating beauty.

Such were the luminous thoughts of the climber of mastheads. Every Sunday morning, he mounted his pulpit and poured into the ears of his congregation, willing or unwilling, large draughts of intellectual day. His eyes grew wider and wider as he spoke, and the little figure seemed to grow taller and taller. One saw him in the streets, at public meetings, ubiquitous, alert, robed in his blue camlet cloak, a shawl about his neck, with his drawn, ethereal face almost lost under the enormous hat; or at Newport, at his summer home, "Oakland," surrounded by its gracious lawns and gardens. There, like Lamennais in his retreat,—for Channing, too, had written his *Paroles d'un Croyant,* even his *Essai sur l'Indifférence,*— he gathered his younger followers about him, discussed and read philosophy and history, in the summer-house or on the wide verandahs, Plato's *Timæus,* perhaps, or Coleridge's *Biographia Literaria,* Schiller, Wordsworth, Shelley, *Wilhelm Meister,* or led them to some seat among the rocks, where Berkeley had also talked with his disciples. He rose at Newport earlier than ever. One heard his quick step on the gravel walk, as he strolled among the shrubs, with the dogs gambolling beside him, or in and out of the green-house, where he studied the plants and flowers. Often the children joined him, trooping along the paths, for Channing was a friend of all the children. "A child's little plan should be respected," he wrote in one of his note-books. To say of a child or a man, as they often said in Boston, "There is a great deal of human nature in him," did not mean to Channing what it meant to so many others. He had a large opinion of human nature,—so large that people thought he was romantic,—even when its powers were in eclipse. Every day, for years, it was known in Boston, he fed with his own hands two poor old women who fancied that people wished to poison them and would accept their food from him alone.

Everyone could see, in after times, that Channing had been the great awakener. By raising the general estimate of human nature, which the old religion had despised, he gave the creative life a prodigious impulse; for, if human nature was a thing so precious,—however enslaved, insane, depraved, degraded,—how could one hesitate to emancipate it? How could one fail to fly to its assistance? How could one fail to offer it the means by which to achieve the beauty that was proper to it? Channing was the father of half the reforms that characterized the Boston of his age.* Moreover, he harrowed the ground for literature, first by his harrowing of the ground for life, and also by his intuitive understanding of the function of art and letters. He knew his country and he knew the poets, and he knew what his country and the poets needed. Independence, he was well aware,—the basis of all enduring greatness,—was something that had to be earned, and that could be earned. It was for the poets and thinkers to earn it. "A people," he wrote in one of his essays, "into whose minds the thoughts of foreigners are poured perpetually, needs an energy within itself to resist, to modify this mighty influence . . . It were better to have no literature, than form ourselves unresistingly on a foreign one . . . A country, like an individual, has dignity and power only in proportion as it is self-formed." † That the true sovereigns of a country are those who determine its mind, its modes of thinking, that writers are the originators of all those currents of thought by which nations and peoples are carried forward,—this was Channing's constant theme and vision. Mind, mind required all one's care.

* Among the many well-known reformers who drew their impulse largely from Channing were Dorothea L. Dix, once a governess in Channing's household, who devoted herself to improving conditions in the prisons and asylums, Elizabeth Eaton, founder of a society to help the poor foreigners who were appearing in Boston, 1830–1840; Elizabeth Peabody, the "grandmother of the kindergarten," etc.

† *On National Literature.*

CHAPTER VI

THE NORTH AMERICAN REVIEW: SPARKS, BANCROFT

THE LITERARY mind was astir in Boston. Not like thunder, not with a roll of drums, but with a little chirrup here and there, the dawn had slowly broken. In Channing, in William Tudor's books of essays, in the *Travels of Ali Bey,* modelled on the *Lettres persanes,* Boston had become self-critical. Dozens of minds were asking themselves the questions that had found words in the *Monthly Anthology.* Hundreds issued the summons, —which was to be repeated for a hundred years, on each new frontier of the American mind,—for a literature that was really American, "redolent of the soil," "purged of old-world influences." In later years, when people spoke of the "renaissance" in New England, they spoke with a measure of reason; for in Boston, as in Florence, four hundred years before, there was a morning freshness and a thrill of conscious activity. The New England imagination had been roused by the tales of travellers and the gains of commerce, the revival of ancient learning, the introduction of modern learning, the excitements of religious controversy. After the long winter of Puritanism, spring had come at last, and the earth reappeared in its beauty.

Ever since 1817, the little circle of the cognoscenti knew that something important was in the air. There had been decisive proofs of this. Professor Edward Channing and his cousin, Richard Henry Dana, had been driving from Cambridge into Boston. Channing was the editor-in-chief of the new *North American Review,* and Dana was his assistant. As they drove along, side by side, Channing read to Dana two poems that had just come into his hands by a young man named William Cullen Bryant, who lived in a village in the Berkshires. One of them was entitled *Thanatopsis.* As Channing continued to read, Dana exclaimed, "That was never written on this side of the water!" His excitement, he said later, was natural, considering what American poetry had been up to that moment. The day before, a middle-aged country doctor had appeared at the office of the review and drawn from his voluminous pocket-book these poems by his son, which he had brought clandestinely to Boston and eagerly showed the editor. Dana, hearing that Dr. Bryant was making a speech before the Legislature, went at once to the State House, to have a glimpse of the father of such a poet. The American world had moved a step forward when village poets could produce such verses and country doctors could be proud and happy to know that their sons were men of genius.

All the circumstances of this event were typical of the moment. First of all, the excited recognition that something had really happened: the time and the place were ready for the poet. The feeling of Bryant's father was typical also, for most of the writers of the coming age were actively encouraged by their fathers and mothers, for whom the career of letters seemed as normal as that of the pulpit or public affairs. Not even in Catholic countries, where almost every peasant family aspired to produce a priest, was there a keener wish, in the poorest household, that a brilliant son might have "advantages" and follow the line of his intellectual interests. Still more symbolic was another fact: a magazine existed,—after so many abortive attempts,—that could provide an outlet for the writers who were appearing on every hand. Ed-

ward Channing and Dana, at this moment, with George
Ticknor, also of their circle, were probably, of all American readers, the best informed on English poetry, from
Chaucer to the new Romantic School. The rest of the
group who wrote the new review, and followed one
another as editor,—Edward and Alexander Everett,
Jared Sparks and John Gorham Palfrey, two young students of history, Greenwood, Dr. Gardiner, together
with Bowditch, Webster and Andrews Norton,—were
all men of the world, more or less, who had kept up with
the literary current and knew what living writers really
counted. They proposed to meet the sneers of the British reviewers in a tone that was neither provincial nor
chauvinistic. They were greatly obliged to Scott, the first
of living writers, in their opinion, who had said, in his
kindly way, that when people once possessed a three-
legged stool they would soon contrive to make an easy-
chair.

The new review was the easy-chair in question. It
was a little angular, perhaps, but no one could have called
it a three-legged stool. Its tone was almost as cold and
tame as that of the *Monthly Anthology.* It had the dry
simplicity, the hard strength, the timid correctness and
those other traits that Goethe said so naturally belonged
to the early period of every art. It was like the old New
England furniture, re-expressed in words. Modelled on
the British reviews, still the foundation of all American
thought, it imitated their magisterial air. The editors
seemed to be on their best behaviour. But the British
reviews also were cold and formal, even when they
"stripped and whipped" their victims. The great Romantic critics had not appeared, to take the starch out of
their pompous manners; and the *North American* had
many virtues. It was aware of all the important writers
in England, France and Germany. It noticed all the
American writers, Cooper, Irving, the poet Bryant, who

was soon to settle in New York, the centre of his future
life and work. It was on guard against the colonial note:
one of the writers condemned a Canadian author on the
ground that no colonial government had ever evoked the
nobility of mind that was essential to greatness. Its standard was severe and thorough: some of its reviews represented five months of study, during which the reviewer
went behind the author, read all the works that he had
read and verified all his citations. In short, with a firmer
hand and greater resources, it carried on the task of the
Monthly Anthology; and, as the years passed and it grew
in strength,—until its conservative policy sapped its
strength,—the public became aware that it had at last a
genuine organ of criticism, one that deserved to rank with
the best reviews in the world.

There was no doubt about its conservatism. If it was
clear, orderly and well-informed, if it possessed all the
scholarly virtues, it was hostile to the forms of feeling,
literary, political, philosophic, that were to characterize
the coming age. It was a Unitarian-Whig review, with all
the temperamental limitations that marked Webster's
class of "solid men." In politics, its aim, as time advanced,
was to keep the tariff up, to keep the Whigs in power
for the sake of the tariff, and to keep on good terms with
the Southern magnates, whose cotton fed the Northern
factories, so that the tariff might serve the Boston bankers. All very simple, like the old curriculum at Harvard.
In literature, it had a marked aversion for the notes of
the new age, enthusiasm, mysticism, rapture. Although it
felt obliged to accept the English Romantic poets, if only
because they were English, it still preferred the eighteenth-century modes. For this reason, the tender-minded
Dana soon broke with his fellow-editors. A Whig, even a
Tory in politics,—in the current American sense of the
words,—a lover of old customs and associations, who
wrote Addisonian "Letters from Town," he was a profes-

sional man of letters, the first of his kind in New England, and the only one of the group, for the *North American* followed the principle of "all gentlemen and no pay." In him, the old idea of "polite letters" had given place to something more profound. He did not think of poetry as a recreation, for he had taken Wordsworth in sober earnest; and he thought there were truths beyond the "understanding" that could not be reached in the usual Boston way. In fact, he preached the high Romantic doctrine. He had written a series of papers on the British poets, defending the Lake School.* He had said that Pope was not a poet at all.† This was too much for his friends, and much too much for Boston. A furious hubbub resounded through the town. Out Dana went, and out went with him any hope that the *North American* would ever understand the new generation.

Alas for Dana, born too soon, not strong enough to break his own path and yet the symbol of a rising world where other poets of a tougher grain were to find their audience waiting. A sensitive dreamer, diffident, self-distrustful, with all the shy and solitary ways that marked the romantic poet as a type, he was to become an ancient Nestor, the only man living, decades hence, when even the Civil War was growing dim, who could still remember Washington's death. As he strolled through the Boston streets, a forgotten ghost, or basked in the sunshine of his Cape Ann garden, his silvery curls reaching to his

---

* In the opinion of Professor John Nichol, these essays were the best that had appeared, up to that time, on the Lake School, either in America or in England.

† The division of feeling in regard to Pope marked the new age more clearly than anything else. See Parson Wilbur's comment, in *The Biglow Papers*, on the youthful Hosea Biglow's view of Pope's verse: "He affirmed that it was to him like writing in a foreign tongue,—that Mr. Pope's versification was like the regular ticking of one of Willard's clocks, in which one could fancy, after long 'listening, a certain kind of rhythm or tune, but which yet was only a poverty-stricken *tick, tick,* after all,—and that he had never seen a sweet-water on a trellis growing so fairly, or in forms so pleasing to the eye, as a fox-grape over a scrub-oak in a swamp."

shoulders, he would speak of the British essayists of old and the charm that lingered round their memory; but he had lived his life as a recluse, sending forth shoots of prose and verse that had very rarely grown or flowered. He had written a long poem, *The Buccaneer,* the fruit of his early rambles on the Newport beaches, poems modelled on Coleridge and Byron, verses that were not as good as Bryant's, tales of the "darker passions," after the manner of Brockden Brown, *Tom Thornton, Paul Felton,*—young men doomed to live in a world that cannot comprehend their aberrations. Not one of his poems or tales could have been called conclusive. He had started a magazine, *The Idle Man,* filled with his own musings and his friends' verses, and lapsed into an unembittered silence, hoping that perhaps the day might come when an American author would be valued as much as an argand lamp. Thirty years of writing as a profession had brought him less than four hundred dollars. No man, he said, could go on forever without some little response from the world about him.

The circle of the *North American* could hardly have been described as sympathetic. These positive minds, however, had other qualifications. Their interests were historical and political, their gifts of a purely critical order. Dana's ablest work was his criticism, and many essays in the magazine were as good as the best in the foreign reviews of their time. One might mention, as an instance, the essays of Alexander Everett, whose mind was livelier and more vigorous than that of his more famous younger brother.* Criticism, oratory, history,—

* As Minister to Spain, Alexander Everett had studied the South American republics, which were revolting against the mother-country. In his surveys of America and Europe, translated into German, French and Spanish, he showed a remarkable understanding of the post-Napoleonic political era. His literary papers on *Gil Blas,* Voltaire, Mme. de Sévigné, Chinese manners, etc., lucid, learned, often witty, revealed the *North American* at its best. He translated Theocritus and Goethe and passages from the *Brahma Purana,* among the first examples of Oriental studies in

oratory, the statesman's instrument, and history, the record of his achievements,—these were the forms of literary expression in which, at the moment, America most rejoiced. In the early days of Rome, with which New England had so much in common, the orators had come before the poets, the chroniclers before the dramatists. To the little statesmanly world of the Boston patricians, of which the *North American* was a spokesman, the noblest, the most honourable career, after making history, was to write it. Or, better still, to speak it. Had not Luther said: "Whoso can speak well is a man"? *

In fact, all over the country, in the Middle States, in the South, as well as New England, during these opening decades of the century, the historical mind was extraordinarily busy. Old men who had fought in '76 gathered the children about their hearths and told them tales of Lexington and Concord. People thronged to Plymouth Rock, which Webster had signalized in his great oration. The neglected chronicles came to light. Growing boys and girls rediscovered Mather's *Magnalia,* wonderful stories about their country that made them feel the very ground they trod on was consecrated by Providence. Hundreds of local histories, histories of states and counties, histories of towns and villages, proud of the parts they had played in the recent wars, poured from the rural printing-presses. It was a symptom of a world-wide movement, for everywhere Napoleon's campaigns had roused the sense of nationality. In England, Macaulay, Grote, Carlyle and Milman, in France, Thiers and Guizot, in Germany, Niebuhr and Ranke were only a few of the notable men who were immersing themselves in historical studies. The archives

America. Among the early *North American* writers, one might also mention Caleb Cushing, the statesman who coined the phrase "man on horseback." Cushing's *Reminiscences of Spain* compare well with Washington Irving's writings.

 * "If ever a woman feels proud of her lover, it is when she sees him as a successful public speaker."—Harriet Beecher Stowe, *Dred.*

in the European capitals were searched and brought to light, and tens of thousands of dusty documents were scrutinized and passed from hand to hand, even from country to country. The historians formed a princely brotherhood, forwarding one another's investigations,— like the men of science of the future. Niebuhr had set an example and a standard for critical scholarship in historical writing, first in the search for materials and secondly in the examination of them; and there had never been a time when a new and distinguished contribution to history received such universal appreciation. England, like America, stirred by the great continental scholars, had awakened from its age-old isolation and begun to study the history of other peoples, and the English historians were developing, thanks to the recent revival of classical studies,—at Oxford, as at Harvard,—a new and fresh feeling for composition, for the artistic virtues of the ancients. Upon all the English-speaking historians, Sir Walter Scott had a profound effect. He gave them a sense of local colour. He taught them to reproduce, in their narrations, the atmosphere of the times with which they were dealing.

The American school of history, established in New York by Washington Irving, was one of the phases of this world-movement. For its culmination in Boston there were various reasons. The first large library in the town, that of the Massachusetts Historical Society, founded in 1791 by Jeremy Belknap and others, was almost exclusively stocked with historical works. The Athenæum and the Harvard Library were both especially strong on the side of history. Young men with literary tastes were drawn into historical research largely for want of other choices. There was little else for them to read. This was the "accident," as Palfrey called it, that gave rise to the New England school, soon to fulfil the prophecy of Horace Walpole that Boston was to produce a Thucydides. But the circumstance was not an accident. Everything had prepared the Boston mind to centre its thoughts on history, as it had chosen theology in the past; and the general interest that filled the libraries with all this apparatus of research animated the young historians and gave their works a sympathetic welcome.

The accumulation of private wealth in Boston, thriftily guarded by the canny Whigs, also served the historians. Prescott, Motley and Parkman were men of large means. So was George Ticknor. Bancroft, who was relatively poor, found himself obliged, and contrived to spend, in the preparation of his earlier volumes, almost three times as much as the President's salary. Ticknor's *History of Spanish Literature* cost as much to produce as a public building. In these formidable bills of expense, the assembling of books and documents was the largest item; for the public and semi-public libraries grew very slowly. Prescott, as late as 1839, said that an American historical writer had to create a library of his own if he wished to write even on American themes, much more if his theme were Spain or Holland. In another twenty years, all this had changed, and the wealth that had made it possible for a few scholars to command the means of study provided the means also for the poor. In 1857, the German, Kohl, describing the private libraries of Boston, which were largely open to students, spoke of the American "author-princes" who flourished side by side with the merchant-princes. Even in London he had scarcely found such splendid collections of books or studies that were arranged so picturesquely, with busts, paintings and curiosities, spaciously illumined from above. Many of the merchants were bibliophiles. One of them owned twelve hundred Bibles, including several that were very rare. Another collected engravings, hundreds of fine examples of every school. Another had a collection of Americana, first editions of every known work relating to the early history of the country. Thomas Dowse, a journeyman leather-dresser who, in the days of his poverty, when he did not own a pair of boots, possessed "six hundred books, well bound," bequeathed a great collection to the public. There were many rivals for the distinction of owning the finest library in Boston. No doubt, George Ticknor's outshone them all; but by some the honour was claimed for Theodore Parker, the great preacher of the eighteen-fifties, whose library was a river of books that flooded his house from attic to cellar. The libraries of Everett and Prescott were renowned. The books of Rufus Choate, the Salem lawyer, who settled in Boston in 1834, filled his large house from floor to floor, in spite of all the efforts of his wife to stem the appalling tide.

With all these new facilities, the studies of the historians made rapid progress. For a number of quiet readers, more or less in Boston and more or less in touch with one another, were preparing a series of monumental works, George Bancroft, the son of Aaron Bancroft, the well-known minister of Worcester, Jared Sparks, William Hickling Prescott, J. G. Palfrey * and Richard Hildreth, editor of the Boston *Atlas.* Rufus Choate's friends thought he was better fitted for history than any of these professional historians. The dream of Choate's life was to write a history of Greece; and, in preparation for this, he made a translation of Thucydides, never choosing a word,—or so he said,—until he had thought of at least six synonyms. But the busy lawyer, whose mind dwelt in Athens, had no margin of time for meditation. There were plenty of others to take his place. Half the men of letters in New England were spreading out their notes and documents in emulation of Robertson and Gibbon. To

---

* Palfrey, the author of the *History of New England,* published, in 1821, an article in the *North American Review,* pointing out the use that writers of fiction might make of early American history. The first New England historical novel, Lydia M. Child's *Hobomok,* was written in response to this article.

be sure, they were few at first. Jared Sparks, even in
1840, wrote home from the British Museum, where
he was examining manuscripts, "In the reading-rooms
are daily congregated more than a hundred readers and
transcribers, of all nations and tongues, plodding scholars,
literary ladies and grave old gentlemen with mysterious
looks. When shall we see the like in the Athenæum?"

Boston was not London; but at least in the Athenæum
one might have seen, even years before, the well-known
Hannah Adams, working on her history of the Jews, the
lady of whom one heard so many stories, as that they
were obliged to lock her in, because it was not polite to
lock her out. Living, Miss Adams was the only female
who ventured to claim her statutory right to browse in
these, to her, celestial pastures. Dead, as she was soon to
be, she was the "first tenant" of Mount Auburn, or so
her gravestone said, though a Boston lawyer, pondering
the inscription, remarked, "She cannot properly be called
a tenant." One had seen Miss Adams at the Athenæum;
one saw the Everetts, Ticknor, Palfrey, Sparks, the pillars
of the *North American*. One saw Richard Hildreth, a little
later, a tall, thin, aging man in black, deaf, absorbed, sitting at his table in one of the alcoves, with his books and
papers before him, rising from his chair only to consult
some work of reference. The vogue of historical writing
increased day by day, in this still air of delightful studies;
and the regular Boston dinner-hour, three or four o'clock,
lent itself to long, laborious mornings. In 1840, Charles
Francis Adams, the famous diplomat of years to come,
brought out the *Letters of Mrs. Adams*. John Quincy
Adams, Abigail's son, expressed the feeling of a thousand
readers when he said that his mother's letters affected him
till the tears streamed down his face; and the editor of the
book, Abigail's grandson, already touched to tears by these
old papers, exclaimed, "Happy are those who pass through

this valley with so much of innocence!" * The new generation was engrossed in history, not in American history
alone, and not exclusively on the highest level. J. S. C.
Abbott, the brother of Jacob Abbott of the Rollo Books,
represented an army of popular writers. Of his *Life of
Napoleon,* Emerson said later, "It seems to teach that
Napoleon's great object was to establish in benighted Europe our New England system of Sunday schools." †

In Cambridge, in the middle thirties, the boys and girls
of the university circle were permitted to dive and delve,
with well-washed fingers, into the great boxes, eight in
number, where lay the unpublished letters of Washington.
There were forty thousand of these letters, which the
great man had written or received, many of them in
the spacious study where they were now assembled, in the
Craigie house on Brattle Street, Washington's study during a long winter. Jared Sparks had moved out from Boston, bringing with him the famous correspondence, which
he was preparing for the press, and had rented a suite of
rooms from Mrs. Craigie. Sparks, the "American Plutarch," was working on his "lives," the *Library of American Biography,* a series of twenty-five volumes, written by
various hands, including his own, describing a whole Pan-
theon of American heroes. He was soon to be more widely
known as the "patriarch of American history." ‡ He was
already engaged in his great campaign, along with George
Bancroft and Peter Force, to collect, preserve and publish the documents of the period of the Revolution.

His writings, however useful, were hardly exciting, at

* Charles Francis Adams maintained the literary habits of the most artic-
ulate of American families. Brought up in the White House as a boy, he
kept an Adams diary, like his father, for more than fifty years. He contributed seventeen articles to the *North American Review,* on Aaron Burr,
Lord Chesterfield, etc.

† E. P. Whipple, *Recollections of Eminent Men.*

‡ After his appointment, in 1838, as the first Professor of History at
Harvard,—at any American college,—a date that marked an era in historical studies.

least, to later readers; and yet they represented a life as exciting as that of an Arctic explorer. Indeed, Sparks had wished to be an explorer, like the hero of his first "life," —the best of all his lives,—John Ledyard, the old Connecticut Yankee, Captain Cook's corporal of marines. He had risen from the ranks, the poorest of the Connecticut poor, supported himself as a carpenter, walked three hundred miles through northern New York, trying to find a school where he could teach. He had battled his way through Exeter, where he had written an essay on the subject, "Intense application to study not detrimental to health." He had battled his way into Harvard at twenty-two and found a position as tutor at Havre de Grace. His Harvard friends protested. How could a man endure existence hundreds of miles from Boston?—considering that, from the point of view of Boston, civilization came to an end at Worcester. But Maryland was the making of him. The inn where he lived was on the post-road, and half the notabilities of the nation stopped there on their way to Washington.* At the time of the War of 1812, he saw the British sack Havre de Grace. They burned the great houses where he worked as a tutor, and the British admiral commandeered the finest coach in the town and sent it aboard his ship. Sparks was prepared to write with feeling when he came to consider the days of '76.

In this wider American world, he soon lost his New England particularism. He was appointed chaplain of Congress, and, with an interest already aroused in history, found himself surrounded with those who make it. Reading Mungo Park, he dreamed of exploring Africa. The plan came to nothing, or, rather, it led him to discover

* Josiah Quincy, who was then in Congress, stopped at the inn one day with Dr. Channing, who had also been a tutor in the South. Quincy and Channing liked the young man and remembered and helped him later. It was Quincy who, as president of the college, called him back to Harvard, and Channing preached at Sparks's ordination, when he became a minister, at Baltimore, the sermon on "Unitarian Christianity" on which his own fame as a theologian was so largely based.

Ledyard's papers and remains, including parts of the
journal that Ledyard kept, describing Cook's death in
the Sandwich Islands. Then, having followed Ledyard
in imagination, he turned to the exploration of another
world, almost as dark as central Africa, the world of
American history. He had had enough experience of public life to know where his materials were to be found. He
visited all the Southern States, examining the papers in
the archives and those in private hands, as often as not in
the old family dwellings of the men he had met in Washington. Then he went abroad, to England, Holland, Germany and France, searching the public offices, with Lafayette's assistance, arranging with Guizot and others to
publish translations of his *Washington*. One of his aides
was Henry Stevens, the "Green Mountain boy," a biblio-
phile in London, who introduced into Europe thousands
of American books and made the British Museum a world-
centre for American historical research.

Now, in his Cambridge study, in Washington's own
chambers at the Craigie house, he was engaged in the
great work of his life. About his standing desk, on every
side, heaps of papers lay, not only Washington's letters
but the letters of Jay, John Adams, Gouverneur Morris,
the statesmen and diplomats of the great war-years. Simple as a child, with his gentle, winning voice and grave
smile, he was the boast and delight of scholarly Cambridge. Everyone knew the story of Washington's letters, how Sparks, having found them at Mount Vernon,
had arranged to carry them up by ship to Boston. Everyone knew the story of the other letters, Gouverneur Morris's, Franklin's. Some of them Sparks had been just in
time to save. He had found two large trunks of Franklin's
letters in a Pennsylvania garret, where they had been lying
for forty years. Another mass of Franklin's letters and
papers turned up in a London tailor's shop, on a shelf,
in loose bundles. One of the manuscripts had already been

cut in the form of a sleeve-pattern. One shuddered to think what might have happened if Sparks had not possessed the explorer's eye. Two or three years more, and it might have become forever impossible to write a correct history of the Revolution.

It was true that he "embellished" all these papers. He could not let the father of his country speak of "old Put": he changed the phrase to "General Putnam." He could not allow Washington to speak of a sum of money as a "flea-bite." The sum was "totally inadequate to our demands." In short, he bowdlerized the political fathers, in the spirit of a neo-classic age. He had in mind the marble bust, after the timid fashion of Canova, the bust that later times, too cynical, were to find little better than plaster. For this there were certain excuses. Science had not regulated history. No settled standards existed anywhere in regard to documentation. Quotation-marks had no precise value, and the greatest historians did not hesitate to revise their quotations without comment. There were other local excuses that were not so sound. In the days of Andrew Jackson, those who cherished manners, grace and form had some reason to feel, as the Romans felt in the days of the Gothic invasions, that all the amenities of life were threatened. The amenities received a double sanction, all the more because, in America, there was no prescriptive class to defend them. The famous "genteel tradition," of which one was to hear so much later,—so very much too much, when the phrase ceased to be used with any discretion,—largely dates from these days of Jackson, who brought the Wild West into the White House; and the high-minded Sparks, who, for the rest, had made his own way in a world that worshipped manners, could hardly have been expected to underrate them. The wonder was that he remained so candid. His Washington had to be a correct example, in harmony with the feelings of the thirties and forties; but he took pains to see that the causes of evil fell on the right heads.*

As for the nature and value of his writings, they were excellent *mémoires pour servir*. Sparks preserved the materials for later writers and placed them in a position to correct himself; and those who, in days to come, visited the library at Harvard looked with respect at the carved mahogany chest, modelled after the tomb of Scipio, in which reposed the Jared Sparks papers. The fame of his work showed what an audience awaited the coming historians, and what a social function they fulfilled, a function as vital as that of the orators, the ministers, the scholars and the portrait-painters.† For the twelve volumes of his *Washington,* orders came from the remotest hamlets in Georgia, Alabama, Illinois. Two hundred sets were sent to the Red River. The *Franklin* was translated presently into one of the dialects of Hindustani.‡ But Sparks's vogue was slight beside that of Bancroft, whose *History of the United States* began to appear in 1834. Never before had anyone attempted to tell the whole story of the nation, and the poor little dry chronicles and annals, Dr. Abiel Holmes's and so many others, that stood for American history were swept from the shelves by Bancroft's enterprise. There were reasons for Bancroft's renown. He was a conscientious student, laborious, open-minded, enquiring, zealous, with the strong will of an old Puritan

* Sparks, in his bowdlerizations, followed a general practice of the time. Similar cases can be found in every European literature. The heroes of the early eighteen-hundreds, conceived by readers of Plutarch, had to be heroes at any price.

† The first necessity of a new nation is to believe in itself. To create this self-confidence was the function of the early American orators and historians. "The only nations which ever come to be called historic are those which recognize the importance and worth of their own institutions." —Tolstoy, *Anna Karenina.*

‡ This was the greatest period of Franklin's universal fame. "The Greeks admire the character of Franklin. His name is far more familiar to them than that of any other American, not excepting Washington. Many of the 'sayings' of the philosopher are in the mouths of their instructed men." —Samuel G. Howe, *Historical Sketch of the Greek Revolution,* page 264.

settler. He had the imagination to see and present the life
of the South and the West, as well as New England. He
was learned enough to place American history in the main
stream of historical events. His style was often picturesque
and moving, irradiated with a solemn glow. It was true
that, in the first editions, before Bancroft "slaughtered the
adjectives," the book was like a Fourth of July oration,
like one of Everett's speeches long drawn out, with the
Stars and Stripes streaming from the author's hands.*
This was the note of the nation in Jackson's time, when,
with little reflection or criticism, the "giant of the West,"
rejoicing in size and numbers, growing, mounting in wealth
and population, building its turnpikes, railroads and canals,
heaping up its factories, bounded towards its "manifest
destiny." For Bancroft, God was visible in history, and
history culminated in the United States. No wonder his
"epic of liberty," with its solid merits, was also acclaimed
for other reasons.

He was well prepared for his task. He had grown up in
a scholarly circle, and, when he was six years old, his
father, Aaron Bancroft, referred to him a question in
Roman history which two friends of the house, one of
them Chief Justice Theophilus Parsons, found themselves
unable to settle. He had known Sparks at Exeter. At Harvard, Edward Everett and Andrews Norton had taken him
under their wing. The college had sent him to Germany.
Another grand tour, like that of his predecessors. Wherever he went, in England, Italy, France, the first question
that everyone asked was "Do you know Everett and Ticknor?"—who had been so diligent and so attractive. Bancroft was prouder than ever of his country; and he was en-

* "Come, children of sorrow! You on whom the Old World frowns;
crowd fearlessly to the forests; plant your homes in confidence, for the
country watches over you; your children grow around you as hostages, and
the wilderness, at your bidding, surrenders its grandeur of useless luxuriance to the beauty and loveliness of culture."
The pruning of these unnecessary feathers of the newly-fledged American
eagle was Artemus Ward's special joy and task.

gaging, too, with his black hair and firmly cut features, his eager air and obvious earnestness. Humboldt wrote to a friend, "He belongs to that noble race of young Americans for whom the true happiness of man consists in the culture of the intelligence." With all his exciting adventures, his meetings and visits with Byron and Benjamin Constant, Manzoni, the Princess Borghese, Lafayette, whose house was hung with engravings of American scenes, he never lost sight of his object. At Göttingen, along with his Latin and Greek, he studied Hebrew and Syriac. He met students from every country, Poles, Hungarians, Netherlanders. He learned to waltz, he learned to ride on horseback: one saw in him already the little sprightly man with the Santa Claus beard who, at eighty-eight, two generations later, pranced about the roads at Washington, with a big red rose in his buttonhole. At the same time, as a Christian devotee, a more than passive Unitarian,—in short, as that species of minister, sometimes ordained, sometimes not, under the guise of which so many young New England men of letters made their first appearance before the public,—he preached to the country congregations about the town of Göttingen, always speaking in the German language. He spent much of his time with Schleiermacher, the great court preacher at Berlin, listening to his lectures on education,* and made a study of the German schools.

Bancroft's heart, however, was far from simple. Still less simple was his outward manner. Returning home, as tutor in Greek at Harvard, who wished as much as Everett and Ticknor to introduce the German thoroughness, he found himself thwarted at every turn. This was not merely because of the Harvard indifference that also thwarted Ticknor. Bancroft was a vain young man and even more ambitious than Everett, in the less engaging

---

* The influence of Schleiermacher was apparent in the mystically religious passages in Bancroft's history.

sense of the term. He had neglected to observe Bacon's admonition in regard to travel, which all good Americans regarded as sound, that one should not change one's country manners for those of foreign parts, but only prick in some flowers of that which one has learned abroad into the customs of one's own country.* He had half forgotten the English language. French, German, soft Italian phrases blossomed on his lips, a flaunting of the dulcet strain that was much too much for Brattle Street. Bancroft's apparel and gestures were a scandal. He greeted his old protector Andrews Norton by planting a large kiss on each of his cheeks. There was a Cambridge tableau! It was the beginning of the end for Bancroft. But this young instructor was resourceful. He took himself off to Northampton and founded the Round Hill School with Cogswell, another peacock in the eyes of Cambridge. Indeed, there were anchors on every side of Bancroft's little ship. A diligent scholar, who worked for his school, he worked still harder for his own advancement; and the good Sparks, who welcomed his contributions to the *North American Review,* felt obliged to chide him for his foibles. He urged him not to use too many words like "emotions, love, affection, sensation, feeling," which carried him sometimes "into more soft abstractions." This was the counsel of a severe student with an eye for the rigours of language, who knew, as Bancroft did not know, the perils of a turgid rhetoric. And Sparks, with even greater penetration, told him frankly that he was too greedy after the treasures that the moths enjoy. "After what else, pray, should a man be greedy?" Bancroft had replied, with equal frankness. It was all very well to talk about "filthy lucre." A young man, the son of aged parents, had to be up and doing. "The only way," as the young man said, "to show you are fit for a better world is to show yourself not unfit for this." And

* This useful piece of wisdom was sadly misplaced in later American epochs.

Bancroft made the most of all his opportunities. No "musing with unseen spirits" for him, no folding his hands in contemplative indolence. He was ready to risk the chance that this was the way to rival Tacitus.

In short, with motives that his friends suspected, he had joined the Democratic party. He had little to fear from censorious Cambridge and Boston, when he had the growing will of the nation behind him. A Democrat in Boston was a social outcast; * but Bancroft had allied himself with powers which, as he well knew, and as Boston surmised, had the future with them. He had transcended the sectional mind of New England. From an equally obvious point of view, he had placed himself in the practical line of advancement; for the Democrats of New England were so few that any distinguished member of the party was sure to be rewarded in the end.† This prospect was certain in the case of Bancroft, a practical man with a gift for administration, almost the only scholar in the party, a learned Harvard man who had had the courage to smite the Boston Whigs with his scorn,—the Whigs who had smitten him, in the person of Andrews Norton,—even one who found in the people's hero, Jackson, the "nursling of the wilds," the hand of God himself. Bancroft, visiting Washington, drew his chair "close up" to the powers that were, as he said in one of his letters. Jackson and Martin Van Buren liked a man who could shape their political views in eloquent words, who was "easily first in literary improvements," as the "kitchen cabinet" called him. Bancroft's career in politics followed as a matter of course.

---

* William Henry Channing recorded later that, as a boy, he had heard with utter amazement,—as if such a thing could scarcely be conceived,—the remark of an old Bostonian, "A Democrat may be honest in his convictions."

† "A Massachusetts man has little chance of success in public life unless he starts a Federalist; and he has no chance of rising above a certain low point unless, when he reaches that point, he makes a transition into Democracy."—Harriet Martineau, *Society in America.*

No doubt, his association with politics was useful to a writer of history. Who, moreover, could impugn a man for taking sides against the Whigs? The party that Jefferson founded and Jackson maintained was grounded in the welfare of the nation, as some of the best Whigs had begun to see; and the Adamses had always agreed with Bancroft that Hamilton's aristocratic policy, shaped in the interests of the few, had no base in principle and morals. Bancroft's sympathy with the popular will was honest, beyond all question. Aside from his political associations, most of his European associations confirmed him in his faith that the Democrats represented the all-American cause for which the Revolution had been fought. Byron had sided with the Democrats. The Democratic party upheld the convictions that Lessing, Herder and Klopstock had in mind when they spoke of the "lodge of humanity" in the West; and yet, alike in Bancroft's life and mind, there was that element of self-deception which often dogs the spokesman of popular interests. The sentimentalist was marked in Bancroft. The conservative Prescott detested the Mexican War,* as a travesty of American principles. It was the Democrat Bancroft, the voice of the people, by no means including the Mexican people, who, as acting Secretary of War, ordered Taylor to march into Texas and gave the command to seize California,—in order to extend the "area of freedom" for those who did not rightfully own the country. Literary men indulge in humbug only at a price, and Bancroft abounded in humbug. "Did he believe what he was saying?" Anthony Trollope remarked in later years, after one of Bancroft's swelling speeches. Emerson had asked the same question when he said that Bancroft was a "soldier of fortune" who would "take any side and defend

* "The impolitic and iniquitous war in Mexico . . . mad and unprincipled . . . The patriot would rather see us go ahead by the arts of peace than war, as better suited to the permanent prosperity of the republic."
—Prescott, *Correspondence*, 648, 658, 668.

it." Who can say how much a man believes, when he has an actor's temperament and a demagogue's faith in numbers? *

And yet Bancroft's work was impressive and made him "one of us," as Ranke said. All too keen for the cloud of witnesses, very imperfectly a man of letters,† insomuch that, after revising his work, pruning its highly-coloured feathers, he gave it an effect of truncation and bareness, he was an indefatigable student, with a grandiosity that was sometimes grand. He had first conceived the enormous task during his years at Göttingen and had exercised himself, to prepare for it, in a series of shorter studies, most of them on historical themes, the Economy of Athens, the Decline of the Roman People, the Wars of Russia and Turkey, some of them on German literature.‡ Meanwhile, he had steeped his mind in the legendry of the country, and, as the years went on,—the fifty years during which he was occupied with his twelve volumes, each one emblazoned on the back with the well-known phrase of Berkeley, which summed up the note of the days of Jackson, "Westward the course of empire takes its way,"—he mastered every corner of his field, as far as a

* "Bancroft talked of the foolish *Globe* newspaper. It has a circulation of 30,000, and, as he said, each copy is read by ten persons, so that an editorial article is read by three hundred thousand persons, which he pronounced with all deep-mouthed elocution. I only told him that I wished they would write better if they wrote for so many. I ought to have said what utter nonsense to name in *my* ear this *number,* as if that were anything. Three million such people as can read the *Globe* with interest are as yet in too crude a state of nonage to deserve any regard. I ought to have expressed a sincere contempt for the Scramble newspaper."—Emerson's Journals, IV, 410.

† His later writings, *The Life of Martin Van Buren* and *The Life and Character of Lincoln,* are always either commonplace or tumid, sometimes ridiculously so.

‡ Printed in the *North American Review.* Jared Sparks, as editor, had spoken up for nationalism in Italy, Greece and South America, and the magazine was widely read abroad. A dozen copies a month were sold in Calcutta, and the Bourbon king, Louis XVIII, caused to be prohibited in France this tribune of popular liberties. Bancroft's essays on Goethe, Herder and Schiller were among the first in America on these subjects. Goethe thanked him heartily for the paper he had devoted to himself.

contemporary could have done so. He had laid out a plan on the scale of Gibbon. He carried on a voluminous correspondence with every man and woman he could reach, north, south, east and west, who was able to give him any information or any unpublished letters. He opened up veins of tradition, collected half-forgotten anecdotes, travelled up and down the Mississippi, set his agents to work in London and Paris, searching the archives for him. After his first volume had been published, the whole world of scholars was ready to help him; the libraries and manuscript collections of almost every family in Europe that had had associations with America were freely opened to him. No one questioned his thoroughness. After forty years, he was still alert for any new material that he could use in some fresh revision of his work. The hardy old man, at eighty-five, still rose in the night, lighted his fire and candles and read his Gibbon and sometimes toiled for fourteen hours on end.

This was the great life-pattern of New England,* and Bancroft's work was not unworthy of it. One still recaptures, as one turns its pages, the pride that thrilled the bosoms of the forbears for whom the glowing historian first unrolled the panorama of the national epos. The forbears shared Bancroft's fervour. The young republic shared it; and the republic saw itself reflected in Bancroft's flattering mirror. There, like a river-system seen from a lofty mountain, the whole American story stretched its length, down to the adoption of the Constitution: the founding of the colonies, the struggles with the European peoples, the Puritans, the Cavaliers, the Quakers, the red men and their ways, the slave-trade, the early wars, the wonders of the Western wilderness,—the elk, the stag, the bear and Daniel Boone, pausing to rest in the golden thickets,—the savage forests and the great planta-

* "For fifty years he rose before the sun," as President Kirkland of Harvard said of John Adams.

tions, the gathering of the forces in the Revolution, the nation rejoicing in its strength, all in connection and relation, God the cause, Progress the effect. Happy days when Plancus was the consul, remote as Rome itself, when the young republic delighted the soul of Tocqueville and every American morning was a Fourth of July! Who would smile, in the sweep of such a vision, at the touchy, self-important little man who served as its rhapsodist and its hierophant, the little leader with his buttonhole who called the steps in the barn-dance of Progress?

CHAPTER VII

PRESCOTT'S
FERDINAND AND ISABELLA

SUDDENLY, in 1837, out of this throng of historical studies, honest and laborious, some of them fervent, none of them august, a great work appeared, like a wonder of nature, as it seemed to American readers,—*The Reign of Ferdinand and Isabella*. It was a brilliant performance, as any child could see and no scholar was ever to deny. Its limitations were obvious enough. It was not a philosophical history. The author had no great leading views, nor any profound feeling for human motives. There were depths upon depths behind and beneath the story that he had never plumbed. But, as a work of art, a great historical narrative, grounded at every point in historical fact, and with all the glow and colour of Livy and Froissart, it was a magnificent success. Its outlines were as firm as those of a cartoon of Raphael, and its pageantry of picturesque detail was calculated to feed as never before the starved imagination of the country. The book had been planned like a battle and built as stoutly as a Salem clipper, destined to sail through many enchanted minds for generations to come.

It was the work of William Hickling Prescott, Ticknor's young friend, the charming, amusing son of Judge Prescott, who lived in his ample house in Bedford Street, overlooking a beautiful garden. Prescott?—who could believe it? He was partly blind, and he had an extravagant love of jolly parties. He talked with a joyous abandon,

running over with animal spirits, laughing at his own in-
consequences, with always some new joke or witty sally.
He could be happy in more ways, in spite of his defective
eyes, and happier in every one of them, than anyone else
his friends had ever seen. One met him in the street, with
his rosy air, with his gay blue satin waistcoat, tall, graceful, with light brown hair and a clear and ruddy complexion. He seemed to look younger every day. It was known
that, for twenty years, he and a group of his friends,—writers in the *North American,*—had carried on a literary club,
reading their papers over a merry supper. He had printed
a few essays in the review. But this was in a dilettantish
spirit, everyone supposed. One of his relatives, meeting
him on the street, not long before his book appeared,
urged him to undertake some serious task. It would be so
good for him. It would be more respectable than leading
this unprofitable life.

Every evening the light from his study-window glimmered through the pear-trees in the garden. But only
George Ticknor, outside the household, knew that, for at
least ten years, Prescott had been hard at work, harder,
perhaps, than any Boston merchant. And, if everyone
bought his book for a Christmas present, it was only because the author was so attractive. One of his cronies, who
was not a reader, rose before dawn, on the day it was published, to buy the first copy; but, while everyone saw at once
that it was good, no one was aware how good it was. There
were scarcely twelve men living who were able to know.
Within a year or two, the electoral returns came rolling
in, from England, France and Spain. The book had been
born a classic.

It was a conquest of personality. Prescott was a first-
rate human being, exuberant, gallant, wilful, firm, devoted, far removed from the clerkly sort of scholar, pains-
taking but wanting in vigour and sinew, who, in a world
in which the most virile types adopted careers of enter-

prising action, ruled over the sphere of books. He was an artist-cavalier. His temperament fitted him to understand an age of courageous exploits, and yet—as if in his veins flowed in equal parts the blood of the old colonel of Bunker Hill and that of the mild and philosophical judge, his father and his grandfather—he was a just and sensitive referee, whose verdicts could be trusted. Whatever he did was sure to be decisive. For the rest, he was happiest on horseback and might have been a soldier.* He did not like to get up in the morning and had to instruct his servant, the faithful Nathan, to pull away his bed-clothes. He did not like to work. He had to make bets with his secretary that he would write a certain number of pages or carry out some other resolution. He was always making resolutions, never too old to make them; and he was never old enough to keep them. He had formed this habit at Harvard: resolutions about the number of hours he was going to spend in study, about the number of times a week he was going, or not going, to balls and theatres. When he broke too many resolutions, he introduced into his reckoning sets of fixed exceptions, amendments on amendments; then he scored them all off and opened a new account. By this means, and others, he made himself a casuist, able to comprehend the Spanish mind.

The refractory horse makes the most mettlesome charger. Prescott had a formidable will, and his gay inconsequence gave it buoyancy. Underneath his mock self-scrutiny, he formed the habit of self-examination; and he had bridled and harnessed his indolent nature. Every morning, in the dead of winter, to wind himself up for the day, he mounted his horse and rode to Jamaica Plain, to see the sun rise from a certain hill. As for his blindness,

---

* Several of the New England authors, Bancroft, Longfellow, Parkman, etc., were, like Prescott, excellent horsemen.

"The absolute tyranny of a human will over a noble and powerful beast develops the instinct of personal prevalence and dominion . . . It makes men imperious to sit a horse."—Holmes, *Elsie Venner.*

which was never total, he made an advantage of it. One might have thought that blindness was a blessing. He could not read for more than ten minutes,—an hour or two a day at the best of times. And how could a blind man write a history, based on unpublished documents, in two or three foreign languages?—for Prescott, who was unable to study law, had fixed his mind on history. Dr. Johnson had said it could not be done, a very good reason to prove that it could, as two of Prescott's later friends, two of the great historians of Europe, Thierry and Capponi, were to prove as well. He made his ears do the work of his eyes, with the aid of a friend and a sister and later of a competent secretary. Blindness had always favoured contemplative habits. Had not Malebranche closed his shutters in order to drive the sunlight out? Had not Democritus, as the legend said, blinded himself deliberately to stimulate his thinking? Saunderson, Euler, Huber all were blind. The blind town-crier of Salem, where Prescott had spent his earliest years, had performed most of the functions of a daily paper. Blindness was good for invention, as many poets proved, from Homer to Milton. The blind were famous for their patience, especially for their feats of memory. One dwelt on passages that were read aloud.

Prescott, who was no fatuous optimist, summed up these thoughts in one of his essays. He taught himself to use a noctograph, by means of which, with the aid of an ivory stylus, pressing on a sheet of carbon-paper, he took his notes and wrote his manuscripts. The secretary copied the notes in a large, round hand, which Prescott was sometimes able to read. Meanwhile, he had learned to memorize, composing in his memory to such an extent that he could often carry in his mind as many as three chapters of one of his books, seventy-two pages of printed text. He could hold it there for several days, turning it over and over, remodelling every sentence. One chapter he thus remodelled sixteen times, before committing a word to pa-

per. His blindness had another effect. No reader of his
histories ever imagined that, however he dealt, perforce,
in a wholesale fashion, with the butcheries of the Spaniards,—"the Inquisition dogs and the devildoms of Spain,"
—Prescott was an impassive man. He had sat at the feet
of Channing, for whom no sparrow fell to the ground in
vain. His blindness increased the sensitivity that lay behind the judgments he conveyed—as an artist ought to
convey them—by subtle modulations of tone and style.
He spoke of the careless indifference with which men who
would never abuse a dog crushed, without a thought, insects whose bodily agonies were imperceptible to the
naked eye.

He had first acquired these mental habits when, as a
young man with failing eyesight,—the victim of an accident in college,—he had been sent abroad, to London and
Paris, to consult the doctors there, and had spent a quiet
winter in the Azores, where his mother's father, Mr.
Hickling, was consul at Saint Michael's. People were surprised, in later years, that Prescott, who had never visited
Spain, or Mexico or Peru, knew so much about these tropical scenes and was able to fill his books with such glowing
pictures,—Spanish gardens, myrtles, laurels, lemons, the
box-tree and the rose, mountain vistas, wildly picturesque, the Cordilleras and the Sierra Nevada, with con-
vent-bells ringing in the valleys. Through his writings, to
the very last, even to the final portrait of Charles the
Fifth, dying in his garden-monastery, breathed the fragrance of the orange-trees, flowering in the southern sunshine. A young man who had grown up in Boston, under
cloudy skies, lashed by the east wind, would have had little
imagination if he had not received vivid impressions during these June-like months at "Yankee Hall," on the outskirts of Ponta Delgada, with a grand old patriarch like
Mr. Hickling, as warm-hearted and merry as his grandson, and a gay brood of half-Portuguese cousins. And sup-

pose this young man, surrounded by so many marvels,—
castellated country-houses, gorgeous churches, crumbling
nunneries,—passing enchanted hours in mule-back rides
over the volcanic mountains, had yet been obliged, in his
blindness, to spend half his time in a dark room, walking
scores of miles from corner to corner, throwing out his
elbows to feel the walls till he wore away the plaster, till
he knew what a dungeon felt like and might have been
himself, even he, one of the victims of the Inquisition,—
would he not have preserved these impressions of what
his eyes had beheld? One takes a good look when, for all
one knows, it may be a last look. One takes two looks at a
tropical scene when one has lived in New England. It was
in this dark chamber, singing as he walked, to keep his
courage up, that Prescott learned the art of memorizing.
He composed a long poem for one of his friends.

The rest of this European journey also had its consequences. A young historical student, one who is going to
write about soldiers and statesmen, cannot see too soon,
at close range, a few good specimens in the flesh, not to
speak of the scenes of which the Romans had written.
In Italy, with his Livy and his Horace in the net of his
travelling-carriage, he crossed the great battle-fields, those
of the Gran Capitan, which he was to describe in *Philip II*.
In Paris, he paid his respects to Lafayette, like all the
other good Americans, some of whom, alas, were eating their hero out of house and home.* There, in his darkened room, where, at a crisis of his illness, he seemed to
be at the point of death, he renewed the friendship with
Ticknor that was never to lapse for forty years. And in
London, face to face with the Elgin Marbles, images of
classical form that left long traces in his mind,—traces
a little too long, perhaps, for there was too much marble

---

* Lafayette collected a fund to restore to their own country various penniless Americans who overran La Grange. Thus early the new world began
to turn the tables on the old. See John Neal, *Wandering Recollections*.

in Boston already,—he spent his days with John Quincy Adams, who was acting there as minister. It was in Adams's private library, the great collection of books which he had deposited in the Athenæum, that Prescott had browsed as a boy, the turbulent boy who could not control his laughter and who had infected one of his sober professors, insomuch that, when the professor rebuked him, the more he looked at Prescott the more he laughed, till the class dissolved in tears. In those earlier days, Prescott, who had the run of the Athenæum, had spent half his time reading books of adventure and romances, like Southey's *Amadis of Gaul,* wishing that he could have been a knight-errant. He read French, Spanish and Italian; and he and a friend played at mimic battles, first with bits of paper and then dressed up in old fragments of armour, which were kept as relics in the Athenæum. On their way to school, they told each other stories, improvising epics of adventure, in the manner of Ariosto. Prescott's head was full of the wildest fancies.

At that time, the Peninsular War had been raging over Spain. The newspapers were full of it; and Prescott, as a grown man, could not recall a day when feats of arms amid Spanish scenes had not filled the foreground of his mind. Now, restored to Boston, after his taste of the Azores, and with his feeling for history quickened and sharpened, he was to find another stimulus to follow up this interest of his boyhood. His friends rallied about him in his blindness and read to him aloud, six or eight hours at a time, especially the inseparable Ticknor, absorbed in the study of Spanish literature, on which he was lecturing at Harvard. Ticknor, to amuse him, read his lectures to him, three or four afternoons every week, along with his favourite classics and historical works and the old English romances; and, together with an exiled Italian scholar, who was spending a year in Boston, they read the Italian poets. The friends wrote to each other in Spanish. On a snowy day, when they could not meet, Prescott defended his belief that Petrarch's Laura was a real woman. Ticknor was more sceptical, much as he loved Petrarch, whom he had read at Vaucluse, on a spring day beside the fountain. Ticknor was almost the only friend one had, in this bustling, money-getting American world, who, having the means, had the time, as well as the passionate zest, for these enchanting studies.

Prescott was reading for pleasure, with Ticknor's Spanish library as his hunting-ground. He had in mind no scheme for a composition, but he was planning a literary career, after the manner of Gibbon, for which he proposed to lay a firm foundation. This was one of the solid Boston customs. As John Quincy Adams had laid a foundation for the statesman's life, based on blocks of good political granite, so Prescott put his blocks together, first clearing the ground with a thorough study of the English tongue. Let the suitable subject find him ready, even the suitable field of concentration. He had made up his mind that the age of thirty-five was soon enough to put pen to paper. English grammar first, as if he had never gone to school or college. For style, Sidney, Bacon, Browne and Milton. One hour a day for the Latin classics, Tacitus and Livy for elevation: he knew them by heart already, but this was a different matter. A year devoted to French, from Froissart to Chateaubriand. A year for Italian, another year for Spanish. There he paused, there he felt at home, too much at home to carry on with German. His eyes were not equal to the Gothic script.

Meanwhile, for practice in composition, he wrote an annual essay for the great review. On one of these papers, *The Arabs in Spain,* which he decided to save for his first book, he spent seven months of close work: two hundred and fifty foolscap pages of notes, all carefully indexed. The review had set a pace for scholars. These essays, which he continued to write and later collected in his *Mis-*

cellanies, dealt with themes suggested by his reading, Molière, Cervantes, Scott, Irving, Bancroft, Scottish Song, Italian Narrative Poetry, the Poetry and Romance of the Italians. It amused him to note that Corneille's friends, like his own friends in Boston, had sat with him for six months at table without suspecting that he was at work on a *Cid.* He wrote a short biography of Charles Brockden Brown, who had found so much of poetical interest under the prosaic surface of American life. Brown had attracted him, perhaps, because he had planned to write two epics on the conquests of Mexico and Peru. As for the general quality of these essays, they were such as one found in all the reviews, the "Old North," as it was called already, as in those of England, Scotland and France, neither better nor worse than Southey's or Lockhart's. They were scholarly books in miniature, learned, lucid, rather like Macaulay's, without the prejudices and without the genius,—for Prescott's genius was for story-telling. They showed his temperamental limitations, those of the Boston Whig point of view, in its most attractive form,—positive, somewhat obtuse, clear, just, full of romantic feeling, with scarcely a shred of intuition.* He did not like the idea of looking for mystical meanings in *Don Quixote;* and for him, as for all his school, the French Revolution had been fought in vain. His essays were best when they touched upon Scott, and Ariosto and Tasso. Prescott understood, no one better, these poet-story-tellers of chivalrous times. He belonged to the same family of minds.

Out of these related studies, his great theme rose with a sort of inevitability. For a while, he thought of writing a history of Italian literature. But, no, an Italian subject

---

* Prescott remarked, however, in one of his letters: "I don't know how it is, but our critics, though not pedantic, have not the business-like air, or the air of the man of the world, which gives manliness and significance to criticism . . . They twaddle out their humour as if they were afraid of its biting too hard, or else they deliver axioms with a sort of smart, dapper conceit" (Ticknor's *Life of Prescott,* page 255)—phrases that might have been uttered a century later.

would not be new: Sismondi had covered the ground too well. He wished for a theme that was new as well as great, for he was not planning a history to please unlettered readers who had not kept up with the progress of research. He meant to write for the world, for the guild of historians, first of all, who formed a super-nation, just as he wrote for the pure love of letters. If one pleased Irving, Southey, Thierry, and conquered, for literature and science, a realm that no other mind had conquered, one's work would be good enough for the popular taste; and Spanish history, if it was not unknown, had not been explored at its most vital point, the reign of Ferdinand and Isabella. Theirs was the momentous reign during which the scattered kingdoms had been brought together, —the age of the conquest of Naples, the age of the subversion of the Spanish Arabs, the founding of the Spanish Inquisition, the opening of the Western hemisphere. It was an age of great men, Ximenes, Gonsalvo de Córdoba, Columbus, an epoch that contained, for better or worse, the germs of the modern political system; and, thanks to the present government of Spain, call it liberal, call it anarchistic, the archives had been thrown open to Spanish scholars. They were busily publishing documents, chronicles, memoirs. But the decrepit kingdom, humbled by the loss of its foreign empire, rising from its ancient lethargy, was yet in too chaotic a state to foster any vigour of expression. Spain, with all its historiographers, had not produced a master-mind who could assimilate for a greater purpose all these documents that had come to light.

The great theme was at Prescott's disposal. For the books and manuscripts that he required, he could count upon Alexander Everett, the minister at Madrid, who had aroused Irving's interest in Spain. In order to feel surefooted in the language, he went over his Spanish grammar again. Then he began to read all round the subject, beginning with the general laws of nations, the constitutional history of England, the histories of the continental countries, France, Italy, Germany, Portugal, the general history of Spain, before he settled on his special field. For a few weeks, each summer, he went to Nahant, where his father had a cottage, "Fitful Head," perched on a wild sea-cliff. Strolling under the chestnut groves, and among the silver poplars that throve in the salt sea-breezes, he often met the Muse of History there. But this old resort of Boston fashion, about which Willis had written his sparkling stories, was full of mundane souls. He worked better at Pepperell, in the plain old salt-box farmhouse, the home of his Prescott forbears. There he had always spent his best summers, close to the "Fairy Grove," with its woodland streams. Behind the house, looking towards Monadnock, a shady path wound beside a pond, where he composed many of his chapters, sauntering back and forth. Sometimes he composed on horseback, especially when he wished to describe a battle, shouting his favourite ballad along the wood-paths, to rally his impressions,—"O give me but my Arab steed." He felt as he had felt, years before, dressed in fragments of armour at the Athenæum.

Many were the bets he had to make, and the forfeits he had to give, to keep his wits screwed up to the proper pitch. The book was a ten-years' task: * three and a half years of study before he wrote the opening sentence, three months for chapter one, seven months for the final chapter, two years for condensing and abridging. He had the text set up in type and caused four copies to be printed, for his friends to correct and criticize. But who would have dreamed that a book on such a subject could have been received with such hosannas? Not Prescott, who, as he painfully scrawled his chapters, writing the lines twice over in his blindness, never guessed how hungry his coun-

* "If you wish to be happy, always have ten years' work laid out before you,"—a phrase of Prescott's father that Ticknor was fond of quoting to his classes. No doubt, the phrase had its effect in the lives of many of Ticknor's pupils.

trymen were for the brilliant glow and colour that he gave them, the pageantry of kings and queens and battles. This was the romance that America longed for, as if the tapestry-makers of Bayeux had suddenly reappeared in sober Boston. Nor had Prescott guessed how eagerly the English, who had won the Peninsular War and were keenly interested in Spain, welcomed tales of soldiers and empire-builders.

The book was a universal triumph, one that even grew, as the years advanced, as the progress of historical research proved that Prescott's skill and documentation had left him the master of his field. The freshness and the freedom of the descriptions, the unity and proportion of the structure, the quiet and modest authority of the apparatus, the lustre of the language were new notes in American history-writing, different indeed from Jared Sparks's bareness and Bancroft's grandiosity. As for the author's style, a little over-formal, in the good old Boston way, Prescott presently took it in hand. He knew that American writing was archaic, like all colonial and provincial writing; he knew that the style of the new generation in England had grown more personal and more familiar. He wished to write the "prose of the centre," of which one was to hear in later days; and, in preparation for his future work, he searched and reviewed his own prose, to make it the natural vehicle of his mind. The sympathy with which he presented his heroes, always judging the action, not the actor, was even more of an innovation, although he had certainly pictured Isabella somewhat in the guise of a Boston lady, in whom a Boston man could find no blemish. Or, rather, a Boston boy, for whom a lady could not be a bigot. For Prescott was a boy, from first to last, a charming, virile and romantic boy, with a scholar's conscience and an artist's genius. One might well ask for different things, but one could scarcely ask for anything better.

CHAPTER VIII

LONGFELLOW IN CAMBRIDGE

THE CRAIGIE house in Cambridge had grown accustomed to distinguished lodgers when, in the summer of 1837, a young man of thirty, Henry Wadsworth Longfellow, the new professor of modern languages, applied at the door for chambers. Jared Sparks had lived there, Edward Everett had brought his bride there. Dr. Joseph Worcester, the lexicographer, was living there at present, working on his *American Dictionary*. Dr. Worcester had recently moved from Salem, where he had been a schoolmaster and had had among his evening pupils the new professor's friend and Bowdoin classmate, the young Nathaniel Hawthorne. The dictionary on which he was working now was a counterblast to Webster, his fellow Yale-man, who had removed from the language, in the interest of American independence, so many of its ancestral elegances. In matters of quantity, numbers of words and the like, together with the excellence of his definitions, the utilitarian Webster had won the day, even against the English dictionaries. In matters of quality, he was much at fault. Dr. Worcester saw no reason why the speech of his countrymen should lose its inherited succulence and fullness. In the name of Massachusetts, he wished to protest against the Connecticut school, with its thin and calculated rigours.*

---

* Worcester remained for a generation the dictionary of the best New England writers. See Holmes, *The Poet at the Breakfast Table:* "Mr. Worcester's Dictionary, on which, as is well known, the literary men of this metropolis are by special statute allowed to be sworn in place of the Bible."

Early as one rose in Brattle Street, Dr. Worcester was up and out already. One saw him on his black horse, jogging along in the shadows of dawn. Then he vanished into his cave of notes. The new professor was equally unobtrusive. It was true that he had a rakish air. With his rosy cheeks and china-blue eyes, he wore his hair in curls. He was fond of colour in his raiment. His neckties and his waistcoats were open to question; so were his gloves and his cane. Mrs. Craigie, much as she loved Voltaire, regarded him with suspicion. But she had read the extravagant *Sorrows of Werther;* moreover, she had read a recent book, *Outre-Mer* by name, the work of the young professor, a sort of all-European continuation of Washington Irving's *Sketch Book.* She liked the book, she liked the young man. It was plainly another case, like Bancroft's, of having studied abroad, and the new professor, unlike Bancroft, was willing to live it down. He got his own tea and toast for breakfast, quietly went about his college duties and buried himself in his rooms. And he soon exchanged the garments of his heart for a broad-brimmed black hat, a black frock-coat and a black cane.

Change his skin as he might, the young professor could not change his spots. He was a romantic soul. He was a born poet whose every fancy clothed itself in images and rhymes as naturally as an apple-tree in May clothes itself with blossoms. He was a poet like those Troubadours, those early-morning "finders" of poetry, who found it on every bush and sang as the vireo sings in summer, about whom he was lecturing to his classes. For he was also a scholar, the man in all America best fitted to fill Professor Ticknor's vacant chair. Ticknor, who wished to resign, in order to visit Europe again and write his history of Spanish literature, had virtually appointed his successor. He had seen some of the young man's translations; and eleven years before, when Longfellow had set out for Europe to fit himself to teach at Bowdoin College, he had given him letters to Southey and Washington Irving, advising him to study at Göttingen. Longfellow had spent three years wandering over the continent, taught at Bowdoin six years more and gone back to Europe for another year, in Germany and Scandinavia, in preparation for his new position. He had shown the practical sense that makes the professor, worthy of the son of a Portland lawyer who had been Dr. Channing's Harvard class-mate. He had formed an acquaintance with various eminent men in every corner of Europe, Lafayette in Paris, who remembered his family pleasantly in Portland, the Swedish poet Nicander, whom he met at Naples, Thomas Carlyle in London, Grillparzer at Salzburg, Bryant, who was already known as the "father of American poetry," with whom he shared long walks at Heidelberg. He had taken a leaf from Sir William Jones's letters and learned not only the usual languages, all that Ticknor knew, but also Finnish and Swedish, and had published several text-books, French and Italian grammars, and a Spanish reader. But he was a poet all the time. As a boy, he had written ballads of the Revolution, songs of the Maine woods, elegiac verses about Indian hunters whose race was falling like the withered leaves when autumn strips the forest. He had planned a series of poetic sketches dealing with aspects of New England life, the taverns, the village customs, the parson, the squire, the husking-frolics and the Indian dances, the French-Canadian peasants. And in Europe, where others were to be so conscious of all that America lacked,—the castles and cathedrals and ivied ruins,—he had recalled the corn-fields of New England, garnished with yellow pumpkins, the green trees and orchards by the roadside, the bursting barns, the fences and the well-poles, the piles of winter firewood, the fresh, cheerful, breezy scenes of home. Everywhere, the Europe that he witnessed,—the Europe of the "Romantic Reaction,"—

had gone back to its national origins, and the poet had
become the skald again, the bard, the singer and the
story-teller, the moulder and hierophant of the national
life, the people's aspirations. Longfellow had felt this
world-impulse.

Settled now in Cambridge, in the gracious mansion, so
like an Italian villa, the young professor, who was always
ready to draw forth some scrap of song or story to entertain some fair Angélique, found willing ears also in his
classes. Beside the round mahogany table in University
Hall, he sat among his pupils, discoursing with a silvery
courtesy,—how different from the harsh, monastic fashion of most of the older professors,—in a style that was
far too flowery, the older professors thought, but with a
feeling for the romance of letters that was much more
intimate than Ticknor's. In Ticknor one felt the glow of
a marble surface. This lecturer was a painter and a poet.
All the tones of his voice were soft and warm. He was a
master of the pastel shades, whose mind was suffused
with the light of Claude Lorrain. The facts, the details,
the philology he left to his large corps of young instructors,—for the university, having abandoned itself to
these degenerate modern languages, wished to do it hand-
somely. His task was to provide the general outlines, to
give the aroma, the bouquet; and in what corner of the
house of song was there a chamber where he had not
lived? From the mouldering walls of the Anglo-Saxon
bards, weather-stained and ruined, he passed to the courts
and gardens of the French Trouvères, *en route* for the
Minnesingers and the Mastersingers. (One had to use
these French words now and then, silly as they seemed in
Cambridge ears.) He told again the ancient Frankish
legends, the Chansons de Geste, the story of Reynard the
Fox, souvenirs of far-off springs and summers that
seemed to have a sort of occult relation to these early-
morning days of the young republic. One heard the New

England birds in the old French gardens, the songs like cherry-blossoms, drifting through an air of dawn, notes of expectation. Were some of the ballads rather grim and ghostly for a bright May morning in the college yard? The lecturer knew how to win his pupils . . . How joyously this ballad opens! It is the Feast of Pentecost. The crimson banners wave on the castle walls. You see how well-arranged the contrast is. The knight appears in his black mail, the mighty shadow trembles in the dance, the faded flowers drop. However, this ballad tells its own story. It needs no explanation. Here is something in a different vein, *The Castle by the Sea*. A somewhat sombre piece. Would you like me to read it? . . . Grim as the poem might be, it was inviting beside the Paley, the Locke or the mathematics one heard in the other class-rooms.

Warmly, too, with what a gift for colour, the young professor spoke of his life in Europe. This was not the cold, old classical Europe that everybody knew or had read about, the Europe that one crossed in a travelling-carriage, on grand tours, with letters of introduction. It was a garden of memories, songs and tears, softly bright as a spring bouquet, tinted with rose and apple-green, pale canary-yellow and the palest blue. One followed the professor on his travels, whether one had read his book or not, shared his pipe in homely Flemish inns, floated with him in a Dutch canal-boat, through meadows laden with tulips, played on his flute, like Goldsmith, on the Loire, among the peasants busy in the fields. One stopped for a month or two in a Spanish village, ambled through Tyrolese valleys, over the blossoming carpet, lay beside him on a flowery ledge, drenched with a summer silence that was broken only by the sound of evening bells. One walked through the still Swedish forests, heard the hemlocks murmuring, watched the sunlight on the waterfalls; one saw the yellow leaves drifting over Denmark. One called upon old Dannecker, Goethe's friend, the great

Canova's pupil, the sculptor of the charming "Ariadne," and shared the young man's thoughts on his homeward stroll,—whether he too might not accomplish something, bring something permanent out of this fleeting life, and then, serenely old, seat himself in his garden, like the artist, wrapped in a flowered morning-gown, and fold his hands in silence.

The young professor often spoke of Goethe. Once he dreamed that Goethe came to Cambridge. The professor gave him a dinner at Willard's Tavern and told him he thought Clärchen's song in *Egmont* was one of his best lyrics. The god smiled. He liked to speak of Heidelberg, where, to the music of the nightingales that flooded the castle garden, he had filled his heart with the old German lore. His friends there dwelt in a land of fancy where brooklets gushed and hemlock-trees were faithful, where maidens' bosoms were not always faithless, where graves were the footprints of angels and all things that lived sang together, the roses, the tulips, the birds, the storms, the fountains. The flowers melodiously kissed one another, keeping time with the music of the moonbeams. Many were the talks the young men had about fame and the lives of authors. Where should the poet and the scholar live, in solitude or in society, in the green stillness of the country or in the grey town?—urgent problems to be passed along to the young men at Harvard. There were admirable examples at Heidelberg, students with their sixteen hours a day and men of letters with retired habits: Thibaut, poring over his Pandects, and that wild mystic who spent his nights reading Schubert's *History of the Soul,* while his own soul dwelt in the Middle Ages. There, with his German Minna, lived the French poet, Edgar Quinet, who, having helped to revive the long-forgotten Chansons de Geste, had written his fantastic *Ahasvérus,* with its Holy Roods and Galilee-steeples, its arabesques and roses, hoping to do in words what Stras-

bourg Cathedral had done in stone. Lives of great men
to remind one . . . toiling upward in the night. One had
to learn patience, especially in the world that surrounded
Harvard, where the pulse of life beat with such feverish
throbs. At Heidelberg, one heard tales of Richter, of
Goethe, Hoffmann, Schiller, who loved to write by
candle-light, with the Rhine-wine always on his table.
What more could a professor do, for his aspiring pupils,
—and who was not aspiring at Harvard?—than to picture all these French and German scholars, toiling, in
want, in pain, sickness, sorrow, familiar with the weeping
walls of dungeons, to carry out their noble purposes? But
for them, who would have kept alight the undying lamp
of thought? But for them, the flapping of some con-
queror's banner would have blown it out forever.

Thus the professor discoursed, beside the mahogany
table, while the shadows of the elm-trees in the Yard
danced on the white pilasters of the class-room. His mind
was like a music-box, charged with all the poetry of the
world.* Ballads that rippled with the River Neckar.
Ballads of summer mornings and golden corn, blossoms,
red and blue, leafy lanes and hedge-rows. Spanish, Swedish, Danish ballads. Epics and fragments of epics, like
Frithiof's Saga, by the mad Scandinavian bishop, Esaias
Tegnér, half pagan Viking, half Lutheran priest, who
had revived the chants of the ancient skalds in the pastoral setting of a Swedish Wakefield. Sagas of ships and
sea-craft and laughing Saxons, dashing their beards with
wine. Songs of Norwegian chieftains, proud of their flowing locks, night-songs, songs of childhood, Christmas
carols, stately Italian sonnets. The music-box unrolled its
coloured stream; but the lecturer was not an antiquary.
He was a poet and teacher of poets who spoke with a
mildly apostolic fervour. He had published an essay de-

* For the range of Longfellow's knowledge of poetry, see his prodigious
collection, *The Poets and Poetry of Europe,* 1845.

fending his vocation. Poetry did not enervate the mind or unfit the mind for the practical duties of life. He hoped that poets would rise to convince the nation that, properly understood, "utility" embraces whatever con, tributes to make men happy. What had retarded Amer, ican poetry? What but the want of exclusive cultivation? American poetry had been a pastime, beguiling the idle moments of merchants and lawyers. American scholar, ship had existed solely to serve the interests of theology. Neither had been a self-sufficient cause for lofty self, devotion. Henceforth, let it be understood that he who, in the solitude of his chamber, quickened the inner life of his countrymen, lived not for himself or lived in vain. The hour had struck for poets. Let them be more national and more natural, but only national as they were natural. Eschew the skylark and the nightingale, birds that Audubon had never found. A national literature ought to be built, as the robin builds its nest, out of the twigs and straws of one's native meadows. But seek not the great in the gigantic! Leave Niagara to its own voices! Let the American poets go back to the olden time, studying not the individual bard but the whole body of the world's song. They could only escape from their colonial heritage in this all-human testament of beauty.

Sufficiently mild words with which to announce an era. Twenty other poets and orators were saying the same things. Longfellow spoke for them all and only spoke with more authority because, with his chair at Harvard, he had an ampler sounding-board behind him. He repre- sented the new school. But what was the older school? Who were the living poets of New England, most of whom were destined to fade and vanish within a score of years? Who were those poor "self-deluded" creatures, pictured by the disappointed Dana, "seated, harping, on some weedy knoll, and fancying it the mount of all the Muses"? Self-deluded or not, their name was legion. The bolder talents, Bryant, Halleck, Willis, had gathered round Washington Irving in New York, but enough remained in New England to constitute a timid air of springtime. Pale, shy little books of poems blossomed on every hand, like the anemones of an April woodland. Connecticut had most to show, for the best-known Boston poet, after Dana, Charles Sprague, author of the "odes,"—odes in the marmoreal style, which he produced for every Boston "occasion,"—was a survivor of the days when Pope and Dryden were the reigning writers.* Connecticut had its little school, with Lydia Huntley Sigourney at Hartford and James Gates Percival at New Haven. John Quincy Adams, watching the skies, wrote in his famous Diary: "It would take nine such poets to make a Tate."

In fact, there was not a poet in New England, except perhaps Maria Gowan Brooks, who could have written a stanza of the translation with which the Cambridge professor had shown his mettle. Longfellow, in days to come, might have been thought, by some, tame and faded; but the beautiful tone of the *Coplas of Manrique,* the old Spanish funeral ode,—an act of high talent, if there ever was one,—sounded like full summer, in its music, beside the pallid poems of the thirties. Mrs. Brooks, who had lived in Boston, although she had, decidedly, not been read there, had written with this bell-like depth of tone.†
It was true that her poem, *Zophiël,* partly composed in Cuba, where, on her coffee-plantation, Mrs. Brooks had built a Grecian temple, over-abounded in the female vein. This lady's personal charms, as the reader gathered,—as the reader, in fact, was virtually told in Mrs. Brooks's story, *Idomen,*—had not been appreciated by her Boston

---

* Sprague had the luck to see one of his odes published in Calcutta, a few years later, with its American names cleverly altered, and afterwards reprinted and praised in London, as the work of a British officer.

† So well that Charles Lamb, when Southey showed him a copy of *Zophiël,* said that there had never lived a woman capable of anything so fine.

husband, a cold-blooded merchant. She had redoubled the
spell, in consequence, ransacking half the libraries of
Paris, plunging into the Talmud and a Persian grammar
for perfumes, precious stones and passion-flowers, for the
irritated comments of monks and saints on the secrets of
the toilet, on women's hair, lutes and bridal bowers, serpents and fallen angels. Her notes were an armoury of
exotic learning. Her fancy, like a Cuban jungle, rioted
with Byron and Thomas Moore. But Mrs. Brooks possessed an energy that triumphed over all these fripperies.
The good-hearted Southey, who gave her a lift—and
opened himself to the vulgar levity that always pursues
relations of sentiment—never wearied of quoting the
lines that began, "And as the dove from far Palmyra
flying." Of *Egla's Song,* he said again and again that it
was "far superior" to Sappho. The poem as a whole had
a glow and movement that made it one of the best of a
short-lived school, on either side of the ocean. The song
was destined for a longer life.

Energy was the one desideratum of all this poetry of
the New England thirties. Longfellow's *Coplas* possessed
it, Mrs. Brooks's *Egla's Song* possessed it. Where could
one find it in the other poets, especially in the other
"female poets"? For these were the days of the female
poets, that soft and sprightly brood. These were the days
of "Peter Parley" Goodrich, the Jack who built the house
of the female poets, the Tokens and Ladies' Portfolios,
the Souvenirs, Albums, Pearls and Caskets of Gems, a
family of magazines more fecund, as one of the critics
said, than any of the animal tribes. Connecticut knew
them well, the annuals and the female poets, almost as
well as New York, better than Boston, the home of
Katherine Ware's "Bower of Taste;" for none of the
brood mildly raged to the tune of Mrs. Sigourney, whose
writings filled fifty-seven volumes. Mrs. Sigourney's little coterie abounded in the balmier mental graces, soft

as the breath of gazelles; but among the virtues of their "moral pieces" energy was not preëminent. Mrs. Sigourney's poems, as a critic said, were "more like the dew than the lightning;" and Sarah Edgarton, Hannah Gould, Sarah J. Hale,* and Eliza Townsend, shadows and shades of shadows, blossomed in other corners as if to prove that "annuals" were not perennials. Nor was Percival's masculine vigour of a hardier kind. This man of prodigious learning, who versified in thirteen languages and who thought that he might have been happy if he had got a cell in Tasso's mad-house, whose life and personal attributes, like Poe's, fulfilled the romantic pattern, wrote as if to prove another fact, that masculine vigour is not energy. If the pattern, not the poems, made the poet, Percival, like Poe, would have been immortal; but all his vigour ran to commonplace.† Fluent commonplace engulfed the rest, John Pierpont,‡ John Neal,§ who was so desperately anxious to "show" the British.

* Author of "Mary had a little lamb."
† Percival is the classic American example of the almost-good in poetry. A typical "manic-depressive," whose life was a mass of pathetic oddities, he was an admirable geologist and died as State Geologist of Wisconsin. He was one of the most remarkable American philologists of his time, and, as a linguist, a rival of George Borrow and Burritt, the "learned blacksmith." He wrote a report on the Basque tongue and spoke and read Sanskrit, Gaelic and six of the Slavonic languages. He made interesting experiments in Greek and German metres. The small house he built for himself at New Haven had no door or windows at the front.
‡ The grandfather of John Pierpont Morgan, a Connecticut man, a minister in Boston, an admirable reformer, who pawned his family spoons to pay the printer of his well-known *Airs of Palestine.*
§ The Portland "Down-Easter," John Pierpont's partner for a while in business, a shop-keeper, clerk, teacher of drawing and fencing, auctioneer, merchant, editor, lawyer,—in short, a typical Yankee handy-andy,—a journalist in England, for a time, who tried to show the British what the Americans were made of by talking about the "charter of greatness" written on our cataracts and mountains. Neal was a good-hearted soldier of fortune who "bounded" with the bounding years of Jackson. His once well-known poem, *Niagara,* was described as a "swash of magnificence." He wrote many slapdash novels, one of them, *Seventy-Six,* in three volumes, which he composed in twenty-seven days. His only book of value, *Wandering Recollections,* contains amusing glimpses of the American Grub Street of his time, together with a description of Jeremy Bentham, with whom he lived for three years in London, 1824–1827.

Pierpont's odes and songs, in the manner of Moore and Campbell, shouted and stamped by schoolboys,—

> Stand! The ground's your own, my braves!
> Will ye give it up to slaves?—

filled the air at public ceremonies with a sound as of horns and trumpets. But these poets came and went as the orators came and went: not one of them left an enduring line.* It was their unconsidered dash and go that carried them all into the void together.

What they needed was not praise, alas, but a more stringent kind of criticism, a lack which the Boston mind had begun to repair. They were overpraised, as a rule, as Poe remarked. Many of them passed through three editions, and the magazines that published their work rose like the waves of the sea.† The good "Peter Parley" befriended them all.‡ Pierpont's *Airs of Palestine* had

---

* Some of Pierpont's lines lasted as long as the nineteenth century. There were schoolboys in 1898 who knew *Warren's Address to His Soldiers at Bunker Hill*, although they never guessed who wrote the poem.

† One student has counted 137 periodicals "of a literary character"—and he knows of others—established in the United States within two decades of the War of 1812.—W. B. Cairns, *On the Development of American Literature from 1815 to 1833*.

‡ "Peter Parley," Samuel Griswold Goodrich, the tireless book-purveyor, the reformer of juvenile literature, an honest, courageous, simple-minded man, has left, in his *Recollections of a Lifetime,* the best account of many of these early minor writers. He was kind to Percival and Brainard; he published Trumbull's *Poems* and paid the author $1,000 for them, about the sum of his own ultimate loss. While his other books have no intrinsic value, the *Travels, Voyages and Adventures of Gilbert Go-Ahead*—who "wasn't made a Yankee for nothing"—reflects the Connecticut popular mind of the time. The hero, a pedlar of clocks in China, Java, Siam, etc., suggests Mark Twain's "Connecticut Yankee." His adventures enable the author to unfold an "educational" panorama of travel like that of the Rollo Books. In his *Sketches from a Student's Window*, Goodrich enumerates, as the works in demand, in a typical book-store of the eighteen-thirties, *Thaddeus of Warsaw, The Scottish Chiefs, Young's Night Thoughts* (of which thirty editions were published, in a generation, in the United States), *Sandford and Merton, Paradise Lost, The Mysteries of Udolpho, Caleb Williams, The Lady of the Lake, Cœlebs in Search of a Wife,* and *The Castle of Otranto,* along with Webster's Spelling-book and a large assortment of hymn-books and Bibles.

an honest vogue among the devout. Numberless readers
looked for Percival's "P" in the newspapers and magazines. Brainard's *Niagara,* written in twenty minutes,
sped through the country. If there was nothing decisive
in their work, nothing or so little,—Brainard's *Connecticut River* was a good poem,—what was to blame but a
national frame of mind that rather welcomed hasty composition, the strained voice, the high key, the midnight
fervours of the adolescent? Even in Boston itself, where
the angel of intellect had stirred the waters, criticism was
only half awake. One found cases in point on every side,
in Cambridgeport, for instance, across the river, where
Washington Allston wrote his poems and nursed his
dreams of Titian under a cold and distant sky. Allston
was idolized as a human being. Everyone loved the silvery old man in the red-lined velvet robe. He was a
charming talker, with his great, soft, luminous, dreamy
eyes and the white curls that clustered about his neck, so
vehement, so gracious, so refined,—for the rest, so well-
bred and well-connected. The Boston people liked to stop
and see him, in his painting-room at the port, an awk-
ward-looking house with a great north window. They
read his poems, they sometimes bought his pictures, usually hanging them in a cramped back-parlour between a
deadly cross-fire of lights; they marvelled over the dust
on his studio floor, thick as a heavy snow-fall, just as it
ought to be in an artist's den! They never came back
from Europe without a higher opinion of his genius, they
were to lecture about him when he was dead. But anyone
might have seen with half an eye that Allston's great
talent had run to seed. Cambridge was a depressing place
for painters.* Even more to the point was the want of criticism, or rather the quality of the criticism, along with
various other deprivations. The people who adored poor

* "Cambridge is like Kaulbach's pictures. It is all literature."—William
Morris Hunt.

Allston's genius said that he made his women much too plump. These intimations of carnality disturbed their quiet minds. They did not like their limbs to be flesh and blood, they liked their limbs to be metaphysical, though how one was to be another Titian *without* the carnal reminder,—and they wished to think that Allston was another Titian, they wished to think that Boston had produced the last great man of the Renaissance,—might have puzzled even the metaphysicians. This would have mattered less if Boston had given Allston a few carnal models; but, wherever he turned for a model, he only found another metaphysician. Everyone talked metaphysics, everyone praised the artist because his work was metaphysical,—"etherealized and sublimed by religious fervour." * His mind, bathed in the fluid mist, grew thinner and thinner every day.

Allston was the case in point that later generations best remembered. A painter, a man of letters,—a man of energy, beyond a doubt,—he had planted himself at the cross-roads, midway between Boston and Cambridge, where everyone was aware of his existence. Hundreds of young men passed his door, drank the enchantments of his conversation, took him for a symbol. He was the "eagle tied to the roost," over whom Horatio Greenough mourned. That he was an eagle no one questioned. The only question was about the roost, and this question loomed as the years advanced. He was a man of high talent. His portrait of Coleridge was enough to prove it, aside from his beautiful drawings. His prestige and his legend were imposing. The first enquiry every foreigner made—unless he asked for Channing—was, Where is Allston's studio? All the friends of his European years, Irving and Fenimore Cooper, Thorwaldsen, Vanderlyn, Leslie, Turner, Coleridge, whom he had known in Rome, —walked with them under the pines of the Villa

* James Russell Lowell.

Borghese, talked out the nights at the Caffè Greco, the haunt of the northern barbarians,—cherished and honoured his name and his work. He had praised the greatness of Turner when everyone in England laughed it down. He had taught Leslie to see Titian's colour, when people laughed at Titian as they laughed at Turner. The traits which the American mind revealed, at the very first encounter, in Allston, as in Bulfinch and Washington Irving, were a congenital sense of style and form, refinement and elevation. But something had gone amiss, the young men gathered. He had never ceased to paint and write,—fine sonnets on the Old Masters, grand letters to his brother-artists. His talk was enough to fire anyone's brain. And yet he had spent twenty long years trying to paint a picture he could not finish, the baleful "Belshazzar's Feast," the nightmare of his life. He had brought the picture back from London, in the far-off days of his youth, thinking it needed only a few touches; and Gilbert Stuart had shown him, all too plainly, that his perspective was not right. He had never outgrown those first misgivings. The picture had been bought in advance, he had mortgaged his life to finish it, and he had grown feeble with his doubts and fears. All the fault of the roost, the young men thought. All Boston's fault. A generation later, Henry James, puzzling over the unfinished masterpiece, "the mask of some impenetrable inward strain," was to draw his own deductions from the painter's nostalgia, "the grim synthetic fact of Cambridgeport." William Wetmore Story drew them first, the young poet, the sculptor of the future, Justice Story's son, a student of law in Cambridge, who, as he watched the eagle moulting, made up his own mind to fly to Europe. Allston had been starved, he wrote in one of his letters,—the rich and beautiful nature, he in whose veins the South had run so warm, born to have grown and spread such fragrancy. With nothing congenial outside him, he had been forced to feed upon himself. He had drained his memory dry.

At Longfellow's very door! Times had changed when tragedies like this pressed themselves on one's attention. The younger generation was making demands which the older generation had never dreamed of. What were the right conditions for artists and writers? The portrait-painters, the orators, the historians had had no occasion to ask such questions. The young republic had given them their conditions, given them freely and fully, in the very fact of its existence. It wished for oratory, it wished for history. The statesmen wished to have their portraits painted. Oratory, history, portrait-painting were all connected with statesmanship; they had a *raison d'être* in politics and throve in an age of nation-building. But art and letters of an absolute kind, the kind that has no mass-demand behind it, had always given birth to the subtlest problems, problems of the artist's life, influence, environment, education. In two thousand years, the human mind had scarcely attacked or begun to solve these problems; and now they had risen before the American mind, portentous, all but insoluble, alarming. Young men who could see that Allston's failure had aspects that applied to painters only, or workers in the plastic arts, asked themselves if writers were not involved. For if Allston had gone astray, as the young men saw, how about the poets? —Allston himself as a poet, Neal, who had scattered his talents beyond redemption, Brainard and Carlos Wilcox, broken reeds, Percival, the walking suicide, feasting on his Connecticut moonshine, "brooding over the wrecks of celestial longings"?* No doubt, they had natural disabilities. They were victims of persecution-mania, Percival, at least, Brainard and Wilcox in a less degree. Were they not also victims of a social order that was still too immature for poets? Was not even Dana such a victim, Allston's brother-in-law and special crony, always an-

* Preface to Percival's collected poems.

nouncing projects, even planning the famous book on Allston, after Allston's death, which, like all his plans, came to nothing? Dana had lost heart. For years his mind had been dying of inanition. Were writers and painters in the same plight? Allston's friends in England had besought him not to return to America, where there was no "antagonism of talent" to make him toe the mark; and what American artist had ever lived, aside from the portrait-painters, to prove that their advice had been mistaken? But Bryant, Irving and Cooper seemed to show that writers were in a different case, with human nature everywhere to study, with books as aids in the study of human nature, books, the only instructors in style and form. The question rested on a few examples.*

Great talents largely create their own conditions. At least, they may be said to crystallize tendencies that exist in the air about them,—tendencies that have gradually come to exist,—of which lesser talents have been unaware. Cambridge, like all New England, like New York, was ready for its poets and its tellers of tales. Cambridge was ready for literature, and Cambridge men were ready to provide it. The world had flowed their way. Allston's disabilities were as nothing,—the metaphysics and the want of models, the poverty under the pressure of which, he said, his pictures crumbled away,—beside the fact that he had lost the world, his world, the world-current of painters and painting. He had followed the wrong tune, as Stuart might have told him, Stuart who saw the dangers of "elevation" and ridiculed Benjamin West's "ten-acre pictures," filled with apostles and prophets. A painter's business, Stuart always said, was to paint what he saw with his eyes and leave the elevation to the poets; and Allston had followed West, against his eyes. No one doubted his elevation. It was his painting that had gone

* These doubts and dilemmas of the younger generation are indicated in several passages of Emerson's early *Addresses*.

to pieces, and anyone in Paris could have told him why.*
There was the fault of the famous "provincial conditions" of which the future was to hear so much. In painting,
Cambridge and Boston were out of the world. In
literature, they were in the world, even a little too much,
it might have been thought, by those who disliked the
world of the thirties and forties. Whether or not one
liked this world, the world of Alfred Tennyson and
Tegnér, of Lamartine and Ferdinand Freiligrath, was a
matter of time and taste. Whether one liked or rejected
all its poets was a matter of time and taste. But no one
was able to doubt beyond a decade that Cambridge and
Boston wrote for the world, or that the world was represented in Cambridge as it was represented in Rome and
Oxford.

For Cambridge had ripened, in these few short years,
as a well-tended garden ripens in June. All in a mist of
birds and honeysuckle, the literary mind had put forth
shoots. Thoughts were growing, books were growing
under the quiet boughs of the ancient elm-trees, in the
fragrant shadows of the locusts, the perfume of the
daphne and the lilac. Robins darted down the leafy paths,
orioles swung on their nests; one heard the murmur of
bees and doves and the bobolink's song in the meadows
along the river. The scent of the syringa filled the air.
These were the scholastic shades that poets had always
loved; and books, whether in verse or prose, were springing from the Cambridge mind, thick and fast as the grass
in the Cambridge door-yards. The old guard clung to its
chimney-corner. Allston and Dana put their heads together and talked about the Waverley novels. Allston

---

* Even Delacroix, who continued to paint historical canvases but who
knew that the time for this *genre* had long passed. See his comments on the
case of Gros, so strangely parallel to that of Allston. (Delacroix, *Œuvres
Littéraires*, II, 195 *et seq.*) Gros, like Benjamin Robert Haydon, the English
painter of "ten-acre pictures," tried to carry on the grand style in a world
that had ceased to be "grand," and both, in despair, committed suicide.

had written a novel of his own, *Monaldi,* full of Italian souvenirs,—artists, bravos, convents, jealous husbands,— with a few charming pages of description. The hero was a painter, like himself, whose mission was to revive the grand style, in its Raphaelesque roundness. Allston had pencilled on his studio-walls various "texts for reflection." * At "Shady Hill," the redoubtable Andrews Norton rejoiced in his gladiatorial Indian summer, playing out his game of "evidences," which left him leisure for a little whist. One saw Dr. Popkin in the square, with his great caped coat and his ruddy visage, looking like an eighteenth-century beadle. Dr. Popkin's historic umbrella was a symbol of the old regime, the Harvard whose severity and simplicity seemed to be rapidly passing.

Everyone in Cambridge appeared to be writing a book. The Holmeses, the Lowells, the Channings, the Wares, the Danas were turning into literary families, expanding like rivers as they advanced. Dana's young son, Richard Henry II, who had spent two years before the mast, was assisting Edward Channing as instructor in English. Jared Sparks and his friends of the *North American* trudged back and forth between Cambridge and Boston, with bags under their arms stuffed with papers. Henry Cleveland was editing Sallust and writing a life of Hendrik Hudson. George S. Hillard was editing Spenser, with elaborate annotations. Cornelius Conway Felton, the jolly giant, the new Professor of Greek, who had edited Homer, with Flaxman's line-drawings, was making a translation of Menzel's *History of German Literature.* Felton was one of Longfellow's special friends. Another

---

* These sentences were preserved by Anna Jameson, who called upon Allston in 1838 and copied them, with the painter's permission. Some of them deserve to be remembered, e.g.:

"The most common disguise of envy is in the praise of what is subordinate."

"Fame . . . is only known to exist by the echo of its footsteps through congenial minds."

"The only competition worthy of a wise man is with himself."

was Charles Sumner, Hillard's partner, a lecturer at the
Law School. The all-attractive Sumner,—the son of the
grim old sheriff who hanged his murderers with his own
hands "because it was disagreeable,"—dazzled even Boston with his legal learning. Only the other day, on a visit
to England, invited to sit with the judges in Westminster
Hall, he had settled a point that arose in the course of
the trial. The Lord Chief Justice, at a loss for a precedent, had asked him if any American decision bore on
the point in question. Sumner had answered that he knew
of none, but that the point had been settled in his lordship's court, and he had given the citation. The incident
had echoed through the world of lawyers.

With Sumner stretched on the sofa at Craigie House,
reading Poliziano or Bossuet, the Funeral Orations that
he loved,—for Sumner, like Hillard, was an orator,—
with Felton to discuss the German poets, with Dr. Beck
and Roelker, the young instructors, to sing German songs
and share his hock, Longfellow had his Heidelberg in
Cambridge. Sometimes, on a sunny morning, Prescott
rode up on his horse to the door, handsome, gay, a little
over forty, astonished to find himself so famous. Sometimes, Longfellow walked into town, to stop at Ticknor's
house or stroll on the Common, lingering on the bridge
to talk with Prescott and watch the kelp and the seaweed
floating by. But the great event of the week was Saturday
evening, when his rooms beheld a gaudy, worthy of
a parcel of good-natured monks. Much as the young professor dreamed of Europe,—villas by the margins of
lakes, city-casements looking on sun-swept squares, when
the perfume, streaming in at his open window, brought
Switzerland back, Italy, the Tyrol,—his mind rode
quietly at anchor. He had his own name for the malcon-
tents who, having tasted the old world, talked of nothing else. They were Frondeurs, difficult as the Fronde of
Louis XIV. Even while he shared their homesick feelings,

he was immune to the virus. He had a shield and buckler in the doctrine that Europe itself had taught him: a poet was the poet of his country. Easy to believe in this pleasant Cambridge, with the city across the bridge and the village about him, tokens of Europe on every hand, ample chambers, filled with books and pictures, with all the sights and sounds of the young republic, the cheerful hammer and the hopeful saw, a population that was up and doing. And when a poet had friends like Samuel Ward, his old Heidelberg crony, who greeted him with a German kiss,—for Cambridge was losing its rigours,—drew a bottle from each of his pockets, gave him all the gossip of New York and carried off his poems to Fitz-Greene Halleck, who liked to see him "resplendently coruscate" in Park Benjamin's paper, how could he not rejoice in his native land? His native land rejoiced in him, and, if it liked his poems all the more, the more they suggested Europe, that was the most "native" thing about it. "Europeans" never thought of "Europe." And anyone could see that Longfellow's poems, whatever their subjects were, expressed the young American state of mind.

For softly, without effort, as he sat in the vast shadow at his open window, the poems rose in his mind, like exhalations,—*Voices of the Night*. The black hulks of the trees rode at their moorings on the billowy sea of grass. The stars glistened through the heaving branches, the silver Charles gleamed across the meadow. Stanza by stanza, the poems came, sometimes all at once, songs, reveries, echoes of German verses, mingling with the whispers of the summer wind,—youthful regrets, youthful aspirations, psalms of a life which, on such an evening, might well appear a dream, though far from empty: *Footsteps of Angels, The Light of Stars, The Reaper and the Flowers, Hymn to the Night*. On these very evenings, at their open windows, thousands of young men

in Hollis Hall, at Bowdoin, Yale, Princeton, in Cincinnati, up and down the Hudson and the Mississippi, in
England, Scotland, Holland, in far-off Russia, beside the
Neva as beside the Danube, heard the trailing garments
of the night, shared these reveries of the New England
springtime that Longfellow was putting into words, with
such a lucid, natural, velvety sweetness,—verses drifting
through the poet's mind as the yellow leaves drift from
the trees in autumn and silently fall to the ground.

In later days, when other fashions came, when the
great wheel of time had passed beyond them, one saw
these poems in another light. They seemed to lack finality and distinction, whether in thought or phrase. But no
one could quite forget their dreamy music, their shadowy
languor, their melodious charm, their burden of youthful
nostalgia; and the world of the Age of Revolutions,
which knew the Romantic poets, shared this poet's mood
of exaltation. A day was to come when a Chinese mandarin transcribed *The Psalm of Life* on an ivory fan, and
a dying soldier at Sebastopol repeated the stirring lines.
When *Excelsior* appeared in a German version, the students of Innsbruck, meeting the translator, thronged
about him and embraced and kissed him, with such joy
and transport, as he said, that he always looked upon
that moment as the happiest of his life. These were the
days when to be "up and doing, with a heart for any
fate," seemed, after the drought of Calvinism, the
drought of monarchism and reaction, in the continental
Europe of '48, when people had thought they were pow-
erless, a miracle and a sudden inspiration; and Longfellow spoke for the youth of all the world. He spoke for
the young in his verses, even in his prose *Hyperion,* the
romance of the American student who looked like Harold
the Fair-hair and bore the name of an old German poet.
This was his own romance, more or less, in the high-
flown style of Richter. Many and many a reader, as the

years went by, readers in English, Swedish, Dutch and French, followed in the footsteps of the hero, sought out the inns where Paul had slept, the Star at Salzig, the White Horse at Bingen, turned aside for a Sunday at St. Gilgen, lingered, book in hand, under the lindens and wept over the night at Heidelberg when the lovely star, Emma, fell from heaven.

Such were the "voices of the night." The voices of the day were firmer and clearer. On these summer mornings at Craigie House, when the birds were carolling in the trees, when insects chirped in the grass and the sunlight and the perfume of the flowers poured through his open windows, Longfellow's mind went back to Sweden, to the still Scandinavian woodlands, carpeted with blossoms at this balmy season, where, in a simple, primeval world, like that of his own Maine, the leaves and ribbons streamed from the lofty May-poles, and the old pagan gods awoke once more, and one heard the hammers of the Vikings, so like the hammers that one heard in Portland, building their oak-ribbed ships. That was his great discovery, after all, that was the brightest feather in his cap: other American writers and scholars were rediscovering Italy and Spain, recapturing France and Germany. He was the first who had visited, amply, at least, with a living imagination, the lands of the skalds and the sagas, where one found traces of one's forbears, in the days of the Danish invasions, forests like one's own New England forests, builders of boats with masts of the lordly pine, the Baltic dashing on the northern strand, desolate as one's own North Shore, village ways like the New England ways, houses of hewn timber, white-painted churches, maidens with flaxen hair, brown ale worthy of King Olaf, apples such as a village blacksmith loved, poets, too, like the mad Esaias, scarcely concealing under his bishop's gown the robe of the chanting gleeman, chanting now not the deeds of blood but the wild freedom of the days of old. There, in those northern lands, the ballad, like the ancient yeoman's life,—the life that was fit for free men and simple, fishermen, farmers, sailors, fit for Nantucket men and Portland men, as for the men of Gottland and Malmö,—there the epic and the story-poem still played living parts in human lives, not as mere survivals and revivals, as they were in the rest of Europe. One of the best of Longfellow's translations,—perhaps, like that of the Spanish funeral hymn, it could not have been better,—was *The Children of the Lord's Supper,* in which Tegnér had revived for Swedish ears, as Goethe had revived it for German ears, in *Hermann und Doro-thea,* the metre that Homer had used and Longfellow was to use in *Evangeline.* He had passed into this north-ern mind by such a line of sympathy that the old poet-bishop found his versions of *Frithiof's Saga* the only ones that fully satisfied him.

In Sweden, or in Scandinavia,—for he found in the Finnish *Kalevala* the form he was to use in *Hiawatha,*—he had gone to school to better purpose than elsewhere in his multi-coloured Europe. Before his eyes waved, and were to wave, the mingled shapes and figures of the past, the myths and scenes of European legend, "like a faded tapestry," faded then, how much more faded later. The Scandinavian world had given him something far more vital, rhythms that signified a secret kinship, deeper than a student's acquisitions, between the pastoral children of the Vikings and the child of Maine for whom the sea and the forest possessed an unfailing magic. The Scandina-vians had given him a feeling for the value of the forms, —the ballad, the folk-poem, the epic fragment, vehicles of the national sentiment that had come to life in Amer-ica, as it had come to a second life in the North,—through which his mind was to flow with its greatest vigour. All his evocations of feudal Europe, of the mediæval world that haunted him, of the biblical world and the world of the Renaissance, what were they ever to mean,—these incidents of an endless panorama, which the patient and facile showman unrolled for a generation before the eyes of his enraptured public, a Panorama of Athens, such as they had set up in Cambridge, extended over the history of the world's culture,—beside a handful of ballads and two or three narrative poems, redolent of the vast American woodlands, the prairies, the prodigious Mississippi, the sylvan solitudes of Canada, the gusty New England sea-coast, poems fragrant still with hemlock, spruce and balsam, the salt breeze of the rocky shore, the wild-brier, the rose and the syringa, breathing a tonic piety, as of paternal altars and forest gods?

Such were the voices of the day, which the poet heard, with a soft excitement, as he took his morning walk at sunrise, or, when evening came, lighted the long candles on his upright desk.

CHAPTER IX

THE YOUNGER GENERATION OF 1840

THESE WERE the days of the "march of intellect."
The movement started in England by Lord Brougham "to promote useful knowledge" found the tracks
laid for it in Boston. In a comedy produced at the
Tremont Theatre, Master Burke, the "Irish Roscius,"
played the part of a professor who taught every subject
known to man. The comedy was meant to satirize the
much-talked-of march of intellect, and the Boston people
saw the point and smiled. But, if their hearts had been
opened, there would have been found, engraved within,
the talisman Education. Education was the word in Boston, as a generation later the word was Culture.*

Whatever could be done by education, Boston proposed to do; for this was the age of "internal development," mental as well as commercial. The merchants had
largely relinquished the maritime commerce that had
created so much of the city's wealth and turned their
energies to manufacture; and the effort of the Southern
and Western magnates to build up what they called the
"American system," at the expense of New England,
drove the Boston mind all the harder. The wheels of the
cotton-factories revolved at a furious pace, and the
Southern slave-drivers plied their whips to feed the Yan-

* "We are all becoming cultivated up to the eyes . . . *tiers état* and all.
A daughter of an old servant of ours, whose father is an Irish bogtrotter
that works on the roads, told me yesterday, 'she had nearly completed her
English education, was very well in her French, and should only give one
quarter more to her music and drawing.' "—Prescott, 1840, *Correspondence,*
121.

kee mills with Southern cotton. The more the prosperity
of New England came to depend on cotton, the closer
the propertied classes drew to the Southern planters,
with whom they felt obliged to ally themselves, yielding
to them in all political matters. At the same time, to
compete with the South and the West, they developed a
system of closer communication between the capital and
the hinterland. A network of railroads spread over New
England, binding the six States together.*

This material growth was reproduced in the intellectual sphere. The rise of the Lyceum lecturing system, in
1826,—the work of the enthusiast, Josiah Holbrook,
who went about the country lecturing on geology and
natural history, urging the villages to form collections,—
was only one of the educational movements that brought
Boston and the rural centres into closer touch with one
another. Webster, Edward Everett and Nathan Hale
established the Useful Knowledge Society. Various other
institutions followed. The Natural History Society, the
Mercantile Library Association, the Mechanics' Appren-
tices' Association, the Lowell Institute diffused their currents of intellectual impulse. New England soon acquired
the lecture-habit, the fruit of Edward Everett's enterprise, for Everett's public lectures on Greek antiquities
were the first of their kind in America. There were constant courses in every town and village,—where Rollo
and Lucy sat at the feet of Jonas,—on chemistry, botany,
history, on literature and philosophy; and almost every
eminent man in New England joined in the general effort
to propagate knowledge.† A season-ticket for a course,
ten to fifteen lectures, usually cost two dollars. In Boston,

* This development came quite suddenly. About 1831, Nathan Hale, the
father of Edward Everett Hale, was considered a fanatic as a railroad-
prophet. He suggested in a speech at Faneuil Hall that, if people could
come from Springfield to Boston in five hours, an average of nine people
would come every day. This was regarded as a preposterous statement.

† It was a practice of Dr. Holmes, after an evening lecture, to write a
poem that was suggested by it.

all the boys and girls went to the Lowell lectures. As
many as five hundred at a time learned that acids were
not alkalis and that Homer did not write the Iliad.* It was
quite the rage. The boys invited the girls, and after the
lecture they walked home together, ending the evening
with an oyster-supper.

Boston, all New England respected learning. No New
England boy was allowed to question that he was destined to succeed in life, provided he knew enough; and
Boston was determined that the boys and girls, and the
blind and insane as well, should have an opportunity to
know enough,—schools based on the best current theories, reform-schools that really worked reform, schools
for the blind that caused the blind to see. Was not Dr.
Howe's famous pupil, the blind, deaf and dumb Laura
Bridgman, a proof that education was the mother of
wonders? Boston had taken Channing at his word and
really believed in perfectibility. It was true that at first
the Boston pedagogues resented the assaults of Horace
Mann, who had no use for their old-fashioned ways. But
no one could resist this human cyclone, the tall, humour-
less man in the long frock-coat, so anxious, so exacting, so
dogmatic, with the will of a battering-ram, who founded
the State Board of Education in 1837. Having closed his
law-office with the reflection, "Let the next generation be
my client," Horace Mann found Boston thoroughly
roused to a sense of the vital importance of public instruction. But what could be done with the country common schools, the merest "dormitories," as he called
them, at least in comparison with the Scottish schools,
which he had visited on a tour of study? The administra-
tive features of the Prussian system seemed to him the
best, and he adopted them largely, much as he detested,

* The "Wolfian theory," long since exploded. "Poor old Homer was rele-
gated to the world of myth. As a schoolboy, I used to hear the belief in the
existence of such a poet derided as 'uncritical' and 'unscholarly'."—John
Fiske, *A Century of Science.*

in the Prussians, the "blind acquiescence" that enslaved the mind. For eleven years he travelled night and day, stopping in every hamlet in Massachusetts, forming conventions of teachers and school-committees. To make an impression on Berkshire County, he said, was like battering down Gibraltar with one's fist, and the Cape Cod mind was solid sand. Nothing new would grow there. But he knew how to deal with sand and granite, having so much of both in his own composition. He counted on the instinct of a people who thought there was nothing odd in asking a stranger if he was "learned in roses."

A Boston man had to be learned in something, and the passion for learning on the upper levels soon spread through all the other strata. Harvard set the pace. Thomas Wentworth Higginson was not unique as one who, at the time of his graduation, read French, Spanish, Italian, Latin and Greek, who later acquired German and Portuguese, Hebrew, a little Swedish, and always hoped for a chance to study Russian. Theodore Parker, the minister, somewhat older, the Roxbury Friar Tuck, the Lexington farmer's son who was able to carry a full barrel of cider, read Dutch, Danish and Russian, along with the others, Coptic, Chaldaic, Arabic, Ethiopic, and was found by one of his friends deep in a grammar of Mpongwe.* Here and there, some workman followed suit. Elihu Burritt of Worcester, the "learned blacksmith," was a typical figure of the moment. This well-known self-taught linguist who, as an apprentice, had kept a Greek grammar in the crown of his hat to study

* Theodore Parker's learning was famous in New England. T. W. Higginson related that he wished to find a certain reference in the Salic, Burgundian and Ripuarian codes before the codification of Charlemagne. Neither Sumner, Justice Gray nor Chief Justice Shaw could assist him on this occasion, but Sumner said, "Try Parker." Parker said at once, "Go to the Harvard Library, and on the fifth shelf in the fourth left-hand alcove you will find a small, thick quarto entitled 'Potgeiser: de Statu Servorum,' which will give you all the information you want." Higginson found his question answered there.—Chadwick, *Theodore Parker.*

while he was casting brass cow-bells, who made a version
of Longfellow in Sanskrit and mastered more than forty
other tongues, toiling at the forge or in the evening, after
a full day's work, affected no singularity, as he said. His
aim was "to stand in the ranks of the workingmen of
New England and beckon them onward and upward to
the full stature of intellectual men." The noble-hearted
Burritt * was not the only man of his kind. Many a boy
walked thirty miles to Cambridge to feast his eyes on the
sight of the college; and many a farmer's son, like
Burritt, might have walked to Boston, a hundred and
twenty miles, from New Britain, with two or three dollars and a silver watch tucked away in a handkerchief,
hoping to catch a ship for India, where he could study
Sanskrit. Sir Charles Lyell and Agassiz were surprised,
when they arrived in Boston in the forties, by the universal interest in education. Lyell had never seen such
crowds of workmen listening on winter nights to learned
lectures on geology and zoology, Shakespeare and Milton. Agassiz was present at an assembly of three thousand mechanics, brought together to form a library and
listening for two hours with rapt attention to a lecture on
the advantages of reading. Dickens was impressed by the
interests of the factory-girls of Lowell, a public that he
knew so well in England. There were joint-stock pianos
in their boarding-houses; the walls of the mills were covered with their poems; they subscribed to the British
reviews; they had classes in German; they all seemed to
know *Paradise Lost* by heart and talked about Wordsworth, Coleridge and Macaulay in the intervals of

---

* A passage from Elihu Burritt's diary, 1837: "*Monday,* June 18, headache; forty pages Cuvier's Theory of the Earth, sixty-four pages French,
eleven hours forging. *Tuesday,* sixty-five lines of Hebrew, thirty pages
of French, ten pages Cuvier's Theory, eight lines Syriac, ten ditto Danish,
ten ditto Bohemian, nine ditto Polish, fifteen names of stars, ten hours
forging. *Wednesday,* twenty-five lines Hebrew, fifty pages of astronomy,
eleven hours forging. *Thursday,* fifty-five lines Hebrew, eight ditto Syriac,
eleven hours forging. *Friday,* unwell, twelve hours forging," etc.

changing bobbins on the looms. Flocks of these serious girls, described by Lucy Larcom in her *Idyl of Work,* afterwards went West as school-teachers and founded "Improvement Circles" on the prairies. The fame of the *Lowell Offering,* which contained their writings,—humorous and pathetic tales, fairy-stories, poems,—travelled round the world. A volume of selections, *Mind Among the Spindles,* was later published in London, and lectures were given at the Sorbonne on this portent of the times.*

In Cambridge, nobody was surprised to hear that the youthful Dana,—before the mast,—had kept his crew of sailors from going ashore, on the California coast, by reading aloud all day from Scott's *Woodstock.* Rough as the sailors were, most of them were Massachusetts sailors, and everyone took it for granted that in Massachusetts reading had a sovereign right of way. At Harvard, the young men read too much, or so it seemed to those who had frugal minds. They were hatching very strange ideas. They sat at their open windows on New Year's Eve and spouted the *Midnight Mass for the Dying Year.* Thomas Wentworth Higginson, the bursar's son, took a vow of poverty: he spoke of putting himself on equal terms with the vast army of the hand-workers. Marston Watson talked of raising pears, a better occupation than raising dollars. George P. Bradford, a brilliant scholar, a descendant of Governor Bradford, was bent on setting up a market-garden and trundling his own wheel-barrow through the streets. William Ellery Channing, the doctor's nephew and namesake, refused to go to chapel. Determined to be a poet at any price, he absconded from

---

* These lectures were given by Philarète Chasles. Recent writers on the Lowell mill-girls, tending to slight their accomplishments, dwell solely on the pitifulness of their wages. Their wages were pitiful indeed,—about three dollars a week. It is to be noted, however, that these wages were more than three times higher than the average corresponding wages in Europe.

college with his clothes and took refuge in a lonely farm-house. All these notions were very disturbing. The young men said that terrestrial love was only a reflection of celestial love. They spoke of "bathing in a sea of thought." They went off mooning in the woods. They refused to talk about railroads, banks and cotton. They had no use for Blackstone and Justice Story. They were unwilling to be "mere" lawyers,—heaven save the cod-fish in the State House! They laughed when their fathers quoted Dr. Johnson. They smiled when their uncles quoted Burke, who had become a very old story. Goldsmith and Pope, to them, were as flat as stale beer. They spoke of the president of the college as President Littlego of Triflecut and referred to Cambridge as "Doughnut." They sneered at Doctor Phosphorus and Lawyer Smealmin and Swippens's Wholesale Grocery concern. They remarked that "the great art of being a merchant is to look wise and ride in a carriage." * Poetry was the only life for them, or painting, or contemplation, if they had to starve in a garret or a hut. And if all this was not the result of reading, where, pray, had they acquired their notions? The mothers and aunts and cousins of young New England,—not to speak of the fathers, who carried on the wholesale grocery business, the cotton-factory and the firm in State Street,—were filled with alarm and dismay.

Not that the fathers and mothers and aunts and cousins were opposed to books and reading. Many of the Boston merchants were authors themselves.† The solid men believed in education. They heartily favoured the great educational movement. It fitted the young men, their sons and nephews, not to forget the meritorious poor, to make the most of all the dazzling chances, legal, technological,

---

* See W. Ellery Channing, *The Youth of the Poet and the Painter,* in *The Dial.*

† See Nathan Appleton on *Original Sin,* and the miscellaneous writings of Thomas Handasyd Perkins, Abbott Lawrence, William Sturgis, Robert Bennet Forbes, etc.

commercial, which the expanding republic offered them. But books of a new kind had begun to appear, French and especially German books, even books by Englishmen and Scotchmen, who should have known better, filled with the wildest sort of metaphysics. These were the books that addled the minds of their sons, as Everett and Ticknor quite agreed,—for Everett and Ticknor, who knew the Germans, shared the opinions of the men of State Street regarding all these "follies of form and style." * The young men who read the new writers,—Thomas Carlyle, George Sand, Richter, Schleiermacher,—saw the matter in another light. If they were drawn to these writers, who spoke of the inner life, it was because the outer world repelled them. They could not share the current of ambition that galvanized the tougher-minded spirits,—the "forth-putting" types, as they said in New England, those that had "faculty," those that knew how to "take hold." What if trade and politics were advancing? Even if they had cared for politics, was it not evident that, with Jacksonism, the noble type of the trained statesman had yielded to the tricky politician? Politics had certainly lost the glamour which the great age of the statesmen had given it.† And commerce, too, had lost its grand role. The old China trade was a statesman's business. The factory was dull and small beside it. And who could ignore the abuses of modern business?— the fraud and perjury at the custom-house, the bribing of

* The *North American* group as a whole was invincibly opposed to the new school, the Transcendentalists and all their works. See Prescott's remarks on Carlyle's *French Revolution*,—"a shower of twaddle . . . newfangled words . . . ridiculous affectations . . . perfectly contemptible . . . both as to *forme* and to *fond*."—Ticknor's *Life of Prescott*, 363.

† This was the standing complaint of Henry Adams, a generation later. Many fine minds anticipated Adams. Josiah Quincy wrote in 1834 that the new race of politicians "steer the ship of state by the winds of popular favour, before which they run, which they never seek to stem, which they dare not resist."—Edmund Quincy's *Life of Josiah Quincy*.

The *Letters of Major Jack Downing*, popular in the thirties and forties, added to the general disillusion. That American politics had returned to the Stone Age was a very natural deduction from this picture of Jackson's "husking frolic" around the Washington "crib."

foreign officials, the sweating of the workers in the mills, the hideous oppression of the sailors? Worst of all, slavery. Was not half the wealth of the Northern mills drawn from the whips of the Southern overseers? Was it not true that in Cuba one slave out of every ten died every year in order to give the Americans their sugar? The ways of trade were unfit for a chivalrous man, unless he could reverse the whole system.

In short, the more sensitive minds of the younger generation, the imaginative, the impressionable, the perceptive, those who characterize a generation,—for the practical people never change, except in the cut of their clothes,—were thoroughly disaffected. The shape of the outward world had ceased to please them. The Fourth of July orations had ceased to convince them that "freedom" had any connection with freedom of mind or that "liberality" in religion had any connection with religious feeling. The aristocrats of trade were essentially vulgar, the "rational" Unitarians were materialistic. The young people were radicals and mystics. They had no interest in size, numbers and dollars. They had begun to explore the inner life, the depths of thought and sentiment. They had returned, on another level, to the mental habits of their Pilgrim forbears. Those who were socially-minded allied themselves with the various cults and movements that were breaking out all over the country, the temperance and non-resistance societies, the vegetarian movement, the no-money movement, the Abolition movement, which was rapidly rising, the Socialist movement, which had come to stay. The Chardon Street Convention gave them a platform.* They sympathized with "Wandering

* The Convention of Friends of Universal Reform, 1840. The Chardon Street Chapel, the haunt of the reformers, was remodelled from the Parkman family's barn. Dr. Parkman, Francis Parkman's father, who did not like reformers,—although, as one of his eulogists said, he was "particularly kind to the unattractive,"—always referred to the chapel as "my mother's barn."

Jew" Taylor, who roamed about the roads and country
lanes and whom one saw, at street-corners in Boston,
standing, bare-headed, offering prayers for the city. They
sympathized with old Father Lamson, with his long beard
and white habiliments. They sympathized even with Abby
Folsom, the well-known "flea of conventions," who ended
each remark with the shrill refrain, "It's the capitalists!"
Those whom a dream had possessed!—mad, no doubt,
but God-intoxicated. The young people whose interests
were social wished to "do good," they wished to be "of
use,"—like the young people in Germany and Russia, in
England, Italy, Hungary and France. For in these late
thirties and early forties, at Harvard, as at Oxford, as
at Warsaw, at Heidelberg, Toulouse and Salamanca, the
young people spoke the same language. And not at Harvard only. At Yale, Princeton, Williams, in New York,
they grieved over the sorrowful disproportion between
their faculties and the importunate work which the state
of the world so patently placed before them.

For, whether their minds were social or poetic, they
all agreed regarding the state of the world. It was a cold,
unfeeling civilization, bred by commercial interests and
isolation, a negative moderation, an excess of prudence,
compromise, provincial good taste. It cast a censorious
eye on human nature, on all the free flights of the picturesque, the goodly growths of fancy. It offered employment to no one but the decorous and the complacent. It
was timid, imitative, tame; worse, it was mean and cruel.
It taught the mind of the young to aim at low objects,—
and never had the young been so unsubmissive. They did
not care a button for common sense. They were bored by
the ideal of the marble statue as a pattern of social behaviour. They did not wish to "get," they wished to
"have." They did not wish to "do," they wished to "be."
As one of them said, in a burst that amused their elders,

> Greatly to Be
> Is enough for me,
> Is enough for thee.

To reaffirm the senses and the soul. To exist, expand, feel, to possess their own uniqueness.* To have, when it came to "having," a flute, perhaps, a little telescope with which to study the tree-tops from Wachusett, a book of Tennyson's poems to sing and recite on long walks over the Andover hills. For Tennyson had just appeared in Boston, a little later than Keats, who represented the purest cult of beauty. If one parted one's hair in the middle and let the locks flow down over one's shoulders, if one wore a blouse or a frock on fitting occasions, one could forget, at least for a day or two, the brutal, monkish regimen of the college.

Here was a "newness" for the New England fathers. They had known ten younger generations who had accepted without sighs or murmurs the yoke of the farm and the counting-house and gladly sought the pulpit and the Senate. All of them had been stable and well-tethered. These boys and girls of the new age were as distinct from their predecessors as young Italians were from the people of Iceland. They had a mania for the "natural." They detested conventional ways. They chose to wander alone, like so many madmen. Stearns Wheeler, one of the tutors in Greek, built a hut in the woods and went to live there. Two young clerks in Boston counting-houses also spent a winter in the woods, reading and writing in their cabin, in imminent peril of an Arctic death. Jones Very, the poet, another Greek tutor, the son of a Salem skipper, lost his mind for a time and had to be placed in the McLean Asylum. A few fled frantically to Europe,

---

* "I want my place, my own place, my true place in the world, my proper sphere, my thing which Nature intended me to perform when she fashioned me thus awry, and which I have vainly sought all my life-time."
—Hawthorne, *The Intelligence-Office*.

where they could lose for a while their sense of oppression. Others committed suicide. Young women indulged
in fantasies, one of them about a *femme fatale* who ran
through the woods half-naked, bathed under the moon
in icy pools, enticing men in order to repel them. The
mal du siècle was in full career, though it usually assumed the most innocent forms. A "band" of aesthetic
youths and maidens gathered in Cambridge and Watertown. They read Keats and Tennyson together, copied
their own poems in manuscript-books, which they passed
from hand to hand, and talked about women's rights
and Socialism. The girls composed flower-pieces and
painted in water-colours. The young men read Saint Augustine and Plato, traversed the cycle of religious faiths
and thought they would like to join the Catholic Church;
and, between a winter in Rome and a summer in Paris,
they echoed the Plymouth tutor, Robert Bartlett, who
said that they should make their own country "classic to
themselves": the American mind should cease to replen-
ish itself with the mighty wonders of Europe and find its
fire within. When they could not meet, they corresponded,
enclosing an anemone or a mallow-blossom. How swiftly,
like magic, the spring was advancing!—every dry twig
bursting forth, covering itself with beauty! Why should
not the dry hearts of men burst forth in a similar way?
Some new and hidden fount of life was about to revivify existence. The young girls read the young men's
characters by holding the young men's letters against
their foreheads. It was all rather bashful and indirect,
as if they were a little ashamed to confess that they were
interested in these mundane matters. They marvelled over
their sensibility. One of them read character by the form
of the letters, another by the merest "contact with a person." They made all sorts of discoveries, as that sometimes words came into one's mind that had a deep
meaning for oneself, although they conveyed nothing to

anyone else. Their thoughts seemed to come too fast for expression. They asked one another questions: "Has your impressibility returned?"—with a sort of breathless virginality, as if they were on the brink of some great secret. The strange, dire planet called Human Nature, hitherto so dark and almost baleful, had swum into their ken. It seemed to portend an age of novel-writing.

In Boston, these new feelings had a focus in the various institutions of art and music that were appearing now on every hand. The C-Minor Symphony of Beethoven was played in the Odeon in 1840, a flowering of the Handel and Haydn Society, which had put to rout the old psalms and glee-tunes. The young men walked in from Cambridge, in parties of three or four, deliciously thrilled by the darkness of the road and the chance of meeting a footpad. The Athenæum displayed its collection of casts, the gift of Colonel Perkins, the Brimmer collection of Italian drawings, collections of gems and engravings, Stuart's florid merchants, Allston's dreamy women, Copley's grim ladies, clad in satin, landscapes by Cole and West, an Annibale Carracci, a Murillo, a few half-fabulous Raphaels and Luinis. The galleries became a rendezvous, where art and love blossomed under the skylights. One could almost feel, in the tranquil air, that one had embarked for Italy, with a best-beloved companion. Sometimes in a single day a little group of youthful amateurs enjoyed a double wonder, a glimpse of "Belshazzar's Feast" and an hour of Mozart. Sometimes they met at the rooms of the *cognoscente* who had upon his door a blazing sun, with gilded rays running in all directions, bearing the motto, "Universal Unity,"—for the young man was a Fourierist,—and underneath the black-and-white inscription, to bring one's mind back to Massachusetts, "Please wipe your feet." Sometimes they found aid and comfort at Dr. Channing's "Club of the Jacobins," in Jonathan Phillips's rooms at the Tremont House, where the two old friends liked nothing better than to greet a Harvard man who was not "indifferent." Or they spent an afternoon of early summer on the spreading lawns of one of the Brookline merchants, with music and a game of battledore, a punch-bowl and a bowl of plum-like cherries, a Reynolds and a Ruysdael to look at, and possibly Prescott in the middle distance, or Daniel Webster sitting under an elm-tree. At night, beside their argand lamps, they pored over albums of engravings, Piranesi, Raphael Morghen, discussed the German poets and read the springtide writers, Chaucer, Boccaccio, Dante. They talked about spiritualism and mesmerism, phrenology and animal magnetism, all the dark problems of the human mind over which the sun of hope seemed to be rising.

Across the hinterland, through the rural centres, the new mood spread like the flowers of May. One heard the flute in the fields. Farmers and village tailors stopped to watch the birds building their nests. They went on woodland walks. They recorded the days when the wildflowers opened. They observed the little tragedies of nature that no one had noticed before, a cat springing on an oriole and marching proudly off with her golden booty projecting in all directions from her mouth. They gathered the first hepaticas, the trailing arbutus that had bled unseen under the boots of their fathers. In hundreds of hamlets the neighbours assembled awe-struck while the night-blooming cereus opened its petals, standing hushed in the presence of the marvel, as the connoisseurs of Florence had stood in the presence of a new Botticelli. It filled them with romantic associations to think of these splendid flowers opening in the night of the Mexican jungle, where there were no eyes to look at them but the agate eyes of lizards and serpents. The cereus was their Boston Athenæum, and all the airs of Mozart sang in its petals; and the young men and women, like those

of Boston, graduates of the female seminaries, of Middlebury College, Dartmouth, Williams,—where Mark Hopkins sat on the end of his log,—also wrote their poems
and their meditations. It was true that the country ministers still preached on the Dangers of Beauty. Hiram
Powers, the sculptor of the future, attracted crowds with
the panorama of hell which he exhibited in the villages,
an orgy of sulphuric flames, the livid faces of children
and devils with pitchforks,—a sermon such as one might
have heard in Rome. The old faith survived in force, and
here and there some youthful minister, seduced by the
Boston Unitarians, felt like a Hindu who has lost his
caste and moaned through his house, "Oh, where shall
rest be found?" He found his rest by "aiming at the
stars" or writing a parable about the boy who climbed the
Natural Bridge. For the old faith, like the new, contributed to the mood of exaltation. Life ought to be consecration, labour, worship! All the young aspired who
had read *The Psalm of Life* and knew the meaning of the
"strange device" that Longfellow might have invented
for Ibsen's Brand.

Poetry spread like fox-fire through the woodlands.
Every village had its Gifted Hopkins, author of *To
Myrtle Awaking* and *To Myrtle Retiring* or *Contemplations in Autumn,* after Pollok. Many a village had its
youthful sculptor, who modelled figures of "Innocence"
in snow, and a Pantasophian Society that served as a
medium of exchange for minds that would otherwise have
blushed unseen. Over his native Connecticut hills and
meadows scudded the haggard Percival, the poet, with
a wild glitter in his eye, startled at the approach of a
fellow-creature, wrapping his rusty camlet cloak about
him, silent, never smiling, the "old rock-smasher," as he
was called by the farmers; for the poor rhymester-vagrant,
with his sinister air, had taken to studying minerals and
was to do in geology, in the end, what he had failed to

do in poetry. Other and younger poets, destined for a happier flowering, or a happier life, at least, dreamed under the stars, perhaps in a hammock, swung between two elm-trees,—a boy who longed to be a Marcus Curtius and leap into a gulf to save his country, a girl, born in India, on a voyage, in the midst of tropical scenes that returned to her with the breeze of her sandal-wood fan. They were to have their say, they were to have their hour at the Tourney of Poets, when New England began to reveal its "portfolio" writings, the Thoughts on Art and Thoughts on the Scholar's Calling, the Musings of a Recluse, the "rapture-feelings" that were to fill *The Dial.* Here and there, a judge or a factory-owner, the great man of the village, touched by the note of a beauty-loving day,—a little confused as regards the fundamentals, though not more confused than the city-people,—built the Greek temple with the green shutters that was to be known as the "house on the hill."

For this, already for a generation, was the day of the Greek revival. Grecian dwellings rose on every Main Street, Parthenons of painted wood, churches and banks vaguely suggesting Athens, with variations in the Egyptian vein. Everett's lectures had borne fruit at Harvard, Byron had contributed a strain. The Greek struggle for independence had caught the imagination of the people, and Dr. Howe's romantic adventures in Greece,—whence he had returned with Byron's helmet,—appealed to the general mind.* The casts in the Athenæum played their part; so did the writings of Walter Savage Landor. A school of American sculptors had appeared and found a home at Florence, where they carried on the tradition of Canova: Horatio Greenough, who, as a boy, had learned to cut his chalk in the Athenæum, soon to be followed by Thomas Crawford, the carver of mantel-pieces in New

* See *Historical Sketch of the Greek Revolution,* by Samuel Gridley Howe, 1828, a vigorous and memorable book.

York, and Powers, who came from Vermont, where the ridges of the hills were of solid marble and marble pigsties rose on lonely farms. The children, brought up on Flaxman's outlines, knew their mythology as they knew the Bible; they were prepared for Emerson's Platonism and the *Wonder-book* and *Tanglewood Tales* of Hawthorne. Everyone talked mythology, as everyone had begun to discuss the history of religion; and the best New England novels, at the turn of the forties, those of William Ware, *Zenobia, Probus, Julian, or Scenes in Judea,* presupposed a feeling for ancient Greece, as they also took for granted a circle of readers who were steeped in the Bible and the Latin authors. Classical stories ran side by side with the realistic stories of New England life that Catherine M. Sedgwick was writing at Stockbridge, *Hope Leslie, Redwood, A New England Tale,* truthful, simple, sometimes too-too simple, after the fashion of Maria Edgeworth, in praise of the duties of home and the virtuous poor. Miss Sedgwick was a highly intelligent woman, a friend and correspondent of Sismondi; she was cultivated, bountiful and good, and her household was the centre of the Berkshires. The naturalness of her style was a kind of triumph, and she prepared the way for the writers who followed by stimulating the interest of her readers in their own landscape and manners; but no one could have supposed that her work would live. Her fellow-philanthropist, Lydia Maria Child, the editor of a magazine for children, the author of a novel of Puritan times, of the first important antislavery book, of *The Progress of Religious Ideas,* of lives of Madame de Staël and Madame Roland, produced a classical novel among the rest. *Philothea* followed *The Frugal Housewife,* a feminine *Poor Richard's Almanac,* a treasury of New England household lore that showed, with an abundance of quaint detail, how one could live on less than a dollar a day. *Philothea* was a dream of Greece, of Pericles, Plato and Phidias, in which a New England maiden in a peplus tries to reform Aspasia. It was a virginal vision, like Powers's "Greek Slave." But William Ware's novels were well-wrought and solid. This Unitarian minister, the son of Dr. Henry Ware of Cambridge, who had visited Greece and the Holy Land, well knew the world of which he wrote, the Roman Empire of the early Christians, and had the imagination to relive it. If his heroes and heroines savoured a little too much of Dr. Channing's circle, Ware was an artist notwithstanding. His novels were to remain for those who enjoy a style that reproduces, with their scenes and subjects, the enchanting rhythms of the ancient authors.

The interest in modern languages, meanwhile, had thriven under the influence of Coleridge. Professor James Marsh of Vermont had published editions of Coleridge's prose writings, but long before this the poet Dana had introduced his critical ideas, and the increasing numbers of American students who flocked to the German universities were spreading them far and wide. The doctrine of "following nature in variety of kinds" had led to an intellectual revolution; for, if nature was inexhaustible in variety, so were the possible forms of the human mind. This key had opened the worlds of letters that lay behind the modern languages. It had destroyed the "rules" that measured everything by the classical standards. The critic was no longer in a position to sit on a lofty throne and send to Gehenna authors who did not conform to these obsolete rules. He had to yield to times and circumstances. He was obliged to submit to other tests than the tests of the "savage and tartarly" Jeffrey and Gifford and the strip-and-whip school of the previous age, with its arrogant insularity. The critic had to "characterize" the author, to understand him and interpret him, asking, From what point does he look at life?

These catholic and supple views of Coleridge, derived from the writings of A. W. Schlegel, whom Ticknor had known in Paris, marked the new era in criticism. All the American writers of the future who had any claim to be considered central shared these views as a matter of course; and the writers of the *North American* group, learned but narrow in their range of feeling, dry, mechanical, timid, subservient to the abstract laws that had governed the eighteenth century, children of Burke and Johnson, gradually lost influence as they spread. In the dialect that Coleridge propagated,—also the fruit of his German studies,—the old school was the school of the "understanding," the new school was the school of "reason." These were the Transcendentalist categories for which the New England mind was so well prepared, for they corresponded with the generations, the older and the younger generations, or, rather, the temperaments of these generations, which were at open war with one another. The "understanding" was the faculty that observed, inferred, argued, drew conclusions. It was the Lockian faculty; it assumed that everything in the mind was drawn from the experience of the senses. Exactly! It was the lawyer's point of view that governed conservative Boston, the cold, external, practical notion of life that guided the merchants in their counting-houses and the Unitarian ministers in their pulpits. The "reason" was the faculty of intuition, warm, perceptive, immediate, that represented the mind of young New England. It assumed, it actually *knew,* that the mind contained powers of its own, not derived from the senses. In the theological sphere, Transcendentalism was a reaction against both Unitarianism and Trinitarianism, neither of which possessed any belief in the self-sufficiency of the human mind outside of revelation. It spoke for an order of truth that transcended, by immediate perception, all external evidence. "God becomes conscious in man," as Fichte said.

"the philosopher man, the man of reason, in whom the absolute being recognizes himself. The reason gazes immediately on the eternal realities." This was the gist of Schleiermacher's teachings, which shocked Andrews Norton,—the phrase, "the soul's sense of things divine." Herder, in the *Spirit of Hebrew Poetry,* translated by Dr. James Marsh, had extended the conception to literature. Writing of the Jewish prophets, he had abolished the distinction between the sacred and the secular, transferring to the credit of human genius all that had been ascribed to the divine. In the bards of Israel, all bards were glorified, a notion which, to the candid mind, far from drawing angels down, raised mortals to the skies. It recognized the creative powers of man. Coleridge had prophesied that a golden age, in letters, art, religion, social ethics, would follow the spread of Transcendentalism; and from various German thinkers, Jacobi and Fichte, the new generation in New England was receiving special impulsions, towards heroism and towards mysticism, that appealed to the youthful mind.

For the influence of Germany grew apace. It had passed quite out of the hands of the earlier students, Everett and Ticknor, Longfellow even, who scarcely shared the Transcendental impulse. It raged through other students and translators, some of whom, like Frederick Henry Hedge, the Unitarian minister in Bangor, the son of Dr. Hedge who had written the *Logic,* had studied in the land of Kant and Herder. To the hesitant *North American,* Bancroft contributed essays on the German writers. He also helped to popularize the sympathetic writings of Victor Cousin, the French eclectic philosopher, for whom all systems were true in what they affirmed, false in what they denied.* Felton, the anti-

* In the earlier volumes of his history, Bancroft appeared as a champion of the new philosophy, which he identified with Quakerism, the gospel of the Inner Light. See his discussion of Locke and William Penn.

Transcendentalist, translated Menzel's history. Mrs. Lee of Brookline wrote a life of Richter. Charles T. Brooks, the minister of Newport, began the long series of German translations that was to include, as time went on, works by Goethe, Schiller, Richter, Rückert. A collection of minor poems by Goethe and Schiller, in the version of John Sullivan Dwight, appeared as one of a number of similar works. All the young men and maidens read the German authors. They echoed Schiller's great command, "Keep true to the dream of thy youth." They pondered Novalis's *Heinrich von Ofterdingen:* several Harvard students spent a summer rendering this "apotheosis of poetry" into the language of their own hearts. They "longed for Italy" after Wackenroder. They believed in the gospel of *Lucinde* that poetry and life should be one and the same, and shared the despair of the heroine over the discord which they could by no means harmonize. They read the tales of Tieck, Musæus, Hoffmann. They yearned for the "blue flower." They dreamed of Jean Paul's Titan, Roquairol, who longed for an enterprise for his idle valour, the hero, torn by passions and hopes deferred, who did not possess the power to mould his world. They felt within, like Manfred,—

> an awful chaos—light and darkness—
> And mind and dust—and passions and pure thought
> Mix'd, and contending without end or order.

They felt that men should be true and wise, beautiful, pure and aspiring. They worshipped heroism, they worshipped genius. And they believed,—the thought was in the air,—that the way to greatness was through books, not battles. Thomas Wentworth Higginson, who seldom yielded even to moral excesses, said of Mrs. Lee's *Life of Richter* that it set before him, just at the right time, the attractions of a literary life, carried on in an unworldly spirit. "From that moment," he added, "poverty, or at least extreme economy, had no terrors for me, and I could not bear the thought of devoting my life to Blackstone."

Much of this German influence reached New England through the medium of a greater man than Coleridge, greater, at least, in energy, greater as a moral force, Carlyle. The readers of the British reviews,—and every well-instructed student read them,—had long been aware of the author of *Characteristics,* the essay entitled *The Signs of the Times* and the series of papers on the German writers. Carlyle,—the name began to emerge from a Scottish mist of anonymity,—Carlyle, the "Germanic new-light writer," was, in fact, the perfect middleman for this new movement of ideas. One thought of New England and Scotland as almost interchangeable terms. There was an occult relation between these regions, with their immemorial Calvinist past and their instinct for the heroic.* The greatest foreign influence in New England had been, for a generation, Scott, who had also been stirred by the German poets; and Carlyle was to find in New England his first large circle of readers, even a publisher for *Sartor Resartus* before the book appeared in his own country. He represented the romantic spirit on its ethical and religious side, where the New England mind was most at home; and for twenty years, down to the Civil War, his influence was to remain almost despotic. This was before the brutality of his later years grew upon him with his indigestion, till the splendid dreams of his youth were all but lost in the spoiled peasant's worship of lordship and power.

Over the rising school of New England writers, even

* New Englanders have often felt more at home in Scotland than in England. It is significant that little Ellen, in *The Wide, Wide World,* when she inherits her paradise, inherits it in Scotland, not in England, though the paradise is properly qualified as a "Scottish discipline" and she returns to America, with equal propriety, in the end.

over the toughest-grained, Carlyle and Carlylese were
to leave their traces. Even the style of Thoreau was to
be tinged faintly here and there with the rhythms and
locutions of a writer whom lesser minds could not resist.
Lowell was deeply affected by them. The eighteenth-
century style of his Homer Wilbur, the intransigent parson of *The Biglow Papers*, was wrenched, by Carlyle's
influence, even to the extent of whole pages, out of its
normal channel.* Margaret Fuller wrote Carlylean essays. Theodore Parker's *Historic Americans* might
almost have been written by the man whom Thackeray,
Dickens and Ruskin called their master. Sylvester Judd's
Margaret bristled with the dialect.† The picturesque
historical style of Motley was almost as much affected
by Carlyle as Dickens's *Tale of Two Cities*. This was
the greatest magnetic force of an age that was much
concerned with animal magnetism; and writers who seldom wrote greatly rose above themselves when they wrote
of Carlyle.‡ He vindicated, they felt, their celestial birthright, showed them that the current ideals were shams,
ridiculed the respectable, the "gigmen," the heroes of a
mechanical age; he taught the "science of Dynamics," the
"primary, unmodified forces and energies of men, the
mysterious springs of love and fear and wonder." He
gave them faith in their own endeavours. He told them
to quit their paper formulas and know that they were
alive and that God was alive. "Did the upholsterers

* "On whirls the restless globe through unsounded time, with its cities
and its silences," etc.—Lowell, *The Biglow Papers*. See also Mr. Wilbur's
sermon, First Series, No. VI.
† See the exclamations of Margaret, in the scene after the trial: "My
poor murdered brother! Fades the cloud-girt, star-flowering universe to my
eye! I hear the screaming of hope, in wild Merganser flight to the regions
of endless cold!"
‡ See Bronson Alcott's description of the "British Taurus" in *R. W.
Emerson: His Character and Genius:* "Curious to see him, his chin aloft,
the pent thunders rolling, lightnings darting from under the bold brows,
words that tell of the wail within, accents not meant for music, yet made
lyrical in the cadences of his Caledonian refrain, his mirth mad as Lear's,
his humour as wilful as the wind."

make this universe? Were you created by the tailor?"
The old ideal of manhood had been forgotten. To young
valour and the thirst for action, a calculating age of
profit-seekers was deaf, dumb and blind; and yet the
Invisible still existed, and opened itself to the inward
eye, and fought on the side of the seeker of it! That
every man had his own task, his own peculiar inlet into
the sea of Divinity, which, once found, destroyed the
canker of doubt: this was an open-sesame for young New
England. According to the Arab saying, "Every people
has its own prophet." Was Thomas Carlyle this prophet?
So it appeared, for a while. Then it became apparent that
Carlyle was only a part of the atmosphere. The real New
England prophet was another man who dwelt in the little
town of Concord.

CHAPTER X

EMERSON IN CONCORD

RALPH WALDO EMERSON had lived in Concord since 1834. The former pastor of a Boston church and a son of the Reverend William Emerson, he had withdrawn from the ministry. Having a little income, he had bought a house on the Boston turnpike, surrounded with pine and fir-trees. There was a garden by the brook, filled with roses and tulips. In the western window of his study, he placed an Æolian harp. It sang in the spring and summer breezes, mingling with the voices of the birds, fitfully bringing to mind the ballads that he loved, the wild, melodious notes of the old bards and minstrels.

He had been writing essays and giving addresses that grieved and vexed most of his older hearers. Dozens, even hundreds of the younger people, thinking of him, thought of Burns's phrase,

> Wi' sic as he, where'er he be,
> May I be saved or damned.

But, although he had his followers in Boston, he was anathema to the pundits there. Everett sneered at Emerson's "conceited, laborious nonsense." John Quincy Adams and Andrews Norton thought he was an atheist and worse. The Cambridge theologians reviled him: he was a pantheist and a German mystic, and his style was a kind of neo-Platonic moonshine. The Concord prophet smiled at these accusations. He had the temerity to think that the great Cambridge guns were merely popguns. There was nothing explosive in his own discourse. He was a flute-player, one who plucked his reeds in the Concord river. But when he began to play, one saw a beautiful portico, standing in a lovely scene of nature, covered with blossoms and vine-leaves; and, at the strains of the flute, one felt impelled to enter the portico and explore the unknown region that lay beyond. It was an irresistible invitation. As for the smiling musician, he was a mystery still. One thought of him as the man in Plutarch's story who conversed with men one day only in the year and spent the rest of his days with the nymphs and demons.

Everyone had heard of him in Boston, where he was giving lectures. His birthplace there was a kitestring's distance from the house where Franklin was born and the house where Edgar Allan Poe was born. But, although he belonged to one of the oldest scholarly families, with countless names in the college catalogues, most of the signs had been against him. Tall, excessively thin, so thin that, as Heine said of Wellington, his full face looked like a profile, pale, with a tomahawk nose, blond, with blue eyes and smiling, curved lips, he had none of the traits, aggressive or brilliant, that marked his brothers in various ways. At moments, on the platform, he spoke with a tranquil authority, but his usual demeanour was almost girlishly passive. He had not acquired the majestic air, as of a wise old eagle or Indian sachem, that marked his later years. He appeared to be easily disconcerted, for his self-reliance was a gradual conquest. He had drifted through many misfortunes, drifted into and out of tuberculosis, drifted into teaching and out of the Church, maturing very slowly. He had known dark hours, poverty, pain, fear, disease. His first wife had died; so had two of his brothers. The trouble with him was, his elders thought, that he seemed to like to drift. He had no sort of record as a student. At Harvard, even three gen-

erations later, when people spoke of Emerson's "education," they put the word in quotation-marks,*—it was not
that he did not know his Greek and Latin, but that he
was never systematic. He had read, both then and later,
for "lustres" mainly. He had drifted first to Florida and
then to Europe, and finally settled at Concord, the home
of his forbears, where he had often visited at the Manse.
The minister there, Dr. Ezra Ripley, who was Emerson's
step-grandfather and very fond of the young man, felt
that he was obliged to warn the people against this leader
of the Egomites, those who "sent themselves" on the
Lord's errands, without any proper calling. As for the
lectures that Emerson was giving in Boston, on great
men, history, the present age, the famous lawyer,
Jeremiah Mason, when he was asked if he could understand them, replied, "No, but my daughters can."

To the outer eye, at least, Emerson's life was an aimless jumble. He had ignored all the obvious chances, rejected the palpable prizes, followed none of the rules of
common sense. Was he pursuing some star of his own?
No one else could see it. In later years, looking back,
Emerson's friends, remembering him, thought of those
quiet brown colts, unrecognized even by the trainers, that
out-strip all the others on the race-course. He had had
few doubts himself. He had edged along sideways
towards everything that was good in his life, but he felt
that he was born for victory. He had not chosen his
course. It had sprung from a necessity of his nature, an
inner logic that he scarcely questioned. In college, he had
consulted the *Sortes Virgilianæ,* opening at the line in
Dryden's version,—

Go, let the gods and temples claim thy care.

* See President Eliot's *Harvard Memories.* The true Cambridge mind
could never accept such cavalier remarks of Emerson's as that "books are
for the scholar's idle times."

It seemed to suggest the ministry, and he had followed the suggestion, as his fathers had followed it before him. But Unitarianism could not hold him. The walls of this temple, he thought, were wasted and thin, and at last nothing was left but a film of whitewash. Then, gradually, another faith possessed him. Channing, who had helped him with his studies, had mentioned some recent writer who said there were two souls in the human body, one the vulgar, waking, practical soul, the other a soul that never suspended its action and guided the involuntary motions. This hint of German Transcendentalism, savouring of the Neo-Platonists and the Sacred Books of the East, with which his Aunt Mary was familiar, lingered and grew in his mind. What was this involuntary soul, this "absolute being" of the German thinkers, but the "inner light" of the Quakers, with whom he had talked at New Bedford, that indescribable presence, dwelling in every being and common to all, which the contradiction of all men could not shake and which the consent of all could not confirm? Every religion had known it, the Holy Ghost, the Comforter, the Dæmon, the still, small voice, the light, the seed, Channing's moral sentiment, the One of Plato and Plotinus, the Universal Mind of the Yogis and Sufis. One felt this presence at moments only,— Emerson had felt it a thousand times, in the woods and fields at Concord; but there was a depth in these brief moments that gave them a strange authority. He felt a sudden influx of power; the currents of the universal being seemed to circulate through him. Was not all nature saturated with deity, and was he not himself a part of nature? He seemed to see in a flash the laws of life, justice, truth, love and freedom. Why should he not explore these wonderful realms? Why should he not proclaim this Joyous Science?

It was to confirm these intuitions that he had visited Europe. He wished to escape from theological problems, which seemed to him the soul's mumps and measles, and meet the living writers, Carlyle, Coleridge, Wordsworth, Landor, who, having nourished his own vigour, seemed to say that men were of tunable metal. He spent a few weeks at Rome and Naples and studied for a while at the Collège de France. In the zoological gardens in Paris, he underwent a strange experience that was the greatest lesson of his journey. Observing the rocks, the grasses, the fishes, the insects, the lions, vultures and elephants, he felt a conviction stirring in him that all these forms of life expressed some property in himself. He felt the zoöphyte in him, the centipede, the fox. He was moved by mysterious sympathies, such as he had felt in the woods at home. Was he not one with all these creatures? Nature was indeed a living whole, a spiral ever ascending. He had been struck by Lamarck's ideas. What Plotinus said, that all beings, even the plants, even the soil that bore them aspired to attain conscious knowledge, seemed to be confirmed by modern science. He had conceived, in his way, the theory of evolution, which he was to express in all his writings; and he felt that the new age of science represented a further ascent. Men would rise above their conventional notions, emerge from their belief in mere prescription, their blind and ignorant following of custom, as science more and more increased their insight into the laws of nature. They would learn to trust themselves, the universal soul within themselves, casting off their "old clothes," walking the earth at last as supermen,—for this was Emerson's notion before it was Nietzsche's. It was Carlyle's belief as well, and Emerson had visited Carlyle. He had spent a day and a night at Craigenputtock. He was "the one of all the sons of Adam" who, as Carlyle wrote later, "completely understood what I was saying and answered with a truly human voice."

In no haste to publish his reflections, Emerson, settled

in Concord, "put his ear close by himself," as Montaigne had done before him, and held his breath and listened. He liked the phrase of Simonides, "Give me twice the time, for the more I think the more it enlarges." Was not America full of puny scholars, clamorous place-hunters and village brawlers, whose talents were only for contention? Was it not a country of small adventures, short plans and daring risks? For patience, for great combinations, for long, persistent, close-woven schemes, where could one look in all this fuss and bustle? Was it not true that Americans lived on the surface, a poor, thin, plausible existence? Their vice, their national vice was imitation; they copied foreign forms in their manners and writing, forms that were merely capricious, as if these were permanent forms of nature. The scholars and the thinkers and the writers, as shallow and as frivolous as the rest,—able as they might be in special tasks, —had no advice to give in vital matters, and the public disregarded them. For the public had its own public wisdom: what it asked of the thinker was something else, the private, the universal wisdom of which it had been defrauded by its own dwelling in the street. Was it not time to be dumb for a while, to sit with one's hand on one's mouth, a long, austere, Pythagorean lustrum? Inner independence was what the thinker needed, and the life of the cottage and the woods,—insulation of place,—only had value as an aid to this. But in solitude, Emerson found, his faculties rose fair and full within, like the forest trees and the field flowers. He did not wish to print his thoughts until he had something to say that men would be obliged to attend and hear.

He knew and would know no such thing as haste in composition; and he was determined to keep his freedom, even at the risk of uselessness. A course in which clear faith could not go might well be worse than none. Besides, although he did not know his way, he felt that the

current knew it. There was a pilot within him, and, when
he did not know how to steer, and dared not hoist a sail,
he had only to drift. He lectured here and there, in
Boston, in the neighbouring towns, in Concord, in order
to supplement his little income. He travelled further and
further from home, until he was known as a lecturer
throughout the West. He joined in the village life and
served on local committees, and he gave the memorial
address when Concord celebrated its second centennial.
In the village Social Circle he found a suggestion of the
well-known society in *Wilhelm Meister,* in which every
member was a master of one of the arts of life, mechanics, agriculture, medicine, law. He liked to talk with
farmers, millers, tailors, with carpenters and coopers at
their work, horse-trainers, geologists, physicists, chemists, whom he visited in their laboratories, astonished by
their feats of skill, their powers of observation and endurance. He watched with awe the life of his farmer-
neighbours. Were not the men in the cities who were the
centres of energy, the driving wheels of trade and the
practical arts, the sons and the grandsons of farmers?
And were they not spending the energies their fathers
had accumulated in poverty, necessity and darkness, in
their hardy, silent existence, in their frosty furrows? He
looked to life for his dictionary. He wished to master in
all these facts a language by which to embody and illustrate his own perceptions; for the thinker was a man for
whom all men worked,—geologist, mechanic, merchant,
chemist, king, painter, composer,—and a thousand men
looked through his eyes. And why should he travel for
his illustrations? Was it not the secret of the gods that
they came in low disguises? Real kings hid away their
crowns and affected a plain exterior, as Odin dwelt in a
fisherman's hut and Apollo served Admetus as a slave.
In the legends of fairy lore, the fairies largest in power
were the least in size. It was the magic of genius to lift

the curtain from the common, showing us the divinities that were all about us, disguised as gypsies and pedlars, as farm-hands and clerks.

With all this active social life, Emerson guarded his solitude. He bought a woodlot by Walden Pond, a wild, rocky ledge, with a grove of chestnuts, oaks, maples and hemlocks sweeping down to the shore. He trimmed the old path around the pond that had been worn by the feet of Indian hunters. He cut vistas over the water, where he bathed on summer afternoons; and there he strolled and lingered, sitting on the bank, reading Plato or Goethe, writing in his journal. There he was "adjacent to the One." He had always felt like a king in the woods, walking through tents of gold and bowers of crimson, garlanded with flowers, vines and sunbeams, surrounded with incense and music. An active enchantment seemed to reach his dust there, as if he had the keeping of a secret that was too great to be told, as if a god dwelt near him in a hollow tree. Every light from the sky, every shadow ministered to his pleasure. He seemed to dilate with the wind. He felt the blood of thousands in his body, and his heart seemed to pump through his veins the sap of all this forest vegetation. It was as if he had left behind all his human relations and become one with carbon, lime and granite. The frogs piped, the leaves hissed, the far-off waters tinkled, the grass bent and rustled, and he seemed to die out of the human world and enter another existence, a life of water, air, earth and ether. He passed into the trances of the Yogis and Sufis, the mystical state of Samadhi, in which the mind works without desire, objectless and bodiless, superconscious, and one feels free, omnipotent, immortal. In this state of elevation, elation and joy, shared by all the mystics, one feels that one belongs to another species, and the vision of a superhuman race becomes more real than reality. Nietzsche felt so at Sils-Maria, and so

Emerson felt in the woods at Walden. There was a god
in man, an angel in disguise that played the fool! The
millions that called themselves men were not yet men.
They were half-engaged in the soil, pawing to get free,
and they needed all the music that one could bring in
order to disengage them. They seemed to be on the verge
of all that was great, and so they were, indeed, were
they only aware of the faculties that slumbered within
them. Emerson's own path lay clear before him. It was
to look within himself and report his own perceptions
and reveal the powers that lay in the soul of man.

He had brought out a little book called *Nature,* the
germ of his later essays; but he seemed to be more eager
to further his friends than his own interests and ventures. He arranged with Stearns Wheeler, the Harvard
tutor, who had built the hut in the woods and had edited
Herodotus with notes, to copy out from *Fraser's Magazine* the pages of *Sartor Resartus,* which no British publisher would issue; and he had the first edition published
in Boston. Far from shrewd in financial matters, he gathered money shrewdly for Carlyle.* He also edited Jones
Very's sonnets. This excellent Greek scholar, a tall, spin-
dling ghost of a man, was one of the new group of Harvard mystics. As a boy, he had voyaged in his father's
ships, outward bound from Salem, and he had taken
flight, in after years, to realms that Salem ships had never
reached. In the McLean Asylum, where he dwelt for
a while, he had written an essay on Shakespeare, which
had been "told" him by the Holy Ghost. He believed
that he had risen from the dead, that he had ceased to
live in the physical world and had passed beyond earthly
realities; and indeed his voice seemed to come from the

---

* Emerson told Edward Everett Hale that the first money he received
from any of his own books was a cheque, in 1850, for *Representative Men.*
He called on his publishers, Phillips and Sampson, and asked them if he
was free to use the cheque. Mr. Phillips showed him how to endorse it.—
E. E. Hale, *Memories of a Hundred Years.*

tombs, and his face with its web of skin suggested a skull. He valued his sonnets not because they were his, but precisely because they were not, because, as he supposed, God spoke through him. Emerson selected and revised these sonnets, among them *The Stranger's Gift* and *The Barberry Bush*. There was little magic in them. Monotones in silver-grey, sober as a dove's breast, they were true poems, none the less. They had a sort of solemn incandescence. They were like frosted orbs of electric light. One caught their dim glow of religious feeling three generations later, partly thanks to Emerson's revisions; for no one knew better than he the importance of skill. He had a passion himself for rhetorical studies. He had aped the styles of various authors, Chateaubriand, Montaigne, Bacon, Browne, during his years in college, and had been drawn to the styles that were "rammed with life," in Ben Jonson's phrase, those that were pregnant and laconic, unlike the starched or flowing styles that were popular and current in his youth. His own prose diction suggested the seventeenth-century authors who had never stooped to explain their thoughts. In his verse he avoided the conventional forms, drawn from English poetry, which all the other American poets accepted, the sonnet, the romantic tale, the song. He liked to write gnomic lines, epigrams and rules of life, conveyed in a lively image, after the Greek or Persian fashion, sometimes contained in a single stanza,—

> Though love repine, and reason chafe,
> There came a voice without reply,—
> ' 'Tis man's perdition to be safe,
> When for the truth he ought to die.'

Occasionally he wrote some longer poem,—the magical *Give All to Love* and *Bacchus*,—in a free-verse style of his own invention. But most of his poems were composed

in the couplets of Milton's *L'Allegro,* which he filled with
a sunny sublimity.

The poet Very was one of the neophytes who felt the
fascination of the Concord prophet. Emerson's address,
The American Scholar, followed by his *Literary Ethics,
The Method of Nature, Man the Reformer* and others,
appealed to the younger generation more intimately than
Carlyle and the German writers. These speeches and
Emerson's essays, appearing at the same time,—*History,
Self-Reliance, Compensation,*—were filled with their problems and dilemmas, which Emerson seemed to have
shared. Unlike the professional orators, he addressed himself to the thinking classes, especially to students and beginners in life; and, instead of preaching the popular virtues, of which they had heard so much, and the value of
conforming to the world about them, he spoke to the individual in each of his hearers. Popularity was for "dolls,"
he said; and the "bloated vanity called public opinion"
should have no weight against the private will. He spoke
of the "maxims of a low prudence" which they would hear
every day, suggesting that the first of all their duties was
to get land and money, name and place. They should turn
a deaf ear to these base counsels, knowing that the search
after the great was the proper occupation of youth and
manhood. All young persons thirsted for a real existence,
for something they could do with all their heart. And was
it not true that each had his own vocation, some bias or
talent or special executive skill, by feeling and obeying
which alone he could rightly find his place in the world?
Every man had his magnetic needle, which always pointed
to his proper path, with more or less variation from other
men's. He was never happy or strong until he found it,
and he could only find it by trusting himself, by listening
to the whisper of the voice within him. Was it not the chief
disgrace in the world not to be a unit, not to be reckoned
one character, not to yield that peculiar fruit which each

man was created to bear, but to be reckoned in the gross, in the hundred, or the thousand, of the party or the section to which one belonged? If one paid no attention to the world's opinion, but followed one's own *proprium,* as Swedenborg called it, if one lived wholly from within, planting oneself on one's instincts and standing firm, the world would come round to one at last; for one's inner voice was the voice of the "collective psyche," as later writers called the Over-soul,—the term that Emerson used,—which imparts a common rhythm to all existence.* One would be acting in harmony with the laws of life, to which the phenomenal world is obliged to bow.

Emerson was proclaiming in these speeches and essays the doctrine which, according to William James, has marked all the periods of revival, the early Christian age and Luther's age, Rousseau's, Kant's and Goethe's, namely, that the innermost nature of things is congenial to the powers that men possess. That everything that ever was or will be, as he said in his essay, *Self-Reliance,* is here in the enveloping now, that he who obeys himself is a part of fate,—this challenged the natural faculties of his hearers. It stirred them to take life strivingly in full belief that what man had done man could do, that the world was all opportunities, strings of tension waiting to be struck, especially perhaps by thinkers and writers, to whom Emerson spoke most directly. Why were young Americans so imitative, so timid, tame, compliant? Why did they so easily lose their aims? Why did they look backward and renounce their hopes and yield to the conventions that turned them to stone? Why did they care so much for foreign opinions?

---

* See C. G. Jung's description of the "artist" as a type: "We see that he has drawn upon the healing and redeeming forces of the collective psyche that underlies consciousness with its isolation and its painful errors; that he has penetrated to that matrix of life in which all men are embedded, which imparts a common rhythm to all human existence, and allows the individual to communicate his feeling and his striving to mankind as a whole."—C. G. Jung, *Modern Man in Search of a Soul.*

Who bides at home, nor looks abroad,
Carries the eagles, and masters the sword.

Could they not see that the near was as great as the far,
that every drop of water was a little ocean, that the
clay with which the Persians and the Greeks moulded
their noble symbols was common lime and silex, the clay
that one held now in one's foolish hands and threw away
to go and seek in vain in sepulchres and mummy-pits in
Europe? It was the deep today that all men scorned, the
poverty that men hated, the heaving of the lungs and the
heat of the blood. All art was yet to be created, all literature yet to be written. All nature was new and undescribed.
America had listened too long to the muses of Europe. It
had met the expectations of mankind with little but the
exertions of mechanical skill. Why should not Americans
enjoy an original relation to the universe? A poetry of insight and not of tradition? A religion by revelation to
themselves? Did the discontented souls who flocked to
Europe expect to find anything essential there which they
had not found at home? Wherever they went, they could
only discover as much beauty or worth as they carried
with them. America's day of dependence, its long apprenticeship to other lands was drawing to a close. The millions who were rushing into life could not always be fed
on the sere remains of foreign harvests. Events were aris-
ing that had to be sung and that would sing themselves.
Who could doubt that poetry would revive and lead in the
continental America of the future?

The effect of these essays and lectures on the younger
people was like that of the sound of a trumpet. It was a
high and solemn music that dissolved the knots in their
minds, roused their wills, enlarged their affections, filled
them with a new illumination. It seemed to justify their
glittering dreams, even as it brought to their support the
authority of their own unconscious natures. They felt
themselves no longer "pinched in a corner," as Emerson

described their former state, but potential benefactors and redeemers, advancing on chaos and the dark. For Emerson pictured America in a way that made them feel how much the scholar counted. This careless, swaggering, shallow nation of theirs, this great avaricious America, boasting of its crops and the size of its cities, indifferent to the kind of men it bred, heedless of its liberty and other people's, gambling away the charters of the human race for a petty, selfish gain, this country needed them to calm and guide it, to see the right done, to check self-interest, to give it repose and depth. The feats it bragged about were of no great moment, telegraphs and steam, gas and ether. Its immense mechanical apparatus turned out little more than Nuremberg toys. But who doubted what the mind could do, seeing the shock given to torpid races by Mahomet, by Buddha, or by Newton or Franklin? All that was requisite, at any time, was a few superior men to give a new and noble turn to things; and Emerson summoned his hearers to the task. The path was a difficult one that lay before them. In stressing this, he won them all the more. They must be ready for bad weather, poverty, weariness, insult and repute of failure. The ease, the pleasure of treading the old paths they must surrender in making and walking their own, with the self-accusation and the faintness of heart, the uncertainty and loss of time and effort that always entangle the feet of the self-directed. Their reward would lie in exercising the highest functions of human nature, raising themselves from private considerations and breathing and living on public and illustrious thoughts. They would be the world's eye and heart, resisting the vulgar prosperity that retrograded to barbarism.

Such was the word of the Concord seer who had thought of calling his essays "Forest Essays;" for he had scarcely ever had a day-dream on which the breath of the pines had not blown.

CHAPTER XI

HAWTHORNE IN SALEM

WHILE BOSTON and little Concord were moving forward, Salem, like most of the other seaports, stricken by the War of 1812, had lapsed into quietude and decay. Beside its dilapidated wharves, where grew the fat weeds, the windlass chanty and the caulker's maul no longer broke the silence. The water-side streets were no longer thronged with sailors, "all right" for shore, with their blue jackets and checked shirts, their well-varnished hats and flowing ribbons, with bundles under their arms from the cannibal isles, or from India or China. One seldom heard the lively "Cheerily, men!" while all hands joined in the chorus. The grass choked the chinks of the cobblestones over which the drays had clattered. An occasional bark or brig discharged its hides. One saw some Nova Scotia schooner, drawn up at Derby's Wharf, unloading a cargo of firewood. A few idle seafaring men leaned against the posts, or sat on the planks, in the lee of some shabby warehouse, or lolled in the long-boats on the strand. But the great days of the port were a tale that was told, over and over, by the ancient skippers, who dozed away their mornings at the custom-house, with their chairs tilted against the wall.

Salem had an immemorial air, the air that gathers about a town which, having known a splendid hour, shrinks and settles back while its grandeurs fade. But Salem was old in spirit, aside from its faded grandeurs. The past that hovered there had much in common with that of the ancient ports of northern Europe, where the Gothic fancies

of the Middle Ages have not been dispelled by modern
trade. Salem was still Gothic, in a measure. In its moss-
grown, many-gabled houses, panelled with worm-eaten
wood and hung with half-obliterated portraits, dwelt at
least the remnants of a race that retained the mental traits
of a far-away past. In its isolation from the currents of
world-thought and feeling, it seemed to be only a step
removed from the age of the Dance of Death. In the mansions of Chestnut Street and Federal Street, one found
the traces of a livelier culture, the books that were read
in Boston, together with the Oriental spoils brought home
by the Salem navigators. But over the quiet lanes and leafy
side-streets, where the graveyards lay, brooded the hush
of many generations. Queer old maids with turbaned
heads peered from behind the curtains, quaint old simple-
minded men hobbled along under the sweeping elms,
"pixilated" creatures, many of them, as they said at
Marblehead,—bewildered by the fairies,—half dead and
buried in their houses, or buried in the morbid family pride
that flourishes where life runs low.

There was vigour enough in Salem, there were plenty
of stout merchants and politicians. One saw swarms of
boys and little girls, in blue, yellow, green and crimson
dresses, bursting from church and school-house, like gar-
den-beds of zinnias or water-colours of Maurice Prendergast. It was only in comparison with Lynn and Lowell,
those near-by towns whose enterprising burghers, faced
with the decline of shipping, had built their factories for
internal trade, that Salem seemed somehow grey and sad.
The Prescotts, Story, Pickering, Choate and Bowditch,
the great circle of earlier days, had long since departed.
At a stone's-throw from the Essex Institute, one almost
heard the silence. One caught the tinkling of the bell at
the door of some little cent-shop, even the quiver of the
humming-birds darting about the syringa bushes. The rattling of the butcher's cart was the only event of the day for

many a household, unless perhaps one of the family hens cackled and laid an egg. Spiders abounded in these houses, eluding the vigilant spinster's eye. Indeed, there were so many cobwebs that it might have occurred to a doctor,— some old Salem doctor, as odd as the rest,—to gather the webs together and distil an elixir of life from the dusty compound. In the burying-ground in Charter Street, where the Gothic emblems flourished,—death's-heads, cross-bones, scythes and hour-glasses, such as one found in Dürer's woodcuts,—the office of grave-digger passed from father to son. Just so passed the household legends, behind the bolted doors, grimmer with each generation. Beside the kitchen fires, old serving-women crouched as they turned the spit and darned the stockings, always ready to tell the children stories. Some of them seemed to remember the days of the witches. Their stories were as dusty as the cobwebs.

For Salem, like the whole New England sea-coast, bristled with old wives' tales and old men's legends. No need to invent stories there: one heard them in the taverns, from the sailors, from charcoal-burners who looked like wizards, from the good-for-nothings on the water-front. One heard of locked closets in haunted houses where skeletons had been found. One heard of walls that resounded with knocks where there had once been door-ways, now bricked up. One heard of poisonous houses and blood-stained houses, old maids who lived in total dark-ness, misers who wallowed naked in heaps of pine-tree shillings. One even heard of Endicott's dreary times, when the stocks and the pillory were never empty. One heard of the magistrates who awoke each morning to the prospect of cropping an ear or slitting a nostril, stripping and whipping a woman at the tail of a cart, or giving her a stout hemp necklace or a brooch in the form of a scarlet letter. One heard of the grey champion who emerged from nowhere to rebuke the tyrannies of the British king, of children who had sprung from the loins of demons, of the wastrels of Merry Mount and the grizzled saints who had stamped out their light and idle mirth, clipping their curls and love-locks. Would they not have stamped out the sunshine and clipped all the flowers in the forest in order to clear a path for their psalms and sermons? In these quiet towns, where nothing happens—except an occasional murder—to agitate the surface of existence, history is ever-present, lying in visible depths under the unstirred waters; and who could have known in Salem what to believe or not? However it might have been on Chestnut Street, the fringes of Salem society were superstitious. If the ring that Queen Elizabeth gave to Essex had appeared in a collection-box on Sunday, it would not have seemed surprising to some of the people. There were plenty of old souls in the lanes and side-streets who never knew where to draw the line. They half believed the tales they told the children. Were there not hollows in the hills close by where the Devil and his subjects held communion? Were there not ill-famed men in the western mountains who were condemned to wander till the crack of doom? All these tales had their truth, and so did the Indian legends, which the farmers repeated. There was an element of fact behind them. Was there a carbuncle in the Crystal Hills that gleamed like the westering sun, as the Indians said? Or was it the sun itself? There were men still living down in Maine who had never settled the question. Carbuncle or not, they had certainly seen it. At least, they had caught its radiance, far up the valley of the Saco.

Salem was a centre for these legends. The mediæval mind had lingered there, in the absence of recent enterprise; and, while the town as a whole was sufficiently modern, there were odd corners and shadowy households where symbols and realities seemed much the same. The young men and women knew the difference, but sometimes it amused them to ignore it. They did not believe in ghosts, but mesmerism had become the fashion: they let their fancies play on the border-line. They sat up at night and told tales of ghosts, largely in default of mundane gossip. Occasionally, they even thought they saw one. The Hawthornes, who lived in Herbert Street, under the shadow of a family curse, were often troubled by an apparition that seemed to haunt their yard. The only son of the household, Nathaniel Hawthorne, who lived like a ghost himself, haunting a little chamber under the eaves, appearing only at nightfall, could not count the times he had raised his head, or turned towards the window, with a perception that somebody was passing through the gate. He could only perceive the presence with a sidelong glance, by a certain indirection; if he looked straight at the dim thing, behold, it was not there. As no one ever passed through the Hawthornes' gate, it may have been Elizabeth, his sister, who also appeared only when dusk had fallen. In fact, one could live for two years under the same roof with this spectral sister and see her only once. That was the way with the Hawthornes. The father, a Salem skipper, had died of yellow fever, years ago, in far-off Surinam; and no mortal eye had penetrated, or was to penetrate for forty years, the Castle Dismal on the second floor where the mother of the family had taken refuge on the day she heard the news. Her meals were brought up and left outside the door, as they were at Elizabeth's door, and Louisa's door,—at least, as often as not,—and, one flight further up, at Nathaniel's door. When twilight came, one heard the sound of footsteps echoing on the stairs, and a door that must have been opened was certainly shut. Elizabeth went out for a little walk. Then Nathaniel went for a walk, alone, in another direction.

All day long, every day, or almost every day, for twelve years, he had sat in his flag-bottomed chair in his little room, beside the pine table, with a sheet of foolscap spread out before him. He was writing stories that rose in his mind as mushrooms grow in a meadow, where the roots of some old tree are buried under the earth. He had no love of secrecy or darkness, uncanny as he seemed to the handful of neighbours who knew that he existed; he was merely following the household pattern. His family, prominent once, had been almost forgotten, even in Herbert Street. No one came to see him. He had few friends, aside from the circle of his Bowdoin class-mates, with whom he had almost ceased to correspond. As a boy, he had often said he was going to sea and would never come back again; and he sometimes remarked to an acquaintance that he thought of disappearing, changing his name, escaping from the orbit of the postman, as if he had not sufficiently disappeared merely by staying at home. He had lapsed into this solitary life, half through a kind of inertia, and half,—he had always known he was going to write,— as if to protect a sensibility that was not yet ready to yield its fruits. His nickname had been Oberon at college, a reference to his shy, elusive ways. He had a massive head; his eyes were black and brilliant; he walked with the rolling gait of a sailor; he had a somewhat truculent voice and presence. Standing, he could leap shoulder-high. He liked to look at himself in the upright mirror and make up stories about the image he found reflected there. This image was dark and picturesque, tall and rather imposing. There was something vaguely foreign in its aspect.

He felt like a man under a spell, who had somehow put himself into a dungeon and could not find the key to let himself out. He had seated himself by the wayside of life, and a dense growth of shrubbery had sprung up about him, and the bushes had turned into saplings and the saplings into trees. Through the entangling depths he could find no exit. His style, his personality, his habits had been formed as far back as he could remember. At six he had read the *Pilgrim's Progress*. The first book he had

bought was the *Faerie Queene*. To see the world in terms
of allegory, or in the light of symbols, was second nature
with him. At twelve, in a note-book his grandfather had
given him, urging him to write out his thoughts,—a few
every day,—he had described a child named Betty Tarbox
as "flitting among the rosebushes, in and out of the arbour, like a tiny witch,"—phrases that might have occurred in the tales he was writing now. At sixteen, he had
written a poem, precisely in the vein of some of these tales,
about a young man dying for love of a ghost. He had certainly not acquired from Godwin's novels, however they
intensified the taste, the feeling for romantic mystery that
had sprung, for him, out of the Salem air. The novels of
Scott had only excited further what seemed to be an in-
born predilection for the history and the scenery of New
England. All he knew was that these habits of mind, already formed in Salem, had been fostered in Maine,
where he had spent a year, during his boyhood, on a
lonely farm in a border hamlet. He had heard all sorts
of stories from the farmers, tales of the supernatural,
tales of ghosts, legends of the old colonial wars. He had
heard the story of Father Moody of York, who had worn
a black veil over his face. In summer, he had seen the
Indians, on the Penobscot River, in their birch canoes,
building their wigwams by the mill-dams. Round about
stood the pine forests, bordering the northern lakes. He
had skated all winter in the moonlight, alone and silent.
He loved the black shadows cast by the frozen hills.

He might well have been thought uncanny. He was certainly "deep," as the country people said, deep as a night-
scene by Albert Ryder. His mind was bathed in a kind of
chiaroscuro that seemed to be a natural trait; and yet it
was a trait that he cultivated, half by instinct, half by delib-
eration. He had a painter's delight in tone. He liked to
throw a ghostly glimmer over scenes that he chose because they were ghostly. It was a taste like Claude Lor-

rain's for varnish. He liked to study chimneys in the rain, choked with their own smoke, or a mountain with its base enveloped in fog while the summit floated aloft. He liked to see a yellow field of rye veiled in a morning mist. He liked to think of a woman in a silvery mantle, covering her face and figure. A man's face, with a patched eye, turning its profile towards him; an arm and hand extended from behind a screen; a smile that seemed to be only a part of a smile, seen through a covering hand; a sunbeam passing through a cobweb, or lying in the corner of a dusty floor. Dissolving and vanishing objects. Trees reflected in a river, reversed and strangely arrayed and as if transfigured. The effects wrought by moonlight on a wall. Moonlight in a familiar sitting-room, investing every object with an odd remoteness,—one's walking-stick or a child's shoe or doll,—so that, instead of seeing these objects, one seemed to remember them through a lapse of years. Hawthorne could never have said why it was that, after spending an evening in some pleasant room, lighted by a fire of coals, he liked to return and open the door again, and close it and re-open it, peeping back into the ruddy dimness that seemed so like a dream, as if he were enacting a conscious dream. For the rest, he was well aware why he had withdrawn to this little chamber, where there was nothing to measure time but the progress of the shadow across the floor. Somewhere, as it were beneath his feet, a hidden treasure lay, like Goldthwaite's chest, brimming over with jewels and charms, goblets and golden salvers. It was the treasure of his own genius, and it was to find this precious treasure that he had sat at his desk through summer and winter. The snow-flakes pelted against the window-panes, the casement rattled in the December gusts, clouds of dust blew through the open window. Seasons and years rolled by. He had his doubts. Was he tearing down the house of his mind in order to find the treasure? In the end, when the house was de-

stroyed, for all he could say, there might be nothing in
the chest but rubbish.

Sometimes, in summer, on a Sunday morning, he stood
by the hour behind the curtain, watching the church across
the way. The sunrise stole down the steeple, touching the
weather-cock and gilding the dial, till the other steeples
awoke and began to ring. His fancy played about this conversation carried on by all the bells of Salem. At twilight,
he would still be standing there, watching the people on
the steps after the second sermon. Then, as dusk set
in, with a feeling of unreality, as if his heart and mind had
turned to vapour, he ventured into the street. Sometimes,
he was out all day, for the sake of observation. He would
spend an hour at the museum, looking at the black old
portraits that brought back the days of Cotton Mather.
These portraits explained the books that he was reading,
histories of Maine and Massachusetts, the *History of
Haverhill,* Felt's *Annals of Salem.* Or he walked over to
Marblehead and Swampscott, where the old salts gathered
in the store, in their red baize shirts and oilcloth trousers,
enthroned on mackerel barrels. He felt a natural bond
with all these Yankees, fishermen, cattle-drovers, sailors,
pilots. Some of them could steer with bandaged eyes into
any port from Boston to Mount Desert, guided by the
sound of the surf on every beach, island or line of rocks.
He liked to sit with them in the bar-rooms, alive with curiosity, over a steaming hot whiskey-punch. He studied the
coloured prints on the tavern walls. He noted the gate-
ways in the crooked streets, the whales' jaw-bones set like
Gothic arches, the bulging windows in the little shop-
fronts, filled with needles, fishhooks, pins and thimbles,
gingerbread horses, picture-books and sweetmeats. He
stood at the toll-house on the Beverly bridge, watching the
procession of carts and sulkies that rolled over the timber
ribbon under which the sea ebbed and flowed; or he
strolled on to Browne's Hill and traced out the grass

grown hollows, the cellars of Browne's Folly. Occasionally, he spent a day in Boston, haunting the public-houses
in Washington Street. He penetrated behind the sober
shop-front that masked the old Province House. Oftener,
setting out at dawn, he rambled over Endicott's Orchard
Farm, over the witchcraft ground and Gallows Hill, or
perhaps Phillips's Beach, exploring the coast from Marblehead to Gloucester. He would bathe in a cove, overhung
with maples and walnuts, pick up shells on the water's
edge, skip pebbles on the water and trail the seaweed after
him, draw names and faces in the sand. He would sit on
the top of a cliff and watch his shadow, gesturing on the
sand far below.

Occupations worthy of a poet who knew the value of
reverie. These idle, whimsical movements absorbed his
body while his mind pursued its secret operations. One
had to be bored in order to think. Passivity was Hawthorne's element, when it was not curiosity. Usually, in
the summer, dressed in his blue stuff frock, he undertook
a longer expedition, to Maine or the Berkshires, perhaps,
or to Martha's Vineyard, or along the Erie canal, as far
as Detroit, where the old Connecticut poet, John Trumbull, was spending his last years. Nothing escaped him
then; he had resumed his habit of keeping a note-book.
He would stop for commencement at some country college, at Williams, so like his own Bowdoin, and mingle
with the sheepish-looking students, half scholar-like, half
bumpkin, fidgeting in their black broadcloth coats. He
would spend a day at a cattle-fair, among the ruddy,
round-paunched country squires who, with their wonderful breadth of fundament, waddled about, whip in hand,
discoursing on the points of the sheep and oxen. He fell
in with big-bellied blacksmiths, essence-pedlars chattering about their trade, old men sitting at railway stations,
selling nuts and gingerbread, oblivious of the rush and
roar about them, wood-choppers with their jugs and axes

who had lived so long in the forest that their legs seemed
to be covered with moss, like tree-trunks, pedlars of
tobacco, walking beside their carts,—green carts with
gaily painted panels,—conjurors, tombstone-carvers,
organ-grinders, travelling surgeon-dentists, the queer con-
fraternity of the road. He would exchange a word with
a tavern-keeper, reading his Hebrew Bible, with the aid
of a lexicon and an English version. If it was a rainy day,
the toddy-stick was in active use and the faces gleamed
about the bar-room fire. He would stop at a farm for a
glass of milk or linger in the market-place at Pittsfield,
among the buckboards and the farmers' wagons, while
the stage-coach discharged its passengers. Opening his
note-book in the evening, he jotted down his observations.
Why these trivial details? He had seen a tame crow on
the peak of a barn. A half-length figure had appeared at
a window, with a light shining on the shrouded face. A
little boy had passed him on the road, lugging a basket of
custard-cups. An intrusive reader, looking over his shoulder, might have wondered why it was worth his while to
record such trifling items. To Hawthorne they were anything but trifling. Every one of these notes possessed for
him a golden aureole of associations. Traits of New England life, aspects of New England scenery: a stone wall
covered with vines and shrubs and elm-trees that had
thrust their roots beneath it, a valley like a vast bowl,
filled with yellow sunlight as with wine, the effect of the
morning sun on dewy grass, sunlight on a sloping, swelling
landscape beyond a river in the middle distance, an afternoon light on a clump of trees, evening light falling on a
lonely figure, perhaps a country doctor on his horse, with
his black leather saddle-bags behind him. Dark trees,
decaying stumps, a cave in the side of a hill, with the sunlight playing over it. How like the human heart, this cave,
with the glancing sun and the flowers about its entrance!
One stepped within and found oneself surrounded

with a terrible gloom and monsters of divers kinds.

Once, before turning homeward, he pressed on to Franconia Notch. This was the artery over the mountains through which the groaning wagons from the seaports carried the goods of Europe and the Indies to northern New Hampshire and Vermont. There stood the Great Stone Face. One dined on bear's meat in these northern woods, echoing with the notes of horn and bugle. Under some avalanche an ambitious guest, a young story-teller, for example, might have been crushed at Franconia Notch. Who would ever have heard of him then, his history, his plans, his way of life? Or suppose this young writer had frozen to death on the summit of Mount Washington? The mountain would have been a pedestal, worthy of a story-teller's statue. Hawthorne roamed up and down the Connecticut Valley. He fell in with a group of vagabonds, on their way to the camp-meeting at Stamford, a book-pedlar with the usual stock,—a handful of gilded picture-books and ballads, a Life of Franklin, Byron's Minor Poems, Webster's Spelling-book, the New England Primer,—a degenerate Indian with his bow and arrows, willing to turn a penny by shooting at it, an Italian conjuror with a merry damsel attired in all the colours of the rainbow. A travelling puppet-show had joined the troupe. The grave old showman, in his snuff-coloured coat, turned the crank of the organ, and all the little people on the miniature stage broke into lively movement. The blacksmith's hammer fell on the anvil, the tailor plied his needle, the dancers whirled about on their feathery tiptoes, the soldiers wheeled in platoons, the old toper lifted his bottle, the merry-andrew shook his head and capered. Prospero entertaining his island crew! It was a masque of shadows that seemed as real as any other world that Hawthorne lived in. Would it not have been a good idea for a young story-teller to join this group and become an itinerant novelist, like the Oriental story-

tellers, reciting his extemporaneous fictions at camp-
meetings and cattle-fairs, wherever two or three were
gathered together?

Most of Hawthorne's journeys, to be sure, were journeys *autour de sa chambre*. He was never away from
Salem long. His note-books, however, filled along the
road with incidents and casual observations, were precious memorabilia. They gave his ideas a local habitation. One saw this in the stories he was writing, sketches
of actual life, historical tales and allegories. He thought
of these as "twice-told" tales because, in several cases, he
had heard them first before he had worked them out
himself. How did he feel about his work? It seemed to
him easier to destroy it than to court an indifferent public. He had thrown into the fire the *Seven Tales of My
Native Land,* for which he had failed to find a publisher,
and he had burned every available copy of his little published novel, *Fanshawe*. There was a devil in his manuscripts! He saw it laughing at him as the sparks flew upward. As for his recent stories,—the annual magazines
had begun to accept them, the *Souvenir* and Peter Parley's *Token*,—they seemed to him to have an effect of
tameness. They had, he felt, the pale tint of flowers that
have blossomed in too retired a shade. If they were read
at all, they should be read in the twilight in which they
were written. They had been concocted from thin air;
but it was this that gave the tales their magic. Some of
them were really insubstantial, dim as ghosts basking in
the starlight; in others, the apparently insubstantial was
a new and original substance. In Tieck's and Hoffmann's
Germany, where the Gothic mind had reawakened, in
harmony with this mood of spectral Salem, even in Poe's
New York, one found similar tales of the listening dead,
of graves and flitting shadows and lovers knocking at
each other's tombs. Processions of mourners passed with
measured tread, trailing their garments on the ground.

One saw figures melting in mist. Black veils, boys with bandaged eyes, bridegrooms dressed in shrouds. Pools paved with marble and mosaic. Images shimmering in water. One heard the cries of children lost in the woods. Young men slept in the road-side shade, oblivious of the fates that might have been theirs if they had been awake; for fortune, crime and love hovered about them.

They were tales like evening moths or butterflies, light as clouds or flowers of early May, blooming in a wood-land solitude. Out of them rose, when they were gathered together, an opalescent world that was strangely old, yet fresh and unfamiliar; it was like Prospero's island, half terrestrial, half an ethereal fabric. It was a new creation, this world of Hawthorne, with a past in Merry Mount and the Province House, in Howe's Masquerade and Esther Dudley, a present in pedlars and Shakers, in vagabonds and white old maids, in sunny Connecticut valleys and forest hollows, in snowstorms and ambiguous lime-burners, a future in little puckish boys and girls at play in the flickering sunshine. All very simple, it appeared, simple as the brightly coloured leaves that drift over a sedgy stream, only that too often, before one's eyes, the stream sang its way out of the meadow and carried its bright burden into the forest, where all grew dark and baleful.

Such was Hawthorne's world, as it rose in the minds of his readers. No other American writer had revealed such a gift for finding his proper subjects; no other had so consciously pursued his ends. Hawthorne had jotted down four rules of life: to break off customs, to meditate on youth, to shake off spirits ill-disposed, to do nothing against one's genius. He had shaped a poetic personality as valid and distinct as Emerson's; but the "spirits ill-disposed" were not easily conquered. He was drifting towards a cataract, he felt. "I'm a doomed man," he wrote to a friend, "and over I must go." He was threatened with melancholia, and he knew it. Out of this fear had sprung, or were to spring, the themes of many of his other stories, *Wakefield, The Man of Adamant, Ethan Brand,* tales of the unpardonable sin that consists in losing one's hold of the human chain. The Man of Adamant turns to stone, Ethan Brand forfeits, in his lonely bleakness, the key that unlocks human nature, Wakefield, who leaves his family and lives for twenty years in a neighbouring street, makes himself an outcast from the world without being admitted among the dead. Hawthorne repeated this note in twenty stories, tales of minds and hearts like chilly caverns, hung with glittering icicles of fancy. Tales of hyper-sensitive recluses who find themselves in white-washed cells. Tales of diabolical intellects,—*Rappaccini's Daughter* and *The Birthmark,*—which, in the name of some insane abstraction, destroy the life that they have ceased to feel. Tales like that of Lady Eleanore who, wrapped in pride as in a mantle, courts the vengeance of nature. Tales of diseased self-contemplation, of egoists who swallow serpents and sleepers who have missed their destiny. What traits, or, rather, what predicament, what fears did these tales reveal in the mind that conceived them? Hawthorne had lived too long in this border-region, these polar solitudes where the spirit shivered, so that the substance of the world about him hung before his eyes like a thing of vapour. He felt as if he had not lived at all, as if he were an ineffectual shadow, as if, having stepped aside from the highway of human affairs, he had lost his place forever. One night he had a dream that told him this. He seemed to be walking in a crowded street. Three beautiful girls approached him and, seeing him, screamed and fled. An old friend gave him a look of horror. He was promenading in his shroud.

Luckily, Hawthorne had another self, a sensible double-ganger. This other Hawthorne, this prosaic Hawthorne, the son of a Salem skipper, was interested in his own self-preservation; and, while he would never have taken too much trouble to keep himself afloat, he was glad to listen to his friends in matters of worldly wisdom. Eleven years were enough in a haunted chamber, filled with thoughts of suicide and madness. In 1836, this other Hawthorne entered the publishing house of "Peter Parley," wrote his *Universal History* for him and edited his *American Magazine*. Then, having broken the spell and gone to Boston, this matter-of-fact, substantial, physical Hawthorne accepted a position at the custom-house.

To the end of Hawthorne's life, these separate personalities dominated his destiny in turn. When one of them came to the front, as fishes, in pursuit of oxygen, rise to the surface of the water, the other vanished or concealed himself behind the nearest curtain. The story-teller scarcely knew the practical man of business who worked on the steaming docks, amid the coal-dust. Was this resolute, forcible being really himself, or was it someone who assumed his aspect and performed these duties in his name? Which was the true Hawthorne, which the phantom? The story-teller lived in a trance as long as the automaton carried on. His writing was accomplished in the happy seasons when the automaton was packed away, in the box where he belonged, when custom-houses, ships and offices lay like dreams behind him.

Both these personalities, meanwhile, had focussed themselves on a single object. Hawthorne had fallen in love. One saw him at the Boston Athenæum, where the ghost of Dr. Harris shadowed him, or moving silently through the Salem streets, enveloped in the cloak with its high-cut collar that almost concealed his features. Vain disguise! Life had reconnoitred him and love had tracked him out. He had become involved with the Peabody family, whose house in Salem overlooked the graveyard where, among so many bones, the dust of ancestral

Peabodys and Hawthornes mingled under the trees. Dr. Peabody's daughters believed they were descended from Boadicea. Whether it was true or not, the sisters possessed a store of nervous energy; and this, like youthful and impassioned nuns, they were devoting to the "higher life." Elizabeth, the oldest, the genius of the American kindergarten, was already known in Boston, where she was teaching, as the inexhaustible friend of all good causes. She was Dr. Channing's literary assistant, she was the confidante of Washington Allston, she was Bronson Alcott's aide at the Temple School. Of all these adventures of the mind she was to leave descriptions in her books.* The second sister Mary was engaged to Horace Mann. Sophia, the youngest, was Hawthorne's inamorata. A neurasthenic invalid, waiting on her couch for the magician who would command her to arise and walk, Sophia was witty and charming, as well as a clever linguist. When her sister married Horace Mann, she said that no doubt the first Peabody grandchild would open its mouth at once and utter a school-report. Her own avocations were artistic. Sometimes, while plying her needle of an afternoon, she would read a little Fénelon in French, a little Isaiah in Hebrew, a dozen pages of St. Luke in Greek and two or three scenes of Shakespeare. When she was not otherwise occupied, she spent her days modelling and painting. She had a pretty studio at the top of the house, and there she had made a medallion of one of Emerson's brothers,—for the Emersons knew the Peabodys and sometimes came to visit them,—and a bust of Laura Bridgman. Her work had been warmly praised by Allston and Channing. Meanwhile, she had passed three years in Cuba, in the hope of reëstablishing her health.

It was Elizabeth Peabody, on one of her visits from

---

* *Reminiscences of William Ellery Channing, Last Evening with Allston, Record of Mr. Alcott's School.*

Boston, who had disinterred Hawthorne from his living grave. With her unfailing scent for remarkable minds, she had followed his work in the magazines. A new and unique style united these often anonymous tales and sketches. Miss Peabody, who had caught this thread, wondered who the author was; and, behold, the clue led straight to a door in Salem. She drew Hawthorne out, induced him to see Sophia, inveigled him into the Transcendental circle that met on Saturday evenings at Miss Susan Burley's. Miss Burley was an amateur of antique gems and the cleverest hostess in Salem. She had even drawn Jones Very, that other Salem solitary, out of his shell. Hawthorne, caught at last in a drawing-room, stood motionless, not knowing what to do, his face pale and stricken. He picked up a knick-knack that lay on the table, to soothe his agitation. His hand trembled so that he almost dropped it.

No matter, he was "out," and out to stay, in a sort of low relief, like Sophia's medallions,—for no one was ever to see around him; and the Peabodys were determined to keep him out. The ever-active Elizabeth, who had introduced Jones Very to Emerson, called upon her friend George Bancroft, the historian-collector of the port of Boston, and obtained for him the post at the customhouse. Meanwhile, Sophia drew pictures for one of his stories, in the style of Flaxman's outlines. These delicate line-drawings of the English sculptor, so cool, so pure, so rhythmical, so graceful, were to leave long traces in American art. The Peabodys and their friends spent many an evening poring over the drawings for Dante and Homer, which they had borrowed from Professor Felton. Sophia had a passion for them, and Hawthorne's stories seemed to lend themselves to the treatment that she knew so well. It was a happy augury that Flaxman's genius, with which Hawthorne had so much in common, presided over the fate of this pair of lovers.

CHAPTER XII

ALCOTT, MARGARET FULLER, BROOK FARM

JUST AT this moment, the Peabodys moved to Bos‧
ton. They rented a house at 19 West Street, which
soon became a rendezvous for the younger intellectuals,
those who were conscious of the "new day." In one of
the rooms on the ground-floor, Dr. Peabody opened a
shop for the sale of homeopathic remedies. In the front
room overlooking the street, Elizabeth and her mother
sold foreign books. Mrs. Peabody was herself at work
translating Goethe's *Hermann und Dorothea*. "God
takes care of us" was her constant motto. She saw no
reason not to be high-minded "even in selling a book."

Along with *Blackwood's* and the *Edinburgh,* which
everyone read religiously at the Athenæum, they sold the
German and French reviews and the writings of the continental authors whose thoughts were in the air. Miss
Peabody, with her multifarious interests, chiefly in the
"gardening" of children, who, she felt, should be "artists
from the beginning," was publishing juvenile books on
her own account, among them the three little volumes of
Grandfather's Chair, which Hawthorne contrived to write
in the intervals of measuring coal at the custom-house.
There Margaret Fuller was giving her Conversations;
and there, on occasion, Jones Very read his sonnets
aloud to a chosen few. Eager school-girls flocked into the
shop and bought more pencils than they could use for a
chance to see Miss Peabody or Miss Fuller. And there,
on almost any afternoon, one saw some of the new illu-

minati, Emerson, Alcott, Frederick Hedge, who had studied in Germany with Bancroft and had settled as a minister at Bangor, John Sullivan Dwight or George Ripley. Hawthorne came often to see Sophia.

This shop, so called, though most of its frequenters were bent on "reforming out" the principle of commer‑ cial enterprise, this intellectual caravansary was the live‑ liest spot in Boston. As a matter of course, the literary Tories, George Ticknor's circle, for example, called it the Hospital for Incapables. It was, in fact, a nest or kindergarten where newly-born thoughts were received and fostered. Thence they emerged as books or social movements. Miss Peabody's second Bible was Gerando's essay, *On Moral Perfection and Self-Culture,* and no one was admitted to the circle who did not accept its teach‑ ings,—that life was a process of education, of which per‑ fection was the proper aim. Miss Peabody exemplified this faith. Her sister Mary had founded a kindergarten in the very year when the German Froebel opened the first school that bore this name; and she herself wrote text-books and lectured on the history of religions. In her paper, *The Dorian Measure,* she urged the impor‑ tance of dancing, not the sort that one learned from Signor Papanti but the mystical Grecian ballet, the folk‑ dance, the rhythmical allegory. This dancing would give the Bostonians a feeling for the customs of other nations. The Dorians had a message for enlightened Boston: severe without austerity, simple and dignified in their private relations, they yet dressed the festival of life, worshipping Apollo in the sunshine, with garlands of flowers and leaves. Perfection in all its forms was Miss Peabody's vision, and at present she busied herself in supplying wants that seemed to indicate a desire for it. The want might be Kraitsir's Lectures on Language, or Bern's Historical Chart, some of the artist's materials that she kept in stock, at Washington Allston's sugges‑

tion, a book on the new philosophy, or something more conclusive,—a plan for a desirable social system; for this was a magical shop, the kind one read about in the fairy-tales, where, in the guise of a book or a lecture-ticket, they sold Aladdin's lamps and rings of Gyges. James Freeman Clarke, another frequenter, a Unitarian min-ister in Louisville, who had come back to Boston for a summer visit, was astonished at the "state of fermenta-tion" he found among his friends. "New ideas," he wrote, "are flying high and low." The centre of the whirl was the shop in West Street.

Miss Peabody was Channing's Eckermann. As a child, she had heard the doctor preach, and she had never for-gotten her mother's words, "It takes genius to reach children," words she had pondered for years until she learned their meaning from Froebel's writings. She had applied for a post as Channing's secretary; and the doc-tor, in order to test her, read to her aloud from Plato, raising his devouring eyes to make quite sure that she understood it. All had gone well after this. She dined at Channing's table every evening; she copied his sermons for the press. He had been greatly struck by Emerson's lectures, which seemed to set the young men on fire; and almost every morning he appeared at the book-shop, sometimes bringing Washington Allston with him. He wished to keep in touch with the new ideas, although he had his doubts about socialism, the Fourieristic notions that flourished there; the trend of life, he thought, was towards individuality of expression, and individual prop-erty expressed this law,—it was the "lowest expression," but still an expression. The doctor was solicitous about the future, and the West Street shop represented the future. As for Miss Peabody's future, one could see it already. One pictured her, forty years hence, drowsing in her chair on the lecture-platform or plodding through the slush of a Boston winter, her bonnet askew, her white hair falling loose, bearing still, amid the snow and ice, the banner of education.* If, perchance, you lifted her out of a snowdrift, into which she had stumbled absentmindedly, she would exclaim, between her gasps, "I am so glad to see you! Can you tell me which is the best Chinese grammar?" Or she would give you the news about Sarah Winnemucka. "Now Sarah Winnemucka"— this was the maligned Indian princess who was collecting money to educate her tribe. Or she would ask if you had read your Stallo. She took down every lecture she heard, although she seldom wrote what people said: most of her reports were "impressions." † She was known to have lived in Europe for two years on $200, passed on with the utmost dignity from one enlightened household to another, invariably losing the railway ticket that found itself, by a miracle, in her hands. She had mislaid the ticket in somebody's *Reminiscences,* but what conductor or purser could disbelieve her?

This was a generation later, but already Miss Peabody was the salt of Boston. With Margaret Fuller as a fellow-worker, she had been assisting Bronson Alcott, another leader of the West Street circle, the Socrates of the Temple School. Alcott, for calling in question the gods of the city, for corrupting the minds of the young with the "new ideas," had had to drink his hemlock. A tall, mild, milky, passionless man, with a singular gift for understanding children, he had had five years for his ministrations. Then

> straight a barbarous noise environed him
> Of owls and cuckoos.

---

* "Miss Peabody is the most dissolute woman in Boston," William James remarked in his sprightly youth. Henry James denied that he had the "grandmother of Boston" in mind in drawing Miss Birdseye in *The Bostonians,* but the likeness was unmistakable.

† "I saw it," Miss Peabody said, when she walked into a tree and bruised her nose. "I saw it, but I did not realize it."

The red-faced sheriff knocked at the Temple door. In vain, Alcott's daughter, little Louisa, striding across the room, assailed the Vandal: "Go away, bad man, you are making my father unhappy!" Down from the walls came the pictures, the maps and the blackboard, Guido's "Flight into Egypt" and the portrait of Channing; the busts came down from their pedestals, Plato, Socrates, Milton; the comely desks, the charming cast of Silence, the dozen or more of Johnson's dictionaries, all these appropriate emblems, so carefully chosen to stir and elevate the dawning mind,—down they came and vanished. And Alcott, leading a child in either hand, followed them down, with mournful steps and slow.

He might have been crushed, if anything could crush him. But the school, that Academe for nascent Boston, was only one of Alcott's paradises. Sheriffs with flaming swords might drive him forth, but who can expel a man from the Garden of Eden that exists behind his own brow? Not for nothing had he schooled himself as "one of the last of the philosophers." One of the last? He meant to be one of the first. He had, indeed, a philosophic mission, to restore the fabled innocence of man and root it in the soil of Massachusetts. He had never doubted the doctrine of pre-existence, the lapse of the soul from its primordial state, with its native creative powers, never since the days when he had first read Plato and found that Plato's cloud-land was, for him, far more solid than the United States. Coleridge had shown him clearly that the elements of the human consciousness were not to be sought in impressions of external nature, but rather in the self-existent spirit, spontaneous and outside of time and space. "Before time was, I am;" and birth was but a sleep and a forgetting. Then wherefore not awaken and remember? Why not recover what the race had lost, fatuously exiled in the realms of sense? Such were the views upon which his school was founded;

such was the faith that he had cultivated, watching over the growth of his little daughters. They had a natural pleasure in beautiful things, a happy trust and affection, free and direct as they were. In them the avenues to the Over-soul were all wide open. How dim were the perceptions of most of their elders! How cold their sympathies were, spoiled and spotted by their mundane interests! How had they fallen from their high estate! They could not become as little children. And Alcott meant to see that the little children did not become like them.

Such was Alcott's theory of education. Every great man of Greece and Rome had had a philosopher as a teacher, and his own purpose in teaching had always been, not to inculcate knowledge,—at least by the method of the pump and bucket,—but to develop genius. Was not every well-born child a genius? By the Socratic method, as it seemed to Alcott, by posing the proper questions, one could elicit from a group of children all the thoughts of Plato. He tried to reach his pupils from within. No forcing, no cramming, no rod or ferule. He had made the schoolroom gracious and attractive and devised recreations and amusements, plays, physical exercises, even a system of self-government. He encouraged the keeping of journals. Children must know themselves to become themselves and escape from the tyranny of custom. With his own little Anna, aged four, he had held intellectual conversations that seemed to him not unworthy of Plato's disciples; and Louisa had been writing her daily journal before she was able to join her letters. He had begun himself when he was twelve, making his own ink out of maple and oak-bark, steeped in alum and indigo; but he had had to fight for his education. A poor farmer's son, like Horace Mann, he had learned to write in a copy-book, forming his letters after the master's phrase, "Avoid alluring company." He had spent his youth as a pedlar, travelling through Virginia with his

horse and wagon, with his tin trunk full of Yankee notions, pins, scissors, combs, thimbles, puzzles, with a self-
respect presumably unknown to the silken sons of pride
and dissipation,—always on the lookout for a school
where he could exercise his theories. He had learned his
best lessons along the road, from some of the Southern
planters, who had taken him into their houses and taught
him manners. He had fallen in with the Philadelphia
Quakers, whose "inner light" he soon identified with the
Brahma of the Oriental Scriptures. Among them, for a
while, at Germantown, where his daughter Louisa was
born, he had conducted a school, before he opened his
great campaign in Boston.

What matter if the Temple School had failed? He
had other careers ahead, this Indra of the seven incarna-
tions. He knew that future times would vindicate him.
There were plenty of closet-philosophers: Alcott was a
philosopher in action for whom the object of life was to
be oneself. Be what you were meant to be! If you were
a crooked stick, go through the world as an oddity, to
your own merriment, at least, if not to that of your contemporaries. Character was a fact, and that was much in
a world of pretence and concession. If Boston was not
ready for such a teacher, so much the worse for Boston.
Was he going to repine and hedge and distrust the powers that always upheld the virtuous and the wise? When
a confidence-man asked him for five dollars, and Alcott
gave him ten, the groundlings laughed at his simplicity;
but the confidence-man, stricken with remorse, sent the
money back. One could trust the law of compensation.

The school was a misadventure, though more for
the children than for Alcott. So was the fate of his book, the
enlightened *Conversations on the Gospels*, most of the
copies of which had been sold to be used for trunk-linings.
This book had largely caused the trouble. It was a record
of Alcott's dialogues with the little sons and daughters

of patrician Boston, in which, in connection with the sacred story, he had tried to replace with clear ideas the fabric of traditional association. The parents were alarmed, but the children, most of them eight or nine years old, were entranced with these religious dialectics. Little Josiah Quincy spoke like an infant prophet. Rapt attention had reigned in the beautiful class-room, as the master sat in his pulpit, his pupils gathered in an arc before him, in the soft light that streamed through the Gothic windows. There were special classes for Latin, for sums and spelling, and the children of three and four had desks in the corners. They drew on their slates and learned the art of silence. Sometimes the poet Dana appeared and gave a quiet reading from Coleridge or Wordsworth, for an audience of children pleased him best. If the day was cold, the master read aloud Thomson's *Winter* and analyzed the poem on the blackboard. A dialogue might ensue on winter sports, on the nature of coasting and skating, or the master divided the words he had just been reading into their various classes, as the names of objects, qualities and relations. Or perhaps he would read one of Northcote's *Fables,* or a chapter of the *Pilgrim's Progress,* or a passage from *The Castle of Indolence.* What did it represent? There were passages that excited the moral feelings, fear, pity, courage; others called into play the intellectual faculties, reason, perception, judgment. The master followed his readings with suitable questions. Language had to be picturesque and lively to clothe these thoughts in words! What was the purpose of going to school? To learn good behaviour? What was behaviour, what was the purpose of manners? What was the purpose of the imagination? What was the meaning of a definition? One had to use one's wits at the Temple School.

Boston, hitherto so cold and formal, had begun to receive the gospel of Conversation. This was the message

of the Temple School. It was the message also of Margaret Fuller, who, with Elizabeth Peabody, assisted
Alcott. Miss Peabody kept the log-book of the school,
reporting its operations word by word, while she was
reading Greek with Dr. Channing. Margaret Fuller also
assisted Channing: she spent one evening of every week
reading aloud to him in German. But the doctor was too
restricted to suit the impetuous Margaret. He was always
looking for the moral in works of creative genius. She
preferred the abandon of the poet. She liked to duck, dive
and fly for truth. Besides, as an impassioned feminist,
she wished to minister to the minds of women. What
woman ever had a chance, among the few men who enjoyed this fortune? What were the legitimate hopes of
women? Why should they all be constrained to follow
employments for which only some of them were fitted?
While men were called upon, from their earliest youth,
to reproduce everything they learned, women never reproduced their learning except for the sake of display.
It was partly the fault of society, and partly their own,
because they were so unconscious, victims of domestic
preoccupations. Better to have one's curtains and carpets
soiled than to soil one's mind with such paltry thoughts
and feelings! Better, the fragrant herb of wit, and a
little cream of affability, than all the pretty tea-cups in
the world! As for American men, they were tame enough,
with their everlasting business, their little games of local
politics, with only two or three tunes in their music-boxes.
One wound them up, and they tinkled about "the office,"
they tinkled again about the next election, and that was
the end of their music. They never added a new tune
after five-and-twenty. No spirit, no variety of depth and
tone! Why should American men and especially women
be satisfied with the common routines of living? Why
should they not be capable of such relations as those of
Landor's Pericles and Aspasia? They should look for

their hidden gifts. They should be satisfied with nothing less than Goethe's "extraordinary generous seeking." Genius, Margaret thought, would be as common as light if men and women trusted their higher selves. She had never questioned her own vocation, and she was just on the verge of thirty when, towards the end of 1839, she opened her Conversations in the West Street house. It was on a Saturday, at noon, her regular weekly hour. She appeared, with a regal air, with various books of reference on her arm and a huge bouquet of chrysanthemums. The lorgnette was much in evidence.

An electrical apparition, this "queen of Cambridge." She had seen men "bristle," as they frankly said,—the foolish little creatures, youths of untouched heart, shallow, as yet, in all things,—when she crossed the threshold of an evening party. She frightened them with her magnetic powers, the depth of her eye, the powerful onward motion that announced the presence of the mysterious fluid. So, at least, she felt. But most of these men had nothing to fear, the dry, cold, sordid money-getters. Margaret knew at a glance the minds that belonged to her, and she was "sagacious of her quarry." So she wrote in her journal. As the daughter of Timothy Fuller, Member of Congress, who had surrendered his income and profession in order to write a history of his country, she had lived in a great house in Cambridge, surrounded by the cleverest Harvard students, who had never seen a girl of her complexion. Her father had taught her Latin as soon as she could speak, and her infant prayers had begun, "O God, if thou art Jupiter!" Occasionally, she had prayed to Bacchus for a bunch of grapes. She thought of herself as a princess, who had been left by mistake on a Cambridge door-step. At boarding-school, at Groton, she had first revealed her insatiable will-to-power. Unable to rule by affection, she had ruled as the demon of discord, swooning at tactical moments, setting the girls by one another's ears, striking her head against an iron hearth, falling into fits of melancholy, until, by one method or another, she had reduced the school to servitude. As for the girls, they raved about her. She was the "bandit's bride" of the trashy novels they read behind their desks. No one had such hair as hers, dressed with a tropical flower, such wild, strange, lively ways, such flashes of the eye. There was always something odd in the way she wore a sash or a necklace. Her simplest frock had an air of fancy dress. The girls delighted in paying her homage. They placed wild flowers beside her plate; and they felt that she was born to be misunderstood by everyone but her lover. As for the unhappy teachers, not one of them, as Margaret said, had ever asked herself an intelligent question about the nature of her earthly mission. Margaret's own mission was to "grow." She felt that her impulses were disproportioned to the persons and occasions she encountered and rightly carried her beyond the reserves that marked the appointed lot of women. She looked with envy at Flaxman's picture of Hesiod sitting at the feet of the Muse. Where could she find an intellectual guide? At fifteen, she rose at five, walked for an hour and practised on the piano; then she read philosophy and French. From half past nine till noon, she studied Greek, practised again, lounged for half an hour, read for two hours in Italian, then went for a walk or a drive; in the evening, she played or sang and wrote in her journal. As between Madame de Staël and the useful Miss Edgeworth, patterns that one might follow, she had no difficulty in choosing. Over her head, as over Madame de Staël's, had risen the sun of Goethe. She, too, would have liked to provoke an emperor's wrath.

She had passed through dreams of romance, hours of yearning and passion. She threw herself into Goethe's life. Should he have given up his Lili? She lived through the rapturous days of the heroines of mythology and drama, Iphigenia, Antigone, the Scandinavian world-mother Frigga, George Sand's Consuelo and Corinne, invoking them in her diary: "Antigone, Iphigenia, you were worthy to live! . . . Iphigenia, I was not born in vain, if only for the tears I have shed with thee." She saw herself as the goddess Isis, dazzling the eyes of her votaries. She might have been the Countess Emily Plater, the Polish Joan of Arc. Among her chosen men were Alfieri, the Countess of Albany's lover, and George Sand's Count de Rudolstadt, aristocratic democrats who shared the culture of the fortunate classes but longed for the welfare of all. Carlyle's was the grand method of education!—idolatrous hero-worship of genius and power. She did not expect to be happy. How could a woman of genius conform to the world about her, or find her mysterious impulses understood? She remembered how as a child she had stood at a window from which she could see an eagle chained, on one of the neighbouring balconies. She had seen people poking it with sticks, and her heart had swollen with indignation. The eagle's eye was dull, and its plumage was soiled and shabby, yet with what a mien the monarch-bird endured these paltry insults. In its form and attitude, all the king was visible, even though dethroned and degraded. Such was the fate of genius in a world of pygmies. They censured her in Boston because she filled the girls, who flocked about her, with her own romantic nonsense. She made them wish to marry Alfieris, as if State Street lawyers were not good enough,—not to mention cotton-merchants and codfish-packers with an eye on the Legislature. They laughed at her superstitions, her faith in demonology, omens, foresight. They smiled when she said that "Margaret" meant "Pearl," the gem that is cradled in slime, in disease and decay, like all that is noblest in the human soul. Only the experienced diver knows the pearl.

Who could comprehend her aspirations, the demands she made upon life, her struggles and conflicts? She would lie all day on the shore at Nahant, with the waves washing about her, looking up at the turrets and jagged cliffs bathed in prismatic light. Prometheus, or Promethea, among the rocks, or perhaps Andromeda chained, waiting for her unknown Perseus. Beethoven, at least, would have understood her. She wrote him a midnight letter. With the Boston girls, her pupils,—for she was obliged to teach, to pay for the education of her brothers and sisters, the father's death having left them in distress,— she read her beloved Goethe, Schiller and Lessing, together with Petrarch and Tasso in Italian. With her chosen friends, meanwhile, James Freeman Clarke, with whom she had first studied German, Frederick Henry Hedge, Samuel Gray Ward, and Emerson, her last and greatest conquest, to whom Harriet Martineau had introduced her as the most brilliant talker she had known, she gathered the spoils of culture,—a little meagre still in frosty Boston, but amplified by her enthusiasm,—portfolios of drawings and engravings, designs from Raphael, architectural sketches, the Athenæum casts, the Brimmer collection. In each of her friends she seemed to divine the law of his own interior growth. She gave them to themselves, or so they felt, drew out their unsuspected faculties. Many of these friends, in later years, traced to some conversation with her the moment when they had seen their way before them, when they had formed some resolution from which their careers had sprung. It was true that she had an influence in hundreds of lives. Long after her death, the painter Hunt saw on a table in Florence a copy of Mrs. Jameson's *Italian Painters*. Margaret had written on the margin, beside a passage on Correggio, "And yet all might be such." Hunt said, "These words struck out a new strength in me. They made me set my face like a flint."

She aspired to write, dry as writing seemed beside the excitement of conversation. The six historical tragedies she had planned had all come to nothing, and she could not afford the time to finish the life of Goethe for which she had gathered a mass of notes and sketches. Meanwhile, she translated the *Conversations with Eckermann,* Bettina von Arnim's *Günderode* and hundreds of pages of Uhland, Novalis and Körner, with poems of her own as commentaries. But conversation was her medium. She liked to see the effects of her mental efforts, and the Saturday classes in West Street were responsive. Half the feminine *élite* were there, Elizabeth Hoar from Concord, Lydia Maria Child, the three Peabody sisters, Mrs. Emerson, Mrs. George Bancroft, Mrs. Theodore Parker, Maria White, who was engaged to James Russell Lowell. The subjects were Greek mythology, "What is Life?", the history of art, the meaning of the various dances. Margaret had the true Boston passion for pigeon-holes and categories, for putting everything in its proper place. Wordsworth was the "poet of reflection," Jupiter stood for "the will," Bacchus for the "terrene inspiration." It was all sharp and clear, like so many definitions from a legal treatise, ready to be gathered in a note-book. Margaret's ideas had good square corners, like building-blocks that fitted at the edges. Set side by side, in just the right arrangement, they formed a solid architectural structure, a true temple of culture, as unmistakable as a Boston bank. One of the ladies kept the class in order with her unswerving eye for Christian morals, which might have been lost in aesthetic divagations. Sometimes the Gothic genius seized the reins of Margaret's fancy, and she would ride like a Valkyrie over the clouds of German metaphysics. Then, before the eyes of her worshipping hearers, the cold New England landscape melted into a dreamland of romance. One dwelt for a moment in

Valhalla, among the Scandinavian gods and heroes, as erstwhile in Athens of the violet crown.

In West Street, one could buy over the counter, in exchange for a little good will,—or a thousand dollars, in case one happened to have it,—a share in the Utopian community that was rapidly taking shape at Brook Farm. This was George Ripley's contribution to the educational movement of Massachusetts. For fourteen years, with no great zeal for the Unitarian cause, Ripley had been preaching in a Boston pulpit; and now, having resigned, he was already living at the farm, at West Roxbury, nine miles out of town. He was a cheerful, hearty, faithful soul, ready for any task, for whom the opinion of the world was but a "puff of empty air." He had always expected to be poor and rather preferred obscurity to fame. "Give me philosophy!" was all he asked. He had heard the call of "association," of the communists and Christian socialists, the Owenites and the Fourierists, followed by the Icarians and Cabet, who were establishing their communities in every corner of the young republic. Almost every month the port of New York welcomed some new boat-load of Europeans who had come to found a "Harmony" or a "North American Phalanx." Ripley, while planning the farm, was editing a work in fourteen volumes, *Specimens of Standard Foreign Literature,* translations of Cousin, Jouffroy, Goethe, Menzel, Benjamin Constant and others. He had recruited many of his translators from the West Street circle. In the winter of 1840–41, the whole group discussed Ripley's project.

It came into existence in the spring, and building was added to building, the Hive, in the shade of an ancient sycamore, the Eyrie, the Nest, the Cottage, the Pilgrim House, and member was added to member, until, at the end of six years, there were more than a hundred and forty associates. Of the circle of the Transcendentalists, most of the ablest members remained aloof, as benevolent neutrals and visitors. "Doing things in crowds" seemed to them too youthful; they were self-sufficient. As Margaret Fuller put it, in her somewhat airy dialect, "Why bind oneself to a central or any doctrine? How much nobler stands a man entirely unpledged, unbound?" This was Emerson's feeling. For Alcott, the plan was not austere enough. All three dissented from the idea behind the association, "As the institutions, so are the men," preferring to think, with Goethe, "As the men, so are the institutions." But Hawthorne, who had no theories, hoped to find at the farm a practical basis for his married life. John Sullivan Dwight, who had translated for Ripley the *Minor Poems of Goethe and Schiller,* and Charles A. Dana, fresh from Harvard, later known as Dana of *The Sun,* were members for a longer period. So was Isaac Hecker, of the "Hecker's Flour" family of New York, the German-American priest of the future, who founded the order of the Paulist Fathers. George William Curtis and his brother Burrill and George P. Bradford were other members. Bradford, whose *Selections from Fénelon* was another volume of Ripley's series, later moved to Plymouth to realize his dreams of the simple life. In the intervals of teaching Greek, he carried on a market-garden, selling his own vegetables from the cart. This was the charming and sensitive Bradford whose New England conscience was such a nuisance. Once, during one of Webster's out-of-door speeches, he was swept up to the front of the crowd. "I have no ticket," he exclaimed, "I have no right to be here;" and, much to the discomfort of the crowd, but much to the comfort of his conscience, he shoved his way back to the outermost rim. Charles King Newcomb, another member, was an individualist of a different sort. In his high room with the French window, this young Providence mystic kept a wooden crucifix on his table, between portraits of Xavier and Loyola, with freshly gathered flowers at the foot. One often heard his voice, in the midnight hours, chanting the litany or reading Greek. Newcomb lived a strange, secret life, prolonged for half a century in Paris, devoted to the writing of a private journal, as long as Amiel's journal, or even longer, that lay unpublished in a Rhode Island attic fifty years after his death. There were farmers and artists among the members, working-men and Brahmins, girls with hazel eyes and extravagant moods, several Harvard students, an English baronet's son, a Spaniard, two Filipinos, the son of a Louisiana planter, "Omniarch" Ryckman, "Camilla" and "Sybilla," —for nicknames were in vogue,—"Chrysalis" List and "Old Solidarity" Eaton.

In the broad entry of the Hive, Ripley's library filled the shelves until, to raise more money for the venture, the master sold his books to Theodore Parker. Ripley, the ever-faithful "Archon," steered the unsteady ship with unwavering eye. He was up before the dawn, dressed in his blue tunic and cow-hide boots, milking, cleaning the stalls, blacking the shoes of some member who was going to town, carting off the vegetables to market, directing the field-operations, writing diplomatic letters, giving a Sunday lecture on Kant or Spinoza, or, on a winter evening, when the stars were bright, gathering the members about him in the snow, while he discoursed on the constellations. His wife, Sophia Ripley, Richard Henry Dana's younger sister, who was soon to join the Catholic Church, cheerfully toiled beside him, ten hours a day in the muslin-room, washing, scrubbing the floors, much to the annoyance of her kindred. The school was more than admirable. Ripley taught philosophy and mathematics. Mrs. Ripley had a class in history and a class for Dante in Italian. Charles A. Dana had classes in Greek and German. The bashful, slender, beaming little Dwight, the dictator of musical Boston in later years, carried on the classes in music. He, too, had had a Unitarian pulpit, and had had a way of forgetting to write his sermons. He had a "want of fluency in prayer," for his mind was entirely filled with Mozart and Haydn. He started his "mass clubs" at the farm. There were classes in botany and geology, carried on among the rocks and trees. All the studies were elective; the rule was to "follow one's attractions." The young men wore blouses and hunters' frocks, belted at the waist, of plain brown holland or a gayer chintz, with little tasselled caps; the girls wore muslin dresses, with flowers and ribbons. The single men lived in Attica, the garret of the Hive; and the vegetarians had a Graham table. George William Curtis trimmed the lamps; Charles A. Dana was the griddle-master. There was much sitting about on stairs and floors, and the conversation,—analytical often, bristling with the new philosophy, with "intuition" and "the analogous," the objective, the creative, the receptive,—sometimes assumed those painful forms of wit that flourish among the intelligentsia. There were many jokes about "affinities," puns of the frostier kind that make one feel so sorry for the punster, animadversions on "morbid familism," *clichés* of a dire facetiousness: "Is the butter within the sphere of your influence?" But there were merry dances every night, picnics on Cow Island or in the grove, boating parties on the Charles, close by, Shakespeare readings, Elizabethan pageants, tableaux, charades, plays, scenes from Byron's *Corsair* and Sheridan's *Pizarro*. Occasionally, in the evening, little groups walked or drove to Boston, to a Beethoven concert or an Emerson lecture,—the interest in Beethoven seemed to flourish in minds that had been quickened by Emerson,—or an anti-slavery meeting at Faneuil Hall. They filled the big farm-wagon, or Jonas Gerrish's stage, which, twice a day, plied between the Hive and Scollay Square. Their favourite rendezvous in the afternoon was Elizabeth Peabody's book-shop. At night, they gathered in Mrs. Harrington's cake-shop, and the younger men and the girls walked home under the stars.

The stage from Scollay Square brought visitors, a few, at first, those of the inner circle, then hundreds and even thousands of "civilisees," as the farmers called the rest or the population. Margaret Fuller came to conduct a Conversation on Education, on "What can we do for ourselves and others?" Impulse was the subject on one occasion, an appropriate theme at the farm, where spontaneity was so much in order. Throwing oneself on the floor was not so bad, but yawning was a little too impulsive. Georgiana Bruce burned pastilles to perfume Margaret's room and brought the morning coffee to her bedside. For Margaret had become another Pauline Wiesel, the heroine of the German Romantics, whom Humboldt walked thirty miles to see.* Emerson often came to lead the talk; sometimes Bronson Alcott. Theodore Parker, who lived close by,—he had a church at West Roxbury,—walked over often for a chat about philosophy or farming. Orestes Brownson dropped in, shouted and pounded on the table and strolled with Isaac Hecker in the grove. They were both on the road to Rome, like Mrs. Ripley; and Brownson's coming always occasioned a talk on Catholicism, Pascal or Port Royal. This was a theme that pleased Charles Newcomb, whose favourite author was Saint Augustine. Brownson, the rustic giant from Vermont, who had passed through so many religious phases, was not a welcome guest. That there was method in his truculence, no one had any reason to suppose; and he had taken up his Greek and Latin, to satisfy his Catholic advisers, at a time when his mental bones had set. He made sad work of his spondees and dactyls, which the patient

* One of Pauline Wiesel's friends wrote of her, in the vein of Margaret's friends, "I look upon her in the light of a phenomenon of Greek mythology." She herself had written, much in Margaret's vein, "Every means, every possible preparation for living, and yet one must never live; I never shall, and those who dare to do so have the wretched world, the whole world, against them."—George Brandes, *The Romantic School in Germany.*

George Ripley would not have minded if Brownson had not appeared to be showing off. As for George Bradford, the ever-gentle, who had learned his Greek and Latin in the cradle, he could not sleep for the misery that Brownson caused him. False vowels and wrong measures were as painful to him as a saxophone would have been. He dreamed one night that he was a Catholic convert and that Brownson, appointed his confessor, obliged him to repeat, after himself, a Latin psalm from the Vulgate. Bradford awoke in agony.

This was a pity, for Brownson, who was honest as the day, was a man of really imposing gifts. He appeared to be unstable enough. He had passed from sect to sect, changing his ministerial coat as many times as the Vicar of Bray, although always in response to a new conviction. Every thinker he read, Lamennais, Jouffroy, Comte, Saint-Simon, Owen, overthrew all his previous views, and he rushed from one position to another, with a headlong, headstrong vehemence, telling the world each time how right he was. With a vigorous, enquiring mind that was anything but sensitive or subtle, he had a warm and generous imagination. He had founded the "Society of Union and Progress," chiefly for the advancement of the workers, and he had preached class-warfare, the death-struggle of rich and poor, as a step towards the "Church of the Future," after the Comtian pattern, of which he saw himself as a John the Baptist. He longed for a new Catholicity until he found a home in the old one. To further his ideas and reflect their changes, he carried on a quarterly review, first the *Boston Quarterly*, afterwards *Brownson's Quarterly*. In this he "aimed to startle," as he said, taking pains to be paradoxical and even as extravagant as he could be; and this method was rather accentuated after he had joined the Catholic Church. The Bishop of Boston lamented the timidity of the Catholic population, most of whom were recent immigrants, of the depressed classes, in a society that was hostile to them. The Bishop urged

Brownson not to hide his light under a bushel. As well
urge a bull not to pretend to be a lamb! The rugged, fiery
Brownson was happy to learn that truculence had an apostolic value. On ferry-boats between Chelsea and Boston, in
barber-shops, in butcher-shops, wherever he happened to
find himself, he engaged all and sundry in religious discussions. Once at an inn at Andover, where he was giving a
lecture, he loudly commanded the waiter to send for the
landlord. "Landlord," he exclaimed, in a voice that was
meant for all the guests, "why don't you have something
in your house that a Christian can eat? Why don't you
have fish? No Christian eats meat on Friday."

This was one of the little things that people seldom did
at Andover. They kept a special corner of hell-fire there
for travellers with Brownson's views. But Brownson
was a courageous man, in the Church as well as out of it,
whom the Brook Farmers learned to respect in the end;
for, having been too Catholic for the Yankees, he was too
Yankee for the Catholics, at least for the Church as he
found it, and he stormed against the Irish domination. He
wished to make the Church an American Church, to counteract the powerful influence that tended to make it Irish;
and no one spoke more forcefully than he against the cor-
ruptions of Tammany. He was under a cloud in Dublin
as well as in Boston, and Cardinal Newman was forced
to withdraw the invitation he had sent to Brownson to
lecture at his new university there. He was the first lecturer that Newman invited, and he was asked to choose
his own subject, geography or "opossums," if it suited him
best; for Brownson's multifarious writings on history,
sociology, religion, on politics, art and philosophy had
given him a world-name. His standing was high in the
Catholic world,* and his gifts, from the point of view

* "You alone can prepare us for the great controversies by founding
among us a school and arming it with the principles of a sound philosophy."—Letter of Lord Acton to Brownson, 1854. See also the long corre
spondence with Montalembert in the *Life of Brownson* by his son.

of any school, his versatility and his breadth of knowledge, his energy and lucidity, were those of a first-rate publicist. Something more than a journalist, something less than a sage, Brownson was a Catholic Theodore Parker. In one book, *The Convert,* the history of his religious life, he left the best account that has ever been written of the spiritual cross-currents of the forties and fifties.

Of the other guests at Brook Farm, two were especially welcome, William Henry Channing, the doctor's nephew, a minister, albeit with many scruples, better known as a Christian socialist, a thrillingly eloquent preacher, and the tall, slight, graceful Christopher Cranch, with the picturesque head and curling hair, the son of a judge in Washington, who, having ample means and mundane tastes, had gradually "sunk the minister in the man" and followed the call of the muses. He was a landscape painter and a poet; he sang and played the flute and violin; he was a clever actor on occasion and the cleverest caricaturist in New England. In fact, he was the victim of too many gifts, no mere Janus with a double head but a sort of accomplished Hydra. He had taken Emerson at his word and planted himself on his instincts, wherever they led him. They had led him into the pulpit and out again; they led him to Louisville, Kentucky, where he took the place of James Freeman Clarke as editor of *The Western Messenger.* With his flute as his constant companion, he had drawn there his comic illustrations for some of Emerson's essays, such as the "Man expanding like a Melon." These drawings, suggesting Thackeray's, shocked some of the Transcendentalists. In years to come, he was to use this talent in the pictures for his charming books for children, *The Last of the Huggermuggers* and *Kobboltozo,*—years during which he lived as a wandering artist, in London, New York, Paris, Rome and Cambridge. What could an artist do, he would write from New York, in a money-getting world? People rushed in from the streets and stopped for a moment in his studio, only to hurry-scurry out again, eternally driving, driving. In Cambridge, he found a congenial circle, and there he translated the *Æneid;* but whenever he came back from Italy he was struck by the look in people's faces, the hard, weary expression about the mouth, the quick, shrewd eye, the anxious air. Everyone seemed to be worried; and back he would go to Rome, to join the circle of William Wetmore Story, write a few more poems and paint from the costume-models.

His painting was nothing out of the way, but some of his poems had a firmer touch. There are poets who survive in a single line. Cranch was destined to survive in two, from the poem called *Enosis,*—

> We are columns left alone
> Of a temple once complete,—

which hundreds of men have quoted in their latter years. At Brook Farm, where he came to visit his friend and fellow-lover of music and German, his Harvard classmate Dwight, he was the all-attractive entertainer. He drew amusing pictures of the Harvard mill grinding its grist of ministers. He performed astonishing feats of ventriloquism. William Henry Channing was more austere. He was a self-tormented creature, earnest, hypersensitive, torn by doubts, a "concave man" who was always retreating, as Henry Thoreau remarked, like a fair mask swaying from a bough. For the rest, he was a man of the world, as all the Channings were, and a preacher unexcelled when the spirit moved him. In later years, he was to live in England, where his daughter married the author of *The Light of Asia.* At the moment, he was editing in New York a magazine called *The Present,* to propagate his socialistic views. What to do for the race? was his constant question; but he was involved in metaphysics, of a sadly tenuous kind, and he was convinced, as a friend remarked, that "Christ did not understand his own religion." He had spent a season in Rome, vainly hoping to get himself converted, and the engravings on his study wall were arranged in the form of a cross. He wrote an occasional poem and various tracts and had recently translated Jouffroy's *Ethics;* but the great project of his life was a work on Vittoria Colonna, a study of the Italian Renaissance. He meditated this for many years, enthralled as he gathered his memoranda, until the enormous task of preparation became a life-work in itself. He never began the book. A mystical enthusiast, like Dr. Channing, but without his uncle's will, irresolute, introspective, the victim of innumerable intentions, a talker and taker of notes who longed to be "useful,"—such was the "evil times' sole patriot," as Emerson called him in a well-known poem. Of all the Brook Farmers, guests or members, William Henry Channing was the symbol, as later times recalled the enterprise. Whatever the facts might be, whatever happened, he could never persuade himself that the world's salvation did not lie just around the corner. He always felt, when he rose from his bed, that the "one far-off divine event" might well occur before he sat down to breakfast.

CHAPTER XIII

EMERSON: WOOD-NOTES

IN THE days of King Philip's War, the Indians had spared the town of Concord. They burned the neighbouring settlements, Sudbury, Chelmsford, Stow, but one of their chieftains said, as they glanced over Concord from a hill-top, "We shall never prosper if we go there. The Great Spirit loves that town." This was an Indian legend, and one could well believe it. Plain, low, quiet, the village had no obvious distinction. The enterprising Yankees passed it by. It had no port, no trade, no water-power, no gold, lead, coal, oil or marble. The granite was better at Fitchburg, and even the Concord ice had bubbles in it. As wood and grass were its only staples, Emerson advised his fellow-townsmen to manufacture school-teachers and make them the best in the world.* The village air favoured this, as it favoured meditation and contemplation. The hills and woods, not too exciting, afforded a gentle stimulus to genial and uninterrupted studies. One recalled in Concord the words of the old Chinese painter: "Wherein do the reasons lie that virtuous men so love *sansui*, landscape? Landscape is a place

---

*A staple for the South and West. Edward Everett Hale relates that a certain French investigator, sent by Napoleon III to study American education, found that virtually every teacher in the West and South had come from one small corner of the country, either Connecticut or Massachusetts. He asked Hale to explain this fact, which he said was unique in history. Hale, to settle the question, enquired of a leading citizen of Massachusetts how many young people of his town, when they left school, began as teachers. "He heard me," says Hale, "with some impatience, and then said, 'Why, all of them, of course.'"—E. E. Hale, *Tarry-at-Home Travels.*

where vegetation is nourished on high and low ground, where springs and rocks play about like children, a place that woodsmen and retiring scholars usually frequent, where birds cry aloud their joy in the scene."

Concord abounded in *sansui*. One found peace there and the flourishing days in which minds are high and joyous, the days that Kakki desired for the landscape-painter. There one could have good feeling and beautiful taste; one could create the *Yu,* the wonderful and mysterious. Emerson found it so, in his woodland walks. Once he had left his study, once in the fields, with the lowing cattle, the birds, the trees, the waters, the satisfying outlines of the hills and the ponds, he seemed to have come to his own and made friends with nature. He found health and affinity there,— no petulance, no fret, but eternal resource, a long tomor-row rich as yesterday. The stems of the hemlocks, pines and oaks gleamed like iron on his excited eye. The thrill-ing leap of the squirrel up the long bough, the softness and beauty of the summer clouds that seemed to enjoy their height and privilege of motion, the millions of sheeny fliers with green body and crape wing that over-hung the grasses and the waters, the chickadees in the piny glen filled him with cheerfulness and courage. He was embosomed in beauty and wonder. The very cattle lying under the trees seemed to have great and tranquil thoughts. The songs of the birds, the sunlight full of gnats, the crickets in full cry, the goldfinches eating the seeds of the thistle, scattering the leaves in their excitement, the hedges of barberry, whitethorn, woodbine and ivy were a cornucopia of golden joys. Out upon scholars, he said to himself, with their pale, sickly, etiolated indoor thoughts! Give me the out-of-door thoughts of sound men, thoughts all fresh and blooming.

Much as the village meant to him, it was in the woods and fields that he knew the joy of the Brahmin. Concord, indeed, was a school for the study of human nature. One learned all the trades and professions by talking with the blacksmith, the grocer, the plumber. All history repeated itself in Concord. The wealth and goods of the Indies and China streamed through the village in the trucks and wagons that carried the wares of Boston to Vermont and New Hampshire. One had only to mix a little imagination with all these sights and sounds of the common life: then one found the whole world in any least corner of it, one found Asia and Europe, past and future, within the circle of one's daily walks. The large mind in small conditions, the high mind in low conditions, everything in leasts: why should not Concord be one's Rome, one's world? A tent, a little rice and asses' milk, or, say, the farmer's scale of living, plain plenty without luxury or show; for the rest, health, the south wind, books, old trees, a boat, two or three friends,—what could a poet wish that life did not shower on him there? His sunshine was Susa; Ecbatana, his shade; and he could rest assured that, if he asked them, every one of the gods would honour his feast.

It was for no private ends that Emerson sought privacy. His ends were universal, his ends were public, like those of Michael Angelo, like Dante's, who seldom dined in company. Swedenborg's best of angels, those that dwelt in the midst of heaven, did not live consociated, but separate, house and house; and Ossian's Cathmore lodged in the wood not only to avoid the voice of praise. If the seeker of truth needs solitude, and almost a going out of the body to think, should a poet apologize for the isolation that breeds Olympian thoughts? Steadily to prefer one's native choices, against all argument and all example, defending them against the multitude, even as much or more against the wise, was not this the burden of Emerson's teaching? Should everyone be busy and useful? Was it any merit in a man to make his own stove, or boil and bake his dinner, when others could do it better than he? His virtue was to carry into action his own dearest ends, to dare to do what he believed and loved, were it only the carving of a cherry-stone or the forwarding of a handful of friends. How much more was it a poet's virtue to solve his own questions, though he died, even if he died of lotus-eating! Therefore, for the poet, idleness, as others chose to think it, leisure for meditation and contemplation. He who could hope to catch the wingéd thoughts that thrilled and agitated humankind, restored youth and sanity, dissipated the dreams under which men reeled and staggered and gave heroic aims to the nations was not required to explain his means. Emerson paid his way by lecturing. For the rest, he abandoned himself to his own caprices. The writer, like the priest, had to be exempted from secular labour, for his work demanded a frolic health; he had to be at the top of his condition. Anyone who challenged Emerson's freedom would have discovered that his village mildness masked, like any woodland creature's, a sharp retractile claw.

He scarcely had a *modus vivendi*. His moods were too variable for this; and he did not wish merely to write. He wished to say only essential things, the things that could not be omitted, the things that his genius uttered,—he did not care to cultivate his talent; and his genius ebbed and flowed and ebbed again. Yesterday, Caesar had not seemed so great; today, he was a dunce. The fruit of his brain was abortive, cramped or mildewed. He was as torpid as a clod. He felt like a ship aground, and suddenly some tyrannous idea, emerging out of heaven, seized upon him. The rigid fibres relaxed; life returned to a finger, a hand, a foot. A river spread over the shoals where the ship lay aground, uplifting the timbers on its waters, and the ship put forth its sails and turned its head to the sea. Were these moods in any degree within control?—for the fruits of these moods alone were all he wished to gather. Were there any tonics for the torpid mind? The electric machine would not work, no sparks

would pass; and then the world was all a cat's back, all
sparkle and shock. A flash of light, a long darkness, then a
flash again. Where was the Franklin with kite and rod for
this celestial fluid?—he who could command it and convey
it into the arts of life, inspire men and take them off their
feet, withdraw them from the life of gain and trifles and
make the world transparent. For to Emerson nothing
seemed incredible, nothing, neither miracles nor magic,
when he had experienced an insight. He longed for the
consecutive, not the single glimpse but the panorama. A
fuller inspiration, as it seemed to him, would cause the
point to flow and become a line; it would bend the line and
complete the circle.

To experience this genius and communicate it, to detect
and watch the gleam of light that flashed across his mind
from within, was Emerson's dream and hope; and this
alone governed his method of living. Not by forethought,
not by calculation, had paradise ever been gained. The
"stairway of surprise" mounted thither, and this was not
to be compassed by rules. To live in the hour, extempore,
free as an Arab, was the only way to be ready when the
gods arrived. All measures of economy were ugly: the
manners of the bard should be above them. And yet was
there not a kind of prudence that had its negative value?
He who respected his ends had to respect his means, however he cloaked and screened them; and, if all high states
of mind were transient, like every other form of inspiration, still, there were methods of inducing them, and
prudence lay in making use of these. One had to have a
measure of worldly wisdom in order to keep one's freedom; and no one was shrewder than Emerson, when it
came to this. Well he knew what crippled and untuned
him, and his stimulants and purgatives were many: the
fire, as it burned in his chimney,—a kind of muse,—air,
landscape, exercise, a page or two of Proclus or Plotinus.
He passed into the Elysian Fields the moment he opened

these authors; the grand and pleasing figures of gods and demons sailed before his eyes. These rare, brave words filled him with hilarity and spring; his heart danced, his sight was quickened, he beheld shining relations between all things; he was impelled to write and almost to sing. Proclus was his opium. But solitary converse with nature was his special *modus* of inspiration. On spring days, at summer dawns, in the October woods, by flood or field, in natural parks of oak or pine, where the ground was smooth and unencumbered, he heard sweet and dreadful words that were never uttered in libraries. The hills began to dislimn and float in the air. The atoms of his frame began to dance. He came into new circulations; the marrow of the world was in his bones; the opulence of forms poured into his intellect; he seemed to be dipping his brush into the paint-pot with which birds, flowers, the living rock, the landscape and the eternal sky were painted.

Away with prudence then! Allah never counted the days the Arab spent in the chase. The one real prudence was concentration, as the one evil was dissipation. One's work would take care of itself if one lived enough; and as long as one's genius bought the investment was safe, although one spent like a monarch. To be profligate was not to spend, but to spend off the line of one's proper life; and to fill the hour was Emerson's life, to fill the hour and own the day. Him to whom works and days were offered, no god could ever rebuke for taking works. The days came and went like veiled and muffled figures, sent from a distant friendly party; but they said nothing, and, if one did not use the gifts they brought, they carried them as silently away. What fairy or what demon possessed such power as he who used the gifts?—

Bread, kingdoms, stars, and sky that holds them all.

It was in search of this power,—call it the poet's madness,—that Emerson set out for the woods and pastures.
He was an abandoned lotus-eater. All he asked was that
the days should be, for him, as full as centuries, loaded,
fragrant. He had various favourite walks, from the
Manse down the river to Peter's Field, to the Estabrook
farm, with its straggling orchards, where the apple-trees
strove to hold their own against the encroaching forest,
to White Pond, a little Indian basin, where one could
almost see the sachem paddling his canoe in a shadowy
cove, to Walden, where he had his own pine garden and
the chickadees flitted through the branches and the
waterflies seemed full of happiness. There, as he sat on
the bank, he had read most of Goethe,—to please Carlyle,
—fifty volumes or more. Sometimes the warm south wind
drew him to the summit of the ridge above the Boston
turnpike. Sometimes he rose before the light and waited
for the dawn over the forest, sitting on a course of dark
rock that had been worn by a glacier. Often he went for
walks at night, when the moon was making amber of the
world and every cottage pane glittered with silver and
the meadows sent up the rank smell of all their ferns and
folded flowers in a nocturnal fragrance. The little harlot
fireflies of the lowlands sparkled in the grass and in the
air, and he heard the voice of the wind, so slight and
pure and deep, as if it were the sound of the stars
revolving.

How many were there who could see the charm of
close, low pine-woods in a river-town? Was Walden anything more than a "prettyish pool," as a travelling poet
remarked? One had to have musical eyes to see what
Emerson saw in these meadows and streams, in the waving rye-fields and the quiet hemlocks. He saw what others
heard: all the soothing, brisk or romantic moods that
corresponding melodies awoke in them, he found in the
carpet of the wood, in the margin of the pond, in the

shade of the pines, in the infinite variety and dance of
the tree-tops. To him, a skiff on the water was a piece
of fairy timber, which the light loved, the wind and the
wave. When he struck the water with his paddle, he
fancied he had never seen such colour, the hue of Rhine
wines, jasper and verd-antique, topaz and chalcedony,
gold and green and chestnut and hazel, in bewitching succession and relief. In the hard clouds he saw what sculpture!—what an expression of immensity in the dotted and
rippled rack, firm and continental, then vanishing into
plumes and auroral gleams, all without crowding, boundless, cheerful, strong. On Indian summer days, he saw the
Indians under the trees in the wood. In his neighbour
Edmund Hosmer's oxen, the beasts that ploughed his
fields, he saw the camels of the faithful Hassan, beside
whom even Tamerlane seemed a slave. The railroad at
Walden, prosaic enough to others, seemed to him a
shuttle, shooting across the forest, the swamp, the river,
over the arms of the sea, binding city to city. In an apple-
tree, he saw the sun painting itself in glowing balls and
leaves,—in apples, the social fruit, in which nature had
deposited every flavour. Whole zones and climates were
concentrated in apples, barrels of wind and half-barrels
of cider. In the oaks and pines, he saw vessels of health
and vigour. They were imperfect men, groping upward,
bemoaning their imprisonment, rooted in the ground. Beside these plants, hardy in their weakness, he had a sudden sense of relief and pleasure, observing the mighty
law of vegetation.

On evenings when the moon shone, the thrifty Concord folk turned out the street-lamps. Emerson did not
need even the moon; he could see well enough in the dark.
He saw honour in scamps and justice in thieves. He could
see energy in beggars and elegance of manners in a peasant. He could see benevolence in misers and grandeur in
porters and sweeps. Why this was, he could never have

told; for he who had leisure for everything else had no
time for introspection. Besides, if he saw in the dark, he
preferred the sunlight. None of his moments ever seemed
empty in which he had given heed to some natural object, a
gentian, a wild-apple-tree with fruit that hung like berries,
a thorn-bush with its red fruit, the musical, streaming south
wind that turned all the trees into wind-harps, the fall
of snow-flakes in the still air, the blowing of sleet over a
sheet of water. He felt that he was emerging from an
egg-shell existence when he saw the great dome that
arched above him. An everlasting Now reigned in nature,
which hung the same roses on his bushes that charmed
the Chaldeans in their hanging gardens.

Often, as he walked, he hummed or whistled the
rhythm of some ballad, some song of Herrick's, a fragment of Taliessin, the old Welsh bard, or a strain of
Persian poetry, Hafiz or Saadi. It struck him that these
metres were organic, derived from the human pulse, beating with the beating of the blood, and therefore natural
and universal. There was a charm in the cadences, heroic,
pathetic or plaintive, that seemed to set him searching for
the words to fill these vacant beats. Rhymes enchanted
him, too, in a way he could not explain but had always
felt. They suggested the correspondence of parts in nature, acid and alkali, body and mind, character and history, action and reaction. These iterations in the natural
world, as in the world of art, had always given him
pleasure: the doubling of rocks and trees reflected in
water, the repetition of pillars in a colonnade, in a row
of windows, or in wings, the symmetrical contrast of
garden beds and walks. Rhymes to the eye, such as shadows, explained the charm of rhymes to the ear; and the
inner life also had its rhymes, perception and expression,
ebb and flow. Rhyme and rhythm measured for him the
latitude and opulence of poets. If they were limited and
unskilful, one saw it in the poverty of their chimes. But

Spenser, Marlowe and Chapman flew far and wide for their weapons: there was no manufacture in their rhymes and rhythms, but a vortex, a musical tornado that whirled the materials of their minds into the same grand order that planets and moons obeyed, and seasons, and monsoons.

He loved rhyme and return, period and musical reflection, rhyme that suggested not restraint but rather the wildest freedom. At Walden, on a winter day, he would stand on the edge of the pond and throw stones across the frozen surface. It charmed his ear as the stones fell and fell again on this crystal drum, repeating the note with just the right modulation. The rhyming and the chiming of this ice-harp filled him with exultation. Well he could understand why poetry had been called the *gaie science,* why sailors worked better for their *yo-heave-ho,* why soldiers fought better for the drum and trumpet. He could understand the building power of music, as the ancient myths described it. He could feel how the walls of Thebes had risen to the music of Amphion's harp. The excitement which the Persian bards produced exceeded that of the grape: they had driven warriors to combat, like Taileffer, who rode out at Hastings, singing the *Chanson de Roland,* challenging the Saxons. Well he could understand why bards and minstrels had been taken for makers and givers of laws, they who had stood for liberation, for courage, freedom, victory. In the myths, they restored the dead to life; they met the approbation of Allah in heaven. They made men, they added and affirmed. They set the intellectual world in action. They sang old ideas out of people's heads and sang new ideas in. They introduced fresh images and symbols that built up the world again in thought. They threw down the walls of circumstance. They awakened in other men the sense of universal relation and power.

Emerson thought of the poet as Adam in the garden

again, new-naming the beasts in the field and the gods in
the sky, calling aloud to the children of morning that all
creation was recommencing. Among partial men, he stood
for the complete man. All the forms of life were in balance in him; he saw and handled that which others
dreamed of, the whole scale of experience. He was the
representative of man, having the largest power to receive and impart. Were not most men like the shepherd
who, lost and blinded in the snow-storm, perished in a
drift outside his door? Were they not like minors who
had not come into their own and did not know what
wealth was rightly theirs? They clung to the wearinesses
of their daily life, their trivial forms and habits, their
petrified social scale of ranks and employments. They
were inferior to their proper selves and did not use the
powers they possessed. Who but the poet could redeem
them from all these routines and idolatries? Their money
was a second best, their alcohol, their politics. Which of
them would not give his lands and houses for a touch of
the perception that stirred the will? Life was a dance,
as Plotinus said, in which the bodies were moved in a
beautiful manner, as being parts of the whole. But most
men could not sustain this order. They were too lumpish
and opaque, for their souls had not been awakened. There
lay the poet's province. For him the world was always
virgin soil; for him all men had their sovereign moments,
as every clod contains its germs of life. It was the poet's
office to unfold them. He was the master of the dance of
life, who knew that every man would begin to move when
the music reached and touched his imagination.

The poets who had shown this power most clearly
were the great religious awakeners, Zoroaster and Plato,
the bards of the Vedas, of the *Vishnu Purana* and the
Bhagavad-Gita. For Emerson, these came first, or such as
these; they were never out of his mind, and he judged
other poets in the light of these commanding oracles. In

his reaction against the Church, and all that savoured of official goodness, he seldom thought of the biblical writers. But, even more than the givers of laws, he liked, or at least he liked to think of, the Norse and the Cymrian bards, Taliessin and the mythical Ossian and Merlin, together with Hafiz and Saadi, the Persian poets. It was evident that his notion of these was coloured by his reading of the Eastern scriptures; but even as they were,—as they survived in fragments,—he found them inspiring and tonic. They spoke to him of the vast, of health and courage. The rude strains of the Northern bards, struck out white-hot with love or grief, pleased him all the more in his own recoil from all that was academic in the English classics; and the cheerfulness and force of the "fortunate" Saadi were the fruits of a situation like his own. For Saadi and Hafiz, in Persia, had escaped from Mohammedan fatalism, just as he had escaped from Calvinism. Their joy was a joy of liberation. He liked to think of the Persians and Arabs. In the absence of other intoxicants, as travellers often noted, poetry and flowers were their wine and spirits: a couplet was equal to a bottle and a rose to a dram. Poetry had its highest effect among them. It was also in his wish to escape from the sway of European tradition that Emerson cultivated the Persian poets, who left so many traces in his writings. The luxuriance of their imagery, the breadth of the Eastern modes of thinking refreshed his New England imagination. The bold Oriental muse had an electric power that animated and unbound his mind.

Much as he loved poems of every kind, it was these poets of the early ages, the springtime bards and seers that he loved the best, they who spoke with authority and not as the scribes, who spoke of the morning of the world, whose words stood for things, for the simplest feelings,—not gifted men who sang, but the children of music, whose scope did not lie in exhibition, whose aim was to serve the gods. "Thus saith the Lord" began their songs. Their utterance was large and their language final, as if it came from the Eternal mind and had not been arbitrarily composed by the writer. The Greek Gnomic poets, the Persian poets, whose words might have been engraved on sword-blades, Pindar, with his grand strokes, firm as the tread of a horse,—among his own contemporaries, Landor, whose epigrams recalled the Greeks: these were his special favourites. They seemed to him the result and the justification of the ages in which they appeared: they made him think lightly of histories and statutes. In their verse, the iron lids of Reason, usually heavy with slumber, were unclosed for a moment. The individual mind became in them the vent of the mind of humanity.

In poetry, Emerson asked for the greatest. He asked that the poet should omit all but the important passages: Shakespeare was made up of such,—Shakespeare, who was like Damascus steel, hammered out of old nails. He was not interested in talent. He loved the charm and skill of execution that he found in Herrick, Collins, Gray and Landor, the elegance that suggested health, the ease that went with mastery. But for external graces he had no use. He thought with Heraclitus that "harmony latent is of greater value than that which is patent"; and Wordsworth's great design, the plan of *The Recluse,* the *Ode to Dion,* pleased him better than all the enamelled poets. None of your parlour or piano verse! None of your carpet poets, content to please! None of your sonneteering, your bookmaking and bookselling; none of your cold spying and authorship! The muse should be the counterpart of nature, exuberant and tranquil. True poetry, Emerson thought, betrayed in every word miraculous presence of mind, quickness, perception of relations. One found it seldom in current letters, even in the history of letters. In a dozen alcoves of English poets, one found only nine or ten who were still inspirers of their race. For literature warped away from life, and the power to transubstantiate the world was the test and measure of poetry. Its mark was contemporary insight, in one's own America as in Pindar's Greece. Easy enough to repaint the mythology of the Greeks, the mediæval Church, the feudal castle, the martyrdoms and crusades of former times. To point out where the same creative power worked in one's own dwellings and public assemblies, to convert into universal symbols the energies acting at this hour in New York, in Chicago and San Francisco, required a subtle and commanding thought. Could one read the poetry in affairs and fuse the circumstances of today? Could one take the hour, with its cares and fears, and hold it up to a divine reason, until one saw that it had a purpose and beauty? Then one would be doing what Pindar did, and Shakespeare and Milton in their times. The dry twig would blossom in one's hand.

Poet that he was in all his prose, it was this other harmony that he longed to compass. He toiled endlessly over his verses; and, in fact, he had developed a style of his own, as marked in his poems as in his essays, a lean, spare, quick, intellectual style that could only have emerged, one felt, from Concord. In his more flaccid verses, one caught here and there glints of Shakespeare, Collins, Gray and Wordsworth; but the Emersonian style at its best had none of the derivative Cambridge note, nor any of the smooth and facile charm of most of the other American writers. In his preference of the "latent" to the "patent," as a protest against the sort of jingles one "put round frosted cake," as he said, Emerson sometimes purposely roughened his verses, throwing in a dissonance or an ill-matched rhyme. Anything rather than rhetoric, for himself. As a matter of fact, with others, he was easily pleased. For all the severity of his conscious standard, anything in rhyme was apt to catch him, provided the feeling was noble. He never took the word for the deed, in the work of other poets, but he often took the deed for the word. The anthology that he published, *Parnassus,* a large collection of his favourite poems, showed the inequality of his taste. In choosing his own poems to publish, he revealed a similar weakness; for at his own worst his work was bad as no merely talented writer's could be. Even the *Threnody* was not really good, and the commonplace or doggerel of much of his writing would never have passed muster with the Cambridge poets. One wondered at the childlike innocence that could have led him to publish some of these verses, for his work was only good when it was great; but he who could write pages of artless lines, with nothing but their sincerity to redeem them, fairly shook the stars when he wrote at his best. One turned the page of *The Adirondacks,* smiling at his ingenuousness, and caught one's breath at his sublimity,—for *Brahma* lay on the next page. So it was with the poet of *Merlin* and *Bacchus,* of *Uriel, Terminus* and *Give All to Love.* At best, he had an intensity like nothing else in American verse. Then, as the Emersonian stars shone forth, over a world peopled with gods and heroes, he seemed like the god of wealth himself, opening power in everything he touched; and one saw that he was one of his own immortals,—

> Olympian bards who sung
> Divine ideas below,
> Which always find us young
> And always keep us so.

Emerson's poems were *sui generis.* They were like Poe's in this, however remote from Poe in their lonely whiteness. Of Poe's melodious magic, Emerson had scarcely a touch. Of colour, he had none, or next to none, except when at moments, behind his verse, one seemed to catch a sort of polar splendour, as of an aurora borealis. There was something bleached and dry, in the best of this verse, like that of an age-old wisdom, exposed for thousands of years to sun and wind, and a strong, clear, bracing mountain air seemed to have blown upon it. Emerson's, at these moments, seemed

> the pen
> Which on the first day drew,
> Upon the tablets blue,
> The dancing Pleiads and eternal men.

CHAPTER XIV

CONCORD: 1840–1844

AT EMERSON'S house, from time to time, the so-called Transcendental Club assembled. Never a club, in the proper sense, never calling itself Transcendental, it was a group of men and women, interested in the new ideas, who met now and then to discuss them. The first meeting had taken place at Ripley's house in Boston, and Ripley, Dwight, Miss Peabody, Margaret Fuller, Alcott, Jones Very, Orestes Brownson, James Freeman Clarke and Theodore Parker were among the occasional members.

Sometimes it was called Hedge's Club, because Frederick Hedge, who lived in Bangor, where he preached to the Penobscot lumber-merchants, made sudden descents upon Boston that resulted in calls for a meeting. Hedge, with Sampson Reed, the Boston druggist, had introduced Swedenborg's writings to his friends. In his snow-bound study in the north, he smoked and read his German. He was preparing there his *Prose Writers of Germany*. Many of the members, like himself, like Emerson, Everett, Ripley, Dwight and Cranch, beginning their lives as ministers, were settling down as simple men of letters. Their vocations were fading out like daguerreotypes.* Others, ceasing to be Unitarians, had become

---

* This was a general symptom of the time. "When I lived in the West, there came a phrenologist to the town, and examining the heads of all the clergymen in the place, found us all deficient in the organ of reverence. More than that, we all admitted that the fact was so; that we were not, any of us, specially gifted with natural piety or love of worship. Then he said, 'You have all mistaken your calling. You ought not to be ministers.'" —James Freeman Clarke, *Self-Culture.*

the same thing without the name. But James Freeman
Clarke and Theodore Parker, whatever their doubts or
deficiencies, were never to abandon the priestly calling.
Clarke's *Self-Culture,* written years later, was a characteristic expression of the West Street circle. His *Ten
Great Religions,* a standard book, also published after
the Civil War, was an example of the comparative
method that Agassiz had popularized in Cambridge. Another warrior of the pulpit who came to meetings of the
club was the hallelujah Methodist, Father Taylor. This
was the scarred old prophet who walked his quarter-deck
at the Seamen's Chapel, where the gay blue flag flew from
the roof,—"bounding like a roe over the hills of spices."
The greatest natural orator in Boston, who had adopted
all the sons of the ocean, the pleading, grieving searcher
of souls, so tender and so volcanic, whose rebukes were
like broadsides from a frigate, he was a master of unconscious style. Everyone flocked to hear him, Webster and
Channing, Dickens, Jenny Lind; for, although, as he said,
he sometimes lost his nominative case, he was always on
the way to glory.*

Father Taylor was ready for any discussion of the
lukewarm spirit of the day. This, in its hundred aspects,
was the leading topic at the club: the American genius,
the causes that hindered its growth, the indifferentism at
Harvard and the like. But the talk was often wire-drawn
and misty. What was the True, the Beautiful, the Good?
What was the Highest Aim? What could be done with
an artist who was not an artist? Could sculpture express
as well as painting the notion of immortality? Emerson
found it rather unrewarding. One did not learn to use
one's tongue in a lonely country parsonage, and the mental hinges of some of the members fairly creaked with

---

* "I have never heard but one essentially perfect orator," Walt Whitman said, referring to Father Taylor. He and his preaching are reproduced
in Father Mapple's sermon in Melville's *Moby Dick.*

rust. Not by words like these could one captivate the
great American Lilliput, great in land and resources, in
coal and corn, but all a village littleness, as Emerson
thought. Most of the members were better at writing
than talking, though this was far from true of Theodore
Parker. If there was any man in the Boston pulpit,—for
Parker had begun to preach in Boston,—who added
cubits to the Lilliputians, it was this poet-preacher, reformer, scholar, who found fifty hours a week to spare
for other than parish work.

It was for Parker's essays on manual labour, on Phari-
saism, on German thought that readers bought *The Dial,*
the new review with the lilac covers. This was the mouthpiece of the West Street circle, a product of Miss
Peabody's shop, and Margaret Fuller was the editor.*
Dr. Channing was so excited when he heard the news
about *The Dial* that he lay awake for three nights. He
rejoiced in all these signs of life that represented reforms
on his reform; and in fact *The Dial* was a gallant venture. It rallied the younger poets and writers and gave
them an adequate focus, as the *North American Review*
had rallied the historical students and critics. Margaret,
—for so she was called, as people said Bettina or
Corinne,—was in her element as the guiding spirit; for
the new illuminati were all her friends and she had correspondents all over New England, younger men and
girls, aspiring students, lovers of Goethe and Schiller,
most of them neophytes and shy beginners. They felt that
Margaret carried a hazel twig, for she seemed to divine
their hidden springs. They spread their portfolios out
before her. Had some young man, who wished to write,
watched Stearns Wheeler at the Athenæum transcribing
the magical chapters of *Sartor Resartus?* Margaret had

---

* The editor's salary, which was never paid, was $200 a year. The
number of subscribers never exceeded three hundred. Miss Peabody's later
venture, *Æsthetic Papers,* which had only fifty subscribers, was discontinued after the first number.

seen the young man watching. She knew he had something to say for *The Dial;* and Wheeler, who had gone to Heidelberg, was glad to send her letters on German affairs. She appealed to Emerson, Alcott, Theodore Parker, Hawthorne, Cranch and Newcomb. Dwight contributed essays on music, others on archæology, Boccaccio, Shelley, notes on architecture, travel-sketches, voyages to Jamaica and Porto Rico. There were essayists of a single essay, poets of a single poem, sometimes composed at Brook Farm, where the poet plucked weeds to the rhythms of Keats and Browning. Some of the poems were obscure, for Transcendentalism had ways of its own. Others suggested Mary and her lamb. Ellen Sturgis Hooper wrote:

> I slept and dreamed that life was beauty,
> I woke and found that life was duty,—

lines that later readers recalled as embroidered on their grandmothers' pillow-shams. Little remained of *The Dial* that pleased these readers, for where it was not too simple it was often vague. Much of it was green and immature. But it stood for a moment of history. It even stood for certain frames of mind, certain ideas and convictions that were to mark Americans perhaps forever.

Meanwhile, Bronson Alcott had settled in Concord. If the world was not ready for him, be it so. It was no mean subterfuge, no ignoble surrender. He trusted in the majesty of goodness and called no man master. What did Bacon say?—"Overt and apparent virtues bring forth praise, but there be secret virtues that bring forth fortune." These were the virtues that they knew in Concord, —"certain deliveries of a man's self" that have no name or fame. Alcott was not to be embittered if the lottery went against him. A blank was as good as a prize, if one

had the equanimity to take it without whimpering or discontent.

It was true, he had no material resources, which made
it hard for his wife and the little Alcotts. The Emersons
suggested that the Alcotts should live with them, forming
a double household, even as Fichte planned to live with
the brothers Schlegel. But the wives of the brothers
Schlegel had not been congenial. Would the wives of the
Concord philosophers have been more so? The Alcotts,
at least, had plenty of apples; and a basket of pearmains
or golden russets, standing on his table, was almost all
that a sage could ask for. Snatch as one might wildness
from the woods, shrewdness from cities, compliments
from courts, one best betook oneself, for sovereign sense,
for subtlety of thought and the joy of colour, for the
graces of diction and behaviour,—

> Where on all sides the apples scattered lie,
> Each under its tree.

And, to fill the little mouths of the Alcott household, to
provide their bread and potatoes, their boiled rice and
grated cheese, Alcott resorted to the spade and saw. He
worked for his neighbours by the day, delved like any
farm-hand, chopped their wood. Wise and friendly eyes
looked on. There was something emblematic in these
labours. They suggested the annual ploughing of the
Emperor of China, and Dr. Channing, who had longed to
witness the union of labour and culture, remarked that
Alcott at the chopping-block was the most inspiring object in Massachusetts. As for Mrs. Alcott, after a good
talk and a crying spell she recovered her usual cheerfulness. Her husband's tatters, she said, were the rags of
righteousness, and there were others in a sadder plight.
Her cousins, who came for a visit, were obliged to bring
their own tea and pepper; but, as soon as the Alcotts

could count on their rice and turnips, they cut their meals down to two a day to provide for the neighbour with the drunken husband. There were those who laughed at Alcott. They said that his intemperate love of water made his mind hazy and cloudy. If he had eaten a little meat or fish, it might have had more marrow and substance. But Emerson, who knew his foibles well, loved him for his copious peacefulness and for the mountain landscape of his mind, with its darting lights and shadows.

He was preordained for the philosophic life, a life which, hospitably taken, was a very simple affair. What did he ask for his wealth and estate? A fireside and a spring, a stream to stir one's blood in the morning, the "frequent cold water" of Agathias, a web of cloth, friends and books, a chosen task, health and peace of mind. For thought, the study; for metaphors, a walk; hills for ideas; for force, a glimpse of the ocean, and over and through all the changing seasons, surcharging mind and body, rendering them primitive and elemental. Fields, streams, groves and country houses, rustic recreations, farmers to talk withal, whose wits were level with the world they worked in. Woodlots, the pleasing homestead, forest paths to foster meditation, alleys and graceful gates opening into a wood. Trees of ancient standing, vines like firm friends and royal neighbours. Orchards of Academe, suggesting the ripest learning of accomplished Greece. A garden, first of all.

> Who loves a garden still his Eden keeps,
> Perennial pleasures plants, and wholesome harvests reaps.

An occupation friendly to every virtue, the freest from covetousness and debasing cares. For the rest, a solar diet. Let the groundlings laugh as they might, they had not heard the word of the Samian sage, "A cheerful and a good heart will have a care for his meat and drink;"

and who knew better than Pythagoras how to preserve
one's powers of divination, one's purity and sweetness of
disposition, one's grace of form and dignity of carriage?
Cherish the justice that animals claim at thy hands, nor
slaughter the cow and the sheep for thy food or profit.
Shun the succulent flesh that beclouds the soul. Preserve
thy taste for wisdom and elegant studies. Good humour,
flowing spirits, a sprightly wit, and diffidence as the
flower of the rest,—these were the virtues of the Orphic
life, nourished by fair water and fragrant fruit, by grains,
next in the scale, and medicinal herbs, and roots as a last
resort. Nor should one forget the loyal lettuce, by choosing which for a name one of the great families of ancient
Rome raised itself to nobility.

The candid Alcott almost wished at times,—pleased as
he was with Concord,—that he had lived in the days
when groves were temples, when sylvan priests and chaste
philosophers, clad in robes of linen, wise in the pastoral
arts, plucked their learning from the golden bough or
sauntered in the Grecian portico. Towards what was
civilization tending? Had it improved upon the state of
things described by the rural poets, Virgil, the sweet
bucolic, the friend of every honest husbandman, Herrick,
Izaak Walton? Were not the fading customs of the Yankee forbears, generous, hearty, pious, better, a hundred
times, than these modern ways? What was to be the end
of all this pother about steam-boats and telegraphs and
railroads?—inventions that ought to be dropped or made
short work of, as a squirrel dispatches a nut, that the
intellect might be won to worthier occupations. For himself, he proposed to live as if the golden age had come
again, or, rather, as if it had never ceased to be. Let
other men follow other patterns, the English gentleman
or the Roman statesman. His was another model, better
drawn by Iamblicus than Plutarch. Virgilian Concord afforded a setting for it.

It was true, he had done his best, with ill success, to fabricate a more extensive Eden, the colony at Harvard village, Fruitlands. Cheering news had come to him from England, as he toiled away at the saw and the scythe. His educational theories, abhorred in Boston, had found supporters in that older world. A school had been established in his honour, Alcott House, near London. The masters had invited him for a visit, and Emerson had gladly filled his pocket with a purse of golden sovereigns. But what could anyone expect of England, choked as it was with smoke and cynicism? The school had died in its cradle; and Emerson's friend, Carlyle, had behaved like an angry peasant in the presence of the man of herbs and onions. Alcott, with potatoes for his breakfast, mixed his strawberries with them, till the juices ran together on his plate. The sage of Chelsea dropped his knife and fork and stormed about the table in disgust. Alcott, blithe as ever, had brought the "English mystics" home. One of them, Charles Lane, had a little money, enough to buy the land at Harvard village, and he brought his library with him, in all a thousand volumes, a notable collection of mystics and poets, Pindar, Alcæus, Quarles, Spinoza, Behmen. They planted their Eden with high hopes, to restore the Orphic life in its pristine beauty. Austerity was to be the note of Fruitlands, though not without a touch of continent mirth. Persons fit and few, twelve at the outset. At early dawn, the silent reveille. Libations, baths, morning walks alone, music,—for Lane had brought his violin,—melodies to subdue the passions, anger, despondency, complaint, dancing of a composed and Doric order, to pacify distempers of the soul, rural rites, repasts of native grains, water, herbs and fruit, to the end of edifying the healthy body. Labour, attractive labour, after the fashion of the *Works and Days,* with the spade and the glistening sickle. For raiment, canvas shoes and linen tunics. Conversation of an interior kind.

A life that knew no indurating toils, but such as Adam's family might have known, with a little advanced instruction.

Seven beautiful months, of mingled leisure, labour, recreation,—the whole of a grasshopper's lifetime, as the plodding ants made haste to say. For ants and busybodies have no love for these green isles in the sea of platitude. Then the December blasts swept through the paradise lost. Charles Lane took refuge with the Shakers. Alcott turned his face to the wall. For three days he refused to eat; then he arose, new-born, and went back to Concord. Was he going to waste his life, that fine essence housed in the handsome dust? He who possessed the richest gift of heaven, the power of contemplating eternal things? And the joys of earth as well,—the names of the herbs, for instance, that so refreshed him, mint, fennel, sweet-cicely, celandine, dill, caraway, lavender, thyme? He could make poverty interesting, with Mrs. Alcott's highly skilled assistance. His journal was a resource. For income, he could count on Conversations, at Emerson's house, later perhaps in Boston. For ennobling and refining the manners and senses, there was no discipline to be compared with the Socratic dialectic, under the wise care of a thoughtful instructor. The dollars, few enough, were yet sufficient to enable him to refuse to pay his taxes,— $1.50 a year,—to a government that protected slavery and was plainly misbehaving on the Mexican border. Alcott was overseeing the children's lessons when Sam Staples, the constable, his neighbour, regretfully came to say that he would have to carry him off to jail. "Very well, Samuel," said Alcott, "if you will wait a moment till Mrs. Alcott can put some food in a basket." The prison fare was too rich for him. Mrs. Alcott brought the basket, and down they walked slowly to the jail. At the door the matron met them and said she was very sorry but Mr. Alcott's cell was not made up yet. "Very well,

Samuel," said the sage. "I will go back and resume the children's lessons, and when you want me you can come for me." In the meantime, Squire Hoar paid the taxes, with no regard for principle whatsoever.

One might have supposed that in Concord the philosophic life would be understood. But, no, these Roman fellow-citizens were as hard-headed as the other Yankees. They smiled at Cranch's drawing of the indolent magus, lying on the sofa, with a copy of *The Dial* on the floor, and his wife sitting beside him, blacking his boots. But suppose they had seen Alcott,—who did not wear boots but canvas sandals,—on the steps of the Boston Court-house, when the mob attempted to seize Anthony Burns. There he stood, at ease, cane in hand, calm as Plato in his portico, another Grey Champion, come from nowhere, to vindicate the honour of the State. No one, indeed, denied his courage, he who had been the first, with Samuel May, to shake the hand of Garrison, lodged for the night in the jail in Leverett Street, with the marks of the rope about his neck. And there were Greeks in Concord along with the Romans, who, for the rest, prized the antique virtues. For one, besides Emerson, there was Hawthorne, who had rented the old Manse from the Ripley family,—although Hawthorne had the darker temperament which Alcott regarded with suspicion. Alcott had a passion for the blond complexion worthy of those who, in times to come, were to preach the mystical virtues of the Nordic race. Blue eyes and fair hair, he thought, were signs of the angelic type, determined in a former state of existence, while the dark eye and the swarthy face betokened the demonic, a remnant of the brute in human nature. But Hawthorne, who had married his Sophia, was obviously, by disposition, friendly, the helpless victim of his twilight mood, with a tender and hesitant voice: and Alcott soon forgave his dusky air. He, too, had come to Concord by a natural attraction that seemed to reside in the tranquil atmosphere. He was like the wise man of Plato, who resolves to stand aside under a wall, shielded from the wind and storms of dust, and keep still and mind his own business.

He, too, had his Eden at the Manse, under the silvery mosses, where he was writing—living as he wrote—*The New Adam and Eve.* Sophia, with her ever-busy paint-brush, had worked a miracle there. The dim, dusty, dismal priestly dwelling had vanished at her touch, under the yellow-papered walls, behind the bronze jar filled with ferns, the gift of Margaret Fuller, the vases of dewy rose-buds, the dishes of golden apples and purple grapes, the floods of morning sunlight. At night, in the soft rays of the hanging lamp, the lovers read their Shakespeare or gave each other lessons in German; or, if the evening was mild, ran races up and down the drive, in the light of the moon streaming through the ash-trees. They were up at sunrise to watch the dawn. Then Sophia painted for an hour or two. She decorated the beds and chairs with outlines after Flaxman,—Endymion, Venus rising from the sea,—while Hawthorne groaned in his study. They dined on bread and milk, with a little fruit, and Sophia danced beside the music-box.

Now and again, Sophia went away, to spend a few days with the Peabody household, and Hawthorne gladly took the vow of silence. He trudged through the snow and slush, with his rolling sailor's gait, never speaking a word to man or dog, perhaps on his way to the village reading-room. Sometimes the snow on the drive was untrodden for weeks by any foot but his. He read the tales of Tieck, Voltaire for the sceptical note, the dash of salt one's fancy had to have, in a world so full of reformers, Rabelais for a little well-fed humour. The ghosts had followed in Hawthorne's wake and sometimes forced themselves on his attention. He had no use for these apparitions, but they were a part of his aura, provided for the pleasure of his guests. It was Mrs. George Hillard, not himself, who, as they sat together on a Sunday morning, felt the touch on her shoulder, and Hillard who heard the rustle of the silken robe passing through the room. He was the ghost himself, at times. More than one caller at the Manse, charmed by the gay Sophia, saw him gliding swiftly through the entry, with his hat over his eyes. He was not unwilling to be thought uncanny. It served him as a shield and palisade.

As he went for his early swim across the meadow, beyond the flags and rushes, or strolled in the winding wood-paths, or worked among the crook-necks in the garden, admiring their graceful shapes, happy visions coursed with airy tongues through his enchanted brain. The summer days were full of bright conceptions, tinged and streaked with darker hues, gleaming in his mind like the butterflies that danced in the air about him. He was writing stories of a larger sweep than his earlier tales and sketches, and some of them were equally sombre, filled with a pervasive sense of evil, the snake that lurked even in Concord gardens. The more he had seen of re-formers, and saw them still, drifting about the village, moths attracted by the Concord Pharos, the Emersonian beacon, the more aware he was of the pestilent serpent that ate the very eggs of Reform itself. The human heart,—there was the sphere wherein the original wrong subsisted of which the crime and misery of the world were merely outward types. Reform from within, in Goethe's sense: that was the only kind he understood. Was not any plan, ignoring this, destined to prove a chimera, a masquerade, like Brook Farm itself, dissolving before one's eyes like a summer cloud? Not that he was hostile to the reformers. He had joined the Brook Farmers in all good faith. He had worked at the farm in a practical way. Hawthorne was not the man who hoed up the corn and carefully formed the hills about the burdocks. It was another member,—no doubt, some executive genius,—who milked with one hand, while he held the cow's tail with the other. Hawthorne had the common sense that men of imagination usually have, when they deal with these affairs of Caesar. He had toiled like a dragon, as Ripley said, until he had begun to ask himself what part in his own economy these feats of the barn and dung-heap represented. He had not become a vulgar sceptic. He did not think that what the socialists wished was to change the ocean into lemonade. But he had brooded, brooded, sitting by himself in the hall of the Hive, after the day's work, holding a book before him, while the young people gossipped in the moonlight. He had been meditating at the picnics, under the maple-trees, watching the masques of Comus. There was a worm in the rose-bud of life, a grub, unseen by the others, at the root of the tree, as at the roots of all these touching endeavours to perfect the social man. If the human heart were purified, then, and then alone, the evil shapes that haunted the outer sphere, and seemed almost the only realities, would vanish. They would vanish of their own accord.

There was the poet's function. Who but he could reach the heart? His task was to rouse the imagination, creating magnetic images of the nobler world in which his own imagination dwelt. As for the world that lay without, the system against which the reformers protested, what could it mean to Hawthorne? No one had less faith than he in the gods that his countrymen had set up for worship. In *The Hall of Fantasy,* for instance, he ridiculed the god of machines. He pictured a great world's fair where all the new machines were shown, one for distilling heat from moonshine, one for condensing mist into building granite, one for transforming the sunset clouds into dyes for women's dresses. Hawthorne was not deceived by Feathertop, the citizen his countrymen admired, the solid

man of politics and business, living in good repute, never
seeing himself, never seen, as what he was, a scarecrow.
Hawthorne's were the eyes that satirized, in *The Procession of Life,* the shallowness and falseness of the clas-
sifications imposed on men by society, the artificiality of
the badges the world considers genuine characteristics
and that hide the true relations of human souls. No one
knew better than he the failure of a man like Everett
who, misled by vanity, acclaimed by all, had abandoned
the scholar's vocation in order to become an empty name
that brawling parties bandied to and fro. No one said
more clearly that the individual seizing of land and gold,
of benefits that all enjoy and all should have their share
in, was a trait of undeveloped intelligence. No one was
more ready than he to rid the world of its trumpery. This
was the point of his tale, *Earth's Holocaust,* retold a dozen
times by H. G. Wells. The Titan of Innovation was
Hawthorne's invention. The earth groaned under its burden of rubbish, and the titan set a match to the pile. He
threw into the bonfire all the old title-deeds, the royal
crowns and robes, the bonnets and faded finery, the guns
and battle-flags, the headsman's axe, the guillotine, the
gallows, even the marriage-certificates and the Bibles,
certain that, after the holocaust was over, everything
would be found among the ashes that really deserved to
survive.

Hawthorne was ready for any change, in social customs, politics, modes of worship, trusting that better
systems might result. He had the American taste for
innovation that characterized the reformers themselves,
as he had the American habit of restlessly moving, wandering to and fro like the palmer-worm that knows no
single diet or abode. Old houses and antiquated customs
charmed his imagination, but he dwelt on the poisonous
influences that gathered about them. That towns should
be purified by fire every fifty years was one of his fixed

opinions; and who delighted more than he in the fresh paint that covered the walls of the Manse? But of what importance, after all, were Hawthorne's views and habits? He scarcely thought of the world as real, either to be seen or touched or lived in, or, for the rest, altered or improved. It was a film on the breast of Maya, the goddess of illusion. No plummet could ever sound the depths of Hawthorne's scepticism. He felt that, in so far as the world existed, it should wish not to exist. It should recline its vast head on the first convenient pillow and take an age-long nap. For himself, he was happy enough, living as if in eternity, happy as Drowne, who made the wooden image, in this brief season of excitement, which had been kindled by love.

The music-box at the Manse belonged to Thoreau, Henry David Thoreau, the pencil-maker, Emerson's *protégé*, who had gone to Staten Island for a visit, to tutor the children of Emerson's brother William. It was a gift of Margaret Fuller's brother to the youthful poet-naturalist who, as one of his friends said, was "getting up a nose like Emerson's." Hawthorne had skated with him on the river, wrapped in his long cloak, and marvelled at Thoreau's dithyrambic dances and Dionysian leaps over the ice, while Emerson pitched along in the weary rear. Hawthorne had bought from Thoreau the fisherman's dory, green with a border of blue, the "Musketaquid," in which Henry and his brother had spent a week on the Concord and Merrimac rivers. Thoreau had changed his name. Dr. Ripley had christened him David Henry, and he had reversed these appellations, after the Concord fashion. For Emerson had altered the name of his wife from Lydia to Lidian, Alcott had revised his native Alcox, and Hawthorne, years before, had inserted the w in his father's "Hathorne." This practice of the Concord authors symbolized their love of independence and, better still, their love of euphony; for

all these Concordians were Pythagoreans, and the followers of Pythagoras have a taste for pleasing and musical names.

The green dory, moored among the reeds, lent itself
to other excursions. Hawthorne loved to drift in the indolent river, watching the reflections in the water. They
were composed, like pictures, far more lovely than the
stark and upright landscape. The leaves of the over-
arching boughs attuned his thoughts with their quiet
sound. Sometimes he drifted further, on a little rowing
journey with Ellery Channing,—William Ellery Channing, the poet, another of the doctor's nephews,—who
dropped in at the Manse, now and then, with an armful
of novels and reviews. For Ellery Channing, too, had
come to Concord, drawn there by Emerson's presence.
He had married Ellen Fuller, Margaret's sister, and
taken the red cottage off the turnpike, on Ponkawtassett
Hill. Ellen had opened a school for little children, and
Ellery, half in earnest,—for he was "chiefly engaged in
doing nothing,"—made shift to cultivate his acre of land.
He preferred to smoke his pipe, read his seventeenth-
century folios, stroll with his dog and write an occasional
poem; for this racy talker, this lover of landscape-
painting, this woodsman second to none, this learned
farmer, who exchanged quotations in Greek while others
did the ploughing and the planting, had sworn that he
would never desert the Muse. He was a professional
poet or nothing, and he had contributed to *The Dial*
more than anyone else. Some of his poems, *The Wood-
man, The Swallow is Flying Over,* the *Epithalamium* of
later years, *The Field-bird's Nest, The Spider,* were
among the best of the Concord school. Light in touch,
natural and lucid, with passages that were worthy of
Cowper or Wordsworth, they were touched with magic
here and there. Everyone remembered Channing's line,—

If my barque sinks, 'tis to another sea.

The Lonely Road was a fine poem. Native wood-notes wild, in every sense, these poems were the despair of Channing's friends, who felt that if he had only taken pains he might have been able to write immortal verses. Emerson edited his first collection, as he had edited Jones Very's sonnets. Channing was to be known in later years not so much for his poems as for a prose volume of the rarest charm, *Thoreau, the Poet-Naturalist*.* He had struck up a friendship with Thoreau, the best Greek scholar in Concord, and had soon become his only crony. He made himself agreeable to Hawthorne.

This Ellery Channing was a moody soul, erratic as the sky in early spring, gay as a troubadour, full of salty gossip, then suddenly reserved and enigmatic. He had always been a problem, and was to be, during the sixty years he lived in Concord, with various "disappearances," outliving all the other Concord worthies. A typical Boston eccentric, quite unlike the usual crooked stick one saw in the village streets, he was perverse and unstable enough. He was a thorn in the side of the Channing clan. He had refused to take his degree at Harvard and had wandered off to the West. He lived in a log hut, which he had built, in northern Illinois, on the prairie. He had studied law and flitted East again and flitted back again to Cincinnati, where he had met and married Ellen Fuller. Margaret was much disturbed, for she had little hope that her sister would ever be happy. Why had he come to Concord? He laughed at the "gigmanity" of Boston, but he laughed still more at the rustic village ways. He would rather have settled, he said, on the icy peak of Mount Ararat. He would have liked a villa in the Euganean Hills, or in Florence, or in Malaga or Cuba. He swore at the cook and damned the butcher. He fell into

* Properly to be read in the final edition, 1902.

dark rages that lasted for days. He passed one on the street with a stony look. Nobody dared to question him; one had to deal with him at arm's length. He seemed to take pleasure in hurting his friends. Then the sun would break, and Ellery nodded and smiled again, smoking away and joking as he smoked. He came and went like the summer clouds, professing not to know where he had been.

Ellery Channing and Hawthorne went fishing up the river, sometimes turning into the Assabet. There, in a silent cove, they drew the boat up under a leafy bower, kindled a fire with pine-cones and driftwood, spread their supper out on a moss-grown log and tired the sun with talking. For Hawthorne liked to expand at times and fly away on the wings of speculation, and Ellery's whimsical prattle broke over the stillness of the wood like eva-nescent spray.

CHAPTER XV

THOREAU

IN EMERSON'S white house on the Boston turnpike, Henry Thoreau had taken up his quarters. He occupied the room at the head of the stairs, a little room, but he was a little man: his nose and his thoughts were the biggest things about him. Emerson, and especially Emerson's children, had formed a warm affection for their difficult Henry, difficult, that is, for the rest of Concord but a treasure for the household of a sage. He was short, lean, frail, although nobody guessed it, he was so tough and muscular, with a meagre chest, long arms falling from the collar-bone, a workman's hands and feet, a huge Emersonian beak, rather like Julius Caesar's, bright blue eyes and flaxen hair. He walked with the swinging stride of an old campaigner. His manners were of the homespun sort, different indeed from Emerson's. But, after the first encounter, one perceived that, if Henry Thoreau was a thorn-bush, he was the kind that bears the fragrant flowers.

He was the son of the pencil-maker, who had his little house and shop on Main Street: "J. Thoreau and Sons." The Thoreaus were a mercantile family of small pretensions who had seen better days. They were well-connected in the Channel Islands, where the French Thoreaus were prosperous wine-merchants. Their maternal forbears, the Scottish Dunbars, had taken the royalist side in the Revolution. As a barefoot village boy, Henry had driven the turkeys and the cow to pasture, and Emerson had vaguely heard of him as a poor student at Harvard. He had written to President Quincy, suggesting Henry's name for a scholarship. Later, Henry walked in to Boston, eighteen miles from Concord, to hear Emerson speak, and walked home again after the lecture. Emerson, touched by this, was still more touched when, after one of his Concord lectures, his sister-in-law, who was boarding with Mrs. Thoreau, said to him, "Henry Thoreau has a thought very like that in his journal." A friendship had soon sprung up between them, and when, one day, the Emersons went on a picnic, to the Cliffs on the Concord river, they asked Henry to join them and bring his flute. The village people looked askance at him because he was so pugnacious. He had queer ideas about teaching school, refusing to use the ferule; for with children and simple folk he was always gentle. With others, he was obstinate and harsh. He liked to administer doses of moral quinine, and he never thought of sugaring his pills. He had withdrawn from Dr. Ripley's church with a thesis more defiant than Martin Luther's. He liked to speak of a cold spot as "sultry," and he had a way of calling the woods "domestic." But at boating and camping he was a master-woodsman, skilled as Ulysses, shrewd as any fox. The redskins had forgotten the arts he knew. Arrowheads and Indian fireplaces sprang from the ground when he touched it. He charmed the snakes and fishes. Wild birds perched on his shoulder. His fingers seemed to have more wisdom in them than many a scholar's head.

This young Briareus of the hundred hands was something more than Emerson's factotum. There was nothing he could not do in the matter of painting and papering, building walls, repairing chicken-houses, pruning and grafting fruit-trees, surveying, tinkering, gardening. But these were trifles in his bag of tricks, useful to pay his way in the world and justify his creed of self-reliance. He was a master of other arts that Emerson also knew, and a scholar of unusual distinction; and he wished to be a philosopher, not a mere thinker of subtle thoughts but one who, loving wisdom, lived a life that was simple, magnanimous, free. In fact, he recalled those ancient sages who, when an enemy took the town, walked out of the gate empty-handed, without a care for the morrow. Why should one be burdened with impedimenta? Henry liked the soldier's life, always on the stretch and always ready for a battle. Each of his mornings brought its strenuous sortie. He lived "for to admire and for to see." He had spoken his mind in his college themes about the "blind and unmanly love of wealth" that actuated most of his fellow-beings. The order of things, he said, should be reversed. The seventh should be man's day of toil, wherein to earn his living by the sweat of his brow; he should keep the rest of the week for his joy and wonder.

These views delighted Emerson. In fact, the two agreed on so many subjects, always with an edge of difference, that one might well have supposed the relation between them was that of master and pupil. Emerson was fourteen years the elder; and it was true that Henry had acquired some of his traits and mannerisms: his handwriting, his voice, even his nose seemed to have gone to school to Emerson. There was something contagious in Emerson's aura; everyone was affected by it, nobody seemed able to resist it. Alcott was more than a little Emersonized; and as for Ellery Channing, what did the lady say who heard him lecture?—that his gait, his inflections, the very turn of his eyebrow were Emerson to the life. Henry Thoreau had felt this influence, as he had felt the influence of Carlyle. He had his own form, none the less. Emerson and he had grown in Concord, as two flowers grow in a common bed, one of them larger and more luxuriant, the other with a much more pungent odour; but they stood in different corners of the bed, with an ample space between them, so that the breeze could blow upon each of them freely. They were different enough in temperament, as in their personalities; and Henry phrased their common points of view with a sort of acidulous accent that was never heard on Emerson's lips.

They were of one mind in a dozen matters, not least in regard to the reformers. "As for these communities," said Henry, expressing their joint opinion, "I had rather keep bachelor's hall in hell than go to board in heaven." Much as he liked Alcott, the "best-natured man" he had ever met,—"the rats and mice make their nests in him,"— he turned up his nose at Fruitlands as well as at Brook Farm. He meant to bake his own bread in heaven, and wash his own clothes there. And suppose, he said, these grievances do exist? So do you and I. And the universal soul prefers the man who sets his own house in order first. A foul thing, this "doing good," observed the con- temptuous Henry, instead of looking after one's own life, which ought to be one's business, taking care to flourish, and taste and smell sweet, refreshing all mankind. He had had encounters with reformers that filled him with abhorrence. They would not keep their distance. They tried to cover him with a slimy kindness that fairly took the starch out of his clothes. These "lovers" of their kind were almost more injurious to their kind than the feeble souls that met in drawing-rooms, fabulating and paddling in the social slush, and going to their beds unashamed, to take on a new layer of sloth.

Henry had plenty of acid in his composition. He had taken a few suggestions from Zeno the Stoic,—for one, that he had two ears and a single mouth, in order to hear more and speak less,—as Alcott had followed Pythagoras and Emerson, largely, Plato. Emerson, older and riper, with a fund of sunny benevolence, the fruit of a happier culture and a fortunate bringing-up,—Emerson deplored this hedgehog's posture, the spikes, the spines, the quills

that made his Henry a John Quincy Adams of the village.
But time would certainly soothe and rectify him. Meanwhile, he was a living illustration of all his own ideas, endowed with hands and feet. Henry described himself, or
his hope for himself,—"stuttering, blundering clodhop-
per" that he said he was,—in words that seemed to have
their truth already. He was prepared for a glorious life;
he had laid out an avenue through his head, eight rods
wide; he had got the world,—much more, the flesh and
the devil,—as it were by the nape of the neck, and held
it under the tide of its own events, and let it go down
stream like a dead dog, till he heard the hollow chambers
of silence stretching away on every side and his own soul
expanded and filled them. He could not help taunting his
fellow-Yankees. Seek first the kingdom of heaven! Lay
not up for yourselves treasures on earth! What does it
profit a man! Think of this, Yankees, think twice, ye who
drone these words on the Sabbath day and spend the
other six denying them! "Doing a good business!"—
words more profane than any oath, words of death and
sin. The children should not be allowed to hear them. If
most of the merchants had not failed, and most of the
banks as well, Henry's faith in the laws of the world
would have been sadly staggered; for what was the
sweetest sight his eyes could see but a man who was
really fulfilling the ends of his being?—maintaining himself, as he could, if he wished to do so, paying the price
in terms of simplification, by a few hours a day at manual
labour. Was he a little impatient and a little narrow? If
there was anything wrong with his angle of vision, there
would always be plenty of others to correct it. For himself, he wished to live deep. He wished to suck out all
the marrow of life, to cut a broad swath and shave close,
to put to rout all that was not living. If the days and the
nights were such that he greeted them with joy, if life
emitted a fragrance like herbs and flowers, if it was more

elastic and more starry, that was his success and all he asked for.

No use to pretend that, for Emerson, he was a balm, however much a blessing. No, but he was medicinal,—as a gadfly, good; as a goad for an indolent writer, who felt that he ought to dig in his own garden, Henry was even better. As a teacher of natural history, for a lover of nature who, as a matter of fact, scarcely knew a robin from a crow, Henry was better still. Best of all, as a fellow-seeker of wisdom and a man of impeccable taste, competent to help him with *The Dial,* which Margaret Fuller could not wrestle with and had asked her Concord friends to carry on. Henry was a capital editor. He had a sharp eye for the faults of *The Dial,* the phrases,— well one knew them,—that had to be pulled open, as one opens the petals of a flower that cannot open itself. The style of *The Dial* annoyed him as much as the weak and flowing periods of the politicians. He liked to see a sentence run clear through to the end, as deep and fertile as a well-drawn furrow. If only writers lived more earnest lives, their minds would pass over the ground like ploughs, pressed down to the beam, like rollers that were loaded, not hollow and wooden, driving in the seed to germinate. It was the height of art, in his opinion, that, on the first perusal, plain common sense should appear,—a law that gave short shrift to much of *The Dial;* truth on the second perusal, beauty on the third. One had to pay for beauty.

The two friends had much in common, in spite of all their differences. Emerson had never built a boat, nor had he shared the Argonautic life that Henry had enjoyed with his brother John,—the John who had built Emerson's bluebird-box,—rounding the capes and sailing before the wind on the Concord and Merrimac rivers, with their cotton tents and buffalo-skins, bringing back their unexpected news of the foreign folk who lived on the

upper reaches. Nor had he roamed over the moors and
meadows, with the fishing-rod and gun that Henry loved,
before he perceived that it was not for him, as a follower of the Brahmins, to "effect the transmigration of a
woodchuck." He was not at home in the wilderness. He
could never have whittled a wooden spoon, better than
the factories made, to eat his rice with. He could not
make a fork from an alder-twig, or a Wedgwood plate
out of a strip of birch-bark. Nor, in the matter of teaching school, had he known such good fortune as Henry,
who had kept the Concord Academy with his brother
John, profiting by Bronson Alcott's methods, taking the
children walking, rowing, swimming. But they both liked
to lecture at the Lyceum, where Henry acted as secretary,
and every citizen who had something to say was expected
to give his lecture. Moreover, they loved the same authors. Henry had a preference of his own for works of a
local kind, ancient gazetteers, State and county histories,
histories of New England towns, farmers' almanacs,
agricultural pamphlets, out-of-the-way books on birds and
flowers, chronicles of old explorers, the Jesuit Relations,
reports on Indian tribes. His mind bristled with antiquarian lore. But when it came to Froissart's bold beauty
or Bacon's bolder terseness, to the voyages of Drake and
Purchas, to Raleigh and the earlier English poets, there
they were both at home. Nothing had attracted Emerson
more than Henry's manifest knowledge of Drayton,
Daniel, the Fletchers, Cowley, Donne, poets, little known
in the eighteen-forties, whose naturalness and vigour
Emerson cherished, and who, as Henry said, were as verdurous as evergreen and flowers, rooted in fact and experience, unlike so many florid modern poets who had
the tints of flowers without their sap.

They agreed that in literature only the wild was attractive, and that dullness was only another name for
tameness,—the wildness of the Iliad or of *Hamlet,* with

something fresh and primitive about it, something ambrosial and fertile. All the Greek poets had this trait, wild in their elegance, wild in their conciseness. Henry had studied Greek with Jones Very, for a time his tutor at Harvard, as he had studied German with Orestes Brownson, with whom he had spent a winter in a Boston suburb, tutoring Brownson's sons. Greek was his second language. He had translated *Prometheus Bound* and *The Seven against Thebes,* with many pieces of the minor poets, Anacreon, Simonides, ivory gems of an ethereal beauty like that of summer evenings. One could perceive them only with the flower of the mind. How still and serene life seemed amid these classical studies! Often, walking along the railway tracks, he listened to the harp of the telegraph-wires, putting his ear to the posts. Every pore of the wood was filled with music, and he could find a name for every strain, every swell and change or inflection of tone in one of the Greek poets. Often he heard Mimnermus, often Menander. Emerson had the same impressions when he listened to his ice-harp at Walden; and Henry, as much as Emerson, delighted in the Oriental scriptures, which he read in the French and German versions. The Bible had lost its bloom for both; but the Vedas, the Bhagavad-Gita came to Henry like desert winds, blown from some Eastern summit. They fell on him like the light of the moon when the stars are out, in the furthest reaches of the sky,—free from particulars, simple, universal, uttered with a morning prescience in the dawn of time. What rhythms, what a tidal flow! Beside these ancient Asiatic books, with their truths like fossil truths, clean and dry, true without reference to persons, true as the truths of science, the literatures of the European countries seemed to him partial and clannish, presumptuous in speaking for the world when they spoke only for corners of it. Henry liked to remember that the barnyard cock was originally, the wild Indian pheasant, such as the poets of the Upanishads knew.

As they worked over *The Dial,* Emerson, with Henry's concurrence, took pains to include some of these Eastern writings. Emerson chose a group of passages which he called *Ethnical Scriptures.* Henry, who had translated for his own amusement *The Transmigration of the Seven Brahmins,* selected some of the Laws of Manu. Emerson also insisted on printing some of Henry's own writings, which Margaret Fuller had had doubts about. Henry was indifferent to publication. The only audience he really cared for was his own taste and judgment. He wished to write well, to warrant every statement and each remark, till the earth seemed to rest on its axle in order to back it up. Hold the bow tight! was his motto. He longed to write sentences that would lie like boulders on the page, as durable as Roman aqueducts. Sentences kinked and knotted into something hard and significant, which one might swallow like diamonds, without digesting. Sentences nervous and tough as the roots of the pine, like hardened thongs, the sinews of the deer. He wrote best when his knees were strong, when the juices of the fruits that he had eaten, ascending to the brain, gave him a heady force. Margaret Fuller had not liked *The Service,* his manual for the spiritual soldier, suggested by the talk about non-resistance of the mealier-mouthed reformers. But his essay, *The Natural History of Massachusetts,* was beyond cavil or praise. Into *The Dial* it went, with *A Winter Walk.* Henry revised and revised, until his page was a mass of blots and blackness.

Into *The Dial* went also some of his poems, the verses that he had ceased to write. These poems were of a home-spun kind, well-woven, but indifferently cut, like Henry's raiment, not intended to please. They were sound and scholarly doggerel, for the most part. The smoke obscured the flame, but now and then a jet rose out of the smoke, and Henry wrote a line or two that shivered its way up the spinal marrow. Sometimes the smoke itself, in a handful of lines, suggested by the Greek Anthology, suddenly turned to incense, and the incense became an Icarian bird, melting its pinions in its upward flight. *Smoke, Mist, Haze* were lyrics not to be forgotten. Nor could one forget *A Winter Scene,* not Greek but Anglo-Saxon,—

> The rabbit leaps,
> The mouse out-creeps,
> The flag out-peeps
> Beside the brook,—

or, for the iron strings, the lines called *Inspiration,*—

> If with light head erect I sing,—

to the end of the third stanza, or, if one insisted, to the end of the seventh, but not a syllable further. There spoke the poet who, for the rest, wrote his poetry in his prose journal, in blank-books bought on those rare occasions when he could find a book with clean white pages, not ruled, as most of them were, for records of dollars and cents. If his poems were often disjointed, like his prose, it was because of this habit of journalizing. He jotted down his paragraphs and verses, a thought or a stanza at a time, and waited for a cooler moment to patch them together,—a good way for epigrams, a good way for the gnomic style, but fatal for the poetry of feeling, and none too good for prose. He was a methodical journalizer, much more so than Emerson. He kept his notes as his father and his father's father, the old French merchant from the Channel Islands, had kept their business-ledgers. He had inherited their plodding habits, akin to the sod as he also was, partaking largely of its dull patience. He sometimes felt that he was in danger of living for his journal, instead of living in it for the gods, his regular correspondents, to whom he sent off daily bulletins. His journal was a calendar of the ebbs and flows of the soul. It was a beach on which the waves might cast their pearls and seaweed.

These were happy months for the seekers of Brahma, not to be repeated. From Emerson's house, in 1843, Henry went to Staten Island. Later, in 1848, when Emerson went abroad again, Henry installed himself for a second visit, as counsellor and helper of the household, in the little room at the head of the stairs. But, later still, a shadow fell on the glowing intercourse of the two crusaders. Through whose fault but Henry's? His journal teemed with innuendoes against the friend who "patronized" him. Emerson was too "grand" for him. Emerson belonged to the upper classes and wore their cloak and manners. He was attracted to Plato, but he would not have cared for Socrates, whose life and associations were too humble. Emerson would never have been seen trundling a wheelbarrow through the streets. He would have thought it out of character. Henry was a commoner, as he liked to say. He thought there was something devilish in manners, —and Emerson had had no right to praise him.* "One man lies in his words," Henry wrote, "and gets a bad reputation; another in his manners, and enjoys a good one." But what about Alcott's manners, so gracious and courtly, consisting with such artlessness of soul, such frank, open, unaffected goodness? Alcott had no reputation, surely. Was there nothing in beautiful manners but foppery, prudery, starch and affectation, with false pride overtopping all? Was the noble merely the genteel? Henry's notion of the art of living was not too comprehensive. Nor his notion of friendship, either, exacting all and giving back so little.

What he gave was solid. As for the rest, the less cared he. When people spoke of the social virtues, he asked

---

* "Praise begins when things are seen partially. We begin to praise when we begin to see that a thing needs our assistance."—Thoreau's *Journal*.

about the virtues of pigs in a litter, lying close together
to keep one another warm. As for friends, what were
they, for the most part? Bubbles on the water, flowing
together. Very few were ever as instructive as the silence
which they shattered with their talk. When it came to
sharing his walks, Henry was rather particular. Alcott
served for a stroll, but the real art of walking was beyond
him. He always wished to perch on the nearest stump.
Hawthorne was even more annoying. One led him to one's
loveliest swamp, and Hawthorne stood on the brink, disconsolate. "Let us get out of this dreadful hole," he said.
He never even noticed the naked viburnum rising above
the dwarf andromeda. Besides, he said that company was
a "damnable bore." After all deductions, Emerson was
still one's best companion, best but one, Henry's only
crony, the moody, witty, generous Ellery Channing, riding his whims like broomsticks, as naturally capricious as
a cow is brindled, tender and rough by turns, another
social antinomian, even a social outlaw, by his own desire.
He was always teasing Henry about his legs, double legs,
not cork but steel, which ought to be shown at the World's
Fair, he said; and he had a Rabelaisian streak and took
pains to shock the sober Henry. There were strange, cold
pockets in the air of his mind into which one swam unwittingly. One never knew where one stood with him. But
he was crammed with poetry that glittered through the
darkness of his reserve like gems in a mine revealed by
the gleams of a lantern, or flashed, in his happier moods,
like gems in the sunlight. Some of his moods, moreover,
were much like Henry's. He wished to be let alone. "If
you go to the post-office once," he said, "you are
damned."—"No," said Henry, "you are only damned if
you get a letter." For Ellery loved solitude. He would sit
on the Cliffs by the hour, among the lichens. Then, in the
dusk of evening, one saw him flitting past on noiseless
pinion, like the barred owl, as wise as unobserved.

Henry, to be sure, had other friends, with whom he exchanged a few words, perhaps on his way to look for mud-turtles in Heywood's luxuriant meadow. There was old Haines, the fisherman, for one, wearing his patched coat of many colours, who represented the Indian still, "Polyphemus" Goodwin, of dubious fame, the one-eyed sportsman of the Concord river, and the crooked old curmudgeon Ebby Hubbard, dressed in his blue frock. There were the musquash-hunters, poets of the wild, up and out early in the wet and cold, ready for any risk at the call of their muse. They were gods of the river and woods, with sparkling faces,—late from the House of Correction, as often as not,—with mystic bottles under their oilskin jackets. How good of George Melvin to follow his bent and not spend all his days in Sunday School! Henry thanked his stars for George Melvin and thought of him with gratitude as he fell asleep. The gawky, loose-hung Melvin, dragging his feet as he walked, who was such a trial to his mother, pleased Henry like an oak-tree on the hill-side. He was one tribe, and Henry was another; and they were not at war. Henry could not deny that hunting and fishing, in spite of his brahminic preferences, were as ancient and honourable trades as the sun and the winds pursue, coeval with the faculties of man. As for his friends, he had some who were wilder than Melvin, the breams, who nibbled from his fingers, while he stroked them gently and lifted them out of the river, the muskrat that emerged from the hole in the ice. The muskrat looked at Henry, and Henry looked at the muskrat, wondering what the muskrat thought of him,—safe, low, moderate thoughts, of course. Muskrats never got on stilts, like some of the Transcendentalists. Once he conversed with a woodchuck, three feet away, over a fence. They sat for half an hour, looking into each other's eyes, until they felt mesmeric influences at work over them both. Then Henry moved closer and spoke to the woodchuck,

in a quasi-forest lingo, a sort of sylvan baby-talk. The
woodchuck ceased to grit his teeth. Henry, with a little
stick, lifted up his paw and examined it; then he turned
the woodchuck over and studied him underneath. He had
a rather mild look. Henry spoke kindly to him and offered
him some checkerberry-leaves. The woodchuck was one
of the natives. His family had certainly lived in Concord
longer than the Emersons or even the Hoars.

For the sort of friends who never hurt one's feelings,
one did not have to look far. Sometimes, in the midst of a
gentle rain, Henry felt an influence about him that was
suddenly sweet and beneficent. Every sight and sound,
the very pattering of the drops, was filled with an unac-
countable friendliness. It was to seek this, and all it meant,
that he went for his daily walk, with note-book and spyglass in his pocket, and the hat with its lining gathered
in the middle to make a little shelf, a botany-box. He was
another Linnæus, setting out for Lapland, though he did
not wish to be a "naturalist." Looking at nature straight
in the eye was as fatal as to look at the head of Medusa.
The man of science always turned to stone. Henry wished
to look at nature sidewise, or to look through nature and
beyond it. Too many observations were dissipating. One
had to be the magnet, in the midst of all this dust and all
these filings. Sometimes he rose at two o'clock, for a walk
to the Cliffs, to wait there till sunrise, or to watch the fog
on the river. He loved those valleys in the fog in which
the trees appeared as if at the bottom of the sea. Sometimes he spent the whole of a moonlight night roaming
the lonely pastures, where the cattle were silently feeding,
to the croaking of the frogs, the intenser dream of the
crickets, the half-throttled note of a cuckoo flying over.
The bushes loomed, the potato-vines stood upright, the
corn grew apace. One's eyes were partially closed then;
the other senses took the lead. Every plant emitted its
odour, the swamp-pink in the meadow, the tansy in the

road. One caught the peculiar dry scent of the corn, which was just beginning to show its tassels. One heard the tinkling of rills one had never detected before. The moonlight over the village, as one stole into the street, seemed to bring antiquity back again. The church, with its fluted columns, reminded one of the Parthenon. The houses had a classical elegance.

Sometimes, even in the morning, usually sacred to reading and writing, the wind fairly blew him out of doors. The elements were so lively and active, and he felt so sympathetic with them, that he could not sit while the wind went by. His regular time was the afternoon, from two-thirty to five-thirty, the hour for a voyage to the Leaning Hemlocks, along the Assabet river, or perhaps to examine an ant-hill, nearer home. He had observed it the day before, with its little galleries, wide as a match, covered with the sluggish, crawling ants. In the early spring, the stalks and grasses, left from last year, were steeped in rain and snow, and all the brooks flowed with meadow-tea. Then came the May-days of the warm west wind, the dream-frog, leaping, willowy haze-days, when anything might happen and one thought that next year, perhaps, one might be a postman in Peru, or a South African planter, or a Greenland whaler, or a Canton merchant. Better still, a Robinson Crusoe on some far-off isle of the Pacific. Henry sometimes stood under a tree half a day at a time, in a drenching rain, prying with microscopic eyes into the swarming crevices of the bark, or studying the leaves at his feet, or the spreading fungi. He would watch for an hour a battle of ants, struggling on a chip, a black ant with two red adversaries, till the black ant severed the heads of the others, losing its own feelers and most of its legs,—a second Concord fight, no doubt with as just a cause. Or, catching sight of a fox, in some woodland clearing, he yielded to the instinct of the chase, tossed his head aloft and bounded away, snuffing

the air like a fox-hound, spurning the humanitarians and
the Brahmins. For he felt as wild, at times,—he who
preferred a vegetarian diet,—as if he lived on antelope-
marrow, devoured without benefit of fire.

The midsummer days came, when the yellow lilies
reigned in the river. The painted tortoises dropped from
the willow-stumps as he walked over the bridge. The
pickerel-weed sent up its blue and the vireo sang incessantly; the poison-sumach showed its green berries, all
unconscious of guilt, the breeze displayed the white sides
of the oak-leaves and gave the woods a fresh and flowing
look, the rush-sparrow jingled her silver change on the
broad counter of the pasture. Henry sometimes felt, on
days like this, as if he were nature itself, looking into
nature, as the blue-eyed grass in the meadow looks in
the face of the sky. He would stand for hours, up to his
chin, in some retired swamp, scenting the wild honeysuckle,
lulled by the minstrel mosquitoes: for he liked to subject
his body to rougher usage than a grenadier could endure,
and he dreamed of still remoter retirements and still
more rugged paths. He walked to Second Division Brook
and watched the yellow pebbles gleaming under the water-
cress,—the whole brook as busy as a loom, a woof and
warp of ripples, with fairy fingers throwing the shuttle,
and the long, waving stream as the fine result. Just the
place for a hut, with a footpath to the water. Or he
strolled over to Boon's Pond in Stow, when the haze
seemed to concentrate the sunlight, and he walked as if
in a halo, while the song-sparrow set the day to music, as
if the sparrow were itself the music of the mossy rail or
fence-post. Or perhaps along the Price Farm Road, with
its endless green-grass borders, with room on each side for
the berries and birches, where the walls indulged in freaks,
not bothering to run parallel with the ruts, and goldenrod
yellowed the path. On these old, meandering, uninhabited
roads, leading away from towns, these everlasting roads

where the sun played truant, one forgot what country one was in. One waved adieu to the village and travelled like a pilgrim, going whither? Whither, indeed? On the promenade deck of the world.

Days to sit in one's boat, looking over the side, when the river-bottom was covered with plants, springing up in the yellowish water, and little sparkling silvery beads of air clung to the axils of the submerged leaves. Days to watch the pout in his flurry struggling to escape from the turtle that held him. In these few inches of mud and water, what ironies, what tragedies, what growth and beauty! In one's ears sounded the roll-call of the harvest-fly, just as it sounded in Greece, in Anacreon's ode. Henry was amphibious, he felt. He could see himself swimming in the brooks and pools, with perch and bream and pout, and dozing with the stately pickerel, under the pads of the river, amid the winding aisles and corridors that were formed by the stems of the plants. And what a luxury, in a warm September, to muse by a wall-side in the sunshine, cuddling under a grey stone, to the siren-song of the cricket. He could always hear in the atmosphere a fine Æolian harp-music, like the mellow sound of distant horns in the hollow mansions of the upper air. The critics seemed to think that music was intermittent. They had to wait for a Mozart or a Paganini. Music was perpetual for Henry. He heard it in the softened air, the wind, the rain, the running water. To his expanded ear what a harp the world was!—even if another sound reached his unwilling sense in the midday stillness, a tintinnabulation from afar, the rumour of his contemporaries. It was of little moment, in these autumn days, when a young man's limbs were full of vigour, when his thoughts were like a flowing morning light, and the stream of his life stretched out before him, with long reaches of serene ripples. Thoughts like wild apples, food for walkers.

CHAPTER XVI

CAMBRIDGE: LONGFELLOW,
DANA THE YOUNGER, LOWELL

DICKENS had come and gone, with two red roses in his buttonhole. Half the households of Beacon Hill had asked him to call on Sunday, after tea, on the day of his arrival, and share their pews at the evening service. They took him in their carriages to Mount Auburn Cemetery, the favourite Boston drive; and the great Boz dinner at Papanti's Hall, presided over by President Quincy of Harvard,—for Quincy had succeeded Dr. Kirkland,—was the greatest event of the kind the town had seen.

Longfellow had returned Dickens's visit. The admiring Charles Sumner had scattered in London handfuls of *Voices of the Night,* and Longfellow found that he was an English poet, almost as renowned as Tennyson. He found that he was a German poet, too, after another summer on the Rhine, largely spent with Freiligrath, who had translated his poems, and with whom he read the *Kalevala,* the Finnish folk-epic. The Boston and Cambridge authors were multiplying their ties with the world beyond the Atlantic. They visited Maria Edgeworth in her home in Ireland, and the Nortons imported a gardener from the Edgeworth place. They had memories of moonlight evenings with Mrs. Hemans in the ruins of Melrose Abbey. They brought back roots and ivy from Miss Mitford's garden and sent her little boxes of American plants, the fringed gentian and the scarlet lily. Letters

sped back and forth between Beacon Hill and Brattle
Street and Edinburgh, Geneva, Bonn and Paris.

Fostered by these reciprocities, a mild haze of Europe
spread over Cambridge that gradually deepened as the
years went on. The customs of Brattle Street grew softer
and warmer. At sewing-bees at the president's house, they
still preserved the good old rustic ways, the baskets of
cake, the flowing pitchers of milk that foamed as cheerfully in the Spartan air as the punch-bowls on the worldly
lawns of Brookline. Cambridge was not likely to forget
the Washington Elm, the blacksmith's spreading chestnut,
about which Longfellow had written a poem; and good
Cantabrigians liked to remember that, in the storm of
1815, the last year of the war with England, the English
elms had been battered and broken, while the American
elms outrode the tempest, proud and free as Commodore
Perry's ships. Cambridge was a Yankee village, dyed as
deeply in its proper essence as ever the indigo-bird in its
native blue. But foreign streaks appeared upon its surface,
blending and melting into one another. One heard Spanish songs to the guitar. There were concerts by the
"Germania," fifteen young Germans; there were musical
parties, with Chopin, Liszt and Schubert, balls with lamps
in the trees, flowers and ices. On June evenings, scented
with the new-mown hay, one caught under the moon the
strains of Pergolesi's Stabat Mater. Hampers of game
arrived from England, grouse and venison from the Scottish moors; and many a capacious Cambridge cellar
nursed its racks of cool Johannisberger, spread the pro-
tecting cobweb over the hock and the wine that might
perhaps have been Horace's Massic. Longfellow represented the changing order that blurred the lines of
Norton's checker-board.

Longfellow, too, had married a merchant's daughter,
fair as a Portland figurehead; and Craigie House, bought
for the youthful couple, soon became the rival of "Shady

Hill." There was something Goethean in its air of ele‹
gant simplicity and space. Never was a poet more calmly
happy. He laid out a garden behind the house, shaped
like the seven-chorded lyre. Rising early, brewing his
own Mocha, standing at his desk by the southern window,
he opened the day by translating some lines of Dante. It
was like running a ploughshare through the soil of his
mind: a thousand germs of thought started up that otherwise might have lain and rotted there. Then came the
lectures and the college work. In the afternoon, a horseback ride or a stroll through Cambridgeport, to the
mouth of the river, where the tide-waters spread like the
sea, flashing and freshening the air; or perhaps, to slake
his thirst for foreign travel, he took the stage to Boston,
to the markets, where the colours and scents of the vegetables in the carts carried him to Italy and France. Or,
walking to town for exercise, he dined with Sumner and
Hillard at the Parker House, a chance for a talk about
Goethe and the subdued tone that he recommended, the
best for artists in song as for artists in painting. Sometimes he went to Newport, where the sea spoke Italian;
often he went back to Portland. There the sea spoke
Norse on tempestuous days. The tide gurgled under the
wooden piers and softly spread its fans upon the shore,
and the sails of the ships gleamed in the vapoury distance.
There he recovered his youth, in the beautiful harbour.
For, behind the tapestried mind of the Cambridge professor, filled with European shapes and figures, lurked
the Portland boy whose longest thoughts were filled with
the Atlantic, the driftwood and the seaweed, the lighthouse on its rocky ledge, the wings of the gulls and the
whitecaps, the clattering hammers in the busy shipyards,
piled with timbers of the lordly pine from the deer-haunted
forests of Maine.

Now and then, at almost any moment, after a morning's work on his Dante lectures, under his apple-tree, in

the rustic seat, or as he rode on the beach at Newport, where *The Skeleton in Armour* had come to him, or stood with his back to the autumn fire, a poem rose in his mind, stanza by stanza, and whipped itself on paper with arrowy speed,—a song or a sonnet, a ballad of the sea-coast, suggested by some event in the morning paper. He had written his *Poems on Slavery* on shipboard, mainly to please Sumner, who had joined the Abolitionists, and much to the displeasure of most of his friends, who wished to let sleeping dogs lie; but *The Slave's Dream* and *The Slave in the Dismal Swamp* were picture-poems with a child's feeling, for indignation was not one of the chords of Longfellow's garden-lyre. Everything that passed into his mind turned into music and pictures. This was the weakness of *The Spanish Student,* the first of several poems in dramatic form without a dramatic moment; but this was the charm of the poems of cities and legends, *Nuremberg, The Belfry of Bruges,* in a generation for which "Europe," even to itself, was only a half-told tale. "Filled was the air with a dreamy and magical light," as of golden leaves and autumn afternoons, for those who, holding the book in their hands, mused over the scenes of ancient splendour that came to life again in the poet's rhymes. *Evangeline,* too, was a picture-poem. No one could forget the Acadian village, the murmuring pines and the hemlocks bearded with moss, the forest scenes, the lagoons of the Mississippi, the haunts of trappers and hunters and *coureurs de bois,* the far-away Indian lodges in sunny clearings, the swaying branches and the rushing torrents. But *Evangeline* was also a story-poem, the roundest and the ripest that Longfellow wrote. The first King Leopold of Belgium caused to be cut on a seal the word Atchafalaya, the name of the lake where the lovers passed each other, each unaware of the other's presence, because "life is like that." Longfellow felt this and conveyed the feeling. It was a feeling that will preserve a poem which has so much simplicity and grace.

Longfellow's mind was never far from the sea. Even on the hills above the valley of Grand Pré, the "sea-fogs pitched their tents." No Massachusetts mind was far from the sea. At one of Margaret Fuller's Conversations, James Freeman Clarke had spoken of the beauty of American ships. Essays, he said, should be written about them, as people wrote of the art of the Greeks, for the ship was the loveliest object in the modern world. The proof of the American search for beauty was the graceful prow and swelling hull, the tall, tapering mast, the shrouds of shredded jet, the bellying canvas and the patron saint who watched the waves from the stem. Ship-building followed the laws of fitness: to bring the form of the ship into the right relation with wind and wave was to find perfect harmony and beauty. Emerson had agreed with Clarke. What New England writer would not have agreed?* Horatio Greenough, the sculptor, when he returned from Italy a little later, exclaimed, as he looked at a clipper-ship, "There is something I should not be ashamed to show Phidias!" The group of Boston men with whom he was talking had never thought of a ship as a work of art. But Emerson and Clarke would have understood him; and so would Rufus Choate. As Choate lay dying at Halifax, looking over the harbour, he said, "If a schooner or sloop goes by, don't disturb me; but

---

* Most of the New England authors wrote well about ships and shipping. See the fine passage on ships in Harriet Beecher Stowe's *The Pearl of Orr's Island* (Chapter XXX): "Who that has seen one bound onward, with her white breasts swelling and heaving, as if with a reaching expectancy, does not feel his own heart swell with a longing impulse to go with her to the far-off shores? . . . On these romantic shores of Maine, where all is so wild and still, and the blue sea lies embraced in the arms of dark, solitary forests, the sudden incoming of a ship from a distant voyage is a sort of romance. . . . What a wonder! There comes a ship from China, drifting in like a white cloud,—the gallant creature! How the waters hiss and foam before her! With what a great, free, generous plash she throws out her anchor, as if she said a cheerful 'Well done!' to some glorious work accomplished."

if there is a square-rigged ship, wake me up." Longfeilow shared these feelings, no one more so,—the author of *The Building of the Ship,*—except, perhaps, Richard Henry Dana, who was also living in Cambridge. Dana's *Two Years Before the Mast,* an Odyssey of the days of the brigs and the clippers, when half the American merchant-marine was manned by young New Englanders, was a poem about the beauty of ships. It had opened a new world for story-tellers.

This younger and bolder Dana, the son of the poet, was the boy who had almost lost an ear at school and who had so much to say on the subject of flogging. He was one of the Cambridge boys for whom the old sloop "Harvard," moored in the river, had seemed like a Viking ship. He had practised navigation on the Winthrop duckpond and sailed away, as a Harvard junior, whose studies were interrupted by failing eye-sight, on the voyage to California that had made the brig "Pilgrim" famous. With all the positive traits that his father lacked, robust and self-reliant,—he had been one of Emerson's pupils,—he was a day-dreamer, like his father, and capable of mystical ecstasies. Returning from the voyage to finish his studies, he had assisted Professor Channing, whose lectures he edited later, and opened a law-office in 1840, the year of the publication of his book. He was already known as the sailors' lawyer, and his office smelled like a forecastle, crowded as it was with men from the ships. He battled like an avenging angel for the seamen's rights and alienated all his paying clients, for the lords of the sea, like the "lords of the loom and the lash," as Charles Sumner called them, did not like a man who called attention to the wrongs of sailors and slaves. Dana, an aristocrat in every sense, fastidious in all his tastes, excelled in the fastidiousness of conscience. He had compiled a seaman's manual to help the sailors in their fight for justice.

He had kept a journal on the voyage and written out his notes at the Law School, and he had read the manuscript aloud to his father and his uncle, Washington Allston. Horace Mann, who had also read it, offered to have it published as a tract if Dana would only add a few statistics, talk a little more about imports and exports, cut the descriptions out, make the book useful, with tables of facts, and draw a moral lesson on every page. Horace Mann preferred the "Rollo" style; but in Liverpool two thousand British sailors bought the book in a single day, and the old connoisseur, Samuel Rogers, said that it had more poetry in it than almost any modern verse. It was the real thing, as the sailors knew, the first book written about the sea, not from the bridge or the cabin, but by one of the hands, one who had shared in the humblest form of sailing. To sail for furs to the Northwest coast was a gentleman's occupation, but it was ignoble to go for hides. This was the current opinion. To say that one saw the horns sticking out of his cargo was the sharpest taunt one skipper could give another.

But a reader did not have to be a sailor to be swept along by the book. One did not even have to know the meaning of a jigger, a bunt or a knight-head, a larboard or a starboard watch, a cross-jack yard or a mizzen topsail. To small-pull a main top-gallant yard, to well it, to twig the fore might mean no more to one's etymological sense than if one were engaged in hunting the snark. The "heave ho" and the "heave and pawl," the "heave hearty ho" and the "heave with a will," the "cheerily, men," while all hands joined in the chorus, blew one's mind awake. The book, like the vessel, leaped over the seas, trembling to the keel, while the spars and masts snapped and creaked; and one felt oneself in a wholesome and bracing climate, with spray and the smell of tar and salt, scrubbed wood, glistening brass, the sunlight glancing on the bright blue waves. It was as taut as a rope from end to end, with sheer high spirits and masculine vigour, with studding-sails alow and aloft, sharp on the wind, and manned by a genius "going strong" and decidedly going somewhere. No one could fail to perceive that the ship was a symbol of life, since the first part of the voyage was spent in getting it ready for sea and the second part in getting it ready for port. The book was full of overtones and symbols, and all the details of the sailor's life were noted with the bold veracity that springs from a heightened state of consciousness, a tension, well controlled and even calm, that passed at moments into exaltation. Such were the moments when Dana, at the helm, witnessed the breaking of day over the ocean, the sighting of the iceberg, near Cape Horn,—the enormous mountain-island, with its dark cavities and valleys, its pinnacles glittering in the sun, rising and sinking at the base while its points nodded against the sky, crumbling, tumbling, thundering in the sea,—or the still, foggy night, near the Falkland Islands, when the dark silence was broken by the slow, long-drawn breathing of invisible whales, drifting to the surface or lying at full length, unseen, beside the ship.

For thirty years and more, in Harvard Square, promptly at eight o'clock every morning, one saw Dana, green bag in hand, waiting for the Boston omnibus. He was always telling tales of the sea; and everyone knew that his book had done as much for the sailors as Dickens had done for the debtors and orphans of England and *Uncle Tom's Cabin* for the slaves. The dream of his life was to make some contribution to international law. He had left far behind him the episode of his youth, with the pumps and white stockings and the white duck trousers, the blue jacket and the varnished hat and the silk handkerchief flying from the outside pocket. Once again only he wrote about the sea, in a little book, *To Cuba and Back,* which was read by tourists in Havana. But he never forgot the tropical nights, the soft trade-

wind clouds under the stars, "the seas and floods in wavering morrice moving." He said that he was made for
the sea and that all his life on shore was a mistake, that
he should have been a traveller, with no profession or
home, roaming over the world like a gypsy.

Meanwhile, the son of another Cambridge worthy,
James Russell Lowell, who lived at "Elmwood,"—his
father's house, the last in Tory Row,—had also appeared
as a man of letters. A little younger than Dana, he had
similar traits, although he was tethered to Cambridge not
by conscience but by an affection for the *genius loci*. With
the same animal spirits and boyish charm, he loved the
soil as Dana loved the sea. He felt the thrill of the earth
under his feet and soaked in the sunshine like a melon.
Short, muscular, stocky, shaggy,—his friend William
Page had painted him with long blond curls and a pointed
beard, a black jacket and a lace collar, as if he were something more than a reader of Shakespeare,—he liked to
think that his ear suggested a faun's. He had an air of the
world, although he was rather self-conscious, even a little
jaunty. He seemed to be pleased with himself and his early
success, mercurial, impressionable, plastic; but under the
romantic, susceptible surface there was something timid,
hard and wooden that was to show in the grain at certain
moments. There was a streak of jealousy in him, an irre-
ducible *amour-propre,* an over-hasty zeal for "the niche
and the laurel." He was much at ease in all the Zions,
and there were those who even thought him shallow and
found his self-confident air very provoking. In fact, he
was exuberant and impulsive, and, if there was something
wooden in him, there was also something rich and buoyant. His fancy was luxuriant. He was the cleverest young
man in Cambridge, and even the most intelligent. He
had the makings of a first-rate scholar. But his leading
trait was a gift of pure enjoyment, whether of books
or garden-flowers, walking, talking, smoking, drinking,

reading, a gusto that was new in Brattle Street. He was a
capital idler. He could lie on his back for days on end,
dreaming in the fragrant air or conning some Elizabethan
poet. Moreover, he, like Dana, had his trances, every
year, when June, from its southern ambush, "with one
great gush of blossom stormed the world."

"Elmwood" was the hub of Lowell's Cambridge, the
large, square Georgian house with the tall pilasters, the
old-fashioned garden, the meadows at the rear, where he
liked to pitch hay on summer mornings. There, as a little
boy, he had fallen asleep to the rhythms of Shakespeare
and Spenser, read to him by a sister who had brought
him up, Miss Mary Lowell, one of those Cambridge
women who knew a dozen languages and who had learned
Hungarian and Polish. He had had hallucinations as a
child. Mediæval figures from the *Faerie Queene* had
walked beside him on his way to school. He had bur-
rowed among his father's books and rescued from the
attic the old prints of Socrates, Plato and Seneca that
had adorned his great-grandfather's study. His Latin was
as fluent as his English.* To the *Natural History of
Selborne,* for which his father had an old affection, he
felt especially drawn; and he liked to record the events
of the garden, the visits of the cross-bills, the battles of
crows and robins. His father had led him out to the barn
to watch the swallows on the roof, taking counsel together before their yearly migration, as Gilbert White
had noted years before; and he had counted seven orioles
flashing about the lawn all at once. He had studied the
cedar-birds in the hawthorn-bushes and learned where to
look for the king-birds, building their nests in the orchard. He had seen a cherry in full blossom, beside his
study-window, covered with humming-birds that had been
benumbed by a fall of rain and snow. He knew the
plaintive may-be of the goldfinch when it was stealing his

---

* See the macaronic Latin verses in *The Biglow Papers.*

lettuce-seeds. He had listened to a pair of indigo-birds singing all day long to one another. He had heard the cuckoo strike the hour, like a Swiss clock, through the night.

Along with the birds, in much the same fashion, he had studied the English poets, observing their notes and their plumage. He could remember the time and the place when each of them had flashed into his mind, Landor, for instance, whom he had read in the old arched alcoves in Harvard Hall. He had made a collection of fragments from Rogers and Campbell, who had written of home as if they had lived at "Elmwood." He had been the member of the "band" who had copied out Tennyson's early poems and shown the manuscript-book to the other members, and he had steeped himself in Shelley and Keats,—of whom he had planned to write a life, in the days when Keats was still a morning star,*—till his mind was a music-box of impressions and rhythms. With his philological instinct, a natural Cambridge trait, he liked to trace the origins of words, the earliest use of phrases, the history of archaisms and colloquialisms; and this had led him to study the Yankee speech, which he knew as Tennyson knew the "northern farmer's." He felt that "the tongue of the people in the mouth of the scholar" was the right motto for poets, and the Yankee tongue was in his blood. He had heard it all about him in his boyhood, on muster-fields, at cattle-shows, at noonings in the hay-fields at "Elmwood," when he had sat with the hired men over their jugs of blackstrap, talking in the shadow of the ash-tree. Yankee was his mother-tongue, the tongue that some of his forbears had brought from England, while others had brought the scholar-dialect. He had revelled in the Yankee speech at Concord when, as a senior in college, he had been rusticated and packed

* Eighty-five years later, this project was carried out by Amy Lowell. the grand-daughter of Lowell's first cousin.

off thither, to study with the Reverend Barzillai Frost. The people were forgetting it in Cambridge, but it throve on the Concord farms. For Emerson, who took him on strolls to the Cliffs, he had acquired a feeling later. In fact, he was one of the neophytes who walked to Boston to hear Emerson lecture and who caught the sound of the trump in his silvery voice. He was thrilled by one of Emerson's phrases, "The walls of the mind's chamber are covered with scribblings, which need but the bringing of a candle to render them legible." That one should sit alone and meditate was almost a new idea to a college boy whose mind was running over with animal spirits. Emerson appealed to the *exalté* in him. But it was Mr. Frost, the minister, who excited his fancy in Concord. Mr. Frost, the rustic Harvard scholar, was reappearing in *The Biglow Papers,* which Lowell was dashing off in his usual way, with lucky hits up and down the pages. The minister was Parson Wilbur. Concord was reproduced in some of the idyllic scenes as well as in the Yankee dialect. This was Lowell's happiest tongue in verse.

With his boyish air and his worldly air, his radical sympathies and his Tory habits, his antiquarian tastes and his love of nature, his sudden enthusiasms and his constant affections, his volatility and his love of puns,—similes made of Semele,—together with his industry and patience, his high romantic poses and his zest for old garrets, desks, pipes and friends, Lowell was a complicated soul who left on the mind not one but a hundred impressions. He was compact of incongruities, like many another humorous Yankee, and some of the readers of his earnest poems were shocked by his inconsequence when they met him; for, while he had a streak of the mystic in him, he also had a pantagruelian streak. He was warm-hearted and cold by turns, as many other men in Cambridge were. He would rejoice in a friend and snub him in the next breath. He had a way of setting one gently right.* Even his spontaneity had a method, for, while he was really spontaneous, he wished to be more spontaneous than he was. He would step, in the Yard, in the midst of some grave discussion, vault over one of the great stone columns, clap his hands and crow like a cock, and then resume the argument. If, as occasionally happened, he failed to leap the column, he was annoyed. He would keep on trying until he succeeded, saying, with a wry smile, "I commonly do that the first time." One had to be gay, or appear so, in spite of one's forbears. This note of the *voulu,* the factitious, which was marked in his personality, appeared in his poems also. His liveliest effects were often forced, and some of his sublimities as well.† The mixed impression that his poems left, the inconclusiveness of his critical thinking suggested that he had never thought anything out, and that he even felt with reservations. Had he ever found his own "average point," ‡ or made up his mind in regard to any question? There was much of the chameleon in his nature, together with much that was firm and strong. For the solid and even chunky physical frame housed a substantial Yankee, shrewd, enquiring and tenacious, with a mind which, however inconclusive, liked to coil about its acquisitions. Lowell had what the phrenologists called inhabitiveness and adhesiveness. He inhabited Cambridge, he adhered to books. No one "stayed put" better than he. He had a rare feeling for style, though his taste was less perceptive

* Said Howells, "Who in the world ever heard of the Claudian Emissary?" Said Lowell, "You are in Cambridge, Mr. Howells."—Howells, *Literary Friends and Acquaintance.*

† This was what Emerson had in mind when he refused to review Lowell's *Cathedral.* "I like Lowell," he said, "but I think he had to pump."

‡ Lowell described himself when he said, in his *Moosehead Journal:* "It is as hard for most characters to stay at their own average point in all companies, as for a thermometer to say 65° for twenty-four hours together. I like this in our friend Johannes Taurus, that he carries everywhere and maintains his insular temperature, and will have everything accommodate itself to that."

than gustatory. Where others only read, he read with passion. He had a feeling for the romance of letters that only Longfellow shared; and, if one knew his open-sesame, one found within something warm and winning. If one could rise to the charms of Mount Auburn or cap Fresh Pond with a good quotation, if one had something to say for the elms and the willows, or knew how to look at a peewee pursuing a fly, or an oriole building its nest, if one could speak with discretion of Chaucer or Dante and open an Elzevir with affectionate fingers, if one loved black-letter as one loved a meerschaum, or even understood how to be idle, one found oneself at home in Lowell's heart.

Longfellow and he had never met until, one day in 1846, they found themselves together in Lowell's study, the upstairs study at "Elmwood," discussing the anti-slavery question. Lowell was an Abolitionist. This was one of his many tinges, for he was a polychromic nature; but there were various reasons for it. His father and his grandfather had had the Boston negroes on their conscience, and Lowell's young wife, Maria White, a poet like himself,—one of the Watertown girls, a pupil of Margaret Fuller, who had belonged to the "band,"—was deep in all the democratic movements. The two young people had written for the Pennsylvania *Freeman,* and Lowell was contributing a weekly paper to the *Anti-Slavery Standard* in New York. He was full of the zeal of the convert, for all his instincts were conservative. He had ridiculed and satirized in college, like any clever boy, the uncouth ways of the reformers and the causes he was defending now, woman's rights and total abstinence, Abolition, Transcendentalism; and, if he was attacking the Mexican War, respectable Whigs like Prescott also attacked it. But he was in a state of exaltation and found it exhilarating to have an object that was outside and beyond his art. Behind his work was all the moral fervour that characterized a New England boy. His literary facility was surprising. *The Biglow Papers, A Fable for Critics,* scores of shorter pieces in verse and prose were pouring from his mind at once. Four volumes of his work appeared together, in the "year of revolutions," '48. He could hardly write slowly enough to develop his thought; he could hardly write fast enough to record his impressions. Moreover, he was a lion at twenty-nine. He was the "best launched man of his time," as N. P. Willis said. The word had gone round among the reviewers that Lowell was the poet of the future.

Of all the younger writers, he was the most adroit and the most accomplished. He seemed to be a master of all the poetic forms, ode, song, epigram and sonnet, the narrative poem, the elegy, the idyll. Everyone knew *To Perdita Singing, The Rose* and *Rosaline,* as presently *Prometheus* and *Rhæcus, The Shepherd of King Admetus* and the *Ode to France, An Indian-Summer Reverie,* with its charming scenes of Cambridge, especially *The Vision of Sir Launfal.* Longfellow and Poe alone, among the American poets, wrote with the colour and music, the skill and taste that Lowell exhibited in all these verses. His artistry was highly conscious. He had studied all the current models. He was almost as good as Keats and Shelley, as Tennyson, Landor and Hood. The question was, when Tennyson and Landor, when Keats, Shelley and Hood were better known, how much would be left to make a Lowell?—for his poetry, undoubtedly good, seemed to be largely at second hand. His titles, like his poems themselves, savoured of other poets,—so much so that one asked if Lowell's writing was not wholly prompted by his reading. Comparing him with Longfellow, Emerson, Poe, one saw that Poe, like Emerson, was unique, while Longfellow claimed little and pretended little. Longfellow's tone was humble, unlike Lowell's. He seemed to write for the joy of sharing his treasures, as if ne were glad to be thought a mere translator, a simple story-teller, a nursery minstrel. This was both disarming and deceptive, for Longfellow had an original mind. He was an innovator in metres and rhythms; he introduced new modes of feeling; he touched his world with a magic that was mild but unmistakable. He had a poetic personality, an individual temperament, tame and even flat as it was at moments, scarcely ever intense. He had his own colour-box and varnish, and all the Longfellow pictures, large and small, bore the signature of the Cambridge artist.* Longfellow asked for less than his due, while it appeared that Lowell asked for more; for, with his greater energy and depth of thought, his air of accomplished maturity, one looked in his work for the signature almost in vain. Lowell took the colour of his subjects, or, rather, of the poets he had absorbed, and only a phrase here and there,—some outburst of New England moral feeling, some reference to American birds and flowers,—broke one's impression that his work was a medley of English poetry. For each and all of his poems, except *The Biglow Papers,* one found a model somewhere in England's Parnassus, in *Locksley Hall,* in *Don Juan,* in *English Bards and Scotch Reviewers,* Browning's dramatic monologues, the *Faerie Queene,* Shelley's *Prometheus,* Coleridge's *France: an Ode,* Keats's *Endymion,* Shakespeare, Gray or Spenser. In fact, to the end of his life, in Lowell's verses, lines cropped out and passages appeared that obviously belonged, in style and feeling, to Tennyson, Wordsworth or Keats.

That Lowell was a sort of shadow-poet, in spite of all his taste and cultivation, became too evident as the years went on. Even at his best, in *The Present Crisis,* that classic of radical orators, he was rewriting *Locksley Hall;* and would he have written *A Fable for Critics* if

---

* To feel the originality of Longfellow's style, one has only to see it reflected in Lowell's *The Changeling.*

Byron had not suggested the form? Tennyson gave him the model for *Sir Launfal*, a touching and popular poem, even deservedly popular, for all its jerkiness and air of haste, as a genuine expression of its time and place, the humanitarian Cambridge of the eighteen-forties. As American poets multiplied, and English poetry grew more familiar, Lowell's reputation slowly sank. Of the splendid mass of Victorian verse, the most bewildering since the age of Shakespeare, could anything be expected to survive that was not entirely fresh? "Desiring this man's art and that man's scope" seemed all too plainly Lowell's state of mind; and that his verse was good, and more than good, with its charming air of literary breeding, that his technical agility was surprising,* that his tone was often noble, all this had to face the final question, What did it add to the sum of things poetic? That it added much to other sums, local, moral, political, hardly affected the question. That the drop of Lowell's reputation implied a holocaust of lesser poets was to be taken for granted. The fact remained that one forgot his poems. One read them five times over and still forgot them, as if this excellent verse had been written in water.

Lowell was scarcely the "maker" he longed to be. He was even a little presumptuous, saying of his "kind of wingéd prose" that it "could fly if it would," when obviously the case was otherwise, since poets always fly when they can. That he was a rhetorician, according to the definition of the poet Yeats,† was closer to the truth. He deceived himself, and his contemporaries were deceived about him. In taking him for a first-rate poet, however, his contemporaries were unjust to what he was. They were no less unjust in taking him for a "radical" poet. It

---

* E.g., *An Oriental Apologue.*
† "Rhetoric is the will trying to do the work of the imagination."— *Ideas of Good and Evil.*

was observed, after his wife's death, that his radical phase rapidly passed; and those who preferred him in this aspect thought of him as a renegade. Three generations later, this view persisted. It was unfair from the first, for the shift in Lowell's point of view might have been taken for granted. Leopards do not change their spots, and Cambridge boys are Cambridge boys even when they marry Maria Whites. The radical note in Lowell's work was a kind of inverse ventriloquism, in which the voice appeared to come from the poet, while actually the speaker was his wife. It was her influence that induced his fervour, for Lowell was highly suggestible, and the influence and the fervour passed together. His radicalism was only a phase that little in his nature sustained or encouraged. It was true that this phase represented his solidest writing. Witness the poem on Garrison and *The Present Crisis,* for all its form was borrowed: witness, especially, *The Biglow Papers.* It was the glory of *The Biglow Papers,*—which made the book almost a folk-creation,—that Parson Wilbur and Hosea Biglow were brothers under their skins. That literate and illiterate in New England met on a common ground of feeling, that they were at one in essential matters, religious and political alike, that their regard for human rights, their hatred of war and false ideas of empire, sprang from their common principle,—this was the burden of *The Biglow Papers.* It was the most profound of Lowell's works because of its instinctive presentation of the folk point of view from which it sprang, for Lowell's moment of radical fervour carried him to the depths of the popular mind.

The Biglow Papers remained as a permanent landmark. No other work compared with it, either then or later, for showing the homogeneity of New England, its common stock, its common faith. But works like *The Biglow Papers* can spring from a divided mind. A heated

imagination can produce them, a sudden and momentary
dramatic impulse, while part of the man remains in reserve; and a large part of the man remained in reserve
in all of Lowell's poetry. For Lowell as a secondary
poet, much, however, remained to be said. His brooding
love of country was a noble trait. If the patriotic odes of
his later years, the *Ode for the Fourth of July,* the *Ode
Read at Concord,* the better-known *Commemoration
Ode,* seemed, in after times, too much like Websterian
speeches rewritten in verse,—one felt in them, too much,
the lapsed occasion, the rhetoric that required the proper
moment,—passages remained that touched one still and
longer passages that convinced the mind how Lowell
must have touched those who heard him. *A Fable for
Critics,*—at its lowest value, the classic illustration of
"college humour,"—was something new under the Yankee sun. No one could know how good it was, how frank,
fresh, perceptive, who had not read the critics of the
eighteen-forties. Beside the New York and Boston reviewers of the "Independent Press," which Lowell satirized in *The Biglow Papers,* in the series of burlesque
notices, *A Fable for Critics* had the virtue that Longfellow's poems possessed in the previous decade. Whatever
Lowell promised as a critic, no one could deny that he,
with Poe, had opened an era in critical practice: he and
Poe were the first American critics to exercise their judgment freely. If, among Lowell's qualities, judgment was
the one that developed least, if he was prejudiced and
hasty, still *A Fable for Critics* marked an epoch. It
formed reputations,—Lowell did not wait till they were
formed. It dealt with American letters directly,—Lowell
did not wait for English opinions. Aside from this, and
The Biglow Papers, his descriptive poems were the best.
A book of American verse could scarcely omit *An Indian-
Summer Reverie,*—

What visionary tints the year puts on,
When falling leaves falter through motionless air
   Or numbly cling and shiver to be gone!
How shimmer the low flats and pastures bare,
   As with her nectar Hebe Autumn fills
   The bowl between me and those distant hills,
And smiles and shakes abroad her misty, tremulous hair!

And what could be more veracious than these lines from *Pictures from Appledore,* for another example?—

   the blind old ocean maundering,
Raking the shingle to and fro,
Aimlessly clutching and letting go
The kelp-haired sedges of Appledore,
Slipping down with a sleepy forgetting,
And anon his ponderous shoulder setting,
With a deep, hoarse pant, against Appledore.

Everything that was rich and sunny, all that was loving, strong and true, in Lowell's heart and talent, spoke through his *Under the Willows* and *The Fountain of Youth, Sunthin' in the Pastoral Line,* the "June" of *The Vision of Sir Launfal,*—with every leaf and blade "some happy creature's palace." The Lowell of May and June was the joyous Lowell, the poet and the lover, off-guard for once and all the time, transfigured with the coming of spring and summer.

CHAPTER XVII

THE BOSTON HISTORIANS: MOTLEY

THE LAST traces of the Doric age were passing away in Boston. The antique severities were gone, along with the floridities of Gilbert Stuart, and a bland and learned elegance had taken the place of the harsh, austere or stately ways of old. The worthies who remembered the Revolution, the open-handed merchants of Stuart's portraits, who had laid down their annual pipe of Madeira, the frugal Romans who, at public dinners, perhaps to celebrate some splendid gift which they had offered to the city, departed so far from their usual rule, when the dessert was passed, as to take three almonds or a fig, the hearty old souls who, at church, sang with might and main, blowing their noses till the rafters rang,—all these types were vanishing one by one. In the old Puritan town, swept by the air of the world, one heard less of Cicero and Plutarch, more of modern Rome than of ancient Rome and much more of London than of Athens.

One by one, the faces that Stuart had painted disappeared from the Boston streets. Judge Joseph Story was dead. So was John Pickering, who had known Chinese and Cochin-Chinese, once so useful in Salem, who had studied the Polynesian dialects and collected the Yankee words and phrases that Lowell had taken up in turn. Dr. Channing had gone before them, in a country inn at Bennington. The frail little invalid's body had been placed in Mount Auburn, while the bell of the Catholic cathedral tolled, as for the passing of a saint; and every good Bostonian wrote in his journal that a generation had been buried with it. For Channing had been the father and bishop of Boston, with a truly paternal love for all that was human. The tomb of the apostle of self-culture, the friend of the slaves and the workers, the scourge of the selfish, whose name had headed all the petitions and who had fought for liberty and grace, was designed by Washington Allston; and Allston, his friend and kinsman, was the next to go. Six hours before his death, he had been working on "Belshazzar's Feast," the unfinished and unfinishable masterpiece. He was carried in the evening to the churchyard, on the edge of Harvard Square, in the flaring light of the torches borne by a crowd of students.

Of the senatorial ancients a few remained, survivors of the old three-bottle days when young men grew up on Pope's Homer, followed the Ciceronian injunctions and fell in love, by candle-light, with damsels who were singing the songs of Burns. Harvard stood firm with President Quincy, that Pharos on a rock; but John Quincy Adams, his noble kinsman, the aged statesman, the aspiring poet, had but a few more lines to write. He still rose at five on winter mornings, groped for his old-fashioned tinder-box,—for he despised the new Lucifer matches,—lighted his candle and fire and took his cold sponge, as once, in the days of his presidency, twenty years before, when he was almost sixty, he had swum across the Potomac and back and walked home under the winter moon. He still toiled over his rhymes and orations, fighting the slave-power, arousing interest in canals and roads, prompting scientific expeditions and founding institutions of research. He had laboured for weeks on a speech on astronomy; he had journeyed to Cincinnati, at seventy-seven, sleeping on the floor of a canal-boat, to lay the cornerstone of an observatory. His hope was to kindle an interest in science in the West. He rejoiced in the spread of German studies, even in Richter and Tieck, who had addled the brains of the young. During the Congressional recesses, one found him at the old house at Quincy, pruning his garden or among his books. Every day, twice a day, one saw him standing in the portico, holding his watch in his hand, timing the rising or the setting sun. And every night, kneeling beside his bed, he repeated, "Now I lay me down to sleep," which he had learned from the lips of Abigail Adams. He had said it every night of his life, in Holland, Prussia, Russia, France and England, in Washington, Boston and Quincy. "I say it out loud always," he remarked, "and I don't mumble it either."

Oratory and history were still the central interests of the Boston mind. The Bostonians had been trained to distinguish the fine points of eloquence; and, as this was still a political Age of Faith, the orators were their tribunes and standard-bearers. The commentators delighted in analyzing the styles of the various speakers,— Webster, whose vocabulary was more Teutonic than Macaulay's and far less Latinized than Burke's, Edward Everett, Webster's under-study, and Rufus Choate, who shared Webster's gift for making his clients feel like heroes and martyrs, so that they wept when he described their actions and saw themselves as Sophoclean figures. Choate was a fiery speaker, witty, weighty, plain and grand by turns, an orator for the thinking few, unlike the mellifluous Everett and the popular Webster. His wit was more than legal. Everyone had heard his phrase about Chief Justice Shaw: * "I always approach Judge Shaw as a savage approaches his fetish, knowing that he is ugly, but feeling that he is great." Thus Choate, when his learned sock was on; and, when he wore the buskin, then from his lips came noble words. Everett was the figurehead of Boston. In the years that had passed since he exclaimed, "Welcome, Lafayette!" and greeted

* The father-in-law of Herman Melville.

President Jackson at Bunker Hill,—placing two cannon-balls in the President's hands, as if this happy thought had dropped from heaven,—he had become the bust on the prow of the ship that beamed upon every passing sail. Who could present the keys of the city, or eulogize a hero or a guest, with more resplendent grace than Everett? No one, facing a crowd of mechanics or farm-ers, could picture the charms of their lot and their occupa-tions with an air that was more engaging or reassuring. He made one feel that all was going well. But Webster was still the unrivalled leader. His eyes were "catacombs of ancient wisdom," as his admirers said, even though his virtue, like stern Cato's, often warmed with wine, was also, and more often, warmed with brandy. Webster had grown sluggish with adulation, and the Fugitive Slave Bill was to drain away much of his local glory. It was not wisdom, it was prudence that dwelt in the catacombs of Webster's eyes; but prudence, after all, was a statesman's business, and Webster had done much to preserve the Union. Moreover, the second Bunker Hill oration had shown that he was still the master-speaker.

The dignity of history and its importance were con-stant themes of Everett and Webster. History was the passion of Rufus Choate, when it was not law or Massa-chusetts, and in his fine speech, *The Age of the Pilgrims,* he expressed the feeling about the past, the origins and greatness of New England, that filled the minds of the younger writers.* The stream of historical interest

* Another of Choate's speeches, *The Power of a State Developed by Mental Culture,* expressed the feeling of renascent Boston. Choate liked to think of the boast of Themistocles, that he knew how to make a small State a great one,—by making the State wise. How was Massachusetts to main-tain its lustre, with its young men drifting westward? Was it destined to fade as the nation grew? Massachusetts had it in its power to retain its intellectual leadership. People had thought too much of banks and cotton, and far too little of the culture that made Athens paramount in Greece, moulding the taste and opinion of Greece and Rome, then of the modern world. This was all that Massachusetts needed to hold its place, and more, in the future.

spread wider and wider. Everett's most attractive trait was an eagerness to help his fellow-scholars, even political enemies like Bancroft. On his journeys abroad, he collected notes for Prescott, examining the libraries of Paris and Florence, the Guicciardini and Medici family archives, the reports of the ambassadors of Venice, the archives of Vienna, and interested Metternich and the Marquis Capponi in the efforts of his Boston friend, learning much that served himself, no doubt, in his own diplomatic career. He exerted his influence to obtain for Bancroft, whose history was advancing from volume to volume, the use of collections of letters and papers in England, although he had broken with Bancroft and sent back his own letters, as if to put an end to their relations. With a spirit like this prevailing in Boston, all the historical writers advanced together. Before the end of the forties, Sparks, Bancroft, Prescott and Ticknor had published a dozen new volumes, Richard Hildreth had written his *History of the United States,* John Lothrop Motley, a younger student, had set to work on *The Rise of the Dutch Republic* and Francis Parkman had written *The Oregon Trail.* Hildreth, a prolific journalist, had shown imagination in a novel, *The Slave, or Memoirs of Archy Moore,* which he had written in Florida, a book that thrilled the younger generation. He was the spectre of the Athenæum, the tall, grey, silent man who had been seen for years haunting his alcove, but who, in truth, was very far from spectral. He was a blunt, hard-headed hater of shams. He detested the "patriotic rouge" of Sparks and Bancroft's pyrotechnics. His history, soberly good, was rather tame, a colourless work in six large volumes, written in a plain business style. It carried the story down to 1820 and pleased the conservative and the matter-of-fact. Entirely free from Bancroft's nonsense, it also lacked Bancroft's picturesqueness, as well as the charm of Prescott; and it lacked the original documentation that made these other historians important.

In Beacon Street, lovely in October, overhung with golden elms, with crimson creepers on the balconies, Prescott had built a new house, facing the Frog Pond and the fountain. Over the drawing-room, he arranged his study, a lofty apartment reached by a winding stairway through a secret door behind a book-case. There he kept, over the mantel, crossed, the swords of his father's father and his mother's father, who had fought on opposite sides in the Revolution, the swords that Thackeray saw, when he visited Boston. These swords suggested to Thackeray the idea of *The Virginians,* the story of the brother who fought for the king and the brother who fought for Washington. Prescott spent hours there, under the portrait of Cortez, the busts of Washington Irving and other friends, turning over his manuscripts, the twenty thousand folio pages, gathered from every corner of Europe, the books that had come by ship from Cadiz. He had been idle for a while, after his first great effort. He had earned an interlude for loafing. He played blindman's buff with his guests and children. He amused himself with his cats, for he often had a cat in his lap. He visited Niagara Falls, the wonder of the world in the eighteen-forties, where every traveller was baptized again with a touch of Byronic emotion. In summer, he went to Nahant and Pepperell, where he kept up the old family farm. As much as his eyes permitted, he read Cooper and Dumas, who refreshed his mind. He thought for a time of writing a life of Molière.

Then plans had risen in his mind, shoots from the stock of his Spanish studies. Why should not he, like the Spaniards, gather gold in Mexico and the Andes? Everything combined to push him forward. His blindness, his cheerfulness, his frankness, his youthful high spirits, his engaging mind had, caught the imagination of other scholars. Guizot, Mignet, Thierry, Lord Holland and Milman, Humboldt in Germany, Navarrete in Spain plied him with offers of assistance. Irving, hearing that he was at work on the exploits of Cortez in Mexico, his own cherished theme for many years, on which he counted for his bread and butter, gladly gave him the right of way. With all these well-wishers working for him, there was nothing for Prescott to do but to go ahead. Much as he loved Dumas, Marcus Aurelius was his favourite author; and Alfieri's example roused the spark. No need to look for the drama in his subject. The drama of *The Conquest of Mexico* shaped itself; and to use, in building the story, he had eight thousand sheets of manuscript, beautifully copied from the Spanish archives, all the original documents, diaries, letters, never yet published, never even seen, except by a few chroniclers and amanuenses. He had Navarrete's manuscript collection, dealing with Peru and Mexico. The Spanish Academy helped him. The old Spanish families opened their chests of papers, which no other writer had asked to see. Thierry sent him books. The Spanish minister in Mexico City sent him information about the Aztecs. Four copyists in Madrid gathered materials for him. Another friend delved in the British Museum. To study the trees and the birds, the landscape and the customs of the country, which had not greatly changed since the days of Cortez, he did not have to go to Mexico. Madame Calderon de la Barca, who had lived as a governess in Concord and for whose *Life in Mexico* Prescott wrote a preface, filled the lively letters that she sent him with sketches of Mexican scenes and manners, enough to satisfy Humboldt, who knew the country, that the half-blind Prescott had also seen it. There was enough diplomacy involved in gathering the materials for his work to have founded a small republic.

No need to rope himself to his chair, as Alfieri was

obliged to do. He found it easy, in the zest of work, even
to master mathematics, which had always baffled him
before and which he had to know to characterize the
astronomy of the Aztecs. He read various books of martial exploits, Voltaire's *Charles XII* and lives of Columbus and Hannibal. Then he set the stage with a panorama
of Montezuma's empire. From the moment when Cortez,
burning his boats and landing at Vera Cruz, began his
march to the capital, the story moved on to its final result with the frightful inevitability of some drama of
nature. The Aztecs, like the Incas, in *The Conquest of
Peru,* the work that rapidly followed, were painted as the
chroniclers had seen them. Their "feather-cinctured
chiefs and dusky loves" were a little operatic, for no
archæologist had as yet revealed the reality of these
builders of civilizations that crumbled under the terrible
feet of the Spaniards. But generations passed before anyone challenged the truth of the picture that Prescott drew
of the conquest, grandly in the Mexican book, only less
grandly in the tale of Peru,—shorter, slighter, much less
unified, as the little black ruffian Pizarro was a lesser man
than Cortez. Pizarro's conquest was achieved at once, and
the rest of the story was an anti-climax: Prescott had to
create his drama out of the sordid squabbles of the seekers of gold, who were little better than bandits. *The Conquest of Mexico* was a natural epic, while all that gave
unity to the other work was that the characters were few.
But everything that Prescott wrote had the same solidity,
and he told these two great stories with an air of effortless ease. Massive but alive in all their parts, they were
full of colour and vigorous movement. They were partly
composed on horseback. Prescott mentally wrote the final
chapter in a gallop through the woods at Pepperell.

While these two books were under way, Prescott and
George Ticknor were always together. Ticknor was also
at work on his *History of Spanish Literature,* lingering

over it with such affection that he could hardly bear to
part with it. Ticknor had grown more and more important,
with his imposing house and his great position, of which
he was by no means unaware. It was he who occasioned
Longfellow's remark that "every Bostonian speaks as if
he were the Pope." His large head was "full of cold
brains," to quote his own phrase about William Godwin;
and the more he advanced in life, the more his voice became an affront to strangers. He was a useful citizen,
however, the builder of the great collection of books in
the Boston Public Library, Prescott's friend and confidant, indeed the willing friend of every scholar. On his
second visit to Europe, after resigning his professorship,
he had been received in every quarter with the *éclat* of
an ambassador. Humboldt had greeted him as an old
acquaintance. He had visited Lamartine and Guizot,
spent a happy evening with Sainte-Beuve, discussed philological questions with the blind Thierry, passed two days
with Wordsworth, and met the youthful Ruskin, who
had shown him the beautiful drawings he had made from
nature. With his history constantly in mind, he had consulted countless men of letters and formed a lasting
friendship with the model scholar, the Crown Prince
John of Saxony, who was translating Dante into German. In Dresden, the prince had invited him to hear
Tieck read aloud from his translation. The listeners followed, with the original text, and, at the end of every
canto, gave their candid comments on the version. This
incident was to have its consequences, for when, years
later, in Cambridge, at Longfellow's instigation, the
Dante Club was formed, the members, who were all
friends of Ticknor and had undoubtedly heard him tell
the story, followed the same procedure. Ticknor had
travelled through Europe with his own coach and foot-
man and four post-horses, very much *en prince;* and at
Rome, at the Princess Borghese's, he might have joined

six cardinals at whist, if a Boston man could have played on a Sunday evening.

With many of these scholars and men of letters, he kept up a regular correspondence. Milman, Hallam, Pasqual de Gayangos were always on the watch for information that might serve him in his great work. Everyone knew that he was writing it, and he could taste his glory in advance; for the universal success of Prescott's writings indicated what his own might be. But might it not be with him as it was with Gibbon, after his task was accomplished,—would he not find the days long and empty and life short and precarious? He had laboured on the work for twenty years, removing all the traces of his lectures, growing more fastidious all the time, verifying his facts again and again, weighing every authority, more and more indifferent to publication. Great was his reward when it appeared, in three handsome volumes. It was the literary event of 1849, the one book of the year that Macaulay recommended to the Queen. There were not six men living who were competent to review it, as one of the possible five remarked, and Hallam, who was another, said that it could never be superseded by any writer who was not a Spaniard, or even by any Spaniard, unless there was a radical change in Spain. Its erudition was impeccable. It was firm and clear in composition. Everything that knowledge and will could give the work possessed in overflowing measure, and edition followed edition, and translation translation, long beyond the day of Ticknor's death; for it always lay open on his study-table, ready for new revisions. He liked to remember what was said of Plato, that, even when he had passed the age of eighty, he combed and curled and braided the locks of his writings. The limitations of the work were the limitations of Ticknor himself, a lack of the spontaneity and imagination that Prescott had so amply. It was cold and hard in tone and treatment, the fruit of a carefully trained intelligence that never knew the madness of the poet.

Years later, Francis Parkman, the strenuous man of genius, a half-blind semi-invalid like Prescott, but with an explorer's or soldier's instincts, deplored the lifeless scholarship of New England,—"void of blood, bone, sinew, nerves and muscle." * It was not Prescott that he had in mind; scarcely even Ticknor. He was referring to Everett, whom he described as the most finished example of this devitalized scholarship, "with many graceful additions." He might have chosen John Gorham Palfrey, that other *North American* writer, the author of the *History of New England,* which appeared a few years later than Ticknor's work,—a man of multitudinous occupations, Everett's successor at the Brattle Square church, Andrews Norton's successor at Harvard, editor of the great review, postmaster of Boston, member of Congress, a "Christian lawyer" in his theology, a theologian in his literature. A Puritan of an earlier day, in type, without the fire that burned in the ancient settlers, unimaginative and unmagnetic, a kindly, modest, conscientious man,— recalled by Henry Adams, in his *Education,* with variouᵖ pleasant phrases, as one of the members of his father's circle,—he was an active Abolitionist. Along with Dana and Sumner, he endured the sneers and snubs of Ticknoɪ and his State Street friends. He was a thorough and trustworthy scholar, and he spent more than thirty years writing the well-known history, which long remained the authority in its field. It was a monumental work, in five large volumes. If it was almost wholly political, this was the author's intention; it was not too provincial in its point of view; it was written in the firm historical style

* According to Parkman, this was the result of an old New England custom. In households of small means, the privilege of going to college usually fell on the son whose feeble health unfitted him for ruder labours. The "narrow-chested hectic Benjamin" was chosen for the sedentary life, with sad results.in the world of books and thought.

which all the Boston writers had developed in common.
And yet the vitality of the work was low. Students were
obliged to consult it, but few could have relished the adventure.

Boston, however, which had produced a Prescott,
brought forth another writer in the eighteen-fifties whom
readers were to enjoy for generations. John Lothrop
Motley, the son of a merchant,—who wrote some of the
Jack Downing letters, those of the second series,—had
much in common with his predecessor. Born in similar
surroundings, a few years later, in one of those households where Scott was the staple of reading and Irving
and Channing were read as American classics, Motley
was a high-spirited boy of whom the last thing to be
expected was the drudgery of a scholar's life. Tall and
graceful, with hyacinthine hair,—so handsome that Lady
Byron, when she saw him, said that Motley looked more
like her husband than any other man she had seen,—
impetuous, wilful, rather vain, decidedly supercilious, he
had an air that suggested a thoroughbred horse when
he flung back his head and a wild look flashed in his eye.
He was plastic and fickle, or appeared to be so, too clever
to be industrious and too fastidious for a dull routine. He
had learned to read French easily at eleven, and had
studied German with Bancroft at the Round Hill school.
He had entered Harvard at thirteen. Wendell Phillips
and T. G. Appleton, better known in later years, had
been his best friends as a boy. Every Saturday afternoon,
in the garret of Motley's house, the three friends, dressed
in cloaks and doublets, had acted impromptu melodramas.
Pretending that they were bandits and heroes of Byron,
they spouted scraps of poetry to one another.

All these three boys played later parts that had associations with the Motleys' attic. There was a strain of the
actor in Wendell Phillips, T. G. Appleton was always
Byronic, and Motley's love of costume and dramatic ef-

fect,—he had made and played with miniature theatres also,—appeared in his writings from first to last. Prescott, at the same age, dressed in a helmet and breastplate at the Athenæum, had shown the same romantic tendency, common enough in boys but not so common in historians. Motley had gone to Germany to study, like Ticknor, Longfellow, Bancroft and so many others. At Göttingen, where he made a translation of *Faust,* he had lived in the closest intimacy with Bismarck, whose "dear Jack" he remained for two generations, perhaps the closest of all Bismarck's friends, the one to whom he wrote with least constraint and whom he always welcomed with the warmest affection. They took their meals and exercise together. Bismarck rejoiced when Motley sat with his red slippers thrust out of the window; and Motley, in *Morton's Hope,* his first novel, left a picture of Bismarck,—peppered all over with freckles, scarred, with an eyebrow shaved, in his chaotic coat, without collar or buttons, and with his iron heels and portentous spurs,—that showed his early skill in descriptive writing. Later, in Motley's diplomatic years, when Bismarck still sang the American songs he had learned from his friend at Göttingen, the two saw much of one another, and Bismarck recalled that Motley had "never entered a drawing-room without exciting the curiosity and sympathy of the ladies." By the time he was twenty-seven, when he went to St. Petersburg as an attaché, he had met Prince John of Saxony, Ticknor's friend, the Goethe family at Weimar, Tieck, who was translating Shakespeare, and Guizot, who wrote an introduction to his *Dutch Republic,* in the French translation which he supervised. Years before, Cogswell had sent to Goethe's daughter-in-law an essay that Motley had written on Goethe while he was still in college. She had replied, "I wish to see the first book that young man will write." On Motley's second visit to Weimar, Ottilie von Goethe had heard of his novel, but he refused to tell her the name of the book.

No one else expected much of Motley. He had studied law, which he never practised; he had interested himself in politics and even served a term in the Legislature. But this had led to nothing, and *Morton's Hope,* the novel he had published, showed little promise. It was a childish fantasy, carelessly written, with no regard for probabilities. The scene was laid half in Boston, before the Revolution, and half in the Göttingen of Motley's time, between which the hero spent his youth. The pictures of German student-life had a certain air of reality,—the aesthetic tea-party, for one. They were merry enough in tone, with happy strokes here and there; but the author did not seem to be in earnest. In the garden of "Morton's Hope," a Brookline house, built by an old China merchant, the lizards "shot to and fro in the patches of sunlight." Young Morton, however, was Motley himself. He, too, burned with dreams of glory. His inflammable nature was filled with a boundless ambition. If he had not breakfasted with a pen behind his ear, or dined with a folio as big as the table, he had longed to write history, like Morton. He, too, had devoured the English poets, from Chaucer and Gower downward. immersed himself in Latin chronicles, read every historical work that he could find, in German, French and Spanish, and all the books to which the notes referred; and, whatever the book was, on whatever subject, he had planned to write a better one himself.

Merry Mount, Motley's second novel, was a very different affair, although no one seemed to know it, then or later. It was a charming picture of early New England, in its more Arcadian aspects, a fantasy of the greenwood, the story of Morton's crew at Wollaston. Hawthorne had sketched the theme in his *Twice-Told Tales,* which Motley had refrained from reading, in order not to confuse his own impressions; and *Merry Mount,* in

some of its scenes, might have been written by Hawthorne. It pictured the dim, unsettled time, at the dawn
of Massachusetts history, when various men who seemed
like apparitions, as they flitted through the early chronicles, played parts that later historians had forgotten.
Who were those pale and misty figures, Blaxton, the first
settler on the site of Boston, Morton and his comrades
of the may-pole, wanderers from Elizabethan England
whom the colony harboured in its sylvan depths? The
forest scenes, the hawking scenes, the scenes in the woodland fortress, the portrait of the hermit of Beacon Hill,
of Miles Standish and the giant blacksmith, of the mysterious knight, Sir Christopher Gardiner, were Motley's
reply to the question. There was an element of historic
fact behind every detail of the vivid picture, and it was
all suffused with a glow and feeling that brought back the
Shakespeare of *As You Like It*.

Meanwhile, in the middle eighteen-forties, Motley
wrote a number of essays for the *North American Review*. One of these papers, on Balzac, who had begun to
be widely read,—Hawthorne, for instance, had read
him,—made a great stir. It was a lively defense of the
artist as man of letters, the sort of defense that Poe was
making and that Hawthorne might have made, but that,
in fact, had not been made by any other writer in New
England. Motley envied the French their freedom of
speech, praising Balzac for his disregard of ordinary notions of the "nasty" in his passion for detached observation. In this he agreed with Fanny Kemble, who
constantly protested, when she lived in Lenox, against
the silly prudery of American women, which took the life
out of novel-writing. This prudery, a recent thing, at least
in circles that knew the world,—for the Boston folk of
old, like other Americans of an earlier day, rejoiced in
Fielding and Smollett, who spoke their own language,—
was to spread like a film for generations over the work

of the novelists, to break in the end with a vengeance
that might have been foreseen. Motley had registered his
protest, and he had carried it further. He praised the
detachment of Balzac as the proper attitude of the artist
in letters, and he uttered a phrase that resounded
through New England, "Certainly the world should be
reformed, but not by novel-writing." Few readers
thought of novelists as artists, in spite of Hawthorne's
presence and example; and Motley, following Prescott,
was soon to show that history also was a form of art. For
Motley, whose early motives had been confused, had
embarked on historical writing. His essay on Peter the
Great, perhaps suggested by his year in Russia, first revealed his gifts in this direction.

The essay appeared in 1845, when the rage for Carlyle was at its height, and Peter the Great was a typical
Carlyle hero. This "strong, silent man," who had carved
a nation out of a Scythian wilderness, who had tried to
Europeanize Russia and turn it into a modern civilization, who "preferred to go to the ocean rather than wait
for the ocean to come to him" and who raised his capital
in the northern marshes, was another Oliver Cromwell,
in his way. Better still, he was an empire-builder, one of
the men who "do" things and who were doing them for
the Anglo-Saxons in all the four quarters of the globe.
He was even, one might have thought, a Russian Yankee,
an Abbott Lawrence on a larger scale, this prince who
worked as a carpenter, in his apron, in a shipbuilder's
yard at Amsterdam, learned his trade from the bottom
and laid down and built, from his own draught and model,
a sixty-gun ship. Peter was a Portland or Salem hero, the
kind they understood in the Yankee seaports, the self-
made man *nulli secundus,* the sort that makes things hum,
who had made Russia hum like another New Hampshire,
multiplied by two or three dozen Maines. Motley, like
Carlyle, admired the type, much as he disliked its brutal

aspects, those that Carlyle came to admire the most. It represented what the age called Progress. Motley did not labour the point. Perhaps he was scarcely aware of it. But, shorn of its barbarian elements, this was the type that had built his own republic.

What was the history of this type? Where had it first emerged? How had it emerged from the mediæval world that held it back? At what point in the history of Europe had the enterprising man declared himself, demanded the free institutions that gave him scope, cast off the burden of privilege? Where had the merchant, the burgher, the craftsman, the sailor, the builder of civilization in its modern form, the man who believed in freedom of thought and action, first come to grips with the old regime? In Holland, where Peter the Great had learned his trade and the Pilgrim Fathers from England had found a refuge before they sailed for America. Just why Motley chose the history of Holland none of his friends knew. When his essay on Peter the Great appeared, they felt that history was his real vocation, and one of them found him at work, soon afterward, with a huge Dutch folio and a dictionary. He had turned to another use than novel-writing his art of painting scenes and characters, but few could have seen the connection between the history of Holland and the history of the American republic. For Motley, the United Provinces, in their struggle to liberate themselves from Spain, suggested the struggle of the United States. William the Silent, for him, was a prototype of Washington. But behind this political aspect, there was another. In celebrating the rise of the Dutch Republic, Motley was celebrating the modern man, the American type in its first historic appearance.

This was the larger meaning of Motley's work, the motive, scarcely expressed, that gave him his vast popularity. It was the tendency of all his writing. American readers felt that he was defending their kind of man,

almost as much as Bancroft. For the rest, they were interested in Holland. It was a camp of the Pilgrims, it was
the battle-ground of Protestantism, it was the home of
many of their forbears; and Holland had been the
laughing-stock of Europe long before America became so.
Motley had not chosen the theme, which had become his
life-study. He felt that the theme had chosen him, before
he knew that Prescott was planning to cover almost the
same ground. Prescott, to whom he described his design,
treated him as kindly as Washington Irving had treated
himself in a similar situation; he welcomed Motley's
rivalry and even thought of giving him the manuscripts
he had gathered for himself. Motley had hoped to write
his book at home. In fact, he had begun it at Nahant, in
an old house in the village street, overhung by two great
willows, where Longfellow later spent a summer. Prescott's presence gave Nahant an atmosphere for historical
writing. Motley did not know, when he undertook *The
Rise of the Dutch Republic,* what hours of dusty labour
lay before him.

It was ten years before the book appeared, years that
were largely spent in Dresden, Berlin, the Hague and
Brussels, where Motley worked obscurely in the archives,
turning up almost as many unpublished papers as Prescott
had read for his Spanish histories. These were the
original documents, in all their native crabbedness, not
neatly copied as Prescott's were. Thousands of them had
never been read by any Dutch historian, and sometimes
they were indecipherable.* Motley felt, at times, as he
toiled in the subterranean depths of black-letter folios in
Latin and German, as if he were working in a coal-pit,
grimy, dark and cheerless. His life reminded him of a
Dutch canal, slow, silent, stagnant. But the novelist in
him never slept, as he fed upon the musty mulberry-

---

* Motley's work was instrumental in stirring the Dutch historians to publish these original documents.

leaves of which he was afterwards to spin his silk. At
night, as he walked the streets of Leyden and Brussels, he
lived over the scenes of the day's reading and seemed to
see Egmont and Horn, Granvelle, the Duke of Alva and
William of Orange in the ghosts that flitted over the
moonlit squares. In one of his letters, writing of Rubens,
who did not appear in the *Dutch Republic*,—one of the
weaknesses of the book, in fact, was that it omitted all
mention of the flowering of Dutch and Flemish art,—he
showed his delight in the glowing colour that appeared in
his own writing. His friendship with Bismarck, meanwhile, whose career he watched with a natural interest
and rather more benevolence than the case required,
sharpened his understanding of the European statecraft
that formed the principal theme of all his volumes.

In later life, as minister to Austria and England, Motley was immersed in politics. *The History of the United
Netherlands* and *The Life and Death of John of Barneveld,* in which he continued his unfinished series,—for he
planned to tell the story of the Thirty Years' War,—were
all too much concerned with statesmanship. At least, they
were little concerned with anything else. They were
largely compilations of documents, like Bancroft's later
volumes. Where was Dutch life, one might have asked,
the life of the people, their art, their thought, their customs, in the history of the United Netherlands? Even in
The Rise of the Dutch Republic, one found too little of
the common scene, in its multifarious aspects, for which
the battles were fought and the statesmen existed. Only
the great individual interested Motley, and, generally
speaking, only the man of action, although the escape of
Grotius, in *Barneveld,* was one of his liveliest episodes;
and his psychology was so simplified that his great men
were supermen or devils. His William of Orange was a
boys' hero, his Philip was a nightmare. The characters he
understood the best were those whom he might have met

in Boston; for the lawyers, manufacturers and bankers who founded the Dutch Republic were such as he had known in his father's circle. John of Barneveld would have felt at home with Amos and Abbott Lawrence, Webster and Choate. These were types that Motley knew, and his imagination scarcely moved outside their burgher atmosphere. His sympathies were all with oligarchies, such as the Essex Junto had represented,—a legal and commercial world. He had little feeling for the people, and less for saints, poets, artists and thinkers. But Motley was a preëminent story-teller. For sheer narrative power, the dense, moving mass of the *Dutch Republic* stood with the greatest of its kind; and some of Motley's scenes and incidents,—the executions of Egmont and Horn, the defeat of the Spanish Armada,—were destined to live with the best of Prescott and Parkman.

CHAPTER XVIII

DR. HOLMES

MEANWHILE, the son of another historian, Dr. Abiel Holmes, had made his appearance as a poet. As far back as 1830, Oliver Wendell Holmes, a young student of the Harvard Law School, who was soon to abandon law for medicine, had written a poem called *Old Ironsides*. He had composed it with a pencil, standing on one foot in the attic of his old house in Cambridge. The battle of Bunker Hill had been planned in this house, and one saw the dents of the muskets on the floor. The frigate "Constitution," in the Boston navy-yard, was about to be dismantled and abandoned. The poem, reprinted on hand-bills from a newspaper in Boston and scattered about the streets of Washington, saved the ship and made the poet famous.

He had "sneaked in," as he later said, in the same year with Tennyson and Darwin, the man of science and the man of rhymes whose natures he was to share in equal parts. His father, a moderate Calvinist, had still defended the faith of Jonathan Edwards, who said that little boys were more hateful than vipers. Against this faith the son was to fight with the diligent wit of a doctor who knew that such ideas were very harmful. But the father, kinder than his creed, a lover of books and the art of living, was also a poet in his fashion. One evening, when the children were in the parlour, he had stepped to the frost-covered window and sketched on the pane with his knife-blade a cluster of branches and stars. Above, he

had written, *Per aspera ad astra.* The family had come
from Connecticut, but they had Boston connections,
enough to cause a boy to feel that he was one of the boys
with the family portraits. Among these portraits was one
of Dorothy Quincy, about whom Holmes was to write a
poem. Another of his forbears was Anne Bradstreet, the
old New England poetess whose blood ran in the veins
of so many writers. Wendell Phillips was one of his
cousins. Others were the Channings and the Danas.

To the end of his life, the rhythms of Moore and Pope,
softened and sweetened in Goldsmith, were to ring
through Holmes's poems, together with those of Byron,
Hood and Campbell. These were the favourite poets of
the Cambridge household. He had gone to the little school
in Cambridgeport, where his younger cousin, Richard
Henry Dana, had had so much trouble with the master.
One of his fellow-pupils was Margaret Fuller, who was always reading "naw-vells," as she called them, and whose
long and flexible neck looked like a swan's,—that is to say,
if one liked her, for it looked like a snake if one didn't.
But he had learned something from Margaret Fuller. He
happened to see one of her themes, which began with the
phrase, "It is a trite remark." Having learned that trite
remarks existed,—for the word was entirely new to him,
—he was better prepared never to make one. He found it
easy to elope from school to see Revenge and Prospect on
the race-course; for, although he loved learning as he
loved his country, he also loved horses, observing that,
wherever a trotter went, he carried in his train brisk omnibuses, lively bakers' carts, and therefore hot rolls, the
jolly butcher's wagon and the cheerful gig. Every New
England deacon, Holmes reflected,—the more he had occasion to study the species,—ought to see at least one
Derby Day to learn what sort of a world it was he lived in.

After he had won his degree at Harvard, in the class
of 1829, and having dropped the law for medicine, he

found his father eager to send him abroad,—equipped with
a good Dutch liquor-case, filled with six kinds of strong
waters,—to study for a year in Edinburgh, the favourite training-school for American doctors, and two years
in Paris. The class of 1829 included the author of "My
Country, 'Tis of Thee." Holmes had his own ideas about
this poem,* but he thought the class worthy of endless
odes, to warm and hearten its members,—other people
were not obliged to read them,—odes and odes, stretching
from decade to decade, till the poet himself had reached
three score and twenty and the first line had to begin,
" 'Tis sixty years since." As for the years in Paris, aside
from all they meant for a medical student, they sharpened
the wit of this ingenious Yankee, confirming the natural
bent of his mind as the softly romantic sentiment of the
Rhineland confirmed Longfellow's natural bent. For the
rest, the evenings at the Trois Frères, when the Chamber-
tin or the Clos Vougeot came in, and the Scotch-plaided
snuff-box went round the table, had their effect on a mind
that loved gracious living and was to claim the rights of
gracious living on behalf of his somewhat frost-bound
countrymen.

Certainly, a good slice of Paris sandwiched between
two slices of New England created a sense of contrast
that enlivened his critical spirit. With other scenes in mind,
the returning pilgrim observed the well-known vista in the
high relief that is always the fruit of comparison. He observed its lovelier aspects and other aspects that were not
so lovely,—for instance, the acidulous Yankee voice, acidulous and stridulous, bred by commercial habits, east
winds, a lean soil and too much enterprise. The young
medical student never forgot the soft and liquid inflec-

* "Sam Smith will live when Longfellow, Whittier and all the rest of us
have gone into oblivion. And yet what is there in those verses to make
them live? Do you remember the line 'Like *that* above'? I asked Sam what
'that' referred to. He said 'that rapture'!" And Holmes made one of his wry
little faces.—See M. A. DeW. Howe, *Memories of a Hostess.*

tions he had heard in France, so winning, so delicious, with so much woman in them. The voices of the brave Yankee girls,—too often at least, he thought,—would not be among the allurements the Enemy would put in requisition were he planning another assault on Saint Anthony's virtue. But most of his impressions were happy enough. He had said to himself, with joyous confidence, in Florence and Pisa, as in the streets of Paris, "I am a Cambridge boy!": and he was to remain a Cambridge poet. His lays were

> of one whose natal star
> Still seemed the brightest when it shone afar.

They dealt with the homeliest facts of the Yankee world, washing-day, the spinning-top, the katydid, the gale, the dinner-bell, the oysterman, the churchyard, the family portrait, the unmarried aunt, scenes and subjects touched by a fresh and original mind, however composed in forms that English and Scottish poets had made familiar. Well he knew how to dress the fable

> in which genius poured
> And warmed the shapes that later times adored.

However this genius seemed in times still later, it was a revelation in a day when foreign writers ruled the imagination. It evoked, for the Yankee ear and eye, the train of associations that made it classic.

The medical student soon became a doctor, established in a modest street in Boston. He also became a professor at the Harvard Medical School; and, as if to enlarge his field for the study of human nature, he gave Lyceum lectures in the country towns on some of the English poets, Wordsworth, Keats, Shelley, Moore. For his animal spirits superabounded,—his curiosity likewise. He kept a

rattlesnake in a cage to study its manners and habits. He
kept a little gold in his house, to handle now and then, in
order to analyze a miser's feelings. He was known to have
inhaled a dose of ether, to record his sensations and
thoughts. In Springfield and Pittsfield, where he spent his
summers, they liked to see the lions and hear them roar;
and the doctor, who belonged to the lion family, as one of
its younger members, was willing to be seen on all occasions. He was a poet laureate by avocation, always prepared to present his bouquet at a banquet or an ode at a
county fair. He knew the vexations of lecturing all too
well, the cold parlours, the cold apples and water, the cold
beds in the cold hotel bedrooms, the cold congratulations
of the committees, to whom his remarks had given "satisfaction." He was placarded and announced as a public
performer and saw his name stuck up in letters so large
that he scarcely dared to appear in the town by daylight.
Well he knew the dangers of lecturing, too,—for he was
aware of everything: one would have had to get up very
early to take the doctor in,—the danger of talking down
to muddier wits, the danger of shaping one's thoughts in a
popular mould. How often the lecture-platform was a
slippery slide down to the Avernus of the windy bores.
But, if you knew yourself as your maker knew you, knew
even that you had your vanities, and if you knew where to
draw the line and picked out the most intelligent faces,
and talked only to them, lecturing had its rewards for a
student of human nature. One learned, for instance, the
law of averages. Two Lyceum assemblies of five hundred
each were much the same in Springfield as in Boston, and
perhaps the doctor would have added Paris. And one
learned to know the tribe of the Pooh-Poohs, so called
from their leading expression. No doubt this tribe served a
useful purpose in keeping down the noxious animals, the
thinking, or rather talking and writing ones. Beyond this,
they were of small value; and they were always retreating

before the advance of knowledge, facing it and moving backwards, with their inextinguishable war-cry, Pooh-Pooh!

A good corrective, lecturing, for a mind a little too ready to think a little too much of its own time and place. Nor was this the only egg that was dropped into the doctor's intellect by the solemn fowl Experience, fed by so many crumbs from the lecture-platform, a fowl which, amid its idle cacklings, sometimes cackled in earnest. One of the doctor's whims was to think of all New England, and even all America, as a large and friendly boarding-house, a house with an ample break-fast-table, at which, for a number of years, he found himself appointed to preside. The role of an autocrat had been thrust upon him, for had not fate endowed him with a luminous mind, the same fate that had endowed New England with a hunger and thirst for knowledge? Well, what an opportunity these lectures gave him to study his fellow-boarders, the schoolmistress, just below the plat-form, whom he always found so sympathetic, the divinity student, whom he could tease a little about the One-Hoss Shay of Calvinism,—which had long since dropped to pieces, "all at once, and nothing first," in Boston, but was still a handsome carriage in these country districts,—the old gentleman opposite, who brought him down with a joke or a volley of facts if he became a little high-falutin, the landlady's daughter, lockets and ringlets and all, and Benjamin Franklin in the back row. This Benjamin Frank-lin, Junior, was the symbol of the rising generation, still up and coming, unversed in the *suaviter in modo* but bent on acquiring his French and science and prepared for the words of Erasmus on religion and morals. Was not the doctor himself an Erasmus or Franklin, who was planning a new *Poor Richard's Almanac* for more advanced stu-dents? There they all were, all the boarders, even the lady in black bombazine with the soul-subduing decorum, and the sad-eyed gentleman in the Spanish cloak, he of the fluted cheeks, worn by the passions of the melodrama, the symbol of the poor old Yankee theatre. What an opportunity for the doctor to take them into his confidence and plant in their minds a few well-chosen seeds,—seeds of moral etiquette, for instance, and even etiquette without the morals, Erasmian seeds, Confucian seeds, seeds of a worldly wisdom that was based on all the Commandments, and even some that Moses knew not of. When a doctor, thanks to his Creator, possesses such a store of sense and wit, and tempers it to the lambs that know not Boston, when he has learned how to approach his patients so that they swallow his pills with high good humour, when they feel better for his doses, why should not a spade be called a spade? Why should he not be called an Autocrat?

The doctor did not possess the gift of silence, and, possessing the gift of wit, he meant to use it. What would be the state of the highways of life, he said on one occasion, if we did not drive our thought-sprinklers through them, with the valves open? He enjoyed his journeys through the rural districts, where, pursuing his mission, spreading the light of the metropolis, he learned so much about his countrymen. Whether in man or tree, as he soon discovered, the provinces did not know a first-rate thing, even when they possessed it, and constantly took the second- and third-rate for nature's very best, for they had no standards of comparison; and, filled with the love of excellence as he was, he was always looking for it, and always making notes of it "when found." He carried in his pocket a measuring-tape, as Emerson carried a compass. This tape, thirty feet long, was long enough to encircle the largest brain, even Daniel Webster's; but the doctor commonly used it to measure trees. In his younger days, when he was much devoted to the young-lady population of Rhode Island, he had measured the great Johnston elm on the Providence Plantations, and with time he had formed the acquaintance of every considerable tree in New England. He knew the grand willows down in Maine, and the grand elms up the other way, the West Springfield elm, the noble Hatfield elm, the Sheffield elm, the great tree on the Colman farm at Deerfield that was living on its past reputation, the poor old Pittsfield elm, the horse-chestnut tree near the Rockport station, as well as all the elms on the Boston Common. Some of these great trees looked very meek when they saw the fatal measure begin to unreel,—like one of those politicians in the country towns who had puffed themselves up to look like Webster. They had never been measured before by a metropolitan eye when the little doctor approached them. The American elm, he observed, was tall and slender, and drooped as if from languor, while the English elm was more robust, and held its branches up, and carried its leaves longer than the native tree. Was this symbolic of the creative force on the two sides of the ocean? Did it indicate that Dr. Knox was right in thinking that Anglo-Saxons could not survive, outside the mother-country, that they were destined to die out unless they were kept up by fresh supplies? The doctor did not wish to decide a point that filled him with misgivings, although he argued stoutly the other way.

As for the "great tree" on the Boston Common, it belonged in the second rank, like the tree at Cohasset. The doctor admitted this without hesitation, for where Boston was concerned he was always candid. He had, of course, a modest pride in Boston, and, when some impertinent New Yorker asked one of his friends how he could endure the fulsome things that were constantly said of the town, he was rather inclined to agree with his friend's reply, "Because we feel that they are *true*." Boston was the hub of the solar system: you could not pry this out of a Boston man if you had the tire of all creation straightened out for a crowbar. But how did the New Yorkers feel about New

York? Did not the axis of the earth stick visibly out
through the centre of every city? Did not the smallest
village of Massachusetts read, to its own advantage,
Pope's well-known line, "All are but parts of one stupendous HULL"? In his weaker moments, the doctor admitted that Boston men ran a certain danger of taking
their local scale for the absolute scale, an error that was
natural enough, since Boston was so bright and wide-
awake. But when he was his own cheerful self, he forgot
these doubts and compunctions. Why not regard the Common as the unit of space, and the State House as the standard of architecture? Boston, of course, was just like other
towns, except for its excellent fish-market; but one had to
remember its fire-department, its admirable monthly publications, which everyone acknowledged, together with its
use of the English language, which everyone ought to
acknowledge. What was the real offence of Boston? One
had to say this without fear or favour. It drained a water-
shed of intellect with which no other could be compared,
and it would not let itself be drained in turn.

This was the open secret that gave the doctor's face its
honest glow. This, and another secret, if it was one: the
doctor loved his Boston with an affection that deepened
as the wonder of it grew. Had he not, in his daily travels,
bored this ancient city through and through? He knew it
as an old inhabitant of a Cheshire knows his cheese; and
when, with his mounting fortunes, a few years later, he
moved into Beacon Street,—the last of his "justifiable
domicides,"—whence he could see Bunker Hill, from his
window facing the bay, and Cambridge across the water,
his cup ran over. There he could indulge his whims at last.
At the Medical School, he continued to give his lectures,
darting about the laboratory as nimbly as a cat, while his
pupils laughed and cried as he told his stories, as often
pathetic as witty, running out of the room when a rabbit
had to be chloroformed, beseeching his assistant not to let

it squeak. He was always tinkering at something, developing photographs or "mending things," breaking a chair or
table to put it together better. He invented the best of
stethoscopes and wrote a medical classic on puerperal
fever, an essay that saved as many lives as Bowditch's
Practical Navigator. He shut himself up with his violin
and fiddled away industriously until he could play "Auld
Lang Syne" so that anyone could recognize the tune. He
never missed a horse-race and knew all the points of the
favourites and winners,* as he knew the virtues of a sportsman,—to pay up, own up and shut up, that is, if you
were beaten. He liked to go to the circus and the side-
shows and chat with the freaks and the giants and measure their chests with his tape; for, being small himself, he
had a relish for size, whether in trees or men. He knew
the deeds of the prize-ring. Charles Freeman, who fought
the "Tipton Slasher,"—a very superior type of American
giant,—granted him confidential interviews; and the
double-headed daughter of Africa allowed him to question **her on the delicate subject** of avoirdupois equivalents.
Prudence and propriety and all the other pious P's had
very little interest for the doctor; and, as only a good
anatomist can, he loved to see a man prepare for box-
ing. Where could one find a handsomer spectacle than a
fine Boston citizen resolving himself into the primitive
elements of his humanity? If only the manly art of self-
defense had been introduced among the reverend clergy,
humankind would have had better sermons.

For the doctor never forgot that he was a doctor, even
when he felt most the poet. And he never forgot that he
was a poet. Sometimes, in the early morning, before the
sun was up, he put out from shore in his little skiff, his
"water-sulky," as he liked to call it, and glided round the

---

* Emerson, who admired skill, whether in men or horses, as much as
Holmes, once corrected the doctor in a matter of horse-racing. It was a
quarter of a second difference in the record of the trotter Flora Temple
at Kalamazoo, 1859. The time was 2.19¾.

bay, up the Charles to Watertown or about the wharves, under the stern of some tall Indiaman, rubbing against the hulls of the old wood-schooners, propelling himself swiftly over the water or drifting with the tide. Only in his poems could he tell the delights of those sweet June mornings, when the bay was as smooth as a sheet of beryl-green silk, as he lay in his shell motionless over the flats, as he watched the crabs crawling in the shallows, the sculpins wavering silently under the boat, as he rustled through the long, harsh grass that led the way up some tranquil creek and paused there, moored unseen, in a loneliness so profound that the columns of Tadmor in the desert could not have seemed more remote from life. A city of idiots Boston seemed to him then, not to have covered this glorious bay with gondolas and wherries,—this bay where a poet might almost find a chambered nautilus, or at any rate might be reminded of one, brought back perhaps in that tall Indiaman, to write a poem about, one poem, at least, to make his name immortal.

For the doctor was a poet, for all he could "write so funny," a solid poet whose fruit was never green. He had observed that American poets did not commonly ripen well. They lacked severe standards; they had no sound thermometers for gauging their talents; and surely, the doctor thought, the United States furnished the greatest market in the world for the green fruit of the intellect. There were certain things, he felt, that were good for nothing until they had been kept a long while, and some that were good for nothing until they had been long kept and *used:* wine, meerschaum pipes and violins. A poem was like a violin, the parts of which were strangers to one another till they had learned to vibrate in harmony. A poem was as porous as a meerschaum,—in order to be good, it had to absorb the essence of one's own humanity. One had to keep one's poem until its sentiment harmonized with all the aspects of one's life and nature, until one had contrived to stain oneself through all its thoughts and images. That was what made poems, real poems, so much like buckwheat cakes, as the young fellow said at the breakfast-table, buckwheat being decidedly scarce and high.

So it was with the doctor's poems. Whatever else they were, they were always ripe. If they were largely occasional, and largely local, what else could be expected of a harper who could never refuse the appeal "by request of friends"? He knew his audience;

> All the gay and young
> Love the light antics of a playful tongue;

and he cheerfully plied the strings on all occasions, Commencement feasts, meetings of fellow-doctors, birthdays of eminent citizens. Would he just this once comply? Be the truth at once confessed; he wavered, yielded, did his best. And why not, when, from his nimble tongue, as from no other American tongue or pen, tripped the phrase, the epithet, on each occasion, that fired in every mind the appropriate train? These rhymes of an hour were fresh, adroit, correct. The doctor never said, in flowery language, that life was full of trials. He never said that youth was like the dewdrop. Moreover, he often glowed with intenser feeling. Well he recalled the moments when a "lyric conception" had struck him like a bullet in the forehead, when the blood dropped from his cheek and he felt himself turning as white as death. Once or twice only he had had this feeling,—as when he wrote *The Chambered Nautilus,*—a creeping as of centipedes running down the spine, a gasp, a jump of the heart, then a sudden flush, a beating in the vessels of the head, then a long sigh—and the poem was written. For the rest, his happiest vein was that which most resembled his conversation, when he felt like a jockey on the race-course, a good Yankee jockey, re-

joicing in his own vernacular, and confident, old as his
horse might be, that he would win the bet.

In this vein, he always won the bet. Had he not, in his
Rhymed Lesson, that *Essay on Man,* or rather essay on
manners, rewritten for another time and country, revealed
himself as a Yankee Pope, even as he revealed his limitations? Prickly pears are also edible, along with the other
varieties, and most of the doctor's prickles were salutary.
There were more things, it was true, even in Boston than
the doctor's philosophy dreamed of, more in the "bores"
and "earnest sages," whom Pope would have disliked as
much as he, more in Bronson Alcott,—

> groping vague and dim,
> Whose every angle was a half-starved whim;

more in Emerson, too, something he never gathered even
when he knew the "wingéd Franklin," whom he loved and
wished to comprehend and even "explained," years later,
in a patient study as good as a clever intellect could make
it. Far less could he understand those uncouth heroes,—

> such as Homer's, who, we read in Pope,
> Dined without forks and never heard of soap . . .
> Such as May to Marlborough Chapel brings,
> Lean, hungry, savage anti-everythings,
> Copies of Luther in the pasteboard style.

The reformers were not for him, any more than the
"genuine article," Luther himself, or Luther's disciples,
rather, were for his dear Erasmus. But has not history,
which Erasmus fills, a case to make also for the doctor,
whose "Reformation," though of a mundane kind, also
brought its blessings? Was he not also a reformer who,
with his ass's jawbone, slew in a thousand households the
pestilent lion that masked itself in a Geneva gown? He

was a reformer in medical matters, bent upon destroying,
root and branch, the nostrums and the notions of human
nature that a narrow past had bred in the Yankee mind,—
even a reformer of the art of living, the lack of any real
sense of which had given birth to these nostrums and
notions. How many lines of reform can a man pursue
without losing that fulcrum in common sense which gives
his lever purchase? Great is the office of wit, ye deluded
reformers, whose reforms are all in the air because your
feet have no firm ground to stand on! Great is the office
of wit, O optimists, who take so much for granted!—ye
who will never know

> Some doubts must darken o'er the world below
> Though all the Platos of the nursery trail
> Their 'clouds of glory' at the go-cart's tail!

Because your forbears saw only the evil, can you see only
the good? You must see the black squares on the checker-
board, as well as the white squares, if you wish to play the
game to any purpose. And you must learn to write, like
men of this world, if you are going to change the world
by writing, you Transcendental authors who foist upon
your readers

> Mesmeric pamphlets, which to facts appeal,
> Each fact as slippery as a fresh-caught eel . . .
> Poems that shuffle with superfluous legs
> A blindfold minuet over addled eggs . . .
> Essays so dark Champollion might despair
> To guess what mummy of a thought was there,
> Where our poor English, striped with foreign phrase,
> Looks like a zebra in a parson's chaise.

What if, afflicted by these effusions, a wit should

> spread them to the smiling day
> And toss them, fluttering like the new-mown hay,
> To laughter's light, or sorrow's pitying shower?—

would it not be, for you and your readers' good, to send you back to school where *you* might learn how to win the bet?

No doubt, the doctor had his incomprehensions, along with his little vanities. It was his passion to define himself, and those who define themselves too readily are men whose imagination has its limits. He disliked some of the friends of progress because of their muddy brains, or because of their Sunday frowns. Some of them he thought were moral bullies. He also disliked them for their dingy linen, a pardonable distaste, and yet it encroached a little on the comic spirit, or, shall one say, the tragic spirit, of which the imagination is all compact, and which, in minds of a larger calibre, resolves these lesser discords. But the doctor seldom lost his sense of proportion. He never professed to see with the eye of God, and he was well aware of his limitations. The essence of wit, he said, consists of a partial view of whatever it touches. It throws a single ray, separate from the rest,—yellow, red or blue,—upon an object, never the white light: that is the province of wisdom.

There were men wiser than he, and well he knew it; but in all America there was none more witty. No one else could have written *The One-Hoss Shay, The Morning Visit, The Moral Bully,* or *How the Old Horse Won the Bet.* That was the region where the doctor's rhymes were safe from all rivals and invaders, where the rhymes added a relish to the doctor's talk. For talk was his native element and his mission. Who knew, as he,—

> the little arts that please,
> Bright looks, the cheerful language of the eye,
> The neat, crisp question and the gay reply?

Who had such a festive air of finding life interesting and full? Who liked people to speak their minds so fully?

Who opened a conversation with such a look of expecting something good from his next-seat neighbour? He rejoiced in every kind of conversation, the kind that floated safely over the shallows, the kind that floated over a few fathoms, the philosophical parley, better still, that called for a deep-sea line to reach the bottom, and best of all the contact of two minds when they were off soundings in the ocean of thought. The doctor was never a monopolist. Well, hardly ever. It was his rule to talk only of subjects he had long had in his mind, and to listen to what others said of subjects that he had only recently studied, for knowledge, like timber, he felt, should not be used until it was properly seasoned. Who could have censured him if, in later life, he talked about all subjects, and most of the time, considering that he had had them all in mind longer than anyone else? He never made puns, unless the occasion enjoined some very rare pun in Old Italian, the well-known tongue invented by Andrews and Stoddard. He considered conversation one of the arts, from which one ought to refrain—inasmuch as listening also was an art—unless one could match one's glass of wine with an equal glow of light and warmth and colour. He was a master of the art himself. At moments, when conditions favoured him, when the candles shone in the deep mahogany, his spirits rose like mercury under the summer sun and flashed like the Shah's regalia. His talk was the eighth wonder of the Boston world. In later years, on one of these occasions, Henry James the elder said to him, "Holmes, you are intellectually the most alive man I ever knew." And the little doctor replied, and he almost danced as he spoke, "I am, I am! From the crown of my head to the sole of my foot, I'm alive, I'm alive!"

CHAPTER XIX

THOREAU AT WALDEN

HENRY THOREAU had built a hut at Walden. In March, 1845, he had borrowed Alcott's axe,—which he took pains to return with a sharper edge,—and cut down some tall, arrowy pines for the timbers, studs and rafters. For the boards he bought a shanty from one of the Irish labourers on the railroad. The hut was ten feet by fifteen, shingled and plastered, with a garret and closet, a trap-door below, a brick fireplace, windows at the sides and a door facing the cove. The cost, all told, was $28.12½,—less than the annual rent of a student's room in Cambridge. There was a bean-field, close by, with a patch of potatoes, corn, peas and turnips. As a quasi-Pythagorean, Thoreau seldom indulged in beans. He exchanged his crop for rice in the village. Rice was the proper diet for one who loved so well the writings of the Oriental sages.

He had long cherished the notion of a forest-life. Ellery Channing had built himself a hut on the prairie in Illinois, and Henry's college class-mate, Stearns Wheeler, who had just died in Leipzig, had also built a rough woodland cabin, over at Flint's Pond, where he had lived for a year to save money, to buy Greek books and pay his way to Germany to study. Henry had spent six weeks in Wheeler's cabin, sharing one of his bunks of straw. There was nothing new in his own adventure, and he could not understand why his friends thought it was so peculiar. Some of them spoke as if he had gone to the

woods in order to starve or freeze. Emerson had bought
land on both sides of the pond, intending to build a summer-house, and Henry had carried out the project. Alcott,
who liked to tinker at rustic architecture, helped him with
his saw and hammer, along with the young Brook
Farmer, George William Curtis of New York, who was
boarding at Edmund Hosmer's in the village and working as a farm-hand. Henry felt at home in his sylvan
dwelling. It made him think of some of those mountain-
houses he had seen on his inland excursions, high-placed,
airy, fragrant, with a fresh, auroral atmosphere about
them. It was quiet, clean and cool, fit to entertain a
travelling god. For company, birds flitted through his
chamber, red squirrels raced over the roof, chickadees
perched on the armfuls of wood he carried. There were
moles living in the cellar. He had occasional visits from
a hare. As he sat at his door in the evening, he remembered that he was descended from the Greeks of old. He
was a wanderer, too, one of the crew of Ulysses. The
shore of the cove was another Ithaca.

There was nothing about his "experiment," as his
friends liked to call it, to arouse such curiosity and contempt. It was a common-sensible undertaking, and only
a slight departure from Henry's usual mode of living.
His average weekly outlay, for necessaries he could not
supply himself, was twenty-seven cents. A few days at
manual labour, building a boat or a fence, planting, grafting or surveying,—six weeks of work out of the year,
when he had grown extravagant and had to have a
microscope,—gave him an ample surplus. Why should
anyone live by the sweat of his brow and bore his fellow-
men by talking about it? Why should not everyone live
with an ample margin?—as anyone could do, provided
he followed the path of simplification, logically and ruth-
lessly enough. The mass of men led lives of quiet despera-
tion. Why, if not to maintain a "standard of living" that

every law of the universe controverted? Did they not
know that the wisest had always lived, with respect to
comforts and luxuries, a life more simple and meagre
than the poor? Had all the philosophers, Hindu, Greek
and Persian, lived and taught in vain? Had anyone
measured man's capacities? Was it fair to judge by precedents, when so very little had been attempted? Who
could say that if a man advanced, boldly, in the direction
of his dreams, endeavouring to live the life he had
imagined, he would not meet with a success that he had
never expected in common hours? Henry believed, and
wished to prove, that the more one simplified one's life
the less complex the laws of life would seem. Why all
this pother about possessions? He liked to think of the
ancient Mexicans, who burned all their goods every fifty
years. Hawthorne, in one of his stories, had pictured a
similar holocaust; and this was the kind of reform that
Henry thought was worth considering. He meant to have
his furniture, actual and symbolic, as simple as an Indian's
or an Arab's. There were three bits of limestone on his
table. They had to be dusted every day, while the furniture of his mind was still undusted. Out of the window,
quick!

If he had had the wealth of Crœsus, Henry's mode of
living would not have been different. Space, air, time, a
few tools, a note-book, a pen, a copy of Homer, what
could he wish more than these? A bath in the pond at
sunrise, a little Spartan sweeping and cleaning, then a
bath for the intellect, perhaps in the *Bhagavad-Gita,* the
pure water of Walden mingling in his mind with the
sacred water of the Ganges. The day was his, for any
wild adventure. Sometimes, on a summer morning, he
would sit for hours in his sunny doorway, amid the pines
and hickories and sumachs, in undisturbed solitude and
stillness. The birds flitted noiselessly about him. He
could feel himself growing like the corn. He knew what

the Orientals meant by contemplation and the forsaking
of works. He was a Yogi, too, a forest-seer, who might
have composed the Upanishads. His Reality was also
Brahma, not the actualities of the world, but its poten-
tialities. What did he care for temporal interests? It was
his vocation to discover God. His days were no longer
days of the week, bearing the names of pagan deities, nor
were they minced into hours or fretted by the ticking of
a clock. He felt like a Puri Indian or a Mexican. If you
had put a watch in his hand and asked him what the hour
was, he might have looked at the dial and said, "Quien
sabe?" The sounds of the railway rose and died in his
ears like the distant drumming of a partridge.

His life here seemed to flow in its proper channels. It
followed its own fresh currents, and he felt himself lurking in crystalline thought as the trout lurked under the
verdurous banks. Not so much as a bubble rose to the surface. At sunset, he jumped into his boat and paddled to
the middle of the pond. There he played on his flute,
while the charmed perch hovered about the stern, and
the moon travelled over the floor of the pond, strewn
with the wrecks of the forest. The wildest imagination
could not conceive the manner of life he was living, for
the Concord nights were as strange as Arabian nights.
He struck the side of the boat with his paddle, filling the
woods with a circle of sound. What a pleasant mission
it would be to go about the country in search of echoes!
He knew where to find the prophetic places, the vocal,
resounding, sonorous, hollow places, where oracles might
be established, sites for oracles, sacred ears of Nature.

What could he say to a man who feared the woods,
who shuddered at their solitude and darkness? What
salvation was there for such a man? Did he not know
that God was mysterious and silent? Henry could never
have wearied of the woods, as long as he could visit a
nighthawk on her nest. He could hardly believe his eyes

when he stood within seven feet of her. There she was, sitting on her eggs, so sphinx-like, so Saturnian, so one with the earth, a relic of the reign of Saturn that Jupiter had failed to destroy, a riddle that might cause a man to go and dash his head against a stone. No living creature, surely, far less a wingéd creature of the air. A figure in stone or bronze, like a gryphon or a phœnix. With its flat, greyish, weather-beaten crown, its eyes were all but closed with stony cunning; and yet all the time this sculptured image, motionless as the earth, was watching with intense anxiety, through those narrow slits in its eyelids. Wonderful creature, sitting on its eggs, on the bare, exposed hill, through pelting storms of rain or hail, as if it were a part of the earth itself, the outside of the globe, with its eyes shut and its wings folded. It was enough to fill a man with awe. Henry thought for a moment that he had strayed into the Caucasus, and that around the hill, on the other slope, he would find Prometheus chained to the rock.

Round and round the pond, Henry followed the footpath worn by the feet of Indian hunters, old as the race of men in Massachusetts. The critics and poets were always complaining that there were no American antiquities, no ruins to remind one of the past, yet the wind could hardly blow away the surface anywhere, exposing the spotless sand, but one found the fragments of some Indian pot or the little chips of flint left by some aboriginal arrow-maker. When winter came, and the scent of the gale wafted over the naked ground, Henry tramped through the snow a dozen miles to keep an appointment with a beech-tree, or a yellow birch perhaps, or some old acquaintance among the pines. He ranged like a grey moose, winding his way through the shrub-oak patches, bending the twigs aside, guiding himself by the sun, over hills and plains and valleys, resting in the clear grassy spaces. He liked the wholesome colour of the shrub-oak

leaves, well-tanned, seasoned by the sun, the colour of
the cow and the deer, silvery-downy underneath, over the
bleached and russet fields. He loved the shrub-oak, with
its scanty raiment, rising above the snow, lowly whisper-
ing to him, akin to winter, the covert which the hare and
the partridge sought. It was one of his own cousins, rigid
as iron, clean as the atmosphere, hardy as all virtue, tenacious of its leaves, leaves that did not shrivel but kept
their wintry life, firm shields, painted in fast colours. It
loved the earth, which it over-spread, tough to support
the snow, indigenous, robust. The squirrel and the rabbit
knew it well, and Henry could understand why the deer-
mouse had its hole in the snow by the shrub-oak's stem.
Winter was his own chosen season. When, for all variety
in his walks, he had only a rustling oak-leaf or the faint
metallic cheep of a tree-sparrow, his life felt continent
and sweet as the kernel of a nut. Alone in the distant
woods or fields, in the unpretending sprout-lands or pastures tracked by rabbits, on a bleak and, to most, a cheerless day, when a villager would be thinking of his fire,
he came to himself and felt himself grandly related. Cold
and solitude were his dearest friends. Better a single
shrub-oak leaf at the end of a wintry glade, rustling a
welcome at his approach, than a ship-load of stars and
garters from the kings of the earth. By poverty, if one
chose to use the word, monotony, simplicity, he felt solidi-
fied and crystallized, as water and vapour are crystallized
by cold.

All praise to winter, then, was Henry's feeling. Let
others have their sultry luxuries. How full of creative
genius was the air in which these snow-crystals were generated. He could hardly have marvelled more if real stars
had fallen and lodged on his coat. What a world to live
in, where myriads of these little discs, so beautiful to the
most prying eye, were whirled down on every traveller's
coat, on the restless squirrel's fur and on the far-stretch-

ing fields and forests, the wooded dells and mountain-
tops,—these glorious spangles, the sweepings of heaven's
floor. He watched the men cutting the ice on the pond.
Some of this ice, stowed in the holds of ships, was going
over to India; and many a seeker of Brahma in Calcutta
was destined to drink from his own Walden well. If
winter drove one in-doors, all the better. It compelled
one to try new fields and resources. Days of merry snow-
storms and cheerful winter evenings by the fire. Evenings
for books of natural history, Audubon, for one. It was
pleasant to read about the Florida Keys, the flowering
magnolia, the warm spice-breezes, while the wind beat
the snow against one's window. Days to sit at home over
one's journal, in one's own nest, perhaps on a single egg,
though it might prove to be an egg of chalk.

These were the days for writing, days to speak like a
man in a waking moment to others in their waking moments. For Henry was hard at work. He was writing
articles, which Horace Greeley placed for him. He had
begun to write a book, and he wished to pay his tribute to
Carlyle, who had liberated the English language, cutting
away the fetters imposed upon it by the pedantic writers
of the British reviews. The frigid *North American* was
even worse, a venerable cobweb that had escaped the
broom. He liked to think of Carlyle, on his vacations,
riding on his horse "Yankee," bought from the American
sale of his books. His own book, rewritten from his journal, was the *Week on the Concord and Merrimac Rivers,*
the story of the journey with his brother, never to be forgotten, when they had doubled so many capes and run
before the wind and brought back news of far-away men.
He did not propose to crowd his day with work, even if
the book had to be written. A writer, he thought, should
saunter to his task surrounded by a halo of ease and
leisure, and the labour of his hands should remove from
his style all trace of sentimentality and palaver. One did

not dance idly at one's writing when one had wood to cut
and cord. As the strokes rang cheerily through the wood,
so the stroke of the pen should ring on the reader's ear.
Was the voyage an old story, eight or nine years old, and
only a week at that? It represented a lifetime's memories.
No boy who had grown up on the Mississippi recalled
those floating enchantments, the river-boats, and the
fabulous river-men, with more of a thrill than Henry
felt, remembering the canal-boats of his childhood. The
news had spread through Concord that one of these
boats was stealing through the meadows, silent as a cloud,
with its crew of "foreigners" from New Hampshire, and
all the village boys had flocked to see it. Henry wished
to write a book that would be saturated with his thought
and reading, yet one that would not smell so much of the
study, even the poet's cabin, as of the fields and woods.
He dreamed of an unroofed book, lying open under the
ether, a book that could hardly be forced to lie on a shelf.

He was not by nature a hermit. He might have frequented the bar-rooms, he thought, if he had had any
business that called him thither. Almost every day he
walked to the village, to trade his beans for rice, to get
a boot repaired, to collect the news of the family. Sometimes he returned late at night, with a bag of rye or
Indian meal, sailing back under the moon to his harbour
in the woods. It was only that he was wary of gossip. He
did not wish to lumber his mind with the rubbish that
most men seemed to rejoice in, the details, for example,
of some case in court. One day he was arrested in the
village for refusing to pay his poll-tax. He felt as Alcott
felt. The government supported slavery, the government
was backing the Mexican War; well, he would not support the government. He did not wish to trace the course
of his dollar until it bought a man, or bought a gun to
shoot a Mexican. He spent the night in jail,—a fruitful
night. It inspired his essay on *Civil Disobedience*. He

wished to establish a principle, that one man locked up in
jail for refusing to countenance slavery would be the end
of slavery, or, to express it on a broader basis, "If the
alternative is to keep all just men in prison, or give up
war and slavery, the State will not hesitate which to
choose." A foolish notion, many people thought, but
some of them changed their minds, in later years, when
one of Henry's Hindu readers, Gandhi, acting on the
principle, disturbed the British Empire for several
months. The next morning, Henry, released from jail,
gathered some of the boys and girls for a huckleberry
party, on a hill, whence the State was nowhere to be seen.
He never fastened his door at Walden, though sometimes,
in his absence, he had unwelcome visitors. How did Mrs.
X happen to know that his sheets were not as clean as hers?
But nothing was ever stolen, except his copy of Homer.
One had to keep one's eye on bookish people.

He had other guests, especially in April, when all the
world seemed to be on the move. A runaway slave appeared, then Alek Therien, the French-Canadian wood-
chopper, a true Homeric peasant who had learned a little
Greek from his priest in the north, then Hugh Quoil, an
Irish soldier, who had fought at the Battle of Waterloo.
Old Quoil, with his wife and his jug, was patiently waiting for death in a hut in the woods. The shanty-Irish folk
along the railroad sometimes came to see him. Henry
thought them shiftless enough, with their women washing under the trees and the pigs poking about among the
tubs. He eyed them with a vague hostility, as the red
men had eyed the first settlers, and with as much reason;
for were they not the first wave of the sea that was to
sweep away so many landmarks? Among the little raga-
muffins that swarmed about these cabins, there were some
in whom the prophetic eye might have seen the masters
of the future, the lords of Greater Boston, mayors, governors, captains of police, even, perhaps, a cardinal.

Henry had one good friend among them, little Johnny Riordan, with his quaint "old worthy" face, behind the sober visor of his cap, plodding to school through the snow in his next-to-nothing, facing and routing it like a Persian army. A great sight, Johnny, in his rags, beside the well-fed villagers, waddling about in their furs and finery. Emerson also came, of course. Henry read aloud to him some pages from his book, while they sat under an oak beside the pond. Alcott arrived one night, struggling through the snow. Ellery Channing spent a fortnight with him. When the poets and sages came, he was glad that his dwelling was so spacious. As the conversation assumed a grander and loftier tone, they shoved their chairs further and further apart, until they touched the walls in opposite corners. This left plenty of neutral ground for their sentences to deploy in martial order.

Once Henry left his house for a fortnight's excursion. He had cousins in Bangor, Maine, one of them in the lumber-trade, a good excuse to visit the northern woods. He wished to study the Indians in their forest wilderness, and he wished to climb Mount Ktaadn. He never travelled without prayer and fasting, for he did not wish to dissipate his mind. With all the industry of a busy life, how could one hope to know, really know, an area more than six miles square? Isaac Hecker had asked him to go to Rome, the two of them together, Hecker to pay the expenses, for Hecker, who had tried Brook Farm and Fruitlands, was boarding with Mrs. Thoreau for a taste of Concord. He hoped to carry Henry over to Rome, in more than one fashion. Later, another friend, an Englishman, invited him for a visit in England. In both cases, Henry said, No. If Europe was much in his mind, and became more and more to him, Concord might become less and less; and what sort of bargain would that be? He did not wish his life to lose its homely savour. If the fields and streams and woods that he loved so well, and the simple occupations of his townsmen, ever ceased to interest and surprise him, what culture or wealth could ever atone for the loss? He did not wish to go to Europe, nor did he wish to go—like the farmers—west. What could he think of this foolish American habit, going east or west to a "better land," without lifting an honest finger to till and redeem one's own New England soil? As for the rush to California, it was a disgrace to humankind,—digging gold, the merest lottery, a kind of toil, if it deserved the name, in no sense beneficial to the world. A startling development, this, of the ethics of trade and all the modes of getting a living. It filled Henry with a cold scorn. For the rest, he had his own western horizon, towards which he was always moving, pitching his tent each day nearer the Golden Gate. But the really fertile soils and luxuriant prairies lay on one's own side of the Alleghanies, wherever a man minded his own business. Were not all the essentials of life to be found in Concord, ten times found if one properly valued them?—which a man could only do if he stood his ground. Henry had something to say to the men in the covered wagons, who were running away from something besides the rocks. If the men in the covered wagons had no ears for Henry, he would be glad to wait for a few generations. The great-great-grandsons of the covered wagons would be ready to listen to him.

Nobody knew the riches of Concord. As for natural history, he had found some of the Arctic phenomena there, red snow and one or two Labrador plants. Still, a little travel now and then was not so bad to give one's mind an airing, especially if it offered him a chance to observe the ways of the Indians. For the Indians had a special charm for Henry; they suggested a simpler mode of life and a greater nearness to the earth. Were there not two eternities, one behind him, which the Indians represented, as well as one before? Wherever he went, he trod in their tracks, yet only a few poets remembered them. Here and there, one saw their lonely wigwams, on the banks of some quiet stream, like the cabins of the muskrats in the meadows,—an old squaw, perhaps, living in her solitary hut, with her dog, her only companion, making baskets and picking berries, insulted by the village boys and girls. Henry dreamed of writing a book about them; * for their memory seemed to him to harmonize with the russet hue of autumn that he loved. A race that had exhausted the secrets of nature, a race tanned with age, while the young, fair Anglo-Saxon slip, on whom the sun had shone for so short a time, was only just beginning its career. As sportsmen went in pursuit of ducks, and scholars of rare books, and all men went in pursuit of money, Henry went in search of arrowheads, when the proper season came round again. He often spent whole afternoons, especially in the spring, when the rains had washed the ground bare, pacing back and forth over a sandy field, looking for these relics. It might have rained arrow-heads. They lay all over the surface of the country, sometimes mingled with arrowheadiferous soil, ash-coloured, left by Indian fires. They were like so many fossil thoughts to Henry, forever recalling the far-away mind that shaped them.

To Maine, then!—where the Indians grew with the moose. A fortnight in the forest, the home of the bear and the caribou, the wolf, the beaver and the Penobscot redskins, where the wild fir flourished and the sprucetops, seen from an elevation, were like the odour of cake in a schoolboy's nostrils. Hemlocks and cedars, silver and yellow birches, watery maples, damp and moss-grown rocks, real woods, these, wild and bearded. One caught the whistle of ducks on solitary streams, the flicker of the darting chickadee, the loon's desolate laugh.

* Thoreau left eleven manuscript volumes, about 3000 pages, filled with notes about the Indians for the book he had hoped to write.

Sometimes, through the moss-clad aisles, one heard a dull, dry, rustling sound, as if smothered under the fungus-covered forest, the falling of a tree, like the shutting of a door in some distant entry of the dark and shaggy wilderness. There one could feel at home, shooting the rapids in one's birch canoe, like a bait bobbing for some river monster, darting from side to side of the stream, then gliding swift and smoothly. This was the place to sing the "Canadian boat-song," or to play on one's flute, at night, under the stars, while the wolves howled about, in the darkness of the continent. Henry watched Joe Polis, the Indian guide, glued to the bank on his stomach, talking to the muskrats in their sylvan language. Sometimes, by the fireside, Joe Polis also sang, a mild and simple nasal chant, like the dawn of civilization over the woods. The white man's brow was clear and distinct, but over the brow of the Indian lingered a haze or mist. For the Indian, the white man's noon was four o'clock in the morning.

A journey like this was only a foretaste, too rewarding not to be repeated. Henry was writing about his travels, and one of the magazines was glad to print his essay on Ktaadn. Later, on two occasions, he went to Maine again. He wished to visit Chesuncook, the Allegash and the East Branch. He was in his element in the woods, as Richard Henry Dana on the sea, as an old French-Canadian *coureur de bois*. Was he not a Frenchman as well as a Yankee, who might have run wild with Du Lhut and harried the woods for beavers? In the meantime, he had left his Walden cabin. Why? For as good a reason as he had gone there. He had other lives to live, and he had no more time to spare for this one. He wanted a change, he did not wish to stagnate. About two o'clock in the afternoon, he had felt the world's axle creaking a little, as if it needed greasing, as if the oxen laboured with the wain and could hardly get their load over the ridge of the day. Who would accept heaven on terms like this?—and a ticket for heaven had to include, for Henry, tickets for hell and purgatory also. Walden was only a bivouac in his campaign. He had other journeys in mind, to Cape Cod, for instance, with Ellery Channing, and later a jaunt to Canada, Quebec and Montreal. (Total expense, two guide-books included, $12.75.) Ellery was not a man for camping out,—that was an art one had to acquire slowly; but he shared Henry's taste for a simple equipment. And Henry would no more have thought of dressing,—dressing for a journey!—than he would have blacked his boots for fishing. Honest travelling was dirty work. A pair of overalls was the proper costume, a grey sack, corduroys perhaps; and as for this blacking of boots, he despised it on all occasions. In this, he was like some of the Harvard professors, who, as Mrs. Story was shocked to note, on one of her visits from Italy, did not have their boots blacked even for Commencement. Henry, who always carried a piece of tallow, in order to keep the water out of the leather, looked like a wood-chuck or a musquash. This was his desire, at least,—the more like a quadruped the better, tawny, russet, yellow-brown, the colour of the sands. Vermont grey was not so bad; and once he had had the perfect suit, a skilful mix-ture of browns, with light and dark cleverly proportioned, and a few threads of green. He had looked like a corner of a pasture, with patches of sweet-fern and lechea. He had been able to glide over the fields, as unperceived from the farmer's windows as a painted cruiser through a spyglass. The wild animals thought he was one of them. Ellery, who was not so systematic, shared Henry's feel-ing in the matter of hats. His own hat was old and weather-beaten and had plenty of holes around the brim. It was as rare and high as a good Stilton cheese. As for the rest of Henry's outfit, a handkerchief served for a bag, or a firm, stout sheet of brown paper, well tied up. What else? An umbrella, of course, a knapsack, with partitions for books and papers, a music-book for pressing flowers, a field-glass and a measuring-tape. A fish-line, spoon and dipper, a little salt and sugar, tea, Indian meal and a slice of fruit-cake. If anyone asked him along the way to do a little tinkering, that was a tribute to his common sense.

So Henry tramped to Provincetown. Having seen the woods, he wished to see the ocean, and Cape Cod was surely the place to see it. There, on the stretches of sand blown clean by the wind, he could forget the towns, where he felt so unspeakably mean and disgraced. He could forget the bar-rooms of Massachusetts, where the full-grown were not weaned from their savage and filthy habits, sucking cigars and guzzling whiskey-punch. On the Cape, one saw wholesome faces, well preserved by the salty air, faces bleached like old sails, hanging cliffs of weather-beaten flesh. The Cape Cod boys leaped from their leading-strings into the shrouds; it was only a bound from their mother's laps to the masthead. They boxed the compass in their infant day-dreams. They could hand, reef and steer by the time they flew a kite. This was a country almost as thrilling as Maine. Henry had three books more or less on the stocks: *The Maine Woods,* full of the scents of the forest, *Cape Cod,* redolent of the sea, even *A Yankee in Canada.* The well-known publishers, Time & Co., could be trusted to see that they were safely printed. One of his neighbours wrote about Human Culture. Why should he not write about Cape Cod, another name for the same thing, and hardly a sandier phase of it? Or Canada, for that matter? He wrote an opening paragraph, with both hands clenched: "Read my book if you dare!"

CHAPTER XX

WEST OF BOSTON

AFTER EIGHT years of ups and downs, Brook Farm had come to an end, not without important consequences. There were not wanting well-informed observers who were to assert, in later years, that from the farm had sprung the movement of organized labour in New England and even throughout the nation. It had other results of a personal kind. Two well-known journalists of the future, Charles A. Dana of the New York *Sun* and John Sullivan Dwight of the *Journal of Music,* received their first training as editors of *The Harbinger,* the magazine published at the farm. *The Harbinger* had opened with a translation of George Sand's *Consuelo,* and almost every writer in New England contributed an essay or a poem. But the farm had not long survived the coming of the Fourierists, Owen, Horace Greeley and Albert Brisbane, who had translated Fourier's writings. Brisbane wished to turn it into a phalanstery, where all the ideas of the master were to be applied. With certain modifications, the plan was adopted, and the members were divided into "groups" and "series." But something went out of the life of the farm. Ceasing to be voluntary, it ceased to be poetic; and when disaster fell, the farm fell with it.

Dwight, the chief of the "Festal Series," was all but broken-hearted. The music-master was a pretty sight, surrounded by his class of singing children. He was happy to hoe the corn on Sundays, paying his regards to the Puritan sabbath by breaking it in every way he could; and, although he did not like to hoe on week-days, he had contrived to put up with the new routine. He did not know what to do when the sad news broke. He struggled on for a time in Boston, trying to maintain a "combined household" for some of the Brook Farmers. He never lost his faith in association; he felt that a communal life was the only life for humanity and that society must be set in order before the individual could be himself. The organization of labour, the abolition of competition, this was the road to the future, as Dwight conceived it. It was not until 1852 that he was able to start the *Journal of Music,* which he was to conduct for thirty years. This was the journal that set the musical standard of Boston. It published the musical news of Italy, Paris, Germany, England, Liszt's *Life of Chopin,* a serial life of Mozart, hundreds of original compositions. It even led the musical thought of the country, till the editor's dislike of Brahms and Wagner gradually destroyed its influence. This was in the far future, when Dwight was the dictator of music. He had made his way by lecturing and writing, carrying on, in Boston and elsewhere in New England, the "mass clubs" he had started at the farm.

"Archon" Ripley went to New York, with Dana, to work on Greeley's *Tribune.* It was a sad descent, sitting all day long in a little office, on the fourth floor of a huge, dirty building, reached by winding, narrow, littered stairs, with machines whizzing and clanking about him, paragraphing and clipping for *The Tribune.* One never heard the vireo there, and Utopia seemed very far away. Every night he plodded home to Brooklyn. He shared a single room with his wife in a shabby boarding-house in a dingy street. In this room his wife died of cancer, while, Ripley, at his table in the corner, worked away for dear life,—the modest, laborious Ripley, too humble to collect in volume-form the clear and scholarly essays he wrote for his paper on Lessing, Voltaire, Rousseau, Hartmann, Spencer.

These essays, like Dwight's,—never collected either,—deserved a place of honour in the literature of criticism. Two decades were to pass, in this Grub-Street twilight, while he composed, with Dana, the *New American Encyclopædia,* before the sun rose again for Ripley. He had a brief, happy second youth, with means, a little travel, a brougham to drive about in Central Park. For even Brook Farmers come to gigs at last.

Two notable women, members of Ripley's circle, had gone to New York, at least for a while, before him. Lydia Maria Child, the novelist, had written thence her *Letters from New York, 1841–1844,* an unpretentious picture of the city that was to have its interest in later years. Mrs. Child was at home in the rural outskirts, the charming villages on the New Jersey shore, the woody banks of Weehawken, a wild garden of early flowers. In the Hoboken meadows, she found violets nestling in moss-grown stumps. New York itself was too much in a hurry-scurry, and there was something brutal in its life. The dog-catchers trooped down the streets, their clothes bespattered with blood; they had clubs over their shoulders to beat to death every dog they found without a master. She had never seen such sights as this in humanitarian Boston. She studied the prisons, the care of the poor, the Swedenborgian meetings, the meetings for the discussion of mesmerism, the popular acclaim of Ole Bull, who had just arrived from Norway. New York was not like Boston. It never entered the head of a Wall Street merchant that he was himself responsible for the evils of the town; and, although she found "Transcendental muslins" advertised in the Bowery, she never met with the well-known cult in any other form. Was she herself a Transcendentalist? She had certainly used the phrase "highly gifted"; and yet she had been mystified, in some of the Boston circles, where she had had to bite her finger to be sure it was really solid. She felt a good deal of sympathy with the plain man of business, and she drew a kindly, generous, motherly picture of the town that he had built for his habitation. But, as for his toleration of slavery and a thousand other abuses, she did not abate a word of her honest abhorrence.

Margaret Fuller, with her intenser mind, had also surveyed the metropolis. She had gone there in 1844 to join the staff of *The Tribune*. She lived in Horace Greeley's house and carried on raids of observation into the territories of the prince of darkness, Sing Sing, Blackwell's Island, the Five Points, even the salons of the literati. Greeley had been attracted by her books, which had appeared in *The Dial*,—the well-known feminist treatise, *Woman in the Nineteenth Century,* and the notes on Western travel, *Summer on the Lakes.* He felt that hers was the sort of pen to make his own paper a living force; for this female Montesquieu, as her followers thought her, who had given her own sex its title-deeds, seemed ready to forward every enlightened cause. She had written well of the West. With James Freeman Clarke's artist-sister, she had spent the summer of 1843 in Cleveland, Chicago and Wisconsin. She had mingled with the New England pioneers, bent on seeking their fortunes, the fathers and mothers of a race to come. What had been their one preoccupation? Alas, from the oldest man to the youngest child, they talked not of what they were going to do but of what they were going to get, ease and money. Could anything more be hoped of the Germans and Swedes, who were flocking into these beautiful wildernesses, amid the prairie flowers and the lowing cattle? The scene, she knew, had a mighty meaning, and she hoped to divine the law by which a new poetry and order might be evoked from this chaos. She liked the outdoor festivals of the pioneers, the huskings and the hop-gatherings, as merry as the Scottish harvest-home or the Italian vintage, the groups of men and girls filling their baskets with the gay festoons. But everywhere she saw, in germ, the fatal spirit of imitation, a reference to European ways. She noted the fine taste the Indians showed in the sites of their clustered lodges on the lakes and streams. Let the white men blacken the Indians as they might, talk of their filth and brutality; she could well believe that an Indian brave, rambling on these paths, in the beams of the sun, might be mistaken for Apollo. The Indians had loved the French. How could they love the Protestant missionary, with his niggardly conceptions, his unfeeling stare? As for the general prospects of these regions, whatever the future might bring she was bound to say, "There is nothing real in the freedom of thought at the West. It is from the position of men's lives, not the state of their minds."

Now, in New York, on *The Tribune,* she was writing on current literature. She hoped to clarify American thought, in its dim and struggling state, and introduce the new European writers. She paid no attention to the magazine-stories, "written for the press, in a spirit of imitation and vanity, the paltriest offspring of the human brain." What was her criterion? "Most men, in judging another man, ask, Did he live up to our standard? To me it seems desirable to ask, Did he live up to his own?" She added that Goethe's faults fitted him all the better for the part he had to play. She interpreted the more significant writers, looking to the day "when our population shall have settled into a homogeneous national life, and we have attained vigour to walk in our own way, make our own world and leave off copying Europe." Her judgments were remarkably just,* and some of her general intuitions gave her work a measure of permanent interest. She contrasted the boyish crudity that marked so many American writers, timid and boastful at once, with the tempered, manly equipoise of the thoroughbred European; and,

---

* E.g., in regard to Longfellow, that "the ethical part of his writing has a hollow, second-hand sound," as also in regard to Emerson, that "he raised himself too early to the perpendicular and did not lie along the ground long enough."

regarding the larger aspects of civilization, she spoke for
the longer time as well as the shorter. "Since the Revolution," she observed, "there has been little, in the circumstances of this country, to call out the higher sentiments.
The effect of continued prosperity is the same on nations
as on individuals,—it leaves the nobler faculties undeveloped. The superficial diffusion of knowledge, unless attended by a corresponding deepening of its sources, is
likely to vulgarize rather than raise the thought of a
nation, depriving it of another sort of education through
sentiments of reverence, and leading the multitude to believe themselves capable of judging what they but dimly
discern . . . . In a word, the tendency of circumstances has
been to make our people superficial, irreverent and more
anxious to get a living than to live mentally and morally."
A statement that could hardly have been challenged ninety
years later.

In 1846, Margaret Fuller set out for Europe. She had
read the invisible ink in many minds and lives, in Hawthorne's, for one, the American writer whom, after Emerson, she most admired. Hawthorne had returned for three
years to Salem. His friends, Horatio Bridge and Franklin
Pierce had gone to Concord, to the Manse, to see him.
They found him chopping wood in the shed, dressed in
his old blue frock and troubled over the problem of earning a living; and they promised to use their influence with
Bancroft, who had risen in the political world and was
Secretary of the Navy, to find a post for him that would
give him an income. Horatio Bridge himself was in the
navy, and he had written a book, with Hawthorne's help,
the *Journal of an African Cruiser,* a collection of lively
impressions of the African Gold Coast, Liberia, Sierra
Leone, the Canaries. Hawthorne went back to Salem with
a heavy heart, as the new surveyor of the custom-house.
A botanist who lived in the town had recently noted that
the English white-thorn, the hawthorn of the poets, had

slowly naturalized itself in Salem. It was otherwise with
the flower of Hawthorne's mind. The mud, the dust, the
east wind, the petty trickeries of the politicians, the chilliness of the social atmosphere—"Who ever heard of the
Hawthornes?" one of the ladies of Chestnut Street remarked—benumbed and befogged his senses. He went
about his work with the dogged and silent practicality that
always characterized his mundane life, testing the rum
that was sent to the Guinea Coast,—for he meant to see
that the darkies had good, strong rum,—while the poet
slept within him. Three years of an outward stupefaction,
years in which the shipmaster's son, who might have
quelled a mutiny, obliged his incompetent staff to toe the
mark. In the evenings, he read De Quincey with his wife.
What music, what perfection of style in the less laborious
passages! How could Hawthorne talk to the Salem
people? Why should he talk, indeed, when the presence
of an uncongenial person caused an almost physical con-
traction of his great masculine frame?

At the end of the three years, he moved to Lenox. He
had written *The Scarlet Letter* in Salem, the book that
had won his freedom; for under his mask of insensibility
the poet had been alive and brooding there. In this winter
of his discontent, he had also written a few fables and
sketches, worthy of one whose first American forbear had
brought from England with him a copy of Sidney's
Arcadia. The tone of *Main Street* and *The Great Stone
Face,* like that of *The Snow-Image,* was of a dove-like innocence that often cloaked the wisdom of the serpent. No
one else in New England had written such stories, or only
one man, William Austin, the Boston lawyer, Dr. Channing's class-mate. This well-known Harvard scholar and
legislator, who had studied law in London, where he had
known Washington Allston and written the *Letters from
London,* which all the American lawyers read because they
contained such good descriptions of the British lawyers

and statesmen, had published a handful of tales in the eighteen-twenties that were almost prophetic of Hawthorne. In *Martha Gardner,* Austin, a Democrat and a radical, castigated the modern corporations that fed on the miseries of the poor. Better than this was *The Man with the Cloaks,* based on a German fairy-tale. The best was *Peter Rugg, the Missing Man.* Austin had a robust, Rabelaisian humour that ran to the gigantesque, as in the story of the hungry teacher who wandered about the country drinking all the cows dry and cutting steaks out of the living oxen. *Peter Rugg* was a great invention, or one of those bold formulations of ancient inventions, the Flying Dutchman, the Wandering Jew, which, like *Rip Van Winkle* and *Peter Schlemihl,* come to the same thing. This tale of the man who disappeared from Boston and was constantly seen on the roads for fifty years, desperately whipping his horse, trying to find his way back, had all the overtones of the true folk-legend, the haunting suggestions of a symbolism that is always lending itself to some new turn of affairs. There were many Peter Ruggs, in days to come, trying to find their way back to Boston, the good old Boston of 1820; and the story was retold by later writers as if it had been a popular myth.* The ambiguous atmosphere of the tale, the mingling of the dubious and the real, the play of light and shadow suggested Hawthorne. So did the old New England setting and costumes. Hawthorne was familiar with it. Peter Rugg appeared in one of his own tales. He was the door-keeper in *A Virtuoso's Collection.*

At Lenox, the air was scented with sweet-grass and clover; and there, in the little red cottage on the lonely farm, Hawthorne had his year of wonders. There he wrote *The House of the Seven Gables* and planned *The Blithedale Romance;* and, while his wife made tracings of

---

* Peter Rugg was the subject of a ballad by Louise Imogen Guiney and a prose-poem by Amy Lowell.

Flaxman's outlines on the dull-yellow painted chairs and tables, he told the children stories that explained the drawings, *The Wonder Book, The Tanglewood Tales*. Tanglewood, as the children called it, was a wild spot in the woods close by where they all went for picnics in the summer and autumn. Hawthorne played the magician there. He was a great tree-climber, up in a flash to the topmost bough, showering nuts all over the floor of the forest. From old door-knobs and strips of shingle, he carved little yachts and figures, a pugilist who swung his arms in the wind. In winter, he made images of snow. The image in the tale he wrote was singularly like a man of genius, a moral that he neglected to point. The father of the children who made the image, a man of common sense and kind intentions, wished to make the image comfortable, even in spite of itself. He carried it into the warm room, where it rapidly melted away beside the fire. Alas, for the poor snow-image that loved the cold, the frosty air, the north wind! The children had known very well it could only live under the stars that glimmered in the arctic night.

Hawthorne had become a father-confessor. Letters poured in upon him from unhappy souls who had been touched by his books. Secret criminals sought him out and came to him for counsel and relief. Most of his Berkshire neighbours were less exacting. Miss Sedgwick, the aging novelist, lived at Lenox. At Mrs. Sedgwick's school, Harriet Hosmer, the merry little gnome, the sculptor of the future, was one of the pupils. Hawthorne was to meet her again in Rome; still later, he described her in *The Marble Faun*. The Sedgwicks pervaded the Berkshires. Even the grasshoppers chirped, "Sedgwick, Sedgwick!" as one of their friends remarked; and Mrs. Sedgwick said, with a measure of truth, "En France tout arrive." Everything happened at Lenox, and everyone came there. Close by lived the lovely Fanny Kemble, whose Shakespeare readings in Boston were events of the forties and who also ap-

peared in one of Hawthorne's novels.* Samuel Gray
Ward had another villa. This dearest of Emerson's
friends, not to be confused with Longfellow's friend,
Samuel Ward of New York,—Julia Ward Howe's
brother, who was later known as the "King of the
Lobby,"—was a Boston banker and patron of art. His
youth, before he entered business, had been devoted to
painting, literature and German studies. He had translated a volume of Goethe's essays and had written a paper
on Boccaccio that was one of the best in *The Dial*. His admirable essay on criticism, in Elizabeth Peabody's *Æsthetic Papers,*† contained two phrases, "creative criticism"
and "significant form," that other men in later generations
were to render more than familiar. Ward had bought
Legendre's mathematical library and had paid for the
publication of the poems of his old friend and school-mate,
Ellery Channing.‡ At Pittsfield, which had once been
Wendellboro, named after his forbears, Oliver Wendell
Holmes spent his summers. There he planted seven hun-

---

* In the character of Zenobia, in *The Blithedale Romance,* also drawn
partially from Margaret Fuller.

† A projected magazine, 1849, discontinued after the first number. In addition to Ward's essay, it contained papers by Dwight, Miss Peabody,
Emerson, Thoreau and Hawthorne. In Emerson's contribution, the essay
on War, one finds the following observation: "The manhood that has been
in war must be transferred to the cause of peace, before war can lose its
charm, and peace be venerable to men." This was perhaps the germ of
William James's later essay, *The Moral Equivalent of War.*

‡ Samuel G. Ward was the "friend" of Emerson's *Letters to a Friend,*
edited by Charles Eliot Norton. His essay on criticism contained the following observations: "Our first misfortune is, that there is a reference to a
standard from without, viz., England. As the spirit that dictates it is, from
many causes, unfair and depreciating, a natural consequence has been to
cause all our own criticism to take the opposite ground, to over-praise that
which is felt to be undervalued or invidiously regarded . . . . Although
all original literature comes from and refers to the heart of the people,
it cannot, except in a rude age, address itself to that people except through
a class capable of receiving it. If great works do not find such a class in
their own age, they wait till time and their own influence create it . . . .
We believe a conscious greatness inseparable from critical literature, and
such, therefore, we look for in this country;—a literature and art based on
thorough criticism, and thorough knowledge of what already exists in the
world."

dred trees and built himself a snug little villa on a knoll on the old Wendell farm; and there he wrote his best bucolic poems, *The Ploughman,* for one, for he liked to play his part at the Berkshire agricultural fairs. At Broadhall, the old Melville house, where Major Thomas Melville had lived,—Holmes's "Last Leaf,"—Longfellow spent a summer, with Ex-President Tyler and Charles Sumner, for it was now a boarding-house. Major Melville's grandson, Herman Melville, was living at "Arrowhead," on the outskirts of Pittsfield. Melville was composing *Moby Dick,* and the great white whale was in his flurry. He was attracted to Hawthorne and wrote an essay on his books, and he often drove up to the little red cottage, with his big Newfoundland dog in the buckboard beside him. He told tales about the South Seas that were more exciting than Dana's. Once, describing a fight there, he laid about him as if with a club. It was so real to the Hawthornes that when he had gone they all asked, "What became of the club?"—which Melville had neither left nor taken with him. Melville and Hawthorne liked to lie in the barn, on piles of new-mown hay, discussing time and eternity.

Not far away, at Northampton, where Bancroft, at the Round Hill school, had taught Ward, Motley and Ellery Channing, another writer had spent his childhood, the Hawthornesque novelist, Sylvester Judd. This hypersensitive, humble, shrinking soul, a Unitarian minister at Augusta, Maine, bred in the rigours of Calvinism, had passed through the Transcendental movement. His doubts and ecstasies had deranged his nerves.* As a student of theology in Cambridge, he had been stirred by Goethe and Carlyle. He wished to destroy the barriers of the sects, and

* It was of Judd that Emerson wrote: "I once asked a clergyman in a retired town who were his companions? What men of ability he saw? He replied that he spent his time with the sick and dying. I said, he seemed to me to need quite other company, and all the more that he had this; for if people were sick and dying to any purpose, we should leave all and go to them, but, as far as I had observed, they were as frivolous as the rest, and sometimes much more frivolous."—*The Conduct of Life.*

exhibit the errors of false theology, war, capital punishment, the prison system. His *Margaret* was a Utopian
romance, the story of the daughter of a German musician,
brought up in an old New England village, who ends by
transforming the village into a Mons Christi, with fountains like those of the Tuileries, belvederes and gardens,
music-rooms, observatories, halls of art, where the barren
lands bloom with rye and corn, and statues of Peace and
Truth and marble muses line the Delectable Way, where
industry, economy and love, simple fare and attractive toil
create an earthly paradise and men of all nations meet as
brothers. This Fourieristic fantasy, more than a little
drawn from *Wilhelm Meister,* with a heroine often suggestive of Mignon, was quite in the Brook Farm spirit.
It symbolized the feeling for art that was dawning in New
England, the messianic socialism, the inspiration of German studies; and Judd's poem, *Philo,* a metaphysical epic,
found readers who believed it would convert the world.
Margaret was obscure and confused, but many pages and
even chapters were vividly picturesque and charmingly
written. Judd had studied New England. He had filled his
note-books with observations of old houses, costumes and
village ways, the talk of the farmers, the husking-bees,
Thanksgiving, the pedlars and hawkers of ballads at country fairs. His best scenes were almost as good as Hawthorne's. There was a touch of ecstasy in some of his
descriptions, the thunder-storm, the winter scenes, the
snow-storm, the sunny clearing in the summer forest, the
coming of the flowers in spring, the horse-tails with their
storied ruffs, the fleecy mouse-ear buds, the straw-coloured
blossoms of the bell-wort, the little polypods with their
feathery fronds and the young mulleins, velvety, white
and tender.

These were the scenes that Hawthorne knew at Lenox.
Never quite at home away from the sea-shore, he still
had hours there, on summer evenings, when he felt as if

he could climb the sky and run a race along the Milky Way. Free at last after the leaden years he had spent at the Salem custom-house, his mind was at its fullest flood. His bones were astir, even to the marrow. Salem, the ancient seaport of his boyhood, never loved by him, shunned indeed, and yet his own so deeply, seen afresh after his life at the Manse, which had given him a standard and a measure, Salem, dust of his own dust, and with it the Boston of Puritan times, pressed against and filled his consciousness. The scarlet letter A that had haunted his mind ever since he had written the *Twice-Told Tales,* the witch, whisked up the chimney on a broomstick and flying away to a devil's communion far in the depths of the dark, still forest, the old colonial governors, the ruffed physicians, the ministers godly and of ungodly fame, the women not to be repressed, the inquisitorial deacons, the elfin children of that Gothic world, prolonged from the Middle Ages, the Boston he had imagined, the Salem he had known, the queer gabled houses and the queerer people, the cobwebs visible and invisible, cobwebs of family pride and secret fraud, bloodstains telling tales and beams of innocent sunlight piercing through: all this had waited for the dam to break, for the moment of leisure and freedom, for his dismissal from the custom-house, another of those politicians' tricks,—a score that he could repay by picturing his enemy in Judge Pyncheon,—to be written out at his desk with the secret drawers, the haunted writing-desk with the tiny panels. He had painted these little panels with impish faces, staring and smiling, while he sat in his purple writing-gown, covered with golden palm-leaves. The dam had burst, in Salem, with *The Scarlet Letter.* The overflow was *The House of the Seven Gables.*

Years before, in Hawthorne's youth, in Salem, when he had written his tales in the little chamber, there had always seemed to be a driving snow-storm on the other

side of the casement, or a cloud of dust in summer, a
film, a veil. When he had stood at the window, on Sunday mornings, studying the church across the way, watching the sunlight stealing down the steeple, he had always
stood behind the curtain. To see the world with a sidelong glance, by a certain indirection, was second nature
with him; and this was the mood his romances conveyed,
as if, in spite of all their air of daylight, he had never
looked straight at Boston or Salem, as if he had always
seen them over his shoulder. It was this that gave him his
effect of magic and made these beautiful books, with
their antique diction, something other than novels and,
if not greater, more intimate in their spell than novels
can be. They clung to the mind like music, like Gluck's
mournful strains of the land of shades or the solemn joy
of Mozart. Or, better still, like masques written for
music in the far-off days in England of which one caught
the dim reverberations in the scene of *The Scarlet Letter*.
Round about the players in the greenwood, one felt and
saw the encircling darkness gather. The deepest shade
covered *The Scarlet Letter*. But the flickering play of the
sun and the leaves set the note of *The House of the Seven
Gables*. The story moved in a soft September light, melting like a happy dream of Shakespeare.

CHAPTER XXI

THE ANTI-SLAVERY WRITERS

OUT OF the depths of the country, far from Beacon Hill and Brattle Street, one "heard as if an army muttered."

> And the muttering grew to a grumbling,
> And the grumbling grew to a mighty rumbling.

The Anti-Slavery movement was on its way. Not from the churches, not from the men of property or culture—or from them only on second thought—came the call to reform. It was the village centres that grumbled and rumbled, the back streets of the manufacturing towns, the tailors' shops and rural printing-presses, the Quaker farms and solitary homesteads. Thence came those that troubled Israel. There the *Pilgrim's Progress* and the *Book of Martyrs* were much more living facts than all the culture of the later epochs. There dwelt, unchanged, the spirit of the Puritans and the Friends, the stiff-necked sectaries of Cromwell's army who had been glad to stand in pillories and suffer their ears to be cropped rather than put bread in the mouths of priests, men who had fought for the right to wear their hats where others stood uncovered, fought for a beard as they fought for a principle and chosen the *peine forte et dure* if they were asked to surrender their opinion regarding some phrase in the Scriptures. Such were the readers of *The Liberator*. In their bones, as Garrison spoke, stirred the fires of the days of Pym and Hampden. "I am in earnest, and I will be heard!"

This was very far from the tone of Boston, far from the tone of Cambridge. It was the voice of the plough-man, the mechanic, the humble cottagers of the home-spun class whose minds were steeped in Bible and Quaker tracts. Out of these circles Garrison had come. In them he remained, in his little room with the dingy walls, bespattered with printer's ink, living on snatches of bread, fruit and milk, sleeping on his table for a bed, with his printing-press beside him. Thence had come, in minds of a similar stock, the dream of the pedlar Bronson Alcott, the vision of the Concord pencil-maker, who had built his hut at Walden. Thence came N. P. Rogers of New Hampshire, tenth in descent from the Reverend John Rogers, the first martyr of Bloody Mary's reign, and the "acts of the anti-slavery apostles," those whom neither courtesy nor money, nor hard words, eggs, blows or brickbats ever deterred from prophesying. The age of Queen Elizabeth had reawakened in the scholarly Cam-bridge mind. The age of Laud and Charles the First had reappeared in the minds of harness-makers, village bar-bers, farmers, tavern-keepers. They drove about the country in borrowed buggies, speaking at the Lyceums and meeting-houses, faring on a few cents a day, a hand-ful of biscuits and raisins, courting the lampblack and the tar and feathers. They lived among revelations and ghostly voices. An old New Hampshire Quaker farmer wrote down a vision that befell him as he stood in his field at noonday. Darkness fell upon his sight and cov-ered the whole earth. He saw the nation divided in civil war.

Under the Boston mind worked the same leaven, but much more complicated thoughts restrained it. The fears of the "cotton interest" inhibited many; so did the social ties of the merchant families, which bound them to the

families of the planters. The Whigs, who had taken
Webster for their leader, followed him in all his com-
promises. They followed Everett, who followed Webster,
and who, with his eye for the "good in everything,"
found something good in slavery: he had visited a plantation in Louisiana, and he was happy to report that the
quarters of the slaves were neat and clean and the beds
were furnished with mosquito-nets. This was reassuring
to Christian souls who counted on the slaves for their
bread and butter. Beside these bread-and-butter fears,
moreover, there was a motive that deserved respect, the
fear of the disruption of the Union, which had been established against such odds. Dr. Channing had expressed
this fear, and no one suspected Channing of partisan
interests. He had shown how the Union preserved the
States from wasting and destroying one another, how the
country would be broken by disunion into restless, grasping sections, all the more hostile to one another because,
as one saw in South America, a common language multiplied jealousies; and Europe would make use of this
dissension to break the nation further for its own advantage. This was enough to sober Boston minds that had
not forgotten the Revolution.

Even in Boston, however, as in the inland regions, the
question worked like madness in the brain. Channing's
little treatise on slavery had made a measure of opposition to it almost a condition of self-respect. This book
was embarrassing to the prosperous classes, who for a
generation had nursed the illusion that, having won their
independence, they had solved the problems of the world.
The educated mind could not ignore a calm analytical
essay that set the theme in a philosophical light. It
showed, as no writer had shown before, the disastrous
effects of slavery, both on the slaves and on the masters,
and thenceforth no one who professed to think defended
the "peculiar institution" without reservations or misgiv-

ings; and the more the South advanced its claims, in the
new States of the West, terrorizing the central government,
and forcing the Fugitive Slave Law on the North,
the more the New England mind rose against it. Officially
both Church and press took sides with the merchants and
the lawyers; but the Abolitionist cause made rapid progress
even among those whose tastes and feelings Garrison
most offended. The converts ran unpleasant risks. One
might be a popular author, like Mrs. Child, but, if one
published a plea for the slaves, one's fame went out like
a candle. Nobody bought one's next book, one could not
get a ticket for the Athenæum and a well-known lawyer
might pick one's pamphlet up with a pair of tongs and
fling it out of the window. One might have sixteen Boston
quarterings and a gallery of Copleys and Stuarts, but, if
one uttered a phrase with "colour" in it, one's cousins
would cut one dead in Beacon Street. One appeared in
the press as an "aristocrat," but also as a "hyena" and a
"squash." In the morning mail one might receive a bulky
anonymous letter from the South, containing a withered
ear and a piece of rope. The ear had been cut from a
slave who had tried to escape. The rope was for the
Boston gentleman, in case he crossed Mason and Dixon's
line.

But this was the sort of embarrassment that animated
generous minds. While the bankers and politicians grew
colder and colder, the poets and the literary men, always
in search of a cause, a just and proper focus for their
feelings, could say Ha! Ha! once more to the sound of a
trumpet. Some of the lawyers joined them. Not all, as
Charles Francis Adams said, were "broken in to the cotton
interest." Richard Henry Dana, the sailors' lawyer,
whose natural instincts and interests were all on the conservative
side, threw prudence to the winds. In the name
of the old Northern gentry, who had always stood for
freedom, and to show how he despised the Boston cring-

ing to the Southern oligarchy, he never lost an opportunity to act as counsel for the runaway slaves. Rockwood Hoar, the judge of later times, who had twice swum the Tiber, like Horatius, made a famous speech in the Legislature, saying that the conscience of Massachusetts had a right to be represented as well as its cotton.* Thenceforward there were two kinds of Whigs, the "cotton Whigs" and the "conscience Whigs," and most of the writers belonged to the second group. It was true that George Ticknor and his circle,—all but the tolerant Prescott,—"Hunkers" of the darkest hue, to whom all agitation was abhorrent, closed their doors to Dana and Charles Sumner, snubbed them on all occasions and cut them on the street. Ticknor grew bitter and vindictive. Sumner, he said, was outside the pale, and he even snubbed the charming Edmund Quincy, the son of the Cambridge Cato, who had betrayed his caste. But Quincy was of bluer blood than Ticknor's. He represented the oldest Boston strain, not only in its love of liberty. He had a cavalier's disregard of the interests of money and property. He scorned the cold respectabilities of the upper-bourgeoisie of Beacon Street. A man of the utmost elegance, with the easy grace of a *grand seigneur,* a lover of ancient customs, with little taste for a mercantile world, he had a paternal affection for the negroes, like that of the old Virginians of the days when they wished to free their slaves. His mind was filled with the lore of colonial times, which he had heard as a child at his father's table, stories of Boston drawing-rooms of old, tales of the Massachusetts negroes; and although, as an active Abolitionist, he wrote to further the cause, his sketches, *Lewis Herbert, Dinah Rollins, Two Nights in San Domingo* and several others, *Mount Verney, Old Houses,* were admirable from any point of view. His

---

* It was Rockwood Hoar who described the three stages of the too-enterprising Yankee,—"to get on, to get honour, to get honest."

short novel, *Wensley,* better known, a Thackerayan picture of New England life, with touches from *Don
Quixote,* excellent in character and setting, missed its
mark in a commonplace plot; but *The Haunted Adjutant*
was a first-rate story. Quincy, a brilliant amateur, with a
humorous eye for human traits, wrote with a dash and
colour, an ease and freshness that were later to be known
as "modern."

In this Abolitionist campaign, which was dividing
households, as the Unitarian movement had formerly
done, the orators especially had found a cause. They
were in need of a cause, for the tale of the Revolution
and the patriot fathers had grown rather stale, flat and
thin. Eulogies of Washington and Adams, profitable to
Edward Everett, rang hollow in the ears of the new generation. What was the meaning of these declamations,
this cant about the inalienable rights of men in a country
where it was known that Jefferson's nephew had chopped
a slave to pieces with an axe, where beating, branding,
mutilating slaves, selling them, kicking them, killing them
was all in the nature of the situation? * The ancient art of
oratory, the pride of ancestral Boston, had become an
abuse. It was breathing out its vacant life in words,
empty as a cloud, cold as the frozen Frog Pond; and
suddenly, as if by a blood-transfusion, its slow pulse
began to beat again. Oratory once more possessed a function. It touched the springs of action, for the voices of
Charles Sumner and Wendell Phillips were voices to
which Boston was obliged to listen. Their doctrines, their
ideas were scarcely new. What was new was their personal style, their passion, their conviction, their sense of
fact. They were members of a family of minds that had
appeared in all the Western countries, in Italy, in Germany, in France, to defend the religion of liberty, poets

---

* See Mrs. Stowe's incontrovertible evidence in the *Key to Uncle Tom's
Cabin;* also Mrs. Child's *Plea for that Class of Americans Called Africans.*

militant, intellectual men who were glad to fight and die
for their beliefs, figures that were appearing in flesh and
blood on battlefields and barricades in Europe. Brothers
of Mazzini, heirs of William Tell, men of the world
themselves and men of culture, they roused the indifferent
minds of the thinking masses and made the American
anti-slavery movement a part of the great world-struggle
of darkness and light.

A century later, reading Phillips's speeches, one could
still feel the moral passion that seemed to rekindle the
eyes of the watching portraits when he invoked the
fathers in Faneuil Hall. One could still feel the electric
excitement that played about the speaker's head. It was
known that the careless, courtly Phillips, so buoyant, so
disdainful of the mob, the son of the first mayor of the
city of Boston, was a convert to the cause. As the college
friend and champion of the Southern students, with a
touch of the actor in his make-up, as a brilliant and promising lawyer, he had not suggested the reformer. It was
not known that at college he had made a profound study
of English history at the time of the Civil War, and had
read every document connected with it, every novel, play,
speech and memoir, from Clarendon to the days of William Godwin. This was the arsenal of learning from
which he drew when he had found his cause. With his
patrician air and his flashing wit, his volleys of historical
allusions, he magnetized the crowd, although he carried
his life in his hands when he walked home after a stormy
meeting. He seemed to say that threats were beneath
contempt. There was no room for rhetoric in his fiery
style. Phillips's mind was like a gatling-gun. Sumner was
a siege-gun beside him, less effective in direct attack,
although Sumner, his fellow-lawyer, born in the same
year, had gifts that a legal world was bound to respect.
Phillips, with his colloquial manner, something new in
Boston that killed the Edward Everett style forever,

raked the audience with his sudden sallies. Sumner obliged them to reason. Rather a lecturer than an orator, he piled his legal precedents mountain-high. His speeches were vast oral essays, bristling with quotations and citations. A little grandiloquent, compared with Phillips, but solid where Everett was hollow, he had appealed to thinking men by his speech on *The True Grandeur of Nations.* This was an attack on war, and he had shown that every warship cost as much as a college to build and keep. Each port-hole cost as much as one professor. This was an argument that impressed New England. Sumner had suggested a world-court and a League of Nations.

Many a New England schoolboy knew by heart Webster's philippic against the slave-trade, delivered in the far-off days before the great question had threatened the Union. But Phillips and Sumner had kept the "prejudices" that Webster was begging men to conquer. As they advanced, with Garrison,—Phillips as a free-lance, Sumner as leader of the "conscience Whigs,"—the movement rent society more and more, leaving wealth and power on the Southern side. One by one, however, the men of letters, the poets first of all, joined in the crusade, even those for whom "emancipation" was not a simple matter of blacks and whites, those who had other slaves to liberate, the "white slaves" of the North,* and other forms of slavery to contend with, not to be abolished by Acts of Congress, the slavery of popular indifference, timidity, sloth, stupidity, the slavery of shabby-mindedness and callous dollar-worship. What could emancipation ever mean unless there was a world worth living in? And what was a world that lacked the imagination without which freedom and slavery were empty words? Emerson was not the only writer who, when he deserted his proper studies, found that the Muse, not to be trifled

---

* "Northern gentlemen think to govern us by our black slaves; but, let me tell them, we intend to govern them by their white slaves."—John Randolph.

with, put chaos and confusion in his brain. He had his
work to do, like Prescott and Hawthorne, although for
him, too, the hour came,—when the Southerners seized
and enslaved free-negro citizens of Massachusetts. Meanwhile, for simpler and more emotional minds, the cause
was a kind of benefaction; and when volunteers from
Germany, Italy, France, exiles and revolutionists, joined
in the guerrilla war in Kansas, when Walter Savage
Landor wrote an ode and eloquent voices rose all over
the world to hearten the Abolitionists, they felt that
great days had come again, like the days of '76, that
America had once more become the focus of the world-
old struggle for liberty. "One learns in a single day,"
wrote one of the New England men who were taking
part in the Free-soil drama, "more about Greeks and
Romans and English Puritans and Scottish Jacobites and
Hungarians and all heroic peoples, than any course of
history can teach. The same process is producing the same
results before your eyes, and, what is most striking, the
same persons whom you saw a year ago in Boston, indolent and timid, are here transformed to heroes." *

Whatever in the way of stimulus the movement afforded the poets, the poets repaid ten-fold. Even the
angular Garrison wrote sonnets, in the gravest style of
Milton, composing them in his midnight walks across the
bridge to Cambridge; and John Greenleaf Whittier, his
lieutenant, had long had cause to know that words, in
times like these, had consequences. One of Whittier's
anti-slavery pamphlets, *Justice and Expediency,* had
caused the death of a friend. Merely for lending it to a
brother-physician, Dr. Crandall of Washington had been
put in prison, where his health had given way in the
dampness and darkness. In fact, in the Whittier of these
feverish years, there was more "deed" than "word,"
strangely in a Quaker non-resistant who clung to the old

* Thomas Wentworth Higginson.

Quaker ways that enabled him to get "into the quiet." But the lithe, quick Whittier, tall and eager, with his black hair and burning eyes, was anything but passive. As a child, in the "snow-bound" Haverhill farmhouse, he had seen or heard of a neighbour melting a minister's image in wax to send his soul to hell; and he himself had not read for nothing the journals of the old fighting Quakers who had wrestled with men and angels in Cromwell's day. He liked to face a mob. His black Quaker coat had been pelted with eggs, and he had seen his newspaper-office, the office of the *Pennsylvania Freeman,* burned over his head. Garibaldi was one of his heroes. Moreover, he was a skilful politician. It was Whittier who had induced Charles Sumner to stand for election to the Senate. There was no lobbyist like him at the State House, when it came to pulling wires "for righteousness' sake," in behalf of the Indians or woman's suffrage, the blind, felons, animals. This befitted the only man of his time who had read all the Utopias. Whittier had had no connection with the Brook Farm movement, but no one in America more than he longed to realize Milton's "true commonwealth."

Whittier was a shoot of the oldest New England. His family had lived in the Haverhill farmhouse since 1688, and no one had known, or was ever to know, the lore of the Merrimac Valley better than he, the legends of Essex and Middlesex and the woods of lower New Hampshire. His forbears had been farmers for six generations and had married the daughters of farmers, and his mind was steeped in local associations, tales of witches, tales of the Indian wars, the gossip of wandering farm-hands and gypsies. A Scottish farmer lived near by who wrote in the manner of Burns for the Haverhill paper. He had often stopped at the Whittier house and sung *Highland Mary* in the kitchen, over his bread and cheese and mug of cider. There were no Yankee pastorals, he had said.

The domestic life of New England had not been hallowed by tender associations. Yet how poetic was the
farmer's life!—the scent of the hay-mow, the breath of
the cattle, the greenery by the brookside, the huskings,
berry-pickings and winter sleigh-rides. These were the
days when scriptural themes and scenes had occupied the
American poetasters and Jared Sparks and Bancroft had
just discovered the romance of American history. Whittier was prepared for Burns and Scott. He had written
his first verses in chalk and charcoal on the beam of his
mother's loom and had hidden his manuscripts in the
farmhouse garret. He longed to escape from farming,
for exposure and over-exertion had broken his health.
The rigours of the New England winter had left in Whittier's mind impressions that tougher boys would have
forgotten. Then Garrison had discovered the "star of
genius" who had sent a poem to his paper. He had driven
out from Newburyport to find him, and, while Whittier
hastened to change his clothes,—he was burrowing under
the barn in search of eggs when the great man appeared
at the gate,—had begged his father to give him an education. Why make war on a young man's nature?

Whittier's reputation was that of a newspaper-poet. In
Cambridge, they had forgotten or scarcely known that
his *Legends of New England,* published in 1831, was the
first collection of poems of the young New England
school. He had versified stories from Mather's *Magnalia,* anticipated Longfellow's *Hiawatha* with ballads of
Indian exploits, written tales of the colony times that
suggested a metrical Hawthorne. Before these writers
had been heard of, Whittier had been widely known. But
he had abandoned his early subjects, and there were
reasons why he was not remembered outside the obscure
and humble public that always cherished him most at the
best of times. He had written with a reckless facility, in
the well-worn metres of Scott and Campbell, with almost

no distinction of language. Aside from a word here and there with a local tang and value,—lug-pole, chimney-lug,—his diction had no nap or freshness: it was a thread-bare diction, and so remained. His associations had never been literary. Among the New England poets his only friend had been Mrs. Sigourney of Hartford, where he had lived for a while. His active life had been spent with orators and reformers, editors, propagandists and politicians. He was regarded as an unlettered rhymester, an anti-slavery journalist in verse. When he asked in one of his poems—

> And wilt thou prize my poor gift less
> For simple air and rustic dress,
> And sign of haste and carelessness?—

what could one say in reply? His senses were defective. He was totally colour-blind and partially deaf. When he looked at an apple-tree, he could not distinguish the leaves from the apples, and once, in a moment of affluence, he bought a carpet that was garishly bright and showy, supposing it was a mild grey and brown, suitable for Quaker feet to walk on. His eye and ear were imperfect. His rhymes were often a scandal. Two hundred years of silence, as he put it, had "taken all the sing" out of the Quakers; and widely as he read, in later years, and carefully as he worked over his poems, he never knew when to cut them short. It was as if, having broken silence, he could not say enough. His technical methods were stereotyped. The simplest and most conventional ballad metres, the sentiments, phrases and rhythms of other poets served him to the last. He had no pride of artistry. When editors revised his manuscripts, Whittier accepted their changes without remark.

In certain aspects, he suggested a lesser Thomas Hood. But Whittier had a verve and flow as notable as

Hood's, a force of moral passion, a fund of feeling. Spirited improvisation was his special gift. Moreover, he had something to say that no one else had said, something that many others after him, true bards and simple, or bards who were merely simple, could only repeat and echo. There was even a touch of grandeur in him, the fiery zeal of a Puritan prophet, the fruit of a passionate nature that "strove in chains." The girls had led Whittier many a dance. In the days when he had longed for wealth and glory, before he became a reformer, it was the worldly girls who attracted him most. They had snubbed him for his poverty and rustic manners and teased him to the brink of suicide. No doubt, this increased his love of money, for Whittier dearly loved to turn a penny, much as he liked others to think him poor; and one of his favourite themes was the happy after-life of a high-born lady who has married a farmer's boy. The girls had made a mistake, he seemed to say, when they had jilted Whittier. For the rest, he had had his compensation, for his virginality fed his poetry. He was a philanderer all his days and could scarcely hold back the flood of "pilgrims" that threatened to engulf his later years, the lady-poets who sent him snips of their dresses, begged him for intimate souvenirs, proposed to marry him on two occasions, built houses near his own, with room for two, and popped in and almost gobbled him up, till he had to set a spring-trap at his door to warn him that they were coming and give him a chance to escape at the rear of his house. These were the days when he always put on his hat before he answered the door-bell, so that he might appear to be going out. He spent whole afternoons roaming the streets, trying to lose the curiosity-seekers. "I had hard work to lose him, but I have lost him," he would say to his sister when he reappeared. "But I can never lose a *her*." But who had encouraged the "pilgrims," the lady-poets, as if he wished to keep the fires burning? He kept the fires burning and thriftily banked them up a single chimney. Poetry was Whittier's vestal altar.

As time went on, he returned to the scenes and subjects that had characterized his early verse; and, while he continued to write for the Abolitionist cause, he became more and more the rural poet. Whittier and Longfellow, whom he scarcely knew, were rivals in popular fame, after he had published the *Lays of My Home*. Longfellow's mind was of a higher cast. Whatever it lacked in intensity, it was poetic in grain. Whittier's mind was sandy and thin beside it, though it had more spontaneity than Lowell's. It glowed with moral feeling, if only here and there with imagination. But Whittier's best work was still to come, in the early eighteen-fifties. Meanwhile, he enlarged the little cottage into which he had moved at Amesbury. He built the garden-room, always filled in season with harebells and laurel, where he liked to read his poems aloud to his friends, while his sister, Elizabeth Whittier, who was also a poet, guarded the vestal flame. In the afternoons, he sat in the village store, perched on a sugar-barrel, joining in the local gossip and putting in a word now and then to turn the vote of the farmers. No other writer had done so much to arouse public feeling for Abolition; and *Ichabod,* the poem on Webster, and *Massachusetts to Virginia* were a part of American history, as everyone felt. But he was only at home in the cause during its prophetic phase. As it entered the violent phase that preceded the war, he grew more and more quietistic and even broke with his old friend Garrison. There were limits beyond which a Quaker poet could not sincerely follow the path of action. This was the period of his prose papers, on Bunyan, Ellwood, Baxter, the notes on the Quakers of Cromwell's time, whom he defended against Carlyle's attacks. Of these the best was the essay on the old New Jersey Quaker, John Woolman, whom Lamb had urged his read-

ers to "get by heart" and who had largely started the
anti-slavery movement,—for Garrison was a disciple of
one of Woolman's followers. Whittier's longest prose-
piece, *Margaret Smith's Journal,* was a picture of the
New England settlements in the days of the Salem
witches. In a semi-archaic style, composed in tone and
only less intense than Hawthorne's pictures, it conveyed
the state of mind of the Pilgrim settlers with a haunting
particularity. One saw the witchcraft working in the
lonely cabins, the irons jumping into the pots, the tools
flying about the rooms, the baskets dropping from the
chimneys, the goodwives flocking to Boston to see the
hangings, while the merry birds carolled in the trees and
the white and yellow flowers besprinkled the banks.
Through the bedevilled air, one caught the scent of the
mayflower, the trailing arbutus, the symbol of a springtime innocence.

This was Whittier's element, and more and more the
"wood-thrush of Essex" sang the summer pastorals and
the songs of home that had so much of New England in
them:

> Along the roadside, like the flowers of gold
> The tawny Incas for their gardens wrought,
> Heavy with sunshine droops the goldenrod,
> And the red pennons of the cardinal-flowers
> Hang motionless upon their upright staves.
> The sky is hot and hazy, and the wind,
> Wing-weary with its long flight from the south,
> Unfelt; yet, closely scanned, yon maple leaf
> With faintest motion, as one stirs in dreams,
> Confesses it. The locust by the wall
> Stabs the noon-silence with his sharp alarm.
> A single hay-cart down the dusty road
> Creaks slowly, with its driver fast asleep
> On the load's top. Against the neighbouring hill,
> Huddled along the stone-wall's shady side,

The sheep show white, as if a snow-drift still
Defied the dog-star. Through the open door
A drowsy smell of flowers—grey heliotrope,
And white sweet clover, and shy mignonette—
Comes faintly in, and silent chorus lends
To the prevailing symphony of peace.

In rudely vigorous ballads, he told the old legends of the
sea-coast, *Skipper Ireson's Ride, The Dead Ship of
Harpswell.* In his *Songs of Labour,* recited at working-
men's meetings for three generations, he glorified the
trades that he knew so well, shoemaking, lumbering, ship-
building, droving, fishing; and his husking-poems and
corn-songs, his idylls of the village and the farm, *The
Old Burying-Ground, Telling the Bees, In School Days,
The Barefoot Boy, My Playmate,* redolent of sweet-fern
and clover and meadows ripe with corn, brought back to
countless readers the world of their childhood. They saw
once more the old roads winding, the gap in the wall, the
stepping-stones in the brook,—

Glimpses of chimneys and gabled eaves,
Through green elm arches and maple leaves.

The night-hawk's sullen plunge in the woods of New
Hampshire, the grey fort's broken wall on the coast of
Maine, the rocky capes, the heavy hay-boats crawling, the
salt sea-scents along the shore, the quilting-parties and
the winter sleigh-rides, the pumpkins and the huckleberry-
thickets lived again in the songs of the "barefoot boy."

CHAPTER XXII

NEW ENGLAND AT LARGE

UNDER a tree in front of his house at Marshfield,
Daniel Webster lay in his open coffin, dressed in
his blue coat with the brass buttons, his right hand over
his breast, the sun full in his face. It was 1852, a warm,
hazy October day. As far as one could see from the
slopes of the hill, a multitude as of grasshoppers covered
the land, and the fields were filled with wagons, chaises
and sulkies, omnibuses and coaches. Over the silence of
the vast assembly, one heard the cattle lowing in their
barns.

To the remotest hamlet of the Androscoggin, New
England hummed with tales of the fabulous man, how,
when he knew that he was dying, he sent his faithful
black servant William to hang the lantern at his shallop's
mast-head and raise the colours there, saying, "I want to
keep my flag flying and my light burning till I die." This
was the grand style of a day that was passing, the epoch
of the building of the Union, the confident young republic; and even the Abolitionists remembered that Webster,
whether "Ichabod" or not, was a great New England
worthy, perhaps the greatest, a masterpiece of Yankee
blood and sinew whose life had been connected at every
point with the interests and hopes of the people. He had
thriven with their progress and their success, their farms,
their mills, their schools. He symbolized their energy and
triumph. Countless boys, like John Fiske, who lived at
Middletown, Connecticut, felt that life had grown sud-

denly small and lonely and wondered how the sun could rise without Daniel Webster.

"I still live"—Webster's last phrase—was engraved on the Sheffield razors that hundreds of farmers used on Sunday mornings. New England was more alive than ever, in the towns, in the manufacturing centres, but farming life had begun to decline. The old farmers were dying out, or so it seemed to those who loved the country,—the men whose hoeing was a sleight-of-hand, who made their own ox-yokes and axe-helves, chopped their three cords of wood a day, knew every medicinal herb that grew in field or stream and knew how to select a piece of timber, chestnut or oak or walnut, that measured a given amount, cut it and score it and load it. These tamers of the wilderness were vanishing from the land. They were hewing their way to the West, along the Great Lakes, while the young men were turning to the cities, learning to pronounce their "ben" as "bin," and sometimes even "bean," and rising with the factories and the railroads.

As wealth advanced and the towns increased, the region grew more self-contemplative. Novelists were appearing here and there, picturing local manners, with an interest in social relations that was aroused by the spread of urban standards. One had to tolerate human nature first, a thing that Calvinism had scarcely encouraged, before one could find it amusing. Landscape-artists appeared in the train of the poets. Thomas Cole, Kensett, Church and others were painting up and down the coast, sketching in the Berkshires, tramping the White Hills and the Green Mountains, looking for the picturesque, catching the scent of Indian legends, following the lead of the landscape-poets; for Whittier, Longfellow, Lowell and Holmes had filled the country with associations. Every waterfall and stream and hilltop, Ossipee, Winnepesaukee, Hampton Beach, Chocorua's horn, the

Kennebec, the Saco, every ancient house and rocky ledge was the theme of some ballad or sonnet that called for the pencil. Summer visitors at Nahant noted in their journals the little scenes that pleased the landscape-painters, the cows going over the beach at sunset on their way to the cow-yards at Lynn, their red hides reflected in the wet sand and lighting up the grey of the sky and the surge. The influence of Ruskin had begun to spread, and people spoke of the beauty of rocks and the sacredness of colour. They compared the effects of changes of air in the mountains and wondered just how much of the vague and dreamy, in the matter of mist or spray, a scene had to possess to be sublime. Intervale was a favourite spot, where artists and tourists gathered. Connoisseurs of landscape from Boston or Hartford, parties from Worcester and Burlington drove on the tops of stages or in private buckboards through the Franconia Notch, observing Mount Webster and Lafayette as if they were two pictures in different styles by the hand of the same master. They scrutinized Wachusett from Monadnock; they looked at Franconia from the Pemigewassett. They studied the slopes and the cliffs, the Flume and the Profile, an older piece of sculpture than the Sphinx, climbed up to the Nose or the Chin, botanized with Asa Gray in mind and longed for a little talk with Agassiz. For Agassiz had made these scenes exciting, even more exciting than Ruskin made them. Speaking as a geologist, he had said that New England was the oldest spot on the earth's surface. They sprang out of their beds at the Mountain House when the porter, walking through the halls, rang his big bell and shouted, "Sunrise!"—assembling on the piazza to see the Franconia Mountains at earliest dawn. They tried the echo on Echo Lake and quoted Tennyson on the "horns of Elfland." They noted the yellow fields of rye and the beautiful cone of Mount Washington, yielding harvests of colour.

The more the ancient rural life receded into the background of men's lives, the more it roused their feelings of romance. The farm, the village ways, harsh enough in actuality, seemed, to the barefoot boys who had gone to New York or were making their fortunes in State Street, merry and jolly or softly sweet as Goldsmith's scenes of Auburn. They liked to remember their school-days, the wadded hoods, the knitted caps and mittens, the snowbound evenings under the lamp, the games, the slates and pencils, rosy apples in the dish, nutting-time, coasting-time. Sawing wood in the frosty air had surely seemed less dull than adding figures. This was the theme of a hundred poems and stories that multiplied with time, as the farm became a universal symbol,—the farm, the weather-painted house and barn, the well-sweep, the orchard, the sandy field surrounded by the woods, the small blue lake at the foot of the hill. No New England boy or man could ever forget the country, the cider-making days of old, the heaps of golden apples under the trees, the cider-mill worked by the plodding horse and all agush with autumn juices. The new generation of city-dwellers longed to be reminded of these rural scenes, and the popularity of the "household poets" rose with the exodus from the "household" setting, the homestead and the farm. This was the secret of Whittier's fame. He was the emblem of Thanksgiving, when two or three New Englanders gathered together, or a houseful of scattered uncles and aunts and cousins, in far New York or on the Western plains. He brought back the painted autumn woodlands, the pumpkin pies of old, the succotash, the doughnuts and the chowder, the wild grapes, the tubs of maple sugar, the school-house, the old-fashioned winter that seemed so different from the modern winter because of the modern devices that had softened its rigours. The pioneers carried Whittier with them, as emigrant Scotsmen carried the poems of Burns. *Snow-Bound* was their image of Pallas, the safeguard of their memories. It was the touchstone of their past.

For New England men were scattering far and wide. They were sowing schools and colleges over the West. In the South Sea Islands, in China, in Burmah, they were planting Orthodox churches and mission-centres, writing their versions of the Bible in half the tongues of Asia. Some of the missionaries were learned men, two or three were great men.* They remembered Thanksgiving Day in the Himalayas and read their *Snow-Bound* on the Yang-tse River. New England seemed romantic in the distance, as Shanghai and Canton had seemed in their barefoot boyhood. The Rollo Books, to be sure, were not romantic, even to the remotest Yankee, redolent as they were of the barn-yard and pasture, the hired man, the chopping-block, early hours and earnest aspirations, nor were Elijah Kellogg's tales of boys in the good old days in the "State of Maine,"—as Maine men liked to call it, to remind the world that their State was no longer a "District." † If the fathers of Jacob Abbott's generation enjoyed the adventures of Rollo as much as their children, it was for a more substantial reason than that which drew them to the household poets; for Rollo was the model boy, in whom the model parent saw himself, the leading manufacturer in his earlier stages. Here the New England passion for self-improvement, as it was understood by the plainer folk, found its completest record. How to be dutiful, how to be conscientious, how to be genteel and well-informed, in order to be right on all occasions and able, especially, to set others right, this was

* Of the original writings of these New England missionaries,—Adoniram Judson, Hiram Bingham, S. Wells Williams, etc.,—an admirable example is *The Middle Kingdom,* a survey of the Chinese Empire. The author, S. Wells Williams, wrote two Chinese dictionaries and was later professor of Chinese at Yale.

† Kellogg's *Lion Ben of Elm Island* and other books for boys, lifeless and wooden enough, are filled with authentic details of pioneer life on the coast of Maine.

Jacob Abbott's open secret. In Rollo, the reader beheld in all its phases the shaping of one of Webster's "solid men."

No one could have doubted Rollo's future. He was destined to rise in the world, with the other factory-owners and cotton-brokers who had left their ancestral farms in Vermont and Maine, the farms that seemed idyllic in their fancy as they drowsed in their office-chairs at the end of the day. "Ik Marvel's" books, *Reveries of a Bachelor* and *Dream-Life,* appealed to this nostalgic mood. One went to the city, accepted the ways of the world, made one's pile and married for advantage, while all the while, in one's heart of hearts, one clung to the simple, wholesome dreams of childhood. Such was the burden of these romances, composed in a style that suggested Irving and Lamb. The fields, the trees, the brooks, the sweetheart whose name one had cut on the bark of the birches were much more real than the noisy, ambitious life of the changing, bustling town, the sharp transactions of the business day, all blaze and vanity. Rain in the garret, as one recalled it, school-dreams, first love, fishing, boy-romance and first ambition were the stuff of the bachelor's reveries. That the bachelor who thought of nothing but marriage was the best of advocates of the married state, that all his dreams were "pipe-dreams" added to the charm of the make-believe. That he acquiesced in what he assumed to reject, the reader quickly gathered. These aspirations and visions were only "smoke," a comforting reassurance for the practical man who had left them far behind him. For the rest, Ik Marvel's enormous vogue showed how many people desired in books the opposite of what they desired in life. It was the busiest souls, those that were eager for all the latest inventions, who most rejoiced in this philosopher, this lover of old ways who never used a watch to measure time, preferred a burning taper to a gas-jet and lighted his cigar with coal and tongs.

But Ik Marvel,—Donald G. Mitchell,—was an engaging writer. His charm of style, his gentle bookishness, the slightly archaic flavour of his mind carried these youthful romances round the world; and long after men had ceased to read them, they were to survive as books for boys, who found their vague feelings, doubts and passions reflected in the bachelor's dreams. Mitchell's later books, *My Farm at Edgewood* and *Wet Days at Edgewood,* were of a hardier quality. Written during these years when rural life was falling into decay, when the city was attracting the ambitious and many farmers were moving West, they pictured the art of husbandry, its pleasures and its benefits, as Alcott was picturing it in his Concord essays, but with more system and practical knowledge. Mitchell, a graduate of Yale, a former consul at Venice and a landscape-gardener by avocation, who had laid out the grounds of Princeton College, had retired in poor health to a farm at New Haven, where he lived among his books. His mind was filled with garden associations, the literary farmers of Greece and Rome, Hesiod, Pliny, Virgil, the old British authors and country story-tellers, from Piers Plowman to the Ettrick Shepherd; but he was a practical farmer, too, who longed to revive the dying interest in the oldest of New England occupations. He rebuked the shams of the farmer's life, the blinded front-parlour that was only entered once a month or so, to consult some gilt-bound dictionary, while it engrossed the best half of the house; and he made no false claims in regard to farming, its profits and advantages. His observations on bees and the care of cattle, on dairying, on the orchard and the garden, on the treatment of grapes, plums, apples, pears, on the dwarf trees that had to be fondled and humoured, on rural decoration, crops and markets were as shrewd and precise as

Evelyn's, or Walton's observations on the angler's art, which, with Jeremy Taylor, Browne and Bunyan, had left their traces in his style. Ik Marvel was at his best in these country essays; and Elihu Burritt, the "learned blacksmith," also wrote eloquent papers on pastoral life. Burritt, who had left his Worcester forge and made a new career for himself as a philanthropic lecturer, had organized congresses of the Friends of Peace at Brussels, Paris, Frankfort and in England, where he served as American consul at Birmingham. With his farm at New Britain, Connecticut, always in mind, he visited farms in every corner of England, making careful notes and observations, in the hope of improving rural conditions at home. His *Walk from London to Land's End,* suggesting Cobbett's *Rural Rides,* was filled with unassuming information. Burritt's account of his visit to the Queen's dairy at Windsor Castle was a more rewarding travel-sketch than most of the current essays on the Coliseum. It was a model dairy, but Burritt thought the milk-pails were too heavy. In exchange for all he had learned, he would have liked to send the Queen some of the light, white-cedar, seamless pails which the farmers used in New England.

Alcott, Burritt, Mitchell, three Connecticut men,—for Burritt was born in New Britain, as Alcott was born at Wolcott, ten miles to the west,—were the three outstanding writers of their time on pastoral life and farming. Frederick Law Olmsted, who had begun to write in the fifties, was also a Connecticut man, the son of a Hartford merchant. This local development was not surprising, for Connecticut was more rural than Massachusetts, where town-life and shipping had occupied so many minds. But even in fertile Vermont, most pastoral of all the States, factories were appearing here and there, at Burlington, especially, on Lake Champlain, where the well-known Minister to Turkey, the lawyer-scholar, George Perkins Marsh, who had been offered Sparks's chair at Harvard, carried on his studies and wrote his books. Marsh, a life-long friend of his fellow-Vermonter, the sculptor Hiram Powers, and a class-mate at Dartmouth of Rufus Choate, a stalwart, inquisitive man and a notable linguist, had published a grammar of Icelandic and was known far and wide as a Scandinavian scholar when Longfellow was studying Swedish and Finnish. The library of Scandinavian books that he kept in his Burlington house was the most complete in the world outside the Scandinavian countries; and he had printed, in 1843, an essay called *The Goths in New England,* suggested by the Northern myths and sagas, that was one of the many forerunners of the modern "Nordic" movement. With none of the animus that later writers, the Houston Stewart Chamberlains and their kind, imported into the Nordic cult, Marsh traced all the virtues of New England to the Gothic element in its forbears. What was the age of the Puritans, which had given birth to New England, but that in which the Gothic strain in England had cast out the Roman element? The Goths were the noblest of races; it was their blood that flowed at Bunker Hill. Whatever the Anglo-Saxons possessed of intellectual power and moral grandeur, they owed to the Gothic mother. Their grasping ambition, their materialism, their spirit of exclusive selfishness were due to the Roman nurse.

This represented one of those germs of feeling, innocent at the outset, like Bronson Alcott's preference for the blond complexion, that sometimes flower in sinister ways. Marsh, who had a scientific mind, would have been horrified if he had foreseen the use that later anthropologists, in the interests of tribal factions, were to make of his Gothic theory. His object was to preach the ancient virtues and simplicities, not to make invidious distinctions. Besides, *The Goths in New England* was only a pamphlet. Marsh wrote several more important works,

an entertaining study of *The Camel,* filled with curious
and amusing lore gathered in his Oriental travels, two
philological books on the English language, based on lectures that he had delivered at Harvard, and the masterly
Man and Nature, better described by its later title, *The
Earth as Modified by Human Action.* This was to remain
a classical work in the field of modern geography, for
Marsh was one of the first to understand the relation
between man and his physical setting. He was almost the
first to protest against the wanton way in which man disturbed the harmonies of nature. It is true that, long
before, a writer who remained anonymous contributed to
Miss Peabody's *Æsthetic Papers* an essay, *Vegetation
about Salem,* describing the reckless fashion in which the
American forests were being destroyed. "Posterity must
feel the consequences" was the moral of this unregarded
paper, a moral that no one drew till the "conservation
movement" of later years. Marsh was the prophet of this
movement. No one had written with such breadth of
knowledge of man as a geological agent, who can upbuild
or destroy his home, the earth. No one had shown before
how man had played the destroyer and what he could do
to reëstablish the partnership between himself and nature.

Marsh, who died in Italy, at Vallombrosa,—he was
the first American minister to the newly-established kingdom,—was the chief contributor of Vermont to the "literature of knowledge." To the "literature of power"
Vermont made a modest contribution, a novel that
belonged to the school of Cooper and was destined to be
read as long as Cooper. Daniel Pierce Thompson, the
author of *The Green Mountain Boys,* was a lawyer and
judge at Montpelier, where he edited *The Green Mountain Freeman.* One saw him shuffling through the streets
in his battered carpet-slippers, on his way to the newspaper-office where he had printed his book; for, although
he was a local dignitary and lived in a clapboard Parthe-

non, he was a jolly old sloven whose greatest pleasure
was to go hunting and fishing with the boys. They all
knew that he had been born in Charlestown, in the shadow
of Bunker Hill; but at the age of five, in 1800, he had
been brought to Vermont, and there was not a worthy in
the State who knew as much about it as the judge. He
had grown up on a farm near Montpelier, where he had
watched the building of the State House, and had seen
the youthful commonwealth emerge from its old border
life, which resembled that of Cooper's New York and the
Scotland of some of the Waverley novels, into a thriving
republic. He had gone through Middlebury College and
studied law in Virginia, where he had met and talked
with Jefferson on the grounds of the university he was
building. As they stood together, the old President, who
was almost eighty, took a chisel out of the hand of one
of his Italian stone-cutters and showed him how to turn
the volute of a capital; then he leaped on his horse and
galloped away. Thompson was full of these tales of the
men of the Revolution. He had wandered all over Vermont, with his horse and his fishing-rod and gun, shooting wolves and catching trout, chatting at farmhouse
doors, talking with the pioneer settlers, listening to yarns
about Ethan Allen. A born antiquarian, like Scott, a
lover of ballads and folklore, he kept careful notes of
these conversations. Every client of the country lawyer
gave him an anecdote or a bit of gossip.

In these little towns of Vermont, surrounded by rolling
pastures and groves of maples, far from the bustling sea-
coast, the eighteenth-century mind lived quietly on. The
new-fangled Boston books seldom reached Montpelier,
and country judges and editors read Pope and Fielding as
if the good old world had never changed. Thompson, a
born story-teller, although he never became a professional
author, wrote his first book in the manner of Smollett.
First and last, he wrote many books, all of them, save

one, surpassingly dull, and all, even the best, amateurish;
for he had few relations with other authors and scarcely
knew the meaning of criticism. Like most unprofessional
writers, he never knew where his strength lay and constantly tried his hand in directions where he was foredoomed to fail. But he had not read Scott and Cooper
for nothing, he had steeped himself in the legends of
Vermont, and, if he was a man of one book, this book,
which he largely wrote on his father's farm, sitting under
a pine-tree, was a most engaging performance. *The Green
Mountain Boys* was a home-grown product, if ever literature saw one, as unpretentious as a log-cabin, but it was
built on such a good model that no faults of style or
execution counted in the final result. It was the classic
picture of Vermont, in the days of its struggle for independence, first from New York and afterwards from
England; and the picture was undoubtedly true in its
atmosphere and feeling. One saw the beaver-hatted
mountaineers, the bold, high-hearted borderers, handsome and fearless, Seth Warner and Ethan Allen, threading their way through the greenwood, like Robin Hood
and his band, bearing the noble buck on their shoulders;
one heard their whistle echoing through the sylvan
glades. One saw the fond and spirited young ladies, imprisoned in block-houses and woodland cabins, ready for
brave escapes and enchanting elopements; and over all
one breathed the fragrant air of pine, spruce and balsam, a
world of sparkling lakes and flashing trout-streams,
youth, adventure, freedom and true romance.

This was a Yankee tale as brisk and wholesome as any
mountain-ballad. It was a border-song in prose, and these
were the days when the Yankee ballads throve as never
later. Catch a "real, green, live Yankee," as Father
Taylor liked to say, and you always caught a man who
could sing a song, especially on the sea-coast. In Maine,
among the old fish-houses, where they still used words

that one found only in Chaucer, there were men who could sing all night, seven score songs in succession, and count up to two or three hundred. On the Isles of Shoals, near Portsmouth, where "Old Bob," the spectre, one of Captain Kidd's men, haunted the coves and the wharves, and Celia Thaxter lived at Appledore, where her father kept the lighthouse, one might have heard an old shoaler, who had fought at New Orleans in 1815, singing by the hour, while he sat bent forward with his arms on his knees, or played on a cracked old fiddle, with his wrinkled eyelids screwed tight together. Where had his queer tunes come from? They were like the creaking and groaning of masts or the whistling of the wind in the cordage of a clipper.* *Lord Bateman* was a favourite with these singers, who added their own variations, or the deeds of "Brave Wolfe," or

> With sixteen brass nineteens the Lion did growl,
> With sixteen brass twenties the Tiger did howl.

There were minstrels and rural singers all over New England, and often a well-known poem became an anonymous ballad. Such was Walter Mitchell's *Tacking Ship off Shore*. This was adopted by the fishermen, who had never heard of the author. Dr. Holmes's *Ballad of the Oysterman* was sung up and down the coast, with hundreds of alterations and elaborations.

Aside from Thompson's tale of Vermont, few New England novels of the moment could have been described as brisk or wholesome. *The Wide, Wide World* of Susan Warner was a swamp of lachrymosity. It was a malarial book. So was *The Lamplighter,* by Maria Cummins, the story of another Cinderella, which had, however, something vigorous in it that *The Wide, Wide World* totally lacked. One felt and saw the Boston slums,—for slums

* See Celia Thaxter's *Among the Isles of Shoals.*

had appeared in Boston with a vengeance,—the street-
lamps and the snow, suggesting Dickens's London. What
was real in both these books, as pictures of their time,
was the pervasive presence of. religion.* Little Ellen was
a prig, but when she was dazzled by the array of Bibles,
of which her mother had promised her one, "so that her
wits were ready to forsake her," and when she spent her
evenings singing hymns, and "hymn succeeded hymn, with
fresh and varied pleasure," she was behaving as Harriet
Beecher Stowe certainly behaved at sixteen; and Mrs.
Stowe had never been a prig. Her large, frank, fiery,
generous nature had nothing in it of the goody-goody; and
hymns, in the passionate world in which she lived, were as
much a part of the atmosphere as ballads ever were in time
of war. All the New England poets were writing them, following Dwight and Barlow, and the best American
hymns that have ever been written appeared when Mrs.
Stowe was in her heyday.† In the two hundred years that
had passed since Governor Winslow refreshed himself
"with singing of psalms, making joyful melody," New
Englanders had exulted in hymns. Mrs. Stowe, as a child
in Litchfield, had listened with ecstasy to the "fuguing
tunes," those billowy compositions which they sang in
church, when the four parts of the choir took up the song,
and went racing round after one another, each singing a
different set of words, till at length, by some inexplicable
magic, they all came together again, and sailed smoothly
out into a sea of harmony. She had looked with wonder
from side to side when treble, tenor, counter and bass

* The religious note entirely dominated R. T. S. Lowell's *The New Priest
in Conception Bay,* a novel of Newfoundland, with a few good scenes of
sea-coast life. The author, an Episcopal clergyman, was a brother of James
Russell Lowell.

† E.g., Holmes's "Lord of all being, throned afar," Whittier's "Dear
Lord and Father of mankind," E. H. Sears's "Calm on the listening air of
night" and "It came upon the midnight clear." Samuel Francis Smith, who,
at twenty-four, wrote "America" in half an hour, produced almost one
hundred and fifty hymns.

were thus roaring and foaming, and it verily seemed as if the psalm were about to be wrecked among the breakers. And then, to her delighted sense, every verse emerged whole and uninjured from the storm.

Harriet Beecher Stowe was one of the volcanic souls whom the Abolitionist movement brought to the front. As the daughter of Lyman Beecher, she had lived through the days of her father's "Revival." She had studied at Hartford, at her sister's school, where Catharine Beecher wrote her well-known essay refuting Jonathan Edwards on the Will, learning French and Italian there, and had answered with a "yes" her father's question, "Do you feel that, if the universe should be destroyed, you could be happy with God alone?" At twelve, however, hearing of Byron's death, she had wandered off to a lonely hillside, laid herself down in a field of daisies, looked up at the sky and wondered about Byron's soul. The vehemence and intensity of Byron's feeling fascinated all the Beechers, who felt the Calvinistic inheritance in him, and Harriet, who adored *The Corsair,* had sung "Fare thee well" with the other schoolgirls, who felt that they would never have let Byron go. Many years later, in her *Vindication of Lady Byron,* in which she turned against the poet, she showed how deep these early impressions were. Her father, who did not approve of novels, made an exception of Scott, whom his children had to read; and Harriet found the *Arabian Nights,* in the family garret, in a barrel of sermons. She dreamed of some heroic cause, some mission or crusade, that would call out her powers of devotion.

She had visited in Boston, as a girl, when Lyman Beecher, at the Park Street church, had pelted the Unitarians with his sermons, and had followed him in the rout to Cincinnati. Boston was past redemption by any Connecticut method, but the "capital of the West" received him gladly. He preached revival sermons all the way. It was there that Harriet married Calvin Stowe, a teacher in her father's seminary, "rich in Greek, Arabic and Hebrew" but as poor as other missionaries in everything else. There, during a cholera epidemic that was like the black plague of the Middle Ages,—nine thousand people in the city died in three months, and there were ten thousand cases of smallpox,—she wrote a tract that was widely read, *Earthly Care a Heavenly Discipline*. Of care she had enough herself, but there were compensations in Cincinnati. The town was half made up of New England people, with a literary club and a magazine. She began to write stories and essays, often on the kitchen table, surrounded by pots and pans, with half a dozen children asking questions. These stories, elementary enough, paler than Miss Sedgwick's, pleased a circle of readers for whom the visible world had begun to exist and the simplest observations were all-sufficient. But Dr. Stowe knew that she had a power of which these tales gave little evidence. He told her that she could form the mind of the West.

It happened that her father's seminary was an Abolitionist centre. Runaway slaves who appeared there were kept and passed along to the north, and just across the river, in Kentucky, were large slave-plantations. Mrs. Stowe spent several days on one of these plantations, which she afterwards described as Colonel Shelby's; and, although she had never lived in the South, she heard so much about it, and met so many Southern men and women, that she was prepared to picture it as no Southern writer had ever done. The moment for this came later, when she moved to Brunswick, Maine, where her husband was asked to teach in Bowdoin College. The Stowes lived there in a house where Longfellow had lodged as a student. The Fugitive Slave Law had just been passed, and letters came pouring in upon Mrs. Stowe describing its tragic consequences, the separations of husbands and wives, the scattering of mothers and their children. Her mind became suddenly incandescent. She felt she had an apostolic mission to put an end to slavery once for all; she felt that it was not herself but God who wrote the tale of *Uncle Tom's Cabin*. If this book was not the cause of the Civil War, as Lincoln said later, it was at least one of the major causes, for it blocked the operation of the Fugitive Slave Law. As a literary event, it was the greatest since Prescott's *Ferdinand and Isabella*. It was a world-event, in fact. Macaulay, Heine and George Sand reviewed it. Three Paris newspapers published it at once, and Uncle Tom's Cabins rose all over Europe, as restaurants, creameries and bazaars. It appeared in thirty-seven languages, and three times over in Welsh, into which Scott and Dickens had never been translated; and it sent Heine back to his Bible and made such an impression on Tolstoy in Russia that, when he came to write *What is Art?*, he took it as an example of the highest type, with Dostoievsky's *House of the Dead*, and much of Victor Hugo. In all the history of the printed book, the Bible alone had appeared in so many versions.

Was Tolstoy right in his opinion? On the whole, yes, ten times right; and this was not only because of the moral force that carried *Uncle Tom* around the world. Everything in Mrs. Stowe was large, her experience, her humour, her feeling for justice, her passion for the realities of human nature. Her mind had the swing and rhythm of the great story-tellers, like Dickens, Cooper, Scott and Victor Hugo, and she showed in her later novels, *The Pearl of Orr's Island* and *The Minister's Wooing*, how little she needed a moral thesis to bring all her gifts into play. "A work is great," says Mr. Joad, "when it has ceased to matter that it is bad." Dickens was great enough to be "bad," and so was Mrs. Stowe, who was also of the technically rough-and-ready, for her characters were not only real, boldly conceived and presented, but they were involved in

situations of a crucial and primary kind. She had a panoramic eye and a just and truthful feeling for human relations that carried her out of the sphere of propaganda.
There was no touch of cant in her moral feeling, no disposition to blame the South; she made one like the Southerners
more than ever, and she chose a native Vermonter, Simon
Legree, to symbolize all that was worst in a national evil.
Removed from the atmosphere in which it was written,
Uncle Tom's Cabin remained a great folk-picture of an age
and a nation. For one saw the Quaker colonies in Indiana
and the far-away farms of Vermont bound up with the
slave-plantations and the Mississippi, the camp-meetings,
the negro life; and the characters, St. Clare and Miss
Ophelia, Uncle Tom, Topsy and Simon Legree, were
drawn with a force that made them types and symbols.
Mrs. Stowe's New England novels, written with the same
rude strength, established a school and a method. It was
her New England, not Hawthorne's, that gave later
writers their point of departure. She set the stage for
Sarah Orne Jewett. But the final proof of Mrs. Stowe's
power was that she created the Southern novel,—as distinguished from the Southern romance,—and that, three
generations later, Southern writers still had to reckon
with her picture.

CHAPTER XXIII

CONCORD IN THE FIFTIES

EMERSON HAD revisited England in 1847. Carlyle had urged him to lecture there, and he had spent nine months, in London, Manchester and Scotland, talking and taking notes. In his pocket he carried a compass. "I like to hold the god in my hands," he said.

He had reached a solstice in his life, one of those dead points when one requires some foreign force in order to avoid stagnation. He had travelled for a whip for his top, and his top had come home spinning. Never had the "parlour Erebus" encountered so many first-rate thinkers and writers, eupeptic studying-mills, cast-iron men, whose powers of intellectual endurance compared with those of most Americans as a steam-hammer with a music-box. He had always wished to measure his valour by his ability to cope with giants, who aroused one's own central courage of insight. He wished to observe the hygiene, the gymnastic, their experience suggested and approved; and he longed to be challenged and frightened, if anyone could frighten him, to put his own thoughts to the proof. In his depressed hours, when his mind was ebbing,—

> Doomed to long gyration
> In the sea of generation,—

America seemed of a village littleness; and it was hard to go beyond one's public. Carlyle, Macaulay, De Quincey, Faraday, Tyndall, all of whom he had met and who had heard him, had roused in him anew the fire of emulation. Tyndall said that he owed to *Nature* all that he had done in the world, and Emerson found that in Oxford he had stirred and heartened Clough and Matthew Arnold, who had been bewildered by Carlyle. He had visited Wordsworth again at Rydal Mount and had spent a month with Clough in Paris, observing the first movements of the new revolution. He had come home filled with fresh ideas. Better still, the need to express himself so that a foreign audience would understand him, the challenge of so many sceptical hearers had led him to define his thoughts more closely. His style grew more and more concrete; the Franklin in his nature grew more apparent, the wisdom of the man who had dealt with men. He was preparing to write his finest books, *English Traits* and the great *Conduct of Life*. Best of all, much as he liked the English, he felt as never before the hope and faith of America. He had returned with joy to the Concord woods and pastures.

> Caesar of his leafy Rome,
> There the poet was at home.

Henry Thoreau, meanwhile, had gone to live in his father's house, the new yellow house on Concord Main Street. He had his den in the attic. There he kept his collections, the birds' nests, mosses, plants and arrowheads. His books were arranged on shelves he had built himself, using the driftwood on the river-banks. Concord was the old coat he wore, his morning-robe and study-gown, his walking-dress and suit of ceremony. If he had had to spend all his days confined to a corner of this attic, like the big spider on the rafter, he would have felt at home there. The world would have been just as large to him, as long as he had his thoughts.

He cultivated poverty like sage, the best of the garden

herbs. What poverty and obscurity meant to him, no one could ever have told,—a more than princely leisure, a poetic leisure, without care, without engagements, fancy-free. How many springs and summers he had lived, how many autumns and winters, with nothing to do but to live them, imbibing the nutriment they had to yield! Two years with the flowers, for instance, observing when they opened. He could afford to spend a whole fall watching the changing tints of the elms and the maples. He could record the drama of the month of March, when the woodchucks' holes were still choked with leaves and he saw the first bluebird two days earlier than the year before. Or had Ellery Channing seen it first? Henry Hosmer saw the first geese, honking over the Sudbury meadows, or so, at least, George Minott said, the same George Minott who was always asking, "Seen a robin?" Henry amused himself, now and then, imitating the geese. He found himself, one day, flapping his sides with his elbows and uttering *mow-ack* with a nasal twang and a sudden twist of the head.

Poverty had given him all this wealth. The leisure to spend a day, whenever he chose, walking twenty or thirty miles, or voyaging about the river in December, when the drops froze on his oars, pleased with the silvery chime of the icicles against the stems of the button-bushes. Leisure to visit his birches and tap them on an April afternoon, while he sat on a rock in the warm, sunny swamp, waiting for his vessels to be filled, watching the great black butterflies, with their buff-edged wings, dancing and fluttering about him. Leisure for a day in Gowing's swamp, where the hairy huckleberries grew and he paddled like Socrates, barefoot, in the Ilyssus; leisure to note the temperature of the springs and ponds, or look for Indian soapstone pots or mouse-holes in some hollow, or watch the flying-squirrels by the hour, skimming their way like hawks between and around the trees; leisure to stop at a grist-mill and observe the cobweb-tapestry, engaging the miller by questions while his eye sought the cobwebs on the miller's hat. Leisure for all his pursuits and contemplations, and more than amply paid for. Did some of his neighbours think that he sat on his father's shoulders? They should have seen him in the family work-shop, taking his turn, and more than his turn, at the pencils. It was he who saved the business when the German pencils threatened to drive their own out of the market. He solved the problem, bought the German clay, contrived machines for cutting the hardened paste and drilling the blocks of wood. He even supplied the Harpers of New York with their plumbago for electrotyping.

Across the way dwelt Ellery Channing. He had moved from Ponkawtassett Hill and bought an old house for himself on Main Street. He was living all alone there, with only his dog for company, to stir up the air of the room when it grew too deadly quiet,—for he experienced awful solitudes. He had fallen out with his family. He continued to write his verses, Wordsworthian meditations, winter wood-scenes, with all his old whimsical zest, and he had published his *Conversations in Rome*. This was a dialogue between an artist, a Catholic and a critic, for Ellery had visited Italy in 1845 and had almost been converted to the Roman church. He had something to say about Italian farming, as well as Salvator Rosa and Montaigne, and he was the Catholic in the "conversations." He had found himself murmuring prayers with the best of them. But for all his frequent petulance with Concord, he said the New England folk were his own flesh and blood; and he and Henry Thoreau were thicker than ever. Ellery was the rustic rhymer who had walked to Walden, after Henry deserted his hut, and hung up the verses on the wall; and Henry had actually seen a man buying a copy of Ellery's poems at Little and Brown's book-shop in Boston. Alcott was living in town, more or less, though he often came out to see his friends. The ever fresh and jubilant Alcott had built a summer-house on Emerson's lawn, rejecting the angular timber that others used, preferring the rustic branch. He had even added a second story, hung with beautiful mosses. It was a philosophic, a Euclidian structure, rather metaphysical than real, designed to exhibit the nature and value of curves. For it seemed, when Alcott walked in the woods, as if nature had looked for his coming and grown all his materials in the brush, along the lines of the fence-rows, where the young pines, bent by the snow or the axe, described, in their efforts to regain their natural rectitude, every graceful form of curve or spiral that he required for his rustic works. They lent themselves to varied combinations. Others might compose their poems and pictures. Alcott composed arbours. None knew better than he the romance of gardens. Why should not Emerson's garden have an additional touch that recalled the Garden of the Hesperides?

Henry, lending Alcott a hand, and sitting on the ridge-pole, had felt that he was "nowhere, doing nothing." Henry was a practical man, all for straight lines; he had no use for the "natural curve" in branches, men or women. No matter, Alcott also was a man who knew what nature meant him to do with her, a Virgil, a White of Selborne, a Yankee settler, wrapped in a single frame. He loved sage, too, sovereign sage, excellent for longevity, and often spoke of Pliny's good housewife who went to her herb-garden for her seasonings, instead of spending money at a spice-shop, and thus preserved the health of her family, the while she saved her purse. He had his knock-down answer for anyone who questioned his qualifications, "If Pythagoras came to Concord, whom would he ask to see?" His only faults were faults of worldly wisdom,—the truthful, candid, always magnanimous man. There were precious goods on his shelves, as Emerson said, but he had no show-window. Were you a child or a beggar, a lunatic or a Boston gentleman, you got the same reply from Bronson Alcott. He had his innocent foibles. He was much concerned with his genealogy. At fifty-four, why not? He liked to think of his old Connecticut forbears and had just revisited Wolcott. He had copied the inscriptions on the grave-stones and the records of fifteen towns, and he sometimes pulled out his long note-book and read them aloud to his friends. He had found an epitaph that he thought would interest Henry,—one of his own forbears,—and made a copy of it. What a preoccupation for a lover of wisdom!

But his chief preoccupations were the same as ever, keeping the famous journal and holding his Conversations.* The journal brimmed over with his thoughts, many of them thin, diffuse, abstract, others nutty and pregnant, phrased in a rare, flowing, antique style, on rural affairs and recreation, friends, books, philosophy, childhood, literary courtesy, hospitality, with a store of apt quotations. The habit of journalizing had been for him a lesson in the art of composition. Alcott no longer wrote in the vague, inadequate fashion of the "Orphic Sayings." He had learned to expand and express these tight conceits. He had slept on his writing and reviewed it on his walks, and *Concord Days* and *Tablets* were the fine result. Time had ripened his life and mellowed its fruits. His Conversations in Boston were difficult still, for there he rode his hobbies, but Emerson and Thoreau went in from Concord, Garrison sometimes came, and Theodore Parker, Lowell, Elizabeth Peabody, James Freeman Clarke, various travelling foreigners. He spoke on "Self-knowledge" or "The Times." He began by reading aloud a poem, George Herbert's *Man*, or some of his own philosophical verses, selected from the red-covered note-book. Then he

* Alcott's manuscript journal, fifty volumes or more, is still preserved in Concord. Louisa Alcott had it bound in stout black leather.

unfolded his favourite doctrines, diet, complexion, race, the "demonic man." A real demonic man appeared one evening, with blazing eyes and swarthy face, the kind of man who lives on beef and brandy, smokes black cigars and possibly builds a railroad. This was a little embarrassing. Objectors sometimes came, as if for the purpose of throwing him off his track. Another trouble-maker was Theodore Parker, who quoted Scripture as he walked away, "The multitude separated, and no man knew wherefore they came together." What could one do with these dogmatists who take delight in shooting balloons and asking a man for proofs when revelations are his stock-in-trade? Would they catechize the s'byl in her cave? Would they ask the Delphic oracle for a demonstration? No doubt, if they lived on Beacon Street or preached in a Unitarian pulpit.

Alcott was not himself in these urban surroundings. He was at home in the country, amid the woods and waters, under the sun and stars, turning about his grounds, sauntering by a brook-side. He was a pagan after Henry's fashion, much as he loved good manners. He was very different from Margaret Fuller, who had found her soul in the world of affairs and who had just lost her life, at forty. Henry had hastened down to Fire Island, on behalf of the Concord circle, to investigate the shipwreck. Margaret had sailed with many misgivings, and the voyage from Italy had been mismanaged. The little boat had broken up at once: the hold was laden with Italian marble and Hiram Powers's statue of Calhoun. Charles Sumner had lost a brother; he had already arrived and left, with William Henry Channing. They found Margaret's desk on the beach, with some of her papers in it, a carpet-bag of the Marquis Ossoli's, the body of the child. Nothing else, no trace of the tragic lovers, no trace of the great history of the siege of Rome.

The book was a loss. The Brownings and Landor

agreed that no Italian had known Mazzini better, and
Ossoli's family connections had given Margaret the other
side of the story. No doubt, the substance of the book,
however,—*Italy in 1848–'49*,—appeared in Margaret's
letters to *The Tribune*, soon to be collected in *At Home
and Abroad*, letters that brought the siege before her
readers as if they had seen it for themselves. She was a
journalist in grain and fibre, none more brilliant, none
more sympathetic, but scarcely a historian or a critic; an
energetic, perceptive soul, not a great writer, but certainly
a great woman writing. This was the fact that her friends
wished to proclaim. Carlyle, who had been so kind to her
in London, had summed up her qualities. He had
small faith in his wife's friend Mazzini. He thought that
Italy needed an Oliver Cromwell; he would have been
delighted with Mussolini. No matter what happened in
the back parlour, provided there was "order" in the
front. But he said that Margaret's courage was "high
and clear," and that she had "a truly heroic mind, altogether unique, so far as I know, among the writing women
of this generation."

The logic of events had sent her home. Mazzini's cause
had failed, and thought and speech like hers were contra-
band in Italy. No matter, she had lived and left her record, in England, France and Rome. She had had her full
taste of the "artist life," so long and happily dreamed of.
She had found *The Dial* widely read in England. Chopin
had played for her; she had met George Sand. She had
had her say about the American artists who were flocking
to Rome and Florence, their minds filled with American
subjects, of whom she had written with understanding.
She had described the American tourists, the colonists and
foreign residents, the servile types, the parasites, the brag-
garts and "booby truants,"—"Jonathan in the sprawling
state,"—as well as the thinking Americans whom she admired; and at last she had found the cause for which she

had been waiting, to lavish all her powers of devotion,
Mazzini's "God and the People." She had met Mazzini
in London, where she told him that the best friends a man
of ideas could have were necessarily women. How could
Carlyle have comprehended him?—Carlyle, with his old
Scandinavian berserker mind, following its impulse as a
hawk its prey. Mazzini had taken Margaret at her word
and put her on her mettle. She had shared in the drama
that she had longed to witness, a heroic passage of history, a nation rising up like Milton's eagle, mewing its
mighty youth: Italy cured of its hasty boasts and meaner
adulation, learning to prize and seek realities. She had
thought of her own America, stupid with the lust of gain
and the sloth of slavery, the criminal greed of the Mexican War, the aims of its politicians petty and selfish, its
literature venal and frivolous. In Europe, a nobler spirit
struggled, a spirit that animated and cheered her own.
She had heard earnest words of faith and love and seen
the deeds of brotherhood, all that made up the America
of which she dreamed. She could not distrust her country
deeply. America was not dead, it was only sleeping. She
had thought of the Abolitionists, whom she had found
so tedious, so narrow and so rabid in their tone. They
had their lofty motives. There was something eternal in
their desire and life; and they, too, understood Mazzini.
In the end, she had had her great romance, just as it
might have occurred in the novels that once enchanted
her,—lived those high, tumultuous hours, married her
Count de Rudolstadt, played the part of Countess Emily
Plater. It had led to sorrow, anxiety, toil and death.

   In Concord, as in Rome, they had understood her; and
Emerson made haste to write a memoir that would convey his feeling for her, an ode in prose outrivalling the
ode that Landor wrote in verse. She was the Ugly Duckling who had died too soon to counteract the legend of
the barnyard; but the poets and the novelists never for-

got her. The Boston Aspasia who had corrupted her sex
by means of intellectual orgies lived again in Hawthorne's
pages and Holmes's *Elsie Venner*.* Elizabeth Hoar, in
Concord, and Sarah Ripley had many of Margaret's
qualities, although without her fire of intellect. In Concord, even the farmers were writing books, Minot Pratt,
for one, whose son married a daughter of Alcott. He had
helped to manage Brook Farm and was carrying on botanical studies for an ambitious work on the local flora.
In 1855, another writer settled in the village, the future
Boswell of the Concord worthies. Frank B. Sanborn was
a sophomore at Harvard when he had first walked out to
call at Emerson's house. Not long afterwards, Emerson,
looking about for someone to take charge of a school for
the Concord children, suggested the plan to Sanborn,
who was delighted with it. He rented a room from Ellery
Channing and took his meals at Mrs. Thoreau's, and he
spent an evening every week at the Manse, reading Greek
aloud with Mrs. Ripley. No one could have said, in years
to come, that the long, lank Sanborn with the rosy cheeks
did not know the Concord he wrote about. He was a born
antiquarian; nothing pleased him more than to pore over
old family papers; and Mrs. Ripley showed him the dusty
records preserved in the "prophets' chamber,"—old Dr.
Ripley's memoranda about half the souls who had lived
in the village. Sanborn, with his hero-worshipping instincts, soon knew more about the Concord people than
most of them had ever known themselves. He was preparing himself for the many books he wrote in later
years. His school became a Concord institution. He followed the methods of Alcott, in a measure, his special
friend and master, taking the children for walks in the

* Hawthorne did not wish to admit that he had drawn his Zenobia
from Margaret Fuller, with certain touches suggested by Fanny Kemble,
but no one ever questioned the fact. That Dr. Holmes had Margaret Fuller
in mind is evident from a passage in *Elsie Venner*. It was natural that she
left some sort of trace in almost every imaginative mind of the time.

woods and fields, with picnics, plays and boating parties, and skating carnivals at Walden Pond. First or last, he had among his pupils Emerson's son, Hawthorne's son, two daughters of John Brown, Horace Mann's sons and two of Henry James's.

It was Sanborn who, a few years later, brought John Brown to Concord, where the anti-slavery cause had many friends. It was from Sanborn's house that Brown set out for Harper's Ferry. Sanborn knew his plans, of which Emerson, Alcott and Thoreau knew nothing. He was arrested after the raid. A posse came out from Boston to seize him, but he spread his arms like a windmill and braced his feet against the sides of the carriage; his sister roused the neighbours, and the church-bells rang the alarm. Judge Hoar issued a writ of *habeas corpus,* and the posse disappeared. The whole town assembled, the following morning, to protest against the outrage. Ever since 1844, when Emerson made his speech on Emancipation, and Henry Thoreau rang the bell for the meeting, Concord had been an anti-slavery centre. Emerson, Alcott and Mrs. Thoreau had special rooms in their houses for fugitive slaves, and John Brown, the Connecticut Yankee, had more friends there than he had in Kansas. When people said he had thrown his life away, "Which way have they thrown their lives?" Thoreau remarked— these figureheads on hulks, with livers in the place of hearts.

Sanborn was even a member of the Walden Pond Association. So the "Sunday walkers" were called in the village,—Emerson, Alcott, Thoreau and one or two others who never sat in pews. One had to pass a stringent test to belong to this society, severer than the Athanasian creed. There were only two or three persons with whom Thoreau, for one, felt that he could afford to walk, his hours were so precious. Was Emerson less exacting? He was only more polite. In the presence of cranks and bores,

he masked his irritation. Henry trampled on them. Two
yards of courtesy did not make society for Henry; and
when, by chance, a bore shadowed him on one of his
walks, he took every ditch at a run, hoping to shake the
shadow off. He detested these mere strenuous pliers of
legs, these broachers of mighty arguments who spoiled
one's day and talked the bobolinks under. With his long
swinging gait, his eyes on the ground, his hands clasped
behind him, his legs like steel springs and his arms as
powerful as a moose's antlers, thrusting the brush aside,
with his wary glance, his earnest energy, as if, on the
lookout for squirrels, rabbits and foxes, he was in the
thick of a day's battle, Henry was no man to trifle with.
He was impatient even with the farmers, who were always
standing on their good behaviour, moralizing and philos-
ophizing, instead of giving a brisk report of their crops.
He preferred the sportsmen and loafers, or anyone who
had seen a painted tortoise, or taken a good look at a
flying lark, or who shared his feeling about the encroaching railroad, that seventh abomination. Henry had grown
so formidable, in fact, that the village-folk had ceased to
call him Henry, especially now that he was earning a living, by lecturing, writing, surveying, by means that anyone could understand. He was Mr. Thoreau, the surveyor,
who gave you fair warning to keep your distance.

No use to attempt to join the Sunday walkers unless
you were able to meet the test. Were the woods for you
full of solicitations, were there forms and colours everywhere, powers on every hand, locked away from ordinary
Christians, to which your wit afforded you the key? The
churches on the square were ready to welcome the dry
souls whom life, as Ellery said, had put away on the
shelf like so many rinds of cheese. You had to be up to
the mark to keep pace with the Walden Society, Emerson,
twirling his stick, while he drew rhymes from the upper
air, Ellery touching off his sudden fuses, dressed in his

red flannel shirt, suggesting an indolent bandit, Thoreau with his taut mind and wound-up muscles, ready to crush you with a merciless phrase. He tied his boots in a hard lover's-knot, while Ellery, half the time, went about with his shoe-strings dangling, or even wore no laces,—just as he wrote his poems, loosely strung, to the scandal of his conscientious friends. He should have been compelled to write in Latin, Henry said and Emerson agreed. Then he would have used a dictionary and written firmly and clearly, instead of in the dangling-shoe-string style, the sublimo-slipshod style, as Henry called it. But Ellery would not pay the going-price, he would not stoop to conquer. Henry, as they walked, pulled out his note-book and jotted down his careful observations. Ellery halfheartedly followed suit, scrawled away for a moment, then drew some hasty sketch and stuffed the book in his pocket again. He had no use for the "definite" and left the "facts" to Henry. Only the "ideal" was good enough for him.

No matter, he was a virtuous walker. He had eyes for every line and every colour, for every fleet of yellow butterflies, ears for every sound, the wood-thrush pitching his notes in the pine-alleys, the oven-bird beating his brass in the heated shades of noon, the partridge's feathery roll-call, the gossiping dialogue of the brown thrashers, a comforting sound, this latter, enough to cure the heartache of a world, on one of those summer days when the sky bends over a walker with a face like Jerusalem Delivered. A fit companion, Ellery, for a dozen poets, or two, at least, Emerson and Henry, or any combination of two or three. What was the programme for the afternoon? A stroll to Conantum, perhaps, or White Pond, or to Round Hill in the Sudbury meadows. Thus the talk flowed.—We'll stop at Duganne's spring and get a drink. —Or suppose we go to Flint's.—Agreed.—That country with its high summits is good for breezy days. And we must not forget the mountain view from the Three Friends' Hill, beyond the pond. Across the pastures, in any case, the broad, healthy new-springing pastures, ornamented with apple-tree pyramids, the pastoral architecture of the cow, and the waving saxifrage and the delicate houstonia, the dark belts of pines stalking over the landscape.—The air is fairly spotted today with the rigmarole of the bobolink, buttery, scattery, wittery, pittery, a few yellow, a few black feathers, a summer-warming song.—Soaring over the tallest pine, the fierce hen-harrier screams and hisses.—And see the peach-trees yonder. Montaigne took pains to be made a citizen of Rome. I should much prefer to have the freedom of a peach-orchard.—Or of an accommodating trout-stream, such as Goodwin loves, the one-eyed Ajax.—What do you think of the farmhouse we are passing? Aren't the clapboards needlessly stiff? Is there not too little ornamentation? In Italy and Switzerland and England, the picturesque seems to spring from the soil, in the shape of barns and buildings, as naturally as the trees and flowers. —Moderate your words, dear Gilpin. Utility lies at the bottom of our village architecture. The structure springs from that. The simple edifice you see, created out of white-pine boards, a mere casing of shingles and clapboards, as it appears to you, appears to its owner, who built it and lives in it, anything but ugly or unpicturesque. It fits him like a shell. Comfort, economy, use, a dry, warm cellar, a sweet, airy milk-room, a barn with its cellars and accommodations, all in the solidest style,— these matters make the study of the farmer.—I say that beauty must have an equal place with utility, if not the first place. Your farmer shirks architecture and landscape-gardening, with his one leg in the barn and his other in the kitchen, and the compost-heap in the midst. And his highest ambition is to have a patent-leather top to his carriage.—Go to, you libel my jolly countryman. He is no such thieving rat as this. O brother Gilpin, hearken ere you die. Those prejudices of yours for Inigo Jones have left you too little sympathy for the industrious yeoman of New England. He stands like a king in the midst of the general penury.—Have you read those old farmers Cato and Varro? "Study to have a great dung-heap. Carefully preserve the dung. Break it up fine." There speaks the New England yeoman. If you would understand him, read this manual of the Roman farmers, how they got their living, what they did from day to day.— But, come, here's the brook. Let me rest a fraction on the bridge.—I am your well-wisher in that. The manners of water are beautiful, playing its sweet games, all circles and dimples and lively gleaming motions.—The brook, the petted darling of the meadows, wild minstrel of an ancient song, poured through the vales forever.—And those eddying pools, where the old experienced trout sleeps on his oars.—Rest a little longer here.—Are not those gulls yonder, gleaming like spots of intense white light far away on the meadow?—And observe that ridiculous colt, the colour of sugar-gingerbread, set upon his four long legs and swishing a bald tail, laughing at us men-folks nibbling our crackers and herring.

Thus the talk rambled, while Peter, Ellery's dog, capered through bush and brier, plunging into the brook with his smiling tail. Peter lived as Henry aspired to live. As the Indians had amused the Jesuits by sitting all day naked on the ice, fishing through their holes, as if they were lolling on feather-beds, so Peter would sleep all night on a snow-bank in January. It was enough to make one shiver to think of, on a day like this, by Clematis Brook, when the ants, bees and millers kept open shop, when the woodchucks sat up at the mouths of their houses, when the Maryland yellow-throats and the bull-frogs and robins performed their operas all day long, and the learned advocate, the *Mephitis chinga,* probed the

roads for beetles. A day for three friends to expand their
fancies. Anon they took their way to the Estabrook
country, or embarked on some riparial excursion, a walk
along the river-bank, or a paddle in Henry's boat, leaving the boat, perhaps, for an inland stroll, at the rear of
the blacksmith's house, five miles up the river. Sometimes
they went for a voyage in the pinnace as far as the Port
of Lilies, along the river which, in its glassy folds, laid
its unswept carpet over the fragrant meadows. Anon they
set forth on a wintry day, under a lead-coloured sky, to
the steady, silent, windless fall of the snow, when all the
pines and oak-leaves were moulded in silver. Sometimes,
after dark, they dropped in to see Perez Blood, the
farmer-astronomer, over towards Carlisle, sitting in his
wood-shed, in his astronomical chair, with his skull-cap
on his head and his short Northern figure, a Concord
Tycho Brahe. They peeped through his telescope and
saw Saturn's rings and the shadows of the mountains on
the moon. If it was spring or summer, they reappeared in
the village streets with flowers and rare insects in their
hats and pockets. They might have been Linnæus and his
pupils on one of their "herborizations."

Thoreau was in danger of losing his solitary habits.
What with lecturing, what with surveying, what with the
acclaim that followed his *Walden,* he was becoming
almost a man of the world. He had had to spend ninety
days surveying to pay for his *Week on the Concord,* but
Walden was actually selling. It was finding the kind of
friends that make a classic. He had had his name posted
for public lectures, two or three a year, wherever—in
Worcester, Nantucket, Salem, Plymouth—they absolutely
required his presence. Not that he wished for "experience": one might as well have advised a bear to leave his
hollow tree and run about all winter, scratching at all the
hollow trees in the woods. The bear would have been
leaner in the spring than if he had stayed at home and

sucked his claws. But Henry was willing to go, to make a few dollars, whenever it was convenient to drop his work, provided it was clearly understood that what he said on the platform was nobody's business. It was just another chore, like surveying. Nothing one did for money was ever worth doing, but one had to pay one's way and hold one's peace. As for the surveying, it was like Haydon's portrait-painting. Haydon had wandered over England, painting the portraits of the country gentry. Henry went about in a similar fashion, to the houses of the farmers and the squires. With his staff and chain, he, too, had to paint his portraits, while his mind was filled with more important matters.

Still, he acquired thereby, and through his writings, a number of new acquaintances who were almost as rewarding as the muskrats. Agassiz, the great professor in Cambridge, was studying the American fishes. Henry was glad to send him four firkins of Concord fish, including one and probably two species that Agassiz had not seen. Agassiz, greatly pleased by this, came out to Concord and examined turtles with him. The lecturing-business also took him to Nantucket, where, as the natives said, you had to strike a whale before the girls would dance with you. This was no great news, to be sure, for Henry. That a young woman had regular features might be a reason for looking at her, but it was no reason for talking to her. Still, it was something to meet the natives; and surveying was a pleasant occupation when one had good friends to set up the staff and carry the chain. Henry was glad when Alcott offered to do so, and it was a question of surveying "Hillside," Marston Watson's country-place at Plymouth. Alcott was in his element there, for Marston Watson, having the means, had had an inspiration. On his beautiful slope overlooking the harbour, he wished to lay out a park and garden, and he proposed to build a summer-house, with front gables facing south and east, and a lookout with winding stairs, all of rustic wood. Alcott gathered the timbers, with plenty of knots and sylvan ornaments, and soon constructed the bower, a riot of natural curves, fit for a Pythagoras to talk in; and he and Watson carried Henry's chain. As they trod the warm, sandy Plymouth wood-roads, or lingered on the slope, they talked over the virtues of pears and apples, golden russets, Tolman sweetings, greenings. Pears were too aristocratic, Henry thought. He much preferred the democratic apples that were left to the hired man to gather and barrel, while the land-owners plucked their own pears and had their daughters wrap them in separate papers. Judges and ex-judges,—Squire Hoar, for instance, —were connoisseurs of pears and named them after emperors and kings, queens and dukes and duchesses,— glout-morceaux, Bonne Louise. Henry thought they were less poetic than apples, the apples that children dream of. He meant to wait for his pears until they got American names.

But when one writes a *Walden,* one has to be prepared for consequences. Much as Henry preferred the republican apple, Marston Watson sent him a gift of pear-trees. Somebody else, in Brattleboro, sent him a box of mayflowers. Another friend in Worcester sent him a humming-bird's nest. All in two days. In Worcester, they were developing a Thoreau "cult." There Thomas Wentworth Higginson lived, the literary minister, one of the active Abolitionists. There lived Theophilus Brown, the literary tailor, who sent forth sparkles of wit as he bent over his measuring-tape and scissors; and there, above all, dwelt Harrison G. O. Blake, a terribly conscientious Harvard man, who, as Emerson said, would even return a borrowed umbrella and who was Henry's firmest partisan. Attracted by Henry's writings in *The Dial,*—the essay on Persius first,—he had persuaded him to go to Worcester, to give a sort of annual parlour-lecture, so

that his friends could really look at him. He had led
Henry into a correspondence, which was conducted on
the highest plane; for "Mr. Blake" was so Transcendental that Henry had to walk on stilts to please him. But
he was a loyal adherent. The moment the postman arrived
with a letter from Concord, he gathered his neighbours
together and read the letter aloud at the breakfast-table.
Blake and "Theo" Brown were also virtuous walkers.
They came to Concord now and then to take walks with
Henry, even as far as Wachusett.

One of Henry's expeditions took him to New Jersey,
where he surveyed the two hundred acres at "Eagles-
wood," Perth Amboy. Marcus Spring was founding a
colony there, with the Grimkés and the Welds and other
Abolitionists. They wished to propagate, in combination,
radical views and old-fashioned culture, and Henry laid
out the streets of the village they were planning. Alcott
joined him there, and they spent a night with Horace
Greeley and went over to Brooklyn to see Walt Whitman, whose *Leaves of Grass* Henry had just been reading.
He wished to pay his respects to the great new poet, whom
Emerson had recently greeted, although he had small
use for the politicians whom Whitman included in his
cosmos. He meant to make his feelings clear. He had all
manner of reservations in regard to this great America,
and he also thought that Walt was a little rank,—although, when it came to that, if you blushed when you
read the *Leaves,* at whose thoughts were you blushing,
your own or Walt's? He felt that Whitman had written
a great primitive poem, as wonderful in its way as the
Bhagavad-Gita. It was an alarm or trumpet-note, ringing
through the American camp.

Meanwhile, he had found another friend, sufficiently
near home to pay him an annual visit, a Quaker and poet,
like Whitman, albeit quite unknown in the world of letters. This was Daniel Ricketson, who lived at "Brook-

lawn," his ancestral home at New Bedford. The Quaker ship-owners in the famous whaling metropolis were shrewd, quick-witted traders. Ricketson had inherited some of their money, but none of their mercantile instincts. He was a naturalist and a man of letters, whose favourite authors were Virgil and Cowper and who had corresponded for many years with Howitt and William Barnes, the Dorset poet. A lover of Gilbert White and William Gilpin, he lectured now and then, especially on "Cowper and His Friends." He liked the ancient saying, "A spare diet and clear skies are Apollo and the Muses." He was at home with partridges, quails and rabbits, and had tramped thousands of miles through the winter woods; and he looked after his farm, his fruit-trees and garden, avoiding forms and ceremonies, seeking a simple, quiet life. A quick man, quick in heart, quick in all his movements, with a taste for free thinking and social reform, he liked to get hold of some outcast and hold him up by the chin and whisper weighty matters in his ear; and, as for the anti-slavery movement, how could he listen to the woodland songs, or look at the great clouds and the starry heavens, and not be a friend of the poor and the oppressed? In the midst of his rural pursuits, he fought for justice. He hoped to see the quarrels of nations settled by arbitration, the factory-system humanized, the prisons without tenants. He longed to see machinery, now so destructive of life, turned into safe and useful channels. An inveterate journalizer, the author of a *History of New Bedford,* a rural poet with a clear vocation, Ricketson was one of those happy readers who create for other men of letters an atmosphere in which they can breathe and work. "In proportion as we see the merits of others, we add to our own," he said. Thoreau had been touched by the word of greeting that Ricketson sent him after reading *Walden.* The modest and perceptive Ricketson had also built a shanty, like his own; and when Ellery Channing went to New Bedford, to write for one of the papers, Thoreau had a double reason for visiting the town. Where was Ellery living there? In his usual fashion, he wrote that he "did not know." Thoreau went down to bring these friends together.

They had high times in Ricketson's shanty, then and every year thereafter, especially when Alcott joined the trio. They went for walks in the neighbouring woods, and Henry found marine plants he had never seen before and an old Indian woman, living alone in her hut, the last of the Nemaskets. The shanty recalled his Walden days. It was much the same in size and style, bristling with evidences of Ricketson's hobbies, twenty rustic walking-sticks, a dozen pipes, a spyglass, Indian relics, stuffed birds, old guns and swords, slips of paper pinned on the walls with verses in praise of country life. In the surrounding woods, the quails incessantly whistled, and morning and evening one heard the strain of the bay-wing. There the happy sages sat, like so many gymnosophists of old, ready to stamp on the ground if any Alexander thrust himself in at the door. Ellery smoked his pipe and joked with Alcott, and Ricketson stood boldly up to Henry. One day, Walton Ricketson, the sculptor-son of the house, named after Izaak Walton, made a medallion of Henry, wearing the full black beard he had recently grown; and, as if to belie his beard,—on another occasion,—Henry, unable to contain his joy, jumped out of his chair and began to dance. He pranced and leaped about, like an Indian in the forest, taking pains to step on Alcott's toes.

CHAPTER XXIV

CAMBRIDGE IN THE FIFTIES

THE GREAT months in Cambridge were June and October. June was Lowell's month. When the trees were heavy with leaves and the gardens full of blossoms, when the insects chirped in the grass and the white clouds sailed aloft, Lowell, pitching his hay in the meadow at "Elmwood," felt the metres of Chaucer, Shakespeare and Keats pounding in his blood. Longfellow loved October. He always uttered the word with a curious pleasure. Every year, when the leaves turned scarlet and yellow, his mind stirred with thoughts and fancies. "Welcome, O brown October!" he wrote in his journal. "Like a monk with a drinking-horn, like a pilgrim in russet!"

At the rear of Craigie House, he had laid out a more elaborate garden, following a Gothic pattern, with borders of box. He made a little pond under the willows. It was 1854, and he had resigned from his professorship. In his brief novel, *Kavanagh,* the story of a minister in Maine, —who might have been Sylvester Judd, for his aim was to remove all prejudices and bring about a union of all the sects,—he had pictured his own predicament. Kavanagh, the youthful poet, who had been brought up on the lives of the saints, was forced to teach grammar for his living, while his mind overflowed with verses; interrupted and hampered by trivial things, he postponed his great designs from year to year and never found the courage to begin. The tale was feeble enough, for Longfellow's mind was poor and thin without its mantle of verse;

but it expressed his feeling at the moment. His college work was like a great hand laid on the strings of his lyre, stopping their vibrations. He was the Pegasus in Pound of whom he wrote in one of his poems. Still, he had written *The Golden Legend,* based on a story of the minnesingers, in form suggesting *Faust.* It was an evocation of the Middle Ages, softly melodious and picturesque, redolent of ivy and ancient ruins, with a fervent strain of religious feeling. Some of the scenes were among the best in the Longfellow picture-gallery, especially the scenes of monastic life.

The first result of Longfellow's freedom was the Indian idyll, *Hiawatha.* This was an October poem, floating in an air of Indian summer, a haze of yellow harvests and autumnal quiet and the smoke of camp-fires and far-away lodges. Ever since his boyhood in Maine, Longfellow had felt the poetry of the ancient forest people. He had seen the last of the Algonquins, stragglers in the Maine woods, and he had never forgotten the words of the Choctaw chief who said that his tribe would hear the news of his death "like the sound of the fall of a mighty oak in the stillness of the forest." He had entertained an Ojibway chief who was lecturing in Boston, and one of his students who had returned from the West and told him legends of the lodge and camp-fire had urged him to weave them into a poem. He had ploughed through Schoolcraft's collection of Indian folk-lore, and then he had remembered the *Kalevala,* the Finnish folk-epic that he had read during his summer with Freiligrath. There was much in common between these primitive peoples and their legends. Many of their metaphors were the same, and the repetitions of the *Kalevala* were characteristic of the Indian songs, so like the wind in the pine-trees. The vague myth of a sunset land, a paradise in the West, where the mountains and forests were filled with deer and the lakes swarmed with fishes, the happy hunting-ground of

the Indian braves, swept through his mind, when autumn
came, with the sighs of the south-wind, Shawondessa. He
saw it all in a wondrous light, in the mist of leaves, in
the flash of the river. The Indians that emerged in the
poem were not the warrior-stoics of flesh and blood. They
were not Indians even as Concord saw them, for Longfellow was not Thoreau. He had reshaped the legends to
suit himself, omitting all the savagery and malice. He had
softened and simplified and humanized them, picturing
the father of the lodge, the patriot, the sportsman and the
hero. There was a touch of Channing in Hiawatha,
the bringer of light, peace and the household arts, and
the elements of romance were European. The mild humanitarian glow of the poem savoured of the poet's Cambridge circle. But why not? Of what did the Indians
savour in *Atala* and *René,* if not Chateaubriand's circle
across the ocean? There was a quiet magic in the story,
a golden languor as of afternoon, of corn-fields in the
setting sun, purple vapours and the dusk of evening.

It was not for children that Longfellow wrote, although
children were his best readers always. *Hiawatha* travelled
round the world; Cardinal Newman's brother translated
it into Latin, and Freiligrath, the German translator,
amply defended Longfellow's use of the metre. He had
been accused of plagiarism, as erstwhile by the author of
The Raven, which had occasioned the lines that he wrote
in his journal,—

> In Hexameter sings serenely a Harvard professor.
> In Pentameter him damns censorious Poe.

Everybody read him, and the critical public recognized
that in his use of metres he had shown himself an original
artist. Still, the children liked him best, and Cambridge
and Craigie House were full of children. Dr. Worcester
had built the house next door, and the Longfellow boys,

perched on the fence, swooped down on the lexicographer's pears and apples. Then Dr. Worcester, roused from his studies, issued from his cave of notes and told the little boys what they were made of. Their father knew already. He had composed a jingle on the subject and also asked what little girls were made of. The Longfellow girls were more discreet. Longfellow wrote several poems about them. Brattle Street, in fact, was a garden of girls, quite in the Tennysonian vein, and Longfellow liked to go to balls in Boston, where he could see them, fair and slender, waving, like lilies on their stems, to the music as to a wind. At Craigie House, they were always reading aloud, every day at the children's hour, often by the cozy fireside, while they looked over pictures from Florence and Dresden. There were many new authors to keep up with, Hawthorne, who had gone to Liverpool, to serve as American consul there, Thackeray, Charlotte Brontë, the Brownings, Ruskin. Longfellow watched the moon, through the open window, rising in the autumnal air. Like a delicious perfume, like far-off music, floated through his mind, as through parting clouds, glimpses and visions of Tyrolean lakes.

But Europe was drifting more and more to Cambridge. Every Cunarder brought some visitor, Agassiz, Adam Gurowski, the terrible count,—the one-eyed Pole who called himself "the homeless,"—Ole Bull from Norway, Frederica Bremer from Sweden, gathering notes on the "homes of the New World," Thackeray, Clough the poet, Luigi Monti, the Italian scholar,—the Sicilian of Longfellow's *Wayside Inn,* who presently married the sister of the poet Parsons,—or Professor Sophocles, the scholar-hermit, bred in a monastery on Mount Athos, a strange Diogenes with a wild, grey beard who looked like Byron's Corsair, who lived like a monk of the Thebaid in his room in Holworthy Hall, where he did his own cooking, and whom one encountered on his lonely walks.

Felton, the great professor of Greek, Longfellow's closest friend and the friend of Dickens, the huge, hearty old-fashioned scholar who liked to apply the epithet forcible-feeble to those who simulated his own robustness, and who often reminded his hearers that Agamemnon had honoured Ajax with a whole sirloin after his fight with Hector,—for he shared the Homeric enjoyment of eating and drinking,—was lecturing at the Lowell Institute. In Zurich, on his way to Greece, he had put on a suit of armour at the Zeughaus, to the delight of the keeper, and laid about him with a battle-axe, for he wished to know how the crusaders had felt, as well as the heroes of Homer. He had made his own collection of Swiss folk-poems and had visited Jacques Jasmin, the barber-poet, who lived in the south of France and whose *Blind Girl* Longfellow translated; and in Greece he had made friends with farmers and sailors, travelled through the mountains in search of ballads and met all the living Greek writers, whom he brought out in a book of selections. He took the modern world-historical view in his great courses of lectures, which later appeared as *Ancient and Modern Greece,* a delightfully readable work. At Harvard, everything was "comparative" now; the studies overlapped one another. With the humorous, copious Felton, all fire and energy and poetic feeling, with Asa Gray, the botanist, with Peirce the mathematician and Jeffries Wyman, with Agassiz in the chair of natural history, the lines and angles of the checker-board had gradually faded out. There was a genial glow in the Cambridge air. Agassiz had brought full summer with him.

The great Swiss professor had settled in Cambridge in 1848. A sort of Johnny Appleseed of science, sowing trees of learning wherever he went, he had lectured to vast crowds from Boston to Charleston, making the great types of the animal kingdom, articulates, radiates, molluscs, as

real and vivid as historic figures. Talking with his enchanting verve and drawing his illustrations on the blackboard, so that one saw the insects and fishes bursting
from their eggs, he infected everyone with his zeal for
nature. Museums rose over-night as the great showman
of science passed through the country, and, as his fame
grew, every strange rock that was unearthed, every queer
creature that anyone caught, in pond or stream or forest,
was sent to the professor for an explanation; and when
he issued a circular, asking for collections of fresh-water
fish, specimens came in from every quarter. He could
scarcely handle his correspondence. He was never without
his blackboard and his bit of chalk and was always ready
to teach at a moment's notice, in camp, on the road, on
the shores of lakes. All creation was his lecture-room. He
carried snakes in his pockets; every room in his house
was a laboratory; garret and cellar were filled with his
collections. Everyone quoted his sayings. He had never
known a dull hour. He had never been a dollar ahead in
the world and never expected to be. He had no time to
waste in making money! This made a great impression
in New England; and everyone heard how he rejoiced,
for science, when a book appeared that demolished a
theory which he had been toiling for years to establish.
It was known that, to keep his chair at Harvard, he refused the directorship of the Jardin des Plantes, offered
him by Napoleon III, and a seat in the French Senate, a
rank equal to Cuvier's. Nothing kept the Americans back,
he said, except a consideration for the opinion in which
they were held in Europe. He hated to see an American
man of genius elated by some foreign recognition, taking
it as a mark of honour that set him apart from his countrymen. Contemptible provinciality! America could so
easily be a centre if it once discarded the foolish notion
that Europeans were its proper judges.

Agassiz, with his joyous magnetism, for whom all the

species of human beings, emperors, farmers, scientists and poets were so many bipeds and bivalves, save for his impetuous affections, who made science a national cause and charmed money out of the politicians with which to found museums, as if they were asylums for the blind, Agassiz, the Pied Piper of Cambridge, soon became Longfellow's alter ego. He took his class one summer to Nahant, where Longfellow had a cottage, not far from Prescott's. Agassiz caught nature "in the act," while Longfellow rejoiced in the northeast storms, the fringes of the foam about the rocks, the wet sails struggling in the wind, the kale, the seaweed and the waste of waters, the scent of the wild roses about the cottage mingling with the odour of the sea. This was Longfellow's element. He was at home with the ocean, like Ole Bull, the Norwegian violinist, who had come to Cambridge, where he was to find his second wife. Ole Bull had swept through the country, a musical Agassiz with his "storm-organ," the whirling spray of sound in which one heard the thunder of the northern avalanches, the wind in the pines and the sun-flecked hollows of Norway, filled with gnomes and elves. All the young girls had heard his music, like the mist scattered by a fountain, and wrote about him in their diaries. They thought he was like Adam in Paradise. He had shared in the Norwegian national movement, working with Ibsen at the Bergen theatre. There, as in America, a fresh, youthful spirit was in the air. Norway had declared its independence and separated from Denmark, and the Norwegian writers were building a literature of their own, one which they hoped would express the dreams and hidden talents of the people. P. A. Munch was their Bancroft, and Ibsen wished to be the national poet. He was writing odes for the May 17th celebrations, much like the American Fourth of July, and festival poems such as Dr. Holmes was writing for the Berkshire cattle-fairs,—even so, Ibsen, the author of *Ghosts,* who said that culture was "unthinkable apart from national life." He was gathering folk-tales among the fjords, as Hawthorne had gathered them on his excursions.

Ole Bull spent a winter at "Elmwood," which he had rented during Lowell's absence; for Lowell, appointed to Longfellow's vacant chair, had gone abroad for a year of study. At Craigie House, he would talk half the night about Paganini, Malibran and Liszt. He played and chanted his old Norse melodies, like one of Longfellow's gleemen of the Viking days, and spoke of his childhood in the northern forests, the flower-clad valleys, filled with singing birds, the rocky coast, the rushing cataracts, the glittering lakes of Norway, so like the woods and valleys of Maine and New Hampshire. He might have been born in Portland, as Longfellow might have been born in Bergen. Hawthorne was more like Ibsen in the sense of fate that wrapped his folk-tales in a Gothic darkness. Hawthorne, too, had appeared at Craigie House, during the years before he went abroad, coming and going like a shadow, hiding behind the curtains, where he spent whole evenings undisturbed, a Viking under a veil. Arthur Hugh Clough, the English poet, who spent a winter in Cambridge, also had a touch of the Viking in him, sadly compromised by introspection. He had written his poem, *The Bothie,* largely suggested by *Evangeline,* filled with a feeling for the out-of-doors, high-spirited youth and the wildest nature. His Scotland was another Maine or Norway. He stayed at "Shady Hill," as a friend and guest of Charles Eliot Norton, Professor Andrews Norton's only son, coaching a few young men in Greek and making a revision of Dryden's Plutarch. The calm and repose of Cambridge soothed his mind, torn and bewildered by scruples and speculation, and brought back his earlier days at Oxford.

Then suddenly who should appear but Horatio Greenough, just returned from Florence. The tall, handsome,

fiery Boston sculptor, a Viking or a Greek, as one chose
to see him, had come home to superintend the erection of
one of his monuments at Washington. As a Boston and
Cambridge boy, two of whose brothers were also artists,
he had copied Roman coins in the Athenæum and a
marble Phocion in his father's garden, studied anatomy
under a Boston doctor, modelled in butter, wax and chalk
and spent his happiest hours with Washington Allston,
during his years at Harvard. In Rome, he had worked
with Thorwaldsen, and Cooper had given him his first
commission, for the well-known "Chanting Cherubs," the
first marble group that had ever been made by an American sculptor. For twenty-three years he had lived in
Florence. He had introduced Emerson to Landor, his
vehement friend and fellow-republican there, and he had
written to the younger Dana, "America has always acted
towards her artists like a hen that has hatched ducklings.
She cannot understand why they run to the water, instead
of thriving on the dung-hill, which only asks to be
scratched in order to feed them. She will learn better, but
not yet." But he had not been able to endure the repressions of Italian life since '48. He had come in a blaze of
vigour, braced by the American air, with little respect
for the Tories he found about him. He made the rounds
of Boston, Concord and Cambridge before he settled in
Newport for the winter.

The lectures he presently gave amplified the exciting
ideas which he had been spreading among his friends.
They were fragments of a book that he was planning. It
was he who surprised the Boston people by praising the
clipper-ship as a work of art. He said that the American
trotting-wagon and the bald, neutral-toned Yankee farmhouse were actually closer to Athens than the Grecian
temples that people were building for banks. This seemed
odd enough, but there was a method in Greenough's madness, as those who heard his lectures soon discovered. He

wished to explain what was the proper basis for a native
American art, and that the true way to follow the Greeks
was not to transplant their forms,—a kind of impotent
dilettantism,—but to accept their principles and build
from the needs of one's own climate and country. This
was the strength of the clipper-ship, the type of what our
architecture should be. It perfectly fulfilled its natural
function. All its details were organic. Would anyone retain a bellying sail, however picturesque it was, however
it pleased one's sense of association, when a flat sail went
closest to the wind? That was the strength of the farmhouse, too. It seemed to belong to the ground on which it
stood, as a caterpillar belongs to the leaf it feeds on. The
monuments of the Egyptians and the Greeks were sublime
as expressions of their power and feeling, but what did a
Greek temple express in State Street? Money and osten-
tation, nothing else, like a frock-coat on an African king.
Nature provides a form for every function; and all the
absurdities of modern usage were due to the fact that
they were non-organic. Instead of adopting the outward
shape first, for the sake of the eye or of association,
without reference to the inner distribution, forcing the
functions into a general form, one should begin with the
heart and work outwards.

Three generations later, one was to hear much of this
"functional" theory, which Greenough preached up and
down the country, with a Yankee wit and a foreign culture mixed, as he said, like the matrix and pebbles in the
pudding-stone of Roxbury, Massachusetts. It all came
down to the doctrine that the one principle of structure
was "the principle of adaptation of forms to functions."
The obelisk was the simplest type of this. Its function was
to signalize a spot that was memorable in history, and
how completely it achieved its end! It said but a single
word, "Here!"—but everyone heard this word and understood it. Greenough's "Artist's Creed" summed up his

faith. There were three things he had seen in man worthy
of love and thought, Beauty, Action, Character: "By
beauty I mean the promise of function, by action I mean
the presence of function, by character I mean the record
of function." A stirring combination of New England
ethics with an aesthetic point of view that was to grow in
meaning.*

At "Shady Hill," Charles Eliot Norton was also preparing to preach the gospel of art. There, in the gracious
house with the wide verandahs, surrounded by its rolling
lawns, the beeches and the willows, filled with the clatter
of crows, the Cambridge circle met, over a game of whist,
for music or for conversazioni, suggesting the "Dante
evenings" of the future. There old Professor Norton beguiled his leisure with Shakespeare, Pope and Scott; and
there, or at the house they had built at Newport, where
they passed the summer months and where Greenough
suddenly died before he could finish his book, the Nortons
entertained their younger friends. Among these were
Clough, Rowse the artist, who was making his red-chalk
portrait-drawings of literary celebrities, William J. Stillman, the painter and writer, the editor of *The Crayon*,
the first American art-journal, and later the friend of the
Rossettis, Thomas G. Appleton, Longfellow's brother-in-
law, and Francis J. Child, the collector of ballads. Charles

* See Louis Sullivan's phrase, "Form follows function, function creates
form," and the writings of Lewis Mumford. In the light of these recent
discussions, one should read Greenough's lectures, *Æsthetics at Washington, American Architecture, Structure and Organization* and *Criticism in
Search of Beauty* in H. T. Tuckerman's *Memorial of Horatio Greenough.*
See also Emerson's comment on Greenough: "His paper on Architecture,
published in 1843, announced in advance the leading thoughts of Mr.
Ruskin on the *morality* in architecture, notwithstanding the antagonism in
their views of the history of art. I have a private letter from him—later,
but respecting the same period—in which he roughly sketches his own
theory: 'Here is my theory of structure: a scientific arrangement of spaces
and forms to functions and to site; an emphasis of features proportioned
to their *gradated* importance in function; colour and ornament to be decided and arranged and varied by strictly organic laws, having a distinct
reason for each decision; the entire and immediate banishment of all makeshift and make-believe.' "—*English Traits,* I.

Eliot Norton, a young man of low vitality, always a semi-invalid, a born collector of autographs and coins, books, engravings, paintings, with ample means to satisfy his tastes, with an acute sense of his social duty, devout, fastidious, learned, a careful scholar, was cautiously feeling his way towards the world of art. He and Clough had sworn eternal friendship, and, in fact, Norton's talent for friendship was the most remarkable thing about him. He was a hero-worshipper by instinct, who only asked that his heroes should be authentic,—good museum-pieces in flesh and blood, classified and certified,—for he had an extreme distrust of anything new.* He was a born confidant. Everyone told Norton everything, for he was the soul of discretion; and one could be sure that, if he wrote one's memoirs, nothing would appear that was not in the best of taste. He had whispered to his mother, at the age of ten, in the midst of a desperate illness, "I wish I could live, so that I could edit Father's works." He was to live to edit Carlyle and Ruskin, who, like Lowell and George William Curtis, made him their literary executor. Nature had preordained him for this work, as it made other men explorers and poets. With a conscientious longing to be useful, Norton felt sure that he had a mission.

As a child, he had been taken to England, where he had met his father's friends, especially Joanna Baillie and Mrs. Hemans, the cultivated Low Church circles that read Andrews Norton's books. Wordsworth had taken him upon his knee and given him a blessing. He had had a taste of the India trade, in the counting-house of his maternal uncles, before settling down to a scholar's life. He had sailed to India as a supercargo. There he had

* It must be added that Lincoln and John Brown were among his heroes. Their photographs, in later days, stood on his mantelpiece at Ashfield. Norton, somewhat timid and imitative on his imaginative side, was highly independent in his moral nature. In John Brown he saw "one of those men who thought themselves commissioned to do the work of the Lord." This was the spirit of his own teaching.

found readers of his father, as well as of Everett's speeches and Longfellow's poems, and had passed much of his time with the poet Dutt and his Harvard classmate, Fitzedward Hall, the Oriental scholar.* He found good friends in several rajahs, but India struck his New England taste as "showy," and it was not till he reached Venice, travelling round the world, that his aesthetic feeling came to life. Even in Europe, on this first visit, for which he was well equipped with introductions, thanks to George Ticknor, who was one of his uncles, his social and political observations occupied him more than matters of art. Returning home, he drifted out of business, edited a volume of hymns, opened a night-school for the poor of Cambridge, busied himself with model lodging-houses, to meet the new problems of immigration, and published an anonymous book, *Considerations on Some Recent Social Theories*. This was a counterblast to the radical doctrines that interested the Concord thinkers, the theories that had come to a head in 1848, Fourierism, Kossuthism, nationalism, the "offensive declamation" of Mazzini. The British rule in India, Norton thought, was better than any native rule could be. Republicanism as such was not important; and what was the use of trying to change conditions unless the people themselves had "character"? That character was what they did not have was the evident moral of their degradation,—which gave the upper classes their Christian function. Norton was a tender-hearted man who felt that he was personally bound to rescue the world from its folly.

It was on his second visit to Europe, in 1855, that Norton's real career began. His ship-mate, James Jackson Jarves, already known as a writer on art, gave him a letter of introduction to Ruskin, who, although he was nine

* Professor of Sanskrit and English in the government college at Benares; later professor of Sanskrit and Hindustani in King's College, London. Hall was the first American scholar to edit a Sanskrit text, the *Vishnu Purana*.

years the elder, soon thought of Norton as his "first real
tutor"; for the bright-eyed Cambridge student with the
musical voice, who had steeped himself in *Modern Painters,* knew classical literature better than he, showed a surprising knowledge of Italian painting and introduced him
to the *Fioretti.* Ruskin, who was still a Calvinist, might
have grown up in New England, in spite of his exuberant
temperament. His shrewd, sensible, prosperous merchant-
father, his grim, repressive mother, who trampled on
every innocent pleasure, the atmosphere of piety, thrift
and culture in which he had passed his early years, his
tours in a travelling-carriage over Europe, the father
sympathizing with the son's ambitions, all suggested Boston. Ruskin and Norton became fast friends at once.
Ruskin showed Norton his Turners and Rossettis, Norton gave Ruskin the writings of his American friends,
Lowell and Dr. Holmes. They travelled together in
Switzerland and climbed the mountain meadows of Sal-
lanches. They met again in Italy. Together they stood at
the fountain in Siena, under the same arches where Dante
had stood, drank of it together and walked together on
the hills above, as Ruskin wrote later in his memoirs,
where the fireflies among the scented thickets shone fitfully in the still undarkened air, like starlight through the
purple leaves.

Thus began the transatlantic friendships that gave Norton much of his later fame. His second great friendship
was with Mrs. Gaskell, the Unitarian minister's wife who
had described in *Cranford* a village life that also suggested New England. After Mrs. Gaskell, whom he met
in Rome and to whom he recited Lowell's poems, while he
gave her lessons in Italian painting, he named one of his
daughters. In Paris, he met Lamartine, Vigny and Tocqueville, and he was glad to find that Ary Scheffer, like some
of his acquaintances in London, thought Longfellow the
greatest living poet. Ruskin, whose passion was the Mid-

dle Ages, said that Longfellow, in *The Golden Legend*, had entered into the temper of the monk more closely than any historian or theologian; and Scheffer proved to Norton's satisfaction that the most poetic imagination was always accompanied by sound sense and practical understanding. Norton was not one of those dreamers who found in Italy a romantic solace. Recalling his social interests at home, he scrutinized the Italian charities, the evening schools for boys, the work of the Misericordia. Finding Keats's grave in sad disorder, he had the stone firmly set and planted myrtles and violets around it, with the same New England instinct for tidying-up that he brought to bear on the impulsive Ruskin,—to "keep him strictly and busily at his work." Rome was falling to pieces; it was all a helpless mass of weeds and ruins. All the more reason for a Protestant grave-yard to set it a good example.* Curious about modern Rome, which seemed to him as gaudy as Calcutta, wanting in simplicity and taste, he talked with scholarly priests and architects and went to meetings of academies where cardinals sat on gilded chairs, where seminarists recited hexameters on the Sacrifice of Isaac, in excellent Latin, and charming young countesses read their poems on Dante's Beatrice and Petrarch's Laura. He took notes on the early painters, Giotto, Fra Angelico and Perugino, whom Ruskin was interpreting for the modern mind and whom the Pre-Raphaelites were imitating, with a new feeling for colour which, in England, following the Oxford Movement, represented a recoil from rationalism and Puritanism. He began his version of the *Vita Nuova,* the first of the long series of Dante translations that were to spring from Cambridge. This was more literal than Rossetti's version, and marked by the same delicate feeling; for Norton, in truth, was an exquisite scholar. He and Rossetti

* Keats's grave was tidied again, about 1874, by the daughter of W. W. Story.

met, as friends of Ruskin, and Rossetti painted a picture for him, "Dante meeting Beatrice." He also began the study of mediæval cathedral-building, the subject of his most important work. The first part of the book he was soon to publish, *Notes of Travel and Study in Italy,* dealt with the Cathedral of Orvieto. Later readers were to find this passage as good as Henry Adams on the building of Chartres.

Norton returned to Cambridge, like another Ticknor, with the same sort of apostolic fervour that had filled his uncle's mind. He was the opener of another door, the world of aesthetic studies. For half a century, as a teacher at Harvard, he was to expound the gospel of taste, the doctrines of Ruskin, Dante, Italian painting, the history of architecture, sculpture, Turner, as his father had expounded the Scriptures,—taste as a means of salvation. He who was called "Pope Charles" by his early friends was destined to outlive the days of the New England papacy; but, even in these first few years, before he became professor of the history of art, he was an autocrat in aesthetic matters. Weak in aesthetic feeling, but skilled and learned, as Ticknor, weak in literary feeling, was also skilled and learned, he had the same responsible sense of an intellectual mission. As Ticknor felt, in his heart of hearts, that all the great writers were of the past,—Ticknor, who lived out his days around the corner from Emerson, Hawthorne, Thoreau, scarcely aware of their existence,—so Norton, who made an exception of Ruskin's friends, Turner and the Pre-Raphaelites, felt that the Renaissance was the end of art. He apologized, in later years, for a Corot that hung in his hall, left him by a friend to take care of. But as Ticknor had sent boxes of his books to enquiring students in Georgia and Maine, and was always ready with counsel for every scholar, so Norton carried boxes of Turners with him, when he gave lectures in the country towns, and left them for the boys and girls to study. He was always lending his gems and precious vases, fragments of sculpture, engravings, drawings, wherever he saw a chance to spread his gospel. Hearing that someone in Portland was interested in Turner, he sent a box of his water-colours there. His tenderness and goodness to the poorer students, his constant wish to be useful and helpful soon became proverbial in Cambridge. He was an archæologist by nature who had learned the alphabet of art after his mental tissues had dried and hardened. He often seemed like a learned and elegant priest discoursing of the sacred mysteries of which he had scarcely felt the inner fire. But as a teacher, a sage, in days to come, a moralist, an expounder of manners, a master in the art of discrimination, he was the most potent of the Brahmins. No one left more of a stamp on Cambridge than Charles Eliot Norton.

CHAPTER XXV

THE ROMANTIC EXILES

AT LIVERPOOL, in his consul's office, Hawthorne spent four dull years. He had to deal with the beggars and impostors that haunt the official in foreign ports, the brutal skippers, the imbruted sailors for whom the gallant Dana was fighting at home. American claimants called upon him, "lost heirs" of English estates, usually mad or spurious, occasionally some visionary soul,—for instance, Delia Bacon,—on some phantasmal mission. One day Herman Melville came, his old friend in Lenox, wandering in a cloud, drifting to Constantinople. At the Unitarian chapel, William Henry Channing had found a pulpit. There the sunny mist of the Brook Farm doctrines mingled with the smoky fog of England.

Hawthorne plodded through the day's work with his usual mask of impassivity. Most of his troublesome visitors came and went like apparitions of smoke and fog, like figures in some romance that he would have written if he had had the energy to write. The poor, shy, proud Delia Bacon, a Hawthorne figure in real life, was a more insistent problem. As a friend of Elizabeth Peabody and Mrs. Stowe, she had written a few historical tales and novels and conducted classes in history, like Margaret Fuller, first in Connecticut, then in Boston and Cambridge, unfolding an idea that became an obsession. She had become convinced that Shakespeare's plays, actually written by a group of scholars gathered about Sir Walter Raleigh, contained a system of thought, concealed by ciphers, the

deepest wisdom of the greatest epoch, a science that the
world was waiting for. The question of the authorship of
the plays was of the least importance in her mind. Her
mission,—she was a missionary's daughter,—was to
reveal their esoteric meaning. Carlyle had treated her
with the utmost kindness, struck by her personality and
her knowledge, and she had obtained, or thought she had,
permission to unseal the tomb of Shakespeare, where she
believed the final clues were buried. She had haunted the
church at Stratford, at midnight, with her lantern, hovering about the grave, then lost her courage with her confidence, lost the last remnants of her reason, and shrunk
into the final stage of madness.

Hawthorne might have invented the story. Later, he
told it in his book on England. Without accepting Delia
Bacon's theory, he had written a preface for her book,
The Philosophy of Shakespeare's Plays Unfolded. This
vast, chaotic treatise was only an introduction to the subject, but the style was impressive, here and there, in the
midst of its incoherence, and some of Delia Bacon's intuitions, especially in the passages on *King Lear*, deserved
a place in Shakespearean criticism.* But, as for Miss
Bacon's romantic feeling for England, Hawthorne could
not share it. This tendency to wander back again, to the
old home of the Pilgrims, this appetite for English soil,
struck him as blind and pathetic. He seemed to be thrice-
armoured against the charm that more and more of his
countrymen felt, proud to be at odds with it, proud of his
New England prejudices, as if he had turned the tables on
Mrs. Trollope and wished to see only the too-much beef,
the gloom, the slums, the poverty. He was too deeply
planted in his own old world across the water to suffer the
beguilement of the "claimants," or so it seemed at first.

---

* Delia Bacon was the originator of the "Shakespeare-Bacon" movement.
For a conclusive refutation of the Baconian theory, see John Fiske, *The
Bacon-Shakespeare Folly*, in *A Century of Science*.

For him the Warwickshire elms could not compare with those that had overhung his village street.

Gradually his feeling changed. His old zest for taking notes returned. He spoke of writing an English romance and even found a clue at Smithall's Hall, an ancient house in Lancashire. A few stage-properties were enough to start the machinery of his imagination, a coffer filled with golden hair, a silver snuff-box, a bloody footstep. *Doctor Grimshawe's Secret* began to take shape in his mind, the novel, begun in Rome, never finished, that struck a new note in American fiction. For was not Redclyffe, the American heir, the first of the transatlantic *revenants* that were to fill the novels of Henry James? Irving and Longfellow, many another, had felt the spell of the old world, but Redclyffe's nostalgia was something else than theirs: "The thought thrilled his bosom that this was his home—-the home of the wild Western wanderer, who had gone away centuries ago, and encountered strange chances, and almost forgotten his origin, but still kept a clue to bring him back . . . He began to feel the deep yearning which a sensitive American,—his mind full of English thoughts, his imagination of English poetry, his heart of English character and sentiment,—cannot fail to be influenced by,— the yearning of the blood within his veins for that from which it has been estranged, the half fanciful regret that he should ever have been separated from these woods, these fields, these natural features of scenery, to which his nature was moulded, from the men who are still so like himself, from these habits of life and thought which (though he may not have known them for two centuries) he still perceives to have remained in some mysterious way latent in the depths of his character, and soon to be resumed, not as a foreigner would do it, but like habits native to him, and only suspended for a season."

In days to come, this feeling, which Hawthorne had begun to share,—a feeling that unsettled him, indeed,—was

to play a part in American culture as marked as that of the
"wanderers" of Pushkin's Russia. The most exotic writers,
hitherto, had had the unquestioning instinct of homing
pigeons, which brought them back from every foreign
journey. The great tradition of the Revolution, the feeling of the national destiny, the prevalence of the classical
studies that always made the mind its "own place," had
rooted them in the Western soil. They had felt that they
were building a civilization; and, in fact, it was not until
after the Civil War that the great diaspora began and
with it the tradition of deracination. Then, as the old
causes grew dimmer and dimmer, as the European peasants arrived in thousands, as wealth advanced and tourists
multiplied, as the human imagination felt cramped and
thwarted in the vast industrial beehive, as classical studies
declined and young men forgot the Plutarchian patterns,
then this yearning for an older homeland rose in people's
minds and men of sensibility flocked to Europe, not to
study, as in former days, and carry their spoils back, like
travelling Romans, but as if they could reascend the river
of time.

The mood that found expression in Hawthorne's Redclyffe was to reappear not only in Henry James but in
dozens, even scores of other writers who somehow felt
estranged from their native life when the thread had once
been broken. The elm-scattered meadows, the hawthorn
hedges, the lawns, the castle-towers, the stiles, the heavy-
timbered manor-houses, the Norman churches uplifting
themselves among the stately trees touched some deepest
buried nature in them, as of their English progenitors, a
nature that seemed to have lain unchanged under the
snows and leaves of ten-score winters and summers, layers
of new customs and institutions that melted away in a
night. They greeted these English scenes with a sudden
flash of recognition. It was like a coming home after an
absence of centuries. These intimations of a previous

state, almost suggesting Plato, this sense that one had "been there before" was partly due to the reading of English books, partly to the maintenance of English customs in households across the Atlantic. There were thousands of families in New England, as in New York and the South, that had never ceased to be English, for all they had accepted the Revolution. They had fought for English rights against the redcoats. They had defended their country against their country because it was an English trait to do so. Not to be patriotic was not to be English, and they were Americans because they were English. Meanwhile, Wordsworth and Byron, Thackeray, Dickens, *Punch* and the British reviews had shaped their minds. A thousand times, in fancy, with Dr. Johnson, they had turned at a corner into Fleet Street. A thousand times they had walked down Piccadilly, among the yellow chariots of Vanity Fair. Shelley's larks were still more real to them than all the bobolinks of their native pastures, and they saw Oliver Twist and Little Nell even under the trees of their village lanes.

There had always been good Bostonians, like Edmund Quincy, for whom their first pilgrimage to London was like the Musselman's visit to the tomb of the Prophet. They saw it as the ancient Jews beheld their holy city after the years of bondage in a foreign land. Deep in their minds lurked the feeling that T. G. Appleton ascribed to the Yankee: "Europe is the home of his protoplasm, of the long succession of forces which make him what he is." It was against this feeling that Emerson fought, or rather against its consequences, in everything that he said of the "tape-worm of Europe." Those who had made England what it was had done so by sticking where they were, regardless of their own atavistic instincts, which might have led them back to France or Denmark. When would Americans cast out the passion for Europe by the passion for America that would give them repose? Old and new coun-

tries were all the same to one who looked at the world
with the eye of wisdom. Why this superstition for a mush-
room Europe, which only had gravity and domestic rest
because it lived a self-contained existence? Emerson, who
travelled and believed in travel, whenever there was a
reason for it, said that one should fill a place at home before one tried to find a place abroad. Who provoked pity,
he remarked, like that excellent family just arriving in
some foreign city, in its well-appointed travelling-carriage,
as far from any honest end as ever? Each nation had
asked successively, "What are they here for?" until they
were all embarrassed, expecting to be asked the same question at the gates of every town. But this idle and pathetic
nostalgia for Europe, which had always existed in the
Yankee mind, was a minor strain before the Civil War.
Two hundred years had left their stamp on almost
every American, and those who had amply shared the life
of their country were as self-possessed as any European.
The eminent Americans of the forties and fifties confronted England with a serene aplomb. Proud of their
nation, proud of themselves, proud of their own good
work, objective in their point of view, contemptuous of
trifles, they were eager for the welfare of the world and
convinced that America had a mission.* The apologetic
note of later years was wholly absent from their tone and
manner. They met the Englishman as Greek met Greek,
as men who spoke their minds on all occasions, as the
Romans of Spain met the Romans of Rome.

The relations between America and England had
reached a sort of equipoise in the eighteen-fifties. The
acrimony of earlier years had largely passed away, the
Civil War had not yet revived it; and English and American writers and statesmen found that they had more in

* "Why do foreign lands regard us with this intensity of interest? Is it
not because the whole world looks hopefully toward America as a nation
especially raised by God to advance the cause of human liberty and religion?"—Harriet Beecher Stowe, Letter of 1853.

common than at any time before or since. A dozen Amer‚
ican authors of the moment, Prescott, Longfellow, Mot‚
ley, Mrs. Stowe, Emerson, Hawthorne and others were
greeted in England with the kind of *éclat* that Dickens met
in America, the kind that English authors have always
met in America but that American authors in England
never encountered in later times. Sydney Smith had said,
before Prescott's visit, that a "Caspian sea of soap"
awaited him. The English admired his pluck and his
glorification of the life of action; but even Prescott's
triumph was a trifle beside the royal progress of Mrs.
Stowe. Hundreds of thousands, like the Queen herself,
had been stirred and moved by Uncle Tom and Dred.
They had wept over the death of Nina and shared the
Queen's annoyance that fate had not chastised Tom Gordon. Mrs. Stowe, like Prescott and Sumner, found her
portrait in English castles, and crowds trooped after her
carriage as if she had been a prima donna. Much of the
cordiality that united the countries was of a purely social
kind. Outside the political sphere, Sumner, Dana, Charles
Francis Adams found everything in English life congenial;
and Sumner cultivated his English connections all the more
because his political views had made him an outcast in
social Boston. His pockets were always full of letters from
duchesses and noblemen, and his diaries in England suggested Ticknor's, almost as copious and entertaining. But
behind this social interest lay another, the humanitarian
feeling that England and New England shared in common. Channing, Garrison, Whittier, Mrs. Child had
spoken the language of Wilberforce and Clarkson. Their
unaffected, intelligent goodness had touched thousands of
English hearts. Philanthropic England, the England of
the great liberal circles, busily building model dwelling-
houses, raising the condition of the poor, occupied with
popular education,—in a spirit, often pharisaical, that
was sometimes saintly,—rejoiced in these American allies,

of whom Mrs. Stowe was the largest-hearted. The Anglo-American friendships of this time, Mrs. Stowe's friendship with Lady Byron, with Mrs. Browning and George Eliot, Norton's friendship with Ruskin, Emerson's with Carlyle,—a reformer of another stripe,—were fruits of this moral solidarity. Another fruit was Emerson's *English Traits,* the best of American travel-books and one of the great and permanent works of its kind. Every candid English reader, Thackeray, Browning, Clough, felt that Emerson over-praised England; but everyone felt that the praise was the praise of a master and that Emerson spoke as befitted a sage. In point of composition, *English Traits* was Emerson's masterpiece, the only book, save one, *The Conduct of Life,* that he ever really composed. What made it sovereign, as a book on England, was its realistic grasp of essential facts, its Olympian air of detachment and self-possession. It was the work of an intellect that was always dominant and always open. One felt as if the eye of God had fallen upon England, after having refreshed its impressions of India, Egypt, Greece.* If God had a special regard for England, that was his own affair.

The romantic-pusillanimous view of England was the product of a later generation. Italy, meanwhile, was the goal of those who sought, without benefit of Argo, the golden fleece of the past. Paris, for twenty years, the years of the Second Empire,—the Paris of the Empress Eugénie's hats,—was all that London later became as a goal of American fashion, of those who never trod their native shores without a steamer-ticket in their pocket; and other Americans, on special errands, flitted all over the continent, collecting twigs for their nests at home. Lowell

---

* "England has inoculated all nations with her civilization, intelligence and tastes; and, to resist the tyranny and prepossession of the British element a serious man must aid himself by comparing with it the civilizations of the farthest east and west, the old Greek, the Oriental, and, much more, the ideal standard, if only by means of the very impatience which English forms are sure to awaken in independent minds."—*English Traits.*

Mason wrote, in 1852, his *Musical Letters from Abroad,*
—reports on the state of music in Germany and England,
—before he returned to Massachusetts with an apostolic
mission like Ticknor's and Norton's. Jacob Abbott's Rollo
and Mr. George were types of a thousand other tourists
who roamed over Europe for their improvement, visiting
silk-mills and iron-foundries, marble-quarries, mosaic-fac-
tories, gathering hints for their future in Fitchburg and
Lawrence. They did not neglect the sights, the Dying
Gladiator and the Coliseum, but they never lost their
practical sense of proportion.* They felt that their minds
should be furnished but not upholstered. If Rollo had his
doubts at times, he always saw that Mr. George's view
was reasonable and right.†

For those who were tropical by organization, who
longed for the myrtle and orange, Italy was another matter. In Rome and Florence, when Hawthorne went there,
in 1858, little bands of exiles dwelt already, grouped
about the sculptors and the painters, precursors of the
colonies to come. These were new types, lovers of the picturesque who, far from seeking another homeland, wished
to be strangers and sojourners. For them, the charm of
Italy was its strangeness, not the familiarity that one
found in England. Fugitives from the land of calculation,
from the east wind, the "whip of the sky," as T. G. Appleton called it in one of his poems, the greyness and
chilliness of coast and headland, from "cold roast Boston"
and expectant Concord, which asked them either to be
men of business or to make bread of the stones in their
native pastures, they found balm and solace in the weeds

* "The Coliseum may have cost the most labour," said Mr. George, "but
the Great Eastern is far above it, in my opinion, in every element of real
greatness."—*Rollo in Rome.*

† "We are travelling for improvement, not for play. We are making
a tour of Scotland for the purpose of learning all we can about Scotland,
with a view to obtain more full and correct ideas respecting it than we
could obtain by books alone. So we must attend to our duty."—*Rollo in
Scotland.*

and the ruins, the lichens and the ancient walls, the colours and the forms that caressed the eye, the flowing life, the *dolce far niente.**

> Nature abhors what housewives love—the clean,
> And beauty hides when pail and brush come in.

So William Wetmore Story, the sculptor, wrote,—the son of Justice Story, who had settled in Rome,—recalling his native Salem. All his fellow-exiles shared this feeling. Some of them, like Story, in taking flight, had been warned by the example of Washington Allston, whose mind had withered away in Cambridgeport. Depressed at home, humbled before the men who were building towns and railroads, turning villages into factory-centres, they revelled in a world that was tumbling to pieces. They had heard too much about the "improvement" that seemed to signify only money and comfort; they were weary of the "perfectibility" that left their sensuous needs unsatisfied Emerson had talked too much, they thought, about the "rococo toy of Italy." He did not understand painters and sculptors. He had seen the case in too abstract a light, as one of them told the sage on a visit to Concord. Nature, he said, might be the same on the banks of the Kennebec and the banks of the Tiber, but, however it might be with writers, who had their books to study from, artists, whose books were pictures, needed Europe. Concord, for them, was another Patagonia.†

In fact, the colonists in Rome and Florence were all painters and sculptors rather than writers, or writers whose principal interest was painting and sculpture. James

---

* "It is this which makes Rome so admirable as a residence for an artist. All things are easy and careless in the out-of-doors life of the common people,—all poses unsought, all groupings accidental, all action unaffected and unconscious. One meets nature at every turn,—not braced up in prim forms, not conscious in manners, not made up into the fashionable or the proper, but impulsive, free and simple."—W. W. Story, *Roba di Roma.*

† Elihu Vedder, *The Digressions of V.*

Jackson Jarves lived in Florence, where he was to remain
for a generation. A man of more vigorous mind than Norton or Story, though less accomplished than either, he was
producing a series of books on art that had a sort of missionary value. He had settled in Italy about 1850, after a
stay in Paris and a long and adventurous youth in the
South Sea Islands. The son of Deming Jarves, the glass-
maker, the "Father of American Glass," who had founded
the glass-works at Sandwich to utilize the fine Cape Cod
sand, he had inherited a little fortune, most of which he
spent in collecting pictures. He had passed several years
at Honolulu and written a standard *History of the Sandwich Islands* and two amateurish novels,—with a few
good pages of description, sketches of Polynesian scenes
and manners,—before he happened upon his real vocation. A lively, shrewd, unworldly, honest soul, with a rare
aesthetic taste, a born collector, familiar with the New
England country auction, at which, as a boy, he had spent
his pocket-money, buying books, especially histories,—he
had a passion for Prescott,—he was engaged in a nine-
years' search for his great collection of Tuscan paintings.

These were the days when the Primitives were still regarded as of dubious value, when gold-background pictures of Carlo Crivelli were burned for the sake of the
gold one found in the ashes and Walter Savage Landor
was called a madman for wasting a handful of silver on
such rubbish. At least, if this fabulous hour had passed,
largely thanks to Ruskin's eloquent writings, one still
found an occasional "Muse of Cortona" used by a peasant
to stop a hole in an oven, a Titian, painted over by some
bungler, that sold for six dollars, a Correggio, tattered
and torn, in the hands of an old-clothes dealer. The age of
wild buying had begun, the forgers were busy, the couriers
were swindling millionaires who proudly carried back to
New York and Boston their false Murillos, Claudes and
Leonardos. With no fixed standards of authentication, the

art-market was a house of darkness. Jarves taught himself to see in the dark. He tramped through villas, palaces
and convents, picked up a canvas here and there, cut from
its frame, in a pile of earth and rubble, or tossed aside in
a lumber-room, and slowly formed the collection, so famous later. It was a triumph of discrimination. It was a task
of devotion, like Agassiz's, for Jarves had no thought of
personal gain. He was an Agassiz of art-museums, one
who found, however, that his country, ready as it was for
the gospel of science, was far from ready for this other
gospel. Neither New York nor Boston would accept his
collection, though Norton tried to find a place for it. The
critics laughed at Jarves's "wiry madonnas" and called
him a scamp for all his pains; and the pictures found their
dwelling-place at Yale,—where a little gallery existed, the
first of its kind in America, founded in 1832,—only
through a comedy of errors. But Jarves was a patient
man. Italian art was the fruit of a working epoch, not unlike his own, an age of democratic energies; and he
thought that the same faith was preparing his country for
a similar efflorescence. He bequeathed collections of
textiles and Venetian glass to the New York museum and
Wellesley College. He studied the glass-making at Murano and tried to introduce the Venetian methods into the
works at Sandwich.

In the books that Jarves wrote in the fifties and sixties,
Art Hints, The Art-Idea, Art Thoughts, Art Studies,— a
highly intelligent history of Italian painting, with illustrations from his own collection,—he preached like one of
the missionaries with whom he had spent his youth at
Honolulu. He urged the cause of art-teaching, museums,
galleries, schools of design. He explained the success of
the British efforts to introduce art into manufacture and
asked why river-banks and public buildings, parks, shop-
windows and railway-cars should not have their beauty
and interest. In a strain of religious feeling that beclouded

his style, for his thoughts were often wrapped in ethical phrases, he asked, in fact, more questions in his field and made more intelligent observations than any other writer of his time,—"an epoch," as he described it, "of monstrous plaster figures, daubed with crazy paint, of mammoth cast-iron wash-basins, called fountains, of cast-iron architecture and clumsy gate-ways to public parks, of shoddy portrait-statues and inane ideal ones." His writings were full of astute perceptions. Like Greenough, he praised the clipper-ship and the old-fashioned farmhouse. They were appealing and true because their style was suited to the realities behind them, the climate, the materials at hand. They were as successful in their way as the Greek temples and the Gothic churches. Why? Because the American merchants and farmers took pride in a work that really met their needs. Had any American patron of painting or sculpture shown the kind of feeling the merchant expressed in Longfellow's *The Building of the Ship?*—

> Build me straight, O worthy Master,
>   Staunch and strong, a goodly vessel
> That shall laugh at all disaster,
>   And with wave and whirlwind wrestle!

Well might the poet say:

> The merchant's word
> Delighted the Master heard,—

for this was the tone of Lorenzo de' Medici, in days when painting had really mattered, too. Jarves, who predicted that architecture would be the first great American art, said that it could have no healthy growth until it represented the people's life and shaped itself in conformity to local causes.*

---

* One of Jarves's early books contained an excellent sketch of Hokusai, who was all unknown to Ruskin. This was the first suggestion of his later handbook, *A Glimpse at the Art of Japan.* Jarves was one of the first students, with Millet, Whistler and La Farge, who, when Japan was opened in the early fifties, became aware of Japanese art.

With a somewhat forbidding style, all thumbs, too often, Jarves was an independent critic who did not spare
the feelings of his friends, the American painters and
sculptors in Rome and Florence. Greenough had gone home
to die, but Powers lived in Florence; and, in Rome, Story,
Crawford * and Harriet Hosmer, a pupil of the English sculptor Gibson, who gave her one of the rooms where
Canova had worked, carried on a school of Yankee sculpture that showed what will could do, if little else. Eager
workers all, anxious to justify their expatriation, they
turned out busts and heroic groups, statues of American
statesmen, histories in granite and romances in marble,
such as the "Greek Slave" and the "Libyan Sibyl." These
story-telling figures possessed every accessory and association that spoke for literature as it spoke for learning and
uttered an occasional word for sculpture. Zenobia was a
favourite subject, the heroine of William Ware's novel,
a true New England woman born too soon. The drapery
of Cleopatra, as Story conceived her, was almost a novel
in itself. The school excelled in allegories, representing,
for instance, the struggles of genius, a sculptor in despair,
while a hand pours oil into his dying lamp. The hand was
the hand of the patron, and patrons were not wanting, after all. Commissions came from Congress, from Cooper,
Sumner, Ticknor, and the fame of Powers's busts had
gone abroad. Thorwaldsen had said that his bust of Webster was the best work of the kind in modern times.
Powers's vogue was world-wide, and travelling magnates
from across the sea, manufacturers, diplomats and scholars, haunted his Florentine studio. No European journey
was complete unless one carried home a bust by Powers.

To warm themselves in one another's presence, the artists in Rome met at the Caffè Greco, the dark and dirty
haunt in former days of Allston, Cooper and Turner.

---

* Crawford's figure of Beethoven, erected in the Boston Music Hall, in
1856, is said to have been the first statue raised in America to an artist.

Little groups of aspiring students went for moonlight rambles in the Coliseum. They strolled through the Forum, singing "Hail Columbia" in chorus. They stopped at the Fountain of Trevi, where Lord Neville had talked with Corinne. They sallied forth with sketch-books for picnics on the Appian Way. They pored over one another's portfolios and wrote "Campagna bits" in their journals and letters. They gathered for musical soirées, perhaps in Charlotte Cushman's rooms, for the great Boston actress with the "thoughtful" style often spent her winters in Rome. They talked about Guido's "Aurora" and Canova, who seemed to have brought back the repose of the Greeks, and the mystery of Beatrice Cenci. They sat on ruined columns, with their colours beside them, sketching some model with dishevelled hair, a beard that suggested Moses or a well-turned arm that might have belonged to Apollo. Some of them aired their distaste for the Puritan ways that had made their life at home so drab and sober. In others, the New England strain seemed only accentuated in the foreign air. They clung to their Calvinistic views and lived in the Rome of the Popes as they had lived in Lynn or Brattleboro. Powers cultivated his Yankee speech, as if it gave him a dramatic pleasure; and he and Joel Hart abounded in mechanical shifts that would have made their fortunes in Lawrence or Lowell. The tone of the little colonies, of all the foreign artists in Rome and Florence, set by Thorwaldsen and the German painters, Overbeck and Cornelius, was rigidly moral and highly religious. One might well have found some Yankee maiden, like Hilda in *The Marble Faun,* living in her tower among the doves and trimming her evening lamp at the Virgin's shrine.

This was the little world that Hawthorne found. Story, his old acquaintance in Salem, had come to spend his life in Rome and Florence. Others came and went, Lowell to visit Story, Norton taking notes on Giotto and Dante,

Bryant the poet, George Stillman Hillard, Hawthorne's old friend and Sumner's partner, who published, in *Six Months in Italy,* a glorified and even glorious guide-book that was destined to serve a generation of tourists. Story, who took Hawthorne under his wing, a slight, wiry, nervous little man, witty, swarthily handsome, abounding in every social grace, clever at acting, singing, sketching, writing, passionately ambitious as a sculptor, had passed his earlier years as a lawyer in Boston. He had written his father's life and various legal treatises; he had shared in Margaret Fuller's Conversations and dreamed and talked of art and Rome, with Longfellow, in Lowell's study. Everything in New England annoyed and bored him, even the growing interest in German thought, for Italy had captured his imagination. His closest friends there were the Brownings and Landor, who had taken refuge with the Storys when, like King Lear, at eighty-four, he had been turned adrift by his wife and children. Browning had encountered the grand old poet, as terrible as he was grand, wandering aimlessly in the streets in Florence, under the burning sun, with a few coins in his pocket, and he had joined the Storys in Siena, where he continued to write his Latin verses attacking Napoleon III. Browning took lessons in modelling from Story, who remained his intimate friend for forty years. Once, at the Palazzo Barberini, Story's house in Rome, he recited *The Pied Piper* to the Story children; Hans Andersen read *The Ugly Duckling,* and Story, playing on his flute, headed a march of the children about the house. But, as a poet, Story followed Browning like one of the children who had heard the piper.

Hawthorne surveyed the scene of *The Marble Faun* with a certain distrust and suspicion. For strangers, he felt, the Italian air had something sinister in it. The years were empty. Postponing the realities of life, one had no

present, and gradually one ceased to have a future.* The
artists "linger," he wrote, "while their originality dies out
of them, or is polished away as a barbarism." This was
surely true in Story's case, at least in the matter of his writing. What Story might have achieved under other conditions as the poet that he always wished to be remained
an open question. His first Italian poems were certainly
better,—if only because he was older,—than those he had
written at home, the pale Tennysonian verses, the imitations of German ballads that had given him a little name
in Boston. In fact, his *Castle Palo,* his *Orestes* and some of
his dramatic monologues, *A Roman Lawyer in Jerusalem,
A Jewish Rabbi in Rome,* would have been surprising in
their power if they had not been virtually written by
Browning. Story was the cleverest of chameleons, an
actor, a ventriloquist in verse, and several of these poems
were brilliant sallies. But less and less one found in his
work the quiet, truthful, natural note that marked such
earlier verses as *The Locust;* and the same thing was true
of his writing in prose. His *Roba di Roma,* the fruit of his
first impressions, charmingly pictured the surface of
Roman life. It was a treasury of the sort of scenes, caught
by an eager artist's eye, that appeared on a thousand canvases of the eighteen-fifties, the *panem et circenses* of the
streets and the markets. This was the work that Story was
to live by, one that he never equalled in later years. His
pretty little novel, *Fiammetta,* like some of Henry James's
early tales, suggested that Story ended where James began. The *Conversations in a Studio,* filled with sophisticated schoolboy-talk,—on Shakespeare, on capping quota-

---

* "The years . . . have a kind of emptiness, when we spend too many of
them on a foreign shore. We defer the reality of life, in such cases, until a
future moment, when we shall again breathe our native air; but, by and
by, there are no future moments; or, if we do return, we find that the
native air has lost its invigorating quality,—and that life has shifted its
reality to the spot where we have deemed ourselves only temporary residents. Thus, between two countries, we have none at all, or only that little
space of either, in which we finally lay down our discontented bones. It is
wise, therefore, to come back betimes, or never."—*The Marble Faun.*

tions, on spirit-rapping,—bespoke a mind that never found its focus, a snapper-up of trifles, not unconsidered, but without the justification of a point of view.

Was Hawthorne right in feeling that "it needs the native air" to give a writer's work reality? Rome had provided him with a fairy setting for the last of his own romances,—the last he was ever to finish,—the tale of Hilda, Miriam and Donatello, the dusky Miriam of the shrouded past and the delicate wood-anemone of the Western forest. This dance of Yankee girls and fauns and spectres was like a Pompeiian fresco or something immobilized on a Grecian urn. A bituminous light suffused it, as of an afternoon in the realm of shades. One caught in the shifting groups the magical, mythological grace of Poussin. One heard Mignon's song rising from the depths in the fitful measure of a wind-harp. Hawthorne had drawn enchantment from the Roman air; and yet, for all the spell of *The Marble Faun,* it was hardly comparable with *The Scarlet Letter* or *The House of the Seven Gables.* The orchidaceous existence of most of the exiles seemed to bear him out in his distrust. One could dream forever in these Roman gardens, under the cypress and ilex, while all one's mental muscles atrophied. Norton, with his acute social conscience, his sense of a mission at home, probed under the surface of Italian life. The repressive political system disturbed him, and he had understood, from his own observation, the sorrows of Petrarch, Dante and Alfieri, who had mourned over their country and its degradation. Norton's critical faculties were alert; he had ridiculed the old romantic guide-books and the cold and pretentious work of the German painters who were dominant in modern Rome. He had cared for the realities of Italian life, as Greenough and Margaret Fuller had cared before him. The others did not wish to care. It was to escape from the prose of existence that they had left America. If their writing lost all grip and bottom, was not this the reason and the explanation?

CHAPTER XXVI

THE AUTOCRAT

THE WELL-KNOWN house of Ticknor and Fields was the publishing centre of Boston. William D. Ticknor, the senior partner, a cousin of George Ticknor, had built up a large business with English authors by paying for their books, an act of justice that was not required by any law of copyright. He had attracted Tennyson and Browning, Coventry Patmore and others, in several cases creating a public for them when they were still unknown at home.* The younger partner, James T. Fields, a man of letters in his own right, was a big, jovial creature, always dressed in Scotch tweeds, with a full beard, abundant hair, keen, twinkling eyes and a hearty manner. The Old Corner Bookstore in Washington Street, where Fields sat behind his green curtain, laughing and manufacturing reputations, was already an institution. There was always some author in Fields's cozy nook, Longfellow, Mrs. Stowe or Emerson, sitting on the window-seat in a litter of books and papers. The shop was crowded with

* Many English authors of the time bore witness to the American "general gift of quicker and more subtle recognition of genius than the English public,"—as Coventry Patmore described it in talking with Hawthorne. Miss Mitford said to Fields: "It takes ten years to make a literary reputation in England, but America is wiser and bolder, and dares to say at once, 'This is fine.' "—Fields, *Yesterdays with Authors.*

See also Richard Garnett's remarks in his introduction to Lowell's *My Study Windows:* "Americans far surpass us English in the prompt recognition of excellence. Carlyle, De Quincey, Coventry Patmore, James Martineau, found their first considerable audiences across the Atlantic. Americans are quicker to discover the merits of a foreign author, more thorough in naturalizing him, and demand a higher standard of excellence in the translation of his works."

visitors, poets, historians, actors and singers, for concert and lecture-tickets were also sold there, country lawyers and ministers, on their annual journey to town, and here and there some elderly judge or merchant in search of a calf-bound set of Burke or Gibbon.

James T. Fields was a sort of liaison-officer between the European celebrities and the literati of Beacon Hill and Cambridge. He had a grand idea of the publishing business. As a Portsmouth boy, a shipmaster's son, like Hawthorne and Jones Very, a passionate lover of reading, he had watched the rise of New England letters and made up his mind to forward it. He had served his apprenticeship as a bookseller's clerk and had startled all the other clerks by guessing, whenever a customer entered the shop, the sort of book the customer presently asked for. His hero-worshipper's instinct would have pleased Carlyle. He knew the London publishers and bookmen as well as he knew New York and Boston, and he had visited all his British authors, Leigh Hunt, Miss Mitford, Wordsworth, Barry Cornwall. He had gathered together De Quincey's scattered writings and published the first collected edition of them. In rare-book rooms and auction-rooms, Fields was a familiar figure. He had read all the marginal comments in Wordsworth's little library. He had lovingly handled Lamb's own copies of Marlowe, Drummond and Drayton and the literary magnificoes at "Elmwood." There was nothing he did not know about first editions. His house, which overlooked the Back Bay, was a temple of busts and portraits, autographs and souvenirs of authors, drawings by Blake, heads of Pope and Dickens, Thackeray, Wordsworth, Hawthorne. In later years, inspired by these portraits, all of them painted from life, he was to write his *Yesterdays with Authors,* a notable memoir filled with veracious gossip. He liked a rough tramp in the Adirondacks or a camping-trip to Moosehead Lake, where one slept on the ground for a mattress with a bundle of faggots under one's head. At present, while he wrote his poems and essays,—the papers collected in *Underbrush* and various songs and ballads,—he gave most of his thoughts to business. He had a shrewd eye for the winning author that would have made the fortune of a racing-man.

The chief reader of Ticknor and Fields was Edwin P. Whipple, a self-made man of letters, like Fields himself, who had been a broker's clerk when Fields was a clerk in the bookshop. The two had been inseparable friends since the days when they had met, as fellow-bookworms, in the rooms of the Mercantile Library. Whipple was a short, slight man, always dressed in black, with a square, prim face and a manner all precision and decorum. Beside the exuberant Fields, with his overflowing air of the world, there was something ministerial in his appearance. He was extremely myopic and excessively shy, and yet this bespectacled man had a vigorous mind that often suggested Macaulay, who had praised him highly. His reputation was already brilliant, in England as well as America, and some of this reputation was deserved. As a writer for the *North American,* he had formed a method of his own, discriminating, acute and often subtle, with none of the ponderousness of his early models; and he was discussing, in his essays and lectures, such subjects as wit and humour, the ludicrous side of life, genius, intellectual health and disease, character, success and its conditions. His estimates of the early American writers were undoubtedly over-friendly, but his papers on the English dramatists and the Scottish and English critics were the best of the kind in America, by far. He had summed up Francis Jeffrey to perfection, and some of his essays, on Fielding, Thackeray, Dickens, were admirable characterizations and definitions. His only American rivals were Poe and Lowell. Whipple, at the moment, was highly regarded; his volumes went through eight and ten editions, and he was to live obscurely as one of those writers whom people rediscover with surprise.

This very intelligent, shy and modest Whipple had long been moving about in Boston and Cambridge, watching the unusual men who lived there and noting their conversation and personal traits. He had formed this habit as a boy in Salem, observing Rufus Choate in his pew at church, so strangely different from the stolid merchants, and had later followed and studied in similar fashion Webster, George Ticknor and Charles Sumner, Prescott, Agassiz, Emerson, Alcott and others. He had a way of meeting them on the street at moments that revealed their oddities, stopping to see them when some bit of news had thrown them off their guard, catching two or three of them together when something in the air satisfied his eye for character. As a bank-clerk, in the Transcendental days, he had been struck by Emerson's sound sense, as compared with the delusions of the Boston merchants. The manias that possessed the business men, who bought up waste and worthless lands and recklessly sunk their millions in hopeless railroads, convinced him that Emerson knew the laws of trade better than Amos Lawrence. And so with all these other remarkable minds. He felt he was living at a historic moment, that a group of worthies had appeared who were to be of interest in the future. Scarcely observed by them, he was the chiel among them taking notes. These notes appeared later in his liveliest book, the excellent *Recollections of Eminent Men.*

That the New England mind had crystallized, that there was a renaissance in Boston,—one of those "heats and genial periods" of which Emerson spoke in *English Traits,* "by which high tides are caused in the human spirit,"—had not escaped the firm of Ticknor and Fields. In fact, they were the practical centre of it. The publishers of Emerson, Hawthorne, Holmes, of Longfellow

and Mrs. Stowe were able to feel that they were creating
classics; for their authors were becoming national figures,
and even international. Their little brown editions were
known wherever books were read; and the day had long
passed when Andrews Norton, making up a list of American writers, had placed Emerson, Longfellow and Hawthorne as minor figures in the second fifty. In Russia, even
in India, even in China, all these names were favourably
known, and lecturers in the West, like Whipple and
Alcott, found that in St. Louis and Chicago they had an
almost sovereign reputation. Seen from a distance, the
New England writers appeared like fixed stars in a constellation that grew more brilliant with every decade. In
fact, they were widely scattered. Aside from the groups
in the capital, they rarely met. The Cambridge authors
never went to Concord; the Concord authors seldom
went to Boston; Whittier, Mrs. Stowe, Thoreau and
others revolved in worlds of their own, and Ticknor's
circle scarcely crossed the circles of Holmes and Lowell.
Connecticut and Massachusetts were like different nations. Their unity was an abstraction still, largely so to
remain, in fact; but Fields, the clever impresario, made a
reality of it. He issued souvenir volumes of "Boston
Authors," with plates of Craigie House and Lowell's
"Elmwood," Webster's house at Marshfield and Ticknor's
in Park Street. His "blue and gold" editions stamped his
poets with authority. Willis wrote to Fields, in his flowery
way, "Your press is the announcing-room of the country's Court of Poetry." From this press the English
writers and the New England writers came together, and
each drew something from the general glamour. Browning and Longfellow, Emerson, Tennyson, Hawthorne,
Holmes, De Quincey, Mrs. Stowe presented a common
front as standard authors.

One of Fields's jokes was about the Boston man who
read Shakespeare late in life but found him far beyond

his expectation. "There are not twenty men in Boston who could have written those plays," he said. More than twenty were engaged at present in work that Boston men were fitted for. Sparks's aspirations for the Athenæum seemed almost to have been fulfilled. There were dozens of more or less productive students in the alcoves that had once been empty; and Prince Jerome Napoleon, visiting Boston, surprised by the freedom of opinion, the absence of Puritanism that he found, remarked that the New England capital had much more intellectual movement than any other part of the country. Among the recent minor men of letters were several whose names were to be remembered. The librarian of the Athenæum, William Poole, was at work on a well-known compilation. As one of the librarians at Yale, he had started the custom of keeping on slips of paper notes on current periodicals that might be useful in student-debates, and this was developing in Boston into *Poole's Index*. Thomas Bulfinch, the architect's son, a class-mate of Prescott at Harvard and a clerk at the Merchants' Bank, whose rooms, overlooking Scollay Square, were piled high with books, published *The Age of Fable* in 1855. In this same year, another book appeared that was equally useful. "Ask John Bartlett" was the phrase in Cambridge when anyone wished to find a familiar quotation. Bartlett owned the University book-store. A notable angler, a lover of whist, who edited Izaak Walton and later wrote a concordance of Shakespeare, he made his shop a centre for literary gossip and wished to live up to his reputation. He had kept for years the voluminous commonplace-book that finally emerged as Bartlett's *Familiar Quotations*.

The founding of the *Atlantic Monthly*, in 1857, marked this high tide of the Boston mind.* In the "new

* The American mind in general reached high tide at about this time. Samuel G. Goodrich ("Peter Parley") presented in *Recollections of a Life-*

magazine," as it was called from Maine to Minnesota, all the established writers appeared together. Lowell, the editor, assembled for the first number contributions from Emerson, Motley, Holmes, Longfellow, Norton, Whittier and Mrs. Stowe. It seemed, from a distance, like a family party, in spite of the diversity of these minds, and murmurs were heard in other regions against the self-complacency of Boston and the mutual admiration that flourished there. But, as Dr. Holmes remarked of his commensals, if they had not admired one another they would have shown a singular want of taste. It was true that at this moment the New England mind began to reveal signs of degeneration, traits that in later years grieved or vexed those that knew not the Boston Zion, and sometimes did not even wish to know it. The "breaking of the seedling tulip into high-caste colours," as Dr. Holmes described this hour in Boston, was not without unhappy consequences. It destroyed the noble unconsciousness of the past. But the note of *The Atlantic* was not self-conscious, in spite of Lowell's tendency to be so. The magazine was born mature. The regard of the writers for one another sprang from an impersonal respect for their characters and their work; and, if they over-valued one another, they set a better example than most of the other American writers and artists, who were all too prone to self-depreciation. They increased the self-respect of their fellow-craftsmen; they won for American letters and art the respect that American letters and art had

time the following statistics of American book-manufacture: In 1820, American authors, 30%, British authors, 70%; in 1830, American authors, 40%, British authors, 60%; in 1840, American authors, 55%, British authors, 45%; in 1850, American authors, 70%, British authors, 30%; in 1856, American authors, about 80%, British authors, 20%. In 1800, American school-books were wholly of English origin; by 1820, they had been adjusted to the needs of American readers; in 1856, they were wholly American. Goodrich added, "We produce annually more school-books than the whole continent of Europe."

always needed.* It was observed, moreover, that, sooner or later, almost everything *The Atlantic* published, essay, poem and story, found its way into a book and had at least a measure of permanent interest; and, as time went on, and Ticknor and Fields took over the publication, and Fields became the second editor, and the Civil War came, and Howells followed, the scope of the magazine grew broader and broader. It became a national institution.

Dr. Holmes had named *The Atlantic Monthly,* as Alcott had named *The Dial;* and he was the first contributor. He had had little time for writing prose in his active professional life, but he recalled that many years before he had published two papers entitled *The Autocrat of the Breakfast-Table.* Nothing could be salvaged from these old essays, but the venture had given him a good idea, to carry a note-book with him and jot down his own conversation. A Boswell writing out himself. Two other contributions to the monthly, evoked by the Civil War, were the *Battle Hymn of the Republic* and *The Man Without a Country.* Julia Ward Howe and Edward Everett Hale, a nephew of Edward Everett, were destined to outlive the century and write their memories of a hundred years. Hale, whose father was Nathan Hale, the editor of the *Daily Advertiser,* the oldest of New England daily journals, remembered seeing his mother rock the cradle in which reposed his sister, the infant Lucretia, who wrote *The Peterkin Papers* in after years, while Webster and Justice Story dictated to her the speeches that were to appear in her husband's paper. To write a book, for one of the Hales, was as natural as to breathe; the father, the mother, the sisters, Lucretia and Susan, were all authors by instinct and almost by

---

* "We every day too easily undervalue our own artists. It is sad to say that to a remark of Thackeray they owe some of the consideration they enjoy. 'Never neglect or forget Trumbull,' he said, and poor America accepted the boon of praise, and thought better of her Revolutionary artist." —T. G. Appleton, *A Sheaf of Papers.*

habit; and Edward Everett Hale, a minister, whose
mind was ingenious and alert, breezy and even salty, had
begun to write for the press at seventeen. He was quite
outside the literary currents that had irrigated the Boston mind. His models were the familiar essayists, and
his mode was evangelical journalism. But he had a "new
idea" once or twice, in *My Double, and How He Undid
Me,* and especially in *The Man Without a Country.* New
ideas are rare in story-telling, and Hale's Philip Nolan,
like Rip Van Winkle, became a folk-figure, a national
myth. That the story appeared at a moment when
patriotic feeling was at a pitch, when men like Thoreau,
whose interests were universal, felt for the first time that
they had a country, accounted for its impression on the
public mind; but it was a bold and fresh conception. Julia
Ward Howe, a banker's daughter from New York, a
clever and charming young woman with a passion for
learning, had met Dr. Howe, the teacher of the blind, on
one of her visits to Boston. He was riding on a black
horse, and she had straightway fallen in love with him.
Miss Julia Ward's friends in New York thought that her
pink stockings should have been blue, for she had herself
roped to her chair, in the manner of Alfieri, during her
hours of study. In Boston, they understood these matters better. As the universal reformer of the future, ready
for every new crop of "causes," almost the only person
who knew the New York "four hundred" as well as the
Boston "forty," she was a more gracious Margaret
Fuller.

Half a century later, Mrs. Howe and Dr. Hale had
become folk-figures in actual life. They were almost as
mythological as Philip Nolan, so many associations had
gathered about them. These were the days when every
child in Boston had sat on Dr. Hale's knee, when the
patriarch who looked like Homer was chaplain of the Senate at Washington and the romantic old sibyl, travelling

with her lecture, her cap and her laces tucked away in her hand-bag, recited the *Battle Hymn* on every occasion. They were the last leaves of the flowering thorn-bush, the Boston, historic, prehistoric, of the eighteen-forties and fifties. Dr. Holmes had fallen long before them, and Holmes had flowered late. He had outlived the life-span of Goldsmith when he appeared in prose in *The Atlantic*. No matter, the pear-trees had reassured him. Some were ripe at twenty, the Jargonelles, and one had to make the most of them when they were young, for their day was soon over. Others came into their perfect condition later. These were the autumn pears that lasted better than the summer fruit. Best of all were the Winter Nelis, hard and uninviting until all the rest of the pears had had their season. Long after the frost and snow had nipped and wrecked the orchards, the Winter Nelis got their glow and perfume. How much worm-eaten fruit, how many windfalls the doctor had seen under the boughs when the sap in his own tree was just beginning to stir!

Thus it was that, at the breakfast-table, the Autocrat resumed his seat one morning and found himself addressing his fellow-boarders, the schoolmistress, the divinity-student, the landlady's daughter, Benjamin Franklin, all the characters he had known so well, in Boston or the "huckleberry districts," during his lecture-tours. The boarding-house was a microcosm of a larger world, for what American did not find himself suggested in one of the characters? The Autocrat had earned his right to speak; he had plucked the flowers of life and come to the berries, and who could say that he was not a teacher fit for a great occasion, he who had fed with the fox in the matter of knowledge and used such Machiavellian astuteness in passing on all that he had learned? What was his mission? It was very simple: the mission of conversation. Was it not very bad to have thoughts and feelings, which ought to come out in talk, *strike in,*

as people said of certain diseases? There was the great
American evil, morbid introspection, class-distinctions
that were unconfessed, scruples of conscience, secrets that
ought to be exposed to common sense, forms of speech
and phrases, ugly and distorted, the outward and visible
signs of the twisted life within. Fruits of the old religion
of Calvinism, fruits of isolation and provincial conditions, fruits of unconscious living. Out with them, and talk
them over! The boarders knew they could trust a family
doctor who read them through and through, who saw
their maternal grandfathers in the way they held their
tea-cups, and who would never abuse their confidence, a
doctor who was used to dealing with secrets and who,
without hurting their feelings, could give them the right
prescription to set them on the road of mental health.

The boarders listened like a three-years' child. All
America had begun to listen, and well the doctor knew
it. Did people think that talk was merely a tool with
which to chop a path for one's primitive wants? Did they
think that absolute truth, in the form of rigidly stated
propositions, was all that conversation ought to admit?
Did they not see how difficult it was for two persons engaged in talk to make the most of each other's thoughts,
when both had so many? (Here the boarders stirred and
looked as if they wished for an explanation. They did not
know they had so many thoughts, never having put them
into words.) Conversation must have its partial truths,
even its exaggerated truths,—the boarders stirred again,
—if, as one of the fine arts, it is to serve a greater art,
the art of human relations. It must not merely express the
"logical mind" that builds a bridge of asses over chasms
that wit leaps across.

Thus, in his diplomatic way, the Autocrat attacked all
the mental habits of his hearers. What was this "logical
mind," the fruit of generations of preachers and lawyers,
but the One-Hoss Shay of Calvinism? The doctor had

no use for Calvinism, and he knew that, while they laughed at the one-hoss shay in Boston and at Harvard, it was no laughing matter in the country. He was determined to break it up,—if laughter failed, by other means, by quoting half a dozen sciences, by the use of analogies and comparisons, by every method but controversy, since controversy equalized the foolish and the wise and no one knew this better than the fools. For what was the "logical mind" of Calvinism but the parent of all injustice, the *a priori* and the *parti pris,* narrow judgment, rigid condemnation, all those moral plagues, in other words, from which the American mind so patently suffered? Did he mean to weaken moral obligations by drawing up the blinds of this dark chamber and letting in the light? His object was merely to define them; for the light he let into the dark chamber was the light of common sense, a doctor's view of the problem of cause and effect as it really expressed itself in human nature. Was some question of crime involved? The "logical mind" spoke of original sin and anathematized the doctor. The rational mind spoke of the effect and anathematized the cause. As for the fruits of the old religion, many of the minister's patients were fools and cowards, and all too many of them were also liars. (Immense sensation at the table.)

The doctor was prepared for the sensation. The religious weeklies and monthlies, all over the country, began to throw brickbats at him. The Autocrat was imperturbable. One cannot turn over any old falsehood without a terrible squirming and scattering of the unpleasant little population that dwells under it. No one can ever say anything to make his neighbours wiser or better without being abused for doing so; and, if there is one thing that people detest, it is to have their little mistakes made fun of. The Autocrat continued, with calm good humour, always ready to talk as long as a few boarders remained at the table, twirling their knives, perhaps, balancing their spoons on

the edge of their tea-cups or tilting on their chairs against
the wall. Was he named Holmes for nothing? A holme
is a meadow surrounded by brooks; and, as long as two
or three brooks, were they only trickles, fed it with their
attention, how could a meadow run dry? Now, these
little mistakes, this tilting of chairs against walls, this
pronouncing the name of one's town as if one did not
know that it ought to be "Norridge," this calling an entry
a "hall" and a buggy a "kerridge," this saying "Yes?"
when somebody told one something,—did they think these
vulgarisms were trivial matters? Was it not plain enough
that a man with a future had to get rid of all these odious
tricks? What hope could he have when he said "How's
your health?" when people liked to hear "How do you
do?" Did not Sydney Smith say that no public man in
England ever got over a false quantity uttered in early
life? And might it not be similarly said that the woman
who "calc'lates" is lost? Worldly wisdom, merely, not at
all the wisdom of the angels; but surely the woman who
"calc'lates" is not an angel, and, since she is given to calculating, she might calculate to better purpose. And what
was one to say about those rural visitors who do not know
how to get out of a room when their visit is really over?
They wish to be off, you wish them to be off, but they do
not know how to manage it. One would think they had
been built in one's parlour and were waiting to be
launched. One had to contrive for them a sort of cere-
monial inclined plane and back them down, stern foremost, so to speak, into the great ocean of out-of-doors.
What was one to say of the "terrible smile," the smile
of those persons whose mouths, the moment they see us,
begin to twitch with an uncertain movement, conveying
the idea that they are thinking about themselves and
thinking that we are thinking that they are thinking about
themselves? What was one to say of the pretty women
who do not understand the law of the road in regard to

handsome faces? Nature and custom agree, the Autocrat remarked, in granting all males the right of at least two distinct looks at every comely female countenance, one to define the person, one as an appreciating homage. The lady of whom he approved was she who left at home her virtuous-indignation countenance, knowing that the street is a picture-gallery where pretty faces framed in pretty hats are meant to be admired, and everybody has a right to see them.

Trifles, perhaps, but not unkindly mentioned. Was not the art of living made up of trifles? And were these awkward postures and rustic phrases as merely superficial as one might think? Were they not the signs of inner dislocations, the rigidities, false reserves, distortions, torments that render human relations so difficult and make men so unhappy? Expression was the greatest need of this unexpressed New England, which almost seemed to enjoy its cold and taciturn ways, ways that concealed what tragic depths! Emotions that can shape themselves in language open the gate for themselves into the great community of human affections. That was why the Autocrat loved words, expressive words, euphonious and pleasing, just as he loved song. As long as a woman could talk, or had some musical utterance, there was nothing that she could not bear. How many a tragedy had found its outlet in a strenuous bravura or a fierce roulade on one of Jonas Chickering's pianos! Therefore the Autocrat loved to hear the all-pervading tum-tum issuing from the window of the unlovely farmhouse, with the brown stream flowing beside the door, in which Almira or Louella might have been found floating, face downward, had she not been able, in these harmless discords, to throb her wild impulses away.

The boarders listened, all America listened, as the Autocrat unfolded his amusing wisdom, unrolled that inexhaustible scroll which only those possess who have kept

their wits alive by constant use. Never had they heard
of such a man for breaking up the ice of mental habits,
for harrowing people's minds and planting in them flowers that out-shone even "Macaulay-flowers." They listened round the table, reading *The Atlantic,* drawing
virtue from it, as hot water draws the strength of tea-
leaves; for society, as the Autocrat said, is a strong solu-
tion of books. The old gentleman opposite smiled
benignly, and Benjamin Franklin gathered some valuable
hints. As for the theological remarks, the divinity-student
honoured himself by the way in which he received them:
he did not swallow them at once, neither did he reject
them, but he took them as a pickerel takes the bait. He
carried them off to his cranny upstairs to ruminate over
them at leisure. The schoolmistress pondered these things
in her heart and presently passed them on to her flock.
All Young America, sooner or later, heard her say that
"those who ask your opinion really want your praise and
will be contented with nothing less." Did she not remark,
"Sin has many tools, but a lie is the handle which fits them
all"? Did she not refer to the cubes and spheres, the little
cubes of Truth that are always white and the spheres that
have "lie" written on them but that roll so easily and so
pleasantly, although they are always rolling into the
wrong corner? One had no real excuse for mistaking the
cubes, because they always stayed where they were left;
but Timidity and Good-Nature and Polite-Behaviour insisted that Truth must roll, and they filed and polished
away the snow-white cubes till one could hardly tell them
from the spheres,—a sad mistake, since Truth is always
square. No doubt, there were members of the rising generation who did not hear this fable in their youth; but
they were not born under the Stars and Stripes.

For schoolmistresses, Dr. Holmes had a tender feeling.
He was well aware of the part they played in a nation and
generation in which the men shirked the tasks of culture.

Who but the schoolmistress, and usually the New England of the species, followed the pioneers wherever they went, even to the remotest corner of the Rocky Mountains, and sowed the furrows they ploughed with the seeds of education which, but for her, would have remained unsown? Well the doctor knew this heroism, and he knew it imposed on the heroine a biological handicap. "The great procession of the Unloved" filled him with compassion, for he was a match-maker on all occasions. Besides, they belonged, as often as not, to the Brahmin caste of New England, that mystical brotherhood and sisterhood in which the doctor took a special pride and which he was the first to designate. He grieved when people supposed that he meant by the Brahmins a bloated Boston aristocracy. His innocent and serviceable caste was no such thing. Its members were commonly sensitive, pallid and shy, and their only birthright was a taste for learning. Bred from races of scholars, descended from gentle souls who had stepped off the "Mayflower" or the "Arbella" with books in their hands, races that had acquired, by the repetition, generation after generation, of the same unworldly influences, a distinct organization and facial type, they took to their books at school as a pointer or a setter to his field-work. Their names were constantly rising to prominence in connection with some learned labour, and the nation owed to their devotion countless unrequited benefits. Indeed, they were a caste to which only a niggard could wish to refuse a decent homage; for, in exchange for all their lofty efforts, what were their worldly claims, their prescriptive titles?—that they wore white linen by inherited instinct, that they were able to pronounce the sacred word "view," a word not to be spelled or, by others, pronounced, the touchstone of New England Brahminism. Dr. Holmes was not to be blamed if other times brought other customs, if, in days to come, the Brahmins ceased to per-

form their function and, in proportion as they lost their
vigour, advanced their worldly claims.

Everybody listened to the Autocrat, except a little group
of thinkers who also described themselves as Humanists.
Perhaps they were not in the room when he remarked:
"Beware of making your moral staple consist of the negative virtues. It is good to abstain, and teach others to abstain, from all that is sinful and harmful. But making a
business of it leads to emaciation of character, unless one
feeds largely also on the more nutritious diet of active,
sympathetic benevolence." Perhaps this little group considered the doctor frivolous, with his marked distaste for a
"soul-subduing decorum." But everyone else was prepared
to listen when he wrote a novel, *Elsie Venner;* for he had
long believed that every intelligent man had the stuff of a
novel in him, and therefore why not he? In fact, he wrote
three novels, as he wrote three books about the breakfast-
table, proving his theory about continuations, that they
were not always justified. Good jockeying, he thought, was
important for authors. One should let the public see one's
horse only just enough and not too much, hold him up
hard when the market was too full of him, always gently
feel his mouth, never slack and never jerk the rein. He
let his own horse out only when the horse grew too impatient, and sometimes with not too much success. His
novels were "medicated novels"; and, as the doctor was
always a talker, he strolled about from page to page, airing his views about his characters, dismissing them at times
with a turn of the hand as if they were so many cases at a
medical meeting. His composition was very untidy. But he
always had a new story, even when it was only a ghost of a
story, as in the breakfast-table series, and he always had
a problem to deal with,—hysteria in a young girl, a young
man's misogyny, morbid religious excitement and its effects. There were happy streaks in all his writings, and
striking applications of modern science; and his essay on

Mechanism in Thought and Morals, the "underground workshop of thought,"—the unconscious,—was a brilliant anticipation of Dr. Freud. In fact, although *Elsie Venner,* of all these later books, was the only one that seriously counted, the doctor knew so much about human nature, and had such a tang of his own, that one could read him at his worst with pleasure.

He was always putting two and two together, and *Elsie Venner* stood for a large sum in this species of multiplication. He had taken one of his twos from the old medical books over which he was constantly poring, Schenckius, Andreas Baccius and Cardan, books that amused the imagination. They were full of Æsculapian gossip concerning girls who had fed on poison and who acted out the influence of the poison, gossip about men, bitten by serpents, who became the fathers of daughters whom serpents could not harm, however the daughters might mistreat the serpents. *Christabel* and Keats's *Lamia* were favourites with the doctor; and recent experiments had seemed to suggest that snake-bites might produce an influence over the moral faculties of the victim. But all these mythical and half-mythical data merely served to fertilize the doctor's fancy. He was out for larger game when he imagined the beautiful, cold girl with the glittering eyes who was destined for a tragic end, the gliding, sliding Elsie, with diamonds on her breast, and her asp-like bracelet, and the barred skirts in which she liked to dance, to the rhythm of castanets. She was still and dangerous and watchful, silent in her anger and swift in vengeance, and the village folk believed that she was able to twist herself into all sorts of shapes and tie herself in a knot. In short, she suggested the rattlesnake that Dr. Holmes kept in his cage; and the story was that a snake had bitten her mother, just before Elsie was born. Was it a case of physical cause and effect? How could any honest doctor say so, even if he liked to tease his readers? Besides, there were plenty of Elsies in New England whose mothers had not been bitten by rattle-snakes. Several of them had been hanged as witches; and who but Margaret Fuller had narrowed her lids, just as Elsie did, till her eyes were small and bright as diamonds? The doctor was interested indeed in the subject of prenatal influences, but not in quite so simple a way as this. He wished to test the doctrine of original sin, which was still raging in New England, or, to place it on a larger ground, the doctrine of human responsibility for the aberrations of a disordered will. Was Elsie "shapen in iniquity," as the farmers and the country parsons thought? Not if one saw her life as the doctor saw it and did his best to make his readers see it. Was she a subject for wrath or a subject for pity? The rattlesnake's bite was only a figure of speech for any kind of untoward circumstance,—a couple of drunken grandfathers, abuse in childhood,—that might explain anyone's aberrations of will. If one saw this clearly in Elsie's case, what about all the other unhappy creatures who were born with poison in their system?

This time the doctor cast a bombshell into the circle of his fellow-boarders. Every breakfast-table in the country resounded with *Elsie Venner*. Were you a Unitarian or a Calvinist, or any other variety of Jew or Christian, were you interested in the recent theories about heredity and environment, in medical and therapeutic questions, philosophy, criminology, education? Then *Elsie Venner* had something to say to you, and sometimes it was not a pleasant message. If, as a good Unitarian, you liked to think of the soul as an "unstained white tablet," then Elsie with her wicked little powders was an awkward nut to crack. The question whether Elsie could help herself was even more of a dose for the Orthodox. If you were a Pharisee, you fared still worse; for, if Elsie was not responsible, if she could not be accused of sin,—however one might punish her for crime,—what became of your own pretensions? Were you not obliged to see that your valour and justice, your strength, truth and virtue were merely the result of your happy fortune? What was your aristocracy but a sum that began with a one in tar and a two in tallow, and perhaps a three in whale-oil, however maintained by pluck? Your elevated type of face and figure were due not to you and your father's virtue, beyond a certain measure, but to the money made from the tar and the tallow that bought the air and sunshine, the healthy, happy summers, the good nursing and doctoring, the best cuts of the best beef and mutton, which enabled your father, and his father and his, to grow up in such a kindly fashion and, when they were grown, to afford the costly luxury of beauty and marry the finest specimens of the other sex. This train of reasoning went a long way when the valour and the truth, strength and virtue were so obviously poisoned *out* of a race by the food of the bushman in his forest, by the foul air and darkness of the tenement-houses where half one's fellow-Christians were constrained to live. Just how far it went, the doctor might not have cared to think, for the "sunny street that holds the sifted few," the "swell-fronts and south-exposure houses" had a singular charm for him, as for other mortals, and the people who lived inside these houses were not only just as good as other people but the pleasantest for a doctor to take care of. "Why not take the tops of your sparrowgrass? Somebody must have 'em,—why shouldn't you?" Such was the doctor's advice to a young disciple; and, in fact, he never pretended to be a sage, too lofty for these trifles. He knew that a certain amount of glass was mingled with the bricks in the house he lived in, a knowledge that disarmed the caster of pebbles; and meanwhile he had discharged a thunderbolt that fairly rocked the walls of Philistinism. Who, after reading *Elsie Venner*, could talk about "total depravity"? Who was to condemn? Who to judge? Or pride himself too much on his family portraits? Or think that God had given him his lands and chattels in recognition of his Christian virtue? Dr. Holmes, perhaps unwittingly, had played into the hands of Dr. Darwin. He had played into the hands of Dr. Freud. He had played into the hands of another doctor of whom he had never heard, Dr. Marx. One never knows how far a doctor's table-talk may carry him.

CHAPTER XXVII

THE SATURDAY CLUB:
LOWELL'S ESSAYS

PRESCOTT died in 1859. Almost totally blind, at the last, and racked with rheumatism, able to read only a few lines in the artificial twilight of his dark blue curtains, lying flat on the floor, with his noctograph before him, when any other posture was impossible, he had never ceased to work at the vast *History of Philip II,* of which three volumes were completed. "My spirits," he said, "are always as high as my pulse, about fifteen points above normal." He was merry and laughing as usual a day before the end. Longfellow's last remembrance of Prescott was a sunny smile at the corner of the street.

The faithful Ticknor, inconsolable, recalled the happy times at Pepperell, the drives and walks with Prescott in the "Fairy Grove" or along the Nashua river, when they had filled the woods with their laughter, the evenings when they had read *The Antiquary,* with two generations of children to share the pleasure. At Lynn, where Prescott had also had a villa, looking over the water towards Nahant, an old cherry-tree stood near the house. Round and round this tree, to protect his eyes in the shade, Prescott had walked every day until he had worn a path in the greensward. The traces of this path remained for years, worn by no foot but his, while Ticknor, touched by all these memories, slowly composed his *Life of Prescott.* This was a rare biography, picturesque and circumstantial. New England had produced no other that could be placed beside it; for Ticknor's affection for his subject had brought out all the skill, the gift for observation and characterization that made his own Jour-nal so entertaining. The unfinished *Philip II* contained some of Prescott's most splendid writing, the Battle of Lepanto, the Siege of Malta. It was a history of Europe in the latter half of the sixteenth century, when the doc-trines of the Reformation were dividing the world; and Prescott had had to spread his investigations over the whole continent. On his visit to Europe in 1850, he had spent several weeks in Belgium and Holland, studying the topography of the country, the scenes of Philip's reign, the spot where William the Silent had fallen at Delft. He had had the help of Pasqual de Gayangos, the great professor of Arabic at Madrid, who translated Ticknor into Spanish. Gayangos searched for him the manuscript collection of Sir Thomas Phillips, twelve thousand pages, gathered in boxes and closets in Phillips's house, some of them under his bed; and Prince Corsini also assisted Prescott, collecting documents in Italy. The archives of Simancas, which no historian had even seen, Philip II's own original papers, two hundred and eighty-four dusty bundles, rolled up at random, that lay like bottles of forgotten wine in the lumber-room of a Span-ish castle, were sorted and scrutinized for him, along with the archives of Leyden, the Hague and Paris. In all, there were eight thousand sheets to be turned into threads for the Gobelin-loom in Boston, where the tire-less Prescott wove his tapestry.

Never again perhaps were historical works to excite so much attention as at present. A generation later, Parkman's great books appeared in little editions of seven hundred copies. Only a handful of readers noticed them. Prescott's *Conquest of Mexico,* a large and expen-sive work in three volumes, had sold four thousand copies in four months, and *Philip II,*—like *Charles V,* Robertson's famous work, which Prescott revised and continued, to fill the gap in Spanish history between Ferdinand and Philip,—was published in England in four simultaneous editions. These splendidly printed books,—for Prescott and Ticknor took pains to appear in the grand manner, —put Peter Parley out of countenance; and the interest in history grew with the interest in public affairs, which were rapidly shaping for the Civil War. Ticknor had returned from his last European journey, with a great new collection of books for Boston. The rival Astor Library in New York, with Cogswell at its head, had filled him with apprehension. Unless something similar were done in Boston, the literary culture of New England would follow trade and capital to the rapidly-growing metropolis. Ticknor had taken the lead for the Boston Public Library, collected lists of necessary books from every interested citizen, established agencies in Florence and Leipzig and bought books in London, Paris and Rome. He had made Boston, once for all, a centre of historical research.

Prescott's example had also had its effect. He had won for Boston the interest of historians everywhere and had opened up facilities for others; and his winning personality and heroic labours made history still more attractive to younger men. Of his own generation, Bancroft, who had withdrawn for a while from public life, carried on his work from volume to volume. He had long since settled in New York, but he kept a place in New England for his household gods, a summer villa at Newport, "Roseclyff." There he planted his fruit-trees and took special pride in his roses. He corresponded with rosarians all over the world. Every evening, at Newport, he read to the ladies of his household the pages he had written during the day, asking for suggestions in regard to style; for the more the flowers grew in his garden, the more he plucked them out of his prose, which soon became monotonous and bare. Everett, who had helped both Prescott and Bancroft, had also retired from politics, adopted a coat-of-arms for a bookplate,—which he was happy to find reproduced on the china and glass of the Everett House in New York,—and withdrawn to his "temple of peace" on Summer Street. His brief term as president of Harvard had not been too agreeable, for the kindly old soul, as vain as he was kind, had grieved because the undergraduates did not touch their hats to him enough. But the aging figurehead of the Boston ship, beaten by so many storms, made of soft pine instead of oak, still Apollonian in its wrinkled beauty, was ready for another voyage. Fearing that a civil war was coming, Everett did what he could to stave it off. Washington's house at Mount Vernon was dropping to pieces. The columns of the portico were falling, the offices were in ruins, the floor of the summer-house was gone, there were pales missing from the staircase. The magnolias had been whittled away by tourists and even the tomb was in decay. Everett, who had tried in vain to save Franklin's early home in Boston, hoped to unite the North and the South in one last touch of common sentiment. He composed an oration on Washington, which he delivered in every part of the country, and helped to save Mount Vernon with the proceeds. The day had passed for Everett's oratory, but there were always crowds to applaud a speaker who held his glass of water aloft and slowly and dexterously spilled it as he spoke of the cleanliness of Washington's soul.

The wheel of time had turned again. On winter afternoons, in Beacon Street, when George Ticknor passed, strolling in the sunlight, with his air of conscious importance, one recalled the days of Gilbert Stuart. The renaissance in Boston had scarcely existed for Ticknor. It scarcely existed for the elder Dana, the author of *The Idle Man,* who had outlived his little fame and whom

one also saw, on sunny days, warming his bones in the
Common, although the Saturday Club, recently organized
by the younger writers,—touched by his charm and silvery courtesy,—elected him an honorary member. The
old guard looked askance at the reigning talents, which
were too informal to please them. Emerson's high-flown
manner offended them still. They did not like Holmes's
style, his way of referring to "Roxbury and Dorchester
boys." This made the younger people feel akin, but it
struck their elders as too familiar. It was almost as bad
as Whittier, so plain that he might have been common.
Lowell was too clever to be sound. If Burke and Johnson
were no longer read, what was more to blame than
Lowell's brilliance? * Thackeray had scandalized Boston, on his reading-tour, by driving to the lecture-hall
with his long legs thrust out of the carriage-window. His
friends had had to repress his jollity, as he ploughed
through the snow on Beacon Street with *Henry Esmond,*
just issued, under his arm. The old Bostonians knew that
Englishmen often behaved like this, but they had never
expected to see a Boston man cutting undignified capers;
and Lowell's puns and Holmes's boarding-house almost
savoured of the vulgar.

The temperature, if not the tone, had risen; and no
one from other regions ever complained that the Boston
tone was low. When Thackeray wrote to Fields, "I always consider Boston my native place," he was referring
to the temperature, the warm and genial air of the Yankee Athens in these days of its efflorescence. Agassiz's
beaming face at the Saturday Club, and Longfellow,
benign, all unconscious of the spell he wove, at the other
end of the table, set the pitch of the gatherings. If the
club had not existed, Dr. Holmes would have invented
it, for such an association, in his opinion,—a club strung

---

* Professor Bowen, editor of the *North American Review,* rejected
Lowell's earlier essays because they were "too brilliant."

like a harp, with a dozen ringing intelligences, each answering to some chord of the macrocosm,—was the crown of a literary centre. What would literature and art have been if Shakespeare had not had his Mermaid Tavern, and Addison and Steele their coffee-house, not to speak of Dr. Johnson, Goldsmith and Gibbon? It was one of the doctor's convictions that a handful of men, at any given moment, carry in their brains the ovarian eggs of the future, and that one should talk with them in order to seize in advance these germs of thought, not yet developed, germs that were moulded on new patterns which had to be long and closely studied. For no fresh truth ever got into a book: an egg once hatched was already old. There were jobbers of thought and retailers of thought; but he wished to know the producers of thought. That was why he loved his club so dearly. One could listen to Asa Gray on botany, Peirce on mathematics and Lowell on language, Agassiz on geology and fossils, Motley on history, Norton on cathedrals. If one followed for a dozen years any line of knowledge, every other line would intersect it; and here all the lines intersected, the doctor was happy to find,—in this carnival-shower of questions, replies and comments, axioms bowled over the table like bomb-shells from professional mortars, while wit dropped its explosive trains of many-coloured fire and pelted everyone who exposed himself. Emerson enjoyed the club for much the same reasons. Of the lonely men of Concord, he was the only member, with Judge Hoar, who drew any virtue from the meetings; for Hawthorne, who joined the club after his return from Italy, sat with his eyes fixed upon his plate. Thoreau's feeling in regard to clubs might have been described as detached.* But Emerson, who said that he fed on genius

---

* "As for the Parker House, I went there once, when the Club was away, but I found it hard to see through the cigar smoke; and men were deposited about in chairs over the marble floor, as thick as legs of bacon in a smoke-house. It was all smoke, and no salt, Attic or other. The only room

and who liked to see feats of every kind, feats of mathematical combination, of memory and the power of abstraction, who rejoiced in a gymnasium and a swimming-
school, where one saw the power of the body, a
race-course, a training-ground for horses, a laboratory, a
surgeon's demonstration, who never heard of any skill or
vigour without fresh resolution,—Emerson sat like a
child at the meetings. Every word that was dropped set
free his fancy. He talked, but rarely; he preferred to
listen.* His was Goethe's gift, the "highest to which man
can attain," wonder.

Lowell walked in from Cambridge to his office at *The
Atlantic*. Once his hat blew into the river, as he was
crossing the bridge, with a hatful of rejected manuscripts.
He scarcely had to look for his contributions beyond the
Boston, Cambridge and Concord circles. The Porter-
house steak at the Porter House, the Parker-house rolls
at the Parker House, guinea-fowl and venison on all occasions, and wine, "the grand specific against dull dinners,"
as Dr. Holmes called it, sped the festive enterprise; and
even the abstemious author of *Snow-Bound,* who had
never entered a theatre and who cared as little for dinners as the men of Concord, caught the contagion of the
magazine and grew more and more the man of letters.
Lowell published a series of Agassiz's essays, which
spread the popular knowledge of science. A poem that

in Boston which I visit with alacrity is the gentlemen's waiting-room at
the Fitchburg depot, where I wait for the cars, sometimes for two hours, to
get out of town. It is a paradise to the Parker House . . . A large and respectable club of us hire it (Town and Country Club), and I am pretty
sure to find someone there whose face is set the same way as my own."—
Thoreau, *Familiar Letters.*

* "I sat by the side of Emerson, who always charms me with his delicious voice, his fine sense and wit, and the delicate way he steps about
among the words of his vocabulary,—if you have seen a cat picking her
footsteps in wet weather, you have seen the picture of Emerson's exquisite
intelligence, feeling for its phrase or epithet,—sometimes I think of an ant-
eater, singling out his insects, as I see him looking about and at last seizing his noun or adjective,—the best, the only one which would serve the
need of his thought."—*Life and Letters of Oliver Wendell Holmes.*

attracted much attention, *On a Bust of Dante,* was the
work of a Boston dentist, Thomas W. Parsons. It was a
good poem, although notable chiefly as an expression of
the *zeitgeist,* the ever-growing interest in Dante studies.
Dr. Parsons, at seventeen, had spent a year in Italy,
where he had formed his life-long love of Dante. He had
learned the *Paradiso* by heart in Florence and had translated the *Inferno* years before Norton began his studies.*
Some of his other poems were good, especially *The
Shadow on the Obelisk.* They represented a kind of verse,
graceful and correct, that was rapidly multiplying. Often
the expression of poetic natures, of cultivated and scholarly minds, usually written with taste but almost if not
quite devoid of magic, this verse, which would have
seemed miraculous a generation before, was a staple of
every journal in later days.† In the country towns, as in
the Western cities, thousands of eager faces, by the
evening lamp, scanned each new issue of *The Atlantic,*
thrilled by a new poem of Whittier or Lowell, perplexed
by Emerson's cryptic rhymes. "If the red slayer think he
slays" was better than a hundred cross-word puzzles. A
paper by Thomas Wentworth Higginson, *Letter to a
Young Contributor,* fluttered a breast in Amherst that
was to sing to better purpose than most of the famous
poets of the eighteen-sixties. To Emily Dickinson, "moving to Cambridge" seemed "like moving to Westminster
Abbey, as hallowed and as unbelieved, or moving to
Ephesus with Paul for a next-door neighbour."

Cambridge still had much of the village look. A mighty
elm shaded Harvard Square, and the groups of youths
and maidens in summer dresses who danced on the green,

* A copy of Parsons's *Inferno,* translated in 1843, was placed under the
cornerstone of the monument to Dante in the Piazza Santa Croce.

† American poetry has had its own "law of acceleration." Rufus W.
Griswold, the anthologist, said that he had read all the American poetry
published before 1850. He estimated this at about five hundred volumes.
Three generations later, at least as many volumes appeared every year.

on Class Day, in front of Holworthy Hall, brought back the May Day of merry England. Old Royal Morse, the driver of the stage in the days of President Kirkland, still haunted the square to tell his tales of a time when President Kirkland had scarcely been heard of. Agassiz strolled across the Yard, smoking his cigar, oblivious of the university statutes. Agassiz represented all that was new. Old Cambridge was John Holmes's special province. For Dr. Holmes's shy and modest brother, whose occupation was friendship, the period since 1832 was "margin" and sometimes "leavings." A "ripe local man," as he wished to be, he lived in a little house on Appian Way, full of cats and birds. "I sha'n't have better quarters," he said, "till I have a better half." For a bit of foreign travel, he went to Nantasket. He even made three short trips to Europe, where he could find nothing to compare with Cambridge. Every day in Venice he repaired to a spot that reminded him of a corner of the port, where Broadway and Cambridge Street met. Besides an occasional poem, he wrote a series of letters to one of his nephews about Goliath Tittle, the Kennebunk sailor. Goliath was tattooed in circles by a tribe in the South Sea Islands, and then he was captured by another tribe who changed all the circles into squares. John Holmes's only ventures into print were addressed to esoterics in Cambridge lore, those who could answer the following questions: "Where was the old Court House? The old jail? The Market House? Where was the college wood-yard? Where was the old hay-scales? Where was the little brook that ran over gravel toward the Charles and, like the two princes, was stifled in its bed?"

In Cambridge, as in Concord, where the "little women" and the "little men" were about to appear in books, children filled the scene. All the New England writers understood them and wrote about them, sometimes with exquisite feeling.* *Uncle Tom's Cabin* was composed, under the lamp, on a table surrounded by children conning their lessons, in a hum of earnest voices asking questions. Hawthorne's stories were as full of children as ever the summer woods were filled with birds; and Whittier's shy affections and Holmes's salty humours were addressed as often as not to boys and girls. Lowell, so self-conscious in most of his letters, only showed how deep his feelings were in these domestic relations. Perhaps they were deep only in these relations, like the feelings of Henry James. In later times, when boys and girls were "problems," and most of their fathers and mothers were also problems, more problematic than the children, when the old cultural forms had broken down, and literature was produced by childless rebels,—or largely so produced,—against the abuses of the older culture in the hour of its rigidity and decay, when the nation had lost much of its faith and even so much of its will-to-live that "race-suicide" was a pressing question, one found it difficult to return in fancy to Longfellow's "children's hour," when life flowed so freely between the generations. This ever-present consciousness of children, in minds so unconscious of themselves, spoke for a culture at its highest tide, a community that believed in itself, serenely sure of itself and sure of its future, eager to perpetuate its forms.

Longfellow had bought an orange-tree, with a hundred buds and blossoms. It flourished in his window beside the lemon-tree, which, for the last ten years, had kept the

---

* "Pliable as she was to all outward appearance, the child had her own still, interior world, where all her little notions and opinions stood up crisp and fresh, like flowers that grow in cool, shady places. If anybody too rudely assailed a thought or suggestion she put forth, she drew it back again into this quiet inner chamber and went on. . . . There is no independence and pertinacity like that of these seemingly soft, quiet creatures, whom it is so easy to silence, and so difficult to convince."—Harriet Beecher Stowe, *The Pearl of Orr's Island*.

See also Emerson's remarks on children, in the opening paragraphs of his essay, *Domestic Life*.

summer blooming through the winter in his white-panelled study. A springtime fragrance of Italy filled the
room. On his table stood Coleridge's ink-stand, the gift
of an English admirer. A Tintoretto hung near by. One
saw an agate cup of Cellini. The folding doors opened
into the spacious library, with its two Corinthian columns. There was something large, bland and sweet,
something fresh and sunny in the atmosphere of the house
that reflected the soul of the generous poet, he whom
neither fame nor the praise of kings could ever spoil or
alter. A fathomless calm of innocent goodness brooded
in the air that spread with Longfellow's poems over the
world.* Nothing disturbed the poet's magnanimous mildness, neither the vanity that he never knew nor the fools
whom he suffered gladly. By no effort of any man could
any malicious phrase be drawn from his lips. Were you
pulling some rhymester to pieces, Longfellow had culled
and was ready to quote, in the poor bard's favour, the
only good line he had **ever** written. Did you beg him not
to waste his time on the cranks who were always beset-
ting him. "Who would be kind to him if I were not?"
was Longfellow's only possible answer. As his fame
spread like the morning sun over the English-speaking
peoples, with its notes of domestic affection and the love
of the sea, of landscape and legend, till twenty-four English publishing-houses brought out his work in competition and ten thousand copies of *The Courtship of Miles
Standish* were sold in London in a single day, as the
royalties of his poems rose till they rivalled those of
Byron and even those which, in ancient Rome, Tiberius
lavished on his poetasters,—four hundred thousand
sesterces for a dialogue,—the flood of interruptions be-

---

* "I had many things to say about the sense I have of the good you
might do this old world by staying with us a little, and giving the peaceful glow of your fancy to our cold, troubled, unpeaceful spirit. Strange,
that both you and Norton come as such *calm* influences to me and others."
—Ruskin to Longfellow.

came so great that he longed for a snow-storm to block
the door. A stranger who came to see Washington's
rooms asked him if Shakespeare did not live near by.
Some of his visitors thought he was greater than Shakespeare. An Englishman stopped to see him because there
were no American ruins to visit. Longfellow smiled when
a Frenchman asked him for *révelations intimes* regarding
his domestic life, to appear in a Paris newspaper; but he
gave a loaf of bread to every beggar, even when the
beggars, disappointed, left the loaves upright on his gate-
post. Now and then a great man came of whom Longfellow had never heard but who had heard of Longfellow,
perhaps in Russia. One day, in 1861, Bakunin arrived at
noon. He had escaped from Siberia. Longfellow asked
him to stay to lunch. "Yiss, and I will dine with you,
too," Bakunin replied, and he stayed till almost midnight. There was another Cambridge tableau.

Walking in his garden, among the birds, to the trill-
ing of the frogs in his pond, like the chorus of a Grecian
tragedy, Longfellow revolved in his mind the stories he
was telling his children, passing them on to a larger
world that was an extension of his household. He told
them with a childlike air of trust, as if he knew in advance that the listening earth shared his faith in true
love and homeland, his hatred of cruelty and his joy in
nature,—the humble sweetness of a courteous heart. He
ranged, in the *Tales of a Wayside Inn,*—the old Sudbury
tavern, on the post-road to New York, where he assembled, in fancy, in imitation of Chaucer, some of his
friends, the poet, Dr. Parsons, the Sicilian, Luigi Monti,
the landlord, Mr. Howe,—over New England, Norway,
Italy, Spain. Most of these tales were of the pretty kind
in which the romantic poets abounded. Longfellow, who
liked to say, "To stay at home is best," who had nothing
of the adventurous in him and did not like extremes or
excess, the extreme of heat, the extreme of cold, treated

the tragic in the tales with the guileless impassivity of
a Florentine monk picturing the miseries of the damned.
He, whose eye had never missed an old stone church or a
winding lane, an unusual tree, a wall, a crumbling house,
in his own American country, by which to endow the
scene with associations, paused at every page of the story-
book of history and read it again aloud with a smile of
his own. But in the New England stories, *Paul Revere's
Ride, The Courtship of Miles Standish,*—"full of the
name and the fame of the Puritan maiden Priscilla,"—
another tone appeared in his voice. He spoke with a
spirit or a tender conviction that sprang from the blood
within him. One heard this note in *My Lost Youth;* one
heard it in the sea-poems, the ballad of *The Cumberland,
The Warden of the Cinque Ports.* One heard it in *The
Saga of King Olaf,* the songs of the Norsemen. In these
runes and rhymes one heard

> the ocean's dirges,
> When the old harper heaves and rocks,
> His hoary locks
> Flowing and flashing in the surges!

Longfellow's soul was not an ocean. It was a lake,
clear, calm and cool. The great storms of the sea never
reached it. And yet this lake had its depths. Buried cities
lay under its surface. One saw the towers and domes
through the quiet water; one even seemed to catch the
sound of church-bells ringing like the bells of the city of
Is. Transparent as this mind was, there were profundities
of moral feeling beneath the forms through which it
found expression, the fruits of an old tradition of Puritan culture, and, behind this culture, all that was noble
in the Northern races. If Longfellow's poetic feeling had
had the depth of his moral feeling, he would have been
one of the major poets, instead of the "chief minor poet

of the English language,"—a phrase of Arnold Bennett's
that strikes one as happy, if "minor" is understood as
"popular," popular in the high sense, not the machine-
made popular of later times. Longfellow's flaccidity debarred him from the front rank; but his work possessed
a quality, a unity of feeling and tone, that gave him a
place apart among popular poets. Of all the sons of the
New England morning, save only the lonely men of Concord, he was the largest in his golden sweetness.

In Lowell, too, there was something large, or, shall
one rather say, robust; for the noble unconscious New
England of old had begun its decline in Lowell. The
"clever" note that had appeared in his earlier verse and
prose, along with Holmes's cleverness, was the first
streak of decay in the "high-caste tulip"; and Lowell,
unlike Holmes, was self-consciously clever. Something
uneasy and insecure lurked in the depths of his soul. The
serene aplomb of Longfellow, Prescott and Holmes,
well-seasoned men of the world, the equipoise of Emerson and Hawthorne, citizens of the over-world, was just
the thing he never knew. His judgment seemed to have
no bottom. He never struck a balance between his radicalism and his Tory instincts.* His schoolmasterish
pleasure in snubbing others, one of the unlovelier traits
of the Cambridge mind,†—so marked that Ruskin protested against his "all-knowing attitude," ‡ was matched
by his capacity for feeling snubbed by those whose superiority he recognized. Emerson, Longfellow, Hawthorne never felt, as reflecting on themselves or their

* "I would not give up a thing that had roots to it, though it might suck
up its food from graveyards."

† "What a delightful, generous and human sound Dr. Holmes's letters
have, especially in contrast to the self-conscious Lowell. It makes one understand father's enthusiasm for the Doctor, who, he used to say, was worth
all the men in the club put together; and how indignant he used to be
with Lowell's manner of snubbing him, and admiring of the perfect way
the Doctor took it."—*Journal of Alice James.*

‡ "Lowell speaks of Dante as if Dante were a forward schoolboy, and
Lowell his master."—Ruskin to Norton.

country, the "certain condescension in foreigners" that troubled Lowell all his life. When foreigners "condescend," the weakness lies in the foreigners, for condescension is a form of weakness; whatever else it also means, it signifies an inferior understanding. Lowell could never feel this. A sense that he had been patronized lay behind the animus that made him a "defiant American," * when he was minister to England. The English knew why he was defiant, and the Romans of Rome who had known the Romans of Spain knew that Lowell was not one of them. He was uncertain of his own values. Something in him doubted the ground he walked on, and this accounted for the painful way,—painful because it was so self-conscious,—in which, in later years, he "wore a top-hat and looked askance at the Common." † Lowell must have blushed when his eye fell on the sentence, in his essay on condescending foreigners, "I am a man of the New World and do not know precisely the present fashion of Mayfair,"—in the days when he had abandoned the "round hat and sack-coat business" and wished Howells to "feel all the honour" involved in the admiration of "some titles" who had enjoyed his books.‡

This draws the curtain of another age, the age that followed the Civil War. "One thing seems clear to me," Lowell wrote, when the new age was under way, "and that is that the Americans I remember fifty years ago had a consciousness of standing firmer on their own feet and in their own shoes than those of the newer generation. We are vulgar now precisely because we are afraid of being so." § Lowell, who was referring to Henry James, included himself in the "we" with a measure of reason. The high-caste tulip was in full decay, in these days of

* Leslie Stephen.
† John Jay Chapman.
‡ Howells, *Literary Friends and Acquaintance.*
§ Letter of Lowell, 1870.

the "furtive apology," * when people forgave the self-
conscious because it was conscious, forgetting that the
noble is only noble when it is unconscious. All that was
grand in the older America, the simple elevation, the
magnanimous faith, which Lowell had praised in his essay
on Quincy, withdrawn from the foreground of the national mind, had passed into the keeping of the Remnant,
—the Remnant that hides in its bosom the esoteric values
of the race. The soil took its revenge on the Yankee
mind, as the Yankee mind abandoned the soil. The Yankee mind ceased to be proud of its country,—that is to
say, in a measure, since all these things are relative,—for
a rootless race has no country; and, having lost its basis,
it lost its values. Then the values of England resumed
their sway, as nature abhors a vacuum. There were other
elements in the situation that became significant in later
times, when urban life spread, with its special demands,
and the old American social forms, adequate for a patriarchal world, could not meet the new requirements. The
"problem" of Henry James was more complex than any
problem that Lowell encountered; but Lowell, whose
roots had never been deeply planted, as the roots of the
men of Concord were, whose youth had been fundamen-
tally literary, foreshadowed the beginning of the end of
the old New England culture. The weakness of his position, evident from the first, was reflected in his verse and
prose, the rhetorical factitiousness of most of his poems,
the exalted commonplace, so essentially empty, of most
of his political writings. His essays on democracy, written after the Civil War, inspired a generation of credulous readers, who had lost their sense of fundamental
values. To later ears, his sentiments rang hollow. What
reality could there have been in the democratic feelings
of a man who said, when he had had a taste of England,

* Robert Grant, in reference to Henry James.

that his servants were "to do as they were bid"? * Those who do not profess to be democratic can assume this attitude with a whole-souled coolness. In Lowell's tone one feels the irritation that springs from an accusing conscience. "Harsh is he that is new at his lordship," Æschylus remarked, and he might have been speaking of a bookman who had become an ambassador. Such a phrase on the lips of a man like Lowell brings to the ground with a crash many balloons of rhetoric.

But this was only an aspect of Lowell. Lacking the largeness of the whole-souled men, he had his own ingenuousness and warmth. He had a dozen literary virtues and practised them in all sincerity. It was a pity that he went to England. He was not sufficiently mature. In this, his case resembled Motley's. The ambassadorial habit, to which American writers are prone, has spoiled many a good man of letters who was not well-seasoned enough to survive the test. Emerson or Holmes, as minister to England, would have remained the men they were before. The adventure relaxed the fibres of Motley and Lowell, who had an exaggerated sense of the value of honours and the "flattering conditions of life abroad," as Lowell described them to Howells. Neither of them wrote as well after the experience as before it. Motley might have been another Gibbon, he could certainly have been another Prescott, if, instead of spending years floating about in drawing-rooms,—"suitable for women and people of rank," in Goethe's useful phrase,—breaking his heart because he lost his post, he had buried himself in his own mind; and Lowell would have been a sounder man if he had never left his cherished Cambridge. His Cambridge sometimes irritated others, and his capacity, in Paris, for making the Rue de Rivoli a mere continuation of Brattle Street was sometimes amusing at Lowell's expense. But his Cantabrigianism was his stoutest vir-

* Howells.

tue. His way with his calves and pigs, and his melons and pears, his making hay when battles were on, even the Battle of Gettysburg, his honest bookishness and his wholesome pleasure in all who loved books like himself, —this bespoke the worthy Lowell. His worldly strain did not run deep. It was evoked by situations to which he felt unequal. There was something transparently simple in him, the boyish frankness that his friends enjoyed.* One saw the "green, live Yankee" under the cosmopolitan surface, like freckles under a coating of rouge. This was the racy Lowell who had written *The Biglow Papers;* and Lowell's bookishness was a Cambridge trait. If one smiled away the shell, or pierced the armour with a shaft of wit, if one held the key that unlocked the door, one liked and rejoiced in the man one found inside.

This was the Lowell whom everyone liked and respected, the compact little man in the velvet jacket who loved his pipe and his fire of logs and turned round *rounder* than anyone else, as Howells said in later years, when he turned to take a book off the shelf. This was the Lowell who sat in his study, winter and summer, for years on end, feeding like a silkworm on his books, only stirring abroad for his daily walk. Lowell was a bookman, pure and simple, born and bred in an alcove; and he basked and ripened in the sun of books till he grew as mellow as a meerschaum. He hardly professed to be a critic, except in textual matters, in which he was both learned and conscientious. He would spend a week, at twelve hours a day,—a fortnight, if need were,—writing a six-page notice of a dictionary. He would run through the whole of Ovid and Lucan to find a word for one of his poems. From dawn to dusk in summer, oftener in winter, in the "tumultuous privacy" of a snow-storm,—for

* "My temperament is so youthful that whenever I am addressed (I mean by mere acquaintances) as if my opinion were worth anything, I can hardly help laughing. . . . A boy of twelve behind a bearded vizor."— *Letters of J. R. Lowell, I, 117.*

he drew all the virtue from Emerson's line,—he read his Boccaccio, and his Hakluyt and Purchas, his old French metrical romances or all he could find on the Yankee dialect. Ever since 1855, when he had lectured on the English poets, at the Lowell Institute in Boston, he had been regarded as a man of letters who had no equal in the United States, for literary knowledge and grace of style; and all this, combined with his animal spirits, made him a capital teacher. Ticknor and Longfellow had explored for Cambridge the foreground of the history of letters. Lowell's task was one of interpretation; and, if his own mind was not quite in the grand style, he still communicated a feeling for it.* He loved his books and he liked his students. He asked them to read with him privately in his study.

Such was the notable Cambridge bookman, the literary recluse and the teacher of letters. When you dropped in and found Lowell reading a play of Calderon or a canto of Dante, you knew you were in the presence of something real. It was not the reality of a critic and made small pretence of being so. The critic's seat is not an easy-chair. Its rushes are iron spikes; and he who writes about books in relation to life, or life in relation to books, distrusts that "precious feeling of seclusion in having a double wall of centuries" † between himself and the world in which Lowell revelled. The rounded curves of a velvet coat are not for him whose proper atmosphere, as Emerson said of the scholar, is "poverty and reproach and danger." Lowell, as a critic, was not important, in spite of the golden opinions he won from those who had

* "Thirty odd years ago I brought home with me from Nuremberg photographs of Peter Vischer's statuettes of the twelve apostles. These I used to show to my pupils and ask them for a guess at their size. The invariable answer was 'larger than life.' They were really about eighteen inches high, and this grandiose effect was wrought by simplicity of treatment, dignity of pose, a large unfretted sweep of drapery."—*Latest Literary Essays.*
† *Library of Old Authors.*

a right to give them,* and all his authority in other circles, wherever the English tongue was spoken.† Those who compared him with Sainte-Beuve forgot Sainte-Beuve's psychology and his feeling for life,—not to speak of his scope and massiveness,—the life that in Arnold, Taine and Renan, even in Walter Pater, served as a touchstone in the world of books. Lowell, who had no philosophy, whose general ideas were so few that only two of his essays may be said to contain them,—the essays on Rousseau and Swinburne,—had no psychology either, and wished to have none; or, rather, he had enough when the subject pleased him, when it conformed with the local proprieties, but none when it shocked the proprieties. He said it was "fortunate" that we know so little about the lives of Shakespeare and his friends, "literary bohemians, living from hand to mouth," but he could hardly know too much about the virtuous Gray and the innocent Walton. It pleased him to contemplate the latter; it shocked him to contemplate the former, the evil in whose lives his conventional mind, all too conscious of the fig-leaf, greatly exaggerated; ‡ and sometimes he was disingenuous in his suggestion that these prejudices had an objective basis.§ All this was to breed

* "I think he is altogether the best critic we have; something of what Ste. Beuve is in French."—*More Letters of Edward Fitzgerald,* 212.

† "My father, who would never accept the authority of an encyclopædia when his children got him in a corner on some debated question of fact, held James Russell Lowell as the supreme judge of letters, from whom not even he could appeal. (It is true, he had never heard of Sainte-Beuve, and regarded Matthew Arnold as a modern fad.)"—Arnold Bennett, *Your United States.*

‡ "Is it not after the discreditable particulars which excite a correspondingly discreditable curiosity that we are eager, and these that we read with greatest zest? So it would seem if we judged by the fact that biography, and especially that of men of letters, tends more and more towards these indecent exposures . . . There are certain memoirs after reading which one blushes as if he had not only been peeping through a key-hole, but had been caught in the act."—Lecture on Chapman.

§ "The so-called realist raises doubts in my mind when he assures me that he, and he alone, gives me the facts of life . . . But are they the facts? I had much rather believe them to be the accidental and transitory phenomena of our existence here."—*The Old English Dramatists.*

a reaction in later generations, when the *cache-sexe* that
emphasized the sex was rudely torn away, and the spot-
light fell on the sex that had fallen on the fig-leaf. Sometimes, in Lowell, a whim of taste triumphed over the
convenances, as in a casual remark on Fielding; * but
psychology and the objective were the last of his cares.
Life had to be as Brattle Street desired, though the
heaven of intellect fell. It had to be as nobly good as
Longfellow really was, and as others wished to think it.

Conventional minds are always timid because they cannot trust their own judgment. As they never exercise
their judgment, preferring to follow accepted ideas,
how can they judge, indeed? Their intellectual muscles
are necessarily flabby. The instability of Lowell's mind,
when he had to judge for himself, was as marked as the
narrowness of his understanding. His sympathies were
exclusively literary, or politico-literary; and, in his rare
digressions into other fields, painting, for example, or
architecture, he showed an ineptitude that was almost
surprising. He said that Paul Potter's "Bull" could no
more be compared with Rosa Bonheur's "Horse Fair"
"than a stuffed and varnished dolphin with a living one,"
a judgment that suggests Mark Twain; and in Rome he
had "doubts about domes," which seemed to him "the
goitre of architecture." † Only a Boston or a Cambridge
man could ever have "doubts about domes,"—despite the
shades of Bulfinch and the State House. Lowell's words
on Michael Angelo,—one part truth, ten parts misapprehension, which he retracted in the sequel, indicated
his want of intuition, the vacillating nature of his
mind, and, more than all, his fear of the great and the

* "He painted vice when it came in his way (and it was more obvious in
his time) as a figure in the social landscape, and in doing so he was perhaps a better moralist than those who ignore it altogether, or only when it
lives in a genteel quarter of the town."—*Literary and Political Addresses.*
† *Fireside Travels.*

vital.* With the great and the vital he felt unable to cope, except when he was aware of the stream of tradition that backed him up in his authority. Hence the insinuation of a grudge in the tone with which he spoke of the great and the vital, the unconsecrated great, the newly vital. He felt that the great must be "exaggerated"; the original was original by "conscious intention." Of the stream of tradition in the plastic arts, Lowell was unaware, if only because he lived in Cambridge, the Cambridge of the pre-Nortonian era. Besides, a certain levity of judgment in regard to the plastic arts was quite in the form of his age, in London as in Cambridge. Lowell's free-and-easy way with domes and Michael Angelo was all of a piece with that of other writers who spoke the word of God where literature was concerned. Carlyle was a case in point. But Lowell's tone in literary matters, where he could not feel the stream of tradition behind him, was equally presumptuous and inconsequential. The list of his ineptitudes, in relation to all that was vital, all that was original and strong in the world of his day, where he had to think for himself, was more than surprising. His instinctive response to Whitman,† Poe ‡ and Swinburne,§ their personalities and their work alike, never corrected in regard to Whitman,‖ scarcely in regard to Poe and Swinburne, since the essay on Swinburne

* "Shall I confess it? Michael Angelo seems to me, in his angry reaction against sentimental beauty, to have mistaken bulk and brawn for the antithesis of feebleness. He is the apostle of the exaggerated, the Victor Hugo of painting and sculpture. I have a feeling that rivalry was a more powerful motive with him than love of art, that he had the conscious intention to be original, which seldom leads to anything better than the exaggerated." —*Fireside Travels.*

† "No, no, the kind of thing you describe won't do. When a man aims at originality, he acknowledges himself consciously un-original."—*Letters,* I, 242.

‡ "He probably cannot conceive of anybody's writing for anything but a newspaper reputation, or for posthumous fame."—*Letters,* I, 100.

§ "I am too old to have a painted hetaira palmed off on me for a Muse." —*Letters,* I, 377.

‖ Apropos of *Leaves of Grass:* "A book I never looked into farther than to satisfy myself that it was a solemn humbug."—*New Letters,* 115.

was non-committal and Lowell could never speak of Poe without qualifications and disclaimers, as if he were eager to forestall any misapprehension of his admiration, were in keeping with his verdict on Thoreau, that "his whole life was a search for the doctor,"—not merely false but singularly stupid,—and his final remark on Emerson's poems,* in which the impression left in one's mind obliterated the truth that it contained. A critic who regards the truth may well retract and qualify in order to present his theme in all its ramifications; but a substantial critic never leaves the reader in doubt about his final judgment. What was Lowell's real opinion of Poe, Swinburne, Emerson, Thoreau?—since we know his opinion of Whitman. Fine pages do not make a verdict, and Lowell wrote many fine pages about Thoreau and Emerson. But the *I-am-afraids* and the *Shall-I-confesses,* the doubts, the hesitations and the doublings, the notes of patronage and condescension, the reluctances, the conventional phrases, the foolish condemnations, the unworthy suspicions that marked Lowell's critical essays concerning living men proved that his judgment had no sure footing. He was the father of a school of American essay-writers that blossomed in the age that followed him. These lesser Lowells exercised a style that shambled and wobbled self-consciously in a welter of qualifications. One might call this style the Indian-giver style, for it took back everything it granted. The mock-modest pretence that one does not know, in writers of this stripe, covers a certainty that one knows indeed. But it meets an equal certainty in others that one knows, really knows, nothing.

Boston was to produce, as time went on, many minds of this sort. What these minds could never see was that their knowing humility, their treating great men as re-

---

* "As for Emerson's verse (though he has written some as exquisite as any in the language), I suppose we must give it up."—1883, *Letters,* II, 275.

fractory children, disqualified not others but themselves.
The pride of Boston gave birth to the pathos of Boston.
What was real in Lowell, then? Much, if one looked for
it in the right direction; and even the father of a doubt‧
ful brood had the importance of a father. As an editor,
he played a historic role. He brought to the work his
learning and his taste; and his understanding of the national feeling, in the years before the Civil War, gave
him a double authority. It was true that, if *The Atlantic*
was full of cream, he had the top of the bottle; true, that
when manuscripts came to him which could not be
weighed in the scales he knew, he had a way of missing
them. He thought that Rossetti was "too foggy" to be
printed in his magazine. His merit was that he did not
doubt the value of the men he understood and found
about him. For the rest, he was a bookman beyond compare in literary America. How does a bookman differ
from a critic? He differs in that he assumes as given the
whole sphere of values. The bookman does not judge,
nor is he asked to judge. He appreciates, he enjoys, he
communicates pleasure. In the world of the bookman,
taste is the main affair, enthusiasm, gusto, relish; and it
was in these that Lowell excelled. When he felt behind
him the stream of tradition, when he did not have to
judge for himself, when he could follow his whims and
prejudices, his preferences, his instinctive admirations,
when he could let out sail, without any danger of reefs and
shoals, then one saw the master. Who asks for judgments
of Dante and Shakespeare, of Chaucer, Spenser, Dryden,
Gray and Walton? Humanity judged these authors long
ago and found them worthy of enduring fame. What one
is asked to do, if one writes about them, is to evoke new
aspects for appreciation. This was Lowell's gift. Here lay
his glory.

"In my weaker moments," he said, "I revert with a

sigh, half deprecation, half relief, to the old notion of literature as holiday, as

'The world's sweet inn from pain and wearisome turmoil.' " *

His weaker moments were his stronger moments. When he abandoned the sphere of the critic, which called for stronger muscles than he possessed, when he gave up the attempt to judge, for which he was not mature enough, and yielded to the secondary role for which his talent equipped him, the cold, self-conscious Lowell of the world became the winning Lowell of the study. He "deprecated" it, but it "relieved" him; for his efforts as a critic were conscious efforts, while all the force of the unconscious Lowell lay behind his bookishness. His mannerisms vanished at once, all that was facetious, arch and coy in the essays where he stood on his good behaviour. In his zest for letters, miracles happened. The indecisive Lowell, the conventional Lowell, the condescending Lowell, the defiant Lowell,—all these Lowells were absorbed in the passionate lover of reading. In love, one feels the world "well lost," even when the love is the love of books. What joy, what shy delights this man revealed when he wrote of the authors he loved! And even, let us add, what judgment! He who could never judge when he had to judge judged like the best when no one was looking.

There one had the Lowell that lives and breathes, the Lowell that lives in *The Biglow Papers*. If the fresh and courageous note of the *Fable for Critics* has died out of the picture, the note of the young man who spoke his mind, regardless of what anyone thought or said, the critic hitting and missing, with the rashness of youth, often hitting well and always trusting his own opinion,— if this note has vanished, another note has taken its place.

* *Latest Literary Essays,* 148.

This later Lowell has abandoned a role for which he was ill-fitted by nature and training. He has stooped to conquer, but he conquers. Take him on his own ground! Do not remind him of his old pretensions. Do not embarrass him with questions. Forget the radical views of his earlier days. Let him rejoice in royalists and churchmen, lovers of good ale and seasoned pipes who would have had small use for Abolition. Do not trip him up with insinuations about his inconsistencies and his timid aversions. There are plenty of timid people in the world, and plenty of others who are inconsistent. But men are not born every day who can write such essays as Lowell's on Walton and Dryden.

When one takes Lowell as one finds him, yields to his tastes and preferences, then one begins to share his pleasures. His animal spirits have returned. He revels in Spenser's charms and in Chaucer's beauties as he has revelled in puns and Yankeeisms. His muscles grow springy and his lungs dilate in this atmosphere of books, as in his winter walks through the streets of Cambridge. Even his puns have a respectable meaning because his beloved Elizabethans used them. Was not Queen Elizabeth an ardent punster?—and is not Lowell's love of puns, even more extravagant than Browning's and quite in the tone of his time, a symbol of his delight in reaching back, behind his Puritan heritage, to the warm and sunny world of Shakespeare and Spenser? You would hardly know this glowing Lowell, this tipster of the library! He loses all his reserves in the joy of books. Warmed with Villon and Marlowe, he gladly admits that Poe is a genius. He is all for Emerson the man, even if he has doubts about the poet. He says the happiest things about Thoreau,—"as if all out-of-doors had kept a diary and become its own Montaigne." No doubt, he would have liked Whitman also, if he had cared for Blake. In his felicitous insights and luckier phrases,* in the tone and texture of his style, Lowell deserved his fame and still deserves it.

* On Dryden: "We always feel his epoch in him, and that he was the lock which let our language down from its point of highest poetry to its level of easiest and most gently flowing prose."

On Carlyle: "He goes about with his Diogenes dark-lantern, professing to seek a man, but inwardly resolved to find a monkey."

CHAPTER XXVIII

CONCLUSION

THE CIVIL WAR brought to a head, however inconclusively, a phase of American culture that later times described as the New England "renaissance." This movement of mind continued in the generation that followed, and many of the writers who embodied it long outlived the war. Some of them produced their best work, or work, at least, equal to their best, during this later period. But all had given their measure before the war, and several had disappeared before it. That they stood for some collective impulse, exceptional in the history of the national mind, no one questioned later or has ever questioned. Whether this impulse was a "renaissance" or only an "Indian summer," as Mr. Santayana has called it, a "golden age" or a "golden day," the impulse existed and the movement was real. The question is only one of its general meaning and what it signified in itself.

It is obvious, almost strikingly so, that this movement of mind in New England followed the typical pattern of the "culture-cycle," as Spengler has convincingly described it. Setting aside the question of scale, one finds in it the same succession of phases that one finds in the great culture-cycles,—for Spengler, in this, at least, has made a case that is so suggestive as to seem conclusive. Here we have a homogeneous people, living close to the soil, intensely religious, unconscious, unexpressed in art and letters, with a strong sense of home and fatherland. One of its towns becomes a "culture-city," for Boston, with

Cambridge and Concord considered as suburbs, answers to this name, which Spengler accords to Florence, Bruges and Weimar, as no other town has ever answered in either of the Americas. There is a springtime feeling in the air, a joyous sense of awakening, a free creativeness, an unconscious pride, expressed in the founding of institutions, intellectual, humanitarian, artistic, and—at first a little timid, cold and shy—the mind begins to shape into myths and stories the dreams of the pre-urban countryside. There is a moment of equipoise, a widespread flowering of the imagination in which the thoughts and feelings of the people, with all their faiths and hopes, find expression. The culture-city dominates the country, but only as its accepted vent and mouthpiece. Then gradually the mind, detached from the soil, grows more and more self-conscious. Contradictions arise within it, and worldlier arts supplant the large, free, ingenuous forms through which the poetic mind has taken shape. What formerly grew from the soil begins to be planned. The Hawthornes yield to the Henry Jameses. Over-intelligent, fragile, cautious and doubtful, the soul of the culture-city loses the self-confidence and joy that have marked its early development,—it is filled with a presentiment of the end; and the culture-city itself surrenders to the world-city,—Boston surrenders to New York, —which stands for cosmopolitan deracination. What has once been vital becomes provincial; and the sense that one belongs to a dying race dominates and poisons the creative mind.

Not to press a formula too far, is not this the story of New England, as the New England mind confesses it, from the days of Channing and Webster to those of Henry Adams and Barrett Wendell? In religion, the springtime faith of Channing, with its feeling of a world to create and redeem, yields to the conception of religion as hygiene in the valetudinarian Mrs. Eddy. In politics, the robust and confident Webster gives place to the querulous Lodge. The scholars and historians lose themselves among their documents; and the cheerful, unconscious, generous note of the essayists and poets of the eighteen-fifties makes way for the analytical and the precious. No doubt, the New England mind exaggerates its own decline and decay. There are times when the visitor in New England feels that it is destined for another growth that will be more vigorous than its first, and the age that followed its "golden day" is richer and fuller to the enquiring eye than its own or other historians have supposed. But that it has passed through a cycle, and some such cycle as Spengler pictures,—this grows more and more apparent.

"Men are free," said D. H. Lawrence, "when they are in a living homeland, not when they are straying and breaking away. Men are free when they are obeying some deep, inward voice of religious belief. Obeying from within. Men are free when they belong to a living, organic, believing community, active in fulfilling some unfulfilled, perhaps unrealized purpose." This was the case with the New England authors, in the epoch of the building of the nation. Perhaps it was never more truly the case with any group of authors, all question of intensity aside. They were as completely of their people as any authors of the oldest nations; and they saw, if not themselves,—for they were not self-conscious,—at least their profession as having a Promethean role to play. They were teachers, educators and bringers of light, with a deep and affectionate feeling of obligation towards the young republic their fathers had brought into being. That New England was appointed to guide the nation, to civilize it and humanize it, none of them ever doubted, a motive that was evident in all their writings, from Emerson's early addresses to the table-talk of Holmes, from Longfellow's *Hiawatha,* in which an Indian myth conveys the poet's notion of his role, to the prophecies of *Uncle Tom's Cabin*. Sometimes they suggested Miss Ophelia reforming Dinah's kitchen; but there was so little of the condescending, so much of the humble and fraternal, in their state of mind and point of view, and they threw so many ideas into circulation and wrote so sincerely and so well that they came to be accepted as fathers and sages.

What was the cause of this transfiguration? The breadth of their conscious horizon, the healthy objectivity of their minds, their absorption in large preoccupations, historical, political, religious, together with a literary feeling, a blend of the traditional and the local, that gave the local wider currency while it brought the traditional home to men's business and bosoms. They filled the New England scene with associations and set it, as it were, in three dimensions, creating the visible foreground it had never possessed. They helped to make their countrypeople conscious of the great world-movements of thought and feeling in which they played parts side by side with the intellectual leaders of the older countries. In their scholarship, their social thought, their moral passion, their artistic feeling, they spoke for the universal republic of letters, giving their own province a form and body in the consciousness of the world. Moreover, there was something in their temper that made them seem friends of the human spirit. They stood for good faith and fair play and all that was generous and hopeful in the life of their time. The hold they gained and kept over the nation possessed an extra-literary sanction, as if they were voices of the national ethos. If they found themselves "done up in spices, like so many Pharaohs," as Holmes remarked in later years, it was because they were looked upon as classics,—

In whom is plainest taught, and easiest learnt,
What makes a nation happy, and keeps it so.

This process of canonization went hand in hand with the spread of New England culture over the country. As the New England strain died out in the West, with the second and third generations of the pioneers and the growth of a native point of view, the reputations of the New England authors had to face another test. They encountered an increasing neglect and indifference, and even a widespread hostility. This was partly due to the reaction against the romantic authors in every country; but it was inevitable that the West should have turned against New England. In order to establish its independence, it was obliged to do so, as the East had turned against the mother-country. Of the popular writers, Longfellow, Whittier, Holmes, something seemed destined to survive in the general mind of the nation, when the life of all the regions, taken together, formed a final synthesis; but much of their work was ephemeral, and most of it was so bound up with regional modes of feeling and local traditions that it could only endure in the regional mind. For the rest, there are two kinds of classics, the popular and the esoteric, those that yield their meaning at the first encounter and those that we have to discover by effort and insight, the classics of the intellectual surface and the classics of the spiritual depths. The popular New England authors, whom every child could understand, remained as classics indeed, but mainly for children; while the handful of esoteric authors,—Hawthorne, with his cloudy symbols, whom one could only see through a glass, darkly, Thoreau, who "listened behind him for his wit," and Emerson, who, in life, never gave a direct answer and said that one should speak in parables,—came more and more into their own. Ironically enough, it was Boston and Cambridge that grew to seem provincial, while the local and even parochial Concord mind, which had always been universal, proved to be also national. Whatever doubts the country at large

felt regarding the other New England authors, Hawthorne, Thoreau and Emerson were clearly of the main
stream, with Emily Dickinson, Whitman, Poe and
Melville.

*
*   *

Thoreau died in 1862. He had caught cold from over-
exposure while counting the rings of some trees on a
snowy day and had fought for a year and a half with
tuberculosis. He had outlived his juvenile-braggart phase
and had grown more and more to seem the sage, whose
life and opinions might have appeared in the pages of
Diogenes Laertius. In an effort to regain his health, he
had journeyed to Minnesota and had made friends with
some of the Indians there. Then, knowing that nothing
could save him, he had settled down among his papers,
with an Indian's indifference to the future, completing
some of his lists of birds and flowers and finishing *The
Maine Woods*. No more walks to Bateman's Pond, to
Becky Stow's swamp or Nine-Acre Corner. But he said
he enjoyed existence as well as ever. His thoughts had
entertained him all his life, never so much as at present.
Fields, the second editor of *The Atlantic,* had asked him
for some of his essays, and he spent his last months
revising these.

His friends could hardly imagine Concord without
him. Solitude peered out from the dells and wood-roads,
and the bobolinks seemed to sing a minor strain. One
had thought of Henry Thoreau as a part of nature,
destined to be transformed perhaps at last into a mossy
rock or a leaf-strewn spring. At least, he was like the
hour-glass apple-shrub of which he had written in his
journal. By the end of October, when the leaves had
fallen, one saw the wild yellow fruit growing, which the

cows could not reach over the thorny hedge. It was so
with the rude, neglected genius of the Concord woods
and meadows. He had suffered many a check at first,
browsed upon by fate, springing up in a rocky pasture,
the nursery of other creatures there, and had grown up
scraggy and thorny, not like the sleek orchard-trees whose
forces had all been husbanded. When, at first, within this
rind and hedge, the man shot up, one saw the thorny
scrub of his youth about him; but, as he grew, the thorns
disappeared, and he bore golden crops of Porters and
Baldwins, apples whose fame was destined to spread
through all orchards for generations, when the thrifty
orchard-trees that had been his rivals had long since
ceased to bear their engrafted fruit. It was true that
Thoreau's fame was slow in growing. Emerson and
Ellery Channing brought out his posthumous books,—he
had published only two during his lifetime; and Emerson
collected his poems and letters. But only his friends could
imagine why anyone should wish to see his journal.
Emerson was convinced that, if it was published, it would
soon produce in New England a "plentiful crop of naturalists." This was true a generation later. When volumes
of selections from the journal appeared, a school of lesser Thoreaus sprang up at once; * and

> The happy man who lived content
> With his own town and continent,

became a teacher of wisdom, even in Asia.

Two years after Thoreau, Hawthorne faded out of
the Concord picture. He had come home from Italy and
England just before the outbreak of the war and had

* Thoreau's manuscript journal consisted of thirty-nine blank-books of
all shapes and sizes, packed in a strong wooden box built by himself. It
was bequeathed by Sophia Thoreau to H. G. O. Blake, who brought out
four volumes of selections, 1881–1892. The complete journal was edited by
Bradford Torrey and published in fourteen volumes, 1906.

taken up his life again at "Wayside," the house he had bought from Alcott, where a man was said to have lived who believed he was never to die. Hawthorne built a tower over the house, a reminiscence of the Italian villa in which he had stayed in Florence. There he had his study, reached by a trap-door, with a standing desk fastened to the wall. With England still fresh in his mind, he composed from his note-books the beautifully rounded chapters of *Our Old Home,* a book that was somewhat unhappily named; but a sudden change seemed to have come upon him with his return to America, a blight as of winter, a deadly estrangement even from his own imagination. Had he been too old to be transplanted, so that he could never take root again? He made a few halfhearted efforts to gather up the threads of his former life. He appeared at the Saturday Club for a few of the dinners; but even Alcott and Emerson seldom saw him. Once, at Emerson's house, he picked up some photographs of Concord, the common, the court-house and the Mill-dam, which he passed in his walks every day, and asked what the pictures represented. The sight of a friend or a stranger approaching his house drove him up the hill into the woods. Along the top of the ridge, among the pines, between the huckleberry and sweetfern bushes, he walked to and fro, brooding over the novel he could not finish. He fancied that the grass and the little shrubs shrank away as he passed them because there was something in his broodings that was alien to nature. Seventy-five years later, one could still trace the path that Hawthorne's footsteps wore on the tree-covered ridge.

He had wasted away and the glow in his eyes had vanished; and, hard as he tried to write, pulling down the blinds and locking his door, he could not bring his mind into focus. The novel became two novels, and the two became four. He could not fix upon a single setting: Salem, Concord, England, "Wayside" and Smithall's

Hall drifted in confusion through his mind, their outlines melting into one another. Even his theme eluded
him. Was it the unpardonable sin, the "ancestral footstep," the man who believed he was never to die? He
made four beginnings, constantly changing his perspective, until he could scarcely bear to touch his blurred and
meaningless manuscripts. A few of the scenes took form,
with all his old perfection, with the sculptural repose of
his earlier writing and a touch of the Gothic imagination that seemed to connect America with the Middle
Ages. But life shook before his eyes, like the picture on
the surface of a pond when a stone has disturbed its
tranquil mirror. His mind had grown like Melville's in
Pierre, groping in a fog for the firm conceptions that
turned to vapour as he tried to grasp them. Then, one
day in 1864, the news reached Concord from Plymouth,
New Hampshire, that he had died in his sleep at the
village inn. For years, he had been in the habit, while
idly scribbling, of writing the number 64, which had, he
felt, some fatal meaning for him. He had not disappeared, like Septimius Felton, crushed by the failure of
his dream, but he had wandered away with as little purpose, knowing perhaps that he would not return.

The Alcotts had settled in "Orchard House," next
door to Hawthorne's. Alcott had rebuilt it, leaving the
old beams and rafters, making arched alcoves of the
ovens and ash-holes; and, over the chimney-piece in Alcott's study, Ellery Channing's lines were inscribed,—

> The hills were reared, the valleys scooped in vain,
> If Learning's altars vanish from the plain.

Alcott had been made superintendent of the public
schools in Concord. His vindication had come late, and
one could only think what he might have accomplished
if he had had this chance when he was younger. Louisa

had begun to write the stories that were to carry his name around the world. Meanwhile, now that Thoreau was gone, Emerson was the master of the Concord revels. He liked to pile the children into the haycart, which they had bedecked with flowers and mosses, and carry them off for a swim and a picnic at Walden.

Emerson was travelling, on his lecture-tours, further and further westward. He was still an impossible puzzle in the popular mind, even a national joke, a byword of the country paragraphers. No matter, there were always a few of his hearers for whom all mythology spoke in his voice, the Indian gods and the gods of the North, who felt that the beautiful and the good must also be the true, if only because Emerson had said so. He seemed to have made his own all the victories of genius, which he invited one to share, he who had never doubted the riches of nature, the gifts of the future, the wealth of the mind. Whatever one's occupation was, mechanics, law, the ministry, he broke the spell of one's routine, relating one's craft and task to the laws of the world: one felt how one's life was intertwined with the whole chain of being. He spoke for magnanimity and the power of thought. In *The Conduct of Life* he had met the objections of those who found his optimism too facile. He had fully recognized the existence of evil, the brutal and barbarous elements in the core of the world, the habits of snake and spider in human beings, the snap of the tiger, the crackle of the bones of his prey in the coils of the anaconda. Even as men rose in culture, fate continued to follow them, as Vishnu followed Maya through all her ascending changes. While their checks and limitations became finer and finer, the ring of necessity still remained perched at the top. But fate had its lord, limitation its limits. It was different seen from above and seen from below. For, if fate was immense, so was power. Man was a stupendous antagonism, and as long as he thought he was free.

It was true, there was nothing more disgusting than the crowing about liberty by slaves, as most men were, and the flippant mistaking for freedom of some statute right to vote by those who had never dared to think or act; yet men had the power to look not at fate but the other way. The practical view was the other. Well had the oracle said, "Look not on Nature, for her name is fatal!" as Hafiz described the phrase on the gate of heaven, "Woe unto him who suffers himself to be betrayed by Fate!" Instead of cringing to facts, one could use and command them. Every jet of chaos that threatened extermination, one could convert by intellect into wholesome force. The water drowned ship and sailor. But, if one learned to swim and trimmed one's bark, one clove the water with it, and the waves were obliged to carry it, like their own foam, a plume and a power.

Thus Emerson spoke to the active forces waiting in his hearers, eager for the word that would set them free. For himself, he found that the more he spent the more he had to spend, the more he communicated the results of his thinking the more new thoughts he had. His zest and curiosity grew with the years; and, for all the discomforts of his lecture-tours, he liked to get away from the Eastern sea-board, where the American current was so superficial. He learned the resources of the country, going to school to the prairies. He had no fear of the future, he did not distrust the rough, wild, incalculable road America would have to travel to find itself. As between the civil and the forcible, he had always leaned, in his sympathies, to the latter. The Hoosiers and the Badgers of the West, the hard heads of Oregon and Utah, the rough-riders and legislators in shirt-sleeves, let them drive as they might. Better than to quote English standards and miss the sovereignty of power. Out of pirates and berserkers the English race had sprung, and no strong nation could ever develop without its own strong, wild will; and the power of the buffalo-hunters, bullying the peaceable and the loyal, would bring its own antidote at last. For liberty in all its wildness bred iron conscience; the instinct of the people was right in the end, and natures with great impulses had great resources and could be trusted to return from far.

There, in the West, he thought, lay nature sleeping, too much by half for man in the picture, with its rank vegetation of swamps and forests, steeped in dews and rains. In this great sloven continent, in its high Alleghany pastures, in the sea-wide, sea-skirted prairie, the great mother still slept and murmured. Man had as yet made little impression upon it. But there, where stars and woods and hills abounded, with all things still untried, could one not foresee a social state more excellent than history had recorded, one that turned its back on musket-worship and lived by the law of love and justice? Let men but know that every day is doomsday, and let them look within, in the populous, all-loving solitude which they left for the tattle of towns; for there *he* lurked and hid, he who was reality, joy and power. So Emerson felt, in the streets of New York, or at Concord, as he strolled through grove and glen. Others, as they saw him, tall and slender, leaving the village behind him, might have said to themselves, with the Swedish poet, "The last skald walks over the meadows."

INDEX

NEW ENGLAND:
INDIAN SUMMER
1865–1915

To

LEWIS MUMFORD

CONTENTS

CONTENTS

CHAPTER I

DR. HOLMES'S BOSTON

IN THE early spring of 1866, a young man named
William Dean Howells quietly slipped into Boston.
He was twenty-nine years old, slight, with a black moustache, mild in his manner and modest in appearance. One
saw that he had delicate perceptions and a shrewd gift of
observation, and he gave one a marked impression of will
and purpose. The brooding look in his eyes betokened a
future.

This young man had realized a bold ambition. The
editor of *The Atlantic Monthly,* James T. Fields, had
given him a post as coadjutor. Six years before, he had
come to Boston, commissioned by his paper in Ohio, with
hopes that he had openly confessed. In the Western Reserve, where he had lived, Boston was a sort of holy city.
The people had largely come from New England, and
those who cared for letters regarded Boston as many of
the Bostonians regarded London. It was the hub of the
universe, as Oliver Wendell Holmes had said, and the
intellectual world revolved about it. Howells, a reverent
pilgrim, aspired to be the "linchpin in the hub." His only
recommendation was a poem in *The Atlantic,* and Boston
had nothing to offer him at the moment; but before he
returned to the West, after this flying visit, an incident
occurred that foreshadowed his future. Lowell invited
him to dinner, to meet Holmes and Fields, in a little
upper room at the Parker House. The talk lasted four
hours, and Holmes said to Lowell, "Well, James, this is

something like the apostolic succession. This is the laying
on of hands."

The doctor's little joke was prophetic, as time was
soon to show. The young man had impressed the Boston
and Cambridge Olympians. "Howells is sure to be somebody if he lives," Lowell had written to Fields, who had
called him back six years later; and Charles Eliot Norton, struck by the papers on Venetian life he had published in the Boston *Advertiser,* exerted himself to find
and helped him to buy a house on Sacramento Street in
Cambridge. There, with his wife, whom he had married
in Paris,—for he had been living abroad, as consul in
Venice,—Howells passed the first of the twenty years
that he was to spend in New England. A sweet-brier
grew over the door and pine-trees flanked the gate. There
were pear-trees in the yard and tangles of grapes and
blackberries. When he was not in his office, reading proofs
and writing reviews, or jogging back and forth on the
horse-car that ran from Harvard Square, or working on
his essays and travel-sketches,—for he had scarcely begun
to think of himself as a novelist,—he fed his eyes and
ears with the Boston scene. Three years in Venice had
not dispelled for Howells the charm of New England.

He had acted with a strategy that marked his life for
fifty years. A campaign biography of Lincoln had brought
him his appointment as consul at Venice, and he had set
his cap at Boston as the indisputable centre of American
letters. Later he was to show the same clairvoyance when
the centre passed to New York, or when, as people said,
he carried it with him. At present, surrounded by men
who aroused his ambition, in an atmosphere that stirred
his imagination, he felt his every faculty on the stretch.
He had been just in time, on his earlier visit, during the
two days he had spent in Concord, to see Thoreau and
Hawthorne, who had passed him on to Emerson with a
friendly note; and the sage had opened his door for the

young man from the West and looked at him with a vague
serenity. The exaltations of Concord were not for Howells, whose appetite was all for visible facts, much as he
revered these luminaries, although Hawthorne, whom he
adored as an artist, said what Howells felt: he longed to
see an America that was free from the shadow of Europe. But he had not forgotten his excitement when, after
meeting Dr. Holmes, he had walked the streets and the
Common till two in the morning. He had approached
New England by way of Quebec and Portland, where he
had first seen the ocean, and the meadows, newly mown,
and the grey stone walls, the crumbling forts, the half-
deserted harbours had evoked the American past of the
histories and poems, as the great square mansions of
Portsmouth and Salem, withdrawing themselves in reserve from the quiet streets, suggested a more complex
civilization than he had known in the West. Marblehead
meant Whittier's ballad, Nahant recalled Longfellow,
while the gaunt old hip-roofed houses brought back the
magic of Hawthorne; and Boston had overwhelmed him
at the first encounter. Was it not a legend in the West
that everything noble and grand, in the national life,
everything magnanimous and enlightened, had originated
in Boston?* There was the "cradle of liberty," Faneuil
Hall, a symbol of the days when there were giants, and
there the genius of freedom had risen again in Garrison,
Charles Sumner and Wendell Phillips. There King's
Chapel stood, and Bunker Hill, the State House, the Old
Corner Bookstore, the Hancock House, the Quincy Man-

---

* See the attitude of Dr. Ellison, of Eriecreek in western New York, in
Howells's *A Chance Acquaintance.* Kitty, his daughter, had always heard
her father and uncle "talking of some indefinite, far-off place they called
Boston, in terms that commended it to her childish apprehension as very
little less holy than Jerusalem, and as the home of all the good and great
people outside of Palestine . . . Boston had always been Dr. Ellison's
faith . . . A little formal, perhaps, a little reserved, but excellent men;
polished, and certainly of sterling principles."
This was the attitude of Howells's father. It was also the attitude of
Hamlin Garland's father, as reflected in *A Son of the Middle Border.*

sion, the Granary Burial Ground, renowned in poems. There Cornhill ran its crooked length, the resort of the antiquaries and the bookworms, and the back of Beacon Hill was an architectural jumble that rivalled Dr. Johnson's haunts for quaintness.* One saw the Franklin tomb, the black old gravestones of the sixteen-thirties, the Park Street Church at Brimstone Corner, the Frog Pond, the Long Path, where the Autocrat had asked a well-known question; and there whole shelves of the books of one's childhood strolled about the streets in flesh and blood. Faces rose out of the crowd, at casual moments, that one had known for years in pictures, the Autocrat's quizzical visage, or Richard Henry Dana's; or possibly one saw Emerson descending from a horse-car, or the scarcely less fabulous Dr. Howe, the husband of Julia Ward Howe, who had written the *Battle Hymn of the Republic.* The "sailors with bearded lips" sauntered about the waterfront, as if they had stepped straight out of Longfellow's poem; and even the Yankee tang and gait and accent satisfied one's thirst for recognitions. History was visible and tangible in Boston. Was it not known that Copley's daughter still lived in Beacon Street, the painter's dearest Betsy, the sister of Lord Lyndhurst, three times chancellor of England? † Mrs. Greene, born in Boston, had heard Burke's opening speech at the trial of Warren Hastings. She had known Sir Joshua Reynolds, not as a child but as a grown young lady. As her father's reader and constant companion, in the painting-room in London, she had talked with Fox and Pitt and Mrs. Siddons. She re-

* " 'I didn't suppose you Western people cared for these things,' Mr. Arbuton once said; 'I thought your minds were set on things new and square.'

" 'But how could you think so?' replied Kitty, tolerantly. 'It's because we have so many new and square things that we like the old crooked ones.' "—Howells, *A Chance Acquaintance.*

† Mrs. Greene, born Elizabeth Copley, died at the age of ninety-six in Boston in 1866, the year of Howells's arrival.

membered meeting Charlotte, the heroine of *The Sorrows of Werther*. Then, marrying a Boston man, she had
witnessed every event in the town since the year of her
return, 1800. Nor was Mrs. Greene the only person who
recalled the building of the State House. Venerable figures and things abounded in Boston. There was something harmonious and mellow, something old or odd, at
every turn of the picture, and, best of all, perhaps, the
"Boston look," a blessing for the budding man of letters.*

The aspirant from the West had arrived at the psychological moment. Ten years before, the city of light
and learning could scarcely have offered a foothold to the
stoutest invader. Dominant, abundant, efflorescent, it was
all too well supplied by its own New England, as twenty
years hence the stout invader might not have cared to
scale the Boston wall. At present, with the breach the war
had made, and with all the treasure still within the city,
Boston was ripe for invasion, and most of the younger
writers throughout the country shared Howells's feeling
about it. New England ideals and examples had a commanding influence wherever people cared for thought and
writing, and eastern Massachusetts was hallowed ground
for thousands of the rising generation. Many a pilgrim
like William Winter walked out to Cambridge in the
moonlight merely to touch the latch of Longfellow's gate.
Many walked to Concord for a glimpse of Emerson's
woodpile, wishing they had the courage to knock at the
door. Others, like Forseythe Willson, who had written
The Old Sergeant, admired and praised by Longfellow,
Lowell and Holmes, too shy to announce their presence,
installed themselves in lodgings, in order to be near these

---

* The "Boston look" was a near-sighted look, occasionally assumed or
affected, that presupposed an interest in all things intellectual. It was a
favourite subject of the comic artists, especially in New York, where it
was supposed that Boston people wore spectacles in their cradles.

famous men.* Edward Rowland Sill, a student at the
Divinity School in Cambridge, later well known as a poet,
whose chosen themes were music and science, hungrily
followed Agassiz's lectures and hovered about the music-
hall, where the Boston illuminati often gathered. One felt
the presence of these worthies, whom younger men revered as the Greeks of old revered their early poets,—

> old Hesiod, teaching us husbandry,
> Ploughing, and sowing, and rural affairs,
> Rural economy, rural astronomy,
> Homely morality, labour and thrift.†

They were "high priests," as *The Atlantic* was a "temple," in the eyes of Emily Dickinson, who lived at Amherst. Miss Dickinson, a lawyer's daughter, a somewhat
rebellious young lady, whose friends left books for her in
hiding-places, had visited during the war in Boston and
Cambridge. She had dreamed of meeting Tennyson in the
office of Ticknor and Fields, and Cambridge for her was
rather like Westminster Abbey. In the West, the older
writers were oracles and sages.‡ Meanwhile, for those
who were merely romantic, the atmosphere of Boston had

---

* Forseythe Willson's poems, of no permanent merit, dealt with Civil
War themes. Lowell read *The Old Sergeant* in a Western newspaper. He
wrote to the poet and presently found that Willson was living in Cambridge, in a house facing his own.

† Aristophanes, *The Frogs.*

‡ "I stopped [about 1869] with my father over a night [at Garfield's]
in Hiram, Ohio, where we found him at home from Congress for the
summer. I was then living in Cambridge, in the fullness of my content
with my literary circumstance, and as we were sitting with the Garfield
family on the verandah that overlooked their lawn I was beginning to
speak of the famous poets I knew when Garfield stopped me with 'Just a
minute!' He ran down into the grassy space, first to one fence and then
to the other at the sides, and waved a wild arm of invitation to the neighbours who were also sitting on their back porches. 'Come over here!' he
shouted. 'He's telling about Holmes, and Longfellow, and Lowell, and
Whittier!' And at his bidding dim forms began to mount the fences and
follow him up to his verandah. 'Now go on,' he called to me, when we
were all seated, and I went on, while the whippoorwills whirred and
whistled round, and the hours drew toward midnight."—Howells, *Years of
My Youth.*

much of the bookish charm of Charles Lamb's London. The auctioneers quoted Shakespeare; and, if you entered a corner grocery, perhaps to buy a codfish, the man would ask you how you liked *Lucile,* while he was tying it up. Many a queer old soul haunted the book-stalls, in quest of some ancient print or musty pamphlet, a relic of Fisher Ames's days, or the days of Benjamin Franklin, or Swift and Pope. Another young writer who had settled in Boston, in the same year as Howells, after having lived in New York, wrote to one of his friends, "The humblest man of letters has a position here which he doesn't have in New York. To be known as an able writer is to have the choicest society open to you . . . A knight of the quill here is supposed necessarily to be a gentleman. In New York—he's a Bohemian!—outside of his personal friends he has no standing." *

In short, the "American Athens" still deserved its name, seldom as one heard this any longer. In 1855, Theodore Parker had called the town the "American Dublin," which was almost more to the point, for the Irish power was rapidly rising with other strains of foreign birth.† There were signs that the building days of New England were over, and all things were ripe for change in Boston. But the Yankees were omnipotent still, in numbers, wealth and prestige, and Boston had no second as a seat of culture. In some of the country districts, where culture had less glamour, and more primitive traits of character had larger sway, the natives, whose necks were usually stiff, challenged the pretensions of their Athens. "Boston folks are full of notions" was a proverb in Rhode Island;‡ and culture itself, in other parts, where good sense abounded, scanned with a doubtful eye

* Thomas Bailey Aldrich.

† In 1857, according to Bliss Perry, in *Park Street Papers,* Massachusetts reckoned about one-fifth of the population as either foreign-born or the children of foreign-born. In 1908, only 32% of the population was Protestant.

‡ Thomas Robinson Hazard, *The Jonny-Cake Papers.*

the cant of culture.* In New York, where nothing annoying to Boston was ever out of order, it was said that, to enter the city, you had to pass an examination, and that when you left it, if you passed, you were given a kind of degree. The New Yorkers could afford to talk thus lightly, for the goddess of Boston was none of theirs; but for those who had to recognize the goddess,—alien writers, artists, lecturers,—the Boston test was formidable, and sometimes alarming. For Mark Twain, who lectured there in 1869, a Boston audience signified "4,000 critics;" † and a Boston man's mere presence, in many a rural household, struck terror into the heart of the local performer.‡ Some of the younger Bostonians, feeling the danger that lurked in this, more for themselves than it lurked for the local performer, fled the city for other parts, through fear of being a "Boston prig," an intellectual prig, the worst of all.§ Complacency, a pride of power that had not sufficiently tested itself, was, as it remained, the bane of Boston, a consciousness of righteousness, a consciousness of culture that others found insufferable or funny; and many a visitor shared the feeling expressed by one who came to stay, when he said that a group of Bostonians with whom

---

* "Cousin Susan says, 'My dear, the greatest objection I have to Boston is that there is always some word which everybody uses. When I was there last, the word was *culture*. Every chit of a girl who came to see Bessie talked about *culture*. I got so tired of it I forbade Bessie to use it in my presence. In my young days we talked about *education* or *cultivation*.' Mary suggests that to say culture, after these, is to substitute guano for the common manures."—1869, *Letters and Memorials of Thomas Wentworth Higginson.*

† "Tomorrow night I appear for the first time before a Boston audience —4,000 critics."—Mark Twain, *Letters,* I, 168.

‡ "He asked her to play to him.
  " 'No,' she said, 'you are a Bostonian.'
  " 'But not a critic.'
  " 'Impossible!' "
  —Elizabeth Stuart Phelps, *Doctor Zay.*

§ "I care a great deal to prevent myself from becoming what of all things I despise, a Boston prig (the intellectual prig is the most odious of all) . . . Anything which takes a man morally out of Beacon Street, Nahant and Beverly Farms, Harvard College and the Boston press, must be in itself a good."—Letter of Henry Adams, 1875.

he had talked were "simmering in their own fat and putting a nice brown on one another." * The Boston folk, who were always frank, confessed to shocking orgies, in which their favourite vices had full play, dancing while they discussed "foreknowledge" or pondered the lessons of Beethoven's symphonies, or pursuing the "holier than thou" to an *altitudo*.† These confessions were sometimes humorous, sometimes not; but in humble minds and witty minds, and minds that were also cultivated, in other regions, they left unfortunate impressions. For Boston had earned its good name; and, as for the unkind things that were said about it, one usually found some Boston man who had said them first and better. As the "little man" remarked in *The Professor,* Boston had opened, and kept open, more turnpikes leading to free thought and free speech and free deeds than any other city in the country.‡

The focus of culture in Boston was the Saturday Club, the club that Dr. Holmes would have invented if spontaneous generation had not produced it. There, once a month, the illuminati, the Autocrat and Emerson and Lowell, Longfellow, Dana, Asa Gray and Sumner, Agassiz and Charles Eliot Norton, Charles Francis Adams, on occasion, or the other diplomat, Motley, met for the talk in which the town excelled. For Boston abounded in good conversation. Experienced outsiders, guests of the club, or perhaps of *The Atlantic,* at one of its dinners, or at some private dinner for public men, were struck by the

* Henry James the elder. This trait was also described by Howells, in *The Rise of Silas Lapham,* as "the willingness Boston men often show to turn one another's good points to the light in company."

† Edward Everett Hale spoke of a dance at which Lowell, while dancing, discussed with his partner "the significance of the 5th Symphony of Beethoven in comparison with the lessons of the 2nd and the 7th, and another partner in the quadrille would reconcile for him the conflict of free will and foreknowledge."—Lilian Whiting, *Louise Chandler Moulton.*

Dr. Hale was recklessly inaccurate, and perhaps this was one of his jokes. But it is typical of the countless stories that formed the popular legend about Boston "culture."

‡ *The Professor at the Breakfast-Table.*

quality of this conversation. Sometimes, at two successive dinners, the same men talked for eight hours, without a sign of fatigue, and the conversation never fell off in interest.* If Dr. Holmes was not the centre of it, the others mostly had their centres elsewhere, in Cambridge, in Concord, in Washington or London, while the Autocrat was not only Bostonian but more than anything else a talker. His poems were versified conversation, he had Boswellized himself, and, in his airy way, he had scattered freely, more freely than the profounder minds, the ideas that had made his town a centre of culture. It was he who had named the Brahmins and described their function as leaders of learning and bringers of light. It was he who had spread the gospel of modern science. It was he who had smitten the Philistines hip and thigh and routed the tribe of the Pooh-Poohs with clouds of arrows, and, withal, as a wise old family doctor, he treated the Yankee household with a heart that was full of pity for human nature. Could one hold his incomprehensions against this lover of excellent things, who was always so bright and wide-awake? He was certainly unfair to the reformers, and there were other doctors, well instructed, who felt he was setting up the old caste-idol, who resented his assaults on rustic manners and, still more, on the Orthodox faith, the better sides of which he knew not of; for *The One-Hoss Shay* and *The Guardian Angel,* which

* Describing his first visit to Boston, in 1865, Raphael Pumpelly thus spoke of a dinner given by Anson Burlingame, the American Minister to China, to the new British Ambassador, Sir Frederic Bruce. The guests included Holmes, Longfellow, Sumner, Lowell, etc. "We stayed at table until 4 A.M. and even I was surprised at the great amount of wine that, under the influence of the brilliant talk, disappeared with only the happiest of results. The next day it was interesting to see what an impression these best representatives of American intellect produced on perhaps the ablest Englishman that had been in America. He told me later that he had never before been at a table where he had heard such a delightfully easy flow of conversation . . . Of these notable dinners I remember only that the talk never fell off in interest. What impressed me strongly, too, was the fact that at two closely successive dinners the same people could keep up an equally easy current of talk through eight hours without a sign of fatigue."—Pumpelly, *Reminiscences,* II, 551-2.

aroused the indignation of thousands, true as they were, were not the truth regarding the depths of the old religion.* Many of Dr. Holmes's constant readers found much that was hard to bear in what he said, and, in fact, he was a wit and not too wise. One had to go to Concord for the sages. But what was Voltaire, what was Erasmus? —with whom he had so much in common, as a highly intelligent man, the most intelligent man in New England. He laid trains of thought that later became abuses, as the Boston mind developed under other conditions; but whose heart, with all its foibles, was more innocent than his, or, even more truly religious? His hymns were sincere, with a touch of sublimity. No one loved life more, or fought for it more gallantly, as he fought for the sports that stood for health and the poems that stood for expressive living. He loved all sorts and conditions of men, as he loved prize-fights and trotting-horses, trees, good cattle, boats and violins.

The Autocrat stood for Boston in its hour of triumph. For Boston was indeed triumphant. Its conversation bore witness to this. The town possessed authority in every sphere. If it was ripe for change, for assaults from without and within, if the Civil War perhaps had struck its hour, the war had been "Mrs. Stowe's war," in President Lincoln's phrase, and, if Mrs. Stowe was not a possession of Boston, at least she appeared at *Atlantic* dinners, wearing her wreath of laurel. Charles Francis Adams, who lived at Quincy and had always quarrelled with Boston, belonged more to Boston than to anything else, and, if Adams had not caused the war, he had certainly helped to win it: he had helped almost as much as Grant or Sherman by holding the British at bay. Motley, the Boston historian, represented his country at two important posts. Sumner, the Boston statesman, was unique in the Senate.

* See Harriet W. Preston's *Aspendale,* pp. 123-157, in which the old country doctor attacks Dr. Holmes, an interesting and powerful statement.

He was the one man there, as even his enemies said, who, during the war-years and after, kept in view the interests of thought and science; for, if Boston had power and prestige in public matters, which gave an additional tang to its conversation, much more was this the case in affairs of the mind. It set the tone of American speech.* It held in equal scales "the Yankee's 'haow,' the stammering Briton's 'haw';" † and its great new technological schools, its quarterlies, monthlies and weeklies, the Lowell Institute and other centres, not to mention the "Boston Symphony," soon to be founded, were institutions of national significance. The *North American Review* was recapturing its leading position. The supremacy of *The Atlantic* was unquestioned. To have published a poem in it, as the case of Howells showed, was to be known among writers all over the country. It was a force indeed throughout the country, setting the critical standard and spreading suggestions.‡ Boston excelled in the machinery of culture, as well as in culture itself.

In days to come, the Saturday Club, where the Boston Olympians gathered, reflected all the changes of the Yankee mind. Consisting chiefly of authors, at first, acknowledged leaders of national thought, it altered when it alteration found. Local worthies, eminent men, but eminent mainly as men of Boston, replaced the original members, who possessed an all-American sanction. As the scope of the membership altered, so did the types, and lawyers and judges, professors of science, economists, physicists,

* "[Edmund] Quincy affected me as the finest patrician type I had ever met . . . His manner was beautiful, his voice delightful, when at our first meeting he made me his reproaches in terms of lovely kindness for having used, in my *Venetian Life,* the Briticism *directly* for *as soon as.*"—Howells, *Literary Friends and Acquaintance.*

† Holmes.

‡ One of its articles is said to have been the seed of Smith College. Another caused the opening of the University of Michigan to women. These instances might be multiplied in other spheres. Its authority in literary criticism is illustrated in Mark Twain's remark, thanking Howells for his review of *The Innocents Abroad,* "I felt like the woman who was so glad her baby had come white."

chemists largely supplanted the men of letters, who spoke for the soul as well as the mind of the race. If Howells, after his first visit, observing the Boston of 1860, felt that he must keep himself "in cotton" till he had a chance to see it again, one knew what he meant and understood it; and the day had not yet come when all men said, the Bostonians most of all, "Ichabod, the glory is departed." Two centuries lay behind the New England writers, and, if they largely ruled the national mind, if they were *voces populi,* there were reasons for it. They had grown in the great tradition of the Revolution, they were closely connected with the soil, they were readers and students of the classics,—three elements, deeply related, that explained their power and accounted for their prestige outside the country.* As heirs of the Revolution, they spoke for the liberal world-community. As men who loved the land and rural customs, they shared the popular life in its roots, at its source. As readers and students of the classics, they followed great patterns of behaviour, those that Europeans followed also. In short, as magnanimous men, well seasoned, they wrote with a certain authority and not as the scribes. If they believed in progress, and felt that America led the way, they professed their faith in a fashion that commanded respect, for they had known doubts and struggles, wars and vigils, and they made their profession of faith as men who had won it, not without years in the wilderness and days of blindness. They had cultivated their gardens, they knew the country, the sea-coast and the homestead, the lakes and mountains, where they

* In regard to their standing in England, Godkin ranked the American authors as follows: "The supreme American literary reputation in England is that of Longfellow . . . He has more readers than any living English poet. Next in renown to Longfellow and Irving, and in about the order given, are the names of Hawthorne, Emerson, Prescott, Lowell, Dr. Channing, Bryant and Theodore Parker."—E. L. Godkin, *Critical and Social Essays,* 1867.

Howells said, in *Italian Journeys,* 1867, that all cultivated Italians knew at least four American writers, in this order: Cooper, Mrs. Stowe, Longfellow and Irving.

had wandered as boys and lived as weather-wise men, familiar with plants and animals, the ways of nature, the trades and occupations of the people. Emerson, Lowell, Holmes and Norton had their Sabine farms, and some of them, like Sumner, resembled Webster in their knowledge of common farming and all the species of cattle, domestic and foreign; and they knew ships and shipping and the forest as well as they knew men and cities. Their books were full of all these human interests, this deep sense of the local earth, a sense that was fed by their classical studies; for the Greek and Roman authors, most of whom were countrymen, had treated rural life with affectionate understanding. The reading of Virgil and Horace, who abounded in genial pictures of it, had always gone hand in hand with respect for the farmer. The decline of classical studies and the loss of respect for rural life concurred, in the age to come, with disastrous results.

The Saturday Club, as time went on, witnessed many changes. Already, more and more, with the rise of the railroads, with the growth of the factory-system, the Brahmins were going into banking, retaining their titles as Brahmins and abjuring their function; for this handsome appellation pleased the patricians, who had sometimes done little to deserve it, but who were not unwilling to appear as tinctured with the well-known Boston culture, as patrons and even protagonists of it. The acquisitive instinct that marked the Yankees, diverted into other channels, where it had produced such victories of the mind, was returning to its original channel; and trade itself was losing its wide horizons. The stately commerce of old, the India and China traffic,* had been ruined by

---

* "The grandest shipping in the world. Beautiful ships, clean as silver, manned by honest Yankee crews. There were gentlemen's sons before the mast, with their share in the venture, going out for the excitement of the thing; boys from Harvard, fellows of education and spirit. Forecastle filled with good Toms and Jims and Joes from the Cape, chaps whose aunts you knew, good stock through and through, sound to the core."— Captain Butler, in Howells's *A Woman's Reason.*

steamships and tariffs. This trade of an earlier day had
connected Boston with the history of Samarcand and
Venice and given it some of the splendour of Lisbon and
Antwerp, and the young men who sailed before the mast,
—perhaps reading Prescott in the maintop,*— or went
as supercargoes to Sumatra, had lived the sort of lives
that were pictured in Homer. The days were past forever
when the Danas and the John Lowells roamed the world
as argonauts or wrote their wills among the ruins of
Thebes; and the young Boston men who were scattering
westward were mostly to end their lives at desks in State
Street, hugging their stocks and bonds and "standing
pat." This day had not yet come, though it was coming,
as alien races pressed on the native race, as new religions
rose, with alien faiths. Then the city lost interest in the
country, except as a field of exploitation, for business or
for holiday-making, and problems of immigration and
factory-problems replaced the older problems of good
and evil, and men, immersed in money, ceased to read,
and the "feminization of literature" was a haunting question. One could foresee a New England turned in upon
itself, while Boston, sulking in its tent, refused to play
with Denver and San Francisco.

At present, outside the Saturday Club lay social, financial and "earnest" Boston, three Bostons known to fame,
and all represented in it, that stretched far beyond in
widening circles. Nor should one forget the other Bostons, religious Boston, often earnest, musical Boston, artistic Boston, even the scholarly Boston that lived apart.
Webster was dead, with Everett and Prescott. George
Ticknor, in himself a circle, ignored the Saturday Club.
This grand and chilly old scholar, who had written the
History of Spanish Literature and whose handsome Geor-

---

* "It was in the maintop of the bark Young Turk that I read Prescott's
Ferdinand and Isabella and Irving's *Tales of the Alhambra*."—Arthur
Sherburne Hardy, *Things Remembered.*

gian mansion * faced the State House, belonged to an age
that was past and had small interest in present or future.
When Howells, venturing into his study, remarked that
the Civil War might be good for the South, Ticknor, who
was gracious, waived the point and sighed, "Perhaps,
perhaps." The old days, slaves and all, had been good
indeed for Ticknor, and, though most of the recent writers who had made Boston famous had been trained in
modern languages in his Harvard department, he took
no interest in them, their lives, their books, their talk. A
more illustrious writer, Francis Parkman, who sometimes
appeared at the club, moved in a world of his own for
other reasons. An impetuous, active, strenuous man, vehement and reserved by turns, with keen, grey eyes and a
military figure, and a chin thrust notably forward, Parkman had wrecked his health in his Western adventures,
when he tried to live like an Indian, and he had to follow
a careful regimen. He was partially crippled by arthritis
and partially blind, and he suffered from chronic insomnia
and nervous disorders. As long ago as 1849, he had published *The Oregon Trail.* Like Dana's *Two Years Before
the Mast,* this account of his journey across the plains had
opened a new world for story-tellers; and Parkman's candid, cheerful nature, his martial tastes and his Spartan
habits suggested Dana's traits in many ways. He had
written, a few years later, *The Conspiracy of Pontiac,*
and he had been preparing ever since, when he was able
to work, for his later series of volumes on the "old
French war." His life had been broken by years of pain
and blindness; but in 1865, when he was forty-two, he had
resumed the thread of publication. A greater writer perhaps than Prescott, who had shared his physical disabilities, and certainly greater than Motley, whose work,

* Sometimes called the "Ticknor iceberg." When someone asked "Tom"
Appleton where he had spent an afternoon, he replied, "I've been calling
on the Jungfrau, the Tête Noire and the Mère [*sic*] de Glace,"—Mr. and
Mrs. Ticknor and their daughter Anna.

since *The Rise of the Dutch Republic,* had lost itself in a welter of documents, Parkman was the climax and the crown of the Boston historical school, which was soon to shift its ground and its point of view. The last romantic historian, in a world that was turning scientific, deriving his impulse from Scott, as he drew his design from Gibbon, Parkman was a lonely man who stood outside his epoch, an aristocrat, a stoic and an artist.

The other Bostons, aesthetic and "earnest," were also represented by men who left good books and better talk behind them. The Boston Art Museum had not yet been established, and Norton had tried in vain to interest the town in James Jackson Jarves's Italian collection, the Bellini, the Pollaiuolo and others that had recently found a home at Yale. The demand for museums, however, was rapidly rising,* and the day had passed when it required courage to hang a painted Venus in the Athenæum.† Even young men from the country ceased to ask, "Is this respectable, sir?" as they opened the door of the reading-room and beheld the casts. No one spoke for this change of feeling better than Thomas G. Appleton, the brother of Longfellow's wife and the son of a notable manufacturer. This early friend of Motley, with large means and expansive tastes, was a gourmet and also a spiritualist, and a lover of purple and gold and all things edible, visible, touchable, including Persian rugs and downy sofas. A bachelor and a globe-trotter, a yachtsman and a book-collector, "Tom" Appleton was the only man who could ride over Holmes and Lowell and talk them down. There were many who cherished him for this, although Holmes

* "The presence of twenty first-rate pictures in one of our great cities would save a great deal of going abroad, and help to form a sincere and intelligent standard of aesthetic judgment . . . We should have a Titian, a Rubens, an Andrea, a Paul Veronese, and so on."—Julia Ward Howe, *From the Oak to the Olive,* 1868.

† "In an early exhibition [William] Page had had the courage to hang there a Venus—at which visitors glanced hastily, quickening their steps." —*Later Years of the Saturday Club,* edited by M. A. De Wolfe Howe.

was not among them; for Appleton got the credit for
some of the doctor's "good things." His wit was excellent
and famous, and he loved all kinds of art and artists,
beginning with cooks and ending with Corot and Millet.
He encouraged the taste for French art that William
Morris Hunt was also promoting. For Hunt, the painter
from Vermont, had settled in Boston recently, as the
apostolic successor of Copley and Stuart. His portrait of
Chief Justice Shaw, which hung in the Salem Court House,
had given him this position almost at once; although Hunt,
who was also a landscape-painter, a figure-painter, a
painter of horses, for which he had a passionate affection,
chafed at the time he wasted on Boston eyebrows. Somebody's fourteenth cousin was always thinking that his
eyebrows should turn up a little more. Hunt had returned
to America in 1855, after years in Barbizon and Paris,
and he had lived at Newport before he came to Boston.
In Boston, as at Newport, his "art class" was a centre of
light. He radiated an influence like Agassiz's in science
and Ticknor's in the old days at Harvard; and "what
Hunt said" passed from mouth to mouth, even when he
swore like a trooper.

In Hunt, in Tom Appleton, even in Dr. Holmes's talk,
the energy of Boston was already following new directions. The old love of learning persisted, with much of
the old religious feeling, which the doctor expressed in his
hymns; and the emphasis that was placed upon culture
was certainly stronger than ever.* But the cause of the
other-worldly and the cause of reform had lost much of
their former impulse, and the triumph of the banking interest was accompanied already by a growth of conservative feeling and all things mundane. The

* "A Greek got his civilization by talking and looking, and in some
measure a Parisian may still do it. But we, who live remote from history
and monuments, we must read or we must barbarize."—Bromfield Corey,
in Howells's *The Rise of Silas Lapham*.

solid man of Boston,
A comfortable man, with dividends,
And the first salmon, and the first green peas,

presided over an Israel at last untroubled. The days of
the great crusades were over. The Unitarian movement
had spent its force, nor had any cause of equal strength
taken the place of Abolition. People who loved goodness
had ceased to "adore" it, with the burning heart of the
saint who lay in Mount Auburn; and, ceasing to adore,
they ceased to struggle. Emerson, it appeared, was right,
—the Unitarians, born Unitarians, had a pale, shallow
religion; * and, as Channing had been born something
else, so something else was to take his place, as the Catholics rose in power, before Phillips Brooks appeared and
the light of an Episcopalian pulpit outshone the long-
dimmed lamps of the "Boston religion." The Orthodox
faith had passed in Boston, in the minds of the more conscious classes, and no one supposed any longer that the
simple and logical creed of Channing, which had lost
Channing's genius once for all, would ever sweep the
South, as Jefferson had predicted, or even sweep Boston
in the future. But outwardly Channing's religion was still
triumphant. With Theodore Parker out of the picture,
the stirring and troublesome Parker, it was even more
respectable than ever; nor were excellent ministers wanting, admirable men, intelligent, humane, with ample
hearts. The two great divines were Dr. Clarke and Dr.
Hale, James Freeman Clarke, who had studied German
literature with Margaret Fuller, and Edward Everett
Hale, the author of *The Man Without a Country*. They
represented a liberal faith with few, if any, doctrinal elements that might have been described as ethical culture.

* "The Unitarians, born Unitarians, have a pale, shallow religion; but
the Calvinist born and reared under his vigorous, ascetic, scowling creed,
and then ripened into a Unitarian, becomes powerful, as Dr. Channing,
Dewey, Horace Mann, Wasson, Garrison and others."—Emerson, *Journals*,
IX, 408.

Both had been anti-slavery men, both were experienced writers, both applied their faith to social questions. They were "practical" theologians both. Clarke's temper was more spiritual, and he was more of a thinker than Hale; he was also more of the past, as Hale was more of the future. While his *Ten Great Religions* became, and remained, a standard book, in the field of comparative studies that was rapidly growing, his lectures on *Self-Culture* were an outgrowth of the Peabody circle, in the days of Brook Farm and the "Newness." Hale, an exuberant journalist with a touch of genius, wrote more than sixty books. With his large, cheerful, breezy mind, he was famous for his picturesqueness. In time, he became the "grand old man" of Boston.

If, in these useful characters, religious Boston showed, with whatever advances, a falling off, in zeal, in essential energy,—for neither Hale nor Clarke compared with Channing or Parker,—this was true as well in the sphere of reform. The moral passion of the old reformers, those who still survived, had largely lost its aim and its momentum. Wendell Phillips, however, continued to fight for all the new reforms; and there were others, Miss Peabody, Mrs. Howe and Dr. Howe, the well-known "Cadmus of the blind." In the good Elizabeth Peabody, the sister-in-law of Hawthorne, whose spectacles were often on her chin, whose bonnet was usually smashed, as if in some fresh encounter with the powers of darkness, while her white hair hung loose, like her opinions,—in the genius of the American kindergarten the passion for justice and progress fermented as ever, though her eyes were faded and strained by the dim lamps of lecture-halls. Miss Peabody was one of the old reformers who never lost her zest, and Julia Ward Howe and Dr. Howe resembled her in this respect. Samuel Gridley Howe had had two careers. As the surgeon-general of the Greek navy, he had played a great part in the revolution in

which Byron lost his life. He had fought with the Turks
hand to hand, a nineteenth-century Yankee Cervantes,
sleeping under the stars with the mountaineers, dressed
in snowy chemise and shaggy capote, with only his cloak
for a mattress. He had risked his life in Paris, in the
July revolution, and shared in a Polish revolt, and had
later been imprisoned in a Prussian dungeon; and the
fund he had raised for the Cretans had paid for the education of a whole generation of Cretan children. His second career, meanwhile, had made his name a household
word, with the name of his famous pupil, Laura Bridgman. For Dr. Howe, as for Wendell Phillips, the cause
of reform was never-ending, nor was it ever to end for
Mrs. Howe. In Washington, in '61, working in the army
camps, she had driven one afternoon with Dr. Clarke.
The soldiers tramped beside the carriage, singing *John
Brown's Body*. Her nerves and her blood were beating
with the rhythm when she woke in the middle of the
night, and suddenly the words came that Dr. Clarke had
asked for and she wrote the *Battle Hymn* in half an hour.
If she never reached this pitch again, the "good hope of
humanity" was the theme of her life, and for decades and
scores of years she sang it and talked it until she became
a national institution.

As long as Mrs. Howe lived, there were always a few
apostles left to vindicate the name of earnest Boston. A
small, shapeless woman, at present, who had once been
exceedingly pretty, with an air of unmistakable distinction, she radiated bonhomie and wisdom. While her hat
was often askew, she abounded in wit, and her reddish
hair suggested a fiery temper; but she overflowed with
intelligent goodness, warmth of heart, romantic feeling,
even as she excelled in common sense. Above all other
jewels, she prized plain speaking. In this, she resembled
another woman, also born in New York, who represented
the later Boston as Mrs. Howe represented the earlier.

For Mrs. "Jack" Gardner already lived in Beacon Street, where she spent all her mornings in bed, though she was to rise betimes and gather culture in a fashion that astonished even Boston. In those days, a third woman, Mary Baker Eddy, was also to figure largely in the Boston scene, which had heard a great deal about "feminization,"—with effects, remote from the world of Holmes, that suggested an even remoter New England, the days of the evil eye and Salem witchcraft. Mrs. Eddy also, a seeress from New Hampshire, had spent seven years in bed, the victim of hysteria and depression; but she had been cured by a miracle at Swampscott and was leading a desperate life at the moment in Lynn, driven from lodging to lodging, while she toiled at a manuscript in which she hoped to reconcile her message with the teaching of the Scriptures. The doctrine of progress in the future was complicated by certain facts of which Dr. Holmes's Boston was unaware, in the days when Howells surveyed the scene, when the "American Athens" rejoiced in its strength, in its statesmen and historians, wits and poets, all in the pride of security.

At present, these complications were remote. Mrs. Stowe had called New England the "seed-bed" of the great republic, adding that its people were "called and chosen for some great work on earth." This still seemed a reasonable statement. Moreover, if New England was the seed-bed, Boston was the hothouse. There the rarer seedlings came to blossom.

CHAPTER II

CAMBRIDGE AFTER THE CIVIL WAR

CAMBRIDGE, when Howells settled there, had much of the village look of old. A low rustic fence surrounded the buildings of Harvard College. The pump stood in the square. The horses stopped to drink at the trough beside it, and cows were pastured in the vacant lots that lay beyond the Common. The agitation of one of these cows, stung by an undomesticated gadfly, was quite an event in the eyes of Howells, who knew the importance of trifles. When a large dog appeared at his gate, or two men walked up Oxford Street, or a man drove past in a trotting-buggy, Howells was really excited; and John Holmes, Dr. Holmes's brother, who lived in Appian Way, said that when two cats crossed the street all the neighbours rushed to the window. In the tranquil Cambridge atmosphere, so confident and simple, lingered still, after so many changes, the fresh morning spirit of the young republic. The Civil War had come and gone and left its tragic wreckage there as elsewhere. But the cheerful note of an earlier day survived in a timeless air of delightful studies.

The population consisted of authors, or so it was supposed in other regions. In this, the scholastic suburb resembled Concord, where, the rumour ran, in every household, they read the Rig-Veda at the breakfast-table. You could not shoot in any direction, a visitor from the West remarked,* without bringing down the writer of two or

* Bret Harte,—a little later.

three volumes; and a Cambridge lady said that, when she met a Cambridge man and found herself at a loss for conversation, she had only to ask, How is your book coming on? to receive a voluble answer. When one little girl said to another, "Your grandfather is a poet, is he not?" the natural reply could only be, "Why, yes, isn't yours?"—unless the ancestral vocation was history-writing, or editing Aristophanes or Sallust. One might be a corrector of the press, like the late "Harvard Aldus," Charles Folsom, or Ezra Abbott, son of the author of *Rollo,* the "deadly foe of error on the printed page." * There were three historic Cambridge printing-presses. But, whether as a scholar or a poet, an essayist on science or a storyteller, the chances were that any Cambridge stroller, on Brattle Street, the Square or the Common,—which John Holmes called the "Philosophers' Camp,"—had some connection with books and writing. The Cambridge authors were quite distinct, as Howells soon found, from the Boston authors, but there were almost as many of them. Longfellow, Lowell and Dana, popularly known as the "Duke of Cambridge," were the first of the numerous clan; but Agassiz, John Gorham Palfrey, the author of the *History of New England,* and Francis J. Child, the collector of ballads, were only less eminent than these. Nor could one forget Asa Gray, whose *Flora* and *Botanical Manual* were classical works. No one had done more than Asa Gray to spread the knowledge of natural history, and countless flower-lovers throughout the nation knew their Gray's *Manual* as they knew their Shakespeare. "Craigie House" and "Elmwood," the abodes of the poets, were the Delphian caves of Cambridge; but Dr. Holmes's gambrel-roofed birthplace still faced the Common, and even more exalted in its prestige was the dwelling of the Nortons, "Shady Hill." There, shrouded in his leafy park, the son of the "Unitarian Pope,"—so

* Horace E. Scudder.

called by Thomas Carlyle,—pursued his studies. Charles
Eliot Norton, as an infant, had sat on Wordsworth's
knee, and there were little boys and girls who thought the
great man had written a poem about this somewhat awe-
some Cambridge household. For whom did he have in
mind when he composed *The White Doe of Rylstone; or,
The Fate of the Nortons?*

At the moment, the centre of literary Cambridge was
the Dante Club that met at "Craigie House." The tragic
death of Longfellow's wife had driven him to seek, for
consolation, a long, laborious task; and, like Fanny Burney's father, a century before, under the same conditions,
he had turned to Dante. For many years he had cherished
this project, as far back as 1843, when, rising early, he
had opened his day translating two or three lines of the
poet, after lighting the spirit-lamp under his coffee. The
exercise, he found, aroused his mind and set him in a
mood for composition; and now, as age came on and his
fancy flagged, this old resource was more than ever useful. One had to keep one's mental muscles working: the
worn-out horse fell down the moment he stopped. Moreover, the interest in Dante studies had grown apace in
Cambridge, in the years that had passed since Dr. Parsons published his *Inferno*. Norton, who had translated
the *Vita Nuova,* was at work on the *Convito* at this moment. Lowell was lecturing on Dante, preparing for his
essay on the poet; and a more or less Italianate circle surrounded "Craigie House," an Accademia Dantesca, however informal, suggesting King John of Saxony's, Ticknor's friend. Christopher Cranch was sometimes there,
the poet who had lived in Rome and Florence and was
soon to translate the *Æneid;* Dana, who later died in
Rome, where he was buried near Keats and Shelley;
Thomas G. Appleton, with a steamer-ticket always in his
pocket, and George W. Greene of Rhode Island, who had
spent twenty years abroad and served for eight years as

consul at Rome. Longfellow and Greene had met at
Naples, in the far-away days of their youth, near Virgil's
tomb and Sannazaro's ashes, and Greene was at work at
present on the admirable memoir of his grandsire, the
great Nathanael Greene of the Revolution. In Italy he
had collected materials for Prescott, and, with his gentle
manner, discreet and suave, he was rather like some old
Italian house-priest, quoting Goldoni and Manzoni with
an exquisite Roman accent. He related faded anecdotes
of the Pincio and the Corso and seemed to know all the
Italian poets by heart; and, when he visited Longfellow,
whom he adored, Howells was always invited to join the
circle. For the former consul at Venice, who had written
Venetian Life and *Italian Journeys,* was a match for any
student of things Italian. If *Venetian Life* was not what
Lowell called it, the best thing ever written on the subject, this book could only not be so described because no
book could ever deserve the description.

The object of these meetings,* soon transferred to
Norton's House, was to verify and revise Longfellow's
version. They took place in the white-panelled study,
where the father of his country had held his councils in
the anxious days of 1776. Beside the southern window, at
the upright desk, the poet stood in hours of composition;
and here and there, in the spacious room, some literary
relic caught one's fancy, George Crabbe's inkstand, the
inkstand of Coleridge, Thomas Moore's waste-paper basket, the fragment of Dante's coffin, in its little glass box,
the gifts of friends in Italy and England. It was a pleasure to bestow these trophies on one who felt so keenly the
romance of letters. Each of the visitors, ten or twelve,
held in his hand an Italian version, while Longfellow

---

* Strictly speaking, the Dante Society was not organized until 1880. It has
published a long series of works connected with the poet. Longfellow's
blank-verse translation follows the original line for line, and almost word
for word. It appeared in 1867. Norton's fine prose translation was published twenty-five years later, in 1891-2.

read aloud a canto from his proof-sheets, first discussing
the canto of the previous evening. The poet sat at his
round table, under the shaded drop-light, and he read, as
Howells remembered, "with a hollow, with a mellow
resonant murmur, like the note of some deep-throated
horn," while the fat terrier snored at his feet. He read
very slowly, pausing at doubtful passages, alert for any
word of dissent from the others; and the circle debated
the various readings and weighed obscure words, while
Longfellow took notes and made corrections. Lowell's
knowledge was accurate, Norton's even more so; but the
benign poet was ready to learn even from babes and suck-
lings. His manner, as he looked about the table, suggested
that the humblest person present was uttering the most
delightful things. When the meetings and the suppers
were coming to an end, Lowell expressed the general feeling. Why could not the poet translate some Indian epic,
of a hundred thousand lines, to prolong the pleasure?

The Dante meetings at the Craigie house had a symbolic significance, for these post-war years were an age
of translation, as the post-Revolutionary epoch, a generation before, was an age of historical writing. As a rising
Boston critic observed, it was the rule for literary movements to inspire fresh translations of the major classics; *
and the close of the romantic epoch, a gradual close, in
America, was marked by translations, not only of Dante,
but of Homer, Virgil and various others.† There was
something noble and fitting in these gallant celebrations
of the great of the past, this chorus of hail and farewell,
in which the generation that was passing acclaimed its

* "It is curious to notice how every new literary movement inspires its
supporters with the desire to make a new translation of the great classics."
—Thomas Sergeant Perry, *English Literature in the Eighteenth Century.*
Perry refers specifically to the age of Dryden.

† Among the American translations of these post-romantic decades were,
—in addition to Longfellow's and Norton's Dante,—Bryant's Homer,
Cranch's Virgil, T. W. Higginson's Epictetus, George Herbert Palmer's
Odyssey and Bayard Taylor's *Faust.*

teachers and models, its masters and pastors, We who are about to die salute you. Other ways were coming, and other seasons, not without heights and depths of thought and feeling; but the spring days of the young republic, with all their aspirations and resolves, the Virgilian days, the Homeric days, were passing with the poets who expressed them.

In Cambridge, where Howells had settled, soon to be joined by the Jameses, where the young John Fiske was already creating a stir with his early essays, where Henry Adams taught a few years later, one saw the new age rising as nowhere else. The leaves had scarcely fallen when the buds began to form, but many of the leaves lingered late, and the sweetness of a ripe October clung to the Cambridge landscape. The sun rose there for many with healing in his wings. Some of Longfellow's finest poems, *Keramos,* for one, and the best of his sonnets, were still to come in the eighteen-sixties; and, if his more ambitious works, *Judas Maccabæus,* suggested by Handel, *Christus, Michael Angelo: A Fragment,* were inferior to the beautiful works of his prime, the story-poems *Evangeline* and *Hiawatha,* they still exhaled the personal charm, or shall one say the moral magic, that was always Longfellow's note rather than genius. This was the magic that Bret Harte felt, as he walked with the poet in the moonlight, the charm that Ruskin also found so rare.* Agassiz shared this charm, and, in fact, the two friends had much in common. Longfellow's position as a poet was at least like Agassiz's in science. The days were approaching when Longfellow's defects appeared more striking than his virtues. So it was with Agassiz, the "romantic" man of science, when he fought against the stars in their courses, opposing the theories of Darwin. His innocent

* Ruskin said to Longfellow, at their last meeting, "It's very strange, I cannot understand it. I hate Americans, and yet you and Norton, both Americans, are the only two men with whom I feel thoroughly happy, sympathetic and at ease."

vanity, then, his *réclame* and his looseness, the traits of
the scientific wholesale-dealer, the jobber, the showman,
the actor, who could not endure to be alone and who
liked to be surrounded with admiring crowds, as he dined
with a cigar in either hand or drew the long bow on the
lecture-platform, talking in his large, lax fashion, abounding in anecdotes and illustrations and leaving ample
spaces for applause,—all this, which had pleased the less
critical world of the years before the war, offended the
scrupulous minds of the age that was coming. Agassiz's
pupils turned against him. They all became Darwinians at
once and favoured Asa Gray, the friend of Darwin; and
only the most perceptive recognized that Agassiz, with
all his faults, remained the unrivalled leader. The labora-
tory-biologists called him superficial, but William James,
for one, knew better. The time had surely come for other
leaders, with other virtues, other traits and methods; but
Agassiz's matchless sympathy with the living world, his
temperament, his breadth of soul, his unction, made later
investigators seem poor and small.* Henry Adams owed
more to him than to all the rest of the Harvard instructors,—it was Agassiz's geological lectures that aroused
in Adams his lifelong interest in the subject.† Through
this old Humboldtian explorer, a generation had turned a

* "Agassiz came before one with such enthusiasm glowing in his countenance,—such a persuasion radiating from his person that his projects
were the sole things fit to interest man as man,—that he was irresistible.
He came, in Byron's words, with victory beaming from his breast, and
everyone went down before him . . . The secret of it all was, that while
his scientific ideals were an integral part of his being, something that he
never forgot or laid aside, so that wherever he went he came forward
as 'the Professor,' and talked 'shop' to every person, young or old, great or
little, learned or unlearned, with whom he was thrown, he was at the same
time so commanding a presence, so curious and enquiring, so responsive
and expansive, and so generous and reckless of himself and his own, that
everyone said immediately, 'Here is no musty *savant,* but a man, a great
man, a man on the heroic scale, not to serve whom is avarice and sin.' "
—William James, *Memories and Studies.*

† "The only teaching that appealed to his imagination was a course
of lectures by Louis Agassiz on the Glacial Period and Paleontology, which
had more influence on his curiosity than the rest of the college instruction
altogether."—*The Education of Henry Adams.*

corner; and so it was with Longfellow, Agassiz's friend. With all his defects, his flaccidity, flat and trite as he often was, Longfellow stood for poetry as no one else.* He knew it, he lived it, he taught it, he wrote it, with a joy, a breadth of learning, a devotion that caught the imagination of high and low. Was he a great poet, was Agassiz great as a man of science? One rather observed how different they were from others who were not great. They were Emersonian men, magnanimous men, speaking through poetry and science.

While science, in the coming generation, was to play a larger and larger part, the poetic impulse flagged and was flagging already. But poetry was still dominant in Cambridge, where the two most famous objects one saw on the street were Longfellow's brown overcoat and the great blue cloak-coat of Lowell. One met Lowell striding across the Common, a short, stocky, competent figure, with a slouch hat on his head and a chamois stick in his hand. He had had a great effusion of poetry during and since the war, in *The Biglow Papers,* second series, in the Harvard *Commemoration Ode,* but his interest in political writing somewhat overshadowed this, and especially his absorption in scholarly studies. He was preparing the essays that presently appeared in *Among My Books* and *My Study Windows,* the fruits of the college lectures in which he stood, and spoke, with wit and feeling, as a man of letters. These were Lowell's best years of prose, the finest critical prose that had ever appeared in the country. His radical ideas had lost their edge, and the taste for the old and the established that had marked his conservative youth reasserted itself as the poet languished within him. He lighted his pipe with flint and

---

* Much has been said about Longfellow's plagiarism, but it might be observed that Baudelaire, according to his own statement, plagiarized Longfellow in two passages of *Les Fleurs du Mal.* Baudelaire's poem, *Calumet de Paix,* was also a translation or paraphrase of a passage of *Hiawatha.*

steel, despising the new-fangled friction-matches, and an interviewer found that Lowell had forgotten he had ever written poems for *The Dial.** He had begun to suffer from gout, the "stamp of respectability," as Norton called it, which removed him from the ranks of the dangerous writers, for gout and good investments go together; but his contagious affection for the authors of the past, the wealth of his intelligence, his gusto forestalled what Plato well described as the "hard little eye of detraction." There was much in his manner that repelled some of his ablest students, who were excellent judges of men, N. S. Shaler, for example; † but for others, Henry Adams, Barrett Wendell and George Edward Woodberry, the poet, Lowell was the incomparable teacher. He was the voice of the many-sided culture that made their vision clearer and keener in particulars, the broad, impartial view that frees the mind from specialties and brings them into relation with the rest. He represented, his pupils felt, the studies that irradiate the reason by kindling, first of all, the imagination, giving the mind repose, imparting measure and symmetry and making life noble and generous.‡

Among the friends of Lowell, and especially Norton, who appeared at the Dante Club, was Francis J. Child, the ballad-collector. "Stubby" Child, with the reddish hair that kinked and curled all over his head, a stocky little man with fresh blue eyes and skin as pink as an infant's, was the greatest living master of Anglo-Saxon. A sailmaker's son from the water-front in Boston, he had been "discovered" in his boyhood, sent through Harvard as Norton's classmate and shipped off to Göttingen to study. When Edward Tyrrel Channing died, Child had been appointed to succeed him, as the Boylston professor

* See *The Prose of Edward Rowland Sill.*
† See the *Autobiography* of Nathaniel Southgate Shaler.
‡ See Lowell's speech on the 250th anniversary of Harvard, in *Literary and Political Essays.*

of rhetoric, the chair that had once been held by John Quincy Adams and that Charles T. Copeland held later. Odd as a gnome and gay as a cherub, with a brain that bubbled over with quaint conceits, he had a heart as light and warm as if he had lived in the greenwood, as if he were the merry man in Robin Hood's band who wrote the ballads that he was so busy collecting. When you saw him, with the children, in a barn, tumbling in the hay, or sitting on the grass and telling stories, you could scarcely believe that Child was a great professor; and, in fact, he liked to mimic the professors, the solemn souls, with brows bent, who strolled about with their arms in the breasts of their waistcoats. But if you had seen him in his class-room, you would have perceived what stores of knowledge can exist in the crotchety mind of an erudite angel. You might have seen an angel lose his temper, when he sent flying through the window a costly copy of Chaucer. The book had been bowdlerized by an unclean hand. Evil be to him who evil thinks! Toiling over Chaucer, on whom he wrote his classic *Observations,* editing Spenser's poems, he carried out his great work, *English and Scottish Popular Ballads,* which reappeared in new editions over a stretch of forty years. He had scoured the British isles for traces of ballads; and before he died, in 1896, he examined every manuscript that was known to exist. He printed all the variations, all the traditional versions of all the ballads, comparing his methods, in a long series of letters, with those of Svend Grundtvig, the other great "ballad man" in Denmark. His final edition of 1894 remained the definitive collection.*

* The "authoritative treasury" of English and Scottish ballads, the *Encyclopædia Britannica* calls the collection. It is said that no genuine ballad has since been added to Child's three hundred and five. See the Child-Grundtvig correspondence (1872–1883) in *Ballad Books and Ballad Men,* by Sigurd S. Hustvedt.

Child's work, carried on by George Lyman Kittredge, was influential in later efforts to collect the "vagrant" American verse of the Southern mountaineers, the Negroes, the cowboys, the Maine lumberjacks, etc.

If Child was not a poet, he was so nearly a poet that most of the actual poets were Philistines beside him. His notes, in keeping with the ballads, were flowers of the mind, befitting one whose motto was *peu de choses, mais roses*. Child among his three hundred roses, in the garden, with its borders of box,—he was scarcely taller than the bushes,—was the most engaging sight in Cambridge. He felt about his roses as he felt about his ballads. You heard him reading Robin Hood, reciting, almost singing, with an air as shy as it was jealous. Were you certain that you felt it? Were you sure you understood it? "Do you really like it?" he asked, with an anxious glance. People flocked to see his roses, as they flocked to hear him read, but few had a call to look at roses. They were mostly good souls, Child remarked, *bonnes mères de familles probes,* as Madame Le Clerc said of the women of Cambridge, but, with respect to roses, ignorant or frivolous. Of the rose, as of love, he added, the true grand passion, all other pleasures were not worth its pains.*

Child and Lowell had memories in common. "Did you ever lick molasses on the wharves?" one of them asked the other. Lowell, as a boy, had walked in from Cambridge, just for this, and to see the ships; for Lowell had a lively palate. One felt this in his critical essays. Child, who was born and bred in the "forest of masts,"—which had ceased to be a forest, as Howells observed, and become a "gentleman's park," so great was the decline of Boston shipping,—Child had known the taste of molasses before he heard of Robin Hood. He knew the old warehouses better than any Cambridge boy, although Lowell, as well as he, had boarded the East Indiamen, and the sailors had given them both rattans and bamboos for fishing-poles. Their common friend Norton had never been

---

* See the little book, *A Scholar's Letters to a Young Lady,* edited by M. A. De Wolfe Howe. These were the letters that Child described as "affection in spray."

a boy at all. He had dreamed of editing "Father's works" when these more adventurous youngsters who had turned out poets were storing away impressions of the visible world; but Norton, as a Cambridge man, shared their interest in birds and flowers. If there, as in everything else, he was mainly the scholar, his knowledge of natural history, in certain aspects, was equally profound and precise. He proved this, years later, in *The Poet Gray as a Naturalist,* a little book designed to show Gray's prodigious learning and observation. The author of the *Elegy* had interleaved his copy of Linnæus. He had drawn, in pen and ink, on these blank pages, animals and plants, birds and insects, with notes and remarks of his own, in Latin, French, English and Italian, enough to form a whole additional volume. Ruskin had owned this copy of the *Systema naturae,* and, after Ruskin's death, it was given to Norton, whose compilation of Gray's jottings, intended as a tribute to the poet, revealed his own exactitude of habit. The grounds of "Shady Hill" were a study for a naturalist, with Norton's Irish gardener in the foreground, the gardener from the Edgeworth place who remembered "Miss Maria" in his childhood. Moreover, as if to prove that he loved the country, Norton had abandoned his summer home at Newport. He had bought an old farm at Ashfield, "Lilliput,"—Farmer Lilly's,— among the hills of western Massachusetts. He had remodelled the house, where he held his harvest festivals in after years. A trout-stream ran through the farm, with deep woods of beech and maple and rocky ledges covered with moss and fern. There, with an orchard on the sunny slope, and meadows smooth and green, one could live a luxurious life on a German professor's salary. Norton was not yet a professor. He was maturing slowly. He had scarcely opened the career that made him famous later, as Ruskin's chief apostle and, more than this, as one of the teachers of Ruskin and even a teacher of his country. At present, he was editing, with Lowell, the *North American Review*. The two friends were reviving the great days of the "old North," to meet the problems that had risen during and since the war.

No one saw Norton and Lowell in a truer light than Howells, with more affection or with more discernment. The young apprentice-novelist, who had not yet shown what he was made of, knew their foibles well, for he had a wonderful eye for character; but he also loved their magnanimous traits, Norton's simple and helpful way with students and beginners, Lowell's liberality and prodigal wit. They, in turn, found in Howells a cultivated intelligence that was both poetic and critical, steeped in all their literary interests, a fresh, perceptive, curious mind and the deferential manner that they liked. Howells faltered at Lowell's gate and walked up the path with anxious palpitations, like Bacchus at the door of Pluto's house. As a young man who knew his place, he had found his *Atlantic* post a thorny problem. He had had to play the censor over the creators of this journal, and his reverence and his literary conscience were at variance more than once. He had discovered an error in one of Sumner's Latin quotations and was obliged to endure the Sumnerian rumblings, when he could not evade the task of pointing it out. He had even had a taste of Emerson's wrath, when he placed a poem of Holmes in a position that sheared the Concord Pharos of its rightful beams. This ire in heavenly breasts had given him pause. A child among the autocrats, he was distressed and puzzled, and had finally concluded that his duty was not to diminish their self-esteem, a view that Lowell considered entirely fitting. The veteran and the aspirant had gradually formed a warm alliance. Almost every week they walked together, in the sunshine, in the rain, in the snow, exploring the unkempt outskirts of Cambridge, the Charles River flats, the Irish slums, strolling as far as the port or

across to Boston. Lowell, who fed on his books for days
together, was also a tireless walker, with a wholesome
strain of indolence in his composition. He was a lover of
whist and regularly played with his cronies, Estes Howe,
John Holmes, John Bartlett of the "Familiar Quotations;" and he liked to have a younger friend to idle his
time away and keep him from his work, now and then.
Howells had brought him, from Venice, an inkstand in
the shape of a lobster,—an object of a fearful mien, he
was all too ready to think it; and Lowell, as they strolled,
talked over with Howells the discoveries which the
younger man had made, and stored away for future use,
in the Yankee speech that Lowell knew so well. Lowell
was not always pleased when Howells had observed some
turn of phrase or accent that he had not remembered.

. The young man himself, with his gifts of observation
and perception, was a fit recruit for scholarly Cambridge;
for, although he was a novelist *en herbe,* for whom scenes
and persons were all-important, he was at present an essayist and poet. He was alert for impressions, and little
escaped him. A Cambridge or a Boston horse-car was
alive with tragi-comedy for Howells, as a battle of ants
had been for Thoreau. The sight of a household moving
or an auction in a mean street left lasting traces behind
his eye. Nothing was too trifling for him if it exhibited
character. He noted the anxious, sidelong glance that a
woman gave her skirt when she shook it out. He went
once or twice to the Boston police-courts, not that he felt
obliged to look for life; he watched the crowds on the
ferry-boats, the excursion-boats to Nantasket Beach,
most of them shrewd and friendly, ready for humorous
intimacies with all and sundry. Of the dramas of domestic
life, in a modest suburban dwelling, Howells missed nothing,—the relations of the mistress with her maids, the
stories of which one caught vistas when a pedlar appeared
at the door: and he noted quite as keenly the foibles of

the Boston patricians, how they somehow proposed themselves as examples and models, as if no such examples existed elsewhere, surrounding themselves with an ether of potential disapprobation in which they suffered strangers to gasp and perish. For, although they had good hearts and would have rescued a stranger, if they had known how, from common kindness, they did not know how,— and this was the real trouble with Boston. Howells saw stories everywhere. He had seen them in Ohio, he had seen them on the Hudson, he had seen them especially in Venice. There, in his consul's office, in the shabby old palace on the Grand Canal, with the garden full of roses and oleanders, in years of measureless leisure,—for few Americans went abroad while the Civil War was on,— he had studied the few Americans with a vigilant eye. He had seen them distinctly against this alien background. He had seen the Italians, too, as the travel-books had never presented them; for what compares with keeping house, on a thousand a year,—the less the better,—for introducing a foreigner behind the scenes?* He had found the Venetians not less unique, nor less a mystery and charm, because he saw them in a different light from that of the old romancers. In Venice, as at home, for Howells, the muse sang mild, domestic lays, truer, to him, than those she had sung for Byron,—which made *Venetian Life* something new under the sun of travel. He had an extreme aversion to melodrama. But his countrypeople, old and especially young, and especially in their aspect as young ladies, aroused his interest most. As the husband of one of these young ladies, one of the Meads of Brattleboro, a family connected at various points with the public

---

* See Kipling's remark on the four years he spent in America: "I had known a corner of the United States as a householder, which is the only way of getting at a country. Tourists may carry away impressions, but it is the seasonal detail of small things and doings (such as putting up fly-screens and stove-pipes, buying yeast-cakes and being lectured by your neighbours) that bite in the lines of mental pictures."—Kipling, *Something of Myself.*

life of the country,* he had a good example close at hand.
Mrs. Howells knew the world better than the consul, who
felt that he had come from a simpler sphere; and, in fact,
this marriage was a canto in the great unwritten epic, the
epic of Eastern wives and Western husbands. The canto
in question was happy: one saw this in the serenity of
Howells's work. The wife was as well-informed as the
husband was observant; and she told him, in the solitude
of these years of exile, all about the New England people.
He might have lived in Brattleboro. He felt how deeply
rooted he was in American life and was desperately homesick for it, in spite of the pleasures of Italy.

In time, all these feelings and impressions emerged in
the sunny, friendly world that revealed itself in Howells's
many novels. In Venice, he had tried his hand at fiction,
but the long, quiet hours of his life there, and the pressure
of the Italian scene, had thrown him back on study as a
central interest. He might have been his own Professor
Elmore, in *A Fearful Responsibility,* who was writing a
history of Venice; † and some of the Americans he met
might well have encouraged this ambition. Motley, for
one, his chief, the Minister to Austria, deep in *The
United Netherlands,* appeared there, a "figure of worldly
splendour," as Howells recalled him later. The consul
and the minister drifted about in a gondola, and Howells
aided Motley in his work in the archives, obtaining copies
of documents for him, the relations of the Venetian am-

---

* Mrs. Mead's uncle, John Humphrey Noyes, was the founder of the
Oneida Community. Of her brothers, one was Rutherford G. Mead, the
architect, of the firm of McKim, Mead and White, and another, the
sculptor, Larkin G. Mead, was professor of sculpture in the school at
Florence where Michael Angelo had taught. It was through Howells's connection with President Hayes, who was Mrs. Howells's cousin, that Lowell
received his appointment as Minister to Spain.

† Howells long planned to write a history of Venice, and as late as
1900 he negotiated on the subject with the editor of *Harper's Magazine.*
The book was never written, but he drew up an outline of it. This was
printed in his *Letters,* II, 122-124. A later New England history of Venice
was written by William Roscoe Thayer.

bassadors. One of his fellow-consuls, under Motley, was the Boston historian Hildreth, at Trieste, a tired old man now, absent-minded, silent, who could not be roused from his reading of *Paradise Lost*. Howells thought vaguely that he might fit himself for a chair of modern languages at home, for he knew German, French and Spanish as well as he knew Italian. He had learned them all in Ohio, and one of his earliest projects had been to write a life of Cervantes. He sent Lowell an essay, *Modern Italian Comedy,* that appeared in the *North American Review,* and he made a careful study of the Italian poets of the years before and during the Risorgimento. He wrote the papers on Alfieri, Foscolo, Leopardi and others, who had roused the Italian people against their drowsy despots, that later formed his *Modern Italian Poets*. With competent translations, they were excellent essays, in spite of Howells's marked distaste for some of the traits of his poets, their high-flown sentiment and their vaguely aristocratic faiths. He had a temperamental suspicion of all romantic tendencies, including his own. Meanwhile, he wrote poems himself, some of which *The Atlantic* printed, poems suggesting Heine, or Whittier, or Browning. The monologue *Pordenone* was a capital piece. The most interesting of these poems were stories in hexameters, *The Movers,* an Ohio tale, *Louis Lebeau's Conversion, The Pilot's Story*. His mind drifted homeward, in Venice, and he saw the West again, the Mississippi, the pioneers, the boatmen and Indian hunters, incidents of the river-life, episodes and village idylls. He even wrote a novel in verse, *No Love Lost*. In all these narrative poems, his model was *Evangeline;* and one felt the originality of Longfellow's talent, seeing it thus reflected in a later writer. Howells was trying his hand at the sort of themes he was afterwards to use in his novels, and at intervals throughout his life he returned to the writing of verse.

Perhaps he wrote only one really fine poem, the lovely
In Earliest Spring,—

> Tossing his mane of snows in wildest eddies and tangles,
>   Lion-like, March cometh in, hoarse, with tempestuous breath.

Thus Howells had appeared in Cambridge first of all
as a student and poet. With almost no formal education,
he was prepared for the Dante Club as only a handful
were in this centre of scholars. Alone, with a sensitive
wife, for years, in Venice, he had been his own university;
and his Cambridge friends would not have received with
displeasure the statement that the Howellses, married in
Paris, had gone "at once to see the Louvre." As a child,
in a little village in southern Ohio, the son of a country
journalist and printer, he had set type before he learned
to write, and a group of neighbouring farmers, proud of
his studies, had offered to send him to Harvard. He had
chosen to stay with his family, who needed his help. They
shared his own precocious love of reading. They were
kindly, simple, gentle-hearted souls who had kept, in their
backwoods clearing, the tastes of the civilized world from
which they had come, German Pennsylvania and far-off
Wales. The father, a Swedenborgian, who had written
religious tracts and an English grammar and had published a magazine, *The Gleaner,* composed of extracts
from his favourite authors, had built with his own hands
their small brick cottage and fashioned a Welsh harp. An
anti-slavery man, who also sympathized with Robert
Owen, he dreamed of a "true state of things," in which
men would be kind, free and equal. He took over a paper-
mill, which he ran on coöperative principles;* and his
editorial articles brought him the regard of all the well-
intending politicians. He was a friend of Garfield. He
bought a Spanish grammar from a soldier of the Mexican

---

* Howells told the story of this venture in *New Leaf Mills.*—"turning
over a new leaf."

War, and he often read aloud from Swedenborg's *Heavenly Arcana*. His best-loved English poets were those who pictured the happy life of villagers and rustics. This elder Howells understood a boy whose day-dreams, as he toiled at the type-case, sometimes setting up his own stories, composing them over the types, were all of a great career in letters.

The family had pursued various fortunes that took them from town to town, and at last they had settled in Columbus. Howells's passion for literature had led him far. He had mastered three languages and passed through many phases, influenced by Goldsmith, Irving and Heine, Tennyson, Dickens, Cervantes. With a nature outwardly mild and inwardly humble, with a flexible mind and a will that was strong and tenacious, he loved form, he loved style and diction. Chaucer had given him a feeling for the Anglo-Saxon weft of his native language, and the grace and ease of Heine convinced him that the best writing springs from the common speech. Chaucer's cheerful temper pleased him more than the "tigerish play of sattire," as he described it; and the free and simple design of *Don Quixote,* with its large and noble lines, seemed to him the ultimate form in fiction. His work showed these influences later. At the moment, the political reporter,— for this he had become in Columbus,—had also a burning interest in human nature and a gift for "elective affinities." He met Artemus Ward and Horace Greeley, and he published with J. J. Piatt, who was afterwards consul at Cork, his first book, *Poems of Two Friends.* But he had a particular feeling for the Lilys and Julias and Sallys with whom he spent his evenings in the summer, sitting on the steps of the big brick houses that stood in their ample lawns on the wide, shady streets. For their mothers and fathers he had an eye, and even for their less enlightened brothers; for he was already writing little sketches of character. But the girls were much more

interesting in conversation. They were always waiting to
be called upon, on the front steps and piazzas, or beside
the soft-coal fire on winter evenings. They had all read
the latest novels, and they liked nothing better than to
discuss them with the only young man who had also read
them. One could spend an evening over *The Marble Faun*
and the mystery of Donatello's ears, not to mention Kenyon's studio and the spectre of the catacomb and Miriam
whose heart was as dark red as blood. Decidedly, the
young man thought, and was to think always, with a mind
that passed through other modifications, the young girl
was the most triumphant fact of American civilization.

In after years, Howells's mind drifted back to this
earlier time. Many of his books recorded the scenes of
his childhood. In some of his finest prose, he celebrated
the forest clearings, the old village life that he remembered and the people he had known in Columbus. At present, his place was in the East, where everything favoured
his budding ambitions. He had written to his father from
Venice that he could not go back to Ohio.* In this he had
shown good judgment, and, better still, when, after trying New York, he had fixed upon Boston. In New York
and elsewhere, he had met Whitman, Bayard Taylor,
John Hay, Stedman and Stoddard; but literary New
York, with Washington Irving dead and gone, was at a
low ebb in the early sixties. "Better twenty years of Boston than a cycle of New York," he thought, and he was
right, for twenty years. With his deeply affectionate nature, however, he never lost his loyalty to the places and
the persons of his youth. If they menaced his ambitions
at the moment, they occupied the centre of his heart, and
for this he was rewarded in the end; for the West rose

* "I do not conceal from you that I have not yet in the three years
shaken off my old morbid horror of going back . . . I must seek my fortune at the great literary centres . . . A three months' residence in Ohio
would dissipate it all."—*Life in Letters of William Dean Howells,* I,
89-90.

in his mind with a wealth of understanding that showed
how profoundly he had loved it. The depth of his attachment to his father found utterance in his work as well.
The elder Howells's vision of a "true state of things"
expressed itself in the son's unworldly nature. It enlisted
his interest in the Shakers and their communistic system.
It drew him to Bellamy and Tolstoy. But this was in the
future. His passion now was to understand New England.

It was from Columbus that he had gone to Venice,
from Venice that he had come to Cambridge. He had
come to venerate the luminaries who had shone so bright
in his Western obscurity, and he was already a lesser star
himself. He knew his own mind, he had carried the day
as a journalist, and he had as much to give as to receive.
He had a craftsman's hand and a friendly eye for everything that Boston loved and cherished. He was equipped,
by aptitude and training, to share in promoting its mission as a centre of culture; and, since fate had ruled the
merging of New England in the nation, he was prepared
to carry on the cross-fertilization with the best available
seeds from other regions. He knew already half the rising
authors, in New York, in Philadelphia, in the West,
whom he was to attract to *The Atlantic*. With his ir-
refutable talent and engaging presence, he had reason to
rejoice in his good fortune. In the evening, as often as
not, he went to a little party at "Elmwood," or perhaps
some less exalted abode of letters, sacred or profane, but
always a little profane, if it was sacred, and always a
little sacred, if profane, where the dish of scalloped
oysters, always present, always knew its place, and he
knew his place as well as the scalloped oysters. Although
he was not yet thirty, he could almost see himself as an
heir apparent.

As time went on, and he rose in authority, and the
novels poured from his pen, and people were forced to
exclaim that, with all abatements, no one had ever

scanned the country with such an all-observing eye, then, as the wonder grew, the more one saw that the "apostolic succession" was his by right. It had ceased to be anyone's gift, or in anyone's power to withhold. But this was the result of a transposition of forces that no one could foresee at the moment. One could only say that, so far as letters went, and letters went very far in Cambridge, Howells was an heir of the ages. Was he not, as Lowell observed, the living image of Chaucer, minus the beard, as anyone could see from Occleve's portrait? This was enough for Lowell, and enough for New England.

CHAPTER III

AMESBURY AND CONCORD

IN THE sea-bound region north of Boston, Essex and Middlesex counties and the tip of New Hampshire, all that was idyllic in New England found its focus after the war. In Concord, graver thoughts prevailed, and the hay-carts, decked with flowers and mosses, into which Emerson piled the children, to carry them off to Walden for a swim or a picnic, bore other invisible burdens. The trees in Concord were offshoots of Yggdrasil. In "Whittierland," they were simple pines and maples; and little more profound than the pathos of association gathered round their natural picturesqueness. The depths of human affection and religious faith underlay this pathos, but the forms they assumed in prose and verse were artless and largely impermanent. However, they marked a moment, in some respects a more than fleeting moment, in the history of the conscience and the race.

From Salem to Portsmouth and Kittery, and up the Merrimac river, where the White Mountains rose in the northern distance, the legends throve with the wild flowers that raged over the land in summer and autumn. Lake Attitash and Ramoth Hill, Ipswich, the Powow river and the Isles of Shoals, nine miles from Portsmouth out at sea, were stories in themselves and fertile mothers of stories and poems, the work of scores of writers, past and present;* for this region was an old world, em-

* A volume called *Poets of Portsmouth,* published in 1865, contained the work of forty poets who lived in Portsmouth alone.

bedded in the new world, with a depth of local history
that was scarcely paralleled elsewhere. Most of these
writers, like Whittier, never left their country. Europe
had only a vague existence for them, except when some
cause, Mazzini's cause in Italy, or Garibaldi's, or some
heroic figure, like Kossuth or Gordon, stirred a responsive chord in their bosoms. The humanitarian movement
in New England had found them all responsive. The
Abolitionist cause had flourished there, for Newburyport
was Garrison's birthplace, and Whittier lived at Amesbury, and the name of the poet Lucy Larcom, the Beverly
shipmaster's daughter, had appeared on all the petitions
in the anti-slavery days. George Edward Woodberry, the
poet of the future, who was also born at Beverly before
the war, remembered these old reformers. A touch of
their moral fervour lingered in him two generations later.
Whittier, like Lucy Larcom, never lost his interest in the
great human questions of his time, which related him to
the larger world; and, if this sympathy greatly exceeded
his care for the art of poetry, to which he was somewhat
indifferent, it kept him nevertheless, in spite of all his
peasant foibles, the reverse of selfish or petty. Except for
this, the poets of Whittier's group were local in their interests and their feelings. They lived between two horizons, the mountains and the sea, with the Merrimac flowing between. One might have seen a rose-bush in one of
their gardens, or an apple-tree perhaps, brought by the
Pilgrims from England, still bearing apples and roses.
The English pimpernel, which was not a native, grew on
the Isles of Shoals, planted there by the early settlers;
for the stream of history, in this region, which had known
few changes, flowed on serenely. The English mind of an
earlier day also lingered on there. One felt the note of
Pym and Hampden in Garrison and Whittier; and the
mayflower, the trailing arbutus, delicate, fresh and shy,
with its ineffable scent and virginal sweetness, recalled

the story of Priscilla, the Puritan *As You Like It*. Among
the youths and maidens of Whittier's country there were
many John Aldens and Priscillas. But in this dim bond
with Shakespearian England they were wholly uncon-
nected with modern England. The ties of first and second
cousins, which even the Atlantic had not broken, had become the ghostly ties of unknown cousins of the seventh
or the eighth generation.

A line of drowsy seaports faced the ocean, northward
from Salem and Cape Ann, pervaded with salty odours
and dense grey fogs. The gables and roofs were covered
with rust, and the worm-eaten wharves, with their armour
of shells and beards of floating eel-grass, brought back
the days of the China trade that had left so many relics
in these towns. The crazy old warehouses were filled with
coils of rope and bales of sail-cloth, blocks, tar-kettles,
casks and hawsers. Here and there a mansion stood, perhaps with a Copley in the parlour, boasting a cellar large
enough to stable thirty horses. The black slate head-
stones in the graveyards, with scythes and hour-glasses
and fat-faced cherubs, symbols of the Gothic past, fed
the imagination of boys and girls who were not too young
to remember the last town-crier. With his "Hear all!"
and his bandy legs, and the bell that was almost as big as
a church-bell, he had cried auctions, funerals and mislaid
children. Little shops, kept by "dames," dotted some of
the humbler streets, and retired East India merchants,
who were sometimes oldest inhabitants, came forth to
enjoy the flowering chestnuts in May. The railroads were
destroying the reign of the "local character," but now
and then some scholarly recluse, in shabby coat of antique
cut, emerged from the Reading-room or the Athenæum,
and battered old fishermen boiled lobsters on the beach
or passed their days whittling on the wharves. Sometimes
they carved a Chinese pagoda, or even a full-rigged ship,
or perhaps they merely exercised their fingers, while the

seagulls sat in rows on the rocks or soared and screamed above them. On the calm, blue sea lay dreaming schooners, and gundalows passing with lateen sails carried one's mind to the Mediterranean; but the sea was the "dreadful sea" to the fishermen's wives, for whom the reefs were reefs of Norman's Woe. They were always watching * and waiting for those who went and came not back, and tales of lovers lost at sea, of spectre ships and mysterious beacons that lured imprudent sailors to their doom haunted the minds of the children who clambered over the granite ledges and made caves and castles of the planks and timbers. At Gloucester, on the cliffs, they listened for the roar of the devil, which Cotton Mather had heard among the rocks; and the devil was busy on stormy nights in all these angry harbours. In almost every town, some boy or girl, a poet or a story-teller later, who had played in the sparkling foam and wandered over the tops of windy headlands, had heard a knocking at the door at night that signified the presence of the devil. It was the knock of a neighbour, with sorrowful news. There was scarcely a household on this northern shore that had not given its hostage to the sea. Woodberry, the poet, remembered how he was held at his Beverly window and told that his father was somewhere "out there." This was his earliest recollection. At Newburyport, Harriet Prescott Spofford drank in this dread of the sea, where the curlews called and circled. Thomas Bailey Aldrich, who was born at Portsmouth, had lost one of his playmates, who drifted away in a rowboat and never returned. Celia Thaxter lived on the Isles of Shoals, the bleak little heaps of granite that lay on the eastern horizon. Her father, the lighthouse-keeper, who had been disappointed in his youth, had vowed he would never set foot on the main-

---

* In *The Madonna of the Tubs,* Elizabeth Stuart Phelps spoke of the "curious watching look" of the Gloucester women,—as if they had spent their lives "peering for the dory before dawn, or searching for the sail at dusk, or scanning the headland by moonlight."

land again, and she herself, from the age of five, had never seen a town till she was married. Her world was Appledore and Smutty Nose, White Island and Star Island, with its tiny stone church in the hamlet of Gosport. The Hebrides and the Orkneys were not more lonely, and there one knew the terror of the sea. But there, too, as in all this region, the flowers ran riot over the rocks, the little stars of crimson sorrel, the crowfoot blossoms and the purple beach-pea, the goldenrod, the rose, the spiked germander. If they were not more lavish than on the mainland, they flourished in the salty air. They glowed among the rocks like masses of jewels.

The wild flowers set the note of Whittier's country, the scene and the poems that sprang from it, especially in these post-war years, the calm that followed the storm. The pastoral stretches along the rivers, with their long lines of barns and sheds, blossomed with the shadbush, the "shadblow," for April in these valleys was the time for shadding, and the fish gave its name to flower and bird. In Essex County, the flicker was sometimes called the shad-spirit, for its note was thought to indicate the day when the fish first ascended the streams. Some of these northerly valleys led to New Hampshire, where Winnepesaukee lay, and the Pemigewasset, the mountain-encircled lake and the silvery river, a land of sundered rocks, cascades and pines. Crag and meadow, stream and island, this was Whittier's world and the world of his friends; and even Boston seemed remote in Whittier's Amesbury cottage, with the harebells in the garden-room in spring. There he had written *Snow-Bound,* when the death of his mother and sister brought back his early days in the Haverhill farmhouse, where the family had lived since 1688; and there he liked to read his poems to Lucy Larcom and Celia Thaxter and other ladies, gifted and less gifted; for his women friends were as numerous as the poet Cowper's. One or two of these other ladies, with pity for his

single state, suggested themselves as partners in a closer
relation. The breezy journalist, "Gail Hamilton," properly Mary Abigail Dodge,—a sort of Margaret Fuller
watered down, and also peppered up,—who was buzzing
about the country, interviewing Grant and Sherman and
others whose names were in the papers, built a little house
for a poet and his wife and hoped that her good friend
Whittier would share it with her. She was not the only
one who embroidered slippers for him, but the poet preferred to ride at anchor. He had his little vanities and
liked a mild philandering, but a game of croquet was as
far as he would go. He was the pride and joy of his neighbours. He met them in the tailor-shop, or he sat on a
sugar-barrel in the village grocery and discussed the affairs of the day for hours together; and sometimes, recalling his hair-breadth escapes, in the anti-slavery days,
he would fight the battles over again. The old man would
leap from his seat, remembering these adventures,—how
he dashed with Thompson to the carriage, through the
side-door of the hall, while the lynchers waited at the
front. He had been pelted with stones in Concord, New
Hampshire. His happiest times were the "laurel parties,"
when all the Whittier circle, old and young, visited the
laurel grounds, every year, at the end of June. They
breakfasted at Newburyport and sailed up the Merrimac
as far as the grove on the banks. There they picnicked
among the pines, surrounded with the glory of the laurels.
Speeches and songs followed the luncheon. Whittier, who
was always there, usually wrote a poem for these occasions.

In the very heart of this region, along the river, the
scenes of the laurel parties, the factory-towns, Haverhill, Lawrence and Lowell, were spewing smoke, wealth
and desolation. Thousands of immigrant working-people,
Poles, Italians, French Canadians, slaves of the "lords
of the loom" who had lured them hither, were slowly

transforming the landscape. More and more, as the factories spread, the owners abandoned the region, loving it less the less they laboured for it, and ruled their slaves from Boston through the whips of agents. The whips were no less real because nobody saw them, and the lords in no way owned the Boston State House less because they ruled by legal methods. The horrors of the industrial system, visible in later days, were blighting the region already, and poets and story-tellers, already appearing, were soon to throw the light of truth and justice over the ghastly scene. Who was to care for Ramoth Hill, for the sites and scenes of Whittier's poems, when the pretty streams were fouled with oil and the laurels were blasted with coal-smoke? Not the Italians and Poles, who had their own associations; not the sons of the old inhabitants, who had forgotten these woods and meadows. Whittier's fame and Whittier's country were all but doomed together, so closely linked they were in a common fate; but Whittier and his friends were scarcely aware of these horrors. Their minds were open to social questions, and Whittier laboured as long as he lived for pacifism, disarmament and penal reform; but he saw the workingman's life in the terms of an earlier age, when he had made slippers for Boston ladies and Lucy Larcom toiled as a Lowell mill-girl. For the rest, how many fight in two crusades who have given all their energy to one? He had more than earned the repose his nature needed. In the quiet of his afternoon, he recalled the thoughts of his early morning. Then rose from him again, transformed, the psalms that had sanctified the Quaker household, hymns like gentle flames, tales of devotion, memories of the barefoot boy and the vanishing world of pasture and meadow and cottage.

In days to come, Whittier's poems, the poems of all the Whittier circle, found little favour in critical eyes, even less than the poems of Cambridge. Too many were relics of lapsed occasions, while others seemed as merely pretty as the wild rose, the goldenrod, the laurel; and the wintry winds of the modern mind blew them off the landscape. But the goldenrod rises again in its season, and the folk-poem recovers its meaning when the heart of a nation, grown old, returns to its youth. Literature abounds in special sanctions, those that govern national anthems and other expressions of faith,—hymns, folk-poems and ballads,—where the only point that essentially matters is whether the feeling, being true, is also sufficiently large and important. Whittier possessed this immunity, and Lucy Larcom shared it with him, as one of the glowing moons of this mild planet. Later, when the smallest poets were masters of their art, but few conveyed the feeling of a world behind them, one still felt, in *Skipper Ben,* as in her personal record, *A New England Childhood,* sincere, direct and truthful, the heroic life of an earlier day, as of wild flowers nursed in granite.

Most luminous of these little moons, Celia Thaxter dwelt in her far sky-parlour; or, rather, on the Isles of Shoals, where the bells tolled on their rocking buoys, she moved in an orbit of her own. In the vast wooden barrack, with its long piazza, the Appledore hotel, kept by her brothers, she lived with her poems, her music and her friends, surrounded by books, ferns, flowers, shells and seaweeds. As a child on White Island, where her father guarded the lighthouse, she had often kindled the lamps on the lonely rock. Her only companions were the goats that browsed by the little stone cottage. Until she was sixteen, the fanciful girl,—the "pretty little Miranda," as Hawthorne called her,*—ranged over the ridges and gorges, haunted with tales of ghosts and pirates, raced with the sandpipers, played amid the kelp and dulse, hung

---

* The account of Hawthorne's visit to the Isles of Shoals is one of the most interesting passages in the *American Notebooks,* edited by Randall Stewart, 256-275. At that time, 1852, the Portsmouth-Appledore boat was called the Fanny Ellsler, after the dancer.

over the pools with their bright sea-treasures, beaten by
foam and spray, as wild and free herself as a gull or a
curlew. Then Levi Thaxter appeared, and the two were
married. Thaxter, a Harvard friend of Thomas Wentworth Higginson, and a cousin of Lowell's wife, Maria
White, who had also belonged to the "band" in the days
of the "Newness," was a teacher of elocution and a public reader. He had studied under Charles Kean, hoping
to go on the stage, and he had come to Appledore to find
a lonely spot where, like Demosthenes, he could declaim
to the waves. He was already known as a reader of
Browning.* He had joined with Celia's father in building
the hotel, for invalids, if they had to come, for poets, if
they could and would. One burst all links of habit there,
and the writers and artists came apace, Hawthorne in the
early days, and John Weiss, the Transcendentalist, the
author of the life of Theodore Parker. Then Whittier
came, and came again, at first with his sister Elizabeth,
who was also a poet. He liked to watch the pretty Celia,
with her necklaces and bracelets of seashells, reading
Dante and peeling squash, or mending her Æolian harp,
or painting on her porcelain at the window,—barberry
clusters or apple-blossoms, autumn leaves or goldenrod,
—while the wild birds on the sills twittered and fluttered.
He read his poems aloud and she read hers. The visitors
came in crowds, as the years went on, writers, musicians
and landscape-artists,† to hear Mrs. Thaxter read her
poems, in the long, light, airy room, with its glass doors
and ten windows, its tables and sofas and screens and

---

* The immense and early American vogue of Browning, as later of
Edward FitzGerald, was largely the result of Thaxter's readings. Browning wrote the inscription for Thaxter's grave, 1885.

† Childe Hassam was one of these constant visitors. A Dorchester boy,
born in 1859, Hassam painted his first landscapes in the environs of Boston,
where his studio adjoined George Fuller's. He spent many summers at
Appledore, where he painted the crags and the surf. One of his first commissions was to illustrate and decorate Celia Thaxter's book, *An Island
Garden*.

rugs, and the plants and the twinberry-vines in dishes of moss. Eastward lay the open sea, and westward, as the sun poured in, one saw the peaks rising, a hundred miles away.

Celia Thaxter's poems were literary water-colours, the counterparts, in theme, vein and style, of her paintings on paper and porcelain. They were graceful, touching, fragile, evanescent. The best were her verses for children, *Jack Frost* and *The Great White Owl;* but her prose was better than her poems, two or three of the tales for children and one book written to last, *Among the Isles of Shoals.* She liked to quote Keats's remark that his intensest pleasure had always been to watch the growth of flowers, and some of her delight in this expressed itself in *An Island Garden;* but *The Spray Sprite,* fresh and crisp, and *Madame Arachne* had Hans Andersen's magic in them. The child at the lighthouse window, watching the spiders, had felt herself inside the spider's mind, and the lonely girl who had roamed the rocks, among the tumbling billows with their flying spume, while the wind blew about her and the gulls rose and dropped, knew the spray-sprite well and had often seen her. No one had ever known these isles as Celia Thaxter knew them,—sad, bleak isles to others, to her enchanted,—from Captain John Smith's cairn to the farthest gorge or boulder, the rocks which the islanders thought were split at the time of the Crucifixion. A hundred men living in Portsmouth, when she was a girl, had dug for buried treasure on the islands, following their divining-rods and scraping the chests at times, they said; and some had seen "Old Bob," the ghost, with the ring about his neck and the face that was pale and dreadful. Celia Thaxter knew them, as she knew the ancient graves and ruined cellars, the church that was built from the wrecks of Spanish ships, as she knew the lean, brown old shoalers and the ballads they sang to their fiddles, the spinning-women who smoked their pipes or crept about with canes gathering herbs. She had rowed from island to island as an amateur doctor, helping at the births of children. She had watched the olive-green sea, swollen and angry, streaming with vapour from the cold, when a sudden rift in the mist revealed a vessel driving to sure destruction towards the coast; and many a night she had opened the door to shipwrecked men who had struck on a ledge, when the wharf was a mountain of ice. *Among the Isles of Shoals* was a permanent picture of all these old, unhappy, far-off things, and of much that was lovely also, and unchanging. A hooked rug in prose, one might call it, woven of pure materials, in harmonious colours.

*
* *

If "Whittierland" was idyllic, so was Concord, though the Concord idyll had other tones. There, too, the wild grape flourished, and the hemlock and savin, the walnut, spruce and pine, and the ground was strewn in season with the kindly fruits of the earth. The quiet river, the groves and meadows, the thrifty ways of the farmer-folk, who sent their milk and firewood to Boston, suggested a tranquil happiness that knew no inordinate affections.

Concord was "without crime," in the somewhat violent phrase of one who was born there.* The only prisoner in the jail, the only one whom anyone remembered, begged,

* The painter Edward Simmons, one of the Ripley family, who was born in the Manse. He was a nephew of George P. Bradford, the old Brook Farmer who translated Fénelon and was Emerson's intimate friend. The limitations of Concord, from an artist's point of view, are suggested by Bradford's remark to Simmons, "Edward, anything but the physical or the material." The whimsical Edward Simmons was famous for his loquacity. When a lady begged his pardon once for interrupting him, he said, "Madam, no one can *speak* without interrupting me." It was in reference to this trait that his friend Oliver Herford posted a card by the fireplace in the Players' Club, New York. This card bore the words, "Exit, in case of Simmons."

when he was released, to be allowed to live there. He sat on the steps, on summer evenings, a great pet of the Emerson household, who was hired to play the fiddle at all the dances; and as for other odd fish, when the Concord people saw one passing, they were resigned to saying, "Oh, that's a philosopher." In Concord, as in Whittier's region, they had hidden fugitive slaves in their ovens, or built secret rooms in their attics to foil the inquisitive sheriff; and one or two Concordians had been tarred and feathered for a speech or a sermon in the South. But the tar was long since washed away, and the ovens had resumed their normal function. Bronson Alcott, building an arbour, or sitting on his rustic seat, absorbed in his Plutarch or his Plato,—or Evelyn, Donne or Cowley,—evoked the note of this later Concord. Sometimes Alcott bestirred himself to plant another row of trees, or a pleasance for his children by the brookside.

Simple as it appeared, however, Concord was very far from simple; and the wiser a visitor was the more he was puzzled. If the Sphinx was not an inhabitant, she seemed to have been a guest, at least, who had left her riddle behind her; nor had any Œdipus yet appeared, from the Theban world without, to solve or even approach the heart of the riddle. Concord was a formidable fact; and, when one tried to place one's finger on it, the fact turned out to be different from what one thought it. How was one to specify it? How was one to designate it? Most of the descriptions recoiled upon their authors. For instance, people called it the "American Weimar," as Boston had once been called the "American Athens,"—a singularly inept phrase. To have called Goethe's town the "German Concord" would not have been less appropriate; for nowhere were Goethe's claims more essentially challenged. Clever people had given up the attempt to classify Emerson. They never hit the nail on the head, and the reason for this was plain enough: Emerson was not for the clever. Nor was Emerson or the dead Thoreau a subject for the innocent. Whittier spoke of *Walden* as a "wicked and heathenish book," a phrase that merely described Whittier,—it did not describe Thoreau at all. There were others, like the young Henry Adams, the son of Minister Adams, who parried the riddle with irony, not attempting to meet it;* but Adams made good his position by denying the Concord premises. Idealism, for him, was a foolish thing; but, if one accepted idealism, where was the force of the irony? The irony cheapened the ironist. Goodness without intellect and intellect without moral perception were helpless in the face of the Concord riddle. It was true, there were those who could read it, though they did not bear the names of Theban princes. Obscure as they often were, these were the children of light, innocent as doves but wise as serpents.

Concord was deep, in other words, deeper than any country well, and the water of life that filled it was clear to the bottom. The difficulty was that one saw the bottom only at fleeting moments, when the sun was high overhead and one's own eye was quite unclouded. Three men of genius had lived in the town, Emerson, Hawthorne, Thoreau, not to speak of the gifted Alcott and the poet Ellery Channing,—uncrystallized geniuses both, one might have called them. If the air was full of cross-vibrations, if it was opalescent, it shone with a clear white light, most of the time, that signified a harmony of all these colours; and, if there was mystery in it, the deposit of genius, there was also a singular clarity, a clarity of per-

---

* "Adams approached it [Concord] in much the same spirit as he would have entered a Gothic cathedral, for he well knew that the priests regarded him as only a worm. To the Concord church all Adamses were minds of dust and emptiness, devoid of feeling, poetry or imagination; little higher than the common scourings of State Street . . . He perpetually fell back into the heresy that if anything universal was unreal, it was himself and not the appearances; it was the poet, and not the banker; it was his own thought, not the thing that moved it."—*The Education of Henry Adams.*

ception and will that sprang from older sources than
Plutarch or Plato. It was this that made Goethe irrelevant in Concord. All the Concord writers knew their
Goethe. Emerson had read him from end to end, though
mainly to please Carlyle. *Wilhelm Meister* had gone the
rounds, and all the young girls were fascinated by Goethe's
correspondence with Bettina von Arnim. This appealed to
their instinct of hero-worship. It led them to form attachments for older men, naively but excessively romantic.
Louisa Alcott, under the spell of Bettina, left flowers on
Emerson's doorstep, as a young New Hampshire girl had
laid siege to Theodore Parker. Louisa, stirred again,—
she who sat in the cherry-tree, singing to the moon at
midnight,—sang Mignon's song in German under Emerson's window. Emerson had written of Goethe with sympathetic comprehension, but he stood outside him and, in
certain respects, behind him; for he judged him by an
older and deeper standard than that of nineteenth-century
culture. Mighty genius that Goethe was, mightier in genius
than any American writer, he who counted his medals and
used the world to promote his own vainglory and his personal ego, who vaunted egoism and made of this his message, while he bowed to the princes of the earth, was
small if one measured him by the wisdom of Egypt and
India; and Emerson spoke by the oldest book in the
world. The tablets of the Nile were behind him; and, as
for the Concord "criticism," if it was very deficient aesthetically, it possessed a more venerable sanction than
any modern aesthetics. Most of the classical treatises
ratified its findings. Emerson, the sage, who was only sec-
ondarily the writer, fallible in his literary judgments,
uttered first and last things on the life that underlay, as it
also transcended, all the expressions of life. He was often
astray with "phenomena," he was seldom or never astray
with "noumena,"—at least less often astray than anyone

else in his time.* Kant's "two things," the "two things"
of Beethoven,—"the starry sky above me and the moral
law within me,"—filled his soul and armed his words, as
they had armed the words of all the prophets since the
beginning of man.

This was the secret of Emerson's power. In a day when
the greatest geniuses spoke for their time, he spoke for
the timeless things, goodness, not in defence, the intellect,
not with emotion, as one and the same; and he spoke with
the calm clairvoyance of one who merely revealed a truth
which the innermost mind of his hearers, responding,
confirmed. For things were so and not otherwise. No
doubt, the time had come for other teachers, who were
not so fatalistically optimistic, for critical and reflective
minds that grappled with secular problems. Too much of
the Emersonian bred an indifference to the hard facts of
American life,—which might come right in eternity but
was certainly going wrong in time. This life had never
gone so wrong as immediately after the war. Emerson's
voice was lost in a babel of other voices, many of them
prophesying doom. His words were overlaid, as the walls
of a house are overlaid with fresh layers of paper. But
what did the Ripleys find in Concord when they repapered
the Manse? Stripping off layer after layer, till they
reached the original paper, they found it was printed on
old French journals of the time of the Revolution. It was
covered with the speeches of Mirabeau and Danton. So
Emerson's words were written on the walls of the nation.

* This was the point of Matthew Arnold's lecture on Emerson, in which,
after saying that Emerson was "not a great writer," he observed that
Emerson's essays were "the most important work done in prose . . . in
our language, during the present century." This was an application of
the classical law according to which the ultimate standard in writing is
one that underlies the aesthetic.

It should be added that Arnold's approach to Emerson's poetry does not
lead to the centre of the subject. The point is not how far Emerson fell
short of Gray or Cowper, in their spheres, but how far they, in his sphere,
would have fallen short of *Bacchus, Terminus* and *Give All to Love.*

Whenever, in decades to come, the house was renovated, and the old layers of paper were stripped away, these words came to light again; and America once more saw the star of promise first seen in its early morning.

The Hawthornes had vanished from Concord. Thoreau was gone. At the Manse lived Mrs. Ripley, who was found in the attic once, rocking the cradle, with a Sanskrit book in her other hand, apologetic because she had to look a few words up and because she could not think in Sanskrit. Frank B. Sanborn, John Brown's friend and helper, who later wrote the lives of the Concord worthies, carried on the Concord school and contributed letters on books and authors to Samuel Bowles's paper, the *Springfield Republican*. These letters, with their news and gossip of the literary world, were a staple of conversation in the Berkshires. They kept Emily Dickinson well posted. Mrs. Hawthorne had taken her children to England. Julian, the son, who had lived as a boy in Liverpool, when his father was consul, was to pass many years in England; and there he began his life as a novelist. Before this, however, he had studied engineering in Dresden and worked for a while in New York as an engineer. One found a reminiscence of Dresden in his *Saxon Studies,* an acute but captious picture of German life, and in his later novel, *The Professor's Sister,* a spiritualistic romance with a German setting, involving hypnotic trances and astral forms. For a number of years, Julian Hawthorne reviewed books for the London *Spectator,* and for more than half a century he continued to write, as a novelist and a journalist, pursued by misfortune. His earlier novels, *Archibald Malmaison, Fortune's Fool* and *Noble Blood, Garth, Idolatry* and others suggested the later vein of the elder Hawthorne, the unfinished *Dr. Grimshawe* and *The Ancestral Footstep. Garth* was the tale of an old New Hampshire house with a gloomy legend. In *Idolatry,* an Egyptian palace rose on the banks of the

Hudson, and the story was like the dream of an opium-eater, with hoopoe birds, enchanted rings, eccentric uncles, mysterious murders and a vague young Dane who was somehow descended from Thor. Others were tales of "American claimants" in England, of whom Nathaniel Hawthorne had met so many, in the consulate, when Julian was a child, stories of changelings, ambiguous baronets and wandering American artists, of English manor-houses with secret panels, locked doors, dusky apartments, towers with ghosts and faces at windows. These stories were heavily documented as a tribute to the realism that more and more prevailed as the years went on, but in essence they were melodramatic; and one found less and less in Julian Hawthorne's later stories that indicated a personal style and vision. One saw this writer best perhaps as a rather ineffectual link between the greater Hawthorne and Henry James.

As for the Alcotts, settled at last in Orchard House, their world was agreeably altered by Louisa's success. For the big, bouncing, ardent girl, who was almost six feet tall, with her "force and temerity of will,"—which Alcott had noted in her at the age of four,—had followed her father's injunction: she was acting out her genius with a vengeance. No longer were the neighbours, asked to tea, obliged to bring their little baskets with them, to fill the pot with souchong and the bowl with sugar. "Duty's faithful child" had changed all this. Louisa had entranced her public as a chronicler of the Alcott household, which had cast its bread upon the waters and found it after many days. She published *Little Women* in 1868. In the same year appeared her father's *Tablets;* and *Concord Days* and *Table-Talk* followed, all in the train of Louisa's good fortune. Alcott's books no longer went a-begging; and, when he set out for the West, the "American Plato," with his brand-new trunk and gloves and cambric shirts, was able to count upon thousands of

auditors. His "conversational tours" were prospering as
far away as Iowa, where he lectured on Webster, Garrison, Greeley and Parker. He brought New England back
to the homesick minds of the exiled Yankees; and those
who had never understood why Emerson thought so well
of Alcott had only to read his books to solve the puzzle.
They had much of the charm of Whitman's *Specimen
Days*. The essay on Emerson, the "favoured of the Nine,"
his genius and personal influence, was a moving tribute;
and the papers on gardens and orchards, their poetry and
philosophy, were signs that Concord well deserved its
name. Not in vain had the rural muse traversed these
meadows, woodlands, fields and brooksides; and, while it
sounded deeper notes in others, Alcott wrote for the
future as well as Thoreau. With him the American wilderness had passed its savage and animal stage, and the
gardener, not the hunter, was the man it called for.* It
was finding this man in Olmsted, and Alcott was one of his
prophets. He had led the way with his arbours and Virgilian woodpaths, which Olmsted translated into parks.

Louisa Alcott's life spanned all the great days of Concord, for she was born in 1832, a year before Emerson
settled in the town of his forbears. She had witnessed, as
an infant, her father's removal to Boston,—from Germantown, which happened to be her birthplace,—and the
rise and fall of the Temple School and Fruitlands. She
had built her first play-houses with diaries and dictionaries
and had learned to use them both at four or five; for her
father, a "child-psychologist," as people said in later
years, analyzed and examined the minds of his daughters
before they were able to speak and encouraged them to

---

* "I came as naturally to the spade, the plow, the scythe and sickle as
to book and pen.
"The mind needs to come into tender relations with the earth and
treat that most intimate of all spots with something akin to piety, since
a personal pressure is diffused through every part of it, and divinity there
awaits to meet us always."—*The Journals of Bronson Alcott,* edited by
Odell Shepard.

shape their thoughts in diaries and stories. At Fruitlands, reading Plato with the others, she was used to discussing such subjects as "What is Man?" She liked to
watch the moon. She had good dreams. She had pleasant
times with her mind.* Moreover, she was physically
hardy. She liked cold baths at five in the morning, and she
throve on a fare of plain boiled rice, apples and Graham
meal without sugar or butter. She was a Dorian girl, if
Elizabeth Peabody wished to see one, who had undergone a training as severe as a boy's, and she knew how to
leap, run and wrestle. At six years old, in Boston, she had
driven her hoop without stopping all round the Common,
and in Concord she jumped off roofs and vaulted fences
and outplayed the boys at break-neck tag. She would have
nothing to do with any boy whom she had not outplayed.
She thought of herself as a horse, for she liked nothing
better than to race through the fields, tossing her head to
sniff the morning air. She had grown up tall, thin and
brown, with a yard and a half of chestnut hair, a towering, hoydenish, moody, stormy creature.

She had shared the Concord life in all its aspects. She
had gathered moss for Alcott's arbours and browsed in
Emerson's library, where she read Shakespeare, Dante,
Carlyle and Goethe. She had roamed the fields with
Thoreau, studying the birds and the flowers. She would
have liked to camp out with Thoreau and Ellery Channing, like Sylvia, in her first novel, *Moods,* the restless
girl who lived by "impulse,"—she had not learned to
live by "principle,"—and who joined three men on an expedition, with a cockle-shell stuck in her hat. Sylvia was
in love with the leader of this party, a tall, bronzed hero

---

* From Louisa Alcott's diary at the age of twelve:
"I wrote in my Imagination book, and enjoyed it very much. Life is
pleasanter than it used to be, and I don't care about dying any more. Had
a splendid run and got a box of cones to burn. Sat and heard the pines
sing a long time. Read Miss Bremer's *Home* in the eve. Had good dreams,
and woke now and then to think, and watch the moon. I had a pleasant
time with my mind, for it was happy."

who suggested Thoreau, as a young girl might have seen him, although Warwick usually went to the polar regions instead of Boon's Pond and Heywood's meadow. Warwick was a master of woodcraft and Indian arts, and his grip filled everyone with life and courage. Sylvia's expedition with these companions recalled the woods of Maine and Thoreau's *Week;* and Louisa, who liked to think of "affinities," and wrote this book to express her feelings, —in a Hawthornesque style that was also Goethean,— shared all of Sylvia's impulse and indifference to trifles.* She longed to be an actress, she longed to be a novelist, and she meant to live her own life, whatever the neighbours and cousins might say. She thought nothing of walking to Boston for a play or a lecture; and, when she made a "battering-ram" of her head, to force her way in the world and earn her living, she ignored the conventional notions that governed her sex. She went to the war as a nurse, or, rather, like Whitman, to amuse the wounded soldiers with games and stories; and in Boston she lived alone in boarding-houses, paying her way as a governess, a housemaid, a seamstress. Sewing sheets and pillowcases, neckties and handkerchiefs, she wrote plays and stories in her attic, lying awake and planning chapters of novels and sometimes working fourteen hours a day. One of her plays was produced at the Howard Athenæum. She was so depressed that she thought for a while of suicide. She was saved by the ministrations of Theodore Parker, who appeared as Mr. Power in her novel, *Work*.

Miss Alcott was an experienced story-teller when she finally wrote *Little Women*. Her first book was the *Flower Fables* she had told the Emerson children, in the style of Frederica Bremer or perhaps Jean Paul. But long before this she had written the melodramas and fairy-tale plays, with giants, pumpkin-coaches, harps and castles, water-

---

* "I like original people who speak their minds out and don't worry about trifles."—Sylvia, in *Moods*.

falls, thunder and armour, that she and her sisters had played in the barn at "Hillside,"—no doubt, the first of all the little theatres that rose in New England barns in days to come. As for *Little Women*, it was the author's high spirits that captivated the world in this charming book. She invested the Concord scheme of life with the gaiety and romance of a Robin Hood ballad.

CHAPTER IV

THE NEW ENGLAND SCENE

THE New England scene, in general, at the close of the war, was a battle-ground of permanence and change. The elements of change were appearing already, but the elements of permanence, also present, were as marked, if not equally striking. All that made New England, and was to make it, as long as New England endured, was sufficiently patent; but one had to seek it in devious ways, by a somewhat circuitous path, because the New England mind was shy. Bold enough, aggressively bold, in trade, in agitation, in religion, it was singularly delicate in essence; and this delicacy, the fruit of a long tradition of ethical culture, was more and more accentuated as the years went on. Change came over the world, and outward and material things swayed the human consciousness more and more; and then the New England mind retreated, withdrawing into itself. The esoteric note of the Concord authors, anomalous in earlier days, became, with Emily Dickinson, Henry Adams and many another writer, the note of the region. The Greek phrase "Hide thy life" was the motto of the later years. This was a gradual process, but already the seeker of New England found it best by a roundabout method. One had to begin at the surface to reach the core.

One saw the surface best perhaps at Newport, for visibility there was a fact and a virtue. Besides, at this well-known watering-place, the old and the new regime dwelt side by side as nowhere else. While the ancient wharves

and warehouses spoke of the past, the "Avenue" spoke
of the future; and for every black old hulk that lay in the
harbour, recalling the China trade or the trade with the
Indies, there were a dozen yachts. The vast hotel with its
sweeping piazzas echoed with the strains of the waltz and
the polka; and in the afternoon, on the leafy streets, great
fragrant haycarts and loads of onions brushed the tandems and four-in-hands, the donkey-carts and goat-carts
and the basket-wagons driven by pretty girls. One saw the
ruined fort and the Mill, the tower like the tomb of
Cæcilia Metella, the mansions of the eighteenth-century
merchants, with their fine square fronts adorned and
carved, their eagles and urns and pineapples, over against
the haunts of modern fashion, rising along the sea-walk,
the mansard villas and wooden chateaus, with their crenel-
lations and turrets, cottages aspiring to be castles or castles disguising themselves as democratic. A soft yellow
haze, the breath of the Gulf Stream, lingered over the
scene.

Everything at Newport suggested leisure. The mouldering old mastyards, littered with spars and timber,
broken rudders, rusty anchors, windlasses and kettles, the
lofts, with their coils of rope and empty casks, the pigeon-
holes with faded labels bearing the names of forgotten
ships, told the tale of a past that had ceased to compete
with the present. An occasional stately bark, spreading
its sails, might have belied this impression, but the air of
the population seemed to confirm it. Everyone sauntered
in Newport, and, if one hastened one's steps, perhaps to
catch a train, curious heads appeared at the doors and
windows. Hitching-posts had been removed all over the
town, to get rid of the multitude of old men who spent
their days leaning against them. So, at least, a shrewd observer said. It was true that the yachts and four-in-hands
and tandems, the Italian opera troupes and the great
hotel referred to something else than leisure elsewhere, to

Wall Street and State Street, Western mines and oil-wells, cotton brokers' offices and railroads, but only as these referred to spoils and vacations. The Point was a sort of artists' quarter; for the undulating land, the rocky ridges, the marshy valleys opening on the sea, the pic-turesque decay of the wharves and the shipping, the little dark gambrel-roofed houses, the tottering masts that Channing had climbed as a boy, attracted the landscape-painters. They pitched their easels along the sands where Channing had strolled with Dana and Washington All-ston. They rejoiced in the Paradise Rocks, where the great Bishop Berkeley had written his *Minute Philoso-pher*. The thinker's stony seat had witnessed since many a moonlight flirtation.

Close by the vine-clad Mill, Miss Jane Stuart lived in a little cottage, crammed with old furniture and pictures. The long-surviving daughter of Gilbert Stuart, who had passed his own youth at Newport, was almost as old as the Mill and quite as famous. A relic of the world of 1812, the world of Channing's youth and the painter Malbone, with a headful of legends and scandals as old and quaint as the tiles in the merchants' mansions,—the beaux and coquettes, bewigged and hooped, the priests, dancers and beggars of the days of Hogarth,—she had watched the growth of the watering-place; for this old resort of the Southern planters, whose households min-gled there with the families of New York and Boston bankers, had become a cosmopolitan centre, the unrivalled summer seat of American fashion. As an aspiring painter, in earlier days, she had been seen in Boston, perched on a stool, copying her father's portraits. At present, she was pursuing another ambition, expressed in her weekly re-ceptions: she hoped to supply the missing link between the world of fashion and the world of art. Miss Stuart had to resort to desperate methods. Although she told for-tunes like a gypsy and excelled in lurid stories of ghost;

and murders, she found herself obliged to stoop to conquer. She begged to be included in the humblest charades,
even in the part of a gorilla; and, as her fickle followers
fell away, she was always changing the bait with which
she hoped to win them. She would pose a pretty girl in an
oaken armchair, under a coloured window, to remind her
guests of Keats's Madeline, or she would place a bench
on the piazza, surmounted with a milkpan and a pumpkin, intended to create a rural air. "Rusticity," Miss Stuart said, "rusticity is the dodge for me." It was old New
England's charm for modern Newport.

Rusticity was the note of Lawton's Valley, where Julia
Ward Howe and Dr. Howe, Bostonians at other seasons,
spent their summers. But Mrs. Howe was innocent of
dodges. With no pretensions to smartness, she had an
appetite for the gay and lively. She liked a whiff of fashion now and then, as she liked to rebuke its vanities, and
she "rumble-tumbled" as she chose through all the Newport circles, with a jingle or a lecture or a sermon. The
Howes had bought a farmhouse in a neighbouring glen,
with a rocky gorge, a dam and a mill, and Dr. Howe had
planted a garden, beside the little stream, and built seats
and tables under an ash-tree. A rugged knoll sheltered
the nook, where Mrs. Howe conducted her out-door
salon; and there, on summer days, as nowhere else, religion, fashion and poetry met and mingled. In the mornings, in her alfresco study, under the Norway firs, Mrs.
Howe communed with Kant and Spinoza, as if she had
never heard of Washington Square; or she organized her
"picnics with a purpose," perhaps at the Paradise Rocks,
a clambake with a seaside lecture, an hour or two of
botany, or an astronomical evening, if the stars were out.
Mrs. Howe often read a paper, on sex and education, for
example, or she spoke on the value of character and the
dangers of wealth, the ease with which money bought the
press or the folly of marrying titles, a subject that was

apropos at Newport. She and Colonel Higginson, her
neighbour,—Thomas Wentworth Higginson,—formed a
Town and Country Club to remind their more frivolous
friends of the duties of culture. The meetings attracted
many writers who lived in the town or were visiting there,
the veteran George Bancroft, still working on his history,
James Parton, the author of the "lives," Fanny Fern, his
wife, the sister of Willis, the Reverend Charles T. Brooks,
the translator of Schiller, and Katherine P. Wormeley,
the translator of Balzac.* Bancroft spent every summer
at his villa, "Roseclyffe." Dr. Holmes came down from
Boston, and Charlotte Cushman was often there, with
Thomas G. Appleton and Charles C. Perkins, whose summer home was called "Bruen Villa." Among the younger
men were Alexander Agassiz, the son of the great professor, John La Farge, the painter, and Clarence King.
Helen Hunt, "H. H.," who was one of Higginson's pro-
tégées, was writing her poems at Newport, where she
passed the winters. Her father, an Amherst professor,
had recently died in Jerusalem, whither he had gone in
search of health, and her husband, an army officer, had
left her a widow. She had lived for years at military
posts, and she went for her summers to New Hampshire,
whence she returned in October laden with chests and
trunks. They were full of pressed ferns and autumn leaves,
which she dispensed to her friends. Her poems were redolent of these spoils of the mountains.

* Beginning in the early eighties, Miss Wormeley translated the whole
of Balzac. She lived for many years at Newport, but her later years were
spent in New Hampshire.
  "This year I have lost one of my dearest older friends, Miss Katherine
Wormeley . . . A delightful 'great lady,'—daughter of an American
mother and an English admiral, who fought in the Peninsular wars, . . .
Miss Wormeley had seen much of the world all her days, but her last
years were spent in a quiet house among our White Mountains, where
she busied herself with French translations, Balzac, etc. . . . She lived as
if she lived in London, but for months she heard few sounds beside the
wind and the mountain brooks and the foxes barking on the hills."—1908,
Letters of Sarah Orne Jewett.

Just beyond Lawton's Valley lay "Vaucluse," the stone colonial house with the large white columns, flanked by two wings, where Thomas Robinson Hazard lived, the Howes' nearest neighbour. This great grey relic of the past, surrounded with its gardens and arbours and hedges, where the rose and the myrtle ran riot, was a picture of decay and desolation. Green streaks of mould and moss covered the joints of the stones, and the long-closed shutters of most of the windows were half-hidden by creepers. From the deep-arched porch at the rear a weed-grown gravel walk led to the far-away knoll where the Hazards lay buried; and the woods stretched down to the sea, with miles of labyrinthine drives and paths. There were bowers and ruined summer-houses at the intersections, with jungles of box and ivy. The farmers still remembered the gaieties of old, when the windows of the dwelling blazed with lights and starry lanterns hung from the shrubs and the trees. All night the roses had heard the flute, as the dancers danced in tune. In those days, "Vaucluse" had been thronged with children, and scores of guests filled the paths and arbours; and even now, in June, it came to life and the soft air blew away the mouldy odours. The solitary gardener did his best to reclaim the lily-beds and the peony-bushes, and old "Shepherd Tom," on state occasions, opened his mildewed wardrobes, took out some garments of his gayer time and put them on and let them hang about him. Behind his closed shutters, most of the year, he lived among ghosts and shadows, for the old man was a spiritualist and a liberal patron of mediums. The spirits allowed him, for remembrance, to cut off locks of their hair.

Grey and thin as he was, however, "Shepherd Tom" Hazard,—so called to distinguish him from Nailer Tom, College Tom, Little Neck Tom and thirty-five other Tom Hazards, who were scattered about Narragansett, in castles, on farms,—had plenty of sap left in his veins and his bones. He had not yet written *The Jonny-Cake Papers,* a work of his eighty-third year, and he could still spin a better yarn than any of the woollen mills at Peace Dale. A rich old crotchety Quaker, he had retired from these mills, after making his fortune, and he spent his last years indulging his hobbies, reforming the asylums and the prisons and the treatment of the poor of Rhode Island. Tall, with a grizzled beard, he was a master-hand at controversy, and his two commandments were to love one's neighbour and to hate all Puritans with a perfect hatred; for, when even the dogs of Rhode Island, as strangers sometimes noted, still kept the spirit of Roger Williams,* how could he make his peace with Massachusetts? He laid about him in dozens of pamphlets, for he liked to smite the Pharisees and those who ground the faces of the poor. As a young man he had raised sheep and brought them through the snow of the bitterest winters, and for years he had ridden on horseback, all over the country, from Benny Rodman's Horsewhip to Pint Judy, vulgarly called Point Judith, delivering carded wool at the cottages of the spinners and carrying the yarn back to the mills. He rode thousands of miles through sun and storm, over bogs, stone walls, rocks and streams, till he knew every farmhouse in the state and every old wives' tale and old man's legend, from the days when Gilbert Stuart was a boy and Oliver Hazard Perry had never been heard of. He knew the Gargantuan feats of the Narragansett worthies,—Little Neck Tom, who brought down fifty-one teal with a single sweep of his duck-gun, and Stout Jeffery Hazard, who carried for several rods the sixteen-hundred-and-twenty-pound weight of the blue stone one

* "I know not whether anyone, even in New York, is so hardy as to laugh at Rhode Island, where the spirit of Roger Williams still abides in the very dogs . . . The small commonwealth, with its stronger and fuller flow of life, is more native, more typical, and therefore richer in real instruction, than the large state can ever be."—E. A. Freeman, *Impressions of the United States.*

still saw at Peace Dale. In those days, Rhode Island men
lifted their barrels of cider for a drink at the bung, and a
forty-pound Narragansett cheese attracted so many rats
to the palace of the King of Surakarta that the king and
queen had to jump out of the window. "Shepherd Tom,"
like Howells, knew the importance of trifles. What caused
the island in the Tiber but a bull's hide lodged in the current? Did not a mighty war result from the theft of a
diamond necklace? In the same way, old black Phillis also
caused the French Revolution, as Shepherd Tom's readers were aware. How the Rhode Island greening was line-
ally descended from the Tree of Knowledge, how Commodore Perry whipped the British tars and why roasting
and baking, in Phillis's kitchen, were arts the modern
palate never knew,—these questions Shepherd Tom alone
could answer. Although he imposed at times on the reader's patience, with his long-drawn-out parentheses and
whims, *The Jonny-Cake Papers,* with its twenty-six bak-
ings, was a classic of Rhode Island Yankee folklore.

The farmers still recalled "Shepherd Tom" driving his
handsome span of buckskin horses, with his three pretty
daughters grouped about him, to the old Quaker meeting-
house at Portsmouth, where George Fox preached in ages
past. Only the other day, he had sent the Howes a barrel
of cats that almost clawed their Boston house to pieces.
This "cat story No. 3," in the vein of *The Jonny-Cake
Papers,* was a sample of the mediæval humour for which
the old Rhode Island folk were noted. In Newport, milder
ways prevailed. There one studied the Middle Ages. One
did not act them out like "Shepherd Tom" and some of
the Renaissance popes. Among the Newport circles, remote from the "town," and almost as remote from the
world of fashion,—at least, the part that savoured of
New York,—was one that knew its Florence, Rome and
Venice as other Yankees knew their native duck-ponds.
This was the circle of the cognoscenti who had drunk too

deep of "Europe" ever to feel at home in their native pastures. For those who, having means and cultivation, had also the wandering habits of lovers of art, who wished to be in their country but not of it,—when they were not in Italy or England,—Newport was a point of reattachment that left them still detached; for the bustling American world seemed far away under the springlike sky of the Newport winter, in the soft, warm zephyrs of the Gulf Stream. There everyone had memories of the Brownings, of conversations with Landor and the haunts of Dante, and ladies who fell into reveries woke with a start and exclaimed, "Oh, I was in Italy." They lived again their days in Story's Rome. They were always "going back," with smiles of deprecation, although most of those who went returned again; for, after all, after all, there was so much to say for America! They sailed as they had sailed on the Bay of Naples, they sketched as they had sketched on the Campagna; and they gave occasional readings in the parlours of the great hotel, in which the Renaissance was often mentioned. Some of them studied with Hunt, who had settled in Boston.

Among Hunt's Newport pupils had been John La Farge and William James, the son of the theologian, Henry James, who had also come from New York; or, rather, the Jameses and La Farge had all returned from Europe, where they had lived at intervals for several years. Henry James, the elder, weary of a wanderer's life, had felt the attraction of New England, and, meeting Hunt in Paris, he had followed him to Newport so that William might have the benefit of Hunt's instruction. Turning one's back on Paris to study art in America struck his second son, the younger Henry, as a somewhat original procedure. People stared and laughed when they spoke of their plan; but the Jameses were always original, and also Irish,—they were members of a Hudson river clan. As for John La Farge, he built a hut on the Paradise Rocks that was almost as lonely and bare as Thoreau's at Walden. He liked to withdraw to this retreat, to meditate while he painted, for La Farge was a thinker and writer as well as an artist. His subtle mind, brooding and profound, was to find its best expression, perhaps, in his books, in which almost every sentence was a picture. A Catholic of French descent,—his father, a San Domingo planter, had settled in New York in 1806 and made a fortune in real estate, like Henry James's father, up the Hudson,—he had a foreign air that suggested by turns a cavalier, a priest and a dandy. There was something prelatical about him. Dressed in cool white canvas or a velvet jacket, he was always leaning forward, musing and peering, with the thick glasses and prominent eyes that were somehow vaguely Oriental. Catholic as he was, he admired Confucius and sometimes had the look of a Chinese sage, and later, in Japan, he understood the Buddhists as if he had known their doctrines in the cradle. Born and brought up in New York, in the French emigré colony, an atmosphere of wealth and cultivation, he had gone as a young man to Paris, where he lived with his mother's cousin, Paul de Saint-Victor. Among this well-known critic's friends, with whom he had been constantly thrown, were the Goncourts and Sainte-Beuve, Baudelaire and Flaubert. Like Hunt, he had studied with Couture and was drawn to the Barbizon painters, when the name of Delacroix, who was their precursor, was still a gage of battle, and he had met men who had known Greuze and hailed the dawn of David and for whom Rousseau and Millet were mere beginners. He had posed for Puvis de Chavannes and begun the study of old French glass, which he was to carry far in later years. Then, drifting into an artist's life, returning to New York, he had joined forces with Hunt and come to Newport. He and William James acted as Hunt's assistants, preparing his work, in the cool grey studio in Church Street.

In after years, La Farge, who was always an "old New York,"—he clung all his life to Washington Square,—maintained this early connection with Newport and Boston. As a boy, he had dreamed of decorating the rude, bare New York churches. Longing to renew the old alliance of all the ecclesiastical arts, he had studied mural painting in relation to architecture, sculpture and glass; and Boston was to give him, with Trinity Church, a splendid opportunity to reveal his powers. This church was the beginning of American mural decoration; and later the architect, H. H. Richardson, opened the way for La Farge's windows, for he grew more and more absorbed in the making of glass. It was he who invented opaline glass, but his mind expressed itself in many forms. Curious and versatile, as cultivated as Delacroix, he thought in colour and line, or with his senses, so that half the charm of his writing, a painter's writing, consisted in its difference from a writer's writing. Often indirect and always subtle, he expounded a philosophy of art as the love of proportions and relations, in thought, in the influences of nature, in the actions of men.* He insisted that the artist was a workman, the healthy view for himself, the healthier the more literally he held it, for it kept him out of circles where he lost his personal dignity and made him inaccessible to fashion, the destroyer of the higher taste and style. At Newport, in these early days, he devoted himself to landscape-painting, to the beauty and harmony of nature. He had brought back from France a multitude of water-colours, sketches of peasants, costumes, interiors, landscapes.

For William James and Henry James, his juniors by

---

* *An Artist's Letters from Japan* was perhaps La Farge's finest book. While his *Reminiscences of the South Seas,* composed on another journey with Henry Adams, was distinctly inferior to this, all his books were admirable,—*Great Masters, Considerations on Painting, The Higher Life in Art,*—lectures on the Barbizon painters, suggested by the memories of his youth.

almost a decade, John La Farge embodied the gospel of
art. Later, he embodied it for Henry Adams also. At
Newport, both the Jameses had studied with him, for
William James had a passion for painting, and even the
younger Henry, deep in Balzac, had worked with his
brother under Hunt. He made a careful drawing of one
of Michael Angelo's Captives. La Farge brought back
for him the world of Paris, from which he had been so
rudely snatched away,—La Farge, who had known the
writers he was reading, Gautier, Baudelaire, Flaubert, as
familiars in the household of his kinsfolk. At La Farge's
suggestion, he translated Mérimée's *La Vénus d'Ille.*
The younger Henry James never forgot these hours of
art at Newport. He was always at home in the studios of
painters, as many of his stories were to show; and William James,—a twelvemonth older,—might have gone
far as a painter.* He returned to his first love, science,
too soon for this. In the years when the Jameses were
living abroad, wandering from place to place and from
country to country,—in Bonn, Boulogne, Geneva and always Paris,—in school-rooms, in pensions, in hotels,
William James had been constantly busy with what he
called "experiments." His fingers were stained with mysterious liquids. His chosen toys were those that emitted
smells. He played with galvanic batteries and chemicals
and drugs and strange marine creatures that floated in
jars. He had an inexhaustible interest in the possible
queer effects of things. He had given all this up in a rage
for painting, and the rage had passed as suddenly as it
came.

* "His capacity was as extraordinary there as it has shown itself later
outside. He had the promise of being a remarkable, perhaps a great
painter. Even many years afterward the drawings I have seen him make
to illustrate some point of anatomy have a character as a memory of
Leonardo."—John La Farge, quoted in *Later Years of the Saturday Club,*
edited by M. A. De Wolfe Howe.
    An excellent example of William James's painting, the portrait of his
cousin, Miss Katherine Temple, is reproduced in Henry James's *Notes of
a Son and Brother.*

The Jameses had gone to Boston, and finally settled in Cambridge. Newport was only a halfway-house, for them, as for all the summer people and most of the artists and writers who found a perch there. The town had its own life, like all the other New England seaports, New Bedford, Salem, Gloucester, Portsmouth, Portland, and Thomas Wentworth Higginson, for one, shared this life abundantly. He was writing a novel, *Malbone,* and stories about it. But the little world of the colonists, fashionable or otherwise, touched it at few points and touched nothing else there but the somewhat exotic life they carried with them; for nowhere else did the springs and sources of American civilization, in business, politics, religion, seem vaguer or more remote than they seemed at Newport. If one saw some of the flowers there, one looked in other places for the roots and the plants. For this reason, Norton had moved his summer home to Ashfield, where the roots and plants were visible, if not the flowers; while the younger Henry James, who cared little for roots and plants, and who had scarcely seen the country elsewhere, rejoiced in his memory of Newport.

Not far away, at Providence, Sarah Helen Whitman lived, the widow of a lawyer who had practised in Boston. "Poe's Helen" had long outlived her hopes and her fame. Higginson remembered Poe. During his college days at Harvard, when all the students, deep in the *Tales,* were agog to see the author, the dark little man had appeared in Boston and given a public reading. He had recited *Al Aaraaf* in a thin, clear, tremulous voice that was somehow like the finest golden thread. Higginson and his friends had walked back to Cambridge feeling that they were under the spell of a wizard. That was in 1845, on the very trip to Boston when Poe, "on desperate seas long wont to roam," had seen this second Helen "once, once only,"—in her garden, among the roses, in the moonlight. He had seen her again at Providence, four years later, after attempting suicide in Boston, and implored her to save him from his doom; and there they were betrothed, amid cries, vows and swoons, in an atmosphere of laudanum and ether. There they had said farewell, a month before Poe's death, and Helen had remained in her scarlet parlour, with her veils and her memories and sighs, still sprinkling her garments with ether, still writing songs for the guitar that floated with Italian airs, conversing, through her medium, with the world of spirits. The time had passed for poetesses, clad in silken draperies, who wrote on locks of Mrs. Browning's hair, passing a curl about their circle and composing songs for each of its threads; but Mrs. Whitman still pursued her mission. For twenty years she devoted herself to defending her poet-lover against the attacks of Griswold and other traducers. Her *Edgar Poe and His Critics* was a skillful and generous little book, and she corresponded with Ingram, who wrote the English life of Poe, and Mallarmé, the French translator. She left no stone unturned to establish a truthful picture of Poe. Among the younger writers who had known Mrs. Whitman at Providence was Howells's friend, John Hay, the Western poet. As a student at Brown University, he owed to this romantic lady his initiation into the world of letters.

One had to look far afield, meanwhile, for the more essential Yankee traits, for the roots and the springs and sources of New England. One found them in Concord, one found them at Andover, where the old religion flourished as nowhere else. Thence, in times past, had gone forth the missionaries who made New England a power all over the world, the five apostles of 1812 who planned the Christianization of Asia and sowed the seeds of a modern China and Turkey; the founders of schools in the seven cities addressed in the Book of Revelation, in Antioch, Tarsus, Smyrna and Ur of the Chaldees, the colporteurs who had scattered the Bible up and down the

Nile, the scholars who had set up printing-presses,—the
first in Bulgaria, the first on the island of Malta,—and
translated the Scriptures into Tamil, into Mandarin, Burmese, Armenian, Turkish and the tongues of the Marshall and Gilbert islands. If Andover was not the mother
of all these feats of the old religion, the theological
seminary, of which Austin Phelps was president now, symbolized the impulse that lay behind them, the last great
wave of the Puritan faith, its final crusade to redeem the
world.* This faith had begotten the zeal for reform, the
passion for education that marked New England, for the
teaching of the black man and the red man, the education
of women, the reform of prisons; and the Andover theology, with its proselytizing spirit, had spread this passion over the West as well. Many a Western college,
modelled on Bowdoin, Amherst and Williams, had sprung
from the inspiration of the Andover doctrines. In the
strait sect of the Andoverians, the little boys played
"preacher" as their chief amusement, and ecclesiastical
humour was alone permitted; and Mrs. Stowe, living
there, had always lived apart, for someone passed the
rumour about that she had been seen in a Boston theatre.
Emerson was regarded as a wicked cynic, although, when
he visited the town, it was duly noted, his clear-cut, sar-
castic lips assumed the well-bred curves of conformity.
The Andoverians knew that Emerson was a traitor to the
faith of the forbears. Even the little girls were obliged
to study theology there. They listened to lectures on pro-
bation, on sanctification and eschatology, mingling with
their notes hurried portraits of their favourite academy
boys; and Elizabeth Stuart Phelps, the president's daugh-

---

* For a good picture of a missionary school,—at Beirut in Syria,—see
John W. De Forest's novel, *Irene the Missionary*, 1879. The minister, Mr.
Payson, who directs the school, says, "God has removed wisdom and
knowledge from the East." He conceives it as the mission of New England
to bring back God and letters to the lands that forgot God and letters
after giving them to the rest of the world.

ter,* had mastered the "Andover argument." Miss Phelps, —already writing stories,—could answer most of the Andover questions, whether everlasting punishment was the same as eternal and whether one act of sin was an infinite wrong. Was the whole race responsible for the guilt of Adam? The "chemistry of heaven" was another engrossing Andover topic. Was the body after its resurrection the same as it was before, or was the blood perhaps extracted from it? The tortured conscientiousness of Miss Phelps's novels reflected the Andover atmosphere. One of her young girl friends whom a young man dared to kiss had wept in expiation for twenty-six hours.

It was true that the Andover type of thinking had already begun to lose its force, and the strength of the old religion was failing with it. For this intellectual seriousness was a firm support of the old religion. Miss Phelps's stories reflected the transformation. In her first book, *The Gates Ajar,* which she wrote as a girl of twenty in the barn and the attic, she showed the growth of aesthetic feeling in the little world of Andover, where a dish of Baldwin apples on a cold winter day was as far as one had gone in the way of entertainment. She saw this book translated into French, German, Dutch, Italian, and countless American families that had lost sons in the recent war rejoiced in the youthful heroine's meditations; for, although she too had lost a brother, she still communicated with him, and what she discovered was consoling. The life to come abounded in modern improvements. There were all sorts of things in heaven, along with the palms and the golden cities. There were flowers and trees for New England nature-lovers; and they even had pianos in the heavenly mansions. That religion should be more aesthetic was the moral of this tale; that it ought

* Miss Phelps's grandfather, Moses Stuart, a former president of the seminary, was the author of the first Greek lexicon prepared in America. His Hebrew grammar was republished in England by Pusey.

to be far more practical was the moral of others. *A Singular Life,* for instance, was the story of a seamen's preacher who put the theologians to shame. They were aghast at his success in saving the wrecks and the waifs at Gloucester, when they had cast him forth as unfit for the pulpit. Miss Phelps's novels were problem-stories that sprang from the Andover mind, expressing its new developments and its natural bent; for they dealt, in a missionary spirit, with dress-reform, anti-vivisection, woman's rights and other humanitarian themes and causes. Her short stories, *Fourteen to One,* were often poignant and skillful; but the tone of her work in general was too consciously righteous.

The new type of Orthodoxy was represented by Horace Bushnell, the great theologian of Hartford. Bushnell, distrusting the Andover doctrines, had evolved a fresh point of view by denying that language and logic could state religious truths exactly. An intuitive, imaginative mind, he clung to the ancient mysteries, while softening their Calvinistic rigour. He, too, stressed the aesthetics of religion; and indeed the day had already arrived when most of the Protestant doctrines were dissolved in an Emersonian ethical culture.* Even Harriet Beecher Stowe, who was also living in Hartford now, had withdrawn from the Andoverian faith of her fathers. Mrs. Stowe had gone back to Connecticut and built a spreading mansion there, with towers and gables, a fountain and a greenhouse. At this very moment, in *Old Town Folks* and *The Minister's Wooing,* she was recalling the poetry of a bygone era, the fears and sorrows of heart of the Puritans whom she had known as a child for the perfect church and state they had hoped to establish. In these books, as nowhere else, one found the roots of the

---

* In 1878, Dean Stanley told President Eliot that he had heard most of the eminent American preachers. His general impression was that the sermon was always by Emerson, no matter who the preacher happened to be.

Yankee mind, in the Hebraistic air of an earlier epoch, when all were of one blood and race and the sentiments of justice and moral indignation, in view of cruelty and crime, were uncomplicated as yet by mundane interests. In *Old Town Folks,* especially, the spirit of her grand progenitors rose in Mrs. Stowe's mind at moments, and she was often inspired and often happy; but she herself had broken with Beecherism and all its works in favour of the "insidious paw" * of the Scarlet Beast. Like others who, in former times, would have joined the Unitarians, —like the poet Lucy Larcom, for example,—she was won by the "balm of devotional liturgy" and the "shadowy indefiniteness" of the more aesthetic Episcopal form of worship. The growth of aesthetic feeling, marked in Boston, was reflected in these transformations in the sphere of religion.

Through all changes of thought and feeling, the old New England love of learning persisted in the most unlikely corners. Was not "I want to know" the Yankee watchword? No one was surprised by the mystical worship of culture that prevailed in the larger towns throughout the region, those towns that abounded in clusters of sisters who were always called "the girls" and were often also known as maiden aunts. Classes in German were universal, botany classes, French classes, led by some friend perhaps of Auguste Comte, and there were rumours of Gaelic classes, conducted by a Highland chieftain,—the last of the MacIvors or whatever,—and Sanskrit classes in charge of East Indian princes. For occasional Hindu readers of Emerson and Channing came to survey the land of these cosmic thinkers. There was a class of young girls, in the town of New Britain, as late as the middle seventies, studying Sanskrit. Their leader was the "learned blacksmith," Elihu Burritt, the

* The Episcopal Church, as the old ladies call it in Mrs. Stowe's *Poganuc People.*

former consul at Birmingham, who had organized the
first Peace Congress in Paris, in 1849, and persuaded
Victor Hugo to act as chairman. Burritt, the living and
lasting symbol of the Yankee passion for self-improvement, had retired to a farm in the evening of his days,
and there he prepared his *Sanskrit Handbook* and his
grammars of Arabic, Persian, Hindustani and Turkish.
But all this might have been taken for granted. What surprised the traveller was the learning one found on farms
and along the road. One heard all manner of anecdotes
about the rustic Yankees who confounded the wandering
scholar with their erudition. Such was Frank, in *The
Jonny-Cake Papers,* who ferried the British Minister
across to Newport. When the minister and his Newport
host, disputing over a passage of Virgil, were able to
come to no conclusion, the ragged, red-faced boatman
raised his voice and repeated the passage correctly, singing it to a camp-meeting tune. This long-dead Frank had
many successors, like the Massachusetts farmer who corrected Norton. Driving about with another professor,
Norton stopped to water his horse. As the two friends
waited, one of them said, "According to Montaigne,"
and gave a quotation, whereupon the farmer, who was
holding the bucket, remarked, "'Tweren't Montaigne.
'Twere Mon-tes-ki-ew.'" "And 'twas," said Rudyard
Kipling, to whom Norton afterwards told the story. The
day had not yet passed when country parsons tutored
bright farmers' boys in Greek, while the neophyte paid
for his tutoring by doing the chores, plucking the parson's geese and washing his sheep and helping him to
make his soap and candles. No doubt, there were other
boys like Bliss Perry's father, who left his Latin grammar
at the end of a furrow, after glancing at the declensions
and conjugations, repeating them aloud as he ploughed
the furrow down and back, then turning the page and
ploughing with another lesson. There were boys like

Charles Dudley Warner, who memorized hundreds of poems while he was milking and who named the cows after Latin numbers, Unus, Duo, Novem and Decem. There were country stores where one of the farmers related in serial form the books he was reading, so that half the young men in the village heard most of the Waverley novels. For a long generation to come, many a Western college president was drawn from this bookish world of the Yankee farm, from households that read the Bible with Josephus and cherished a Christian life in the clefts of the rock. With all this hunger for knowledge, however, one still found traces here and there of an older than mediæval superstition. In times of drought, when the wells were dry, one saw the dowser at his priest-like task, with the forked twig of hazel in his hands, moving slowly across the fields, invoking the aid of Thor,—though he may not have known the name,—in his search for water. As late as the eighties, in Vermont, the body of a woman was exhumed to prevent her from killing her family, and remedies were still used in lonely households that recalled the pharmacopæia of the Pilgrim fathers, mullein-root in cider, tansy, burdock, sowbugs tickled into a ball and swallowed before they uncurled again, dried rattlesnake-flesh, the powder of a red squirrel, baked alive, pounded in a mortar and consumed while fasting.

The pictures of rural New England that lasted best for later minds were those of Mrs. Stowe and Mrs. Cooke,—Rose Terry Cooke, who was also living in Hartford. There had been earlier writers,—Catherine M. Sedgwick, for one,—who described the humble life of the country-people, but before these admirable realists, with their homely art, no one had truly conveyed its colour and savour, its rude strength and depth of feeling. In Mrs. Stowe's books one found most of the "chestnut burrs" that became the stock-in-trade of New England fiction, the philosophical sea-captains, the stubborn farmers and wild young men, the regiment of Yankee spinsters, infinite in variegation. These types were living realities in her pages; and a young girl in Maine who was soon to write about them, with an art that Mrs. Stowe had never dreamed of, had been led to observe her world by Mrs. Stowe. For Sarah Orne Jewett, who lived at South Berwick, *The Pearl of Orr's Island* was a revelation. This was the book that opened her eyes, as she drove about the country with her father, the doctor, calling at fishermen's cottages and lonely farms. But before Mrs. Stowe wrote this novel, Mrs. Cooke was writing her short tales; and it was she who established the type of rural story that other writers developed more dexterously later.* Rose Terry Cooke was the founder of the school that produced Miss Jewett, Miss Wilkins and Alice Brown.

As one glanced in later years at this series of authors, one observed the transformation of the Yankee scene. In Mrs. Stowe one saw it in its power and fullness, before the land was sapped by the westward migration. Miss Jewett and Miss Wilkins described the Yankee ebb-tide, a world of empty houses and abandoned farms, of shuttered windows, relics, ghosts and silence. In Mrs. Cooke, the tide was still at flood, or perhaps one ought to say that one saw it turning. Between the lines of her tales one perceived already the draining and denuding of the land, the movement of the young men westward and, more evident still, the inner decay of the region. Everyone remembered the little boy in Granville who shed such bitter tears in the rocky pasture because he could not find earth to bury his seeds. Since those days, countless thousands had left their farms, in search of the fertile prairies, in Ohio, Minnesota or "Westconstant," with their clocks and spinning-wheels and covered wagons, and their studded horse-hair trunks hung on behind. They had

* One of Mrs. Cooke's stories, *Sally Parsons's Duty*, appeared in the first issue of *The Atlantic*, 1857.

cleared the forests and bridged the streams and founded
cities and commonwealths, in the name of New England;
and on many a Western river-bank they had reproduced
their ancestral villages, the church, the school, the common, fringed with trees. For every one of their dwellings,
with its white-washed fence, and its pot of baked beans
on a Saturday evening, there stood some counterpart in
the Yankee homeland, a weather-worn house with a
maiden aunt and rooms that ached with loneliness, a mass
of tumbling wood or a brick-filled hollow where the lilacs
bloomed in Maytime, where

> naught remained, the saddening tale to tell,
> Save life's last wrecks—the cellar and the well.*

This world that was left behind, with its bramble-draped
cellar-holes and dim trails leading through the woods,
was to breed a peculiar miasma, as the years went on;
and one found prefigurations of Mary Wilkins's haunted
scene in the village life that Mrs. Cooke observed. How
many traits of a lowered vitality were evident in this village life, how many nagging wives and sullen husbands,
what covetousness and meanness with all its courage. But
still, in these western New England hill-towns, straddling
granite ledges covered with pines, these Stoneboros, New-
fields and Wingfields, with their mountain valleys,—
where the devil gave his name to glens and gorges, to
bridges and punch-bowls and pulpits,—one also found
youthful ambitions and romping lovers, Gargantuan
feasts, high spirits and the joy of living. When a young
man went to California, in one of Mrs. Cooke's tales,
there was always another young man to take his place,
a smart Yankee with plenty of "faculty;" and, with all
that was grim and terrible in the best of these tales, the
enveloping air was elastic. One heard through the night
the cheerful bells of sleighing-parties; there were husk-

* Holmes.

ings, barn-dances and quilting-bees. One was never far from the brisk little scene of the prints of Currier and Ives.

It was Mrs. Cooke's tales, perhaps, that Henry James had in mind when he said, "I hate old New England stories—which are lean and pale and poor and ugly." Mrs. Cooke's world was singularly charmless, and few of her stories transcended its leanness and paleness. Her Aunt Nancys and Miss Semanthas, her Aceldamas and Sary Anns, her Amasas, Celestys, Philurys and Sallathiel Bumps, with their liver-complaints and rheumatism and their moral angles and mental spikes, had little indeed to please the roaming fancy; and one heard too much, in these artless narrations, about camel's-hair shawls and black alpacas and best satin-finished black silks, about stuffy spare bedrooms opening out of kitchens and darkened parlours smelling of ill-dried feathers. People who will not "jaw" at table, and whose feelings and meditations are not distinguished, can expect to find few lovers on this crowded planet. Like the deaf adder, the reader stoppeth his ear against them and will not hearken to the voice of charmers, charming never so wisely; and Mrs. Cooke too often described them in terms of a provincial scene for which all amenities were snares. But as history, some of these tales, with their note of harsh veracity, were never to be replaced by later authors; and as tales, in their bleak finality, two or three,—*Too Late* and *Some Account of Thomas Tucker,**—were all but beyond comparison. In the course of two generations, a series of writers, Miss Jewett, Mary Wilkins and Edith Wharton, Robinson, Frost and O'Neill, were to find their account in this old New England, with its desperate passions and wild regrets. They knew what volcanoes, strewn with vines, lay under the placid hollows of its human surface. In *Too Late,* at least, Rose Terry Cooke foreshadowed all their stories and their plays and poems.

* In the volume called *The Sphinx's Children.*

CHAPTER V

THE POST-WAR YEARS

IN JULY, 1868, Charles Francis Adams and John
Lothrop Motley returned to Boston. For many years
they had lived abroad, in the diplomatic service, but
Adams's mission in England had come to an end and
Motley had retired from his Austrian mission. Both had
reappeared to recover their bearings in the new American world. Adams's younger son, Henry Adams, who had
spent the Civil War years in London, acting as his father's secretary, recorded their first impressions in words
that were famous later: "Had they been Tyrian traders
of the year B.C. 1000, landing from a galley fresh from
Gibraltar, they could hardly have been stranger on the
shore of a world, so changed from what it had been ten
years before."

The adventures of Henry Adams in this world, transformed by the recent war, were to take place largely outside of New England; but no one observed his age more
keenly, whether in New England or elsewhere. A shy,
self-conscious little man, inordinately proud, with a restless, introspective, probing mind, he had taken it for
granted, as an Adams, that he had a career before him,
the sort of career that Adamses always had.* For three
generations his family had had their hand on the lever of
power. They had all been at home in the White House

---

* The Adamses were the first family that Francis Galton chose to illustrate his method in *Hereditary Genius*. Galton ended his list with Henry
Adams's father.

ever since it was built, and Henry Adams had half thought
he owned it. That he should some day live there was almost a matter of course with him.* It had never occurred
to him, till his return, that the days of the Adamses were
over.† He had had a taste of politics, the politics of the
new age, that somewhat disillusioned him in London, for
the British statesmen seemed to him highly disingenuous
and very unlike the Adamses in this respect; but he had
never supposed that America would dispense with its
best-trained statesmen and cast its lot for politicians who
took their orders from bankers. That statesmen could
be obsolete, this was a conception the Adamses could
scarcely comprehend; for, without a thought for themselves, for three generations, they had sacrificed personal
interests and local interests to the welfare of the country
as a whole. They had really believed in the cause of advancing mankind, and for three generations the family
had fought for the country against the British and against
the bankers,—Downing Street, Wall Street, State Street,
—and triumphed in most of their struggles; and Charles
Francis Adams, as Minister to England, had foiled the
British again and kept them out of the war. He had
raised to its highest pitch the prestige of American policy; but the bankers had prevailed in his absence. They
had won the war for the North and demanded their
pound of flesh, if they had to kill the country to obtain it.

* "The Irish gardener once said to the child: 'You'll be thinkin' you'll
be President too!' The casuality of the remark made so strong an impression on his mind that he never forgot it. He could not remember ever to
have thought on the subject; to him, that there should be a doubt of his
being President was a new idea. What had been would continue to be . . .
A President was a matter of course in every respectable family."—*The
Education of Henry Adams.*

† They were not as much over, politically, as Henry Adams liked to
think, for he thoroughly enjoyed his disillusion. His father was at least
considered for the presidency, and his brother, John Quincy Adams, was
nominated for the vice-presidency. His elder brother, Charles Francis, as
president of the Union Pacific railroad, was as much of a statesman as
he wished to be. His nephew, the third Charles Francis Adams, was Secretary of the Navy.

John Quincy Adams, who had formed the faith of his sons and grandsons, had had a noble vision of the country's future. He had hoped to develop the national wealth on a collective, not a competitive, basis. He thought there was a volume of energy stored within the Union, enough for the prosperity of all: if this could be brought into use in accordance with the laws of science, it would lead the population to perfection.* For this reason, John Quincy Adams had promoted the study of science, while he fought with all his might against the bankers, who stood for competition and disruption. And now it appeared that science itself, applied in machinery and railroads, had stimulated nothing but ambition and greed.

With some such thoughts as these, and such misgivings, Henry Adams returned to the homestead at Quincy, the retreat of all the Adamses for three generations in times that called for study and meditation. Only six months before, he had been expecting to begin a career in the press at home as the champion and the confidant of a bold and honest American government. He had prepared in London for a publicist's life, working at financial theories and John Stuart Mill; and his ears were still ringing with his father's exhortations.† The fourth generation of Adamses was to carry the Adams banner forward.‡ At moments

---

* See Brooks Adams's *The Degradation of the Democratic Dogma.* Henry Adams spoke correctly when he said of himself, in the *Education,* "By rights, he should have been also a Marxist,"—that is, as well as a Darwinian. John Quincy Adams's economic thought, the basis of the faith of the family, was distinctly a form of socialism, in the voluntary pre-Marxist form.

† See the letter of Charles Francis Adams to his older son, written on June 17, 1864, the anniversary of the Battle of Bunker Hill: "The labour of extricating us from our perils will devolve upon the young men of the next generation who shall have passed in safety through this fiery furnace . . . Great will be the responsibility that devolves upon you! May you acquit yourselves of it with honour and success! The great anniversary has inspired me to write to you in this strain."—*A Cycle of Adams Letters.*

‡ Henry to his brother Charles, 1862: "It will depend on the generation to which you and I belong, whether the country is to be brought back to its true course and the New England element is to carry the victory, or

he had dreamed the sensation of wielding unmeasured power, a sense that came like vertigo. He knew how his forbears had felt, in the spacious upstairs study, as they sat in the President's chair, at the writing-table; but he felt that he was "for sale, in the open market . . . to be bought at the price of a mechanic." The old order had passed, and his dreams of power passed with it. He would have to make his way as best he could, in a world in which his quality scarcely counted. At the moment, prepared as he was for the press, he went at once to Washington, although he foresaw already "a life of wasted energy," as he observed later in the *Education*. Grant's administration was beginning, and it had no use for reformers; but it seemed to be a law of Adams's nature to gravitate to centres of power, and all he could do was to go and try his luck there. His brother, Charles Francis the second, struck for the railroads. A brigadier-general after the war, who had studied law with Dana, he became in the end a historian; and he made of the railroad business a learned profession, in the good old Adams way. The energy and daring of New England, once devoted to foreign commerce, was turning to the developing West, and the capitalists of Boston were building railroads. The Adamses knew railroads from the cradle,* for the first line in the country was the Old Colony line, built to carry the

whether we are to be carried on from war to war and debt to debt and one military leader after another, till we lose all our landmarks and go ahead like France with a mere blind necessity to get on, without a reason or a principle."—*A Cycle of Adams Letters.*

* And felt the poetry of them. "The Chicago express glided in as gracefully and silently as though it were in quite the best society, and had run a thousand miles or so only for gentle exercise before dining at Delmonico's and passing an evening at the opera."—Henry Adams, *Esther.*

Emily Dickinson, too, felt the poetry of railroads,—*I like to see it lap the miles, etc.*

Emerson's writings abounded in references to railroads, e.g., "It is not prosaic, as people say, but highly poetic, this strong shuttle which shoots across the forest, swamp, river and arms of the sea, binding city to city. The Americans take to the little contrivance as if it were the cradle in which they were born."—Emerson's *Journals,* VI, 336.

Quincy granite for the Bunker Hill monument; and
Charles Francis Adams approached this business as his
grandfather had approached the career of a statesman,
laying down solid blocks of knowledge, historical and
financial, with which to meet the problems of the Union
Pacific. The coming generation, as Henry Adams saw, was
"already mortgaged to the railways," and everything they
implied, capital, banks, machinery, mines, together with
new ideas and habits, social and political, to fit the new
scale and suit the new conditions. If the Adamses were
foredoomed to failure, as they were always saying, it was
largely because nothing could seem like success in the light
of their family history. For the rest, they understood their
generation, which Henry Adams described as a "bankers'
Olympus."

Years passed before the books of the Adams brothers
revealed this diagnosis of their age, an age of the utmost
confusion to most of those who were living in it. To
Henry Adams, in Washington, trying to understand it,
both political parties were corrupt, as the public seemed
indifferent. All he desired was "something to support,"
something that would let itself be supported; and the
presidency of Grant, which opened in 1869, "outraged
every rule of ordinary decency." * The Fisk-Gould "gold
conspiracy," which all but involved the President's person, and about which Adams wrote an essay, was the symbol of a state of affairs with which he could not contend,
and the "Crédit Mobilier" scandal seemed to prove that
a similar state of affairs existed in Boston. Gone were
the days when directors were also trustees; the new business men were jobbers and robbers, and no one seemed to

* "Every hope or thought which had brought Adams to Washington
proved to be absurd. No one wanted him; no one wanted any of his
friends in reform; the blackmailer alone was the normal product of politics as of business . . . Grant avowed from the start a policy of drift;
and a policy of drift attracts only barnacles . . . Grant had no objects,
wanted no help, wished for no champions."—*The Education of Henry
Adams.*

care.* The Adamses wrote together, in *Chapters of Erie,*
a sharp attack on "Caesarism in business," the Drew-Fisk-
Vanderbilt war.† Then, though they did not surrender
their hopes of reform, they faded more or less from the
public picture. Failures in their own eyes, in the eyes of
others eminent successes, they carried on existences, partly
subterranean and partly broken, the real meaning of
which appeared only after both were dead. Meanwhile,
the new age, with its new symptoms, established itself in
New England. The elements of change in this long-
settled country were not as marked at first as in other
regions; nor were they ever as marked as they were in
the West. The elements of permanence were much more
firmly fixed than later writers supposed in New England
itself.

Such as they were, the signs of change were sufficiently
marked already, with the war, the growth of the railroads and the factory-system, the spread of wealth, the
spread of immigration, which implied the spread of poverty,—with these and the time-spirit ‡ as primary causes.
The war, in a measure, uprooted the native population,
with whom wandering habits had been growing for decades. The opening West attracted them. The gold rush
of '49 had already increased this tendency, and, after the

* Thomas G. Appleton suggested in *Windfalls* that "a gallows con-
veniently placed at either end of Wall Street might be useful."

† "Vanderbilt is but the precursor of a class of men who will wield
under the State a power created by the State, but too great for its control."—*Chapters of Erie.*

‡ Aside from local New England causes, or even the broader American
causes, one must reckon with the time-spirit of Western civilization. Bene-
detto Croce, in the following passage, describes the whole of Europe, after
1870, in terms that apply to America and, specifically, New England:
"When the great political battles were over, the new generations, and
even the old patriots and combatants, devoted themselves to business; and
competition and the struggle for markets, in their turn, helped to suggest
the primacy of energy, force, practical capacity, over ethical and national
motives. The great economic prosperity that was supposed to supply new
and plentiful gifts to the work of human ideality seemed, on the contrary,
rather to suffocate it."—Croce, *History of Europe in the Nineteenth Century.*

war, the newly poor and those who, being poor, had never felt so, under the old conditions, went West in greater numbers for a better chance. At the same time, the rich, the newly rich, or those whom leisure filled with a taste for culture, and those who merely had the taste for culture, flocked in growing hordes to Europe. With the opening of the transcontinental railroads, the economic centre of the country gradually shifted westward; and New York, with more and more of the Western trade, increasingly drew the foreign trade from Boston. The Asiatic trade had already dropped away, and in 1868 the Cunard Line also shifted from Boston. The mail and passenger steamers from Europe made New York the main port of entry.* Thus Boston was isolated, as compared with New York, both from the West and from Europe, although it grew richer and richer from the factory-system. It profited by the growth of the West, creating goods for the pioneers, who sent their own products to New York. Meanwhile, with these economic changes, changes took place in the population, thinned by the westward movement and the war. With the growth of machine-industry, the handicrafts were fading out. The Sandwich glass-works, for example, with its glowing chimneys and smoking forges and swarms of well-trained craftsmen, was destroyed by the war, and the cheap machine-made pressed glass replaced the beautiful glass of old. The household arts were dying. The mills supplanted the spinning-wheels and hand-looms, as photography supplanted portrait-painting, the reaper took the place of the scythe and the cradle, the village cobblers vanished, and the village tailors; and new workers were coming in to tend the machines and till the soil by methods they had learned in other countries. Everyone remembered the coming of the Irish, who had dug earthen shanties to live

* The Cunard Line and others reëstablished Boston later as a secondary port of entry.

in. The French-Canadians had crossed the border in the decade after 1840, in groups of a man and a woman, ten or a dozen children and two or three bundles. At the old "north end" of Boston, the Irish superseded the Yankees and slowly gave place to Italians and Russian Jews; and all these races, and others, spread through the smaller towns.* The factories offered some of them openings, and others took up abandoned farms. The more they swarmed, the more the "oppressed of Europe" became, in the Yankee mind, the "scum of Europe," with results that were often tragic and always fateful.

All this was to change New England appreciably. Gone was the day when foreigners were as rare as in Scotland, and poverty twice as rare, when few were rich and few produced for profit, while all but the very few produced for use, when almost every man was a craftsman, skilled in hand and brain, and everyone knew his place, on the farm, in the village, where his fathers had lived before him. The new civilization abounded in practical benefits, railroads and steamships and gaslight, telegraph-wires and friction-matches, sewing-machines and reaping-machines and what not. Its disastrous effects, however, were apparent at once. With the growth of the stock-exchanges and the corporations, the great centralized industries, the factory-owners moved to the cities and lost their connection with the country. They ceased to feel responsible for the welfare of their workers, as they had felt in the days of the little private factory, when their wealth had been anchored in the soil, when they had seen the workers and their dwellings, workers of their own race whom they knew and partially understood. As absentee directors, they ruled a foreign population. The bond between the masters and the workers, wholly ab-

---

* It was to catch the spray, as it were, from a wave of immigration that Mrs. Alcott opened an intelligence-office in Boston. As might have been expected, all the Alcotts, father, mother and daughters, caught smallpox from an immigrant family whom they invited into their garden and fed.

stract and financial, was full of the seeds of the class-war
of the future, and the factory-towns became "hell-holes,"
in Cobbett's phrase. A similar movement followed in the
rural regions. Everyone had laughed at Orestes Brownson when, about 1850, he predicted that the landlord-
system was going to supplant, in New England, the universal system of local and personal ownership.* This
change came slowly, it is true. As late as 1883, Matthew
Arnold asked Whittier, "But where do the tenants, the
working people live?" There were few visible tenants,
but this condition gradually passed. The smallest towns
soon had their slums, and countless farms were mortgaged: the farmers were tenants of the banks. The evils
of the landlord-system rose with the evils of the factory-
system; and the "summer people," the "city folks," who
flocked in growing numbers to the shore and the mountains, brought with them the class-distinctions of the outside world. The rural folk became self-conscious, and the
younger people, already uprooted, added the evils of the
city to the evils of the country. Meanwhile, the great web
of the national railroads, destroying the sectional feeling,
destroyed the sectional pride that had always redeemed
it; and a sharp decline of patriotic feeling accompanied
the decline of sectional feeling. The war had exhausted
the nation, as even Emerson felt and said. The old idealism had been burnt away, the hopes of the patriot fathers,
the youthful and generous dreams of the early republic.
The war, with its fearful tension, draining the national
vitality, had left the mind of the people morally flabby.
The indifference to the public welfare was as marked as
Henry Adams thought, and a low type of "business
ethics" prevailed over the old ethics, in a larger and
larger measure, as time went on. Visions of sudden wealth
possessed the people. Promoters and gamblers in stocks
swarmed over the country, with tales of fabulous silver-

*Thomas Wentworth Higginson, *Book and Heart.*

mines and coal and iron properties in the West; and war-
profiteers, Jay Gould, Jay Cooke, Jim Fisk and others,
set the pace for younger men whose minds were adrift
among unknown forces. Wasteful and prodigal habits
grew, in reaction from the past, with its parsimony and
narrow frugalities, the legacy of hard early days; and a
world that was used to vulgarity had scarcely seen anything more shocking than that which sprang directly from
the Yankee farm-life.* The most popular New England
men, in all walks of life, during these decades, Ben Butler,
Beecher, Barnum, D. L. Moody, when they were not
venal, were singularly coarse, as compared with the earlier leaders. Money and "numbers" governed all their
thoughts, even, and even especially, in the sphere of religion. For who could imagine a greater contrast than that
between Moody and Beecher and the great religious leaders of the previous age, Theodore Parker and Channing?
Where Channing and Parker, learned men, had devoted
themselves to advancing thought, to art, philosophy, reform, these men were political routinists, at home in Wall
Street and all but devoid of intellectual interests. They
thought in terms of quantity, very seldom in terms of
quality, and their "publicity methods" resembled Barnum's.†

These changes in the New England scene were reflected
in literature almost at once. The stories of the younger
writers, whose books were already appearing, abounded
in the problems of the moment, the shifting population,
the abandoned farms, the evils of immigration and the

---

* E.g., the case of Jim Fisk, born and bred on a farm in Vermont.
† "Numbers is the king of our era," said Harriet Beecher Stowe, ten
years before Matthew Arnold said it. "Numbers" was certainly the king
of her brother and Moody, who "sold" religion as he had once sold shoes.
Both were religious wholesale-dealers, and the thought of money was
never out of their minds. Beecher's first thought, when he met Mark
Twain, was to tell him "what to do and how to do it" in the matter of
making a fortune. It was he who also manœuvred John Fiske into the
hands of a lecturing-agent. As a result of this, Fiske wasted himself in
giving lectures of a more and more popular type.

factory-system, the increasing corruption in politics, the
rise of the newly rich, the feeling that the region was declining. Elizabeth Stuart Phelps was among the first to
respond to these various problems. She had been roused
to a sense of the wrongs of the factory-workers by the
great mill-fire in Lawrence in 1859, when scores of New
England girls were burned to death. She studied the
wretched conditions that produced these horrors, the
lives of hands who scarcely saw the sun, who went to the
looms by gaslight and returned by moonlight, who subsisted on bread and black molasses and died of the "cotton cough." In *The Silent Partner, Hedged In* and other
stories, she described the growing slums and their human
wreckage. Other changes were reflected in these writers,
changes in education, in religion, in family life, the relations of the sexes, alarming enough at first and significant
later. One of these great changes was the surplus of
women. There were fifty thousand "extra" women in
Massachusetts alone,* women who were widowed by the
war, or whose lovers had died in the war, or who had
been left behind in the movement of the young men westward. The "glorious phalanx of old maids" that rejoiced
the heart of Theodore Parker was to dominate New
England for an age to come, the age of the "strong-
minded women" that might have been called the age of
the weak-minded men. Hawthorne had complained, years
before, of the "damned mob of scribbling women" who
were swarming all over America; † and the clan of women
writers grew apace. The resounding success of Mrs. Stowe

---

* Census of 1870. In 1880, the number had risen to 75,000. According
to the census of 1900, the surplus of women in Massachusetts was greater
than in any other state.

This surplus of women was only less marked in the other New England
states. In New Haven, the story was told, during the Civil War, that "a
student threw a stone at a dog and, missing him, hit seven old maids."—
John W. De Forest, *Miss Ravenel's Conversion.*

† "America is now wholly given over to a damned mob of scribbling
women."—Letter of 1855, quoted in Caroline Ticknor's *Hawthorne and
His Publisher.*

had opened the way for the women writers, with the multiplication of magazines for stories. These women writers
all but outnumbered the men, with results that were far
from happy; but for this who and what was most to
blame? The women won their influence by default. In the
new frenzy of speculation, the excitement over oil and
railroads, the absorption of young men in business,—in
the Hecla mine, the Buckeye Company and hundreds of
other enterprises,—literary and ethical interests and those
involving human rights gave place to questions of trade,
finance and commerce. Gone were the days when Yankee
boys aspired to be sailors or missionaries, pedlars or
poets. All these occupations had stirred the imagination,
and so, in its way, had the life of the farm and the forest.
The farmers of old, who had known their Bible, had often
been readers of Plutarch also, and most of them had read
Webster's speeches. The business life was hostile to all
these interests. It encouraged the reading of newspapers
and occasional books on engineering, but the world of
thought and feeling impeded its action; and the tendency
of the younger men was more and more to withdraw from
this world, which remained, with books and reading, in
the hands of women.* That women were ill prepared, if
only by their education, for this dominance in the world
of thought and feeling, no one was better aware than a

* "Speaking generally of the mass of business men,—and the mass are
business men in this country,—have they any habit of reading books? . . .
Look at the drift of things. Is the feminization of the world a desirable
thing for a vigorous future? Are the women, or are they not, taking all
the vitality out of literature? Answer me that. All the novels are written
by, for, or about women—brought to their standard . . . They write most
of the newspaper correspondence—and write it for women!

"In the large cities the women's clubs, pursuing literature, art, languages,
botany, history, mythology are innumerable. And there is hardly a village
in the land that has not from one to six clubs of young girls who meet
once a week for some intellectual purpose. What are the young men of
the villages and the cities doing meantime? . . . Is it comfortable for the
young man to feel that laughing eyes are sounding his ignorance"?—
Charles Dudley Warner, As We Go.

See also the remark of the poet Stedman about the post-war period:
"For ten years the new generation read nothing but newspapers."

few of themselves.* But they were not consulted. They acted on a *fait accompli*. The "feminization of literature" was a foregone conclusion.

Thus opened the somewhat dreary epoch in which the poet Whitman said, "Genuine belief seems to have left us." The decline of culture, marked throughout the country, was visible almost at once throughout New England. All that was mundane in the Yankees, already sufficiently marked, even in various leaders of culture,† came to the fore and took the helm; while Longfellow, Parkman, Norton, Higginson and many other anxious observers noted the alarming changes in the public mind. Longfellow and Norton deplored the decay in the interest in literature.‡ Higginson remarked that nine lectures in every ten were merely stump-speeches in the old Lyceums. Parkman was disturbed by the sudden debasing of standards, the disregard of cool thinking except in connection with business, the desire for sweeping statements or "something funny," the passion for amusement and excitement, in lectures and even in the pulpit. Flatulent writing, he said, was growing at the expense of pregnant writing. Was not moral and intellectual greatness the true end of man, to which material progress should be only a means? To men like Parkman, the violent activity of an age of speculation was abhorrent. It was all but fatal to their hopes and interests. Meanwhile, as the cause of culture

* "The education of our girls is extremely timorous and one-sided. Ignorance may be 'bliss,' but it is not necessarily innocence, and I doubt whether it is ever really 'folly to be wise.' "—Harriet W. Preston, *Aspendale*.

† "Horace Mann lamented that in European exhibitions the fine arts were always assigned a more conspicuous place than the useful arts. Theodore Parker complained that in Rome the studios were better than the carpenter-shops. Both exulted in the thought that in America these things were better ordered."—Thomas Wentworth Higginson, *A Plea for Culture*, 1867.

‡ "Longfellow was complaining the other day of the decline in the interest in literature and in the taste for it, nor was he mistaken,—this generation is given over to the making and spending of money, and is losing the capacity of thought. It wants to be amused, and the magazines amuse it."—Norton to Carlyle, 1873.

lost ground in New England, the region itself lost ground
in the life of the nation. Perhaps the New England statesmen were the first to feel the change, for they were un-
horsed at once and, it seemed, forever. What Henry Adams feared soon came to pass, for the West, in the person
of Grant, cared little for Boston. Did it matter that
Charles Francis Adams had also saved his country? That
Sumner, Motley and Rockwood Hoar were masters of
public affairs? These patriots of the old type, these statesmen and diplomats were "highbrows," who did not like
the methods of the cave-man. Rockwood Hoar was too
good to exist, from the point of view of Grant's friends,
and Sumner wore English clothes, and Motley "parted
his hair in the middle." * Grant disliked them one and all
at sight. Motley had been recalled from both his foreign
missions, in circumstances that almost broke his heart;
and Rockwood Hoar was marked for an early slaughter.
As for Charles Sumner, he was the last New England
statesman who played a national role for a generation.
The balance of power in politics had shifted westward,
and the tastes of the West, and its choices, won the day.

In the sphere of education, the spirit of the new age
declared itself immediately and clearly. Charles William
Eliot, an energetic chemist, had turned Harvard over
"like a flapjack." The phrase was Dr. Holmes's, and
Charles Eliot Norton's cousin turned over many flapjacks
as the years went on. The higher education of the country was largely remodelled on his ideas, for no one knew
better than he what the country desired. Harvard had
"struck bottom," he said, with a series of ineffectual presidents, who reflected the indecisiveness of the national
mind. This mind halted between two opinions, the old
classical system and the new technical system; and the

* "Mr. Fish afterwards told Adams, with the rather grim humour he
sometimes indulged in, that Grant took a dislike to Motley because he
parted his hair in the middle."—*The Education of Henry Adams.*

cry had been going up for instruction on special, vocational lines. Technological schools were rising to meet the new demands, with chairs of geology, engineering, mining, schools for bridge-builders and railroad-builders, chemists to work in the factories, geologists to develop the mineral wealth of the West.* In the colleges, where the "man of thought" had always ruled as a matter of course, the students debated the question, "Resolved, that the man of action is more important." Eliot replied with a new regime that marked the decisive change, a change that was soon reflected in the minds of writers.†

A Channing Unitarian of the Boston-Puritan-Roman type, serene as Cato, cheerful as a boy, Eliot was marked by a passion for the practical and a singular grandeur of nature. He was redeemed from Philistinism by a delicate ethical instinct and a feeling for the values he did not understand in others, unlike himself, whom he respected. A daring pilot and skipper, he loved skill, as Emerson loved it, and he shared Emerson's faith in human nature. He was a Puritan formed on the classical model, elevated, simple, grave and patient. Abounding in all the

---

* The opening, in 1861, of the Massachusetts Institute of Technology was the most notable symptom of this general movement. Eliot became president of Harvard in 1869. At about the same moment, the "young Yale" movement began, for college reform at New Haven. It was in 1870 that W. W. Phelps made the well-known speech that created such a furor at Yale: "Harvard takes great poets and historians to fill its vacant professorships—Yale takes boys who have proved their qualifications by getting their windows broken as tutors." The modern Yale is said to date from this hour of self-examination.

† In the mind of Henry Adams, first of all. The lesson of the Civil War, as he saw it from London, was that the great new forces were science and mechanics. The success of the American ironclads, the offspring of science, in the Battle of the Rams, caused the English to perceive in three weeks that their wooden navy was antiquated and useless. Great Britain's sea-power was "knocked in the head" by modern science. "I tell you," Adams wrote to his brother Charles, "these are great times . . . Man has mounted science, and is now run away with. I firmly believe that before many centuries more, science will be the master of man. The engines he will have invented will be beyond his strength to control. Some day science may have the existence of mankind in its power, and the human race commit suicide by blowing up the world."—*A Cycle of Adams Letters.*

Plutarchian virtues, which he liked to celebrate in his inscriptions,—for his words were fit to be carved in granite,*—he liked Martha better than Mary, and he served
a generation that shared this taste. Eliot took for granted
the Emersonian doctrine that the young should follow
their stars without let or hindrance. That he himself and
Emerson had only begun to follow their stars after a long
immersion in the wisdom of others, in the good old
Yankee way at home, in the good old classical way at college,—that this immersion, in fact, was education,—did
not disturb his faith that human beings instinctively knew
and followed the good-for-them. They could scarcely be
trusted too soon for this,—the belief that lay behind the
"elective system;" and perhaps at other periods the system might have worked in the interest of a broadly human
world. At the moment, the "stars" which the young were
prepared to follow, the stars which they observed in the
sky outside them,—and the sky offered them less and less
of any other kind, as the sources of other stars grew dimmer and dimmer, with the decline of religion, with the
decline of classical studies,—were largely materialistic
and often mean; and Eliot's elective system, which prepared them to follow these stars, worked against other
objects and other causes. It was true that this system promoted efficiency in many socially useful professions. It
opened a great new epoch in science, medicine, engineering.† But one saw the total effect in time, as the other

* Among Eliot's multifarious writings, the most characteristic were his
inscriptions. Towards the end of his life, it became the custom, all over
the country, when a new post-office was erected, or some other public
building or monument, to ask him for an inscription to be cut in the
marble or granite. These inscriptions, redolent of the Roman authors, on
whom he liked to dwell, and also of the Puritan tradition, in which he
lived in good faith, conveyed, while often describing others, the note of
Eliot's own mind.

† "We have but a halting faith in special training for high professional
employments. The vulgar conceit that a Yankee can turn his hand to anything we insensibly carry into high places where it is preposterous and
criminal. We are accustomed to seeing men leap from farm or shop to
courtroom or pulpit, and we half believe that common men can safely use

universities followed Harvard and lost sight of human ends in means. Then it became apparent that civilization was losing its soul, as education had lost its soul already.

The first step at Harvard was to throw the classics overboard and promote the "specialist" system the age demanded. Thus died the old American college; the European model was discarded; the American university came into being. The classics, not too competently taught, went down before the new engrossing interests;* and this marked, in literature, almost the greatest of possible changes. The change in literary style was not the most important, although this was sufficiently striking.† The

the seven-league boots of genius . . . This lack of faith in the prophecy of a natural bent and in the value of a discipline concentrated upon a single object amounts to a national danger."—Eliot's inaugural address, 1869.

In these words, the American mind turned a corner. To Eliot is largely due the immensely increased efficiency in American professional life, along with the efficiency of business. But this was accompanied by a sharp decline in most of the extra-mundane activities, the literary life among them.

* It is true that the study of classical philology gained greatly under Eliot, along with everything else in the specialist system, but this concerned only the special student. Eliot led the way in dropping required Greek and Latin, and the pattern set by him was almost universally followed. "It is a hard saying, but Mr. Eliot, more than any other man, is responsible for the greatest educational crime of the century against American youth,—depriving him of his classical heritage."—S. E. Morison, *Three Centuries of Harvard.*

President Eliot's "five-foot shelf" was largely a realization of Emerson's theory that everything good in the classics may be gleaned from translations. Emerson and Eliot alike were excellent classical scholars, and one of the amusements of Emerson's old age was to compare a translation of Plutarch with the original Greek; but it was an effect of their joint teaching that in another fifty years one had to look far for a college man who could read either Greek or Latin with ease or pleasure. The "five-foot shelf" was an admission of this, and also a justification of the theory which was the cause of this effect. It was a symbol of a social order, materially aristocratic, that was also intellectually plebeian.

† Disregarding secondary writers, all the first-rate writers of the later age, even those who knew the classics well, suffered, as regards their style, from a vital indifference to the classics. Few of their books have the authentic ring that marks the best pages of Thoreau, Dana, Hawthorne, Motley, etc., who were steeped in Greek, Latin and the Bible. The "vices" of their style were almost as marked as the "beauties": the thin facility of Howells and the earlier Henry James, the obscurity of the later Henry James, the excessive colloquialism of William James, the perversity of Emily Dickinson, the awkward, metallic or inexpressive quality of much of Henry Adams's writing, especially the later chapters of the *Education.*

study of the classics had always been connected with accurate linguistic training and the study of form, while the modern tongues were loose in their construction; but, what was even more important, the classics had made spacious men and men prepared to meet great problems. None of the abundant cant that was uttered on this subject, both at the time and later, altered the fact. They kept alive great patterns of behaviour, which all the American people had seen in action in the ample minds and characters of the earlier leaders, most of whom were steeped in Plutarch's lives and the legends of Greece and Rome. The close association of intimate studies had made these patterns real, and the patterns had made great writers as they made great statesmen. They appealed to the instinct of emulation, an instinct that in later days followed the patterns set by industrial leaders, by bankers and by millionaires whose only ideal was the will to power and who ruled by the blind force of money.*

Meanwhile, the coming age was represented by a number of Eliot's appointments. As William Morris Hunt said, Cambridge was "all literature;" and whatever at this hour spoke for Cambridge spoke for American literature also, even, and perhaps especially, when it spoke for science. Of the new "university lecturers," Chauncey Wright and Charles S. Peirce were influential in shaping

---

* "What is the American ideal of greatness?" one of the characters asked in Howells's *A Traveller from Altruria* (1894). The banker answered: "I should say that within a generation our ideal had changed twice. Before the war, and during all the time from the Revolution onward, it was undoubtedly the great politician, the publicist, the statesman. As we grew older and began to have an intellectual life of our own, I think the literary fellows had a pretty good share of the honours that were going; that is, such a man as Longfellow was popularly considered a type of greatness. When the war came, it brought the soldier to the front, and there was a period of ten or fifteen years when he dominated the American imagination. That period passed, and the great era of material prosperity set in. The big fortunes began to tower up, and heroes of another sort began to appeal to our imagination. I don't think there is any doubt but the millionaire is now the American ideal." If, thirty years later still, Americans had no ideal, who was to blame for this,—which generation?

the mind of the future. Howells stood for the modern languages, the interest in which was rapidly growing, and Eliot also appointed Emerson,—of all the older men of letters the most sympathetic to men of science.* The younger Oliver Wendell Holmes was instructor in constitutional law. But perhaps the most representative of all these teachers was the young Connecticut Yankee, John Fiske, who lectured on positivism and Darwinism, the most engrossing topics of the moment. Fiske had seen in Emerson a prophet of the new ideas that Darwin and Herbert Spencer had begun to establish.† That man had risen from inorganic matter, instead of being "specially created," that he had not fallen from perfection but had only begun his journey towards perfection, this was the notion that Fiske set out to preach; and, although he was under a cloud at first and taught in the teeth of Agassiz, the defender of "special creation," he made rapid headway with the doctrines that were universally held in later years.

This "great, simple, learned child," as one of his friends described him, was the son of a Hartford journalist who had once been Henry Clay's secretary. Fiske, whose original name was Green, had grown up at Middletown, a lanky, goggle-eyed boy with red hair and freckles who was also a prodigy of learning. Fond of sports, fonder of music, he composed a mass and an opera later, and his flowing high spirits were as marked as his deep strain of religious feeling. His zest for study was astounding. He seemed to know all about all the sciences by the time he

* This appointment, one of Eliot's first, marked the reconciliation of Emerson and Harvard. During the years in which Emerson had become a writer of world renown, the college had never forgiven him for his Divinity School address of 1838. His lectures were published as *The Natural History of Intellect*.

The subject of Howells's lectures was modern Italian literature.

† Spencer also saw in Emerson, who had read Lamarck, a herald. of the evolutionist point of view. During his visit to America, in 1882, he made a pilgrimage to Emerson's house at Concord. This is said to have been the only occasion on which Spencer paid tribute to another thinker.

entered college, and half a dozen languages as well; and one of his classmates asked him why he had bothered to come to Harvard. What did any college have to teach him? He might have answered, Hebrew, Sanskrit, Gothic, Icelandic, Roumanian, Dutch, for he presently added them all to the rest of the list. His teachers were astonished at the breadth of Fiske's knowledge, his grasp of history, philology, philosophy and science, and, what was more unusual, his gift for thinking. For with all this receptiveness, his mind was an active and powerful engine. His learning was the fuel that drove it forward.

In the slight, long-legged, self-conscious student one scarcely discerned the later Fiske, the form that became so famous on the streets of Cambridge, the huge, hearty, hirsute creature with the bushy beard and the gold-rimmed spectacles who looked like a German professor. But one had a prevision of this in his tastes and his habits, in the long-stemmed meerschaum pipe that he smoked, for example. He would slowly produce and assemble this pipe from various recesses of his person, slowly fill it and light it slowly, with a great sigh of contentment, while he rounded up his thoughts for conversation. He was one of William James's men who could sit over a pot of beer, lost in the depths of his mind, for hours together; and his first little book, *Tobacco and Alcohol,* defended his predilections against all and sundry. On behalf of drinking and smoking and their physiological value, he marshalled authorities in half the tongues he knew, Latin, German, Spanish, Dutch, Italian; but long before this he had shown his varied powers. He was a formidable writer and a stormy petrel. He had studied law, enraptured with Blackstone, as with everything that called for a mental tussle, and had even set up as a lawyer in Boston; but his writing gave him little time for practice. While he was still an undergraduate, he had written and published several articles that aroused the attention of readers even in England. One of these, a review of Buckle, interested Herbert Spencer and Lewes, who were soon to know much more of their youthful author. One, on the evolution of language, revealed the genius for exposition that marked Fiske's work for forty years.* Ticknor, Child, Lowell and Norton had all been struck by this model student, whose method and tone were like those of the "great reviewers;" and when Lowell and Norton took over the moribund *North American* they gave him a free hand for reviews and essays. Fiske wrote with equal competence on Longfellow's Dante, on Taine and Motley, on politics, religion, education, on philosophy, anthropology, history and music. His methodical, orderly mind moved like a stone-crusher, reducing the boulders of thought to a flow of gravel that anyone could build a mental road with. He simplified the knottiest points, he made the most difficult abstractions as lucid and easily grasped as a nursery-story, and all without any sacrifice of substance. He was supple, readable, human, direct, and, although he was seldom original and seldom suggestive, he was equally instructive and entertaining. Moreover, he was imaginative. He felt the magic power of myths, and once he saw the devil, or believed he saw him, actually sitting in his study, with hoofs, horns, fiery eyes and all. The big, warm-hearted, exuberant Fiske, whose wit was somewhat elephantine, was vehement and cheerful in manner, both in writing and in speaking. A first-rate popularizer, he was filled with the zeal of a propagandist. Evolution for him was a new religion.

His interest in this new theory dated from his college days, when his mind was full of Humboldt, Comte and Buckle. In Boston, at the Old Corner Bookstore, he had happened on a prospectus of Spencer's writings. This was

* "I never in my life read so lucid an expositor (and therefore thinker) as you are."—Letter of Darwin to Fiske, on the publication of *Outlines of Cosmic Philosophy*. Darwin further said that he had never been able to understand Spencer until Fiske elucidated Spencer's doctrines.

in 1860, when Spencer had just begun to publish the series
in which he rounded out his system. Fiske was enthralled
at once by Spencer's programme, and his interest in the
subject was confirmed when Spencer's friend Youmans
called upon him. The remarkable E. L. Youmans, who
founded the *Popular Science Monthly* and whose life
Fiske wrote in later years, was a New York farmer's boy
who had educated himself by heroic efforts and become
the American prophet of modern science. It was he who
introduced to American readers, through his *International
Scientific Series,* the writings of Darwin, Bagehot, Buckle,
Helmholtz, Huxley, Lecky and Tyndall.* Convinced that
the theory of evolution was about to remodel modern
thinking, he saw in Fiske the perfect expositor for it; and
it was Youmans who introduced Fiske to Spencer, for
whom he had raised a subscription to enable him to carry
on his work. Up to that moment, science was a mere collection of facts and rules, with no coherent body of governing truths, while the new conception of the unity of
nature bound all these facts together in a web of causa-
tion. It seemed possible to write nature's history back to
the primitive chaos, and one saw that all its phenomena,
instead of being unrelated and produced by the Creator's
personal whim, were parts of an unbroken chain of cause
and effect. Suns and stars, plants and animals had followed one law of development from a common source,
and man was also a part of this cosmic drama. Through
all the vast sweep of time, from the primordial vapour to
the multifarious world one knew today, one saw the various forms of nature evolving from previous forms. The
simile of Paley's watch was no longer valid. The simile
of the flower was a better description. For the universe

---

* The declining of this series by Ticknor and Fields, to whom, in 1860,
Youmans offered Spencer's *Education,* was one of the first indications of
the passing of Boston as the intellectual centre of the country. As a result
of this first refusal, all these works of science, which dominated the mind
of the coming epoch, were published by the Appletons of New York.

was not a machine,—it was an organism, with an in-dwelling principle of life; and man had not been made,—he had grown and developed.

Such was the great Spencerian vision that Fiske ex-pounded at Harvard, with his own interpretations and amplifications. Spencer had ignored previous systems, to which Fiske related the new philosophy. To the general notion of evolution, he contributed one idea of his own, the effect of the prolongation of infancy in forwarding human development; and he published his lectures pres-ently in *Outlines of Cosmic Philosophy*. For the rest, he found in evolution an ethical and religious meaning that scarcely existed in Spencer's original statement. For Spencer's Unknowable he substituted God, as the well-spring out of which flows the unfolding cosmos, so that progress was not only the working out of natural laws but a process that was controlled to beneficent ends. In this way he reconciled science and religion, and one saw in the end that Fiske was a religious thinker who had given the New England faith a firmer basis. But at first he was considered an atheist, and the feeling against him rose so high that he was never appointed to a chair at Harvard. He remained as assistant librarian, and he soon turned to the writing of history, approached from the evolu-tionary point of view. But everyone remembered that the great debate over evolution began, in America, at Har-vard, and that Fiske had been the centre of the storm. It was the greatest debate since the Reformation.*

While all these Harvard lecturers left their mark on the coming age,—Fiske, Holmes, Wright, Peirce and Howells,—none exerted a personal influence stronger than that of another man whom Eliot's predecessor had appointed. Raphael Pumpelly, the first professor of min-

---

* In 1869, the New York *World* reported in full Fiske's Harvard lec-tures. There has never been any other case in American history of such a popular interest in a philosophical controversy.

ing, remained only two years in Cambridge; but he fired
the imagination of many a student. In a day when the
young New England men were scattering over the world,
looking for "opportunities," for mines to develop, for
the romance of travel or mere excitement, this Huguenot-
Yankee Marco Polo was a highly symptomatic figure. A
dashing, dramatic geologist, with a beard like a shower
of gold, an explorer and mystic whose life was already
a legend, Pumpelly appealed to many minds, those who
were bent upon making money, those for whom the West
and Arizona, Mongolia, China, Japan were El Dorados,
lovers of pure science and lovers of adventure who sought
their adventure now in the outer world. For the day of
the inward adventure was passing, and men who, fifty
years before, would have found their adventure in books,
like Ticknor, or, like Thoreau, in their minds,—the wildest sort of adventure,—looked for it in the physical scene
and found in Pumpelly a guide and a stimulus. There
were others, such as Howells and the brothers William
and Henry James, who found their adventure in observation, anywhere and everywhere; but, even among the perceptive, these were few. Henry Adams was only one of
the many restless younger men whose minds were touched
by Raphael Pumpelly.

Both inwardly and outwardly, Pumpelly's personality
was a striking illustration of the times. As a boy in western New York, the child of a great land-owning family,
with many farms and forests, mills and stores, a patriarchal clan of the semi-feudal type, he had found in Hugh
Miller the "wonders of geology" and gone abroad to
study in his youth. With a mind that was alive to music,
painting and poetry, as well as technology and science, he
had a zest for wild life like that of the irrepressible moufflon which he led all over Europe as a travelling com-

panion.* Between periods of study in Germany and Paris, he spent five months in Corsica, with the bandits and the mountaineers; and there, as later in the Rockies and the Urals, pursuing his geological work, he fell into moods of exaltation.† Returning to America, at the opening of the Civil War, he went to Arizona as a mining engineer. Thence he proceeded to Mexico, and then to Asia, to survey Japan and China for their mineral resources; but his great opportunity came at the end of the war. The East buzzed with tales of the West and its iron, gold and copper, and there were few trained experts to develop the mines; and Pumpelly made geological surveys of the Michigan copper and iron regions and reported on the routes for Western railroads. Where Agassiz showed the significance of geology for science, he showed its significance for industry and business; and, while he contributed to scientific knowledge, he made and lost fortunes and caused the making of larger fortunes. In the great game of exploiting the West, Pumpelly had one of the whip hands, the hand on the lever of power that fascinated Henry Adams; for men who had money to invest were obliged to rely on his judgment. As one who knew the sources of wealth, he hobnobbed with princes and kings and the powers of the earth. Adams's friend, Clarence King, was another young man who discussed with Pumpelly the future of the Rockies and Asia, and John La Farge rejoiced in his hundreds of Japanese prints and the bronzes and bits of jade he had brought from Japan and China. Like Washington Allston, in earlier years, he sat where the young men passed at the cross-roads in

* The "moufflon story" is a lively passage in his ever-lively *Reminiscences*. Pumpelly said he had told this story in English, German, French, Italian and Japanese.

† His excellent books, *Across America and Asia* and the later *Reminiscences*, abound in expressions of "cosmic feeling," as people used to call it. John La Farge wrote the chapter on Japanese art in *Across America and Asia*. This was the earliest of La Farge's published writings.

Cambridge; but he pointed towards other goals and in other directions.

If Pumpelly was not in Cambridge long, this in itself was symptomatic. He was off, he was always off, to the ends of the earth, to the "old Yuma trail" or the coal-fields of China, an example for the restlessness of others. He made New England seem small; and, if it was true that this small New England had given birth to great ideas, there were many who were prepared to risk the future. What if a greater New England were to give birth to small ideas? Ideas, to them, were less important than numbers of other goods which the future promised. As for Pumpelly himself, he was far from small. His charm was his spaciousness, his feeling for horizons; and if, as another Pied Piper, he led the children up a mountain that opened and closed again and left them in the dark, it was his music that led them, and the music was real. The darkness was the cave of money to which the adventure usually led. But the music was adventure itself, the joy of a whole generation.

CHAPTER VI

THE RADICAL CLUB

THERE were other musicians, luckily, to lead the dance of the post-war years, though their music was relatively sombre. E. L. Godkin had founded *The Nation* in 1865. With the prophetic eye of a sensitive alien, who loved the old American traditions, Godkin had foreseen the tendencies of the coming age and organized his journal to combat them. *The Nation,* a weekly review, was one of the few periodicals that become historic, as *The Dial* and *The Atlantic* became historic, because they focus the mind of a new generation; and, while it was published in New York, it was closely connected with Boston and Cambridge, where Parkman, Lowell and Norton were its constant advisers.* Parkman made it the vehicle of much of his occasional writing, and many of the contributors were younger Cambridge men. Howells had worked for a time on *The Nation* before he joined *The Atlantic,* and he and the brothers James and Henry Adams were among the regular reviewers. Eliot had offered Godkin a professorship of history, and at various times in the future he lived in Cambridge. It was there he found his first editor, John Dennett, a Harvard man, before he assumed the editor's chair himself, and his literary editor for almost forty years was Wendell Phillips Garrison, the Liberator's son. In times that were difficult for conscientious thinking men, with all the heavy

* Of the capital of *The Nation,* one half was raised in Boston, a fourth in New York and a fourth in Philadelphia.

metal turned against them, at least they had an organ in *The Nation.*

Godkin, an Irishman, the son of a Presbyterian minister, had settled in America in 1856. He had studied law in England and had crossed the Atlantic, drawn by a deep regard for the republic. A disciple of Mill and a well-trained journalist, he had watched the disintegration of the public life upon which he had built his faith and hope. Educated Americans were losing all interest in public affairs and considered them disagreeable and even repulsive, and he resolved to rally the younger generation and revive the ideals of the country. In short, he represented a regenerative impulse, a reaction against incompetence and corruption. The daily press were hurried and partisan, the weekly press superficial and narrow. Thinking men found no account in either, and Godkin, who knew that America abounded in critical minds, proposed to create a medium that would bring them together. *The Nation* was modelled on the London *Spectator,* and in certain ways Godkin's policy harmonized with President Eliot's. Eliot preached the doctrine of special training for special work, as against the Yankee man-of-all-trades method. Godkin applied this doctrine to public affairs. He championed civil-service reform, or the cause of special training in politics, as opposed to the rampant spoils system; and he stood alone for this at first, for civil-service reform was regarded as a "European whimsy" or "something Prussian." The public had forgotten John Quincy Adams, for whom the career of a statesman was a learned profession, and Godkin made small progress at first or later; for although the spoils system, introduced by Jackson, had come to such a shocking head with Grant, it was firmly fixed in the popular mind of the country. But Godkin, who appealed to the cultivated classes to work for the restoration of the old republic, succeeded in winning the minds of the younger university men, for whom he was an unexampled leader.

In days to come, Godkin was the most influential American journalist, with Horace Greeley, Dana and Samuel Bowles, the editor of the *Springfield Republican*. The latter were "personal journalists" and popular spokesmen, whether for good or ill. Godkin was impersonal; he was all but unknown to the public, but he influenced the public indirectly. *The Nation* was read by other editors, and Godkin's ideas, which were seldom acknowledged, reached the general mind through a hundred channels. It was true that these ideas found little acceptance. The Jacksonian ways, upheld in the West, had saturated the mind of the masses, and Godkin, who hated the West, was hated by it. The public was indifferent to corruption because it was immersed in money-making, and money-making throve in the loose and unscrutinized system of things that Godkin brought to book in all his writings. He was called "un-American" because his mind was critical at a moment when the critical mind impeded the orgy of money-making; and it made no difference whatever that he was defending the old ideals. The mores had shifted away from the old ideals. They had even reversed these ideals,—to defend them had become "unpatriotic." * Godkin tried to break down the system of party-organization, as the source of the worst corruption; but the party-organization had become the great American shibboleth. Godkin and *The Nation* fought against all the American shibboleths, the love of display, the love of conquest, the defence of war, the contempt for peace, the flouting of national creeds once held sacred, high tariffs, graft and greed, machine government, boss government, ostentatious wealth and shoddy thinking. Godkin's

* For the classic explanation of this paradox of American history, see William Graham Sumner's *Folkways*.

sympathies were narrow and his temper was harsh, but no mind of his time was more tonic. He held a unique position in American cultural history. He originated, if not a school, at least a type of American minds, the journalist-intelligentsia of the future.* *The Nation* was the parent of *The New Republic*.

Important in politics and the world of education and science, *The Nation* marked an epoch in reviewing. American reviewing, outside the *North American,* had been almost wholly personal in tone.† George Ripley, on *The Tribune,* the idol of the young, was the leading reviewer; and Ripley, except in his longer articles, devoted to established writers, was more active in heart than in mind. He was too eager to encourage those who wished to write or paint to promote the abstract welfare of art and letters. *The Nation* established at once a severe and expert standard, with no regard for persons whatsoever. It began by wiping the slate clean of the Knickerbocker school, the last decrepit relics of Irving's time. This set by the ears the literary and publishing world, which *The Nation* faced with grim determination. Merciless to private interests, it built up a staff of trained reviewers, who established its authority at once;‡ and most of the serious writers of the coming generation owed much to its wisdom and rigour. In literary matters, Wendell Phillips Garrison was as influential as Godkin in the world of affairs. In temperament a stoic, in taste a purist, he gave *The Nation* its stamp in style and form. He translated

---

* The journalist Ford, in Howells's *The Undiscovered Country,* is an excellent early portrait of this type, so familiar in America later.

† "The great mischief has always been that whenever our reviewers deviate from the usual and popular course of panegyric, they start from and end in personality, so that the public mind is almost sure to connect unfavourable criticism with personal animosity."—Godkin, *Critical and Social Essays.*

‡ "Outside of Cambridge and Godkin, it appears to me that our literary review-writing world is only one vast Tuckerman . . . *The Nation* hasn't pronounced yet . . . Horrible, isn't it, to have only one critic for 40,000,000 of people?"—*Life in Letters of William Dean Howells,* I, 138, 144.

Petrarch and Carducci, but he wished to remain obscure and behind the scenes, upholding the standards of literature and moulding its tone. Even less known to the public than Godkin, Garrison made *The Nation* the leading literary journal of the country.*

*
*   *

In Boston, meanwhile, the reformers had lost their major impulse. The public was tired of oratory; and, while there were many new causes, they lacked the charm of the old campaigns in the days of Abolition. In an epoch of milder antagonisms, one ran no risk of tar and feathers, one could not expect to be locked in a Georgia jail; and those who had spent their youth roaming through the South, carrying the Bible to the slaves, or on platforms, in phalansteries, in conventions, running the "underground railway," in the more exciting years before the war, found all these later causes rather tame. There were no more showers of eggs: only temperance lecturers in Irish circles were ever greeted with missiles. The great days were past for the Boston crusaders. The "new truths" had no such lightning in them, and many an old reformer felt like Moorfield Storey, who regretted that he was born to ignoble times, when the devil was handcuffed and muzzled.

Earnest Boston had lost its focus, for the cause of the wage-slaves was not as simple as the cause of the chattel-slaves had been. One could not sum it up by saying to the masters, "Let my people go." When slavery was abolished, most of the Abolitionists felt that all the battles had been won for freedom. This had been Garrison's

---

* Aside from his father's life, written in collaboration with his brother, Garrison's only published work was *The New Gulliver*. This amusing satirical fable was written in defence of Darwinism. The life of William Lloyd Garrison, in four volumes, remains the standard history of the Abolition movement.

feeling, when he discontinued *The Liberator,* and Whittier had withdrawn more and more into the Quaker calm of his Amesbury cottage and the memories that he expressed in *Snow-Bound.* Edmund Quincy spoke for them when he said to Wendell Phillips, with a happy sigh, "No more picnics, Wendell." For Phillips, as it happened, the picnics never ceased. He continued with his old crusading zeal. "Welcome, new duties!" he had said, when the Abolitionist movement ended. "We will not say 'Farewell,' but 'All Hail';" and for twenty years he fought to raise the status of the workers, defending the Russian nihilists before a Harvard audience, praising the Paris Commune, the "vanguard of the Internationals of the world." To replace the profit-system by coöperation, to "crumple up wealth" by enormous taxes, to restore the old ideals of the republic was the programme of this Ishmael of Boston, whose home, as he said, was the sleeping-car, with the brakeman and porter for comrades; and men who hated his doctrines were carried away by the spell of his voice and presence. One Bostonian was observed muttering under his breath, as Phillips spoke, "The damned old liar, the damned old liar!" while he clapped his hands in violent applause. But Phillips, who represented the faith of the forties in an age that was mad for money, was a lonely man indeed and almost friendless.* Most of the old reformers were exhausted. They had no energy left for fresh campaigns, although Boston, prolific in causes, swarmed with friends of progress and new reformers rose with other movements, the cause of peace, the cause of woman's suffrage, dietary reform and Darwinism, the cause of the short-skirts league and the short-haired women who amused profane

---

* "I remember Nora Perry, the poetess, who knew him well, telling me of his meeting her once and asking her where she was going. 'To see a friend,' she replied. 'Ah,' he said, 'you remind me of the Frenchman who received the same answer and said, 'Take me along, I never saw one.'"
—G. E. Woodberry, *Heart of Man and Other Papers.*

New York for a generation. Nevertheless, of the old reformers, only one was an active cynic, Charles A. Dana
of *The Sun*. Dana, for whom Brook Farm had once been
the hope of the world, was the enemy, in days to come,
of all it stood for: he ridiculed civil-service reform, opposed the control of monopolies, fought for high tariffs
and huge land-grants for railroads and defended the
banking control of the money-system. Brook Farm itself
had been used as a soldiers' camp in the war, and the
spirit it expressed had been trampled under foot with the
wild flowers that grew there in the spring. But Dana
alone, of the disillusioned farmers, seemed to take a bitter joy in reversing his former convictions.

Boston, Henry Adams thought, had ceased to believe in
itself any longer, and many a sign of the times confirmed
this feeling. The national-political element had faded out
of the Boston picture. The foreign element faded with it,
on the intellectual level, for Boston was less and less the
port of call it had been in the days of the old Cunarders.
Once every enquiring traveller had visited the town, attracted by its statesmen and its writers; while now, with
less hope of reward for the trouble, one had to make a
special journey thither. The religious element also appeared to be waning. The secularizing tendency of the
Concord writers spread rapidly in the rising generation.*
As Henry Adams said, the young men threw off Unitarianism and "never afterwards entered a church." † Mean-

* "My respect for clerical people, as such, and my faith in the utility
of their office, decreases daily."—Hawthorne, *American Notebooks,* edited
by Randall Stewart, page 165. It was very seldom indeed that Emerson
or Thoreau appeared in church.

† Many were agnostics, like Parkman and Norton.

It may be added that Howells's faith in revealed religion was destroyed
in boyhood when he read Strauss's *Life of Jesus.* "Until, in middle age,
he was walking near Florence with James Bryce and Stillman, the correspondent of the London *Times,* he had taken it for granted that no well-
read man had any faith. His happening to say so astonished his companions, and to learn that many educated men believed in God came to
him, as he described it, like a blow."—Owen Wister, *William Dean
Howells,* in *The Atlantic Monthly,* December, 1937.

while, all manner of quacks were abroad, purveying substitutes for religion. Nostrum-mongers gathered about
the sincere reformers, battening on their doctrine of the
"open mind." Mesmeric healers and trance-speakers
throve amid waiting circles in darkened rooms, where
taps were heard on the walls and tables and flowers rained
from the ceiling and dim things flitted in the dusk,—
a humanitarian gypsy-band to which the "new truths"
often lent themselves.* The decay of the ancient faith,
with its firm grasp of human realities, its feeling for
values and standards, filled the air with noxious emana-
tions; and the critical spirit gasped for breath in a world
of lady-mediums and lady-preachers, of lecturers, editors,
writers, mostly women; † for the age of Elizabeth Cady
Stanton and Susan B. Anthony and their Boston friends
and disciples was on the way, and what could one reply
when Mrs. Stanton asked, "Where will you poor men
stand in another fifty years? You will be crowded off the
horizon." The currents of society were certainly setting
in this direction, and few denied that women had a valid
axe to grind. But the critical spirit was baffled in this
over-feminine atmosphere. It scarcely knew where to
draw the line; and even the Radical Club was not immune
to the inspirations of witches and wizards. The Radical
Club, in Chestnut Street, the house of the Sargent family,
was the intellectual centre of earnest Boston; and to one
of its members, at least, the most earnest of all, the

---

* The classic pictures of this phase of Boston are Howells's *The Undiscovered Country* and Henry James's *The Bostonians.*

† "The whole generation is womanized; the masculine tone is passing
out of the world; it's a feminine, a nervous, hysterical, chattering, canting
age, an age of hollow phrases and false delicacy and exaggerated solici-
tudes and coddled sensibilities, which, if we don't soon look out, will usher
in the reign of mediocrity, of the feeblest and flattest and the most pretentious that has ever been."—Basil Ransome, in Henry James's *The Bostonians.*

"The talk, the social life were so completely in the hands of the ladies,
the masculine note was so subordinate . . . like a country stricken by a
war, where the men had all gone to the army."—Henry James, *A New
England Winter.*

swans and the geese looked much alike. This was Elizabeth Peabody, who had fumbled for too many years in her satchel for papers. She had signed too many petitions and attended too many conventions. She longed to think that all the frauds were heroes.

But the Radical Club did its best. As the only heir and successor of the Peabody house of the forties, as a relic of the Transcendental Club, it harboured the liveliest minds in Boston. Emerson, Garrison, Wendell Phillips were among the older frequenters, with Dr. Hedge and Dr. and Mrs. Howe, Thomas Wentworth Higginson and the elder Henry James, who loved a good club as he loved his Maker. Whittier came on his visits to town, and Frank B. Sanborn appeared from Concord. Dr. Holmes read to the club his paper on Jonathan Edwards, and John Tyndall spoke, fresh from London;* while among the younger members or speakers were John Fiske and Thomas Davidson, the peripatetic Scottish philosopher who had recently come from St. Louis.† In a spacious

* John Tyndall addressed the club in 1873, when he was giving his Lowell lectures. He was astonished to hear that Emerson had not been asked, and would not be asked, to lecture at the Lowell Institute. "If anyone can be said to have given the impulse to my mind," he remarked, "it is Emerson. Whatever I have done the world owes to him."—*Sketches and Reminiscences of the Radical Club.*

† See William James's essay on Davidson, in his *Memories and Studies, A Knight-Errant of the Intellectual Life.* This learned and picturesque philosopher conducted summer schools at Farmington, St. Cloud, New Jersey, and Hurricane in the Adirondacks. Later he founded the Educational Alliance in New York. "He denounced me," William James said, "for the musty and mouldy and generally ignoble academicism of my character . . . The memory of Davidson will always strengthen my faith in personal freedom and its spontaneities, and make me less unqualifiedly respectful of 'civilization,' with its herding and branding, licensing and degree-giving, authorizing and appointing, and in general regulating and administering by system the lives of human beings."

"Thomas Davidson was really a remarkable man; that was clear to me even on a first meeting . . . I came away feeling that this was the most remarkable man, the most intensely alive man I had ever met; I am not at all sure that I should not say so still."—Havelock Ellis, *My Life.*

Davidson established in London the Fellowship of the New Life,—with Havelock Ellis, Edward Carpenter, etc.,—from which sprang the Fabian Society.

closet in this house, all the remaining copies of all the
anti-slavery tracts were neatly arranged on shelves. One
drew a long breath as one opened the door, thinking of
all the thunders that lay asleep there. It was almost as
impressive as the Tower of London, Thomas Wentworth
Higginson felt,—filled with the relics of wars that were
fought for freedom. This closet, he thought, should be
kept as a sacred place, like the Old South Church and
Faneuil Hall. The meetings of the Radical Club could
hardly rise to the old heights; but, if they had an air of
Indian summer, suggesting brighter seasons of the past,
they showed that plain living and high thinking could
still exist in unheroic ages. One speaker said that Margaret Fuller in many respects resembled Sappho, a tribute to Sappho's genius, from the point of view of Boston,
that did full justice, however, to Margaret's morals. But
the tone of the discussions was seldom local. The topics
were usually those that were agitating the modern mind,
heredity, peace and war, the freedom of women, coöperation, hygiene, Darwinism. Was science antagonistic to
religion, in spite of all that John Fiske could say? Now
and then, a spell descended on the company, and one of
the members suggested a silent meeting. Those who best
construed, in the long years to come, the ideals of the
older reformers were Thomas Wentworth Higginson and
Julia Ward Howe. Colonel Higginson, living at Newport, often appeared in Boston, before he settled at last
in his birthplace, Cambridge. Mrs. Howe, with Dr. Howe,
had left "Green Peace," their home on Dorchester Bay,
near the Perkins Institution; but when they were not at
Newport they were always somewhere on Beacon Hill.
Mrs. Howe never lacked the courage to rise in her seat
and say, "Mr. B., you are uttering falsehoods."

Wherever the Howes lived was a cosmopolitan centre,
for the "Cadmus of the blind" attracted to his Institution whatever curious foreigners still came to Boston.

"Green Peace" had swarmed with refugees, Greeks, Hungarians, Poles and dwellers in Mesopotamia, some of them learned men like Count Adam Gurowski. Dr. Howe found employment for them, for the one English word they knew was "lessons." When this word was uttered, they beamed with joy, like the Russian, the Turk and the Spaniard in *The Peterkin Papers,* who had all come to Boston to give lessons but who could not explain themselves till the Lady from Philadelphia divined their purpose. They taught Dr. Howe's children, and the five little Howes could scarcely remember a time when they had not known half the tongues of Europe.* But Boston abounded with Agamemnons and Solomon Johns, who were eager for all their wares, beginning with Sanskrit.† It was a privilege to receive an exile,—so Elizabeth Peabody felt, and the Howes agreed.‡ Kossuth and many others had once stayed at "Green Peace." The rambling old house, a farmer's cottage, with two or three modern additions, was full of odd turns and crooked stairways. On the green hattree in the entry, Byron's helmet hung, with its floating plume, and the walls of the great square dining-room were covered with old masters, from "Uncle Sam" Ward's New York collection, the "Boar Hunt" of Snyders, the Domenichino, the Rembrandt that nobody ques-

---

* All the five Howe children later wrote books.

† "Mr. Peterkin suggested they should each take a separate language. If they went abroad this would prove a great convenience. Elizabeth Eliza could talk French with the Parisians; Agamemnon, German with the Germans; Solomon John, Italian with the Italians; Mrs. Peterkin, Spanish in Spain; and perhaps he would himself master all the Eastern languages and Russian . . . Mr. Peterkin made some enquiries about the Oriental languages. He was told that Sanskrit was at the root of all. So he proposed they should all begin with Sanskrit. They would thus require but one teacher, and could branch out into the other languages afterward.

"Mrs. Peterkin was afraid it would be like the Tower of Babel, and hoped it was all right."—Lucretia Hale, *The Peterkin Papers.*

‡ "Western Europe was civilized by the exiled Greeks . . . Why should not our citizens form such noble friendships as Lorenzo de' Medici and the rival princes of Italy formed with the learned Greeks?"—Elizabeth Peabody.

tioned, the Poussin that no one had to question. There lay the Gobelin carpet from the Bonaparte house at Bordentown. From the slope, with the terraced garden and the little classical temple that Dr. Howe used as a seed-house, one had seen the Cunarders steaming into Boston. The grand old doctor-cavalier had ridden about on his black horse, directing the work and play of the Institution, while Mrs. Howe conducted her "Hôtel de Rambouillet," which she carried on wherever she was, in Boston or at Newport in the summer season.

A Bostonized New Yorker, who had grown up in a banker's family, addicted to the world and Paris fashions, Mrs. Howe supplied the link, missing hitherto, between the somewhat hostile rival cities. She filled this role in a way of her own that scarcely fitted at the edges, for she was too earnest to please New York, too earnest even for social Boston, and she had her own frivolities,— to make the case a little odd,—that sometimes offended the reformers. But Mrs. Howe went her way serenely, plucking the golden fruit of all these gardens. As a young girl in New York, who was singularly pretty, she had learned Italian at sixteen, as later, living in Rome, she had studied Hebrew. Later still, she mastered Greek at fifty. Her special joy was German thought; and, when she was not running downstairs for "fun," she was often upstairs reading Kant and Hegel. "I have followed the great masters with my heart" was Mrs. Howe's motto, and she loved Goethe, Schiller, Aristophanes and Dickens and had also studied Catherine Beecher's cook-book.

> My practised hand the loaf can mould,
>   with careful touch and swift,

Mrs. Howe wrote in one of her poems, for she had a high regard for the household arts. A poet on all occasions, an *improvisatrice,* of the good old Italian type and manner, she had written the *Battle Hymn* in a moment of genius. This genius never burned again, either in *Passion Flowers* or in *Later Lyrics*,—poems of summer nights and lofty causes, or in the plays she wrote with small success;* but Mrs. Howe's ambition was not exacting. She faithfully strummed her lyre for fifty years. In many of her poems she seemed to be rebuking the remnants of Eve in herself, the vanities of the wicked world for which she had retained a lingering fancy.

As Dr. Howe's companion, she had roamed over Europe, collecting funds and talking with other reformers, not without moments of joy in the pomps of the flesh. A deeply religious nature, she had sat at the feet of Theodore Parker, who had been interested in her early verses. He had urged her to appear on the lecture-platform. Theodore Parker's brain reposed in a box in a closet at the Perkins Institution. It had been sent to Dr. Howe by Parker's Italian physician, when the great preacher died and was buried in Florence. The Howes regarded the box with horror, not knowing what to do with this fearful relic; but Parker's mind lived on in Mrs. Howe. She lectured in Unitarian pulpits, she preached in a Negro chapel in San Domingo. She was quite as ready to preach to the worldlings at Newport, whose hearts were set on diamonds and yachts. She reproved the worship of wealth and the vulgar aesthetics of luxury. Never more at home than in "the chair," promoting another cause or another hero,—the Armenian cause, Stepniak, Russian freedom, —she founded clubs as Agassiz founded museums. Study-circles rose in her path, peace associations and women's unions,. as she scratched her furrows and dropped the seed, ready to wait for results till the Day of Judgment. She established a club in New Orleans; she reminded the

---

* Mrs. Howe's play, *Hippolytus,* written for Edwin Booth and Charlotte Cushman, was first performed after her death by Walter Hampden and Margaret Anglin.

ladies of Athens that "women are people," as Lucy Stone
had recently remarked.* If, in her philosophical writings,
character masqueraded as intellect, the character at least
was real and potent. In her drawing-room, she delighted
in contrasts. She confronted all the worlds with one another. When nothing else availed, she would set her
guests to work translating Mother Goose into Greek and
German.

At the Radical Club and elsewhere, Thomas Wentworth Higginson was Mrs. Howe's associate in all these
causes, peace, universal suffrage, Russian freedom, the
higher education of women; for even the Digger Indians,
whom he had seen in the West, had not destroyed his
faith in human nature. A true disciple of Channing, a
liberal Unitarian, who had lived through the period of
the "Newness," Higginson had grown up in Cambridge.
His father, the bursar of the college, had planted the
elms in the Yard, and all his early memories were connected with Harvard. At dancing-school, at the Nortons'
house, he had cut off little Charlie's front hair. His nurse
had married Longfellow's "village blacksmith." In the
days of Brook Farm, when Thoreau was living at Walden, he had planned as his own experiment the cultivation
of peaches. The only true free man, he thought, was he
who could "live on a little." † Then he had entered the
ministry, at Newburyport and Worcester, and become
involved in the cause of the fugitive slaves. An active
Abolitionist and a lover of nature, he had walked and
talked with Thoreau, who praised his essay, *Snow,* in
The Atlantic; and at Worcester he had lived near Harrison G. O. Blake, Thoreau's correspondent who had later
become his executor. Higginson was one of the neigh-

* On her third triumphant visit to Greece, after Dr. Howe's death.
Mrs. Howe founded the Women's Peace Association in London, 1872.
† Ellery Channing told Higginson that the Hawthornes lived in Concord
on $300 a year. The rent of the Manse was $75 a year, which they paid
from the apple-crop.

bours who gathered round the breakfast-table when Blake
received a letter from his friend in Concord, and he recognized bits of these letters when they appeared in *Walden*. In Kansas, he had shared in the Free-Soil struggle,
standing on real stumps to make his speeches; and, after
the war broke out, he had organized a regiment of
Negroes and fought in South Carolina for two or three
years. His friends were reminded of Cromwell's days
when this minister descended from his pulpit, drew on
his jackboots and rode off to the war. In 1864, the fighting colonel had been invalided to Newport, where he
lived as a simple man of letters. He had published a
translation of Epictetus, a rebuke to the new ideas of
luxurious living. He wished to remind the world that
slaves had been philosophers. He recalled that Epictetus,
his fellow-stoic, was also Toussaint L'Ouverture's favourite reading.

Colonel Higginson still bore, indeed he bore for life,
the scar of a sabre on his chin. It was a souvenir of the
day when he and Dr. Howe had forced their way into the
Boston court-house, in their attempt to rescue Anthony
Burns. A generous, valorous, hopeful soul, he was always
ready to write or speak on subjects suggested by the
zeitgeist,—the function of culture, the manners of tourists, the future of country towns, domestic service. He
had produced one book of permanent interest, *Army Life
in a Black Regiment,* a first-rate human document of the
Civil War. This was the story of the "military picnic"
of the First South Carolina Volunteers. Higginson had
looked for the arming of the Negroes for six years before the war began, ever since the days of the Kansas
troubles, and he had already raised a Massachusetts company when he was placed in command of the camp at
Beaufort. His mind was filled with military matters, but
the training of eight hundred slaves,—the first Southern
regiment of Negroes, as Colonel Shaw's, in Boston, was

the first in the North,—might well have taxed the skill
of Grant or Sherman. They felt they were fighting with
ropes about their necks, for the officers and soldiers of
all the Negro regiments suffered a felon's death when
they were captured. Higginson kept a diary in camp, as
Dana had kept a diary on the "Pilgrim," and the story
of this "gospel army," fighting for its freedom, had much
of the spirit and charm of Dana's book. It was filled
with grotesque and dramatic adventures, like those of
Marion's band in the Revolution, when the "old swamp
fox" eluded his foes in these same forest-paths of Carolina, in the pine-barrens and muddy creeks, embosomed
in blossoming shrubs, where the mocking-birds sang in the
magnolias. There were foraging expeditions up the rivers,
—up the Edisto, for one, to destroy the bridge on the
railroad,—where the cotton-fields were white with fleecy
buds and the air was full of hyacinthine odours. Never
could one forget the fascination of these nocturnal ascents
of unknown streams, leading far into the enemy's country, as one slipped in the moonlight through the meadows,
passing the picket-fires on the silent banks,—the rippling
water, the veiled lights, the anxious watch, the whispered
orders, while the reed-birds wailed overhead and one
heard the yelp of a dog on some distant plantation. Nor
could one forget the nights on picket, under the live-oak
branches with their trailing moss, among the wax-myrtles
and the oleanders, the japonicas, oranges, lemons, the
date-palms and fig-trees, in the endless bridle-paths of
the flowery forests.

In retrospect, the colonel saw himself adrift on a
horse's back in a sea of roses. He had spent scores of
nights in the saddle, in the starlight, in a mist or densest
blackness, while the chuck-will's-widow droned above and
the great Southern fireflies rose to the treetops or hovered
close to the ground, till the horse raised his hoofs to
avoid them, riding through pine-woods and cypress-

swamps, or past sullen brooks and clustered tents, or the dimly seen huts of sleeping Negroes. He had spent a whole night swimming in one of the rivers, alert for every sound on the glimmering shore; and often, returning from rides on the plover-haunted barrens, he had silently entered the camp in the midst of a "shout." The dusky figures about the fire moved to the rhythm of the dance,—the kind of scene that Winslow Homer loved,— chanting, sometimes harshly, but always in the most perfect time, a monotonous refrain, *Bound to Go* or *When the War is Over.* Higginson loved the Border ballads that Child was collecting in Cambridge. He had always envied Scott the delight of tracing them out and writing them down; and here was a kindred world of unwritten songs, as indigenous and simple as those of the Scotsmen, usually more plaintive, almost always touching and often as essentially poetic. He listened to these spirituals, *Wrestling Jacob, Hold Your Light, My Army Cross Over, One More River,* and jotted down the words, as best he could, and carried them to his tent, like captured birds or insects, to study them and print them at his leisure. Had Europe or America seen an army so religious since Higginson's own forbears fought with Cromwell? The fatherly colonel thought of the Negroes as the world's perpetual children, docile, lovable and gay. The regular troops were mundane and rough beside them.

In later years, Higginson never rose again to the literary heights of some of these chapters, the superb *Up the Edisto* and *A Night on the Water.* He had written one of those rare books that recall a passage of history as the works of the formal historians cannot recall them.*

---

* *Army Life in a Black Regiment* deserved to be remembered with Stephen Crane's *The Red Badge of Courage.* Higginson later recognized at once the "extraordinary freshness and vigour" of Crane, whom he described as second only to Tolstoy in his pictures of war. See Higginson's *Book and Heart.*

Meanwhile, he had thrown himself into miscellaneous writing and was one of the chief supports of *The Atlantic*. A linguist and an excellent scholar, he had never known a moment of boredom, nor could he imagine such a thing while there was still a language or science to learn. He remembered a time when a prison-cell would have looked rather alluring to him if he had had a copy of Laplace to read. He wrote historical essays, papers describing Newport,—*Oldport Days,*—a romance called *Malbone,* rather feeble, and pleas for literature and culture that were tonic in their effect on younger writers.* In *A Charge with Prince Rupert* and *Mademoiselle's Campaigns,* he was almost as good as Carlyle in a similar vein; and he followed Thoreau in his essays on birds and flowers. But the interests of women were his special study, as befitted a friend of Margaret Fuller who had spent days on the Rhine visiting the scenes that recalled Bettina and the spot where Günderode died. *Ought Women to Learn the Alphabet?* was one of his essays; and in *Saints and Their Bodies* he preached the gospel of out-door life, quoting Catherine Beecher's remark that in all the vast acquaintance of the Beechers there were not a dozen healthy women. He formed a collection of books on the status of women, the Galatea collection, which he left to the Public Library in Boston.

Mrs. Howe and Higginson were voices of a Boston epoch that might have been described as a "second growth." This feminizing Boston, this Boston that followed the war, wished to believe in itself rather than did so. But Mrs. Howe and Higginson still believed, with the faith of old and some of the force, in this resembling also Dr. Hale; and, if the faith had waned a little and lost its old effectiveness, it was full of generosity and

---

* It was one of these papers of Colonel Higginson that caused Emily Dickinson to write and ask if he would be her "master."

goodness.* For the rest, one of Higginson's hobbies was discovering talent. He had offered a prize at Newburyport, the bait that caught Harriet Prescott Spofford. He was one of the earliest friends of Celia Thaxter. It was he who sent Elizabeth Stuart Phelps her first letter of praise. He called upon Rose Terry Cooke at Hartford, when she was still unknown, living in a sort of moated grange, a mile out of town, an old brick house with an air of decay, where she dwelt with an old grey father. He discovered Emily Dickinson. He encouraged "H. H.," later known as Helen Hunt Jackson, Emily Dickinson's friend as a child at Amherst, who was Higginson's neighbour at Newport.† If the new age of writers was largely an age of women writers, Higginson was the first to find them and read them.

As for the elder Henry James, who had moved with his family to Cambridge, the Radical Club had no more faithful member; for, although this wandering New Yorker was a stranger in Boston, he had many friends among the old reformers. Besides, he was not wholly a stranger there. He had run away to Boston and supported himself as a proof-reader, while he was still a student at Union College. He had quarrelled with his father, a rich Albany merchant, of the straitest sect of Presbyterians, who disapproved of his wild habits, his love of cigars and oysters, and perhaps his friendship with an actor. For the young man abounded in animal spirits. But he had returned to college and had studied theology at Princeton, where he had met George Ripley as a fellow-student; and he had become a Fourierist in the days of

---

* Higginson said of Mrs. Howe, in words that might be applied to them both, barring his best book and her best poem: "Generally she feels about her editorials as if she were a pair of tongs that could not quite reach the fire. This she said to me and it well describes them."—*Letters and Journals of Thomas Wentworth Higginson.*

† Higginson also discovered George Edward Woodberry, whom he recommended to Lowell.

the "Newness" and a lecturer on this new philosophy. As
a friend of most of the Brook Farmers, he shared their
socialistic aspirations, agreeing with Fourier that men
should follow their natures and that natural appetites
and passions were meant to be enjoyed. He was convinced
that property was not a final fact of history, since men were
ashamed of the deference they paid it; and he dreamed
of a new social order, a new church, a new world that
would spring from the reconciliation of spirit and flesh.
He was full of an impulsive love of humankind. He had
met Thoreau and Alcott in New York, and Emerson had
visited him often and admired him greatly, describing this
New York friend as a "sub-soil plower." When William
James was born, his eldest son, Emerson bent over the
cradle and gave him a blessing. This was at the Astor
House, the infant philosopher's birthplace; for hotels
were a constant element in the life of the Jameses. The
family had large means, and the elder Henry James preferred a detached existence on behalf of his children. He
was vaguely opposed to their going to college, opposed
to their forming any attachments that might perhaps lead
to their undoing; for so many of his brothers and cousins
had come to grief that he was afraid of America, or
afraid of New York, as a nursery for the younger generation. Generally speaking, however, he adored his country; and although, in America, he often longed for Europe, he longed much more for America as soon as he
got there. In his youth, he had visited England with the
great Joseph Henry, who had filled him with a permanent interest in science; and there he had undergone a
religious conversion. Fear had come upon him, and a
trembling in his bones; and he felt that the writings of
Swedenborg had saved his reason. Much in England rejoiced him, its ease and convenience, and the charm of
which he sometimes spoke with rapture; but he felt that
American disorder was sweet beside European order,—it

was, as he said, so full of promise. He could not abide
the class-distinctions that fossilized the English mind and
caused his own heart to dance with glee, as he recalled
his Nazareth across the Atlantic; * for the hope of mankind, as he saw it, was the hope of social equality, and,
feeling the weight of the past in Europe, he pined for
the land of the future. Emerson had given him a letter to
Carlyle, who impressed him as a "literary desperado." †
The sage of Chelsea ridiculed reformers and talked "as
if the temple of his friendship were a hospital, and all
its inmates were scrofulous or paralytic." His scorn for
humankind disgusted James, who later wrote an essay on
"cantankerous Thomas." ‡ For James was a mystical
democrat. He once remarked that a crowded horse-car
was the nearest approach on earth to the joys of heaven.
Like Whitman, he preferred the company of stage-
drivers to that of "our" literary men, the "vain, conceited nobodies" whom he knew in New York. As for
the family, before they arrived in New England, they
had roamed for several years all over Europe, with a
faded set of Swedenborg as a part of their luggage; for
the elder James, like Howells's father, was faithful to
Swedenborg, though in this, as in everything else, he
remained a dissenter.

In a few short years, the Jameses had settled into the

* "I venture to say that no average American resides a year in England
without getting a sense so acute and stifling of its hideous class-distinctions
. . . as makes the manners of Choctaws and Potawatomies sweet and
Christian, and gives to a log-cabin in Oregon the charm of comparative
dignity and peace."—Henry James.

† "Carlyle is the same old sausage, fizzing and sputtering in his own
grease . . . He names God frequently, and alludes to the highest things
as if they were realities; but it almost looks as if he did it only for a
picturesque effect, so completely does he seem to regard them as habitually
circumvented and set at naught by the politicians."—Letter to Emerson,
1856.

‡ "He"—Carlyle—"was Mother Eve's own darling cantankerous Thomas,
the child of her dreariest, most melancholy old age; and he used to bury
his worn, dejected face in her penurious lap, in a way so determined as
forever to shut out all sight of God's new and better creation."—Henry
James, *Recollections of Carlyle*.

Boston world as if it had been theirs from the beginning. The two younger brothers, Robertson and Wilkinson, had gone to Frank B. Sanborn's school in Concord. They had enlisted and fought through the war, while William and Henry, as invalids, were too frail for this. Alice, the sister, was also an invalid; indeed, she remained the victim of a nervous disorder. Later, she lived in England near Henry the younger, and her journal revealed a literary gift as marked in its way as that of her father and brothers.* Henry, who had spent a year at the Law School, was known already as a writer. He reviewed novels for *The Nation*. Norton had encouraged him to work for the *North American* also, and Howells, on *The Atlantic*, welcomed his stories. When William, who had gone to Germany to study, returned in 1869, Henry went to Europe for a year, the first of the several journeys that took him across the Atlantic before he made up his mind to live abroad. William had gone through the Scientific School, and later the Medical School. His bent was all for science, and he had passed from chemistry to the biological sciences, with a voracious interest in other studies, literature, philosophy, history and art. He was

---

* "Henry, by the way, has embodied in his pages many jewels fallen from my lips, which he steals in the most unblushing way, saying, simply, that he knew they had been said by the family, so it did not matter."— From Alice James's journal in England.

Alice James died in England in 1892. So strong was the literary habit of the family that she was revising her journal during the hours of delirium that preceded her death. This journal abounds in fine passages, as, for example, the following: "She . . . told me that she was going to my land,—whilst my highest privilege, shrivelled and rickety, was to go to bed in hers! What a tide of homesickness swept me under for a moment! What a longing to see a shaft of sunshine shimmering through the pines, breathe in the resinous air, and throw my withered body upon my native earth, bury my face in the coarse grass, worshipping all that the ugly, raw emptiness of the blessed land stands for,—the embodiment of a huge chance for hemmed-in humanity; its flexible conditions stretching and lending themselves to all sizes of men; pallid and naked of necessity; undraped by the illusions and mystery of a moss-grown, cobwebby past, but overflowing with a divine good-humour and benignancy, a helping hand for the faltering, an indulgent thought for the discredited, a heart of hope for every outcast of tradition."—*Alice James, Her Brothers, Her Journal*, edited by Anna Robeson Burr.

turning to psychology, which soon became his main field, but he had studied physiology in Germany, where he had seen much of Hermann Grimm. Emerson, with an avuncular fondness for the sons of his old friend Henry James, had given William a letter to his German translator, and he followed William's development and that of the younger Henry with an anxious pride and joy in their gifts and their progress. William was also reviewing for *The Nation,* but he was living at home in Cambridge in a desperate state of neurasthenia. He passed from crisis to crisis, suffering from insomnia, digestive disorders, mental paralysis, eye-strain, panic fear. He was consumed with a sense of futility, and this suicidal melancholia continued for three or four years before it left him. Meanwhile, he had interrupted his medical course to go to Brazil with Agassiz, the most exciting of all his Harvard teachers. Agassiz wished to explore the Amazon and conquer it for science, and the Emperor, Dom Pedro, rejoiced in his coming; for this Portuguese Harun-al-Rashid, who had liberated the slaves in Brazil, admired the New England scientists and poets.* Dom Pedro enthusiastically advanced the plan. Agassiz had organized a travelling school of science as Sherman organized his army: he divided his assistants into groups, some to explore the interior, others the coast, and he lectured on the downward voyage, preparing them for the work to come. All day long, on deck, with his joyous gusto, he talked about the Gulf Stream and its seaweeds, the South American fishes, the wonders of the world they were to see; and one moonlight night on the river, as they swung in their hammocks, Agassiz turned and whispered, "James, are you awake? *I* cannot sleep. I am too happy. I keep thinking of these glorious plans." William James learned

---

* Dom Pedro translated into Portuguese a number of poems of Longfellow and Whittier. He visited New England in 1876 to study its educational and scientific institutions. There are interesting accounts of this visit in the authorized biographies of Agassiz, Whittier and Longfellow.

much from this expedition. The collecting and geologizing bored him. He was not cut out for a field-naturalist, much as he enjoyed pure adventure; but Agassiz's loving eye and outdoor instinct and his sympathy with living nature left lasting traces in James's mind. They taught him the importance of "concrete fullness" as opposed to what he called "abstractionism." This was the leading trait in all his writings.*

During these years, the elder James brooded over his children's problems, for he was a parent, perhaps, above everything else. He was one of those uncrystallized geniuses who are often the parents of real geniuses, with a largeness and power of nature that everyone felt; and if, in the autumn of his days, he had come to Boston, it was mainly for the welfare of his offspring, much as he enjoyed himself the Radical Club and the Saturday Club and the chance to abound in his own humour. He had reacted against a Presbyterian father who tried to crush, as he felt, his natural instincts, and he diligently fostered these instincts in his children as what he considered divine educational forces. That one should obey these instincts, as Emerson said, was the first of his articles of faith. He was an absolute libertarian for whom all evil was "fossil," the result of diseased institutions and the pride of selfhood, the conceit of his moral endowments that led the individual to feel he was not as other men. His pet aversion was "flagrant morality," or any sort of conscious virtue. He preferred the sinner to the prig, and giving the Sabbath a "black eye" was one of his favourite amusements. He liked nothing better than to whip the "pusillanimous" clergy, whose narrowness

* "Behind the minute anatomists and the physiologists with their metallic instruments, there have always stood the outdoor naturalists with their eyes and love of outdoor nature. The former call the latter superficial, but there is something wrong about your laboratory-biologist who has no sympathy with living nature. In psychology there is a similar distinction." —William James, *Memories and Studies.*

afflicted him like charcoal-vapour.* It was not because he took religion lightly. Religion was the theme of all the books to the writing of which he devoted his passionate thought. By social reform, by destroying selfhood, by abandoning the existing sects, the way would be opened, he felt, for the great consummation, the establishing of the true relation between mankind and its Creator, the revelation and presence of God on earth.

* See his letter to the Swedenborgian editor: "The old sects are notoriously bad enough, but your sect compares with these very much as a heap of dried cod on Long Wharf in Boston compares with the same fish while still enjoying the freedom of the Atlantic Ocean . . . Your mature men have an air of childishness and your young men have the aspect of old women . . . [As for your paper] I really know nothing so sad and spectral in the shape of literature . . . It cannot but prove very unwholesome to you spiritually to be so nearly connected with all that sadness and silence, where nothing more musical is heard than the occasional jostling of bone by bone. Do come out of it before you wither as an autumn leaf, which no longer rustles in full-veined life on the pliant bough, but rattles instead with emptiness upon the frozen melancholy earth."

CHAPTER VII

AESTHETIC BOSTON

WHILE the cause of reform in Boston languished, another symptom soon appeared that characterized the coming generation. This was a recrudescence of the old colonial feeling towards Europe that had seemed to be utterly extinguished. New England had lost its political leadership, and many of the New England men had lost their old connection with the soil. They were uprooted and adrift in a world they did not understand and found more and more uncongenial, and even some of the older men who had been ardent patriots were uncertain of their moorings and their bearings. They felt as if the labours of their fathers had been mocked, as if their country had been wrested from them;* and they looked across the sea again, despairing of a nation that had passed beyond their powers of comprehension. In their breasts rose once more a hankering for the ancient homeland, as if three generations of history had gone for nothing.

Scores of Southern families shared this feeling. Many of the Charleston Huguenots returned to France.† Embittered by the war, discouraged by the new regime, they abandoned their country forever and flocked to Paris; and they tried to grope their way back to the heart of the old French culture from which they had been weaned for generations. Others returned as suppliants to Eng-

---

* "The Land of Promise?" said Lowell. "The Land of Broken Promise." See also Lowell's *Letter to George William Curtis.*
† See the Probert family in Henry James's *The Reverberator.*

land. This movement resembled the Russian hegira that also occurred in the sixties, after the emancipation of the serfs, when many disgusted aristocrats withdrew from their estates and cast themselves adrift in western Europe.* The movement was widespread along the Eastern seaboard, in the class that had once so largely controlled the country; and it was strongest in Boston, perhaps, where the leading families felt most keenly the loss of their old political power and prestige. This power and prestige had shifted into Western hands, and Boston was left high and dry; and, moreover, the state of mind of the post-war years was bewildering to cultivated people. They could not understand the vast, shambling new republic, with its scandals, its corruption and its greed. To minds that were formed on the ancient plan, intellect and character were the ends of existence, and many troubled observers noted that intellect and character, with the shattering of the older culture, were no longer respected. The decline of political life was marked and shocking. The maggoty lobbyists of the "special interests" bribed their way all over it and destroyed its fibre, and a new tradition rose in which it was a merit not to know that politics existed. The respectable classes conspired to ignore them, as Godkin had observed with indignation. They even ceased to vote, in many cases. As the years went on, scores of novels deprecated this turn of affairs, urging good men to enter public life or showing how hopeless it was for them to do so; † but, except in so far as they kept the conscience of thousands awake, these novels were ineffective, like the writings of Godkin. Nothing availed to turn the tide, and the general mind, averted from politics, immersed itself in private affairs alone.

* These were the exiles described in Turgenev's *Smoke*.

† Among New England novels, or novels about New England, concerned with this theme, were John W. De Forest's *Honest John Vane,* Henry Adams's *Democracy,* F. Marion Crawford's *An American Politician* and Winston Churchill's *Coniston* and *Mr. Crewe's Career.*

Men drove further into business, with less regard for the public welfare. Their old sectional pride was broken, their national pride was still unformed; and they had little left to be proud of, aside from their success in money-making.

To many of the older Americans, in Boston and in the South especially, this national frame of mind was repugnant and alien. Proud of their country once, they were doubtful now; and some were ashamed of their country. Even Mrs. Stowe could have said no longer what she had said in the fifties, that the world looked hopefully towards America as a nation especially raised by God to advance the cause of liberty and religion. The day had gone by when New England ambassadors plumed themselves in foreign courts on the virtue of American institutions. Bancroft's salutary impudence was a relic of the past;* and, as for American institutions, many a Boston ear was open to the worst that English travellers said about them. Godkin's abhorrence of the West was shared by "stuck-up Boston folks" † who withdrew in proud reserve from their countrypeople, a reserve that was more and more jealous the more it was challenged; ‡ and

* When Bancroft was minister to Berlin, the British ambassador asked him why American ministers appeared at court "all dressed in black, like so many undertakers." Bancroft replied that they represented "the burial of monarchy."

† "Ohio people are sensitive about 'stuck-up Boston folks.' "—*Letters of Mrs. Henry Adams.*

"Such is the tendency of democracy to a general. mingling of elements, that this frigidity is deemed necessary by these good souls to prevent the commonalty from being attracted to them, and sticking to them, as straws and bits of paper do to amber. But more generally the true-blue old families are simple and urbane in their manners; and their pretensions are, as Miss Edgeworth says, presented rather intaglio than in cameo."—Harriet Beecher Stowe, *Pink and White Tyranny.*

‡ "I think Americans who are jealous of their reserve are even more so. than Englishmen,—perhaps because in a democracy it is a more conscious prize and has to be fought for."—*New Letters of James Russell Lowell.*

"A line of respectable connections, being the harder to preserve where there is nothing in the laws to defend it, is therefore the more precious when we have it really to boast of."—Redclyffe, in Hawthorne's *Dr. Grimshawe's Secret.*

meanwhile America ceased to interest many Americans, who closed their minds to their country and all its problems. The "best people" did not talk about it, as travelling foreigners noticed in the flesh and in fiction; or they only referred to their country to abuse their country. They preferred to talk about Europe, and especially England.* For they agreed with Matthew Arnold that America was not "interesting" and that for lovers of "elevation" the sky there was of brass and iron.† This verdict was unworthy of a thinker, although they did not see this; for, if every country should interest a thinker, what should one say of a country about which hordes of travellers were writing books? ‡ American conditions,

* "This not talking of America at all," or talking only to abuse, was a puzzle to many Europeans. "Very curious," says Lord Rainford, in Howells's *A Woman's Reason,* "I can't get the people I meet to say a good word for their country. They all seem ashamed of it, and abuse it, no end . . . I find your people, your best people, I suppose they are,—very nice, very intelligent, very pleasant,—only talk about Europe. They talk about London, and about Paris, and about Rome; there seems to be quite a passion for Italy; but they don't seem interested in their own country. I can't make it out. It isn't as if they were cosmopolitan; that isn't quite the impression, though—excuse my saying so—they try to give it. They always seem to have been reading *The Fortnightly,* and *The Saturday Review,* and *The Spectator,* and the *Revue des Deux Mondes,* and the last French and English books. It's very odd, upon my word, at one dinner the Americans got to talking to one another about some question of local finance in pounds, shillings and pence . . . I don't understand it."
See also the remark of the journalist Ford in Howells's *The Undiscovered Country*: "If I went to this lady's house . . . I should have to be just arrived from Europe, or just going . . . My talk should be of London and Paris and Rome . . . of English politics and society; my own country should exist for me on sufferance through a compassionate curiosity, half repulsion; I ought to have recently dined at Newport with poor Lord and Lady Scamperton, who are finding the climate so terrible . . . You see that's quite beyond me."
† "And so I say that, in America, he who craves for the *interesting* in civilization, he who requires from what surrounds him satisfaction for his sense of beauty, his sense of elevation, will feel the sky over his head to be of brass and iron."—Matthew Arnold, *Civilization in the United States.*
"The trouble about Matthew which sets so many against him is the entirely needless priggishness of his tone . . . His ultimate heads of classification, too, are lamentable. Think of 'interesting' used as an absolute term!"—William James, Letter of 1888.
‡ Some of these books were discerning. A few, like James Bryce's *The American Commonwealth,* were more than discerning. Most of them de-

American institutions were matters of burning concern
to most of these writers. Almost every liner brought some
Englishman or Frenchman who was bent upon solving
the puzzle and threading the maze; and, if Arnold's sense
of the interesting did not include what interested them,
what was one obliged to think of Arnold? And, as for
"elevation," those who had heard the Gettysburg speech
were on fairly intimate terms with this emotion. As for
the "sense of beauty," they agreed with Arnold. They
agreed when he called attention to their Briggsvilles and
Higginsvilles, those remnants of their too "Hebraic"
past. In this sphere, all he said was salutary, and Americans heard him gladly, young and old. But regarding
"elevation" they had their doubts. They had little to
learn in this respect from travelling rhetoricians, especially one who gravitated, as if by a natural instinct, to
Barnum and Andrew Carnegie, a few years later.* They
felt they knew more about this than their British advisers; for many besides the Adamses were shocked by
the low tone of British politics. There were nice old
ladies who pitied Thomas Arnold in his heavenly mansion
for begetting this impudent Matthew. But the confidence
of others had been shaken. They did not wish to parry
Arnold's charges. They were interested in Europe, and
Europe alone.

It was useless, in these circles, to quote Emerson's ob-
jurgations against their attitude of mind, their "mendi-
cant, curious, peering" ways, itinerant and imitative,
studious of other countries and ignoring their own. Emer-

served Josiah Quincy's phrase about Basil Hall and Mrs. Trollope:
"These birds of passage have skimmed over this country like vultures
over the surface of the Carolinas, pouncing upon whatever is corrupt,
and passing by whatever is sound or healthful, as adapted neither to
their taste or scent."

* Matthew Arnold was the standing illustration of Bromfield Corey's
generalization, in Howells's *The Rise of Silas Lapham,* regarding the
travelling Englishmen, that they are "more curious about the great new
millionaires than about anyone else, and they respect them more."

son could not share their feeling, indeed he was scarcely aware of their feeling, rapt as he was in his dream of America's future; * and most of the older writers, such as Longfellow and Holmes, were as firmly rooted as Emerson in the soil of the country. Longfellow had just returned from his final visit to Europe, and "Holmes, sweet Holmes," as the students called him in England, was soon to make his last triumphal journey, with a day at the Derby and a day measuring Tennyson's elms and days with four generations of London beauties. Longfellow had visited at Windsor Castle, and, in Rome, Liszt set to music, in his convent rooms, a part of *The Golden Legend*. There Longfellow was crowned as a shepherd of Arcadia. These two old poets were lifelong lovers of Europe, but to them the new colonialism, the recrudescent Anglomania, with its disregard of America, was utterly foreign. Their minds went back too far for this. They remembered the growing days of the young republic, and they had always seen themselves as builders of a great, new, hopeful western civilization. They did not measure themselves by other countries, for they felt they had their own sufficient centre; and the younger men whose interests were all in the country continued to feel as their fathers and grandsires had felt. It was other-

* "The young men in America at this moment take little thought of what men in England are thinking or doing. That is the point which decides the welfare of a people, *which way does it look?* If to any other people, it is not well with them. If occupied in its own affairs and thoughts and men, with a heat which excludes almost the notice of any other people,—as the Jews, the Greeks, the Persians, the Romans, the Arabians, the French, the English, at their best times have done,—they are sublime; and we know that in this abstraction they are executing excellent work. Amidst the calamities which war has brought on our country this one benefit has accrued, —that our eyes are withdrawn from England, withdrawn from France, and look homeward. We have come to feel that 'by ourselves our safety must be bought,' to know the vast resources of the continent, the good-will that is in the people, their conviction of the great moral advantages of freedom, social equality, education, and religious culture, and their determination to hold these fast, and, by them, to hold fast the country and penetrate every square mile of it with this American civilization."—Emerson, *Letters and Social Aims.*

wise with younger men whose local attachments were not deep. It was otherwise with Motley, Lowell and Norton, who were more disposed to feel the degradation of public life because their political interests had always been strong. They were lovers of New England whose hearts had scarcely embraced the nation and who loved New England less in its decline; and, as the immigrant races began to rival the Anglo-Saxon, they were drawn to an Anglo-Saxon England. Boston, for the rest, was closer to Europe than other American cities. There appeared *Every Saturday* and *Littell's Living Age,* compiled from European papers, and the French and English magazines were staples of conversation at every dinner-table and in all the clubs. "Boston is very well up in all things European," Henry Adams noted in 1873, "but it is no place for American news;" and, as the interest in things American rapidly dropped away, the relish for the old world grew apace. The return of the colonial feeling was a part of this.

In later years, Henry James exemplified this feeling more fully than anyone else, before or since; but James's curious Anglicism was only comprehensible in the light of the social context in which it arose. His sponsors abroad were Lowell and Norton, who introduced him to English society, and Lowell and Norton, with Motley, were members of the New England group that was most disaffected at home. They were acutely sensitive to the sudden drop of the national prestige and more or less abashed by their country, and they gravitated towards England in this frame of mind. Motley settled there and never returned to America, where he had been discredited and hurt. He became an Anglophile of a type his country had never known in the days when it gave scope to seasoned statesmen. Save in his technical allegiance, Motley became wholly English, and almost as completely the author of *The Biglow Papers* reverted to the pattern of English culture. Lowell, who had said, "We are worth nothing except so far as we have disinfected ourselves of Anglicism," * was the first to be reinfected as time went on. Socially and personally, he fell in love with everything English; and, after he had lived in England, he went back every year, and he formed closer ties there than he ever formed again at home. He never returned to his old simplicities of costume, manner and voice, and the "defiant Americanism" for which he was noted in England was the protest of his nature against his taste. Norton, who had left America to spend five years abroad, returned to fight it out at home; but his constant tone of exasperation showed how far, in doing so, he violated his taste and his inclinations. All these men found in England "the perfection of human society," Motley's phrase for the London dinner-table and the English country-house; and Henry James met this society under the wing of these men, in a state of mind that was influenced by their example. They were disappointed in their country, smarting from its disrepute, and inclined to apologize for themselves as Yankees; and they were disposed to see the English as somehow larger than life, the more they saw their countrymen as somehow smaller. If they did not feel inferior, this was because, as eminent men, they could always fall back on their achievements; although, for the matter of that, their self-esteem was involved in their esteem for their country. Younger men, like Henry James, had nothing to fall back upon and shared their mortification and chagrin. Of course, James felt, shall we say, uneasy, as everyone is bound to feel who cannot believe that his country possesses a standard. He may have felt that Americans were morally better than Europeans, but in other respects he felt that his country was "negative"

* *On a Certain Condescension in Foreigners.*

or nugatory.* This was to have strange consequences in James's writings.

*

*   *

Meanwhile, in Boston the interest grew in things aesthetic. The Museum of Fine Arts was founded in 1870, the symbol and crystallization of this movement of feeling; and half the domestic walls of Boston blossomed with Fra Angelico angels, with photographs or prints of Mona Lisa, or perhaps The Last Communion of Saint Jerome. Lounges appeared in houses that were studies in colour, hung with purple curtains, with rooms that were harmonies in green or melodies in blue; and even the Roman nose that had flourished in Boston was losing its severity of outline. On all sides, the question rose, What place was art to have in the satisfactory human life that Boston was trying to realize? Already a species of art-cant, as sharp observers called it, was displacing the commoner cant of religion and culture, and one heard on every hand the phrase, "He is a true artist," or "She has not the feeling of an artist." Everything was "artistic" or "inartistic." The great question "Love or Art?" filled many a youthful imagination that had fed upon Mrs. Browning's *Aurora Leigh*. While Aurora found that "love is more," she was desperately certain that "art is much;" and in this there were many Bostonians who agreed with Aurora.

The outburst of aesthetic feeling that expressed itself in the new museum was part of a wider movement of emotional growth. One saw this in religion, in all the fields of social habit; one saw it in the changing names of children. A generation of Mauds and Enids, of Alices, Daisys and Daphnes, of Isabels, Mariannes, Elaines and Graces

----

* "When one approached her [London] from the alien positive places (I don't speak of the American, in those days too negative to be related at all)."—Henry James, *The Middle Years.*

was growing in the garden where once the fresh New
England flowers had borne such names as Abigail and
Hannah. The new age was Hellenistic as it was also Tennysonian: it scarcely required an Arnold to spread this
taste. Steeped as it was in all the poets, Greek, German,
French and English, it was losing the Hebraic flair, although it preserved the Hebrew names when these were
euphonious also. Esther, Ruth and Eva vied with Penelope and Imogene in the parental fancy. One observed
a similar change in the country districts, where the Hebraistic imagery was dying also. The country-people had
vaguer standards, but they too longed for something
pretty and were not concerned to scrutinize its source and
value. They sometimes invented names that struck them
as having associations with the classical world or the world
of the poets and romancers. In these less critical regions,
one encountered such names as Liverius, Lurella and Lu-
cina, Levina, Zepheretta, Loretta, Zerrilla.*

This indicated a tendency that was equally marked in
the sphere of religion. With the breakdown of the old
theology, the rural churches only flourished by meeting
the mundane demands of the congregations. The spiritual
element was generally submerged in the social, humanitarian, aesthetic, in music, dancing, lectures and oyster
suppers. It was held in effect that salvation must not be
made to appear depressing or the young would lose all
interest in their souls; and the ministers, for whom the
ancient faith had lost its outlines and its dogmas, preached
about "flowers, stars, love and crystal springs." † They
floated in a mist that was vaguely romantic and vaguely
poetic. In the more conscious classes, the growth of Epis-

---

* "Where the Puritanism has gone out of the people in spots, there's
the rankest growth of all sorts of crazy heresies; and the old scriptural
nomenclature has given place to something compounded of the fancifulness
of story-paper romance and the gibberish of spiritualism."—Howells, *The
Lady of the Aroostook.*
† Rose Terry Cooke, *The Sphinx's Children.*

copalianism corresponded to this development in the simpler people. All the "best families," it was sometimes said, were either Unitarian or Episcopalian. Dr. Holmes had remarked in *Elsie Venner* that they were "expected to be," a phrase that offended some of his readers; and it was Dr. Holmes who explained the decay of his own faith, of which the Episcopal Church was the advancing rival.* The dignity of man and the beauty of virtue had ceased to excite the thrills of old, and the religion of reason had starved the senses: it could not compete any longer with the rapidly rising Catholic Church and the Anglican Church that stole the Roman thunder with its choirs and illuminations, its colour and music. No use to protest that rites and forms were shallow, where the feminine mind especially had grown so strong.† They appealed to the aesthetic depths, they appealed to other emotional depths which the old New England faiths had left unsounded; and it only required a preacher of genius, who appeared at once in Phillips Brooks, to establish the Episcopal Church in the heart of Boston.‡ What Channing had once been, Phillips Brooks became, the typical divine of an epoch; for this fuller-blooded Channing, this muscular Christian, exuberant, robust and cultivated, had all the traits that made the Boston leader. A kinsman of Wendell Phillips, he revived the moribund art of the

* " 'The beauty of virtue' got to be an old story at last. 'The moral dignity of human nature' ceased to excite a thrill of satisfaction after some hundred repetitions."—Holmes, *Elsie Venner*.

† "Something in its favour"—in favour of the Episcopal Church,—"is the influence that every ritualized faith has with women. If they apprehend these mysteries, more subtly than we, such a preference of theirs must mean a good deal. Yes; the other Protestant systems are men's systems. Women must have form. They don't care for freedom."—The Rev. Mr. Waters, in Howells's *Indian Summer*.

It was symptomatic of this moment in New England that Hawthorne's daughters entered religious orders. Many others followed Una Hawthorne, who became an Anglican nun. Rose Hawthorne later became a Catholic nun and was famous later still as Mother Alphonsa.

‡ Phillips Brooks became the rector of Trinity Church in 1869, the year in which Grant became President and Eliot became president of Harvard.

orator in a world that was less concerned for social reform and more concerned for science, art and travel. He
spoke for an age that was saturated with Tennyson and
Browning, with the gospel of *In Memoriam* and "the
larger hope."

If, in all these ways, the New England mind had cut its
ancient moorings, it was also drifting literally in the paths
of travel. The time had long since passed when a voyage
to Europe was like a voyage in Charon's ferry-boat, when
friends and families gathered with sobs and tears to speed
the adventurous wanderer and letters from across the
sea were like angels' visits. Where handfuls had followed
once in the footsteps of Byron, seeking out the consecrated sites and dilating with appropriate emotions, thousands were accustomed now to "hopping backwards and
forwards over the Atlantic," as Matthew Arnold's "Boston informant" put it. Travel-books no longer began by
telling why one took the journey and how it felt to be
rocked by the ocean waves. They no longer described the
condition of Shakespeare's tomb, or the busts in Westminster Abbey, or the Bay of Naples. These were old
stories to the new generation of travellers,* who were
often familiar with Syria, Egypt and Greece. Others
roamed over America, exploring the Florida scene and
straying to Quebec and Montreal, which had begun to
seem as historic as Europe; for Irving had made the Hudson classic ground and Parkman was garlanding Canada
with associations. They roved through Evangeline's country and the village of Grand Pré. Naturalists like Wilson
Flagg sought for birds in Tennessee, and Saint Augustine
and Summerville, as rising winter resorts, vied with the
Campobello of July and August. It is true, there were
certain Bostonians, like Howells's Mr. Arbuton, who were

* A new American type, after the Civil War, was the travelling-companion, hitherto not unknown but certainly rare. Louisa Alcott went abroad
in 1865 as a travelling-companion.

not convinced that America was entitled to legends. It
struck them as presumptuous for this raw country to assume the prerogatives of Europe; and, as for the exaggerations of American nature, were they not in rather
bad taste? Were not the cliffs of the Saguenay excessively
high as a feature of river scenery? In a world of such
well-bred streams as the Thames and the Tiber, they felt
they had to snub the Mississippi, to maintain the Bostonian sense of proportion and fitness; and travel in Europe
was growing so common that many felt obliged to snub
the ingenuous souls who "did" the standard sights. But,
sooner or later, one and all, however disdainfully, went
the rounds from the scenes of *The Belfry of Bruges* to
the Mer de Glace, from St. Ursula's church at Cologne
and the Lion of Lucerne to the tomb of San Carlo Bor-
romeo. They read *Hyperion* on the Rhine, they read *The
Marble Faun* in Rome, and in Florence they quoted Longfellow's sonnet about the Ponte Vecchio, with the twisting
dragon of the Arno underneath it. They strolled through
the Via de' Bardi, where Romola lived, and they visited
the grave of Theodore Parker, who resembled Savona-
rola in certain respects. They rowed into the Blue Grotto,
climbed Vesuvius, drove to Amalfi; they were punctual at
St. Peter's on Palm Sunday. They spent a day at Fontaine-
bleau, a day at Rambouillet, an hour in front of Rubens's
Descent from the Cross, and perhaps a week at Vevey or
Baden-Baden; and they lingered at Gibbon's house in
Lausanne and the Iron Virgin of Nuremberg and the
organs of Freiburg and Haarlem. They snuffed the fog
of Johnson's London and visited Chester and Coventry,
where they faithfully murmured Tennyson on the bridge,
rejoicing in the random corners and the feasts of crooked-
ness that satisfied their passion for the picturesque.* The

* "If the picturesque were banished from the face of the earth, I think
the idea would survive in some typical American breast."—Henry James,
Transatlantic Sketches.

English lawns, the castle towers, the woods, the village churches brought tears of recognition to their eyes, as of the previous state that Plato spoke of; and, eager as they might be to improve conditions at home, there were no such tories—in Europe—as travelling Yankees. They longed for the picturesque at any price, regardless of dampness, injustice or any abuses.* But most of them, after a year or a summer, also longed for the keen air, the active life, the stimulus of home; and they came back laden with table-tops and paper-weights, with Psyches and Hebes and Graces in alabaster, and with caskets, lockets, picture-frames and laces. It was only a question of time before they also brought home façades of Venetian palaces and castles in boxes.

For this vogue of travel went hand in hand with the ever-growing rage for art that characterized the younger generation. Young men of means roamed over Italy, inspired with a wish to see sincerely, the fruit of their reading of Ruskin. They copied Roman inscriptions in their pocket notebooks. They studied Siennese architecture and Tuscan sculpture; and they went to Verona to examine the Lombardic pillars, often with a mounting scorn of all things modern. As they sat in Santa Maria Novella, they pored over *Mornings in Florence,* wondering how far they should follow the hectoring Ruskin. Most of the younger American artists were turning away from Italy,

* "The American who, in his own country, is in feverish haste to improve conditions, when he sets foot in Europe, becomes the fanatical foe of progress. The old world, in his judgment, ought to look old. He longs to hear the clatter of wooden shoes. If he had his way he would have laws enacted forbidding peasant folk to change their ancient costumes. He would preserve every relic of feudalism. He bitterly laments the division of great estates . . . He is enchanted with thatched cottages which look damp and picturesque. He detests the model dwellings which are built with a too-obvious regard for sanitation. He seeks narrow and ill-smelling streets . . . He frequents scenes of old murders, and places where bandits once did congregate . . . A heath ought to be lonely, and fens ought to be preserved from drainage . . . The religious pilgrim does not expect to find the old prophets, but he has a pious hope of finding the abuses which the prophets denounced."—Samuel M. Crothers, *The Toryism of Travellers.*

and those who travelled abroad to study now more often
went to Düsseldorf or Paris; but remnants of the circle
described in *The Marble Faun* still basked in the golden
air of Rome and Florence, where Powers died in 1873.
One still found sculptors working on allegorical figures,—
perhaps "The Pacific Slope," for San Francisco,—and
painters for whom Venetian priests and peasants remained the last word in picturesqueness. They were
mostly happy and innocent souls and fervently American,
however dim and vague about their country, using the
slang of the pre-war days, mingled with Italian phrases,
dim and vague as they were about Italy also. Most of
them were poor and driven, for their statues and their
pictures had little appeal for the new generation of tourists. William Wetmore Story lingered on in Rome, where
Charles C. Perkins, who had returned to Boston, had
given his musical soirées in the days of Mazzini. Story
had left the studio that Hawthorne pictured as Kenyon's.
Still living in the Palazzo Barbarini, he had built a larger
workshop, with a garden full of trees, flowers and vines,
strewn with broken statues and fragments of friezes; but,
although his ambition grew and his work increased, the
day was already passing for literary sculpture. Harriet
Hosmer's "Clasped Hands of the Brownings" retained a
sentimental interest, but Story's sculptures seemed like
bad translations; and the Sibyls and Cleopatras that had
charmed the eye of an earlier age more often aroused an
unkind mirth at present.* Meanwhile, two American boys,
both born in Italy, who were later to be known in art and
letters, were growing up more or less in Story's circle.
John Singer Sargent, whose father had come from
Gloucester, was carried as a child all over Europe, to

---

* "We went to Mr. Story's studio, and oh! how he does spoil nice blocks
of white marble. Nothing but sibyls on all sides, sitting, standing, legs
crossed, legs uncrossed, and all with the same expression as if they smelt
something wrong. Call him a genius! I don't see it."—*Letters of Mrs. Henry
Adams*, 1873.

Spain, France, Germany and England; but the family
lived in Florence, Sargent's birthplace. Francis Marion
Crawford was the son of Thomas Crawford, Story's associate and rival as a sculptor in Rome.*

This Italianate circle was closely connected with Boston, and there the rage for art was all-engrossing. Days
that had once been merely misty were described now as
"Corot days," and Giotto and Cimabue, as themes of conversation, vied with castled crags and historic landscapes.
The copies of Guido and Carlo Dolci, the fruit of earlier
grand tours, were displaced by the sort of pictures that
Ruskin approved of,—a Turner, perhaps, that was sold
upside down, and "no one found it out," as Miss Alcott
remarked. All these pictures were eagerly discussed. Their
merits and authenticity were as carefully canvassed as the
qualifications of new professors at Harvard, although
sometimes the most meritorious were the most disturbing. One heard of a little girl who remarked, as she
looked at Correggio's Magdalen,—a copy, in this instance, to be sure, "Why, that lady is dawdling! She is
reading a book when she ought to be dressing." Others
were troubled by Rembrandt's coarseness: his heads were
so un-Emersonian that one shuddered at them. But the
taste for art had come to stay, and Elizabeth Stuart
Phelps, in *The Story of Avis,* advanced the thorny problem of the woman artist. Avis had studied painting in
Florence, in a bare little studio-attic, like Hilda, in *The
Marble Faun,* among her doves, and had won Couture's
praise in Paris. Then her career was wrecked by an invalid husband. Should woman artists marry? Should Avis
have married? The question reverberated in many a
feminine breast in Boston; and many a reader rejoiced
in Miss Phelps's conclusion. Avis's daughter, please God,

* Marion Crawford was born at Bagni di Lucca, 1854. Sargent, born in
Florence in 1856, began his career in Paris, 1874, as a pupil of Carolus
Duran.

should be only an artist! One found this zest for art on the humblest levels. Young girls, obliged to earn their living, no longer took up teaching as a matter of course. They painted hollywood boxes, fans and vases, or, like the dutiful Ruth Felton, in Harriet Prescott Spofford's *Azarian*, they searched the rhodora marshes for flowers to paint, while their fancy roved in Italy and Greece. Mrs. Spofford's romances and tales expressed this lowlier phase of Boston. *The Amber Gods, Sir Rohan's Ghost, Desert Sands, In a Cellar,* were day-dreams that struck her readers as new and daring, for they dealt with artists who lived in Paris, cellars stocked with wondrous wines, ladies in gowns of Genoa velvet with peacocks' feathers of green and gold and painters who longed for the languors and heats of the desert. Their fanciful, airy style was full of a kind of aesthetic feeling, kindled by Keats and Tennyson, Browning and Hawthorne; and their high-flown phrases and recklessly chosen exotic words, "chatoyant" eyes and "sprinkles" and "spatters of splendour," were protests against the bare, the cold, the rigid. In two tales, *In a Cellar* and *Circumstance,* especially, Mrs. Spofford emerged from her flowery mist. *In a Cellar* suggested Poe, but *Circumstance* was all her own and a highly original story, though perhaps too long. This tale of the pioneer woman, in the wilderness of Maine, who saved herself from the lynx by singing to it,—for she had heard that music charms wild beasts,—was singularly real and thrilling. The idea was fresh and brilliant, and Emily Dickinson in Amherst was struck by this story.* In her

* "The only thing I ever read," Miss Dickinson wrote in a letter, "that I didn't think I could have imagined myself! Send me everything she writes." There were phrases and images in other stories by Mrs. Spofford that seem to have left their traces in Emily Dickinson's mind,—"A daintiness of morning costume but recently indulged . . . The solicited events of centuries transpired unnoticed beside him . . . On the soft soil of the avenue, the sound ferried the silence" (*Sir Rohan's Ghost*). These stories of Mrs. Spofford's were the rage in the sixties, according to Howells, and *Sir Rohan's Ghost* appeared in *The Atlantic,* which Miss Dickinson read religiously. Is it an illusion that one catches in these turns of speech the

general mood of romantic extravagance, Mrs. Spofford
showed how far the New England mind was starving for
colour and splendour.

As if in response to this demand, a group of remarkable artists appeared, two or three of whom were men
of genius. Winslow Homer, George Fuller and Albert
Pinkham Ryder were born in Massachusetts, one and all,
and an artist of another type, Frederick Law Olmsted,
was already at work in landscape architecture. Homer,
a Boston boy who had grown up in Cambridge, had gone
to the Civil War as an illustrator. Later, he had settled
in New York, whence he returned in the eighties to the
coast of New England to paint the Gloucester fishermen,
the rocks and the waves with a magisterial grandeur of
touch and feeling. As long ago as the Brook Farm days,
Homer, who lived near the Washington elm, in a house
that overlooked the Cambridge Common, had fished in
Fresh Pond at four in the morning, and his drawings of
barefoot boys and berry-pickers, of corn-huskings and
barn-dances were as full of New England feeling as
Whittier's poems. His first oil-paintings were campaign
sketches, based on his powerful drawings for *Harper's
Weekly,* and he knew the Virginia Negroes and the war-
time camp-life as well as the northern woods and rivers,
the sailors and the fishermen, the loggers and the deer-
stalkers and even the idlers and girls at the summer-
resorts who appeared in the novels of Howells. Like
Howells, he knew that little things mattered, and he saw
the details of army life that professional military painters had never noticed. Again, like Colonel Higginson, he

peculiar Emily Dickinson stamp and ring? One of Mrs. Spofford's heroines
had "sherry-coloured eyes" before Miss Dickinson discovered that her eyes
were "like the sherry in the glass that the guest leaves."

In her later stories, Harriet Prescott Spofford followed the tendency to
realistic writing. The short pieces in the volume called *A Scarlet Poppy,*
largely dealing with conflicts of husbands and wives, were among the best
of the delicate sketches, sufficiently real but of no great moment, that were
common in New England in the nineties.

was drawn to the Negroes, and his Caribbean water-
colours, with their Negro figures, recalled to many observers Whitman's line, "I behold the picturesque giant
and love him." As for his early paintings, fine as they
were, in their somewhat harsh veracity and candour, they
were only dim presentiments of the later Homer, the
great prose-painter as Ryder and Fuller were poets. Fuller was an itinerant portrait-painter who had gone into
practical farming to save his ancestral acres in the village
of Deerfield. There, with his own hands, he reclaimed a
tract of swamp-meadow, exchanging the plough for the
brush whenever he could, developing the unique style that
suggested the figures and scenes of Hawthorne, with its
veils of ambiguity and haze of distance, its Indian summer mists and depth of tone. Fuller was the painter of
October afternoons in the fertile harvest-lands of the
interior valleys. Ryder's world was midnight on the sea,
where lonely ships challenged the watery abysses and
ragged storm-clouds sped across the moon. Ryder, like
Winslow Homer, had gone to New York, where he lived
for the rest of his life, but his chosen scenes were those
of his native New Bedford, where Melville stopped before he set forth on his whale-hunt; and he spent many
summers in the Cape Cod harbours, "soaking in the moonlight," as he said. The impulse that was flagging in the
poets seemed to have been reborn in these three painters;
and meanwhile Olmsted also symbolized the times and
the rise of aesthetic feeling in the towns and cities. Olmsted, a Hartford man, had been one of Godkin's advisers
in the founding of *The Nation*. He had written three
studies of the South, in its economic and social aspects,
that Godkin had used as guides on a horseback journey.*
Godkin thought these books far surpassed Arthur Young's

---

* *A Journey in the Seaboard Slave States, A Journey in Texas* and *A
Journey Through the Back Country.* The best parts of these three books
were later combined in *The Cotton Kingdom.*

for vivid actuality in travel-writing; and Olmsted, in fact, was a first-rate observer who left a permanent record for historical students. As pictures of the old South, his books were irreplaceable: no one else had examined the scene so shrewdly. At that time, Olmsted was just beginning his great career as a landscape-architect. At a moment when the younger men were flocking to the cities, abandoning the soil and the farms, Olmsted's career was symptomatic. It was a reaction against the decline of rural life in the conscious cultivation of parks and gardens. An adventurous boy, the son of a prosperous merchant, who had wandered all over New England, hunting and fishing, and who had sailed to China before the mast, Olmsted had studied chemistry at Yale and become a Connecticut farmer and nurseryman. Then he had taken up landscape-gardening, for which his observations had prepared him, for on walking-trips and drives with his father, up the Connecticut valley and through New Hampshire, he had made a careful study of scenery. He had observed the dells and slopes, the grouping of trees and the vistas, the aspect and position of the homesteads, the arrangement of buildings, the relation of copses and woodlands to ponds, streams, meadows, rocks and mountains; and in Europe, where others haunted museums, he had spent his time in parks, till he knew their every aspect in London and Dublin, in Paris, Brussels, Berlin, Vienna and Rome. He was widely known as a writer on agriculture and scenery before he put his knowledge to the test in designing the park for New York. Central Park was the first of many, for the great Connecticut landscape-architect designed sixteen other parks, from Brooklyn to Stanford University. He made the name of his art a household word. Olmsted kept alive in a world of cities the values and associations of rural life.

The founding of the museum and the rise of art-schools were natural effects of the moment. So were the activities

of a number of writers on art and music who appeared in
the sixties and seventies, chiefly in Boston, "Tom" Appleton, Charles C. Perkins, William Morris Hunt and
William Rimmer. During these years, the consul at Trieste, Alexander Wheelock Thayer, who was born at
South Natick, was writing his *Life of Beethoven.* No
doubt, Hunt stirred aesthetic Boston more than anyone
else with his *Talks on Art,* but he shared the field, as a
talker and teacher, with Rimmer, whose art-school was
the first in New England.* This reserved and elusive physician, who had been a village shoemaker and was later
a doctor at Quincy, where he worked among the quarry-
men, had taken up sculpture and used the Quincy granite,
with which he had made a remarkable head of St.
Stephen. A self-instructed artist, who never went abroad,
he produced the grand figure of Hamilton, vaguely suggesting a figure-head, that stood in Commonwealth Avenue, overlooking the Common. A draughtsman of great
power, as one saw in his beautiful Blake-like drawings, he
lectured on art-anatomy, the subject of his ablest book;
and he had among his pupils John La Farge and Daniel
Chester French, the Concord sculptor. A solitary, proud
and silent man, Rimmer had none of the traits that made
the magnetic Hunt a Boston favourite, though his influence was scarcely less important.† These two together led
the Boston art-world. Hunt was an artist with a mission.
That the present was a great artistic epoch, that Americans, who were poets, should also be painters,—this was
"what Hunt said" on all occasions. If some of his other

* So it was said in the circular announcing the school, 1864. The Yale
School of the Fine Arts, the first of its kind attached to a university, was
founded in the same year.

† Rimmer was a man of mystery whose father, a French immigrant, had
assumed this name. See Truman H. Bartlett, *The Art-Life of William
Rimmer.*

The character of Dr. Bhaer, in Louisa Alcott's *Little Women,* is said to
have been drawn from Dr. Rimmer, with whom May Alcott studied ana-
tomical drawing.

sayings, which passed from mouth to mouth, were far from complimentary to Boston, they nevertheless expressed his faith that every place was another Hymettus when people looked for the honey in the flower that grows.

Hunt, before settling in Newport and Boston, had lived for many years abroad and had once been Couture's favourite pupil. Then he discovered Millet, who was still unknown, and went to live in Barbizon beside him. For two years he wore a blouse and sabots and walked in the afternoons in the fields with Millet, who showed him how to look at a cart by the roadside. They would stand for hours before this cart, observing how it sagged or how the light fell on the wheels, or perhaps they discussed the Bible, which they knew by heart. One might have thought that no one had ever read it as one heard this French peasant declaiming its phrases. "Now the famine was great throughout all the land,"—what a description, that, what breadth, said Millet. He saw the book of Ruth from a painter's standpoint. The story went about that an English collector was buying up all Millet's pictures, and the dealers in Paris began to be interested in him; but Hunt was the man who bought them, when no one would have "The Sower" for $60, as he also bought Barye's unknown bronzes and persuaded his American friends to buy them. It was Hunt who had since made Boston,— where Millet's brother Pierre was living, the brother who served as a model for the figure in "The Angelus,"—a focus for all the artists of the Barbizon school. There seemed to be an occult relation between these men and the Yankee mind. No doubt, the New England poets had prepared the ground, with their love of landscape, nature and the Bible.

A rangy, spare, muscular man, with a bony nose and flashing eyes, Hunt looked like Don Quixote or an Arab. He had kept his own horses in Paris, tall hunters and

fast trotters, and every day at Newport he had galloped
on the sands, with the air of a Moorish sheik in a Fro-
mentin picture; or one saw him spinning along in a racing-
buggy, with velvet jacket and scarlet sash, and a beard
like a fountain in the wind. In Boston, with his art-classes,
he stirred up a rage for charcoal-drawing, especially por-
trait-heads and cat-tails; and he liked nothing better than
to tease the Boston people, whose niggling conscientiousness annoyed him. He would set his soup-plate on his
head at restaurants, to save the waiters trouble, or throw
his arms about some pompous lawyer, who had never
seen a man like Hunt before. An actor, a mimic, a fiddler,
whose violin had belonged to Balzac, he would meet an
organ-grinder on the street, seize the organ and play
it and collect the money, while the forlorn Italian stood
by astonished; and he said he always voted for the politicians whose figures looked best on the beach. When one
of the Boston critics wrote an attack on Barye, he ran
out at night on the Common and stormed around it several times. These people did not deserve to see his Mil-
lets,—"Their dry eyes would burn holes right through
them;" and, lonely as he was, with no one to look up to,
he welcomed other artists who returned from Europe,
eagerly bought their pictures and gave them exhibitions.
The tenderest and most delicate things, he said, were
snubbed out of the world; for art was like jelly in this,
it was only recognized when it was cold. He had no use
for the lectures on art that his Boston pupils enjoyed so
much,—one might as well try to smell music or eat a
cook-book; and he peppered them with Taine and Hazlitt and begged them to "paint for fun," regardless of
their success or the New England conscience. Draw fearlessly, avoid the kind of finish that rats give to cheese,—
that hide-bound air, that look of goneness, that unmis-
takably empty look which a house presents when the
family has left for the country.

Hunt's *Talks on Art,* with their gibes at Boston, harrowed the ground for many seeds.* Meanwhile, Appleton, who had ·known Hunt in Europe, encouraged the taste for French art that his friend had introduced and that characterized the coming generation.† Appleton, the Boston wit, Dr. Holmes's rival, had crossed the ocean forty times before the Civil War and the deepest of his tastes was for painters and painting. He had studied in Italy and copied in the galleries there, as one of the passing members of Story's circle. His little talent had petered out in a passion for painting pebbles, which he gave his friends to use as paper-weights; for Appleton was like Bromfield Corey in *The Rise of Silas Lapham,*—"It was absurd for him to paint portraits for pay, and ridiculous to paint them for nothing, so he did not paint them at all." But his failure increased his sympathy for other struggling American artists, who were frequent beneficiaries of his sudden fancies. He would see a poor student copying in the Louvre and tap him on the back and say,

* The two series of Hunt's *Talks on Art* were compiled at the suggestion of the English painter, G. Lowes Dickinson, the father of the author of this name. The superintendent of the class stepped behind a screen and rapidly jotted down Hunt's remarks. They were printed in this impromptu form. The following are among Hunt's sayings:
"Boston is a great place for receipts.
"When anybody in Boston sees a picture he likes, instead of buying it, he goes home and tries to paint one like it.
" 'Why didn't you like Cambridge?' . . . Because I love art. Cambridge is like Kaulbach's pictures. It is all literature.
"The mouth is not a slit. It is shaped like a trumpet.
"People go to Europe and bring home second-hand 'old masters.' Get them cheap, and there's a cry over them. But if one of those old painters were living in Boston today, not one of his works·would they buy . . . No, they go about whining because we have 'no art in this country,' and 'we never shall paint like Titian'! . . . Such people are logs across the track.
"If you have painted a sketch in two hours, don't tell of it. If you do, people will say it is horrid. They like the look of work that takes weeks and months. Just as in society you'll hear a lady say, 'See my beautiful embroidered handkerchief. The girl who worked it made herself blind. Isn't it lovely?' 'Oh!' 'Ah!' etc."
† "As our physicians gave up the training of England for that of Paris, so a kind of distaste even of English methods of art, and the keenest enjoyment of that of the best French school, has of late come about."— Appleton, *A Sheaf of Papers,* 1875.

"Come to Egypt with me;" for he had a special feeling
for Egypt and wrote a charming book about it.* He told
the Italian picture-dealers to cheat him as much as they
could, well knowing that he himself knew more than they
did.

A poet on occasion, Appleton was an essayist, abounding in good sense and shrewd ideas. It was he who said,
"Good Americans, when they die, go to Paris." He suggested tying a shorn lamb at a certain corner in Boston, to
temper the wind. He was a gourmet, and some of his best
essays dealt with the virtues of mutton, trout and white-
fish and the horrors of Puritan cooking. He was chiefly
interested, however, in the cause of advancing art in Boston, along with his fellow-founder of the museum, Charles
C. Perkins. Appleton gave the museum a collection of
Tanagra figures.† Perkins worked devotedly over all the
collections. A nephew of Colonel Perkins, who had given
the Athenæum its collection of casts and one of whose
other uncles had discovered Rimmer, he had lived for
many years in Rome and Paris, where he had studied
painting with Ary Scheffer; but he had surrendered this
ambition to become an art-historian and had published
Tuscan Sculptors in 1864. This first of Perkins's several
books, with its technical knowledge and charming style,
and its illustrations etched from the author's drawings,
had become an authority at once. It was followed by
Italian Sculptors, dealing with other than Tuscan subjects, by *Raphael and Michael Angelo* and the later *Historical Handbook of Italian Sculpture.* Perkins's last
book, *Ghiberti et son école,* was written in French. A
writer far superior to James Jackson Jarves, though with-

* *A Nile Journal.* See also the beautifully printed book by another Boston
art-lover, Martin Brimmer's *Egypt.* Brimmer, like Appleton and Perkins,
was one of the founders of the museum.

† See Appleton's charming story-essay, *The Artist of Tanagra,* in
Checquer-Work. It was Appleton who said of the museum,—the building
replaced in 1908,—that, if architecture was "frozen music," this was
"frozen Yankee Doodle."

out the provocative opinions that made Jarves exciting,—
for his work was descriptive rather than critical,—Perkins was one of a family of minds that included Symonds
and Pater in England. His *Tuscan Sculptors* ranked with
Norton's *Church Building* and Henry Adams's *Mont-
Saint-Michel and Chartres.*

Meanwhile, the interest in music was rapidly growing
in the home of Jonas Chickering, Oliver Ditson and the
Mason and Hamlin piano; for John Sullivan Dwight and
his *Journal of Music* had had a profound effect on the
Boston mind. Perkins was involved in this development
also. He had studied music in Germany, like Henry Lee
Higginson, and he wrote the history of the Handel and
Haydn Society, of which he was conductor for a time. It
was he who had given the music-hall Crawford's statue of
Beethoven, the first statue of any artist erected in the
country. The Beethoven cult dated from the forties, when
the young Brook Farmers had walked in to Boston to
listen to the "Emerson of music;" * and during all these
years the more or less Bostonian Thayer was at work on
his life of the composer. The effect of all these influences
on the younger generation was almost as marked as that
of science.

It is true that Thayer's biography appeared in English
when most of this generation was dead and gone. But the
first volume was published in German in 1866, and the
work was a characteristic product of the Yankee mind of

* Beethoven and Emerson were closely associated in the young New
England mind of the eighteen-forties.
Two incidents connected Beethoven with Boston. In 1822, the Handel
and Haydn Society commissioned the composer to write an oratorio for it.
Beethoven referred to this in one of his letters: "If God gives me back my
health, which has at least improved somewhat, I shall yet be able to comply with all the requests which have come from all parts of Europe, and
even from North America, and I might yet feather my nest."—Thayer,
Life of Beethoven, III, 87-88. One of Beethoven's last requests, when he
was dying, was to see the full report of Channing's address of December
12, 1826, of which he had read or heard an abstract.—Thayer, *Beethoven,*
III, 283.

an earlier decade when the cult of hero-worship flourished
in Boston. Alexander Wheelock Thayer had conceived his
passion for Beethoven while still at Harvard. All the existing accounts of the composer were a tissue of romantic
tales and errors, and Thayer resolved at once to write
the great biography, the first of all authorities on its subject. He went abroad in 1849 and spent two years in re-
searches in Bonn, Berlin, Prague and Vienna, and this
was the beginning of the forty years of labour and poverty at the end of which he left the task unfinished. He
acted for a while as Motley's private secretary, when
Motley was engaged in his Austrian mission, and then
for thirty years he was consul at Trieste, where he was
Hildreth's successor. From this convenient base he carried on his exploring tours with a single-minded zest and
perseverance. He roamed over the continent, examining
archives and libraries and talking with all the composer's
surviving friends, whether among the musicians or the
"princely rabble." He interviewed Grillparzer; he had
many conversations with Bettina von Arnim; he visited
Sir George Smart in England, who gave him his journal
to transcribe. In Paris he saw Thalberg, and he studied
the correspondence of Prince Galitzen. He called on old
violinists and singing-teachers who had known and remembered the composer, gathering anecdotes and records. He found some of Beethoven's letters in a London
music-publishing house and others in the hands of auto-
graph-dealers, and he made transcriptions of Beethoven's
conversation-books, deciphering the scrawls and hiero-
glyphics. At last he finished the first volume. He could not
afford to go home to oversee the printing of it, and he
knew it was not the custom at home to publish books in
parts; so he gave it to Dr. Hermann Deiters, the musical
court councillor at Bonn, who translated it and published
it in German. The appearance of this first volume roused

many other students, for he had opened up lines of research and pointed out subjects for special study. Old men gave up their memories and hundreds of other documents came to light, and Thayer in the end had enough materials to spend the rest of his life arranging and sifting. Long before he died, in 1897, he had finished three volumes of the work; but the old Yankee consul with the patriarchal beard found himself unable to complete it. It weighed on his mind like an incubus, while the musical world pursued him, eager for the results of his final studies; but an hour or two of thought on the subject brought on a racking headache and he had to stop. He turned for distraction to other themes and wrote a book on the Jews in Egypt, and another against the Bacon-Shakespeare theory, with various essays and tales for children, while others, using his papers, concluded the work for which Thayer himself never received a penny.*

Aside from a handful of friends and students, this grand old scholar's careless country knew little about his work and never saw it. Thayer's *Life of Beethoven* had long been a German classic when it first appeared in America in 1920. The author had been dead for twenty-three years, but the guild of musicians had not forgotten him, and the story of this publication suggested the devotion with which the work itself was conceived and written. Thayer, with his calm and logical mind, scrupulous, magnanimous and spacious, was a scholar of the other dispensation. He had set out to describe for posterity the great

* The final German edition of Thayer's *Life of Beethoven* was issued in five volumes in 1908–1911. It is said to have involved the labours of more than eighty men, who were stimulated by Thayer's investigations. The American edition, the first in English, was published in three volumes, 1920–1921, by the Beethoven Association of New York. A group of American musicians devoted to this purpose the proceeds of a winter's season. The editor was H. E. Krehbiel, who revised and completed the work from Thayer's papers. Thayer had known Krehbiel through his own connection with the New York *Tribune,* on the staff of which he had worked in Greeley's day.

man as he was and lived, as Cromwell had wished to be
painted with all his warts; and his patient realism and all
but inexhaustible industry had created an irreplaceable
and masterly portrait.

CHAPTER VIII

FRANCIS PARKMAN

DURING these years, Francis Parkman was at work in his Boston study. He was a lonely man, detached from his time and place and their interests and causes. A classmate of Hunt, with whom he had travelled in Italy, he was also an old friend of Norton, who had helped him with the proofs of *The Oregon Trail*. He was indifferent to painting and sculpture, however, and European opinion meant nothing to him. He was still more remote from everything Higginson represented, or all but his admiration for Epictetus and his love of out-door life. Parkman detested reformers, though he also detested the worship of money. He despised the "morality of commerce," and he had made common cause with Godkin in his efforts to save the republic. He had no use for "flintlock business men." He was a soldier in all his instincts, although fate had made him something else, a writer, and one of the greatest of his age and country. The state of his health had prevented him from taking part in the Civil War, and for him the post-war years were so ignoble that he wished for no part or lot in their concerns. He was only at home in his own mind, where he lived with explorers, borderers, adventurers and woodsmen.

Some years before the war, Parkman had published a novel bearing the name of the hero, *Vassall Morton*. This Morton was a rich young man with a preference for young ladies who were wild and lawless. He did not admire the tamer virtues that prevailed in his little Boston world. He refused any fixed and stated calling. Ardent and energetic, a lover of hardship, with a mind formed for action, he planned to devote his life to the study of primitive races, resolving to gain his ends at any cost. In this he succeeded, the reader was led to suppose, but only after encountering incredible odds and disasters. He spent four years in an Austrian dungeon, and he was condemned to die and imprisoned again, a "death in life," a "slow-consuming horror." But he hardened his heart, in this inferno, against himself and his own troubles; and, when he escaped at last and returned to Boston, he felt he was proof against all further woes. With a mind that had ripened in solitude and suffering, he was ready to face the future with golden hopes.

The novel was one of those still-born books that no one reads but the friends of the author. When the author is a man of genius who has put his worst foot forward, these books are always interesting, however; and Parkman's friends saw at once that he had pictured himself in Morton.* This impetuous young man, who had learned to be patient,—strenuous, eager, proud, confident, manly, —was certainly the son of Dr. Parkman, the minister, the friend of Dr. Channing, who had lived in a spacious old house in Bowdoin Square. It was Dr. Parkman's brother, the physician, who had been murdered by Professor Webster in the laboratory of the Harvard Medical School. In college, Francis Parkman, the grandson of a rich old merchant, had constantly read Cooper, Scott and Byron. He had "Injuns on the brain," his friends remembered, and he had crossed the plains, on the Oregon Trail, when it was as dangerous to do so as ever it was for Columbus

---

* It may be noted that Morton is also the name of the hero of Motley's first novel. Perhaps in both cases this name was suggested by that of the rebel of "Merry Mount," who disliked the ways of the Puritans as much as Parkman and Motley. These two Mortons were totally different, but both were rough self-portraits of men who found their vocation in historical writing.

to cross the Atlantic. The book he had written about his adventures was boyishly vigorous, fresh and frank, and he wrote as if he rather wished his pen had been a sword. One saw in Morton all these traits of Parkman, with his ethnological interests and his plans for historical writing. Parkman had published *The Conspiracy of Pontiac* five years before he wrote the novel. But even his friends might have been puzzled by some of the scenes in *Vassall Morton*. If the picture of the Tyrolese woods and mountains was highly circumstantial, they were aware that Parkman knew the Alps. He had visited the wilder Alpine regions, which recalled to him at once the American woods. No forester knew these woods better than Parkman. But what about Morton's anguish in the Austrian dungeon? What gave these prison-scenes their unmistakable air of reality? Had the writer of this novel been in prison? Or was the dungeon a symbol of something else? One could only say, though one said it with conviction, "Eccovi, this child has been in hell."

It was true. Parkman had lived in hell, and his life, at best, remained a purgatory. As a delicate, sensitive boy, with a passion for adventure, he had lived in a state of constant tension. Fascinated by Cooper's heroes and Byron's wanderers and outlaws, he was bent on surpassing the Indians in strength and endurance. He had spent all his summers in the woods, with his rifle, "Satan," riding the wildest horses without saddle or stirrups. He had tried to crush, in the Indian fashion, every personal weakness; and, while his will and energy were super-normal, his constitution could not bear the strain. He had broken down at one point,—overtaxed his heart,—then at another and another. His eyes had given way from excessive reading. To rest his eyes, while studying Indian life, he had undertaken the Oregon journey. This had destroyed his digestion and given him chronic insomnia. Arthritis attacked his knee and left him crippled, and, finally, a

nervous disorder engulfed his mind. At any attempt to
think or write, he felt an iron band about his head that
seemed to contract with force. He could not enlist in the
Civil War, the bitterest disappointment of his life, and
the doctor he consulted in Paris threatened him with insanity if he ever tried to use his brain again. He was reduced to the kind of inaction that men of his type can
least endure; for, while he exulted in danger and almost
exulted in suffering, he could not bear stagnation and confinement. For two long periods, one lasting four years, he
could not use his mind for any purpose; and at best he
was able to work two hours a day. Two or three hours,
of the twenty-four, was the most he ever slept. He could
not read continuously for more than five minutes, and he
usually read a minute at a time. "Prescott could see a
little," he wrote in one of his early letters; "confound
him, he could even look over his proofs, but I am no
better off than an owl in the twilight." He had composed his first books, *The Oregon Trail* and *Pontiac*, pacing back and forth in the garret of the old colonial house
in Bowdoin Square. Sometimes he sat in the dark, with
bandaged eyes and drawn curtains, memorizing his work,
chapter by chapter, dictating or using his writing-machine;
for he had what he called a "gridiron," like Prescott's
noctograph, a wooden frame with horizontal wires, with
which he could write in pencil,—at an average of six lines
a day,—when he could not even see to write his name.
Then, for fourteen years, he published nothing, or nothing but the novel, *Vassall Morton*, which showed, at
least, his gift for story-telling. His mind ran riot in the
darkness.

Not until 1865, when Parkman was forty-two, was he
able to resume his historical writing. Then appeared *The
Pioneers of France in the New World*, the first, or the
first but one, of his great series. He had published *Pon-*

tiac, the last of the series,—in chronological order,—as if he feared he could never round out the subject; and he had been preparing ever since, when he was able to work, for the other volumes. He collected his books and documents and had them read aloud to him. He jotted down his notes, which were later deciphered and read to him again till he knew them by heart. It was wonderful to follow his dictation, to watch the scenes unfold and the persons come to life out of the crabbed notes that he held in his hand. Although he could scarcely see these notes, he had lived them, in a sense, from his earliest boyhood; and he had formed a plan for his life during his student-years at Harvard. This plan was to write what he called the "history of the American forest,"—the history of the "old French war,"—the contest of the Indians, the French and the English for the control of the continent. He had met with little encouragement. No one seemed to care about this old French war, a dim and squalid struggle, as people supposed it, between savages and bush-rangers, with nothing but a wilderness as the stake; and even *The Conspiracy of Pontiac* had aroused little interest in it.* But this war had decided the fate of the continent, and Parkman knew how important it was. Moreover, he knew that he had a chance, the last and only chance, to picture, in the Indians, who were disappearing, —at least, in their primitive form,—authentic American men of the Stone Age, the forbears of civilization. No

---

* In spite of the success of Bancroft's American history, the reading public long remained indifferent to the subject of it. John Fiske referred to an incident, in this connection, that occurred about 1875: "A gentleman in a small New England town was asked if some lectures of mine on 'America's Place in History' would be likely to find a good audience there. He reflected a moment, then shook his head gravely. 'The subject,' he said, 'is one which would interest very few people.' In the state of mind thus indicated there is something so bewildering that I believe I have not yet recovered from it."—John Fiske, *Essays Historical and Literary,* II, 126.

"The preferences of sentient creatures are what *create* the importance of topics."—William James.

one could have been better prepared to carry out this project, nor was any project ever achieved with a more tenacious will.

From his earliest childhood, Parkman's tastes and interests had converged to form this will. For, while he was a man of the world, he was a woodsman born. As a little boy, he had caught horned pouts in the Frog Pond,— a stone's-throw from Prescott's later dwelling,—and broiled them over a fire in his father's garden. At eight, he was taken to live on his grandfather's farm at Medford, in the woods of the Middlesex Fells, with their cliffs, ravines, marshes, streams and lakes, a patch of primitive wilderness that still remained within eight miles of Boston. He had four years of freedom in the fields and forest, riding, shooting, trapping, fishing, camping. He carried snakes in his pockets, he botanized; he even raised silkworms for a while. He knew all the animals and imitated their calls. In Boston, he was observed, on a Sunday morning, following his father and mother on their way to church, carrying by the tail a rat which he meant to take home and stuff. Then one day Cooper's novels came alive in Boston: a party of Sacs and Foxes, in deerskins and feathers, performed a war-dance on the Common. His college rooms at Harvard were the rooms of a sportsman. He spent all his summer vacations tramping through New England, western Massachusetts, New Hampshire and Maine, crossing the Canadian border, following the Indian trails, tracing the routes of the French and the *coureurs de bois*. He kept careful diaries on all these journeys.

He was highly systematic, though not by nature. With his temperamental zest for adventure, he found research repulsive.* He despised "emasculate" scholarship all his

* In this he resembled Prescott and Motley. The tension created by this repulsion is characteristic of first-rate minds. No good writer has ever liked drudgery, nor has any good writer ever permitted anyone else to do his drudgery for him.

days. But he forced his tastes to gain his ends. He was ferociously accurate and savagely thorough. No one was ever more reckless, as *The Oregon Trail* showed, and no one was more methodical in pursuing an object. He directed his travels and reading like a Jesuit novice. He divided his time in college between rhetoric, history and gymnastics; and when he was sent abroad, at nineteen, to spend some months in Italy, for the sake of his health, he stayed for several weeks at a convent of the Passionists, near the Coliseum in Rome. The monks did their best to convert him, but Parkman was intractable. Neither then nor later was his positive mind open to religious exaltations. He had an extreme distaste for the clergy at home, in spite of his excellent father. He had fallen away from the faith of Channing, although he was drawn to Theodore Parker, with whom he climbed Vesuvius and talked in Rome. Parker was a muscular man, who preached a robust religion, while Channing had always been Parkman's special aversion,—because he was frail and small and his habits were too sedentary and he preached the superiority of mind over muscle. Parkman thought the clergy as a class were soft, gushing, vague and spoiled by women. He liked to describe them as "vermin;" and, having small use for the Puritans, he had still less for the Catholics. He was an agnostic, somewhat harsh in temper. Then why did he visit these amiable monks and get himself presented to the Pope? Because he wished to carry out his plan. He haunted the churches and monasteries, in Italy and Sicily, because to write his history, as he knew, he had to understand the Church, the methods of the missionaries, the ecclesiastical system, from top to bottom. He wished to live in a monastery and see it from the inside, as later he wished to live in an Indian lodge.

In the same systematic way, he studied human nature, to learn what he called the springs of emotion and action. His journal bristled with accurate sketches of soldiers,

sailors, farmers, priests and scholars. He went through
the Law School, not for the sake of the law, but to study
history and statesmanship and, still more, human character; and in Boston, after his breakdown, when he could
not sleep, he rose and prowled all night in the open,
watching the tramps on the Common. Just so, he had
watched the reformers in the days of the "Newness." The
Chardon Street Chapel, the haunt of the "Friends of
Reform," had once been the Parkmans' family stable,
and Dr. Parkman, who disliked reformers quite as much
as his son, always spoke of the chapel as "my mother's
barn." Parkman abhorred these eccentric people,—he
called the Brook Farmers the "she-philosophers,"—but
he went to their meetings just the same. He had no shred
of sympathy with their causes, but they were types to
examine. Visionaries, idealists, fanatics,—they were all
one to Parkman,—had played a part in Canadian history,
and he took pains to observe them. He had a contempt
for physical weakness that grew with his own infirmities
and suggested the "hard-boiled" mind of a later epoch.
"How I hate 'em!" he would say, referring to men who
were frail or sickly; but he noted their manners and motives, and their conversation, and set them all down
among the rest. What he really hated was the weakness
in himself, in this resembling all the "hard-boiled" writers.
Of Thoreau, in later years, he spoke with respect, for
Thoreau had known the Indians as he knew the woods;
but he was too self-conscious and introspective to please
this Boston Spartan. Wordsworth he could not abide.
Everything that savoured of speculation, the dreamy, the
sentimental, the philanthropic,—philosophy, metaphysics,
the inward eye,—was antipathetic to Parkman. He disliked the words "culture" and "refinement" because they
suggested the artificial. What he called the "improved
savage" was Parkman's favourite type, delicate in his

feelings and decent in behaviour and also virile, natural, resourceful and strong.

Such was this lover of action, this literary soldier who was to picture himself in describing his heroes, Frontenac, La Salle, Lord Howe and Wolfe. His element was the Border, and the life of the Border, where the primitive and the civilized were in conflict, where civilization prevailed, but only by means of the primitive virtues, and human nature appeared in its utmost starkness. In Italy, on Lake Como, he had written, "Give me Lake George, and the smell of the pine and fir!" He had preferred Vesuvius to all the ruined temples; and in England, with its smooth green hills and hedges, he had longed for the shaggy mountains, the cedars and the scrub-oak, the "fiery glare of the sun . . . its wild and ruddy light." In Scotland and Switzerland alone, among the crags and cataracts, he had felt at home. No one knew better than he the depths of the forest, dim and silent as a cavern, the cedar-bordered streams of the northern lakes, with their water-girdled rocks and verdurous islets, where the muskrats swam and plunged, the rock-maples rearing their shadowy masses, the sombre balsam-firs, the coves where the wild ducks dived beneath the alders, and the moose, neck-deep in water to escape the flies, vanished among the trees with clumsy trot. Many a time, on Lake Champlain, as the sun set behind the western mountains, piled in mist along the sky, he had watched some dead pine stretching its arms athwart the burning heaven, with a crow perched on its top like an image carved in jet. He had observed the night-hawk, circling in its flight, pitching through the air, on whirling wing, for the unseen prey that flew beneath it. To the farthest outposts of Canada, to the Rocky Mountains, Parkman knew the wilderness, the savage forests and the open woodlands, the mighty rivers and the lakes and prairies; and he knew the inhabitants of all these regions, the Indians, the half-breeds and the traders, the settlers, soldiers, trappers and pioneers. Before he was twenty-three, he had seen most of the Indian tribes from Maine to Colorado and Nevada and had visited many of the spots he described in his books. He had explored the sites of the Indian towns and villages, measured the ruined forts and talked with the oldest settlers. He had gathered from survivors of the tribes the legends of the Ojibways and the Mohawks, the Iroquois, the Foxes and the Hurons. An ancient brave at Old Town, Maine, patching his canoe, had described the attacks of the Mohawks, as the tribe recalled them: they had roasted the children on forked sticks like apples. He had heard fireside tales and wild recitals of necromancy and witchcraft, tales of the magic drums of the conjurors, of grisly weendigoes and bloodless geebi, of evil manitoes in the dens of the woods and malignant sorcerers dwelling on lonely islands, in lakes they had bound with spells. He had heard of pygmy champions, mighty in soul, who had subdued the monsters of the wilds, and heroes who had achieved marvellous triumphs over the brute force of their assailants. He knew the secret places of the woods where the Indians had held their councils; and he read the signs of the forest himself, the whistle of a bird that stood for danger, the rustle of a leaf that stood for death. In the perilous depths of the mountains, he had lodged with lonely trappers, in time-worn buckskins, gripping their rifles in sinewy hands, sleeping on the rough earth, with dried meat and water for their food and drink. The wild, hard life of these pioneers had for him a resistless charm. He had even found *coureurs de bois,* still dwelling beyond the solitudes of the northern lakes, unchanged in life and character since the far-off days when the Sun-king claimed this cheerless empire.

By the time he was able to write again, Parkman was

almost ready to carry out his whole ambitious plan,—for all his historical writings, taken together, were to form a single work in eleven volumes. Now and then he went abroad, to extend his investigations, for his studies were based on original manuscript sources. He made four visits to Paris. He had to take a secretary into the libraries with him and listen while the documents were read aloud; and all the income from his books scarcely paid for the copyists who collected manuscripts for him in Paris and London. But most of his notes were assembled in 1865, and he was already prepared for his double task: to picture the forest and its history and drama and to "realize a certain ideal of manhood,—a little mediæval," as he called it. He had been all the better fitted to live the story that he wrote because, like La Salle, he was a "man of thought, trained amid arts and letters." * Meanwhile, unable to use his eyes, and threatened with insanity, he turned aside for a while into horticulture. He took refuge in his garden at Jamaica Plain; and there, confined to his wheel-chair, he rapidly moved about, sowing seeds, raking and weeding, planting and cutting his borders and splitting wood. Active and methodical, as elsewhere, he studied the art of gardening. He even served for a year as professor of horticulture at the Bussey Institute. He developed the "Parkman lily" and brought out new varieties of larkspur, phlox and poppy. He was a famous grower of roses, like Bancroft and Prescott before him, and like John Fiske and Henry Adams and Henry Cabot Lodge.

* "The pioneer of western pioneers was no rude son of toil, but a man of thought, trained amid arts and letters."—*La Salle and the Discovery of the Great West.*

Parkman observed in a note appended to this: "A Rocky Mountain trapper, being complimented on the hardihood of himself and his companions, once said to the writer, 'That's so; but a gentleman of the right sort will stand hardship better than anybody else.' The history of Arctic and African travel, and the military records of all time, are a standing evidence that a trained and developed mind is not the enemy, but the active and powerful ally, of constitutional hardihood. The culture that enervates instead of strengthening is always a false or partial one."

He had a thousand varieties of roses. He even wrote a
handbook on this flower of historians, describing its
groups and families, its cultivation and propagation.
Parkman was severe with roses as with men, an aristocrat in horticulture, an aristocrat in human culture. He
would have liked to subject his race to the methods that
governed the growing of flowers. If it was good for roses,
why not for men? He expressed his social faith in *The
Book of Roses.**

Thenceforward, at 50 Chestnut Street, where he always spent his winters, one might have seen Parkman
forever at work in the shadow of his third-floor study.
Two of the walls were covered with books; the others
were hung with portrait-engravings. The light from the
north windows was subdued. A few Indian relics stood
on the mantel, with statuettes of animals by Barye, whom
Hunt, his friend, had more or less discovered. One saw
two or three photographs of the statue of Colleoni,
which he kept for the sake of the subject, not for the
sculpture. Colleoni was never out of his eye or mind. Solitary and silent mostly, usually sleepless, often in pain,
stoical as an Indian struck by an arrow, he could be
amusing with his daughters,—his wife and son were
dead,—who knew he had a capital sense of humour. He
appeared on the streets, at a rapid gait, a tall, slender
figure in a long grey coat, with the fur cap that rose in
winter over the prow-like chin. But he was obliged to re-
strain his passion for action, and he who could so ill
endure confinement, and who studied as it were against

---

* "The art of horticulture is no leveller. Its triumphs are achieved by
rigid systems of selection and rejection, founded always on the broad
basis of intrinsic worth. The good cultivator propagates no plants but the
best. He carefully chooses those marked out by conspicuous merit; protects
them from the pollen of inferior sorts, intermarries them, perhaps, with
other varieties of equal vigour and beauty; saves the seed and raises from
it another generation. . . . Thus the rose and other plants are brought
slowly to their perfect development. . . . We cultivate the parent, and look
for our reward in the offspring."—*The Book of Roses,* 95-98.

the grain, could not relax indeed but had to sit. Or, rather, he rode his chair as if it were a saddle. He had to sublimate his love of danger, he had to repress his energy to save his nerves. His mind was like a bow, too tightly strung; and this tension appeared in his work, in its frequent speed and picturesqueness. One felt the virile force of the writer, his pleasure in the savage and the vast, while his eagerness, transformed into patience, made him thorough and accurate.* One felt his impetuosity in the drive of his writing. With his cordial dislike of Puritanism, which he thought narrow and bookish, he retained its passionate fervour and its rigorous tenseness. No doubt, the isolation and strain of his life intensified his natural harshness. He loved hard truth, and he neither gave nor expected praise or pity; but this, with his positive mind, his New England practicality and liking for the useful, limited his sympathies and imagination. Of all the figures in his books, the one he most resembled was La Salle, the stern and self-reliant Roman Frenchman, masterful, martial, serious, austere and shy. For all his distaste for priests, he admired the courage and heroism of the Jesuit martyrs, and he followed the priestly model in his own career. The heir of a long line of divines, like many of the New England writers of the previous age, he shared their sacerdotal temper and all their pride of learning and pride of power. Parkman was a Brahmin of the Brahmins.

This mediæval strain of the priest and soldier, marked in Parkman's nature, fitted him for the theme that filled his life. He had something in common with all the types, English, French and Indian, that appeared in the drama, and the drama itself was mediæval, or, rather, it covered

---

* See, however, the strictures of Charles Francis Adams the second on Parkman's account of the capture of Quebec, a matter in which, according to Adams, no one could have been right who had not actually taken part in military operations.—C. F. Adams, *Lee at Appomattox and Other Papers,* 347-354.

the whole age, from Champlain to Montcalm and Wolfe,
during which the mediæval became the modern. It was a
conflict, as Parkman revealed it, between the past and the
future, the old and the new, between feudalism and monarchism, an autocratic Church and State, and the democratic freedom that replaced them. That all the fervour
of the Middle Ages revived in the enterprise of Montreal, with the spirit of Godfrey de Bouillon, that the set-
tlement was another crusade,—a movement of faith that
became a political movement, as the economic motive
grew in power,—Parkman was the first to show, in any
conclusive fashion, while he showed the meaning of the
old French war as a cause of the American Revolution.
He understood the protagonists, French and English,
who had shared his romantic feeling and his feeling for
action, and his imagination failed him only with the Indians, whose virtues, for the rest, he admired and knew.
His Indians were visibly real. They were not operatic,
like Prescott's, or the noble savages of Cooper. Parkman
had lived with them, and his Indian scenes and portraits
were drawn from life. But he had preconceived ideas
about them, and he took no pains to keep up with later
investigations and observations. Ethnology scarcely existed at the time when he began to write, and the Indians
he had known best were the Sioux, at the very worst
period to judge them. He had approached them, moreover, as a young New England man whose mind was
filled with legends of Haverhill and Deerfield. He saw
them as Miles Standish might have seen them, with his
inelastic nature, from the outside only. His ungenerous
treatment of Pontiac was a case in point. He had made
up his mind in regard to racial and moral questions and
he never expanded or changed it. He had no feeling
whatever for evolution. But as, volume by volume, his
work advanced till the series came to an end in the early
nineties, everyone became aware that he was a great his-

torian, the greatest perhaps who had ever appeared in the country. While *The Conquest of Mexico* was finer than any of Parkman's books, as a masterpiece of historical story-telling, he was more original than Prescott or Motley, for he had established the taste by which he was read.* He had made Champlain and La Salle historic figures like Charlemagne, Peter the Great and Robert Bruce. Until he wrote, students who thought the Tudors all-important saw nothing in the conflict in the forest that had made the American nation what it was; and Parkman, who had discovered his theme, or first perceived its real significance, created a form that matched his theme in grandeur.

* According to John Eglinton *(Irish Literary Portraits)*, the question, "Is Prescott or Motley the better writer?" was one that George Moore liked to spring on his friends in Dublin. Parkman was never included in this question, in Ireland or anywhere else in Europe. This was because Europeans were not interested in his subject-matter. They did not care for American themes and persons.

To a large extent, their subject-matter determines the vogue of novelists also. Granting that Henry James was greater than Howells, the all but total oblivion that befell the latter after his death could only be explained on these grounds. The English did not care to read about Americans in their natural state, and "sophisticated" Americans of a later time did not care to read about their forbears. They were apt to prefer Anthony Trollope, not because he was infinitely better than Howells but because they were fascinated by Trollope's people.

CHAPTER IX

THE YOUNGER GENERATION OF 1870

THE young men were scattering in all directions. Their imagination was caught by the West, and scores who might have been writers in the days of *The Dial* were seeking their fortunes in railroads, mines and oil-wells. During the war, as Emerson noted, in every house and shop, a map of America had been unrolled and studied, and thousands for whom the country had once been as vague as Australia were well-informed about its means and prospects. The colleges, meanwhile, were pouring out new types to meet the new conditions, mining engineers and railroad experts, geologists and technicians. Most of these young men, born for action, lived undivided lives. What was remarkable, in the new generation, was the number whose lives were divided and sometimes ruined.

"Boston seemed to offer," as Henry Adams said, "no market for educated labour." To many young men for whom it was a centre the future offered nothing there but idleness and slow defeat. They were dispersing in exile, cattle-raising in Colorado, sheep-ranching in California, farming or growing cotton in the South. Two of Henry James's sons took up an orange-grove in Florida. Henry Lee Higginson, who founded the Boston Symphony later, had settled in Georgia for a time before he turned his mind to Western oil-wells. He and George Bancroft's son had planned to live in Virginia and cultivate the vine and the olive.* Edward Simmons joined an oil-firm in Pittsburgh before he went to Paris to study painting. Julian Hawthorne entered engineering. Edward Rowland Sill, the young Yale poet, had gone to California round the Horn. He worked as a postal clerk at Sacramento, as a ranchman, as a bank-clerk, as a teacher. Later he returned as professor of English at the new university in Berkeley, where Josiah Royce acted as his assistant. Others threw themselves into Western railroads. For westward lay the world of riches and adventures, as once, for young Bostonians, it had lain in China;† and Agassiz's son Alexander, the son who was born in Switzerland, had made a fortune in the West before he returned to Harvard and science. As a young engineer, he had gone out to Michigan, and there he had organized the Calumet and Hecla mines. In many ways, his life was like Pumpelly's, although, in making his fortune, he had ruined his health. As an oceanographer later, and one of the greatest, an authority on deep-sea fauna, he was said to have done more permanent work than his father. Alexander Agassiz, Henry Adams wrote, was "the only one of my generation whom I would have liked to envy." For the rest, the Agassizes, father and son, marked all the difference between the generations. Eminent, both, in science, and competent writers,‡ and lovers of writers and artists, they had scarcely another trait in common. To the reckless, exuberant father, warm-hearted and open-handed, utterly indifferent to money, innocently vain, with a hearty love of popularity and a great Humboldtian zest for life,

* Higginson and the younger Bancroft conceived this plan as a result of reading Olmsted's books, *A Journey in the Seaboard Slave States,* etc.

† "The West is the place for a young fellow of spirit to pick up a fortune, simply pick it up; it's lying round loose there . . . The richest land on God Almighty's footstool . . . If I had my capital free, I could plant it for millions."

"To the young American . . . the paths to fortune are innumerable and all open; there is invitation in the air and success in all his wide horizon." —Mark Twain, *The Gilded Age.*

‡ See Alexander Agassiz's *Three Cruises of the Blake.*

optimistic, liberal, unexacting, the dark, spare, tall son,
retiring and reserved, was a singular contrast. Scrupulous
in details, introverted, realistic, he detested notoriety, as
his father loved it. He hated the teaching his father enjoyed, preferring a life of quiet research; and yet as a
man he was far more essentially worldly.* One saw this
contrast repeated in many other fathers and sons, the
two Henry Jameses, for example, as the older generation, rooted in the soil, or at least in the popular life,—
genial, emotionally profound, unconscious,—yielded to
the younger generation.† Alexander Agassiz was restless,
like all the unanchored men of his time. He spent half his
life, another Pumpelly, wandering over the seven seas,
and died at last on shipboard.

The type of all these restless men was a graduate of
Yale, Clarence King. A Newport boy, of a merchant family, whose father had died in China, King was a geologist
and a mining engineer who had studied with Louis Agassiz and Whitney. He was a born mountaineer who had
rambled as a boy in Vermont, and in time he became the
first director of the National Geological Survey. A brilliant, a "radiant" creature, as Henry Adams called him,
with a quick step and a charm of person that made him
irresistible, he had crossed the plains on horseback, in
1863, and shared in the survey of the Rockies. It was he
who surveyed the Yosemite Valley and first defined its
boundaries. He named Mount Tyndall and Mount Whitney, after two of his masters, and he might have named a
mountain after Ruskin, whose descriptions of Alpine

---

* "I remember being shocked by a story told me by a lady who had sat
next to Alexander Agassiz at a lunch party . . . Agassiz had said to the
lady, 'Why, if it were a question of bribing a State Legislature, I should
regard it in the same light as the removal of a bank of sand.' "—John
Jay Chapman, in M. A. De Wolfe Howe's *John Jay Chapman and His
Letters.*

† In one way or another, with variations, one saw this contrast in the
Adamses, father and sons, in the Danas, the Hawthornes, etc. Turgenev's
Fathers and Sons, a novel much read at the time, marked a parallel change
in Russia.

scenery affected his own. His *Systematic Geology* ranked
as a contribution to science with the younger Agassiz's
work on deep-sea fauna; and his *Mountaineering in the
Sierra Nevadas* was as fine as *The Oregon Trail* or *Before the Mast*. Neither Parkman's book nor Dana's had
anything better in it than King's sketches of mountain characters, the Newty family, the Digger Indians, the "Pacific
Slope Bonheur," or the spirited chapter, *Kaweah's Run,*
in which he described his escape from the Mexican bandits. What made the book unique, however, as Parkman's
and Dana's in their fields,—one for the plains, one for
the ocean,—was its special feeling for the mountains.
John Muir alone in later years approached in veracity and
splendour King's pictures of the ice-fields and the gorges,
the granite corridors filled with the tumult of water, the
arrowy rushing of brooks and the grandeur of snow-storms, the cold, still peaks and the lake-basins, silent and
black at night, like the void into which Dante looked
through the bottomless gulf of Dis. King had a painter's
eye,—he "fitted into the ways of thinking of artists," as
John La Farge said later. He had rejoiced in the sapphire
sky of the stark and glaring desert; and he never tired of
gazing down long vistas where the shafts of pine stood
in stately groups, each with its own tinting and finish, its
feathery branches waving, while broad streams of light
poured in, gilding the columns of purple and red and falling in bright paths along the floor. Above the spires of
golden green, as through the dark, cool alleys, he saw the
winding roadways of the Sierras; and the mountains, observed from a summit, shaped themselves like the ruins
of Gothic cathedrals. There he perceived the sharp roof-ridges, the buttresses and pinnacles and statues, the receding doorways with pointed arches carved into blank
façades of granite, doors that were never to be opened,
cruciform peaks. He could not doubt that the Alps had
furnished the models for the early Gothic builders.

In after years, to many observers, the brilliant, mercurial Clarence King was the symbol of his American generation. When Henry Adams met him, in 1871, at the door of a Colorado cabin, he fell into King's arms, he said. Adams had known Lyell in England, and he had reviewed Lyell's *Geology*. He shared King's interest in this subject and had gone West with a field-party; but, quite aside from this, he was drawn to King,—they might have been friends in the Stone Age. In his wit and his bubbling energy, his youth and his charm, Clarence King suggested Alexander, all-conquering and to conquer.* He seemed the "ideal American" that all his friends wished to be, the "richest and most many-sided genius of his day," as Adams wrote later in his memoirs. They all agreed in this, La Farge, John Hay, for whom King was the "best and brightest" of his generation. They were ready to drop all other plans to go with King to the ends of the earth; and, in fact, he was always "going," like most of the others, to London or Paris, to buy pictures,† to Spain, to find the helmet of Malbrino,—Don Quixote's barber's basin, which he found, or liked to think he found, and about which he wrote an amusing story,—to Mexico, the

---

* "King had everything to interest and delight Adams. He knew more than Adams did of art and poetry; he knew America, especially west of the hundredth meridian, better than anyone else; he knew the professor by heart, and he knew the congressman better than he did the professor. He knew even women; even the American woman; even the New York woman, which is saying much . . . King's abnormal energy had already won him great success. None of his contemporaries had done so much, single-handed, or were likely to leave so deep a trail."—*The Education of Henry Adams.*

† John Hay took King, in Paris, to the studio of Gustave Doré. King disliked Doré's sensational effects, but "in five minutes" the two "were brothers and were planning an excursion to Arizona to sketch the war-dances of the Apaches." Hay also related how King made the acquaintance of Ruskin at an auction in London. The two were standing side by side and King, not knowing to whom he was talking, argued on a number of subtle points. Ruskin, who was delighted with him, invited him to Coniston and offered him his choice of two fine Turners. King always gave and took with equal generosity, and the story is that he said, "One good Turner deserves another," whereupon Ruskin gave him both.—See *Memorial of Clarence King.*

Windward Islands, Cuba. It seemed to Henry Adams, his companion in Cuba, that he knew the whole population, the Spaniards, the Indians, the planters, the Negroes, with whom he spent his nights at Voodoo dances. He fraternized with the revolutionists, and his special friends were the old Negresses, whom he liked "because they were not academic." He sat with them for days in their cabins, drinking coffee and talking the Negro-Cuban dialect with them. When Adams joined him for this journey, —years later, in 1894,—King had been discharged from an asylum. He had made and lost fortunes and wrecked his health; and at last, alone and uncared for, he died in an Arizona tavern.

If King's life had a moral, as all his friends seemed to feel, if it was symptomatic and symbolic, of what was it the symbol? The waste of the brightest faculties unemployed by civilization, the *zeitgeist,* the time and the country. Henry Adams, in later years, drew this moral for all to see, Adams, who knew his age from the beginning and had foreseen its tendencies. A civilization that could not employ such men as Clarence King,—except for a dozen years as technical experts,—that allowed their capability and god-like reason to fust in them unused, or used so little, challenged the critical mind; and the critical mind itself failed and fainted in the want of a living air to bear it up. The old culture had broken down, the old causes were dead and forgotten, and no new ideal had arisen to rally the minds of the younger men; and, while many turned westward, almost as many turned towards Europe, in despair of the civilization they saw before them. Of these, the younger Henry James was the great exemplar in years to come; but there were numbers of others, from New England and elsewhere, who also sought for haunts of ancient peace. Most of them travelled in the spirit of Montaigne, from a "lack of relation to the present conditions of our country;" and most of

them were interested in art. Many collected pictures, like
Clarence King and Henry Adams, Alexander Agassiz,
John La Farge, like Pumpelly, Perkins, Appleton, Jarves
and Norton. A few, like Henry James's Rowland Mallet,
"looking round for something to do," and having ample
means with which to do it, went abroad with plans to buy
old masters and provide their native towns with art museums. Naturally, the artists themselves, the painters,
sculptors and architects, were those who felt most powerfully the attraction of Europe. Sixty years before, after
the War of 1812, the painters who had lived abroad had
mostly returned to America. Vanderlyn, Morse and Trumbull, Peale and Allston had been full of hope for a life at
home and a country that had established its independence;
and their portraits, at least, were full of native character,
while some of their genre painting abounded in it. Their
impulse in returning home was justified in this, although
otherwise their lives were often thwarted; but after the
Civil War the artists flocked abroad again. At a time
when even the farms and villages, which had lost their
old political interests, were awakening to the appeal of
art and science,—brought in, as often as not, by the
"summer people,"—this was only natural; and it was also
natural that a cosmopolitan point of view should have
governed the minds and hands of migrating artists. The
element of "native character" that had given strength to
the earlier artists and that strengthened the home-grown
artists of the age to come had little weight for Whistler,
for instance, and Sargent, predestined cosmopolitans, like
Henry James. Sargent, who was born in Italy, saw America first at twenty; and Whistler, who had been taken to
Russia when he was nine years old, was at home as a boy
in England also, where his sister had married Seymour
Haden. Both these artists, however, like James, were
American in their inmost fibre, and both had connections
with New England. Sargent had grown up in a wander-

ing household that preserved its New England traits through all its travels. The legend of the American navy was as much a part of Sargent's childhood as the legend of West Point was a part of Whistler's; and Whistler, who "wouldn't" be born at Lowell, had lived at Stonington, Pomfret and Springfield, following his father's appointments as an engineer. In this first great age of American painting, Whistler and Sargent, like Henry James, achieved preëminence even in Europe as masters of technical processes. It was as if the virtue of the old Yankee craftsmen, the men who had built the clipper-ships, had passed into them, to reappear in new forms, just when the clipper-ships were disappearing. The brilliance of these artists no one questioned, and for many this virtuosity was all-sufficient. For others, it was insufficient, either then or later; they saw that Whistler and Sargent, like James, were light-armed soldiers of art, who travelled so far and so fast for an obvious reason. Relieved of the impedimenta that burdened the heavy-armed soldiers, who had their "native character" to deal with, they could turn their whole attention to technical questions. It was natural that Whistler, Sargent and James should have excelled in technique all but the greatest of the Frenchmen. But the French were always a step ahead of all the cosmopolitans, for they kept their "native character" as well.

This became poignantly evident as one followed the life of Henry James, for whom the "drama of Europe in American breasts" remained for fifty years the central problem. For most of the other sentient New Englanders of the generation of 1870, this problem, if not central, was important. Europe meant much to Howells also, to William James and Henry Adams, all of whom, like most of their friends, had lived there.* For most of them,

---

* "In old times I used to notice every window, door-handle and smell as having a peculiar and exotic charm, every old street and house as filled with historic life and mystery."—*The Letters of William James.*

for most writers, the question of facing the new America, with its worship of "bigness" and numbers, seemed overwhelming. The lesson of *The Man Without a Country* had served well in time of war, when the national mind was focussed on a single object. But the national mind was dispersed at the moment. It was clearly focussed only on the things of Mammon; and nothing was more difficult than to comprehend the country,—enough to create aesthetic patterns from it. How could a novelist handle this chaos? How could a philosopher synthesize it? How could a young political thinker, with all political thought behind him, cope with a public life that suggested the Stone Age? Henry Adams, an "estray" already, a "flotsam or jetsam of wreckage," was facing this problem; and the others were to meet it, one by one. Godkin predisposed them all,—all, that is, but Howells,—to look with suspicion on the West; and, in any case, the West was a menace for *les délicats,*—Ernest Renan's phrase for the tender-minded. The tough-minded throve there and returned with treasures of gold and oil; but for sensitive intellectuals, like Clarence King and the younger Agassiz, the reckless life which the West implied, its hardships and fever of speculation, meant ruined health and broken souls and madness. Was not Francis Parkman an earlier case in point? Even Charles Francis Adams,—Henry's tougher older brother, who was soon to win all the prizes which the West could give,—was to turn in the end in disgust from his life of money-making with the feeling that he had wasted his existence.* Certainly, for all these men, who were all at home in the modern languages,—for whom French and German, at least, and often Italian, were almost as native as English,—Europe might well have been a refuge. There was something else, moreover,

* "I should have settled myself systematically down on the development of my aptitude,—the art of literary expression."—*Autobiography of Charles Francis Adams.*

that made it seem so. Writers, as a class, follow the aristocratic pattern, follow it, that is, when they do not create it,—for they follow the "free will" that makes all patterns,—and the aristocratic American mind, disturbed and disrupted after the war, had reopened the trail to Europe for artists and writers. What held most of the young men back was their essential Americanism, with all that this implied in regard to Europe. It implied a divided life for them, almost as much as the West; and deeper than all this was the general feeling that America, at its lowest reach, was better than Europe. Howells and Mark Twain, the Western writers, were those who took this feeling most for granted; but even Henry James confusedly shared it. Sargent shared it also, and so did Whistler, who remained, with all his blague, a "West Point man." The faith of these men who had chosen Europe was very often shaken, and often their conscious minds denied this faith; for they had exposed themselves to conditions that shook it, and they were not well-armoured like the men at home. But in the depths of their souls they believed that the "real right thing," the essentially noble thing, was an American secret. For William James, with his "two souls," it was an open secret; and in even Henry Adams, a generation later, an ember of the faith still glowed under the polar ice. For Howells, as for Emerson and Whitman, the fact was as plain as the sun or the moon. Merely to picture his people was to show it.

These problems, the West and Europe, confronted all the younger minds, although most of them soon arrived at practical conclusions. New England, or the East, might be the frying-pan, but at least it was better than the fire. It was better than either fire, the West or Europe. The question of the West was further settled by the ablest of the younger Western writers, who were settling in the East, like Howells, as the price of survival. Mark Twain

was living in Hartford, where he could break the bread
and eat the salt of hospitality without any interference
in his opinions.* John Hay had joined *The Tribune* in
New York, where Bret Harte also lived before going
abroad. As for the question of Europe, the painters settled this most easily. They enjoyed the immunity of painters,—they did not have to think the question out. They
followed the still small voice that governs painters. Those
who were not deeply attached to the country, and whose
interest was primarily in technique, sailed for Europe at
once without doubts or regrets. Those for whom technical problems were of secondary interest, and whose local
attachments were deep, remained without regrets or
doubts at home. The painters, unlike the writers, were
not obliged to argue with the still small voice, and no one
was more indifferent to Europe than Homer, Fuller and
Ryder, who had scarcely seen it. They felt that whatever
painters gained in Europe was less than what they lost by
living there,—what all the American painters had lost
since Copley lost his edge in England, the grim force of
the native character that vanished under his later bravura.† It was true that the conditions with which these
artists had to deal destroyed the weaker men and crippled the strongest. They were unable to profit by the
great growth of art-schools that followed the Centennial
of 1876; and they were obliged to live divided lives, as
shoe-makers and sign-painters, village doctors and practical farmers, tobacco-growers, cartoonists in popular
papers. They suffered and struggled alone, neglected and
poor. It took two generations for Americans to see that
they were the primary painters and always had been, these

* "Fortunately a good deal of experience of men enabled me to choose
my residence wisely. I live in the freest corner of the country."—Mark
Twain, 1876, Letter to a Western friend.
† "Don't you know how many New York and Boston artists have gone to
Europe and hermetically sealed themselves up somewhere to ferment into
greatness like a jug of cider turning into vinegar in a farmer's cellar?"—
Arlo Bates, *The Pagans.*

deep, unworldly souls who loved the scenes they painted, while Sargent and Whistler carried the world before them.

It was those who remained in the frying-pan and paid the full price of their courage that later times revered as noble grandsires. For great works are great not, first of all, for technical reasons, but because they express the ethos of the race behind them. The great technique only confirms the greatness; and this becomes apparent when an age of manifold snobberies is followed by an age that seeks the real. *Noblesse oblige* was never truer than it was with men like Homer and Ryder, who cast their bread upon the waters, who gave their country bread in return for stones. They accepted the local conditions and built upon them; and in this they were like two other men of the generation of 1870, the founders of American architecture. For Richardson and Sullivan well deserved this phrase: it distinguished them from the earlier architects, whose work was almost wholly derivative. H. H. Richardson, a Harvard Louisianian, who had returned from Paris at the close of the war and later came to Boston from New York, was creating a style of his own that suggested his person. It was florid, luxuriant and massive, reflecting the bold, exuberant Southerner, the teacher of Charles McKim and Stanford White. Exotic as his style was, what made this man important was that he faced the problems of the world he lived in. For instance, for an age of travel, he designed railway stations that made it a positive pleasure to wait for a train. In this respect, Louis Sullivan, a Boston boy born and bred,—one of the first fine shoots of the Boston Irish,—was to go far beyond Richardson, as the teacher of Frank Lloyd Wright and the father of an organic architecture.* Studying first in

* Louis Sullivan, born in Boston, was the son of an Irish dancing-master. One of the exciting causes of his career was a series of lectures on botany by Asa Gray. His *Autobiography of an Idea,* a sort of Whitmanian rhapsody, was written in the third person, perhaps on the model of *The Educa-*

Boston and later in Paris, he found his field in Chicago, where he met the conditions of a crowded business-district by developing the steel-framed skyscraper. These men and their followers soon met most of the local conditions, the conditions of a democratic world. They undertook to solve the problem of erecting banks and office-buildings, warehouses, ice-plants, factories and garages. They were builders in the line of Emerson and Whitman, who had established the principles on which they built; and they too were ancestors rather than descendants, like the mediæval and classical architects who created most of the public buildings. They showed that a native integrity was better than any borrowed nobility, the triumphs of which, if more obvious, were far more facile; and one might add that the generation of 1870 provided the country with ancestors also in music. There were abler composers than John Knowles Paine, the first professor of music at Harvard, in the years that followed his appearance; but Paine at least established a tradition for native composers to react against.* In 1881, Henry Lee Higginson, —Colonel Higginson's cousin,—founded the Boston Symphony orchestra. This banker whose imagination always remained his dominant trait had longed to devote himself to music, which he had studied in Germany. A patron of many good causes, he was also a forbear of modern America, for the orchestra that he founded and led, in all but the literal sense, was the parent of all the American orchestras later.

So much for the men who remained in the frying-pan,

tion of Henry Adams. Fanciful, emotional, mystical, rhetorical,—call it what you will,—it was incoherent; but it was written when Sullivan was a broken man, and it suggests the original mind of its author.

* Paine's oratorio, *St. Peter,* the first composed in the country, was performed at his birthplace, Portland, Maine, in 1873. John Fiske, himself a composer and a competent judge, said that at that time the Portland Choral Society was "the most thoroughly disciplined choral society in this country." The Bethlehem Choral Union was organized in 1882, the Bethlehem Bach Choir in 1900.

who faced the national problems and strove to solve them. So much, that is, for those who preferred the state of their minds to the state of their fortunes, in Richard Steele's phrase; for even Major Higginson, the banker, was always more concerned for the state of his mind. Those who preferred the state of their fortunes sailed before the wind. But even men of this type, when they are young and tender, rejoice in the pattern-maker who points the way, and Harvard, prolific in leaders, provided them with a pattern-maker in the Unitarian minister, Horatio Alger. As a young man, Alger, who had lived in Paris, had tutored boys in Greek and French in Cambridge. He had organized them into a boy-scout group that was known as "Alger's army of up-and-comings." He moved to New York in 1866. The streets swarmed with drummer-boys who had run away to the war and wished, after the war, to see the city, where they were blacking boots and selling papers. Their centre was the Newsboys' Lodging-house, and Alger went to live there, secretly visiting Chinatown, when he was bored with the boys, on errands that were far from edifying.* At Harvard, he had read *Moby Dick,* which seems to have inspired him to take up writing, and he soon set to work on his *Luck and Pluck* series, to show Ragged Dick and Tattered Tom how easily they might rise to fame and fortune. For many who began their lives as bootblacks and newsboys, by sweeping out the store or by carrying parcels, and who rose to be captains of industry, the Horatio Alger theme was a joy and a solace. It showed that a young man who was too good to be true was also bound

* The life of this strange creature, who was born in Revere, Massachusetts, where his father brought him up to be a "spiritual leader," has been written by H. R. Mayes,—*Horatio Alger, a Biography Without a Hero.* Alger kept a diary in which he took delight in recording his prudish amours and furtive orgies. He had his first taste of the literary life in Paris. He related how, sitting in a café with his mistress, he was told of the death of Murger, the author of the *Vie de Bohème.* This news caused his face to be "stained with tears."

to be successful, a moral that history vindicated in the
eighties and nineties. Alger was one of the men who all
but effaced the New England tradition, for he vulgarized
Emerson's *Self-Reliance* and turned into a laughing-stock
Longfellow's *Excelsior* and *The Psalm of Life*. He made
virtue and purity odious for thousands of the following
age, who, having been taught to "swim," preferred to
"sink." How good customs corrupt the world was the
moral of his work, for he was the lineal heir of Jacob
Abbott; and he spoiled the Rollo-philosophy by adjusting
his mind to conditions that turned the Rollo-philosophy
inside out. Where Abbott had written for country boys
whose central motive was self-improvement, and who
wished to advance, indeed, but as excellent men, Alger
wrote for city boys whose only motive was self-advance-
ment and whose "excellence" was hypocrisy and humbug.
In adapting the Yankee morality to a motive essentially
vulgar, he made the morality itself a reproach and a byword.

Meanwhile, the younger thinking men, who disdained
the "bitch-goddess Success," and who never knew the
name of Horatio Alger, were confronted with difficult
problems. The *tempo* of their age was all against them.
The *tempo* of the age favoured other types, the business
man, the practical man and the scientific man of a practical turn who served the interests of business. Whatever
ideality lurked in the country,—and it lurked, in fact, in
almost every corner,—was hidden from all eyes but the
most perceptive. Politics were a closed door,—only the
toughest-minded could push it open; and the young men
felt there was nothing to hold them up. There were no
expressed ideals for them to cling to, and even the heroes
had failed them, for Lincoln, whom everyone worshipped,
was dead, and Grant, who might well have been a hero,
had lent himself to every defamation. He had further
corrupted good manners by appearing at the Boston Jubi-

lee as the guest of the gaudy Jim Fisk. Only the older writers whose prestige was passing remembered Mazzini and Kossuth and the patriot fathers; and even the women had ceased to praise the men who "got up insurrections," who had once been so dear to Mrs. Stowe, or other recklessly chivalrous types of living.* Those who, like the Adamses, were born to rebuff the prince of darkness, and his minions in State Street and Wall Street, found their consciences moving in an empty chamber: there was nothing for them to resist. No one denied that the times were evil; the times had never been so evil. Everyone cheerfully said so, and no one cared.†

No wonder the younger men were baffled. No wonder they felt themselves at sea. It was all very well, in these conditions, to repeat the word of the forties, "Be true to the dream of thy youth." What was the dream of youth, what could it be, in a day that had witnessed nothing but war and destruction and the sordid scramble for money that followed the war? The commercialization of life had thinned the emotional atmosphere. It had almost destroyed the disposition to quarrel with public wrongs; ‡ and one of the new developments that Parkman observed in the country was a mixture of cool emotions and excit-

* "How do you account for it," said Anne, "that the best-developed and finest specimens of men have been those that have got up insurrections in Italy, Austria and Hungary?"—Harriet Beecher Stowe, *Dred,* 1856.

† "Society was not disposed to defend itself from criticism or attack. Indeed, the most fatal part of the situation for the poet in revolt, the paralyzing drug that made him helpless, was that society no longer seemed sincerely to believe in itself or anything else; it resented nothing, not even praise. The young poet grew up without being able to find an enemy."— Henry Adams, *Life of George Cabot Lodge.* Adams was writing here of Boston in the nineties, but he might have been writing of the seventies just as well.

‡ "When I think of the versatile and accommodating habits of America, it seems like a land without thunder-storms. In proportion as man grows commercial, does he also become dispassionate and incapable of electric emotions? . . . On the whole, I . . . find myself surmising whether a people who, like the Americans, put up quietly with all sorts of petty personal impositions and injustices, will not at length find it too great a bore to quarrel with great public wrongs."—Lowell, *Literary Essays.*

able brains. In the past, the men with the calmest minds had been those who possessed the deepest feelings, while the younger men, compared with them, were shallow and hypersusceptible.* No doubt, in addition to the war, the change from country living to city living had much to do with this, for almost all the younger men were born to an urban civilization and had lost the sanitary influences of rural life. The older writers, like Dr. Holmes, felt as if to be too urban was an all but ignominious state of mind, and most of the men of his generation had loved their country places, where they kept in close touch with the population. Many of them were bred on the Greek and Roman authors, who abounded in sweet and genial pictures of rural life and the rural people. But the prestige of the country had passed, as the balance of power had also passed from agriculture to industry and business, and the younger men no longer read the Greek and Roman authors, who had once afforded the models that stirred the young. They read, along with works of science, the new French novelists and playwrights, who pictured city life as the only life for ambitious men and described the life of the province as dull and silly. This change in reading habits was decisive; for, while those who had known their Plutarch and Virgil had grown up to spacious lives in villages, in hamlets and on farms, as the older statesmen and writers abundantly proved, the young men, steeped in modern books, were almost all uprooted before they read them. This reading confirmed their habits as déracinés. They could no longer feel that "the mind is its own place," when the place where the mind existed was the country or the village. Indeed, they feared the "local habitation," which meant for them obscurity and worse; and Emerson's noble saying, "Make much of your own place," became for them a menace and a byword. Thrown back upon themselves, they lost the inherited ties that

* Compare, e.g., Josiah Quincy with Henry Cabot Lodge.

bound them to the rest of the population; and, inasmuch
as the population was urbanizing, like themselves, and
was filled with strange, new elements of every kind, they
did not even wish to know it. Parson Wilbur and Hosea
Biglow were brothers under their skins, but what was one
to make of a city proletariat, with its alien racial strains
and unknown ways? The young men of 1870, bred in an
Anglo-Saxon world, could scarcely have read the riddle
of immigration. They would have had to know the tongues
of Babel, in addition to their Dante and their Goethe;
and, moreover, the urbanized Yankees were a difficult
problem. For these Yankees had ceased to be the men one
knew on their farms and their ships. Many were turning
into Cornplows and Babbitts,—they were Philistines, in
Matthew Arnold's phrase. What had once been "plain"
was growing "common," as often happens when simple
folk who have thriven in simple conditions are subjected
to complex conditions that cheapen their minds,—for they
cannot live up to these conditions, to which they are not
accustomed, without discarding some of their moral bal-
last. The people were changing as much as the writers,
and the writers regarded the people with a hostile eye;
and thus arose the mood of the modern intellectuals, and
their motto, "No compromise with the public taste." To
recognize a rift between writer and public became almost
the corner-stone of their self-respect. Inevitably, the writers were far less "young" than the young men of the
previous age, which had given young men the openings
that youth demands,—causes that aroused their faith,
dreams of bettering humankind, adventures that stirred
their souls and made them men. Having no roots in the
popular life, they were restless, cynical, sceptical, doubtful, self-conscious, apprehensive and torn by scruples,
the scruples that devour a mind which has no large impersonal interests or any instinctive connection with primary things.

Such was the general character of the younger writers of 1870, and such were the conditions that produced it. Henry Adams knew what the writers needed, as he knew that, at the moment, it was out of the question. "What we need is a *school*," he had written to his brother. "We want a national set of young men, like ourselves or better, to start new influences not only in politics, but in literature, in law, in society, and throughout the whole social organism of the country,—a national school of our own generation. And that is what America has no power to create. In England the universities centralize ability and London gives a field. So in France. Paris encourages and combines these influences. But with us, we should need at least six perfect geniuses placed, or rather, spotted over the country and all working together; whereas our generation as yet has not produced one nor the promise of one. It's all random, insulated work, for special and temporary and personal purposes, and we have no means, power or hope of combined action for any unselfish end." *
Was not this indeed foreordained? The school that Adams had in mind, in the nebulous state of the nation, was a daydream and a castle in the air; for the West was too busy at primitive tasks to lend itself to such a plan and the times were unpropitious in the older regions. The South was broken and hostile, New York was given over to money-making, New England was lastingly weakened. A "national set of young men to start new influences" was in fact an impossibility under these conditions, though the dream had been partially realized in 1865 when Godkin established *The Nation*. No wonder the young men were apprehensive. They knew they were doomed to fight their fights alone,† in a world that was more than likely to divide and destroy them. Some, like Henry Adams,

* 1862, *A Cycle of Adams Letters.*
† "Somehow the men of my generation never seemed to get acquainted with one another."—*Letters of George E. Woodberry.*

were all but born discouraged. Others, like Henry James, were to spend ten years trying to solve the question where to live. William James was also to pass ten years consumed with a sense of futility, although in the end he developed a faith like his father's. William James and Howells, who had come from the West, retained the buoyant mood of the early republic; but most of the others were cautious and conservative, cool and disillusioned on the surface, with the knowing air of men who expect to be swindled, who cannot trust the society in which they live. They were guarded, for they were surrounded with pitfalls. They had to struggle for their integrity in an age that was littered with failures. In conscious revolt against all things romantic, as young men always are in post-war years, they were as much concerned to react against the world about them as they were to coin the metal in themselves. To coöperate with this world was almost out of the question for them. If many of the younger minds that led the age seemed often morbidly scrupulous and over-refined, one had to remember how far the popular personalities were governed by numbers and money. In reaction against a public life that had grown corrupt and vulgar, they cultivated the "private life" and deliberately sought the unpopular. They exaggerated the "little" to shame the "big." These were a few of the traits that characterized the generation, producing its anomalous effects.

CHAPTER X

HOWELLS IN CAMBRIDGE

TO HOWELLS, living in Cambridge, absorbed in his writing, the new age, dawning in the country, was one of peace, prosperity and content. The scandals of public life, the abuses of business were remote from the little world in which he dwelt. Coming from the West, he had found a haven in Cambridge and Boston when the young men who had grown up in this region were most inclined to feel its limitations. Others might hanker for Paris and London: for him the New England capital was all-sufficient. Besides, he had known much more of America than most of the young New England men and had more reason to think it essentially sound. He knew New York and the Hudson river, Ohio and the Mississippi. He had seen Quebec and Montreal. His four years in Europe were incidental. As a child of the Western Reserve, he had shared the old political faith that Emerson and Whitman serenely embodied; and the atmosphere of his family had shaped his mind. His Quaker and Swedenborgian forbears had never questioned the "inner light." He was predisposed to be unaware of evil.

Howells was a happy man. The others were restless and anxious: he was tranquil. Even the Civil War was vaguer in his mind than it was in the minds of Boston men who had seen its woes at close range. In his Venetian consulate, he had caught only rumours of it; and, while he felt responsible for having missed the war,* it was like a

---

* "Every loyal American who went abroad during the first years of our great war felt bound to make himself some excuse for turning his back on his country in the hour of her trouble."—Howells, *A Fearful Responsibility.*

dream for him, as for some who had fought.* Moreover,
while most of the other young men were groping for a
foothold, Howells had found his vocation and was
launched upon it. How could he not have been happy?
He was prepared to accept the "true American gospel,"
that everything was coming right in time.† Years later
Howells questioned this gospel. He awoke to the evils of
his day far more than Henry James or Henry Adams,
who had seen these evils at once; and he really faced the
problem, which few of his generation faced,—what was
a good American to do about them? Howells, happy, was
also honest; his moral perception was deep and real. But
he was predisposed to trust his country, and he rejoiced
in the lull that followed the war. He rejoiced in his work,
he rejoiced in his countrypeople, he rejoiced in the noble
realities he found about him. Were not the poets and
scholars as real as Wall Street? The Cambridge air was
kind to the flowers of thought: it carried its burden of
pollen from mind to mind. Sufficient unto the day were
his misgivings. As the wife said in Tennyson's *Sea Dreams,*
"Let all evil sleep." He felt as if the troubles of the
world were settled.

In the house he had built on Concord Avenue, with the
Eastlake tiles and the book-lined study, he carried on his
work for *The Atlantic.* His travel-papers, reviews and
stories were giving place to novels, slight at first, expanded sketches, then gradually more and more ambitious. Meanwhile, he explored New England in the
summer season. With his manuscripts and his magazine-
proofs, he went for a month or more to the sea or the

---

* "Of all things of the past a battle is the least conceivable. I have heard
men who fought in many battles say that the recollection was like a dream
to them."—Howells, *Their Wedding Journey.*

† " 'Ah,' said the old man gently, 'it will all come right in time.'
" 'You preach the true American gospel,' said Colville.
" 'Of course; there is no other gospel. That *is* the gospel.' "
                              —Mr. Waters, in Howells's *Indian Summer*

mountains, to Kennebunkport, Conanicut, Bethlehem, Jaffrey, to the farm boarding-houses and the summer hotels that were rising all over the region. One spring he spent at Lexington, where the fathers of the village, who were proud to have an author in their midst, gave him the town-hall to use as a study. He spent a few days at Campobello, and he passed one summer at Nahant. There he rented an old place with a forsaken garden and a belvedere that overhung the sea, a relic of the romantic days, half ruined, that watched the tides crawl over the shining sand. Once he stayed at Shirley among the Shakers and went to meeting there with the brothers and sisters, dressed in their neat, white kerchiefs and clean, stiff caps and their Quakerish coats and shoes of 1780. One of the brothers wrote mystical tracts, such as Howells's father had also written; another had a system of musical notation, which he employed in hymns of the angelic life. Elder Fraser cultivated his grapevines and blackberries, and others made baskets, palm-leaf hats and rugs. There was much in this Yankee communism that appealed to Howells. It reminded him of his father's ideas. It confirmed his deep belief in equality as the guiding ideal of American life. The Shakers soon began to appear in his stories.

Indeed, the scenes of all these wanderings soon appeared in Howells's stories, the harvest of an all-perceiving eye. At the beaches, he observed the ladies, with their needlework beside them, sitting and talking in rows on the long piazzas. Sometimes they sat in the shelter of a cliff, and one of them read aloud while the others knitted, —Felix Holt or Middlemarch or the Evening Transcript. Occasionally, one of the ladies rose and trailed her shawl behind her, perhaps to pick up a spool that had fallen from her lap. Pursuing the spool, she dropped her scissors and thimble. Then all rose at once and scattered, for the time had come to lie down. While the older ladies were lying down, the young ladies were most in evidence, perhaps on the croquet-ground in front of the hotel or out in the rowboats on the river; for all these summer resorts abounded in loverless maidens, enough to provide a novelist with heroines forever. There were hammocks strung between the birches with young ladies in them, reading novels. They were always doing something to their hair, and all of them seemed to be prepared for what were called "attentions." They were the summer girls of the summer hotels, and it always seemed to be summer in Howells's stories. At the hotels in the mountains, the table-girls were school-teachers, who were adding to their income in vacation, and sometimes, in the afternoon, in their fresh, bright dresses, they played the piano in the parlour. The clerks were usually college boys, and often young men from the hill-towns, with their girls in the buggies beside them, drove over for supper. Now and then, a landscape-painter appeared with his easel and colours,—he was making studies of goldenrod and granite and spread them about in the parlour for the guests to see. The great event of the day was the hop in the evening. When a Boston family arrived, or a bride and groom, the plot began to thicken. The waitresses straightened their hair, the ladies looked up from their knitting, and everyone knew that something was about to happen. What happened was a Howells story. It had to occur before it was written, but the chances were that, next summer, the young ladies in their hammocks were reading this. For the chances were that Howells had seen what happened. It might have been invisible to others, or nothing more than a breath or a ripple, the sort of thing that novelists seldom noticed. To Howells, who noticed everything and who seemed to be ubiquitous, this "nothing" that happened—for others—was the best of all. That he made something out of this nothing was the marvel of his mind and art; and moreover the something in question was highly important. It was love, in its American phases, love in the American form; and what, for American readers, was more important?

Sometimes, in his wanderings, Howells stopped at Hartford, a halfway house on the road to New York, where Mark Twain lived, near Mrs. Stowe. Howells had first met Clemens in Boston, when the latter's lecturing-headquarters were at Redpath's office. He had reviewed *The Innocents Abroad* and Clemens had called to thank him; and since then the two ex-printers, both of whom had pilot forbears and who had much else in common in their Western boyhood, had struck up a lasting friendship. Howells had introduced Clemens to the readers of *The Atlantic* and was publishing his stories and sketches; and Clemens, convinced that he lived at last in "the freest corner of the country," liked Boston better than New York.* His cronies there, besides Howells, were Fields and Aldrich. He would storm into Cambridge in his great sealskin coat, with his tousled red hair and wild moustache, and fall asleep in a bed at Howells's with a lighted cigar in his mouth. Once he took a room at Parker's and left the gas burning for two or three days, while he wandered about in his evening clothes, muffled in his overcoat. Most of the Cambridge circle looked at him askance, while another Western genius from San Francisco, who had burst on the world at the same moment, was received with open arms in Cambridge and Boston. Bret Harte was entertained by Longfellow, Lowell, Agassiz, Fields. He was as much of a lion as Dickens, who had reappeared in 1868,—when Howells and the younger Henry James had met him; and Harte disrupted dinner-parties and arrived as late as he chose at luncheons and seemed to be all the more popular the more he did so. But Howells gloried in

* See Howells, *My Mark Twain*. Referring to *The Atlantic,* Clemens wrote to Howells in 1874: "It is the only audience that I sit down before in perfect serenity (for the simple reason that it doesn't require a 'humorist' to paint himself striped and stand on his head every fifteen minutes)."

Mark Twain, and Norton and Child shared Howells's pleasure in him.* Later the two friends wrote a play together,—or, rather, they tried to do so,—on the story of Colonel Sellers from *The Gilded Age.* This novel, which Mark Twain composed with Charles Dudley Warner,— his neighbour, who was editing the *Hartford Courant,*— was only redeemed by its leading character. Sellers was a great creation of American folklore, while the book was otherwise without form and void, although Warner's hero, Philip Sterling, was a more or less lifelike sketch of the type of young New England men who were going West to seek their fortunes. Howells, visiting Hartford, sometimes stayed with Warner also. This son of a Massachusetts farmer had practised law in Chicago before he returned to New England and began to write. He had made a name for himself as a commentator on rural life in his weekly contributions to the *Courant.* In *My Summer in a Garden,* with woodcuts by Darley, followed by *Back-Log Studies* and *Being a Boy,* he described the repose and the happier aspects of the old New England country scene in a charming, natural style that suggested Irving's. He had known all the Indian trails in western Massachusetts in the days when the gate of the sea was at Boston and the gate of the West was at Albany; and, passing through the Western gate, he had lived for a while in Missouri, where he had worked as a surveyor. There he had had a chance to observe the "land and railroad operations" that he and Clemens described in *The Gilded Age,* and he well understood the ambitious young Yankees for whom every Western path was a path of fortune. He had seen Philip Sterlings by the dozen in Chicago, but his own ambition

---

* At the time of the Whittier birthday dinner, Child wrote to Mark Twain, praising his well-known speech as "the richest piece of humour in the world." Norton's admiration may also have been spontaneous. It seems more likely, however, rather more in character, that Norton was drawn to the work of this far from Nortonian author by his friend Charles Darwin's delight in Clemens. At the time when Norton was seeing much of Darwin, Mark Twain was the latter's favourite bedside reading.

was all for a life of letters, and he spoke in his earlier
books for the interest in farming and gardening that
Olmsted was reviving in his parks. His *Being a Boy* followed Mark Twain's *Tom Sawyer*. It was full of the
aromatic scents of the hill-pasture and green meadow and
the joys of the farmhouse attic on rainy days. Later,
Warner was better known for his mildly critical social
essays, in defence of high thinking and plain living, together with his useful compilations; * but he had already
appeared as a second Bayard Taylor, the author of a
series of books of travel. *My Winter on the Nile* was perhaps the best. These somewhat literal records, packed
with information, were tokens of this first great age of
tourists, when Americans were swarming abroad, hungry
for every crumb of knowledge, and the "beaten path"
was still a wild adventure.

Warner and Mark Twain,—ardent, optimistic men,
with an all-American vision like Howells's own,—were
comrades-in-arms, with him, in a great crusade. The war,
in breaking down the sections, had rendered a unified nation possible. The sectional schools of writing had passed
or were passing,—the New England school, the Knickerbocker school, the South Carolina school and others,—
and the Middle West and the Far West were finding
voices in Hay and Harte that suggested an all-American
point of view.† Howells, Warner and Mark Twain, who
had lived all over the country, were at one in their desire
to promote this movement; but, while this bond was deep
and real, the three had little in common otherwise. The
irony of Warner's fate lay in his having worked with
Clemens,—the man of talent collaborated with the man
of genius. The result was that this excellent writer, this
competent, ready, industrious craftsman, was only re-

* Warner edited the *Library of the World's Best Literature* and the
American Men of Letters series.
† Sectionalism reappeared in the new form of Regionalism in the Ameri-
can literature of the 1930's.

called in later years for the weakest work he ever did. *The Gilded Age,* in fact, was a failure for both, although its name survived as the name of an epoch; and Warner's failure was remembered because Mark Twain was connected with it. As for Mark Twain, he knew that Colonel Sellers was the only strong figure in the book, and he wished to revive this figure and give him a separate existence. It was to help him in this that he called upon Howells, a far more skillful craftsman than himself. In the end, he succeeded alone with his play, when Howells, unlike Warner, found that he could not work with Clemens,—a proof of the independence of Howells's talent. It was as if Vermeer had tried to work with Rubens, as if Jane Austen and Henry Fielding had attempted to write a novel together. But the incident was important for both these writers. While it threw Mark Twain back on his own resources, Howells had not wasted his energy. At this very moment, he was writing plays himself, and the failure of his attempts to work with Clemens undoubtedly cleared his mind. One only understands oneself by learning what one cannot do. Howells tried his hand at plays, as if to make sure of his proper form before he committed himself to novel-writing. He had tested himself, just so, as a poet and critic, and he carried on all these lines to the end of his life. He knew they were minor lines, but he was competent in them all, and no doubt his experience with them enriched his mind. As for his plays, they were comedies, and the best were farces.* Like his own Maxwell, in *The Story of a Play,* he disliked the the-

* Howells's one fine comedy was *A Counterfeit Presentment,* the story of a girl whose heart is broken by an unworthy lover but who is cured by falling in love with his double. The situation in *Out of the Question,* another of Howells's comedies, might well have been suggested by Mark Twain's marriage. It is "out of the question" for the young girl to marry the Western steamboat-mechanic until the mechanic himself, by proving himself a natural gentleman, makes it "out of the question" for her to refuse him.

atre as much as he liked the drama.* The conditions of
the stage were repugnant to him. This indicated that
Howells was not a playwright born; but he had a gift for
private theatricals,—dramatic chamber-music, as one
might call them. In *The Elevator, The Register, The
Parlour-Car, The Sleeping-Car,* he exploited the possibilities of these inventions. One overheard conversations
through registers, and strange things happened when
elevators refused to budge between the sixth and seventh
floors. Parlour-cars and sleeping-cars lent themselves to
situations. In after years, Howells's farces recalled a moment of history when all these modern toys were excit-
ingly new.

Howells's friendship with Mark Twain had various
repercussions, for each served the other as a foil. Each
became better aware of his quality in contrast with the
other mind, as always happens when men of high talent
meet. They defined themselves in this relation, and, while
both were pliable up to a point, each learned something
from the other. Mark Twain confirmed Howells's American consciousness, which might otherwise have been over-
borne by Boston; and his scorn for all things European
precluded any danger that Howells would follow the
course of Henry James. On the other hand, Mark Twain
deferred to Howells in matters of form and style. In this
he profited greatly, for his feeling for aesthetic values
was uncertain and weak. Howells's delicate taste and skill
checked his genius of improvization, which was always
running wild in absurd caprices. But Mark Twain also fell
a victim to Howells's limitations, for he seldom questioned
the right of his friend to censor and alter his work.

These curious limitations of Howells, his tendency to
the namby-pamby, his prudery and his timorous over-
niceness, were partly temperamental and partly due to

---

* Howells's attitude towards the theatre was much like Henry James's,
who was similarly repelled by the "sawdust and orange-peel business."

circumstances, his editorship, his marriage, the place and the moment. With a taste for the "cleanly respectabilities," he had avoided "abhorrent contacts," * while still a reporter in Columbus, the contacts with police-stations, saloon-keepers and ward-politicians who represented the seamy side of life. He had a morbid horror of the sordid and ugly; † and this squeamishness had grown on the tender-minded Howells with his life in Venice and later in Cambridge and Boston. In Venice, alone with his wife, he had known few men; and, in fact, Mrs. Howells was more and more a nervous invalid who required, if she did not exact, his continual devotion. He wrote much more for her than for anyone else, and his mind was unconsciously governed by her distaste for all that was disagreeable and unpleasant. He had whimsically complained to Norton that he suffered from "too much female society;" ‡ and, for all his literary friendships, he

* Howells, *Years of My Youth.*

† Edmund Gosse related that in 1882 Howells was planning a novel with scenes laid partly in Hong-Kong. As he bewailed his ignorance of China, Gosse, with much trouble, procured and sent him a detailed report on night-life in Hong-Kong. Howells did not acknowledge this. Later he admitted that he had received it but was so disturbed and horrified that he had burned the report. He dropped all thought of writing about Hong-Kong.

This, however, is not the whole story. Howells, in any case, on second thought, would probably have dropped the idea of writing about China. He never wrote well of things he had not seen. The most incongruous episode in all his fiction is the description of Fenton, in *A Woman's Reason,* cast away on a South Sea island. This was so unreal that it must have taught Howells never to stray again from his chosen world. Similarly, he always failed in verisimilitude when he departed too far from the middle ranks of society. The general feeling was that he failed in his portraits of Boston patricians, as he failed in his portraits of tramps *(Out of the Question)* and Boston working-girls *(A Minister's Charge).*

As for Howells's squeamishness, see his statement about Mark Twain's "Elizabethan breadth of parlance." He would hide away in holes and corners letters from his friend that he could not bear to burn yet could not bear to look at. While he exercised in many ways a beneficent influence over Mark Twain, he was undoubtedly prudish in toning Clemens's language down to the taste of a feminized public.

‡ "I think my state is partly attributable to too much female society; and what becomes of literary men in Paynim lands, where wives, nurses and grandmothers are indefinitely multiplied in households, I couldn't in my enfeebled condition guess."—Letter to Norton, 1868.

was never thrown closely with men. To see the world through the eyes of women, to humour them, to share their interests, to avoid whatever shocked their prepossessions, this was an instinct and a tendency in Howells that his life on *The Atlantic* had confirmed. He had been an editor before he began to write novels, and his mind was further shaped by this ordeal; for the new age of readers was mainly an age of women readers, and his mind was naturally in harmony with this obvious condition.* As an outsider, as one who revered *The Atlantic* and was anxious to forward its interests, he was eager to be so. Thus the editorial habit, with its feeling for the prospective reader, determined the novelist's mind as it were in advance.

All this qualified Howells's realism. His view of life was severely limited, although he was scarcely aware of these limitations. "Nuns fret not at their convent's narrow room;" and there was something nunlike in Howells's Quakerish innocence and simplicity of heart. A deeply truthful nature, both honest and courageous, he shared the

---

* "The man of letters must make up his mind that in the United States the fate of a book is in the hands of the women. It is the women with us who have the most leisure, and they read the most books. They are far better educated, for the most part, than our men, and their tastes, if not their minds, are more cultivated. Our men read the newspapers, but our women read the books."—Howells, *Literature and Life.*

See also the remark of Fulkerson, the promoter of *Every Other Week,* in *A Hazard of New Fortunes:* "We've got to recognize that women form three-fourths of the reading public in this country, and go for their tastes and their sensibilities and their sex-piety along the whole line."

Henry Adams agreed with Howells in his description of the reading public. "I suspect that women are the only readers—five to one—and that one's audience must be created among them. As I see the American man here, he is a negligible quantity. If a *dix-neuvième* is to be built up for America, it must be for—or by—the women."—*Letters of Henry Adams,* 1892–1918.

"It"—*Mont-Saint-Michel and Chartres*—"was meant only for nieces and women, for men no longer read at all, and I've given only to men who asked for it. Indeed I've not given it even to my brothers or nephews. They borrow it from their women-folk if they want it."—Henry Adams, Letter of 1905.

romantic American worship of women.* This did not prevent him from deriding their foibles, but to accept their
"sex-piety," as the editor Fulkerson called it, was second
nature with him as a man and a writer.† His mind was
bathed in a feminine atmosphere, and the air of his stories was sometimes close. He was singularly preoccupied
with domestic matters,‡ and he had a tendency to fuss,
to make too much of trifles, that was also characteristic
of Henry James. The tendency to fuss had always been a
New England trait,§ and the decay of its larger public interests had revived in the Yankee mind this spinsterish
habit. Howells was obliged to reflect it, but he often
seemed to humour the trait. He lent himself to the point
of view of people who magnified scruples and quibbles
into problems of conscience, who thought for days about
some peccadillo that a larger mind would settle and dis-
miss at once. Could a young man offer himself in the waiting-room of a railway station? Was it not wicked to go
driving with a girl one did not "quite respect"? Misunderstandings over such trifles abounded in Howells's
weaker novels, and often formed the substance of the
story. In some of his moral-obstacle races, the obstacles
were cobwebs that a breath of common sense would have
blown away.

Howells's mind, for all this, was large, alert, observant

* "They were Americans, and they knew how to worship a woman."—
Howells, *The Lady of the Aroostook.*

† How honest and courageous Howells was he showed in 1887 in his agitation on behalf of the "Chicago anarchists." This may be contrasted with
his action at the time of the notorious Gorky dinner. He had instinctively
accepted the taboo regarding sexual matters that characterized the mores of
the time, but he was reckless of consequences when he clearly recognized
a call for courage.

‡ There was something indescribably feminine in Howells's burning interest in domestic arrangements and comforts. See the innumerable pages
in *A Hazard of New Fortunes* devoted to the problems of apartment-
hunting, etc. *Their Silver Wedding Journey* abounds in the wildest excesses of domesticity.

§ Ever since John Cotton set all Massachusetts agog over the question
whether women should wear veils.

and witty, and the world that appeared in his novels was a revelation. For here was the real American scene, reflected in a burnished mirror, as no American eye had ever perceived it. This was not the romanticized scene of Cooper, or Hawthorne's crepuscular world, or the rudely drawn reality of Mrs. Stowe, still less the distorted scene of the ordinary novels, those formless, artificial, sentimental inventions that passed, in 1870, as reflections of life. There were no heroes or heroines here "dying for each other," no turgid flights of fancy or exaggerations, but a manifold assemblage of Yankees, New Yorkers, Southerners, Westerners, all in their habits as they were, going about their business in the morning sunlight. Aware as Howells was of Europe, which often appeared in these novels, he saw his people in terms of themselves and their country, moving in their own orbit, under their own American sky, in all the actuality of their daily existence; for he had followed Emerson's counsel, not seeking the great, the remote, the romantic, but sitting at the feet of the low and familiar. His work was an ample reply to those for whom America was not sufficiently rich and complex in its types to provide a novelist with subject-matter. In range and variety, his portrait-gallery was second to none; and so truthfully drawn were all his people that every reader exclaimed at once, Yes, this is right, how well I know them! They all assumed flesh and blood at once. For Howells's eye for detail in their costume and appearance was as subtle as his knowledge of their motives. And how natural were his conversations, what an ear he had for shades of distinction in tone between regions and classes, the rustic and the urban, the Western, the Virginian, three or four kinds of Bostonians and the people of Maine! Add to this Howells's style, so limpid and precise, so animated, gay, adroit and fresh, and one could understand the joy with which his American readers acclaimed this panorama of their charms and their foibles.

While New England, for a number of years, was Howells's central *mise en scène,* his mind from the first was continental. If he had a purpose, this was to reconcile sections and classes in a broadly democratic feeling for life; and, in order to bring them together, he often presented his people as travellers, who meet in hotels, in stations, on trains, on steamboats. One gathered from his novels that Americans were always moving, always going or coming, abroad or at home; and, in fact, in this respect, these novels reflected the post-war years and Howells's own habit as a constant tourist. In one of his tales, the girl was married in a storage-warehouse. She had been meeting the young man there for years, for the families had been twenty times "in and out of storage." But how, except as travellers, in a country so diversified, could Howells have assembled so many varieties of people? Where could Kitty Ellison of Eriecreek, New York, have met Mr. Arbuton of Boston except on a Saint Lawrence river-boat? Where, save on the "Aroostook," could Lydia Blood have fallen in with Staniford and Dunham? Only in Venice could Lily Mayhew have told the Austrian officer that her home was in Patmos, New York; and only in a station or a summer hotel could the South have encountered the West in the casual, natural fashion of Howells's novels. Accordingly, for settings, he liked these fortuitous meeting-places, where his fellow-Americans gathered on a neutral ground; and he shared all their pleasure in the bustle of travel, in the chaos of docks and wharves, in the rattle of baggage, in the jolting of stages and coaches, in the views from the trains. How charming, as one sped past, the sight of a woodcutter's shanty, losing itself among the shadows in a solitude of the hills! How amusing to sit in a waiting-room and establish fanciful relations with people whom one saw for half a minute! Howells delighted in these adventures, in the hissing and coughing of locomotives under the flaring gas-jets of a

station at night, in the odour of paint and carpet that prevailed on the steamboats, in the tinkle of the ice-water
pitchers, in the cinders on the trains, in the Negro waiters, the porters, the conductors, the drummers, whom he
viewed with Walt Whitman's benevolent eye. What joy,
as he conveyed it, to receive your stateroom-key an hour
before departure on the Albany night-boat, well knowing
it would be light enough until you reached West Point to
see the best scenery on the river! How pleasant, on a
summer evening, on the Nantasket boat, as you sat on
your camp-stool on the deck, to feel the air freshening,
while you watched the gay life of the harbour, while the
islands of the bay waxed and waned and Boston slowly
vanished in the hazy distance! Was there ever such up-
holstery and music as one found on the Fall River boat!
Such gorgeously carpeted cabins, such a glitter of glass,
such a multitude of plush chairs and sofas! Or such mirrors as one found in the great hotels in Portland and
Boston, such tessellated floors and marble mantels, such
acres of Brussels carpet and glossy paint, so many varnished tables and fluted pillars! Howells's people moved
about their world in the perpetual presence of these mild
marvels, with a chorus of customs officials and condescending hotel-clerks, stewardesses, cabin-boys and consuls.

This was the "young country" that Europeans talked
about, and the moon that overlooked it was of lucent
honey. In the foreground of every American landscape
one saw a bridal pair, at Mount Desert or Niagara, on
the Florida keys; and Howells was an accomplice of all
the lovers. Was not this country a larger Arcady? It struck
him so, at moments, in the presence of all these shepherdesses and shepherds. Wherever he looked there were
brides and brides, charmingly dressed, with ravishing toi-
lets. How small their gloves were, how high the heels of
their little boots, over which the snowy skirts electrically
fluttered! Howells was a born match-maker; he delighted

in a pretty woman; he had an eye for every touch of style, and he liked to show how naturally the simplest American village girl assumed the grace and elegance of the world of fashion. All his "young ladies" were "stylish," wherever they came from, whether the Lapham girls or Helen Harkness, with her vividly birdlike mobility, or Lydia, from South Bradfield, where the village seamstress had studied the paper patterns and *Harper's Bazar,* while she observed the costumes of the summer boarders; and Howells shrewdly noted the trifles of behaviour that so often carried the day in his game of love. A girl ran up the steps of a house with the loop of her train in her hand, or she wore the special "light hat" that settled the question, or she poked with her parasol a shaving on the pavement which the young man was holding with his foot. She changed the bow at her throat from scarlet to crimson, or perhaps she laughed at everything, not because she was amused but because she was happy. She always knew just how she looked; she always knew, like Howells, what she was doing. The parents often stood in awe of these phantoms of delight, deferring to their knowledge of the world; and Howells shared all their tender solicitude for them. He loved to see them piloted into safe harbours. With what distress he hovered over Helen Harkness, when she lost father, house and money and helplessly floundered in Boston to keep afloat! With what anxious care he followed Egeria, in *The Undiscovered Country,* drifting about the roads with the visionary doctor, until she found a haven with the Vardley Shakers!— and he liked to picture Lydia as the idol of the ship, with its pride and chivalrous sentiment revolving round her. When Lydia boards the "Aroostook," what pleasure the fatherly captain takes in making her feel at home in the little white cabin, with the rug that his wife has hooked and the gimcracks left by the girls and all as snug and tidy as a farmhouse kitchen.

Howells's world was a paradise of lovers, though the centre of his picture was not love. He was in reaction against the old romancers who saw love in a monstrous disproportion to the other relations of life. But his earlier novels especially abounded in love-scenes,—love in a blueberry-patch, in a sailboat, a rowboat,—and some of these were exquisitely felt. Such was the scene in *The Undiscovered Country* when the journalist Ford and Egeria, on opposite sides of the grapevine, find each other. No word of love passes between them, and yet, across the screen of vines, as they catch occasional glimpses through the leaves and the tendrils, they establish a perfect understanding. Howells excelled in these idyllic moments, and it was not from any fault of his if a life of endless holidays did not lie beyond them. He knew how often marriages failed,—in *A Modern Instance* he pictured a failure,—but, if he had had his way, the course of love would always have run smooth. Romeo would have saved his Juliet, and somehow Hamlet would have regained Ophelia. In fact, his people were usually happy. His nature obliged him to see them so, as he naturally saw human beings doing the decent, honest thing. His world was one of mutual trust, and Dr. Boynton's faith in people, when this Alcott who never found his Concord set forth on the road without a penny, confident that doors would open for him, was reflected in Howells's general view of life. His Dr. Ellisons abounded in self-respecting candour, his Kittys never imagined themselves misprized for anything but a fault. His policemen were kind and obliging; and if, in his New England, you went out for a walk, and the rain overtook you in the country, you could borrow a waterproof at the nearest schoolhouse. You could leave the waterproof with the station-master, knowing that the stage-driver would safely return it. Howells's Americans were all a natural family, and family loyalty was his favourite theme. His novels were full of loyal

households, the Maverings, and the Coreys, the Gay-
lords, the Laphams, and Howells delighted in testing the
bonds that held them together, conjugal, maternal, paternal and filial. With what pleasure he showed how Dan
Mavering, the young man in *April Hopes,* awoke to his
father's intellectual interests! How proud the Laphams
were of one another, the more they plumbed the probity
in each! Howells grieved over the inequalities that kept
his worthy people apart, and he liked to show how trifling
their differences were. Staniford quickly penetrated beneath Lydia's rustic phrases. Mr. Corey was ready to find
that the bull-headed Lapham was the soul of honour.
Howells resented only those who broke this law of trust
that bound his Americans together,—the arrogant, the
vulgar, the pretentious. He liked to show how far from
vulgar the apparently vulgar could be, how the poetry of
Lapham's paint redeemed him; but he could not abide
presumption, pretension or sham. Profoundly anti-aristo-
cratic, he treated his real patricians, the Bellinghams and
the Coreys, with understanding; but he was merciless to
those who presumed on their caste. With what cold scorn
he pictured Mr. Arbuton, the little Boston prig in *A
Chance Acquaintance,* who slighted the charming, imaginative Western girl! This was the poor young man who
felt that he honoured the farm in Quebec by saying it was
just like Normandy and "expected the cows to be grate-
ful." With what zest Basil March rallied his wife, who
was a bitter aristocrat at heart, when she took for a foreign nobleman the haughty commercial traveller with the
stare that indicated his long descent! It was notable that
Howells's blackguards were often newspaper-men, like
Bittredge, in *The Kentons,* and Bartley Hubbard, who
broke his law of mutual trust with their prying disregard
of human dignity and rights. Like Henry James and
Henry Adams, he detested these glib young journalists
who represented the new publicity. As an old newspaper-

man, he disliked to see this new type pushing aside the
journalist with a feeling for letters.

As Howells advanced, his more serious novels reflected, one by one, the changing conditions and phases
of American life. *The Undiscovered Country* described
the rise of spiritualism at the time when Mrs. Eddy was
settling in Boston, the queer streets where the mediums
lived, with "Madam" on their door-plates, and the air
was full of astral manifestations. Egeria and Dr. Boynton were types of the moment, as Marcia Gaylord was in
A Modern Instance; for the growth of divorce was another sign of the times. *The Rise of Silas Lapham* was
the best of all the pictures of the new self-made millionaires, and *A Woman's Reason* presented another type of
the eighties, the girl setting out to make a living in open
competition with the world of men. Through decade
after decade, Howells followed the life of the nation,
and he caught so many of its phases that as a social historian he had no equal. No doubt, he was most at home
in domestic relations. His portraits of women perhaps
were the best of all, and he aroused a passion of protest
with his realistic record of their foibles and their instinct
for manœuvre. An age of "feminization" was not prepared for this particular aspect of the Howells mirror,
for these women with their strategic headaches, these
mothers who feed on their daughters, who carry on a system of strikes and lock-outs and whose cabins, when they
travel, are smugglers' dens. But Howells's portrait-gallery
was varied and large. He knew the town and the village, the farm and the city, the factory, the business-
office and the lumber-camp, the artisan, the idler, the
preacher, the teacher; and he pictured artists and editors,
shop-girls and students, American scholars in Italy, professors at home, religious impostors, philanthropists,
helpless parents, manufacturers, scientists, journalists,
country squires, hotel-keepers, lawyers, sterile dilettanti,

the hare-brained villager and the village fool. All these people were admirably real, and they recalled in later times a prosperous, buoyant American age when everyone "got on" and most were happy. If there were other stories, these were true also; and Howells himself told some of the other stories. His vision darkened as he advanced in life. But, while he lacked a certain intensity, his writing never lost the charm of a truthful, candid, cheerful, hopeful temper. Howells was the most winning of American writers.

CHAPTER XI

HOWELLS AND JAMES

THE JAMESES had settled in Cambridge a few months after the Howellses, and Howells and the younger Henry James had soon become intimate friends. James was six years the junior,—he was born in 1843; but he had already published several stories when Howells, who was struck by his *Poor Richard,* encouraged him to write for *The Atlantic.* James abashed Howells a little with his air of worldly maturity, but the two had almost everything in common.

For a good part of nine years, while James lived in Cambridge,—he was absent for two or three years on journeys abroad,—the friends had been constantly together.* They walked together at all hours, perhaps to the Botanical Garden, where they sat and talked in the sun on the edge of the hotbeds, pushing their walking-sticks into the sandy path when the talk grew too exciting. On Sunday afternoons, they sometimes strolled to Fresh Pond, where, as they rowed about on the placid water, they discussed the stories they were writing. They rambled at night all over Cambridge, debating methods of fiction, and James told Howells, in the interest of art, the picturesque tale of his uncles and cousins. They read their work to one another under the kerosene lamp at Howells's, where James ate nothing at dinner, or only crumbled a biscuit; for he was a constant sufferer from

* Henry James was in Cambridge during the years 1866–1869, 1870–1872, 1874–1875. He came back again in 1881 and 1882, returning to England in 1883. Thereafter he did not visit America until 1904.

indigestion.* Both were planning American novels, and
their European sympathies were closely related. Howells
was under the spell of Italy, and James loved Italy also,
though his literary predilections were all for France.

While the Jameses had come to live in New England,
they were even more alien there than Howells, whose
mind had been largely formed on the Yankee writers.
Henry James, as a boy in New York, had caught the New
England atmosphere in one or two of his playmates who
had come from this region, a suggestion of apples, nuts
and cheese, of doughnuts and personal toughness, a hardihood that went with Bible-reading; but he had not even
read Hawthorne when he came to Newport,—except for
The Wonder-Book and the *Twice-Told Tales,*—and he
had been moved about so much, in the wandering life of
his family, that he was almost as alien on the banks of the
Hudson. As a child, he had met his father's circle, the
New York illuminati and a few from Boston, Washington Irving, Sumner, Curtis, Ripley. But his "huge queer
country" in general was a puzzle to him. The family had
few associations with the roots of American history. If
their forbears whipped the redcoats in the good old days,
the Jameses apparently never heard it mentioned. Had
they ever heard discussions of Yorktown and Valley
Forge, Mount Vernon, the Tripoli pirates or Lake Erie,
the sort of discussions that flourished in most American
households with a long transmitted interest in the country? There was no evidence of it in the writings of the
Jameses; and they had few rural associations that connect
the mind with the soul of the country,—their Albany
counted for something, but not much. The elder James

* At this time Henry and William James were both semi-invalids. "The
unpublished parts of the correspondence between William and Henry
James are very largely composed of hygienic, symptomatic and therapeutic
details. Their interest in one another's condition of health was equalled
only by their faith in their own remedies."—Ralph Barton Perry, *The
Thought and Character of William James.*

was inveterately urban and was even obliged to live in towns, for, having lost one of his legs, he depended on cabs and adequate pavements. Moreover, the Jameses,— "hotel children," floating vaguely about the world,— knew nothing of politics or business, the primary occupa- tions of their sex. The historical instinct of the country was scarcely in them, though the elder James was Ameri- can through and through.* In later years, William James adjusted himself to this condition; he over-adjusted him- self, in fact, a little. For was not his "plunge into the muddy stream of things" a more or less conscious re- action against this detachment? He might have been de- scribed as more American than the Americans, as Henry James was less, or, rather, different,—he became more English than the English. Both had to fight for a local foothold, and both were constrained to overdo it. Mean- while, Henry was "at sea" about his "native land" and all it represented for a story-teller.†

When he arrived in Cambridge, therefore, James's mind was torn already by a problem that he never really solved. He was bent on becoming a novelist, but novelists always had "native lands:" this was the most obvious fact about them. He recognized this fact in his critical writ- ings,‡ and that he was aware of what it meant in regard

* It should be added that Henry James was deeply impressed by the Civil War, from which two of his brothers, who fought, returned with broken health. See the account of his hour of "consecration," after a visit to the camp of wounded soldiers at Portsmouth Grove, near Newport. Thenceforward he thought of the literary life as "something definitely and firmly parallel to action in the tented field."—*Notes of a Son and Brother,* 317-8.

† "It was a joke, polished by much use, that I was dreadfully at sea about my native land."—Henry James, *Essays in London.*
In *Notes of a Son and Brother,* James described himself as "a young person reaching the age of twenty in well-nigh grotesque unawareness of the properties of the atmosphere in which he but wanted to claim that he had been nourished."

‡ E.g., apropos of Turgenev: "[His] works savour strongly of his native soil, like those of all great novelists, and give one who has read them all a strange sense of having had a prolonged experience of Russia."—*French Poets and Novelists.*

to his own ambitions one saw in his hesitation to leave the
country.* Hawthorne had shown him that one might be
an American novelist without "going outside" about it.†
Indeed, when Hawthorne went outside and wrote about
the Roman scene he seemed to be divested of half his virtue: he "forfeited a precious advantage in ceasing to
tread his native soil," as James observed later in his life
of Hawthorne. This showed that the "American matter"
was vital·to the "American hand," as the English, French,
Russian or whatever matter was vital to the hands he
most admired; while, as for himself, vague as he was
about America, he felt he could scarcely endure an American existence. He had been struck too deeply by the "out-
land dart," he had absorbed the "European virus." ‡ As
a boy in New York, he had missed no contributive image
that went to form a picture of Washington Square,§ and
his later impressions of Boston were equally sharp; but

* This problem was obviously central in James's mind during all the
years that he lived uneasily in Cambridge. It remained central in his mind
long after he had settled abroad. "I know what I am about, and I have
always my eyes on my native land."—Letter to William James, 1878.
    † Notes of a Son and Brother.
    ‡ "A return to America"—in 1870—"was to drag with it . . . the torment
of losses and regrets. The repatriated victim of that unrest was, beyond
doubt, acutely conscious of his case: the fifteen months just spent in Europe
had absolutely determined his situation. The nostalgic poison had been dis-
tilled for him, the future presented to him but as a single intense question:
was he to spend it in brooding exile, or might he somehow come into his
'own'?—as I liked betimes to put it for a romantic analogy with the state
of dispossessed princes and wandering heirs."—Preface to The Reverberator.
    § Washington Square remained to the end of James's life his closest
point of attachment to the land of his forbears. There was a touch of
poetry in all his allusions to it, in spite of the "inexpensive ailanthus" that
garnished the square in his novel about it. It is in lower Fifth Avenue
that Bernard Longueville, in Confidence, scatters the dry autumn leaves.
"He tossed them with his stick as he passed; they rustled and murmured
with the motion, and it reminded him of the way he used to kick them in
front of him over these same pavements in his riotous infancy." This
image and situation recur in James's writings, early and late. Where, in
his childhood, an American has first shuffled his autumn leaves, that is
where his heart lies, there he belongs. James always thought of himself
as a New Yorker, and he called his collected edition the "New York
Edition."

he had heard his parents sighing for Piccadilly, Windsor and Kew, and far more real to him than the scenes about him were those he found in *Punch,* in Leech's drawings, in Thackeray, Dickens and Trollope. Before he happened upon Hawthorne, these English writers had filled his mind, and he knew the names of the London streets as he never knew the streets of New York,—Drury Lane, the Row, Kensington Gardens, with the little boys in Eton jackets, the costermongers, the bathing-machines and all the familiar images of the English picture. At twelve, with infant memories of an earlier visit, he had been taken abroad for four more years. In Switzerland, France and England, drifting from school to school and from pension to pension, he had learned languages, read novels and especially gathered impressions that made a return to his country look like failure. America, for him, afforded no objects of interest to compare with this European "fantastication."

The problem in question remained on James's hands unsolved during all the years that he was to spend in Cambridge. By the nature of the case, he could not solve it. He met it, as he met all his problems, just as his brother did, by "pragmatizing," by acting as if they were solved when he could not solve them. Years later, when William James explained this "way of thinking," he saw how far he had lived in accordance with it,*—how he had let the problem drop, in the hope that it would solve itself, after trying and failing to solve it by direct attack. That he tried hard to solve it one saw in his earlier stories, in which he showed with what determination he strove to meet the exactions of the "native soil," to become an American novelist, a successor of Hawthorne. For, as to his being a novelist, this question was settled,

* "I was lost in the wonder of the extent to which all my life I have (like M. Jourdain) unconsciously pragmatized."—Letter to William James, on the appearance of *Pragmatism,* 1907.

whatever the conditions might be. No one had ever possessed a clearer vocation, and his mind was an inexhaustible well of stories. He could find, not sermons, but
stories in stones, if the native soil, or the foreign, was
beyond his grasp; and it might have been presumed that,
if he could not grasp his own, the soil of other countries
would elude him. He could always count on a fund of
stories, and, as for the art of telling them, this was the
joy of his life and always had been. He had been studying
fiction almost before he attempted to write it. That he
"read too many novels" was the burden of the complaint
against him, in so far as his family circle indulged in complaints, and that one should *not* do as one chose, not exercise one's absolute liberty, was the only real ground of
complaint in the house of the Jameses. No one was better
aware than he of the efflorescence of French fiction that
marked the years when his mind was coming of age. One
of his early tutors was the son of Töpffer, who told him
tales of literary Paris, and John La Farge at Newport
had amplified the picture with his personal recollections
of the later writers. If John La Farge had not known
Balzac, he had met, at his cousin's house in Paris, Flaubert, Gautier, Daudet, the Goncourts and others who had
since become the objects of James's study. Moreover,
James had met Thackeray, his father's friend in Paris,
who had called upon the family in New York. He had
met Dickens at Norton's house, as Howells had met him
at Longfellow's; and he had seen George Eliot on a visit
to England, along with Tennyson, Ruskin and William
Morris. He might have felt that he too was a link in the
"apostolic succession," especially as some of these emi-
nences admired his work.* He spoke with an authority in

* James's early work immediately impressed numbers of the distinguished
older writers on both sides of the Atlantic. Lowell reviewed him with
high praise. William James reported to him in 1869 a remark of Emerson's son that his father "does nothing but talk of your letters,"—James's
travel-letters in *The Nation.* In *The Middle Years,* describing his visit to

his earliest reviews, which were followed by other notes on travel and painting, that showed an extraordinary knowledge of the art of fiction. He also wrote on Swinburne, Whitman, Browning, Morris and Matthew Arnold. His first "consecration to letters" had occurred in 1864, in the golden brown study at "Shady Hill;" and he had been taken up at once by the circle of editorial friends, Norton, Lowell, Fields, Godkin, Howells. James and Howells met as aspirants for American fiction and as students and followers of realism, the great new movement. For realism was coming in, along with "scientific history," as one of the marks of an age that was governed by science.

A mediator between these friends was Thomas Sergeant Perry, who was also deeply interested in the art of fiction. Like others in the Cambridge circle and elsewhere in New England,—the younger women as well as the younger men,—he had seen at once that realism was the art of the future. Perry, a grandson of Commodore Perry,—the "Lake Erie" commodore whose brother had opened Japan,—had known the Jameses well in their boyhood at Newport, where his older sister married John La Farge. He had rambled with Henry James along the beaches and over the Paradise Rocks, discussing Fourier's plan for redeeming the world,—one of the favourite themes of Henry's father; or, as more often happened, painting and fiction. Once Henry, who had been reading Ruskin, carefully copied a leaf with his pencil, and he made a faithful drawing of a rock. Now and again, they had put off in a sailboat, well-stocked for an all-day trip

---

Tennyson, James records that Tennyson "superlatively commended" one of his tales. Ruskin, who was delighted with a paper of James on Tintoretto, afterwards reprinted in *Transatlantic Sketches,* told Norton that henceforward he would "count Harry among the men for whom he should especially work."

with their chosen authors, Balzac, Victor Cherbuliez or Alfred de Musset. Perry had gone to Germany with William James and lived with him at Berlin as a fellow-student, at a time when the Americans at this German university outnumbered all other foreigners put together. There the mercurial William James had ranged over medicine, chemistry, languages, literature, public affairs and the traits of nations, and nothing stirred his mind more than the French and German novels,—the new realistic novels,—which he read with zest. He drew deep draughts of human nature from them. He even reviewed them for *The Nation;* and, from this German vantage-point, while Henry was in Cambridge, he sent his brother suggestions that he thought might please him, urging him to write essays on Balzac and George Sand, which Henry was already contemplating, and especially to read Gautier's travel-sketches. In all this, Perry was William James's comrade-in-arms, for Perry was roaming through literature as William James roamed through life. Perry was an omnivorous reader, as Howells saw at once, when Henry James brought the two together. For William James and his literary comrade had soon returned to Cambridge, where Perry became a tutor in French and German.

Thus Henry James and Howells, deep in the problems of novel-writing, formed a triumvirate with Perry, who was better-informed than either of them. For instance, he had discovered Turgenev at a moment when few writers of English were aware of such a thing as a Russian novel. A first-rate classical scholar, he also taught Sanskrit, and he was scarcely less interested in painting and science. In later years, in France, where he had known Turgenev, Perry became an intimate friend of Monet, and he knew John Fiske as well as James and Howells. His last book was a life of Fiske, and he followed the evolutionary method in his critical writings. He was all but universally curious, and his studies in three literatures were admirable in substance and in style.* Alike in his talk and his writing, he abounded in brilliant *obiter dicta,* and his feeling for modern fiction was clairvoyant. He was the chief reviewer of novels for *The Nation,* and he wrote for *The Atlantic* for several years all its reviews and notices of foreign books. His supple mind, rarely intuitive, divined the currents of modern thought, and he seemed to know the significant works of writers almost before they appeared,—his recognition of them was prompt and final. Howells and Perry, acting together, kept *The Atlantic* well abreast of all the new developments in the world of letters, and Perry wrote articles on Turgenev, Auerbach, Fritz Reuter, Cherbuliez, Victor Hugo, George Sand and others.† He translated several of Turgenev's novels, beginning with *Virgin Soil.*‡ He introduced Turgenev to James and Howells, both of whom, as novelists, were influenced by him as much as by anyone else, native or for-

---

* Perry's most important work was *A History of Greek Literature,* 1890. On a scale slightly smaller, it was incomparably finer in literary feeling than Ticknor's *History of Spanish Literature.* Less useful as a work of reference, it revealed a remarkable breadth of sympathy in regard to art and science and most of the major literatures, ancient and modern. The author's use of the evolutionary method was well shown in the treatment of the Greek drama. Perry's *English Literature in the Eighteenth Century* was rather a discursive essay than a history proper. *From Opitz to Lessing* was a good sketch of German literature in the formative years that preceded its efflorescence. Perry edited with Howells *The Library of Adventure by Sea and Land.*

† Between the years 1868–1883,—roughly, the years of Howells's editorship,—*The Atlantic* also published papers on Stendhal, Dostoievsky, the Goncourts, Flaubert, Zola (three articles), Mérimée, Mistral, Alfred de Musset, Baudelaire, Gautier, Björnson, Bourget, Renan, Sainte-Beuve, Scribe, Dumas the elder, etc. Among the writers of these papers, besides Howells, James and Perry, were Brander Matthews and Eugene Benson, the New York painter.

‡ From the French and German versions. Perry learned Russian later in the days when other New Englanders, Isabel S. Hapgood and Nathan Haskell Dole, were translating Turgenev and Tolstoy directly from it.

eign.* The vogue of Turgenev spread rapidly; † there
seemed to be an occult connection between the Russian
novelist and the young post-war Americans, both men and
women. Nourished, in his far-off Russia, on English authors, Turgenev had grown up in a great wooden manor-
house, like an American Southerner on a primitive plantation. In his student days, he was called "the American,"
because he admired the Western republic, and, although
he was not a reformer in temper, his writings had served
the cause of reform: his *Sportsman's Sketches,* published
in the same year as *Uncle Tom's Cabin,* had paralleled
the American book as an agent of emancipation.‡ He had
followed the growth of American literature, and by 1873
he had read Hawthorne, Whitman, Bret Harte and
Howells.§ Disheartened by the turmoil of his country, he
had settled in western Europe, as many of the new Americans were settling there, because they too were lost in the
transition from an old regime to a new; although, far
from losing touch with Russia, he brooded over all its
problems, so like the American problems in various ways.
One of these resemblances, in the younger generation, lay
in the relation of the sexes. In the disorganized state of

* In *My Literary Passions,* Howells says that he read Turgenev over
and over, more than anyone else. "The man who has set the standard for
the novel of the future is Turgenev."—Letter of Howells, 1877. Turgenev,
in turn, greatly admired Howells. See the letter of President Hayes in
Howells's *Letters,* I, 280. James paid countless tributes to the "beautiful
genius."

† See, in Howells's *April Hopes,* chapter XIII, the conversation on Turgenev among the ladies on the hotel-piazza at Campobello. There is another conversation on Turgenev in Howells's *Indian Summer,* Chapter V.

‡ "You may imagine how Turgenev's eyes stood out of his head on the
day when he met Mrs. Harriet Beecher Stowe . . . who was introduced to
him as being the heroine that had made the chains to fall from the limbs
of the slaves of a continent . . . He said that she seemed to him to be a
modest and sensible person . . . Perhaps the reader will think out for himself all that that amazing meeting signified."—Ford Madox Ford, *Portraits from Life.*

§ See Yarmolinsky, *Turgenev, the Man, his Art and his Age,* 330-331.
It may be added that Emerson and Cooper are among the authors mentioned by the young intelligentsia in Turgenev's *Fathers and Sons.*

Russia, the young men were bewildered. They were ineffectual, divided, hesitant, weak, with all their good intentions, for their function in the body politic was obscure. They were debarred from public life, much as the young Americans were,—for somewhat different reasons, to be sure,—and they were unmanned by this, their morale was low; while the young Russian women, calm, steadfast, passionate, eager for danger and hardship in the name of love, were strong and complete beside them. So it appeared at least in Turgenev's vision, and a similar condition prevailed in America in these days of the "reign of womanhood" and all it stood for. Were not James's and Howells's novels the proof of this? In James more than in Howells, but largely in both, the younger women eclipsed the younger men. Howells's older men were sufficiently potent, but how many of his younger men were light and vague, amateur artists or amateurs in life,— like James's,—irresolute, indecisive, often flimsy, hovering about the girls in hotels or on shipboard, with an air of apologizing for their want of purpose! They seemed to be waiting for a breeze, their sails were flapping, and the women supplied the breeze, for, with all their "tastes," they seldom had any masculine force or motive. In both these writers, the masculine sex appeared to exist, even in England, in order to fall in love with American girls.* The young American men were the victims of conditions that resembled in part the conditions of Turgenev's Russia. There was nothing to hold them up, they were all at sea; and "the sex that discriminates most finely" † had all the honours in American fiction and art as it had in life. The sovereign charm of the young women was the one triumphant fact of an age and a civilization that had little to boast of; and even Henry Adams's Virgin of Chartres

---

* See Lord Rainford in Howells's *A Woman's Reason* and countless other instances in both Howells and James.

† Henry James, *Portraits of Places.*

was as much an American girl in essence * as the heroines of James and Howells and Saint-Gaudens's Diana. The American man was a "failure," Henry Adams thought, and Turgenev's Russian man was a failure also; and Turgenev's enchanting young girls, ardent, shy, all of a piece, seemed much like American girls to American readers. The pages of *The Atlantic* were thronged with letters on these Mariannes and Natalies and Lisas. For the rest, how American were the traits of the Russians in *Smoke,* their tall talk, their liking for new ideas, political, psychological and social, their recentness and the vastness of their country! In 1874, Henry James the elder wrote to Turgenev at Carlsbad, when the younger Henry had published an essay on him. This letter was both charming and discerning. The old man wished to say with what unfeigned delight their Cambridge circle had read Turgenev's novels, what multitudes of Americans read him and how they talked about him often, in the evening, on the piazza, facing the sunset. If ever he crossed the ocean, he must come to Cambridge. Between the fumes of his pipe, he could tell them what his eye divined, either of promise or menace, in their civilization. Turgenev, who was touched, replied that, although he did not smoke, he would enjoy a quiet evening with them.

Turgenev left long traces in American letters. Perry left traces, too, below the surface. An unambitious man, self-effacing and wholly indifferent to fame, he was one of many writers in this epoch who felt no special incentive to continue at work. He produced three or four fine books; then he serenely cultivated his garden in silence. This man of rare intelligence was the friend of many

---

* "She was still a woman, who loved grace, beauty, ornament . . . and liked both light and colour . . . She was extremely sensitive to neglect, to disagreeable impressions, to want of intelligence in her surroundings . . . Her taste was infallible," etc.—Henry Adams, *Mont-Saint-Michel and Chartres.* Adams's Virgin of Chartres suggests in many ways such Henry James heroines as Isabel Archer.

eminent scholars, and he taught for a while in a Japanese university, as professor of English literature, like Lafcadio Hearn. At seventy, enthralled by Chekhov, he mastered Russian. He visited Russia, to see the Moscow Art Theatre, and he ranged with zest afterwards over the whole of Russian literature. He read with his finger-tips. His apprehension was so quick that, while he was cutting the pages of books, he felt obliged to hold them upside down, so as not to absorb them all before he read them. Fifty years after these early Cambridge days, he was alert for new and fine creations.* His insight was prophetic.† But of all his manifold services to American letters none bore better fruit than his influence as a student of fiction on James and Howells.

This widespread interest in fiction, in the new mode of realism, was a natural effect of the moment. Just as in Greece, in the days of Euripides, when the age of the interest in heroes had passed, the popular mind was drawn away from the contemplation of grandeurs and mysteries to the careful observation of human traits. Human nature in all its complexity became a sufficient field of interest, and minds that had once been concerned with principles and lofty teachings devoted themselves with zest to the study of manners. This inevitable tendency of all postheroic ages was reinforced at present by the spread of science, which attracted the mind away from itself to the world of outer experience and all the wondrous fruits of observation. Science revealed the importance of environment, the power of material conditions over the psyche, and the half-romantic Balzac and his realistic French successors gradually brought the novel to terms with science: they proposed to exhibit the types and classes of men as zoology and botany exhibited plants and animals. This

---

* Edwin Arlington Robinson, who edited Perry's *Letters,* called him "one of the great appreciators, without whom there would be no great writers, or artists of any sort."

† See this remarkable statement, written in 1887, in Perry's *The Evolu-*

notion of fiction as one of the branches of natural history
removed all the mystery from life: whatever was romantic, heroic, distinguished was revealed as an effect of natural causes, and more and more the novel devoted itself
to picturing life as ordinary people lived it. As with the
naturalist, so with the novelist, who also called himself a
naturalist soon, the "document," the "fact" was all-sufficient; and a somewhat sober and literal style replaced the
styles of the older writers, as if the facts of life were too
important to be hidden under literary splendours. Realism, naturalism, the child of science and positivism, was
allied with the democratic movement, and it flew the
banner of "truth" on its forward march. Let the truth
prevail, abolish all the mysteries: the facts of life revealed were the whole of life. Such was the art of fiction,
as "history" and as "nature," that an age of science demanded, achieved and worshipped.

This realistic method arose in all the Western countries, spontaneously, inevitably, following similar general
causes. No one invented it: it came. Howells was a realist
before he ever heard the word,—he had written realistic
sketches as a boy in Ohio, sketches "as natural as the
tooth-ache," his father called them. Realism was only
relatively new. In England, Defoe was a realist, and even
Jane Austen. Howells, who knew these writers well, was
also impressed by Goldoni, whose realistic plays, of the
late eighteenth century, had struck his imagination when
he saw them in Venice. Howells had developed his own
realistic method, and Turgenev rather confirmed than de-

tion of the Snob: "It should be said that if *le monde s'américanise,* as
desponding European writers are prone to say, it will alter slowly, for one
peculiarly American quality is its intense conservatism: it adheres with,
on the whole, wonderful tenacity to what has won the approval of Europe.
These questions, it seems, will rather be decided by the Russians, who
appear to be destined to take the place long held by the French; that,
namely, of becoming the Greeks of modern times,—in other words, the people who shall carry out their ideas in action, who put their theories into
practice."

termined this method: he confirmed it with his plotless
novels and his grouping of three or four persons whose
interwoven fates alone concerned him. Turgenev charmed
Howells and James with his poetry and his reticence; but
Howells's own personality ordained his method. By temperament anti-romantic, he was also highly susceptible to
changes of literary weather; and the realistic view of
life, which he drew as it were out of the air, appealed to
his democratic instinct. He did not believe in heroes and
extraordinary people. But science had intensified the realistic impulse, and the Yankee mind in general was prepared for this movement. It had produced realistic stories
before Howells and James appeared, in fact. Mrs. Stowe
had established her pattern before the Civil War, when
Mrs. Cooke had also begun to write, and Elizabeth Stoddard's *The Morgesons, Two Men* and *Temple House*
had appeared by 1867. These three precursors of Miss
Jewett and Miss Wilkins were all realistic, more or less,
although Mrs. Stowe was mainly historical,—she pictured a world that was past or passing,—and Mrs.
Cooke's tales were too often factitious, and Elizabeth
Stoddard's novels were all too dim. This Massachusetts
girl who had gone to New York, as the wife of the poet
Stoddard, had written and published her books during
the war-years. Hawthorne had mildly praised *The Morgesons,* and indeed, in all these cluttered novels, formless
and overcrowded with irrelevant details, one felt the
glow of an ardent nature and a notable gift of observation. In effect, they were pallid imitations of the Brontës,
through which the New England setting glimmered
faintly. But, with Mrs. Cooke's work and Mrs. Stowe's,
they marked a change of feeling, none the less. One of the
clearest symptoms of this change of feeling was Mrs.
Stowe's attack on Byron, which advanced the cause of
realism indirectly. Lady Byron's death in 1860 had renewed the discussions of her marriage: she was denounced

for having ruined her husband's life, and Mrs. Stowe, to whom she had told her story, had poured the story out in defence of her friend. The scandal had rocked *The Atlantic,* in which it appeared. It almost wrecked the magazine, for it alienated hundreds of readers. But Howells had rejoiced in the incident: it put an end, he felt, to the glamour of Byron. That it marked a turning-point in the feeling of New England, where Byron, for all his errors, had been a hero, this, to be sure, was accidental; but it showed how the wind was blowing. Henceforward, the romantic spirit, which had actuated all the poets, was regarded with distrust and suspicion.

New England, meanwhile, had produced another writer whose novels foreshadowed the work of James and Howells. John W. De Forest, who lived in New Haven, had served in the war as a captain, and Howells, who greatly admired his writing, published three of his novels as serials. *Kate Beaumont, Honest John Vane* and *Irene the Missionary* all appeared first in *The Atlantic,* although much finer than these was *Miss Ravenel's Conversion,* which had attracted Howells to De Forest.* As a young man this writer had spent much of his life abroad, in Paris, Florence and Beirut, where his brother had a missionary school; and his first works were travel-books, one of them picturing life in Syria. When the war broke out, he was living in Charleston, but he returned to New Haven and recruited a company there. Later, for a year, after the war, he was stationed in South Carolina. The settings of his novels,—two had appeared before the war,—reflected the various scenes in which he had lived. He wrote them in rapid succession, a dozen or

---

* This was a first-rate novel of the Civil War, published in 1867. It was admirable in its scenes and characterizations. De Forest described himself in Captain Colburne and his adventures in Louisiana and the Shenandoah.

De Forest had read Balzac and Stendhal during his years in Paris, and in Florence he had translated into Italian Hawthorne's *The House of the Seven Gables.*

more. Then, like Thomas Sergeant Perry, he relapsed into silence.

Why De Forest ceased to write was a question that greatly troubled Howells, who tried to find an audience for this interesting author. If the answer was that no-body read him, this added to the mystery; for De Forest's work was remarkable, beyond a doubt. His touch, though sometimes crude, was strong, and he pictured American scenes and manners, in Connecticut, New York, the South, the West, with a breadth of understanding and a truth to actuality that were certainly unique at the mo-ment. While he sometimes lapsed into melodrama, as in the Western novel *Overland,* the story of the Santa Fe trail, with its all-too-wicked Mexican cousins of the all-too-lovely American heroine and its lurid world of bad-men and Apaches, he was usually veracious and observ-ant. He skillfully chose subjects that were typical of the national life. As a picture of Washington politics and their corruption, *Honest John Vane* had few rivals. In a day when foreign missions were of general interest, *Irene the Missionary* gave its readers a lively account of a mission, with a story that brought its elements all to-gether. De Forest knew the Americans in Syria, the wan-dering archæologists, the consuls, the learned and fatherly missionaries and their younger assistants, who taught the children to read English in Irving's *Life of Columbus,* as he knew the Washington lobbyists for whom the republic was the creature and servant of money; and, although he knew best of all the Connecticut Yankees at home, his two South Carolina novels, *The Bloody Chasm* and *Kate Beaumont,* showed that he also understood the South. As a man of imagination who had served in the war, he was eager to reconcile the discordant sections. He had suggested this wish in *Miss Ravenel's Conversion,* in which the Southern heroine lives in New Haven, and that he himself was at home in Charleston his other novels proved,—his portraits of South Carolinians, General Hilton, Colonel Beaumont and the knightly, simple, sensible Colonel Kershaw, were singularly keen and sympathetic. De Forest excelled in portraits of men, and he liked to picture reconciliations: one of his best scenes was the meeting of Beaumont and Judge McAlister, the chiefs of the rival Carolinian clans. In *The Bloody Chasm,* the North and South were reunited in a way that shed honour upon all.

In John De Forest, a writer had appeared with a panoramic eye for American manners. His scenes were vividly realized, the streets of New York, the Southern plantation-houses, the country-seats he loved in his own Connecticut landscape, overlooking the Sound,—a Parthenon on a rocky bluff or a low, wide-spreading house with pointed gables, perched on a turfy hillock with lawns below and parlours hung with portraits and spoils of travel; and, with his marked regard for the world that was passing, the "old-time society" and its patriarchal types, he recognized the new types and filled his novels with them. Side by side with Colonel Kershaw, the "white rose of Southern chivalry," and the Puritan Judge Wetherel, the Connecticut magnate, with his old-fashioned courtesy, unworldly in diction and feeling for all his wealth,* he

* The "master of Sea Lodge," in *The Wetherel Affair,* was one of De Forest's finest portraits. As a specimen of the old New England rural aristocracy, he enabled one to understand the power of the missionaries who founded schools and colleges all over Asia. Judge Wetherel is so steeped in the Bible that whenever he feels strongly his language is naturally biblical. With no suggestion of cant in his patriarchal simplicity, he represents the grand style of the Puritan tradition. See his words of welcome to the missionary's daughter who has come to Sea Lodge as a guest: "The child of God's apostle to his ancient church in the Kurdish mountains shall be a member of my family as long as she chooses to be." A dictatorial soul, grimly authoritative under a consciousness of duty, he is invariably courteous and gentle with the gentle. See, especially, the chapter, "The Judge's Manners and Customs."

De Forest's pictures of the old patriarchal life of America, both in New England and in the South, strangely resemble, in spite of every difference, Aksakov's pictures of the old Russian life in *A Russian Gentleman* and *Years of Childhood.*

described the girls who were "crazy for Newport," the foreigners with titles, often bogus, who were pursuing these girls, the rascally politicians of the post-war years, the Gallicized Americans in Europe, the young men who were going into chemistry and metallurgy, geologizing in California, developing phosphate-beds in the South; and, while his people had a way of meeting in Europe or on shipboard, as in Howells's novels and James's,* their interests were strongly American and characteristic. They were drawn with great vitality and directness. All in all, De Forest's work was a record of his time and country that should have aroused a more than passing interest.

So Howells felt, but the case was hopeless. De Forest did not appeal to women: this seemed to be the reason for his failure and silence. Men had largely ceased to read, and De Forest was a man's writer. His detached, ironical tone was masculine; so were his broad and general interests. If he had been a Bostonian, if the war had not appeared in so much of his work, he might have attracted more attention. But people wished to forget the war, and the larger American scene had little charm at present for women readers. Besides, he aroused the hostility of women readers. With a soldier's taste for dashing young ladies, he was rather disdainfully blunt with the rest of the sex. He had a pitiless eye for their foibles, and he liked to describe superannuated flirts and silly, extravagant wives who wreck their husbands. In a world in which women decided the fate of books, the odds were all against this virile writer.

The literary case of John De Forest was a sign of the place and the moment. While New England was ready for realism, as Mrs. Stowe had amply shown, De Forest

* "In society the mass of people have few startling topics in common, and still fewer interests; but among heroic ruins, solemnizing cathedrals, revered works of art and life-pictures of strange peoples, sensations rapidly sympathize, and thoughts become charmingly interchangeable."—De Forest's *Seacliff*.

showed the kind that New England was *not* ready for.
The impalpably masculine character of his whole performance was the very thing that damned it,—which defined the type that readers were prepared to welcome;
and what else could have been looked for, in the place, at
the moment? The tastes and interests of women determined this type. Wherever realism appeared, in whatever
region or nation, the regional mind remodelled it along
the lines of its own conditions. French realism differed
from Russian, and Russian from Spanish, and Spanish
again from Norwegian, as Björnson showed it. American realism differed from these others, and New England
had its special variation. To reject this latter, one had to
begin by rejecting New England. Each to his own taste,
—why not? But the realism itself could "do no other."
The case was merely a repetition of the case of the previous age, in which romantic poetry was the dominant art
in all the other regions *and* New England; and the dominance of Howells and James in the coming decades was a
proof of the power of realism as the art of the moment.
The delicate, limited mode of these writers, who were in
New England, if not of it,—and they largely wrote in
relation to New England readers,—was peculiarly sympathetic to the feminized public; and most of the women
writers were realistic, although they were even more limited and severely conditioned. Howells and James transcended the others because of their centrality of vision,
the unity of their style and tone and their all-American
subject-matter. For the rest, what poetry had been, the
novel was to be,—the novel or the story,—as a focus of
interest. If the short story proved to be the form in which
the local art of fiction triumphed, this was because it was
better adapted to women with narrow horizons.

These tendencies were already current when Howells
and James had begun to write. They were all in the ambient air of the post-war Yankees. In the novels of Har-

riet Waters Preston,* one read the minds of the younger
women who were largely to form the audience of James
and Howells. It was they, or other young women like
them, who were soon to write the New England stories,
and, while their horizons were certainly narrow, one had
to say it with qualifications. Their lives were restricted,
their experiences were circumscribed; and this determined
the range of their acts and their writings. But their feelings were far from narrow or shallow; indeed, they were
intense and deep, and, tested by the standard of "aware-
ness," these Claras, with their aesthetic teas, these Zoes
who had outlived their follies outrivalled many a damsel
of the years that followed. At times, in fact, in certain
ways, they made the bacchantes of Greenwich Village
look like rustic nursery-girls or milkmaids; and, if there
was something nun-like in them, it was not for want of
positive traits,—they had merely made their peace with
fate and fortune. Some of these girls, advancing in years,
were music-teachers in college towns; others dwelt together in the country; others carried on romances, perhaps in New Hampshire boarding-houses or in literary
circles in Worcester or Boston. Their over-active brains
at times were combined with over-sensitive consciences,
and they sometimes contracted their brows a little too
much and cultivated the "strong" way of speaking. But
all of them, whatever their age, as they read the scientific
monthlies and often went to church in their brown shade-
hats, were wonderfully well aware of the world they lived
in. They canvassed the modern novel from end to end.
They discussed the relations of labour and capital. They
touched upon the "woman question," quoting George

* Especially *Aspendale* and *Love in the Nineteenth Century.* These early
realistic novels resembled in their pallor and thinness the poems that preceded the outburst of the forties. They represented the faint beginnings of
a type that rapidly grew in strength. Weak enough as novels, they have
their special interest as revealing the state of mind of the younger people,
especially the young women of this epoch.

Sand and Mill; and they knew their Darwin as they read
their Huxley. They threshed out all the problems of love
and marriage. Was it ever, ever, "folly to be wise"?
They shared the light of Sainte-Beuve's exemplary ladies.*
How did Madame Swetchine regard these matters? What
did Madame Récamier think about them? If Madame de
Sévigné were living, how would she feel? Were they not
the heirs of twenty more ages than Plato? They knew
Rossetti's diluted Botticelli; and, as for French poetry
and fiction, it was all on the tip of their tongues. Matthew
Arnold led the rest in the matter of moulding their taste,
although even regarding Arnold they were still judicious.
For good sense abounded in their minds, and they were
Emersonian first of all. Was "the temper to which truth
is revealed" as fastidious or as desperate as the supercilious Arnold appeared to think it? They asked themselves if "culture" and "anarchy" were not somehow one,
as shame and fame were all the same to Brahma. If they
were "Hebraists," they certainly had to be "Hellenists,"
and they shared James's joy in Arnold's phrases,—his
contempt for that bane of mankind, *das Gemeine,* the
common, his scorn of the "Philistine" and the "provincial." But, unlike James, they were rather inclined to take
the phrases with grains of salt; for James was much more
credulous than these Yankee maidens, some of whom took
him with grains of salt in the days when they had all

---

* See *The Library of Exemplary Women,* published in Boston about
1873. In addition to writing her novels and poems, Harriet W. Preston
translated three volumes of Sainte-Beuve. Miss Preston's special field, however, was Provençal literature. See her *Troubadours and Trouvères* and
her well-known translation of Mistral's *Mirèio.*

Miss Wormeley, the translator of Balzac, also translated Sainte-Beuve.
Miss Grace Norton, Charles Eliot Norton's sister, discussed Sainte-Beuve's
women in her Cambridge classes. Miss Norton later published three volumes of essays on Montaigne, papers on his style, his reading, his friends,
his travels, etc. A veritable great lady, as John Jay Chapman recalled her,
she was usually, but not always, "boisterously frank." . . . "Grace gave
Mabel Quincy, as a wedding present, a copy of Montaigne with the
'naughty' pages gummed together. Could there be anything more deliciously droll?"—*Journal of Alice James.*

grown old together. Whatever their limitations were, they formed a critical audience,—if the audience had to be feminine,—for writers of novels; and they promised a new order of things in fiction when they, and other women, seized their pens.* As for Henry James himself, he never forgot the day when Matthew Arnold swam into his ken. He had only just arrived in Boston, and Fields had lent him the manuscript of Arnold's *Essays,* with its classic pages smirched by the printer. All day long, as he lay on the sofa,—for he had injured his back, the injury that prevented his enlisting,—his fancy followed the magic lines that carried him to Heine's Germany, to Oxford, to Paris and to Greece. Henceforth, the Arnoldian categories, the common, the provincial, the Philistine, distinction, the cult of the shade, were invested in his mind with a singular world of overtones that eventually led him far from primary facts.

As for realism, both Howells and James, in later years, qualified their strict adherence to it. Howells developed a vein of fantasy, and James's final phase was remote indeed, in effect, from the note of his prime. Moreover, some of James's first stories were exuberantly romantic in their feeling, *Gabrielle de Bergerac,* for instance. But he soon accepted the realistic method, which he and Howells professed to the end of their lives; and one of the last of James's utterances,—the lecture, *The Lesson of Balzac,*—reiterated the views of his earlier essays. Balzac was still, for him, the "father of us all," to whom every road still came back, as the beginning and end of the novel was the art of representation, based upon observa-

* "If ever we *do* come alongside of you, Mr. Journalist, in artistic and dramatic ability, there will be a new order of things in fiction . . . Is it not generally allowed that women read character more readily than men? . . . Dependence has made them very acute. All dependents are acute. How well your servants know you! And besides, women have had only individuals to deal with and think of and plan for . . . but men have had masses, and such as were quite indifferent to them."—Harriet W. Preston, *Love in the Nineteenth Century.*

tion of actual life. That the novelist was a social historian
was always James's doctrine, and therefore the question
of a terrain was one that he could not ignore. If he could
not represent America, what could he represent? Could
he ever understand another country?

Later, James told a friend that before he settled in
Europe he had given his own country a "good trial." It
was true; but his imagination was so Europeanized that
he could only look for a Europe at home. He had seen
his Cambridge boarding-house in terms of Balzac's Mai-
son Vauquer, and he saw all America in terms of his
reading, just as his cousin Robert Temple, newly returned
from Europe, seemed to him a character "in the sense in
which 'people in books' were characters, and other people,
roundabout us, were somehow not." As America failed to
stir his interest on its own account, he could only recreate
it in accordance with patterns drawn from George Sand,
Thackeray, Mérimée or Balzac. Thus, in *Poor Richard,*
the young New England farmer kisses Gertrude's hand
whenever he meets her, while she, a homespun Yankee,
maintains in her parlour the ritual of an English country-
house. In *De Grey: A Romance,* the American Mrs. De
Grey keeps a priest in the house to serve as her confessor.
In *Crawford's Consistency,* the young girl is brought up
"in the manner of an Italian princess" in a "high-hedged
old garden" in Orange, New Jersey. The hero of *Eugene
Pickering* has been pledged in marriage to the unseen
daughter of his father's friend. The family curse that
hangs over some of these households is very different in
accent from Hawthorne's curse, the good old convincing
curse of Salem. It is a Frenchified curse, as the young men
are Frenchified; for they always say *J'ai vécu* and *Nous
verrons,* when even a travelling Frenchman would have
said "We shall see." James shared Mrs. Follanbee's
weakness: he had "a sort of indefinite faith in French

phrases for mending all the broken places in life." * But
he did his best to follow American models, or the only
American model that he felt as germane. The influence of
Hawthorne was marked in his stories,† and perhaps if
there had existed a great American realist to show the
way for him and interpret the scene,—during his formative years,—James's whole career might have been different. As it was, he could make nothing of the country.
"I believe I should be a good patriot if I could sketch my
native town," one of his characters remarks, in *The Impressions of a Cousin*. "But I can't make a picture of the
brown-stone steps in the Fifth Avenue, or the platform
of the elevated railway in the Sixth . . . I can sketch the
palazzo and can do nothing with the uptown residence."
This was the situation of Henry James.

Long afterwards, living in England, James was to find
that he knew America,—or knew, at least, certain aspects
of it,—as he had never supposed when he lived at home.
He was to produce, in *Washington Square* and *The Bostonians,* brilliantly veracious pictures of it. But, during
these years of indecision, with his alienated mind, he was
wholly out of touch with the life of the country. Politics
and business, the forces that were shaping it, lay outside
his horizon, and he sought for it in places like Newport
and like Saratoga, where almost every thought was of
Paris and London. All that was not European repelled

---

* "You don't know, *mignonne,* how perfectly *ravissante* these apartments
are!" etc.—Mrs. Follanbee, in Harriet Beecher Stowe's *Pink and White
Tyranny.*

† *The Last of the Valerii, The Romance of Certain Old Clothes, A Passionate Pilgrim, The Madonna of the Future* (based on a story of Balzac),
etc.

"It also tickled my national feeling not a little to note the resemblance of
Hawthorne's style to yours and Howells's. . . . That you and Howells with
all the models in English literature to follow should needs involuntarily
have imitated (as it were) this American, seems to point to the existence
of some real American mental quality."—Letter of William James, 1870.

As for Howells, the influence of Hawthorne is most marked in *The Undiscovered Country. The Blithedale Romance* affected Howells most, as
James was especially affected by *The Marble Faun.*

and bored him. He liked to be reminded of old-world drawing-rooms, ambassadors, luxuries and splendours, and he found harsh lights and hard lines, a cold, vacant, undraped scene, without shade, without composition, as one said of pictures.* "I shall freeze after this sun," Albrecht Dürer said, returning to Germany from Venice, and this was James's feeling whenever he turned homeward after one of his visits to Italy or England. The Beacon Street windows were "terrible" to him. Like the baroness in *The Europeans,* after a year in America, he felt the annoyance of a swimmer "who, on nearing shore, to land, finds a smooth, straight wall of rock" instead of a "clean, firm beach." He could not scale this wall, and America was too big and too vague! He felt that his only safety lay in flight.

* "It is very hard, very cold, very vacant. I think of your warm, rich Paris . . . I had no idea how little form there was. I don't know what I shall do; I feel so undraped, so uncurtained, so uncushioned; I feel as if I were sitting in the centre of a mighty 'reflector.' A terrible crude glare is over everything; the earth seems peeled and excoriated; the raw heavens seem to bleed with the quick, hard light . . . When things are so ugly, they should not be so definite; and they are terribly ugly here. There is no mystery in the corners; there is no light and shade in the types. The people are haggard and joyless; they look as if they had no passions, no tastes, no senses . . . I want my little corner of Paris; I want the rich, the deep, the dark old world; I want to be out of this horrible place."—Louis Leverett, in James's *The Point of View* and *A Bundle of Letters.*

CHAPTER XII

HENRY ADAMS

IN 1873, Charles Eliot Norton, after spending five
years in Europe, had returned to Cambridge. Having
settled his summer home on the farm at Ashfield, to bind
himself more closely to the country, he had yielded to the
attraction of England, much in the manner of Motley and
Lowell, and had gone abroad, as it seemed at first, to
stay. With his well-known aptitude for friendship, he resumed his old relations with Ruskin and Dickens and was
soon on intimate terms with Carlyle and Darwin, whose
son married Mrs. Norton's sister. At the end of three or
four years, he seemed to be an established part of the
English literary landscape; and, if he had followed his
tastes, he might well have become so. But Norton personified conscience. The tough moral instinct of the old
Puritan first families, with its train of responsibilities,
possessed his mind. His political sense was strong. He had
shared in the anti-slavery movement; he had met the
problems of immigration by agitating for model lodging-
houses. He could not abandon his country to its own devices. He was convinced that America was on the road to
ruin, and its new developments horrified all his feelings.
All the more, for this reason, America needed a Jeremiah,
and Norton returned with the consciousness of a role to
play.

Thus began, at Harvard, in his chair of the history of
art, Norton's long career as a teacher and prophet, as a
scholar, a censor, a sage. To lay down the law was his

nature. He had laid it down to Ruskin in the matter of his unsteady habits, and he set to work at once to regenerate Harvard; for his cousin, President Eliot, was destroying the college, from the point of view that Norton represented, by embracing the abominations of the road to ruin, the materialistic practicalities through which the nation was losing its grasp of all that was noble and worthy in its own tradition. The delicate Norton, a semi-invalid, spoke for the "royal priesthood" that his forbear, John Norton, had once proclaimed; for, although he had ceased to believe in God, he felt that he spoke the word of God. Authority was authority, and the law was the law. He was an agnostic, like Clough and Leslie Stephen, his intimate English friends of the past and the present, and he even considered that Christianity, with its system of rewards and punishments, was debasing. He felt that Protestantism was an utter failure. But the mood of the Puritan clerical caste survived in his tenacious mind, as the mood of the old French priesthood survived in Renan. Norton remained a priest, with a mission; and since art, along with science, was the new religion, and Norton cared little for science, the nature of his mission was aesthetic. His aesthetic feeling was weak and derivative, but his scholarly feeling was strong, while his ethical feeling dominated all the others; and Ruskin had taught him that art had an ethical basis. To preach art as ethics was thus the soul of Norton's mission, and to preach the scholarly virtues as the soul of art. If the modern world was ugly, the modern world was also base: its baseness and its ugliness went together. Taste alone could redeem it, and taste was therefore Norton's gospel. He preached it as his forbears preached salvation.

He had prepared himself in Italy and England, in constant association with Ruskin's friends, Burne-Jones, Morris and Rossetti; and Carlyle's dictatorial temper had strengthened his own. He had spent long afternoons with the sage of Chelsea, walking or smoking with him in his study, while the old prophet, Emerson's friend, who took a special fancy to Norton, told him the story of his youth. Carlyle gave Norton his mask of Cromwell, and, through him, he later gave to Harvard the books he had used in writing his *Cromwell* and *Frederick*. He had grown to feel that he was mistaken in his views about the Civil War,—which had destroyed his authority in America forever,*—and he wished to express his gratitude to the friends in New England who had formed so large a part of his early readers. Like Ruskin, his family appointed Norton his literary executor; and Norton was confirmed by these two masters in his own contumelious, cavilling habit of mind. In Italy, meanwhile, he had carried on the investigations that he had begun long since in his work on Dante. He spent two years there, preparing for his admirable *Historical Studies of Church-Building in the Middle Ages*. This dealt with the cathedrals of Venice, Siena and Florence. In all these cities, as well as in Rome, Norton worked in the archives, studying the political and social conditions under which the cathedrals arose. He was frail and easily tired, and he felt that his task was rather to teach than to write. He bought Greek vases and bits of Pisan sculpture for Ruskin and helped him in the revision of *Modern Painters;* and in Italy, when Ruskin joined him, he introduced his friend to the *Fioretti* and the other Franciscan writings. Immersed in Italian chronicles and *trecento* lives and letters, Norton, as one later

---

* "Each oracle denies his predecessor, each magician breaks the wand of the one who went before him. There were Americans enough ready to swear by Carlyle until he broke his staff in meddling with our anti-slavery conflict, and buried it so many fathoms deep that it could never be fished up again. It is rather singular that Johnson and Carlyle should each of them have shipwrecked his sagacity and shown a terrible leak in his moral sensibilities on coming in contact with American rocks and currents."— Oliver Wendell Holmes, *Our Hundred Days in Europe*.

"The proof that a philosopher does not know what he is talking about is apt to sadden his followers before it reacts on himself."—*The Education of Henry Adams*.

saw in his further translations of Dante, was a master of mediæval studies.

It was a mediævalist, therefore, who preached from the pulpit at Harvard, where the youthful Henry Adams was established already as professor of mediæval history. For Adams, at a loose end after his foray in Washington, had accepted President Eliot's invitation. He was deep in the study of Viollet-le-Duc and the architecture of the Middle Ages. Norton, as a mediævalist, followed Ruskin, for whom the age of Giotto was the golden age, a reproof, a sublime example for a world of machines and money-madness, a paradise of art and social justice. If Ruskin had known more of economic history,—which no one knew when he began to write,—he would have discovered that the modern system he despised had already begun its career in Giotto's Florence. He would have discovered that Giotto was a usurer, who rented looms himself at exorbitant rates, and that the Florentine guildsmen, the most ruthless exploiters in Europe, were already destroying the life of the handicraft-system. In Venice, built on the slave-trade, and Florence, the manufacturing centre, the modern age was beginning,—just there and just then; and Ruskin's Utopia was itself the fountain-head of all the modern evils he condemned. In order to prove that great art expressed a good society, Ruskin chose an example that was far from apt; for Manchester sprang from Florence as the flower from the bud.* But this did not alter the fact that art is related to social conditions. It did not impugn the art of the age of Giotto!—and Norton, who advanced the study of this art, while he railed at existing conditions, was a useful teacher. His temper, to be sure, was that of an archæologist; he had small feeling for art as a living process. But no one aroused the country more to a sense of its general

---

* See Miriam Beard, *A History of the Business Man,*—statements drawn in part from Davidsohn's *Geschichte von Florenz.*

ugliness and a will to create a beautiful civilization. As an enemy of "numbers" * and "President Grant architecture," as a lover of perfection in details and of every craftsman, as the friend of Olmsted, the maker of parks, as the founder of schools and museums,† Norton deserved his fame as a mentor and leader. Henry James was only one of a series of younger men for whom the great brown study at "Shady Hill," with its manuscripts and paintings, its books and medals, was the scene of their consecration to art or letters.‡

A number of younger Cambridge men, more or less in Norton's circle, shared his aesthetic interests in one form or another. William James, who was teaching psychology, never lost his love of painting; and Oliver Wendell Holmes, the jurist of the future, who was lecturing at present in the Law School, had studied art before he went in for law. This Holmes,—the "second edition,"—had attempted etching and had only given it up when he felt that his etchings had no merit. As for the short, bald, bearded Henry Adams, with his multifarious interests, his interest in art was eager, universal and lasting. The first of Adams's lessons was the lesson of colour: he remembered a yellow kitchen floor on which, at the age of three, he had sat in the sunlight. He never forgot the

---

* When his classes grew so large that his lectures had to be given in Sanders Theatre, Norton observed, as he looked over the throng of students,—who had come, as he knew, for no good purpose,—"This is a sad sight."

Cf. Henry Adams: "I am much disgusted at this"—the size of his classes —"and have become foul and abusive in my language to them, hoping to drive them away."—Letter of 1876.

† Norton founded the Archæological Institute of America, the parent of the American School at Athens and the School of Classical Studies at Rome. The Fogg Museum in Cambridge, with its school of museum-directors, was largely an outgrowth of Norton's presence and teaching.

‡ Among the many eminent students whom Norton greatly influenced were George E. Woodberry, Bernhard Berenson and James Loeb, the founder of the Loeb Classical Library. Mrs. "Jack" Gardner went to Norton's classes, beginning in 1878. Norton and Henry Adams made purchases for Mrs. Gardner's collection, which was chiefly formed by Berenson, Norton's pupil.

greens, reds, blues and purples that haloed his childhood
at Quincy; and later, in his student years, at Dresden, he
had learned the gallery by heart. He had passed a whole
day at Nuremberg, in two of the churches, lying on the
altar-steps and looking at the stained glass windows with
their glorious colours. He had even studied the theory of
painting; he had planned a work on art "to smash the
Greeks;" and, during his years in London, he had often
run over to Paris for a talk with H. H. Richardson, his
friend in college, who was studying architecture at the
Beaux-Arts. This early taste of Adams was to find a
splendid expression later,—he was a collector at the moment; and, in fact, in aesthetic perception and feeling,
Adams excelled the scholarly Norton. So, for the matter
of that, did James and Holmes.* But art was only one
of their many interests. What their central interest was,
the interest of the younger men,—whether history, philosophy, science, art or letters,—it might have been hard to
say. Taking "mental photographs," perhaps. This was
Chauncey Wright's favourite game, which he played with
the Cambridge young ladies till 2 A.M., leaving them entranced, amid their "shivers of sleepiness," with the
words, "I see you keep the same late hours." These psychological questionnaires struck the note of the place and
the moment,† the note of James's lectures and his brother's
stories; and, though Henry Adams found Cambridge a
"social desert," ‡ it flowed with intellectual milk and

* "Talk about a green thought in a green shade. Dante's paradise is
white on white on white—like a dish of certain tulips in the spring."—
From a letter of Justice Holmes.

† "Does Mrs. Saintsbury like me?" asked Dan. "Well, she's awfully
nice. Don't you think she's awfully fond of formulating people?"
"Oh, everybody in Cambridge does that. They don't gossip; they merely
accumulate materials for the formulation of character."—Howells, *April
Hopes*.

‡ "Several score of the best-educated, most agreeable, and personally the
most sociable people in America united in Cambridge to make a social
desert that would have starved a polar bear . . . Society was a faculty-
meeting without business."—*The Education of Henry Adams*.

honey. Adams who had spent his youth in the social oasês of London and Paris, at court balls and royal garden-parties, would have found Oxford as much of a desert as Cambridge; and Henry James, whose mind was full of the same oases, was taking steps to leave it, for this reason. "Poor nudified and staring Cambridge" was not for him.* Even William James complained of the "buttoned-up Boston respectable character," the "middle-aged tone" of the club he had formed with his friends. The Cambridge manner was certainly staid, uncomfortably for the older man,† absurdly for the younger and more vivacious.‡ Cambridge was not a social oasis, but the older men, assembled there, had made it a preëminent centre for thinkers; § and the younger men vied with the older. Howells, Thomas Sergeant Perry and Henry James, at intervals, appeared at William James's club, with Henry Adams, John Fiske, Alexander Agassiz, Chauncey Wright, Charles S. Peirce and Holmes. The subject of one of the evenings was John Fiske's *Cosmic Philosophy,* and the author, who was present with his friends, quietly went to sleep under their noses. Once, at a livelier meeting, Charles Peirce announced the name and the doctrine of pragmatism. The principle of this new philosophy lay unnoticed for many years until William James exposed it for all to see.

* "Life here in Cambridge—or in this house, at least—is about as lively as the inner sepulchre . . . [Social relaxation] is not to be obtained in Cambridge—or only a ghastly simulacrum of it. There are no 'distractions' here . . . Likewise 'calling.' Upon whom?"—Letter of Henry to William James, 1867.

† "Dr. Palfrey remarked at Cambridge, when we talked of the manners of Wordsworth and Coleridge, that there seemed to be no such thing as a conventional manner among the eminent men of England, for these people lived in the best society, yet each indulged the strongest individual peculiarities."—Emerson's *Journals.*

‡ See Henry Adams's comment on his meeting with Swinburne: "One felt the horror of Longfellow and Emerson, the doubts of Lowell and the humour of Holmes at the wild Walpurgis-night of Swinburne's talk."

§ "Mr. Charles Darwin once said in a letter that he thought there were clustered round Harvard University enough minds of ability to furnish forth all England's universities."—T. G. Appleton, *Checquer-Work.*

As for William James, who was living with his parents, he developed much more slowly than his brother Henry. More vividly bright, as people said, and prompter in his human responses, he had too many sympathies and interests to be able to focus his mind at once. He had emerged from his long depression, the suicidal state of panic fear in which he had lived for a lustrum. His temperament was psychopathic; he was always subject to nervous breakdowns; he was neurasthenic, at intervals, for the rest of his life. This organization and all it entailed, in the way of experience and insight, opened his mind to the souls of abnormal people. It deepened his moral perception,— *The Varieties of Religious Experience* bore witness to this; * and psychology, in the meantime, gave him a footing. He was already advancing on a firm foundation. He was publishing valuable papers. Years were to pass before he produced a major work, and all his major work, in fact, appeared at a time when he supposed his career was over. He had reason to believe in the "energies of men," the latent powers that one so seldom uses,—it took so long for him to find his own. But all his traits were clearly marked already. Chivalrous, curious, courageous, he was eager and also unstable and easily bored. He seemed to be "born fresh every morning," as Alice James noted in her journal, but he could not stick to things "for the sake of sticking." Impulsive and spontaneous, he was keenly ready for everything new, a lover of adventure, risks and hazards; and, with his tough and sinewy mind, he was quick in his feelings and deeply compassionate.

* "When a superior intellect and a psychopathic temperament coalesce . . . in the same individual, we have the best possible condition for the kind of effective genius that gets into the biographical dictionaries . . . In the psychopathic temperament we have the emotionality which is the *sine qua non* of moral perception; we have the intensity and tendency to emphasis which are the essence of practical moral vigour; and we have the love of metaphysics and mysticism which carry one's interests below the surface of the sensible world."—William James, *The Varieties of Religious Experience.*

As he stooped over a poor dog, strapped on a board for vivisection, he felt that he must pay something back to life for every jet of pain that he was causing. All the dogs were under-dogs to James. He liked to run his own risks. He liked to use himself as a *corpus vile,* experimenting with mescal and nitrous-oxide gas as readily as with Yoga and mental healing. His delight in human nature was acute and unending, and all his doors and windows opened outwards, as he said of the house at Chocorua that he built in the eighties. In his boyhood, Mayne Reid's tales of out-of-door adventure had impressed him with the virtue of field-observers. To Reid, the "closet-naturalists," the collectors and the classifiers, the handlers of skeletons and skins, were contemptible beside the men who observed the ways of living animals; and James, as a psychologist, followed Reid. He had thought, as a child, that a "closet-naturalist" must be the vilest kind of wretch, and Agassiz had confirmed this fixed impression. So James was wary of generalizations, abstractions, preconceived ideas,* and sought for facts voraciously, the tame and the "wild." He sought them in the highways, he sought them in the byways and even in shady corners where conventional thinkers would not have believed their eyes if they had found them. He had a passion for physiognomy. He collected portraits of interesting men, as he praised his friends in proportion as they differed from him. This suppleness and catholicity, joined with his cosmopolitan outlook, were to make him a prince of psychologists, as time went on. Meanwhile, at the core of his being, James was religious. He had a poet's feeling for the marvel of existence, and he had hours of rapture akin to Whitman's. In the woods, in the fields, on the rocks at Magnolia, with the perfume of the laurels

---

* "One must know concrete instances first; for, as Professor Agassiz used to say, one can see no farther into a generalization than just so far as one's previous acquaintance with particulars enables one to take it in"—William James, *The Varieties of Religious Experience.*

and the roses, with the breath of the pines in his lungs and the surf in his ears, he felt, in the beautiful wash of light, the mystical union with Deity that still filled Emerson also with awe and courage.

At the moment, William James had scarcely begun to climb his ladder. Holmes was two or three rungs beyond him, and, as for Chauncey Wright, he had scaled his ladder to the summit. Chauncey Wright's short life was all but over. These novices and friends had much in common. It was William James's hope that philosophers might come to grips, as closely as realistic novelists, with the facts of life. This was Holmes's hope in regard to the law, for Holmes was a realist also; and nothing existed for Chauncey Wright,—the "great mind of a village," as James described him in a later essay,—but facts, facts, facts. The balder and barer the better! He had no use for metaphysics: experiment and description, for him, were the whole of thinking. All three agreed in distrusting abstractions; they all suspected general terms.* Holmes was already preparing his great work, *The Common Law,* in which he described the life of the law as experience, not logic. This idea of jurisprudence,—once a self-sufficient science, with traditions handed down as it were from Sinai,—was to make Holmes later, as John Morley said, "the greatest judge of the English-speaking world." The need of "thinking things rather than words" was the essence of Holmes's teaching, as of James's also, —although Holmes's words, for the rest, were bright new coins. He had been encouraged to mint them in his earliest childhood. His father, the Autocrat, had made it a rule at the breakfast-table to reward a well-phrased observation with an extra helping of marmalade; and Holmes, for ninety years, had things to say, on literature, philosophy, art and science, that were better than almost anything said by others. Chauncey Wright was a

* "No generalization is wholly true, not even this one."—Justice Holmes.

brilliant talker also.* He was famous for his Socratic
sessions with William James and the elder Henry, and
he fascinated the younger Henry James with his searching characterizations of people. A poor young man from
Northampton, Wright was a bosom-friend of the Jameses
and the Nortons and a local sage and character who was
second to none. A tutor and a lecturer, he wrote in the
North American, but he supported himself by computing
for the *Nautical Almanac,* compiled in Cambridge. He
devised new ways of computing, for he was a mathematical genius, and he forced the work of a year into two
strained months. No one saw him then, and he saw neither
sunlight nor moonlight; but he emerged from his cave
with time to burn. He walked and talked for weeks at
Mount Desert; he philosophized all over the Franconia
mountains. Once he went abroad for a visit to Darwin,
who had brought out one of his essays as a pamphlet in
England; and he remarked that "Paris was as good as
Cambridge,"—perhaps to annoy Henry James. A big
man, with mild blue eyes, somewhat sluggish and inert,
he was remote, slow, melancholy, but not unfriended; he
was shy, but he was serene; he was simple and frugal,
and his freedom from all cares and wants, material and
mental, reminded the Cambridge circle of the antique
sages. Like them, and like Emerson, he slighted books
and reading; indeed, as he never read, the wonder grew,
—he seemed to know much more than if he had. This
lonely soliloquizer, with his corncob pipe, excelled by the
sheer, bleak power of unaided thought. But he was a lover
of children, and, like Thoreau, he delighted in entertaining them with magic and juggling. He was a master at

---

* "A lad is a boy with a man's hand on his head." This is almost the
only surviving relic of Chauncey Wright's conversation, which reminded
the Cambridge circle of De Quincey and Coleridge. His phrase "cosmical
weather" also survives. Chauncey Wright's *Letters* suggest, better perhaps
than anything else, the intellectual atmosphere of Cambridge in the early
seventies. His philosophical essays were collected and published by Charles
Eliot Norton.

sleight-of-hand, and he used his mathematical genius to invent and exhibit all manner of puzzles and games. There were no Christmas parties like those of the Nortons at "Shady Hill," where Chauncey Wright was busy with his marvels and Child and his three little girls performed old ballads, which they turned into Robin Hood plays with their gestures and costumes.

Once Wright and John Fiske tired the moon with talking, as they strolled from each other's lodgings, back and forth. A dozen times they made the double journey, till the sun rose over their discourse. Fiske was turning from philosophy to history, as history was also turning from art to science. He was already beginning his historical studies. Indeed, he had begun them years before, and it was Henry Adams's post that he had hoped to have when Eliot dropped Fiske in favour of Adams. Fiske was too "'irreligious" to please the college, and no one knew that Adams was ten times more so.* As for the new historical mode, it harmonized with the Cambridge mind in novel-writing, psychology, philosophy, law. The day of the Prescotts and Motleys and Parkmans was passing. Parkman continued to write, and better than ever, in the shadowy Boston study where he rode his chair. He pursued his Canadian history, volume by volume, and his method, so realistic and so solid, compelled the regard of all. The more one insisted on "documents," the more one had to bow to him, and his thoroughness put the scientists on their mettle. He had six thousand folio pages carefully copied for one of his volumes,—from the French archives alone, not to speak of the English. While all this was true, he had no feeling for evolution; and he had a romantic belief in the "great man theory." He was a lover of heroes, and the kind of heroes,—adventurers,

---

* Like George Strong, in his novel *Esther,*—the geologist who was drawn from Clarence King,—Adams "looked at churches very much as he would have looked at a layer of extinct oysters in a buried mud-bank."

soldiers of fortune,—for whom an age of prose had little use. He, in turn, despised his age, an emasculate generation of policemen and bankers,—but the line of Scott
and Byron could go no further. The bankers, the policemen and the younger intellectuals were bored by sieges,
marches and clashes of arms. Spencer had destroyed the
"great man theory," as John Fiske, for one, rejoiced to
say.* To understand conspicuous men was not to understand their times, and "decisive battles" had ceased to
seem decisive. Meanwhile, Comte had established the
notion of the "laws of historical development," along the
lines of any other science. The environment, the mass-
psyche, the mores of the group seemed more important
now than the intrigues of courts, and the new generation
of students found the turning-points of history in the
cumulative action of causes minute but incessant. They
examined social institutions, legal theory, public law, and
they took the whole of society as their field and their subject. In temper, they resembled the realistic novelists,—
they were sober, objective collectors and arrangers of
facts. They shrank from generalizations as much as William James or Holmes; they distrusted and avoided
moral judgments. They looked at questions from every
side. They scrutinized their witnesses. They tried to
divest themselves of the party spirit, political, economic
or religious. It was their aspiration to let the "sources"
speak for themselves, to present a neutral mind to the
past and its persons. They were to mirror reality in their
placid pages. In short, they approached the phenomena
of history as biologists and physicists approached their
fields. It scarcely occurred to historians for a long generation that they were not, completely, men of science.

This was the note of historical studies when John
Fiske and Henry Adams began their career as historians

* See Fiske's essay, *Sociology and Hero-Worship,* written in reply to
William James's *Great Men and Their Environment,* 1880.

in the Cambridge setting. That history, if not an exact science, might in time become so,—such was the current belief, such was the programme. Years later, Henry Adams thought the laws of history paralleled the laws of physics, obviously and strictly. He even identified history with thermo-dynamics,—he believed he had the science "in his ink-stand." Just then, for various reasons, this theory exploded; and, in fact, neither Adams nor Fiske, in their actual writings,—as historians, not theorists on the subject,—paid any special regard to these fanciful laws. Fiske, as an evolutionist, saw in American history a chance to illustrate his favourite doctrine; and this, although he profited by the "scientific" method, was his only major tribute to historical "science." Fiske's opportunity sprang from his present labours. As one of the Harvard librarians, he catalogued the books and pamphlets that dealt with American history, an immense collection. With his zeal for order, he worked wonders for the library and incidentally read the books and pamphlets. He found himself in possession of a theme forever. In 1878, to enlarge his income, he began to give public lectures in the Old South Church; and henceforth writing American history and lecturing about it became the central interest of his life. As a lecturer, the genial Fiske, the hirsute, bespectacled mammoth with his hearty manner, with his gift for elucidation, was a master-performer. Spencer said he had never heard such "glorious" lectures as Fiske's, when he spoke, under Huxley's auspices, in London;* and the "Fiske season" rivalled Barnum's, in the years to come, when he tumbled all over the country, as far as Denver. He aroused in the population a zest for American history, which the Centennial celebrations had already awakened. The public had lost its interest in the

---

* Huxley, always generous and often just, said that Fiske's first lecture on American Political Ideas was the best lecture he had ever heard at the Royal Institution.

long, close-woven, detailed studies of the writers of the older generation. It averred that what it lacked was the time to read them, though what it really lacked was pride in the country,—it had lost all interest in the past. The vogue of historical writing had vanished. The prevailing indifference to Parkman proved it; for Parkman's histories appeared in small editions, as small as seven hundred copies, where Prescott had had his tens of thousands of readers, and Henry Adams was soon to find how small the public was for works on a scale that Parkman took for granted. Adams's history, all but ignored by the press, never achieved even a second edition. John Fiske was the exception that proved the rule: he found as many readers as Prescott or Motley. For his books were broad surveys that simplified his subjects; and, with his light, attractive, flowing style, he was an unexampled popularizer. He was a relief after the Bancrofts and Hildreths and much more literary than the men who followed, James Ford Rhodes and Edward Channing. Readable, approachable, variously learned, he placed his country in relation to the history of the world, for he knew more than his predecessors about its earliest origins in the primitive life of the continent and the life of Europe. He traced the growth of American institutions as Darwin traced the origin of species. For the rest, his works were episodic, and they followed the exigencies of the lecture-platform. They were written piecemeal in the course of a rough-and-tumble career that left small time or energy for research or thinking. Fiske was unable to carry out his plan for a monumental work to cover American history from end to end; but one of his books, at least, *The Discovery of America,* possessed the weight and scope of a major creation.

All this lay in the future. Fiske had not yet begun his historical writing, and Henry Adams had written only occasional papers when he took up his teaching at Harvard. Five years passed before Adams turned to American history; and he spent only seven years in Cambridge and Boston. Then he returned to Washington to live for the rest of his life and to write the books that made him famous later. Meanwhile, he established the German historical method, and the so-called seminar method, in his classes at Harvard. He had studied law in Germany,— he had even planned to be a lawyer,—and he stressed the legal aspect of the Middle Ages, the early German, Norman and Anglo-Saxon institutions, along with domestic life and architecture. His course, beginning with primitive man, continued through the Salic Franks to the Norman English. In order to arouse his students, he rode roughshod over their prejudices and fixed ideas, and he gave them special subjects, well-chosen for each, to follow and examine for themselves. In 1875–6, he offered a course in American history. In 1877, he resigned. That Adams was a great teacher all his pupils affirmed later, and Henry Cabot Lodge, afterwards the senator, never forgot the stormy careers of the great German emperors and the struggles of papacy and empire. Henry Adams had burned them into his mind. Lodge was one of the pupils who became historians, under the tutelage of Adams; and, although he soon dropped history for politics, he produced a number of competent books.* Adams, who had married in the meantime, continued to pursue his other interests. He travelled, he geologized, he collected,—Palgrave and Woolner in London had encour-

* Henry Cabot Lodge's chief works were *A Short History of the English Colonies in America* and lives of Washington, Hamilton and Webster. He edited the nine volumes of Hamilton's writings. As a devoted Hamiltonian, he carried on the line of the Federalists of an earlier Boston. Shortly after opening his political career, he campaigned against "Ben" Butler's governorship. As Bishop Lawrence said, Lodge was the David who fought on the side of "all the powers of respectability and virtue" and slew this Goliath. Compare with this the later opinion of Adams, who was Lodge's life-long friend: "The true type of successful cant, which rests on no belief at all, is Cabot, who grabs everything, and talks pure rot to order."
—*Letters of Henry Adams, 1892–1918.*

aged this taste. He was a tireless purchaser of water-colours, drawings, Greek terra-cottas, bronzes, Spanish leather. As for geology, Agassiz's lectures had aroused this interest in him, and Lyell, a friend of his family, had confirmed it in England. He spent days and nights geologizing; and this led him to Colorado in 1871, where he met his friend Clarence King. As for travel, his wandering habits of later years were established in this earlier time at Harvard.* But politics transcended these other interests. All the Adams idols had been statesmen, and this was a family inheritance that he could not escape. He had grown up in the shadow of presidents; he had visited the White House at twelve; he had lived among politicians all his life, whether in Washington or London. He had read, as a child, for proof-correction, the writings of John Adams, which his father had been editing for publication; and winter after winter, every day, as he worked at his Latin grammar in his father's study, he had heard the elder Adams, with Dana, Sumner and Palfrey, discussing anti-slavery politics. He had copied his father's speeches for the press, and Sumner and Seward might have been his uncles. He had lived on comradely terms with half of President Johnson's cabinet, and Bright and Cobden in England were familiars of his household. No other young American, except perhaps another Adams, had ever been so steeped in politics, and some sort of connection with politics was inevitable for him. He had received, with his Harvard appointment, the editorship of the *North American,* which had become with time a family trust of the younger patrician Bostonians; and, with Lodge as assistant editor, he found himself deeper in politics than ever before. He even tried to arrange to buy the Boston *Advertiser,* to start an

---

* As early as 1873, Adams referred in a letter to his "fifteen years of knocking about the world, in every city and nearly every wilderness between Salt Lake City and the Second Cataract of the Nile."

independent-liberal party. His "vast and ambitious projects for the future" took him to New York and Washington often. The reformer was still strong in him, and his
first foray in Washington had not convinced him that his
case was hopeless. Indeed, he had high hopes of political
success.* He wished to attack the caucus-system, the heart
of party-organization, as the source of the worst corruption in the existing parties. His was a party of no-party,
representing the nation over the sections, defending free-
trade against the bankers and civil-service reform against
the machines. It was a continuation of the Adams programme. Henry Adams and his friends chose Carl Schurz
to lead this party, but the mores of the time were all
against them. Schurz left them in the lurch and returned
to the Republicans, and Adams recoiled from political
action forever.

Such was Adams's outer life, during these years at
Harvard. The historical writings that followed were outgrowths of it; or, rather, American history was in Adams's
bones, as Puss in Boots, Bluebeard and Cinderella were
bred in the bones of other children. Part of it was Adams
history and most that was not Adams had reached him
through a thousand early channels. His happiest hours
in childhood, in the farmhouse at Quincy, were passed as
he lay, in summer, reading Scott, on a heap of congressional documents,—he day-dreamed on musty documents
as others on hay. Along with the materials, he had the
models. His father's shelves were stocked with historians,
and none of the Adamses ever forgot the haircloth
rocking-chair in the house in Boston where they pored
over Gibbon and Macaulay by the fire in the grate. Henry
and his brothers, Charles Francis and Brooks, had all
read history more than anything else. When, therefore,

* "I look forward to the day when we shall be in power again as not far
distant . . . We will play for high stakes."—Letters of Henry Adams, 1870,
1875.

in 1877, the year of Adams's resignation, the papers of Albert Gallatin were placed in his hands, the retiring professor knew how to use them well. His life of the statesman-financier was published in 1879, together with three volumes of Gallatin's writings. He found this father of American ethnology, who had once been instructor in French at Harvard, a highly sympathetic subject; but he made no reparation to the hero of his following book, a brilliant ancient enemy of the house of Adams. The bitter *John Randolph* appeared in 1882, when Adams was already preparing for his magnum opus, the *History of the United States* * that occupied his mind until it was published at last at the turn of the nineties. After leaving Harvard, he had gone abroad to work in the archives of London, Madrid and Paris, studying the diplomatic aspect of American history of the years 1800–1812. He had a desk, in Washington, at the Department of State, with access to its documents and records. At about this time, George Bancroft, the patriarch of American history, had also returned to Washington for the evening of his days. It was at Bancroft's table in Berlin that Adams had met Mommsen and Curtius; and the old man, retired from diplomacy, though he plodded away at his history still, rejoiced in his vote of admission to the floor of the Senate. Bancroft's position was unique in the capital: he was the only private citizen at whose house the President dined. At eighty, as at eighty-eight, he worked fourteen hours a day; and this tough old survivor of Jackson's times set the pace for other and tenderer Yankees. He was an example to less dedicated spirits,—Henry Adams, for one, whose energy flagged.† Adams, meanwhile, hobnobbed freely with senators, generals, ambassadors, in

---

* During the administrations of Jefferson and Madison, 1801–1817; nine volumes, 1889–1891.

† One of Adams's friends said later that she had stirred him into a spasm of activity by telling him how many candles Bancroft used while writing before breakfast.

whose hands the political history of the present lay. He
was at home in Washington as never in Boston. The
Adamses had always been at war with Boston; they had
always preferred all-American relations and contacts,
and Henry Adams had never felt that he was a true Bostonian,—Boston, for him, was a "bore." He had liked
the Virginians at Harvard: a son of General Lee was
his special friend there. Besides, he had always liked
Washington,—even his father had felt its singular charm.
The summer alone had reconciled him to Quincy in his
childhood, the smell of the hot pine-woods and the new-
mown hay, the peaches, the lilacs, the syringas, the taste
of the pennyroyal and the flagroot, the sweet-fern in the
scorching summer noon. At Washington, the Potomac
squandered beauty, and he loved the soft, full outlines of
the landscape, the sunshine and shadow in May and the
heavy odours, the catalpa, the azalea, the laurel, the
chestnuts. He was at home in the brooding heat of the
profligate vegetation, sensual, animal, elemental, the indolence of the Negro population, the looseness and lazi-
ness and the Southern drawl, the want of barriers and
forms, the absence of pavements, women with bandanas,
pigs in the streets. The freedom and the swagger of nature and man captivated his Yankee imagination. As the
men to whom he was drawn through life were the happy,
unconscious, objective types, men like Clarence King and
"Roony" Lee, as he was drawn, above all and through
all, to women,—to those who did not reason and think
about themselves, who were not introspective like himself,—so he was always and everywhere at home in the
tropics.* He had affirmed in 1860, "I shall make up my
bed in Washington;" and in 1868 he had repeated that
he was settled in Washington "perhaps for life." It was

* "A good, rotten tropical Spanish island, like Cuba, with no roads and
no drainage, but plenty of bananas and brigands, never bores me."—Letter
of 1894.

natural for him to return there, "as stable-companion to statesmen." But he did not break his tie with Massachusetts. As long as his wife lived, he spent the summer in Beverly, where the Adamses had a cottage among the pines. Every day at noon, when he rose from his work there, a few more beautiful pages lay on his desk; for his handwriting was really beautiful,—the letters were carved and interlaced, as in some manuscript of the Middle Ages. In the afternoon, with his wife, he went off riding through the woods. Three terriers tumbled about the feet of the horses.

So much for Adams's outer life. He found history "wildly interesting," and he seemed to be a happy and successful author. Behind this mask, however, another life went on. Adams was deeply dissatisfied. He had not wished to be a professor,* and even historical writing, which he enjoyed for a time, soon palled upon him. His history was a masterly performance. With its easy and confident style, its wealth of portraits, its singularly unprejudiced point of view, with its long historical perspective and its rigorous standards, this monumental work was beyond all praise; or, rather, its only drawback was that the subject,—a passage of sixteen years,—was not sufficiently large for the abundance of the treatment. But Adams wearied of the task before it was finished. Later he explained this lapse of interest by saying that he could "make life work" no longer,† which meant that his life

* "He broke his life in halves again in order to begin a new education, on lines he had not chosen, in subjects for which he cared less than nothing, in a place he did not love, and before a future which repelled."— *The Education of Henry Adams.*
"My engagement [as professor] is for five years, but I don't expect to remain so long."—Letter of 1870.

† "You find my last two volumes more critical—deliberately fault finding?—than the earlier ones. They were written chiefly within the last five or six years, and in a very different frame of mind from that in which the work was begun. I found it hard to pretend either sympathy or interest in my subject. If you compare the tone of my first volume—even toned down, as it is, from the original—with that of the ninth when it appears, you

was not in writing, that he was not a historian as Parkman was; for nothing, neither ill-health, personal tragedy, popular failure, ever destroyed in Parkman the zest of the artist. It was true that Adams continued to write; in fact, in his desultory way, he wrote better than ever. He wrote his best two books towards the end of his life. If he could not "make life work," it was not as a writer. And yet he described himself and his life as a failure. Evidently, to write fine books was not to be a "success," for him. What was his standard, then? What did he wish?

What Adams desired was power, like Mrs. Lightfoot Lee, in *Democracy*,* a very different ambition from that of the artist. The Adamses had possessed power, and the will-to-power was a family trait that governed Henry Adams's every instinct. He had taken the White House for granted as a boy. Did he wish for office? He sometimes said so.† But, generally speaking, what he desired was to rule from behind the scenes; and this was his motive in writing,—it had always been so. Although he liked to write, and had early thought of history and fiction,‡ he had never thought of writing as an end in itself. Liter-

will feel that the light has gone out. I am not to blame. As long as I could make life work, I stood by it, and swore by it as though it was my god, as indeed it was."—Letter of 1891.

* "What she wanted was Power . . . It was the feeling of a passenger on an ocean steamer whose mind will not give him rest until he has been in the engine-room and talked with the engineer. She wanted to see with her own eyes the action of primary forces; to touch with her own hand the massive machinery of society; to measure with her own mind the capacity of the motive power. She was bent upon getting to the heart of the great American mystery of democracy and government."—Henry Adams, *Democracy*. Mrs. Lee did not wish merely to understand these things. She wished to have her hand "on the lever."

† "They [Hay's letters] are interesting to me—more so than my own *Education;* for he did what I set out to do, only I could never have done it."—Letter of 1907.

‡ "But how of greater literary works? Could I write a history, do you think, or a novel?"—Letter of 1859.

ature, beside politics, was small beer for Adams;* he
wished to exercise influence and govern opinion.† Not to
be a power, not to live up to the family pattern,‡ this
was ashes in his mouth; for in all his fantasies, whimsical
or otherwise, he always saw himself as the cock of the
walk. If he dreamed of being a monk, then he was the
abbot; § and he felt that a cardinal's hat might well have
become him.‖ He wrote for "prizes," ¶ he wrote to "win a
place" for himself.** "If he worked at all, it was for social
consideration," and this he even supposed was the motive
of artists,—as if Emerson and Winslow Homer, Ryder
and Emily Dickinson "found their return in the pride
of their social superiority"! *** That one could work

* "Of *Atlantic Monthly* and *Putnam* and *Harper* and the men who write
for money in them, my opinion is short. Rather than do nothing but that, or
make that an object in life, I'd die here in Europe."—Letter of 1858.
See also his later remark in London: "So I am happy and contented to
think that at all events I am not bored by Andrew Lang, and Gosse and
Sidney Colvin."—Letter of 1892. Compare this with his interest in politicians. Every minnow of a politician, economist or diplomat unfailingly
interested Adams.

† He "began what he meant for a permanent series of annual political
reviews which he hoped to make, in time, a political authority . . . Whether
the newspapers liked it or not, they would have to reckon with him; for
such a power, once established, was more effective than all the speeches in
Congress or reports to the President that could be crammed into the government presses."—*The Education of Henry Adams.*

‡ "Were you intoxicated when you wrote that I am to 'combine in myself
the qualities of Seward, Greeley and Everett'?"—Letter to his brother,
1858.

§ "If we lived a thousand years ago instead of now, I should have become a monk and would have got hold as abbot of one of those lovely little
monasteries which I used to admire so much among the hills in Italy."—
Letter of 1863.

‖ "The only thing I wanted in life was to be made a cardinal, and in
Rome I sounded delicately the pontifical ocean to ascertain the bearings of
my hat."—Letter of 1899.

¶ "I am satisfied that literature offers higher prizes than politics."—Letter
of 1877.

** "His object was literary. He wanted to win a place on the staff of the
Edinburgh Review, under the vast shadow of Lord Macaulay; and, to a
young American in 1868, such rank seemed colossal—the highest in the
literary world . . . The position . . . flattered vanity."—*The Education of
Henry Adams.*

*** "Thus far, no one had made a suggestion of pay for any work that
Adams had done or would do; if he worked at all, it was for social con-

for anything but "reputation," even in public life, he could
scarcely imagine;* and in dealing with his pupils he had
urged this motive.† Such was his standard, and, measured
by this, of course he himself was a failure. He had failed
as a king-maker. He failed as a writer, for his publications attracted little attention. Was this not why he could
not "make life work"?

Vanity, in short, was Henry Adams's governing motive,‡ as one saw in the anonymity to which he resorted.
If he could not have fame at once, he would not play. He
had failed in politics because he would not stoop to conquer. He refused to accept the terms of political action.
He wished for "a career in which social position had
value," and without this impossible advantage he refused
to fight. "He wanted it handed to him on a silver plate,"§

sideration, and social pleasure was his pay. For this he was willing to go
on working, as an artist goes on painting when no one buys his pictures.
Artists have done it from the beginning of time, and will do it after time
has expired, since they cannot help themselves, and they find their return
in the pride of their social superiority as they feel it."—*The Education of
Henry Adams.*

* Length of service has much to do with future reputation, and if you
did not take office for reputation, what the deuce did you take it for?"—
Letter to John Hay, 1899.

† "The question is whether the historico-literary line is practically worth
following, not whether it will amuse or improve you. Can you make it
pay? either in money, reputation, or any other solid value ... Now if you
will think for a moment of the most respectable and respected products of
our town of Boston, I think you will see at once that this profession does
pay. No one has done better and won more in any business or pursuit, than
has been acquired by men like Prescott, Motley, Frank Parkman, Bancroft,
and so on in historical writing. ... Further, there is a great opening here
at this time. Boston is running dry of literary authorities. Any one who
has the ability can enthrone himself here as a species of literary lion with
ease, for there is no rival to contest the throne. With it, comes social dignity, European reputation, and a foreign mission to close."—Letter to Henry
Cabot Lodge, 1872.

‡ "For I am, as you have often truly said, a mass of affectation and vanity."—Letter to his brother Charles. This may have been said in irony,—it
was certainly true.

§ "I think of [Justice] Holmes as mostly keeping the doors of his sympathy open, and of Adams as mostly keeping them shut.

" 'If the country had put him on a pedestal,' said Holmes to me once, 'I

without descending into the rough-and-tumble; and, similarly, when publication failed to yield the longed-for prize, Adams ceased to write for publication. He had refused to write anonymously as long as he thought his name might count,* but all his later work was written so, or, if it was not anonymous, it was privately printed; † and that his motive was not indifference one saw in the curiosity with which he watched the sales of his two novels. He was immensely elated by the success of *Democracy,* much as he professed to despise the public,‡ and regarded its wholesale piracy as the triumph of his life.§ One saw the same inverted pride in his attitude towards honours, which he invariably refused in later years. Only a man who cared for them excessively could have found such ingenious reasons for declining these honours. President Eliot understood him well.‖

Writing for Adams was therefore a makeshift, and yet the thing that he was born for. What else could he have

think that Henry Adams with his gifts could have rendered distinguished public service.'

" 'What was the matter with Henry Adams?' I asked.

" 'He wanted it handed to him on a silver plate,' said Holmes.

"Now Holmes had gone after 'it' tooth and nail."

—Owen Wister, *Roosevelt, the Story of a Friendship.*

* "I will not go down into the rough-and-tumble, nor mix with the crowd, nor write anonymously, except for mere literary practice."—Letter of 1869.

† "As you may have noticed, I have not published anything since 1890 . . . I have privately printed, but never published."—Letter of 1916.

His novel *Democracy* was published anonymously. *Esther* was published under the pseudonym Frances Snow Compton. *The Memoirs of Arii Taimai* were privately printed under his Tahitian name. In the *Life of George Cabot Lodge,* his name was printed on the fly-leaf but not on the title-page. The *Education* and *Mont-Saint-Michel and Chartres* were privately printed in very small editions for his friends.

‡ "I hate publishing, and do not want reputation. There are not more than a score of people in America whose praise I want."—Letter of 1893.

§ "As for piracy, I love to be pirated. It is the greatest compliment an author can have. The wholesale piracy of *Democracy* was the single real triumph of my life."—Letter of 1905.

‖ When he refused an honorary degree at Harvard, President Eliot wrote to Adams: "To decline it would require a thousand explanations—to accept it is natural and modest."

done? What could he have been? Certainly not a statesman. He was not aggressive enough for this. Nor was he
in temper a reformer. He had no zest for the role of an
oppositionist; and, disliking the tendencies of the age he
lived in, he still enjoyed their fruits too much to fight
them. He had too deep a stake in the welfare of banks
and stock-exchanges, he was too fond of "luxury as a
steady business;" * and, while he abhorred the politics of
John Hay and Cabot Lodge, these two remained his constant companions and friends. In fact, he developed a
hatred of reformers, and he could scarcely find words to
express his contempt for those who tried to carry out in
action the ideals he had represented in earlier days. Were
not Theodore Roosevelt, La Follette and Woodrow Wilson attempting, in terms of their day, what he had tried
to do in 1870? He regarded them all as bores, insane and
dishonest. But, feeling that he should have been a statesman, that he ought to have been a reformer, that he
ought to have carried on the Adams line, he could not
feel that writing justified him. Writing amused him, and,
because he had a first-rate mind and the pride of an excellent craftsman, he wrote admirable books. But in motive
he was always a dilettante.

* "I am not so easy about the coal-strike and labour-troubles in Europe,
because they may bother me. I keep my eye fixed on the stock-exchange,"
etc. . . . "After all, I do like luxury as a steady business . . . As a man of
sense I am a gold-bug and support a gold-bug government and a gold-bug
society."—From letters of Henry Adams.

CHAPTER XIII

HENRY JAMES

HENRY JAMES had crossed and recrossed the Atlantic, trying to solve his great dilemma, whether
to live at home or to live in Europe. In 1875, he settled
in Paris, and it seemed at first that he meant to remain
there forever. The writers he most admired were living
there, and Paris was the best of meeting-places in which
to view his countrymen abroad. He had concluded that
the "international novel" was the type that he was qualified to write;* and where were the auspices happier for
a writer of novels?

So, for a twelvemonth, Henry James lived in Paris, in
constant association with La Farge's friends, the novelists whom he had studied with rapture at home. Howells
had agreed with his comments on the English novel,
which had everything to learn in the matter of handling,
of artistic treatment and form;† and James had all but
worshipped these French writers, with their instinct for

---

* This "conclusion," practical if not deliberate, was a natural outgrowth
of James's childhood and the atmosphere of the James family. The patriotic father "overflowed with the bravest sort of contradictions," and, while
he disdained what he called "this fumbling in the cadaver of the old
world," he encouraged the comparison of different European countries and
of them all with America. Louis Leverett, in Henry James's *A Bundle of
Letters,* spoke for both Henry and William when he said, "I am much interested in the study of national types, in comparing, contrasting, seizing
the strong points, the weak points, the point of view of each."

† "The novel, as largely practised in England, is the perfect paradise of
the loose end."—James, preface to *The Awkward Age.* Compare Howells's
remarks on Thackeray, Dickens, etc., in his *Criticism and Fiction.*

The Irish writer, George Moore, who had also lived in Paris and who
shared James's admiration for the French art of the novel, carried on
through life a quarrel with English fiction that was similar to James's. He

settings and details, their gift for analyzing the reports of their senses. Art, he had always felt, lives on discussion, the interchange of views, the comparison of standpoints; and in Paris the Goncourts, Flaubert, Turgenev and Zola gave him a place in their circle. He spent mornings at Auteuil, in Edmond de Goncourt's study, and rainy afternoons with Turgenev, whom he always left with excitement, leaping over gutters lightly and stopping to look in shop-windows,—with an air of being struck,—for no reason at all. He felt that all manner of secrets had been placed in his keeping. He dined with Renan, the hideous and charming, and at Madame Viardot's Sunday afternoons he often saw Turgenev again, sometimes on all fours, in a mask and shawl, in some extravagant charade that reminded him of historical games at Concord. The best of these occasions were Flaubert's Sunday afternoons, when the old master, in his Arab blouse, discoursed with his younger disciples, one of whom was Guy de Maupassant. Flaubert was annoyed with James because he spoke with disrespect of Prosper Mérimée's style; but James had never dreamed of such conversation, such confidences about plans and ambitions, such counsels of perfection that spoke of an intense artistic life. The talk was all of logic, lucidity, the clear image, precise observation, the inevitable word,

complained of the English "lack of seriousness," he felt that the great English novelists had scarcely a trace of discipline, unity or artistic direction, and he went to London with the hope of winning "freedom" for English fiction by remodelling it in the style of the great French writers.

While both James and Moore added much to the English art of fiction, both remained unreconciled to the English genius. They were unwilling to accord the English the right to the sort of novels that the English liked. James was as indifferent as Moore to what John Eglinton calls (Irish Literary Portraits) the "vitality and good spirits" of the English novel, "its incomparable sense of romance, its thoughtfulness, its gift of humour, its affiliation to drama and poetry rather than to the arts of painting and drawing."

It may be added that Moore's uneasy relations with Ireland were much like James's uneasy relations with America. Both were always going home to find themselves disillusioned again, and both remained essentially foreigners in London.

grace and felicity, lightness and shapeliness, design, style, manner, the virtues of form. The intelligence of these writers was truly infernal.

All this confirmed James's resolution to carry his art of the novel to a pitch of perfection. How deep this resolution was one saw in his work and his prefaces later, but the themes of many of his stories also showed it. He was passionately concerned with self-education, although the concern of his characters was to educate others. "I believe in you," said Rowland Mallett to Roderick Hudson, as they set out for Europe, "if you are prepared to work and to wait and to struggle and to exercise a great many virtues." Rowland Mallett's hope was to make a great artist of Roderick, and this was Sherringham's object in *The Tragic Muse,* in connection with Miriam Rooth; while Gabriel Nash conceived it as his function to serve as a conscience for Nick Dormer. The theme of *The Bostonians* was the tutelage of Verena Tarrant,— who was to exercise it, Ransome or Olive?—and James's early novel, *Watch and Ward,* described the bringing up of a little waif by her future husband, Roger Lawrence. In the continual recurrence of this motive one saw how much his own development occupied James's mind; * and

---

* James's austerity of purpose was reflected in many of his young men, the youthful Roderick, Rowland Mallett, Longueville, in *Confidence,* and Longmore, in *Madame de Mauves,* who, "like many spirits of the same stock, had in his composition a lurking principle of asceticism to whose authority he had ever paid an unquestioning respect." Compare this passage about Longueville: "It was annoyance that he had passed out of his own control—that he had obeyed a force which he was unable to measure at the time . . . In spite of a great momentary appearance of frankness and a lively relish of any conjunction of agreeable circumstances exerting a pressure to which one could respond, Bernard had really little taste for giving himself up, and he never did so without very soon wishing to take himself back." Compare also these passages from *Roderick Hudson:* "'I believe that a man of genius owes as much deference to his passions as any other man, but not a particle more, and I confess I have a strong conviction that the artist is better for leading a quiet life.' . . . There was in all dissipation . . . a vulgarity which would disqualify it for Roderick's favour . . . The young sculptor was a man to regard all things in the light of his art, to hand over his passions to his genius to be dealt with, and to find that he could live largely enough without exceeding the circle of pure delights."

there were other motives that drove him forward. He
felt that he had to make up for missing the war; and he
felt the "Higginsonian fangs" behind him.* He had to
justify his expatriation;† and he had to counterbalance
his American birth. For James believed that art was a
European secret: he had much more to learn than a
European. Did he not feel, at times,—he later implied it,
when he said the tale was "documentary,"—as the painter
Theobald felt, in *The Madonna of the Future?*—"We
are condemned to be superficial. We are excluded from
the magic circle. The soil of American perception is a
poor little barren, artificial deposit. Yes, we are wedded
to imperfection. An American, to excel, has just ten times
as much to learn as a European. We lack the deeper
sense; we have neither taste, nor tact, nor force. How
should we have them? Our crude and garish climate, our
silent past, our deafening present, the constant pressure
about us of unlovely circumstance, are as void of all that

* "The truth is that Mr. James's cosmopolitanism is, after all, limited;
to be really cosmopolitan, a man must be at home even in his own country."—Thomas Wentworth Higginson.

† James's will and pride were undoubtedly piqued by the numerous gibes
at his expatriation. Typical of these is the following passage from *Rollo's
Journey to Cambridge,* which appeared in the *Harvard Lampoon,* 1879–
1880:

"Now it happened, while this scene was taking place, a foreigner had
got into the car. In his coat-pocket there was a red 'Guide to New England.' He was reading de Tocqueville on America, and had asked Benny
whether Jarvis Field was a prairie, and whether buffaloes (bisons) were
still shot in Cambridge. This gentleman was Mr. Henry James.

"As soon as he saw Dovey, he began to take notes of her with a polyglot
pencil on analytic paper. When the proctor saw this, he fled incontinently.

"Mr. James then enquired of Mr. George, with a strong foreign accent,
whether the lady, his *vis-à-vis,* was *de ses amies.* Mr. George emphatically
disclaimed her acquaintance, though admitting she had been of service to
him the day before.

" 'The gentleman, her *compagnon de voyage,* is I fancy her husband?'
queried Mr. James. 'A most unhappy *ménage.*'

" 'I do not believe it,' said Mr. George.

" '*Tiens!* and can it be the custom in this country for young ladies to
travel unattended, or, still worse, in the company of a young man, from
Cambridge to East Cambridge? I must remember this in my forthcoming
work on the American girl.' "

Turgenev was similarly lampooned in Russia.

nourishes and prompts and inspires the artist as my sad
heart is void of bitterness in saying so." He certainly felt
this at moments; and nothing more actively spurred him
on to prove that his misgivings were not true. The great
craftsman that he became was the product of all these
motives, and he finished his apprenticeship in Paris. He
had been stirred to a passion of emulation, a "rage of
determination to *do,* and triumph."

At the end of a year, however, James moved to London. He had wearied of the company of these French
writers. Much as he had gained from them, he had not
found them congenial: they sometimes reminded him of
a pirates' cave. Aside from their craft, they had no interests, and they struck him as brutal, exclusive, corrupt and
complacent. They had no vision, no humanity, no taste
for the intangible; and, besides, he could not endure their
Bohemian ways. They often shocked Turgenev, the gentle Russian giant, and they shocked this young American
ten times more so. He felt, for the rest, an outsider in
Paris. He felt that he could not establish relations in
France; and to know the great world of Europe, to penetrate its secrets,—this had been James's object in coming
abroad. He had tried Italy before he went to Paris and
found that he could not pierce behind the scenes. "I feel
forever how Europe keeps holding one at arm's length,"
he wrote in one of his letters, "and condemning one to a
meagre scraping of the surface." And again: "What is
the meaning of this destiny of desolate exile—this dreary
necessity of having month after month to do without our
friends for the sake of this arrogant old Europe which
so little befriends us?" On the continent he could not hope
for any initiation,* although he felt he had grasped in

* James undoubtedly expressed his own feelings in the story, *At Isella,*
referring to the old burgher mansions in a Swiss town through which the
narrator is passing: "I wondered of course who lived in them, and how
they lived, and what was society in Altdorf, longing plaintively, in the
manner of roaming Americans, for a few stray crumbs from the native

Italy "what might be meant by the life of art." In *Transatlantic Sketches,* he had pictured his rambles through Tuscany, with a volume of Stendhal in his pocket, his rides on the Campagna and his starlit nights in Venice, amid the accumulations of the festal past; and he often returned to Italy later for its "tonic picturesqueness" and all its "mellowed harmonies of tint and contour." * There he had found the remnants of Story's circle, "much broken up," or "broken down;" and there he had written some of his earlier stories, among them *The Madonna of the Future.* Suggested by Balzac's *Le Chef-d'œuvre inconnu,* this also suggested the life of Washington Allston, before whose unfinished "Belshazzar's Feast," over which the painter had toiled at home, James had lingered long, with sad misgivings. He had "lived it over," the painter's nostalgia, the "grim synthetic fact of Cambridgeport," where Allston's beautiful talent had wasted away. He had also partly written in Florence the first of his important novels, the story of the sculptor, Roderick Hudson; and it was in Florence that he met Sargent, who gave him the idea of *The Aspern Papers.* Sargent had known Claire Clairmont, who had died in Florence, the mother of Byron's Allegra and the friend of Shelley. In the same house with old Miss Clairmont and her middle-aged niece

social board, with my fancy vainly beating its wings against the great blank wall, behind which, in travel-haunted Europe, all gentle private interests nestle away from intrusion. Here, as elsewhere, I was struck with the mere surface-relation of the Western tourist to the soil he treads. He filters and trickles through the dense social body in every possible direction, and issues forth at last the same virginal water-drop. 'Go your way,' these antique houses seemed to say, from their quiet courts and gardens; 'the road is yours and welcome, but the land is ours. You may pass and stare and wonder, but you may never know us!' "

* "I have come on a pilgrimage," I said. "To understand what I mean, you must have lived, as I have lived, in a land beyond the seas, barren of romance and grace . . . Here I sit for the first time in the enchanted air in which love and faith and art and knowledge are warranted to become deeper passions than in my own chilly clime . . . The air has a perfume; everything that enters my soul, at every sense, is a suggestion, a promise, a performance."—James, *Travelling Companions.*

there had lived an ardent collector of Shelleyana, an American, Captain Silsbee of Salem, who longed to procure from Miss Clairmont her jealously guarded collection of Shelley papers. Silsbee, who happened to be in America when Miss Clairmont died, rushed back at once to secure the papers, which the old-maid niece agreed to give him if he would accept herself as part of the bargain. Thereupon Silsbee fled, and lost the treasure. Such was the germ of one of James's finest stories, as he received it from Sargent.*

Meanwhile, James had been drawn to London as one of the many "American claimants" for whom it was a paradise as well as a world. He approached it in a spirit of reverence and awe that somewhat suggested Howells's at the gates of Boston.† Had he not shared all the emotions of his "passionate pilgrim," who felt that England should have been his home? ‡ Could it be his home? Could he understand it? These were questions for the future. At present, so far as introductions went,—James was under the wing of Lowell and Norton,—he was soon in the centre of the picture. He shared the prerogatives of travelling Americans in realms that native writers seldom entered.§ As for the rest, he applied himself to the

---

* *John Sargent,* by Evan Charteris. Captain Edward Silsbee bequeathed his collection of Shelleyana in equal parts to Harvard and to Oxford.

† "He was always the great figure of London, and I was for no small time, as the years followed, to be kept at my awe-struck distance for taking him on that sort of trust."—James, *The Middle Years.*

‡ "I was born with a soul for the picturesque . . . I found it nowhere. I found a world all hard lines and harsh lights, without shade, without composition, as they say of pictures, without the lovely mystery of colour . . . Sitting here, in this old park, I feel—I feel that I hover on the misty verge of what might have been! I should have been born here and not there."—Searle, in James's *A Passionate Pilgrim.*

"I had taken . . . the adventure of my twenty-sixth year 'hard,' as *A Passionate Pilgrim* quite sufficiently attests."—Later preface.

§ "The position of the American of some resources and of leisure was, in European society of the nineteenth century, one of a singular felicity. Without, or almost without, letters of introduction or social passports of any kind, the American 'went everywhere,' everywhere in the world—into the courts of the Emperors of Austria or into the bosom of English county

study of English ways and types with his usual assiduity
and firmness of purpose. Hawthorne in Rome had seemed
to him to prove that a novelist could not "project himself into an atmosphere in which he had not a transmitted
and inherited property." But what could not be done by
observation? It was the doctrine of his friends in Paris
that one could "get up" any subject, that one could master any field or world, provided one lived sufficiently in
one's ears and one's eyes. Zola had recently got up Rome
with a Baedeker and a visit of four or five weeks. If
Hawthorne had been more observant, he might have done
so,—and what could not a novelist do with a lifetime?
James submitted himself to the "Londonizing process."
He dined out almost every evening; by day and by night
he roamed the streets. He "went everywhere," shy, sedate,
grave and watchful, with his guarded, formal manner
and his dark brown beard. He had a flat in Kensington,
but he moved about the country freely. One of his favourite retreats was an inn at Torquay, and once he worked
for a while on the Irish coast; and he stayed on the
Normandy coast, at Bayonne, at Dover. He spent a summer at Broadway with Sargent, Abbey and Millet, the
American painters, and he usually went to Paris for a
month each year. In 1881–82, he returned for a year to
America, and he wandered over the continent between
whiles. *A Little Tour in France,* the best of his earlier
books of travel, was the fruit of a jaunt through Balzac's
country.

Meanwhile, in a rapid succession of novels and stories,
James pictured the world of wanderers that he knew so

families. To know, or to admit an American into your family circle appeared to commit you to nothing. There was the whole immense Herring
Pond between yourself and their homes and you just accepted the strange
and generally quiet creatures on their face values, without any question as
to their origins and taking their comfortable wealths for granted. Thus
Mr. James could really get to 'know' people in a way that would be absolutely sealed to any European young writer whether he were Honoré de
Balzac or Charles Dickens."—Ford Madox Ford, *Henry James.*

well, the Americans in Europe whom he had watched as
a child and whom he was encountering in his peregrina-
tions. Who were these Americans, and what were the
motives that drew them abroad? Most of them were
products of the post-war years. There had always been
Gallophiles in Paris and Anglophiles in London, and
James pictured these older American types as well, along
with the "aesthetic" colonists in Rome and Florence. But
the sudden growth of wealth at home accounted for most
of the travellers, together with the spread of a feeling
for culture.* The drop of the national thermometer had
alienated many, who had lost interest in their country;
and the absorption of men in business had provided their
families with money to spend and driven them abroad
for romance or amusement. While the vast majority lived
at home, just as Howells pictured them, hordes were governed by these motives. They felt they had no function at
home any longer. The men, who existed to make money,
had ceased to care for the public good, and the women
were bored by business and knew nothing about it. They
were no longer required to be mothers of homesteads;
they had been largely absolved from their ancient duties;
and, with leisure on their hands, in a world that made no
provision for leisure, they were drawn to Europe, where
leisure was an art. Middle-class women had always felt
that they had a right to be warriors' wives; they had
wept over romances of knights and princes and followed
the patterns of aristocratic ladies. With their instinctive
love of valour, these women could not be content with a
drab and grubby world of business men; and the more
the American male was absorbed in this, the more the

* In Matthew Arnold's sense of the word. "To care only for the best! To
do the best, to know the best,—to have, to desire, to recognize only the
best. That's what I have always done, in my quiet little way. I have gone
through Europe on my devoted little errand, seeking, seeing, heeding only
the best. And it has not been for myself alone; it has been for my daughter. My daughter had had the best. We are not rich, but I can say that."—
Mrs. Church, in James's *The Pension Beaurepas.*

women dreamed of castles and titles and a brilliant life of social adventure elsewhere. There were thousands of Madame Bovarys in New York and in Boston, as in San Francisco, Milwaukee, Chicago and Denver, and they played in fancy with a frequent theme of the French novel, the story of the young wife, tired of domestic monotony, who exchanges the dullest of husbands for the gayest of lovers. The American men had given up their chance of aristocracy, for they had withdrawn from politics and war; and where were the women to find it, since they had a natural craving for it? Where could they find the elegance they also dreamed of?—which existed at home, to be sure, but in no such measure. America had always had its aristocracy, but this had not evolved in native forms. Its forms had remained European,* and for this reason, and because it was without prescriptive rights, European aristocrats, who embodied the source of all these forms, possessed in American society a special glamour; † and now, with the decay of European aristocracy, together with the growth of American wealth, Europe offered an open field for American social ambition. Was not the example of the Empress Eugénie, the little Spanish girl with the Yankee grandsire, one that all the American girls might follow? The international marriage was one of the striking facts of the moment; ‡ and

* "We haven't socially evolved from ourselves; we've evolved from the Europeans, from the English. I don't think you'll find a single society rite with us now that had its origin in our peculiar national life, if we have a peculiar national life."—The "facetious gentleman," in Howells's *Through the Eye of the Needle.*

† Henry Adams said that his father was "one of the exceedingly small number of Americans to whom an English duke or duchess seemed to be indifferent, and royalty itself nothing more than a slightly inconvenient person."

‡ ". . . The great truth that the star of matrimony, for the American girl, was now shining in the East,—in England and France and Italy. They had only to look round anywhere to see it; what did they hear of every day in the week but the engagement of one of their own compeers to some count or some lord?"—James, *The Reverberator.*

The marriage of Miss Jennie Jerome to Lord Randolph Churchill, 1874, was sometimes described as the "entering wedge."

the American magazines swarmed with stories of girls
who had caught sham nobles, and sometimes real ones,
though more often than not to their sorrow.* For they
were usually pictured as leading a life of domestic misery;
they were often abandoned penniless on some foreign
strand. During the years of the Second Empire, Paris
had had all the prestige.† Americans had praised everything French and were rather inclined to slight everything
English. The Napoleon III moustache blossomed on
countless American faces, and the happy dream of countless women was to appear at a ball at the Tuileries. Paris
abounded with families like the Follanbees; ‡ and the
young girls, as Mrs. Stowe remarked, longed to be "à la
everything Frenchy and pretty," everything "gay and
glistening," like the Empress herself, with their hoops
and puffs and pinkings and ruffles and bows. No one
denied that they succeeded. The legend had arisen that
all American women were charming and that their men
were always plain, awkward and dull. Meanwhile, with
the downfall of Napoleon and Eugénie, the prestige of
London had risen as the centre of fashion. Many of the
American suppliants were flocking thither. Add to this
the romance of Europe, all the more alluring as American life seemed to grow drabber and drabber, add the
rising hunger and thirst for culture, which had become
so largely the province of women, and one could under-

* The grim stay-at-homes retaliated by inventing such comic characters
as Count No-account, Count Screwloose of Toulouse, etc.
† This was the moment of T. G. Appleton's phrase, "All good Americans, when they die, go to Paris."
‡ In Harriet Beecher Stowe's *Pink and White Tyranny.* Mrs. Follanbee
"felt that a residence near the court, at a time when everything good and
decent in France was hiding in obscure corners, and everything parvenu
was wide awake and active, entitled her to speak with authority about
French manners and customs." Mr. Follanbee,—a pedlar who had risen to
untold wealth,—"was one of the class of returned travellers who always
speak condescendingly of everything American, as 'so-so,' or 'tolerable,'
or 'pretty fair,'—a considerateness which goes a long way towards keeping
up the spirits of the country."

stand the great hegira that afforded Henry James the theme of his lifetime.

For this was James's chosen world, the world for which he was foreordained; and he returned to this world in his last long novels. He had even followed the general movement by moving from Paris to London himself, and he pictured Americans in Italy and France before he pictured them in England. Later, when he had largely relinquished his hope of describing English society, he found in this earlier theme a recourse and a refuge, although, just as he attempted to picture the English among themselves, so, in three or four of the novels of his prime, he presented his Americans at home. *The Bostonians* and *Washington Square* were two of his brilliant achievements; and possibly *Washington Square* was the best of them all. The scene of his earliest memories returned to his mind, after he had lived for a while in London, and nothing that he ever wrote was more hauntingly truthful and final than the story of Catherine Sloper, her father, her lover and her aunt Lavinia Penniman of Poughkeepsie. This perfect little novel was an American classic, surely, an irreplaceable picture of old New York, with its sights and its sounds and its odours; and was not *The Bostonians* almost as much so? James had known these phases of his "huge, queer country," with his Cambridge, his Cape Cod, his Central Park, and with Dr. Tarrant, Verena and Basil Ransome, Miss Birdseye, Olive Chancellor and so many others. It was true that outside these circles, and even within them, he sometimes failed in verisimilitude; * and his Boston was the unlove-

---

* Thomas Wentworth Higginson observed that James opened *The Europeans* with horse-cars on the Boston streets ten years before they were introduced; and it was generally noted that it was impossible for such a girl as Gertrude Wentworth never to have seen an artist. Lowell objected that no Boston household like the Wentworths could have been so amazed by the sight of Europeans. "In the new story, when you reprint it, soften Mr. Wentworth's ignorance of European phrases and things a bit . . . I must have known many Harvard graduates of the class of 1809 and I assure

liest of all the Bostons. His American scene was severely
limited, and his American novels were singularly cold
beside the warmth and glow of his pictures of Europe.
It was in their longing for Europe that he sympathized
with his countrypeople; and the ardour with which they
shared this motive quickened them in James's mind. "In
Boston one can't *live* . . . One can't live aesthetically;"
and "the great thing is to *live,* you know." What Louis
Leverett said, in *A Bundle of Letters,* Strether repeated
in *The Ambassadors* later; and living, for James and his
people, meant going abroad.*

What happened to these people? What was the nature
of their adventures? And, first of all, who were they?
There were dozens of types, and they came from all over
America, Washington, Boston, Schenectady, Northampton, San Diego, and one saw them in Florence, in Paris,
at Homburg, at Vevey, in Baden-Baden, Geneva, in
Rome or in London. There were business men who had
made their pile and were out for entertainment.† There
were odious society reporters like Mr. Flack. There were
broken-down husbands who tagged along with their wives
and daughters.‡ There were patient American citizens

you they knew Europe pretty well. You boys fancy that nobody went
thither before the Cunarders began to ply in 1837. In most respects Europe
was better known then than now."—Letter of Lowell to James, 1878, referring to *The Europeans.*

* "The city of Boston be damned!" Ransome said in *The Bostonians.*
The violence with which Ransome rescued his Andromeda was certainly a
reflection of James's feelings. Was not the story a symbol of James, escaping from America with his art?

† "I want the biggest kind of entertainment a man can get . . . I want to
see the tallest mountains, and the bluest lakes, and the finest pictures, and
the handsomest churches, and the most celebrated men, and the most beautiful women."—Christopher Newman, in *The American.*

‡ "Mr. Ruck is a broken down man of business. He is broken down in
health, and I suspect he is broken down in fortune. He has spent his whole
life in buying and selling; he knows how to do nothing else. His wife and
daughter have spent their lives, not in selling, but in buying; and they, on
their side, know how to do nothing else. To get something in a shop that
they can put on their backs,—that is their only idea; they haven't another
in their heads."—*The Pension Beaurepas.*

who were bored by Europe.* There were old American
Francophiles, who worshipped privacy and good manners, and others who said "Mount Blank," "Amurica"
and "Parus;" and there were earnest young men who
had rushed abroad to save some charming creature from
a French deceiver. There were young men, sketching in
Italy, who had not found at home "a great deal to take
hold of," and who, after going back "to see how it
looks," hit upon some plan for returning to Europe.
There were ministers, on summer vacations, with Mrs.
Jameson in their luggage, and young men, passionless,
subtle and knowing, who were always comparing nationalities, contrasting their manners and customs, with a
special regard to the ways of the "baronial class." These
young men sometimes liked to think that they were "as
particular as any Englishman could be;" and they were
as eager to know the geography of other countries as
they were vague about their own. They were analytical;
they went into the "reasons of things," and they were
always trying to get visual impressions. Of what did the
"character" of objects and persons consist? They were as
fastidious about furniture and bric-a-brac as James himself and some of James's women; and this is saying much,
for some of these women were always collecting bric-a-
brac, material and human. They went in for snuff-boxes,
Dresden tea-cups, altar-lace and occasionally some "rather
good old damask;" and sometimes they were satisfied
with members of the other sex whose resemblance to good
old damask was their principal charm.† These women
usually cared a great deal about money, although they

---

* "Bored, patient, helpless; pathetically dependent on his wife and
daughters; indulgent to excess; mostly a modest, decent, excellent, valuable
citizen; the American was to be met at every railway station in Europe,
carefully explaining to every listener that the happiest day of his life would
be the day he should land on the pier at New York."—*The Education of
Henry Adams.*
† Gilbert Osmond, in *The Portrait of a Lady.*

disdained the men who made it, who were lacking in "social drapery," more often than not;* and, if they returned to America, it was to look after their investments, for they felt that their country existed to provide them with money. Some spent money with implacable persistence. Others travelled in order to economize. They had an inexhaustible knowledge of hotels and pensions, and their rooms became dwellings over-night, with the books they spread about, the flowers and the draperies; for they had the housekeeping habits of inveterate nomads. There were some who hoped to "get into society," like Mrs. Headway of San Diego; others, born for society, were trying to find it; others carried their Murray in their laps, even when they went to the tailor; others again were marked by a passion for knowledge. There were American women in Paris who smiled at the "big-footed" English, and there were American wives in London who were better tories than their husbands, and there were others who spent hours looking out of their London windows, longing to "see something of the life." There were small boys, like Randolph Miller, who could not find any candy in Italy,—they usually had pale complexions and sharp little features; and especially there were young girls who were variously enchanting,—there was always some young man who found them so. A few of these young girls were plain: they had been brought up on "nature." † Others were travelling for culture,‡

---

* "Isabel hesitated a little. 'I think I value everything that is valuable. I care very much for money, and that is why I wish Mr. Osmond to have some' . . . She cared nothing about [Goodwood's] cotton-mill, and the Goodwood patent left her imagination absolutely cold."—*The Portrait of a Lady.*

† "She had been brought up to think a great deal of 'nature' and nature's innocent laws, but now Rowland had talked to her ingeniously of culture; her fresh imagination had responded, and she was pursuing this mysterious object into retreats where the need for some intellectual effort gave her an air of charming tension."—*Roderick Hudson.*

‡ "I always have my answer ready: 'For general culture,' to acquire the languages, and to see Europe for myself."—The young girl in *A Bundle of Letters.*

and others for fun. Others again had "modelling" and a
large infusion of colour and mystery; some were brilliant
and dashing; some were flirts. There were prettily innocent Daisy Millers who lived in a round of dressing and
dancing. They had found at Vevey a better Saratoga, and
they flitted hither and thither in their muslin flounces,
with their knots of pale-coloured ribbon and their thin,
gay voices. How light their figures were, how quick their
glances, how rapid were their gliding steps, how coquet-
tish their hats! Their profiles were delicate, their tone
was full of mockery; and the more discreet Americans
wondered where these uncultivated children got their
taste.* For others were chaperoned, well-bred and well-
conducted, often in the care of mothers who knew their
world. Perhaps they had come abroad to learn the art
of wearing a train, present a cup of tea and compose a
bouquet. Sometimes they nursed a secret dream of marrying a son of the Crusaders. There were Francie Dossons,
Bessie Aldens, Pandora Days and Linda Pallants, and
Isabel Archers who moved in a realm of light; and they
were invariably idols of their fathers and mothers, their
lovers and masculine cousins, or their uncles and aunts.
A chorus of Europeans danced attendance on them, English lords, French counts, Italian guides. There was often
some German baroness to forward their matches; and
occasionally some stalwart American male became involved with Bellegardes who "pouted at" the Empire.
But the delightful American girls were the cynosure of
every eye. The world of James, as of Howells, revolved
around them.

Such were James's *dramatis personae,* and dozens
of others surrounded these principal persons, Henrietta
Stackpole, Casper Goodwood, General Packard in Paris,

---

* "She has that charming look that they all have. I can't think where they
pick it up; and she dresses in perfection . . . I can't think where they get
their taste."—Winterbourne's aunt, in *Daisy Miller.*

Miss Flora Finch, old Mr. Touchett, the American
banker in England,—but how could one begin to name
them all? This American world in Europe was almost as
wide as Howells's world and pictured with a more distinguished art; for, while James's sympathies were nar-
rower than Howells's, the quality of his mind was more
intense. And what befell these people? In many cases,
nothing, or something so intangible that only James could
make it count. They drifted about in isolated groups,
satisfied merely to bask in the sunlight of Europe. They
explored their own minds; they studied one another; they
lived in a "passionate consciousness" of their situation.
They met at tea on the lovely lawns of beautiful English
country-houses; they revelled in Italian palaces and
French chateaus. They watched from the outside the
gaiety of Baden-Baden, or they surveyed the riders in
Rotten Row, the shining procession of English beauty
and fashion; or they sat submissive in cafés or on rows
of chairs in the Champs Elysées. They floated on the
edges and surfaces of things. Some were initiated, some
were detached, some were disposed to treat Europe as a
holiday toy, to be thrown away at the dawn of another
convenience; but just to be in Europe, in many cases, made
their drama, and most of them wished, in one way or
another, to merge their lives with the life of Europe. If
they were not bewildered by Europe, they were beguiled
and charmed by Europe. They were charmed and then
they were beguiled; for they were usually innocent creatures, virginal, upright and open-hearted, and in almost
every case they came to grief. The unsuspecting Christopher Newman was trapped and betrayed by the Bellegardes. Daisy Miller was misprized and died. Isabel
Archer was led astray, like Roderick Hudson and so many
others,—for innocence wronged was the theme of James's
work. And this innocence was American innocence at the

mercy of the dark old world that so charmed it, deceived it, destroyed it and cast it away.

Now, what James suggested in all these stories was that his fellow-Americans were morally superior to Europeans. The magnanimous Christopher Newman was the type of them all, the chivalrous, honest, candid soul who submitted his fate to the hands of the Bellegardes and suffered through their cruelty and tortuous behaviour. This was the story of Maggie Verver, this was the story of Milly Theale, in James's last long novels; and he seemed to feel, from first to last, that the world into which they were drawn, the great world of Europe, and especially England, was arrogant, base, corrupt, insolent and greedy. This indeed was James's feeling about the English upper class, as he expressed it in one of his letters to Norton;* yet this was the world that fascinated James, as it charmed and beguiled his American characters. Had he not "roamed and wandered and yearned," like his own Hyacinth Robinson, watching the great company of London fashion, longing for an identification with it that letters of introduction could never supply? † Had he not watched like Lucien de Rubempré in Paris, like all those young men in his own stories whose imagination wistfully wandered, as Hyacinth Robinson's did, "among the haunts of the aristocracy?" His American characters might be nobler, but, if the old world was cor-

---

* "The English upper class . . . The condition of that body seems to me to be in many ways very much the same rotten and collapsible one as that of the French aristocracy before the Revolution—minus cleverness and conversation; or perhaps it's more like the heavy, congested and depraved Roman world upon which the barbarians came down . . . Much of English life is grossly materialistic and wants blood-letting."—Letter to Norton, 1886.

† "I arrived so at the history of little Hyacinth Robinson—he sprang up for me out of the London pavement. To find his possible adventure interesting I had only to conceive his watching the same public show, the same innumerable appearances I had watched myself, and of his watching very much as I had watched."—Preface to *The Princess Casamassima*.

rupt, its glamour outweighed its corruption in James's mind; and, while he upheld his moral standard, the glamour filled his imagination, regardless of all the baseness that might lie beneath it. He admired it socially more than he condemned it morally, and this led to a confusion in his sense of values, so that he later pictured people, actually base, whom he described as eminent, noble and great. Was there not something in it that was "better than a good conscience," as Longmore, envying the baron's manner, felt in *Madame de Mauves*? * All of James's characters were drawn by this glamour, which struck them as mystically superior, whether noble or base. They turned away from other people who represented probity, and whom James usually described as banal or prosaic, and were captivated by Europeans, or Europeanized Americans, although they were often aware that the latter were base. So Roderick Hudson turned from Mary Garland in order to pursue Christina Light, a thoroughly perverse little baggage, and so Isabel Archer turned from Warburton and Goodwood, attracted by the ignoble Gilbert Osmond; and these choices were not presented as matters of passion but as somehow indicating a higher discernment. What seemed to James really important was not morals but manners, which would not have compromised his work if he had not professed to stand for morals; and it was inevitable that, worshipping manners, he should have lost interest in his countrypeople. For they were least interesting in the sphere of manners. In his heart he had always felt that they were scarcely worth writing about, in comparison with Europeans, if one could grasp them; for they were, by definition, provin-

---

* "Something he had, however, which Longmore vaguely envied—a kind of superb positiveness—a manner rounded and polished by the traditions of centuries—an amenity exercised for his own sake and not his neighbour's—which seemed the result of something better than a good conscience —of a vigorous and unscrupulous temperament. The baron was plainly not a moral man, and poor Longmore, who was, would have been glad to learn the secret of his luxurious serenity."—James, *Madame de Mauves*.

cial for James,* and he felt that "luxurious aristocracies"
were superior as subjects.† This was a pity, for his relation
to the latter was always artificial and factitious, while he
possessed his Americans as extensions of himself; and who
cares what race or class a novelist pictures, so long as he is
at home with his world and its types?

* "I don't at all agree with you in thinking that 'if it is not provincial
for an Englishman to be English, a Frenchman French, etc., so it is not
provincial for an American to be American.' So it is not provincial for a
Russian . . . a Portuguese, a Dane . . . to savour of their respective countries: that would be where the argument would lead you. I think it is extremely provincial for a Russian to be very Russian . . . Certain national
types are essentially and intrinsically provincial."—Letter to Howells, 1880.

Everything American, whether literary or social, was provincial for
James. Thus he described Hawthorne as "consistently provincial" and
Thoreau as "worse than provincial—he was parochial;" and he said of
Poe's essays that they were "probably the most complete and exquisite
specimen of provincialism ever prepared for the edification of man."

† Thus he said to Mrs. Wharton, contrasting Tolstoy with *Madame
Bovary,* "Ah, but one paints the fierce passions of a luxurious aristocracy;
the other deals with the petty miseries of a little bourgeoise in a provincial
town."

CHAPTER XIV

ALDRICH AND HIS CIRCLE

IN THE pages of the "Contributors' Club," at the back of *The Atlantic,* the youngest generation aired its problems. This literary confessional hummed with its comments on the grimness of country life and the struggles, earnings and interests of aspiring authors. It abounded in suggestions for translators, discussions of Americanisms, a matter of concern for story-tellers who were eager for verisimilitude, defences of the Boston speech against the vulgar forms of English actors. But the chief preoccupation of these letter-writers, their all-absorbing interest, was the art of fiction. The day had passed when Godkin, in 1867, referring to the production of novels,—about two a week in England,—could speak of it as a "vicious fecundity." The "coming novel," as people called it, the "great American novel," was a matter of urgent importance to scores of writers.*

This interest filled the contributors' letters with questions and reflections. What constituted an "interesting" character? What were the pros and cons of the autobiographical form in fiction? Why should not the American novel develop the dramatic form? One writer said that story-tellers should vary their situations more, for one knew in advance, by heart, what was going to happen. The contributors bristled with comments on Hawthorne and Henry James, whose novels, along with Howells's, were running in *The Atlantic.* If Hawthorne had not been a

* See the "Contributors' Club" during the years 1877–1881. Howells had established this department in the magazine.

story-teller, he might have been a famous chemist, for he was a mental chemist in his method of handling emotions and passions.* Henry James's stories and people were the most exciting topics. Was *Daisy Miller* a loyal service—or was it not—to American girlhood? Should the hero of *The American* have accepted defeat? Was Newman's character really consistent? His idea of equality ought to have triumphed. No, said another contributor, James was right. A third took issue with a critic in *The Nation* who said that James should not have created Newman,—he was "not aesthetically attractive." How *César Birotteau* must have shocked this critic, or Freytag's *Soll und Haben!* A fourth enquired how it was that James's novels had such charm, with so little life, motion or progression. The answer lay in the delicate care of his brush-strokes. A fifth objected that James saw only the ludicrous points of his simpler people, such as Mr. Brand's large feet and his passion for home-made cake. Was he fair, moreover, in *The Europeans,* in picturing *first* the blemishes of the baroness's features? He was following Turgenev, of course; but was it fair?

While James led all the rest, as a theme for discussion, with Howells, who remained in the background,—for the editor selected the letters, and Howells was modest,—the writers ranged far and wide over the field of modern fiction. Howells and James themselves had largely aroused this interest, and their vogue was a stimulus also. They were appearing together in the Tauchnitz series, and one read them on summer tours in Europe, on the plush-covered seats of the railway-carriages or in tea-gardens and beer-gardens, where Baedeker lay on the table and the Lion of Lucerne looked on. It was delightful, in such surroundings, to turn the little square leaves, while Howells and James young men and women strolled among the

* Similarly, a well-known living critic has described James Joyce as an "engineer," because of his marvellous feats of "engineering" in style.

plane-trees. One had only to watch one's fellow-travellers to see how deftly these two writers caught their turns of phrase and their characteristics; and then it was a pleasure to send *The Atlantic* a line of corroboration or objection. James was appearing in German,—he was the "fashionable darling" of the Teuton public, according to the Leipsic prospectus. But for all this charm of James and Howells, the "Contributors' Club" teemed with comments on other novelists, English and continental. Trollope was a frequent theme, and it was noted that English writers dwelt more and more on the charms of American women, —even Matthew Arnold had given them a C+ in his general examination of human types.* George Eliot was much discussed. Was she not too severe with her pretty girls? How many of her Dorotheas had one met? Was Deronda's friendship with Gwendolen true to life? The critics who denied this were obviously men: only women could understand this kind of relation between the sexes. But could any woman really like Deronda? Was Gwendolen meant to be "fast"? So voluble was this discussion that a lively contributor soon proposed the founding of a Deronda chair at Harvard, with a chemical laboratory adjoining the lecture-room to assist in establishing habits of analysis.† The cult of Turgenev continued to rage. To

* "Almost everyone acknowledges that there is a charm in American women,—a charm which you find in almost all of them, wherever you go. It is the charm of a natural manner, a manner not self-conscious, artificial or constrained. It may not be a beautiful manner always, but it is almost always a natural manner, a free and happy manner; and this gives pleasure."—Matthew Arnold, *Civilization in the United States*.

† This was perhaps suggested by the lectures on George Eliot that Elizabeth Stuart Phelps was delivering at Boston University. For other echoes of this rage, see Henry James's *Partial Portraits*,—the dialogue of the young women on *Daniel Deronda*,—and the discussion of *Middlemarch* in Howells's *The Rise of Silas Lapham*, chapter IX.

See also Alice James's comment on George Eliot's *Letters and Journal*: "Whether it is that her dank, moaning features haunt and pursue me through the book or not, she makes the impression, morally and physically, of mildew or some morbid growth,—a fungus of a pendulous shape, or as of something damp to the touch."—Anna Robeson Burr, *Alice James, Her Brothers, Her Journal*.

one writer, Turgenev's stories suggested an unfinished frieze with charming figures painted here and there, in cool greys, blues and whites, with harsh tints and unformed shapes between. Meanwhile, *The Atlantic* published papers on virtually all the modern novelists, French, Norwegian, Russian, English, German. These articles abounded in discriminating comments on the methods and themes of the writers in question, their close observation, rich in shades, their delicacies, veracities, refinements. Even Zola's *L'Assommoir,* with all its washing of dirty linen, was recognized as a stout piece of work. The energy with which the author followed his own straight line was certainly highly respectable.

This lively interest in modern fiction undoubtedly quickened the minds of the novelists.* Each new work of Howells and James was debated through the press as the Waverley novels had been in the eighteen-twenties, and all their characters were as eagerly discussed as if they had been living souls and models. The writers and their public were on intimate terms with one another, as in all the healthy epochs of production; and one could understand the dismay of Henry James when he found that he had lost this public later. Realism had come to stay, in a form that Americans found congenial, and even the older generation, which protested against more intransigent forms, acclaimed and rejoiced in the writings of James and Howells. While realism progressed, however, there were always exceptional cases in which the romantic spirit reappeared. In the early eighties, Marion Crawford began to write; and William Henry Bishop and Julian Hawthorne were producing somewhat colourless romances, with settings in Germany, Italy and France that reflected the current passion for travel, with persons of all nationalities and sometimes their own. Bishop's

* In 1889, there was a summer school at Deerfield, organized for a "general discussion" of "the novel."

The House of the Merchant Prince, a sprightly picture of New York, in the post-war years of trade and fashion, was perhaps the best work of either author. The "rather romantic novel with realistic characters" was Bishop's definition of his work;* and this described the work of Arthur Sherburne Hardy, the author of *The Wind of Destiny* and *But Yet a Woman.* These novels might have been described as just about as good as almost-good French novels, but, when the fashion passed and people continued to read French novels, written by the French about the French, who cared to read about people "just like" the French in novels that were "just about" as good? Neither Hardy, Bishop nor Julian Hawthorne compared with Marion Crawford, whose formula was much the same as theirs, or with Helen Hunt Jackson, the author of *Ramona,* which appeared in 1884. The impulsive, attractive, clever woman who called herself "H. H.," the protégée of Higginson at Newport who was also Emily Dickinson's early friend,† had long been a popular author when she wrote this book, her only work that later times remembered. She had lived at army posts with her officer husband and wandered at home and abroad; and she rivalled Gail Hamilton, as a lively woman journalist, with her "bits" of domesticity and travel. She was universally known as the leading American woman poet in a world that had never heard of her friend in Amherst, and her fluent and fanciful poems were sometimes good. But her prose and her verse were alike undistinguished till she happened on a theme that stirred her to the depths

* Bishop was sufficiently interested in the realistic movement in fiction to call upon Galdos, Valdes and Juan Valera during a visit in Spain. In *A House-Hunter in Europe,* he gives an amusing description of these three writers, whom Howells introduced in America.

† The heroine of her novel, *Mercy Philbrick's Choice,* seems to have been suggested by Emily Dickinson. The "unique and incalculable" Mercy, with the "orchid-like face," is a morbidly diffident young woman who has had an unhappy love affair and secretly writes poems that she will not publish.

and electrified her talent for a moment. She had gone to Colorado, in search of health, and the state of the Indians there excited her pity. As she studied their history, the relations of the races, the conquest of the Indians by the whites, the old crusading zeal of the Yankee Abolitionists awoke in this mind of a later, indifferent New England. While the plight of the Indians was more tragic than that of the Negro slaves had been, since they were virtually outlaws and without protection, the public took no interest in their condition. They who had once been feared were now ignored; and even Mrs. Jackson's *A Century of Dishonour,* a documented history of the Indian question, had no effect on this general apathy. She thereupon determined to write the romance that paralleled *Uncle Tom's Cabin,* the book that roused the popular mind to the sorry state of the conquered race and led to a change of policy in dealing with it. *Ramona* thus became a part of American history, as Mrs. Stowe's book had been before it, though it lacked the crude power of *Uncle Tom's Cabin* and was far more sentimental and melodramatic. With all its faults, however, its excessively simple psychology and theatrical setting, it remained, with its high vitality, a popular classic. "H. H." excelled as a bold and effective story-teller; and this brilliantly coloured romance of the Indian girl and the old California hacienda, the Mexicans, mission priests and American settlers, took its place, as time went on, in the folklore of the West and the nation.

Meanwhile, Marion Crawford had appeared in New England, where he wrote his first romances at the turn of the eighties. A nephew of Julia Ward Howe, he had been born in Italy, the son of Thomas Crawford, Thorwaldsen's pupil, the New York sculptor of the fifties whose circle Hawthorne pictured in *The Marble Faun.* He had lived as a child in this circle in Rome, where many of his later stories had their setting; and every day he had walked past Constantine's basilica, the Capitol, the Forum, the Coliseum, with the pageant of Roman history spread out before him. Towards the end of his life, he returned to this theme in his *Ave Roma Immortalis*. He had been sent to America to school and had studied at three universities, in England, in Germany, at Rome, where he took up Sanskrit; and at twenty-five he had gone to India and stayed there for two years, as editor of the *Indian Herald* at Allahabad. He had joined the Catholic church in India, and, tiger-hunting there and playing polo, he had studied the Zend-Avesta with a Parsee priest and developed his gift as a linguist. He kept his diary in Urdu, and in time he spoke sixteen languages, five or six of which he knew already. At a loose end, in his late twenties, he had returned to America, not knowing what to do but with burning ambitions. He thought of entering politics, he longed to be an opera-singer, he saw himself already as a conquering hero. Handsome, arrogant, clever and young, the centre of an adoring circle of aunts and cousins, he seemed to be universally informed and gifted. He drew, he modelled, he studied singing with George Henschel, who led the new orchestra in Boston; and he was already a journalist with an excellent training. So he began to write for the press, on any and every subject, from Buddhism to politics and railroads.

He was living in Boston, at Mrs. Howe's on Beacon Street, when he was not in New York to be near his uncle, the well-known "king of the lobby," Samuel Ward; but he wrote his first novel at Newport, in Mrs. Howe's "green parlour," the rustic, open-air study under the Norway firs where his aunt communed so often with Spinoza and Hegel. He had made an instant impression as a story-teller. When he had first appeared in Boston, Longfellow and Holmes were enthralled by his tales and anecdotes of Indian life. One of these tales was about a Persian diamond-merchant, a sort of Sir Basil Zaharoff whose name was Jacobs and whom Crawford had known in India, in the mountains, at Simla. This Jacobs had told him the story of his life, an Arabian Nights entertainment in modern conditions, and Crawford wrote the story out and called it *Mr. Isaacs* and found himself instantly famous. Gladstone spoke of the tale as a "literary marvel," and the name of Marion Crawford went round the world. He had anticipated Kipling with his bold pictures of Indian life, and his burst of fame was much like Kipling's later. Still at his aunt's house, in the study facing Beacon Street, he wrote *Dr. Claudius* and *A Roman Singer.* The story of *Dr. Claudius,* a Swedish professor at Heidelberg, who inherits an American fortune and comes to Newport, suggested the philosophical discussions in which Mrs. Howe rejoiced at Lawton's Valley; while *A Roman Singer* was the fruit of Crawford's defeated ambition to conquer the world as an opera-singer himself. For all these first romances were largely transcribed from his own experience. *An American Politician,* a Boston novel, reflecting his political ambitions, pictured the drawing-room of Mrs. Jack Gardner, where Crawford spent much of his time, and the conversations there on finance and Dante. *The Three Fates,* again, was a good description of his struggles as a writer in New York, when, toiling away at articles, in a little hall-bedroom, he suddenly struck the vein that made him famous. The hero of this novel inherited a fortune also; and Crawford's own struggling-time was brief. Three years after his first appearance in Boston, he went abroad again in a blaze of success. This was in 1884, when Crawford was thirty. He spent a winter at Constantinople, where he was presently married, in a cloud of ambassadors, admirals, generals and princes. Then he settled at Sorrento, where he lived for the rest of his life, in the villa that overlooked the Isles of the Sirens.

Thus opened the career of the deft, ingenious story-

teller who was known for twenty-five years as the Prince
of Sorrento. For he lived there in princely style. He liked
an atmosphere of grandeur, with trains of servants and
sailors in Sorrentine dress, with gay masquerades and
parties on the loggia and a cosmopolitan troop of friends
and guests. One of his romances, *With the Immortals,*
suggested the conversation at his dinner-parties, which
ranged over literature, politics and art from the days of
Pliny and Horace to those of King Humbert. The Englishman in the story had bought a villa like his own, a
half-ruined castle on the cliffs, and he invented an electrical device that produced an immense eruption under the
sea. This suddenly caused the reappearance of seven or
eight immortals, Caesar, Leonardo, Pascal, Heine, Chopin and two or three others, who emerged from the mist
after the storm and wandered about the grounds and
joined in the conversation at the castle. For seclusion,
Crawford leased a tower on the Calabrian coast, San
Niccola, a stronghold built as a refuge in the Saracen
times, on a cliff that overhung a little bay, with a dungeon
lashed by the waves in stormy weather; and there he
wrote many of his novels. In his lateen-rigged felucca,
with four sailors, he explored the Mediterranean, sailing
from island to island and along the coast, sometimes with
the youthful Norman Douglas, who obtained the idea of
his first novel from a priest on the island of Elba during
one of these cruises. Later, in a larger yacht, he crossed
the Atlantic. This was in the days when he went to America every year for lecturing tours and winters in New
York, where he turned out hasty novels that no one mentioned seriously to maintain his magnificence at home.

In fact, between this later work and the novels he
wrote in the eighties there was little difference in quality,
in type or in style. He was an improvisator, a story-teller,
natural, nonchalant, easy, and the art of the novel was
always the last of his cares. Personally brilliant, he was

anything but a brilliant writer, and problems of technique and social problems, which occupied the minds of James and Howells, were far from his intellectually simpler world. His fresh, brisk style was in no way distinguished, and his characterizations were general and somewhat blurred. His people were puppets in what he called a "pocket theatre," and one scarcely recalled their traits when the curtain fell. But his narrative gift was astonishing, and his interest in life was eager and inexhaustible, wide and observant. In his historical novels, about ancient Arabia and Persia, the Crusades or the Spain of Philip II, in his novels of modern life in many countries, Germany, Turkey, Bohemia, America, England, in the Saracinesca series, most of all, describing the Roman nobility in the decades after 1860,—the social world he had known from his earliest boyhood,—he seemed to possess in every case the special and accurate knowledge that created a perfect illusion of the *mise en scène*. He could tell you how life on the Bosphorus differed from life in Pera. He knew every street and shop in Constantinople. He could tell you about glass-blowing in the glass-works at Murano and how cigarettes are made in a factory at Munich, how silversmiths conduct their trade and how the Baden tailors are able to make their clothes at a moment's notice. He could take you on a duke's yacht at Newport, or as readily introduce you behind the scenes at an embassy in Petersburg or Paris, a cardinal's apartment in Rome or a rectory in England; or it might be the court of Darius, a tiger-hunt in India, a German professor's household, an Italian castle. He could take you through a duel in all its phases. He knew the cry of the trumpeter swans when they pass overhead in the early morning in Iceland; he knew how a Cossack feels on a bench in exile, and he had at his tongue's end the proverbs and untranslatable phrases of Italians, Russians, Czechs, Arabs and Spaniards. Add to this versatility, which was truly astounding, his lucidity,

his energy, his dash and the zest and the masculine charm
that informed his writing, and one understood the vogue
of Marion Crawford, with his tone of a clever, accomplished man of the world. He was the perfect romancer
of the Tauchnitz series, born to be read on trains and in
Swiss hotels, as one contemplated raids on Munich or
Venice, on Prague, Rome, Heidelberg, Naples or Constantinople. Wherever one proposed to go, Marion Crawford had been there first and had written a charming
story on the scenes in question, a story that gave a third
dimension to Baedeker's dry notations and enabled one's
fancy to share in the life of the people.

With Marion Crawford and "H. H.," following
Howells and James, the interest in fiction steadily grew
in the eighties. Meanwhile, the interest in poetry lapsed,
perhaps because, as Godkin said, the spread of science
"killed the imagination." The poets seemed to be disappearing, as the wild flowers had disappeared, in the
regions where the poets had thriven of old. The arethusa,
the gentian, the cardinal-flower that had bloomed near
Agassiz's museum, the rhodora that lurked in West Cambridge, the Watertown yellow violets and the ginseng of
Brookline had retired before civilization. They had not
even waited for the coming of the suburban streets; they
seemed to feel the danger miles away. They had followed
the Indians into oblivion, and the poets were following
the flowers; for no new poets of equal scope had appeared in the train of the older poets, who were gradually falling silent, one by one. It was true that Emily
Dickinson, in her hermitage at Amherst, excelled in her
special intensity all but the greatest; but Miss Dickinson
throve in conditions that throttled the rest. The great social causes and the spiritual causes that had stirred the
romantic poets of the earlier time, the faiths and the
adorations all were gone; and poetry was left high and

dry in a world that had ceased to nourish poets, who remained as idle singers of empty days.

The best of all these idle singers was Thomas Bailey Aldrich,—for poetry of a kind abounded still. This alert little man, blond, erect, ruddy and jaunty, had arrived in Boston as recently as Howells. Born in Portsmouth, he described himself as Boston-plated because he had lived in New York in his formative years, in the well-known Bohemian circle; and he wore a waxed moustache, a symbol of his mundane tastes, in the style of Napoleon III, the Paris-plated. A journalist, an assistant of Willis, he had gone to the front in Virginia, like Winslow Homer. He had reported the war, as Homer sketched it;* and he had returned to New England in 1866 as an editor under the same roof with Howells. His magazine, *Every Saturday,* reprinted selections from foreign papers, reflecting the new cosmopolitan interests of Boston. It was "eclectic," to use a word that was much in vogue, and Aldrich's own mind was eclectic also,—it borrowed freely from every source that appealed to a roving fancy. A wit as well as a poet, Aldrich had had an early success, in this, and in other ways, resembling Lowell; for, along with his exotic themes, he shared the pure New England feeling that Lowell expressed in his poems about birds and springtime. He was a lesser Lowell, more deft than his master. He was already a "household poet" in 1866; and Howells, in his Western remoteness, had thought of Aldrich as one of the reigning stars of the Boston circle. Aldrich had a cottage in the village of Ponkapog, overlooking the Neponset marshes, south of Boston.

By 1881, when he took the place of Howells, who had resigned from *The Atlantic,* Aldrich's best-known work had already appeared. He was popularly respected as a

---

* Later, Winslow Homer contributed full-page drawings to Aldrich's magazine, *Every Saturday.*

poet and a story-teller whose writing was always accomplished and sometimes brilliant. In his cool and polished prose and verse, he revealed himself as a notable craftsman; and he said he would "rather be censured in pure English than praised in bad,"—which was not true, of course, but let that pass. His writing was undoubtedly distinguished. It was lucid, skillful, crisp and fresh; and the neat-handed Aldrich, who was very seldom commonplace, always knew when to stop, an unusual virtue. The fluent elder poets had not possessed it; and Aldrich's flute-like note was exceedingly pleasant in a world that was used to poets who went on and on. Moreover, he was adroit as well as brief. Dr. Holmes had warned him against verbal epicureanism and his liking for vanilla-flavoured words, the end of which was "rhythmical gout," as the hardy doctor knew, and "incurable poetical disorder." Aldrich scarcely needed this admonition. He was more consciously an artist than Holmes or Lowell, though he lacked their moral force and their wealth of perception, and he soon outgrew his early faults of style. Even his travel-writing, *From Ponkapog to Pesth,* was clear and witty: where most of his travelling friends,—for instance, Warner,—when it came to their "days in Tangier," could never find words enough to convey their impressions, Aldrich's care was not to say too much. These literary virtues marked his stories, *Majorie Daw, A Midnight Fantasy,* the little tales of *Two Bites at a Cherry* and his three short novels or romances. Fanciful or whimsical, realistic now and then, these tales ranged widely in their themes and persons: they dealt with Western gold-seekers, returned soldiers and human oddities, yachtsmen, strikers, misers and insane young women who recover their wits at appropriate moments. Sometimes they were Hawthornesque, sometimes they were arch or coy, sometimes they were impossibly melodramatic; but their touch was almost invariably expert and clever. *Mar-*

jorie Daw, the cleverest, was the novelist's dream of the perfect reader, in a day when the novelist's readers were mostly young ladies. For Marjorie was incredibly lovely; and what was she doing under the trees, lying in her hammock, swaying like a pond-lily? Reading,—and what but a novel?—and a novel by whom? Would not Howells and Henry James have liked to know? While *Marjorie Daw,* of all these tales, was the most original invention, *The Story of a Bad Boy,* the most sincere and natural, was destined, on all accounts, for the longest life. This picture of Aldrich's childhood at Portsmouth was the first of the series of books about boys that his friends of Mark Twain's circle were soon to write. For Aldrich was intimate with Clemens, as with Howells and Warner, and even had something in common with this friend from the West. As a child who had lived in New Orleans, before he returned to Portsmouth, he remembered the steamboat-life on the Mississippi. *The Story of a Bad Boy* started the train of associations that led to the similar books of all these authors, Warner's *Being a Boy,* Howells's *A Boy's Town* and Clemens's *Tom Sawyer* and *Huckleberry Finn.* In this somewhat inglorious post-war epoch, boyhood seemed better than manhood. At least, the leading authors wrote about it with a relish they seldom brought to the rest of life. Aldrich's book was happier than Warner's as an evocation of childhood in the older New England.

For the rest, there was more of New York than Boston in the temper of Aldrich's prose and verse, for all it owed to Longfellow, Hawthorne and Lowell. Aldrich's "surprise endings" reflected the love of effects that was always said to characterize New Yorkers, and his taste for the Second Empire savoured of Broadway. He was a tireless reader of the light French novels that everyone discussed on the banks of the Hudson, and the studio-talk of the New York painters had left long traces in his mind. Many of these painters imitated Isabey, Gérôme,

Fortuny and their scenes of Algeria, Arabia, Spain and Tunis, with odalisques and dancing-girls, snake-charmers and Moorish models, brocaded hangings, minarets and mosques. These pictures reappeared in the verses of Aldrich, which also reproduced their skillful brush-work. He shared the taste for bric-a-brac, for the picturesque at any price that characterized this age of collecting and travel, for knick-knacks and what-nots, Persian carpets, Spanish leather, Turkish brass, vases and German silver, sandalwood, cloisonné, lacquer. His poems were as full of these trappings as the studios and parlours of the eighties.* He carried in his head and transferred to paper what others brought home from Europe in their trunks and boxes.† As for his songs and epigrams, they were fresh and charming. He excelled in the light verse that English writers were also producing in this evening of the greater English poets.

Round Aldrich, as an editor, clustered most of the other poets who spoke for this twilit world of the later New England. One of his protégés was George Edward Woodberry, whom Higginson had introduced to Lowell. Woodberry, the Beverly boy, had catalogued Lowell's library, when he was a student at Harvard. He was one of Henry Adams's pupils and had also studied with Norton; and his first book, *A History of Wood Engraving,* was one of the many products of Norton's teaching. Half

---

* For an account of this phase of household art in Boston, see Harriet Prescott Spofford's *Art Decoration Applied to Furniture,* 1878.

No one in the eighties passed for an artist whose studio was not crammed with objets d'art and such articles of virtu, to use the current phrase, as bits of armour, cups of ruby glass, giant altar-candles, old silver altar-lamps, tall brass flambeau-stands, stuffs from Algeria, weapons from Tripoli and Tunis, musical instruments from Egypt and Spain and pottery from every known land. Most of these objects appear in Aldrich's poems. This was the age, alike in Boston and Moscow, in which Tolstoy was regarded as a saint because, as Lewis Mumford says, his bedroom was "unfurnished."

† "I have come back chock-full of mental intaglios and Venetian glass and literary bric-a-brac generally."—Letter of Aldrich, on returning from Europe, 1875.

its illustrations were from Norton's collection. The remarkable efflorescence of American wood-engraving had suggested this excellent book; but Woodberry was already a poet, and Norton and Lowell considered him the most promising of the rising generation. He had reviewed for *The Atlantic* under Howells, but Aldrich gave him an opening as a regular writer; and Edward Rowland Sill, the Connecticut poet, was another of Aldrich's favourites. Both these men were living at a distance. Woodberry was teaching in Nebraska, and Sill was in California, a professor of English. A more immediate member of Aldrich's circle was John Boyle O'Reilly, who edited the Boston Catholic weekly, *The Pilot*. This romantic Irishman, a schoolmaster's son, had been a trooper in the British army. Imprisoned for republican agitation, he had escaped from Dartmoor and had been recaptured and transported to the Australian penal colony, where he wrote patriotic poems on the walls of his cells. Thence, in 1869, he had escaped again by the aid of a New Bedford whaling captain; and, reaching America, he had come to Boston as the literary centre of the country. Visitors in his Boston study observed a track across the room where he had worn the carpet threadbare. He had been used to pacing up and down his cell and had not lost the habit after years of freedom. A floridly handsome, black-eyed man, warm-hearted, virile and winning, he belonged to the "tempest class," as Whitman said; but he did more than anyone else, as editor of *The Pilot,* to reconcile the Catholics and Protestants in Boston. He was a highly magnetic reciter and speaker. His passion for freedom, which sprang from his love of the Irish cause, enabled him to bring to American causes the libertarian feeling of the pre-war times; and one of his closest friends was Wendell Phillips. Listening to this Irish orator, one felt as if one lived again in the days of the Abolitionists and the Yankee crusaders. He brought back life and fire to the languid eighties. Most of his work recalled the older Irish political poets, with their fluent versification and flowery diction. But he wrote a few songs and lyrics,—*A White Rose* and *The Useless Ones,*—that were lovely and lasting reminders of his delicate feeling.

Edward Rowland Sill shared with Aldrich, although the two had nothing else in common, the leading place among these lesser poets. A slight, shy, diffident man, a graduate of Yale, Sill had gone to California in 1861, where he spent five years in various occupations. Returning to Connecticut, his birthplace, intending to study theology, he went to the Harvard Divinity School for a year. But, finding that he was too sceptical to continue his studies, he soon went West again, with memories of Agassiz's lectures on science and the Boston music-hall that later found expression in his verses. He taught for a while in Ohio, but the greater part of his later life,—he died in 1887, not yet fifty,—was passed in California, at Berkeley, where he left a deep impression as professor of English. Aldrich heard of this "teacher who occasionally wrote verses," as the unassuming Sill described himself, and gave him a free hand in *The Atlantic,* where Sill, who shrank from publicity and preferred to appear anonymously, often signed his poems with a pen-name. In person, he resembled Amiel, and he shared Amiel's mental habits. He was introspective, and the bent of his mind was generally ethical. He was obsessed with the conflict of religion and science, and most of his delicate verses were concerned with this conflict, with doubt and disbelief, a somewhat vague aspiration and a wistful, post-Emersonian nature-worship. At their worst, they were marred by an adolescent mawkishness, and Sill was a poet of low vitality always; but his finest poem, *The Venus of Milo,* with its evocation of Greek serenity, and some of his fables and field-notes were graceful and moving. *The Clocks of Gnoster-Town,* Browningesque in form, was an admirable illustration of Emersonism. Sill's rather fragile essays were often charming, with their notes on humming-birds and the redwood forests where he rode for weeks on horseback in the high Sierras. He translated some of Sully-Prudhomme's sonnets. But his work, as a whole, was pallidly reflective and rather a matrix of poetry than poetry itself. There was scarcely a distinguished line or phrase, or any suggestion of magic, in his flowing verses. He lacked the intensity of another obscure New England poet who was scarcely known at all during his lifetime. Frederick Goddard Tuckerman, born in Boston, a classmate of Higginson at Harvard, who had retired in early life to Greenfield, had died in 1873. Emerson had praised his one book of sonnets, and Tennyson, whom he visited in England, and who gave him the manuscript of *Locksley Hall,* was drawn to the youthful poet and recalled him fondly. But Tuckerman, the shyest of recluses, after the death of his wife, withdrawing to western Massachusetts, had made no further attempts to interest readers. He passed his days in botanical studies and amateur astronomy, adding from time to time to his series of sonnets. It was not until 1931, sixty years after his death, that he found his belated place in American letters. The poet Witter Bynner republished the sonnets of Tuckerman. Admirable in craftsmanship, firm, fresh and clear, these sonnets were memorable expressions of tragic feeling.

Meanwhile, side by side with Aldrich, Louise Chandler Moulton presided over the poets who remained in Boston. This somewhat gushing lady, as Whitman called her, had appeared in the days of the gift-books as "Ellen Louise." A Connecticut girl, she had gone to school, in the village of Pomfret, with Whistler, who had given her some of his drawings. She was a cousin of Stedman and had married a Boston editor, and she wrote Boston let-

ters for the New York papers; then, forming a regular
habit of going abroad in the summer, she introduced to
American readers many of the newer poets of France
and England.* A good-hearted, sympathetic literary go-
between, sincerely devoted to poetry, she collected poets
as others collected old masters; and she passed from
Mallarmé's circle to Lord Houghton's in London, discovering, acclaiming, acquiring and sharing her treasures.
She was eager to rescue and forward unfortunate poets.
Chief among these was Philip Bourke Marston, blind
and beset with calamities, who left her his manuscripts
to publish; and she also assembled the poems of his
brother-in-law, the afflicted Arthur O'Shaughnessy, who
died in his thirties. William Sharp wrote many sonnets
for her. As for her own poems, they were of the facile
kind that several New England women produced in the
eighties, for most of the women novelists were poets
also.† This poetry of women, by women, for women, as
it might well have been called, was a *réchauffé* of Tennyson and Browning, sometimes accomplished, usually flaccid, stereotyped and vague, abounding in hackneyed
phrases and threadbare conceptions. While it occasionally suggested depths of feeling, as in Rose Terry Cooke
and Elizabeth Phelps, it was often sicklied over with the
palest thought and very seldom fresh, direct or vital. All
too literary, it was mostly second-hand; and the characteristic note of the earlier poets, through whom the American scene had found expression, was lost in its general
reversion to English models. The lark and the nightingale reappeared in Mrs. Moulton, as if the American

---

* Two of the latter she introduced were William Watson and John
Davidson.
† Among the New England women novelists who published volumes of
verse were Helen Hunt Jackson, Elizabeth Stuart Phelps, Rose Terry
Cooke, Harriet W. Preston and Harriet Prescott Spofford. Of these, "H. H."
was by far the best poet, but most of the others occasionally wrote good
poems, as, e.g., E. S. Phelps's *Gloucester Harbour*.

landscape and its birds and flowers had never been won for poetry. These singers were the "caged warblers" whom Amy Lowell silenced, in her effort to revivify poetry thirty years later; and indeed, their weary verse, as Miss Lowell called it, devitalized, nebulous, dim, slipping along the path of least resistance, invited, and even demanded, a bold reaction. Meanwhile, in Amherst, another woman poet was preparing the way for this vigorous movement later.

CHAPTER XV

EMILY DICKINSON

THE Dickinsons lived in the principal house in Amherst. A large, square, red-brick mansion that stood behind a hemlock hedge, with three gates accurately closed, it was a symbol of rural propriety and all the substantialities of western New England. Edward Dickinson, the lawyer, had always had his office in the village, and four times a day, in his broadcloth coat and beaver hat, with a gold-headed cane in his hand, he had passed through one of the gates, going or coming. A thin, severe, punctilious man who had once been a member of Congress, a friend of Daniel Webster in his youth, a Calvinist of the strictest persuasion, he was a pillar of Amherst College until his death in 1874. The college had been founded, largely by his father, to check the sort of errors that were spreading from Harvard, and he never abated his rigour in the interests of pleasure. He was said to have laughed on one occasion, but usually he was as cold and still as the white marble mantel in his parlour. The story was told in Amherst, however, that once he had rung the church-bell, as if to summon the people to a fire. The whole town came running, for he rang the bell excitedly. He wished to call attention to the sunset.

Next door, behind the hemlock hedge, another ample dwelling stood, suggesting in its style an Italian villa. Here lived the Squire's son Austin, once his partner, who kept open house for the college. While the Dickinson mansion was somewhat forbidding, with the stamp of the

Squire's grim ways and his invalid wife, the villa was a centre of Hampshire hospitality that shared its rolling lawns and charming garden. Olmsted had visited there, when he was planning Central Park, to examine the shrubs and trees, the plants and flowers, and distinguished guests at the college commencements and lecturers during the winter season were received and welcomed there as nowhere else. Emerson, Phillips, Beecher and Curtis had stayed in this house next door, and Samuel Bowles of the *Springfield Republican* was an intimate friend of all the Dickinsons. In an age when the newspaper was largely taking the place of the pulpit, Samuel Bowles was known all over the country as one who fought for honest politics. He had joined with Carl Schurz in the movement for reform that was also the cause of Henry Adams. The *Republican* was a school for journalists, known far and wide, and travellers,—Dickens and Kingsley among them,—constantly stopped at Springfield in order to have a chat with Samuel Bowles. His paper was a sovereign authority in Amherst, and he often drove over for a call at the villa or the mansion, sometimes bringing manuscripts by well-known authors to show the Dickinson daughters before they were published. His favourite was Emily, who was older than Lavinia, but Emily usually "elfed it" when visitors came. She was always in the act of disappearing. Through the blinds of her western windows, overlooking the garden, she observed the hospitalities of the villa, and snatches of whatever was current in the books and talk of a college town, in the politics and thought of the moment, reached her when the guests had gone away. But even her oldest friends seldom saw her. While sometimes, in the evening, she flitted across the garden, she never left the place by day or night. To have caught a fleeting glimpse of her was something to boast of, and a young girl across the way who watched at night for a light at her window was thrilled if Miss Emily's shadow appeared for a moment. There were nurse-maids who thought she was a witch. They frightened the children by uttering her name, as if there were something malign in Miss Dickinson's queerness.

While her friends seldom saw her, and almost never face to face,—for she spoke from the shadows of the hallway, as they sat in the parlour, or sometimes down the stairs,—they were used to receiving little letters from her. These letters were also peculiar. Miss Dickinson rarely addressed the envelopes. Some other hand, perhaps her sister's, performed this office for her. More often the names of the person and town had been clipped from a printed paper and pasted together, as if it were a sort of violation to expose the strokes of her pen to the touch of the postman. The letters themselves were brief and cryptic, usually only a line or two: "Do you look out tonight?" for example. "The moon rides like a girl through a topaz town." Or "The frogs sing sweet today —they have such pretty, lazy times—how nice to be a frog." Or "Tonight the crimson children are playing in the West." Or "The lawn is full of south and the odours tangle, and I hear today for the first the river in the tree." Now and again, some fine phrase emerged from the silvery spray of words,—"Not what the stars have done, but what they are to do, is what detains the sky." Sometimes her notes had a humorous touch: "Father steps like Cromwell when he gets the kindlings," or "Mrs. S. gets bigger, and rolls down the lane to church like a reverend marble." But her messages often contained no words at all. She would lower baskets of goodies out of the window to children waiting below. At times, instead of a letter, she sent a poem, an odd little fragment of three or four lines, with a box of chocolate caramels or frosted cakes and a flower or a sprig of pine on top, heliotrope, perhaps, or an oleander blossom or a dande-

lion tied with a scarlet ribbon. Her letters were rhythmical, they scanned like the poems, and they were congested with images,—every phrase was an image; and
the poems themselves suggested nursery-rhymes or Dr.
Watts's hymns, broken up and filled with a strange new
content. They might have struck unsympathetic readers
as a sort of transcendental baby-talk. It was evident that
Miss Dickinson had lost the art of communication, as
the circle of her school-friends understood it. She vibrated
towards them, she put forth shy, impalpable tentacles,
she instantly signalized with a verse or a note every event
in their lives. But she did not speak the language of the
world outside her, and one gathered that she did not wish
to touch it. She was rapt in a private world of sensations and thoughts. It was even observed that her handwriting went through three distinct phases and that towards the end the letters never touched. Each character,
separately formed, stood quite alone.

She had been a recluse since the early sixties, and her
family surmised the reason. She had fallen in love with
a married man, a Philadelphia clergyman, and had buried
herself at home by way of refuge. When her supposed
lover supposedly pursued her there, her sister dashed
across to the house next door and exclaimed to their
brother Austin's wife, "Sue, come! That man is here.
Father and mother are away, and I am afraid Emily will
go away with him." Such was the family legend, which
may have been apocryphal. Undoubtedly, the clergyman
came to see her, but probably only to call. Was he in love
with Emily? Probably not. In any case, she did not go
away. She withdrew from all activities outside the household, and her mind turned in upon itself. She had hitherto
been eminently social, or as much so as her little world
permitted. Born in 1830, in the red-brick mansion, she
had grown up a lively girl who was always a centre of
attention. She was a capital mimic. She travestied the

young-lady pieces, the "Battle of Prague" and others, which she played on the mahogany piano, and her odd and funny stories enthralled her friends. Later they remembered that she placed bouquets of flowers in the pews of those she liked best, at church. Helen Hunt Jackson, now a well-known writer, had been her favourite playmate in early childhood. Dancing and card-playing were not allowed in Amherst, but Noah Webster's granddaughter, who lived there, evaded the prohibition on behalf of her circle. She held "P.O.M." meetings for the Poetry of Motion, and Emily Dickinson excelled in this branch of learning. She joined in picnics and walks over the Amherst hills with groups of boys and girls from the town and the college. They had "sugaring-off" parties and valentine parties, and they often climbed Mount Norwottuck where they found ferns and lady-slippers; and sometimes they met at a brookside in the woods, where the boys went fishing and the girls made chowder. Emily was an ardent botanist. She knew the haunts of all the wild flowers in the region, and sometimes she scrambled alone through the forest, perhaps with her big dog Carlo. She was an expert cook. At home she baked the bread and boiled her father's puddings, but her father was difficult to please. He read "lonely and rigorous books," she said, on Sunday afternoons, fearing that anything else might "joggle the mind;" and Shakespeare, the Bible and Dr. Watts's hymns were the reading that he chose for his daughter. He did not like her to work in the garden, or to make visits without him, and when she was too witty he left the table. At fifteen she could not tell the time: her father supposed he had taught her, but she had not understood him, and she did not dare to ask him again or ask anyone else who might have told him. Now and again, she rebelled. She smashed a plate or a tea-cup, and her friends and her brother found ways to provide her with books, hiding them in the box-bush that stood beside the front door or on the parlour piano, under the cover. In one way or another, she contrived to read most of the current authors, especially the Brontës and the Brownings, with Hawthorne, Coleridge, Irving, Keats and Ruskin. One of her special favourites was Sir Thomas Browne, and she loved the drollery of Dickens. For the rest, she read Heine in German and Emerson's poems, and Frank B. Sanborn's letters in the *Springfield Republican* kept her in the literary current. She was by no means passive in this house of duty. Once, at a funeral in Hadley, whither she had gone with her father in the family barouche, she ran away for several hours with a young cousin from Worcester and drove back to Amherst in his buggy. At school, she declared her independence. She had been sent as a boarding-pupil to Mary Lyon's seminary, where she had written her themes on the nature of sin. She had listened to lectures on total depravity as if, like most of the other girls, she had meant to be a missionary's wife; but when, one day, Miss Lyon asked all the girls to rise, all who wished to be Christians, Emily alone refused to do so. She had found that she could not share the orthodox faith. Otherwise her life went on, with a few journeys here and there, like that of any country lawyer's daughter. As a young girl, she had visited Boston. She remembered the concerts and Bunker Hill, the Chinese Museum and Mount Auburn; and later, on two occasions, she stayed in Cambridge, to receive some treatment for her eyes. When her father was serving his term in Congress, in 1854, she spent seven weeks in Washington with him. Her father's friends were struck by her charm and her wit. It was on her way home that she stopped at Philadelphia and received the sudden shock that had changed her life.

This was the whole of Miss Dickinson's story, so far as outward events were concerned, when Thomas Wentworth Higginson entered the picture. Higginson had

written an appeal in *The Atlantic,* addressed to the rising generation. Remembering the days of *The Dial,* when
the hazel wand, waved over New England, had indicated hidden springs of talent in many a country town, he
said that to find a "new genius" was an editor's greatest
privilege. If any such existed who read *The Atlantic,* let
him court the editor,—"draw near him with soft approaches and mild persuasions." Higginson added a number of admonitions: "Charge your style with life . . .
Tolerate no superfluities . . . There may be years of
crowded passion in a word, and half a life in a sentence."
This appeal was anonymous, but many of the Amherst
people knew who wrote the articles in *The Atlantic,* for
Sanborn's literary gossip kept them posted; and presently
Colonel Higginson, who was living in Worcester, received an odd little letter. The letter was unsigned, but
the writer sent four poems, and she placed in a separate
envelope the signature "Emily Dickinson." She begged
this distant friend to be her "master." The poems puzzled Higginson. While he felt a curious power in them,
he was not prepared for a "new genius" who broke so
many rules as this lady in Amherst, who punctuated with
dashes only and seemed to have small use for rhyme and
merely wished to know if she was "clear." She did not
ask him to publish the poems, and he did not pass them
on to the editor, but he wrote her a sympathetic letter
that was followed by a long correspondence. She continued to send him poems at intervals, signing her notes
"your gnome" and "your scholar," but, although she
asked him again if he would be her "preceptor," and he
offered her a number of suggestions, she never changed a
line or a word to please him. In one note she said, "If I
read a book and it makes my whole body so cold no fire
can ever warm me, I know that is poetry. If I feel physically as if the top of my head were taken off, I know that
is poetry. These are the only ways I know it. Is there any

other way?" And once she replied, when he asked her
for a photograph, "I had no portrait now, but am small,
like the wren; and my hair is bold, like the chestnut burr;
and my eyes like the sherry in the glass that the guest
leaves." This feminine mystification piqued the colonel.
He wrote, "You enshroud yourself in this fiery mist and
I cannot reach you, but only rejoice in the rare sparkles
of light." When she told him that her companions were
the hills and the sundown, he replied that she ought to
come to Boston: she would find herself at home at Mrs.
Sargent's. At last, in 1870, he went to Amherst. After a
brief delay, while he waited in the parlour, he heard a
faint footstep in the hallway and a shy, little childlike
creature glided in. She carried two day-lilies, which she
placed in his hand, saying, in a soft, breathless voice,
"These are my introduction," adding in a whisper, "Forgive me if I am frightened. I never see strangers and
hardly know what to say." She spoke of her household
occupations and said that "people must have puddings,"
and she added a few detached, enigmatic remarks. She
seemed to the amiable Higginson as unique and remote
as Undine or Mignon or Thekla. But he was disturbed by
the tension in the air and was glad he did not live too
near this lady. There was something abnormal about her,
he felt. He had never met anyone before who drained
his nerve-power so much.

At that time, Miss Dickinson was forty years old and
had long since withdrawn from the world; and the
friends who came to see her sister were used to the "hur-
rying whiteness" that was always just going through a
door. She sometimes swept into the parlour, bowed and
touched a hand or two, poised over the flowered Brussels carpet, and vanished like a ghost or an exhalation;
but even these appearances had grown rarer and rarer.
Only the neighbours' children really saw her. She had
given up wearing colours and was always dressed in

diaphanous white, with a cameo pin that held the ruching together. She was decisive in manner, anything but frail. Her complexion was velvety white, her lips were red. Her hair was bound with a chestnut-coloured snood, and when it was chilly she wore a little shoulder-cape crocheted of soft white worsted run through with a ribbon. She often had a flower in her hand. She moved about in a sort of revery, flitting "as quick as a trout" when she was disturbed. This was one of her sister Lavinia's phrases. The children knew her "high, surprised voice." They knew her dramatic way of throwing up her hands as she ended one of the stories she liked to tell them. She made them her fellow-conspirators. They followed her upstairs and heard her comments on the guests she had left in the parlour. She would say, with finger on lip, as feminine callers left, "Listen! Hear them kiss, the traitors!" Or, peeping down the stairs, she would say of some man, "Look, dear, his face is as pretty as a cloth pink," or "His face is as handsome and meaningless as the full moon." She remarked, apropos of some scholarly person, "He has the facts, but not the phosphorescence of learning." She said that her own ideal caller was always just going out of sight, and that it made her shiver to hear people talk as if they were "taking all the clothes off their souls." She called herself the "cow-lily," because of the orange lights in her hair and her eyes, and she observed that the housemaid moved about "in a calico sarcophagus." Once she said to her little niece, who was puzzled by her shy ways, "No one could ever punish a Dickinson by shutting her up alone." Meanwhile, her life went on with her flowers and her sister. She had a small conservatory, opening out of the dining-room, a diminutive glass chamber with shelves around it; and there she grouped the ferns and the jasmine, the lilies and the heliotrope and the oxalis plants in their hanging baskets. She had a little watering-pot, with a long, slender spout

that was like the antenna of an insect, and she sat up all
night at times in winter to keep her flowers from freezing. The garden was her special care, and occasionally
one saw her at dusk through the gate fluttering about the
porch like a moth in the moonlight. When it was damp,
she knelt on an old red army blanket that she had thrown
on the ground, to reach the flowers. Usually, on summer
evenings, she sat for a while with Lavinia on the side
piazza, overlooking the flagged path that led to the
villa. There stood the giant daphne odora, moved out
from the conservatory, and the two small oleanders in
their tubs.

Meanwhile, since 1862, Miss Dickinson had been writing poems, although there were very few of her friends
who knew it. They all knew the little rhymes she sent
them with arbutus buds, but they did not know how seriously she pursued her writing, at night, beside the Franklin stove, in the upstairs corner bedroom, in the light that
often glimmered over the snow. From her window she
had caught suggestions that gave her a picture, a fancy,
an image. Perhaps a boy passed whistling, or a neighbour
on her way to church, or a dog with feet "like intermittent plush;" or perhaps she knew that a travelling circus
was going to pass in the early morning, and she sat up to
watch the "Algerian procession." A dead fly on the win-
dow-pane stirred her imagination, and once in the glare
of a fire at night she saw a caterpillar measuring a leaf
far down in the orchard. She saw the bluebirds darting
round "with little dodging feet,"

> The motions of the dipping birds,
> The lightning's jointed road;

and all these observations went into her verses. She wrote
on sheets of note-paper, which she sewed together, rolling and tying the bundles with a thread or a ribbon and

tucking them away in the drawers of her bureau; although sometimes the back of an envelope served her as well, or a scrap of the *Springfield Republican*. But, casual in this, she was anything but casual,—she was a cunning workman,—in her composition. Poetry was her solitaire and, so to speak, her journal, for, like Thoreau in Concord, she watched the motions of her mind, recording its ebbs and flows and the gleams that shot through it; and she laboured over her phrases to make them right. Were they all her own? Were there echoes in them, or anything of the conventional, the rhetorical, the fat? Were they clear, were they exact, were they compact? She liked the common hymn-metres, and the metres of nursery-jingles, which had been deeply ingrained in her mind as a child, and she seemed to take a rebellious joy in violating all their rules, fulfilling the traditional patterns while she also broke them. She was always experimenting with her rhymes and her rhythms, sometimes adding extra syllables to break up their monotony, sometimes deliberately twisting a rhyme, as Emerson did, for the sake of harshness, to escape the mellifluous effect of conventional poems. Many of her pieces were like parodies of hymns, whose gentle glow in her mind had become heat-lightning. For Emily Dickinson's light was quick. It was sudden, sharp and evanescent; and this light was the dry light that is closest to fire.*

The visible setting of these poems was the New England countryside, the village, the garden, the household that she knew so well, a scene, the only scene she knew, that she invested with magic, so that the familiar objects

---

* Why did not Miss Dickinson publish her poems? This question is insoluble and idle. One can only say that, if she had published them, the poems would have been quite different in their total effect. If she had seen her work in proof, she would have arranged the poems in some reasonable order, she would have rectified the punctuation, etc. Her work would have seemed less arbitrary and less eccentric. The poems as they stand abound in misprints; and Miss Dickinson's collected work consists of serious poems, fragments and trivialities confusedly shuffled together.

became portents and symbols. Here were the hills, the
changing seasons, the winter light, the light of spring, the
bee, the mouse, the humming-bird, the cricket, the lonely
houses off the road, the village inn, the lamp-post that became, in the play of her fancy, sublime or droll; and with
what gifts of observation she caught the traits of her
birds and insects, of everything that crept or ran or flew,
—the snake "unbraiding in the sun," the robin's eyes,
"like frightened beads," the umbrella of the bat that was
"quaintly halved." She often seemed a little girl, amusing
herself with childish whimsies, and, in fact, as the ward of
her father, she remained in some ways adolescent; and, as
she dressed to the end in the fashion of her early youth,
so she retained the imagery of the child in the household.
But her whimsies sometimes turned into bold ideas that
expressed an all but fathomless insight or wisdom. She
saw the mountain, like her father, sitting "in his eternal
chair;" her ocean had a "basement," like the house in
Amherst, and her wind and snow swept the road like the
brooms that she had been taught to use,—the brooms of
the breeze swept vale and tree and hill. A journey to the
Day of Judgment struck her as a "buggy-ride," and she
saw a "schoolroom" in the sky. She domesticated the universe and read her own experience into the motions of
nature and the world she observed. The sun rose in the
East for her "a ribbon at a time," and the "housewife in
the evening West" came back to "dust the pond." Clouds
for her were "millinery," mountains wore bonnets, shawls
and sandals, eternity "rambled" with her, like her dog
Carlo; the wind had fingers and combed the sky, and
March walked boldly up and knocked like a neighbour.
Volcanoes purred for her like cats, and she saw the
planets "frisking about," and her Providence kept a store
on the village street, and she thought of death as coming
with a broom and a dustpan. The moon slid down the
stairs for her "to see who's there," and the grave for her

was a little cottage where she could "lay the marble tea." One could not "fold a flood," she said, and "put it in a drawer," but she rolled up the months in moth-balls and laid them away, as she had swept up the heart and put away love; and she saw hope, fear, time, future and past as persons to rally, tease, flee, welcome, mock or play with.

The turns of fancy that marked these poems were sharp and unpredictable, and yet they were singularly natural,—nothing was forced. Miss Dickinson lived in a world of paradox, for, while her eye was microscopic, her imagination dwelt with mysteries and grandeurs. Ribbons and immortality were mingled in her mind, which passed from one to the other with the speed of lightning, though she sometimes took a mischievous pleasure in extravagant combinations of thought, uniting the droll and the sublime, the trivial and the grand. There was in this an element of the characteristic American humour that liked to play with incongruities, and Miss Dickinson maintained in the poems of her later years the fun-loving spirit she had shown as a schoolgirl. To juxtapose the great and the small, in unexpected ways, had been one of her prime amusements as the wit of her circle, and this, like the laconic speech that also marked the Yankee, had remained an essential note of her style as a poet. "Shorter than a snake's delay," her poems were packed with meaning; and, swiftly as her images changed, they were scarcely able to keep the pace with which her mind veered from mood to mood, from faith to mockery, from mysticism to rationalism, through ecstasy, disillusion, anguish, joy. These poems were fairylike in their shimmer and lightness, they moved like bees upon a raft of air; and yet one felt behind them an energy of mind and spirit that only the rarest poets ever possessed. Was not Emily Dickinson's idiom the final proof that she possessed it? Her style, her stamp, her form were completely her own.

Such were the games of solitaire that Miss Dickinson played in the silent room, as lonely as Jane Eyre, in her red-curtained alcove, dreaming over the book with its pictures of the arctic wastes and the rock that stood up in the sea of billow and spray. Miss Dickinson had only this "acre of a rock," and yet what a harvest it yielded of grape and maize. Having but a crumb, she was sovereign of them all, as she said quite truly; for her constant theme was deprivation, the "banquet of abstemiousness," and this sharpened as nothing else her perception of values. When the well's dry, we know the worth of water, and she felt that she knew victory because she knew defeat, she felt that she knew love because she had lost it; and certainly for all she missed she made up in intensity. Where others merely glowed, she was incandescent.

CHAPTER XVI

INDIAN SUMMER

IN THE mild air of the early eighties, a haze of Indian
summer hung over New England. The heats and the
rigours of the past were long forgotten, the passions of
the war, the old crusades, and a mood of reminiscence
possessed the people, for whom the present offered few
excitements. Society had lost its vital interests, and the
Boston mind was indolent and flaccid, as if the struggle
for existence had passed it by. Its ambition seemed to be
atrophied, except on the practical plane, and this was
equally true in the rural regions. Many a clock had gone
dead in hamlets that had hummed with life, where the
men, it was often remarked, were torpid and listless; and
farmers sat in the village stores, wagging their beards all
day, chewing and whittling, as shiftless as Canada thistles.
The old strain was wearing out, or so the Boston people
said; but the region was tranquil and mellow, at least on
the surface. In the absence of motives, its mind was be-
calmed; and Thomas Wentworth Higginson, with his
nose for causes, could find no shield on which to break a
lance. So he jogged about the country with a horse and
buggy. Sometimes he collected ferns. Sometimes he ransacked the farms for spinning-wheels and colonial chairs
and tables.

For the vogue of antiques had begun, both in people
and objects. The story-tellers looked for types, as if the
race were truly dying and one had to gather the relics before they vanished. Others gathered the shells it had left
or was leaving, the grandfather's clocks and the claw-

footed furniture, the pewter plates, the latches, the knock-
ers, the lanterns. They picked up Sheraton highboys and
Hepplewhite lowboys; they even collected wax flowers
and funeral wreaths. The country was becoming a museum or a vast antique-shop; and the sense of the past
was omnipresent, with a feeling of decay and desolation.
Had the Yankee mind really lost its vigour and its hold
on the bounding modern world? It was certainly losing
some of its characteristics. All manner of strange religions
were taking root in Boston, where novel forms of spiritual
dissipation seemed to be the order of the day. The seeress,
Mrs. Eddy, had opened her Christian Science church, and
swamis and mystics from Persia began to appear in drawing-rooms in a town that was ready for everything and
amused by all. It was amused by Mrs. Jack Gardner, who
walked down Tremont Street with a lion in leash, who
hired locomotives when coaches were not fast enough and
appeared at balls with a page to bear her train. The Anglo-
Catholic church had risen, following Phillips Brooks's
rise, and marking the gradual return of the colonial feeling. The new Back Bay streets and apartment-houses also
reflected this change: the names that most of them bore
were notably English, Clarendon, Wellington, Hereford.
In schools like Groton and Saint Paul's, the tendency to
revert to England in educational methods, in sports and
in manners denoted the secession of the fashionable
classes from the democratic forms of the old republic.
The Anglo-Catholic movement had repercussions in literature soon, and it concurred with the growth of aesthetic
feeling, the most recent symbol of which was Trinity
Church. Richardson had built this church in 1877, with
the aid of John La Farge and Stanford White and the
Franco-Irish-American sculptor Saint-Gaudens. Burne-
Jones and William Morris had made windows for it. In
its colour and splendour, it indicated forcibly the break
of the Boston mind with its Puritan past.

Boston was prepared to see itself as others saw it, in this hour of elasticity and relaxation. Its days of storm and stress were past. It was ready to laugh at itself and its oddities and foibles, and Edward Everett Hale's vivacious sister, the witty, the sprightly Lucretia, improved the occasion at once with *The Peterkin Papers*. This book was an amicable satire on the well-known culture that was everywhere associated with the name of Boston, and the Peterkins suggested the literary families that also abounded in Boston and its learned suburbs. They might have been drawn from the Alcotts, the Howes or the Hales. With their innocent pedantry, their breezy gullibility, their high-minded faith in life and utter lack of common sense, they carried the traits of these families to a pitch of the absurd. Their "educational breakfasts" were one of the notes of a nonsense-Boston that might have been conceived by Edward Lear. Their bent for self-improvement, their conundrums at picnics, their zest for the acquisition of Sanskrit and Turkish, their joy in making life an object-lesson,—studying the butter at table and including the cow,—could only have been possible in a world that had known Elizabeth Peabody and the candours of transcendental Concord. But the book that recounted their adventures could only have been written when the day was already passing for these candours and joys.

In Concord itself one found the note of Indian summer, an afterglow of Transcendentalism. Emerson's early dream of a new university had had a late fulfillment at the Hillside Chapel. Alcott, on his lecturing-tours, had met in the West numbers of students for whom the little town was a loadstar and who were flocking thither in the summer, along with their New England condisciples, to sit at the feet of the Yankee worthies and sages. The redoubtable William T. Harris was one of these students, a Connecticut man, like Alcott, who lived in Saint Louis,

where he edited the *Journal of Speculative Philosophy*.*
Alcott and Harris joined hands, and the Concord School
of Philosophy came into being. It was founded to counteract the materialistic tendencies of the current scientific
thought, and there the Hegelian categories, introduced by
Harris, mingled in the lectures and conversations with the
modes of thought and speech of the days of the "Newness." The omnibus, the "Blue Plato," rumbled through
the town, astir with Hypatias in muslin and straw-hatted
Kants; and, sooner or later, two thousand neophytes sat
on the rustic settees or gathered on the grassy stretches
outside the chapel. The trees brushed the open windows,
through which the murmuring summer sounds mingled
with the voices of the speakers.

The school was Alcott's triumph. It had sprung from a
conversation at Orchard House, beside which the Hillside
Chapel stood, with its Gothic doors and windows, and the
hardy old philosopher was the dean and leader. Under
his elms stood the academy, the river was his Ilyssus now;
for Emerson, who remained as a presence, was fading out.
One saw Emerson, slightly stooping, with a shawl about
his shoulders, patiently standing in line at the post-office
wicket. He sometimes appeared at the school, and a reverential student now and then joined him for a stroll to
Sleepy Hollow, perhaps with Elizabeth Peabody and
Ellery Channing. As these ancient luminaries stopped for
discourse at the foot of an oak, or moved from gravestone
to gravestone, they always forgot their portfolios, their
sticks and their hats. The outlines of Emerson's personality remained firm and clear, but the details grew dimmer
and dimmer as his memory waned; while Alcott, at eighty,
was beginning a new career as a poet with a series of excellent sonnets addressed to his friends, the past or pass-

---

* In this first journal in the English language devoted exclusively to
philosophy appeared the first philosophical essays of Charles Peirce, William James, Josiah Royce and John Dewey.

ing worthies of New England, Garrison, Dr. Channing,
Thoreau and Hawthorne, Whittier, Phillips, Emerson
and his daughter Louisa, who decked the Hillside Chapel
with flowers and branches. These sonnets, noble and
touching, had an unmistakable ring of authority, unlike
the skillful exercises of most of the current sonneteers.
Sometimes Miss Peabody presided at the sessions, sometimes Mrs. Howe, who was always at home in the
"chair;" but the younger intelligentsia joined with the
older, and the school was a lively parade of American
thought. It lingered on through nine idyllic summers.
There were courses on Goethe, Emerson, Dante and
Plato, on Buddhism, Homer and Milton; and among the
speakers were Dr. McCosh of Princeton and President
Porter of Yale, Higginson, Frank B. Sanborn, Charles
Peirce and Stedman. Harrison G. O. Blake read from
Thoreau's unpublished journals. William James and John
Fiske, representing Cambridge, lectured on psychology
and religion, and Julian Hawthorne spoke on novel-
writing. Thomas Davidson scandalized some of the stu-
dents by comparing Zola with Christ.*

Thus, for a season, once again, Concord swarmed with
earnest thinkers, as forty years before at the time of *The
Dial.* Young men and maidens, aging sibyls who sometimes wore their skirts inside out, white-haired reformers
and prophets with a gleam in their eye threaded the winding woodpaths, and the glens and hills reëchoed with their
talk. They hovered about the Manse, they visited the bat-
tlefield by moonlight, and they added their stones to the
cairn on the site of Thoreau's hut, while, unconscious of
all observers, Emerson's daughter Ellen ambled about the
roads on her large grey donkey, with her full skirts bil-
lowing in the summer breeze. If they strolled, by chance,
to Walden on a Sunday, they found themselves in the

---

* Similarly an eminent critic of our day has compared D. H. Lawrence
with Christ.

midst of another assemblage, remote from the austerities
of Concord, that was yet not unrelated to the Concord
scene. There, in the grove by the pond, the spiritualists
held camp-meetings, and trance-speakers addressed the
crowd, gathered from buggies and carryalls tied to the
trees, inviting them to "come to spirit-land." Mediums
gave exhibitions of self-expansion and self-compression,
and mesmerists and faith-healers waved their wands and
cast their spells. The connection may have been tenuous,
but still it existed, between this new religion and Emerson's doctrines, which denied the reality of matter, or
seemed to deny it, while they taught the omnipotence of
mind. Had not Emerson said, "Never name sickness"?
Was it not his idea that, since man was divine, evil could
scarcely have any real existence? Alcott had shown an
active interest in Mary Baker Glover,—Mrs. Eddy, as
she was known in Boston,—for whom pain, disease, old
age and death were "errors." Alcott had been struck by
her *Science and Health* and had visited her classes in
Lynn and lectured before them. There was a deep relation
between the Concord point of view and the mind-cure that
was raging through New England; and, beside this cult
and the spiritualism that flourished in the Walden grove,
the School of Philosophy seemed a mere survival.

There was nothing essentially new in this interest in
the "spirit-land" and these other allied phenomena that
excited New England, phrenology, astrology, galvanism,
hypnotism and the study of manifestations and astral
forms; but since the war their vogue had grown immensely. They had thriven from early times in this land
of the Shakers, whose founder, Mother Ann Lee, the
"Woman of the Apocalypse," had lived in the hills near
Mrs. Eddy's birthplace. The founder of phrenology had
died in Boston: it somehow seemed natural that Spurz-
heim should have found a grave in Mount Auburn. Hawthorne had pictured a medium in *The Blithedale Romance;*

Orestes Brownson had written about spirit-rappers; Epes Sargent continued the theme in his novel *Planchette.**
But what had been a casual interest in the fuller days before the war was a much more serious matter in the post-war years. The decay of the old religion had left the religious instinct unsatisfied, and the Yankee mind was lost without the causes that had given it an outlet and a focus. These psychical mysteries filled a void; and, if this was true among thinking people, was it not truer still in a village world that abounded in ailing women and empty houses? Many of the New England authors were interested in spiritualism, from Shepherd Tom Hazard in Rhode Island to Celia Thaxter on the Isles of Shoals. Mrs. Thaxter acted as a medium herself, and even Tom Appleton in Boston was caught by this fashion: he wrote a charming story about Lavater, and no one was more curious than he in all these matters. Mrs. Stowe was addicted to planchette, and she and Whittier sat up many a night discussing manifestations and table-rappings.† For some of these worthies, who had lived through great excitements and who found themselves in a world that was dull and empty, spiritualism afforded new sensations; and life was duller still for the village people. The building days were long past, with all their compensations, their ambitions and interests, the tasks that had filled the present with zest and meaning. The men who had gone to the war and returned to their farms were often idle, slack and discontented; and the hope of a future life seemed vaguer and vaguer. In these stranded villages and lonely home-

---

* William James's review of this book is included in his *Collected Essays and Reviews*. Epes Sargent was a cousin of the painter Sargent.

† Whittier's closing years were attended with "manifestations," in which he always took a lively interest. On the last night of his life, he was dining at Hampton Falls College. There were thirteen at the table, and twice newcomers appeared and guests left the table to break the spell. As he said "Good night" and left the room, the old clock struck one. The clock had not been wound for years, and no one had ever heard it strike, and it could not be made to strike again.

steads, one found countless queer and stricken women, brooding on death and disease, obsessed with their complaints and their troubles and symptoms. If they had "complications" in addition to troubles, they aroused a special interest in their families and neighbours, and many a young girl had tantrums and conniption-fits when she could not attract attention by other methods. Hysteria in all its forms, the fruit of isolation and repression, throve in these regions, and one heard all manner of rumours of miraculous cures. Mediums appeared and conducted séances, mesmerists and men who "pulled out toothaches," like the hero of Henry James's *Professor Fargo*. One of these mental healers was Dr. Quimby, who cured Mrs. Eddy at Portland and died of an "erroneous" tumor shortly after. Partly because the people were sickly and partly for want of other excitements, they amused themselves with leaps in the dark. They played with automatic writing, communing with ghosts in default of friends, they tried to exert magnetic influences, and they talked about clairvoyance and antagonization; and many who seldom spoke aloud rejoiced in the spread of mental telepathy, a new and more entertaining form of silence. These border-line activities, which were neither religion nor science, partook of both; and Mrs. Eddy's rising fortunes showed how far they answered a deep, insistent need of the population. It was riddled with nervous disorders. It was also bored.

The dusky genius of Mrs. Eddy was therefore a sign of the times, a portent of the race, the place, the moment; for only a time of declining vitality, only a region at ebbtide could have given birth to the cult of Christian Science. It presupposed hysteria as the normal condition; for health is the centre of religion only for the sick. More closely connected with Concord was the school of remarkable naturalists who rose with the reputation of the dead Thoreau. While Wilson Flagg perhaps owed little to

this, Bradford Torrey edited Thoreau's journals; and
Frank Bolles made a famous journey up the Concord
river with his fellow-Cantabrigian, William Brewster,
whose Concord home was called "October Farm." Wilson
Flagg, the first of these excellent writers, was a Beverly
boy, like Woodberry, who lived in Cambridge. His interest in natural history was awakened at eight, on a driving-
tour from Beverly to lower New Hampshire, through the
"Dark Plains," a tract of sandy country that was covered
with a primitive growth of pines and hemlocks, such as
later existed only in northern Maine. The music of these
woods, their darkness and silence, their echoes and their
solitude and vastness caused in the boy what he called a
religious conversion, and for many years this doctor who
never practised medicine rambled whenever he could in
the depths of the forest, in Tennessee and Virginia as well
as New England, observing the foraging habits of birds,
sharing the diet of the squirrels, listening to the log-cock,
the red-headed woodpecker and the song, unheard by
others, of the lonely veery. *A Year Among the Trees,
Studies in the Field and Forest* and *The Birds and Seasons of New England* assembled his notes in a fine though
somewhat formal style, unlike the familiar manner of the
later writers. Torrey also roamed through Tennessee and
studied the birds in Florida and North Carolina, as well
as Maine, New Hampshire and Vermont. He carried on
with Celia Thaxter a correspondence about their habits,
and he counted seventy-three species of plants in bloom
in Massachusetts in November. His essays in *A Rambler's
Lease, Birds in the Bush, The Clerk of the Woods* were
fresher and more deft than Flagg's, if also slighter. Both
these writers maintained the Cambridge tradition of Nuttall and Gray, although both were more literary than scientific; and they owed their vogue to the interest Thoreau
aroused, in ever widening circles, as the years went on.
    A more vigorous writer than either of these was the

secretary of Harvard College, the tall, rugged, bearded
Frank Bolles. Bradford Torrey first met Bolles in the
great swamp in Cambridge. In the dark, they could not
see each other's faces, but both had come on the same
errand, to watch the aerial evolutions of the April snipe.
Bolles, who haunted the Belmont meadows, the Bussey
woods and the Waverley oaks, whenever he could escape
from his Cambridge office, had tracked dove-prints in the
snow in Boston, on Rowe's Wharf and in Crab Alley, and
studied the whistler ducks and the gulls in the harbour.
He had a "wren orchard" near Cambridge, and one of his
favourite resorts was the Middlesex Fells, where Parkman had lived as a boy; but his Walden was Lake Chocorua in New Hampshire. At the tip of this heart-shaped
lake he built a cottage, and there he learned the secrets of
the wilder creatures that flitted about his abode on foot
or wing, the muskrat and the fox, the mink, the bittern.
He also roamed in Nova Scotia,—*The Land of the Lingering Snow.* He studied the birds of Cape Breton and
recorded in *From Blomidon to Smoky* his ascents of the
northern summits. But this lake with its oaks in New
Hampshire was his permanent centre. There he kept his
captive owls, eleven of various species, and perhaps the
finest of all his papers was *A Night Alone on Chocorua,*
the horn-like peak that rose above his cottage. He knew
the secret places of the mountains, and once when the
time for meteors came round in August he proposed to
count his meteors from the loftiest point. Clarence King
never excelled his report of the mountain thunder-storm,
when the peaks seemed to fall in noisy ruin, when the
sounds striking here and there on misty promontories
gave out their softened booms and waning rumbles and
the ghost-like clouds slipped over the black abysses. His
canoe-voyage up the Concord with William Brewster recalled the well-known journey of Thoreau's *Week.* Brewster, the ornithologist, had grown up in Cambridge when

farms existed still on Brattle Street, or at least large
barns with horses, cows and poultry. He had first visited
Concord in 1872, to hear a woodcock sing, and he found
woodcocks' nests at Walden. Then he had bought a tract
of woodland at Ball's Hill, near the river, a favourite
haunt of Thoreau; and he carried on his observations at
his eighteenth-century farmhouse and recorded them in
journals like his master's. He made annual trips up the
river with Daniel Chester French, the Concord sculptor,
who had begun his career with the statue of the minute-
man and a seated figure of Emerson, which remained in
the town. It was Brewster who made the first collection
of North American birds, and the journals that he kept
with loving care abounded in excellent descriptions. He
sometimes spent an afternoon perfecting a sentence, in
order to do full justice to some furry battle, perhaps between a mouse and a shrike, or the strange behaviour of
a muskrat or a snapping turtle.*

This interest in wild life steadily rose in the eighties, as
the cities encroached on the country and destroyed its
beauty. Norton·was only one of many who deplored the
dirt and the smoke in the sky, the denuding of the hills,
the cluttering of the seashore, the converting of mountain
streams into factory-sewers. At Ashfield, his summer
home, Norton established an annual festival to combat
these abominations and all the others that were eating
away the roots of American life. He restored the ruined

---

* Two posthumous volumes, *Concord River* and *October Farm,* have
been drawn from William Brewster's journals.

A writer far greater than any of these, W. H. Hudson, the author of
Green Mansions, might also be claimed for New England. Although he
was born in the Argentine and never set foot in America, his father was a
Maine man and his mother was of the oldest New England descent. Hudson settled in London in the early eighties, as much of a stranger there as
Hawthorne had been. For several years he made his living as a genealo-
gist, searching out pedigrees for Americans of English descent.

In connection with these naturalists it might be added that Luther Burbank was born at Lancaster, Massachusetts, in 1849. He perfected at
Lunenberg the "Red rose" potato. Burbank moved to California in 1875.

Ashfield academy, and for twenty-five years his "academy
dinners" threw light on most of the current American
problems. The village band marched up the road, and the
maples glimmered with lanterns on these occasions, and
the wagons thronged the little town with neighbours who
came from far and wide to hear the speeches. Norton
strove to arouse their interest in civil-service and tariff reform,—the causes that were also dear to Godkin,—anti-
imperialism, Negro education and the preservation of
nature and the beauties of landscape. George William
Curtis, Lowell, Howells, Woodberry and Booker Washington were among the speakers. It was Norton who
largely saved Niagara Falls. Meanwhile, as Olmsted's
parks spread over the country, bird sanctuaries arose on
abandoned farms; and Higginson, collecting ferns, sought
eagerly for native plants that were dying out in eastern
Massachusetts. He found at Worcester two or three that
had vanished on the seaboard. Others, already rare at
Worcester, flourished further inland; while the country
abounded with importations,—the dandelion, the butter-
cup, the celandine, burdock, mullein, chickweed and yar-
row,—that had never known the tread of Miles Standish's
foot. New England swarmed with foreigners, botanical
and human, while the native races ebbed and shrank away.
In the botanical sphere, Higginson observed that the ex-
otics were coarser than the indigenous flowers. The children instinctively recognized this and were apt to overlook them, when gathering the more delicate native
blossoms of the woods.* In his nostalgia, the colonel re-

* T. W. Higginson, *The Procession of the Flowers.*
In the human sphere, New Englanders made the same distinction. In
this they resembled the natives of all long-settled regions where a strong
folk-feeling has developed with time. Families from other counties remained "aliens,"—there were said to be people in Concord who considered the Emersons aliens. How much more alien were families that had
one foreign forbear, how infinitely more if they had three! See Kate
Douglas Wiggin, *Rebecca of Sunnybrook Farm:* "The Randalls were
aliens. They had not been born in Riverboro nor even in York County.
Miranda would have allowed, on compulsion, that in the nature of things

gretted the day when every Yankee boy could give intimate details of out-door life from observation. The current nature-poetry was sentimental because it was di-
vorced from the rustic living that had lain behind the
work of the older poets. For the rest, another symptom
of an urbanizing world was the growing charm of the
wilderness for the men of the eighties. The "Philosophers' Camp" of the fifties had been almost unique; and
Emerson, Lowell and Agassiz were pioneers for the rest
of their circle when they shared the unbroken forest with
the bears and the wolves and lived for a while as woodsmen at Follansbee Lake. The simple life had been everyone's heritage, but roughing it was the fashion now, and
life in the Adirondacks was a kind of salvation for William James and other younger men. James had spent his
honeymoon there in 1878, and for many years the farmhouse in Keene Valley, converted into a camp, remained
an inspiration and a refuge for him. There he could enjoy
the "wild animal personal relations" with nature that
were necessary, he found, for his mind and body; and
there later Thomas Davidson, the peripatetic philosopher, conducted the well-known school in which James
rejoiced. Others, like Tom Appleton, whose nerves were
Europeanized, regained their American consciousness in
the Adirondacks. An Adirondack literature soon appeared. One of its first and best books was Warner's *In
the Wilderness,* with an essay on hunting from the deer's

a large number of persons must necessarily be born outside this sacred
precinct; but she had her opinion of them, and it was not a flattering one
. . . 'They used to say' (a villager remarks) 'that one o' the Randalls married a Spanish woman . . . Lorenzo was dark complected, you remember;
and this child is too. Well, I don't know as Spanish blood is any real disgrace, not if it's a good ways back and the woman was respectable.' "
    All this would be taken for granted in Ireland, Denmark, etc. In con-
nection with New England and the South, it strikes Americans as comic
because the American mind in general is not used to the mental habits of
long-settled regions.

point of view. Another was Philander Deming's *Adiron-dack Stories.**

Meanwhile, the "summer people," in quest of the odd and picturesque, invaded the remotest hamlets with their strange, new customs; and painters interpreted the land-scape, while story-tellers explained the "natives" for city-dwelling folk who did not know them. William Morris Hunt, who had turned away from portrait-painting, had built a painter's van for sketching-tours. In this gypsy-wagon, with its team of horses, its bunks and compart-ments for provisions and canvases and easels, he had wan-dered all over the region, developing a new career as a landscape-artist. Hunt, despondent, had drowned himself on the Isles of Shoals, in the pond where Celia Thaxter found his body; but, three or four years before, he had discovered George Fuller in the village of Deerfield. It was the generous Hunt who persuaded Fuller to go to Boston and organized an exposition for him; and there the Deerfield genius, with his great ruddy head, enjoyed a late success with his glows and mists. For two or three years, he lived at Belmont, where Howells was one of his neighbours.† At Dublin, Abbott Thayer had begun to paint Monadnock; and at Gloucester, where Elizabeth Stuart Phelps had a summer cottage, Winslow Homer studied the fisher-folk, the Grand Banks fishermen who frequented the harbour. There tales of ancient mariners abounded, and flocks of pleasure-sails possessed his eye, with lumber-schooners from Machias and coal-barks bound for Boston and fishing-sloops headed for New-

* These vivid little sketches of the lonely mountain and forest folk were published in 1880.

It was at Saranac, in 1887, on a fine, frosty night of stars, "sweet with the purity of forests," that Stevenson conceived *The Master of Ballantrae,* which he wrote in this Adirondack village.

† See the fine biographical sketch that Howells wrote of the painter in *George Fuller: His Life and Works.*

foundland. Homer, the solitary, with all of Thoreau's
love for the tough and the pungent in men, rejoiced in
Gloucester; and his great pictures, "Eight Bells," "Kiss-
ing the Moon," "The Fog Warning," with their oilskins
and sou'westers and towering waves, were full of the feeling that Kipling partially caught in *Captains Courageous*
after he had visited these scenes. Homer had settled at
Prout's Neck in lower Maine, where he built a cottage-
studio overlooking the ocean. He had a painting-hut on
runners, for cold or stormy weather, and he moved it
from spot to spot, where he wished to paint, observing
through the big plate-glass window the tumult of the surf
and the lights on the rocks. Thence he set out for the
northern woods, to sketch deer-stalkers and lumbermen,
as later he went to the Barbadoes to study the Caribbean
and the Gulf Stream. Miss Phelps wrote at Gloucester
The Madonna of the Tubs and other stories of the fish-
ing-people. The humanitarian note in these ran too much
to the sentimental; but Miss Phelps jealously guarded the
self-respect of the natives, who were sometimes patronized by the summer people.

For the summer people were a problem. They were
often as odd as the natives, and troublesome also; and,
although they were of many types, they had one trait in
common,—they seldom understood the country-people.
Numbers had forgotten their rustic antecedents, others
had no forbears in the country, and the villagers were as
strange to them as the roaming Indians who sold their
sweet-grass baskets in the hotel parlours. There were
others who came in a reverential mood, the Western pilgrims, for instance, who returned in the summer to visit
ancestral homesteads and scenes of the past. These pilgrims, who swarmed at the Concord School, were strangers like the rest, though at least there was no vulgarity
in their attitude and feeling. There were some who had
lost all memory of the land of their fathers, as the Yan-

kees had lost their memory of the mother-country; while
in others this homesickness had mounted with the years,
so that the scene was touched for them with magic. They
sought out the sacred objects, familiar by name in their
childhood, of which they had read in Whittier, the "neighbourhood" poet, the lighthouses, the old schoolhouses,
the beaches, more fabulous yet to many who had never
seen the ocean; and often they ransacked some family attic, with its old hoopskirts and broken chairs, relics of the
"hand-made" days and the days of the war, shells from
battlefields, haversacks and bayonets, spinning-wheels,
wrecked portraits and rusty muskets. All this was natural
and touching, and so was the hunger for beauty that was
bred in the city, the eagerness of the summer people for
every tidbit of sea and landscape and all that was quaint
or charming in the ways of the natives, the clambakes and
the fishing-parties, the latticework flakes and the lobster-
pots, the gulls and the flags and the fog and the general
freshness,—lobsters just out of the pot, corn from the
field, eggs from the visible hen, milk from the cow and
chickens half an hour out of their feathers. The girls who
wove rag-rugs were interesting to city-people who were
hearing about handicrafts again;* and who could resist
the charm of the Maine boat-builders, in their airy shops
on sunny wharves, where the children played with the
sweet-scented shavings and the work always ended in
something graceful and useful? The villagers were glad
to share their pleasures. They were proud when some
fellow-native, a great man in the West, turned up again
and spoke at the little red schoolhouse,—the hero of Dis-

* There was a marked revival of interest in the arts and crafts, in textiles, pottery, etc., in the years round 1880. This reaction against machine-
methods was further stimulated by the visit of Oscar Wilde in 1882. Longfellow's *Keramos*, 1877, appeared when the interest in ceramics was
reviving. The poem sprang from Longfellow's memories of an old pottery
near Deering's Woods at Portland. There the poet had stopped as a boy to
watch a potter making bowls and pitchers at his wheel in the shadow of a
thorn-tree.

trict Number Four; and they did not object when the summer people set their bean-pots on the floor and filled them
with clematis and woodbine. Aware that they had neglected the graces, they did not object too much when the
summer people covered their houses with vines, though
the vines attracted spiders and were bad for the paint;
and they permitted their tenants to open the parlour
blinds, though the sunlight was sure to fade the carpets.
But the summer people did not stop at this. They painted
the old grey clapboards of the mouldering houses, they
rooted up the bushes by the wayside, they smartened the
village greens and remodelled the churches, they straightened the winding lanes that were better before.* In
short, they improved the country, a doubtful blessing,
while they looted the furniture and china. The natives
could scarcely protest against this, however they might re-
sent it,—but the visitors went on to improve the natives,
an apple off another tree indeed. They gave Browning
readings to widen their "spheres." They disapproved of
the food that was eaten at picnics. They flaunted their
silks in the morning and abashed the women, who guarded
their one black silk as if it were cloth of gold.† It was bad
enough to have strangers come to play for fun at the sort
of life they lived in sober earnest all year round.‡ It was
worse when the strangers tampered with the village good-
for-nothings and turned these bribable souls into lackeys
and swindlers. But, worst of all, they arrogantly "studied"
the natives, as if natives were curiosities like hoopskirts
and muskets. They regarded selectmen as "types." This
was all very well with Neapolitan *lazzaroni*, but whoever
assumed this attitude with a sovereign Yankee deserved

---

* "Improvement makes straight roads, but the crooked roads, without
improvement, are roads of genius."—Blake, *The Marriage of Heaven and
Hell.*

† Mary E. Wilkins, *The Jamesons.*

‡ "People don't like to have what is practical to them patronized as
amusement by others. It cheapens it in their own eyes."—Edward Bellamy,
Six to One: a Nantucket Idyl.

the contempt and hostility he won for his pains. The result of the confrontation of summer people and country-people was a kind of covert warfare, a real class-war, though the friction never resulted in violence or bloodshed; and the country-people usually triumphed, except in the fashionable colonies where the lackeys abounded, because, as often as not, the summer people, with their city cheapness, were the true grotesques. If this warfare subsided in time, it was largely because of the writers who acted as interpreters and filled the breach. Howells was one of these. With his knowledge of city and country alike, and his perception and charity, he brought together all sorts and conditions of men; and Sarah Orne Jewett, who knew her Howells,* and also knew the natives as a native, established for other interpreters a scale and a standard. Like Howells, she knew the world as she knew the village; and, as an admirable artist, she saw the village in the light of the "scale of mankind." † Her vision was certainly limited. It scarcely embraced the world of men, and the vigorous, masculine life of towns like Gloucester, astir with Yankee enterprise and bustle, lay quite outside

* A passage in Howells's *A Chance Acquaintance* might well have been the germ of Miss Jewett's stories. It expresses a fancy of Kitty Ellison as she strolls with Mr. Arbuton about Quebec. " 'Why, it's Hilda in her tower,' said Kitty. 'Of course! And this is just the kind of street for such a girl to look down into. It doesn't seem like a street in real life, does it? The people all look as if they had stepped out of stories, and might step back any moment; and these queer little houses; they're the very places for things to happen in! . . . I suppose there's a pleasure in finding out the small graces and beauties of the poverty-stricken subjects, that they wouldn't have in better ones, isn't there?' asked Kitty. 'At any rate, if I were to write a story, I should want to take the slightest sort of plot, and lay the scene in the dullest kind of place, and then bring out all the possibilities. I'll tell you a book after my own heart: *Details,*—just the history of a week in the life of some young people who happen together in an old New England country-house; nothing extraordinary, little, every-day things told so exquisitely, and all fading naturally away without any particular result, only the full meaning of everything brought out.' "
One can hardly doubt that Miss Jewett was struck by this passage when she read it in *The Atlantic* in 1873. She had already published one of her stories, but the *Details* that Howells mentions is a sketch in advance of Miss Jewett's first book, *Deephaven,* published four years later in 1877.

† Dostoievsky.

her province and point of view. She spoke for a phase of New England, a scene that was fading and dying, the special scene her experience presented to her. But her people were genuine Yankees and stood for the rest. They all reflected her own transcendent self-respect and put the summer people in their places.

Miss Jewett lived at South Berwick in Maine, up the Piscataqua, twelve miles from Portsmouth. She was "one of the doctor's girls," as people called her. Born in 1849, the daughter of Dr. Jewett, who had once been a professor at Bowdoin College, she had grown up with grandparents and great-aunts and uncles in a world of square, white houses, picket fences,—some of them ornamental, with high posts and urns,—and yards overflowing with larkspurs, petunias and asters, with hollyhocks and borders of box. When the fences were torn down, and the old reserve went with them, she felt that she belonged to an age that was passing; for she had shared in imagination the lives of all these older people who recalled the brisker days when the town was growing. Once an inland port, with a few old mansions, Berwick had carried on a busy trade, bartering timber for rum and West Indian molasses. Its ships had sailed to Russia for iron and cordage. John Paul Jones had recruited his men from the Berwick farms,* and later French prisoners of war had appeared on the river. In those days, ships from many countries had struggled up the channel, and even now two gundalows, fitted for lateen sails, were rotting by the wharf near the sawmill. But one felt as if all the clocks in the town had stopped, and as if the population had stopped with them. The gravestones outnumbered the people, and for those who were left the brooks no longer ran as they used to run, and the snow was not nearly so deep. There were cer-

---

* Miss Jewett's historical novel, *The Tory Lover,* dealt with John Paul Jones and his time at Berwick and the men he assembled for the "Ranger."

tainly no such drifts on the schoolhouse steps as the older folk remembered.

Such was the atmosphere, reflected in many a town and village, that enveloped Miss Jewett in her childhood. Her grandfather had owned the ships the names of which she knew as if they had been members of the household, and everything in the Jewett house, an ample, formal colonial dwelling, spoke of a time, once full, that was full no longer. The carving in the hallway was the work of three ships' carpenters, and the mirrors and the tables had been brought from England. The playroom was a chamber in the barn at the rear with a foresail from some old vessel spread over the floor; and whenever, as a little girl, Miss Jewett had wandered along the river, which separated Maine from New Hampshire, she found herself in abandoned mill-yards, dark-red, weathered ruins and haunted houses where cries were heard at night. The attics were full of yellowing letters, and the houses looked as if they said, "Good heavens, the things that we remember!" The little girl was eager for impressions. She mounted the teams and listened to the talk of the drivers. She scrambled up the great white oaks, swinging from branch to branch and from tree to tree. Once she climbed to the top of Agamenticus, five or six miles away, and saw the White Mountains in the distance. Later, on her horse, she roamed beyond, exploring the woodpaths and clearings, the cellar-holes and abandoned graveyards, the hollows where the lilacs bloomed in Maytime. She found forsaken orchards, with gnarled and tangled apple-trees spreading their shrivelled arms abroad; and often, at the end of some dim trail, she discovered the ghost of a garden, with honeysuckle, sweet marjoram, lilies and mallows. Sometimes, in a clearing, she happened on a lonely dwelling where an old woman sat on the doorstep, or she saw two sisters spinning yarn, stepping back and forth at their big wheels. But many of the houses were deserted and empty, with floors that creaked as she crossed them, and the windows shook in their loosened frames or lay in the grass below. She would build a fire in the crumbling hearth and imagine the life that had once been lived there. She liked these silent, long-lost places, with a few bits of bright colour relieving the green of the woods or the white of the snow. She seemed to die out of the world in this forest quiet, where everything was merged in the life of nature.

When she was not alone, she was often with her father, who liked to take her with him on his rounds. The doctor drove along the country byways, through the low, straggling woods of spruce and fir, stopping here and there at some high hill-farm or some little house, blackened by rain, with its tangle of roses. His daughter, his favourite companion, sat beside him, and he told her the stories of his patients. She heard the secrets of these dwellings, grey as boulders and silent as the mounds in the graveyards, with their front doors locked and guarded by lilac-bushes and every blind shut tight. Secrets, hidden away from curious eyes, that no one knew but Dr. Jewett. She joined him in the smoke-browned kitchens and the darkened parlours, where a whale's tooth stood on the mantel with a ship drawn on it; or she waited behind the horse till the call was over, at the corner of the dooryard fence. Then, as they drove along, they discussed the household, or the doctor described some incident in the family's life. Perhaps the "last of the Jeffreys," a sterile old scholar, was supported by his sister's little shop. Perhaps a lover had gone to sea, forty years before, and had come back as a tramp and no one knew him. Perhaps an old man, as he lay dying, had insisted that the grass in the yard should be cut, so that all this good hay would not be wasted when the folks came to the funeral and trod upon it. A will had been lost, perhaps: the house had gone to the cousins and the true heir, who had gone away to

Boston and made his fortune, had found the will by chance and torn it up. Here was a lonely old woman who thought of herself as the queen's twin, because she had been born on the same day as Queen Victoria and had seen the queen once on a voyage to London; and here a mysterious stranger had appeared at the corners, a man who wore gaudy shirts and liked a dinner of boiled fowl and went every day to the graveyard, or a grey man who never smiled and who cast a chill over his neighbours whenever he softly opened the kitchen door. The doctor was a local historian, although he never recorded these stories, and his daughter might well have been a doctor. She debated his remedies with him, and she read his medical books and his diaries. When later she wrote *A Country Doctor,* describing her father's character, she imagined herself as the daughter who became a physician and greatly shocked the town by doing so. For women doctors were appearing in the country, and Howells and Miss Phelps wrote novels about them, *Dr. Breen's Practice* and *Doctor Zay,* who lived in a Maine village, like Miss Jewett, and cured the young Bostonian, Waldo Yorke. Miss Jewett used her knowledge in other ways. It helped her to understand her people better, and to understand her people was all she wished. For Miss Jewett was a natural story-teller. She saw stories on every side,—in a funny old man in a linen duster on a station platform, in an old country-woman on the train, with her basket and bundle-handkerchief, who had lost her farm, in a poor old soul who had run away from an almshouse. Growing up in Berwick, with music-lessons and German lessons, and with *Cranford* and *Pride and Prejudice* as her favourite stories, she had read *The Pearl of Orr's Island;* and this novel about Maine people living in a decaying harbour had suddenly opened her eyes to the world she lived in. *The Atlantic* accepted one of her sketches when she was not yet twenty, and eight years later, in 1877, she pub-

lished her first little volume. This book, called *Deephaven,* was the story of two Boston girls who came to
spend the summer in a town like Berwick. They opened
the long-closed Brandon house and rediscovered their
family past in the relics and bundles of letters in the drawers of the desks, in the neighbours who made braided
rugs, in sea-chests filled with forgotten treasures, in the
church where the flute and the violin were played in the
gallery still. Miss Jewett found her own world in the persons of these Boston girls, and Howells caught, in the
delicate fancy that marked this youthful book, the note
of a rare new talent.

This little corner of Maine, with the islands northward,
was Sarah Orne Jewett's peculiar realm. She travelled
early and late,—as a girl to Wisconsin, and three or four
times abroad, as far as Athens,—but she always returned
to Berwick and the house and garden where she had lived
as a child and where she died. Her closest friend was
Mrs. Fields in Boston, with whom she formed the habit
of passing her winters, and she visited Celia Thaxter on
the Isles of Shoals. When Mrs. Thaxter came to Berwick, the great event was a drive in the woods and a
glimpse of a hermit thrush, if the friends were lucky, or
a winter drive in the basket-phaeton to Witch Trot or
along a ridge where the bare branches stood out clear
against a cloud or a yellow sunset. Miss Jewett spent
long days on the river in a rowboat, or, driving perhaps
to York or Wells, she rambled about the narrow alleys
where buildings stood cornerwise or had their back doors
where the front should have been, where the roofs had
windows in them and the streets were cobble-stoned and
the grey, rough-shingled warehouses were covered with
lichen. She knew the fishermen's cottages as well as she
knew the farmer-folk, and she talked with the old sea-
captains who basked on the wharves like drowsy flies that
had crawled from their cracks in the spring, as worn as

the driftwood and the ship-timber and rusty iron that were rotting away beside them. Sometimes she went to Tenant's Harbour, where, in the summer, she hired the schoolhouse for fifty cents a week and strolled to her morning's work through a bayberry pasture. In this "country of the pointed firs," with its long frost-whitened ledges and its barren slopes where flocks of sheep moved slowly, she found the Dunnet shepherdess and Mrs. Todd, the herbalist, and many of the scenes and persons of her finest stories,—stories, or sketches, rather, light as smoke or wisps of sea-fog, charged with the odours of mint, wild roses and balsam. There, in the low, unpainted houses, mourners watched with the dead, and sometimes a funeral train wound over the hills, like a company of Druid worshippers or strange, northern priests with their people; or, looking seaward, one saw perhaps an island funeral, a coffin in a rowboat, covered with its black pall, and a line of little boats close behind it. On the shore, old sailors baited their trawls whose eyes had looked upon far-away ports, who had seen the splendours of the Eastern world and painted South Sea savages. They spent their idle times carving ship-models or a model of Solomon's temple, following the Scripture measurements. As for the scattered islands, each had its story. One had its king, like Celia Thaxter's father, who had vowed he would never set foot on the mainland again. On another dwelt two families, divided by a feud, who had not exchanged a word for three generations. A hermit-woman occupied another, who thought she had committed the unpardonable sin. But most of the people were like the trees that grew in the cracks of the rocks and kept their tops green in the driest summer. Miss Jewett knew where to find their living springs. No one since Hawthorne had pictured this New England world with such exquisite freshness of feeling.

CHAPTER XVII

THE WANDERINGS OF HENRY ADAMS

HENRY ADAMS built a big red house in Washington. His friend, John Hay, at work on the life of Lincoln, built an adjoining house in a similar style. Richardson had raised the standing of all American architects, and Adams, who was an old hand at architectural studies, had commissioned this vigorous friend of his Harvard days. Most of the larger American cities had one or more of Richardson's buildings, which had spread across the country like Olmsted's parks. The houses he built for Adams and Hay in 1884 suggested his Sever Hall in Cambridge, the architectural masterpiece whose floors in later years were watered by the tears of countless freshmen.

The sunny rooms of the great red house were hung with Adams's pictures, the English water-colours and Italian drawings, with the Chinese bronzes, the Turner landscape and Blake's Nebuchadnezzar, crawling on his knees and eating grass. The chairs and the sofas were made very low, to fit the diminutive legs of the bearded master. In the greenhouse roses grew, the flower of all the historians, Bancroft, Parkman, Fiske and Cabot Lodge. Here Adams had hoped to finish his history, and his friends were to have a centre here, whenever they found themselves in Washington; for the Adams circle was unique in the capital,—the embassies and the White House were dull beside it. Richardson and John La Farge and Alexander Agassiz occasionally joined the Adams circle, and Henry James, when he happened to be in the country. The nucleus of the circle was the "Five of Hearts,"—the Adamses, the Hays and Clarence King. It was for the "Five of Hearts" that Adams had written *Democracy,* the first of his two little novels. The friends debated it, chapter by chapter, and, when it was published anonymously, the rumour went about, and lingered long, that King was the author of this novel. But King's brief writing days were over, and he flitted hither and thither in pursuit of the fortune that eluded him more and more as time went on. King was a bird of passage. Hay was Adams's constant crony. Every afternoon, when their work was finished, the two set out for a walk, the little, dark, brooding Adams and Hay, who was also a little man, but for whom a generation that blighted his friend had brought, and was to bring, success and fame. They were both deep in American history, and they had been more or less intimate since they had met in Washington at the close of the war, as Minister Adams's secretary and President Lincoln's secretary; and Hay had advanced from triumph to triumph, as a popular author in prose and verse, as a diplomat in Austria, France and Spain, as editor of *The Tribune* and assistant in the Department of State, and finally as the writer of the life of Lincoln. A Western man, untroubled by memories or traditions, he had sailed before the wind with the party in power, while his friend, the saturnine Adams, whom he called "Oom Hendrik," fought against the political stars in their courses.

Adams, who had longed for power, had known for several years that he could not hope to exercise power directly. But he liked the feeling that he was near it * and even exerting it indirectly as the confidant and friend of men in office. Ambassadors came to consult him, and

* "Socially speaking, we are very near most of the powerful people, either as enemies or as friends."—Letter of 1882.

they sometimes followed his advice; and later, when Hay and Cabot Lodge were running the foreign affairs of the country, they had a way of running them in his house. It was even rumoured that Henry Adams wrote some of Theodore Roosevelt's state papers. Meanwhile, he had written his two novels, *Democracy* and *Esther,* before he moved into the great red house,—the first expressing his disgust with politics as he found them, the second bidding farewell to traditional religion. Nimble in style and light in tone, these novels resembled in many ways the earlier works of Henry James and Howells, and in both, as so often in James and Howells, the leading figures were women, who presented Henry Adams's point of view. The charming Mrs. Lightfoot Lee, the heroine of *Democracy,* who had come to live in Washington, was bent upon learning what went on behind the political curtain and taking a hand in reforming public abuses. She was disillusioned much as Adams was. Esther Dudley, the heroine of the other novel, was equally disillusioned with the Church. She fell in love with a clergyman, vaguely suggesting Phillips Brooks, who stood for her as a symbol of modern religion, and found that she was incapable of sharing his faith. The characters in *Esther* were drawn from Henry Adams's friends. The geologist, George Strong, was Clarence King, and there was much of La Farge in the artist Wharton. The story suggested the building of Trinity Church in Boston, which occurred when Henry Adams was teaching at Harvard. He had shared in the discussions of church-arrangement and decoration, matters in which his clergyman, Hazard, was learned. Hazard, in this aspect, was clearly a portrait of Phillips Brooks, as Wharton at work on his murals was inspired by La Farge.

Suddenly, a blow fell from which Henry Adams never recovered. His wife committed suicide one Sunday morning, while he was out for a walk. The mainspring of his

life, he felt, was broken; and, moving into the new house
on Lafayette Square, he could not bear to live in it alone.
He burned his diaries, and his notes and correspondence,
and he commissioned Saint-Gaudens to design the Rock
Creek monument that was to stand henceforth on the un-
marked grave. He seemed to himself as dead as a ghost
or a mummy. Meanwhile, like Mrs. Lightfoot Lee, he
longed for the oblivion of Egypt. Mrs. Lee's nerves had
also been shaken by Washington politics. She also felt
her life had gone awry, and her final word expressed
Adams's thought: "Oh, what a rest it would be to live in
the Great Pyramid and look out forever at the polar
star!"

Thus began for Henry Adams a life of restless wandering that carried him round the world for twenty years.
In time he returned to Washington, and later he finished
his history at Quincy, where his forbears had eaten out
their hearts in disgust and disappointment at the turns of
fortune; but the work had lost its vital meaning for him.
He was ready to join any friend for any sort of expedition, Hay for a camping trip in the Yellowstone, King for
a visit to Trinidad, a casual English acquaintance exploring the West. Sometimes he went alone, when friends
were lacking, perhaps to South Carolina, perhaps to Van-
couver. He wandered over Mexico on muleback, wearing
a sugar-loaf hat and a leather jacket, living with the Indians in their mud-cabins, intimate with their pigs, hens,
burros and babies. King was the friend he joined most
happily. Geology, he found, was tranquillizing. It carried
one's thoughts away from time, and the reckless, active,
adventurous King, unsicklied by analysis, was the crony
he needed.* With King he visited Dos Bocas, a Cuban

---

* "As for Strong,"—Clarence King,—"he was always in good spirits.
Within the memory of man, well or ill, on sea or shore, in peril or safety,
Strong had never been seen unhappy or depressed. He had the faculty of
interesting himself without an effort in the doings of his neighbours."—
Henry Adams, *Esther*.

plantation, rising with the sun and rambling over the hills, geologizing. Adams had a theory there: if they could get down deep enough into the Archæan rocks, they would find President Eliot and all the professors of Harvard College. But he was drawn especially to the lands of Buddha. He felt that longing for the East which proud people often share, when, as Kinglake said, they are "goaded by sorrow." * On the first of his expeditions,† in fact, he went to Japan with La Farge, who had his own reasons for wishing to see it.

This longing for the East was a symptom of the moment, especially marked in New England. Numbers of Boston and Harvard men were going to Japan and China in a spirit that was new and full of meaning. Oriental art was the vogue among Bostonians, and they were filling the region with their great collections. Alexander Agassiz was an early and ardent collector. So was Raphael Pumpelly, for whose first book La Farge had written an essay on Japanese art. Mrs. Henry Adams's brother collected Chinese paintings. Edward S. Morse, the Salem zoologist, ‡ who made three journeys to Japan, collected Japanese pottery; Ernest Fenollosa, the son of a Salem musician, made a great collection of Japanese pictures, and William Sturgis Bigelow brought back from Japan twenty-six thousand objects of Japanese art.§ Some of these col-

* Kinglake, *Eothen.*

† 1886.

‡ Edward S. Morse, a pupil of Agassiz, went to Japan in 1877 to study the brachiopods in Japanese waters. He made two subsequent visits and became professor of zoology in the Imperial University of Tokio. His published journal, *Japan Day by Day,* was filled with careful observations of Japanese life and manners, accompanied by amusing pen-and-ink sketches. His great collection of Japanese pottery was bought by the Boston museum.

§ Morse wrote as follows, regarding his journey through the southern provinces, 1882, in the company of Bigelow and Fenollosa: "We shall see a little of the life of old Japan; I shall add a great many specimens to my collection of pottery; Dr. Bigelow will secure many forms of swords, guards, and lacquer; and Mr. Fenollosa will increase his remarkable collection of pictures, so that we shall have in the vicinity of Boston by far the largest collection of Japanese art in the world."—*Japan Day by Day.*

This prophecy proved to be true.

lectors were detached observers. Morse had no interest in Japanese religion; neither had Thomas Sergeant
Perry, whose grandfather's brother, the Commodore,
had opened Japan and who spent three years as a professor at one of the Japanese universities.* But others
were enthralled by Oriental thought; they were seekers
of salvation in the Buddhist way. Henry Adams was not
the only one who turned to the East for Nirvana, which
was "out of season" in Omaha but not in Boston.† This
word fascinated Boston, and even Tom Appleton named
one of his yachts "Nirvana,"—he who enjoyed the world
so heartily. Japan, for these minds, was a loadstone, and
in several cases its influence was profound and lasting.
Fenollosa became a Buddhist, and so did Sturgis Bigelow,
whose *Buddhism and Immortality,*—his only book, a lecture,—was a relic of the interest he aroused. Bigelow, a
student of medicine who had worked with Pasteur, had
gone to Japan with Fenollosa and studied seven years
with a friendly abbot. He was received into the Buddhist
communion. Three or four decades later, dying in Boston, he summoned a Catholic priest and besought him to
annihilate his soul. He could not forgive the priest for
refusing to do so. He left directions to have his ashes
carried to Japan, where they lie beside Fenollosa's on
the shore of Lake Biwa.

When Adams was drawn to the East, it was thus with
a motive that other New Englanders shared, and for
similar reasons. Still others continued to go as missionaries, who never had a doubt regarding their own possession of the true religion. But the day had passed when the
great scholars shared this faith and acted on it,—the men

* Thomas Sergeant Perry was professor of English literature at Keiogijiku
University, 1897-1900.

† "At Omaha a young reporter got the better of us; for when in reply to
his inquiry as to our purpose in visiting Japan, La Farge beamed through
his spectacles the answer that we were in search of Nirvana, the youth
looked up like a meteor, and rejoined, 'It's out of season!' "—Letter of
Henry Adams, 1886.

who had once translated the Bible into the tongues of
Asia and boldly disputed with the brahmins and the man-
darins. The Tamil and Burmese and Chinese dictionaries,
written by New England men, to convert the Asiatics
through the Scriptures, were the work of an earlier generation. The scholarly mind of New England was torn
with doubts, and when Sturgis Bigelow returned to Boston he found an open field for his message. This was
something else than the teaching of Concord, in which
even the Buddhist texts had been applied to magnify and
stimulate the will. It was a message of resignation, peace,
passivity, inactivity that appealed to the tired minds of
this later New England. In the Unitarian form, the Christian faith had lost its positive content, and the sons of
those who had hoped to convert the Asiatics were wondering if the truth was not in Asia. The old Unitarian
hope had failed, and for many New England itself was a
failure. Boston had grown complex, with the coming of
alien races, and the feverish activity of the rest of the
country seemed senseless to these hurt, bewildered minds.
The optimism that John Fiske and William James maintained in Cambridge was foreign to their mood and offended their taste. It justified the restless striving that
had lost all meaning for them. They longed for quiet,
solace and escape. Sad and fatalistic, feeling that life was
empty, they found a natural haven in the teachings of
Buddha. Blessed for them was Nirvana, where illusion
ceased, where the trials, the expiations and the whirlwind
of life were calmed and silenced and ended in absolute
truth.*

One of these students of Japanese thought was a young

* The character of Dr. Peter Alden, in Santayana's *The Last Puritan,*
may well have been suggested partially by Sturgis Bigelow. Dr. Alden, a
man of means who never practised medicine, had wandered in his youth
through Japan and China, collecting ivory carvings for the Boston museum.
Driven by a "hunger for something less disconsolate," the hypochondriac
Alden roamed the seas in his yacht, the "Black Swan," with two gilded
Buddhas in the cabin, and at last in his own way found Nirvana.

man of fashion, Percival Lowell. This grandson of the poet's cousin, a well-known polo-player, had gone to Japan three years before Henry Adams. He had arrived in Tokio in 1883, drawn by a wish to study the language and people. As a boy, he had gone in for astronomy, and later he remembered seeing the white snow-caps of Mars crowning a globe that was spread with many colours. He returned to astronomy afterwards at Flagstaff, Arizona, and became world-famous as "the Martian," with his theories about life on this favourite planet; but for ten years Japan was his chief intellectual interest, and he wrote three fine books about it. He hired a house in Tokio and set up an establishment, where he lived like a Japanese prince; but at first he stayed for a while in Korea, as a governmental counsellor and guest. His official position gave him a chance to see the Hermit Kingdom as no one from the outside world had ever seen it; and he described, in *Chosön,* the life of the court and the nobles, as well as the arts and the ways of the streets and the people. This picturesque and solid book was unique and permanent, for Japan was soon to destroy the old Korea; but Lowell's *The Soul of the Far East,* slighter in form and more theoretical, was the book that gave the author his reputation. This study of the Japanese mind, its impersonal nature, in family life, in language, art, religion, in which individuality was a transient illusion, attracted many readers who were ready for the message, " 'Tis something better not to be." This impersonality was painful to Lowell. He was not in search of Nirvana, however he ministered to other seekers, and he had before him a strenuous life such as even Theodore Roosevelt might have envied; but he made Lafcadio Hearn in America feel "like John of Patmos." Percival Lowell's little work, "precise, fine, beautifully worded," as Hearn described it in a letter, had much to do with sending to Japan the greatest writer of English who ever lived there. Lowell, moreover, wrote two other books that ranked with Lafcadio Hearn's for perception and beauty. He had made a special study of the Shinto trances, the subject of *Occult Japan;* while *Noto* was a simple book of travel. Only one foreigner before him had explored the mysterious peninsula that bore its name. This isolated region, with its deep-bosomed bays and headlands, stood out to the west of Tokio, a striking outline. It had long caught Lowell's fancy before he undertook the journey that carried him into this world of primeval Japan.

Later, Amy Lowell,—Percival Lowell's sister,—shared in the multifarious fruit of these travels. Amy Lowell, a roly-poly little girl, was twenty years younger than her brother. Not long ago, as a baby in a basket, she had been brought by her father to the Saturday Club; and there she was passed around the table, so that the aging poets might beam upon her. As for fairies, those she knew were fox-sprites and spider-demons, of which she was always hearing from her brother in Japan. He sent her long letters on decorated note-paper, and he told her about these pixies during his visits to Boston. She was already familiar with the two-sworded nobles and the camellia-trees that appeared in her poems. Meanwhile, a more serious student than Lowell who had gone to Japan five years before him was living there when Adams and La Farge arrived. Ernest Fenollosa had settled in Tokio in 1878. He was already engaged in a work that was to mark an epoch in Japanese culture.

This half-Yankee son of a Spanish musician had grown up in Salem, his birthplace. His father, a musical prodigy who had led the cathedral choir in Malaga, had toured the American cities as a member of a marine band and finally settled in Salem as a teacher of music. George Peabody had attracted him there with his great collection of musical instruments, and the elder Fenollosa had married one of his pupils, the daughter of a Salem ship-

ping magnate. The son, at Harvard, was influenced by
Herbert Spencer, whose teachings John Fiske was popu-
larizing, and, when the University of Tokio was opened,
he was appointed professor of philosophy. Fenollosa felt
at home in Japan at once, and he had among his pupils so
many future statesmen that he acquired a name which
meant "Teacher of Great Men." But his interest shifted
away from philosophy. He had always been a lover of
music and painting, and, as Oriental art more and more
became his central study, he was soon involved, as a sympathetic foreigner, in the Japanese aesthetic revival. The
moment was one of confusion. The feudal system had
passed away, and the Japanese, who were adopting the
European dress and customs, were disregarding their
own traditions and methods. In the schools they were
teaching American drawing and studying under Italian
instructors, and the great Japanese works of art, rejected
and despised, were disappearing. Many belonged to dai-
mios who, reduced to poverty, left these treasures to their
servants, through whom they reached the pawnshops; and
collections of paintings and porcelains, lacquers and
bronzes were scattered and sold for next to nothing. The
"foreignists" were burning them as rubbish. Fenollosa
found one of the greatest paintings in the Osaka market,
and he picked out of an ash-barrel a great ceramic head
of Buddha. This was part of a statue destroyed in an
earthquake, the pride of an ancient monastery, and the
monks, tired of keeping the fragment, which they no
longer valued, had thrown it away. Fenollosa's moment
in Japan was like James Jackson Jarves's in Florence,
when, thirty years before, Jarves had collected the primitives that nobody wanted. The Japanese nobles and priests
who had owned these works for centuries seemed to have
lost all feeling for their national past.

But the Yankee-Spanish Fenollosa was not a mere collector. He had become a Buddhist and cast in his lot with

Japan, and he became the centre of a movement to save
this ancient art. He bitterly reproached the Japanese for
throwing away their birthright. He established an artists'
club, over which he presided, and he helped to form the
"Art Club of Nobles," to interest the ruling class in this
great cause. Largely as a result of his insistence, the
Japanese methods of art-instruction were soon restored
in the schools; and he was appointed, in 1886, Commis-
sioner of Fine Arts for the empire. He was the first director of the Tokio Academy and the Imperial Museum. He
was asked to register all the art-treasures of the country
and draw up laws regarding the restoration and export-
ing of works of art. He was authorized to inspect the
godowns and open long-closed shrines. For two hundred years, in certain cases, these shrines had never been
unlocked, and the priests, who thought it a sacrilege, tried
to prevent him. The greatest of all his discoveries was
the standing Buddha of Horiuji, a figure of wonderful
beauty that was wrapped in swathing bands of cotton,
covered with the dust of centuries. For weeks he lived in
monasteries with the kindly priests, studying the great
scroll-paintings and other treasures, haunting the sanded
courts with their mossy stones and their banks of ancient
shrubs and irregular slabs. He sat before the stupendous
rolls, in the light, cool, beautiful rooms, to the murmur
of trickling water, with tears in his eyes. While he studied
these pictures, he studied the Noh-plays, which had risen
from the Buddhist and Shinto rites. Umewaka Minoru,
Fenollosa's teacher, had revived the plays in 1871. This
scholar and poet had found an old daimio's stage and set
it up and trained his sons as actors. He collected costumes
and re-established the ancient drama, with its masks and
choruses and sacred dances. For twenty years, Fenollosa
worked with Minoru, studying Noh, acting and singing,
and he recorded the traditions of this drama, which resembled in certain ways the plays of the Greeks and the English

morality-plays. He prepared translations of about fifty texts. Some of these Noh-plays were remodelled later, from Fenollosa's notes, by Ezra Pound. As *Certain Noble Plays of Japan,* with their art of gesture, dancing and chanting, they influenced the Western theatre, especially through the poet Yeats.* Fenollosa had foreseen this influence. He knew that he lived in what he called a "weak transitional period" in the poetic life of America and Europe and that Japanese and Chinese forms, with their subtlety and condensed power, were bound to affect the work of the Western poets.

In his later years, Fenollosa returned to Boston. The emperor said to him then: "You have taught my people to know their own art." His collection was bought by the Boston museum, where he acted for a while as curator. He lectured all over America, went back to Japan for three more years and died at last in London in 1906. In the summer of that year, in a New York apartment, he made a pencil draught of his one great book. This *Epochs of Chinese and Japanese Art,* compiled after his death, was full of errors, for he had no opportunity to revise it; but it remained as a monument and landmark in the study of Oriental culture. Fenollosa's purpose was to break down the old idea that Chinese civilization had been static by showing the special beauties of all its epochs, along with the relations of the Chinese and Japanese as interlocking phases of one great movement. With his "vistas of strange futures of world-embracing cultures half-weaned from Europe," Fenollosa later seemed a prophet, the somewhat cloudy symbol of a day when East and West were merging for ends unknown. But in his earlier time, as a scholar and awakener, his object was distinct and his work specific; and Fenollosa was in full

* See Yeats's preface to the Irish edition of this book, 1916. The translations from the Chinese in Ezra Pound's *Cathay* were also based upon Fenollosa's notes.

career when Adams and La Farge reached Japan, where
his ashes were to lie, like Bigelow's, in one of the temples.
With the shy, retiring Bigelow, who acted as their cour-
ier, he received the wandering students and took them in
hand. They had brought no books and meant to read
none, for they wished to come "innocently," as La Farge
described it; and the strict Fenollosa, for whom all true
art had ended with the advent of the shoguns, taught
them to discriminate between the classic forms and the
modern imitations and degradations.

La Farge had definite reasons for visiting Japan. He
was planning his fresco for the Church of the Ascension,*
and he hoped to find "certain conditions of line in the
mountains," as he wrote in his *Artist's Letters from
Japan,* that would help him for the background of this
picture. He kept this in mind, and he found a space of
mountain, with rocks and clouds, that exactly fulfilled his
intention. He sketched it many times, and he used it later
in his fresco. But, more than this, the atmosphere suggested the miraculous. One could imagine there the ascension of Christ and feel it in relation to the setting, for
ascensions and disappearances of pilgrim saints were normal events in Buddhist history, and Buddhism joined with
the earthly faith in attaching religious value to mountain
heights and solitary places. Sacredness dwelt in the Japanese mountains, and nature lent itself to miraculous events,
to moods in which the edges of all things blended and man
and the outside world passed into each other. Nature was
not separate, as it seemed in the West, although nature
had never seemed separate to Emerson in Concord. As
Emerson had felt, La Farge felt here,—how little plants
and flowers, grasses, mountains, the clouds that rose from
the water, the drops of water, begotten by nature absolute, great and small, might all become the godhead. And

* In New York.

then, after years of wilful energy, it was a relief to be guided by the "inner light" of Tao. It was good to try again the freshness of the springs, to see if one was capable of the new impressions that had once been so common in childhood.

So La Farge had reasoned, or so, at least, he felt; for he left the reasoning to his companion. "Adams, you reason too much," he said one night. He dreamed, after one of their arguments, that he heard the mind of Adams making a great clatter in the room. He awoke,—it was only a rat. They had taken a little house at Nikko, overlooking a temple and garden, with the Japanese mountains in the distance; and, while La Farge sketched, Adams read Dante's *Paradiso* or walked or rode on pack-horses over the hills. Sometimes he took photographs, or he sat cross-legged on the verandah, overhauling bales of stuffs and lacquers, mounds of books and tons of bronzes, with Bigelow and Fenollosa to guide his choice. The friends rejoiced in the sacred groves, where the god Pan might still be living, the holy trees and stones, the little shrines, the old roads between the walls, broken by turrets and bridges. Here were the "soul-informed rocks" of the Greeks and a world that associated spirits with every visible form of the earthly dwelling. The bareness and coldness of the Japanese interiors, which insisted on the idea of doing with little,—a noble one, certainly, —pleased La Farge: the highest care in workmanship was all that adorned the emperor's palace at Kioto. How civilized, this emptiness, after the accumulations of Western houses! La Farge was in high feather. He discovered in the figures in field and street reminders of the antique world, so dear to the artist. The distinctly rigid muscles of the legs and thighs, the ripplings and swellings of the backs revived his old excitement as a draughtsman. For a painter, Japan was a godsend; while, as for Adams, he found in the statue of Kwannon the image of his quest. Here was Nirvana indeed, achieved in eternal calm, with eternal compassion.

The travels of La Farge and Adams, soon to be continued, left traces in the lives and work of both. Adams's "historic sense," La Farge said, "amounted to poetry," and even Adams's reasoning was full of suggestion. His deductions set La Farge's mind sailing into new channels, and the *Artist's Letters from Japan* owed much to Adams. For his part, Adams developed new faculties under La Farge's influence. He had left the world of public affairs behind him. The author of the *History* underwent a transformation, and the Adams who wrote *Mont-Saint-Michel and Chartres* was, in a measure, at least, La Farge's creation. Adams had always been drawn to art; as a student of things mediæval, he had been drawn especially to architecture; he had had an early passion for stained-glass windows. He had collected pictures, terra-cottas, bronzes. But this was all rather external: his aesthetic feelings were buried under other interests. He was prepared for the spell of La Farge only when the political world had lost for him,—for the moment,—its stirring appeal; and the "spectacled and animated prism," as he called his friend, led him to feel from within the meaning of colour. La Farge had lived in Paris at the time of the battle-royal between the pupils of Ingres and Delacroix. Ingres had held that the first motive in colour-decoration was line, while for Delacroix the great point was colour,— colour, wherever one chose to place it, colour, however one wished to use it, if one's lions had to be pink and one's camels green. So all the French artists had felt in their great days of stained glass, and La Farge, who was trying to work in glass like a twelfth-century artist, was a partisan of Delacroix from the first. He was always talking glass and talking colour, and the feeling that Adams showed for glass and colour, when he came to write *Mont-*

Saint-Michel and Chartres, was largely a result of these conversations. The friends even worked together. During their second journey, to Samoa and Tahiti, Adams tried his own hand at painting.

Between his various expeditions, Adams reopened his Washington house. He returned, he said, "as a horse goes back to its stable." There he remained alone, for he never dined out any longer, while the world ran by with spectre-like silence. He finished his history, volume by volume, but he could not believe it would interest any-one: he did not even send it to his friends. He wandered out to Rock Creek and lurked in the evergreens and holly that surrounded Saint-Gaudens's Nirvana, as he sometimes called it. In his absence, the hooded figure had become a fad of tourists, and he found an ironical pleasure in lis-tening to their comments. Occasionally, he mingled with them, knowing that he was himself unknown, and the resentment that clergymen showed at this figure of denial, —as they saw it,—filled him with a bitter satisfaction. He had lost his own faith in life; but what was their faith and security if a graven image could so provoke and wound them? A faith that could not ignore this challenge was no great loss for him, he felt. They were no more secure than himself, for all their professions.

When La Farge suggested another journey, Adams longed for the East again. He would have liked to sleep forever in the trade-winds under the southern stars, in the void of the dark purple ocean. But once again La Farge had a positive purpose. He was eager to paint the South Sea islands, and Clarence King's phrase about Hawaii and the "old-gold girls tumbling down water-falls" captivated the fancy of both the friends. For the greater part of a year, they wandered from island to island, La Farge with his paint-box and Adams as La Farge's pupil; and again it was La Farge who wrote the book. *Reminiscences of the South Seas,* suggested partly

by Adams's talk, related their common adventures. The
dances and the native feasts delighted La Farge and
amused his companion, who described them at length in
his letters; and both were enthralled by this new world of
colour, which they tried to capture with their brushes.
There were the old-gold girls, like nymphs of streams,
swimming and hiding in the vines, with faces and arms
glancing out of the branches, while the men were a deep
red beside them. There was the velvet-green of the mountains, streaked by long white threads of waterfalls; and
the ferns grew thick on the dripping banks, and the sea
glowed blue through the pandanus leaves. The shores
were fringes of gold and green, and the palm-trees glistened in the moonlight, with their long arms waving and
rustling; and Adams and La Farge went swimming in the
purple light. Adams watched La Farge at work, intoxicated himself with the broad bands of orange and green
in the sunsets, the strong blues, the soft violets, the shifting tints of the ocean, the glow of the mountains. There
was an endless charm in the colour and light of every visible hour in these tropical islands. La Farge splashed in
deep purples over dark greens till the paper was soaked
into a shapeless daub, and yet the next day, with a few
touches, it all came out a brilliant mass. He would see
sixteen shades of red in a sky that was cobalt to Adams;
and Adams wondered vainly how he did it. But he mixed
his own colours by the dozen and splashed away. The
results were certainly feeble, but one could never tell: next
time, perhaps, the miracle might happen. He felt as he
had felt as a boy about fishing. There was always a
chance of getting a bite tomorrow.

With this education of the senses, Adams recovered his
feeling for history. He had long powwows with the
Samoan nobles. These great chiefs, immense, with heavy
arms, who sat with spaces between them, majestic, indifferent, as if for a decoration on a frieze, suggested

Agamemnon or Ajax. Their bodies expressed reserve, and they were as sacred as demigods, intermediaries with heaven. They reduced to the level of stable-boys the aristocrats of Europe: so Adams felt in their presence. But they accepted him as a great man also. The American frigate "Adams" had voyaged through these seas and left his name behind it. He discussed their laws of property and kinship with them, questions he had studied in connection with the Anglo-Saxons and early Germans. In Tahiti, his interest in history returned in full measure. The old chiefess Arii Taimai adopted him into her family, and Henry Adams became Tauraatua. He was named for a forbear of the queen who had once been enamoured of a maiden called Marae-ura, and songs about these lovers still survived. As one of the Tauras, with all the ancestral privileges, he became the heir of an estate of six orange-trees and a mango, and he took investiture of his duchy in the shape of an orange. From this relationship grew in time one of Henry Adams's books, the *Memoirs of Arii Taimai;** for he persuaded the chiefess to relate her family history to him, and he retold it, with his own investigations, as if she herself had composed the story. At certain hours every day he repaired to a cottage behind her palace, shut in by trees that filled the little garden. Then, from some inner apartment, the queen appeared and repeated her legends and songs. Betweenwhiles, with her sister Manihinihi, she prepared the material for these conversations; and sometimes, in the early evening, the sisters walked down to the shore and answered Adams's questions about the past. They sat on the rocks under the palms, in the light of the afterglow, with the blue ocean far away and the shadows moving over the water. The great heights of Aorai appeared and vanished behind the clouds, and nothing broke the stillness

---

* One hundred copies of this book were privately printed in Paris in 1901. It was signed only by Adams's Tahitian name, Tauraatua I Amo.

but the rustle of the surf. The musical voices of the sisters mingled with the murmur of the ripples, into which Manihinihi thrust her bare foot. It might have been a Puvis de Chavannes! Genealogy, in Tahiti, was a science. It ranked with the intellectual work of Europe, and the tale of the Tauras was the tale of Tahiti. Adams brought his historian's skill to the task. He knew the writings of all the travellers who had visited the islands, and he disentangled the complex threads of rumour, legend and fact. But only a few reflections and a few quotations from French and English authors disturbed the reader's illusion that the queen herself had written this charming book.

Meanwhile, La Farge and Adams continued their journey. This took them to Ceylon, where, seated like priests or deities in a sacred ox-cart, on chairs upholstered in red, they were dragged through the woods to Anuradhapura. There, among the stone doorways standing in the jungle, monkeys jumped from branch to branch; and Adams sat for half an hour under the shoot of Buddha's bo-tree. Where else could he ever hope to find Nirvana?

CHAPTER XVIII

HOWELLS IN NEW YORK

ONE by one, the older writers were gathered to their fathers. Emerson, Longfellow, Motley and Dana were gone. In 1886, Emily Dickinson died at Amherst in the red-brick house where she was born. Fifty-six years old, she had been for a while an invalid and more invisible than ever; but one of her pleasures had been to listen while a younger neighbour played the piano for her in the empty parlour. Miss Dickinson hovered in the hallway, a glimmering whiteness. In her isolation, she had never heard Beethoven, Bach or Scarlatti; and she always sent in to the player a glass of wine on a silver salver, with a cake, a flower and a poem, a flash of the moment. At the funeral, Colonel Higginson read *No Coward Soul is Mine,* and Emily Brontë's unknown fellow-poet was carried to the grave by labourers on her father's land.

This youngest of the older writers passed obscurely, while the public fame of the others was in everyone's mouth. She had left word to have her poems burned. She had kept them in envelopes and boxes in her desk and her bureau, rolled like parchment in bundles bound with ribbons. Her sister destroyed her papers; then, struck by the poems, she saved them, in a fever of excitement. She turned them over to Higginson and the friend who had played for Miss Dickinson, and four years later they began to appear in the series of volumes that announced a unique and original American poet. Meanwhile, of the earlier writers a few survived. At Hartford, Mrs. Stowe, who had lost her mind, roamed about her grounds in the

care of a muscular Irishwoman, drifting in and out of
Mark Twain's house. Now and again, on slippered foot,
she stole behind some sleeper and roused him with a sudden Indian war-whoop, or she wandered into Warner's
house and sat at the piano, playing some weird refrain or
quavery hymn. To those who spoke of *Uncle Tom's
Cabin,* she often said, "God wrote it." Whittier had retired to Danvers, where he lived at "Oak Knoll" with his
spinster cousins. There he had revived his old skill in
horticulture and busied himself with flowers, plants and
trees; and there a visitor found him once playing croquet
against himself among the many-coloured autumn leaves.
A vessel built on the Merrimac bore his name, and the
governor and his staff went out to Danvers to celebrate
his eightieth birthday. In Boston, the half-blind Francis
Parkman pursued his Canadian history in his shadowy
study. One met Parkman out of doors, with a walking-
stick in either hand, hobbling at a run along the pavement, then throwing himself, to breathe, against a wall;
for, although he could scarcely support himself, neither
could he saunter. In his mind, for all his crippled body,
he was still on the Oregon trail. Pale, with his desperate
energy and his black-rimmed glasses, moving as if a demon
drove him forward, he frightened the children who came
upon him suddenly, lying in wait on a doorstep. But Parkman's health and eyesight had improved with age, and
he wrote his finest book, *Montcalm and Wolfe,* with his
own hand, in pencil. Howells was only one of an army of
readers for whom Parkman had made Quebec and Montreal "the beautiful inheritance of all dreamers." The
birthdays of most of these aging worthies were com-
memorated throughout the country, and their visages
were almost as familiar as those of the national heroes
on coins and stamps. In the game of "Authors," the
heads of historians and poets eternally rested from their
labours, brow on hand. Dr. Holmes felt like Nestor rec-

ollecting his ancient comrades, Theseus, Polyphemus and the rest; for the Saturday "club" was only a walking-stick now. As a wholesale talker, the doctor kept his end up, and he still presented his keyboard of nerve-pulps, not yet tanned or ossified, to the finger-touch of everything outside him. But the days of the conversational dogmatist, on the imperial scale, were gone forever. Johnsons and Popes were impossible in an age of science. For the rest, the veteran harper of Boston often attuned his strings now to birthdays that foretold a vacant future.

About this time, an English authoress, at a Boston dinner-table, said, "Isn't it a pity, don't you think, that all the really interesting Americans are dead?" The remark might have been phrased more happily, but, after all, this lady expressed what many of the Bostonians were thinking. Their classic age was past, or passing. The "second growth" of New England authors scarcely rivalled the first, and that "interesting" Americans might still be living elsewhere was no great consolation to the men of Boston. Besides, could they be really interesting if they were not Bostonians? * In other fields than literature, in science and philosophy, New England was certainly advancing. William James had long been at work on the *Principles of Psychology,* which was to appear in 1890, and Josiah Royce had been called from Berkeley to Harvard. In California he had been the "solitary philosopher between Behring's Strait and Tierra del Fuego." † Royce, whose head suggested the world poised on the body of the tortoise, was one of those "extraordinary men, too eminent for praise," as his colleague, George Herbert

* When someone mentioned the proposal to publish *Who's Who in America,* Edmund Quincy is said to have asked, "Wouldn't the Harvard Quinquennial Catalogue answer every purpose?"

† "There is no philosophy in California from Siskiyou to Fort Yuma, and from the Golden Gate to the summit of the Sierras."—Royce to James, 1879.—"Your wail as the solitary philosopher between Behring's Strait and Tierra del Fuego has a grand lonesome picturesqueness about it."—James to Royce.

Palmer, called him, who were forming the great philosophical department in Cambridge. These men were new centres of agitation in the intellectual life of Boston, and as long as Holmes and Lowell survived, with Parkman and two or three others, its literary prestige was secure. Writers from afar still came to Boston with veneration and curiosity. A case in point at the moment was Hamlin Garland. When he took the "back trail" from Dakota, reversing the pioneer law of development, even as Royce had reversed it, Boston attracted Garland, not New York. He had come with a feeling like Howells's, twenty-five years before, and was living there on forty cents a day, reading John Fiske at the Public Library, along with Spencer, Taine and Whitman, while his tan melted away with his corn-fed muscle. He lived in Boston several years, studying, lecturing, teaching, and he wrote *Main-Travelled Roads* at Jamaica Plain, where Parkman continued his history in the summer season. He haunted the streets with as firm a conviction that he was at the centre of the world as Henry James felt in the streets of London. But, for all this, the American centre had shifted to New York,—or was rapidly shifting, at least,—and Boston knew it. The literary leaders of the younger generation, Howells and the "Boston-plated" Aldrich, were half outsiders. They were loyal to the Boston genius, but not to Boston without the genius; and Howells had grown restive, although literary Boston had heaped him with all its honours and crowned him with laurels. The town that he adored was dying, the other Boston was none of his, and the young men were growing up dispirited and listless there.* A Harvard student, John Jay Chapman, lay awake at night, "wondering what was the

---

* "The young men of the seventies were told that there was no health in them; that Boston's classic age was gone; and Howells and Aldrich were perhaps none too loath to believe it, and that they were the only successors. They never really liked Boston. Lowell remarked once that Howells always wrote 'as if some swell had failed to bow to him on Beacon Street.'"— Frederic J. Stimson. *My United States.*

matter"—as he put it—"with Boston." Another acute observer explained it later. That Boston had "filled up" was H. G. Wells's diagnosis. Its capacity was just sufficient to comprehend the whole achievement, up to a certain year, of the human mind. About 1875, it had reached an equilibrium. Its finality was a proof of the laws of physics.*

This was partly true, at least, sufficiently so for Howells, who felt an insistent need for pastures new. Boston had been kind to him, and he held a unique position there as the confidant of writers old and young. When Longfellow died, it was Howells who was asked to look over his posthumous poems and make a last selection for publication. When Whittier cast about for someone to write his official biography, Howells was the first to whom he turned. Later, Norton asked him to write the official life of Lowell, who had offered him the Smith professorship. Cambridge could no further go than to add the name of Howells to those of Ticknor, Longfellow and Lowell, or, rather, to suggest this honour, which Howells refused; and, when the Boston writers and artists wished to establish the Tavern Club, he was invited to form it and lead the meetings. Just under fifty, he had vindicated Holmes's joke,—the apostolic succession was in his hands; but he had lost his feeling for New England, as New England was losing itself in the rest of the country. *The North American Review* had moved to New York; so had Edwin Booth, Parkman's neighbour, who had lived so long in the town. Boston had ceased to represent the widest American interests, and the younger American writers were ceasing to come there: they were drawn to New York much more in their

* "The finality of Boston is a quantitative consequence. The capacity of Boston, it would seem, was just sufficient, but no more than sufficient, to comprehend the whole achievement of the human intellect up, let us say, to the year 1875 A.D. Then an equilibrium was established. At or about that year, Boston filled up."—H. G. Wells, *The Future in America.*

dreams of careers, and they carried the widest American interests with them. The Boston writers were local writers, more and more, as the years went on, as the law of metropolitan attraction gradually lost its force there. The centre of poets and thinkers had become the centre of tutors and scholars and followed the path of a greater and earlier Athens. Dr. Holmes was touchy on the subject, and the question mildly raged in the Boston press. It was observed that, whenever a Boston author died, New York at once became the American London. The Bostonians, as Aldrich said, were not thin-skinned about it. They had no skin at all.

Howells had moved from Cambridge to Belmont, and at last into Boston itself. There he had bought a house on "the water side of Beacon Street." In this house he had written *The Rise of Silas Lapham,* and the story of the house that Lapham built was drawn from his own experience here and at Belmont. For Howells cared deeply for architecture.* He had an instinctive feeling for all the plastic arts, and he invariably saw with the eye of a painter.† But he had had his "twenty years of Boston," and the basis of his New England life was

---

* At the time of Howells's eightieth birthday, Cass Gilbert wrote that he had done more to cultivate good taste in architecture than any American architect then living. This architect added: "A single sentence in *Silas Lapham* about black walnut changed the entire trend of thought and made it possible for the architects of the time to stem the turbid tide of brownstone and black walnut then so dear to the heart of the American millionaire."

Howells's Belmont house was designed by his brother-in-law, William Rutherford Mead, of the firm of McKim, Mead and White. John Mead Howells, the architect, was Howells's son.

† "Mrs. Alderling . . . was leaning against one of the slender fluted pine columns like some rich, blond caryatid just off duty, with the blue of her dress and the red of her hair showing deliciously against the background of white house-wall."—*Questionable Shapes.*

See also his portrait of Mrs. Bowen in *Indian Summer:* "There was reason in Mrs. Bowen's carrying in the hollow of her left arm the Indian shawl sacque she had taken off and hung there; the deep cherry silk lining gave life to the sombre tints prevailing in her dress, which its removal left free to express all the grace of her extremely lady-like person . . . She

broken. He was disturbed and unsettled. He had gone
abroad for a year and seen his country once more in perspective. Boston, from the point of view of Florence,—
of the English and Americans there,—was much the same
as Denver, Chicago, St. Louis;* and this was the feeling,
rapidly growing again in Howells, that every excursion
from Boston served to confirm. He went for a winter to
Buffalo; he thought for a time that he might live perhaps
in Washington. Meanwhile, he arranged with the Harpers to publish his books and was writing in *The Century*
and *Scribner's*, the New York rivals of *The Atlantic*. He
withdrew from New England reluctantly and slowly. He
sometimes returned to Boston for a year or a season,
and many of his later summers were passed in Maine.
But henceforth New York was his centre. The world was
still full of novelty and interest for him, and he liked the
huge, kind, noisy, sprawling city.† As an all-American

had, with all her flexibility, a certain charming stiffness, like the stiffness
of a very tall feather."
   This might be a picture by Alfred Stevens or any of a dozen American
painters of the time.
   Here Howells sees Mrs. Bowen as she sees herself, as a psychologist sees
her, and also, very notably, as a painter would see her. This is characteristic of Howells's portraits.
   Howells's aesthetic feeling,—congenital, of course,—attracted him to artists from the outset. The sculptor J. Q. A. Ward was one of his early
friends in Ohio. But this instinct grew with his open sympathies and his
friendship with artists. His essay on George Fuller memorialized one of
these many friendships. It was not an accident that one of Saint-Gaudens's
finest works was the large relief of Howells and his daughter.
   * "Some geographical distinctions which are fading at home had quite
disappeared in Florence . . . He found in Mrs. Bowen's house people from
Denver, Chicago, St. Louis, Boston, New York and Baltimore, all meeting
as of apparently the same civilization . . . The English spoke with the
same vague respect of Buffalo and of Philadelphia."—Howells, *Indian
Summer.*
   † "March could not release himself from a sense of complicity with it, no
matter what whimsical, or alien, or critical attitude he took . . . She"—
Mrs. March—"lamented the literary peace, the intellectual refinement of
the life they had left behind them; and he owned it was very pretty, but
he said it was not life,—it was death-in-life."—Howells, *A Hazard of
New Fortunes.* Mr. and Mrs. Basil March were scarcely veiled representa-
tions of Howells and his wife. These characters, who first appeared in
Their Wedding Journey, reappeared in *Their Silver Wedding Journey*.

mind, sensitive to national changes, he wished to be in touch with the younger writers; and he was forever in search of new types for his work and ready for new points of view.* There were various other reasons for his change. One was the rapid growth of his sociological interests. Another was his desire for a simpler life, for Boston had lost the simple intensity that once had been its charm for him and had grown more reactionary also.† In all this he showed the influence of Tolstoy, who, as he often said, remade his mind.

For Howells was deep in Tolstoy. Eagerly interested in all the new novelists, whom he was introducing to American readers,‡ he was drawn to the author of *Anna Karenina,* as formerly Turgenev had drawn him. In this latter case, it was not merely the artist that drew him. Tolstoy's Christian socialism appealed to him still more and had a profound effect on his life and writings. Howells was prepared for this doctrine. Essentially, it

* From Mark Twain to Robert Frost, over a stretch of fifty years, there was scarcely a good new American writer whom Howells was not the first to acclaim. The list of these authors about whom he wrote is virtually coincidental with the literature of two generations. It includes Hamlin Garland, Stephen Crane, Frank Norris, Mary E. Wilkins, Robert Herrick, Edith Wharton, John Oliver Hobbes, etc.

† "Elinor and I both no longer care for the world's life, and would like to be settled somewhere very humbly and simply, where we could be socially identified with the principles of progress and sympathy for the struggling mass."—Howells, Letter of 1887.

To his wife, in 1906, he wrote of their early days in Cambridge: "The phrase for our life there is, *Intense and simple."*

‡ "I read everything of Zola's that I can lay hands on."—Letter of 1882.

Among the European novelists and dramatists about whom Howells wrote,—in addition to Tolstoy and Zola,—were Galdos, Palacio Valdés, Björnstjerne Björnson, Thomas Hardy, Ibsen, etc.

Howells knew Björnson well in Cambridge, where the latter spent the winter of 1880 in the house of Mrs. Ole Bull. Björnson, an ardent republican, was in disgrace in Norway because he had described the king as a donkey.

It may be added that George Gissing,—also in disgrace, at home, for less creditable reasons,—spent several months in Boston in 1876. There he supported himself by tutoring. Later he drifted to Chicago, where he contributed stories to the Chicago *Tribune.* He returned to England in the fall of 1877.

was not new to him: it was a reformulation, startling in its power, of thoughts that were familiar in his childhood. He had always believed in human equality. His father had nourished this faith in him, and he had grown up in an atmosphere that brought before him every day the ideal of coöperation as a way of living. He believed in the public ends that make men "a family, as private property never does;" * and he desired the good society, as what he loved was personal goodness,—he called himself a socialist because he was one. He had found in the Shakers an emblem of the good society, for all their sometimes squalid limitations. Their primitive Christian-socialist brotherhood held his imagination,† much as he also rejoiced in the world as it was; and, while he never lost this zest,—this delight in the play of human relations,—his conscience laid the train that Tolstoy fired. He was alarmed by the growing division ·of classes, the rift between poverty and wealth. The popular ideal had once been political greatness, while the modern Websters and Clays were the millionaires; and the older America, which had seemed to be tending towards equality, was yielding to another social order. Along with the millionaire, the tramp had appeared on the scene, and the streets were full of beggars and hungry workmen, while the papers recounted the scandals and rascalities of business. Meantime, the trial of the Chicago anarchists proved that Americans could be killed for unpopular opinions.‡ Howells brooded over this case. For two months it filled his mind, as the Sacco-Vanzetti case, in a

* Howells, *A Boy's Town.*

† Howells's mind was haunted by the simple, communal life of the Shakers. They appeared in four of his novels, *The Undiscovered Country, A Parting and a Meeting, The Day of the Wedding* and *The Vacation of the Kelwyns.* See also, in *Three Villages,* his description of the community at Shirley, Mass.

‡ "The historical perspective is that this free Republic has killed five men for their opinions."—Letter of Howells, 1887.

later decade, occupied the minds of other writers; and he cared nothing about the risks he ran, defending the anarchists after their unfair trial. His horror and heart-sickness, the more he dwelt on this, "indefinitely wid-ened" his horizons; * but he felt he could no longer trust his country.† Was America a republic still? ‡ His op-timism had been mistaken. Socialism alone could save the nation. All his major views passed through a sea-change, and even his own success smote his conscience.§ He felt that writers and artists should ally themselves with the toilers of shop and field. They had no part or lot in the secular world; ‖ and they had to confront the "ugly

* Letter of 1887.

† "I should hardly like to trust pen and ink with all the audacity of my social ideas; but after fifty years of optimistic contact with 'civilization' and its ability to come out all right in the end, I now abhor it, and feel that it is coming out all wrong in the end, unless it bases itself anew on a real equality."—Letter to Henry James, 1888.

‡ See his letter to Mark Twain, 1889, at the time of the downfall of the Brazilian empire: "I have just heated myself up with your righteous wrath about our indifference to the Brazilian republic. But it seems to me that you ignore the real reason for it which is that there is no longer an Amer-ican Republic, but an aristocracy-loving oligarchy in place of it. Why should our money-bags rejoice in the explosion of a wind-bag? They know at the bottom of the hole where their souls ought to be that if such an event finally means anything it means their ruin next; and so they *don't* rejoice; and as they mostly inspire the people's voice, the press, the voice is dumb."

§ "He felt the self-reproach to which the man who rises without raising with him all those dear to him is destined in some measure all his life. His interests and associations are separated from theirs, but if he is not an ignoble spirit, the ties of affection remain unweakened; he cares for them with a kind of indignant tenderness, and calls himself to account before them in the midst of pleasures which they cannot share, or even imagine." This instinctive *noblesse oblige,* attributed to Lemuel Barker in *The Minister's Charge,* characterized Howells through life. It marked his rela-tions with his Ohio family, as with all who were less fortunate than himself.

‖ "In the social world, as well as in the business world, the artist is anomalous, in the actual conditions, and he is perhaps a little ridiculous . . . Perhaps he will never be at home anywhere in the world as long as there are masses whom he ought to consort with, and classes whom he can-not consort with. The prospect is not brilliant for any artist now living, but perhaps the artist of the future will see in the flesh the accomplishment of that human equality of which the instinct has been divinely planted in the human soul."—Howells, *Literature and Life.*

realities" also.* The old Howells lived on, the sunny, cheerful, happy man who believed in his countrypeople as much as ever. But the new Howells continued to live with the old. His social consciousness never deserted him. It remained the burden of much of his work, alike in verse † and in prose.

This change,—or this resurgence of Howells's original feeling,—was part of a widespread movement of the eighteen-eighties. Projects of reform were in the air, and the Western plan of Henry George arose with the Massachusetts plan that sprang from Edward Bellamy's *Looking Backward*. Literary Boston was more and more reactionary. As the town had lost its adventurousness and guarded its spoils,—the spoils of the adventures of its forbears,—it returned to the Federalist views of the faraway past; and Aldrich followed Lowell ‡ in this direction. Aldrich was hostile to every movement of social reform. His mind reverted to the French Revolution, and he saw the struggling workers as the "lazy *canaille*." §

* "It is not ill, but it is very well to be confronted with the ugly realities, the surviving savageries, that the smug hypocrisy of civilization denies; for till we recognize them we shall not abate them, or even try to do so."—Howells, *Heroines of Fiction.*

† "Yes, I suppose it is well to make some sort of exclusion,
  Well to put up the bars, under whatever pretence:
  Only be careful, be very careful, lest in the confusion
  You should shut yourself on the wrong side of the fence."
                               —Howells, *Stops of Various Quills.*

‡ Lowell did not "think straight," as William James remarked, but his general political tendency was sufficiently clear. This did not prevent him from saying, in *Democracy:* "Socialism means, or wishes to mean, coöperation and community of interests, sympathy, the giving to the hands not so large a share as to the brains, but a larger share than hitherto in the wealth they must combine to produce—means, in short, the practical application of Christianity to life, and has in it the secret of an orderly and benign reconstruction."

§ "We shall have bloody work in this country some of these days, when the lazy *canaille* get organized. They are the spawn of Santerre and Fouquier-Tinville."—Letter of Aldrich.

This feeling is reflected in Aldrich's stories. Nothing could be more sinister than the union of the marble-cutters in *The Stillwater Tragedy.* In *Shew's Folly,* the retired business man who builds a model tenement is swindled for his pains. Everything happens in life, but an author reveals his tendency in his habitual choice of the things that happen.

All this contributed to Howells's alienation from Boston, though even there the radical movements throve. Boston was the scene of *Looking Backward,* and Tolstoy made a deep impression there.* A Tolstoy Club was organized, largely by Edward Everett Hale, whose "Lend-a-Hand" clubs were spreading through the country. Hale lent a hand to every effort to christianize civilization, and he had a memorable talk with Howells on Tolstoy; † and Thomas Wentworth Higginson, who was called a socialist, said the name was "a feeler in the right direction." ‡ Both Higginson and Hale, meanwhile, favoured Edward Bellamy's movement, with Howells and his friend Mark Twain. § Howells wrote a preface for Bellamy's *The Blindman's World,* and he and this country editor had much in common; for, while Bellamy was a villager,—he lived at Chicopee Falls,—he had seen enough of the world to horrify him. He had spent a year as a student in Germany, and the slums and hovels of

---

* There was much translating of Tolstoy in Boston and Cambridge or by New Englanders elsewhere. The first English version of *Anna Karenina* was that of Nathan Haskell Dole, 1886, who translated many other works of Tolstoy. In the same year, the Bostonian Isabel S. Hapgood translated *Childhood, Boyhood and Youth.* Miss Hapgood also translated Gogol, Turgenev and Gorky and various Dutch, Polish, Italian and Spanish authors. While the standard English version of Tolstoy is that of Aylmer Maude, the most nearly complete edition, up to 1902, was that of Professor Leo Wiener of Harvard.

It may be added that Tolstoy often expressed his admiration for Howells.

† On a train in 1887. Hale wrote to his wife, regarding this talk with Howells: "You know how deep he is in Tolstoy. Tolstoy has really troubled him, because he does not know but he ought to be ploughing and reaping . . . I dare not begin to write down what he said and I, I went nearer the depths than perhaps I have ever done with anyone but you . . . Howells is a loyal Christian, and hates to have anybody say that Jesus made plans or demanded things that are impossible."—*Life and Letters of Edward Everett Hale.*

‡ At this time, Higginson said later, Harvard was almost the only college where even the word could be mentioned.

§ Mark Twain was fascinated by *Looking Backward* and welcomed a visit from Bellamy at Hartford. He sympathized strongly with the organization of labour and regarded the unions as the workmen's only hope of standing up against the power of money. See Howells's *My Mark Twain.*

In his preface to *The Blindman's World,* Howells said that Bellamy moved the nation "more than any other American author who has lived."

Europe haunted his mind. He had never known that such
misery existed, though he found it, on his return, in New
York and Boston. He was convinced that America was
going the way of the old world and losing its democratic
hope and basis. With a deep distrust of city-life, he saw
the villages drifting towards it. He saw the future steadily growing darker. Within a few years, he had written
Looking Backward, with his plan for a better system of
human relations. A new political party sprang from his
teachings.

Bellamy had a fresher mind than even this book suggested, although he began to write as a follower of Hawthorne. He liked to play with the sort of fancies that
were always running through Hawthorne's head,—stories
about homeless ghosts and queer old doctors and young
men who fall in love with portraits.* The atmosphere of
all these tales reflected the Yankee village life that
Bellamy knew so well in the seventies and eighties. This
was Mrs. Eddy's world, a world of lonely people who
had lost their vital interests and were bored and ailing;
and Bellamy's tales mirrored this boredom, as they also
mirrored the shifts by which the villagers tried to escape
it. In trances, through mediums, the characters sought to
retrace the past, or they tried as hard to penetrate the
future. The two old souls in *A Summer Evening's Dream*
convinced themselves that they were young again; and
the boys and girls in *The Old Folks Party* masqueraded
as their future selves, as what they expected to be when
they were old. This scarcely implied that the present was

---

* Of his earlier novels, only one suggested the socialist Bellamy. This
was *The Duke of Stockbridge,* a historical romance about Shays's Rebellion,
the revolt of the debtor-farmers and ex-soldiers after the Revolution. In
Bellamy's own Berkshire region, the seeds of all the present miseries had
been sown at the dawn of the Republic. After this romance appeared, in
the Great Barrington paper, Bellamy withheld it from book-publication. He
wishrd to develop his political ideas, and he meant *The Duke of Stockbridge* to serve as an illustration of them. It did not appear as a book until
after his death.

very exciting; and anything but reality here and now was
the moral of most of these stories. The old maid in *Miss
Ludington's Sister* preferred to build a town for ghosts
rather than dwell any longer in the living Hilton.

In all this, Bellamy, like various other New England
writers,* was merely reproducing Hawthorne's dream-
world. In doing so, however, he soon struck out a line that
was followed by H. G. Wells a decade later. In the small
towns of which he wrote, with all their interest in pseudo-
science, there was an interest in actual science also. John
Fiske's friend Youmans found an eager audience there,
and the *Popular Science Monthly* was a staple of reading. For the Yankees were a race of inventors, and the
marvels of applied science, with its labour-saving devices,
appealed to them deeply. They were prepared to understand the wonderful hints of coming discoveries and
even try them out in their sheds and workshops. In the
cluttered, laborious life of the farm and the village, the
material delights of the cities, with their ease and convenience, possessed a charm that city-people, who took
these things for granted, never dreamed of.† Science
stood for rest and comfort, anodynes for aching bones,
peace for the heavy-laden, hope for all. The heaven pic-

---

* Aldrich, Julian Hawthorne, Barrett Wendell, etc. Aldrich's "Mr. Jaffrey" is an old bachelor who *makes real* the son he has not had. "To such
a man," says the author, "brooding forever on what might have been and
dwelling wholly in the realms of his fancies, the actual world might indeed
become as a dream, and nothing seem real but his illusions." In Julian
Hawthorne's *The Professor's Sister,* the German characters reflected the
New England interest in galvanism, materializations, astral forms, unexpected awakenings, etc. See also Barrett Wendell's *The Duchess Emilia,* a
novel of metempsychosis, and some of Henry James's later stories.

† This explains the vogue of *Looking Backward,* in which Utopia is
cluttered with modern inventions, among the simpler people of the country.
More aesthetic readers, Howells said, were shocked that nothing better
could be imagined than the futile luxury of their own lives; and later, in
fact, when these inventions were realized and widely spread, Utopia was
as far away as ever. With no disrespect for machinery, it may be said that
Hawthorne showed a more enlightened instinct when, in his *Hall of Fantasy,* he satirized this machinery-worship. He knew well how little, beyond
a certain point, machinery could ever mean to man.

tured in the hymns which the country-people knew by
heart was a place where the burdens of farm-life were
gently eased from their shoulders. It was an infinite and
endless Pasadena, and science seemed to promise this on
earth. Bellamy's stories also reflected this interest. They
mirrored this feeling for science, with its vistas of the
future and the worlds of speculation to which it led, in
astronomy, psychology, mechanics and physics. *At Pin-
ney's Ranch* is the story of a man who recovers his wife
by mental telepathy. The dreamer in *The Cold Snap*
enters interstellar space and experiences the ineffable
cold that prevails there. The astronomer in *The Blindman's World* passes into a state of mind in which he is
independent of his body. His consciousness visits Mars
and finds that the Martians have developed beyond the
earth-people: they literally possess foresight and know
the future. In the islands of the mind-readers, in *To
Whom This May Come,* the people do not need to use
their tongues. They live by direct mental vision. In *With
the Eyes Shut,* the people do not need to see. Their books
are phonographed and their clocks talk,—the ear per-
forms the functions of the eye. The physician in *Dr.
Heidenhoff's Process* invents a galvanic-mesmeric device
that extirpates unhappy recollections. Patients whose
lives have been wrecked by the past can have their ob-
noxious thoughts removed and live as if the past had
never existed. The unhappy young girl who undergoes
this prefiguration of psycho-analysis sleeps and wakes
again with a happy mind.

Ten years after Bellamy, H. G. Wells began to write
similar stories. Wells, a student of science in London,
was full of the same ideas. He imagined time-machines
and visits to Mars and trances from which the sleeper
wakes in a world that has changed beyond all recognition. With Wells, as with Bellamy earlier, these fantasies
led to Utopia-building, for both were obsessed with the

miseries of the social system and science seemed to both to point the way to a just and sensible order of things. All one required was a plastic human nature, willing to accept the means of its own salvation; but that human nature was not plastic, or not sufficiently so, had always been the obstacle in Utopia-building. Wells, at first, was unaware of this, and Bellamy died too soon to be disillusioned; or, rather, he shared the American faith in the will, which has never counted costs or consequences, and he saw men as infinitely plastic.* For him, as for Emerson, nothing was fixed in human nature, everything lent itself to transformation; men were naturally good, the will was able to work miracles, and, if mankind desired a reasonable world, why should it not obtain one overnight? This American faith, which outlived Bellamy, had actuated the Brook Farmers. All the revivalists shared it,—sudden changes, for them, were a matter of course; and it sprang from the age-old belief in the millennium that had always lurked in the depths of the Yankee mind. Bellamy mirrored this mind at a moment when the nation was changing so rapidly that everything seemed possible tomorrow.

For Howells, the realist, who knew his human nature, these Alice-in-Wonderland methods were beside the question; but he sympathized with Bellamy and also, largely, with Henry George, to whom Hamlin Garland introduced him. Garland had reviewed his Tolstoyan novel, *The*

---

* To reconstruct a town or a world, to restore the past or build the future, is as simple as saying Jack Robinson to Bellamy's people. Miss Ludington, the rich old maid, who does not like the "march of improvement," thinks nothing of building a town to suit herself. She reproduces the Hilton of her childhood, complete with its country roads and grassy borders, schoolhouse, meeting-house and all. Such things really happen in America. Henry Ford realized this fantasy in Dearborn.

The plasticity of human nature is the theme of many of Bellamy's stories, which are always ingenious and plausible. The young man in *Pott's Painless Cure,* who has made the young girl love him, devises a method of making her un-love him. In *A Love Story Reversed,* the roles of the lovers are inverted with excellent results.

Minister's Charge, and discussed with him the West and its problems. He was writing his own first stories, under Henry George's influence, and, also impressed by Taine, he reminded Howells of the "local colour" movement in the West, the need for writers in every section to deal with the life they knew and the conditions peculiar to their scene and climate. All this weaned Howells further away from the narrowing life of Boston. In New York he was in touch with all these writers; and *A Hazard of New Fortunes* showed how much the metropolitan scene amused and stirred him. He rambled about the East Side, where the streets were picturesque, the docks, with steamers arriving from Spain and France, the Chinese quarter in Mott Street, a paradise for painters, the Bowery, where one still met ballad-sellers. The turmoil of the cars and trucks, the web of the elevated railways pleased his eye, the fields and cellar-holes and old farm-fences one found on rocky hill-sides near the park, where low sheds jostled huge apartment-houses, and goats and hens wandered in and out. He shared Walt Whitman's pleasure in the beaches, in the dime-museums, horse-shows, circuses and theatres, which he had so rarely seen in Boston; and, as he sat on benches in Washington Square and haunted Italian restaurants, he felt once more his old delight in travel. He rejoiced in the touch-and-go quality of the metropolitan life, after his intense identification with Boston; and a whole world of the new types for which he was always in search crossed his path in offices, in the streets, in the shops,—clerks and bankers, promoters, editors, newspaperwomen and shop-girls, publishers, art-students, visiting Southerners, self-made men from the West. This multitudinous life of the city appeared in *A Hazard of New Fortunes,* which caught the note of New York as *Silas Lapham* conveyed the feeling of Boston. But now he saw on every hand poverty and misery. Suffering was lurking everywhere. He grieved over the slum-children, the old women sleeping on door-steps, the hungry workmen searching in the gutters. The world that had seemed to him so full of pretty and pleasant things was overcast with sadness, death, injustice; and he thought of his older America now as a dream of his youth that had passed. That race of shepherds and shepherdesses no longer existed. He had himself grown older, and America had changed; but, more than all, Tolstoy had altered his vision.

For a number of years, in a series of novels, the question of social reform overshadowed everything else in Howells's work. Then his expression of this question grew less and less direct, as the movement of reform waned in the country. With his temperamental optimism, a fruit of the older America, he felt that all was coming right in time,* though he never ceased to share, as a man, in the fight for social justice, and the theme of social injustice recurred in his books. He watched with anxiety the growing of class lines and barriers and the rising power of ruthless business men, establishing inequalities, as it seemed, forever. The earlier types, the Silas Laphams, scrupulous, honest and liberal, seemed to be giving place to more sinister figures, as industry also gave place to gambling in stocks; and he pictured in Dryfoos, in *A Hazard of New Fortunes*, the new kind of despot-financier. Gerrish, in *Annie Kilburn,* was a similar portrait; and the defaulter Northwick, in *The Quality of Mercy,* was a type he saw on every hand. The rascally manufacturer in *The Son of Royal Langbrith,* who had gone through life as the hero of the town, was another proof of Howells's distrust of business; and this novel, which appeared in 1904, was one of many proofs that

* "In America, life is yet a joke with us, even when it is grotesque and shameful, as it so often is, for we think we can make it right when we choose."—Howells, *Their Silver Wedding Journey.*
There were "oceanic depths of ingenuous affirmation" in Howells's nature, as Newton Arvin said of Walt Whitman.

Howells's mind responded to every change in the mood of the nation. For Langbrith's disillusioned son, who had idolized his father, was a type of these early twentieth-century years, when the younger generation, bathed in a false idealism, perceived how much hypocrisy lay behind it. Howells was sensitive to all the currents of thought and feeling that passed, for two-score years, through the mind of the country; and, while his novels of social reform were far from being his best, they caught the leading note of the eighties and nineties. With what delicate perception he showed, in *Annie Kilburn,* the growth of a quiet old New England village into a sprawling modern American town, losing its humaneness and its heritage of freedom as the factory-system rose and gained control. Looking back at Boston, Howells saw its sordid aspects, as he had never seen them in happier years, as Lemuel Barker saw them, in *The Minister's Charge,* when this country boy arrived from Willoughby Pastures. He saw the wretched restaurants where the poor forgathered, the "Misfit Parlours" where they bought their clothes, the confidence-men who robbed them, the benches where they slept at night, the lodging-houses, hospitals and jails. He saw how little official religion was able to grasp their problem, out of touch as it was with the humbler classes, and he saw how pharisaical the upper classes were, beating down their workpeople's wages, while they carried flowers to hospitals and took up subscriptions. Lemuel was the touchstone by which Howells tried Boston, from the point of view of Tolstoy's Christian doctrine; and the minister in *Annie Kilburn* gave up his church and went to Fall River to live with the mill-workers as they lived, to help them as a teacher while sharing their life. But these novels were too evidently prompted by conscience. They were strained and unreal and wanting in verisimilitude. Howells's mind was driven by his will into regions where it never felt at home.

A Traveller from Altruria was therefore the best of his socialist novels, for it made no attempt to be realistic. It was a fantasy, one of the few he undertook, in the vein of William Morris's *News from Nowhere*. Mr. Homos had come from Altruria, an early-Christian republic; and he "felt like a sort of bad conscience," as one of the characters said. He was Howells's conscience embodied, wandering over Howells's world, holding Socratic conversations with ministers, bankers, professors and lawyers, while he surveyed the scenes that Howells had pictured. He visited a summer hotel, where the ladies were always resting, wondering what it was they rested from, and with his air of innocence he challenged the assumptions of the "most advanced country of its time." Its assumptions were those of his own Altruria; its reality was a squalid struggle in which the shrewd was valued more than the noble, in which personal worth had small recognition and the man who needed a dinner was never asked to dine. In the irony of these indolent sketches, Howells, speaking through Mr. Homos, tested the sincerity of American professions; and he was happier here than he was in the novels in which he tried to present the war of the classes. Deep as his convictions were, his nature was too passive to comprehend profound antagonisms. He could not convey the feeling of groups in conflict, and his imagination too generally failed him when he strayed outside the middle class. But of all his later portraits there were none more sympathetic than those of David Hughes, the old Brook Farmer, who saw mankind as "the family," in *The World of Chance,* and Lindau in *A Hazard of New Fortunes*. Lindau was drawn from an old German immigrant through whom he had heard of socialism as a boy in the West.

As he passed into this later phase, Howells's style lost much of its sparkle, the gaiety, brilliance and wit of his earlier novels; and the novels themselves all but lost their old compactness, the perfection of organization they had once possessed. He had become suspicious of conscious style and conscious art, in this again reflecting the teaching of Tolstoy. His longer novels had scarcely any structure. They were aesthetically flaccid; though, occasionally, in some briefer novel,—*Miss Bellard's Inspiration,* for example,—he recovered the verve and form of his earlier years. In these briefer novels there were beautiful pages, —*Fennel and Rue, New Leaf Mills,* in which he returned to the forest scenes of his childhood; and in some of his short stories, *Questionable Shapes,* Howells achieved his utmost in mastery and ripeness. These tales, indeed, were beyond all praise in their effortless movement and quiet grace, the rewards of exact observation and scrupulous candour. His zest for new phases of life remained fresh to the end; and he caught the feeling of all the various groups he entered, the realm of the magazine in *A Hazard of New Fortunes,* the realm of writing and publishing in *The World of Chance,* and, in *The Coast of Bohemia,* the realm of the artists. He saw New York through the eyes of Shelley Ray, the young Western novelist who had come to the city in a mood so like his own of an earlier time. He saw it through the eyes of the young art-student who, in *The Coast of Bohemia,* had come from Ohio; and the New York types of the nineties thronged in these novels, drawn with the subtlest feeling for the place and the moment. Here were the "light" New Yorkers, so different from Bostonians, with all the levity of their old Dutch blood, and, among countless others, the impressionist Ludlow, the painter who had just returned from Paris, eager to report the native American world on canvas and draw as much pathos out of the farm-folk as Millet had ever drawn from the Barbizon peasants. Sometimes the scene shifted, and Howells returned to a summer hotel,—in *The Landlord at Lion's Head,* for instance,—or the grassy-bordered street of a

Shaker village, or Saratoga, now bereft of fashion.
There, sitting on a bench, he had watched the country-
people who had come to "get acquainted" at the great
hotels, where the wooden courts and parlours and piazzas
buzzed with ingenuous flirtations and the "Washington
Post March" blared over all. Howells, who had for-
sworn his old delight in match-making, remained the in-
corrigible Santa Claus of youthful lovers; while, with his
open sympathies and devouring eyes, he had followed
every phase of the life of the country. In his conversations one traced its interests, from the days of Turgenev
and Rossetti to those of Ibsen, Maeterlinck, Lombroso
and Hauptmann; and William James's "will to believe"
and his explorations of psychical mysteries were reflected
at once in Howells's "border-line" stories. These tales of
eidolons and hallucinations, presentiments, metaphantas-
mia, *Between the Dark and the Daylight, Questionable
Shapes,* bespoke in Howells a mystical afflatus that carried one back to the poetry of his early life. They were
touched with an exquisite spirituality; and, indeed, this
lover of all things human, truthful and benign, was always
a poet. Was he shallow? Was he narrow? Here and there,
undoubtedly; and he never sounded the depths of the minds
that are oceans. He was rather like some great fresh-
water lake. If these lakes have their shallows, they are
transparent, and, if they have their narrows, they are also
large; and all manner of living things forgather in them,
as they forgathered in Howells.

CHAPTER XIX

HENRY JAMES IN ENGLAND

HENRY JAMES had remained a stranger in England. Shortly after his arrival, he had met a German who had also come to make his home there. "I know nothing of the English," this man said. "I have lived here too long—twenty years. The first year I really knew a great deal. But I have lost it." So it was, in a measure, with Henry James. Deeply as he had submitted himself to the "Londonizing process," had he become an "insider," except in "that limited sense," as he called it, "in which an American can ever do so"? His earlier impressions had been so sharp that he felt he knew the English character as if he had "invented it," he said. But so it often is with an alien's impressions: after the novelty passes and the first sensations have worn away he perceives that he has scarcely crossed the threshold. James had become with time,—in the phrases of two of his friends,—an "old-established colonist," but a "homeless man." That he had failed to root himself in England was more and more evident every day in his work.

This was the outstanding fact that explained the events of his middle years, the vague anxieties that weighed upon him, the nature of his later work and the strange hiatus in his career in which he abandoned the novel and turned to the theatre. America had faded from him, and he was "deadly weary of the whole 'international' state of mind."* It was clear to him that he must "do England in

* "So that I *ache,* at times, with fatigue at the way it is constantly forced upon me as a sort of virtue or obligation."—Letter to William James, 1888.

fiction;"* and he had attempted to do it in two long novels; and how solidly real were the English characters, —the fruits of his early impressions,—in *The Princess Casamassima* and *The Tragic Muse*. Miss Pynsent, the seamstress, Mr. Vetch, the old violinist, Lady Aurora, the socialist aristocrat, the young revolutionist, Paul Muniment, and Millicent Henning, the Cockney girl, were as clearly alive as Newman or Daisy Miller. So were Captain Sholto, Mrs. Dallow and Nick Dormer and Mr. Carteret, the old politician. Not in vain had Henry James met John Bright and Gladstone, some of whose traits appeared in this fine portrait. But these were his only long novels, except *The Awkward Age,* in which the scenes and the characters were predominantly English; and James returned thereafter to the international theme of which he had grown so "deadly weary." † The stone rejected by the builder once more became his headstone; and would this have occurred if he had felt that he could really "do England"? For James never relinquished his faith that the novelist is a "patient historian, the living painter of his living time," and therefore, if he returned to American subjects when they had faded from him, it was obviously because England had eluded his grasp. Was this not evident in his later English characters, who behaved in a most un-English way? ‡ James felt he had fallen between

* "One thing only is clear, that henceforth I must do, or half do, England in fiction—as the place I see most today, and, in a sort of way, know best. I have at least more acquired notions of it, on the whole, than of any other world, and it will serve as well as any other. It has been growing distincter that America fades from me, and as she never trusted me at best, I can trust *her,* for effect, no longer."—Letter to Howells, 1890.

† "The 'international' is very presumably indeed, and in fact quite inevitably, what I am *chronically* booked for."—Letter of 1904.

‡ As many critics have observed. Thus Ford Madox Ford, who based his claim for James's greatness on his being a "historian," showed that the Gereths, in *The Spoils of Poynton,* if they had been English, would certainly have gone to law. Ford, for this reason, described James as an "un-Americanized American" who was also the "least naturalized of all the English."

two worlds. He was "troubled about many things." * He
had ceased to speak the language of his army of readers;
and he turned for a while to shorter stories and plunged
into the theatre, with results that were calamitous and
futile.

It was after this hiatus that James emerged with the
"later manner" in which he seemed to abandon the objective role. He never did so consciously; he never meant to
do so; he believed he was quite as much the historian as
ever. He still observed the world around him, eager for
"revelations, confidences, guesses," † for "anything that
others could give him from their personal lives . . . food
for his ruminating fancy." ‡ To the last, as Hugh Walpole said, he was "unconsciously using his notebooks;"
but, if he had mastered his English world, would he have
craved in later years for the "vivid and solid *material*"
that he felt a return to his country might give him?
Charmed as he was by England, he had too little in common with it. Politics meant nothing to him, professional
life, the love of the country, sport, school or college, riding, hunting; and, if the tastes of English men were
mostly beyond his horizon, he was scarcely more in rapport with the English women whom he had chosen to
study. Their interests were much like those of the men;
and what did these women care for art? That they did not

---

* "I am troubled about many things, about many of which you could
give me, I think (or rather I am sure) advice and direction. I have entered upon evil days—but this is for your most private ear. It sounds portentous, but it only means that I am still staggering a good deal under the
mysterious and (to me) inexplicable injury wrought—apparently—upon
my situation by my last two novels, *The Bostonians* and *The Princess,*
from which I expected so much and derived so little. They have reduced
the desire, and the demand, for my productions to *zero*."—Letter to
Howells, 1888.

† Edmund Gosse.

‡ "He was insatiable for anything that others could give him from their
personal lives . . . He welcomed any grain of reality, any speck of significance around which his imagination could pile its rings. It was very no-
ticeable how promptly and eagerly he would reach out to such things, as
they floated by in talk."—Percy Lubbock, *The Letters of Henry James.*

care for art at all was the principal thing he noticed in
them. He had not been obliged to share the interests of
his countrymen to understand his countrymen themselves.
By a deep racial instinct he had comprehended Christopher Newman, Isabel Archer, Roderick, Rowland Mallet; and up to a certain point, by observation, he had penetrated the English mind as well. He had had every chance
to penetrate it, and English acquaintances told him things,
because he was American, which they did not confide to
one another. But what, in the end, was the sum of his
knowledge beyond the talk of dinner-tables, anecdotes,
gossip, rumour and tittle-tattle? He was lost, as he said,
in the "fathomless depths of English equivocation."
Hovering about the English mind, circling round and
round it, hankering for some deeper initiation, he was
perpetually baffled, like the people in his later novels who
hovered about one another with the same effect of strained
curiosity. Did they not hover because he had hovered?
Was not this posture of James's people the result of his
own frame of mind? At the same time, in this alien world,
with which his relations were so tenuous, he drifted further and further from life itself. He lost his feeling for
the "vital facts of human nature," as his brother William
said. And William James was not for nothing the greatest psychologist living. He knew whereof he spoke, and
he was right.

Were not these the essential facts that lay behind the
"later manner" in which James triumphed as a craftsman? He triumphed by substituting for his old interest in
character an interest in predicaments and situations, an
interest that he had developed in his work for the stage,
in which the situation was all-important. "Saturation" and
all it implied, a living sense of objective reality, this had
slipped from his grasp, and he was reduced to the "grain
of suggestion," the "tiny air-blown particle" of which his
later novels were amplifications. Did he not say that *The*

Sacred Fount, The Spoils of Poynton, What Maisie Knew
"grew by a rank force of their own" from the short
stories that he had planned?—and what he called the
"long-windedness" of *The Wings of the Dove* and the
"vague verbosity" of *The Golden Bowl* were fruits of the
same kind of unnatural expansion. There was scarcely
enough substance of life in these great ghosts of novels to
fill the novelette in which he excelled; but what concerned
him now was form, almost regardless of content, the
problems of calculation and construction, and he who had
once been unable to think of a situation that did not depend for its interest on the nature of the persons had begun to think of his persons as pawns in a game. Did they
"compose" together? Were they sufficiently foreshortened? The day had not yet come when he forgot the
names of his characters, when, in his scenarios, he referred to "the girl" and "Aurora What's-her-name," or
perhaps to "my first young man" and "my second young
man," to persons who concerned him only as to their size
and weight in the structure he was building. But it was
significant that *The Spoils of Poynton,* the first of his
later novels, was a story of "things." His persons were to
grow dimmer and dimmer, like flames of an exhausted
lamp, while his technical virtuosity worked its wonders.

This technical virtuosity was the "figure in the carpet"
of which Hugh Vereker spoke in one of his stories. It was
the particular thing that Vereker wrote his books most
for, the secret buried in them that no one observed. It
was James's "well in the desert," the something he had
found that he felt was a compensation for all he had lost;
and he was entitled to the pride with which it filled him,
for what novelist had ever revealed such prodigies of
skill? He had taken up the gauntlet that Europe had
flung at the feet of America, as he had seen it in his youth,
he had accepted his handicap, as he also saw it, and
striven with faith and force. He had waked and toiled

while others slept, and the indifference of his readers had
only served to toughen his will the more. Only difficulty
interested him now, as he said in a letter, the problems
of organization, the "secrets of the kitchen," and it was
by this concentration that he developed the method which
remained as a model for novelists in days to come.* The
details of this method were explained in the prefaces that
were collected later in *The Art of Fiction*. There one saw
the conjuror at work with his puppets; and who had ever
devised such arch-refinements or such supersubtleties as
his? But was not this absorption in technique the proof
that James's themes had lost interest for him?

He had emerged as a passionate mathematician of art,
or, shall one say, a huge arachnid, pouncing on the tiny
air-blown particle and wrapping it round and round. For
a new prodigy had appeared, the later style of Henry
James, the style that was the man he had become. He had
remodelled his personality. He had outgrown his American self and largely grown to be the type he loved. He
had disliked the American "thinness" and "paleness," the
something "meagre" about the American type. Its line
and composition had seemed to him wanting in roundness
and richness,† while the English had a "fatter, damper"
nature. He had desired the rich and the round, the fatter,
the damper, the resonant, and he had developed these
traits, or their appearance; for had he not become, in a
sense, an actor, a curiously artificial being who seemed to

---

* But only, or mainly, for those who resembled James in the paucity
and tenuity of their subject-matter. In expounding his doctrine that the
novel is to be judged by its oneness, he admitted that Tolstoy and Balzac
could never have followed his method. "The promiscuous shiftings of
standpoint and centre of Tolstoy and Balzac for instance . . . are the inevitable result of the *quantity of presenting* their genius launches them in . . .
With the complexity they pile up they *can* get no clearness without trying
again and again for new centres."—Letter to Mrs. Humphry Ward, 1899.

† "We are *thin*, my dear Howard; we are pale, we are sharp. There is
something meagre about us; our line is wanting in roundness, our composition in richness."—*A Bundle of Letters*. Did not James speak in his own
person here?

have borrowed a mantle and to wear a mask? One heard reverberations when one tapped this shell. But James's sensibility had grown with all it fed on, and the fabrics upon which his eyes had feasted, the colours that he loved, the soft sounds, the delicate scents had surely left their stamp on the house of his spirit. This house was Henry James's style, and it threw out "extensions and protrusions," as he somewhere called them, "indulging even, all recklessly, in gables and pinnacles and battlements, things that had transformed the unpretending place into a veritable palace, an extravagant, bristling, flag-flying structure that had quite as much to do with the air as with the earth." His senses had been nourished by the collation of types and tones, of signs and aspects and items, the comparison of beautiful objects and degrees of finish; and type and object and form had moulded his style. Wonderful metaphors blossomed in his pages, like air-plants from the tropics.

But other things appeared in this style, the evasiveness and hesitancy of a man who was habitually embarrassed. The cautious ceremoniousness, the baffled curiosity, the nervousness and constant self-communion,—these traits of the self-conscious guest in the house where he was not at home had gone to fashion his personality also. And why the atmosphere of uncertainty that hovered over all these novels, the conscious cultivation of indirectness? Why all those "crooked corridors" and "antechambers" in which he seemed to delight in eluding his readers? Was he not, in reality, hiding from them, as the cuttlefish hides from the pursuer by ejecting the black fluid that assures his escape? All these devices of James, in which he rejoiced as a craftsman, served him as a smoke-screen behind which to vanish; for had he not always been fleeing from something, the American self that he deprecated and that he longed to lose in the European? Then, too, America had always lacked "mystery" for him. It had seemed

to him "undraped" and "uncurtained." He had disliked
its glare of daylight and its "harsh, hard" lines; and were
not his circuitousness and his veils of ambiguity the result of a lifelong desire to escape from these? Perhaps a
childhood in hotels had increased the morbid love of privacy that caused him to shrink with horror from any exposure; and, meanwhile, all these crooked corridors enabled his mind to evade the presentation of moments of
emotional stress. After his long association with people
who merely glimmered for him, in the museum-world in
which he lived, he was no longer equal to this because he
was out of touch with life, with the vital facts of human
action and passion. Did his stories correspond to the "life
without rearrangement" that had always been his standard for the novel? He presented his people as "eminent,"
as "wonderful," "noble" and "great," and most of their
actions belied his professions for them. Thus, in *The
Wings of the Dove,* a "gentleman, generally sound and
generally pleasant," presently appeared as a potential
murderer, without any adequate explanation. The countess
in *The Ambassadors,* supposed to be a great lady, used
her daughter as a scapegoat. The exquisite young girl in
The Spoils of Poynton ridiculed her hostess behind her
back. The "pure, passionate, pledged" radical, the young
man in *Covering End,* married the girl he disliked and
went back on his party in order to retain possession of his
family estate. The guests in the country-house in *The
Sacred Fount* solemnly devoted themselves for days to
"nosing" out the secret of one of the ladies. The two
young men in *The Ivory Tower* refused to read the will,
which they had a perfect right to open, in order to discuss
for hours what it probably contained. Other young men,
supposed to be in love, were presented as admirable beings because they preferred a house to the girl of their
choice; and one of them broke his engagement to devote
his life to discovering an author's "intention." One man

procured as a private preserve an altar in a Catholic church; and a great author died in a country-house, under the roof of a lady who did not respect him, fearing that he would offend her if he went home. Was not this author rather a goose than a lion? All these people acted out of character, or against the nature of things, or in violation of James's description of them; for how could one respect the lover who preferred his furniture to his mistress, how regard as honourable the politician who betrayed his own convictions to save his house? James's "noble" characters peeped through keyholes, and his "perfectly splendid" beauties lied and schemed; many of his "fine" souls behaved like monkeys, and his "eminent" beings were eminent for inquisitiveness only. Was not this odd derangement of values the fruit of a mind that worked in a void, without any clear sense of human cause and effect?

Thus James's world was remote from reality. It was a subjective world, peopled by dim projections of the author's fancy; and more and more these characters spoke with the voice of James himself.* He had become the victim of his own personality. He said, "We take for granted a primary author . . . We forget him in proportion as he works upon us, and he works upon us most in fact by making us forget him." Certainly no one had ever been conscious of James in contemplating the world of his earlier novels. There the illusion was complete: one saw the people, knew them, felt them. But who could forget the manipulator in this vague later world, in which one scarcely remembered the names of the people? James himself filled the foreground; he stood between the reader

---

* How far James had lost the sense of his early characters one saw in his revision of *The American,* for instance. There the frank, shrewd Christopher Newman, emotionally direct and simple, assumed the sophistications of the later James. Thus he was made to remark, in the spirit of a connoisseur, as his final reflection on love, "Fancy this being to be had and—with my general need—my not having it!" All of James's later people took one back to James himself. They spoke with one generalized voice, the voice of their author.

and life; and one might almost say that he made the substance of his art out of his failure to grasp the materials of it. For where the primary novelist begins by possessing his people, whom he then presents in action, James, without possessing them, presented them merely in the act of discovering one another. They formed little groups, detached from all life beyond their circle, and their ruling passion was curiosity. They tried to discover what went on in one another's minds and remained in the end as mystified as they were in the beginning. Nor did the reader know them any better, after all this psychological exploration. One was scarcely conscious of anything but an avid eye, fixed on a human spectacle that barred it out. Everyone watched in James's novels, watched himself, watched the others, "nosed about" for relations, sniffed and pried, and the people were without consistency,—one seldom knew what to expect from them,—they were apt to destroy one's impressions of them at almost any moment. They spun webs about themselves, and, in fact, they were ghosts without interests or attributes, without passions, ambitions, convictions, hearts or vitals; and they drifted about in a curious limbo as insubstantial as themselves. They were made, as William James remarked, "wholly out of impalpable materials, air, and the prismatic interferences of light, ingeniously focussed by mirrors upon empty space."

Was it not largely true, then, as Middleton Murry expressed it, that James "yearned after the fullness of European life, which he could not rejoin again, and had to satisfy his impulse of asceticism in the impassioned formalism of an art without content"? This was only partly true because, with his imagination, as an extraordinary artist and man of genius, James was not wholly dependent on the world outside him. He could turn everything into art. His own perplexities served him well; and, if his people were ghosts, he could make ghosts people. He could make atmospheres palpable. The short stories and novelettes that he poured forth so abundantly were marvellous evocations of their kind; and, playing his labyrinthine games, James remained a happy man, with a sense that, if he was a mystagogue, he was a master. He knew he was teaching novelists in times to come to look for the half-resolutions, the nuances of motive, the velleities, disinclinations, misgivings, obsessions that also govern the mind, along with the decisions and rejections that make for action. For them he extended the sphere of human consciousness, even as he added greatly to the novelist's craft. But a psychologist is not a novelist,—psychology is not the same as character; * and did not James feel that he had somehow missed his way, that he had paid too much for his expatriation? Why otherwise should he have bewailed his "thin, starved, lonely, defeated, beaten prospect"? Why should he have said of Edith Wharton, "She *must* be tethered in native pastures, even if it reduces her to a back-yard in New York"? How much was implied in the letter to Howells in which, looking back on their two careers, he said that Howells had always had the advantage of breathing an air that suited and nourished him, sitting up to the neck amid the sources of his inspiration.† In one of his last, unfinished novels, James was still pondering the question what living in America might make of a man; ‡ and to more than one younger American writer who saw him in his later years

* "The writer must be a psychologist, but a secret one; he must sense and know the roots of phenomena, but offer only the phenomena themselves, as they blossom or wither."—Turgenev, quoted in Yarmolinsky, *Turgenev, the Man, his Art and his Age.*

† "For you have had the advantage, after all, of breathing an air that has suited and nourished you; of sitting up to your neck, as I may say—or at least up to your waist—amid the sources of your inspiration . . . I can only feel and speak for those conditions in which, as 'quiet observers,' as careful painters, as sincere artists, we could still, in our native, our human and social element, know more or less where we were and feel more or less what we had hold of."—Letter to Howells, 1912.

‡ *The Sense of the Past.*

he bitterly regretted the road he had taken. "Don't make my mistake," he said to Amy Lowell. "I have cut myself off from America, where I belonged." He had cut himself off from the culture that had produced him and failed to attain the culture he had tried to acquire. He had come to feel that his work was a "tangle of temporal and local differences that revealed, after all, nothing of the depths, references as fleeting as O. Henry's slang, flavours mistaken for essences, split hairs, not dissected anatomies." * This was in 1913, three years before he died. Fourteen years before, he had uttered the same regrets to Hamlin Garland.†

Certainly, he somehow felt that he had been deluded, like the American characters in so many of his stories. Was this not evident in his tales of the disappointed author, of the "poor sensitive gentleman" who is "too fine for his rough fate"? These tales, among the best he wrote, poured from his pen in the nineties and after, and they presented the plight of the writer in a fashionable world which he has followed in good faith and which utterly fails to understand him. The exquisite artists in *The Next Time, Broken Wings, The Velvet Glove, The Middle Years* and others are all of them "badgered and bothered on the pretext of being applauded," while they are treated as cat's-paws, ignored and misused by people who have no imagination. No one has any conception of what they are trying for. No one knows what they are talking about; and they are driven by their genius to produce hopelessly beautiful books that nobody has in the house and nobody reads. People lose their manuscripts and only the

---

* S. Foster Damon, *Amy Lowell.*

† "He became very much in earnest at last . . . 'If I were to live my life over again,' he said in a low voice, and fixing upon me a sombre glance, 'I would be an American. I would steep myself in America, I would know no other land. I would study its beautiful side. The mixture of Europe and America which you see in me has proved disastrous. It has made of me a man who is neither American nor European. I have lost touch with my own people, and I live here alone.' "—Hamlin Garland, *Roadside Meetings.*

"crazy" admire them, while the authors of the latest shockers have all the honours. All their readers care about is vulgar personal gossip about them. In the world to which they are drawn they have no place. All these exquisite artists, Neil Paraday, John Berridge, Hugh Vereker, Mark Ambient, Ralph Limbert rose, James said in one of his prefaces, from the depths of his own experience, and they were indications of his own disenchantment. And in how many of his other stories some child or some innocent creature was victimized by a callous and malevolent world! Innocence and good will exploited and abused remained James's theme to the end of the chapter. Was it not the story of the Puritan child in himself who had toiled up the slope of the British Olympus and found that the gods had turned into "cats and monkeys"?

In the generation after he died, James's later novels were praised at the expense of his early writings. Their vogue was immense in a world of cosmopolitan aesthetes who saw themselves dimly reflected in James's people, functionless people, like themselves, without objective interests, who spun webs of thought about one another, who analyzed themselves, for want of other occupation, while they collected bric-a-brac, material and human. The great work of James's prime was forgotten or ignored, as he had sometimes seemed to wish himself, the work in which he had celebrated an actual historic drama, the nostalgia of the American for his ancestral home in Europe. All his great novels had dealt with Americans at a time when he had understood them, when he was at home with himself in his own domain, alert, witty, tender, benevolent, freely at play with a world that he saw from above and behind, from without and within. This was his major work, although he remained to the end an artist of extraordinary power and a lover of perfection, with an inexhaustible fund of ideas and subjects and a style that was often magnificent; and those for whom his later novels were grey webs of speculation, peopled with phantoms in a fog, could always rejoice in his shorter tales. There, in *The Pupil* and *Brooksmith,* in *The Author of Beltraffio* and *The Beast in the Jungle,* in *The Turn of the Screw, Glasses* and *The Great Good Place,* flawless and full in their tone and structure, with their softly flowing outlines, one saw him in his clearest autumnal beauty.

CHAPTER XX

BOSTON IN THE NINETIES

WITH the advance of the nineties, the New England mind was steeped in disappointment and chagrin. The impulse that had characterized it seemed to be exhausted, and its mood was sad, relaxed and reminiscent. Boston, absorbing its suburbs, had grown larger and larger; but this huge and cosmopolitan population had little to distinguish it from others. If the old race was not actually dying, if the old culture was not extinguished, there were many who felt it was merely a question of time. The Boston mind, once so cheerful, was full of the sense of last things, as if it hoped for no resuscitation. The older writers were all but gone, as the squirrels were disappearing on the Common; and Barrett Wendell, the Harvard professor, expressed a general feeling that the days of the Yankee folk were numbered. "We are vanishing into provincial obscurity," he wrote in 1893. "America has swept from our grasp. The future is beyond us."

In one way or another, many New England men of letters echoed and amplified this note of Wendell's. Henry Adams, George E. Woodberry, George Cabot Lodge,— the son of Senator Lodge, Adams's friend,—were only a few of these prophets of doom and destruction. For Godkin, always close to the mind of Cambridge, the whole American enterprise had ended in failure; Parkman more or less agreed with Godkin; and Norton, for whom New England had meant so much, was struck by the waste and futility of all its effort. In the face of the foreign inrush, how apparently ineffective were the labours of the earlier

generations! Others were cheerful and hopeful as ever,—
perhaps they were also the wisest; but the evidence seemed
to be against them. William James looked forward calmly.
John Fiske had few doubts. President Eliot serenely confronted the future. The Emersonian Eliot believed in the
future: he had no tears to waste on the past in regrets.
For Howells, as for Justice Holmes, so open in their sympathies, the good could never lose its sporting chance;
and one found no ear for tales of woe on the part of Miss
Sarah Palfrey, the historian's daughter, who, every morning, at the age of seventy-five, took a spin on her tricycle
round Fresh Pond before breakfast. The older were the
bolder in Boston, as elsewhere; and the older and bolder
they were the less inclined to think the world was going to
the dogs. They were tough enough to know that the good
was tough; and, like all true aristocrats, they believed in
their country, if only because their country included themselves. Those who had fought and bled in freedom's
cause, like Justice Holmes and Colonel Higginson, were
prepared to take long views of these ultimate questions;
and so was Edward Everett Hale, the "grand old man
of Boston," and Julia Ward Howe, the romantic old
sibyl. These magnanimous worthies, these generous natures, for whom nothing had ever existed that was common or mean, were destined to see mankind as forever
triumphant. They ignored the signs of the times and lived
above them, as Emerson had lived all his life. But for
those who lived close to the ground the signs of the times
were anything but roseate or auspicious. It was easy for
William James and Howells, John Fiske and President
Eliot to take long views of the future. They were sufficiently realistic, but they were not New Englanders merely.
Howells was not a Yankee at all, James was a Yankee
only by courtesy, and the consciousness of Eliot and Fiske
embraced the nation. Their ships were heavily ballasted
and sailed on broad bottoms. The true-blue Yankees who

were only imperfectly also American sailed in skiffs and found the water shallow. Most of their birds of the hour were of evil omen.

Was the Yankee race really dying? Barrett Wendell felt so, not without grounds for his feeling, both inward and outward.* George Cabot Lodge, who agreed with Wendell, broadened the base of the question. He felt that the whole old American race was dying.† That the Yankee stock which had leavened the nation was somehow wearing thin one saw in Mary E. Wilkins's remarkable stories. If the strength of the flower of Boston sprang from its roots, what was the meaning of these stories, which had begun to appear at the turn of the nineties? What light did they throw on the human soil of the region? Mary E. Wilkins was only one of a number of writers whose minds were preoccupied with the ends of things, families running out, forlorn old women, ramshackle dwellings, lone eccentrics. The almshouse and the village pensioner figured largely in these stories. In Elizabeth Stuart Phelps's *Jonathan and David,* the man had only a dog to share his world; and dogs and cats, the children of the childless, ranked with men and women as *dramatis personae.* All these authors took fag-ends for granted. Their theme was desolation doing its best, or so at least it seemed to Boston readers; and up and down the scale, from roots to flowers, the New England mind repeated its tale of exhaustion. Had Hawthorne perhaps been right when he said to Howells that the apparent coldness of the Yankees was real, that the suppression of emotion for long generations would extinguish emotion at last in the soul of New England?

* "I feel that we Yankees are as much things of the past as any race can be."—Barrett Wendell, Letter of 1893.

† "We are a dying race, as every race must be of which the men are, as men and not accumulators, third-rate."—*The Life of George Cabot Lodge,* by Henry Adams. Lodge's argument was based on biological grounds. It followed the line of Theodore Roosevelt, apropos of "race-suicide."

The Boston mind appeared to have lost its force. It was yielding, inch by inch, to the Catholic Irish; and the time was approaching when a Catholic Irish mayor of Boston was to say that the New England of the Puritans was as dead as Caesar. It was the Irish, he added, who had made Massachusetts a "fit place to live in,"—the Irish had had letters and learning when the forbears of New England were savages living in hyperborean forests. This last remark was largely true; but still it was an unkind cut for the makers of New England. The Puritans who had conquered the Indians had not been so unkind. They had not poured scorn on the red men for their forest-existence, although, it must be added, the Puritans were not rhetoricians,—they were not compelled to assert themselves by means of these floral displays. There were cuts on both sides. The Bostonians resented the Irish, though the case already had its compensations, —the conquerors were bearing gifts for the joy of the conquered. John Boyle O'Reilly was one of these gifts; another, just emerging, was the lovely spirit of Louise Imogen Guiney, the essayist and poet. Miss Guiney was the daughter of an Irish lawyer who had commanded a regiment in the Civil War. Brevetted a brigadier-general, like Charles Francis Adams,—as gallant as all the Irish fighters were,*—he had been hopelessly wounded; and one day in Boston, twelve years later, he suddenly stopped in the street, removed his hat, knelt, crossed himself and died. Miss Guiney's spirit rode forward in her father's stirrups. None of this was lost upon the city of the Puritans. The Bostonians knew a soldier, as they knew a poet. What they had seen in O'Reilly they saw in the Guineys; and the Irish, in the Protestant form, had given them Godkin and both the Henry Jameses and William James. Heaven only knew what future gifts the conquerors had

* "In all the records of the Civil War there was no such thing as an Irish coward."—Thomas Wentworth Higginson.

in store for a later New England; and the Yankees were
not ungrateful to them. Some of Miss Jewett's best stories
were tributes to them, and certainly Miss Jewett knew
the Irish,—she had spent the greater part of a year
among them, once, at Bantry Bay. It was in the nature of
things that the Yankees resented the Irish, but they resented their own impuissance more. They could present
no equal counterforce; they could not hold their end up
any longer. They saw their glory vanishing before the
invaders.

The old New England was slipping away. The rock-
bound coast was stern no longer: its villas, lawns and
gardens suggested the Hudson river or the Isle of Wight.
The Reef of Norman's Woe was merely a rock. The old
public spirit was fading, along with the old religious
spirit, as they had faded away in an earlier Athens. Senator Lodge, the "scholar in politics," the first New England statesman who had played a national role for many
years, the conscious heir of all his predecessors, seemed
oddly small and shrunken in their light. This David who
had slain Goliath Butler and who had been the hope of
the younger Yankees traduced the spirit of his forbears,
though he wore their mask. As virtually a nephew of
Sumner, Motley, Parkman and Holmes, who had called
him "Cabot" from the cradle, he was the scion of all
the old patricians. He owned and worked on Bancroft's
writing-table, he followed Bancroft and Parkman as a
grower of roses; and his speech alone had style, as they
said in the Senate,—he led his fellow-Senators away from
bombast "towards reality and forceful expression." * It
was Lodge who brought about the copyright-bill, deserving, as he won, the praise of authors. In these and other
ways, he carried on the old line, and he went through
all the motions of the older statesmen. But he had none
of their breadth of soul and vision. Sectional interests

* Elihu Root.

and caste-interests really governed his motives, while he
stood as a defender of the nation; and he was merely the
lawyer in his international policies, with none of the understanding of the life of nations that illumined the men
of the past.* The older statesmen had found their models
in Plutarch, while he found his in the busts of the older
statesmen. He was the victim of a day of small things,
and one felt in him the end of a spent tradition.

The religious tradition seemed equally all but exhausted.
There was little to withstand the Catholic power, except
the dubious faith of Christian Science,† and within a few
years the most prominent objects in Boston were the
Catholic cathedral, the dome of the Synagogue and the
dome of Mrs. Eddy's Mother Church. The prevailing
religion was comfort, with accessories, which varied from
mind-cure and easy-going optimism to cults that gave
aesthetic satisfaction; and the leading doctrine of Boston
was not to offend, in the shade of which conviction turned
to dust. The faith-healer had won the day, and invalids
frequented practitioners who silently thought benevolent
things about them. The miracles of mind-cure were naturally numerous, although Fletcherism flourished as a
rival; and people solemnly chewed their food very fine
and slowly to be slender enough to pass through the eye
of the needle. A modish high-Anglicanism led the other
cults, together with drawing-room faiths from Arabia and
Persia; and young men who, in Channing's day, would
have proselytized the West enjoyed a romantic destiny as
high-church monks. The ethical caprices of Boston could

---

* "When working at the language of a treaty, he thought of it as a
document and did not allow his mind to wander far into the country, habits and religions of the people on the other side of the treaty."—William
Lawrence, *Henry Cabot Lodge*.

† "I can't bring myself . . . to blink the evil out of life . . . It's as real as
the good, and if it is denied, good must be denied too. It must be accepted
and hated, and resisted while there's breath in our bodies."—Letter of
William James.

scarcely have been numbered.* They rivalled those of
Los Angeles in a day to come; and anything but Protestantism, anything else than the Puritan past,—this was
their common emblem and their watchword. Anything,
in fact, that was not Boston,—for Boston had its forms
for all these faiths and was bent on rejecting the forms
because it had them. In the Episcopal faith, it possessed
a genius in Phillips Brooks, who had reconciled Anglican-
ism with its inmost fibre; and what, with their beards
and robes, did the Eastern mystics have to say that Channing and Emerson had not said before them in a form
that sprang straight out of the soul of New England?
But Boston, as strangers gathered, no longer wished to
believe in itself, and robes and incense † now made all
the difference. What came from Pusey's Oxford and
somebody's Persia seemed necessarily better than anyone's Boston,—which meant that Boston really believed
in nothing, or so, at least, Bostonians occasionally said.‡
In short, the Bostonians were lost, as a family, in this
resembling the Peterkins, as in other respects; § and they
had no Lady from Philadelphia to tell them to meet at
the Sphinx.|| Whether they could have found the Sphinx

* "We are the children of the Puritans and have inherited a twist toward the ethical and the supernatural so strong that we have to have
these things served up even in our amusements."—Arlo Bates, *The
Puritans.*

† "I am too old to hear religion, I am too old to see religion. But I can
still smell religion."—Mrs. Bell, Rufus Choate's daughter, who, in her later
years, occasionally went to the Church of the Advent.

‡ "As some reactionary backslider has said, the spiritual history of this
region from Channing's day to ours may be summarized as that of a theological progress from certainty concerning what the devil is to uncertainty
concerning what the devil anything is."—Barrett Wendell, *Liberty, Union
and Democracy.*

This moment was appropriate for the founding of the Ingersoll Lectures
on Immortality, 1897. Few indeed believed any longer in immortality, but
there was a general interest in hearing what could be said for it.

§ " 'This time,' Elizabeth Eliza said, 'it is not our trunks that were lost—'
" 'But we, as a family,' said Mrs. Peterkin."
                                        —Lucretia Hale, *The Peterkin Papers.*

|| *The Last of the Peterkins.*

and what the Sphinx might have had to say were questions which they scarcely dared to ask.

All this had happened in Athens as it happened in Boston, though in Athens, when the great days passed, literature remained. Then, in Athens, literature vanished also. Was it vanishing in Boston already? The Bostonians felt so. The bells tolled every year for a great man gone: Lowell in 1891, Whittier in 1892, in 1893 Francis Parkman. Holmes, who died in 1894, had lived to "sing the swan-song for the choir." These were "pitch-pine" Yankees of the stoutest timber. They had withstood the storms that battered down the lesser men, and the second growth had yielded few equals or rivals. Parkman alone perhaps was built for another millennium, but all had produced their planks for the house of the future; and whether their eminence was relative or absolute, this, after all, mattered little. Lowell as a sage was not impressive,* but *The Biglow Papers* counted for much and long; so did a few of his literary essays, and his speech on Coleridge in Westminster Abbey might have made the fame of another man. His wit was as genuine as Holmes's, and this said much. As for Holmes himself, most of his verse had had its day, but his "high-bred amicability,"—Goethe's phrase on Molière,—was a lasting possession. He had permanently enriched the Yankee scene with his genius of good sense and his gaiety and vigour. Green was the golden bough of life for him. At eighty-five, at Beverly Farms, he had found a mammoth elm that was finer than all his other favourites; and the charming little old man in his open carriage, holding his minikin sunshade, perhaps with Mrs. Bell on the seat beside him, had used his amicability to diffuse the sun in

---

* "They"—Americans generally—"are right in feeling that way about Lowell here too,—as a political teacher and wiseacre he surely ought not to be very seriously taken. Doesn't 'think straight,' etc. Charles Norton ditto! with his 'culture,' never forgetting that it is not vulgarity."—Letter of William James, 1888.

corners, unlike his, that were damp and dark. Mrs. Bell, Rufus Choate's daughter, whose mind was also of the kind one spoke, spoke it often and well, as well as he.* Whittier, too, stood lastingly for the gods of New England, the passion for goodness and justice and the household lares; and Parkman, who never drew morals, lived the moral that all his books conveyed. These men had fought good fights in one way or another, and all of them had won the Promethean prize. They had carried their lamps unextinguished to the end of the race.

There were plenty of Bostonians who were never willing to say die, but who was to take the place of these men that had gone? The future echoed the question. There was no reply. That the fortunate bloom of Athens was only a question of fifty years, that Spain's great hour was brief, this mattered little. How long were any of these "heats and genial periods"?—Emerson's phrase for the "high tides" of the spirit. The morning after was always grey and sad; and Boston for twenty years counted its survivors before it reluctantly said, This is the last. It was too chagrined to observe the new generation that was rising in its presence, all unknown. Those who remained to recall the times that people called "heroic" or "Augustan," chips of the older block indeed, were smaller. They were the equals in character of those who had passed, but as writers they were subordinate and mostly humble. On Cornhill, at the Athenæum, in the Old Corner Bookstore, one met these lingering worthies when the sun came out, Edward Everett Hale, Mrs. Howe or the sweetly, sadly beaming little Norton,

---

* "I do not believe Henry James is so silly as to pompously announce that he is no longer an American. He probably said it was a pleasant day in such a roundabout way that no one knew what he was driving at."— Mrs. Bell, at the time of James's naturalization in England. Mrs. Bell, the complete Bostonian, did not like the country. She said to a friend who was setting out for the woods and fields, "Well, kick a tree for me." When a dray passed her house, filled with jangling rails, she said to her sister, "Never mind, it might have been a bird."

with his habit of shaking his head as he smiled and sighed; or it might have been Colonel Higginson, on his high-wheeled bicycle, bolt upright, scorching at five miles an hour through the streets of Cambridge. The great-grandmotherly Mrs. Howe, never at a loss for causes, appeared in her lace hood at every meeting. No meeting could have deserved the name unless she recited the *Battle Hymn,* in her flowered silk cloak and lilac satin. She was never too old to appear at the State House to plead for justice or mercy,—no day without its cause was her constant motto; and, as Holmes had celebrated birthdays, she celebrated centenaries, from Bryant's and Margaret Fuller's to Abraham Lincoln's. As a national institution, Dr. Hale was her only rival. The rough-and-ready Hale, like Mrs. Howe, had kept the faith and gusto of the early republic. With his air of an untidy Pilgrim father, he seemed to say that Gilead still had its balm. Every child in Boston had sat on his knee, from Beacon Street to the byways and lost alleys where he searched for the lame in body and the maimed in spirit; and, moreover, this hardy old Christian, who loved adventure, and who knew all the world as he knew his country, had kept the statesmanly instinct of the ministers of old. "Cradled in the sheets of the Boston *Advertiser,*" he had known most of the statesmen of America and England, and he who was soon to become the chaplain of the national Senate * was one who had not been discouraged by the post-war years. No one knew politics better. No one knew the founders of the country better; † and it was in their name that he took, at the age of eighty-one, the line that others followed in after decades. In his daily edi-

---

* "Do you pray for the Senators, Dr. Hale?" someone asked the chaplain. "No, I look at the Senators and pray for the country."

† After *The Man Without a Country,* Hale's most substantial work was his *Franklin in France,* two volumes, 1888. This was based on unpublished documents and letters. He was an unpretentious journalist in most of his other writings.

torials, he defended the Rochdale coöperative system, the government ownership of coal-mines, old-age pensions, and he asked why all these measures were regarded as novel. Did not the people own the roads, the canals, aqueducts, schoolhouses, lighthouses? Did they not own the libraries, reservoirs, churches? Was not the word "commonwealth" first used by Winthrop for a political organization? Had not the American genius always run in the line of the "government ownership of the essentials"? Was the "ownership of wealth in common" anything so odd? * John Quincy Adams had asked, in his way, a similar question; and Hale, who was not "without a country," knew that the best way to possess a country was to follow the path of justice for the greatest number. Dr. Hale and Mrs. Howe were living illustrations of the truth that New England perhaps was created to show,—that character was what Emerson had called it; and one felt this in Colonel Higginson's presence as one saw the sabre-scar on his chin, a souvenir of the fight for Anthony Burns. Norton, too, had character, though not so simply. When, attacking the war with Spain as "inglorious" and "criminal," he was called a traitor for his pains,† Norton sighed perhaps but he shrugged his shoulders. He had heard all this before, with Lowell and Dana, when the Mexicans instead of the Spaniards were the bone of contention. If Norton lacked the moral sweep of Higginson and Hale, this was because his sympathies were far less open; and for this reason his teaching, fine as it was, was very far from what it might have been. Like his sympathies, his imagination was imperfectly developed, a fact that was all the more glaring because his

* *We, the People,* 1903.

† Among men of letters, Howells, Higginson, William James, Mark Twain, Aldrich and William Graham Sumner equally opposed the Spanish War. "Don't yelp with the pack," William James said to his classes. The Anti-Imperialist League was organized in Boston in 1898 to oppose the annexation of the Philippines, etc.

field was of imagination all compact. So he left the "art" out of art, just as, in following Ruskin, he left out the heart of Ruskin's teaching,—for was not Ruskin a socialist, like Dr. Hale? Strange as it might have appeared, the chaplain of the Senate had more in common with Ruskin than the exquisite Norton.* Norton, perhaps, was not the "real thing." William James was certain that he was not;† and the popular phrase about Norton that, entering heaven, he exclaimed, "Oh, oh! So overdone! So Renaissance!" expressed a general feeling that was true and just. Always an invalid, he had carried his fastidiousness to a point that was all but absurd and unsound as well. As with many dons who glory in their donnishness, his alienated taste was over-ripe; and many an equal of Norton's in culture whose sympathies were open out-smiled the smiling sage at his expense. John Jay Chapman ‡ and Santayana § were only two of these; and indeed there

* "He was a kind of angel gone astray; meant for the thirteenth century, he got delayed on the way, and when he finally arrived was a white-winged anachronism."—Norton's comment on Ruskin at the time of his death. This was a fine phrase but far from true. No man was less an anachronism than the author of *Unto This Last.*

† "Charles Norton, I see, receives the bequest of Lowell's manuscripts, etc. The way that man gets his name stuck to every greatness is fabulous, —Dante, Goethe, Carlyle, Ruskin, FitzGerald, Chauncey Wright, and now Lowell! His name will dominate all the literary history of this epoch. 100 years hence, the *Revue des Deux Mondes* will publish an article entitled 'La Vie de l'esprit aux Etats-Unis vers du XIXme siècle; étude sur Charles Norton.' He is our *foyer de lumières;* and the worst of it is that he does all the chores therewith connected, and practically fills the position rather better, than if he were the genuine article."—Letter of William James to Alice James, 1891.

‡ "The great business of Bostonians was to place values upon everything in the world, with conscientious accuracy. Professor Norton once said to me on the steps of Sanders Theatre, after a performance of Beethoven's 'Eroica Symphony,' that, after all, the 'sentiment' of the funeral march was a little 'forced.' This was charming, too. Of course, it is not great or of the great world. . . . It was Boston's foible to set metes and bounds to everything."—John Jay Chapman, *Memories and Milestones.*

§ "Old Harvard men will remember the sweet sadness of Professor Norton. He would tell his classes, shaking his head with a slight sigh, that the Greeks did not play football."—Santayana, *The Genteel Tradition at Bay.*
There were also professors who told their classes that the Greeks did nothing but play football.

was something preposterous in this winning old pundit,
with his "note as sweet as an eighteenth-century organ." *
Howells had shown the right perception when, years before, Norton had first returned to teach in Cambridge.
He had said that Norton's standard was "dreadfully
high," by which he did not mean that it should have been
laxer, and that the apple-blossoms were worth all the
past of which Norton sighed "to find us disinherited." †
This might have seemed an exaggeration in 1874, but
one saw what Howells meant in 1890, observing the contentment with which Norton told his classes that they too
might have been happy, on one condition,—not to have
been born at all in the age they lived in.‡ There had always been something wrong with a standard that led to
this denial of life, a denial that was sterile and complacent. The "apple-blossoms" taught a better lesson,
and so did the genuine pessimists, unhappy themselves,
who denied life in order to affirm it.§ But those who said
that Norton was precious also said he was powerful, a
teacher "in the mystical and personal sense" ‖ who was
all but unique in his time; and his translation of Dante
in masterly prose,—he felt this befitted the temper of the
age more fully,—was a proof that his scholarship was
vital. This was more important than Norton's writings.
For scholarship and character one never had to look far
in New England, character with salt and scholarship with
wit and poetry. But poetry and wit themselves were an-

* John Jay Chapman.
† Letter of Howells, 1874.
‡ "Professor Norton lectured in Italian 4 this afternoon. The dear old man
looks so mildly happy and benignant while he regrets everything in the
age and the country—so contented, while he gently tells us it were better
for us had we never been born in this degenerate and unlovely age . . . I
wonder if these dear and reverend people realize what an impression they
give the younger ones when they beg them to believe that there is nothing
high and lovely in this country or this age."—*Diary and Letters of
Josephine Preston Peabody.*
§ "If way to the Better there be, it exacts a full look at the Worst."—
Thomas Hardy, *In Tenebris.*
‖ John Jay Chapman.

other matter. Literature proper was evaporating, surely. In Gautier's verses, the bust outlived the city, but in Boston the bust had also outlived the poem.

The Bostonians were convinced of this, whether it was true or not, and those who called the moment Alexandrian knew their history well. On its smaller scale, New England was repeating the conditions of the classical age that bore this name. The Alexandrians could return no longer to their homogeneous early Athenian life. The gods of the State and the household were diminished in stature. Indeed, they ceased to be gods, they were even as men; and men no longer reverenced the temples in their own breasts,—they respected their mundane interests more than their feelings. The bonds that had held them together had fallen apart, and persons were merely persons without the attachments that had given them significance and value. Idiosyncrasies flourished without rhyme or reason, and women assumed the tasks in which men had failed. As in Greece, so in Boston, the logic of cause and effect worked itself out in literature, as in all things human. Literature became merely literary,—to use the phrase of the hour,—because it had lost its native impulse. It was driven to follow models more abjectly than ever, and models that were also arbitrary, unlike the co-ordinated models of the earlier writers, who had borne an organic relation to the men they followed. Learning took the place that poetry had held in a day when men shared heroic passions; and no one better than Bostonians knew what this implied, however their prosperity had grown. They were all Agamemnons and Solomon Johns, when it came to reading encyclopædias, and they knew that these compendiums, which represented human standards, contained a hundred poets for every banker. To be able to compete with Detroit was no great prospect when they had been, uniquely and potently, Boston. If New England was to rise again, it would have to rise

on another basis; and what this basis was few men could
see. It was certain that the pitcher of the past was broken
at the fountain. Cambridge might have its worthies to
the end of the chapter, like old John Holmes, the Autocrat's brother, whose sole occupation had been friendship. John Holmes, blind now, had to put up with an
attendant, who led him out to the Common and left him
on a bench. There he sat alone, basking in the sun, murmuring Homer. Cambridge, Boston, Worcester, Hartford might long have their John Holmeses; but when
would another mayor of a factory-town, stirred by another Yankee poet's death, utter a funeral oration in the
manner of Athens? *

Boston was left to gather up its relics, with a feeling
that its forbears had had "all the fun." † The New Yorkers laughed when Oliver Herford characterized New
England as "the abandoned farm of literature." The
Bostonians did not laugh,—the barb struck home. The
North American Review had gone to New York, and the
Atlantic Monthly was doing its best to forget that it represented Boston. Last things were in order now,‡ and all
the Boston men could do,—or all they thought they could
do,—was to bury the dead. Mount Auburn was becoming over-crowded. Every other Boston book was somebody's *Retrospections,* and *Yesterdays,* cheerful or other-

---

* "To honour the memory of the great, the wise and the good by suitable
expression has at all times and under all conditions of civilization been a
criterion by which to judge of the degree of intelligence, morality and refinement attained. In their ideals we may measure their aspirations and
ambitions . . . In a city preëminent for its devotion to business, this audience is assembled to honour the memory of one the aim of whose life was
higher than the ambition to accumulate wealth. Here may we be reminded
that man is most honoured, not by that which a city may do for him, but
by that which he has done for the city."—From the speech of the Mayor of
Haverhill at the funeral of Whittier, 1892.

† Thomas Sergeant Perry.

‡ Even Dr. Hale wrote a sketch called *The Last Shake,* commemorating
the last man with a hand-cart who was ever allowed to shake carpets on
Boston Common.

wise, flooded the book-shops. Doing the Pharaohs up in
spices, in Dr. Holmes's phrase, was the central occupation of the literati. Dr. Holmes's own life was written
by John T. Morse, Jr.,—almost as salty as his subject,—
the veteran who edited the *American Statesman Series*
and ran like a sugar-maple with wit and wisdom till he
died at the age of ninety-six. M. A. De Wolfe Howe, the
Boston historiographer, also began at this moment the
long career that united the liberality of the old New England with the sunniness and fullness of New England culture. As a Rhode Islander, Mark Howe, so-called universally, saw Boston with an edge of difference; and this,
no doubt, was the reason why, having so much in common
with it, he was able to reveal to others its potent charm.
He performed a historical function in so far as Boston
was itself a historical city; for he was to live through all
the decades in which the country turned against it, and
more than anyone else, in his own person, he led the
country back. Mark Howe possessed the secret that puzzled the burghers, like other Pied Pipers before him. The
biographer of Phillips Brooks, Bancroft, Norton, Moorfield Storey, and later of Wendell, Holmes and John Jay
Chapman, was a poet all the time; and that is why, in
Mark Howe's books, the Pharaohs came to life again, as
they died again in other "lives and letters." He shared in
whatever was human because it was human, so that all
his heroes abounded in their own sense. Most of the other
biographers were dazzled by their heroes, or they were
humdrum themselves; and they so swathed the mummies
of the Pharaohs that it took a generation to unwrap
them.

This mood of retrospection, so closely allied to the
moods of regret and defeat, expressed itself most fully
in Barrett Wendell. He shared Norton's feeling,—he
was born too late in a world too old; and he could not

find his way back to the earlier Boston.* Where was Boston, the Boston of the springtime twenties? He whipped his horse about the roads in vain. For Wendell was Peter Rugg incarnate, and the image of this old man in the yellow-wheeled chaise, who was forever asking, "Where is Boston?" haunted many in these bewildered years. Miss Guiney and Amy Lowell wrote poems about Peter Rugg, who had stepped out of a story and become a folk-figure.† He stood for the seekers of lost trails who abounded in Boston, for those who felt their world had gone awry and who tried to grope their way back to an earlier time when life had been vigorous and hopeful. There were many of these besides Wendell, and, like him, they sorted their family papers, as if in these yellowing documents they might possibly find the secret of the life which they had missed. Might not the virtue flow into them again if they touched these relics of their forbears that spoke of a large and active life in the past?‡ This sorting of family papers seemed to them a public service, though in certain cases the families had scarcely been public and had never played a part in the larger world that called for any general interest in them. In other cases, anxious descendants who longed to live up to a family tradition continued to go through the motions of a pub-

* "The very pleasantest little oasis of space and time was that of New England from about the beginning of the century to about 1825."—Charles Eliot Norton.
   "At this moment, very often, I feel a certain regret that I had not the fortune to be born fifty years earlier. Then I could eagerly have joined in the expression of faith in the future which made New England literature promise something. Now I find my temper doubtful, reactionary. Such moods as mine are not things that literature demands."—Barrett Wendell, 1893.
   † See Amy Lowell's *Before the Storm* and Louise Imogen Guiney's *Peter Rugg, the Bostonian*.
   ‡ The well-known Boston malady, "grandfather on the brain,"—so called by Harriet Preston in *Aspendale*,—reached its crisis in the nineties. This malady, or this mood, spread through the country. It was during these years that the Colonial Dames, the D.A.R., etc., were organized, to restore the fading racial faith and to assert the prestige of the original stock, threatened by the waves of immigration.

lic life on the small private scale that was open to them. If they could not promote bills in Congress, they could write letters to the *Transcript,* declaring war on the sparrows, instead of the British, and urging the protection of the squirrels on the ground that they sucked the sparrows' eggs. The contrast between their inherited tone and the trivial field their world afforded was a fruitful cause of satire, both then and later. Robert Grant's *The Chippendales* anticipated by thirty years the delicate, but sharper satire of *The Late George Apley.**

Barrett Wendell, like so many others, wished he had lived in the great good time when things were a-doing in Boston. He shrank from the "bewildering surge" of a world that seemed "sadly bound nowhither," † and cherished his Harvard memories of a world that was gone. But, if he had lived in the days he longed for, would he have shared in the "faith that made New England literature promise something"? He felt so. He wished to believe it. He was surely mistaken. For the tender-minded Wendell, who likened himself to "a Federalist in Jefferson's time, a sound Whig in Jackson's, or an honest Southerner in Lincoln's," could never have had the root of the matter in him. The "last of the tories," as he also called himself, would have been a tory all the time; but, glorying in this, as he was certainly free to do, how could he have shared the springtime faith? He was hostile to all its premises and all its results. Deploring the French Revolution,‡ he deplored the American Revolu-

---

* By John P. Marquand. The pathos of this Boston type is illustrated best in Bliss Perry's life of Richard Henry Dana III. When Dana was baptised, as an infant, in 1851, the clergyman exclaimed, "May there ever be a Richard Henry Dana to stand before the Lord!" Having, with small capacity, to live up to this,—to live up to the family tradition of sacrifice and service,—Dana spent his life in bewildered efforts to find some way of being useful. As in the case of George Apley, he had the patrician's pattern of mind in a world that had ceased to afford scope for patricians.

† Letter of Barrett Wendell.

‡ Of the results of the French Revolution he said, in *The France of Today,* "More than a little philanthropic purpose was accomplished, they say."

tion,* which had divided the English-speaking world; and, missing the significance of all the Revolution stood for, he had missed the meaning of his country. Indeed, he scarcely pretended to be loyal to the country; † and yet the paradoxical Barrett Wendell saw in himself a defender of "American traditions" ! ‡ By American traditions, he meant a number of things, no doubt, but mainly that good old families had good old glass, Heppelwhite chairs and good Madeira; and he meant that they had been English and should have remained so. Meanwhile, the important traditions were beyond his horizon, for Wendell, travelling over the country, wining and dining at Harvard clubs and sharing in "our funny local life," had certainly never experienced the American present; and only those who experienced the American present were able to comprehend the American past. Had he undergone any experience, for the matter of that, the vital kind of experience that affords one a key either to the past or to the present? The wistful Wendell, who had always yearned for "peace," § had never known, he said, the "stress of life;" and did he know what experience was? What did he mean by the word? Nothing that concerned the spiritual depths; for he observed that the Saviour died too young to have the sort of experience he

* "The American Revolution, then, disuniting the English-speaking world, has had on history an effect which those who cherish the moral and political heritage of our language may well grow to feel in some sense tragic."
—Wendell, *Literary History of America*.

† "The virtue of loyalty has been denied me by a fate which has hardly ever afforded me a sovereign to whom I could conscientiously be loyal."—Letter of 1915.

‡ "I remember . . . how disappointed he became in a certain young man who, presuming to be his follower, said to him, 'But we Americans have no traditions.' If the sense of the remark had been to the effect that Americans should not respect traditions, that he could have borne. The offence of the young man lay in his failure to realize that no man can help having traditions, and also in the indirect affront cast at the quality of American traditions."—Daniel Sargent, *Essays in Memory of Barrett Wendell*.

§ "Peace I have always yearned for. Four or five of my earlier books purposely ended with the word."—Letter of 1919.

knew and valued.* He meant a certain mundane sophisti-
cation; and, when he said that American literature was a
record of "national inexperience," † this was the standard
that lurked in the depths of his mind. The real experience of the country, which found a voice in literature,
was vague and repugnant to Wendell; and naturally he was
half-hearted, therefore, even about its greatest writers,
even in his own New England, to say nothing of the rest.
The defender of American traditions gave them away.

Thus the past, in Wendell's mind, as in others that
shrank from the present, was a sort of phantasmal entity
without life or substance. And not the American past
alone. The remoter past was phantasmal also, as one
saw in his efforts to recreate it; ‡ and it was phantasmal
for an obvious reason, because tradition, like charity, begins at home. One can only reach the background through

---

* "Historically considered, the Gospels tell the story of a remarkable man
who lived under extremely fixed earthly circumstances, remote from any
we know, and died before he was old enough to have much experience."—
Letter of 1919.
  This seems to suggest that all would have been well if the Saviour had
had a taste of London and Paris.
  † "In the flush of its waking, [America] strove to express the meaning
of life; and the meaning of its life was the story of what two hundred
years of national inexperience had wrought for a race of Elizabethan
Puritans. Its utterances may well prove lacking in scope, in greatness; the
days to come may well prove them of little lasting potence . . . We used to
believe them,"—Thoreau, Hawthorne, Emerson, Whitman,—"heralds of the
future; already we begin to perceive that they were rather chroniclers of
times which shall be no more."—Wendell, *Literary History of America*.
  The impression that readers will get from this book, Howells observed
in reviewing it, "is that American literature is not worth the attention of
people meaning to be really critical."
  ‡ In *The Traditions of European Literature*. A comparison of this with
Emerson's *Representative Men* marks all the difference between crescent
and senescent Boston. Emerson, who professed to despise tradition, chose
six great historical figures and made them live for his contemporaries.
Wendell, who worshipped tradition, wished to make Plato and Dante live,
but he completely failed to do so. He represented them merely as manifestations of traditions, not as men who sought truth in their time. Emerson conveyed the substance of tradition, Wendell conveyed only its shells.
Which should a lover of tradition prefer,—one who "despises" tradition or
one who worships tradition for its own sake?
  Wendell's leading thought was much the same as Henry Adams's,—that
the world had been steadily going to the dogs ever since the time of Dante.

the foreground; for what makes the past real except a vigorous present existence that reads itself into the records of times that are gone? It was no accident that the great New England histories appeared in the days when New England was a force and a power. Prescott, Motley and Parkman shared the pulse-beats of a great and developing nation, and their Spain, their Holland, their Canada lived through this. They were participants in the past, and recreators of it, because they were also participants in the age they lived in. That Parkman was a born explorer, like his Canadian heroes, that Motley was a diplomat and statesman, that Prescott had eagerly followed the Peninsular War,—all this counted for something; and one and all had grown up at a time when young New England men were ardently conscious members of a country in the building. No one thinks of defending tradition in days that are making tradition, when people feel the past as a force of the present, an auxiliary, a ministrant, a helpmate. One only defends tradition, one resorts to tradition to fill the void in oneself, when life runs low. And then one grasps only the forms of tradition. Only the husks of tradition remain in one's hands.

Boston, sorting its papers, like a man who is dying, anxious to arrange his affairs, was full of these forms. Its dominant mind was a dry sea-beach where all the creatures of history had deposited their shells. Its tone was elegiac. It abounded in praisers of times past who would never have known their Catullus, had he walked their way, and who savoured the "decencies of comfortable corruption" * while they fondled their costly bindings and their choice mementos. There brooded over the town, as a stranger noted, "an immense effect of finality," as if all intellectual movement had ceased there; † and a horrible

* Barrett Wendell.
† "There broods over the real Boston an immense effect of finality. One feels in Boston, as one feels in no other part of the States, that the intellectual movement has ceased."—H. G. Wells, *The Future in America*, 1906.

sense of conviction overcame this stranger, at a certain
club of Boston bibliophiles. The mind of the world was
dead, he said to himself; and this was a distribution of
souvenirs! "I felt," H. G. Wells recalled, "that all the
books had been written, all the pictures painted, all the
thoughts said." Wells, dismayed, rushed from the room
and roamed through the streets in the moonlight, till he
caught the glimpse of a ray in a bookseller's window;
and there, in fresh covers, lay books that had just come
out. The mind of the world was still alive!—in spite of
the bibliophiles and in spite of Boston.

CHAPTER XXI

THE EPIGONI

WAS New England really dying? Or did it merely wish to think so? Was it dead or simulating death? All these questions puzzled the enquiring stranger. There were evidences corroborating almost every possible view, for the Yankee mind had grown to resemble the Sphinx, the Sphinx of the desert as well as the Sphinx of the mountain. In some respects, it seemed certainly moribund, while in others it maintained a state of suspended animation; but now and then one asked oneself if there was not a hoax at the bottom of it all. For if the Yankee mind was dead it had the best of all excuses for no longer providing the country with statesmen and poets.

Such were a few of the riddles the Yankee mind proposed to strangers, who were sometimes rash in their responses. But the Yankees were companionable. In this they were unlike the Sphinx,—they were willing to discuss the riddles as well as to propose them. They even had their vanities: they encouraged people to talk about them. They welcomed all the unpleasant things that strangers said about them, and even said them first and rather better; and their most admired authors were those whose constant burden now was that they were going to the devil. The Yankees, sometimes vain, were proud. They had stood for intellect and virtue. Even more than the false, they had stood for the real; and, more than any other strain, their strain had leavened the life of the country. Their failure was not merely a failure of persons; and it was not solely on their own behalf that they were filled with anxiety and chagrin. Suppose these authors of theirs were right, suppose their day was over, then much for which they stood was over also. However this might have been, it was not for strangers to smile at the lamentations at the wailing wall. If, as these authors believed, New England was a failure, New England was a tragic failure, truly. It had won the respect of mankind; and the willing suspension of disbelief,—that is, in this belief,—was the mood in order.

Henceforth, at least, for twenty years, the chief pursuit of the Yankee authors, and of most American authors concerned with New England,—was the game of pulling the skeletons out of the cupboards. There were plenty of skeletons in them to pull, for no one had ever done justice to the fund of evil that lurked in the soul of the region. The Yankee mind was beginning to pay for its somewhat cocky optimism, and even for Emerson's noble ignoring of pain. It had had perhaps too easy a victory over a virgin world of nature, where every prospect pleased and man was good; and its energy reverted now to the earlier Calvinistic view that narrowed and all but closed the eye of the needle. New England was searching its conscience, an unlovely task, but one that it had to perform. It was useless to dwell any longer, in the happy older fashion, on the blue-jays that bickered in the hedgerows, on the goldenrod with its splendid plumes, the gentians and the morning-glories and the purple asters nodding on the road-sides. These flowers that had filled the New England poems had once been the symbols of health and joy. They had burgeoned in the Yankee soul, pervading the mind with zest and vigour, in days when all the roads, with their fragrant borders, were roads of generosity, hope and purpose. Whither did the roads lead now? This ominous question shadowed the flowers and muted the songs of the birds, to such an extent that poets.

concerned with this question, the more they were concerned to answer it, turned their backs the more on the flowers and the birds. For the ground of the literary mind was gradually shifting, and the writers of the future were destined for a season to reverse and even deny the writers of the past. Whither did the roads lead? Some led where they had always led, although fewer and fewer minds were disposed to see it. The day was approaching for Irving Babbitt to have his say, for Edwin Arlington Robinson, for Santayana, for Eugene O'Neill and T. S. Eliot, for Edna St. Vincent Millay and E. E. Cummings. It was true that in these writers,—in Robert Frost especially,— New England was to have another springtime. But, first of all, it had to dree its weird. It had to pass through the valley of the shadow. Only then was it ripe for these new revelations.

The nineties were not the day for revelations. They were a day of little faith, the day of the epigoni, the successors, in whom the nineteenth century went to seed. Poets abounded, novelists, critics, in several cases highly gifted, but most of them were discouraged or astray in blind alleys. Like all Alexandrians, they had lost touch with their own tradition, or they resumed this tradition in mechanical ways; and they sought to recover trails their forbears had abandoned or else to follow new trails that were blazed by others. The blazing of new trails was not for them. They symbolized the end of an epoch in which the strongest were incomplete; for, as numbers had withdrawn altogether from the struggle,—such men as Clarence King and T. S. Perry,—so William James never built the arch of his philosophy, John Fiske's historical plan remained abortive, and Henry James and Howells and Henry Adams, great as they were in their way, were somehow qualified successes. All required explanations. None swam free in the crystalline upper air of the genuine classics, however the Jameses and Howells and Adams produced a few books that were built to live. If this was true of the greater writers, what was the natural fate of the lesser? Yet, of these epigoni, George Edward Woodberry, George Cabot Lodge, Trumbull Stickney, Louise Imogen Guiney and various others, all were symptomatic and all had their interest, either as writers proper or as Yankee types.

In the region of aesthetics, the Boston mind was clearly advancing, and all that was most vital in the nineties and after was associated with this advance. Arlo Bates's novel, *The Pagans,* spoke for a group of younger artists who were gifted, fiery and truthful and who really existed. They stood for sincerity in life, in art, in manners, against established formulas, conventions and shams. They opposed the spirit of imitation, and the golden gods of Philistia were not for them. Mrs. Helen Grayson, the heroine of this novel, might well have been Mrs. Whitman, the beautiful, generous creature who had appeared in Boston suddenly,—from "some savage town—Baltimore perhaps," * and who became the sun of the Boston artists. At Mrs. Whitman's salon, William James, Royce and Holmes abounded in the sense of the younger people who only required an eye to seek them out; and what could one say of such a woman, whose spiritual hospitality was this eye,—what more than Sainte-Beuve said apropos of Madame Récamier, with all that was implied in three French verbs? *Elle se sent, elle passe, elle apparait,* and in the presence of her gaiety, her joy of life, her tragic faith, her love of youth and promise, in the presence of these emotions everything changes! So it was with Mrs. Whitman. She was the Wingéd Victory that other Bostonians liked in casts, while others again preferred original statues; and the story of the MacMonnies

* John Jay Chapman, *Mrs. Whitman,* in *Memories and Milestones,*—Sarah Wyman Whitman, a very different sort of person from Sarah Helen Whitman, the betrothed of Poe. See also *Letters of Sarah Wyman Whitman.*

Bacchante, which caused so many blushes,—more than a few at the expense of Boston,—showed how seriously Boston could take a statue. It took the Shaw Memorial seriously, as it took Saint-Gaudens's Phillips Brooks, in which the Franco-Irish-American sculptor showed he was more American than French or Irish. Perhaps it took these things too seriously. At least, it was serious enough, which could not have been said of other cities. It prayed over the Florentine Library and Mrs. Jack Gardner's Venetian palace, and it even made Florence and Venice Bostonian somehow because of its regard for Italian culture. The fact that Boston girls grew up with Botticelli manners made Botticelli almost a Boston painter; and the Library seemed quite at home in a town where Italian studies, fostered by Norton and Longfellow, by Perkins and Lowell, were a part of the atmosphere that all men breathed. Dante,* Petrarch, Ruskin and Browning were Boston citizens in their way, although, for the good of all, they kept their distance; and handbooks on Italian art poured from the Boston presses, together with the reminiscences of New England worthies. Whistler was invited, along with Sargent and E. A. Abbey, not to speak of Puvis de Chavannes, to decorate the walls of the Library; and meanwhile the college settlements ministered to the arts and crafts, and the Copley prints appeared,

---

* The cult of Dante had woven itself into the fabric of Boston life. In 1881, Marion Crawford introduced Mrs. Gardner to Dante. They read the *Divine Comedy* together, and the two copies they had used were interleaved and bound by Tiffany, after a design by Crawford. Somewhat later, in an upper room of the Athenæum, John Jay Chapman read Dante with the half-Italian lady who became his wife.

It is recorded that Emerson translated the *Vita Nuova,* and that Ellery Channing rendered for him the sonnets and canzoni. This version was not published, nor was the translation of the *Inferno* made—of all people in the world—by President Calvin Coolidge in his youth.

The two chief New England continuers of Dante studies were Professor Charles H. Grandgent of Harvard (*Dante, The Ladies of Dante's Lyrics, Discourses on Dante,* etc.) and Professor Charles A. Dinsmore, later of Yale (*The Life of Dante, The Teachings of Dante, Aids to the Study of Dante,* etc.).

and *Poet-Lore*.* There was a rage for poems about Titian's garden. The Symphony advanced from triumph to triumph, and the "sublime sweet evening star" of Wagner eclipsed for the moment Emerson's morning star. The clever Mrs. Gardner did the rest. This "gloom-dispeller, corpse-reviver and general chirker-up," as Sturgis Bigelow called her,—the rival collector,—this reckless, exuberant, witty woman whose motto was *C'est mon plaisir* was filling Fenway Court with the spoils of Europe. As a local Queen Elizabeth, she cut off heads right and left and stuck them on again if it pleased her to do so; and, when the Bostonians called her an upstart, she cut off their ancestral heads by proving that she belonged to the house of Stuart. Norton, her master, had bought Della Robbias for her, and Henry Adams had procured for her the best French window in the country. Meanwhile, Bernhard Berenson, whom she befriended at Harvard, became her regular adviser and expert-in-chief.

All this represented vitality. The question was, What kind of vitality? Did it not rather suggest the "museum of idols" that Mrs. Whitman found in Sargent's fresco, —"all the things without being the one thing," and rather an assemblage of objects than a composition? † The Bostonians were great collectors. They collected religions,‡

---

* There was also at this time a notable movement in Boston in behalf of fine printing and book-making. D. B. Updike established the Merrymount Press, which produced the magnificent *Humanists' Library,* works by Erasmus, Leonardo, Pico della Mirandola, Dürer, Sir Philip Sidney, etc. For an account of this, see Updike's delightful *Notes on the Merrymount Press and Its Work.* Bruce Rogers became, in 1895, the designer of the Riverside Press. Less distinguished in its work, the firm of Copeland and Day excelled in the production of beautiful books; nor should one forget the charming publications of Thomas B. Mosher of Portland, Maine.

† "It"—Sargent's fresco on the stairway of the Library,—"is all the things without being the one thing; clever, decorative, enormously so,—and rich in colour, yet not beautiful in colour; an assemblage of objects rather than a composition; a museum of idols rather than a picture of the world's religions. So it seemed to me."—*Letters of Sarah Wyman Whitman.*

‡ The history of religions was a favourite subject at Harvard.

along with these objects of art; and the archæological manners of the Botticelli girls suggested an even more intimate kind of collection. They also collected political ideas; and, in their revolt from democracy and realism,* their desire to expunge all remnants of the Puritan past, they conceived a monarchist movement, a royalist movement, in which "King Charles his gentlemen" figured largely. They never saw a purple king but always hoped to see one, for the kings they contemplated were purple indeed, and far from the "business kings" of the age they lived in. They organized a local branch of the Jacobite Society, the "Order of the White Rose," namely; and they offered expiation on the feast of St. Charles, drank seditious toasts on all occasions and even corresponded with Queen Mary of Bavaria and also Don Carlos of Spain, the Legitimist sovereigns. Ralph Adams Cram, the archæological architect, who was bent upon reversing evolution, was the prior of the chapter.† This singular Boston royalism, with other admixtures of soberer hue, reappeared in T. S. Eliot two decades later; and meanwhile Mrs. Gardner, with King Charles on her family tree, scrubbed on Good Friday the altar-steps of the Advent. Mrs. Gardner proudly wore religion as the best gem upon her zone. For the rest, her eye, otherwise discriminating, ignored art when it blossomed in the fields

---

* The reaction against realism was marked in New England, as in almost every region in the nineties. It appeared in the most unexpected quarters. Thus the old New Haven realist, John W. De Forest, reëmerged after a long silence with a romantic novel, *A Lover's Revolt,* dealing with Revolutionary Boston. Sarah Orne Jewett produced *A Tory Lover,* and even Mary E. Wilkins wrote a cavalier romance, *The Heart's Highway.*

This romantic reaction, although short-lived, was completely romantic, unlike the similar reaction in the eighteen-eighties. Marion Crawford, William Henry Bishop, Julian Hawthorne and Arthur Sherburne Hardy paid tribute to the force of the realistic movement by mingling realism with their romance. The later writers threw off all pretence of realism.

† "I still treasure my parchment as 'Prior' in those American territories lying between the Canadian border and the Rio Grande."—Ralph Adams Cram, *My Life in Architecture.*

around her. She saw Giorgione's finest points, as she saw
the virtues of Sargent and Whistler, who blazed like
meteors over the world of fashion. But she did not see
the Yankee Giorgiones, Maurice Prendergast, Winslow
Homer, Ryder. The innocent eyes that perceived these
wore no veils.

What, then, was vital in all this connoisseurship, in the
world of art, religion, politics, manners? It was the
scholar's instinct, the historical sense that reënforced the
instinct of the common collector; and even a little magnificence was good for Boston. For the rest, in an age
when vulgarity reigned, when barbarians gambled in pictures as they gambled in stocks, when the passion for
display glutted itself with castles and palaces and raided
the department-store of Europe for million-dollar bar-
gains in the basement, Boston had an advantage over
other cities. Mrs. Gardner was vulgar enough. In the
game of self-glorification, in the game of sensation, she
outglittered even the magnates of Nob Hill; and similarly Cram's Gothic churches gave the village meeting-
houses a dignity that even they had lost. There was
something meretricious in all these manifestations, which
were often sentimental and occasionally silly. Almost as
much as Harry Lehr's Newport, they discredited religion,
politics, art. Alas, for Mrs. Howe's old friendly Newport, where architects and priests were on their knees before the insane vulgarities of the world of fashion. There,
where the old patricians had paid their way in manners,
in kindness, in culture, there ladies supposedly great insulted their guests and daughters blackmailed their fathers,
there savages told beads of jade, moving their lips in
prayer while they hissed insults, and a President of the
nation, surrounded by grooms, was forced to call his own
carriage, while the grooms tittered.* Realities were

* See 'King Lehr' and the Gilded Age, by Elizabeth Drexel Lehr.

wrecked at Newport along with illusions. Mrs. Gardner's
Boston was allied with this Newport, but Boston was
never Mrs. Gardner's, and all that Mrs. Gardner stood
for had a certain dignity because it also stood for thought
and learning. Obliquely as it spoke, it uttered still the
tongue that Blaxton spoke, the learned settler, who had
heard the wolves howling on the site of the State House;
and the good name of Boston survived these orgies, the
name of the Boston of effort, of conscience, of schools.
This note emanated from the Fogg Museum, which was
spreading an influence that was almost despotic as a
school of museum-directors. It produced aesthetic valets
for barbarian collectors. It also gave whatever schools
can give,—and so much the worse for artists if they could
not withstand it, if they could not leave the chaff and
take the grain. Out of this milieu, moreover, the brilliant
and useful career of the expert, Bernhard Berenson, was
just emerging. A protégé of Mrs. Gardner, he had begun
at Harvard his long-continuing studies of Italian painting, and before the end of the nineties he had almost
completed the handbooks, at once profound and charming, that were later assembled in the single volume,
Italian Painters of the Renaissance. These handbooks, so
different from the anecdotal and fanciful writing of most
art-critics of the past, characterized precisely the work
of all the Italian schools in the light of a philosophy of
taste. Berenson had conquered a tendency to follow Pater
before he developed his theory of "tactile values." He
had stood for hours before the Mona Lisa, repeating
Pater's rhapsody over and over, until he perceived that
it had no objective sense. He was already known as one
of the modern students of art who applied the methods
of science in their connoisseurship; and at twenty-six, in
1891, he had expertized the pictures at Hampton Court,
which were hopelessly confused in their attributions. The

great Renaissance names, in all the museums, were sprinkled over paintings by later artists, and Berenson undertook the task of authenticating works and accrediting them to the proper names and schools. While he lectured to classes in museums, he deduced the history of artists from a study of their works; and he also reconstructed unknown artists, as paleontologists with a handful of bones reconstructed the unknown animals to which they belonged. Before the turn of the century, he had settled in Florence, where James Jackson Jarves had lived before him. He was already consulted by museum-directors, collectors and dealers; and the time was approaching when the world of expertizing was divided between Berenson and Wilhelm von Bode.

Boston existed for education, Henry Adams said, and its genius had triumphed again in the field of art. It was collecting the documents of art as it had gathered historical documents. It was concerned, moreover, with theories of art; and, while Berenson was writing his handbooks, George Santayana was lecturing at Harvard on aesthetics. This young Spanish colleague of William James, Royce and Palmer had been brought to America at the age of eight. Born in Madrid, he had grown up in a Boston family, into which his mother had married, a strange, alien, lonely child, a duckling, far from ugly, in whom perceptive eyes foresaw the swan. Louise Imogen Guiney had seen him as a boy kneeling in a neighbouring pew in the Jesuit church; for he was brought up as a Catholic, and he kept his Catholic habits of mind, albeit Catholicism had become for him only a "theoretic pose" or a "vista," as he said, "for the imagination." *
He lived in his imagination, with Greek myths and Latin traditions, for he felt he had nothing in common with

* Santayana, *Soliloquies in England.*

the life about him; and he assumed a calm detachment from this world, which seemed to him foreign and repulsive.* The literature of New England struck him as "all a harvest of leaves;" its liberalism was alien to him, and he scorned its humanitarian impulse. The "agonized conscience" of Protestantism he felt was futile, and he disliked its atmosphere of spiritual striving, its Emersons, Whitmans and Brownings, as if its will and energy availed in the end. For was not progress merely the babble of dreamers? What mattered who ruled the land, or what form of government one had to submit to? And were not classes the normal order of nature? Were not soldiers the natural leaders, with cardinals and engineers? Why quarrel with conventions? Were the standards by which one judged them any truer than they were? And why should one quarrel with nature? Why not rather welcome its fugitive beauties? Why not rejoice in its fair outward ways, detached from the world without hostility to it? Were not repose and serenity the paramount virtues? The Apollonian Santayana, with his "Epicurean contentment," a pagan and a sceptic in his naturalism, was launching into the great soliloquy in which he expressed his hedonism and all his wonder and pleasure in the face of nature. Meanwhile, disliking the taste of academic straw, he preferred the wandering life of the mediæval student; and he usually went abroad in the summer to Spain, France or England, where he lived in later years before settling in Rome. In Cambridge, he wore a long, picturesque cape; and, aloof as he was from the other professors, he was charmed by some of the students.

* "You tax me several times with impertinence and superior airs. I wonder if you realize the years of suppressed irritation which I have passed in the midst of an unintelligent, sanctimonious and often disingenuous Protestantism, which is thoroughly alien and repulsive to me, and the need I have of joining hands with something far away from it and far above it."
—Santayana, Letter to William James, 1900.

Their "animal faith" was sympathetic to him. Amused
and serene as he was, a poet, a writer of exquisite prose,
with a style that was musical and happy, he suggested
a Greek of Plato's time or an avatar of humanistic
Florence. His lectures were published as *The Sense of
Beauty*.

All these interests of Boston and Cambridge were vital
for education, none more so than Santayana's lectures.*
But they were only obliquely related to living art and
poetry; and the ladies who listened to papers on Pico
della Mirandola were not disposed to welcome the artists
and authors who lived in an actual Boston, not a fanciful
Florence. The culture of Boston was higher and dryer
than ever. Having become a religion, it was dying as
culture; and it regarded with a glassy eye the poor little
efforts of poets who struggled beneath it. It identified
itself with Dante, Browning, with Matthew Arnold, Ruskin, Walter Pater, and felt that because it somehow knew
these authors it was entitled to regard with scorn the
ingenuous beings who also tried to write. Did they think
they could write as well as Browning? What nonsense,
then, to try to write at all. It was true, the Bostonians
were not Brownings; but if one has wrestled over the
question, What does the Dark Tower mean? one feels
one has a right to speak for Browning, and Boston, as
everyone knew, was divided into Browning "sections" as
other towns were divided into wards. It proved points
by quotations from Browning, as once it had proved them
by the Scriptures. Poems without Dark Towers could
scarcely be poems; and, unless they lent themselves to
explanations, they were hardly worth the attention of

* Daniel Gregory Mason's earlier books on music,—*From Grieg to
Brahms, Beethoven and His Forerunners* and *The Romantic Composers,*—
were written under the influence of Santayana.—See Mason's *Music in My
Time.*

cultivated ladies. Such was the "readeress's" view of the "babes of Apollo," unless one chose to call it the "scholastic blight." * One had to be a Donne to bear the test.†
And why try to be a poet when it was greater not to try, and so much more refined to live one's works? ‡ Boston, congested with learning, was hypercritical,§ hyperæsthetic, cramped, self-conscious, tortured with notions and problems. Its conscience was always tripping it up, invading spheres where it scarcely belonged, for the mind had lost

* "To what a pass has the ascendant New England readeress brought the harmless babes of Apollo! She seeks to master all that is, and to raise a complacent creation out of its lowland wisdom to her own mountainous folly's level; she touches nothing that she does not adorn—with a problem; she approves of music and pictures whose reasonableness is believed to be not apparent to the common herd; she sheds scholastic blight . . . We lay it all to the ladies; for the old lazy unprovincialized world of men was never so astute and excruciating . . . There were no convenings for the purpose of illuminating the text of Dr. John Donne, although the provocation was unique. Poets were let alone, once upon a time; and all they did for their own pleasure and sowed broadcast for the pleasure of others failed not, somehow, to fulfil itself from the beginning unto the end . . . The man's attitude, even yet, towards a book of poetry which is tough to him is to drop it, even as the gods would have him do; the woman's is to smother it in a sauce of spurious explanation, and gulp it down."—Louise Imogen Guiney, *Patrins.*

† John Donne, a favourite of the Concord authors, Emerson, Alcott and Thoreau, who referred to him often in their writings, became in the nineties in Boston a fashionable poet. Lowell corrected extensively, in regard to punctuation, his own copy of Donne's poems, which had never been properly edited. The Grolier Club of New York published this edition in 1895. See also Norton's collection, *The Love Poems of John Donne.*

‡ "Berri says there are lots of people like that in Boston,—painters and writers and musicians who are really very great, but think it more refined just to 'live' their works."—C. M. Flandrau, *The Diary of a Freshman.*

§ "A remark made to me, last night, by a young woman, apropos of some amateur music at Dr. Wadsworth's, to which we were listening, 'It really seems as if we might develop in Boston, some day, a glimmer of talent.' Your good Bostonian is nothing if not critical, still speaking 'as if he were the Pope,' to quote Longfellow's journal."—*Journal of Thomas Russell Sullivan,* 1898.

Howells, in *Mrs. Farrell,* spoke of "those critical spirits, rather commoner in Boston than elsewhere, who analyze and refine and re-refine and shrink from a final impression, with a perseverance that leaves one in doubt whether they have any opinion about the matter."

the power of deciding simply;* and Boston was full of a sad sterility, the fruit of emotional desiccation, that masked itself in assumptions and sometimes in sneers. Senator Lodge, whose "mastery of the sneer" † was identified with Boston in other regions, where people were unaware of the kindness of Boston, had many followers both then and later. Literary or otherwise, they indulged in a savage contempt for America, which, though they hardly felt it, included themselves.‡

Thus the vitality of Boston turned against Boston. Its Culture-Philistinism sowed the wind; the creators of its culture reaped the whirlwind. The Boston authors, fed on Dead Sea apples, were hungry for nourishing pastures, —they longed to escape. Not all, to be sure, shared this feeling. Numbers remained in the town, and some who were good. Robert Grant, for one, the admirable novelist, was soon to produce *Unleavened Bread,* in which "American womanhood," so generally flattered, was asked to regard the abuses that sprang from its power. Robert Grant's American scene foreshadowed Sinclair Lewis, and his earlier novel, *An Average Man,* and *The Undercurrent,* reaffirmed his remarkable gift as a student of manners. The finest of his books, *The Chippendales,* remained the classic picture of this age of Boston, with all its futilities and foibles and tempests in teapots

---

* " 'Well, well, well!' said Joshua, coming to the door-step, and washing his hands and arms just outside, in a tin basin. 'I thought I see you set down a parcel of oysters—but there was sea-weed over 'em, and I don' know's I could have said they was oysters; but then, if the square question had been put to me, "Mr. Carr, be them oysters or be they not?" I s'pose I should have said they was; still, if they'd asked me how I knew?' " etc.—H. W. Chaplin, *Five Hundred Dollars and Other Stories.*

For "oysters" substitute "Cinquecento Painters" or "Metaphysical Poets" or whatever, and one has the mental pattern of many a New England magnum opus, emerging from learned descendants of Joshua Carrs.

† Owen Wister, *Roosevelt, the Story of a Friendship.*

‡ "I had a classmate at college who had never been far from South Boston, and one evening while dancing at the Dorchester assembly he slipped and fell to the ground. He arose at once with great aplomb, remarking, coldly, 'These cursed American floors!' "—John Jay Chapman, *Memories and Milestones.*

and all that was excellent and solid beneath and behind them. Born and bred in this literary brier-patch, Robert Grant and others held their own; while writers of a local scope produced their deft little sketches and verses in the manner of Thomas Bailey Aldrich. They wrote about the summer people at Mount Desert and the North Shore; and tales of Harvard class-days and adventurous yachtsmen were interspersed with comedies of dinner-tables. They abounded in problem-novels about trouble-some children and lawyers who did not understand their wives. The wives in question were usually goddesses, and the children were often imps of perdition, which threw more light on the authors than it threw on the subjects, for most of the authors were women; and, as some of the children were also authors,—or were to be in twenty years,—one understood their wish to run away. Having ceased to attract outsiders, Boston was repelling its own; and the time was approaching when one might have said, What shore is not filled with its labours save Boston only? Anywhere, anywhere out of the world, the younger people said to themselves, anywhere, at least, out of Boston; and, while some fled bodily, others retreated into their minds, where they escaped to Greece or the Middle Ages. Robert Herrick went to Chicago, and there, in years to come,—as a novelist, a successor of Howells, bolder than Howells and somewhat bitter,—he viewed the Western scene from a New England standpoint. With much of the old Yankee moral fervour, he wrote in terms of pro-test and revolt. Edwin Arlington Robinson had gone to New York from Gardiner, Maine, though he lingered a while in Cambridge to try it out. Robinson, who had acted as President Eliot's secretary, had left Harvard early in his course there. He had returned to Gardiner, where he worked in his room all day till five, emerging with a fid-dle to amuse the children. A silent man, always writing, he spent a summer reading Hawthorne, whose shadowy personality his resembled; and he liked to mingle after dark with the outcasts on the water-front, who were soon to appear in his poems. He had published a little book at Gardiner, and New York eyes perceived his talent, which no one recognized in Boston; but he had reappeared in Cambridge, where he worked in a magazine-office while he was writing *Captain Craig.* He was soon convinced that New York was the place for him. All these writers were lonely, but those who remained were as lonely as candles in bottles.

George Cabot Lodge was extinguished in the bottle. He died, like Trumbull Stickney and Philip Henry Savage, in his early thirties, feeling he had lived in a void.* This son of Senator Lodge had studied in Berlin and Paris, where he met Trumbull Stickney, who, born in Switzerland and brought up largely in Europe, later returned to Harvard as instructor in Greek. Both felt that they were Greeks born out of time. Stickney, whom Henry Adams knew in Paris, and who studied six years at the Sorbonne, was the first Anglo-Saxon who was ever awarded a doctorate in literature there.† He wrote a Greek play, *Prometheus Pyrphoros,* and most of his work was distinguished, although it resounded, like Lodge's, with Victorian echoes. What, in the eighteen-nineties, could

---

* "The gap grew steadily wider . . . This consciousness of losing ground . . . the growing fear that, beyond this narrow range, no friends existed in the immense void of society . . . the suffocating sense of talking and singing in a vacuum that allowed no echo to return, grew more and more oppressive with each effort to overcome it."—Henry Adams, *The Life of George Cabot Lodge.*

† "Well I remember the day when he was examined by the French professors, led by Croiset, the Dean, in the Great Hall of the Sorbonne, under the scarlet picture of Richelieu. With what learning and subtlety he defended himself against their sleight of tongue! How they pricked and tore and tossed his thesis! With his beautiful grey eyes and sad, bewildered face he met them on his own ground and in their own tongue. How carelessly the Greek flowed from his lips, and with what unperturbed French he met all their objections for hour after hour. When the strife was over they were all polite congratulations . . . He was made a doctor of the Sorbonne *cum summa laude.*"—Shane Leslie, *American Wonderland.* Stickney died within a year after his return to America.

odes to Greek liberty mean except that one knew Walter
Savage Landor? Lodge's work was also rhetorical, and
his principal writings were long verse-plays, suggested
rather by Swinburne than by Shelley or Byron. For Swinburne charmed the latter-day New England mind. He
was "capable of passion," as Woodberry said; and his
freedom and extravagance, which had cast a spell over
Henry Adams, enchanted the souls of these other inhibited Yankees. Lodge's poems, *The Song of the Wave,
The Song of the Sword, Ode to the Earth,* were exuberant exercises in Swinburnian rhythms, and they expressed
the various moods of an ardent, adventurous, active young
man who knew the Western plains and the sea at Nahant. Lodge served in the Spanish War as an ensign in
the navy, and he longed to get into the tide of American
existence; but his plays were as remote from this as they
were from the plays of the Greeks, which had none of
their solemnity and abounded with life. In these accumulations of declamatory dialogue, the poet rebelled against
the world he lived in; but there was something autumnal
and sad in Lodge's note and Trumbull Stickney's, too little
native hue, too much pale thought. Lodge received from
Sturgis Bigelow a tincture of Buddhistic thinking, and
Schopenhauer, Lucretius and Leopardi left traces in the
minds of both these friends. The poet Savage was also
elegiac. All were alone against the world, and in all one
felt the weariness of lives "little in joy, little in pain." *

---

* "An important element in the tragedy of Oliver (not in his personality, for he was no poet) is drawn from the fate of a whole string of
Harvard poets in the 1880's and 1890's—Sanborn, Philip Savage, Hugh
McCulloch, Trumbull Stickney and Cabot Lodge . . . Now, all those friends
of mine, Stickney especially, of whom I was very fond, were visibly killed
by the lack of air to breathe. People individually were kind and appreci-
ative to them, as they were to me, but the system was deadly, and they
hadn't any alternative tradition (as I had) to fall back upon; and of
course, as I believe I said of Oliver in my letter, they hadn't the strength
of a great intellectual hero who can stand alone."—Letter of Santayana to
William Lyon Phelps, discussing *The Last Puritan.*—Phelps, *Autobiography
with Letters.*

No less lonely was George Edward Woodberry, who lived in exile in New York. He felt that he was an exile, both in time and in place, an exile from the old humane New England for which, like Barrett Wendell, he was born too late. He did not belong in this "mastodon age of gold;" and he saw his life "going down in the sands of the desert like a river born on the wrong side of the mountains." * A Beverly boy of the oldest descent, he had been a pupil of Henry Adams, and he was also a favourite of Norton's at Harvard. He had been regarded there as a natural successor of Lowell and by far the most promising of the younger poets. Woodberry had often lectured at Norton's Ashfield festivals and had written for *The Nation* under Godkin; and he had gone as a teacher to Nebraska before he settled in New York. He was professor of English at Columbia University, where he carried on a work that paralleled Wendell's. This was to convey to a rootless generation a feeling for the tradition of English letters, and, more than this, a feeling for the race-mind in general, as it had found expression in other great writers. Woodberry, whose critical sense was incomparably finer than Wendell's, was also a magnetic and powerful teacher. With a touch of the old Emersonian fire, he appealed to the poet in his pupils, inviting them to share his exaltation; and he made them feel that literature was a torch they were to carry on, the light of the developing mind of the race. His general papers were often vague,—they suggested a Transcendentalism too far from its source; but this was not true of the critical studies he devoted to Virgil, Cervantes, Montaigne, and to various English poets, Marlowe, Milton, Gray, Scott, Byron, Matthew Arnold. Some of these were masterly essays, overflowing with fresh ideas, the best that America offered, after Lowell's. The only essays that ranked with them were those of Lewis E. Gates, whose two small

* Woodberry's *Letters.*

volumes were drawn from lectures at Harvard. Gates, an
instructor in composition,* was a first-rate critical writer.
He died too soon to give the measure of his fine analytical talent.

In later years, Woodberry drifted back to Beverly and
wandered through the Mediterranean lands. A lost and
bewildered romantic, he was filled with a nostalgia for
worlds that he had missed, he knew not how. All that he
cared for he felt was "dying out of us,"—kindness, the
honour of literature, all were gone. The old ideals had
vanished; nothing was left but the din of traffic; he had
no part or lot in this modern nation.† The desert, he felt,
was the only fit place for him; and perhaps his travel-
papers, after all, were the best of Woodberry's writings.
His mood of self-pity resembled Henry Adams's, and,
like Adams's letters in similar scenes, *North Africa and
the Desert,* with its charming impressions, glowed with a
life of the senses too long denied. Woodberry's poetry,
good as it was,—and so much better than good in poems
like *Wild Eden,*—seemed rather a distillation of all the
other Victorian poets than anything individual or new. It
carried on the line of Lowell at one remove still further
from Lowell's masters, Tennyson, Milton and Keats; and
it suggested that Woodberry, who had lived in books so
ardently, had never lived at all in his age or his country.
His contemporaries scarcely existed for him. In his little
volume, *America in Literature,* he spoke of American
literature as dead and gone. It had passed its prime in
1860,—it lay "a generation, and more, behind us;" and,
as for the "period of dubious fame" in which the writer
himself had lived, he found few names even to mention
in it. Had he heard of Emily Dickinson? Had he heard

---

* Frank Norris wrote much of *McTeague* in Lewis Gates's classes.
Gates's two volumes were *Studies and Appreciations* and *Three Studies in
Literature.* Perhaps his finest essay was *Newman as a Prose-Writer.*

† *"I am not of it,* I am unhappy here, and the country has not the least
use for me, or my books, or for poetry at all."—Woodberry's *Letters.*

of Melville? He had small use for Whitman, and Mark Twain, Howells and James meant little to him. This literature had wholly "failed to establish an American tradition," and it had failed to produce a poet "even of the rank of Gray." *

With teachers like Woodberry, whose note was much the same as Wendell's, the writers who came to maturity twenty years later felt that they were men without a country.† They were the intellectual children of men who had ceased to believe in the country, who had no faith whatever in their place and their time. If this coming generation was rootless, there were certainly other reasons for it, but the nostalgia of its teachers was one of the reasons. Woodberry's mind, like Wendell's, harked back to other times and places in which their imagination felt at home; and especially, in their inmost hearts, they longed again for England, which had more and more resumed its sway over the Yankee mind. No books were more popular than Kate Douglas Wiggin's *Penelope's English Experiences* and *A Cathedral Courtship*. Tours of cathedral towns were more in vogue than ever; and Louise Imogen Guiney was only one of a number of pilgrims who tramped over England with a stick and a pack and an oak-leaf badge in their hats for King Charles the Second. Miss Guiney connected her father with the cavaliers of Stuart times, and felt she was a cavalier's daughter; and from this atavistic fancy, followed in all good faith, she drew the inspiration of her poems and her es-

* "It behooves us, especially, to be modest, for our magnificent America has never yet produced a poet even of the rank of Gray."—Woodberry, Essay on Gray.

† Wendell, in his best book, *English Composition,* invariably referred, in his illustrations, to English authors, never American. He chose De Quincey instead of Hawthorne, Carlyle instead of Emerson, Hazlitt instead of Thoreau, etc., although these American authors were equally classics. Woodberry followed consistently the same half-unconscious policy. It was natural that younger writers growing up under these teachers should have felt that they had no tradition, although Woodberry and Wendell talked tradition, in season and out.

says. She supported herself as postmistress at Auburn-dale, where her friends bought postage-stamps in enormous numbers to make her position more secure; and later she worked as a cataloguer in the Public Library, where Philip Henry Savage had a post. Dr. Holmes had been charmed by her poems and called her his "little golden guinea," although he was dismayed by the two huge Newfoundland dogs with which the pretty young poetess invaded his study. These poems had a fragile beauty that constantly verged on the false-archaic, and her mannered little essays were very self-conscious. She imitated cavalier poems and early Christian ballads, sometimes with mediæval spelling, for her gift was ventriloquistic and intensely bookish. But sometimes her poetic note was true, direct and fresh,* and the prose of her later essays was precise and distinguished.† *A Little English Gallery,* papers on Farquhar, Henry Vaughan, Hazlitt and two or three other less-known figures, abounded in curious learning. She lived in a dream of the seventeenth century, with other Bostonians of her time,‡ who often shared her interest in the Oxford Movement.§

In 1901, Miss Guiney went to live in England. The rest of her life she spent in Oxford, a friend of Lionel Johnson and Alice Meynell, with whom she had much in

* See *When on the Marge of Evening* and especially *A Talisman.*

† "My old friend Lionel Johnson once wrote to me: 'When I'm dead, the colon won't have a friend in the world but you.'"—*Letters of Louise Imogen Guiney.*

‡ Among other seventeenth-century poets, besides John Donne, to whom Bostonians paid special attention, were Robert Herrick and George Herbert, an old New England favourite. The Harvard philosopher, George Herbert Palmer, was named after the latter,—"so that I might always have a friend," as Palmer said in his autobiography. Palmer published an elaborate edition of *The English Works of George Herbert,* 3 vols., 1905. Robert Herrick was the favourite poet of Thomas Bailey Aldrich, who planned to write a life of him. Aldrich's best essay was a fragment of this otherwise unwritten biography.

See also Austin Warren's fine later study, *Richard Crashaw.*

§ One of Miss Guiney's many books was a life of Hurrell Froude. She also made an anthology of the Recusant Poets. This was published in 1939, nineteen years after her death.

common both in mind and in style. She had an American
bust of Keats set up in the Hampstead parish church, and
she paced the crowded Poets' Corner, measuring the flagging and the wall, hoping that Keats's ashes might be
moved there. She tried to arrange for the recutting of
Drayton's epitaph, and she rescued the grave of Henry
Vaughan. These pieties of the romantic American were
much like Delia Bacon's, while they expressed a wish to
make amends for all that religious New England had
represented. Meantime, various other New Englanders,
who were scarcely aware of America, were also writing
in England during these years. Howard Sturgis and Pearl
Craigie,—John Oliver Hobbes,—were hardly American
at all by experience or birth, and yet in certain traits of
mind they recalled their long New England inheritance,
and they were as detached in England as Whistler or
James. Whistler had made a virtue of his rootlessness.
He said, in his *Ten o'Clock,* in *The Gentle Art of Making Enemies,* "The master stands in no relation to the
moment at which he occurs." That the artist was not a
product of any place or any time was the doctrine that he
preached on all occasions, and this enabled him to turn
his sitters into "arrangements" and "harmonies," which
had no sort of connection with the world they lived in.
Swinburne observed that Phidias thought of other things
than "arrangements" in marble, even as Æschylus had
something in mind besides "arrangements" in metre.
But Whistler wished to justify an art that had no roots
in life. Meanwhile, he kept his Yankee twang; and
was not Whistler's butterfly,—the signature of all his
later works,—a reminiscence of Hawthorne and his
early New England? * Whistler was something more
than detached in London. He was antagonistic to the

* "The butterfly came and hovered about his head, and reinspired him,
as, indeed, this creature of the sunshine had always a mysterious mission
for the artist—reinspired him with the former purpose of his life."—Hawthorne, *The Artist of the Beautiful.*

English mind. All England was a bull for him into which he thrust his banderillas, the barbed little notes that sprang from the quills on his table. John Oliver Hobbes and Howard Sturgis, beside Whistler, were English of the English, but one found in their work an alien touch that almost as clearly suggested the world they came from. Howard Sturgis, Santayana's "quasi-cousin," a dilettante of genius, was born in England, the son of Russell Sturgis, the Boston China merchant who had become a partner of Baring Brothers; while Pearl Craigie, born in Boston, had been taken there to live as a child,— her father was an American manufacturer in London.* Sturgis, who wrote *Belchamber,* an admirable novel, might have been one of Henry James's heroes. He lived near Windsor, in a "nest of cushions, of wit, and of tenderness," † surrounded by dogs and a swarm of friends and relations; and Edith Wharton recalled him later lying on a sofa, with a basket of bright silks beside him.‡ For knitting and embroidering were his favourite amusements; he would work for hours at his embroidery-frame. As for *Belchamber,* the sensitive, lame young marquis, who rebelled against his class and its barbarism, suggested, in his vision of universal brotherhood, the Unitarian note of an earlier epoch; and there was a deep ascetic strain in John Oliver Hobbes that savoured of New England quite as strongly. This brilliant, beautiful, witty woman felt, in the world she satirized, that she was "an alien and a stranger," and the theme of her earlier novels was the theme of James. It was the plight of the artist in the

* John Morgan Richards, who, for a while, owned *The Academy,* one of the principal organs of the circle of *The Yellow Book,* with which his daughter was more or less connected.

† "My inimitable friend and quasi-cousin, Howard Sturgis, host and hostess in one, who held court in a soft nest of cushions, of wit, and of tenderness, surrounded by a menagerie of outcast dogs, a swarm of friends and relations, and all the luxuries of life."—Santayana, preface to *The Last Puritan.* It was in Sturgis's garden that Santayana professed to have met Mario Van de Weyer, the young man in this novel.

‡ Edith Wharton, *A Backward Glance.*

world of fashion; and while, with her "knack of uttering literature as though it were conversation," to quote her own phrase about Lord Locrine, she showed that she understood this world, she was "in the wrong paradise," she was not at home there. She felt like "an air-bird in the water."

CHAPTER XXII

COUNTRY PICTURES

WHILE so many minds were turning towards England, an English writer, Rudyard Kipling, turned his face the other way. Kipling, like Stevenson, had married an American and had come to live in Vermont, near Brattleboro. His wife was a sister of Wolcott Balestier, a friend of Henry James's who had gone to London, where this young American novelist died of typhoid fever, a victim of his love of the picturesque. He had clung to his mouldy old chambers until they killed him. Kipling had met Balestier on his triumphal return from India and had written with this friend a romance, *The Naulahka,* a sort of Marion Crawford novel after which he named the ship-shaped house he built when he came to Vermont. In this house, where he spent three years, he wrote the *Jungle Books* and *Many Inventions,* and he hauled the dirt and spread the phosphate over the farm where he dug the well and where he took Monadnock for his weather-prophet.

Meanwhile, he roved about the country, falling in with Henry Adams and forming a strange alliance with Norton in Cambridge. Norton, who hated imperialism and found few other things to please him, wrote with extraordinary praise of the young man's poems. He said that Kipling carried on "the royal line of English poets," —which may have had its grain of truth, indeed, but was yet a surprising statement, coming from Norton. That Kipling was a nephew of Burne-Jones by marriage may

well have been the reason for this singular outburst, for a
tendency had developed in Boston to find a writer interesting because he was somebody's grandson or nephew or
cousin.* Kipling made one or two visits to Gloucester at
the time of the celebrations of the men who were lost or
drowned in the codfishing fleet. With a doctor who had
served in the fleet, he wandered about the water-front,
dining in the sailors' eating-houses, boarding the schooners, examining the compasses and studying the charts old
and new. His head was full of the Grand Banks when he
also visited the old T-Wharf in Boston. Then he wrote
Captains Courageous in his house in Vermont, a prose
transliteration of Winslow Homer that was meant especially for boys. He had his own long thoughts about the
Vermonters. He was struck by the loneliness and the
desolation that other outsiders felt and the Yankees bewailed.† What might have been attributes and powers
were perverted there, it seemed to him, and strange faiths
and cruelties flourished like lichen on sick bark.‡

What Kipling thought about the natives other writers

---

* The witty Mrs. Bell explained the matter otherwise. "Someone ex-
pressed surprise at the admiration of Professor Norton and his family for
Rudyard Kipling's poems. 'Of course they like them,' said Mrs. Bell.
'They never heard a bad word in their lives.' "—*Mrs. Bell,* by Paulina C.
Drown.

There was, at this time, in Boston a distinct reversion to the "vulgar
Quarterly standard,"—as Lowell had described it, apropos of the critics of
Keats,—"measuring genius by genealogies." This was one of Barrett Wen-
dell's foibles.

† See the remark of the woman in the farmhouse on the next ridge. "Be
ye the new lights 'crost the valley yonder? Ye don't know what a comfort
they've been to me this winter. Ye aren't ever goin' to shroud 'em up—or
be ye?"—Kipling, *Something of Myself.* The Kiplings kept the lights
bright on that side.

‡ "The land was denuding itself of its accustomed inhabitants, and their
places had not yet been taken by the wreckage of Eastern Europe or the
wealthy city-folk who later bought 'pleasure-farms.' What might have become characters, powers and attributes perverted themselves in that desolation as cankered trees throw out branches akimbo, and strange faiths and
cruelties, born of solitude to the edge of insanity, flourished like lichen on
sick bark."—Kipling, *Something of Myself.*

Mary E. Wilkins's *Madelon,* the scene of which was laid in Vermont,
prefigured the well-known Kipling feud.

were also thinking, as many a story and poem had begun to show. For, whether in Vermont, in Maine or Massachusetts, this was the view that prevailed at the moment, and later. Few were able to see any longer what Sarah Orne Jewett saw at the ends of the grass-grown cart-tracks, choked by alders. The lights that glimmered in lonely windows suggested thoughts that were far from hers, although her idyllic scenes were sufficiently truthful. All that Miss Jewett saw was there, but how much that was sinister and dark she had failed to see! It was not the desiccation merely that struck the younger writers, but the skeletons in the cupboards, the sombre secrets. They could scarcely imagine a time when this world was alive.

That Vermont itself had been very much alive one saw in Rowland E. Robinson's stories and essays. This blind old man, who had grown up at Ferrisburgh, over by the shore of Lake Champlain, was writing a series of books in the eighties and nineties that recalled the earlier times for the natives themselves. Outsiders found it difficult to read these books,—they were written in the purest Vermontese. Robinson, who had gone to New York as an illustrator after the war, had returned to Vermont with failing eyesight; and, unable to draw any longer, he had taken to writing down his memories, while he supported himself by raising sheep. The best Sheffield shears had once been called the "True Vermonter," because of the fame of the wool that was grown in these hills. But most of the sheep had vanished now, and the cows outnumbered the people, and Robinson pictured the days before the cows came, the days when the pioneers had struggled up the rivers, with a flintlock, an axe and an ox-cart, and the valleys swarmed with bears, wolves and panthers. All this had happened within fifty years in Robinson's childhood; he had known survivors of the time; and he had followed the streams and tramped the pastures when the covered bridges and tanneries and grist-mills were new.

Blind as he was, he rambled over the country still, led by one of his children, and he knew the signs of the forest like an Indian hunter. His sensitiveness to sounds, the gift of the blind, had caused him to observe the varieties of speech he recorded all too faithfully in his dialect stories.* *Uncle Lisha's Shop* was the best of his books, with its scenes of the hearty life of the old Vermonters. The cordwainer, Uncle Lisha, was a kind of Yankee Uncle Remus, at home with the trout and the kingfisher, the muskrats and foxes, and his little shop was the social centre of a world that drew no social lines save that between eaters of white bread and eaters of buckwheat. There, on rainy days, in slack times, on winter evenings, the brotherhood of axe and gun assembled, Sam Lovel, the master of woodcraft, Peletiah, Solon Briggs, Joseph Hill and Antoine, the ingenious Canuck, who saw the axe-helves in the hickory, the baskets in the ash, the planks in the pine and hemlock, before he cut them, as Michael Angelo had seen the statue that lay in the uncut block. They stumbled over the frozen roads and fought their way through blizzards for a chance to sit on Uncle Lisha's sap-tubs; and, while the old man mended their boots, they swapped their yarns of the week's adventure, tales of sugar-making and bears in cornfields. The walls of Uncle Lisha's shop resounded with many a wondrous exploit of the rod and the gun.

This high-hearted older life had followed the frontier westward. Even Uncle Lisha had gone to Wisconsin; and the Yankees with the "real, old-fashioned, downright rustle and razzle-dazzle," with "git up and git," like Kipling's Tarvin, were building towns in Iowa and Colorado. The West attracted the men of Vermont even more than

---

* There are said to be seventeen dialects distinctly recorded in Robinson's books, those of the Indians, Canucks, Quakers, Yankee woodsmen, etc. All the kinds of American speech that were heard in the Green Mountains appear in *A Danvis Pioneer, Danvis Folks, Uncle Lisha's Shop, Uncle Lisha's Outing,* etc.

the other Yankees, and the young philosopher, John
Dewey, who was almost a neighbour of Robinson,—he
was born at Burlington, where he went to college,—had
first gone to Michigan as professor of philosophy before
he established his School of Education in Chicago. For
all the decay of the region, there was life enough in the
Yankee breed. John Dewey alone was enough to prove
it, Dewey whose passion for social democracy sprang
straight out of this rural Vermont. Twenty years later,
the hardy Dewey outrivalled all other Americans as a
leader of thought; and others who were children now,
scattered all over New England, were to show what reserves of energy the region possessed. Conrad Aiken, a
shoot of the oldest Yankee stock, brought to New Bedford from Savannah, lived as a boy in a house overlooking the harbour. He saw the last whaler setting out on its
last adventure, and the scenes of Herman Melville mingled in his eye with the nocturnal images of Albert Ryder.
Eugene O'Neill lived in New London. The son of an
Irish-American actor, he read Dumas from end to end
and swam every day in the Sound in the dead of winter.
He saw that his father's art had been ruined by the old
romantic drama, and he was turning away from the life
of the mask. What lay behind the mask? It was this that
concerned him, and some of this he saw as a schoolboy at
Stamford. He saw still more as a New London reporter.
On the coast of Maine, at Rockport and Rockland, Edna
St. Vincent Millay climbed the waves. She lived in a world
of anchors and shells and ships, and well she knew

> the green piles groaning
> Under the windy wooden piers,

the bell in the fog, the reach of the winter ocean. She had
in her bones the marrow of the Maine sea-farers. Longfellow had had this also, and, as he expressed it in songs
that recalled the Vikings, the scalds and the gleemen, so

she was to revive, in *The King's Henchmen,* the throbbing pulse and breath of Beowulf. Later, too, on this coast of Maine, overlooking the cedar-grown islands, beside the northern winter sea, Elinor Wylie found she was a poet; and T. S. Eliot's poems bore traces of the New England capes and harbours, the grey rocks, the woodthrush calling through the fog. At present, all over the region, with the ascendant summer resorts, colonies of artists were appearing. Howells, with whom the summer hotel was always a favourite *mise en scène,*—it brought so many types of Americans together,—pictured in *A Ragged Lady* and *The Landlord at Lion's Head* the gaieties and diversions of the summer people. Here one found the rustic philosophers who took the ladies for walks and talks, or, as they were called, "Tramps Home to Nature," the picnics that ended with readings from Browning, the chafing-dish parties, the coaching parades at which miracles were performed with cheesecloth and bunting. A young girl swathed in flowers represented the "Spirit of Summer," and the coaches, decked with goldenrod and asters, filed under the flag-draped arch that rose in the street. As for the colonies, Saint-Gaudens had established one at Cornish in 1885. The "Spirit of Summer" appeared in Saint-Gaudens's work, in forms that offended the taste of the sensitive Howells.* Abbott Thayer was

---

* Was not Howells right? Saint-Gaudens, in turn, disliked the realism of Howells.

"Your father was then slowly and desultorily completing the equestrian Sherman, and showed me with particular interest the figure of the Victory, which he said was studied from a young Southern girl. I owned that I did not like the introduction of the ideal in that group and the Shaw monument, but he defended it strongly, and, I have no doubt, effectually.

"Apropos of my realism, he told me a dream he had had about me. We were on shipboard together, and a dispute rose between the passengers as to the distance of a certain brilliant planet in the sky. Some said it was millions of miles away, but I held that it was very near, and he related that I went down to my stateroom and came up with a shotgun, which I fired at the star. It came fluttering down, and I said, 'There! You see!'"— Letter of Howells to Homer Saint-Gaudens, in *The Reminiscences of Augustus Saint-Gaudens.*

the centre of a colony at Dublin; * and at Stowe, in Vermont, Edward Martin Taber, who had studied painting with Thayer, lived and wrote. He sketched the plants on Mount Mansfield and he kept a journal that appeared as *Stowe Notes* after his death, a record of observations that revealed a grave and beautiful mind, with something of Hans Andersen's feeling for winter. Few poems of the nineties were touched with the natural magic of these unpretentious notes of the short-lived painter, scenes of winter nights, effects of landscape, of evening stars quivering over the snow, comments on the changing winds, on the light of the sunset gleaming through icicles or perhaps the glitter of moonlight on the head of an axe. At Shelburne, New Hampshire, in the Androscoggin valley, there was another colony, especially of writers. Paul Elmer More was writing there the first of his *Shelburne Essays;* and Vida D. Scudder and Florence Converse spent their summers in this village. Miss Scudder, born in India, a missionary's daughter,—she had grown up, like More, on the *Bhagavad-Gita,*—was one of the Boston mediævalists, well-known in her later years for her devoted study of the Franciscan writings.† Paul Elmer More had a

* The Winslow Homer of the New Hampshire mountains. Thayer, a naturalist in a world of naturalists, originated the study of protective coloration. (See *Concealing-Coloration in the Animal Kingdom,* a summary of Thayer's discoveries, by his son, Gerald H. Thayer.) The development of camouflage in the first world-war was largely a result of the theories of Thayer.

Near Dublin, at Chocorua, the summer home of the naturalist Frank Bolles and William James, lived Truman H. Bartlett, the sculptor-philosopher, who wrote the life of William Rimmer. For an admirable picture of Bartlett and his circle,—he was one of E. A. Robinson's triumphant failures,—see Daniel Gregory Mason's *Music in My Time.*

† Vida D. Scudder, a follower of Ruskin, Morris and Tolstoy, had studied at Oxford in the eighties. She was one of the first two American women to do so; and there she had formed her lifelong feeling that the Middle Ages, rather than the nineteenth century, were her "natural home." During the eighties and nineties, she shared in the ferment of thought in Boston, excited by Edward Bellamy and the settlement-houses, that seemed to revive the fading emotions of the era of Brook Farm and Abolition. As an active socialist, she sought for a *via media* between the Catholic Church

cabin by the road, with an inscription in Sanskrit over the doorway. More had appeared at Harvard in 1892, and there he had met Irving Babbitt, his brother-in-arms in a future crusade, who had returned to Cambridge after studying in Paris. The two formed together the whole of an advanced class that Professor Charles R. Lanman conducted in Sanskrit,* and they had begun to develop in common an attitude towards literature that grew from this early study of religion and ethics. New shoots of intellectual life were emerging all over the region, and at Derry, in these mountains, Robert Frost established himself on a farm at the end of the nineties. Frost, who was born in San Francisco, had returned as a boy to the land of his fathers, of which he was to become the unrivalled spokesman. He had made shoes and taught school, with intervals at Dartmouth and Harvard, and had written and even published a handful of poems. Two decades were to pass before the public heard of Frost, while he lived the obscure existence of an upland farmer.

Later, Frost affirmed and proved, as no one else for many years, the depth and the vigour of life that subsisted in New England. But he knew how much was morbid in it, and his early poems reflected a world of dearth,

and the teachings of Marx. Miss Scudder's Franciscan writings included two romances, *The Disciple of a Saint* and *Brother John,* and the fine historical study, *The Franciscan Adventure.*

Most of Florence Converse's early books had a Shelburne setting. Miss Converse's best work perhaps was the romance *Long Will,* about Langland and the vision of the Ploughman.

* Another of Lanman's pupils was Arthur W. Ryder, later professor of Sanskrit at the University of California. A Yankee sage and scholar, in some ways like Thoreau, Ryder maintained the traditional bond between the New England mind and the wisdom of the East. As indifferent to renown as Edward FitzGerald, he had much of the literary power of this English translator, and he was widely known for his admirable versions of the *Panchatantra,* the *Bhagavad-Gita,* the poems of Kalidasa, etc. His translations of the *Sakuntala* and *The Little Clay Cart* have been frequently produced on the stage.

Marion Crawford and T. S. Eliot were also pupils of Lanman, whose career as a teacher spanned three generations.

decay and desiccation. What Kipling glimpsed in this
Yankee life, Robert Frost knew all too well. Edwin Arlington Robinson also knew it; and there were summer
visitors, like Edith Wharton, and children who were to
write, like Eugene O'Neill, in whom this desiccation left
lasting impressions. They wondered about the black old
tenantless houses, where the windows lay in the grass and
the roof had tumbled in, the houses, damp and cold, with
people in them, where the rain had rotted the shingles,
the barns with wooden cages in dark corners, the double
houses of brothers who never spoke, the thresholds that
had never been crossed since someone's death. They wondered about the Yankees who had shut out humanity,
like all those sinister characters in Hawthorne's tales, in
whom the force of the past, repressed and turned inward, reeked with suspicion, hypocrisy, hatred and poison. What lay behind the shutters of the white Greek
temples, with the dark shadow-pines beside the door?
What secrets lurked in the graveyards, under the head-
stones, whose inscriptions, for the rest, were sometimes
true? The Yankee sun had shone over the world. It was
time for the moon to have its say, and these younger
writers saw what the moon saw. There were colonies of
savages near Lenox, queer, degenerate clans that lived
"on the mountain," the descendants of prosperous farmers.* There were old women poisoners in lonely houses.
There were Lizzie Bordens of the village, heroines in reverse who served the devil. There were Draculas in the
northern hills and witch-women who lived in sheds, lunatics in attics and men whose coffins hung with their bodies
from rafters, who had thought they could escape the
grass that waited, lapping round the walls, to catch them
when the old barn fell. The Yankee power had spread
over the world. It had launched a thousand clipper-ships;
it had despatched the Mormons to conquer Utah; it had

* See Charity Royall's people in Edith Wharton's *Summer*.

transformed the South Seas with its missions and planted schools all over heathen Asia. Now, having lost its outlet in the Yankee homeland, this power, at last inverted, devoured itself. There were Yankees like Heine's gods in exile, the gods who became diabolic when they could no longer be divine.

How terrible this power could be, turned backward on itself, few readers were aware in the eighteen-nineties. Others had to wait till Eugene O'Neill wrote *Mourning Becomes Electra.** But Mary E. Wilkins, if one read between her lines, revealed, if not its terribleness, at least its strength; and there was a certain truth in Louise Imogen Guiney's phrase,—she was "a sort of sordid Æschylus." There was something fierce and primitive in her view of life, and the Furies existed for her, and for her, in the laws of range sublime, there was a mighty god that grew not old. It was a pity that her later books obscured the stories of her prime. Tragic at first, they became pathetic and often sentimental,—because Miss Wilkins had a village mind. As long as she wrote in terms of the village, she possessed the village integrity and all the grand inheritance of the Puritan faith; and this gave her a profundity that made her point of view, at moments, all but universal. But when she attempted to write novels, for which she was not qualified, and when she dealt with other than village types, she lost her universality and, along with this, the integrity that sprang from her village birthright. She did not understand the types Miss Jewett understood so well, the more cultivated life of the "mansion-houses,"

---

* Edith Wharton's *Ethan Frome* and O'Neill's *Desire Under the Elms* were examples of this drama of the later New England and all that is "warped and twists and eats into itself and dies for a lifetime." The scene of *Mourning Becomes Electra* was laid at the close of the Civil War, but the author's mood was that of his own moment. This play will remain, no doubt, as the classic picture of a singular phase of New England.

Ethan Frome, good as it was, could not compare with the best of Miss Wilkins. Its plot was factitious, and it had the air of a superior person surveying the squalid affairs of these children of fate.

where the women wore "blue-lavender silk" instead of
the calico dresses she knew, or instead of the "one black
silk that stood alone." Her attitude towards all this was
that of the other village women, resentful yet roman-
tically dazzled;* and as, with success, she moved from
her early position and outgrew her resentment of the rich,
her romantic admiration of them took the upper hand
and she lost her hold on the verities for which she had
spoken. She became unreal and self-conscious in the presence of high life, regarding which she was driven to write
too much, and she cut her people to fit the story instead
of letting the story spring out of the people. But in some
of her early tales, perhaps twenty or thirty,† she was an
eminent artist, as eminent as Miss Jewett, and even more
so, because of the depth of feeling that informed her art.
In one sense, Miss Wilkins warranted all the laments of
Boston. She revealed the desolation of the Yankee ebb-
tide. But, better than anyone else, she also pictured the
powers of last resistance in the Yankee soul. Was the
Yankee soul at bay? At least, its lights were burning,—
this was the fact at the heart of Miss Wilkins's tales. It
was quick to fight for its self-respect, and even for perfection, whatever the odds might be and whatever its fate.

Although she had lived for a while in Vermont, Miss
Wilkins was born in a Boston suburb, the daughter of a

* This attitude of the village women was reflected in *The Jamesons,* one
of Miss Wilkins's longer stories. The Jamesons were city-people who settled in the village and tried to "improve" it. They were almost totally
absurd, but Miss Wilkins only partially saw this. She saw that they over-
did the "Browning readings," which were meant to enlarge the "sphere"
of the village mind, but she could not stand up stoutly for the village. She
shared its curiosity and resentment, and also all its dazzled admiration.

Mary E. Wilkins suggested Matilde Serao, as Henry James described
this Italian writer: "Madame Serao is at her best almost in direct proportion as her characters are poor. By poor I mean literally the reverse of
rich; for directly they *are* rich and begin, as the phrase is, to keep their
carriage, her taste totters and lapses, her style approximates to that of the
ladies who do the fashions and the letters from the watering-places in the
society papers."—Henry James, *Notes on Novelists.*

† Mostly in *A Humble Romance, A New England Nun* and *People of
Our Neighbourhood.*

carpenter in Randolph; and she had returned there in 1883, the year in which she published her first story.* Randolph at that time was not a suburb. It was a fading Yankee village, and this was the moribund village,—the symbol of hundreds of others,—that appeared in her stories. In its dilapidated houses dwelt a race that seemed to be dying, as shell-fish on a shoal that is seldom reached by the tide wither and perish at last when deprived of water. To begin with the shells, the houses, they were usually mortgaged. Sometimes they had never been painted and the shingles were falling off like scales, while the roof sagged, with its holes, in a mossy hollow. If they had been painted, only a few discoloured patches remained to prove a fact one seldom guessed. The doors and windows were often awry, and the doorsteps were sunk among the grasses, as if the houses were settling into their graves. The barns were generally deserted, and a few rusty tools and the phantom of a sulky alone suggested that they had ever been used. Most of the apple-trees were too aged and sapless to blossom freely. They had deteriorated along with the houses, and the apples were small, hard and sour. Within, the houses breathed an "icy wind of loneliness," a characteristic phrase of Miss Wilkins herself. The clock had often gone dead, and no one could make it tick any longer. The parlour and the kitchen were the only rooms that visitors saw; and the kitchen was the scene of all the life,—that is, the social life,—which the house admitted. The parlour was commonly used for funerals only, and it sometimes had no carpet on the floor.

---

* Miss Wilkins disclaimed the influence of other writers, though, like Miss Jewett, whom she had not read, she walked in her own way in the footsteps of Howells. She had read Turgenev, and, like others of the nineties,—Stephen Crane and Hamlin Garland,—she felt the need of a realism more drastic than Howells's. She said that she was afraid of reading. She feared that other writers might blur her mental pictures, showing how aware she was that her vein was thin. She knew that she might be overpowered; and as, from other causes, this actually happened, she was right for herself in regard to the cause in question.

There stood the shabby haircloth rocker and sofa, shabby
alike from age and excess of care; for the haircloth had
been house-cleaned through so many seasons that its holes
represented much besides its years. A clove-apple, a nautilus shell shared the shelf with bits of china. Perhaps
there were two or three pieces with lavender sprigs, each
one an heirloom of incalculable value, as precious as a
rajah's ruby to the members of the household. Framed
coffin-plates hung on the walls, together with funeral-
wreaths that had sometimes been woven from the hair of
five generations. A great-grandsire's hair had provided
the acorns, a grandmother's curls had yielded the leaves,
and the lilies had come from the tresses of an aunt, which
had turned a greenish yellow in her last illness. Uncle
Abijah's hair had produced the poppies; the rosebuds
were souvenirs of Lois. On the mahogany table lay Mrs.
Hemans and Mrs. Sigourney, bound in red and gold, and
perhaps a photograph-album with views of the Holy
Land or pictures of uncles and cousins who had died or
gone West. Death pervaded the air, and what remained
of life seemed to have reached a state of fossilization.

Such was the setting, and the people were in harmony
with it. They were mostly old, and mostly women; and
their object in living seemed to be to keep out of the poor-
house and get safely settled in their graves. If they
avowed an object, this was to pay off the mortgage, an
effort that almost always proved to be hopeless. They
were content if they kept one hen that laid one egg a day.
They were village-bound, and they were house-bound. Beyond the horizon of the village, they had no thoughts;
and whether they had thoughts below the village was a
question that strangers asked as seldom as whether or not
they possibly had thoughts above it. As for a social life,
they scarcely knew the phrase existed, although they still
had quilting bees and apple-paring bees and sometimes
did housewifely jobs for more opulent neighbours that led

to an interchange of words. When one of these opulent neighbours sent them some lamb-broth, they responded with a gift of peas or turnips; for there were mansions in the village, two or three big square houses where a ghost of the old prosperity still existed. More often, even there, one found only a lone old maid, who hoarded her burial-money in the musty chambers. Perhaps she had a mania for asking folks to tea, which meant that she asked them once a fortnight. For the rest, the village women wove rag-carpets and braided rugs, and they knocked at one another's doors to borrow a pitcher of milk or return an egg. If one of them went to Boston, she was more than likely to make her will; for how could she count upon surviving a ten-miles' journey on the railroad? The young people, such as there were, had Christmas sings and annual picnics, usually on the Fourth of July; and the brisker girls were often called "fast quilters." But, as if to settle the social question, the secretaries were squarely shut, unless one had to find a will or a deed. Only the kitchen door ever stood open.

The village life was plainly dying. There were very few young men, and the young girls were delicate, ailing and fading. They seemed to be always "going down," condemned to an early death from nerves or consumption. They were often left alone to look after the house. They supported themselves by making shoes or doing the village fancy-work, contriving tidies or lambrequins in red worsted and beads or colouring prints of crosses twined with flowers. They had been taught to sew their square of patchwork or seed and pick over the raisins before their supper, and to knit lace edging for the store and get a reputation for it was the best way to keep them in bacon and butter. Sometimes the young men who had gone West came back after twenty years; and their notion of a pleasant walk was to visit Mr. Sims's grave and see what sort of flowers had been placed upon it. They carried on their courtships in the graveyard,—that is, when they were able to speak their minds; but more often they were the victims of misunderstandings. Occasionally, two lovers sat side by side on a haircloth sofa every Sabbath evening for eighteen years and never reached the point of raising the question. Perhaps they were "too terrible set;" or possibly, after eighteen years, the question of marriage had ceased to have any importance. Often they gave it up for a nervous whim. But now and then a woman waited thirty years for the letter that was always coming and never came,—she stopped the postman every day at noon. Most of the women settled into spinsterhood, and they turned their minds to substitutes for love. They hid their best chemise in the lowest bureau-drawer, where the neighbours could find it and use it to bury them in; and they filled their jars and sugar-bowls with rose-leaves, or they collected cats, or they expressed their thirst for action by changing the position of the books on the table. They shifted the views of the Holy Land from the right-hand corner to the left-hand corner or reversed the china cups with the lavender sprigs. The bony figures of aging spinsters dominated the village scene, where one might have supposed that the end of the world was at hand. Stiff-necked and tough-minded, they seemed to be fighting a losing battle against fire, mortgages and illness and almost as much against life as they fought against death. Beyond them stood the almshouse. Beyond the almshouse stood the graveyard. An air of winter twilight enveloped all.

This seemed to be the whole story. Strangers thought so, readers thought so, albeit a handful of readers received from Miss Wilkins another impression, and of another order. In what way was her picture "sordid"? Sometimes these women were driven to steal; and this had an air of the sordid,—they certainly felt so. They stole a loaf of bread, or a few toys for the children's

Christmas, or a glass or two of milk from a cow in the pasture. They thought this was sordid; but was it not true that they alone had the right to think it? They measured themselves by the highest standard of honour; and, pinched as they were, they drank of the water of life, however the buckets were rusty and the dippers were small. Socially, their days were nil, from the point of view of the city-people, and they clung to the cliff of existence with the tips of their fingers. They were suspicious, and they were superstitious; they were hard, inquisitive and odd, and their actions were often mechanical, or appeared to be so. They tucked pieces of camphor under the wings of stuffed canaries; they spent the whole spring cleaning house, and sometimes they had the boards of the parlour floor arranged so that they could be lifted and cleaned on the under-side. Much of this was morbid, and a boarder needed the help of heaven to survive amid these terrible exactions. But what did these exactions mean? What lay behind these morbid activities? Was it not because the men were absent that the women minded their households to this degree? Besides, these habits spoke of a thirst for perfection that could not command its field of action, or, rather, could command no larger field. The temperament that cleaned the under-side of floor-boards would have cleaned the under-side of a government also, if it had had the government instead of the parlour; and in any larger sphere,—the running of a homestead,—these habits would have had their normal sweep. Indeed, in former days, they had had their sweep. The forbears of these desperate women, two or three generations earlier, had been prosperous farmers, statesmen and mothers of households; and they, in their unmanned sphere, without enterprise or politics, were living up to the sphere in which they had thriven. The situation, not the persons, produced the morbid symp-

toms; and the women who had for their supper one-half
of a cold boiled potato and a spoonful of jelly and saved
their one egg for the morning were contending for something far more important than thrift. As they could not
alter conditions, they lived within them; and, living within
the conditions, they mastered the conditions and kept a
margin for their souls to grow in. Well, then, what a triumph to pay off the mortgage, to become as free once
more as their forbears had been; or, if they could not do
this, to have a black silk dress or a bonnet with black-
thread lace and a tuft of jet. This was really living, and
they lived with zest. To keep up with the neighbours was
to keep up with their forbears, or, one might rather say,
to keep up with themselves; and, if they resented the rich
and were dazzled by them, this implied no loss of self-
respect. It was merely the tribute to *savoir-faire* which
those who do not know the world inevitably pay to those
who do,—at the moment, for the period, of their confrontation; for, in the unsophisticated, this frame of mind
rapidly passes when they return to their sphere and resume their standards. As long as their sphere maintains
its integrity, they are safe, remaining in it. Only when
they lose it do they lose their values; then, emulating
others, they are lost indeed. They have had no preparation for the world. This happened, in some degree, with
Miss Wilkins; and it happened to countless other villagers who became, not sentimental, as she, but vulgar. For
the rest, their aesthetic sense betrayed them. It hankered
after a beauty it had scarcely earned; whereas, on its own
ground, this sense was firm. On its own ground, it throve
on two willow-ware dishes as in few of the tourists who
gaped through the rooms of the Louvre. Whitman understood the lilac in the dooryard, and readers of Miss
Wilkins soon discovered that a rhododendron-bush was a
sacred symbol, or an oleander-tree, pink with blossoms,

the only spot of colour in a shabby old house; and those
for whom these aging women seemed to be creating nothing might have changed their minds if they had seen what
lay behind the bush or the oleander. What lay behind the
yellow stand with its heliotropes and geraniums? In pos-
sibility, what did it represent? Or the lombardy poplar
that signified "company"? Or the blinds that one had always wished for? Or the window facing the road that one
did not have? They were all symbols of life for people
who were filled with a passion for life that was very seldom shared by city-dwellers; for those who prefer to
starve rather than say they are hungry are living as
the well-fed seldom live. All these villagers lived with a
vengeance; and, however the weft of their tapestry was
worn and thin, its warp was as sinewy and as firm as ever.
This may have been the grimmest of all the well-known
Yankee jokes. Both whimsical and grim, it was also grand.

Thus, underneath Miss Wilkins's village something
lurked that was still sublime, although it was true that
the village guarded its secret. It exacted from fate every
last penny of tribute. Those who, like many Bostonians,
were already disheartened found evidence in Miss Wilkins's dun-coloured stories to suppose that Yankeeland
had come to an end. Perhaps it had, on the old basis; and
there was always the chance that it could not react any
longer to new conditions. It may have been pushed to the
wall and beyond the wall. But is it not a law of life that,
the more it is repressed, the more intense the will to live
becomes,—provided it is able to survive at all,—and that
if, at last, it finds an outlet, it expresses itself in proportion to its former repression? What fate was in store for
New England? Were the Barrett Wendells right? Was
its prospect really as dark as Miss Wilkins seemed to
show it? In so far as writers counted, the prospect was
reassuring; for writers emerging all over the region were
to suggest before long that the Yankee stock was hale

and as virile as ever. They were a proof that the real New England was not to be found in the Barrett Wendells or in what Miss Wilkins's stories appeared to show. They proved that the reality was what Miss Wilkins really showed, in her plain, stark, factual tales.

CHAPTER XXIII

THE ADAMSES

THE heyday of the Boston historians had come to an end with Parkman, but a number of other historical writers carried on the school that Bancroft, Sparks and Prescott had established. As a man of letters, only Henry Adams compared with the great triumvirate, Prescott, Motley and Parkman, although John Fiske's art of exposition almost amounted to genius. James Ford Rhodes and Edward Channing were distinctly inferior to these. What one missed in their work was the grand design of the older men, the shaping imagination and the narrative power. Godkin's remark was largely true,—"science killed the imagination;" for where Prescott, Motley and Parkman had recreated the past, these later historians could only describe and explain it.

There were few sparks of the artist in Channing. He scarcely wished to be thought a writer. That history was a form of literature seemed to him to mean that it could not be a form of science, and his work, with all its dignity, was bald and humdrum. For the rest, in scope and massiveness, his *History of the United States,** covered its field better than any other. James Ford Rhodes had come from Cleveland. There, in his early years, in the coal and iron business, he had been Mark Hanna's partner. He had retired to Boston with a fortune, after study-

---

* From the beginning to 1865, six volumes. Edward Channing was the son of Ellery Channing, the poet, the friend of Emerson and Thoreau in Concord. He was also a nephew of Margaret Fuller. He had been one of Henry Adams's pupils, and he had planned in college the work to which he devoted the rest of his life.

ing in Paris and Berlin, and he carried on there for twenty years the work that he had already begun in Ohio. His *History of the United States,* in seven large volumes, covered the years from 1850 through the post-bellum period of reconstruction. It was best in its account of the Civil War, for Rhodes was too much the plain man of business, immersed in current politics and finance, to discuss with imagination a country at peace. Nothing concerned him deeply but questions of tariffs and panics, and his psychology was crude, and his style was a dignified newspaperese. The decline of humanistic interests was notable in these later historians, marked as it was in the audiences for whom they wrote. Bancroft had written for statesmen and farmers, and Prescott, Motley and Parkman for lovers of letters. Channing wrote for his graduate students, whose interests were special and technical, Rhodes for men of business like himself.

Meanwhile, the Adams brothers, Brooks and Charles Francis, were following Henry Adams in history-writing. Charles Francis Adams had always felt that his real vocation was history, and he had retired, like Rhodes, from business, to work over his father's papers. He planned a diplomatic history of the Civil War, and, while this remained unwritten, he felt that any sort of historical writing was like coming "out of the darkness and into the light." He became a local chronicler of the utmost distinction, for, working on a small canvas, he revealed an instinctive taste and skill that were never achieved by the bolder Rhodes and Channing. He saw the men and events of Massachusetts as he saw French or English men and events, with the same realism and the same detachment, and his picture of the bigotry of early New England, which he compared with Spain, was a blow to conventional notions of ancestor-worship. He described as the Massachusetts "ice-age" the period from 1637 to the Boston renaissance of the eighteen-thirties; but, deplor-

ing its religious life, he showed how Massachusetts had
advanced the cause of civil liberty. The finest of all his
papers was the history of Quincy, which remained a model
in its field.* "Otherwise-minded," like all the Adams
brothers, he detested a civilization of business men; † and
he was an anti-imperialist, who did not believe in the
"white man's burden," for he felt that any self-government
of the people involved was better than any government
imposed from without. He regarded his education as a
series of errors, in this, as in other ways, resembling
Henry; ‡ but his historical writing was wholly concrete.
He was not interested in the "laws" of history, and he
contributed little to the well-known Adams philosophy
that kindled so much interest in the years to come.

This Adams philosophy, bleakly fatalistic, expressed
the dominant mood of the later New England. There the
vision of Lucretius appealed to many minds as the only
true one. They rejoiced in the vivid strokes with which
he described the approach of death, lassitude in pleasure,
the fatigue of the will and the final disposition of the
atoms of the soul, lost in the universal flux.§ The only

* *A Study of Church and Town Government,* in *Three Episodes of
Massachusetts History.* It seems safe to say that this is, by all odds, the
finest history of an American town that has ever been written.
  † "As I approach the end, I am more than a little puzzled to account for
the instances I have seen of business success—money getting. It comes from
a rather low instinct. Certainly, so far as my observation goes, it is rarely
met with in combination with the finer or more interesting traits of character. I have known, and known tolerably well, a good many 'successful' men
—'big' financially—men famous during the last half-century; and a less
interesting crowd I do not care to encounter. Not one that I have ever
known would I care to meet again, either in this world or the next; nor is
one of them associated in my mind with the idea of humour, thought or
refinement. A set of mere money-getters and traders, they were essentially unattractive and uninteresting."—*Autobiography of Charles Francis
Adams.*
  ‡ Charles Francis Adams quoted with approval Lowell's remark, "The
Adamses have a genius for saying even a gracious thing in an ungracious
way."
  § Lucretius was constantly quoted during these decades in Boston. Santayana's essay, in *Three Philosophical Poets,* was only the finest of many
utterances about him.

fact was force, irresistible, unchangeable, a conception that spread through the world as the century waned; and this doctrine had a special appeal in New England, where faith in the will and in progress had once been so strong. That the old aspirations were delusions was the teaching of William Graham Sumner, the great Yale sociologist who expressed the mood of the moment better than the novelists and poets. This hard-headed realist, the son of an English workingman, with a voice like a howitzer in action, attacked every cause that New England had stood for. He did not deny the doctrine of progress. He followed Herbert Spencer. He introduced Spencer at Yale, fighting for the right to teach him there as John Fiske had fought ten years before at Harvard. But he scouted all the New England conceptions of progress. He ridiculed "ethical views of wealth," reform, popular education, the "absurd attempt to make the world over." Sumner, for good or ill, was one of the minds that formed the future. He developed, in *Folkways,* the anthropological view of ethics. There were no ethical forces in history, he said, and good and evil had no reality except as expressions of the mores, the customs and habit-patterns of the time and the place. As the father of all the "debunkers," Sumner exposed myths and legends. What Ethan Allen said at Ticonderoga was something very different, as he conceived it, from what the wishful historians had always reported. But, while he attacked cant, he undermined, as no one else, the ancient humanitarian faith of the Yankees. He was a preacher of force in a world of fate.

Now, certainly this was very far from the point of view of William James, a more influential American thinker than Sumner, and William James also expressed New England, or a large and living section of New England feeling. James's conception of life was the reverse of Sumner's, and so was Josiah Royce's conception of life, which differed in so many ways from James's and yet as-

serted quite as much the power of the individual as opposed to fate. Both were deeply religious natures and
ardent humanitarians, and James had quarrelled with
Spencer's fatalism, which lay behind William Graham
Sumner's and which ignored the patent fact that progress
is not automatic but that subjective interests govern it
also. As a psychologist, he had explored the range of
these subjective interests. No one had ever explored them
so thoroughly before; and James had remained an optimist, a convinced free-willist who believed that the power
of the will could redeem the world. Through all the
changes of his time, William James had kept the buoyant
faith of Emerson and the old Brook Farmers; and he had
consistently preached the gospel of individual effort as a
means of achieving personal and social freedom. Detest-
ing every tyranny, the worship of power, the "bitch-
goddess Success," the omnipotence of science, he fought
them and believed in fighting them, believed that the
struggle availed,—fought for the Boers against the English, for the Filipinos against America, for the private
against the officer, for youth against age, and especially
for the new against the old. For he believed in the future
intensely, believed in the reign of peace and justice, believed that human effort could bring it about; and he
believed in the utmost of human variability. Was not the
least of God's creatures worthy of respect? And who was
to judge the value of another creature? Might not the
last prove to be the first? He sought to evoke the potential energies that people possessed without knowing it,
showing that these energies would grow with use; and he
attacked the bosom-vices of modern civilization, swindling, adroitness and cant, and sang the praises of poverty, loyalty and honour. In all this, James was governed
by a passionate faith in human nature and its power to
mould, control and create the world.

James exerted over the country a more effective influence than any of these other New England thinkers. With his wealth of imaginative sympathy, his sinewy mind, his tolerance, spontaneity and magnetism, he threw into circulation more general ideas than any American thinker since Emerson, perhaps. His notion of the stream of consciousness fed the minds of novelists. His "moral equivalent of war" was a memorable counsel. His antithesis of the tough-minded and the tender-minded was one of the fertile suggestions in which he abounded. In his Protean imagination,* his feeling for concrete realities, for all varieties of experience, James was an artist; and he was a "high-hearted freeman," †—one of his phrases,—who imputed to others the power that he found in himself. Moreover, James, who was more humane than any of the Adamses, was quite as realistic as they or Sumner. But, while he expressed the mood of the nation, they expressed the regional mood, or what seemed to be this mood at the end of an epoch.

That man could not control his world was the Adamses' doctrine as well as Sumner's, although Sumner believed that fate worked out for the good. For Brooks Adams, Henry's younger brother, the "law of force and energy" was the only law, and it foreboded no good in a visible future. He had conceived a theory of history, partly drawn from Marx, that in many ways anticipated Spengler, for he saw civilization as proceeding in cycles, propelled by fear and greed, in which the individual counted

---

* "Can we realize for an instant what a cross-section of all existence at a definite point of time would be? While I talk and the flies buzz, a seagull catches a fish at the mouth of the Amazon, a tree falls in the Adirondack wilderness, a man sneezes in Germany, a horse dies in Tartary and twins are born in France."—James, *The Principles of Psychology.*

† Sigmund Freud recalled a moment when he and James were walking together, during Freud's visit to America in 1909,—James "stopped suddenly, handed me a bag he was carrying and asked me to walk on, saying that he would catch me up as soon as he got through an attack of angina pectoris which was just coming on. He died of that disease a year later, and I have always wished that I might be as fearless as he was in the face of approaching death."

for nothing. Fear gave birth to superstition, and this to religion, in turn, and religion produced an accelerated social movement that led to a civilization governed by greed. The instinct of greed supplanted the instinct of fear and gradually dissipated in war and trade the energy that religion had developed. Such were the oscillations between barbarism and civilization, in which the greatest men, like the floods and the whirlwinds, were merely natural forces. No use to regret the past or oppose these mighty revolutions, which were inevitable and automatic. Nations must float with the tide, and men must float with them. Society could never reach a permanent equilibrium, and only change was constant. But, regarding as futile all opposition to natural forces, Brooks Adams claimed the right to express his taste; and he could not forgive an age in which pig-iron was more important than poetry. The times that bred religion bred also the imaginative mind, and the artist and craftsman arose with the warrior and the priest. These were Brooks Adams's chosen ages, and the age of the French cathedrals led all the rest. For Brooks Adams shared his brother's interest in architecture and saw it as the highest expression of religious faith. As the bankers won the day over warrior, priest, craftsman and mystic, the emotional life and civilization withered; and Brooks Adams saw his world at the dying end of one of these cycles in *The Law of Civilization and Decay*.

This book was published in 1895, long before Henry Adams's *Education;* and Brooks had anticipated Henry in applying to history the laws of physics, of acceleration, retardation and mass. Henry adopted the second law of thermo-dynamics as explaining the world in which he lived, the law of the degradation of energy,—the universe was running down, it was losing its vital energy and was headed for death. Was it a universe? It seemed to

him a multiverse, a random manifestation of aimless
forces, of which man was as much the sport as the trees
and the rocks. He had discussed these theories with his
brother, who was living at the old house in Quincy during
his Washington years; and his mind had turned, like
Brooks's, to the age of the French cathedrals as one in
which he might have felt at home. For then, whatever the
universe was, man felt it was a universe, and he held the
highest idea of himself as an active participant in it.

What struck the reader in all this, when Adams printed
his *Education*, was rather his wish to believe it than the
theory itself. Could one apply to history the laws of physics? These laws, in the first place, were constantly changing, and the theory of relativity invalidated soon the laws
that Henry Adams accepted as final. All attempts to cor-
relate history with science were exploded as time went on,
as historians perceived that history, as it actually was, is
not and cannot be known.* Adams's conception, then, was
a vast and intricate rationalization. It was what he wished
to be true; and he evidently wished it in order to find an
excuse for the chaos and futility of his own existence. If
the world was chaotic and futile, it relieved him of all responsibility for the scattering of his own energies, his
defeated ambition, for the unresolved conflict between his
tastes and his inheritance, for the anarchy of the forces
that dwelt within him. Adams's soul was the "multiverse."
He was the chaos.†

For twenty years, Henry Adams, globe-trotting or sitting at home, had been gleefully watching the world going

* For the various reasons why history cannot be correlated with science,
see Charles A. Beard, *The Discussion of Human Affairs,* pp. 85-86.

† Admirably as he wrote on most occasions, there was no unity even in
Adams's style. Except for certain recurrent conceptions and phrases, the
history, the novels, the memoirs of the Queen of Tahiti, the *Education* and
Mont-Saint-Michel and Chartres might all have been written by different
hands.

to the devil.* Dead himself, as he liked to say, "stone
coffin dead," landed, lost and forgotten, he lived alone in
his Washington house, a "long-established ghost." One
saw him on horseback, riding alone in Rock Creek Park,
with his air of an emperor in exile, or out for his daily
walk with Hay. At home he played solitaire, studied physics and read Byzantine books, gloating over the fall of
the Roman Empire. He never dined out any longer, but
ambassadors and statesmen thronged his house; and he
saw himself as an old courtier, "sitting among the mighty,
and sneering at them to their faces." † He had once
thought of himself as a sort of American Horace Walpole, recording the manners of his time, and many of his
letters, when they were published in after years, justified this one of his many ambitions. They abounded in
sketches and flashes of the rarest insight. But this was
not enough to satisfy him. He had "too much ego in his
cosmos," like Kipling's Bimi. He winced when he saw
himself mentioned as "the late Henry Adams," although
for a dozen years he had covered his tracks. He was bitter when the cab-drivers pointed out his house as the residence of the late Charles Francis Adams. "He lives well
that has lain well hidden," Abraham Cowley said; but
this was not what Adams had really desired. The sense
of his obscurity rankled in him, and he was still consumed
with the "insanity of restlessness" that had filled him
ever since the death of his wife. Wherever his friends

---

* "One revelled at will in the ruin of every society in the past, and rejoiced in proving the prospective overthrow of every society that seemed
possible in the future."—*The Education of Henry Adams.*
"To me the crumbling of worlds is always fun."—Letter of 1914.

† "I am sitting here in Washington just as you left me ten years ago. I
have grown so used to playing the spider, and squatting in silence in the
middle of this Washington web, and I have seen so many flies and other
insects caught and devoured in its meshes, that I have now a little the
sense of being a sort of ugly, bloated, purplish-blue and highly venomous
hairy tarantula which catches and devours Presidents, senators, diplomats,
congressmen and cabinet-officers, and knows the flavour of every generation and every country in the civilized world."—Letter of 1899.

beckoned, there he went, to Egypt with the Hays, to Constantinople and Greece with the ambassador Rockhill, with the Lodges to Caen and Coutances. It was in Paris that he fell in with Trumbull Stickney, with whom he discussed Greek philosophy, and saw most of George Cabot Lodge, whose life he wrote when this young poet died; and it was during these years that he rediscovered the twelfth century and made the preliminary studies for the finest of his books. Saint-Gaudens took him to Amiens, and La Farge to Chartres, where again they discussed stained glass together; and Adams spent whole summers in Champagne and Touraine, visiting parish churches, "collecting spires," wandering through the streets of Troyes with Joinville, till he felt he was a "twelfth-centurian." He had begun to realize a prophecy of his earlier years, that art was to give him his greatest advantage and pleasure.* His contempt for the present grew with his love for the past. He wandered from desert to desert and from Ritz to Ritz, "playing with the toys of childhood, Ming porcelain, salons, operas, theatres, beaux-arts;" and everywhere, "dead," but "gay as a rabbit," examining the great hall of Karnak, and the domes of Justinian and Constantine, he saw the jackal creeping down the ruin. England was "cardiacally diseased," Spain was "extinct," Austria was "splayed," France was "rotten." Each year, his "beloved old senile wreck of Europe" was more decrepit than ever.† It was at its last gasp; and, as for his own country, nothing in it seemed to him worth preserving. The illusions of young men occasionally touched him, and perhaps a remnant of faith still

---

* "After all, I shall get most pleasure and (I believe) advantage from what never entered into my calculations, Art."—Letter of 1858.

† "The more I live here in western Europe, the more I am impressed with the sense of decay,—not the graceful and dignified decay of an Oriental, but the vulgar and sordid decay of a bankrupt cotton-mill."—Letter of 1898.

glimmered in his breast.* But, on the whole, for him, it was over and done with, and he was for forcing the pace and speeding the ruin.†

Now, certainly, in the pre-war years, much in Adams's view of the world was penetrating, truthful and prophetic. He felt the nightmare of those years. He sensed the impending calamity. He perceived that the old order was collapsing. He saw that Russia was "sailing straight into another French Revolution;" and he foresaw the collectivized world of the future. Although he did not like it, he knew that a socialist order was bound to follow the downfall of the one he had known; and, while he abused all the statesmen who were trying to bring it about, he even recommended a socialist system as the only one that could work in the given conditions.‡ He felt that even

* When Owen Wister called upon him in 1912, Adams said, "What do you think of the state of things in this country?"

"I shook my head," wrote Wister, "and said nothing.

" 'Our old friend over there,' continued Henry Adams, with a wave towards the White House, where we had spent such unforgettable hours in the days of the Roosevelts, 'did his best. But whose best could save us?'

" 'Oh, well. I don't feel as black as all that about it.

" 'You don't? With that saturnalia going on up there?' And he waved in the direction of the Capitol.

"Again I shook my head.

"He continued to look at me with his most gimlet-like expression. Then, suddenly, his countenance softened. His eyes grew warm, he got out of his chair, came over and laid his hand on my arm, and in a voice quite changed said, 'Keep the faith!' "
—Owen Wister, *Roosevelt, the Story of a Friendship.*

† "Hating vindictively, as I do, our whole fabric and conception of society . . . I shall be glad to see the whole thing utterly destroyed and wiped away . . . My view of the case is always to encourage the big thieves and to force the pace. Let's get there quick! I'm for Morgan, McKinley and the Trusts! They will bring us to ruin quicker than we could do it ourselves."—Letters of 1893 and 1895.

‡ "The world is abjectly helpless. It is running a race to nowhere, only to beggar its neighbours. It must either abolish its nationalities, concentrate its governments and confiscate its monopolies for social economies, or it must . . . founder, at last, economically; while it will founder socially if it does not concentrate and economize."—Letter of 1898.

"All the same, I revert to my political platform of last year. The only possible political party must stand on a well-defined platform of State Socialism. Nothing else can reflect the social movement."—Letter of 1899.

"Society is ready for collectivism; it has no fight left in it; and our class is as defunct as the dodo."—Letter of 1910.

with communism he could exist.* His political divinations
were long to be quoted; and there was a certain grandeur
in Adams's tone as he dwelt on the collapse of the world
he lived in. He perceived it, he rejoiced in it, he feared
it. With his "nose in the champagne brut," cursing his
dyspepsia, he resembled other old men who sat in club-
windows, and there were times when it seemed that his
agony over the fall of the world was merely due to fear
for his investments. He imputed this motive to Brooks
Adams,† and he undoubtedly shared it.‡ But Henry
Adams's feeling was also spacious. There was a deep vein
of poetry in his sense of the ruins of empires. As a historian, he had looked down from the tops of the pyramids over Alexander, Caesar, Napoleon and Lord Cro-
mer, seeing them foreshortened to the same plane, of the
same apparent scale and proportions; and, as a geologist,
he had felt the mutations of history and the insignificance
of the personal atom, lost in the awful vastness of time
and space. On mounds in deserts of the East, he had pondered on dead cities, generations gone and crumbling
kingdoms, and all this mingled in his mind with his feeling of the present and gave it a sombre magnificence. His
style abounded in grand figures, and his geological similes
sometimes imparted to it a majestic sweep. But why did
he rejoice in the downfall of worlds? And why did he entirely fail to see the signs of a new life all about him?
For, truly, he saw nothing, and he wished to see nothing;
and he uttered at the Paris exposition his ironical prayer

* "With a communism I could exist tolerable well, for the commune is
rather favourable to social consideration apart from wealth."—Letter of
1893.
† "*He* considers the world to be going to the devil with the greatest
rapidity quite apart from war; and I endeavour, as you know, to console
him by the assurance that it went there at least ten years ago . . . I am
sorry to say I really think his agony of mind [is] chiefly due to the approaching destruction of all values in the stock-market."—Letter of 1917.
‡ "The imminent peril of the finances of the world weighs on my mind
more than anything else."—Letter of 1904. He described himself during the
"money panic" of 1893 as "the scaredest man this side of the Milky Way."

to the dynamo because he found nothing else in his time to respect.* When the Irish republic was rising, he saw "energy" only in Ulster.† When France was purging itself in the Dreyfus case, he could see only "treason" in Zola.‡ And, as for literature, music, thought and art, he was certain they had vanished from the planet. Literature was "nil." There were "no new books," even in Paris. There were "no books, no pictures." History was "dead." There was "no thought," except in mathematics. There were "no plays,"—Shaw was a "howling" socialist orator,—although he had heard that the Russian ballet was good. There was "no music." There were "no beautiful women or witty men." § There was "hardly anyone living . . . worth writing for;" and, while the young men at the British embassy assured him that "never in history was so much beautiful work being done," he agreed with friends, readily found, for whom literature, art and poetry were as dead as Achilles. No doubt, these were difficult years for old men with settled tastes, and Adams's age in America was a relatively dull one; ‖ although, save for his little circle of friends, Adams had missed in his age the

* "Every afternoon, I went to the Exposition, and prayed to the dynamos. There was nothing else to respect."—Letter from Paris, 1900.

† "The most encouraging sign is Ulster. Those people still retain energy. It cannot last another generation, but it is a measure for us."—Letter of 1914.

‡ On the imprisonment of Zola: "If he did not deserve it for the special offence, he did for his novels; and on the whole I think he had better have joined his friend Dreyfus on the Devil's Island some time ago."—Letter of 1898.

§ "I hear of no books that need writing, or at least reading; no plays that need to be seen, no music that should be heard; no pictures that should be bought. I hear of no beautiful women or witty men . . . Paris is as flat as a flat-iron."—Letter of 1913.

His letters are peppered with similar phrases.

‖ "Nothing tries my lovely nature so much as the startling rapidity with which every form of thought or intellect has vanished in America. Neither science, art nor literature produces anything any longer. Since 1870 we have lived on our previous product, and there is little left. I cannot be mistaken."—Letter of 1896.

finest writers and artists that America produced. Had he heard of Emily Dickinson or Stephen Crane, Winslow Homer or Ryder? He never referred to them in his books or his letters. Had he bothered to read even James or Howells, except for a novel or two? He mentioned them only once or twice.* Convinced that he "knew everybody," that he was "wiser than anyone else," however ironically he said it,† he shrank from meeting even the lights of the Sorbonne, the great authorities on the Middle Ages, whose conversation might have unsettled his mind.‡ *Omne ignotum pro magnifico;* and he was without a rival companioned by nieces, by ladies with whom he went shopping and adoring young men. He closed his sympathies to every sign of life in the world because, if the world was alive, then he was wrong. If there were other men fulfilling their careers, he might have been to blame for missing his. But, no; and, if he was a failure, so must the world be. If Henry Adams was dead, the world must die.

Naturally, therefore, Adams could see in the world no hidden forces to appeal to, the sense of which buoyed his

* "Since the Civil War, I think we have produced not one figure that will be remembered a life-time . . . What is more curious, I think the figures have not existed. The men have not been born.

"If they had existed, I should have attached myself to them, for I needed them bad. As life has turned out, I am dying alone, without a twig to fall from. I might as well be a solitary woodchuck on our old Quincy hills as winter comes on."—Letter of 1911.

† "Between us we know everybody, and those we don't know, know us."—Letter of 1869.

"As you know our role in life has always been to be wiser than anyone else and the consciousness of that is the only reward we are likely to get from it."—Letter of 1917.

‡ "During all those summers spent in Paris, he never made friends or even bowing acquaintance with any of the lights of the Sorbonne or the Collège de France. He might have known Gaston Paris, Gebhart, Langlois . . . all great experts on the Middle Ages. He read all their books but would not meet them, preferring the society of his own little group, consisting almost entirely of Americans."—Mrs. Winthrop Chanler, *Roman Spring.*

friend La Farge.* He had felt the existence of these
forces until he was middle-aged, as long as he had faith
in his will and himself; but when he began to drift the
light went out. For what is our consciousness of the forces
in others, if it is not a sense of the forces in us? When
Mont-Saint-Michel and Chartres was published, Adams
was astonished to find himself a "leader of a popular
movement;" † and how much more surprised he would
have been if he had foreseen the success of the *Education.*
He had taken it for granted that no one could understand
these books, whereas they were just the books that the
moment called for. A younger generation had risen who
shared his despair of the present, and thousands who, like
him, had lost their faith were turning, as he turned, to
the Middle Ages. The hidden forces existed in society,
although he had failed to perceive them. The hidden
forces had even persisted in Adams!—who had simulated
death, and had really died in some respects, but who had
also remained "as gay as a rabbit." His sympathies had
died, but not his senses. He had lived and grown aesthetically with a vengeance; and he who had "yearned for
nothing so keenly," even in his earlier days, "as to feel at
home in a thirteenth-century abbey," had found in his
imagination a refuge and a drug for all the chagrins of
his existence. "Running madly through the centuries," he
had brought up at an age that he had known from the beginning and that had come to seem to him a symbol of the
believing community in which he might have lived to some
effect. Chartres was all that Washington ought to have

* "La Farge . . . seemed held up by an intuitive conviction that society
had hidden qualities which he could appeal to. He had the instinct of a
primitive cave-dweller, who painted hairy elephants on a cave's stone roof.
The God knew how good they were! I always broke down at the door.
After middle-age,—say fifty years of age,—I was satisfied that our society
contained no hidden qualities that artists could appeal to,—that it is really
what it appears on the surface."—Letter of 1911.

† "I, vastly to my surprise, find myself a leader of a popular movement,
with my Chartres as Evangel, and Ralph Adams Cram for St. John Baptist."—Letter of 1912.

been! His old studies of Viollet-le-Duc, his studies of mediæval law were the basis upon which La Farge had wrought;* and he had "hunted windows like hares," he had lived at Chartres, Bourges and Le Mans,—from Quimper to Troyes and Vézelay he had ravaged France. He had lived with the pointed arch, the illuminated missal, the chanson and roman and pastorelle, and had groped his way into the presence of St. Thomas Aquinas, of Abélard and Francis of Assisi, Aucassin, Blanche of Castile and the Queen of Heaven. He had found forgotten treasures of French musicians, love-songs, spinning-songs, songs of crusaders, and had had them all transcribed into modern notation, so that his young nieces might sing them to him; and the age of the Crusades, the monks and abbots, the Courts of Love, the queens of France, the pilgrims had become more real to him than the age he lived in. For days, in the afternoon light, he had sat in Chartres cathedral, reading the open volumes of colour in the windows, till he could all but overhear the talk of the architects and priests who had built this shrine for the Virgin; and there, while the voices of the children chanted in the choir, while the music drowned his ears and his eyes were flooded,—one sense reacting on another until sensation reached the limit of its range,—he could feel a sense beyond the human ready to reveal a sense divine that would make the world once more intelligible. He almost felt the presence of the Virgin, in the depths of feeling that she showed here, in lines, vaults, chapels, colours, chants and legends; and he shared the life he had missed but might have had. He would have known what to do in an age of faith and youthful ardour, light-heartedness, candour, gaiety, simplicity, action.

Adams, as a writer, had verified another prediction,

* "The text of a charter of Edward the Confessor was uncommonly remote from a twelfth-century window. To clamber across the gap has needed many years of La Farge's closest instruction to me, on the use of eyes, not to say feet."—Letter of 1901.

made in his youth to his brother,—that he was going to
"plunge under the stream" and "remain under water"
and come up at last "with an oyster and a pearl." If the
Education was the oyster, *Chartres* was the pearl. After
so many deaths, Adams had triumphed. He had worked
himself into the Middle Ages, grasping so many aspects
of them that *Chartres* was destined to live as a history
and a classic; and in the *Education* he had pictured his
time with a force and a power of suggestion that were
surely unique. Were his representations objectively true?
Was the age of Chartres the "unity" that he wished to
think it? Was his own age as hopeless as he thought?
Would not Henry Adams have been Henry Adams in the
days of Abélard as in the days of Grant? However one
answered these questions, his Chartres was a symbol. It
stood for all the believing communities,—New England
had been one,—in which alone the human spirit thrives;
and it said that men must have an object, men must have
the common faith which the socialized mind of the young
was already embracing. And was not Adams's Dynamo
also a symbol, in a world in which blind power was running wild? The *Education,* with its acrid flavour, struck,
during the war-years, the note of the moment. It appealed to the younger generation, who felt themselves
adrift, and who were in revolt against their past, against
puritanism and its restrictions, the sexlessness of American art, the power-house, the teacher, mechanics and
business. Adams, for many, seemed an older brother, who
had shared their disillusionments long before them; and,
more permanently, the *Education* revealed a phase of
American history with an unparalleled boldness and measure of truth. This was Adams's greatest achievement, this
and the golden glow of *Chartres;* and they assured for
the bored old man, with his cold, old heart, the length of
days he had only desired for Nirvana.

CHAPTER XXIV

THE PRE-WAR YEARS

WITH Henry Adams, the New England mind seemed to have come full circle. It had passed through its springtime, its summer and Indian summer, and Edwin Arlington Robinson was not the only Yankee who saw

> A dreary, cold, unwholesome day,
>   Racked overhead,
> As if the world were turning the wrong way,
>   And the sun dead.

Had Charles Francis Adams's "ice-age" reappeared in this vigorous region, which had produced such abundant fruits of the spirit? The fatalism of Henry Adams was surely ten times darker than Calvin's fatalism had ever been. Was the tale of the Adamses symbolic? One thought of old John Adams, under his apple-tree at Quincy, rejoicing in the prospects of his "Christian Sparta;" and one thought of his great-grandson invoking Nirvana under the sickly shoot of Buddha's bo-tree. How much had waxed and waned in these four generations! Brooks Adams had only to look homeward to find an illustration that seemed to prove the truth of his theory of cycles.

Edwin Arlington Robinson personified winter. Abandoning New England, he had carried to New York an aura of blight, desolation, decay and defeat. His view of the world was wintry,—so was his life,—and his style and his personality were bleak and bare. Had there ever been a poet who loved life less or found so little joy in the turning of the seasons? In the down-east phrase, Robinson was "master chilly." There was something starved and cold about him, as if his clothes were too scanty and his blood were too thin, as if the Maine wind had invaded his marrow. He was like the stranger in his *Tasker Norcross* who confessed that he had "never yet been warm." Taciturn, shy as an owl, diffident, lonely, he could only establish relations with others by drinking; yet everyone confided in him, for he was the most sympathetic of men, as winning as he was aloof, and completely unworldly. Helpless in practical matters, naturally forlorn, he had the will to write but not to live; and he suffered himself to be rescued again and again and reverted again and again to a life in the shadow. Abjuring the "octopus of superficial self-respect," he haunted mean streets and sordid houses, for the only success that he recognized was failure in the eyes of men, and he saw even this as distorted and thwarted. He had become vaguely known as the "poet in the subway," in days when few were aware that he wrote or existed; for he had a post, in New York, in the newly-built underground railway, checking the loads of material that were dumped at the mouths. There, all day, in his long black coat and broad-brimmed hat, he paced the damp, dark tunnel, with its odour of gases. If he saw a light at the end of the tunnel, it was usually choked with mephitic mist: it was not so much a light as a murky glimmer. And this was like the light in Robinson's poems. He seemed to share at moments the old Emersonian faith, which he variously called the "gleam" and the "vision." But, in him, this faith was only a dim conjecture. More often he looked out upon "dark tideless floods of nothingness," where men escaped from their dungeons only to drown.

Robinson brought to the "Town Down the River" a view of life that was formed in "Tilbury Town." He saw

New York as he had seen Gardiner, Maine, in his youth in this moribund port on the Kennebec river. Gardiner, which had once been a thriving shipping-centre, had gone the way of other New England towns, and Robinson, whose father had been a prosperous timber-merchant, had witnessed in his own household the decay of the region. The family fortune, such as it was, had vanished, and Robinson's brothers had fallen on evil days; and Gardiner abounded in men who had once been important and who had no life any longer to shape to their code. Their minds had been formed for a large way of living. They had set the tone for their neighbours and headed their clans. But they had no clans to lead now, and the making of laws was not for them: they were left with the "dusty ruins of their fathers' dreams." They had lost their confidence, as the years went by, and they crept away into their houses and grew queerer and queerer. Eccentricities multiplied on humbler levels also, and misery walked patch-clad through the streets. There was never a more wintry world, as Robinson saw it. The sun rose dull there. Brown weeds grew through the floors of houses. Torn curtains flapped in broken windows. The trees were leafless, a ghostly band in cold array, and the thin leaves skipped on the stones with a freezing whisper. The streets were swept by an icy wind from the river, and the water was black under the piles of the docks. Spring never came there. At best, a late autumnal glimmer lingered by the river-side and warmed the bones of aging men. There were Archibalds and Isaacs on some of the farms, ripe and sweet as the cider they kept in their cellars. There were good old uncles who were good old liars. There were admirable doctors of billiards, "fallen from on high." But these were few beside the lonely men who wandered through the scene, disconsolate shadows. There were outcasts, in broken shoes, sleeping in doorways on Water Street, who had once driven their span of horses; there were skirt-crazed old reprobates, misers and spendthrifts; there were men who had been wrecked by kinks, horrors who had never lived, ruins ridden by fear and killed by terror. There were creepers among catacombs, "whose occupation was to die," there were respected citizens who blew their brains out; and one saw them straggling through the town, stumbling over frozen ruts, in the cold white shine of a dreary day. In short, this population was a whole *Spoon River Anthology,* acting out its epitaphs in the world of the living.

Such was Robinson's picture of Gardiner, where he had seen his future life as a "long and foggy voyage;" and through the cold fog, wherever he went, he saw the old familiar faces. Sometimes the derelicts of Gardiner appeared in New York, and "queer fellows" drifted all over the city. But why were they derelicts? Why were they queer?—and were they not, in any case, more interesting than men who were called successes? They interested Robinson more, as they interested many another young man who was living in New York at that moment and who found a spokesman in Robinson, then or later. Robinson was always drawn to them. Most of his Gardiner friends had been square pegs in round holes, a doctor, for example, who had lost his standing, a disreputable tin-smith, an outcast named Wash Benjamin who kept a mistress down the road. As long as the town did not respect them, they were likely to find a friend in him,—and not at all because he felt a failure. He had no interest in success; and he was quite content when a single suitcase contained all his possessions, including his books. Nor did his kindness explain it, kind as he was: he made an intimate friend of a lighthouse-keeper, largely because he had had a foot wrenched off. He had, he said, a little of the hobo in him; and he sought, by a natural impulse, the despised and rejected, the lost, the maladjusted and the lonely be-

cause, in his time and his place, he was a poet.* Who
were the successful men, on the whole, in a world of business? One might have asked Sinclair Lewis, who was
young just then, and who was so soon to reply with *Main
Street* and *Babbitt.* Whether in New York, in Gardiner
or in Gopher Prairie, the "bitch-goddess Success" repelled
the young. It was noisome to the sensitive, as it had never
been before: even for Horatio Alger it had lacked the
glamour that failure as a symbol had for them. When
Henry van Dyke was a great man and Veblen was a nobody, the Veblens had for the young an extraordinary
charm; and one saw in every "queer fellow" a genius *in
posse,* if not *in esse,*—one knew that if they were geniuses
they had to be queer. To be adjusted to such a world, yet
not to be a Babbitt, implied an all but unprecedented
force of soul; and, as people had ceased to look for heroes
and the young could scarcely believe they existed, they
regarded maladjustment as a sign of grace. Five times
out of ten, in fact, it was so. Most of Robinson's "lost"
souls possessed some spirituality, and it was just for this
reason that they were "lost." The people who were queer
were the people who were real. Such was Robinson's message for an age of rebels.

Now, of course, there was nothing new in this. The
founders of all the religions had known where to look for
their apostles; and Hawthorne, in his *Feathertop,* had
pictured the successful man who had not been able to pass
through the eye of the needle. That successful men could
not pass through it, neither Christ nor Hawthorne said;
but a poet in a day like Robinson's could not dwell on exceptions. Poets had seldom dwelt on these exceptions, well

---

* Long after Robinson had himself become a "success," he gave up his
New York friends and music and went to live in Brooklyn in a dingy
apartment to care for two good friends who were said to have been
"failures." No one else apparently saw anything in them; but how much
more they undoubtedly gave this poet than New York dinner-tables could
ever have given!

knowing that successful men can look after themselves.
In a day when success was the only visible goddess, a poet
could only point out that it signified failure; and Robinson's successful men were Feathertops in every case,
whited sepulchres full of dead men's bones. This, and its
natural corollary, was the whole of his teaching. In all his
long psychological poems, he stripped the emperors of
their clothes,—what was false within always betrayed
them; while he turned the tables on conventional opinion
by showing goodness and genius walking in tatters. It was
the Fernando Nashes and the Captain Craigs, the casta-
ways who "went begging" that really "went giving;" and
this, the oldest of morals for poets, had never ceased to
be new. The novelty had always lain in the local application. Hawthorne had applied it, and Robinson applied it,
each in his own place and time; and Robinson thus revealed a fact which Americans had almost forgotten, that
poetry is always opportune. Emerson had restated this
fact two generations before him, and only Emily Dickinson had revealed it since, in the line of the Yankee tradition; and Robinson carried on their line,—he was their
natural heir,—just as he carried on the line of Hawthorne. And if, in him, the Yankee tradition seemed to be
tapering off, this was characteristic of the moment. The
scene that he pictured was moribund, and the Emersonian
gleam that often appeared in his poems was shrouded
and dim. He could not share the old assurance that life
was part of a purposeful plan, much as he wished to share
it and almost did so. A sad man in a withered world, he
could not believe in the triumph of life, and the best of
his real successes were scarred by their failure. They, too,
all too often, were sterile fruit for the button-moulder,
children of the abyss, impotent and vain.

In later years, after the war, when poets talked of a
"renaissance," Robinson was called its prime precursor.
At a time when American poetry had reached its lowest

ebb, he, in his obscurity, was real and vital; and the "irony and pity" * with which he regarded his victims of fate struck the new note of the novelists as well as the poets. His probing, questioning, doubting mind was the mind of the new generation; and his portraits, even his sonnets, were novels in little. His longer psychological poems continued the line of Howells and James; and his technical development foreshadowed the poets that were coming. He had cast off early the influence of Aldrich, which dominated the magazine-verse of the moment, although, as if to train his hand, he had written his villanelles and ballades. He had reacted against this facile jingling. He had sought for the spoken phrase, for the neat and plain; and, if his style was too prosaic, if it was too bare and cold, it was hard, it was clear and it was honest. Here again Robinson was in the line of Emerson, who liked "dry light and hard clouds, hard expressions and hard manners." Robinson eschewed the nebulous, the blurred and the vague, as he abhorred the fatuous and the stereotyped. In short, in a poetical world of baker's bread and confectionery, Robinson brought forth real bread again.

It might have been foreseen that, after this return to nature, American poetry was destined for a liberation. The "renaissance" that soon occurred was the result of various causes, and Robinson was only one of these. But his austere integrity and his tragic feeling were more than a little influential and his style cleared the ground for other growths; and the time was approaching when no one who was concerned for poetry looked for this year's birds in last year's nests. Robinson, a traditional poet, carried on the New England tradition, together with the classical tradition that lay behind it; but "last year's

* A phrase of Anatole France, much used and even abused in the post-war years. " 'What's all this irony and pity?'—'What? Don't you know about Irony and Pity?'—'No. Who got it up?'—'Everybody. They're mad about it in New York.' "—Hemingway, *The Sun Also Rises.*

nests" in poetry, as the new poets saw them, were the
nests of the romantic mind in its hour of decay. Romanti-
cism had given birth to a verbal fatty degeneration that
revealed the degeneration of the life it sprang from, in a
world whose actual deity was the goddess Success; and
younger minds reacted against such phrases as "reverence for life" and "quest for beauty," because of their
sense of the false and the hollow behind them. The older
poets, in all good faith, had used these phrases because
they meant them. They really reverenced life, they sought
for beauty; while the recent poets, the magazine-poets
used them merely because the older poets had used them.
They did not reverence life,—they only said so; and they
sought for the pretty and the charming but not for
beauty. The passions they claimed were not real passions;
their heartbreaks never broke their hearts. They took in
vain a language that had once been great. In short, they
were "phonographs," as Amy Lowell presently said, or,
as she might have said, ventriloquists, for their voice was
not their own, it was alien to them, and they were either
ordinary children of Mammon or wistful sentimentalists
without strength. What had become of the great old life?
What had become of the great old language? The bitch-
goddess had them in her toils, and the "great words" had
gone down with the great life-patterns.* It was no use to
talk to the young about "sacred" and "glorious" things,
especially when the war had traduced them further; and
the more sacred one felt they were, the more one felt it
was obscene to use the words or even think about them.
The younger writers, growing up in this dying phase of

---

* "It is advertising that has been the death of words.
The word 'Personal' now on an envelope means 'impersonal;'
'Important,' 'unimportant.'
'The Finest,' 'The Best,' 'The Purest'—what do they mean now?
Something somebody wants to sell.
We are a nation of word-killers: *hero, veteran, tragedy,*—
Watch the great words go down."
                    —Edna St. Vincent Millay, *Conversation at Midnight.*

the old society, knew that Robinson was right. Success in
this civilization was inevitably failure, although failure
might be success. The more honest these younger writers
were, the less they believed in the world they lived in,—
they were all rebels at the outset,—and the better they
expressed their minds, the surer they were to express
them in terms for which Robinson had prepared the way.
For just as he had swept the house for all that was truthful and loyal in living, he had swept it for plain speaking,
veracity and candour. As for poetry, he had broken up
the "roof of heaven,"—the cotton-batting roof it had become,—and the "new forms" followed as a matter of
course. The free verse, the new rhythms, the imagism,
the realism, the characteristic forms of the coming decades,—and especially the classicism that was salient also,
—expressed new states of mind and new ideas of which
Robinson was one of the prophets.

These new American states of mind, the new ideas of
the coming epoch, flourished, with unparalleled luxuriance, in New York. Robinson had found New York "the
best town to live in," * as Howells had found it before
him. It was the best town because it was the town of
"life," as Howells had shown in *A Hazard of New Fortunes,* but the life of which Howells had written in the
"age of innocence" had become the life of megalopolis. It
was vital with a vengeance, and the vengeance and the
vitality were equally marked; for, if there one saw the
American eagle "mewing her mighty youth and kindling
her undazzled eyes at the full midday beam," the eagle's
brood were apt to forget their nest there. Most of the
younger writers gathered there, from New England, the
South and the West, because the currents of thought converged in New York that had formerly met in Boston

* "Boston is a good town to write in—perhaps the best, just as New
York is the best town to live in . . . I can't feel at home anywhere
else."—Letter of Robinson, 1905.

and spread from New England. They gathered, and they drank the heady waters, and some grew strong thereby, those in whom the eagle remained undazzled; but in many of the brood, from New England, the South and the West, the heady waters produced delirium tremens. They were constrained to feel provincial, and, feeling their provinciality, they lost their bearings; for never in modern history had any cosmopolitan town presented a more overwhelming chaos. Howells, the ripe old veteran, lived serene there; and Robinson, the tough Yankee, kept his head. His Pierian spring was unsullied by the river of whiskey he drank; and Howells, with his open sympathies, rejoiced in the chaos. He saw it as life, multifarious life, full of hope and promise; and he was inoculated against the poisons, the virus that lurked in the chaos. He had long since taken the serums of Italy, Spain, Germany, Russia,—he had entered all their literatures by an inner line; and the beautiful travel-books that he was writing in his calm old age were a proof of the catholicity of his understanding.* As an old socialist, he was an internationalist also, and for him the cosmopolitan had no poisons. There was nothing to disturb him, there was everything to feed him in the mixture of races in New York; and he who knew so well the American eagle knew it had room for all under its wing. He knew the young West as he knew the old New England; and he who was one of the first to review Robert Frost was the first to review Abraham Cahan. Moreover, this "linchpin" of Boston had linked the two ages of poetry, the old and the new; for he had recognized Emily Dickinson, whose star was about to rise to its zenith, and had passed her work on to Stephen Crane. He had fought for the publication of Crane's *Maggie,* and inviting the young man to dinner,

---

* As Howells had always been a first-rate travel-writer,—ever since his early *Venetian Life,*—so he excelled in the final fruits of his "mental kodak," *Familiar Spanish Travels, Hither and Thither in Germany, London Films,* etc. The vein of these books was psychological.

had read him Miss Dickinson's poems, which had just appeared; whereupon Crane wrote *The Black Riders,* the poems that carried her torch to the poets who followed. In fighting for *Maggie,* the candid Howells had fought for all the new novelists whose realism was paling the light of his own; and this suggested that if he had had the audience of these later writers he might have shared their drastic point of view. For men were beginning to read again, and women were casting off the old taboos; and the "young lady" standard that his time and his place imposed on Howells was going the way of Cooper's "young female" world. Howells was a "dead cult," * although this cult was to live again when the inverted prudery of Howells's successors had gone the way of Howells's prudery. The "he-men" were to follow the "she-women" into the abysm of time; and Howells's complex psychology and delicate art were to win new readers who loved the American scene. Meanwhile, all standards and values were at risk in New York; and, if this explained why Howells and Robinson liked it, still what was meat for them was poison for others. That life has laws to which death pays tribute the strong had always known and were always to know; and, knowing it, they had always rejoiced in life, and the more life the better. But few of the younger writers could afford this risk. The law of metropolitan attraction all but compelled them to take it, but most of them were too soft to bear the strain. They were heirs of the confusion of morals with which the nineteenth century ended, and, besides, they were uncertain about their country. There were some who had listened to teachers, like Woodberry and Wendell, in whom the American tradition had gone to seed; and all of them had seen their country whoring after the bitch-goddess,—they could not

---

* "I am comparatively a dead cult with my statues cut down and the grass growing over them in the pale moonlight."—Letter of Howells to Henry James, 1915.

believe in themselves as Americans any longer. So chaos often overwhelmed them; for every brass tack contradicted the feeble talk they heard about "ideals" and "inspiration," which was drowned by the Babel of voices that rose in New York. Puritanism, once so grand, Victorianism, once so potent, went down like houses of glass at the impact of Freud, who had found incest in filial affection, guilt in generosity, malice in the tender feelings, hatred in love. The facts that Freud revealed were patently present; and what modern ethic was there to defend these feelings, whose substance of reality Freud never attacked? In those who could not meet him with a modern ethic, or with a core of tradition, stoutly maintained, Freud subverted religion and romantic love, which became for them a gloss over animal instincts; so that romantic young men and women,—and all Americans were romantic,—were suddenly confused and deranged at the roots of their being. Better to be honest animals than dishonest men!—though, unhappily, the case was not so simple, and many became dishonest animals also. That Freud met no resistance was not his fault, and nothing met resistance in New York, where the doctrines of all the iconoclasts were sown broadcast. The brilliant journalist James Huneker spread before the younger minds the writings of Shaw, Nietzsche, D'Annunzio, Strindberg, Laforgue, Schnitzler, Wedekind, Anatole France, presenting them all on one level, as equally great, the boulevard-thinkers and drawing-room poets together with the lonely seers who had wrestled with the deepest problems in their cottages and attics. Each of these minds was a logical outgrowth of some one national ethos, personified in New York by an immigrant group, and they could only have been really understood in relation to these groups and their traditions. But the immigrant groups themselves had lost their keys. They had cut themselves adrift from their own traditions and sought for an American

tradition to which to cling, which they could find nowhere
in New York,—any more than Henry James could find
his birthplace when, in 1905, he reappeared. As Henry
James's birthplace had long since vanished, so all the native ideas seemed remote and dim beside this staggering
onrush of new thoughts. These European authors floated
in a vacuum. No critic related them to the native mind,
and Huneker welcomed them all and passed them on with
a sympathy and enthusiasm that knew no standards. Indeed, his impressionism, the prevailing doctrine, invalidated the very conception of standards; for it argued
that taste and thought were subjective and thus destroyed
all objectivity, whether of authority, precedent, scholarship or tradition. Its only standard of value was the reader's pleasure. This universal hedonism, the note of megalopolis, condoned all irresponsibilities; and it marked a
disillusioned, urban, cosmopolitan people who had lost all
sense of their former attachments. This was the note of
the melting-pot whose contents failed to melt because
there was no fire underneath it, no conscious native feeling to fuse its warring elements into a common ethos that
all accepted.

Meanwhile, Boston was hostile to the world-ideas, the
ideas of the coming age that congested New York. *The
Atlantic* was the medium through which these new ideas
had once been announced to America, more often than
not, while Huneker was the medium now, and Huneker
was anathema to the mind that had gradually come to
prevail in Boston. The city remained, in its way, a city of
readers, in a measure that astonished Arnold Bennett,*
but it was also "finished," as Bennett said; and, while by
"finished" he meant complete,—other cities "will be,"
Boston "is,"—this was a more fundamental comment. Its

* When Arnold Bennett visited Boston in 1912, he was amused and
surprised to find in his room a catalogue of the hotel-library, one hundred
and eighty-two pages.—See Arnold Bennett, *Your United States.*

completeness implied a certain complacency, as if, having reached its limit of growth, it had nothing to learn from other quarters; and the Watch and Ward Society was doing its best to prevent it from growing any further. Within a few years, the society prohibited sixty books that were generally accepted in the rest of the country as representing the life and ideas of the time. The Irish, the official rulers, had inherited the Puritanism that was no longer active in the true-blue Yankees; but the Yankees allowed them to have their way, for they had lost interest themselves in ideas that were novel and disturbing. The phrase "banned in Boston" was the novelist's dream of successful publicity, but Boston banned itself in excluding the world; and American writers generally now regarded it with a certain rancour as illiberal, sterile, indifferent, censorious and petty. They were prepared for the Adamses' gibes at Boston,* they shared Mencken's contempt for the "ashes of New England;" and certainly the New England critics, Woodberry and Wendell, had been singularly indifferent to American letters. Both depreciated what the country had done already, neither showed any interest in what it was doing; † and both appeared to wonder why Americans wrote at all or what they found in its life that was worth expressing. When they were not

* "This is the trouble with Boston—it is provincial. Including Cambridge, one finds there what might be called a very good society stock company . . . Socially, however, the trouble with Boston is that there is no current of fresh outside life everlastingly flowing in and passing out. It is, so to speak, stationary—a world, a Boston world, unto itself; and, like all things stationary, there is in it, as the years pass, a very perceptible lack of that variety and change which are the essence and spice of life; it tends to stagnate . . . In the course of my life I have tried Boston socially on all sides. I have summered it and wintered it, tried it drunk and tried it sober; and, drunk and sober, there's nothing in it— save Boston."—*Autobiography of Charles Francis Adams.*
"Boston is a curious place . . . When a society has reached this point, it acquires a self-complacency which is wildly exasperating. My fingers itch to puncture it; to do something which will sting it into impropriety."— *Letters of Henry Adams.*

† Wendell, who had glanced at Crane's *The Red Badge of Courage,* described it in one of his lectures as "sensational trash."

looking backward, they looked across the sea towards Europe; but they were as oblivious of the new ideas that were coming from Europe,—the ideas that were flowing especially through Huneker's mind,—as they were of the life beyond the Charles and the Hudson. They resembled the Anglo-Irish critics in Dublin, Edward Dowden and his school, who were equally indifferent, when they were not hostile, to the literature that was coming to birth in their country. Their necks were awry, their eyes were twisted.* Hamlin Garland, speaking for the West, had recently disowned, in *Crumbling Idols,* these critics who ignored the American scene; † and Boston represented, for the rest of the nation, the blight one felt behind them. Boston was the schoolmarm, and the nation had grown too big for her,—it was altogether out of hand; and the schoolmarm herself had lost her humility and grown, with the waning of her power, arrogant and peevish. The

* "There is a school of criticism in Ireland, a school that knows the work of the finest critics in the world, and knows too, what is more important, the finest literature in the world. This, when dealing with literature in general, adds to the store of fine critical work. This at times encourages and approves good original Irish work. I think it unfortunate, however, that it should have grown with, or indeed before, the original work. Dealing with the monuments of the older literatures,—English, French and the like,—this criticism knows its place, its bearings, its conditions. Dealing with a naissant literature . . . it looks over its shoulder, as it were. Its neck is awry. Its eyes are twisted round. Its feet turn from their known way and stumble. When it does get a clear view of its object, it misses the shapes and forms it saw in other lands and expresses its disappointment.

"Ireland is not the only country that suffers so today. America also has a full-grown criticism and a baby literature. Something of the same relation exists between the two there is in Ireland."—Thomas MacDonagh, *Literature in Ireland.*

† "For fifty years the best writers of England and Europe have been calling for the native utterance of American writers . . . and almost as constantly have the conservative and narrow critics of Boston and New York discouraged the truest, freest utterance of the American poet and novelist . . . Upon the tender springing plant of American literature the frost of conservative culture has fallen.

"It really comes down to a contest, not between the East and the West, but between sterile culture and creative work, between mere scholarship and wisdom, between conservative criticism and native original literary production."—Hamlin Garland, *Crumbling Idols,* 1894.

West would have none of her, and a rising generation that saw itself reflected in Henry Adams, whose quarrel had always been with his educators, found Boston its natural enemy. Why waste words on the definition of puritanism? The fact that it came from New England was enough to damn it. Puritanism was Miss Ophelia, who had reformed Dinah's kitchen; and Dinah had rebelled and thrown her out. For was she not a shrew?—was she not old?—like those two other symbols of Boston, the sphinx-like Mrs. Eddy and the aged Mrs. Gardner, swathed in white. These latter suggested, in their carriages, animated mummies. It was rumoured that Mrs. Eddy was actually dead and had only a pretended existence in the person of a double.

Now, true it was that, all this while, and for all the dry-rot on the surface, the Boston, the New England authors continued to write; and many of them wrote as well as ever. The tough New England intellect and its still tougher moral force were not to be downed by adverse circumstances; and, while William James was at his zenith, the Spaniard-Yankee Santayana had finished his great work, *The Life of Reason*. The Adamses were in full career, Mark Howe was memorializing his New England worthies, and, at Wellesley Hills, Gamaliel Bradford wrote his *Lee, the American,* the first of his long series of literary portraits. Samuel M. Crothers, a follower of Dr. Holmes with a touch of Western "folksiness," was writing his essays; and William Roscoe Thayer produced his magnificent *Life and Times of Cavour,* the fruit of a lifelong devotion to Italian studies. This theme was as congenial to a good New England liberal as the rise of the Dutch republic had been to Motley; and the masterly composition of Thayer showed that for scholarly writing the New England intellect was as strong as ever. Bliss Perry carried on at Harvard the noble Yankee humanism that Lounsbury and H. A. Beers main-

tained at Yale,—despite the militant philistinism of the
formidable Sumner,—its ethical delicacy and its tolerant
candour, together with its steadfast faith in the goodness
of men. With Lounsbury, Beers, Chauncey Tinker and
William Lyon Phelps, Yale had outgrown its earlier indifference to letters,—marked by the obscurity of John
De Forest, who had lived all his life in New Haven, invisible as a treetoad in an oak. De Forest died in 1903;
and in 1911 Wilbur L. Cross founded the *Yale Review*,—
after writing his memorable life of Sterne and before he
wrote the life of Fielding,—the quarterly that was to play
the part which the moribund *North American,* revived by
George Harvey, had largely relinquished. The breeze
that was blowing over literary Yale was to have its effect
on the new generation of writers, brilliant groups of
whom were at nurse there.* When it came to scholarly
writing, nothing could ever down New England, but in
poetry, fiction and drama it was also alive; and, while
Robert Frost pegged away on his New Hampshire farm
and Robinson pegged with him in New York, Amy Lowell was growing up in Boston. There Robert Grant was
publishing his finest book, *The Chippendales,* and Alice
Brown was continuing her admirable stories. *Meadow-
Grass* and *Tiverton Tales* lacked some of Miss Jewett's
poetry, as they lacked the full force of Miss Wilkins's
tragic feeling, but they certainly combined Miss Wilkins's
veracity with a very large part of Miss Jewett's charm.
Miss Jewett died in 1909, and Miss Wilkins had fallen a
prey to the sentimental; but James B. Connolly was writing his fine Gloucester tales and Vida D. Scudder her
Franciscan romances. Amy Lowell was still a beginner.

* Among the future authors who were students at Yale during the years
(roughly) 1900–1920 were Henry Seidel Canby, William Rose Benét,
Stephen Vincent Benét, Sinclair Lewis, Waldo Frank, Thomas Beer, Paul
Rosenfeld, Leonard Bacon, Chard Powers Smith, Robert M. Coates,
George Soule, Clarence Day, Philip Barry, Archibald MacLeish and Thorn-
ton Wilder.

The brilliant apparition of the future was scarcely indicated in her timid verses; but the little roly-poly girl had turned into a tomboy, and the tomboy had become a redoubtable woman, and it only required the warmth of the spring that was coming to reveal the flower in this portentous bud. As a child, she had browsed in the Athenæum, in a quiet nook aloft, gained by a "little painful spiral stair." Her earliest love had been Keats, the favourite poet of her grandfather's first cousin, the preëminent Lowell; and she had lived with her usual verve through the aesthetic nineties in Boston, absorbing Huysmans, Laforgue, Remy de Gourmont and other new French writers already in vogue there. She had grown up with her brother Percival's letters from his far-away Japan, and she was steeped in the Boston Orientalism that flourished with Sturgis Bigelow and Fenollosa. She knew their Japanese and Chinese collections as she knew Mrs. Gardner's Fenway Court; and all these exotic notes were to appear in her later work. The reigning poet, meanwhile, in Boston, was Josephine Preston Peabody, whose fluent and graceful verses were admired to excess. These verses, usually fervent but often insipid, expressed the humanitarian mood and feeling that remained endemic in New England and that Vida D. Scudder and Anna Hempstead Branch also expressed in their poems, romances and plays. All these writers were in revolt against a commercial civilization, as the rebels of the following decade were; but, unlike the later writers, they reacted against the world they lived in by falling back on mediæval themes. In her verse-plays, *The Piper, The Wolf of Gubbio, Marlowe* and others,—all more intense than her poems,—Miss Peabody dramatized the widespread interest in history that filled the New England colleges during these years. Her plays, which ignored the present, except by implication, offered escapes into moments that seemed nobler and richer; although Hamelin, in *The Piper,* might have been Boston,—since the money-bag served it for a heart. This piper who led the children away was not the sinister creature of legend but the poet who saved them from the waste-land. *The Wolf of Gubbio* was a Franciscan play, suggesting Miss Scudder's romances. Anna Hempstead Branch, who lived in New York and New London, was also humanitarian and mediæval. Her work abounded in echoes of Coleridge and Wordsworth and especially in Pre-Raphaelite archaisms, with ballads and plays of court fools, princesses and pages that were popular in the colleges for women.* But her religious feeling was authentic, and she often wrote admirable verse.

Literary Yankeedom was quick enough, in short, however the rest of the country was disposed to ignore it;† and this was particularly true in the case of the drama. The first "little theatre" in the country was established in Boston, the Toy Theatre, 1911; and there, as nowhere else in America, the Elizabethans had come to life. The Elizabethan poets and playwrights had long been a central interest in Cambridge, where their plays were constantly revived; and most of the New England poets of the present and immediate future were full of Elizabethan conceptions and rhythms. Everyone was talking of Webster, Middleton, Beaumont and Fletcher, for whom Gamaliel Bradford had a passion; and Miss Peabody's *Marlowe* expressed a sympathy that Robinson also expressed in *Ben Jonson Meets a Man from Stratford.* This sympathy

---

* Edna St. Vincent Millay's early plays, *The Lamp and the Bell, Two Slatterns and a King,* etc., were in the vein of Anna Hempstead Branch.

† In the revolt against New England that marked the nation's coming of age, the New England authors were almost totally ignored. The Yankee classics were dethroned, and the critics scarcely mentioned such authors as Miss Guiney, Lodge and Stickney. These New England writers were at least as good as the secondary and tertiary precursors elsewhere. In 1925, Miss Peabody's excellent plays were completely forgotten, and Alice Brown and other living authors had passed into an undeserved eclipse. One had to pay for being a Yankee in these great formative years of the national mind.

later appeared in various forms in Edna St. Vincent Millay, Eliot and Cummings, who abounded in Elizabethan
imagery. New England was undergoing a revival of the
drama, which was marked by George Pierce Baker's Harvard "workshop," later transferred to Yale; and the
Provincetown Theatre was foreshadowed in the Greek
plays of Lodge and Stickney and the prose-plays of Robinson and Percy MacKaye.* But, while all this was promising, especially in the field of forms, the spirit of most of
these writers was atavistic. Rebels as they were, like the
writers who followed, Miss Peabody, Miss Branch and
Miss Scudder were more like the "escapists" of the nineties, the seekers of lost trails who wandered back to the
Middle Ages, or to a fanciful Greece or an actual England. They did not like the present, but they did not come
to grips with it, as the writers of the future were obliged
to do, although, by implication, they attacked the present,—and in this they were unlike the writers of the nineties.† They attacked the unlovely present with the weapons of the past, they used the weapons of the past to
abuse the present, whereas the young writers who were
growing up at Harvard were bent upon finding their
weapons in the present also. The latter were realistic,
however romantic they also were; and, disliking the present quite as much as any of the existing writers, they
shared Robinson's frank obsession with it. They did not

---

* Robinson published two plays, *Van Zorn* and *The Porcupine.* Percy
MacKaye's New England plays, like Eugene O'Neill's, were only a phase
of his work. *The Scarecrow* was suggested by Hawthorne's *Feathertop.*
Yankee Fantasies, 1912, were New England folk-plays, dealing with sur-
prising variations of the Yankee psyche. See also Robert Frost's play,
A Way Out, published in *The Seven Arts* magazine.

Josephine Preston Peabody's *The Piper* was produced at the Shakespeare Theatre in Stratford-on-Avon.

Among other more or less New England plays were Marion Crawford's
Francesca da Rimini, produced by Sarah Bernhardt, Paris, 1902, and
Thomas Bailey Aldrich's *Judith of Bethesda,* produced in 1904. One
might also mention here the work of William Vaughn Moody, the
Indiana poet who was closely connected with Cambridge and Boston.

† An exception should be made here of George Cabot Lodge.

wish to escape from the present, for they were of the present. To escape from the present was to escape from themselves, and this, as realists, they could not do. Moreover, they did not wish to abuse the present: they wished to understand it, unravel it, solve it and use it as a foundation for the building of the future. Such was the basis of many of the points of view that characterized the Harvard authors who were coming.

For Harvard, in these pre-war years, teemed with growing writers who were to show that geniuses are "ferments." * This was William James's word, and they were drawn to Harvard by its "persistently atomistic constitution." † Again, the phrase was James's, and the Harvard faculty had grown along the lines of James's department, in which the professors of philosophy were chosen to represent variety, first of all. It avoided inbreeding and aimed at diversity and thus promoted a critical attitude, while it encouraged every private bent; and it maintained, both above and below the various vital ideals it stood for, its own tradition and its "scale of value." A remarkable group of powerful teachers, with nothing in common but their humanity, presented the special subjects that attracted writers, philosophy, psychology, the literary languages, history, comparative literature and the best of

* Among the future writers who were students at Harvard during these pre-war years were Conrad Aiken, Heywood Broun, Witter Bynner, Stuart Chase, Malcolm Cowley, E. E. Cummings, S. Foster Damon, John Dos Passos, Walter Prichard Eaton, T. S. Eliot, Arthur Davison Ficke, John Gould Fletcher, Hermann Hagedorn, Robert Hillyer, Walter Lippmann, S. E. Morison, Charles Nordhoff, Eugene O'Neill, Lucien Price, John Reed, Edward Sheldon, Stuart P. Sherman, Lee Simonson, Harold Stearns, Wallace Stevens, Claude C. Washburn, John Hall Wheelock and John Brooks Wheelwright.

† Why did the "undisciplinables" go to Harvard, that "nursery for independent and lonely thinkers"? William James, considering this question, answered it as follows: "It is because they have heard of her persistently atomistic constitution, of her tolerance of exceptionality and eccentricity, of her devotion to the principles of individual vocation and choice. It is because you cannot make single one-ideaed regiments of her classes. It is because she cherishes so many vital ideals, yet makes a scale of value among them."—William James, *Memories and Studies.*

English; and one could trace in the later work of almost all the coming writers the influence of one or more of these.* William James's realism pervaded the atmosphere, together with all the romance that young men liked; and one gathered that the line of valour was to face the music, whether the music was Bach or whether it was jazz. Harvard was the *Dive Bouteille* of all the intellectual passions. Its motto was *Fais ce que vouldras* and take the risks; and, whether as novelists, poets or playwrights, historians, journalists, critics, as socialists, liberals, aesthetes or radical tories, the Harvard men were often disposed to do so. If they went up alleys of the past, these alleys could not be blind alleys, and, if they lived in the future, they did so with reason; and as moulders of forms and setters of fashions, and even as "movers and shakers," they played an unusual role in the times that were coming.

There were few of these young men at Harvard,— there were still fewer at Yale,—whose destinies were deeply involved with New England. But there were Yankees among them, and others who were partly Yankee, and these young men were in a special case; and this case was marked when they were tough-minded, as they were apt to be, for the Yankee mind was traditionally a mind of wrestlers. The Yankee mind, for hundreds of years, had been wrestling with angels and devils, and it could not take life lightly, in the New York fashion; and the tough-minded Yankees were still wrestlers. There were tender-minded Yankees, there were "white-pine Yankees,"—to abuse a shrewd distinction of Dr. Holmes,—† Yankees

---

* The Harvard teachers of the humanities included during these years the following: Irving Babbitt, George Pierce Baker, L. B. R. Briggs, Charles T. Copeland, Kuno Francke, Charles H. Grandgent, Charles H. Haskins, William James, George Lyman Kittredge, Charles R. Lanman, George Foot Moore, Hugo Münsterberg, William Allan Neilson, Bliss Perry, Edward Kennard Rand, Josiah Royce, George Santayana, Frederick J. Turner, Leo Wiener and Barrett Wendell.

† In *The Poet at the Breakfast-Table.*

of the softer grain, unlike the "pitch-pine Yankees," who were able to follow the line of least resistance. These white-pine Yankees saw nothing amiss with New England. They were not the wrestling kind, they were not concerned with angels and devils, and their comfort meant more to them than the state of their souls. They were easy-going traditionalists, and they were joined by outsiders who were prone to idealize New England in the Western way; for Westerners either hated New England or they loved it over-much, in this resembling Howells in his earlier phase. The literary life of Boston was largely composed in the future of these tender-minded natives and visitors from afar; and certainly it was a happy fact that Boston found appreciators when most of its tougher minds were turning against it. The tough minds were driven to turn against it; for, granting that one was born to wrestle, what was there to wrestle with?—what risks, in this latter-day Boston, were there to take? What was reality in Boston, since one had to face it? Harvard, with its realism, Harvard, with its gospel of risks, had spoiled these New England men for their region and their town. For Boston offered them no resistance, nothing to cut their teeth upon; and wrestlers must find their resistance or they cease to be wrestlers.

There was nothing essentially new in this, for, ever since the Civil War, the Boston mind had been growing softer and softer; and whatever drove the young men forth in the early twentieth century had driven Henry James and Henry Adams. Howells had been driven forth in a similar fashion. As long as the old nobility was dominant in the Boston mind there had remained a rock to cling to, but this had long ceased to be dominant, although it still existed, and much of what was left was Pharisaic; and those who took most seriously the old professions of Boston,—its moral dynamism and its faith in progress, its faith in the goodness of men,—were those who were most disillusioned with the Boston of the present. For they saw a Boston that had suffered itself to be betrayed and that was on the way to betraying them. It seemed smug, flaccid, tepid, snobbish and priggish. It was fatuous in its pessimism, which consisted in throwing up sponges. It was still more fatuous in its optimism; for it abounded in "glad books," and the "Pollyanna philosophy" vied with the sterile despair of the house of Adams.* The tribe of the Pooh-Poohs, which Dr. Holmes had routed,† had reclaimed its ancestral totems in the town of Boston; and everything new was "pseudo" there, from the point of view of Irving Babbitt.‡ Everything new was pseudo to Dr. Crothers. What Holmes would have welcomed as vigorous and fresh, Crothers gently ridiculed in the name of Sir Walter and the good old days that knew no modern science. Everything embryonic for him was pseudo, and he threw out all the babies with the bath. The "new biography," the "new poetry," the "new psychology" or whatever were all so many bubbles for him to prick; and nothing struck him as more absurd than keeping up with the march of mind that New England had once been so willing and eager to follow. For Irving Babbitt there was no march of mind, and he virtually included all contem-

---

* Eleanor H. Porter's *Pollyanna,* 1912, was a characteristic expression of the Boston of the moment.

† "The Pi-Utes and the Kickapoos of the wilderness are hard to reason with. But there is another tribe of irreclaimables, living in much larger wigwams and having all the look of civilized people, which is quite as intractable to the teachings of a new philosophy that upsets their ancestral totems. This is the tribe of the Pooh-Poohs, so called from the leading expression of their vocabulary, which furnishes them a short and easy method of disposing of all novel doctrines, discoveries and inventions of a character to interfere with their preconceived notions. They may possibly serve a useful purpose, like other barbarous and semi-barbarous human beings, by helping to keep down the too prolific family of noxious and troublesome animals,—the thinking, or rather talking and writing ones. Beyond this they are of small value; and they are always retreating before the advance of knowledge, facing it, and moving backwards, still opposing the leaders and the front rank with their inextinguishable warcry, Pooh-Pooh!"—Holmes, *Pages from an Old Volume of Life.*

‡ "I am sorry I need so many 'pseudos' in describing our modern activities."—Irving Babbitt, *The Masters of Modern French Criticism.*

porary tastes when he said, "There are tastes that deserve the cudgel." As for Boston, the old spirit of effort and strife had long gone out of its Emersonianism, and the sons of the patricians who had taxed themselves for the great republic were bent upon nothing so much as evading their taxes. To undo the labours of their fathers was the chief of their cares. The old force had been sadly dispersed, and the famous culture of Boston consisted of vague generalities and empty intentions. So, at least, the younger people saw it. The poets all wore "singing robes," and they all had "mystic illuminations," which meant anything or nothing: they were sentimentally mediæval or, as a rising poet soon said, compounded of "marshmallows and tears." * The festering lilies of Boston smelt worse than weeds.

So it seemed to the younger writers who were growing up at Harvard, especially T. S. Eliot and E. E. Cummings. Eliot had returned from St. Louis to the home of his forbears, and Cummings was the son of a Boston and Cambridge professor and minister, Dr. Hale's successor at the South Church. Both felt as Henry Adams felt about Boston, and there were many others who shared their feeling. Their "fingers itched to puncture it," as their poems were to show, to "sting it into impropriety." It struck them as a "dreary place," a "target for disgust,"—as the ill-fated Harry Crosby presently called it; † and they were irritated by the "Boston virgins . . . with their flat-heeled shoes and tortoise-shell glasses," by the "Cambridge ladies with permanent faces" who lived in "furnished souls," ‡ by the worshippers of "Matthew

* Conrad Aiken.

† "A dreary place (dreary, drearier, dreariest) . . . No concentration here, no stimulus, no inner centrality, no exploding into the Beyond, no Sun. It is a City of Dreadful Night, a Target for Disgust."—*The Diary of Henry Grew Crosby,* published in three volumes by the Black Sun Press, Paris. For an account of Harry Crosby, see Malcolm Cowley's *Exile's Return.*

‡ E. E. Cummings.

and Waldo." * Eliot's earlier poems, the fruit of the years he spent at Harvard, were mostly gibes at Boston states of mind, at Cousin Harriet's *Evening Transcript*, Miss Helen Slingsby, the maiden aunt, the dowager Mrs. Phlaccus and her palace and Prufrock's indecisions and inhibitions; yet Eliot's mind was itself a compound of all the tastes of this latter-day Boston, a scholarly "museum of idols," like Sargent's fresco. There one saw the Boston royalism, the Boston Anglo-Catholicism, the taste for Donne, Laforgue and Remy de Gourmont, the interest in Dante, Sanskrit, the *Bhagavad-Gita* and the Elizabethan dramatists and poets, the classicism of Babbitt and Santayana. Eliot's mind was a mirror of Boston Alexandrianism, and its learned religiosity evoked in him later a singular mode of Christianity,†—small faith, less hope, no charity at all. Was it because he was deeply involved in so much he despised that Eliot's characteristic note was a sneer suggesting the cold east winds at the tip of Nahant? However this may have been, he saw the "waste-land" · first in Boston before he ever described it in terms of London. Here was the sterile and desolate country that was ruled by an impotent king, the rats' alley full of stony rubbish. This waste-land of all the modern cities, where the dry stone gave no sound of water, was suggested to Eliot by Boston when he was in college; and it amused him to contrast its desiccated culture with Sweeney, whom he found in a bar in South Boston. The present filled him with cold aversion. He saw the reality of the modern world in dingy furnished rooms and sawdust restaurants, cocktail-smells in bars, cigarettes in hallways; and E. E. Cummings too saw "putrid windows," disintegrating cigar-stubs lying in gutters and the first star feebly scratching the "sore of morning." Other young writers

---

* T. S. Eliot.

† "The spirit killeth, but the letter giveth life."—T. S. Eliot, *For Lancelot Andrewes.*

turned to low life, which may have been ignoble but was certainly real, unlike the feeble pretensions of the people of culture. Conrad Aiken was soon to picture, in *The House of Dust,* the seething life of the masses in the chaos of the city, and his mind was filled with images of Boston tailors and vaudeville jugglers dying among violins and paper roses; and John Dos Passos, who also haunted the slums, was struck by the lovely face of an Italian woman, suggesting Botticelli amid all the squalor. Sometimes these young men saw low life with compassion, sometimes they saw it with disgust, but they usually saw it as interesting, as actual, as real; and, as Stephen Crane had gone to the slums and found a heroine there in Maggie, so they sought for the primitive and, if need were, the brutal. Had not Synge said that poetry must learn to be brutal, in order once more to be human, as the teeth, after too much sugar, need flesh and gristle? Everywhere writers, in the decay of the old society, were seeking for the "salt in the mouth" and the "rough to the hand." Eugene O'Neill was already doing so; and all these writers, following Robinson, turned their backs on "success," as they turned them on "culture," and looked for life in its nakedness, however raw. What lay behind the "mask" was the object of their quest.

Now, in all this the young New Englanders were at one with the young of the rest of the world, who had generally lost faith in the world they lived in. In England, they were dethroning their Tennyson, and Victor Hugo fell in France, precisely as the Americans of the following decade dethroned their Emerson, Whittier, Longfellow and Bryant; and it only required the first world-war to crush the shams of this liberal culture, which seemed to have become a simulacrum. Was its idealism real, as Emerson had felt, or empty, as the young were constrained to feel it, a humbug that stank in their nostrils? For this idealism had been mouthed too long; it

was an abuse of Pharisees who evaded its tasks, while all
they really cared for was their own success, their pursuit
of dollars, francs, marks and shillings. What had become
a festering lily must have been a humbug always,—such
was the inference of the younger people, who had read
all the idol-smashers that Huneker spread through New
York and who knew the actualities behind the shams.
They were aware of the secrets that lurked behind the
prevailing comstockery, and they turned against their
elders, who seemed to have maintained a conspiracy of
silence about them; and in their need for frankness and
honesty they were impelled to tear down the false roof of
the house in which they had grown. The more, in their
hearts, they believed in progress, the more they denied
this travesty of it; the more sensitive they were, the more
embittered; and it was much the same in London as in
Boston, in Paris and Milan and Dublin. The culture of
the nineteenth century had gone to seed, and the young
were bent on destroying it, root and branch. It was futile,
it was incoherent, it was full of cant. It was so much sentimentality, priggishness and "slop." * Such was the mood
of the younger writers who were growing up in the pre-
war years and who were to find their voices in the years
that followed; and many a Yankee agreed with Eliot and
Cummings. They hated "cheerfulness, optimism and hope-
fulness." † They turned against "education" and ridiculed it.‡ They ridiculed patriotism and patriotic poetry; §

---

* "There is no standard of values in the modern world—it's mostly
slop, priggishness and sentimentality. One had much better be a wild man
in Borneo and at least have a clear and unabashed love for the sight of
blood."—Hart Crane.
   † T. S. Eliot.
   ‡ "O Education: O
      thos cook & son."
                    —E. E. Cummings.
   § "My country, 'tis of you, land of the Cluett Shirt," etc.
   "Listen my children and you shall hear the true story of Mr. Do-
nothing," etc.
                    —E. E. Cummings.

and they sometimes seemed to turn against humanity itself. Many were convinced that society was too banal to write for. They scarcely even wished to communicate with it; and they cultivated an "esoteric literary art" such as Henry Adams had dreamed of in his isolation.* Meanwhile, with showers of Parthian shots, they withdrew from Boston and launched into the chaos of the modern world.

* "As my experience leads me to think that no one any longer cares or even knows what is said or printed, and that one's audience in history and literature has shrunk to a mere band of survivors, not exceeding a thousand in the entire world, I am in hopes a kind of esoteric literary art may survive, the freer and happier for the sense of privacy and *abandon*." —Letter of Henry Adams, 1907.

CHAPTER XXV

SECOND MARCH

IN THE spring of 1915, Robert Frost returned from England, where he had been living for two or three years. He had published there *A Boy's Will* and *North of Boston*, which had been reviewed by Ezra Pound; and, as he left the pier, at the port of New York, he picked up a copy of *The New Republic*. It contained a review of the book by Amy Lowell. This liberal weekly was only six months old, and all these names were new to American readers, Amy Lowell, Ezra Pound and Frost; and it was symptomatic of a change in the country that Frost, who had gone to England obscure and discouraged, should have stepped off the ship a well-known man. America was undergoing a transformation. It was rousing itself like a strong man after sleep; and it was casting off its sloth of literary dullness,—eager, impressionable, receptive, it was vocal also. It had suddenly received a gift of tongues. The signs of a maturing life, self-scrutiny and discontent, that had characterized the confusion of the pre-war years, foreshadowed the revelations of the years that followed. It was generally felt that America was coming of age.

What this meant in the larger sphere the future was to show more clearly. It was certain that a new literature was coming to birth, a poetry more vigorous than had been seen for fifty years, a vital American theatre, a flowering of the novel. Criticism was in high feather, so was American architecture, so, at no distant date, was American painting; and for writers the most striking

change was that men had begun to read,—they had ceased
to regale themselves with newspapers only. The new generation of men actually talked about novels and poetry,
just as men before the Civil War had talked about Webster, Bancroft, Irving and Cooper, and just as in days
that were earlier still they had talked about Fielding
and Smollett, with the same enthusiasm and the same
directness. This was the greatest of possible changes, for
the new writers were in rapport with minds that were
frank, clear and virile; and the new women were almost
as direct as the men. They were almost as direct as
women could be; for the spread of education and popular
psychology had restored their old acquaintance with their
own instincts. Their entrance into professional life had
revived a sense of responsibility which they had lost in an
age of parasitism, and they moved in an open world with
open men. The mists of Victorian gentility were melting
away. It was the lack of masculine readers and feminine
readers with clear minds that had crippled the earlier
novelists, Howells and James; and was it not this that
had brought American poetry to its low estate? Poetry
had been on the way to something when men and women
both read Burns and Byron. For the rest, and this too
was essential, Americans were aware once more how radi-
cally they differed from Europeans. That they should
differ, to be themselves, while maintaining the general
traditions of the civilized races, few had ever questioned
in earlier times. But this realization also had been largely
forgotten. Americans, awake again, were rediscovering
their traditions, the deep, instinctive springs of their own
life. The day was approaching when the great nation was
to revolve as freely and confidently on its own axis as the
little nation had revolved in the days of Commodore
Perry and Andrew Jackson.

Literature reflected, as it had always reflected, more
swiftly than any other art, the temper of the nation. The

West and the South were expressing themselves through novelists and poets who were singularly original, powerful and fresh; and the new poets appeared in the magazine *Poetry,* founded in Chicago by Harriet Monroe. For a few years the claim was made, not without justification, that Chicago was the literary centre of the country; and, while it was true that Boston had forfeited this claim, the claim of New York was not yet fully established. Perhaps it was never to be established, for no one felt at home in New York. Not even the New Yorkers felt at home there. Even the New Yorkers hankered after other homelands, perhaps in old New York, perhaps in the country; and no one from other regions or nations felt that New York was finally home,—the longer one lived there, the more one loved Vermont, or Kansas, or Tennessee, or Sicily, or Poland. It was the practical centre merely, the centre of life but never of lives; and those who were born to love New York loved it for its past or future. For it had no present that one could love. It was "permanently in transition," as Henry James remarked: one could not halt one of its moments to call it fair. Nor was it yet established as the practical centre, as the movements of the younger writers showed, and especially perhaps the writers who came from New England. For New England, too, was finding expression, among the various regions, with a new and vigorous chorus of notable poets. It was not that these young writers remained in New England, although, after their diaspora and as time went on, they were prone to do so, more and more. And it was not that they were "unreconstructed." They had no axes to grind in favour of Boston, which they were disposed to treat with disrespect. But, while a few remained in Boston, and others, like Robinson, went to New York, others still found their way to London, not so much as returning pilgrims, in the manner of Henry James, as because they felt that London was still the centre. For the centre for writers is where their life is most intense. It is the magnetic centre; and, as Boston had ceased to be the magnet, and New York was not the magnet yet, London seemed as magnetic as Paris seemed later. This was the spirit in which John Gould Fletcher, the Arkansas poet from Harvard, had gone to England;* Robert Frost had gone for a similar reason; and even T. S. Eliot had settled in London at the very moment when Frost returned to this country not so much in Henry James's spirit as because of the superior intensity of the literary life there. But Eliot was a special case. He had rejected America and the American tradition and soon abjured his formal connection with them.† Meanwhile, Conrad Aiken felt as John Gould Fletcher felt, and as Amy Lowell felt when she went to London and met there, among others, Pound and Fletcher. Miss Lowell was astonished that she had had to go so far to find two young Americans who cared so much for modern poetry. The literary life in London was more intense than it was in New York at the moment. As for these voyagers, Ezra Pound was the type of them all; and he was never more this type than when he soon abandoned London for Paris. For Paris later supplanted London for most of these American writers who sought for what they could not find at home, an intensity of literary living. Later still, for various reasons, most of them returned to America, and then New York became fully the practical centre. That New York could not be more than

* See John Gould Fletcher, *Life is My Song*. This book is by far the best yet written (1940) on certain important phases of the so-called "renascence of poetry" during these years.

† Eliot rejected the American tradition *in toto*,—the cause of the Roundheads in the English Civil War, the cause of the American Revolution, the consequences of the American Civil War ("The Civil War was certainly the greatest disaster in the whole of American history."—*After Strange Gods*). In *The Use of Poetry*, he spoke of Shelley's beliefs as "beliefs that excite my abhorrence." They seemed to him "childish;" yet these "catchwords of creeds outworn, tyrants and priests" were the basic ideas of the American Revolution. Eliot made good his position by causing himself to be naturalized in England.

a practical centre these writers showed themselves, for
many of them returned to their own regions.

In 1915, this was a decade or more in the future, but
what seemed to be on the horizon already was the ultimate regionalization of American writers. Not of all
these writers. Other motives governed many,—for there
are many mansions in the city of letters. But the tendency to regionalism was a natural effect of the size of the
country; and Hawthorne had spoken for the South and
the West as well as New England when he said, during
the Civil War, "New England is quite as large a lump of
earth as my heart can really take in." There were writers
who felt this way in South Carolina, in New Orleans, in
Virginia, in San Francisco; and, while there were always
other writers, sometimes eminent, sometimes intense, for
whom the *genius loci* scarcely existed, this local attachment was highly important for many. For writers are
moved by love, though they often seem to be moved by
hatred; and they learn to love the more by loving the
less. They come to know the general by knowing the particular, and this particular is often the spot where they
are at home with their own instincts; and there were no
more American writers, and none more universal, than
those who were Southerners, Westerners, New Englanders first. The widest American visions had been village
visions, the visions of Concord, for instance, and the visions of Camden. The time was coming when all the
regions were to have their flowering, when regions that
had never flowered were to burst into bloom; and that
another spring was breaking in New England anyone
could see with half an eye. Within five years this spring
declared itself in a region that for Barrett Wendell had
been "virtually extinct." It had appeared with Robinson,
and Frost was a decisive fact. Edna St. Vincent Millay, a
student at Vassar, had written her *Renascence* in 1912.
T. S. Eliot had appeared in *Poetry* with *The Love-Song*

of J. Alfred Prufrock; and Conrad Aiken, impressed by
Freud, was writing the nocturnes that recalled the haunted
old New Bedford of Melville and Ryder. E. E. Cummings had gone to New York to study painting,—he was
soon to write *The Enormous Room*; and presently Wallace Stevens of Hartford published the polychromatic
poems that suggested Henry Adams's old French windows. For, reading these poems, one felt as if a window
of Chartres had been shattered, and the lovely bits of
colour lay on the grass, and one forgot the picture, which
one could scarcely reconstruct, in the pleasure of letting these fragments fall through one's fingers. Gamaliel
Bradford appeared along with the younger writers, with
his impressive series of literary portraits; nor was Edward
J. O'Brien to be forgotten, an offshoot of the Boston
Irish, like Boyle O'Reilly and Louis Sullivan, with a mind
as mediæval as a gargoyle. This youthful avatar of the
old romantic Irish scholars was to be known later for his
"five-foot shelf," as the President Eliot of the "best short
stories;" and Samuel Eliot Morison was soon to revive,
if not the grand style of Prescott and Parkman, at least
their natural adventurousness and their masculine verve.
One felt on every page of his *Maritime History of Massachusetts* the man who was not the student merely. The
"abandoned farm of literature" was producing in these
writers a crop that all but rivalled the crop of the "Newness;" and this was more than a regional share of the
general crop of the moment, the national revival of letters. For, as Robinson was the precursor of all the new
poets, so also Amy Lowell was their militant leader. In
poetry, Miss Lowell was all that, in other fields, Elizabeth
Peabody and Susan B. Anthony had been. She crowned the
line of the puissant women of Boston.

Now, many of these writers were exiles from New
England. They were exiles from the wintry world in
which they had grown; and, while they might have lost

by this, they had gained more than they lost by attaching themselves whole-heartedly to the life of the country. Most of the tougher New Englanders were all-American minds, such as John Dewey, for example. Such was Gamaliel Bradford; and the Yankee historian Morison was to be another in his time. There was no more all-American mind than that of Robert Frost, who was born in California and named after Lee;* and Amy Lowell, who shared with Frost the intensest kind of Yankeeism, was quite as all-American as he was. But, wherever they went, wherever they lived, these writers carried their aura with them; and, if there were other writers who suffered from exile, there was reason to think that this need not occur in the future. For, behind their backs, new signs of life were appearing all over the region; and one gathered that another generation would find New England what it had formerly been, a sufficient homeland. These signs of life were marked and stirring. The Provincetown Players appeared in 1915 and soon transformed the sleepy fishing-village, which was already known, like Rockport and Gloucester, like Old Lyme and Ogunquit, as a centre of artists. They opened their theatre in a weathered fish-house, and there one saw the first plays of Eugene O'Neill, a lover of the sea who dwelt across the dunes in an old, abandoned coast-guard station. Edna St. Vincent Millay appeared on the boards there, and Robert Edmond Jones was the stage-designer, a New Hampshire boy who had grown up in a grim and lonely farmhouse, like the house in *Desire Under the Elms*. "Bobby" Jones introduced the stage-craft of Max Reinhardt; and soon wharves and barns all over New England blossomed as summer-theatres and concert-halls. Villages and ports that had seemed to be dying bustled with a new activity, and the

---

* It was significant that Gamaliel Bradford began his most serious work with a study of Robert E. Lee, about whom Charles Francis Adams wrote so well. This was an instance of the instinctive effort of the New England mind to nationalize itself at this critical moment.

old handicrafts were coming to life, and local printing-presses were appearing in Vermont, in New Hampshire, in Maine. There was a rapid spread of art-museums, at Andover, Hanover, Worcester, Hartford, Springfield; and the Pittsfield Musical Festivals, at the instigation of Arthur Whiting, were turning factory-hands and farmer-boys into fine musicians. The MacDowell Colony at Peterboro was a haven for writers. There Edwin Arlington Robinson came into his own; and there, as time went on, his life achieved the rhythm that had once been broken and sporadic. The "misfit" became the master-poet in the cabin in the woods that faced Monadnock; and the wintry mind of Robinson burst into summer in a passionate glorification of love and joy. He had his first popular success in *The Man Against the Sky,* which appeared as a part of the general chorus of poets; but who could have expected from the cold and ironical Robinson the vernal glow and emotional splendour of *Tristram*? It was true that one found in this poem, as in those that followed, the old obsession of frustration; and the light that had shone for a moment grew dimmer and dimmer in the long psychological poems that he wrote in the future. But Robinson had felt, if only for a day, that dust and ashes were not the whole of life.

There was more than a little symbolism in Robinson's later development, as if his repatriation in New England had somehow focussed his mind. If he had found himself, was it not significant that he had also found himself once more in living touch with the body and soul of his region? The most traditional of poets, he had been starved in his long exile in New York, which, for the rest, had been so good for him; and this belated spring in Robinson's life, in the presence of his own New England folk, was a part of the general spring of the region itself. For these signs of a new life were not merely aesthetic. The interest in art that was rising all over the country, where art-schools

and museums appeared on every hand, was marked in
New England by many such manifestations as the employment of Orozco by Dartmouth College. But, more
generally, the region was recovering its confidence with
new methods of industry, a new population and the currents of the wide world of thought and feeling that were
passing through the loneliest village and farmhouse. With
the telephone, the radio, the movie, the abandoned districts were on speaking terms with Washington, London
and Paris; and the mood of Eugene O'Neill's New England dramas was already beginning to pass when the
dramas appeared. *Desire Under the Elms* was a truthful
picture. *Mourning Becomes Electra* was both truthful
and great; and there were Cabot farmhouses still and
households like the Mannons, as any New England villager would have recognized at once. They had existed
for generations, especially since the Civil War, when the
ebb-tide of the old pioneering spirit had bred this legacy
of hatred and sadistic lust; and it only required a masculine genius to read this phase of New England in the
light of mythical Greece and its heroines and heroes. All
this was true indeed, but only those who contemned New
England fancied that the pictures of O'Neill were the
only truth. For them,—and there were many during these
years who wished to wreak vengeance on New England,
—a sort of stage New Englander walked the boards who
was comparable to the stage Irishman of the popular theatre. For them all the Yankees were Cabots and Mannons; whereas those who were familiar with the scene
knew that *Our Town* was also true, and that Thornton
Wilder's Grover's Corners, when it appeared on the
stage, was quite as real and typical as the purlieus of
O'Neill. Grover's Corners had always existed also. Presented with far less power, it was equally there; and the
force of O'Neill was not more potent than the force that
emanated from this quiet village, which seemed to be

nothing more than a "very nice town." * While this force
was disguised by its mildness, what was this mildness but
a calm and confident sense of its probity and health?
Tragedies occurred there; the organ-master hanged himself; the graveyard figured largely in the minds of the
people; and, while there had been no burglars yet, everyone knew there were burglars, and the people had taken
to locking their doors at night. But in Grover's Corners
the mortality and birth-rates were constant; nine-tenths
of the high-school graduates wished to live there; the
young men wished to be farmers, the young girls wished
to be farm-wives, and love and youth were the centre and
heart of the picture. There was even as much fresh paint
in Grover's Corners as there had been a hundred years
before; and one felt, as one saw the play, that if the New
England village was moribund this was a moribundity
that never meant death. Perhaps the force of the village
was passive, perhaps it was a feminine force. It was a
force of humility and under-statement; but it aroused the
protective instinct,—it was sufficiently potent for this,—
in those who were predisposed to feel its charm. Who
would not fight, if need were, to save from destruction a
civilization so winning and so worthy to live? Grover's
Corners had always existed, and by 1938 the mood of the
region had changed so that one could see it, as few had
wished to see it seven years before when O'Neill produced *Mourning Becomes Electra*. And this change of
mood followed a change of fact; for many another village, such as Mary E. Wilkins had written about, had
recovered its equipoise and its confidence in life. Alice
Brown's Bromley had climbed again "to a fair degree of
prosperity." It had even ceased to have a poor-house,—
"none of its people were, as of old, on the town." Alice

* "Grover's Corners isn't a very important place when you think of all
New Hampshire, but I think it's a very nice town."—Thornton Wilder's
Our Town.

Brown's development told the story. She had begun, in the manner of Miss Wilkins, with tales of lean-jawed widowers, lorn spinsters and poor-farms, and she had ended with novels that were scarcely less good in which these themes were all but forgotten. Alice Brown was a writer of integrity, and she reflected reality in its changes; and she knew that New England itself was outliving these themes. It was assuming a new lease of life.

This was a far cry from the mood of 1915, though the poems of Robert Frost were a forecast of it. In 1915, it looked as if New England had withered and floated away from the rest of the nation. It was a Wickford Point, sadly adrift from realities, whom there were few to love and less to praise. Its force seemed to have rotted away, it followed random impulses without the repressions that were natural when the force was focussed; it was like a clock that was running down, and those who loved it saw in it a vanity of effort, together with a certain "sadness of predestined failure." * Where was New England in New England? Was it not like Chekhov's Cherry Orchard, where there was nothing left but to put up the shutters, turn the key in the lock and go away? But those who felt this did not know the writers, in whom the prescient saw other signs of the times. For the Yankees were writing again with talent and vigour; and did this suggest that New England was really exhausted? Had they ever ceased to write with vigour? Had they ever ceased to write in the New England tradition? The clock of Wickford Point went on ticking; and the new Yankee writers, ap-

---

* "I can see that Wickford Point was like a floating island that once had been solidly attached to the mainland. I can see it being severed from realities when I was still very young, and drifting off, a self-contained entity, into a misty sea . . .

"The whole place was like a clock which was running down, an amazing sort of clock, now devoid of weights or springs or hands, yet ticking on through some ancient impetus on its own momentum. Always when you thought it was going to stop, it would continue ticking."—John P. Marquand, *Wickford Point.*

pearances notwithstanding, remained in the New England tradition which they seemed to flout. They sometimes thought they were outside it, they sometimes wished to be outside it, but unconsciously they were within it, which was more important; and was it not part of their tradition that they should flout tradition, even as the greatest of the Yankees had flouted it before them? That one should flout tradition was the first of laws for Emerson's heirs. Rebellion was of the essence of the Yankee tradition, which was always concerned for fresh affirmations of life; and the most obvious thing about the new rebels was that they rebelled in the Yankee way. If they derided New England, if they disliked a standardized world, if they opposed the rigidities of the times and the mores, were they not repeating the pattern of 1840, when the young had been rebels at the outset? They all ran true to type in one fashion or another. To invent a "new way of being alive," the motive of E. E. Cummings, was a new way of being Thoreau at Walden; and no one ever vibrated to the "iron string" more than this terrible child, who wrote on the lintels of his doorpost, Whim. The author of *The Enormous Room* was an Ellery Channing with genius; and to turn one's back on banalities, with Edna Millay's force of feeling, was not remote from Margaret Fuller's plan. Amy Lowell played a role that had many a Boston precedent; and Robert Frost revived, for a new generation, the part of the poet-seer of Emerson's day. These writers represented a high degree of intensity, and all the plays of their game were buoyant and fresh; but they were all tarred with the brush of the Yankee tradition. One saw this in the doggedness with which they pursued their careers; and they proved that the Yankee mind was brimming with life.

Amy Lowell's force of will, the secret of her success and failure, was her most markedly racial characteristic. For this was the Yankee will, and she won her victories

by it, and she largely failed by this will in her life as a
poet. Too much of her poetry sprang from the will, not
the poet. But there was no doubt about the will. She was
a Lowell and a Lawrence, and she liked to run things,
whether fleets of clipper-ships or colleges or towns; and,
having the taste, she had the capacity, as dozens of the
Lowells had. She ran right well whatever she chose to
run. She was a born promoter, as masterful as her forbears were, and the shrewdest of salesmen also, like the
old China traders; and, seeing that America was giving
birth to a first-rate product, she put her shoulder to the
wheel and pushed it on the market. The product was
American poetry, which was plainly on the rise again and
which she handled like any other "big business." Was it
good, bad or indifferent? What did it matter? It was
good in bulk, and that was the point. It was another
form of Standard Oil; and Miss Lowell set out to put it
"on the map," as others had put salvation or woman's
suffrage. Agassiz, in just this wholesale fashion, had put
natural science on the American map; and this required
perception, in his case as in hers. For Miss Lowell had
perception, just as her grandfather's cousin had had it
when he saw that American poetry was on the rise and
wrote his *Fable for Critics* in the eighteen-forties.* What
scorn she felt for those who did not have it!—for the
"caged warblers" and "phonograph" poets who thought
they still lived in Victorian times, for those whose work
was not their own but echoes, for those who cowered in
ivory towers and never looked out of the window, for
those who praised the glories of old New England and
could not see the genius of Masters and Sandburg. She

* With less concentration of energy, James Russell Lowell had performed a similar role as the impresario of this earlier movement. Amy
Lowell's *A Critical Fable* repeated her cousin's performance with about
the same measure of success. Her judgments were equally fresh and
shrewd, and the poem abounded in lucky hits, e.g., the portraits of herself and Vachel Lindsay.

scorned Henry Adams, who had thrown up the sponge.
She scorned Henry James and other "traitors." * She
scorned the lady-painters and performers of Chopin, with
their "ghastly nights on cracked hotel-pianos." She was
arrogant enough to impress occasional English observers,
who were full of admiration for her because she reminded them of their own dear betters. She ran ocean
liners and terrorized their orchestras by telling them to
stop their outrageous noise; and she whizzed over the
face of the earth in her claret-coloured motor, reorganiz-
ing hotels where she spent the night. Like Eliot's Cousin
Nancy, she "strode across the hills and broke them;"
and, if she was not bearded, she was full of oaths; and
her bed had eighteen pillows, and she had ten thousand
black cigars and seven megatherian sheep-dogs that
mauled and all but murdered her visitors. This Daniela
Webster was also an actress, whose earliest idol was
Duse, and all her dramatic flair, with her verve and her
gusto, went into the great pitched battle that she waged
for the poets. She fought in the front rank, when occasion called for her, or, as less often happened, behind
the lines, where she mustered her majors and colonels,
her generals and lieutenants.

For literary soldiership, or literary statesmanship,
America had never seen Miss Lowell's equal. Literary
politicians had always abounded, but she was the prime
minister of the republic of poets; and under her control
this republic rose from the status of Haiti and became
an imperial republic of the calibre of France. The poets
had reason to thank their stars that they had a Lowell
behind them, for whom editors and publishers were factory-hands and office-boys. Her telephone had the force
of a dozen Big Berthas; and God might have picked up

* See her portraits of T. S. Eliot and Ezra Pound in *A Critical Fable.*
Amy Lowell was one of those who felt that Henry James made a great
mistake in detaching himself from the life of his countrypeople.

the fragments of those who opposed her,—there was little left of them for men to bury. One could hear the guns go off at the other end of Texas. But the Texans and Nebraskans and the people of St. Paul crowded the window-ledges of their halls to hear her; and the map on which she had put poetry started and trembled under her feet,—the map of poetry blossomed in purple and red. She touched a fuse wherever she went, and fireworks rose in the air; and there were no set-pieces more brilliant than hers, no Catherine-wheels or girandoles or fountains. There was no still, small voice in Amy Lowell. Her bombs exploded with a bang and came down in a shower of stars; and she whizzed and she whirred, and she rustled and rumbled, and she glistened and sparkled and blazed and blared. If, at the end, it seemed like the Fourth of July, it was a famous victory, none the less, though the fields and the trees were littered with the sticks and the debris, with charred frames and burnt-out cases.

Besides, much more was left than people felt on the morning after. Miss Lowell was a pyrotechnist, but some of her scenic effects were permanent; and when she was not permanent she was salutary. Her theory of "externality" was undoubtedly fallacious, and much of her work was factitious, the fruit of the will. As if poetry could ever be "external"! Yet her actual externality was good for the moment. It was a challenge to internality at a time when the "internal" poets were so often sentimental, derivative and soft. When the *fond* was so corrupt and weak, the way to sting it into life was to assert that nothing was important but the *forme*; and all the new poets made much of technique,—they sometimes talked as if nothing else mattered. And what, in the end, did this matter?—though the end perhaps might be long in coming. The poets of the further future were to gain by this immediate future, in which the false remnants of the past were trampled out of sight and in which all manner of new forms were placed at their disposal when they developed the *fond* that was equally worthy. The world could always wait for its poets, and this was a time for tuning the instruments; and the free verse and poly- phonic prose which Miss Lowell adapted and popular- ized provided a whole new orchestra for the poets who were coming. How good this audacity was after so much futile indirectness! After so much weltering in borrowed souls, how good it was to "live in the eye alone"! How good was imagism to sharpen the perceptions, and all this zest for seeing, reporting, recording, this joy in the visible world, this picture-making, after so much wreath- ing and writhing and fainting in coils. How good this "religion of art," the note of the epoch, after so many woolly abstractions and impotent emotions, so many blurred conceptions and mouldy morals! This technical virtuosity, so clean and fresh, this feeling for orchestral colour and verbal music, and this all but morbid fear of the obvious also! These poets reacted against bad tech- nique by making technique an end in itself. What of it! The poets of the future would redress the balance. And they rightly threw out of the window the old New Eng- land classics, with all their Miltonic ideals and all their Victorian nature-worship. No need to fear that they would not come back. Were the Yankees really in danger of losing their ethos? If the classics went out by the window, they were sure to return by the door when the noble mind had outlived the abuse of its virtues. The new generation started with Poe, the first favourite of Frost as of Robinson, with Emily Dickinson's novel perceptions and Whitman, who had discarded the past. The new gen- eration was also redressing a balance.

As a writer as well as a propagandist, Miss Lowell was part of all this movement, so similar in France and England in its causes and effects. For the whole Western world was undergoing the same changes, and Boston was a centre of this world,—as it had been in the eighteen-forties. It had never ceased to be a centre, despite the croakers and despite the dry-rot; and in the darkest hour of Boston and Cambridge world-influences had emanated from these twin cities in the persons of William James and Mrs. Eddy. For all the reactionary forces that opposed new culture, they were still hungry for new culture; and Amy Lowell was as hungry for the culture of this morning as an Omaha woman's club was hungry for the culture of the day before last. She made the Omaha woman's club hungry for it,—and she begged it and borrowed it, stole it, invented it, like all the writer-conquerors, with a high hand and a high heart and the enterprise of a merchant-adventurer.* No doubt, her externality reflected her own extroversion. It was an escape as well from a troubled psyche; for Miss Lowell's inner life knew no repose. She had solved none of her vital problems, and she remained the conventional child that expressed itself in the first of her volumes of poems.† Indeed, she was never a poet, properly speaking,—the poet in her never struggled through,—so she seized on the outsides of things as her only chance of effectuality, and her dramatic instinct achieved the rest. She had awakened suddenly to modern painting and music, and she pillaged them as she pillaged the Boston museums where she had played as a child. Among her objets d'art she

* "My ship has tasted water in strange seas,
  And bartered goods at still uncharted isles.
  She's oft coquetted with a tropic breeze,
  And sheered off hurricanes with jaunty smiles."
      —The Dutch merchant, in Amy Lowell's *Sword Blades and Poppy Seed.*
  † *A Dome of Many-Coloured Glass,* 1912. This book was a curious revelation of Amy Lowell's equipment as a poet in the proper sense. It represented her work up to the age of thirty-eight, after which she developed her "external" method. Conventional and weak in thought and feeling, it was on the level of the writing of most of the current New England poetasters.

was always the child, a Gargantuan child with the reach of a khan or a brigand; and she pillaged books,—she tore the entrails out of them,—and she used in the composition of her rockets and pin-wheels the *alchimie du verbe* of Rimbaud, Verhaeren, Mallarmé and heaven knew how many others. She wrote free verse after Debussy's piano-pieces; she stole the show at aquariums, with their "swirling, looping patterns of fish;" and every place she read about and every place she visited,— whether Mexico, China, Peru, Saint Louis or Charleston, —left in her hand some scrap of a rhythm or a picture. She found a mine in Keats, whom she admired for his fearlessness, straightforwardness, directness, for all he had in common with herself;* but everything served her purpose that gave her a little gold or brass, a beam of sandalwood or a bolt of silk, a flag, a trumpet, a tuba or a box of spices. And she toiled over her poems from midnight till dawn, not as one to whom the muses whispered, but as one who had to wrestle with them and force them to their knees in the sweat of her brow.

Well, was it all for show? Was it merely a night of the Fourth of July? Was it only a parade and swagger of Boston fashion? There was surely enough of the material in Miss Lowell's talent, too much noise, too much excitement; and yet how much remained that was new and crisp, what vividness of colour, what joy of action! One could say much for externals that enlivened the senses; and, when one had given up to time the bric-a-brac, the petals of Chinese flowers whose roots were somewhere else around the planet, one came back to Miss Lowell's story-telling. She was a story-teller, if not a

* Amy Lowell's *John Keats* was the master-work of a powerful mind that suffered from its author's limitations. Miss Lowell saw Keats as primarily a poet of colour. She was largely outside the subject, by the nature of things; but he only can throw stones at this magnificent tour de force who shares Miss Lowell's zest, her learning and patience, her knowledge of the world, her natural authority, her power of concentration and her feeling for truth.

poet, who had studied her art in Chaucer, in Keats and
in Browning, and who, in some of her best tales, followed Miss Jewett and Miss Wilkins, when she was not
touched by Robert Frost. Perhaps this deep Yankee in
her was to live the longest, the Yankee whose tales in
East Wind and the ballad of *Evelyn Ray* refurbished this
old New England *genre* with a note of her own that was
wholly fresh. Her colours here were browns and greys,
but some of her blues and reds were fast; and, among
other pieces, *Can Grande's Castle,* with its cinemato-
graphic style, remained her most characteristic. Perhaps
its excess of vivacity wore one out. It was charged with
enough electricity to burn one's hand off: it was like a
third rail, it was like a power-line, and one had to touch
the wires with circumspection. But there Amy Lowell
exulted in her strength; and her feeling for ships and
battles, for barbarism and heroism, for pageantry, pomp,
dash and fanfaronade, for the theatre of history and the
clash of peoples boiled up and bubbled over with a splendid brio. She was Lady Hamilton, she was Nelson, she
was Commodore Perry in Japan, with his sailor-chanties;
and no New England historian since the great days of
Prescott and Motley had given the world such brilliant
historical scenes.

If Amy Lowell was a Yankee of the Yankees, so were
Cummings and Edna Millay, although both were in
sharp reaction against New England. They delighted in
turning topsy-turvy the house of the mind they had
grown in,* as in decking their "amorous themes with the
honester stenches." † Edna Millay was "the booth where
folly holds her fair," and both had accepted the word of
Blake, in face of their Yankee inheritance, "The road of
excess leads to the palace of wisdom." It sometimes

---

* "Safe upon the solid rock the ugly houses stand:
    Come and see my shining palace built upon the sand."
                            —Edna Millay, *A Few Figs from Thistles.*
† Edna Millay, *Conversation at Midnight.*

seemed as if Cummings's governing motive were to thumb his nose at Cambridge and all it stood for, propriety, regularity, the neat and the tidy;* but what, at bottom, was this motive if it was not the love of freedom that had always marked the Yankee mind? This passion filled *The Enormous Room* and constituted, in *Eimi,* the protest against the compulsions of Soviet Russia, a "joyless experiment," as he saw it, "in force and fear;" and, while a hatred of tyranny actuated both these books, they were much more deeply actuated by a sense of the life that tyranny "bossed and herded and bullied and insulted." For Cummings had a marvellous feeling for life and for the "gods that come in low disguises;" † and he turned away from the tyrants and humbugs to give himself with joyous zest to the wretched and beautiful people whom they misprized. With what gallantry and tenderness he painted, in *The Enormous Room,* the portraits of Jean le Nègre, Mexique, the Zulu, magnificent representations in the Rabelaisian vein that expressed his high animal spirits and his love for men who could not be pigeon-holed. With his burlesque-loving spirit, he saw the world through a child's eyes. He liked, as he said, "shining things," he liked barber-poles and hurdy-gurdies; and he liked to play the clown in the universal circus and knock over ministers, veterans, policemen and bankers. ‡ He was an enemy of clichés, pomposity and cant; and did he not play havoc with the English language as a way of protesting against them? Behind his mockery lay a sense of the infinite worth of the individual, coerced and constrained and menaced by a standardized world; and he showed that the Yankee mind, the more it

* "By being dirtier than usual, I was protesting in a (to me) very satisfactory way against all that was neat and tidy and bigoted and solemn." —E. E. Cummings, *The Enormous Room.*

† Emerson.

‡ See *By E. E. Cummings.*

changed, remained the more irrepressible and the more the same.*

In Edna Millay's high lyrical talent, the Yankee note, which one felt from the first, increased in depth and clarity as time went on, as the flippancy of her earlier verse,—its conscious naïveté mingled with wonder,— yielded to profundity of feeling. She had begun with fairy-tale fancies and travesties of nursery-rhymes, in which she turned the moral inside out; but this mood of an infantile mischief-maker had always been half-rapturous, and the rapture grew together with her force of passion. An accomplished and disciplined craftsman, Miss Millay was a learned poet, with the Yankee love of Virgil, Catullus, Chaucer and especially the Elizabethans whose vein she recaptured in her tragic sense of youth and the brevity of life. She was direct and lucid because her feeling was intense. So had been the feeling of the ballad-makers whose forms she so generally followed; and her gift of music was like theirs; so was her physical perception, her sense of the miracle of consciousness and the things of earth. Her poems were full of the odours and flavours of New England, bayberry, hay, clover, seaweed and sorrel, and the salt smell of the ocean in them, of weedy mussels on rotting hulls, mingled with the rustle of eel-grass in the cove and the tinkling of cow-bells in stony pastures. Thoreau had never felt more keenly the beauty of animal forms and movements, of the buck that stood in the forest "with listening hoof;" and all the old Yankee feeling for justice revived in the cycle of verses which the Sacco-Vanzetti case evoked from this poet.

That the Yankee tradition was still alive one saw in all these poets almost as clearly as in the Yankee classics.

---

* Much of Cummings's symbolism suggested his New England inheritance. His play *Tom* was based upon *Uncle Tom's Cabin,* and *The Enormous Room* abounded in symbols from the *Pilgrim's Progress.*

Cynical as they sometimes seemed, they still maintained the root-ideas that had always governed America and governed New England, faith in the individual, the passion for justice, the sense of the potential in human nature and its world, the love of life, the belief in its ultimate goodness. These traits persisted in the Yankee mind in a world that seemed to be losing all consciousness of them; and in 1915 the day was coming when writers from all the regions were to flock to New England, when Connecticut farms and farms in Vermont were to house recalcitrant souls from the South and the West who had long made their peace with New England. They found New England friendly, and they found it alive. One could be regional there without being provincial; and one could rejoice there in the "sweet American vaguenesses" * of mountain, forest, lake and upland pasture. In those days, even Boston, in the mind of the nation, had ceased to be the city of Pharisees only. It had its Sacco-Vanzetti case; but where were the liberals more in evidence? Where did they picket a state-house with livelier zest? Where were the old Abolitionists still more active in every new cause of truth and freedom?—and, if O'Neill's *Strange Interlude* was banned in Boston, was it not a triumphant success in the suburb of Quincy? The most refractory Westerner was willing to grant the old, proud boast of Massachusetts, that it had surpassed many empires in its contributions to progress and in its great men;† and the nation could not forget New England, could not let the subject drop,—Americans could do anything but leave it

* Henry James, in *The American Scene*.
The most embittered exiles sometimes longed, like Harry Crosby, "for the sunbasking on Singing Beach, for the smell of the woods around Essex, for the sunset at Coffin's Beach, for the friendliness of the apple-trees . . . I would even like (for me tremendous admission) a small farm near Annisquam, with a stone farmhouse looking out over flat stretches of sand toward the sea."—*The Diary of Henry Grew Crosby*.

† "Massachusetts which, though but a small commonwealth, has since 1770 surpassed so many empires, in her contributions to human progress, and in her great men."—*The Letters of William Roscoe Thayer*.

alone. They liked to tease New England, but they were never indifferent to it. They could not have enough of Henry Adams, Santayana's *The Last Puritan,* the novels of Marquand. New England haunted the minds of Americans, who tried to read its riddle, as if for their souls' good they must know what it meant. What was the truth about it?—and there were reasons for this obsession, for, generally speaking, Americans had a stake in New England. They were deeply implicated in it, as the seat of their deepest, their stoutest, their greatest tradition. Their blood was mixed perhaps with other strains, and perhaps they had long lived in other regions, but New England was their ark of the covenant still. How fared this ark? Into what hands had it fallen? Were these hands strong and good, so much the better. Were they good but weak, they must be supported. Were they strong but evil, they must be corrected. For it meant much to Americans that this old region should fare well, as their palladium of truth, justice, freedom and learning. They could not rest until they were reconciled to it, and until it was reconciled to them.

It was Robert Frost's function to mediate between New England and the mind of the rest of the nation, so sceptical of it, yet so solicitous also, eager for its welfare, willing to believe in it, but not without proofs of its probity, its sanity, its health. Robert Frost afforded these proofs. In him the region was born again,—it seemed never to have lost its morning vigour and freshness; and one felt behind his local scene the wide horizons of a man whose sympathies and experience were continental. He had himself discovered New England after a boyhood in California, and he had tramped through the Carolinas and wandered over the West; and he knew how to say that "Yankees are what they always were" in a way that commanded affection as well as respect. A true folk-mind, Frost was a mystical democrat, compassionately filled

with a deep regard for the dignity of ordinary living; and
he was an artist as well as a poet, a lover of goodness
and wisdom, who found them, not by seeking them, but
rather along the path of gaiety. At home, like Hawthorne's snow-image, in the frosty air of polar nights, he
felt the wild and the strange in the low and familiar, and
the stones in his walls were meteors, and the tamarack-
swamps were playgrounds for his boreal fancy. He invested with his white magic the woodpile, the log-road,
the blueberry-patch, the birch-tree, the barn and the
orchard; and through his gnarled poems, twisted and
tough, a still music ran, like the music Thoreau heard in
the poles by the railroad. Sometimes this was like the
music of a hidden brook, lost in the grasses of a pasture,
or the whisper of the scythe, or the whir of the grind-
stone; and it bespoke a tranquil happiness, drawn from
fathomless wells of living, more often tragic than otherwise, but jubilant and hardy. A boy and a sage at once,
Frost carried with him an aura as of infinite space and
time. Yet so paternal was he, and so human, that many
a younger writer felt about him as Gorky felt about Tolstoy, "I am not an orphan on the earth as long as this
man lives on it."

INDEX